Guide to

or

on

DIRECTORY OF SOCIAL CHANGE

Published by
Directory of Social Change
24 Stephenson Way
London NW1 2DP
Tel: 08450 77 77 07; Fax: 020 7391 4804
Email: publications@dsc.org.uk
www.dsc.org.uk
from whom further copies and a full publications catalogue are available.

Directory of Social Change Northern Office
Federation House, Hope Street, Liverpool L1 9BW
Policy & Research 0151 708 0136; email: research@dsc.org.uk

Directory of Social Change is a Registered Charity no. 800517

First published 1986
Second edition 1989
Third edition 1991
Fourth edition 1993
Fifth edition 1995
Sixth edition 1997
Seventh edition 1999
Eighth edition 2001
Ninth edition 2003
Tenth edition 2005
Eleventh edition 2007
Twelfth edition 2010

ISBN 978 1 906294 41 0

British Library Cataloguing in Publication Data
A catalogue record for this book is available from the British
Library.

Cover design by Kate Bass
Text designed by Lenn Darroux and Linda Parker
Typeset by Marlinzo Services, Frome
Printed and bound by Page Bros, Norwich

Contents

Introduction

This edition

Welcome to the twelfth edition of *The Guide to the Major Trusts Volume 1*. Much has changed since the last edition of this book was published in 2007, not least a global recession that few saw coming. In the eleventh edition we compared the grantmaking of the top 25 trusts in 2007 with the top 25 back in 1991, and concluded that the staggering increase in the grantmaking of those trusts during that time may have been due to the recession in the early 90s, as well as how strong the economy was in 2007. How times have changed in just two years. At the beginning of 2010, the UK and the rest of the world were only just starting to show signs of moving out of the worst recession in living memory[1]. It could be argued that because of the current difficult economic climate the information in this publication has never been more useful.

The purpose of this book has always been to get inside the policies and practices of the largest trusts and foundations in the country, and to explain what they are doing with their money, open them up to public scrutiny, encourage transparency and provide information for charities seeking funding for their valuable work. In doing this, the book has had considerable success. As well as being a practical and useful resource for those seeking grants, it has also been an independent review of the work of the larger trusts and foundations. As such, it has enabled readers to compare and contrast grantmakers and how they operate.

We continue to see improvements in the way in which trusts report their activities and the impact that their funding has on the charities they support. The annual reports and accounts of the funders in this book now contain more detailed analysis than ever, and new reporting requirements such as statements on public benefit seem to have given some impetus for more funders to consider their objectives, achievements and performance in greater depth.

In particular it has been interesting, and in many cases encouraging, to read about trusts' individual responses to the recent financial crisis. Many of them have been hit hard – collectively the value of the assets of the trusts featured in this book has fallen by around £4 billion – but many say their intention, at least in the short term, is to maintain levels of grantmaking so that their beneficiaries can continue their valuable work with some of the most disadvantaged members of society.

As reported in the last edition, many large grantmakers now also have helpful and informative websites of their own. Also in the last edition, less than half of the trusts had their own websites – around 56% of the trusts in this edition now have one (around 30 more than last time). This means we are now more able to provide details of upcoming developments, proposed policy changes and revisions of guidelines because information available on trusts' websites is usually more current than information taken from annual reports and accounts. As a result it is hoped that readers will find that this edition remains current and relevant for longer.

Many grantmakers that may have been reluctant to divulge information in the past now realise the value of providing relevant, up-to-date information on their grant-making activities, where their money is spent and what they hope to achieve with it. This is something DSC has advocated for many years – providing as much information as possible on grant-making activities helps potential applicants to target their proposals more effectively, and discourages ineligible applications, rather than increasing the number of requests for funding.

Further details on how DSC aims to promote more effective giving are discussed later (see page ix)

The trusts in this edition gave almost £2.53 billion to organisations during the latest year for which information was available: in most cases the 2007/08 financial year. This is a relatively modest increase on the £2.3 billion in the last edition, although it is significant when considering the current difficult economic climate. It should also be noted that much of the financial information taken from accounts in 2007/08 relates to a time either before the recession or when economic difficulties were emerging. However, comparing these figures with those from the previous financial year when the economy was strong, any increase in grantmaking, however small, is significant.

Much of the increase in grantmaking in this edition is due to the impressive work of the Wellcome Trust, whose grantmaking rose from £324.7 million in the last edition to a staggering £598.5 million in this edition. The work of this trust continues to impress – the impact of its funding is far reaching, including the development of anti-malarial drugs, and funding the Sanger Institute and its work on the Human Genome Project.

Other trusts which have increased their grantmaking in this edition include: the Garfield Weston Foundation, which gave £55 million in 2007/08 compared with £38 million in 2005/06; the Leverhulme Trust, which gave £29 million in the previous edition and £48.5 million here; and the City Parochial Foundation, whose grantmaking has increased from £9.7 million to £11.5 million. Although this is a relatively modest increase, the City Parochial Foundation is a good example of a proactive and dynamic foundation that achieves a great deal with its money – the foundation works with some of the most excluded and disadvantaged people in London and is not afraid to tackle difficult issues. The foundation's annual report is also an excellent example of one in which an impressive amount of detail is given to show the impact of its funding.

Naturally, there are also trusts featured here whose grantmaking has decreased since the last edition (and some which have been omitted as a result), be it because of natural fluctuations in the level of funding distributed each year, or as a result of the recent financial crisis. The Northern Rock Foundation, for example, has seen its level of grantmaking reduce from £27.1 million in 2006 to £10.5 million in 2008, largely due to uncertainty around funding arrangements from Northern Rock plc. The foundation had annually received 5% of pre-tax profits from the bank, but after the bank was transferred into public ownership following its well-publicised troubles in 2007 this arrangement came to an end. The foundation was then guaranteed £15 million each year from the bank until 2010. Hopefully a viable long-term funding arrangement will be in place for 2011 and beyond.

While many trusts have indicated that, where possible, they intended to protect their existing beneficiaries in the wake of falling income levels, some have not been in a position to do so. One of the most high-profile casualties of the recession has been the Lloyds TSB Foundation for Scotland – see page vii for full details.

There are also 18 trusts which are new to this volume, including: Amabrill Limited; the John Armitage Charitable Trust; the Bowland Charitable Trust; the D M Charitable Trust; the Charles Dunstones Charitable Trust; the Stafford Trust; and the Maurice Wohl Charitable Foundation. The trusts new to this edition gave a combined total of over £41.7 million.

As we can see from the table, the top 25 trusts and foundations gave around £271 million more overall than the top 25 featured in the previous edition. Clearly this overall increase is largely due to the substantial increase in grantmaking from the Wellcome Trust, although 15 other trusts in the top 25 also increased their giving.

---

[1] Revised figures released at the end of February 2010 show that the UK technically came out of recession with a 0.3% growth in GDP (http://news.bbc.co.uk/1/hi/business/8538293.stm)

Top 25 trusts*

	Guide to the Major Trusts Volume 1 – 2007/08	Total grants		Guide to the Major Trusts Volume 1 – 2010/11	Total grants
1	The Wellcome Trust	£324.7 million	1 (1)^	The Wellcome Trust	£598.5 million
2	The Football Foundation	£57.6 million	2 (2)	The Football Foundation	£82.1 million
3	Comic Relief	£54.4 million	3 (6)	The Garfield Weston Foundation	£55 million
4	The Gatsby Charitable Foundation	£53.8 million	4 (9)	The Leverhulme Trust	£48.5 million
5	The Wolfson Foundation	£38.5 million	5 (3)	Comic Relief	£47 million
6	The Garfield Weston Foundation	£38 million	6 (4)	The Gatsby Charitable Foundation	£40.9 million
7	The Coalfields Regeneration Trust	£38 million	7 (5)	The Wolfson Foundation	£39.2 million
8	BBC Children in Need	£34.4 million	8 (8)	BBC Children in Need	£36.8 million
9	The Leverhulme Trust	£29 million	9 (13)	The Henry Smith Charity	£26.7 million
10	Esmée Fairbairn Foundation	£29 million	10 (16)	Lloyds TSB Foundation for England and Wales	£23.7 million
11	The Northern Rock Foundation	£27.1 million	11 (-)	The Prince's Charities Foundation	£21.9 million
12	The Lennox Hannay Charitable Trust	£25.5 million	12 (10)	Esmée Fairbairn Foundation	£21.5 million
13	The Henry Smith Charity	£23 million	13 (17)	Wales Council for Voluntary Action	£21 million
14	The Peter Moores Foundation	£22.5 million	14 (25)	Arcadia (formerly the Lisbet Rausing Charitable Fund)	£18.4 million
15	The Health Foundation	£19.7 million	15 (18)	The Tudor Trust	£17.8 million
16	Lloyds TSB Foundation for England and Wales	£19.5 million	16 (21)	The Sigrid Rausing Trust	£17 million
17	Wales Council for Voluntary Action	£18.9 million	17 (-)	The Monument Trust	£16.3 million
18	The Tudor Trust	£17.5 million	18 (19)	The City Bridge Trust	£15.5 million
19	The City Bridge Trust	£16.9 million	19 (-)	The Jack Petchey Foundation	£14.5 million
20	The Shetland Charitable Trust	£15 million	20 (22)	Paul Hamlyn Foundation	£13.4 million
21	The Sigrid Rausing Trust	£14.5 million	21 (20)	The Shetland Charitable Trust	£11.7 million
22	Paul Hamlyn Foundation	£11.6 million	22 (24)	The City Parochial Foundation	£11.5 million
23	Community Foundation Serving Tyne and Wear and Northumberland	£9.9 million	23 (7)	The Coalfields Regeneration Trust	£11.5 million
24	The City Parochial Foundation	£9.7 million	24 (11)	The Northern Rock Foundation	£10.5 million
25	The Lisbet Rausing Charitable Fund	£9.7 million	25 (-)	The Wolfson Family Charitable Trust	£10 million
	Total	**£958.9 million**		**Total**	**£1.23 billion**

*excluding the Big Lottery Fund and Awards for All   ^figures in bracket show position in the previous edition

The current environment

There have been many surveys and reports over the past 18 months that have attempted to assess the impact of the recession on the voluntary sector and charities as a whole, and grant-making trusts in particular. In summer 2009 we surveyed the trusts and foundations in this book and asked them three simple questions.

- Do you have less, more or about the same amount of funding available to give this financial year compared to last year?
- In general, have you noticed applicants asking for less, more, or about the same amount of funding compared to last year?
- Do you anticipate having less, more, or about the same amount of funding available for your next financial year?

Unfortunately, the response rate was disappointing: less than 10%. This may have been due to recession-related survey fatigue, however there were still some interesting results and comments.

Around half of those who responded said that they had about the same level of funding available during the current financial year (in most cases this year was 2008/09) that they had available in the previous financial year. Interestingly, and more relevantly for readers of this book, around half of those who responded also said that they anticipated they would have around the same level of funding available during the next financial year. Around 65% of the respondents said that that they were being asked for similar amounts to, or less than, what they were being asked for before the recession.

Those who chose to make additional comments tended to be those with a slightly more pessimistic outlook:

'Applicants seem particularly interested in unrestricted grants at this time.'

'Some bigger charities are approaching us!'

'The real impact of the recession will be through public sector finances – this has not come through yet.'

'We have more organisations approaching us for funding, many because they are losing Local Authority funding. We are anticipating a tough year with some hard decisions needing to be made as many other

funders [. . .] have ceased to operate or have significantly less funding to distribute.'

Although there were also a few positive comments, such as:

'Whilst there is less income for grants, it is less than 10% down, and so eligible charities should be encouraged to keep applying.'

The following figures emerged from an analysis of the assets, income and annual grant totals of all of the trusts in this guide. We compared data from the latest financial year for which figures were available (mainly 2007/08), with data from the previous financial year:

- 272 trusts (68%) saw a drop in the value of their assets on the previous financial year; 116 trusts (29%) saw the value of their assets increase
  - £4.1 billion drop in assets overall
- 169 trusts (42%) saw their income fall on the previous year; 225 trusts (56%) saw their income increase
  - £126.6 million fall in income overall
- 156 trusts (39%) saw their grant totals fall on the previous financial year; 237 trusts (59%) saw their grant totals increase
  - £165.3 million increase in grants overall since the previous financial year.

Our research for this edition suggests that despite grant-making charities seeing the value of their assets fall and their levels of income reduce overall, they are trying where possible to protect their beneficiaries from the worst effects of the recession by at least maintaining their levels of funding, although many are taking a cautious approach to managing their finances. Below is a selection of comments taken from the latest annual reports of some of the grantmakers featured here. They reflect on the impact of the recession and give a flavour of the trusts' attitudes and outlooks.

'2008 saw a significant increase in the number of applications received by the fund. We were delighted to be able once again to award a record amount in grants to projects, together with a modest increase in grants [. . .]. However, our capacity to deal with a fast growing number of applications, together with the inevitable impact of the recession on our income, has led us to re-examine our criteria, which will lead to a more focused approach in 2009.'

'*Reflecting the turmoil in financial markets, the value of the foundation's investments at the end of 2008 reduced to £89 million from £111 million in 2007. Income dropped from £8.7 million to £6.3 million, as a result of the company making a lower donation than in the prior year. The trustees are adopting a prudent approach to grantmaking in 2009 in the expectation that an extended downturn will have a significant impact on income over the next two years. Unfortunately, the economic crisis has hit many charities, and as a result we have seen some projects abandoned or downscaled. Sadly, a number of charities have failed, although to date we have had little direct exposure to such closures. However, we are being yet more rigorous in assessing applicants' financial circumstances and monitoring their progress during the life of a project. We are also being somewhat circumspect in supporting ambitious appeals which are at an early stage, given our lower income, the tight market for fundraising generally and a reluctance to tie up our grant-making capacity for an extended period.*'

'*The trustees expect to maintain grants at levels similar to those of the current year. Should the returns on its investment portfolio increase then future grant awards can be increased accordingly.*'

'*We have made no changes in light of the stock market falls of late 2008, as we believe that maintaining a consistent, diversified asset allocation is the best way for us to ensure healthy investment returns over the medium to long-term. Although the falls in valuation will have an impact on our grant-making budgets for the next few years, we believe that staying with our current strategy and allocation is the best way forward.*'

'*To offset the effect of the economic downturn on the foundation's assets, the foundation will strive to maximise income through fundraising initiatives and keep costs as low as possible.*'

'*This has been a year of change for the foundation. We, like everyone else, have experienced a shift in the tectonic plates of the financial world. Whilst we were braced for a downturn, the ferocity, scale and unpredictability of events made for an unsettling and disturbing few months. In 2008 the total return achieved on our investment portfolio was -17.6% compared to +5.7% in 2007. This could have been much worse and the economic and financial outlook remains uncertain. However we remain committed to a long term perspective both in our investment choices and our grantmaking.*'

'*In the current economic climate it is important to say something about our spending. We are cautious of what may lie ahead for our investments but have taken a decision for the coming year to maintain spending plans. This is an issue we will need to keep reviewing, but as an independent foundation we believe we have a duty to continue to support organisations whose activities we believe can deliver change, especially as many other sources of funding are declining.*'

'*Despite the current difficulties in the financial markets, the trustees aim to continue to maintain annual income levels so far as is possible and to consider and support the widest range of charitable activity consistent with their objectives and their grant-making policy. They will continue to monitor the demand for existing programmes and to develop new programmes and schemes which will keep the level of commitments to resources in line with policy.*'

'*The change in value of the investment portfolio as a whole since the start of the new financial year has not been sufficiently material to warrant an adjustment to the spending plans approved by the board of governors [...]. Spending plans for the financial year 2009/10 and beyond will be reviewed, as has always been the case, during 2009.*'

So the message from grant-making trusts and foundations is that they are generally not overreacting, in the truest sense, to the economic downturn and its impact on their investments and income – their responses appear to be proportionate. Naturally, however, the severity of the impact of the recession and a trust's ability to maintain its levels of grantmaking depends on where it receives the majority of its income

from and how its activities are funded. For example, the Tudor Trust, whose assets fell by around £70 million in the year to 2008/09, was able to maintain its level of funding due to the fact that it does not have to protect its endowment in perpetuity, and that it can draw on its capital as well as its income if necessary to fund its grants programme. Compare this to the Lloyds TSB Foundation for Scotland, whose income comes from a share of the profits of Lloyds Banking Group (see page vii).

Most aim to take a long-term approach if possible, and are committed to their strategic objectives of helping some of the most disadvantaged members of society, which means that now is not the time to be cutting funding to the charities working on the ground.

A survey carried out by the Association of Charitable Foundations (ACF) in April 2009[2] would seem to back this up. ACF's report on its findings suggests that grant-making trusts and foundations were 'cautiously optimistic' about their long-term funding prospects, with most taking a long-term view of their investment portfolio. More prudent financial controls within the voluntary sector have meant that trusts and foundations may be in a better position to 'weather the storm'.

David Emerson, Chief Executive of the ACF, said of their findings: 'Some of the largest and the smallest foundations in the country are telling us that while not immune to the recession, for the most part it is business as usual, and things are looking brighter over the longer term.'[3]

When asked about their grantmaking in the future, the ACF found that out of the 95 grant-making trusts and foundations that responded to their survey:

- 43.2% will make fewer grants
- 13.6% will make the same number of grants but they will be of a lower value
- 34.1% will keep their current grant-making levels the same
- 20.5% will increase their level of grantmaking
- 11.4% will need to change the way they manage their investments
- 22.7% will need to change their grant-making criteria
- 31.8% don't anticipate a need to change their grantmaking.

These findings are broadly corroborated by a report carried out by Dr Diana Leat on behalf on the Charity Commission in the Spring of 2009[4], which surveyed 19 of the largest grant-making trusts in the UK (all of which are also featured in this book, including the Big Lottery Fund). The report focused on, amongst other issues, how they anticipated their grantmaking would be affected by the economic downturn. Out of the 19 trusts and foundations surveyed, 14 said that the economic downturn had had little or no effect on their grantmaking in 2009, while three stated that their levels of grantmaking had actually increased. Interestingly, however, almost all of them stated that they were being more cautious in their approach to their grantmaking.

For these reasons potential fundraisers have good cause to remain optimistic, at least in the short term. However, most trusts and foundations agree that the picture beyond 2010 remains uncertain, with many citing the inevitable cuts in future public spending[5] as being a significant factor in this uncertainty. The Charity Commission's report highlights that optimism or pessimism about the length of the economic downturn is a contributory factor in how grantmakers view their ability to at least maintain their levels of funding. However, all of the evidence does suggest that there is a will and a desire to try to minimise the impact of the recession on the charities and individuals that rely on their funding.

In conclusion, a further cause for optimism in the midst of all the doom and gloom is that new sources of charitable funding are appearing all the time. While some trusts have disappeared from this book for one reason or another, the 18 trusts new to this edition demonstrate that new money is still out there. It must be said, however, that the full impact of the recession on grant-making trusts may not begin to emerge until the next edition.

---

[2] Survey of Members, Association of Charitable Foundations, April 2009

[3] Press Release, Association of Charitable Foundations, June 2009 (http://www.acf.org.uk/news/archive/?id=&arc=1&eid=2096)

[4] Firm Foundations, Charity Commission, August 2009 (http://www.charitycommission.gov.uk/Library/publications/pdfs/foundationtext.pdf)

[5] £35.7 billion of departmental cuts required by 2013/14: Public Spending Briefing, Institute of Fiscal Studies, December 2009 (http://www.ifs.org.uk/budgets/pbr2009/public_spending.ppt)

Case Study: Lloyds TSB Foundation for Scotland

The 2009 recession had a significant impact across the voluntary sector and grant-making trusts and foundations, which have enjoyed a long period of economic growth, have had to adjust to the new economic reality. The impact has varied, leaving some in severe difficulties, while others have remained largely unscathed, but all have had to reassess their financial situations.

Undoubtedly, one of the headline stories – and the focus of this case study – has been the ongoing dispute between the Lloyds TSB Foundation for Scotland (the Foundation) and the Lloyds Banking Group (the Group), over the future funding of the Foundation.

The Group's current lack of profitability has warranted a need for short-term transitional arrangements to tide the Foundation over until the Group returns to the black. However, the Group appears to be using this as an opportunity to move the goalposts by cutting the covenanted percentage and imposing its own funding priorities, resulting in the current impasse and the danger that one of Scotland's leading charitable funders will be suspending its grantmaking indefinitely.

Background
There are four independent Lloyds TSB foundations covering England and Wales, Scotland, Northern Ireland and the Channel Islands. They were originally formed in 1985 as a condition of the Trustees Savings Bank becoming a public limited company.

The covenant, which sets out the financial arrangement between the foundations and the Lloyds Banking Group, states that the Group should distribute 1% of pre-tax profits (averaged over three years) between the four foundations, with the Foundation for Scotland receiving just under 20% of this amount. The Foundation's income is therefore dependent on the financial performance of the Group.

The Foundation has so far distributed around £85 million to charities across Scotland[6]. The vast majority of this funding follows the successful merger of Lloyds Bank and TSB in 1995.

However, unlike most traditional corporate foundations, the Lloyds TSB foundations have maintained their independence from each other and their parent bank. Like the others, the Foundation has its own independent chair and board of trustees and its grant-making policy is determined by them and not by the demands of the Group.

Impact of the recession
The banking crisis and ensuing recession, coupled with the ambitious takeover of HBOS, left Lloyds Banking Group making a reported loss of £4 billion.[7] This has put the Foundation in a difficult position due to a provision in the covenant which means that, in the event of making a loss, the Group is only obliged to pay a small amount (£200,000 split between the four foundations) instead of the usual 1%. This de minimis payment clause came into effect in 2009 and meant that the Foundation received £39,000 compared to the usual £5–6 million.

In an attempt to tide the foundations over until it returned to profit, the Group offered an interim funding package to all four foundations. At the end of 2009 the foundations for England and Wales, Northern Ireland and the Channel Islands agreed to a new settlement. This guaranteed them an increase in funding over the next four years, but meant their entitlement to the Group's pre-tax profits would halve in the long term from 1% to 0.5%.

The Foundation was offered the same deal, equating to £6 million in funding for 2010–2014. However, the conditions attached to the deal, including reducing the covenant amount to 0.5% of pre-tax profits (half the current 1%) and the representation of a Lloyds director on the trustee board, have greatly concerned the Scottish foundation.

The current position
After taking legal and financial advice the Foundation decided to reject the Group's offer and despite negotiations running throughout 2009, the stalemate between the Foundation and the Group remains unresolved.

The Foundation has argued that the deal will limit available funding in two ways:

Firstly, the proposed cut of 0.5% would halve the original covenant agreement. The Group has defended the move, saying that the merger of Lloyds TSB and HBOS has created a much larger organisation (Lloyds Banking Group), with potentially much higher profits. This means that the Foundation will simply be getting a 'smaller slice of a bigger pie' and should eventually receive more. However, there is no guarantee of future profitability and thus no guarantee that the Foundation and the communities it supports will be better off. In fact, the Foundation has estimated – based on figures provided by the Group – that the current proposal could mean it will lose out on £22 million over nine years.[8]

Secondly, following the merger, the Group wound up the HBOS Foundation. This foundation gave £8.3 million in 2007 in the UK, and so has left a significant funding gap in the sector.

The other key stalling point has been the fact that the financial offer has been tied to other conditions, which would almost certainly shift control of where much of the money is spent from the Foundation to the Group.

It is not unusual for traditional corporate foundations to be influenced by their parent organisation, but it would mark a significant departure from the status quo for the Lloyds TSB Foundations. All four foundations have always had control over their own grant-making policies, allowing them to react to local needs and to fund less popular causes. There can be no doubt that the reduction in the terms of the covenant would see a closer alignment to the fundraising activities of the Group's Scottish staff and its own corporate giving focus, leaving the Foundation controlling a fraction of the income previously available to it.

Mary Craig, Chief Executive of the Foundation, has described this as an unacceptable threat to independence, saying it will turn the Foundation into a 'marketing arm of the banking group'.[9]

In an attempt to find a compromise, the Foundation has made a counter-offer, suggesting that the Group should give the proposed interim funding as an advance on its profits – the idea being that this advance will be repaid by the Foundation when the Group returns

---

[6] A letter from Shane O'Riordain, Director of Communications for the Lloyds Banking Group to Scottish Council for Voluntary Organisations Chief Executive, Martin Sime, accessed 30/11/09 (http://www.scvo.org.uk/scvocms/images/Letter_from_Shane_ORiordain_to_Martin_Sime.pdf)

[7] Telegraph Online, 'Lloyds slumps to loss as bad debts soar to £13.4 billion' 05/08/09, accessed 10/12/09 (http://www.telegraph.co.uk/finance/newsbysector/banksandfinance/5975489/Lloyds-slumps-to-loss-as-bad-debts-soar-to-13.4bn.html)

[8] Lloyds TSB Foundation for Scotland website, Chief Executive's update 9 December 2009, accessed 10/12/09 (http://www.ltsbfoundationforscotland.org.uk/index.asp?lm=193&cookies=True)

[9] Matthew Little, 'Lloyds TSB Foundation for Scotland in row over funding and independence', Third Sector, 27/10/09

to profit, whilst leaving the Foundation's independence intact. However, the Group has rejected this proposal, saying that it would prefer to come to a mutual arrangement with all four foundations.

What does this mean for fundraisers?

In October 2009 Foundation stated that it would honour existing funding agreements, including multiyear awards. However, further grantmaking activities have been suspended for the foreseeable future.

The current impasse means that there are still four possible outcomes: consensus, unhappy agreement, status quo or termination.

Unfortunately the best result for Scottish charities – an agreement which secures the Foundation's income and independence – is looking increasingly unlikely. The fact that the other foundations have reached an agreement with the Group has left the Foundation in a difficult position, while strengthening the hand of the Group. As such, at the time of writing (December 2009), a consensus looked unlikely, despite the damage this may do to the voluntary sector and the Group's reputation in Scotland.

If the Foundation reluctantly agrees to the current proposal, including the reduction in the covenanted income, then a significant proportion of future grantmaking will be aligned to the Group's corporate giving criteria. At present the Foundation's main grant programmes are designed to address essential community needs and in particular to support small under-funded charities. It is unclear to what extent the proposed agreement will affect these funding priorities but it is likely to narrow the grant-making focus and limit the Foundation's ability to work with charities which are most in need. Equally, the desire to concentrate more on staff fundraising priorities, which often favour very large, popular charities, will also limit the level of funding available to a large number of organisations who might previously have been eligible to receive support from the Foundation.

Indeed, the Foundation believes that, taken alongside the Group's proposal to halve the covenanted percentage, it is likely to receive only around 30% of the money it would usually have to fund the grassroots charities which are central to its current grant-making programme.[10]

Failure to reach an agreement with the Group – in other words keeping the status quo – would leave the Foundation with an income of only £39,000 for 2010 and minimal income for the next few years, thus severely limiting its grant-making capacity.

In the event that no agreement can be reached and the Group decides to terminate the covenant, as it has threatened to do, the Foundation could still continue to operate. Any termination of the covenant would require nine years' notice so the Foundation would continue to receive its share of pre-tax profits for that period. After that, the limited voting shares that the Foundation currently holds would become ordinary shares and it would be entitled to an annual dividend like any other shareholder.

To prepare for either of the latter two scenarios, the Foundation has started looking at alternative funding sources: those that would allow it to continue its grant-making programmes until it reaches an agreement with the Group or the Group returns to profit and it can again receive funding through the covenant. The Foundation expects to have a clearer idea of the level of funding available in early 2010.

The outcome of these negotiations will obviously have serious implications for Scottish charities. If the Foundation fails to either reach an agreement with the Group or to raise its own money, a huge pot of funding will have been withdrawn at a time when the sector is already experiencing a significant decline in funding resources. The Scottish Council for Voluntary Organisations has valued this net loss to the Scottish sector at £4 million a year.

In spite of this, the Foundation has continued to receive significant support across the sector from those who believe there is a value in retaining its long-term independence and grant-making integrity.

Please note: The uncertainty surrounding the Foundation and the fact that it has suspended its grant-making programme means that there will be no entry for it in this edition of the guide. For the latest developments please visit the Lloyds TSB Foundation for Scotland's website – www.ltsbfoundationforscotland.org.uk.

*As this guide went to print in early 2010, it was announced that the Group will terminate its covenant with the Foundation following a nine year notice period. The Foundation will continue to operate and hopes to launch a new programme of grants in the second quarter of 2010 that will focus on smaller and harder to fund organisations. The Group will set up a new foundation, the Bank of Scotland Foundation, through which it will distribute grants in Scotland.

---

[10] Lloyds TSB Foundation for Scotland website, Chief Executive's update 9 December 2009, accessed 10/12/09 (http://www.ltsbfoundationfor scotland.org.uk/index.asp?lm=193)

DSC policy and campaigning

Over the years DSC has campaigned on a number of fronts for better grantmaking. We believe that funders have a responsibility that extends far beyond providing funding. The way funders operate and develop their programmes has a huge impact on the organisations, causes and beneficiaries which their funding supports, as well as on the wider voluntary sector. Transparency is a key principle for us: by providing information about funders in this book and other DSC publications we have sought to open up their practices to greater scrutiny. Clearer and more accessible information enables fundraisers to focus their efforts effectively, and encourages open review and discussions of good practice. Our Great Giving campaign has grown out of these long-established beliefs.

We have identified some specific campaigning areas that we wish to focus on as part of an overall campaign for better grantmaking.

1) A clear picture of the funding environment

We think that to enable better planning and decision making from funders and policymakers, more comprehensive information is needed about where money is going and what it supports. Many of the funders in this book are leading the way, although some fall short in terms of the level of detail they provide about their activities and effectiveness.

2) Accessible funding for campaigning

Financial support for campaigning is vital to the role organisations play in achieving social change. Greater clarity from grant-making trusts is needed so that campaigning organisations can find the support they need more easily.

3) An end to hidden small print

DSC is asking all funders to provide the terms and conditions which govern the use of the funds at the outset when people apply and to be open to negotiating terms when applicants request it.

4) No ineligible applications

We know that most funders receive applications that do not fall within the funder's guidelines. Clearer guidelines can help, but applicants also need to take more heed of funder guidelines and target their applications appropriately.

DSC has always believed that clear and open application and monitoring processes are essential for both funders and fundraisers to produce more effective applications and better eventual outcomes. The availability of such information has come a long way since the first edition of this guide. However, an important element of the funding process often remains hidden from wider scrutiny.

The detailed terms and conditions which set out what the applicant is required to do to obtain and retain the grant are too often unavailable until the point at which a formal offer of a grant is made. For an applicant, seeing these terms and conditions for the first time only when there is an offer of money on the table is not helpful. Even if negotiating the conditions is an option, the balance of power is still squarely with the funder. If the funder is not willing to negotiate, the applicant is faced with a difficult decision: should any conditions conflict with their organisation's values or the wider needs of their beneficiaries, they then face a dubious choice between accepting conditions which may threaten their independence, and turning down much needed funding.

We surveyed the largest charitable, corporate and government funders to find out more about the availability and accessibility of their terms and conditions, which culminated in a research report, *Critical Conditions*.[11] This research found that many trusts and foundations were demonstrating what we consider good practice – 72% of those that responded said they made their terms and conditions publicly available, and there were a number of good examples. However, nearly half of trusts that responded stated that their terms were non-negotiable, a stance we consider not in the best interests of funders or applicants. Overall these findings compared favourably to the central government funders that responded. By comparison these funders appeared to be less transparent and more averse to negotiating by comparison. They also tended to have more complicated and lengthy terms.

However, in late 2009 DSC asked similar questions of a much larger sample of trusts and foundations, and the results paint a different picture. In this research only half of respondents said their terms and conditions were publicly available, and a solid majority said they were non-negotiable. The rate of those which said their terms were not publicly available at all was three times greater than in the *Critical Conditions* survey. Some of the variation is accounted for by the fact that the larger sample contained a far greater number of smaller trusts and foundations that do not have any terms and conditions at all (49% of respondents to this survey said they had terms and conditions, compared with 86% in the *Critical Conditions* report). Nevertheless, this further research broadly suggests that there is room for improvement from trusts as regards the transparency of their funding terms and conditions.

Some may argue that providing more information at the beginning of the application process could make things more time consuming and costly, but DSC believes the benefits of greater transparency should take precedence. It is crucial that fundraisers have access to all the information they need to make an informed decision about whether to apply. It is also vital that such information is publicly available so that funders and others can make comparisons and share good practice. Further, in this age of digital communication, there is an ever-increasing expectation that all the relevant information, guidance and application forms will be available online. A link to a web page or a short document outlining the detailed terms and explaining their place in the application process is easy to provide and need not cost anything. Clear instructions should be provided for the fundraiser about the importance of the terms and conditions, why they are necessary and what they mean, along with exhortations to read them thoroughly.

Again the onus is not entirely on the funder – fundraisers have a responsibility to inform themselves as fully as possible and to ask for relevant information if it isn't available or is not clearly presented by the funder. Reading and evaluating the criteria, guidance and detailed terms and conditions is part of making a well-targeted application which is more likely to be successful. More crucially it is about protecting the organisation's independence and building funding relationships that will work well for both parties. The fundraiser, therefore, has an important role to play in scrutinising the conditions of the funding arrangement at the outset, and communicating their views to other decision-makers in the organisation (see www.dsc.org.uk for more advice on terms and conditions for fundraisers).

---

[11] *Critical Conditions*, Directory of Social Change, 2009 (http://www.dsc.org.uk/NewsandInformation/PolicyandCampaigning#cmOW)

Frequently asked questions

How do you get your information?

In general we use the copy of the report and accounts on the public file at the Charity Commission. We then write a draft entry and send it to the trust via email, where possible, inviting suggested additions as well as corrections or comments. New information provided by the trust, and not generally available, is usually put in the form 'The trust notes that... '. In cases where the trust or foundation has a website containing full information on its activities, including downloadable annual reports and accounts, this is the first port of call. In many cases the amount of information available on a trust's website is comprehensive, including guidelines for applicants and detailed information on current programmes, and this information is used extensively throughout this book. The draft entry is then sent to them in the usual way.

Do you print everything the trusts say?

Generally yes, but there are two kinds of exceptions. First, if what the trust says is purely formal and could be said equally of most of the other trusts in this book, we do not feel it needs repeating. Second, some trusts, such as the Lloyds TSB foundations or the Esmée Fairbairn Foundation, now produce literature on such a scale that it has become impossible to reprint it all. Provided it is available there, we often refer to the availability of further material on the trust's website. This is particularly the case where guidelines are under review and liable to change soon after the publication of this book.

Do you investigate further when the information from a trust is inadequate?

No, we just report the fact that it is inadequate. We also try to ignore hearsay and anecdote, whether positive or negative.

What is your policy on telephone numbers?

When we know the telephone number we will normally print it, and will do so even if a trust doesn't want us to (provided it is an office rather than a private number). Where a trust has said that it does not wish to receive telephone calls from potential applicants, or to have its number listed, this is noted in the text of the entry. However, when the available telephone number is simply the head office of a big professional firm that acts as a post box for the trustees, we generally leave it out.

Do you edit the 'applications' information?

No and yes. The content of this section generally comes from the trust if they have a specific document regarding making applications, and we will reproduce whatever they have available. However we sometimes edit it to achieve a reasonable level of consistent presentation from one entry to another. If there is no specific application document available we collate information from annual reports, accounts and websites.

Why do you leave out the letters after trustees' names?

There are so many of them, and we try to present the entries in as simple and straightforward a way as we can. Besides, where do you draw the line? At Captain the Honourable A Anthony, DSO? Or going on to MBE, D Phil, AMCEEE and so on? The additional information might be helpful in identifying one A Anthony from another. However, we do see more and more trusts using simpler systems themselves: Arthur Anthony being more often happy nowadays to appear as such. Nevertheless, we do list titles – Lord, Lady, Dr, Professor and so on.

We are also sparing with capital letters. We use this minimalist style in the interests of clarity and correct editorial rules, but it does annoy some trusts, which go to considerable effort to try to change our usage back to what they see as proper. But reading about Trust after Foundation after Guideline after Application Form can get tiring.

Why don't the figures in the entries always add up?

There are a number of reasons.

- Unclear distinctions between grant commitments and grant payments.
- The fact that grants' lists and totals are often created by trusts quite separately from their audited figures.

- The fact that values for returned grants are included in some totals and not in others.
- The existence of small undisclosed grants: if the discrepancies are large, we go to some effort to clarify the situation. Where they are small, the figures are normally for illustration rather than being the basis for further calculation. If resources were spent on seeking perfect numerical consistency, they would have to be taken from the more useful task of trying to find out and reflect clearly what the trust is doing.
- Grant figures given in the entries are rounded up or down, which sometimes means that there may be a slight discrepancy between figures given individually and sum totals given elsewhere.

What's in a name? Trusts, foundations, funds, charities, settlements, companies, appeals: are they all the same?

The book covers organisations, usually charitable, that give grants to other charities. They may use almost any name; we judge them by what they do rather than what they are called.

Which trusts are in this book?

Roughly, all those that give, or could give £300,000 or more in grants. Smaller trusts are covered in Volume 2 of this book as well as in the local and specialised grant guides also published by DSC.

Why are some grant-making charities omitted?

This book does not generally seek to cover the following grant-making charities.

- **Company trusts** – if they are operated by company staff on company premises, we will usually regard this as a channel for giving by the company, to be reported in our *Guide to UK Company Giving* and on our www.companygiving.org.uk subscription website.
- **Specialised grantmakers** – those that operate in a narrow field where they are likely to be well known and accessible to most applicants. Examples include trusts only funding research on specific medical conditions (these are generally accessible through the excellent website of the Association of Medical Research Charities, www.amrc.org.uk) or only supporting projects designed by themselves.
- **Trusts or charities only making grants for work overseas** – these are covered in the *International Development Directory* or *The Major Charities* (also published by DSC). Many of these organisations, such as Oxfam or Christian Aid, operate on a large scale.
- **Statutory funders, awarding public money** – these sources are covered in our *Government Funding Guide* and on our www.governmentfunding.org.uk subscription website.

What about lottery grants?

We have difficulties about deciding what we should include and have to make compromises. We include the Big Lottery Fund and Awards for All, but we do not cover the arts councils, the sports councils or the Heritage Lottery Fund. Although all Lottery grants are part of public expenditure, subject to review by the National Audit Office and the Public Accounts Committee of the House of Commons, in many ways the Big Lottery Fund looks and acts like a grant-making trust, and a particularly big and interesting one at that.

... and community foundations?

Local community foundations are a rapidly developing part of the voluntary sector. Originally the idea was that they would build up endowments which would enable them to become important local grantmakers. They are still doing this, but only a few have generated enough income from their endowments to earn them a place in this book. However, most of them have also developed two new streams of income. Firstly, they have become a vehicle through which local philanthropists make their donations, usually using a named subsidiary fund. But this is still on a modest scale in most cases. Secondly and more importantly, they have become the vehicles for distributing government money, particularly the Local Network Fund for Children and Young People but also for a range of other local government funding initiatives. We have included brief entries for those giving grants of £300,000 or more, even when most of this is coming from statutory sources. Contact details for all community foundations registered with the Community Foundation Network can be found at the back of this book (see page 407).

How to use this guide

The trusts are listed alphabetically and the indexes are at the back of the book. As well as an alphabetical index, there are subject and geographical indexes which will help you to identify the trusts working in your field and area.

At the front of the book (from page xvi) we have ranked the trusts by the amount of money they give. This list also shows their main areas of interest. If you are looking for grants for your charity, we recommend that you start with this listing and select those trusts which might be relevant – starting with the biggest.

When you have chosen enough to be getting on with, read each trust entry carefully before deciding to apply. Very often a trust's interest in your field will be limited and precise, and may demand an application specifically tailored to its requirements or often no application at all as they may not currently be accepting applications.

Remember to cover all parts of the guide: do not just start at the beginning of the alphabet. It is surprising, but still true, that trusts near the end of the alphabet receive fewer applications.

It is particularly important to show awareness of all the information available from the trust, to acquire up-to-date guidelines where possible, and to target your applications with respect to each trust's published wishes where such information exists.

Inappropriate and ill-considered approaches, especially those that show you have not read the published guidelines, antagonise trusts and damage your organisation's reputation. Of course, many trusts publish nothing useful. If this is the case, unfortunately you are on your own.

We have included a chart to help with the timings of your applications (see page xiii). It shows, for over 100 trusts, the months when trustee meetings are usually held, or when applications need to be submitted.

For those new to raising money from trusts, the box overleaf is recommended as a starting point.

Classification

Serious applicants who will be fundraising from trusts in the long term do best, we believe, if they go to the most promising entries in this book and try to establish specific links between what the trust seems to be interested in and what their organisation is trying to do. The indexes and summary headings in this book are not likely to be enough on their own to identify the trusts that are most likely to have matching interests with a particular charity.

Notes on the entries

The entry headings

Grant total and financial year
The most up-to-date information available is given here. In a few cases the grants commentary in the main text is for the preceding year, as this information for the most recent year was unavailable or it was supplied at the last minute and was too late for inclusion in this guide. Sometimes the information received on a particular trust dates from two different years. For example, most of the entry may contain information from the latest published annual report, but may also include very recent information gained from consultations directly with the trust or taken from its website.

The main areas of funding
These categories have been chosen by the editors from an analysis of the trusts' funding. They are indicative rather than definitive, and useful in a preliminary trawl through the guide. They are no substitute for a close reading of each entry.

The correspondent
This is the lead person. Sometimes this is a solicitor or an accountant handling trust affairs solely on a 'postbox' basis. Other useful administrative contacts may also be given in the 'applications' section, or within the main body of text.

Beneficial area
This is the area or areas – when this is restricted – within which the trust operates, either legally or as a matter of policy or practice. When a trust with a UK-wide remit shows an interest in a particular locality, this is noted. While the information usually comes from the trust itself, it may also arise from a pattern of grantmaking seen by the editors. Where this heading does not appear, the area of benefit is unrestricted.

Information available
This section notes the information available directly from the trust. If there is a website, this is usually the best starting point for information.

The main body of the entry
A summary of the trust's grantmaking usually prefaces the text. Trusts' policy notes and guidelines for applicants, where these exist, are normally reprinted in full. However, there are a few instances in which these are so lengthy that some abridgement has had to be undertaken. More trusts now analyse their own funding in their annual reports and, where available, this material will also usually be quoted in full. Some analysis has also been carried out by the editors based on grants lists accompanying the accounts.

Exclusions and applications sections
These reproduce, where possible, the trust's own information or comments, though edited to suit the format of this book.

It would be useful to mention here why we include trusts and foundations which do not wish to receive unsolicited applications. These are included partly because this book is a survey of the grantmaking of the largest trusts and also to try and save the time and resources of organisations that may otherwise apply for funding in vain.

How to apply to a trust

Although there are complete books on this (for example *The Complete Fundraising Handbook* and *Writing Better Fundraising Applications*, both published by the Directory of Social Change), there is no need to be daunted by the challenge of making effective applications. If your charity's work is good – and of a kind supported by the trust in question – a very simple letter (of one uncrowded page or less, and backed by a clear annual report and set of accounts) will probably do 90% of everything that can be done.

If there is an application form and detailed applications requirements, just follow them. However, because these sorts of trusts make the process easier, they tend to get a lot of applications. You may have even better chances with the others.

1) Select the right trusts to approach
If they fund organisations or work like yours, and if you genuinely fit within any guidelines they publish, put them on your list.

2) Ring them
If the entry makes this sound sensible, ring them to check that the guidelines in this guide still apply and that the kind of application you are considering is appropriate for them.

3) Send in an application
Unless the trust has an application form (many do not), we suggest that the main part of this should be a letter that fits easily on one side of a sheet of paper (back-up materials such as a formal 'proposal' may be necessary for a big or complex project, but are usually, in our view, secondary). We suggest that the letter contains the following points.

- A summary sentence such as: 'Can your trust give us £10,000 to develop a training programme for our volunteers?'
- The problem the work will address: This should normally be the beneficiaries' problem, not your charity's problem: 'Mothers of children with learning disabilities in our area get very little help from the statutory services in coping with their children's day-to-day needs.'
- What you are going to do about this: 'Our volunteers, who have been in the same situations themselves, support and help them, but the volunteers need and want better training, especially on home safety.'
- Details of the work: 'We want to commission an expert from our sister charity Home-Start to develop and test suitable training materials that we will be able to use.'
- Information about your charity: 'We attach one of our general leaflets explaining what we do, and a copy of our latest annual report and accounts.'
- Repeat the request: 'We would be very grateful if your trust can give us this grant.'

And that is all. Keep the style simple and informal. Where you can, handwrite the date, salutation and signature. A charity is not a business and does not impress by trying to sound like one. The best letter comes from a person involved in the proposed activity.

Making the letter longer will often reduce rather than increase its impact, but attaching compelling material is fine. You are not saying they have to read it through. A letter of endorsement might also be nice: your local bishop saying your work is wonderful, for example.

Appearance matters. It is a great help if you have a good quality letterhead on something better than photocopy paper, and if your report and accounts and literature are of appropriately high quality for your kind of organisation. However, you don't want to give the impression that your charity spends unnecessary money on expensive materials rather than on carrying out its work.

Good luck.

Finally . . .

The research for this book has been conducted as carefully as possible. Many thanks to those who have made this easier, especially the trusts themselves through their websites, their trust officers who provided additional information and the trustees and others who have helped us. Also thanks to the Charity Commission for making the annual reports and accounts available online.

We are aware that some of this information may be incomplete or will become out of date. We are equally sure we will have missed some relevant charities. We apologise for these imperfections. If you come across any omissions or mistakes, or if you have any suggestions for future editions of this book, do let us know. We can be contacted at the Liverpool Office Research Department of the Directory of Social Change either by phone on 0151 708 0136 or by email: research@dsc.org.uk

Dates for your diary

X = the usual month of trustees' or grant allocation meetings, or the last month for the receipt of applications.

Please note that these dates are provisional, and that the fact of an application being received does not necessarily mean that it will be considered at the next meeting.

	Jan	Feb	Mar	Apr	May	Jun	Jul	Aug	Sep	Oct	Nov	Dec
The 29th May 1961 Charitable Trust		X			X			X			X	
The H B Allen Charitable Trust		X										
The Architectural Heritage Fund			X			X			X			X
BBC Children in Need	X			X			X			X		
The Bedford Charity (The Harpur Trust)			X				X					X
Percy Bilton Charity			X			X			X			X
The Bluston Charitable Settlement			X									
The Bromley Trust				X						X		
The Clara E Burgess Charity	X						X					
The William A Cadbury Charitable Trust					X						X	
Sir John Cass's Foundation			X			X				X		
CfBT Education Trust			X				X		X			X
The Childwick Trust					X							X
CHK Charities Limited			X							X		
Church Burgesses Trust	X			X			X			X		
The Church Urban Fund			X			X			X			X
The City Parochial Foundation			X			X				X		
Richard Cloudesley's Charity				X							X	
The Colt Foundation			X							X		
Colyer-Fergusson Charitable Trust			X							X		
The Ernest Cook Trust				X						X		
The D'Oyly Carte Charitable Trust			X				X				X	
The Daiwa Anglo-Japanese Foundation			X						X			
Baron Davenport's Charity			X						X			
Peter De Haan Charitable Trust			X			X			X			X
The Drapers' Charitable Fund	X			X			X			X		
The Dulverton Trust		X			X		X			X		
The Dunhill Medical Trust	X			X		X				X		
The Englefield Charitable Trust			X						X			
The Equitable Charitable Trust	X	X	X	X	X	X	X	X	X	X	X	X
The Eranda Foundation			X				X				X	
Essex Community Foundation	X								X			
The Eveson Charitable Trust	X		X			X				X		
Allan and Nesta Ferguson Charitable Settlement		X							X			
The Sir John Fisher Foundation					X						X	
The Fishmongers' Company's Charitable Trust			X			X					X	
The Donald Forrester Trust					X						X	
Four Acre Trust		X		X		X		X		X		X
The Foyle Foundation												
The Hugh Fraser Foundation	X			X			X			X		
The Joseph Strong Frazer Trust			X						X			
The Gannochy Trust	X	X	X	X	X	X	X	X	X	X	X	X

	Jan	Feb	Mar	Apr	May	Jun	Jul	Aug	Sep	Oct	Nov	Dec
J Paul Getty Jr Charitable Trust				X			X		X			X
Simon Gibson Charitable Trust			X									
The G C Gibson Charitable Trust											X	
The Girdlers' Company Charitable Trust	X						X					
The Goldsmiths' Company Charity	X	X	X	X	X	X	X			X	X	X
The Great Britain Sasakawa Foundation		X			X					X		
The Grocers' Charity	X			X		X					X	
The Gulbenkian Foundation			X				X				X	
The Kathleen Hannay Memorial Charity		X										
The Charles Hayward Foundation	X			X			X			X		
The Heart of England Community Foundation	X		X		X		X		X		X	
The Hedley Foundation	X		X		X		X		X		X	
Help the Aged			X			X			X			
Lady Hind Trust			X				X				X	
Sir Harold Hood's Charitable Trust											X	
The Albert Hunt Trust			X				X				X	
Isle of Dogs Community Foundation	X		X		X		X		X		X	
John James Bristol Foundation		X			X			X			X	
Jewish Child's Day				X			X					X
The Anton Jurgens Charitable Trust						X				X		
The Kay Kendall Leukaemia Fund					X					X		
Ernest Kleinwort Charitable Trust			X							X		
Lloyds TSB Foundation for Northern Ireland	X			X			X			X		
The London Marathon Charitable Trust								X				
John Lyon's Charity			X			X					X	
The R S Macdonald Charitable Trust			X						X			
The Mackintosh Foundation					X					X		
The MacRobert Trust			X							X		
The Manifold Charitable Trust	X	X	X	X	X	X	X	X	X	X	X	X
Marshall's Charity	X			X			X			X		
The Henry Moore Foundation	X			X			X			X		
The J P Morgan Foundations			X			X			X			X
The Frances and Augustus Newman Foundation						X						X
The Ofenheim Charitable Trust			X									
The P F Charitable Trust	X	X	X	X	X	X	X	X	X	X	X	X
The Parthenon Trust	X											
The Dowager Countess Eleanor Peel Trust		X				X				X		
The Pilgrim Trust	X			X			X			X		
Polden-Puckham Charitable Foundation				X						X	X	
The Rank Foundation			X			X			X			X
The Joseph Rank Trust		X			X			X			X	
The Sir James Reckitt Charity					X					X		
The Robertson Trust	X		X		X		X		X		X	
Joseph Rowntree Reform Trust Limited			X				X			X		X
The Saddlers' Company Charitable Fund	X						X					
The Francis C Scott Charitable Trust			X				X				X	
Seafarers UK (King George's Fund for Sailors)							X				X	
The Archie Sherman Charitable Trust	X	X	X	X	X	X	X		X	X	X	
The Henry Smith Charity			X			X			X			X
Sparks Charity (Sport Aiding Medical Research For Kids)			X							X		
The Spring Harvest Charitable Trust											X	
St James's Place Foundation							X					X
The Steel Charitable Trust		X			X			X			X	
The Sir Halley Stewart Trust		X				X				X		

	Jan	Feb	Mar	Apr	May	Jun	Jul	Aug	Sep	Oct	Nov	Dec
Stratford upon Avon Town Trust		X					X			X		
The Sir Jules Thorn Charitable Trust											X	
The Tolkien Trust				X								
Trust for London		X			X					X		
The Trusthouse Charitable Foundation		X			X		X				X	
The Douglas Turner Trust		X			X			X				X
The Will Charitable Trust	X							X				
The Harold Hyam Wingate Foundation	X			X			X			X		
The Wixamtree Trust	X			X			X			X		
The Woodward Charitable Trust	X						X					

The major trusts ranked by grant total

Trust	Grants	Main grant areas
☐ The Wellcome Trust	£598.5 million	Biomedical research, history of medicine, biomedical ethics, public engagement with science
☐ The Big Lottery Fund	£558 million	Community, young people, welfare
☐ The Football Foundation	£82.1 million	Grassroots football, community, education
☐ Awards for All	£61.4 million	General
☐ The Garfield Weston Foundation	£55 million	General
☐ The Leverhulme Trust	£48.5 million	Scholarships for education and research
☐ The Gatsby Charitable Foundation	£40.9 million	General
☐ The Wolfson Foundation	£39.2 million	Medical and scientific research, education, health and welfare, heritage, arts
☐ BBC Children in Need	£36.8 million	Welfare of disadvantaged children
☐ The Henry Smith Charity	£26.7 million	Social welfare, older people, disability, health, medical research
☐ Lloyds TSB Foundation for England and Wales	£23.7 million	Social and community needs
☐ The Prince's Charities Foundation	£21.9 million	Culture, the environment, medical welfare, education, children and young people and overseas aid
☐ Esmée Fairbairn Foundation	£21.5 million	Social welfare, education, environment, arts and heritage
☐ Wales Council for Voluntary Action	£21 million	Local community, volunteering, social welfare, environment, regeneration
☐ Arcadia	£18.4 million	The preservation of the environment, heritage and culture
☐ The Tudor Trust	£17.8 million	Welfare, general
☐ The Sigrid Rausing Trust	£17 million	Human, women's and minority rights and social and environmental justice
☐ The Monument Trust	£16.3 million	Arts, health and welfare (especially AIDS), environment, general
☐ The City Bridge Trust	£15.5 million	Social welfare in Greater London
☐ The Jack Petchey Foundation	£14.5 million	Young people aged 11–25 in the London boroughs, Essex and the Algarve, Portugal
☐ Paul Hamlyn Foundation	£13.4 million	Arts, education and learning in the UK and local organisations supporting vulnerable groups of people, especially children, in India, social justice
☐ Comic Relief	£12 million	Social welfare
☐ The Shetland Charitable Trust	£11.7 million	Social welfare; art and recreation; environment and amenity
☐ The City Parochial Foundation	£11.5 million	Social welfare
☐ The Coalfields Regeneration Trust	£11.5 million	General, health, welfare, community regeneration, education, young people, older people
☐ The Northern Rock Foundation	£10.5 million	Disadvantaged people
☐ The Wolfson Family Charitable Trust	£10 million	Jewish charities
☐ The Robertson Trust	£9.9 million	General
☐ The Maurice Wohl Charitable Foundation	£9.8 million	Jewish, health and welfare
☐ The Hunter Foundation	£8 million	Education, young people, children, relief of poverty, community development
☐ The Souter Charitable Trust	£8 million.	Christian evangelism, welfare
☐ Mayfair Charities Ltd	£7.8 million	Orthodox Judaism
☐ The Rank Foundation	£7.4 million	Christian communication, young people, education, general
☐ The Tubney Charitable Trust	£7.4 million	Conservation of the natural environment, welfare of farmed animals
☐ Community Foundation Serving Tyne and Wear and Northumberland	£7 million	Social welfare, general

☐ **The Nuffield Foundation**	**£6.8 million**	Education, child protection, law and justice, older people, and capacity development
☐ **The Charles Wolfson Charitable Trust**	**£6.8 million**	Medical research, education and welfare
☐ **Keren Association**	**£6.5 million**	Jewish, education, general
☐ **Allchurches Trust Ltd**	**£6.3 million**	Churches, general
☐ **The Stewards' Company Limited**	**£6.1 million**	Christian evangelism, general

☐ **The National Art Collections Fund**	**£6 million**	Acquisition of works of art by museums and galleries
☐ **The Joseph Rowntree Charitable Trust**	**£5.9 million**	Peace, democracy, racial justice, social justice, corporate responsibility, Quaker issues
☐ **The Eranda Foundation**	**£5.7 million**	Research into education and medicine, the arts, social welfare
☐ **The Linbury Trust**	**£5.5 million**	Arts, heritage, social welfare, humanitarian aid, general
☐ **The LankellyChase Foundation**	**£5.4 million**	Social welfare, community development, arts, heritage, penal affairs, mental health, prevention of abuse
☐ **The Foyle Foundation**	**£5.1 million**	Arts and learning
☐ **The Clothworkers' Foundation**	**£5 million**	General charitable purposes, in particular social inclusion, young people, older people, disability, visual impairment and textiles
☐ **Help the Aged**	**£5 million**	Welfare, for older people
☐ **The Mercers' Charitable Foundation**	**£5 million**	General welfare, older people, conservation, arts, Christian faith activities, educational institutions
☐ **The Rufford Maurice Laing Foundation**	**£5 million**	Nature conservation, sustainable development, environment, general

☐ **John Lyon's Charity**	**£4.9 million**	Children and young people in north and west London
☐ **The John Armitage Charitable Trust**	**£4.6 million**	Medical, relief in need, education, religion
☐ **Euro Charity Trust**	**£4.4 million**	Relief of poverty, education
☐ **The Fidelity UK Foundation**	**£4.4 million**	General, primarily in the fields of arts and culture, community development, education and health
☐ **The Hintze Family Charitable Foundation**	**£4.4 million**	Education; Christian churches; museums, libraries and galleries
☐ **The Clore Duffield Foundation**	**£4.3 million**	Arts/museums, Jewish charities, education, older and disadvantaged people
☐ **The Community Foundation for Greater Manchester**	**£4.3 million**	General
☐ **The John Ellerman Foundation**	**£4.3 million**	National UK charities supporting health, disability, social welfare, arts and conservation and overseas projects
☐ **The Waterloo Foundation**	**£4.3 million**	Children, the environment, developing countries and projects in Wales
☐ **The Lancaster Foundation**	**£4.2 million**	Christian causes

☐ **AW Charitable Trust**	**£4.1 million**	Jewish causes through educational and religious organisations; general charitable purposes
☐ **The Baily Thomas Charitable Fund**	**£4.1 million**	Learning disability
☐ **The Helen Hamlyn Trust**	**£4.1 million**	Medical, the arts and culture, education and welfare, heritage and conservation in India, international humanitarian affairs and 'healthy ageing'
☐ **The Parthenon Trust**	**£4 million**	International aid, medical research, assistance to the disadvantaged including people with disabilities, culture and heritage, medical treatment and care, education, promotion of civil society and research on current affairs
☐ **The Peter Cruddas Foundation**	**£3.9 million**	Children and young people
☐ **The Freemasons' Grand Charity**	**£3.9 million**	Social welfare, medical research, hospices and overseas emergency aid
☐ **The Diana, Princess of Wales Memorial Fund**	**£3.8 million**	Humanitarian causes Refugees and asylum seekers and penal affairs in the UK Post conflict and palliative care overseas
☐ **The 29th May 1961 Charitable Trust**	**£3.7 million**	Social welfare, general
☐ **The Birmingham Community Foundation**	**£3.7 million**	General
☐ **The Volant Charitable Trust**	**£3.7 million**	General

☐ **Allan and Nesta Ferguson Charitable Settlement**	**£3.6 million**	Peace, education, overseas development
☐ **The Helping Foundation**	**£3.6 million**	Orthodox Jewish
☐ **The Peter Moores Foundation**	**£3.6 million**	The arts, particularly opera, social welfare

☐ Action Medical Research	£3.5 million	Medical research, focusing on child health
☐ Community Foundation for Merseyside	£3.5 million	Community development, regeneration, general
☐ The Joseph Rowntree Foundation	£3.5 million	Research and development in social policy and practice
☐ UnLtd (Foundation for Social Entrepreneurs)	£3.5 million	Social enterprise
☐ Royal British Legion	£3.4 million	Armed services
☐ The Community Foundation for Northern Ireland	£3.3 million	Community, peace building, social exclusion, poverty and social injustice
☐ The Sutton Trust	£3.3 million	Education
☐ Rachel Charitable Trust	£3.2 million	General charitable purposes, in practice mainly Jewish organisations
☐ The M and R Gross Charities Limited	£3.1 million	Jewish causes
☐ Shlomo Memorial Fund Limited	£3.1 million	Jewish causes
☐ The Dulverton Trust	£3 million	Young people and education, conservation, welfare, general
☐ The Dunhill Medical Trust	£3 million	Medical research, older people
☐ J Paul Getty Jr Charitable Trust	£3 million	Social welfare, arts, conservation and the environment
☐ The Goldsmiths' Company Charity	£3 million	General, London charities, the precious metals craft
☐ The Lancaster-Taylor Charitable Trust	£3 million	Educational excellence
☐ The Roddick Foundation	£3 million	Arts, education, environmental, human rights, humanitarian, medical, poverty, social justice
☐ The Wates Foundation	£3 million	Assisting organisations in improving the quality of life of the deprived, disadvantaged and excluded in the community
☐ The Baring Foundation	£2.9 million	Strengthening the voluntary sector, arts and international development
☐ The Sir Jules Thorn Charitable Trust	£2.9 million	Medical research, medicine, small grants for humanitarian charities
☐ The Vardy Foundation	£2.8 million	Christian causes, education in the north east of England, general
☐ The Childwick Trust	£2.8 million	Health, people with disabilities and older people, welfare and research in connection with the bloodstock industry and Jewish charities in the UK; education in South Africa
☐ The Kirby Laing Foundation	£2.8 million	Health, welfare, Christian religion, young people, general
☐ Quartet Community Foundation	£2.8 million	General
☐ S F Foundation	£2.8 million	Jewish causes
☐ Capital Community Foundation	£2.7 million	Community activities
☐ Hobson Charity Limited	£2.7 million	Social welfare, education
☐ The Scottish Community Foundation	£2.7 million	Community development, general
☐ The Sobell Foundation	£2.7 million	Jewish charities, medical care and treatment, education, community, environment, disability, older people and young people
☐ St James's Place Foundation	£2.7 million	Children and young people with special needs, hospices
☐ The South Yorkshire Community Foundation	£2.7 million	General
☐ Clydpride Ltd	£2.6 million	Relief of poverty, Jewish charities, general charitable purposes
☐ Peter De Haan Charitable Trust	£2.6 million	Social welfare, the environment, the arts
☐ Investream Charitable Trust	£2.6 million	Jewish causes
☐ The P F Charitable Trust	£2.6 million	General
☐ Seafarers UK (King George's Fund for Sailors)	£2.55 million	The welfare of seafarers
☐ The Army Benevolent Fund	£2.5 million	Service charities
☐ The James Dyson Foundation	£2.5 million	Science, engineering, medicine and education
☐ The Eveson Charitable Trust	£2.5 million	People with physical disabilities
☐ GrantScape	£2.5 million	Environmental and community-based projects
☐ The True Colours Trust	£2.5 million	Special needs, sensory disabilities and impairments, palliative care, carers
☐ The Alice Trust	£2.4 million	Conservation and education
☐ The Barrow Cadbury Trust and the Barrow Cadbury Fund	£2.4 million	Young adult and criminal justice, migration and poverty and exclusion
☐ The DM Charitable Trust	£2.4 million	General

☐ **The Lord's Taverners**	**£2.4 million**	Youth cricket, minibuses for organisations supporting young people with disabilities and sports and recreational equipment for young people with special needs
☐ **The Samuel Sebba Charitable Trust**	**£2.4 million**	General, covering a wide range of charitable purposes with a preference for Jewish organisations
☐ **The Bernard Sunley Charitable Foundation**	**£2.4 million**	General
☐ **David and Frederick Barclay Foundation**	**£2.3 million**	Medical research, young people, older people, advancement of religion, people with disabilities, the sick and the disadvantaged
☐ **CHK Charities Limited**	**£2.3 million**	General
☐ **Four Acre Trust**	**£2.3 million**	Youth work, respite breaks, mentoring schemes and health related work overseas
☐ **The Hadley Trust**	**£2.3 million**	Social welfare
☐ **The Jerusalem Trust**	**£2.3 million**	Promotion of Christianity
☐ **Sparks Charity (Sport Aiding Medical Research For Kids)**	**£2.3 million**	Medical research
☐ **The Variety Club Children's Charity**	**£2.3 million**	Children's charities
☐ **The February Foundation**	**£2.25 million**	Education, heritage, community-based charities, environment, animals, medical/welfare
☐ **The Headley Trust**	**£2.2 million**	Arts, heritage, welfare, overseas development
☐ **Maurice and Hilda Laing Charitable Trust**	**£2.2 million**	Promotion of Christianity, relief of need
☐ **The Joseph Rank Trust**	**£2.2 million**	The Methodist Church, Christian-based social work
☐ **The Michael Uren Foundation**	**£2.2 million**	General
☐ **The Peter Harrison Foundation**	**£2.1 million**	Sports for people in the UK who have disabilities or are disadvantaged; support for children and young people in the south east of England who are terminally ill, have disabilities, or are disadvantaged; and educational initiatives for children, primarily in the south east of England
☐ **The Trusthouse Charitable Foundation**	**£2.1 million**	General
☐ **The Zochonis Charitable Trust**	**£2.1 million**	General
☐ **Amabrill Limited**	**£2 million**	Orthodox Jewish
☐ **The Bowland Charitable Trust**	**£2 million**	Young people, education, general
☐ **Dunard Fund**	**£2 million**	Classical music, the visual arts, environment and humanitarian causes
☐ **The Charles Dunstone Charitable Trust**	**£2 million**	General
☐ **Global Charities**	**£2 million**	Children, young people and disadvantaged adults
☐ **The Kay Kendall Leukaemia Fund**	**£2 million**	Research into leukaemia
☐ **The National Churches Trust**	**£2 million**	Preservation of historic churches
☐ **The Rayne Foundation**	**£2 million**	Arts, education, health, medicine, social welfare
☐ **SHINE (Support and Help in Education)**	**£2 million**	Education of children and young people
☐ **Voluntary Action Fund**	**£2 million**	General
☐ **The Burdett Trust for Nursing**	**£1.9 million**	Healthcare
☐ **The Church Urban Fund**	**£1.9 million**	Welfare and Christian outreach in deprived communities in England
☐ **The Gosling Foundation Limited**	**£1.9 million**	Relief of poverty, education, religion, naval and service charities and general charitable purposes beneficial to the community
☐ **The Gulbenkian Foundation**	**£1.9 million**	Education, arts, welfare
☐ **Jay Education Trust**	**£1.9 million**	Jewish causes
☐ **Lloyds TSB Foundation for Northern Ireland**	**£1.9 million**	Social and community need, education and training
☐ **The Pilgrim Trust**	**£1.9 million**	Social welfare and the preservation of buildings and heritage
☐ **The Joron Charitable Trust**	**£1.86 million**	Jewish, education, medical research, general
☐ **The Audrey and Stanley Burton 1960 Charitable Trust**	**£1.8 million**	Charities supporting education and the arts; Jewish people/ Israel; social welfare; health; and overseas and developing countries
☐ **County Durham Foundation**	**£1.8 million**	Tackling social disadvantage and poverty, general
☐ **Tees Valley Community Foundation**	**£1.8 million**	General
☐ **Sir John Cass's Foundation**	**£1.7 million**	Education in inner London

☐ **The Albert Hunt Trust**	**£1.7 million**	Welfare
☐ **The Medlock Charitable Trust**	**£1.7 million**	Education, health, welfare
☐ **The Nationwide Foundation**	**£1.7 million**	Social welfare
☐ **The Peacock Charitable Trust**	**£1.7 million**	Medical research, disability, general
☐ **Ridgesave Limited**	**£1.7 million**	Jewish, religion, education, general
☐ **The Ernest Cook Trust**	**£1.6 million**	Educational grants focusing on children and young people for the environment, rural conservation, arts and crafts, literary and numeracy and research
☐ **The Gannochy Trust**	**£1.6 million**	General
☐ **The Charles Hayward Foundation**	**£1.9 million**	Heritage and conservation, criminal justice, hospices, older people, overseas, young people at risk
☐ **Hurdale Charity Limited**	**£1.6 million**	Advancement of Jewish religion, relief of poverty and general charitable purposes
☐ **Jerwood Charitable Foundation**	**£1.6 million**	The arts, education, design, science, engineering and other areas of human endeavour
☐ **The Manifold Charitable Trust**	**£1.6 million**	Education, historic buildings, environmental conservation, general
☐ **The Manoukian Charitable Foundation**	**£1.6 million**	Social welfare, education, medical, the arts, 'Armenian matters'
☐ **CAF (Charities Aid Foundation)**	**£1.5 million**	Capacity building for small and medium sized charities
☐ **CfBT Education Trust**	**£1.5 million**	Organisations involved in education, particularly those concerned with the development and management of schools; managing and delivering effective learning and teaching; overcoming barriers to learning; and projects involving communication, language and multi-lingualism
☐ **Church Burgesses Trust**	**£1.5 million**	Ecclesiastical purposes, education, and other charitable purposes
☐ **The R and S Cohen Fondation**	**£1.5 million**	Education, relief in need and the arts
☐ **Derbyshire Community Foundation**	**£1.5 million**	Social welfare
☐ **The Execution Charitable Trust**	**£1.5 million**	Mainly local multi-purpose community projects supporting social welfare
☐ **The Northwood Charitable Trust**	**£1.5 million**	Medical research, health, welfare, general
☐ **The Steel Charitable Trust**	**£1.5 million**	Social welfare, culture; recreation, health, medical research, environment and overseas aid
☐ **The Westminster Foundation**	**£1.5 million**	Social welfare, military charities, education, environment and conservation
☐ **The Bluston Charitable Settlement**	**£1.4 million**	Jewish, general
☐ **The Cadogan Charity**	**£1.4 million**	General charitable purposes, in particular, social welfare, medical research, services charities, animal welfare, education and conservation and the environment
☐ **Cripplegate Foundation**	**£1.4 million**	General
☐ **The Sir Joseph Hotung Charitable Settlement**	**£1.4 million**	General
☐ **Lloyds TSB Foundation for the Channel Islands**	**£1.4 million**	General
☐ **The London Marathon Charitable Trust**	**£1.4 million**	Sport, recreation and leisure
☐ **The Performing Right Society Foundation**	**£1.4 million**	New music of any genre
☐ **The Schroder Foundation**	**£1.4 million**	General
☐ **Stratford upon Avon Town Trust**	**£1.4 million**	Education, welfare, general
☐ **The Vail Foundation**	**£1.4 million**	Jewish causes
☐ **Entindale Ltd**	**£1.3 million**	Orthodox Jewish charities
☐ **Mercaz Torah Vechesed Limited**	**£1.3 million**	Orthodox Jewish charities
☐ **The Rothschild Foundation**	**£1.3 million**	Arts, culture, general
☐ **The Francis C Scott Charitable Trust**	**£1.3 million**	Disadvantaged young people in Cumbria and north Lancashire
☐ **The Tolkien Trust**	**£1.3 million**	General
☐ **The Worwin UK Foundation**	**£1.3 million**	General
☐ **The Queen's Silver Jubilee Trust**	**£1.25 million**	General, in practice grants to organisations supporting disadvantaged young people
☐ **Cash for Kids Radio Clyde**	**£1.2 million**	Children
☐ **Devon Community Foundation**	**£1.2 million**	General
☐ **The Djanogly Foundation**	**£1.2 million**	General, medicine, education, social welfare

☐ **The EBM Charitable Trust** — £1.2 million — Children and young people, animal welfare, relief of poverty, general

☐ **Essex Community Foundation** — £1.2 million — Social welfare, general

☐ **The Grocers' Charity** — £1.2 million — General

☐ **The Haramead Trust** — £1.2 million — Children, social welfare, education, people with disabilities, homeless people, medical assistance, victims and oppressed people and religious activities

☐ **The Hertfordshire Community Foundation** — £1.2 million — General

☐ **The King's Fund** — £1.2 million — Health and health care, especially in London

☐ **The Henry Moore Foundation** — £1.2 million — Fine arts, in particular sculpture, drawing and printmaking

☐ **The J P Morgan Foundations** — £1.2 million — Education, community, young people, women, the arts

☐ **The Rose Foundation** — £1.2 million — General – grants towards building projects

☐ **The Underwood Trust** — £1.2 million — General charitable purposes, in particular, medicine and health, social welfare, education, arts, environment and wildlife

☐ **Sutton Coldfield Municipal Charities** — £1.16 million — Relief of need, arts, education, building conservation, general

☐ **Baron Davenport's Charity** — £1.15 million — Almshouses; hospices; residential homes for older people; children and young people under the age of 25

☐ **The Alliance Family Foundation** — £1.1 million — Jewish, general

☐ **The D'Oyly Carte Charitable Trust** — £1.1 million — Arts, medical welfare, environment

☐ **Hampton Fuel Allotment Charity** — £1.1 million — Relief in need, health, education of children and young people and social welfare

☐ **The Jane Hodge Foundation** — £1.1 million — Medical care and research, education and religion

☐ **John James Bristol Foundation** — £1.1 million — Education, health, older people, general

☐ **The Sir James Knott Trust** — £1.1 million — General charitable purposes, in practice, support for people who are disadvantaged, the young, older people, the disabled, education and training, medical care, historic buildings, the environment, music and the arts and seafarers' and services' charities

☐ **The Leathersellers' Company Charitable Fund** — £1.1 million — General

☐ **The Lennox and Wyfold Foundation** — £1.1 million — General

☐ **ShareGift (The Orr Mackintosh Foundation)** — £1.1 million — General

☐ **Cumbria Community Foundation** — £1 million — General charitable purposes in Cumbria, in particular grant making to children and young people, older people and their carers, people with disabilities, the unemployed and people on low incomes

☐ **The Dollond Charitable Trust** — £1 million — Jewish, general

☐ **The Drapers' Charitable Fund** — £1 million — General charitable purposes including education, heritage, the arts, prisoner support and textile conservation

☐ **The Heart of England Community Foundation** — £1 million — General

☐ **The Beatrice Laing Trust** — £1 million — Relief of poverty and advancement of the evangelical Christian faith

☐ **Marshall's Charity** — £1 million — Parsonage and church improvements

☐ **The Edith Murphy Foundation** — £1 million — General, individual hardship, animals, children and the disabled

☐ **Joseph Rowntree Reform Trust Limited** — £1 million — Promoting political and democratic reform and defending of civil liberties

☐ **The Sir Halley Stewart Trust** — £1 million — Medical, social, educational and religious activities

☐ **The Harold Hyam Wingate Foundation** — £1 million — Jewish life and learning, performing arts, music, education and social exclusion, overseas development, medical

☐ **Isle of Dogs Community Foundation** — £996,000 — Regeneration, general

☐ **The H B Allen Charitable Trust** — £994,000 — General

☐ **The H D H Wills 1965 Charitable Trust** — £990,000 — General, wildlife conservation

☐ **The Rubin Foundation** — £984,000 — Jewish charities, general

☐ The Donald Forrester Trust	£980,000	Children and young people; older people's welfare; hospitals and hospices, physical disability; blind and deaf; community care and social welfare; medical research; overseas relief; animal welfare, services and ex-services; religious organisations; maritime; mental health; the homeless; arts, culture and sport; environmental heritage; trades and professions; education; general
☐ The Church and Community Fund	£956,000	Church of England, social welfare
☐ Ernest Kleinwort Charitable Trust	£952,000	General charitable purposes – in practice, mainly to wildlife and environmental conservation both nationally and overseas; disability; medical research; welfare of older and young people
☐ The Hedley Foundation	£949,000	Young people, health, welfare
☐ The Schreib Trust	£947,000	Jewish, general
☐ The Golden Bottle Trust	£943,000	General with a preference for the environment, health, education, religion, the arts and developing countries
☐ The Stobart Newlands Charitable Trust	£936,000	Christian religious and missionary causes
☐ The Gerald Ronson Foundation	£930,000	General, Jewish
☐ Charitworth Limited	£913,000	Religious, educational and charitable purposes. In practice, mainly Jewish causes
☐ The Constance Travis Charitable Trust	£902,500	General
☐ The Mary Kinross Charitable Trust	£898,000	Relief of poverty, medical research, community development, young people and penal affairs
☐ Rosetrees Trust	£895,000	Medical research
☐ The Arbib Foundation	£892,000	General
☐ The Equitable Charitable Trust	£892,000	Education of disabled and/or disadvantaged children under 25
☐ Community Foundation for Calderdale	£874,000	General
☐ John and Lucille van Geest Foundation	£872,000	Medical research, healthcare, general
☐ The Robert Gavron Charitable Trust	£863,000	The arts, policy research, general
☐ Sussex Community Foundation	£860,000	Community-based projects, education, disability, health, and the relief of poverty and sickness
☐ Itzchok Meyer Cymerman Trust Ltd	£856,000	Advancement of the orthodox Jewish faith, education, social welfare, relief of sickness, medical research and general charitable purposes
☐ The Bromley Trust	£854,000	Human rights, prison reform, conservation
☐ The Archie Sherman Charitable Trust	£854,000	Jewish charities, education, arts, general
☐ H C D Memorial Fund	£436,000	Health, education, environment and community action
☐ Elizabeth and Prince Zaiger Trust	£836,000	Welfare, health, general
☐ The Sheepdrove Trust	£831,000	Mainly environment, education
☐ The Elton John Aids Foundation	£830,000	HIV/AIDS welfare and prevention
☐ The Hugh Fraser Foundation	£814,000	General
☐ The Valentine Charitable Trust	£814,000	Welfare, the environment and overseas aid
☐ The Debmar Benevolent Trust	£813,000	Jewish causes
☐ The Carpenters' Company Charitable Trust	£812,000	Education, general
☐ The Ashden Trust	£799,000	Environment, homelessness, sustainable regeneration, community arts
☐ The Alice Ellen Cooper Dean Charitable Foundation	£790,500	General
☐ Edward Cadbury Charitable Trust	£789,000	General
☐ The Yorkshire Dales Millennium Trust	£786,000	Conservation and environmental regeneration
☐ Trust for London	£779,000	Social welfare
☐ The Sir James Reckitt Charity	£770,000	Society of Friends (Quakers), social welfare, general
☐ The Jones 1986 Charitable Trust	£769,000	People with disabilities, welfare of older people, welfare of younger people, education and purposes beneficial to the community
☐ The Enid Linder Foundation	£765,500	Health, welfare, general
☐ Lord Leverhulme's Charitable Trust	£760,000	Welfare, education, arts, young people
☐ The Tajtelbaum Charitable Trust	£759,000	Jewish, welfare

☐ **British Record Industry Trust**	£758,000	Performing arts, music therapy, general
☐ **The Allen Lane Foundation**	£756,000	Charities benefiting asylum-seekers and refugees, gypsies and travellers, lesbian, gay, bisexual or transgender people, offenders and ex-offenders, older people, people experiencing mental health problems and people experiencing violence or abuse
☐ **Network for Social Change**	£756,000	Third world debt, environment, human rights, peace, arts and education
☐ **The Booth Charities**	£755,000	Welfare, health, education
☐ **The Bedford Charity (The Harpur Trust)**	£754,000	Education, welfare and recreation
☐ **The MacRobert Trust**	£735,000	General
☐ **Milton Keynes Community Foundation**	£734,000	Welfare, arts
☐ **The John R Murray Charitable Trust**	£734,000	Arts and literature
☐ **The Wixamtree Trust**	£727,000	General – in particular, social welfare, environment and conservation, medicine and health, the arts, education, sports and leisure and training and employment
☐ **The Cross Trust**	£726,000	Christian work
☐ **The Community Foundation for Wiltshire and Swindon**	£725,000	Community welfare
☐ **The Sir John Fisher Foundation**	£723,000	General charitable purposes with a preference for the shipping industry, medicine, the navy or military and music and theatre
☐ **The Architectural Heritage Fund**	£718,000	Loans and grants for building preservation
☐ **Jewish Child's Day**	£717,000	Charitable purposes of direct benefit to Jewish children who are disadvantaged, suffering or in need of special care
☐ **The R S Macdonald Charitable Trust**	£716,500	Visual impairment, cerebral palsy, children, animal welfare
☐ **The Will Charitable Trust**	£714,000	Environment/conservation, people with sight loss and the prevention and cure of blindness, cancer care, people with mental disability
☐ **The Colt Foundation**	£711,500	Occupational and environmental health research
☐ **The Stafford Trust**	£696,000	Animal welfare, medical research, local community, relief in need
☐ **Oglesby Charitable Trust**	£693,000	General
☐ **The Spring Harvest Charitable Trust**	£693,000	The promotion of Christianity
☐ **The Kennedy Leigh Charitable Trust**	£688,000	Jewish charities, general
☐ **The William A Cadbury Charitable Trust**	£685,000	Local welfare and disability charities, penal reform, Quaker charities and overseas
☐ **Richard Cloudesley's Charity**	£683,000	Churches, medical and welfare
☐ **John Moores Foundation**	£682,000	Social welfare in Merseyside and Northern Ireland, emergency relief overseas
☐ **The Barnwood House Trust**	£680,000	Disability
☐ **Rowanville Ltd**	£680,000	Orthodox Jewish
☐ **4 Charity Foundation**	£679,000	Jewish causes
☐ **The Charities Advisory Trust**	£676,000	General
☐ **The Band Trust**	£665,000	People with disabilities, children and young people, scholarships, hospices and hospitals, education, older people and people who are disadvantaged
☐ **The Great Britain Sasakawa Foundation**	£665,000	Links between Great Britain and Japan
☐ **The Reed Foundation**	£650,000	General, arts, education, relief of poverty, women's health
☐ **The David Tannen Charitable Trust**	£645,000	Jewish causes
☐ **The George John and Sheilah Livanos Charitable Trust**	£632,000	Health, maritime charities, general
☐ **The Football Association Youth Trust**	£612,000	Sports
☐ **The James Tudor Foundation**	£607,500	Relief of sickness, medical research, health education, palliative care
☐ **The Richmond Parish Lands Charity**	£604,500	General
☐ **The Jordan Charitable Foundation**	£602,500	General

☐ Achiezer Association Ltd	£602,000	The relief of older people and people in need; advancement of education; advancement of religion; and general charitable purposes
☐ Colyer-Fergusson Charitable Trust	£601,500	Social isolation, exclusion or poverty, community activity (often through churches), church maintenance, environment, the arts
☐ The Dowager Countess Eleanor Peel Trust	£599,000	Medical research, older people, socially disadvantaged people and general
☐ The Staples Trust	£596,500	Development, environment, women's issues
☐ The Girdlers' Company Charitable Trust	£590,500	Medicine and health, education, welfare, youth welfare, heritage, environment, humanities and Christian religion
☐ The M K Charitable Trust	£589,000	Jewish charities
☐ Mr and Mrs J A Pye's Charitable Settlement	£588,000	General
☐ The Fishmongers' Company's Charitable Trust	£585,000	General – in particular education, relief of poverty and disability
☐ The Joseph Strong Frazer Trust	£583,000	General, with broad interests in the fields of social welfare, education, religion and wildlife
☐ The AIM Foundation	£577,000	Healthcare, community development, young people, environmental matters and other charitable activities particularly related to influencing long-term social change
☐ The Triangle Trust (1949) Fund	£574,000	Social welfare, health, people with disabilities, integration and general
☐ Alan Edward Higgs Charity	£572,000	Child welfare
☐ The Glass-House Trust	£358,000	Social housing and the urban environment, art and child development
☐ The G C Gibson Charitable Trust	£556,000	Art, music and education; health, hospices and medical research; community and other social projects; religion
☐ North West London Community Foundation	£550,000	General
☐ The J J Charitable Trust	£540,000	Environment, literacy
☐ The Neil Kreitman Foundation	£540,000	Arts and culture; education; health and social welfare; and Jewish charities
☐ Largsmount Ltd	£540,000	Jewish causes
☐ Closehelm Ltd	£538,000	Jewish, welfare
☐ The Derek Butler Trust	£537,000	Medical, health, arts (particularly music), general
☐ The North British Hotel Trust	£532,500	Health, social welfare
☐ The Sovereign Health Care Charitable Trust	£525,000	Health, people with disabilities
☐ The Norwich Town Close Estate Charity	£517,000	Education in and near Norwich
☐ The Sandra Charitable Trust	£515,000	Animal welfare and research, environmental protection, social welfare, health and development of young people
☐ The Campden Charities	£511,000	Welfare and education (particularly the under-25s)
☐ St Katharine and Shadwell Trust	£505,000	Community development
☐ Basil Samuel Charitable Trust	£498,000	General
☐ Queen Mary's Roehampton Trust	£497,000	Ex-service support
☐ Simon Gibson Charitable Trust	£488,000	General
☐ The Welton Foundation	£487,000	Medical research, health, general
☐ Erach and Roshan Sadri Foundation	£483,000	Education, welfare, homelessness, Zoroastrian religion, general
☐ The Milly Apthorp Charitable Trust	£480,000	Health, older people and young people
☐ The Alan and Babette Sainsbury Charitable Fund	£477,000	General
☐ Polden-Puckham Charitable Foundation	£476,000	Peace and security, ecological issues, social change
☐ The Three Guineas Trust	£469,000	Autism and Asperger's Syndrome
☐ The Kennedy Charitable Foundation	£468,500	Roman Catholic ministries, general, especially in the west of Ireland
☐ The Maud Elkington Charitable Trust	£468,000	Social welfare, general charitable purposes
☐ The 1989 Willan Charitable Trust	£467,500	General – in practice mainly organisations supporting, children, older people, people with mental and physical disabilities and medical research
☐ Sir Harold Hood's Charitable Trust	£461,000	Roman Catholic charitable purposes
☐ The Huntingdon Foundation	£461,000	Jewish education

| ☐ The Daiwa Anglo-Japanese Foundation | £457,000 | Anglo-Japanese relations |
| ☐ The Madeline Mabey Trust | £452,000 | Medical research, children's welfare and education |

☐ Fisherbeck Charitable Trust	£451,600	Christian, homelessness, welfare, education, heritage
☐ Gwyneth Forrester Trust	£450,000	General
☐ Reuben Brothers Foundation	£449,000	Healthcare, education, general
☐ Percy Bilton Charity	£448,000	Disabled, disadvantaged young people, older people
☐ The Hilden Charitable Fund	£446,000	Homelessness, minority groups and race relations, penal affairs and overseas development
☐ Mike Gooley Trailfinders Charity	£439,500	Medical research, general
☐ The Freshfield Foundation	£438,000	Environment, healthcare
☐ Porticus UK	£438,000	Social welfare, education, religion
☐ Nemoral Ltd	£437,000	Orthodox Jewish causes
☐ The Joffe Charitable Trust	£431,000	Alleviation of poverty and protection/advancement of human rights

☐ The Clara E Burgess Charity	£429,000	Children and young people
☐ The Douglas Turner Trust	£426,000	General
☐ Trustees of Tzedakah	£426,000	Jewish charities, welfare
☐ The Saddlers' Company Charitable Fund	£424,500	General
☐ The Stone Family Foundation	£422,000	Relief in need, social welfare, overseas aid
☐ The ACT Foundation	£415,000	Welfare, health, housing
☐ The Mackintosh Foundation	£411,000	Priority is given to the theatre and the performing arts – also funded are children and education; medicine; homelessness; community projects; the environment; refugees; and other charitable purposes
☐ The Roald Dahl Foundation	£409,600	Haematology and neurology conditions affecting children and young people up to the age of 25
☐ Cullum Family Trust	£406,000	Social welfare, education and general charitable purposes
☐ The Englefield Charitable Trust	£405,000	General charitable purposes with a preference for local charities in Berkshire

☐ The Frances and Augustus Newman Foundation	£404,000	Medical research and equipment
☐ The Charles and Elsie Sykes Trust	£404,000	General, social welfare, medical research
☐ The Mulberry Trust	£399,000	General
☐ The John S Cohen Foundation	£393,000	General, in particular music and the arts, education and environment
☐ The Maurice Hatter Foundation	£392,000	Jewish causes, general
☐ The Pilkington Charities Fund	£386,000	General, health, social welfare, people with disabilities, older people and victims of natural disaster or war
☐ Mrs L D Rope Third Charitable Settlement	£381,000	Education, religion, relief of poverty, general
☐ The Anton Jurgens Charitable Trust	£380,000	Welfare, general
☐ The Sir John Eastwood Foundation	£377,000	Social welfare, education, health
☐ The Isle of Anglesey Charitable Trust	£377,000	General

☐ Heathside Charitable Trust	£373,000	General, Jewish
☐ The William Leech Charity	£371,000	Health and welfare in the north east of England, overseas aid
☐ The Balcombe Charitable Trust	£356,000	Education, environment, health and welfare
☐ Impetus Trust	£356,000	The development of charities working with people who are economically disadvantaged; and general
☐ The Ofenheim Charitable Trust	£354,000	General, mainly charities supporting health, welfare, arts and the environment
☐ Childs Charitable Trust	£352,000	Christian
☐ The Brian Mitchell Charitable Settlement	£345,000	General
☐ The Woodward Charitable Trust	£344,000	General
☐ The Tompkins Foundation	£343,500	Health, education, religion, community projects and general charitable purposes
☐ The Mark Leonard Trust	£340,000	Environmental education, young people, general

| ☐ Lady Hind Trust | £328,000 | General with some preference for health and disability related charities |
| ☐ The Privy Purse Charitable Trust | £328,000 | General |

☐ **Brushmill Ltd**	**£324,000**	Jewish causes, education, social welfare
☐ **The Patrick Frost Foundation**	**£310,000**	General
☐ **The Adint Charitable Trust**	**£305,000**	Health, social welfare
☐ **The Tedworth Charitable Trust**	**£301,000**	Parenting, child welfare and development, general
☐ **The Severn Trent Water Charitable Trust Fund**	**£249,000**	Relief of poverty, money advice, debt counselling
☐ **The Kathleen Hannay Memorial Charity**	**£222,000**	Health, welfare, Christian, general
☐ **The Sylvia Adams Charitable Trust**	**£210,000**	Disability, welfare, poverty, children and young people
☐ **The Joseph Levy Charitable Foundation**	**£132,000**	Young people, older people, health, medical research
☐ **The Shirley Foundation**	**£110,000**	Autism spectrum disorders with particular emphasis on medical research
☐ **The Thompson Family Charitable Trust**	**£105,000**	Medical, veterinary, education, general

The 1989 Willan Charitable Trust

General – in practice mainly organisations supporting children, older people, people with mental and physical disabilities and medical research

£467,500 (2007/08)

Beneficial area Worldwide, in practice mainly the north east of England.

Community Foundation Serving Tyne & Wear, 9th Floor, Cale Cross, 156 Pilgrim Street, Newcastle upon Tyne NE1 6SU

Tel. 0191 222 0945 **Fax** 0191 230 0689

Email kg@communityfoundation.org.uk

Correspondent Karen Griffiths, Fund Manager

Trustees *Francis A Chapman; Alex Ohlsson; Willan Trustee Ltd.*

CC Number 802749

Information available Accounts were available from the Charity Commission.

The trust was established in 1989 for general charitable purposes, with a preference for benefiting organisations in the north east of England.

The following information is taken from the trust's annual report and accounts.

In recognition of the origins of the trust fund and the economic impact that the decline of shipbuilding has had on the region, the trustees tend to concentrate their support towards causes which are active in Tyne & Wear and its immediate surrounds. The trustees favour causes which aim to ease social deprivation and/or enrich the fabric of the local community and the quality of life of individuals within that community.

In 2007/08 the trust had assets of £10.2 million and an income of £603,000. There were 149 grants made during the year totalling £467,500.

Beneficiaries included: SAFC Foundation and Cancer Connexions (£10,000 each); Amble Multi Agency Crime Prevention Initiative (£6,000); Durham City Centre Youth Project, The Children's Society and the Calvert Trust (£5,000 each); Chester le Street Youth Centre (£4,000); Different Strokes North East, Northern Roots and People and Drugs (£3,000 each); Leukaemia Research and Coast Video Club (£2,000 each);

Northumberland Mountain Rescue and the Association of British Poles (£1,000 each); and Healthwise and Newcastle Gang Show (£500).

Exclusions Grants are not given directly to individuals. Grants for gap year students may be considered if the individual will be working for a charity (in this case the grant would be paid to the charity).

Applications In writing to the correspondent at the Community Foundation Serving Tyne & Wear. Applications are processed, collated and shortlisted by the Community Foundation on a quarterly basis. The shortlist is then circulated to each of the trustees for consideration and approval.

The 29th May 1961 Charitable Trust

Social welfare and general

£3.7 million (2007/08)

Beneficial area UK, with a special interest in the Warwickshire/ Birmingham/Coventry area.

Ryder Court, 14 Ryder Street, London SW1Y 6QB

Tel. 020 7024 9034

Email enquiries@29may1961charity.org.uk

Correspondent The Secretary

Trustees *Vanni Emanuele Treves; Andrew C Jones; Anthony J Mead; Paul Varney.*

CC Number 200198

Information available Accounts were available from the Charity Commission. A separate 'Grants Awarded' publication was available from the trust.

The policy of the trustees is to support a wide range of charitable organisations across a broad spectrum with grants for both capital and revenue purposes. Some grants are one-off, some recurring and others spread over two or three years. The majority of grants are made to organisations within the UK and preference is given, where possible, to charities operating in the Coventry and Warwickshire area.

The trust gives over 300 grants each year, ranging in size from hundreds to hundreds of thousands of pounds; most

are between £1,000 and £5,000. About half appear to be for work in the Coventry and Warwickshire area. Most grants are now on a three-year basis and will not be renewed without at least some interval.

Grants for 2007/08

In 2007/08 the trust had assets of £108 million, which generated an income of £4 million. Grants were made to 403 organisations totalling £3.7 million. Grants were broken down geographically as follows:

Region	Value
Midlands	£1,490,000
London and the South	£1,173,000
National	£917,000
North	£72,000
International	£19,000
Northern Ireland	£2,000

Grants were further broken down into the following categories:

Social welfare (161 grants totalling £917,000)

The NSPCC received two grants, £100,000 towards the 'Stop Organised Abuse' appeal and £10,000 towards core costs. Heart of England Community Foundation also received two grants during the year, one towards the administration of the foundation (£30,000), the other towards the provision of small grants in the Coventry and Warwickshire area (£18,000).

Other beneficiaries of larger grants of £10,000 or more included: Abbeyfields Midlands (West) Region providing grants to update sheltered accommodation provision (£35,000); Childline towards running costs (£26,000); Birmingham Settlement towards running costs (£25,000); Myton Hamlet Hospice Trust towards core funding (£20,000); Helen Ley Court towards equipment costs (£15,000); and Birmingham Rathbone Society towards refurbishment costs, Chaseley Trust towards the costs of expanding facilities, Home Farm Trust towards providing residential care, Sick Children's Trust towards accommodation provision and Trinity Project towards the costs of a building development project (£10,000 each).

Smaller grants included those to: Childhood First (£7,500); Asylum Aid, Broadreach House, Counsel and Care for the Elderly, Demand, Detention Advice Service, Devon Community Foundation, Elizabeth Fitzroy Support, Gatwick Detainees Welfare Group, MoMo Helps Charitable Trust, NCH Action for Children, One Parent Families, Post Adoption Centre, Royal School for the Deaf, Samaritans and Warwickshire and

1

Northampton Air Ambulance (£5,000 each); Break, Centre 70, Ipswich Housing Action Group and New Jumbulance Travel Trust (£4,000 each); and Age Concern – Coventry, Barnardo's, Camden Society, Deptford Churches Centres, Just 42, National Council for One Parent Families, Northampton Hope Centre, Salvation Army, Tiny Tim's Children's Centre, Turntable Furniture and Vila Maninga (£3,000 each).

Arts and museums (35 grants totalling £866,000)

By far the largest grant, of £220,000, went to University of Warwick towards the running costs of the arts centre, with a further £12,000 given towards sponsorship of the Coull Quartet. There were two other major grants made to Hereward College towards the costs of a new Performing Arts Centre and Royal Shakespeare Theatre towards the costs of a re-development of the theatre (£100,000 each).

Other beneficiaries of larger grants included: Sadlers Wells Trust towards the costs of subsidised tickets (£40,000) and towards the costs of its schools access programme (£30,000); Holbourne Museum towards restoration and extension costs (£25,000); Black Country Museum (£20,000); and Aldeburgh Productions (£15,000).

Smaller grants included those to: Belgrade Theatre Trust, Glasgow School of Art Restoration and Public Catalogue Collections Fund (£10,000 each); Armonico Consort, Dartington Hall Trust and Wales Millennium Centre (£5,000); Living Paintings Trust (£4,000); and Birmingham Royal Ballet (£3,000).

Leisure, recreation and young people (81 grants totalling £501,000)

Coventry and Warwickshire Awards Trust received £100,000 towards the running costs of a sports centre providing facilities for disadvantaged communities. Other beneficiaries of major grants included: Federation of London Youth Clubs towards general funds (£75,000); and Midlands Sports Centre for the Disabled and Warwick Association of Youth Clubs towards running costs (£28,000 each).

Other beneficiaries of larger grants included: Family Holiday Association (£15,000); and Bala and Penllyn Sports and Recreation Association, City of Coventry Scouts County, Fields in Trust, the Lion Club, Pioneer Centre Appeal and UK Youth (£10,000 each).

Smaller grants included those to: Kids (£8,000); Outward Bound Trust

(£7,000); Ackers Trust, Boys Brigade – West Midlands, Coventry Sports Foundation, Farms for City Children, Steps and Willow Trust (£5,000 each); Street League (£4,000); and Bag Books, Bradbury Club, Campus Children's Holidays, Coventry Boys' Club, Crimebeat, Happy Days, Kids in Action, Over the Wall, Sport for Life and Whirlow Hall Farm (£3,000 each).

Homelessness and housing (41 grants totalling £451,000)

Shelter received £85,000 towards the costs of a project to prevent ex-offenders becoming homeless upon release. Other larger grants included those to: Crisis towards core costs and St Basil's Centre towards the costs of providing hostel accommodation (£50,000 each); Connection at St Martins towards running costs and Emmaus UK towards the costs of a deputy community leader (£25,000 each); and Notting Hill Housing Trust towards the costs of the refurbishment of six flats (£15,000).

Other beneficiaries included: Depaul Trust, and Turnaround (£10,000 each); Cardinal Hume Centre (£8,000); Centrepoint, Housing the Homeless Central Fund, Langley House Project, Penrose Housing Association, Providence Row, St Mungos, Thanet Trust and West London Churches Homeless Concern (£5,000 each); and Benjamin Foundation, Central and Cecil Housing Trust, Oasis, Pavement, Second Step and Young Housing Project (£3,000 each).

Employment, education and training (27 grants totalling £426,000)

The major beneficiary in this category was London Business School which received £200,000 towards expanding the executive education theatre. Other larger grants included those to: Coventry Day Care Fund for People with Learning Difficulties towards the costs of providing work experience for people with disabilities in Coventry (£65,000); Gap Activity Projects towards the costs of the West Midlands Global Challenge project (£20,000); and Working Men's College towards the costs of renovation works (£15,000).

Other beneficiaries included: Book Aid International, National Star College and Suffolk School for Parents (£10,000 each); Action for Kids Charitable Trust, Express Link Up, I Can, Reading Matters, Training for Life and Treloar Trust (£5,000 each); UCanDoIT (£4,000); and Devon and Exeter Spastics Society (£3,000).

Medical (26 grants totalling £236,000)

The major beneficiary in this category was Cancerbackup which received £50,000 in core funding for its national cancer counselling telephone line and £40,000 towards the costs of the charity's centre in Coventry. Another larger grant was made to Warwick Hospital – Cancer Ward Appeal towards the costs of providing facilities (£25,000).

Other beneficiaries included: Alzheimer's Society and Building for Babies (£10,000 each); Changing Faces and Wellbeing (£7,500 each); Action for ME, Baby Lifeline, Breast Cancer Care, King's College Hospital Charity and SPARKS (£5,000 each); National Association for Children of Alcoholics (£4,000); and Asthma UK (£3,000).

Offenders (28 grants totalling £195,000)

The largest grant in this category went to NACRO who received £30,000 for core costs. Howard League for Penal Reform received two grants of £10,000 each towards the organisation's work with young adult prisoners and towards the costs of a National Commission of Enquiry into the penal system.

Other beneficiaries included: Adfam, Prison Advice and Care Trust and St Giles Trust (£10,000 each); Counselling in Prison (£7,500); Action for Prisoners Families, Butler Trust, Forgiveness, New Bridge, Prisoners' Educational Trust, Shannon Trust, SOVA and Wakefield Prison Visits Children's Play Facility (£5,000 each); and Synergy Theatre Project (£3,000 each).

Conservation and protection (14 grants totalling £82,000)

The largest grant in this category was £25,000 to Historic Royal Palaces towards the costs of conserving the White Tower at the Tower of London.

Other beneficiaries included: New Orford Town Trust (£10,000); National Memorial Arboretum (£7,500); Suffolk Wildlife Trust (£7,000); Living Environments Trust (£5,000); and Pilgrim to the Sea and War Memorial Trust (£3,000).

Exclusions Grants only to registered charities. No grants to individuals.

Applications To the secretary in writing, enclosing in triplicate the most recent annual report and accounts. Trustees normally meet in February, May, August and November. Due to the large number of applications received, they cannot be acknowledged.

4 Charity Foundation

Jewish

£679,000 (2007/08)

Beneficial area UK and Israel.

54–56 Euston Street, London NW1 2ES

Tel. 020 7387 0155

Correspondent Jacob Schimmel, Trustee

Trustees *Jacob Schimmel; Marc Schimmel; D Rabson; Mrs A Schimmel.*

CC Number 1077143

Information available Accounts were on file at the Charity Commission, without a list of grants.

Set up in 1999, the charity changed its name from Les Freres Charitable Trust to 4 Charity Foundation in January 2008. Grants are made to Jewish organisations for religious and educational purposes.

In 2007/08 the foundation had assets of £10.3 million and an income of over £6.8 million mainly from rents. Grants were made during the year totalling £679,000.

A recent list of grants was not available. Previous grants include those to: the American Jewish Joint Distribution Committee (£78,000); the Millennium Trust (£66,000); Keren Yehoshua V'Yisroel (£43,000); Project Seed (£35,000); World Jewish Relief (£29,000); Menorah Grammar School (£27,000); British Friends of Jaffa Institute (£23,000); Friends of Mir (£19,000); Heichal Hatorah Foundation (£15,000); Chai Life Line Cancer Care (£12,000); Jewish Care (£11,000); and British Friends of Ezer Mizion (£10,000).

Applications This trust does not respond to unsolicited applications.

Achiezer Association Ltd

The relief of older people and people in need, advancement of education, advancement of religion and general charitable purposes

£602,000 (2007/08)

Beneficial area Worldwide.

130–134 Granville Road, London NW2 2LD

Tel. 020 8209 3880

Email genoffice@dasim.co.uk

Correspondent David Chontow, Trustee

Trustees *David Chontow; Sydney S Chontow; Michael M Chontow.*

CC Number 255031

Information available Accounts were available from the Charity Commission.

The trust's objects are to:

- offer relief to the 'aged, impotent and poor'
- advance education, religion and purposes beneficial to the community.

In 2007/08 the trust had assets of £1.8 million and a consolidated income of £739,000. Grants were made totalling £602,000. The cost of generating funds was £191,000 and management and administration costs were £113,000. The accounts for the year do not include the individual beneficiaries of the grants made. According to the trust, a list of grant beneficiaries is 'detailed in a separate publication which is available from the Registered Office'. A copy has been requested but is yet to be received.

In the past, the trust has mainly supported Jewish charities with a few small grants being given to medical and welfare charities. No further information was available.

Exclusions No grants to individuals.

Applications In writing to the correspondent.

The ACT Foundation

Welfare, health and housing

£415,000 to organisations (2007/08)

Beneficial area UK and overseas.

The Gate House, 2 Park Street, Windsor SL4 1LU

Tel. 01753 753900 **Fax** 01753 753901

Email info@theactfoundation.co.uk

Website www.theactfoundation.co.uk

Correspondent Maralyn Gill, Grants Coordinator

Trustees *Paul Nield; John J O'Sullivan; Michael Street; David Hyde; Robert F White; Denis Taylor.*

CC Number 1068617

Information available Accounts were on file at the Charity Commission. The charity also has a clear and helpful website.

The charity was established in 1998, and it provides grants to individuals and other charities, principally in the UK, with the aim of enhancing the quality of life for people in need (specifically those who are mentally and physically disabled).

Grants generally fall into the following areas:

- building – funding modifications to homes, schools, hospices etc.
- equipment – provision of specialised wheelchairs, other mobility aids and equipment including medical equipment to assist independent living
- financial assistance – towards the cost of short-term respite breaks at a registered respite centre.

Projects that intend to be a platform for continuing services will be expected to demonstrate sustainability. ACT would be concerned to be a sole funder of projects that require ongoing support.

The foundation's website states:

ACT's income is derived almost entirely from its investment portfolio and in any year we receive many more applications than we can fund. As our funds are limited we have to prioritise. Not all applications for grants will be successful and some may be met only in part.

General

In 2007/08 the charity had assets of £58.7 million and an income of almost

£16.4 million, mostly from property investments. Grants were made during the year totalling £861,000, including £445,000 to 386 individuals and £415,000 to 74 organisations. In previous years the charity's grant-making has run into several million pounds.

Grantmaking in 2007/08

Its strategic review and recent activities are described in the 2007/08 annual report:

Directors currently focus their efforts principally on disabled children and young adults, forming strategic partnerships with organisations working in these areas, as well as assisting individuals and other smaller charities. These strategic partnerships have approximately eighteen months to run to fulfil the pledges made and are carried forward as creditors in the financial statements.

The Directors meet formally on an annual basis to review the charity's strategic objectives over two days in January. Following the 2007 review the Directors appointed New Philanthropy Capital (NPC) to assist them in determining the focus of future grant giving, specifically to ensure that grants awarded are used effectively and efficiently in meeting the charity's objects. NPC is a registered charity that carries out research into different charitable sectors and the needs within them.

The results of this work have been debated by the Directors over the course of the year, and a new strategic plan was adopted in January 2008. The plan sets out a new five year grant programme commencing April 2009 tying in with an investment strategy directed at providing £15 million in grants to strategic partners and £5 million of small grants over the five year period. The Directors agreed to adjust the focus of their strategic grantmaking to young disabled adults, in particular in the 'transition' following completion of their formal education. Criteria for identifying suitable projects for strategic funding have been agreed with reference to research undertaken for the charity by NPC. [The foundation's new strategic partners are: Autism West Midlands, Core Arts, First Step Trust, Livability, Hollybank Trust, Surrey Care Trust, The Children's Trust, Treloar Trust and Whizz-Kidz].

Objectives for the year

Directors seek to use the income from their investments to further their mission statement by providing the majority of their grant support to building related projects and equipment provision.

The budgets set in respect of the year to 31 March 2008 envisaged £2.4 million of

donations to strategic partners and £600,000 to other general applications. £50,000 was allocated to overseas grants and there was also a £200,000 contingency.

Pledges made to strategic partners brought forward from the previous year were £3.8 million. £1.44 million was paid in the year against these pledges with no new pledges being made in the year. Pledges to John Grooms of £757,000 and Action For Kids of £50,000 included in the brought forward figure were reversed in the year since they are unlikely to be fulfilled in the foreseeable future. Total pledges outstanding at the year end amounted to £1.57 million. The payment of these pledges over an eighteen month time frame will see the fulfilment of the main plank of the stated objectives.

General applications which represent individuals and smaller charities are seen by the Directors as an important and integral part of their grant-making objectives. Grants of this type totalled £857,000 in the year. Such grants provide real positive impacts to the lives and independence of an increasing number of disabled, older and disadvantaged people.

Overseas, objectives continue to be met by the ongoing involvement in Meninos do Morumbi in Brazil with the inclusion of a school building (held by an overseas subsidiary undertaking) being accounted for as functional property. £3,300 of donations were made to other overseas organisations.

Strategies to achieve the objectives

By seeking to establish strategic partnerships with charities working in areas and with beneficiaries that the Directors have agreed to concentrate their grant making activities on, the objectives for the largest part, by value, of the grant making programme are met.

These relationships are typically, but not exclusively, in support of building related projects. This is an area where the Directors have considerable knowledge and experience.

The charity seeks applications from individuals and other charitable organisations by advertising its existence and publicising its application procedures on its website. It is also listed as a grant maker under its beneficiary criteria in a number of other media, as well as with the Charity Commission. The charity receives many more applications than it is able to fund.

Measuring impact

Most of our grant making is reactive and impact is measured against what organisations and individuals tell us they are seeking to achieve. In most cases we are part of a funding consortium and only contribute a portion of the overall funding

need and cannot therefore take sole credit for the many remarkable outcomes that are achieved especially by our charity partners operating in the care and social services sectors for which we have much admiration. We have no generic set of objectives but believe our impact can be measured from the hundreds of thank you letters we receive each year from our beneficiaries, from seeing building projects and facilities delivered months and sometimes years earlier than would otherwise have been possible, from seeing pilot projects flourish and grow when others would not take the risk on funding and from seeing lives transformed with just a very small financial contribution.

Grants also included those to: Hollybank Trust (£50,000); Dame Hannah Rogers Trust (£30,000); Elizabeth Fitzroy Support (£25,000); Treloar Trust (£14,000); Corbet Tey School, Federation of London Youth Clubs, Kent Kids Miles of Smiles and Royal Hospital for Neuro Disability (£10,000 each); Cedar Foundation, Hampshire Autistic Society and Royal Blind Society; and Community Link Up (£2,500).

Exclusions The foundation will not make grants:

- to replace statutory funding
- to pay for work that has already commenced or equipment already purchased or on order
- towards the operating costs of other charities except in connection with setting up new services
- to charities that have not been registered for at least three years
- for projects which promote a particular religion or faith
- to community centres or youth clubs except where those served are in special need of help (e.g. older people or those with special needs)
- to Local Authorities
- to umbrella or grant-making organisations except where they undertake special assessments not readily available from the foundation's own resources
- to universities or colleges, grant-maintained, private or local education authority schools or their Parent Teacher Associations, except if those schools are for students with special needs
- for costs associated with political or publicity campaigns.

Applications The foundation's website states that application by registered charities and overseas charitable organisations has to be by way of letter on the organisation's headed paper and should:

- give a brief description of your organisation including any statutory or voluntary registration
- provide a summary of the work you plan to undertake with the grant, together with a cost breakdown, plans and/or specification if available and a summary of the key milestones for the work
- provide information on why you need to do this work and what would happen if you were unable to do it
- give details of any other UK-based support received or pledged for your project
- specify what you expect the results of the work to be and the number of beneficiaries helped
- explain how you plan to evaluate whether the work achieved its goals
- explain if the work will require capital and/or ongoing operational funding and if so how you plan to meet these costs
- in addition you need to attach the following financial information to the letter:
  - a cashflow projection of income and expenditure budget for the work
  - details of any income already raised for the work and income outstanding and where you plan to raise it from.
  - your latest annual report and accounts.

When to apply
You can apply for a grant at any time. trustees meet four times a year, but you do not need to time your application to coincide with these meetings. Procedures exist to give approvals between meeting dates, where necessary.

We do not publish the dates of trustees' meetings.

What happens to your application
We will send you an acknowledgement letter within one week of receiving your application. If your proposal is either in an unacceptable form, or ineligible, or a low priority, we will tell you in this letter.

We will assess all acceptable applications and we may contact you for further information and/or make a personal visit. In the case of charitable bodies we may also ask for a presentation.

We aim to make decisions on grants of up to £50,000 within one month of receiving your application. Decisions on grants over £50,000 can take up to three months.

If the application is for an emergency you may request a faster timescale and we will do our best to assist.

Action Medical Research

Medical research, focusing on child health
£3.5 million (2008)
Beneficial area UK.

Vincent House, 31 North Parade, Horsham RH12 2DP
Tel. 01403 210406 **Fax** 01403 210541
Email research@action.org.uk
Website www.action.org.uk
Correspondent The Research Department
Trustees *Ms Valerie Hammond; Mrs Karen Jankel; Charles Jackson; Diana Marsland; Prof. Andrew George; Richard Price; Ann Paul; Sir John Wickerson; David Gibbs; Mark Gardiner; Colin Hunsley; Anne Palmer; David Holder.*
CC Number 208701
Information available Annual report and accounts were available from the Charity Commission. The charity also has a helpful website.

The charity was originally set up in 1952 as the National Fund for Poliomyelitis Research, and evolved into Action Medical Research. Since 2009 the focus of the charity has been child health, including problems affecting pregnancy, childbirth, babies, children and young people.

We support a broad spectrum of research with the objective of:

- preventing disease and disability
- alleviating physical disability.

Please note that our emphasis is on clinical research or research at the interface between clinical and basic science. We pride ourselves that our research is both innovative and of a high standard as judged by rigorous peer review.

Within the above criteria, we also support research and development of equipment and techniques to improve diagnosis, therapy and assistive technology (including orthoses, prostheses and aids to daily living) and we encourage applications in the field of medical engineering.

In 2008 the charity had assets of £5.4 million and an income of almost £6.6 million. Grants were made totalling £3.5 million.

Guidelines
The charity's website gives the following guidance on its project grants:

Grants are made to those in tenured positions in a UK university or institution. Research workers who require personal support from a project grant, and who have made a substantial intellectual contribution to the grant proposal, may be named as co-applicants with an established member of staff as the principal applicant.

Grants are provided for up to three years duration in support of one precisely formulated line of research. A two page outline of the proposed research is required before a full application form can be issued. Successful applicants from the outline stage will be sent a full application form. Awards will be made following peer review.

Applications should be of the highest quality as the scheme is very competitive.

The average award we make is in the region of £110,000 and grants above £200,000 would rarely be given. We are happy to consider grant requests at a lower level of funding (below £50,000).

Support covers salary costs, consumables and items of dedicated equipment essential for carrying out the work. The application should not include any indirect costs such as administrative or other overheads imposed by the university or other institutions.

A research team can only apply for one grant per grant round.

Please note that there will be a limit to the number of full application forms that we can send out. Where the work is considered peripheral to our aims, or in cases where demand on our funds is high, we will inform you of our decision not to pursue a full application.

Exclusions The charity does not provide:

- grants towards service provision or audit studies
- grants purely for higher education, e.g. BSc/MSc/PhD course fees and subsistence costs
- grants for medical or dental electives
- grants specifically for PhD studentships (although researchers may independently register for a higher degree)
- grants for work undertaken outside the UK
- any indirect costs such as administrative or other overheads imposed by the university or other institution
- costs associated with advertising and recruitment
- 'top up' funding for work supported by other funding bodies
- costs to attend conferences and meetings (current Action Medical Research grantholders may apply separately)

- grants to MRC Units, other than RTF awards where the training/facilities cannot be offered elsewhere
- grants to other charities
- grants for research into complementary or alternative medicine.

Applications

Outline proposal

All applicants should complete a two page outline proposal form, available from the charity's website, summarising the research and giving an estimation of costs, and email it to the Research Department. The details on the outline form should include the potential clinical application of the work, how it fits the remit of the charity and a description of the work proposed.

The purpose of the outline proposal is to establish that your proposed work clearly falls within the charity's remit and priorities.

If your work is considered peripheral to our aims, or clearly falls within the remit of another funding organisation, and in cases where demand on our funds is high, we may be unable to pursue an application from you.

Full application

If the outline proposal is acceptable, you will be invited to complete a full application form online and you will be advised of the timetable.

Applications are assessed by peer review, first by independent external referees and then by our scientific advisory panel.

The decision to approve a grant is made by the council on the recommendations of the panel.

Closing dates for proposals and applications are available on the charity's website.

The Sylvia Adams Charitable Trust

Disability, welfare, poverty, children and young people

£210,000 to organisations in the UK (2007/08)

Beneficial area UK with a preference for Hertfordshire and its immediate area, national projects

that have a national benefit and the developing world.

Sylvia Adams House, 24 The Common, Hatfield AL10 0NB

Tel. 01707 259259 **Fax** 01707 259268

Email info@sylvia-adams.org.uk

Website www.sylvia-adams.org.uk

Correspondent Kate Baldwin, Director

Trustees R J Golland; M Heasman; T Lawler.

CC Number 1050678

Information available Accounts were available from the Charity Commission.

This trust was set up using the income from the sale of works of art, following Sylvia Adams' death. The trust's aim is to improve the quality of life of those who are disadvantaged, through the alleviation of disease, sickness and poverty.

About 50% of the trust's grant total is given to UK causes, with the remaining 50% going to causes in the developing world. Grants generally range from £5,000 to a maximum of £25,000 and can run over several years.

Grants are made in the following categories:

- people with disabilities
- children and young people
- people living in poverty.

The trust is particularly interested in helping people to become self-supporting and self-help projects. Its UK focus is on enabling people to participate fully in society. Worldwide, the focus is on primary healthcare and health education, access to education, appropriate technology and community enterprise schemes. Both UK causes providing a national benefit and causes local to Hertfordshire are supported, as well as UK charities working overseas.

Grant-making policies

The trust assesses project proposals looking at the strength of the organisation as a whole and the sustainability of the proposed project.

The trust seeks to develop long-term relationships with appropriate organisations offering flexibility of funding in order to target its money where it is most needed. In order to develop these relationships, the charity's grant making is based on visiting organisations, being involved in charity networks and frequent use of new technology to keep in contact at low cost, both in the UK and worldwide. The trust is not prescriptive in its grant making and, whilst having a clear view of the work it wishes to fund, does not

believe its own objectives should distort the work of the charities with which it works. It therefore considers requests for capital projects, revenue costs, capacity building and new developments.

Partnerships

Partnership grants are made over a three to five year period but the trust reserves the right to end the arrangement at any time. Each year there is a significant, full and thorough review of the grant in order to ensure that the grant is being used appropriately. This will involve written reports and visits.

In its 2007/08 annual report the trust listed five partnership arrangements that were in place.

- Basic Needs (£30,000 over 5 years, agreed 2008) to develop the capacity of the organisation to attract non-institutional funding and therefore to become more sustainable. This grant is aimed at developing a franchising model which will enable more people in the developing world to access mental health services.
- Sense International (£30,000 in year 1, £35,000 years 2 and 3, £25,000 years 4 and 5, agreed 2007) this grant is targeted at helping the charity to develop it's international governance.
- VSO (£25,000 over 5 years, agreed 2007) for a five year mental health project in Sri Lanka which will need time to develop as mental health services are at a rudimentary stage in the developing world.
- Shelter (£25,000 over 5 years, agreed 2006) this grant helps to fund the establishment of a Diversity and Equalities Unit.
- NCVO (£25,000 over 3 years, agreed 2006) this grant provides funding for a Collaborative Working Unit assisting voluntary and community organisations to work together more effectively.

Grantmaking

In 2007/08 the trust had assets of £12 million and an income of £474,000. Grants totalled £496,000, of which £210,000 was given to 26 organisations in the UK.

UK beneficiaries included: NCVO, Shelter and ERIC (£25,000 each); Treehouse (£20,000); TB Alert (£15,000); Get Connected and Youth Sports Trust (£10,000 each); Spinal Injuries Association (£7,600); Ehlers Danolos Support Group and Friends of St Lukes – Redbourne (£1,000 each); and Youth Create (£500).

There were 11 overseas grants. Beneficiaries included: Esther Benjamin Trust (£65,000); Camfed (£25,000);

Farm Africa (£20,000); Solar Aid (£15,000); and Pattaya (£10,000).

The trust also decided to allocate a budget of £10,000 per trustee for grants to be made at their discretion. Two 'trustee grants' were made during the year to the Children's Trust and Trade Aid.

Exclusions The trust does not give grants to:

- individuals
- projects in the Middle East or Eastern Europe or the countries of the ex-Soviet Union
- work that solely benefits older people
- organisations helping animals, medical research or environmental causes.

Applications Full guidelines for applicants are available from the trust and through its website; applications can also be made online.

The Adint Charitable Trust

Health and social welfare

£305,000 (2007/08)
Beneficial area Worldwide, in practice UK.

Suite 42, 571 Finchley Road, London NW3 7BN

Correspondent Douglas R Oram, Trustee

Trustees *Anthony J Edwards; Mrs Margaret Edwards; Douglas R Oram; Brian Pate.*

CC Number 265290

Information available Accounts were available from the Charity Commission.

This trust was established in 1972 by the settlor, Henry John Edwards. Most of the grants made are for £5,000 or £10,000 to a range of health and welfare charities, many concerned with children.

In 2007/08 the trust had assets of £6.3 million and an income of £383,000. Grants were made to 54 organisations totalling £305,000.

Beneficiaries included: Fareshare, I CAN, Macmillan Cancer Relief, Royal British Legion and St Giles Trust (£10,000 each); Listening Books (£6,000); Arthritis Research Campaign, Combat Stress, Dementia Relief Trust and Playtime Matters (£5,000 each); MDF Bipolar Organisation (£4,000); National

Society for Epilepsy (£3,000); and Headway London (£1,500).

Exclusions Individuals are not supported.

Applications To the correspondent in writing. Each applicant should make its own case in the way it considers best. The trust notes that it cannot enter into correspondence and unsuccessful applicants will not be notified.

The AIM Foundation

Healthcare, community development, young people, environmental matters and other charitable activities particularly related to influencing long-term social change

£577,000 (2007/08)
Beneficial area Worldwide. In practice, UK with a preference for Essex.

Whittle and Co, 15 High Street, West Mersea, Colchester C05 8QA

Tel. 01206 385049

Email louisa@whittles.co.uk

Correspondent Miss Louisa Tippett

Trustees *Ian Roy Marks; Mrs Angela D Marks; Nicolas Marks; Joanna Pritchard-Barrett; Caroline Marks; Phillipa Bailey.*

CC Number 263294

Information available Accounts were available from the Charity Commission.

Set up in 1971 as the Ian Roy Marks Charitable Trust, this trust changed its name to the AIM Foundation in 1993. The foundation stresses that grant-making policy is highly proactive in seeking out potential partners to initiate and promote charitable projects principally in the fields of healthcare, community development, young people, environmental matters and other charitable activities particularly related to influencing long-term social change, both in the UK and overseas.

In 2007/08 the foundation had assets of £9.6 million and an income of £1.1 million. Grants were made totalling

£577,000 and were categorised as follows:

Youth care and development – grants totalling £145,000
Beneficiaries included: Antidote (£30,000); The Lady Taverners (£10,000); Inside Out Trust and Kids Company (£5,000 each); and Cirdan Sailing Trust (£4,000).

Community development – grants totalling £133,500
Beneficiaries included: Essex Community Foundation and Devon Community Foundation (£50,000 each); Wells for India (£6,000); Families in Focus (£5,000); and Westminster Befriend a Family (£3,000).

Influencing long-term social change – grant totalling £117,000
Beneficiaries were: New Economics Foundation (£65,000); and Network for Social Change (£52,000).

Healthcare – grants totalling £115,000
Beneficiaries included: Health Empowerment through Nutrition (£60,000); Penny Brohn Cancer Care (£10,000); and Traditional Chinese Medicine (£5,000).

Environment – grants totalling £61,000
Beneficiaries included: GAIA Foundation (£30,000); Friends of the Earth (£15,000); and the Soil Association (£10,000).

Miscellaneous – grants totalling £6,000
Beneficiaries included Clare College Cambridge (£5,000) and charities receiving smaller grants totalling £1,000.

Exclusions No grants to individuals.

Applications It cannot be stressed enough that this foundation is 'proactive in its approach' and does not wish to receive applications. 'Unsolicited requests for assistance will not be responded to under any circumstance.'

The Alice Trust

Conservation and education

£2.4 million (2007/08)
Beneficial area Buckinghamshire.

The Dairy, Queen Street, Waddesdon, Aylesbury HP18 0JW

Tel. 01296 653235 **Fax** 01296 651142

Correspondent Fiona Sinclair

Trustees *Lord Rothschild; Lady Rothschild; Sir Edward Cazalet; Hon. Beth*

Rothschild; Lord Cholmondeley; SJP Trustee Company Limited.

CC Number 290859

Information available Accounts were available from the Charity Commission.

The Alice Trust was founded in 1984. Its aims include the preservation, protection, maintenance and improvement of Waddesdon Manor in the Vale of Aylesbury, Buckinghamshire, its lands and contents for the benefit of the public generally, together with the advancement of education in matters of historic, artistic, architectural or aesthetic interest.

Waddesdon Manor was bequeathed to the National Trust in the will of the late James de Rothschild. The Alice Trust manages the activities at the manor on behalf of the National Trust under an agreement dated 3 October 1993. It is the current policy of the trustees to direct their grant-making activity almost entirely to the needs of Waddesdon Manor. Grants are very occasionally made to other charitable organisations.

In 2007/08 the trust had assets of £89 million and an unusually large income of £13 million (£7.2 million in 2006/07). This was mainly due to a gift of shares with an open market value of £4.4 million.

Only two grants were made during the year, totalling £2.7 million. The largest (£2.4 million) was made to the National Trust for Waddesdon Manor's running costs, repair and refurbishment. The other grant of £300,000 went to the Prince's Charities Foundation.

Applications Applications can be made for the advancement of education in matters of historic, artistic, architectural or aesthetic interest, but in view of the commitment of the trust to its principal beneficiary, Waddesdon Manor, it is unlikely that many applications will be successful. The trust states that the trustees meet twice a year to consider grant applications and that grants are occasionally made to other charitable organisations. However, in reality very few grants are made. We would suggest that an informal enquiry is made to the trust before undertaking the preparation of any grant application. The trust acknowledges postal enquiries.

Allchurches Trust Ltd

Churches and general

£6.3 million (2008)

Beneficial area UK.

Beaufort House, Brunswick Road, Gloucester GL1 1JZ

Tel. 01452 528533

Email atl@eigmail.com

Website www.allchurches.co.uk

Correspondent Mrs Rachael J Hall, Company Secretary

Trustees *Michael Chamberlain; Rt Revd Nigel Stock; Fraser Hart; Bill Yates; Nick J E Sealy; The Ven. Annette Cooper; William Samuel.*

CC Number 263960

Information available Annual report and accounts were available from the Charity Commission. The trust also has a helpful website.

The trust makes a large number of small grants each year. Around 600 are awarded to churches and cathedrals and perhaps 50 go to other organisations, many of which also have Christian associations.

The trust's income is derived from its wholly-owned subsidiary company Ecclesiastical Insurance Office plc.

The trustees make grants to the Church and the Christian community. Grants will be considered in response to appeals in support of churches, church establishments, religious charities and charities preserving UK heritage. Grants will be in the form of single payments.

In 2008 the trust had assets of £301.7 million and an income of £18.8 million. Grants were made during the year totalling almost £6.3 million.

Grantmaking in 2008

The trust described its activities during the year in its annual report, including a list of sample beneficiaries:

Category	No. of grants	Amount
Dioceses	110	£5,000,000
Cathedrals	106	£536,000
Parishes and other charities	751	£751,000

Dioceses and cathedrals

The majority of the trust's donations are used to support the dioceses and cathedrals of the Church of England. During the year, the trust made donations of £5.5 million (2007: £5.2 million).

Grants were largely utilised as follows:

- supporting deployment of clergy at parish level, particularly within deprived areas
- funding other staff to support the work of the clergy
- funding new initiatives ranging from supporting parishes to educational work in schools
- maintaining and repairing the church fabric in cathedrals
- funding specific mission and outreach activities.

Anglican churches, churches of other denominations and the Christian community

The trust has a general fund which responds to requests for financial assistance from Anglican churches, churches of other denominations, the Christian community and other charitable organisations in accordance with its grant making policy. In general, the trust supports appeals from churches for building and restoration projects, repair of church fabric, church community initiatives, religious charities and charities preserving the UK heritage.

Special project fund

The special project fund was established in 1999. Its purpose is to support a small number of projects on a larger basis. During the year, the trust allocated funds to the Lambeth Conference, and to the Rural Life and Faith Project at the Arthur Rank Centre.

Overseas projects

During the year, the trust allocated funds amounting to £41,000 (2007: £20,000) to support Christian causes overseas. In addition, a subsidiary company operating in Australia donated £527,000 (2007: £468,000) to charitable causes in Australia.

Some of the grants made

Some examples of recent donations are listed below to give an illustration of the variety of uses to which the grants have been put.

Lambeth Palace Library, London [£3,000]
A further annual donation was made towards the cost of running the library's unique heritage of archives and manuscripts for worldwide use via the internet.

Rural Life & Faith Project [£25,000]
It was agreed to make a financial contribution to this project over a three year period. Funds have been given towards a research worker and the provision of training resources for rural churches and their communities.

Cottingley Cornerstone Centre, West Yorkshire [£5,000]
A grant was awarded towards the cost of building a new church and community centre in a deprived area. This facility will be used by older people, pre-school children and youth groups.

The Children's Society, London [£3,000]
The trust gave financial assistance towards the funding of focus groups relating to The Good Childhood Inquiry, a project which works with young offenders, refugees and disabled people.

Shallowford House, Stone, Staffordshire [£8,000]
A contribution was made towards the building of a new chapel and a meeting room at the Lichfield Diocese's Retreat House. This is a main training centre for Church of England clergy and includes a facility for conferences.

Chester-le-Street, Methodist Church, County Durham [£3,000]
A donation was made towards the rebuilding of the church hall to benefit the church and the wider community. Sure Start and Age Concern use the facility and on a Friday evening a youth group meeting is held there.

St Mary's Church, Shirehampton, Bristol [£3,000]
A donation was made towards the building of a Community Resource Centre at the church to provide cafe and youth facilities.

City Arts Trust Limited, London [£3,000]
Financial assistance was given to this trust to enable it to work with cathedral, abbey and chapel foundations to promote and re-invigorate choral singing across the United Kingdom.

AllChurches Bureau, Wellington, New Zealand [£20,000]
Funds were provided for the Churches Education Commission to be used for school chaplaincy throughout New Zealand.

English Province of the Order of Preachers, Oxford [£1,000]
A grant was made towards the refurbishment of the Order's Priory building, to include the removal of asbestos and the upgrade of utility facilities.

St Mark's Baptist Church, Easton, Bristol [£3,000]
The trust provided financial assistance towards the upgrade of the church building, adding a cafe and facilities for a youth club to support the church and the community.

Christ Church Cathedral, Dublin [£8,100]
A donation was made towards the provision of an occasional orchestra to accompany and develop the cathedral's choir and to fund scholarships for young musicians.

Exclusions The trust is unable to support:

- charities with political associations
- national charities
- individuals
- appeals for running costs and salaries.

Applications cannot be considered from the same recipient twice in one year or in two consecutive years.

Applications An application form is available from the trust's website.

The H B Allen Charitable Trust

General

£994,000 (2007)
Beneficial area Worldwide.

Teigncombe Barn, Chagford, Newton Abbot TQ13 8ET
Tel. 01647 433235
Email mail@hballenct.org.uk
Website www.hballenct.org.uk
Correspondent Peter Shone
Trustees *Helen Ratcliffe; Peter Shone.*
CC Number 802306
Information available Accounts were available from the Charity Commission.

This trust was established in 1985 by the late Heather Barbara Allen, whose family produced the famous Beefeater gin. The trust benefited from just under £10.5 million from her estate and smaller grant-making trust in 2005 (following her death) and 2006. Miss Allen had maritime interests and was a supporter of Padstow lifeboat station, paying for the 'James Burrough' lifeboat (named after the creator of Beefeater gin in the early 1860s and founder of the company). Its recent replacement, 'Spirit of Padstow', was bought by the trust with a £2 million donation to the RNLI in 2006.

Grants, generally for amounts between £5,000 and £25,000, are made to a wide range of national and, occasionally, local charities. Most grants are to charities previously supported.

General

The trustees have no restrictions on them as to the kinds of project or the areas they can support and are generally prepared to consider any field. They do not make grants to, or sponsorship arrangements with, individuals or to organisations that are not UK registered charities.

There is no typical grant size, though the trustees do make a large number at £5,000. Grants can be recurring or one-off and for revenue or capital purposes.

The trustees give priority each year to those organisations to which grants have been made in the past.

The trust notes that many charities do not carry out up-to-date research into its activities and hopes that potential applicants will read the guidelines carefully and, if necessary, make a preliminary call to check their eligibility. The trust's guidelines are available on its website and include the current status of all the grant categories.

Please note: the trust has recently stated that the trustees, 'are now planning to support a major project over the next two or three years. As they are also anticipating a substantial reduction in income this year, they do not expect to be able to support many new applicants in the next year or so'.

Grants in 2007

In 2007 the trust had assets amounting to just over £31 million and an income of £1.3 million. Grants were made during the year totalling £994,000.

Beneficiaries were categorised under a wide range of fields, including: children and young people, general community, medical research, disability, environment and overseas aid. The largest grant was made to the Royal Hall Restoration Trust, Harrogate (£150,000).

Other beneficiaries included: Skeletal Cancer Action Trust (£50,000); Wildlife Conservation Research Unit at Oxford University's Department of Zoology (£40,000); Hebridean Trust (£25,000); Practical Action (£20,000); Children's Hospice South West and AgeCare (£10,000 each); Fight for Sight, Mencap and Bat Conservation Trust (£5,000 each); and Tree Aid (£2,000).

Exclusions No grants to individuals, organisations which are not UK-registered charities or gap-year students (even if payable to a registered charity).

Applications In writing to the correspondent, including a copy of the organisation's latest annual report and accounts. Applications should be submitted by post, not email, although enquiries prior to any application can be made by email.

Please note the following comments from the trust.

Applicants should note that, at their main annual meeting (usually in January or February), the trustees consider applications received up to 31 December each year but do not carry them forward. Having regard for the time of year when this meeting takes place, it makes sense for applications to be made as late as possible in the calendar year so that the information they contain is most up to date when the trustees meet. It would be preferable, from all points of view, if applications were made only in the last quarter of the calendar year. Although, preferably not in December.

The trustees receive a very substantial number of appeals each year. It is not their practice to acknowledge appeals, and they prefer not to enter into correspondence with applicants other than those to whom grants are being made or from whom further information is required. Only successful applicants are notified of the outcome of their application.

The Alliance Family Foundation

Jewish and general

£1.1 million to organisations (2007/08)

Beneficial area Unrestricted, but mainly UK, with some preference for the Manchester area.

12th Floor, Bank House, Charlotte Street, Manchester M1 4ET

Tel. 0161 236 8193 **Fax** 0161 236 4814

Email jridgway@boltblue.com

Correspondent Miss J M Ridgway, Secretary

Trustees Lord David Alliance; Hon. Graham Alliance; Hon. Sara Esterkin; Hon. Joshua Alliance.

CC Number 258721

Information available Accounts were available from the Charity Commission.

The trust's objectives are 'the relief of poverty, advancement of education, advancement of religion and any other charitable purpose'. Most grants are made to Jewish organisations.

In 2007/08 the trust had assets of £14 million, producing an income of £514,000. Grants totalled £1.3 million, of which £91,000 was distributed to individuals and £1.1 million to organisations. The remaining £110,000 was classified as 'sundry general charitable donations'.

Only grants representing 2.5% or more of the total expended for the year were listed in the accounts. These beneficiaries were: Tel Aviv University Centre of

Iranian Studies (£674,000); Imperial College Trust (£100,000); Maimonides Academy Baltimore (£51,000); LR Jiao Research Fund Hammersmith Hospital (£50,000); Centre for Study of Muslim-Jewish Relations (£30,000); and Kabbalah Centre Charitable Foundation, Dor Vador Institution and Centre Forum (£25,000 each).

Applications The trust has previously stated that they will not respond to unsolicited applications.

Amabrill Limited

Orthodox Jewish

£2 million (2007/08)

Beneficial area UK with a preference for north-west London.

1 Golder's Manor Drive, London NW11 9HU

Tel. 020 8455 6785

Correspondent Charles Lerner, Trustee

Trustees Charles Lerner; Frances R Lerner; Salamon Noe; Israel Grossnass.

CC Number 1078968

Information available Accounts were available from the Charity Commission.

The principal activity of this charity is the advancement of education and religious practice in accordance with the teachings of the Orthodox Jewish faith.

The following is taken from the annual report and accounts.

Grants are made both for capital purposes – which can include buildings, equipment and educational material – and towards the general running costs of the grantee institution. Other grants are made for the relief of poverty and these are only made after appropriate certification has been seen. (An independent organisation has been set up in north-west London to verify the identity and means of Orthodox Jewish persons for this purpose.)

In 2007/08 the charity had assets of £3.7 million and an income of £2.2 million, mostly from donations. Grants were made totalling just over £2 million.

A list of grants was not included in the most recent accounts. Previous beneficiaries include: Kahal Chassidim Bobov; YMER; BFON Trust; Beth Hamedrash Elyon Golders Green Ltd; Friends of Shekel Hakodesh Ltd; Friends

of Mir and Parsha Ltd; Cosmon Bels Ltd; United Talmudical Academy; British Friends of Mosdos Tchernobel; Mayfair Charities Ltd; Friends of Toldos Avrohom Yitzchok; Achisomoch Aid Company; the Gertner Charitable Trust; and Higher Talmudical Education Ltd.

Applications Appeal letters are received and personal visits are made by representatives of Jewish charitable, religious and educational institutions. These requests are then considered by the trustees and grants are made in accordance with the trustees decisions.

The Milly Apthorp Charitable Trust

Individuals as well as voluntary and charitable organisations concerned with health, older people and young people

£480,000 to organisations (2007/08)

Beneficial area North-west London, mainly the London borough of Barnet.

Iveco House, Station Road, Watford WD17 1DL

Tel. 01923 224411 **Fax** 020 8359 2480

Email first.contact@barnet.gov.uk

Correspondent Lawrence S Fenton

Trustees John D Apthorp; Lawrence S Fenton.

CC Number 284415

Information available Accounts were on file at the Charity Commission.

Set up in 1982 by Mrs M L Apthorp, her death in November 1989 saw considerable further amounts being left to the trust. The role of the trust is to 'enrich the lives of the community' in Barnet, particularly amongst people who are young and/or disabled.

Most of the grants are made through three specific programmes run for the trust by the London borough of Barnet: the Administered Fund, which caters for a wide spread of needs; the Apthorp Adventure Fund which helps provide character building activities for young people; and the Holiday Fund which provides holidays for the physically disabled and their carers. A fourth general grants programme may stray over the boundaries of the borough since it makes grants from an unrestricted General Income Fund. However, unsolicited applications to this fund are not accepted.

In 2007/08 the trust had assets of £11 million and an income of £1.2 million. Grants were made to 82 organisations totalling £480,000. A further £181,000 was distributed to 377 individuals.

Grants, covering organisations and individuals, were broken down as follows:

Administered Fund

Young people: £272,000 in 115 grants – Grants were given for character-building activities, job training, combating drug abuse and sport.

Sports: £15,000 in eight grants – Successful projects included the development of basketball facilities in the Burnt Oak area and funding for the Saracens Foundation's 'Sport for Health' programme, which aims to enhance the lives of children through sport.

Medical: £87,000 in 86 grants – Grants were made to enable people with disabilities to undertake various courses and training, ranging from art therapy, singing, music, theatre, choir, pottery, drama, floristry, bossing and welding courses. One award was made as a contribution towards extension of premises to allow wheelchair access. Other grants were made for a dyslexia assessment, voice recognition software, a power pack for wheelchair, computers and cookery lessons.

Older People: £46,000 in 30 grants – Support was given to sheltered housing schemes and clubs for annual outings, events and equipment.

General community benefit: £119,000 in 54 grants – Support was given to: environmental projects, arts activities, residents' associations, outings for parents and toddler groups and local churches.

Apthorp Adventure Fund

The object of the fund is to give 'opportunities for personal development and social education to adolescents'. Grants totalling £24,000 were paid in the year to enable 120 individuals to 'embark on character forming and adventurous activities'.

Holiday Fund

The mission of this fund is to enable 'physically handicapped people and/or their carers and families to go on holiday'. In the year a total of £42,000 was distributed to help 40 families go on respite holidays.

General Income Fund

In the year grants were made totalling £53,000 to RELATE, the Samaritans and scout and guide associations.

Exclusions No unsolicited appeals to the General Income Fund.

Applications Applications to the Designated Funds are open to organisations and individuals in the area of the London borough of Barnet, who can apply for the three funds administered by the borough. Organisations must be a registered charity or other non-profit making body which provides a service for residents of the borough and its environs and will normally be based in the Barnet area.

Grants may be for either capital or revenue projects, which are designed to extend existing levels of provision or to develop new services, and which demonstrate a clearly defined benefit to local people. Awards will not generally be made to support existing activities alone. Projects will be monitored and close attention paid to how the grant awarded is meeting its objectives.

UK charities are not eligible to apply but autonomous local branches of UK charities may do so. Applications must be submitted in the approved format and accompanied by latest audited accounts, plus constitution of rules and most recent annual report if one is produced. Projects should not normally exceed three years, and at the end of the funding period should be self financing or have an alternative source of funding available.

Application forms for grants from the designated funds are available from the London Borough of Barnet Libraries, other official buildings and directly from the Grants Unit, London Borough of Barnet, North London Business Park, Oakleigh Road South, London N11 1NP (Tel: 020 8359 2092).

The Arbib Foundation

General

£892,000 (2007/08)
Beneficial area Unrestricted.

The Old Rectory, 17 Thameside, Henley-on-Thames RG9 1BH

Tel. 01491 848890
Correspondent Carol O'Neill
Trustees *Sir Martyn Arbib; Lady Arbib; J S Kirkwood: Annabel Nicoll.*
CC Number 296358
Information available Accounts were available from the Charity Commission.

The foundation's grantmaking is described as follows:

The charity supports the philanthropy of Sir Martyn Arbib, one of the trustees, and his direct family. Much of the funds are donated to the River and Rowing Museum Foundation, and mainly charities with which the trustees have a connection.

In 2007/08 the foundation had assets of £189,000 and an income of £989,000, mainly from the Arbib family. Grants were made to 30 institutions totalling just over £892,000.

Grants were made during the year under the headings of social welfare, medical, education, children's welfare and animal welfare and conservation. The largest award by far went to the River and Rowing Museum Foundation (£600,000).

Other beneficiaries included: Institute of Cancer Research (£100,000); RNIB and Barbados Community Foundation (£50,000 each); Ramsbury Recreational Centre (£20,000); Watermill Theatre Trust (£15,000); Water Vole Project (£10,000); Restore Burns and Wounds Research (£5,000); Mitchemp Trust (£1,000); and Breasthaven Carers (£200).

Exclusions Unsolicited applications are unlikely to be successful unless there is a geographical connection to the foundation.

Applications Please note: the trust has previously stated that unsolicited applications are not being considered as funds are fully committed for the 'foreseeable future'.

Arcadia (formerly the Lisbet Rausing Charitable Fund)

The preservation of the environment, heritage and culture
Beneficial area Worldwide.

Fourth Floor, 192 Sloane Street, London
SW1X 9QX

Email david.sisam@nyland.org.uk

Website www.arcadiafund.org.uk

Correspondent David Sisam, Director of
Administration

Trustees *Charities Aid Foundation; Dr
Lisbet Rausing and Peter Baldwin (Donor
Board).*

Information available Information was
taken from the fund's website.

Formerly the Lisbet Rausing Charitable
Fund, Arcadia was set up in 2001 and
appears to have operated in parallel with
the Lisbet Rausing Charitable Fund until
that fund was officially wound up at the
end of 2008. Full information about
Arcadia and its activities is given on its
website, some of which is reproduced
here:

From 2009 onwards, Arcadia's key mission is
to protect endangered treasures of culture
and nature. This includes near extinct
languages, rare historical archives and
museum quality artefacts, and the protection
of ecosystems and environments threatened
with extinction. Although no longer part of
our remit, we have historically donated to
charities working to protect free societies and
human rights, to encourage education and to
promote philanthropy.

How We Operate

Grants are made only to charitable
institutions. The donor board concentrates
on a few themes. These are identified on the
basis of its members' own scholarly and
practical interests and experience, and
informed expert advice. The donor board is
solely responsible for the choice of
programmes or fields to be supported,
and **we do not consider uninvited
applications**.

The general criteria for a grant decision
include its scholarly and/or practical
importance; the expertise of those receiving
the grant; and the urgency of the relevant
issue. All grants are subject to detailed terms
and conditions. Regular reports are
requested, and careful financial
administration enforced.

Arcadia's mission is to protect cultural
knowledge and materials, such as near
extinct languages, rare historical archives,
and museum quality artefacts. These are
efforts we feel are vital and yet often
neglected. We are also committed to saving
natural treasures, and we support ecological
conservation through organisations including
Fauna & Flora International, Yale University,
Cambridge University, Conservacion
Patagonia, and The Whitley Fund for Nature.

We have historically funded in several areas
that are no longer part of our key mission

work. This includes the defence of human
rights, as demonstrated by our repeat grants
to Human Rights Watch. Other past grant
areas include higher academic training and
research and the promotion of philanthropy.

Recent grantmaking

By February 2009, Arcadia had invited ten
organisations to apply for new grants in
2009 totalling $25.8 million (approx
£18.4 million). Nearly all of these grants are
multi-year commitments, and include the
following:

- $5 million (approx £3.5 million) to each
  university library of Harvard, Yale, and
  UCLA
- $5 million (approx £3.5 million) to The
  Wende Museum
- $1.5 million (approx £1.1 million) to
  Birdlife International
- $1.2 million (approx £857,000) to Royal
  Botanical Gardens – Kew Seed Bank.

One of the most exciting grants for 2009,
although one of the smallest, is an initial
grant of $85,000 to the Early Manuscripts
Electronic Library. This grant is to support the
survey work for a potential five year project
to recover the palimpsests held at St.
Catherine's Monastery at Mount Sinai, Egypt.

Details of Arcadia's grants can be found
on the fund's website as they are
announced.

The fund currently makes grants to
organisations in the fields of
environmental conservation and cultural
knowledge, with large grants being made
to high profile projects and
organisations. As mentioned above, the
fund is keen to stress that unsolicited
applications are not considered.

Applications Unsolicited applications
will not be considered.

The Architectural Heritage Fund

Loans and grants for building preservation

£718,000 (2007/08)

Beneficial area UK (excluding the
Channel Islands and the Isle of Man).

Alhambra House, 27–31 Charing Cross
Road, London WC2H 0AU

Tel. 020 7925 0199 **Fax** 020 7930 0295

Email ahf@ahfund.org.uk

Website www.ahfund.org.uk

Correspondent Barbara Wright, Loans
and Grants Manager

Trustees *Colin Amery; Nicholas Baring;
Malcolm Crowder; Roy Dantzic;
Fionnuala Jay-O'Boyle; George McNeill;
John Pavitt; Merlin Waterson; Thomas
Lloyd; Liz Davidson; John Townsend;
Michael Hoare.*

CC Number 266780

Information available Accounts were
available at the Charity Commission.
The fund also has a helpful and
informative website.

The Architectural Heritage Fund
promotes the permanent preservation of
historic buildings in the United
Kingdom by providing financial
assistance, advice and information to
building preservation trusts (BPTs) and
other charities and by disseminating
information about the work of BPTs to
statutory and non-statutory bodies,
other organisations and the public at
large. BPTs, (charities established to
preserve historic buildings for the benefit
of the nation), operate within defined
geographical areas, usually a specific
town or county.

The fund seeks to achieve its objects
primarily by making grants and low-
interest short-term loans to assist BPTs
and other charities to acquire and repair
buildings which merit preservation for
re-use. The trust makes grants towards
initial options appraisals and certain
other costs, including the cost to BPTs
of employing a project organiser.
Refundable grants towards the cost of
specific professional work to develop a
project and to provide additional
working capital are also available.

In 2007/08 the fund has assets of almost
£13.5 million and an income of
£1.2 million, which included grants from
statutory sources totalling £623,000.
Grants were made totalling £718,000;
loans were made to the value of
£299,000.

Projects supported included those
initiated by: Highland Buildings
Preservation Trust; Glasgow Building
Preservation Trust; Heritage of London
Operations Limited; Heritage Trust for
the North West; Manchester Historic
Buildings Trust; The Vivat Trust; West
Midlands Historic Buildings Trust;
Cadwgan Building Preservation Trust;
and The Strawberry Hill Trust.

The AHF's website features a number of
case studies of projects that have
received support over the years which
potential applicants may find particularly
interesting.

Guidelines

Please note: the upper limits for Options Appraisals Grants and Project Development Grants quoted below were reduced slightly for the 2009/10 financial year; please (as with all applications) contact the AHF Projects Team before you complete your application.

The trust's website offers the following guidelines on its schemes:

Options Appraisal Grant
The AHF offers grants of up to 75% of the cost of an initial options appraisal of a project likely to qualify for an AHF loan. The maximum grant is normally £7,500, but in exceptional circumstances this can be raised to £12,500. In rare cases the AHF may offer grants for options appraisals which examine the feasibility of only one option, but the grant offered will be a maximum of £3,000.

An options appraisal eligible for an AHF grant will look at the key conservation issues affecting the building, examine all options and consider in outline the viability of the most beneficial option. It should also explore all possible sources of funding for the project. The charity must bring together the findings in conservation and financial terms, implementation strategy and the further work that needs to be carried out to develop the preferred option.

Project Development Grant
The AHF's Project Development Grant scheme is only available to building preservation trusts (BPTs). This grant replaces the previous project organiser and project administration grants.

Project development grants are intended to help BPTs with the costs and expenses of developing a project once its viability has been established, and take it towards the point at which work starts on site.

Items covered by these grants could include, for example:

Administration costs: any reasonable administrative costs relevant to the project (e.g. printing and copying, photography, telephone etc) may be claimed, up to a maximum of £4,000;

The costs of a suitably qualified project organiser to develop and co-ordinate a viable project and take it towards the point at which work starts on site. The project organiser is usually someone appointed for a fee from outside, but could be an employee; the grant will not normally exceed 75% of the project organiser's total cost, up to a maximum of £15,000;

Other development costs: a BPT can apply for assistance towards development costs of an eligible project that cannot be recovered from other funders, for example the fee cost of business plans. BPTs with paid staff may claim for their own staff time and overheads to produce such items at cost, up to a maximum of £7,500;

The costs of a mentor to work with a less experienced BPT to help them move their project forward up to a maximum of £7,500; in some cases this help may be available before an options appraisal is commissioned.

Low-interest loans
AHF loans are available as working capital to allow charities to purchase and/or finance the cost of the capital works. The recipient must have, or acquire, title or a long lease for the historic building to be repaired.

Amount
Loans are usually subject to a ceiling of £500,000 and security is required for every loan to protect the AHF's resources.

Interest rate
Interest on loans is charged at 4% simple (6% on loans for acquisition), payable at the end of the loan period.

Duration
The normal loan period is two years, or until the building is sold, whichever is earlier. The AHF will always consider allowing extra time, if this is requested before the loan falls due for payment, but the AHF does not offer long-term finance.

Security
Security can be offered in the form of a repayment guarantee from a bank, local authority or other acceptable institution, or as a first charge over any property (including that for which the loan is required) to which the borrower has a free and marketable title.

More detailed guidance is available from the AHF website.

Exclusions Applications from private individuals and non-charitable organisations. Applications for projects not involving a change of ownership or of use, or for a building not on a statutory list or in a conservation area.

Applications Detailed notes for applicants for loans and grants are supplied with the application forms, all of which are available from the fund's website. The trustees meet in March, June, September and December and applications must be received six weeks before meetings.

The John Armitage Charitable Trust

Medical, relief in need, education and religion
£4.6 million (2007/08)
Beneficial area England and Wales.

c/o Sampson West and Christo, 34 Ely Place, London EC1N 6TD
Correspondent The Trustees
Trustees *J C Armitage; C M Armitage; W Francklin.*
CC Number 1079688

Information available Accounts were on file at the Charity Commission, without a list of grants.

Set up in 2000: 'The principal objective of the trust is to provide financial support for charitable and worthy causes at the discretion of the trustees in accordance with the trust deed.'

In 2007/08 the trust had an income of £21 million, mostly from donations in the form of shares gifted to the trust. Grants totalled £4.6 million. Assets stood at £33 million at year end.

Donations were broken down as follows:

Category	Value
Medical research/medical care	£1,900,000
Relief for the poor, people with disabilities and older people	£1,400,000
Advancement of education	£943,000
Religion	£263,000
Other	£83,000

The following comments were included in the notes to the accounts: 'During the year, the trustees particularly wanted to help further medical research and care and a donation of £1.25 million was made to the charity Seeing is Believing. 11 other donations were made in this area with a total of £1.9 million being donated. The trustees are keen to support existing medical research and care projects.'

In the previous year a major donation was made to the Royal Marsden Cancer Campaign.

Applications Applications received by the trust are 'reviewed by the trustees and grants awarded at their discretion'.

The Army Benevolent Fund

Service charities

£2.5 million to organisations (2008/09)

Beneficial area Worldwide.

Mountbarrow House, 6–20 Elizabeth Street, London SW1W 9RB

Tel. 0845 241 4820 **Fax** 08452 414 821

Email pcummings@armybenfund.org

Website www.armybenfund.org

Correspondent Paul Cummings, Director of Grants and Welfare

Trustees *Gen. the Lord Walker; Guy Davies; Peter Sheppard; S M Andrews; P J Carr; S Clark; A W Freemantle; Mrs A M Gallico; A R Gregroy; M B Hockney; A I G Kennedy; Sir Michael Parker; D J M Roberts.*

CC Number 211645

Information available Accounts were available from the Charity Commission.

Grants are made for the support and benefit of people serving, or who have served, in the British Army, or their families/dependants.

The work of the [applicant] charity/service concerned must be of direct benefit to a number of soldiers, former soldiers or their dependants. Not only should this number be considerable but it must also comprise an appreciable portion of the numbers of people who benefit from the work or service of the charity.

In 2008/09 the fund had assets of £31.5 million and an income of almost £9.6 million from donations, legacies and investments. Grants to other charities totalled £2.2 million plus £2.5 million to regiments and corps for the benefit of individuals.

Around 100 organisations benefit from the fund each year. They include the Army Families Federation, Royal Commonwealth Ex-Services League, Officers' Association, Portland Training College, Royal Star and Garter Home, Thistle Foundation, Alexandra House, Queen Alexandra Hospital Home and the Royal Hospital – Chelsea.

Applications Individual cases should be referred initially to the appropriate Corps or Regimental Association. Charities should apply in writing and enclose the latest annual report and accounts.

The Ashden Trust

Environment, homelessness, sustainable regeneration and community arts

£799,000 (2007/08)

Beneficial area UK and overseas.

Allington House, 1st Floor, 150 Victoria Street, London SW1E 5AE

Tel. 020 7410 0330 **Fax** 020 7410 0332

Email ashdentrust@sfct.org.uk

Website www.ashdentrust.org.uk

Correspondent Alan Bookbinder, Director

Trustees *Mrs S Butler-Sloss; R Butler-Sloss; Miss Judith Portrait.*

CC Number 802623

Information available Excellent annual report and accounts are available from the trust's website.

This is one of the Sainsbury Family Charitable Trusts, which share a joint administration. They have a common approach to grantmaking which is described in the entry for the group as a whole.

Sarah Butler-Sloss (née Sainsbury) is the settlor of this trust and she has been continuing to build up its endowment, with donations and gifts in 2007/08 of £719,000. Total income during the year was £1.7 million including investment income. Its asset value stood at £26.4 million. Grants were paid during the year totalling £799,000.

Grantmaking

This trust's main areas of interest are (with the value of grants paid in 2007/08, including support costs as list in the accounts):

Category	Value	%
Ashden Awards for Sustainable Energy	£351,000	39%
Environmental Projects UK	£178,300	19%
Environmental Projects Overseas	£117,000	13%
Sustainable Regeneration	£93,400	10%
People at Risk	£77,000	8%
Environmental and Community Arts	£62,300	7%
General	£35,400	4%

The following information about the trust's grantmaking in 2007/08 is taken from its helpful and descriptive annual report:

Environmental Projects UK

The trustees initiate and support work that can reduce the speed and impact of climate change including energy efficiency and renewable energy technology, aviation and transport policy, and the wide ranging benefits of sustainable agriculture.

In the area of climate change and sustainable energy, the trustees aim to take a broad approach supporting research, practical action, awareness-raising, education and organisations that aim to influence policy in the field. This year they have supported the Green Fiscal Commission [£10,000] to make the case to policy makers that environmental taxes and incentives must form part of the government's long-term strategy and Green Alliance's report 'The way we run our homes: the buck stops where?' [£15,000] which identifies policies that are urgently needed to drive mass environmental change amongst householders, and to advocate these measures to government and the opposition.

To encourage institutions and individuals to take action on climate change trustees have supported Forum for the Future's work [£20,000] to develop new funding mechanisms that will allow Local Authorities to create their own, innovative responses in order to meet emissions targets and Green Thing's website [£15,000 approved] which makes sustainable living accessible and fun for individuals across the globe.

Environmental Projects Overseas

The trustees continue to support community-based renewable energy projects which aim to equip people with the knowledge and tools to help themselves in an environmentally sustainable way. These projects help to alleviate poverty by using renewable energy technologies for the enhancement of income generation, agriculture, education and health. This year a grant to RETAP [£70,000 over 4 years] will train teachers, school children and managers to grow their own woodlots to provide a sustainable source of fuel for cooking in energy efficient cook stoves. The improved stoves use far less wood and are smoke-free, eradicating the harmful effects of smoke on kitchen staff. Allavida's work [£10,000 approved] in an informal settlement in Nairobi trains and supports young people to develop environmental businesses. The recent conflicts in Kenya following the elections in December 2007 were especially damaging to this community yet these small enterprises offer hope and opportunity to the motivated young people who are involved in the project.

The trust is interested in the uptake of appropriate technology and this year has supported Potters for Peace [£5,000]. This organisation trains local entrepreneurs in Latin America and Africa to produce and sell ceramic water filters. These can be made from local materials and eradicate almost 99.9% of water borne disease agents found in drinking water.

Grants to the Beijing Earth Village [£5,000] and PANOS [£7,500] will train and encourage the reporting of news stories on environmental issues. Despite the fact that climate change will be felt most acutely in developing countries few people are aware of why weather patterns are changing. More stories in local newspapers and radio broadcasts will allow people to understand and take action on this critical issue.

People at Risk
Grants are made to organisations which help people at risk to access support, secure permanent accommodation, regain economic independence and reconnect with important family and social networks.

Over several years the trustees provided considerable help to homelessness projects which recognise that providing housing is only part of the solution, and therefore provide a range of additional support services. In 2003 the trustees commissioned Dreams Deferred from the research company Lemos & Crane, who identified homeless people's own aspirations for personal development. This led to the creation of Support Action Net, a network of agencies working with people at risk, offering toolkits, examples of good and effective practice, and training and organisational development. The trustees encourage this by funding awards for the most effective and innovative agencies.

In this and the Sustainable Development [Regeneration] category, the trustees aim to support projects that are pioneering fresh approaches, such as: self-help and peer support groups, education and training projects, and the provision of employment or work experience for people at risk. This year the trustees have been especially concerned with the needs of struggling young people, preventing early signs of risk developing into long-term health, substance abuse and homelessness problems.

[Notable beneficiaries this year included: Project 58 – Torquay (£25,000), towards the development of the Reversing Trends and Moving On Crew's work; and Broadway (£20,000), towards a model new advice service and training for dealing with people from Eastern European EU accession countries in London.]

Sustainable Regeneration
Funding in this relatively new category aims to bring together the themes of social exclusion and environmentally sustainable development in ways which can help local communities make the most of their resources and develop new skills and competencies. In many cases, projects will reflect the themes of the trust's environmental work, such as the promotion of cycling or sustainable agriculture, and its

work with people at risk, including support for employment and enterprise.

The trustees are keen to support projects which link people to the natural environment in a variety of ways. This year they have funded Farms for City Children [£10,000], Surrey Docks Farm [£16,000 approved] and Food Up Front [£18,000], all of which link fresh food and nutrition to inclusion and regeneration. Farms for City Children introduces pupils from inner-city primary schools to life on a working farm. A typical day for children staying at one of the farms might include milking, egg collecting, mucking out, weeding, fruit-picking and apple pressing all fuelled by meals grown and harvested on-site. Surrey Docks Farm provides opportunities for trainees, volunteers and school children to learn about farming at this working site in Rotherhithe, east London. Food Up Front is a new organisation that supports London residents to grow fresh vegetables on unused pieces of their property – front gardens, balconies, window sills or door steps. Participants have been inspired by how easily they can grow their own salad leaves and have found the networking with other local growers enormously rewarding.

Grants to the Society of St James [£10,000] and Street Shine [£20,000] both support people to move on from homelessness through enterprise and on to employability and regular work. The Society of St James has developed training and job opportunities for hard-to-reach homeless people in a micro-propagation business supplying nurseries and garden centres around Southampton. By going into top FTSE companies with a welcome shoe-shine service from desk to desk, Street Shine's trained traders at last gain a footing on the employment ladder.

Trustees envisage that research carried out by the Development Trusts Association into the level of environmental activity across its member organisations will identify interventions that could see a dramatic rise in community engagement on this issue.

Environmental and Community Arts
The trust continues to promote awareness of the developing field of environmentalism and the arts, and in particular, the performing arts, through its website, the Ashden Directory of Environment and Performance. The directory can be found at www.ashdendirectory.org.uk.

Within this category, the trust has begun to explore ways that arts organisations can collaborate with one another to address environmental issues, to reduce their carbon footprints, and to prepare their public for the implementation of measures which will improve sustainability.

The trust also helps organisations which highlight current environmental issues through the medium of literature and the arts [including: Cape Farewell (£15,000), towards core costs in raising awareness about global warming; and Cardboard Citizens (£15,000), towards a drama-training and performance programme for homeless people and young people at risk to combat and overcome problems linked to homelessness].

Ashden Awards for Sustainable Energy
The Ashden Awards were created in 2001 by the Ashden Trust. The aims of the awards are to contribute to the protection of the environment, the advancement of education and relief of poverty for the public benefit in developing countries, UK and elsewhere by promoting the use of local sustainable and renewable energy sources. The Awards does this through:

- raising awareness of small-scale sustainable energy projects in the UK and developing countries
- demonstrating how best they can be put into practice, using the winners as best practice case studies
- encouraging policy makers, NGOs and other funders, to incorporate small-scale sustainable energy into their agendas
- providing financial awards to outstanding projects which are environmentally and socially beneficial.

The Ashden Awards 2008 comprised eight UK awards (including four second prize award winners) and eight international awards for work in developing countries in the areas of enterprise, food security, health education and welfare, light and power for homes and businesses and enterprise, including an overall energy champion award and an outstanding achievement award. [The trust allocated £200,000 to the awards in 2008.]

UK Awards
Schools category:

- Ringmer Community College, East Sussex
- Sandhills Primary School, Oxfordshire

Local Authority category:

- Leeds City Council
- Arun District Council

Energy Business category:

- Kensa Engineering, Cornwall
- Dulas, mid-Wales

Charity and Community category:

- Global Action Plan, London
- Energy Agency, South Ayrshire

International Awards

- Technology Informatics Design Endeavour (TIDE), India (Energy Champion)
- Aryavart Gramin Bank, India

- Cooperativa Regional de Eletrificação Rural do Alto Uruguai Ltda (CRERAL), Brazil
- Fruits of the Nile, Uganda
- Gaia Association, Ethiopia
- Kisangani Smith Group, Tanzania
- Renewable Energy Development Project (REDP), China

This year's Outstanding Achievement Award went to Grameen Shakti of Bangladesh. The organisation has made a significant contribution to the spread of sustainable energy solutions – to date it has installed 160,000 solar home systems and is adding around 8,000 new systems each month. Since winning an Ashden Award in 2006 it has diversified into the provision of fuel-efficient stoves, which improve living conditions and save fuel; and domestic biogas systems which bring clean sustainable energy to thousands more.

Full details on the Ashden Awards can be found at www.ashdenawards.org.

Exclusions The trustees generally do not make grants in response to unsolicited applications. However, see Applications.

Applications

Who should apply?

If your organisation has a proven track record in supplying local, sustainable energy solutions in the UK or in the developing world then you should read the guidelines for the Ashden Awards for Sustainable Energy, available from the trust's website.

The Ashden Trust is one of the Sainsbury Family Charitable Trusts. Before applying to one of the trusts, please read the guidelines below.

1) The trust does not normally fund individuals for projects, educational fees or to join expeditions. If you apply for a grant in one of these categories, we are afraid the trustees are unable to help. If you are a registered charity or institution with charitable status applying for a grant we must warn you that only an extremely small number of unsolicited applications are successful.

2) Do not apply to more than one of the Sainsbury Family Charitable Trusts. Each application will be considered by each trust which may have an interest in this field.

3) All of the Sainsbury Family Charitable Trusts have proactive grant-making policies and have chosen to concentrate their support in a limited number of activities. If you have read through the Ashden Trust's website and feel your project fits into the trust's priorities we would be very interested to hear from you by post.

4) The trustees generally do not make grants in response to unsolicited applications.

If you would like to apply to the trust you should send a brief description of the proposed project, by post only, to the director.

The proposed project needs to cover:

- why the project is needed
- how, where, when the project will be delivered
- who will benefit and in what way
- income and expenditure budget
- details of funding – secured, applied for
- description of the organisation.

Please do not send any more than 2–4 sides of A4 when applying to the trust, at this point additional material is unnecessary.

AW Charitable Trust

Jewish causes through educational and religious organisations, and general charitable purposes

£4.1 million (2007/08)

Beneficial area Unrestricted.

66 Waterpark Road, Manchester M7 4JL

Tel. 0161 740 0116

Correspondent Rabbi Aubrey Weis

Trustees *Rabbi Aubrey Weis; Rachel Weis; Rabbi Zeev Cohen.*

CC Number 283322

Information available Accounts were available from the Charity Commission.

This trust was established in 1981 for general charitable purposes. The trust's aims are 'to support all worthy orthodox Jewish causes' and it meets these objects by making grants mainly to Jewish education and religious organisations both in the UK and abroad.

In 2007/08 the trust had assets of over £54 million and an income of £11 million. Grants were made totalling £4.1 million.

The largest grant again went to an organisation called TET (£725,000). Beneficiaries of other large grants included: Asser Bishvil Foundation (£287,000); Chevras Oneg Shabbos-Yomtov (£227,000); and Friends of Mir (£225,000).

Beneficiaries of smaller grants included: CML (£98,000); Toimchei Shabbos Manchester (£37,000); British Friends of Kupat Hair (£25,000); Purim Fund (£10,000); Beenstock Home (£5,000); and Zoreya Tzedokos (£1,800).

Applications In writing to the correspondent. The trust considers 'all justified applications for support of educational establishments, places of worship and other charitable activities.'

Awards for All (see also the Big Lottery Fund)

General

£61.4 million available in 2009/10 (England: £45 million; Northern Ireland: £3.5 million; Scotland: £10.5 million; Wales: £2.4 million)

Beneficial area UK.

(See local sections for contact details)

Tel. 0845 600 2040

Website www.awardsforall.org.uk

Information available All information is accessible through the Awards for All website.

Awards for All is a Big Lottery Fund grants scheme funding small, local community-based projects in the UK. Each country in the UK administers its own programme. The following information is reproduced from Awards for All's website.

England

Awards for All England is a simple small grants scheme making awards of between £300 and £10,000.

The programme aims to help improve local communities and the lives of people most in need.

To do this Awards for All England wants to fund projects that meet one or more of the following outcomes:

- people have better chances in life – with better access to training and development to improve their life skills

- stronger communities – with more active citizens working together to tackle their problems
- improved rural and urban environments – which communities are better able to access and enjoy
- healthier and more active people and communities.

You can apply if:

- you are a not-for-profit, voluntary and community organisation, including both registered and unregistered charities, co-operatives, friendly societies, industrial and provident societies, companies that are not for profit businesses and unincorporated associations
- you are a parish or town council, school or health body
- you have a bank account that requires at least two unrelated people to sign each cheque or withdrawal
- you have a governing body with at least three unrelated members
- you can spend the grant within one year.

Contact details:
If you have a general enquiry or want an application form, please contact us on one of the following.

Tel: 0845 410 2030

Textphone: 0845 602 1659

Email: general.enquiries@awardsforall.org.uk

If you need to contact Awards for All England about an application you have made or grant you have received, please use the details provided in correspondence to you or use the following:

For projects where the beneficiaries are based in the **Eastern, North East, North West, South East or Yorkshire and the Humber regions**:

Big Awards for All
2 St James' Gate
Newcastle Upon Tyne
NE1 4BE

Tel: 0191 376 1600

Textphone: 0191 376 1776

Fax: 0191 376 1661

For projects where the beneficiaries are based in the **East Midlands, West Midlands, London or South West regions:**

Big Awards for All
Apex House
3 Embassy Drive
Calthorpe Road
Edgbaston
Birmingham
B15 1TR

Tel: 0121 345 7700

Minicom: 0121 345 7666

Fax: 0121 345 8888

Northern Ireland

Awards for All Northern Ireland awards funds of between £500 and £10,000.

The aim of the programme is to bring real improvements to communities and to the lives of people most in need by funding projects which involve people in their communities, bringing them together to enjoy a wide range of charitable, community, educational, environmental and health-related activities.

We want our money to make a difference by helping:

- people to participate in their communities to bring about positive change
- people to develop their skills and widen their experiences
- people to work toward better and safer communities
- improve people's physical and mental health and well being.

We hope these awards will improve people's lives and will strengthen community activity.

You can apply if:

- you are a voluntary and community organisation, including both registered and unregistered charities, co-operatives, friendly societies, industrial and provident societies, companies that are not for profit businesses and unincorporated associations; or
- you are a statutory organisation.

And:

- you have a UK bank or building society account in the name of your organisation, which requires at least two unrelated signatures on each cheque or withdrawal
- you can meet our requirements for annual accounts
- you need an award of between £500 and £10,000
- you can spend the award within one year
- the people who will benefit from your project live in Northern Ireland
- you have adopted appropriate policies in line with your type of work
- your award will pay for your project-related costs.

Contact details:
If you have any questions, please contact us at the address or telephone number below.

Awards for All
1 Cromac Quay
Cromac Wood
Ormeau Road
Belfast
BT7 2JD

Tel: 028 9055 1455

Fax: 028 9055 1444

Textphone: 028 9055 1431

Email:enquiries.ni@awardsforall.org.uk

Scotland

Awards for All Scotland gives grants of between £500 and £10,000 for people to take part in art, sport and community activities, and projects that promote education, the environment and health in the local community.

We can fund a wide range of activities through the programme and want to support projects that meet our outcomes.

The outcomes for Awards for All Scotland are:

- people have better chances in life
- communities are safer, stronger and more able to work together to tackle inequalities
- people have better and more sustainable services and environments
- people and communities are healthier.

If your project could help us achieve one or more of these outcomes, Awards for All could be the right scheme for you.

You can apply if:

- you are a not-for-profit, voluntary and community organisation, including both registered and unregistered charities, co-operatives, friendly societies, industrial and provident societies, companies that are not for profit businesses and unincorporated associations
- you are a parish or town council, school or health body
- you have a bank account that requires at least two unrelated people to sign each cheque or withdrawal
- you have a governing body with at least three unrelated members
- you can spend the grant within one year.

Contact details:
For advice on completing the application form and any general queries you have about the scheme you can call the Information and Events Officers on 0870 240 2391 and you can also email them at scotland@awardsforall.org.uk

Awards for All
4th Floor
1 Atlantic Quay
1 Robertson Street
Glasgow
G2 8JB

Tel: 0141 242 1400

Fax: 0141 242 1401

Textphone: 0141 242 1500

Wales

Awards for All Wales is a simple small grants scheme making awards of between £500 and £5,000.

The programme aims to help improve local communities and the lives of people most in need.

Awards for All Wales aims to fund projects that:

- support community activity – by helping communities to meet their needs through voluntary action, self-help projects, local facilities or events (by communities we mean people in a local area or people who share a common interest or need)
- extend access and participation – by encouraging more people to become actively involved in local groups and projects, and by supporting activities that aim to be open and accessible to everyone who wishes to take part
- increase skill and creativity – by supporting activities which help to develop people and organisations, improve skills and raise standards
- improve the quality of life – by supporting local projects that improve people's opportunities, health, welfare, environment or local facilities, especially those most disadvantaged in society.

You can apply if:

- you are a not-for-profit, voluntary and community organisation, including both registered and unregistered charities, co-operatives, friendly societies, industrial and provident societies, companies that are not for profit businesses and unincorporated associations
- you are a parish or town council, school or health body
- you have a bank account that requires at least two unrelated people to sign each cheque or withdrawal
- you have a governing body with at least three unrelated members
- you can spend the grant within one year.

Contact details:

Tel: 0845 410 2030

Textphone: 0845 602 1659

Fax: 01686 622 458

Email: enquiries.wales@biglotteryfund.org.uk

Exclusions Generally, organisations with an income more than £20,000 a year (though there are exceptions to this, particularly for projects coming through schools and similar bodies).

Also:

- costs related to existing projects, activities or resources currently provided by your group, for example, ongoing staff costs and utility bills, regular rent payments, maintenance (including maintenance equipment) and annual events
- items which only benefit an individual, for example, scholarships or bursaries
- activities promoting religious beliefs
- activities that are part of statutory obligations or replace statutory

funding, including curricular activity in schools
- endowments
- loan payments
- second hand road vehicles
- projects with high ongoing maintenance costs – unless your group can show that you have the funds/skills to maintain them once your Awards for All grant runs out.

Applications Application forms are simple and straightforward and are available from Awards for All's website.

The Baily Thomas Charitable Fund

Learning disability

£4.1 million (2007/08)
Beneficial area UK.

c/o TMF Management (UK) Ltd, 400 Capability Green, Luton LU1 3AE

Tel. 01582 439225 **Fax** 01582 439206

Email info@bailythomas.org.uk

Website www.bailythomas.org.uk

Correspondent Ann Cooper, Secretary to the Trustees

Trustees *Charles J T Nangle; Prof. W I Fraser; Prof. Anne Farmer; Toby N J Nangle; Suzanne Jane Marriott.*

CC Number 262334

Information available Annual report and accounts were available from the Charity Commission. The trust also has a helpful website.

This is the largest trust featured here dedicated solely to the well-being of those with learning disabilities. It combines one or two major funding programmes with an extensive programme of generally one-off medium and smaller grants. These are divided between revenue and capital costs, and seemingly without the common requirement for applications to be dressed up in 'project' form.

In 2007/08 the trust had assets of £71 million and an income of £4.9 million. Grants were paid during the year totalling £4.1 million.

Beneficiaries receiving £50,000 or more were listed in the accounts and included: King's College – London (£131,000); Autism Cymru and the Calvert Trust (£100,000 each); University of Oxford

(£94,000); CASE Training Services (£80,000); RTR Foundation (£70,000); West Sussex Learning Links (£60,000); and the Children's Trust (£50,000).

Guidelines

The trust gives the following general guidance on its website:

The Fund's Policy

The Baily Thomas Charitable Fund is a registered charity which was established primarily to aid the research into learning disability and to aid the care and relief of those affected by learning disability by making grants to voluntary organisations working in this field.

We consider under learning disability the conditions generally referred to as severe learning difficulties, together with autism. In this area, we consider projects concerning children or adults. Learning disability, thus defined, is our priority for funding. We do not give grants for research into or care of those with mental illness or dyslexia.

Exclusions Grants are not normally awarded to individuals. The following areas are unlikely to receive funding:

- hospices
- minibuses except those for residential and/or day care services for those with learning disabilities
- advocacy projects
- arts and theatre projects
- physical disabilities unless accompanied by significant learning disabilities.

Applications Meetings of the trustees are usually held in June and early December each year and applications should therefore be submitted no later than 1 May or 1 October for consideration at the next relevant meeting. Late applications will not be considered. If your application is considered under the Small Grants procedure then this will be reviewed by the trustees ahead of the usual meetings in June and December. Following the meeting all applicants are contacted formally to advise on the status of their application. Please feel free to submit your application whenever you are ready, rather than waiting for the deadline.

Applications can be made online via the trust's website.

General applications

Funding is normally considered for capital and revenue costs and for both specific projects and for general running/core costs.

Grants are awarded for amounts from £250 and depend on a number of factors including the purpose, the total funding requirement and the potential sources of other funds including, in some cases, matching funding.

Normally one-off grants are awarded but exceptionally a new project may be funded over two or three years, subject to satisfactory reports of progress.

Grants should normally be taken up within one year of the issue of the grant offer letter which will include conditions relating to the release of the grant.

The following areas of work normally fall within the fund's policy:

- capital building/renovation/refurbishment works for residential, nursing and respite care, and schools
- employment schemes including woodwork, crafts, printing and horticulture
- play schemes and play therapy schemes
- day and social activities centres including building costs and running costs
- support for families, including respite schemes
- independent living schemes
- support in the community schemes
- swimming and hydro-therapy pools and snoezelen rooms.

Research applications
We generally direct our limited funds towards the initiation of research so that it can progress to the point at which there is sufficient data to support an application to one of the major funding bodies.

How to apply
Applications will only be considered from established research workers and will be subject to normal professional peer review procedures.

Applications, limited to 5 pages with the type no smaller than Times New Roman 12, should be in the form of a scientific summary with a research plan to include a brief background and a short account of the design of the study and number of subjects, the methods of assessment and analysis, timetable, main outcomes and some indication of other opportunities arising from the support of such research.

A detailed budget of costs should be submitted together with a justification for the support requested. Details should be included of any other applications for funding which have been made to other funders and their outcomes, if known.

We do not expect to contribute towards university overheads.

A one page Curriculum Vitae will be required for each of the personnel actually carrying out the study and for their supervisor together with a note of the total number of their peer reviewed publications and details of the 10 most significant publications.

Evidence may be submitted of the approval of the Ethics Committee of the applicant to the study and approval of the University for the application to the Fund.

An 80 word lay summary should also be submitted with the scientific summary.

Any papers submitted in excess of those stipulated above will not be passed to the Research Committee for consideration.

Before submitting a full application, researchers may submit a one page summary of the proposed study so that the trustees may indicate whether they are prepared to consider a full application.

The Balcombe Charitable Trust

Education, environment, health and welfare

£356,000 (2007/08)
Beneficial area UK and overseas.

c/o Citroen Wells, Devonshire House, 1 Devonshire Street, London W1W 5DR

Tel. 020 7304 2000

Email jonathan.prevezer@citroenwells. co.uk

Correspondent Jonathan W Prevezer

Trustees *R A Kreitman; Patricia M Kreitman.*

CC Number 267172

Information available Accounts were available from the Charity Commission.

This trust generally makes grants in the fields of education, the environment and health and welfare. It only supports registered charities.

In 2007/08 it had assets of £26.2 million and an income of £743,000. Grants were made during the year to 24 organisations totalling £356,000, which is an increase on previous years due to a substantial transfer of assets to the trust several years ago.

Grants made were categorised as follows:

Health and welfare – 14 grants totalling £184,500
The beneficiaries were: Oxfam (£31,500); NSPCC (£25,000); British Red Cross (£20,000); Amnesty International, Cancer Backup and Africa Now (£15,000 each); Leuka 2000 (£13,000); Cancer Care Appeal (£10,000); Family Planning Association (£8,000); Breast Cancer Care (£6,000); Maggie's – Cambridge and

Victim Support (£5,000 each); and Heart of Kent Hospice (£1,000).

Environment – 4 grants totalling £107,500
The beneficiaries were: Durrell Wildlife Conservation Trust (£82,500); Andrew Lees Trust (£15,000); and Wildlife Vets International and Bath Preservation Trust (£5,000 each).

Education – 6 grants totalling £64,000
The beneficiaries receiving more than £1,000 were: Action Aid (£20,000); Royal National Theatre (£15,500); Money for Madagascar (£15,000); Trust for the Study of Adolescence (£10,000); and Blackheath Conservatoire of Music and the Arts Ltd (£3,000).

Exclusions No grants to individuals or non-registered charities.

Applications In writing to the correspondent.

The Band Trust

People with disabilities, children and young people, scholarships, hospices and hospitals, education, older people and people who are disadvantaged

£665,000 (2007/08)
Beneficial area Worldwide, in practice UK.

Moore Stephens, St Paul's House, 8–12 Warwick Lane, London EC4M 7BP

Tel. 020 7334 9191 **Fax** 020 7651 1953

Email richard.mason@moorestephens. com

Correspondent Richard J S Mason, Trustee

Trustees *The Hon. Lavinia Wallop; The Hon. Nicholas Wallop; Richard J S Mason; Bruce G Streather.*

CC Number 279802

Information available Annual reports and accounts were available at the Charity Commission.

The trust was established in 1976 for general charitable purposes and beneficiaries are registered charities in the UK. The trust describes its policy as follows:

The objects of the trust are to aid persons (primarily those who are residents of the

United Kingdom) who are in need of education or care, whether wholly or partially, including those who are ill, disabled or injured, old and infirm or children with special needs. Such aid will be given through making grants to the providers of care such as institutions, homes and to the carers themselves.

In 2007/08 the trust had assets of £21.5 million and an income of £799,000. Grants were made during the year totalling £665,000, broken down as follows:

Category	No. of grants	Value
Children & Young People	13	£179,000
Disabled	12	£121,000
Hospices & Hospitals	4	£110,000
Educational	12	£105,000
Disadvantaged	6	£70,000
Homeless	2	£25,000
Army	1	£15,000
Church	1	£10,000
Older people	3	£8,000
Miscellaneous under £2,000	15	£12,500
Ex-employees	1	£10,000

Beneficiaries included:

Children & young people
PACE (£50,000); The Children's Trust (£25,000); Well Child (£15,000); National Holiday Fund for Sick and Disabled Children (£10,000); and Andover Young Carers (£5,000).

Disabled
Raynauld's & Scleroderma Association (£25,000); U Can Do IT (£20,000); Breast Cancer Haven (£10,000); Vassall Trust Centre (£5,000); and Bag Books (£1,000).

Hospices & hospitals
Chelsea Pensioners' Appeal (£50,000); and Maggie's, British Home and Trinity Hospice (£20,000 each).

Educational
Holburne Museum (£20,000); Friends of the Courtauld Institute (£16,000); Starehe UK Association (£10,000); Chelsea Festival (£6,000); and Tyne River's Trust (£1,000).

Disadvantaged
Fine Cell Work (£30,000); Leonard Cheshire (£15,000); 999 Club (£10,000); and St Mary Le Bow Young Homeless Charity, Barnardo's and Hustbourne Tarrant Development Trust (£5,000 each).

Homeless
Emmaus Hampshire Shelter (£15,000); and Colchester Emergency Night Shelter (£10,000).

Army
Army Benevolent Fund (£15,000).

Church
St Luke's Hospital (£10,000).

Older people
Florence Nightingale Aid in Sickness Trust (£5,000); Barristers' Benevolent Trust (£2,000); and Friends of the Elderly (£1,000).

The trust also awarded two scholarships to the Honourable Society of Grays Inn (£25,000) and the Florence Nightingale Foundation (£24,000).

Applications 'The trustees do not wish to receive unsolicited applications for grants as they themselves identify sufficient potential recipients of grants who fulfil their criteria from information that is in the public domain. If they require further information, they will request this from the potential candidates identified.' No grants are made to individuals. Trustees' meetings are held at least three times a year.

David and Frederick Barclay Foundation

Medical research, young people, older people, advancement of religion, people with disabilities, the sick and the disadvantaged

£2.3 million to institutions (2008)

Beneficial area Not defined, in practice, UK.

3rd Floor, 20 St James's Street, London SW1A 1ES

Tel. 020 7915 0915

Email mseal@ellerman.co.uk

Correspondent Michael Seal

Trustees *Sir David Barclay; Sir Frederick Barclay; Lord Alistair McAlpine of West Green; Aidan Barclay; Howard Barclay.*

CC Number 803696

Information available Annual report and accounts were available at the Charity Commission.

The foundation was established in 1989 by brothers, Sir David and Sir Frederick Barclay. The whole of the funds distributed come from them. The objects of the foundation are wide and the trustees distribute the income at their own discretion, 'for the benefit of charities or charitable purposes'.

In 2008 the foundation had assets of £4,000. Income received during the year amounted to £2.1 million. Grants were made to 13 organisations totalling £2.3 million and to two individuals totalling £12,000.

Grants in 2008 were categorised as follows:

- aid for the sick, people with disabilities and the disadvantaged
- aid for the young
- medical research
- aid for older people
- advancement of religion.

Help for the young
Grants in this category totalled £2 million. By far the largest grants went to Great Ormond Street Hospital and Alder Hey Imagine Appeal (£1 million each). Other beneficiaries included: Make a Wish Foundation (£18,000); Dorset Orthopaedic Limited (£17,000); and Foundation for Conductive Education and British Institution for Brain Injured Children (£5,000 each).

Medical research
Grants for medical research totalled £190,000. The largest grant was awarded to the CFS Research Foundation (£150,000). Other grants went to Nicholls Spinal Injury Foundation and Wellbeing for Women (£20,000 each).

Aid for the sick, people with disabilities and the disadvantaged
Grants in this category totalled £55,000. Two grants were made to The Passage (£50,000) and Farleigh Hospice (£5,000).

Aid for older people
The sole beneficiary in this category was Abbeyfield (Reading) Society (£10,000).

Advancement of religion
One grant was made to St Brides Appeal (£10,000).

Applications Applications should be in writing, clearly outlining the details of the proposed project (if for medical research, so far as possible in lay terms). The total cost and duration should be stated; also the amount, if any, which has already been raised.

Following an initial screening, applications are selected according to their merits, suitability and funds available. Visits are usually made to projects where substantial funds are involved.

The foundation welcomes reports as to progress and requires these on the completion of a project.

The Baring Foundation

Strengthening the voluntary sector, arts and international development

£2.9 million (2008)

Beneficial area England and Wales, with a special interest in London, Merseyside, Cornwall and Devon; also UK charities working with NGO partners in developing countries.

60 London Wall, London EC2M 5TQ

Tel. 020 7767 1348 **Fax** 020 7767 7121

Email baring.foundation@uk.ing.com

Website www.baringfoundation.org.uk

Correspondent David Cutler, Director

Trustees *Amanda Jordan, Chair; Mark Baring; Geoffrey Barnett; Prof. Ann Buchanan; Prof. Nicholas Deakin; Katherine Garrett-Cox; Janet Morrison; Jim Peers; Ranjit Sondhi; Dr Danny Sriskandarajah; Christopher Steane; Prof. Myles Wickstead.*

CC Number 258583

Information available Accounts were available at the Charity Commission. Full details of the foundation's current programmes are available from its website.

Established in 1969, the Baring Foundation's purpose is to improve the quality of life of people suffering disadvantage and discrimination. Its main objective is to help build stronger voluntary organisations, which serve those people, directly or indirectly, both in this country and abroad. The foundation aims to achieve its objective through its three grant programmes which place a high priority on funding organisations through its core costs programmes, whilst continuing to support smaller pieces of work through project funding.

The foundation's stated values are:

We:

- Believe in the fundamental value to society of an independent and effective voluntary sector.
- Use our funds to strengthen voluntary sector organisations, responding flexibly; creatively and pragmatically to their needs and with a determination to achieve value for money.
- Put high value on learning from organisations and their beneficiaries. We seek to add value to our grants by encouraging the communication of knowledge through a variety of means, including influencing others.
- Seek to build positive, purposeful relationships with grant recipients, as well as with other grant makers.
- Aim to treat grant-seekers and recipients with courtesy and respect; being as accessible as possible within clear programme guidelines and maintaining consistently high standards of administrative efficiency.

Grant programmes

The foundation makes grants under the following programmes – potential applicants are advised to check the website for current guidelines and up-to-date information on deadlines for applications.

Arts programme

The programme is closed to applications for 2010. Check the foundation's website for the deadline for 2011 applications and current themes.

Joint International Development grants programme (in collaboration with the John Ellerman Foundation)

The programme is closed to applications for 2010. Check the foundation's website for the deadline for 2011 applications.

Strengthening the Voluntary Sector – independence programme

Guidelines and information about this programme for 2010 were not available at the time of writing (November 2009), but are due to be published on the foundation's website from the beginning of 2010.

The foundation also occasionally funds special initiatives which are not open to applications.

Grants in 2008

In 2008 the foundation had assets of £51.3 million and an income of £1.6 million. Grants were made totalling £2.9 million.

Beneficiaries included:

Arts programme (under the previous theme of Arts and Refugees)

Charnwood Arts (£75,000); Craftspace (£68,000); North East Theatre Trust – Live Theatre (£50,000); and Bridge and Tunnel Voices and Artsdepot (£45,000 each). All awards were for core funding.

Joint International Development programme

Minority Rights Group International (£167,000); Camfed International (£155,000); Akina Mama Wa Afrika (£152,000); Peace Direct (£115,000); and Send a Cow UK (£39,400).

Strengthening the Voluntary Sector – independence programme

Law Centres Federation (£200,000); Coventry Law Centre (£191,000); Avon and Bristol Law Centre (£175,000); and Grapevine Coventry and Warwickshire (£35,600).

Exclusions See individual grant programmes on the foundation's website. Generally, the foundation does not accept applications from:

- appeals or charities set up to support statutory organisations
- animal welfare charities
- grant maintained, private or local education authority schools or their Parent Teachers' Associations
- individuals.

Applications On application forms available via the foundation's website. Potential applicants should check the foundation's website for current guidelines and application deadlines.

The Barnwood House Trust

Disability

£680,000 to organisations (2008)

Beneficial area Gloucestershire.

The Manor House, 162 Barnwood Road, Gloucester GL4 3JX

Tel. 01452 611292 **Fax** 01452 372594

Email gail.rodway@barnwoodtrust.org

Website www.barnwoodhousetrust.org

Correspondent Gail Rodway, Grants Manager

Trustees *John Colquhoun; James Davidson; Anne Cadbury; Richard Ashenden; Simon Fisher; Caroline Penley; David A Acland; Clare de Haan; Sara Shipway; Roger Ker; Annabella Scott; Jonathan Carr.*

CC Number 218401

Information available Detailed annual report and accounts available from the Charity Commission. Full information for applicants available on the trust's website.

Barnwood House Trust was established in its original form in 1792 and is now governed by a Charity Commission Scheme of the 17th April 2000. It is one of Gloucestershire's largest charities aiming to assist people with disabilities, including those with mental disorders, who live in the county. Its current endowment arises principally from the sale of the land upon which Barnwood House Hospital stood until 1966.

Since the sale of the hospital the trust has developed as a provider of facilities and funding for people with disabilities. It offers grants to individuals and organisations and provides supported accommodation and day care, all of which is focused on improving opportunities and quality of life for individuals and subsequently their carers.

The trust's grantmaking objectives are: firstly, 'the relief of persons who have a mental or nervous disorder or a serious physical disability and who are sick, convalescent, disabled, infirm or in need, hardship or distress by relieving their condition or assisting their recovery. Preference is given to those who live, or have formerly lived, in Gloucestershire'; and secondly, 'the promotion of research (carried out within Gloucester) into the cause, prevention and treatment of sickness associated with the above conditions'.

Grants to organisations

Grant applications are open to Gloucestershire-based charitable and voluntary organisations whose services seek to improve the quality of life of local people with long-term disabilities.

Grants for organisations can be awarded for specific capital or revenue costs and typically range from £500 to £20,000. In exceptional circumstances, higher awards may be considered. Start-up costs for a new project, or to expand an existing service and pilot schemes for testing need may also receive funding.

To be eligible for a grant, organisations must be based in Gloucestershire and provide one of the following services to the direct benefit of people with long-term disabilities:

- day care
- respite care
- support services
- occupational therapies
- holidays and play schemes
- social and recreational activities
- transport
- building works to adapt premises for use by a disability organisation
- other related building projects
- pre-employment training
- specialist equipment, such as hoists and baths.

Please note: the trust tends to look favourably on applications that can

demonstrate how the project will continue to function after the grant has been spent.

Grantmaking in 2008

In 2008 the trust had assets totalling £58 million and an income of £3.2 million. Grants were made to 79 organisations totalling £680,000.

Grant requests for sums under £750 are considered under the 15 day fast track scheme. 15 grants totalling £8,900 were awarded to 15 organisations under this scheme. In addition, to enable grants to be assessed quickly, requests for group activities, play schemes and holidays are considered against a pre-agreed formula. A total of £42,000 was awarded to 42 organisations. Grants of more than £750 were approved by the full grants committee.

Only organisations which received grants of over £10,000 were listed in the accounts. Beneficiaries included: St Vincents Centre (£236,000); Forest Pulse (£37,000); Cotswolds Care Hospice (£20,000); Inglos (£18,000); NCH, People and Places in Gloucestershire and the Lions Club of Cheltenham (£10,000 each).

Grants of less than £10,000 were made totalling £205,000.

The sum of £283,000 was distributed in grants to individuals. The trust also lets 39 sheltered housing units and 5 disability bungalows. A riser-recliner chair loan facility is also in operation.

Exclusions Grants are not normally made in the following circumstances:

- to organisations outside Gloucestershire
- for building or adapting private, public sector or social housing
- to start-up or subsidise services purchased or contracted out by the public sector
- where the applicant organisation has significant unrestricted reserves
- where the applicant organisation operates an exclusive policy, e.g. by charging excessive fees
- for core funding to the public sector
- to non-disability organisations seeking to make community buildings more accessible, unless there is exceptional need
- for a management charge applied to a project
- for any work that is not aimed specifically at disabled people.

Applications The trust advises potential applicants to phone before making an application to confirm the

eligibility of their proposal. Grant application forms can be downloaded from the website or requested by telephone or post.

Applications are assessed on a quarterly basis, meaning applicants should not have to wait more than three months for a decision. Applications for less than £750 will be 'fast tracked' and should be processed within 15 days. Please note: holiday and play scheme grants are also fast-tracked and have a dedicated application form.

If successful, applicants have the option of drawing down their grant immediately on production of required invoices, or can ask the trust to hold it open for up to 12 months. Organisations which have received a grant from the trust can also apply for a repeat grant of up to £750.

For further information about grants for individuals, contact the trust, or see *A Guide to Grants for Individuals in Need*, published by the Directory of Social Change.

BBC Children in Need

Welfare of disadvantaged children

£36.8 million (2007/08)

Beneficial area UK.

PO Box 1000, London W12 7WJ

Tel. 020 8576 7788 **Fax** 020 8576 8887

Email pudsey@bbc.co.uk

Website bbc.co.uk/pudsey

Correspondent David Ramsden, Chief Executive

Trustees *Stevie Spring, Chair; Tim Davie; Neena Mahal; Beverley Tew; Sir Terry Wogan; Yogesh Chauhan; Alan Broughton; Susan Elizabeth; Peter McBride; Nicholas Eldred.*

CC Number 802052

Information available Information was provided by the charity.

The charity, registered in 1989, distributes the proceeds of the BBC's annual Children in Need appeal (first televised in 1980). Around 2,000 grants in total may be made in a year. These are allocated in four rounds, in January, April, July and October. Amounts range from a few hundred pounds to a normal maximum of about £100,000.

Grants are made for specific projects which directly help children and young people (aged 18 and under).

In 2007/08, covering the BBC Children in Need Appeal 2007 held in November 2007, it had a total income of £37 million.

The trustees approve all grant awards on the basis of the assessment of applications by third party assessors and the recommendations of eight regional advisory committees. Grants are awarded to properly constituted not-for-profit organisations working with disadvantaged children in the United Kingdom (and The Isle of Man and Channel Islands). Grants are for periods of one, two or three years, apart from holiday projects with overnight stays that can only apply for one year of funding at a time.

Where a grant is awarded for a period of greater than one year each annual instalment is only released after the receipt of a satisfactory report on the prior year's expenditure.

During the year the charity received 3,219 applications for grant aid with a total amount requested of £183 million. Awards were made to 1,327 organisations to the value of £36.8 million.

The following grants made in 2007/08 give an example of the largest and smallest grants made.

- Renfield Centre Children's Fund – Scotland (£346,000). Welfare grants for individual children in need throughout Scotland.
- Women's Aid Federation England – Bristol (£154,000). This project will play a unique national role in advocating on behalf of the needs of children and young people experiencing domestic violence. This continuation grant will fund the salary and on costs, for a further three years for the National Children and Young People's Officer.
- Seaham Youth Initiative – County Durham (£144,000). The project will provide information, support and activities designed to develop young people's social skills and bring together young people from different communities, to break down barriers and prevent conflict. The grant, over three years, will fund two existing part-time Detached Youth Worker posts, plus two-thirds of the running costs of the project.
- Mencap Greenwich – London (£133,000). The Greenlights project will continue to work with children with learning difficulties and

challenging behaviour. This three year grant will fund the Project Workers costs and non salary costs.

BBC Children in Need believes that smaller amounts of money can have a significant impact and so here are some examples of its smaller grants:

- Berwickshire Group Riding for the Disabled (£777). Grant for equipment including riding hats, vaulting shoes, adapted stirrups and blacksmith's tools, for children with a variety of disabilities. This project boosts confidence, improves balance and increases communication skills for children and young people in Berwickshire with a range of physical and mental disabilities, by providing horse riding activities.
- Dumfries High School Home Link Service (£570). This project will help children and young people in transition to secondary school who have been identified as needing additional support. This one year grant will pay the costs of the school holiday project.
- St Paul's Child Contact Centre – Bracknell (£495). The project will provide a safe place for children to meet and interact with their non-contact parents. This one year grant will pay for a Wii entertainment system and accessories.
- Seesaw Playgroup Ballymoney – Northern Ireland (£350). This project will enable children who live in rural areas to go on educational outings.

In 2008 BBC Children in Need launched a one-off grants programme, 'Positive Destinations' which is a £2 million grant programme, additional to BBC Children in Need's normal grants programme, which was undertaken in partnership with The Hunter Foundation.

Positive Destinations has now made three large and two smaller grants to ensure that children and young people achieve a positive and sustained future in terms of education, employment and training. As an integral part of this programme projects will be expected to generate learning and ensure sustainability of their work beyond the life of the programme. The learning from the programme will be disseminated on a continuing basis to help inform practice and policy in this field.

We do not anticipate any further funding to be made available through the Positive Destinations Fund but BBC Children in Need may look to run other specialist grants programmes in the future.

Fun and Friendship
In May 2009 the charity launched the 'Fun and Friendship' programme, for

disabled young people between the ages of 12 and 18, with the following press release:

The £3 million grants programme, Fun and Friendship, was set up following commissioned research revealing a significant lack of opportunity for independent socialising for disabled young people, often leading to feelings of loneliness and isolation. BBC Children in Need are targeting organisations that can provide these opportunities for friendship, and identify and address the barriers disabled young people face as teenagers growing up.

BBC Children in Need intends to award up to 12 three-year grants of up to £300,000 each. The Fun and Friendship grants programme is in addition to BBC Children in Need's general grants.

David Ramsden, Chief Executive of BBC Children in Need says 'Fun and Friendship is aimed at projects that empower disabled young people and work to support opportunities for friendships, fun and social independence.'

The scheme is designed for organisations with the infrastructure and experience to support the participation and leadership of disabled young people, and those who are willing to engage and share with the network of Fun and Friendship projects and others in the field of disability.

Ramsden continues 'We want to increase learning across the wider sector, and with each successful applicant's contribution, work together to promote new and effective ways of doing things.'

The primary focus of applications should be social interaction, with disabled young people actively engaged in determining how that develops, combined with a commitment to sharing what is learned in the process.

Advice for applicants
If at any time you need help with your application please contact the BBC Children in Need helpdesk by emailing: pudsey@bbc.co.uk; or by telephone: 020 8576 7788.

We now have a fully online application system. This enables us to respond more quickly to requests. You can find our grant application form at: www.bbc.co.uk/pudsey.

You will also find lots of helpful information and advice on our website – including simple step-by-step support on how to complete the application form.

Our grants range from a few hundred pounds to over £100,000. We want to fund projects for success and it is important that you ask for the costs realistically needed to change children's lives for the better. Grants can be made for between one and three years, depending on the project.

While we make quite a number of large grants, we also know from experience that very valuable work can be achieved for quite modest sums. We are always keen to encourage applications from organisations seeking smaller amounts.

Organisations apply to us for a wide range of grants. The purpose and amount can vary enormously. From our experience we think that the following information might help an organisation to make a more effective application for a grant.

Our focus is firmly on those children and young people who are experiencing disadvantage. We seek to fund organisations working to combat or alleviate this disadvantage and to make a real difference to the quality of children and young people's lives.

The appeal gives grants to organisations working with disadvantaged children and young people who must be aged 18 years and under, living in the United Kingdom. Their disadvantages will include:

- illness, distress, abuse or neglect
- disability
- behavioural or psychological impairment
- living in poverty or situations of deprivation.

The application should demonstrate how your project will change the lives of children for the better. It should be entirely focused on children. Where possible and appropriate it should take into account children's views and involve them in decision-making. Applicants should be very specific in helping us to understand the nature of the disadvantage they are seeking to address.

The application form is designed to help us make an informed decision about your organisation and although some questions are probably easier to answer than others, you must complete the whole form otherwise we will not have enough information to make a decision.

We are committed to making sure our grants bring about changes for the better in children's lives and we want to support work that can do this.

The most important step in making a good application takes place before you even start to fill in the application form, and that is to plan your project well.

Good planning means:

- identifying in advance what difference you want to make for children
- realistically defining how the project will achieve this difference
- knowing how you will recognise whether the project has made the difference you want to make.

Completing the application form is the starting point. Every eligible applicant will then have the opportunity to talk through their plans with one of our assessors, whose reports assist our local committees to make informed choices.

During the assessment of your application we will want to know more about:

- the background to your organisation and some knowledge of how it is governed
- how you work with other organisations and services in your area
- how your project was planned and what it hopes to achieve for children
- how you monitor/evaluate your work
- the child protection measures that are in operation
- if applicable job description(s), person specification(s) and expected salary level(s)
- the basis for costing equipment, services or activities
- the timing of other decisions with regard to multi-funding or complex projects.

Please note: The above provides only a brief outline of all that you need to consider before making an application. We recommend that you visit our website to read or download the *BBC Children in Need Applicant Guidance* which provides comprehensive advice for would be applicants.

If at any time you need help with your application please contact the BBC Children in Need helpdesk by emailing: pudsey@bbc.co.uk; or by telephone: 020 8576 7788.

Exclusions The appeal does not consider applications from private individuals or the friends or families of individual children. In addition, grants will not be given for:

- trips and projects abroad
- medical treatment or medical research
- unspecified expenditure
- deficit funding or repayment of loans
- retrospective funding
- projects which are unable to start within 12 months
- distribution to another/other organisation(s)
- general appeals and endowment funds
- the relief of statutory responsibilities
- projects for pregnancy testing or advice, information or counselling on pregnancy choices
- the promotion of religion
- additional projects for organisations that already hold a BBC Children in Need grant where funding is not coming to an end.

Applications Straightforward and excellent application forms and guidelines are available from the website

or from the following national BBC Children in Need offices:

England (and general helpline): PO Box 1000, London W12 7WJ.
Tel: 020 8576 7788.

Northern Ireland: Broadcasting House, Ormeau Avenue, Belfast BT2 8HQ.
Tel: 028 9033 8221.

Scotland: BBC Scotland, G10, 40 Pacific Drive, Glasgow, G51 1DA.
Tel: 0141 422 6111.

Wales: Broadcasting House Llandaff, Cardiff CF5 2YQ.
Tel: 029 2032 2383.

There are four closing dates for applications – 15 January, 15 April, 15 July and 15 October. Applicants should allow up to three months after each closing date for notification of a decision.

Application forms must be completed online – visit the website for more information (www.bbc.co.uk/pudsey).

Please note: Incomplete or late application forms will not be assessed.

The charity has recently expressed an interest in receiving more eligible applications from north-west England. The charity is particularly interested in hearing from organisations that have not had funding from Children in Need in the past. Contact Philip Jeffery, Regional Officer on 0161 244 3442 or by email at: philip.jeffery@bbc.co.uk.

The Bedford Charity (The Harpur Trust)

Education, welfare and recreation

£754,000 to organisations (2007/08)

Beneficial area The borough of Bedford.

Princeton Court, Pilgrim Centre, Brickhill Drive, Bedford MK41 7PZ

Tel. 01234 369500 **Fax** 01234 369505

Email grants@harpur-trust.org.uk

Website www.bedfordcharity.org.uk

Correspondent Lucy Bardner, Grants Manager

Trustees *David Palfreyman; Prof. William Stephens; David W Doran; David*

CC Number 204817

Information available Accounts were available at the Charity Commission. The charity has an excellent website.

This trust is one of the oldest described in this resource, and probably one of the oldest in the country. The following is taken from the charity's website.

The Bedford Charity, also known as the Harpur Trust, has been in existence since 1566 when it was founded by Sir William Harpur (1496–1573) a tailor from Bedford and later Lord Mayor of London, who created an endowment to sustain a school he had established in Bedford. The endowment also made provision for the marriage of poor maids of the town, for deprived children to be nourished and informed, and for any residue to be distributed to the poor of the town.

These ideals evolved over the years into the three charitable objects of the Bedford Charity today which are:

- the promotion of education
- the relief of those who are sick or in need, hardship or distress
- the provision of recreational facilities with a social welfare purpose.

Most grants are made to organisations, but there is a very small budget (less than 5% of the total grants budget) for grants to individuals under the education object.

Today, the activities of the trust are still inspired by the vision of William Harpur who saw the real value of education and the real needs to be addressed amongst the disadvantaged, poor and sick in his home town of Bedford.

The trust owns and runs four independent schools in Bedford – Bedford School, Bedford High School, Bedford Modern School and Dame Alice Harpur School. All four provide selective education for a total of over 4,000 children in the age range 7–18 years. It also owns and manages 40 almshouses which provide secure, affordable accommodation for a number of the borough's less advantaged older citizens.

Grant-making policy

The charity makes grants in support of its three charitable objects. The trustees have flexibility to allocate resources to each object according to the perceived need. The charity's main priorities, its grants programme and application processes are set out in the Guidance Notes which are available by post and on the website. They are summarised here under the relevant charitable purpose:

Promotion of education

The Bedford Charity since its inception has had a key role in developing and enhancing educational opportunities in the borough. This interest is reflected in the educational programmes that comprise a major element of the community grants activities. The awards are generally made to support:

- collaborative projects, enabling significant numbers of young people in the borough to have access to new and valuable learning opportunities;
- projects that focus on: enriching the educational experiences of younger people, enabling older people to remain active learners and provision for those with additional support needs to be able to access educational and training opportunities
- innovative and potentially replicable projects initiated by schools in the maintained sector, and other educational establishments, where there is no statutory obligation for funding
- educational projects where an award may help leverage in significant additional funding from other sources.

Promotion of any charitable purpose for the relief of people who are sick or in need, hardship or distress

Requests for funding for staffing, running and capital costs for projects and core services will be considered. The trust advises that competition for grants is particularly fierce within this broad grants programme. Through research and consultation, locally and beyond the borough, the trust continually develops the grant giving priorities to respond to emerging local needs and opportunities.

The trust's grant making activities aim:

- to help establish projects that can enable an organisation to prove the value of developing new, or enhancing existing, services to relevant audiences, particularly potential funders and other complementary service providers
- to encourage collaborative working between organisations to meet the needs of end beneficiaries. This may include the trust's own involvement with developing funding partnerships at the early stages of a project's activities
- under exceptional circumstances, to assist established local organisations with short-term funding to enable

continuity of their services until more sustainable financial support can be secured.

Provision of recreational facilities with a social welfare purpose

Grant giving under this programme has a strong emphasis on projects that aim to address the needs of young and/or disadvantaged people. How a project proposal will act 'in the interests of social welfare' is carefully considered. The focus of this programme is on people, and how a project will significantly improve their access to valuable recreational opportunities and experiences. Successful project requests generally include aspects that complement the objectives of the other two programmes.

The organisation making the application must be a registered charity or other non-profit making body and be based in the borough of Bedford, and/or be conducting specific activities aiming to meet the needs of people who are normally resident in the borough, (the borough comprises the town of Bedford and the surrounding area of North Bedfordshire).

Themed Grants Programmes

In addition to its ongoing responsive programme, the charity has four themed grants programmes:

- Excellence in Education
- Voluntary Sector Infrastructure Support
- Homelessness
- Child and Adolescent Mental Health.

The application process for the themed programmes is the same as that for the responsive programme.

In 2007/08 the charity had assets of £111.4 million and an income of almost £51 million, which included £45.2 million from school fees and £3.1 million from investments. There were 52 grants to organisations totalling £754,000; grants, awards and bursaries to individuals totalled £76,600.

Beneficiaries included: Bedfordshire Alliance of Nursery and Lower Schools (£102,400), for the Mind Mapping Research Project; King's Arms Project (£75,000), towards ongoing support; Autism Bedfordshire (£63,700), for a full time development officer; Cecil Higgins Art Gallery and Bedford Museum (£32,000), for a audience development project; Bedford Prep School and Pilgrims School (£20,000), for the Bedford Maths Academy; Ormiston Children and Families Trust (£15,000), for Children of Offenders – Parenting Programme; HMP Bedford (£14,000), for a feasibility study on the Resettlement Support Project; Bedfordshire Primary Care Trust (£10,000), for the Early Intervention Project; Bedford Chamber Music Festival (£8,000), towards the 2008 festival; Bedford Sea Cadet Corps (£5,500), to replace heating and hot water boilers; Addaction Bedford (£5,000), for the Health, Employment and Lifestyle Programme; Queen's Park Lower School (£2,500), to enhance the playground; Bedford Cricket Club (£2,000), for new nets; and Tavistock Community Centre (£1,000), for flame retardant curtains.

Exclusions Grants are not made:

- in support of commercial ventures
- for any project that relates primarily to the promotion of any religion
- in support of projects that do not benefit the residents of the borough of Bedford
- to cover costs already incurred, although exceptions are considered and this should be discussed with the trust prior to an application being submitted
- for services which are the responsibility of the local authority, for example, a school applying for a grant to cover the cost of employing a teacher is unlikely to be successful. However, the trust could consider an application from a school for a creative arts project that involved paying a voluntary organisation to deliver lunchtime or after school workshops.

Applications The following information is taken from the charity's Funding Guidelines, which are available to download from its website.

Please contact us to discuss your request well before you intend to submit an application. We have a two stage application process which is outlined below. We are happy to provide assistance at any stage during the application process.

Preliminary Proposals (first stage)
We ask you to send us an outline of the project on a Preliminary Proposal form for initial consideration before you submit a formal application. We will share your Preliminary Proposal with trustees at one of their meetings. We will then write to you with their comments and if appropriate invite you to make a formal, second stage application. We will advise you of the next appropriate committee date.

The formal application process (second stage)
We will acknowledge receipt of your application form within a week of receiving it. Please contact us if you have not heard from us within two working weeks of submission.

Our staff will first look through your application. If it is ineligible under our current grant programmes we will tell you at this stage.

We will ask you some additional questions, based on the areas of your application that we believe our trustees will focus on when they consider your request.

Trustee meetings, and when you will be notified of a decision
Depending on the size of grant you are requesting, and the type of project you are proposing, your application will be considered in the following ways.

- the chairman and deputy chairman of the grants committee can make a decision on full applications of up to £5,000. A decision on an application of this size normally takes two to three months from the preliminary proposal submission date.
- The full grants committee can consider applications for grants of up to £50,000 for a single project in any one year and up to £150,000 for a project over a three year period. The committee meets approximately every three months. If the committee requires further information from you to support your application, they may defer making a decision until the next meeting. You can therefore expect to hear a decision on this size of request three to six months after submission of your preliminary proposal. Please allow more time if you are submitting a request that will be processed during the summer months as there are no committee meetings in July and August. Grants awarded by the committee above £50,000 will need to be endorsed by the full trustee body of the Bedford Charity, which meets three times a year. These meetings usually take place in March, July and December. Awards of this size are rare, and the decision making process will almost certainly be longer than for more modest requests.

Please make sure you submit your application well before you need a final decision on your request. Please contact us or see our website for latest submission deadlines.

The Big Lottery Fund (see also Awards for All)

Community, young people and welfare
£558 million paid to grantholders (2009)
Beneficial area UK and overseas

(See **Useful contacts on page 35–36**)
Tel. 08454 102030
Email enquiries@biglotteryfund.org.uk
Website www.biglotteryfund.org.uk
Trustees *Prof. Sir Clive Booth, Chair; Roland Doven; Frank Hewitt; John Gartside; Rajay Naik; Anna Southall; Huw Vaughan Thomas; Diana Whitworth; Sanjay Dighe; Alison Magee; Judith Donovan; Albert Tucker.*

Information available Full details of all programmes can be found on the fund's website, along with application information. Details of all lottery funders can also be found on one website: www.lotteryfunding.org.uk.

Summary

The National Lottery (the Lottery) was launched in 1994 and rapidly established itself as a key funder of the voluntary sector. Since it began, £23 billion has been raised and more than 330,000 grants given out for good causes (2009 figures). However, the assessment process is a rigorous and demanding one. Many organisations commit a substantial part of their fundraising resources in applying for grants from the various Lottery distribution bodies. The Lottery currently funds four good causes and funding is allocated as follows:

- charities, health, education and the environment (jointly) – 50%
- sports – 16.67%
- arts – 16.67%
- heritage – 16.67%.

General

Distribution bodies
Distribution bodies, sometimes referred to as Lottery funders, are the organisations that distribute the good causes' money to local communities and national and international projects. They cover arts, heritage, sport, community and voluntary groups as well as supporting projects concerned with health, education and the environment. They will also be contributing to the

funding of the 2012 Olympic Games and Paralympic Games in London and until at least 2012, the diversion of Lottery funds to the Olympics means that there will be less new Lottery money available. The funding bodies are listed below.

- **Arts Council England**: Arts Council England is the national development agency for the arts in England, distributing public money from government and the Lottery.
- **Arts Council of Northern Ireland**: This is the lead development agency for the arts in Northern Ireland.
- **Arts Council of Wales**: This body is responsible for developing and funding the arts in Wales.
- **Awards for All**: Awards for All is a BIG Lottery Fund grants scheme funding small, local community-based projects in the UK. Each country in the UK runs its own programme (see page 16).
- **Big Lottery Fund**: The Big Lottery Fund (BIG) is committed to improving communities and the lives of people most in need.
- **Heritage Lottery Fund**: The Heritage Lottery Fund uses money from the Lottery to give grants for a wide range of projects involving the local, regional and national heritage of the UK.
- **NESTA**: NESTA (the National Endowment for Science, Technology and the Arts) is a non-departmental public body investing in innovators and working to improve the climate for creativity in the UK.
- **Olympic Lottery Distributor**: The Olympic Lottery Distributor's remit is to support the delivery of the London 2012 Olympic and Paralympic Games. The Olympic Lottery Distributor is not currently running any open funding rounds.
- **Scottish Arts Council**: The Scottish Arts Council champions the arts for Scotland.
- **Scottish Screen**: This agency develops, encourages and promotes film, television and new media in Scotland.
- **Sport England**: Sport England invests in projects that help people to start, stay and succeed in sport and physical activity at every level.
- **Sports Council for Northern Ireland**: 'Making sport happen for you.'
- **Sportscotland – the national sport agency for Scotland**: Working with partners, it is responsible for developing sport and physical recreational activity in Scotland.
- **Sports Council for Wales**: The Sports Council for Wales is the national organisation responsible for developing and promoting sport and active lifestyles.
- **UK Film Council**: As the lead agency for film, the UK Film Council aims to stimulate a competitive, successful and vibrant UK film industry and culture, both now and for the future.
- **UK Sport**: UK Sport works in partnership to lead sport in the UK to world-class success.

The Lottery distribution bodies are independent; however, because they distribute public funds, their policies are subject to a level of statutory control from government. Their grantmaking is also under close public and media scrutiny and is often the subject of wide-ranging debate.

Big Lottery Fund

The Big Lottery Fund (BIG) was launched in 2004 and given legal status on 1 December 2006 by way of the National Lottery Act 2006. It was brought about by the merging of the Community Fund and New Opportunities Fund, and the transfer of residual activities and assets from the Millennium Commission.

There was much controversy surrounding the launch of BIG as the Community Fund had previously operated via 'open-grants' programmes. BIG introduced new programmes based on themes and outcomes set by the government. These were announced by the government, not by BIG itself, and before the relevant consultation period had ended, which led to fears that funds would be used to achieve government ends rather than those of applicant charities.

BIG is the largest of the Lottery distributors and is responsible for giving out 50% of the money for good causes raised from the Lottery, which provides a budget of around £600 million a year. Funding covers health, education, environment and charitable purposes. During 2008/09, £625 million (2007/08 £601 million) was received in Lottery income directly from ticket sales. As stated, BIG normally receives half of the money raised for the good causes by the Lottery, however, government has directed that between 2009 and 2013 £638 million should be transferred from BIG to the Olympic Lottery Distribution Fund (OLDF). On 1 February 2009 the first transfer of £43 million was made.

BIG's mission is to be 'committed to bringing real improvements to communities and the lives of people most in need'. To do this, it has identified seven values.

They are:

- fairness
- accessibility
- strategic focus
- involving people
- innovation
- enabling
- additional to government.

In response to complaints about the short-term nature of its funding, a number of BIG's programmes now provide funding for up to five years. Projects are required to provide a realistic exit strategy that plans out how the project will continue after the funding from BIG has finished. One effect of this is that requests for larger amounts and for longer periods are made, which, over time, might lead to BIG funding fewer projects.

In 2008/09, payments to grant recipients were over £563 million. During that accounting year, £526 million was *committed* across the UK in grants ranging from £300 to £10 million. A further £83 million of awards were, at the time of the annual accounts, waiting grant holder acceptance. The voluntary and community sector received 88 per cent of the funding that was awarded. Operating costs for the year were 8.6% of income (9.1% 2007/08).

Administration of non-Lottery funding
The Act of 2006 also includes powers for BIG to distribute non-Lottery funding and to make loans. Much of BIG's funding is given in grants made directly to successful applicants, particularly those in the voluntary sector, however, BIG also administers non-lottery funds, for example, it is running the Community Assets programme on behalf of the Office of the Third Sector, delivering over £30 million to refurbish local authority buildings in England, which will eventually be given to third sector organisations. It is also administering the myplace programme on behalf of the Department for Children, Schools and Families. Through myplace, BIG has awarded £240 million so far to provide youth facilities, in a programme worth £270 million, the balance of which will be delivered in 2009/10. In 2009 BIG was successful in obtaining £16 million in European Social Fund grants through the Welsh Assembly Government to 'enhance and expand its Lifeskills programme.

Current BIG programmes in England

Changing Spaces
The Changing Spaces programme will invest around £200 million in

27

environmental projects in England, including schemes to improve green spaces, grow local food and help community groups to reduce the amount of energy they use. BIG is working with five organisations that have the skills and experience to run an effective environmental programme on its behalf. Each organisation is running an England-wide, open grants programme.

Changing Spaces: Community Sustainable Energy Programme

Summary
The Community Sustainable Energy Programme (CSEP), run by the Building Research Establishment (BRE), opened in April 2008. The programme will help community-based organisations in England reduce their environmental impact through the installation of energy saving measures and microgeneration technologies (producing heat or electricity on a small scale from a low carbon source). The scheme will also fund development studies that help community organisations to find out if a microgeneration and energy efficiency project will work for them.

Grants available
This programme will award grants of between £5,000 to £50,000 and will provide £10 million to community-based organisations for the installation of microgeneration technologies, such as solar panels or wind turbines and energy efficiency measures including loft and cavity wall insulation. It will also provide £1 million for project development grants that will help community organisations establish if a microgeneration and energy efficiency installation will work for them. It aims to achieve the following outcomes:

- reduction in CO_2 emissions
- increased community awareness of climate change and how changes to our behaviour can reduce it
- increased skills base of local trades (for example, local builders and building-service subcontractors working on renewable energy projects for the first time)
- reduction in energy bills
- reduction in reliance on imported energy and increased independence from commercial energy suppliers
- stronger partnerships within local communities with lasting social benefits
- growth of local enterprise in new technologies.

The grants are awarded as follows:

- capital grants – projects can apply for up to £50,000 or 50% of the project cost (whichever is lower)
- project development grants – maximum grant available is £5,000 or 75% of the study cost (whichever is lower).

Deadlines
The programme is expected to be open until 2010. Please check the Community Sustainable Energy website (www.communitysustainable.org.uk) for information on deadlines for specific funding rounds, the most up-to-date information and where details of all aspects of the grant application process can be viewed.

Capital grants will be awarded on a competitive basis at quarterly selection panel meetings. Project development grants will be awarded on a first come, first served basis until all funds are spent.

Eligibility
CSEP will only award grants to not-for-profit community-based organisations in England. This includes: community groups governed by a written constitution, registered charities and trusts, parish councils, schools and colleges, charitable companies with a community focus, mutual societies, church-based and other faith organisations.

Changing Spaces: Ecominds
Grants: £20,000 to £250,000. This programme is for groups that want to encourage people with experience of mental distress to get involved in environment projects.

Summary
As part of the Changing Spaces environmental initiative BIG has given £7.5 million to MIND to run a grant scheme over five years. Projects will promote what is called ecotherapy, that is, work and experiences in outdoor environments. With this in mind, the programme is for groups that want to encourage people with experience of mental distress to get involved in environmental projects, such as improving open spaces or wildlife habitats, designing public art and recycling. Ecominds has been designed 'to help reduce the stigma surrounding mental distress and help create a society that treats people with experience of mental distress fairly, positively, and with respect'.

Grants available
The programme awards grants of up to £250,000. Four levels of grant were available:

- small – up to £20,000 (open until June 2010)
- medium – from £20,001 up to £60,000 (closed in January 2010)
- large – from £60,001 up to £150,000 (the large grants programme closed in October 2009)
- flagship – from £150,001 up to £250,000 (approximately five grants will be awarded within this category). Note: The flagship grant closed in May 2009.

Currently, however, (November 2009), BIG is looking to award up to £20,000 for smaller projects due to the success of the larger grants. All projects must be delivered by December 2012.

Eligibility
The following England-based groups may apply to Ecominds:

- mental health, environmental and community groups
- commercial organisations running projects on a not-for-profit basis, including community interest companies and social enterprise companies where project profits are reinvested solely into the Ecominds project.

Exclusions
This programme will not fund individuals, statutory authorities (although applications from organisations working collaboratively with them are welcomed), projects aligned with or co-funded by pharmaceutical companies and applicants and projects based outside England.

For more information on this programme and full details of the application process, please visit the Ecominds website: www.ecominds.org.uk. Please note there are two sets of guidance notes for this programme.

Changing Spaces: Local Food

Summary
Local Food, run by RSWT (Royal Society for Wildlife Trusts), opened in March 2008. It funds a range of organisations that want to carry out a variety of food related projects to make locally grown food more accessible and affordable to local communities.

Grants available
This programme awarded grants of between £2,000 and £500,000. Three types of grants were available (small,

main and beacon), ranging from £2,000 to £500,000:

- small grants between £2,000 – £10,000
- main grants between £10,001 – £300,000
- beacon grants between £300,001 – £500,000.

Please note: Beacon grants closed for applications in June 2008 and at the time of writing (November 2009), the Local Food programme had been suspended to all new First Stage Applications. Please visit the website for updates on this.

Deadlines
Local Food employs a two stage application process for all three sizes of grant.

- First Stage Application: A simple open application process for projects to outline their proposals and to ensure eligibility. Visit the website for further details on eligibility.
- Full Application: All eligible projects will be invited to submit a full application. If you are not invited to submit a full application you will be told why.

All funded projects must be completed by March 2014.

Eligibility
Grants will be awarded to not-for-profit community groups and organisations in England, including schools, faith-based organisations, health bodies (such as primary care trusts) and universities. See RSWT's website for more information and full details of the application process – www.localfoodgrants.org.

Changing Spaces: Community Spaces
Summary
Community Spaces is an open grants programme managed by Groundwork UK on behalf of an experienced national consortium. The programme empowers community groups to improve public spaces in their neighbourhood. 'It responds directly to people's aspirations to have better places on their doorsteps – more interesting places for children to play, safer places for people of all ages to sit, greener spaces where people and nature can grow and flourish.'

Community Spaces is a major capital-funding programme designed to ensure that money is spent on making physical and lasting improvements to people's neighbourhoods. Applicants will need to split project costs into revenue and capital expenditure. Small and medium grants will need to ensure that any revenue expenditure does not exceed 25% and capital expenditure is at least 75%.

The Community Spaces programme aims to:

- create better local environments
- increase people's access to quality local spaces for interaction, play and recreation
- increase the number of people actively involved in developing and running a practical environmental project that is visible in their community
- improve partnerships between communities, support organisations and local authorities.

Grants available
This programme will award grants of between £10,000 and £450,000. It will fund community groups that want to improve local green spaces such as play areas, community gardens and parks. Small grants from £10,000 – £25,000 and medium grants from £25,001 – £49,999 are available until January 2011. Large grants from £50,000 – £100,000 and flagship grants from £100,001 – £450,000 are now closed.

Applications
This programme will only award grants to not-for-profit community groups based in England. 'Community group' is defined as: 'A group made up of people living in one particular area or focused on a neighbourhood, who are considered as a unit because of their common interests, background, nationality or other circumstances'. This may include:

- community groups governed by a written constitution
- church based and other faith groups
- 'friends of' groups
- tenants and residents associations.

Applications must show that projects will improve local neighbourhoods and environments. Types of projects can include, for example:

- community gardens and parks
- informal sports areas and multi-use games areas
- nature reserves
- squares and village greens
- churchyards
- ponds and projects which improve the local community's access to green space.

This list is not exhaustive and if you are thinking about a project that isn't listed, it may still be considered if it meets the eligibility criteria. There will be some crossover with BIG's other funding streams. For example, projects looking at play areas, orchards, city farms and woodlands will be considered as long as they meet the general criteria of the programme, although there are other of

BIG's Changing Spaces programmes that will fund these types of projects.

There are two stages to the application process and all community groups that are successful at stage one must agree to work with a facilitator – a trained individual who is able to provide specialist advice and guidance to groups. Facilitators will be able to help groups develop their stage two application form and may be able to help successful groups develop and deliver their project.

Applications from youth groups for youth projects are welcomed as it is considered important for young people to be fully involved in projects and where possible be leading projects of direct benefit to them. However, the main applicant and alternative contact must both be aged 18 years or over. For further information on the application process please visit the Community Spaces website – www.community-spaces.org.uk.

Eligibility
Community Spaces will provide funding for community groups across England that hope to create and improve their local environment. To be eligible to apply for funding groups must meet the following criteria:

- applications must be from community groups
- projects must be in England
- projects must meet the Community Spaces outcomes – see the project outcome/s document provided on www.community-spaces.org.uk
- consideration of your application will depend on your stated outcomes
- projects must be within a two mile radius of a residential area
- projects must be open to the public 'most of the time' – please see the 'Definitions' page on the community spaces website.

Deadlines
Community Spaces' small and medium grants will be open for applications until January 2011 and decisions will be made on regular basis throughout the programme's life.

Exclusions
Community Spaces will not fund:

- individuals
- sole traders
- local authorities
- parish or town councils
- schools
- health bodies
- profit-making organisations and other statutory bodies that have not been mentioned above.

Community groups will not be able to apply for funding for the following:

- costs incurred or monies spent on a project before being awarded a Community Spaces grant
- projects without reasonable physical access for the general public
- activities that promote religious or political beliefs
- the purchase, construction, refurbishment of or access to buildings
- the purchase of land
- formal sports pitches
- projects on school grounds
- the purchase of animals
- projects on commercial property
- vehicles for transporting goods or people
- projects based on statutory allotments
- anything that is the legal responsibility of other organisations
- road improvement projects.

Changing Spaces: Access to Nature
Summary
Access to Nature, launched in April 2008, is run by Natural England on behalf of a consortium of major environmental organisations. It is a £25 million grants programme to encourage people from all backgrounds to understand, access and enjoy our natural environment. It aims to encourage more people to enjoy the outdoors, particularly those who face social exclusion or those who currently have little or no contact with the natural environment. It funds projects in urban, rural and coastal communities across England.

The programme awards grants of between £50,000 and £500,000 to support projects that deliver one or more of the programme's main outcomes. In addition the programme will make a small number of larger grants of over £500,000 (up to £715,000), for projects that have a national significance or impact.

Applications
Before applying for funding for your project, you are advised to read the Access to Nature general guidance notes document to check that what you are planning to do fits the programme. These guidance notes give information on the types of project that will be considered for funding, the types of grants available and full details of the application and assessment processes. The guidance notes should be read in conjunction with the Regional Targeting Plans, which explain the priorities for each region; both can be found on Natural England's website.

The application process is in two stages:

Stage 1 – Outline proposal form
All applicants will be required to initially submit a stage one application form to provide basic information about their project and organisation and there is guidance on the website to help you with this. Receipt of your application form should be acknowledged within five working days. A regional adviser will then contact you within 20 working days to discuss your project in more detail.

NB. Section 4 (the 'Declaration Form') requires original signatures and will need to be posted in hard copy form. Photocopies, fax and email versions will not be accepted and assessment will not begin until the signed declaration has been received.

Stage 2 – Full application form
If your organisation is eligible to apply and your project is something that might be supported, the regional adviser will tell you how to submit a stage two application form. You should read carefully the stage two guidance notes, which can be found on the website and which explain how to complete the form. A grants officer will assess your application and it will then be considered by the project board (for grant applications up to £100,000) or by an independent grants panel (for grant applications over £100,000), who will decide whether to award you a grant.

Deadlines
Grants: June 2010. For up-to-date information on closing dates for the national and flagship projects see Natural England's website.

Eligibility
Access to Nature will only award grants to not-for-profit community-based organisations in England. This includes: community groups governed by a written constitution, registered charities and trusts, parish councils, schools and colleges, companies with a charitable purpose and community focus, mutual societies, church-based and other faith organisations.

Funding will focus on three main themes:

- community awareness and active participation
- education, learning and volunteering
- welcoming, well-managed and wildlife-rich places.

Within these themes, grants will be awarded to organisations which can demonstrate that their project will deliver one or more of Access to Nature's five main outcomes:

1) A greater number and diversity of people having improved opportunities to experience the natural environment.

2) More people having opportunities for learning about the natural environment and gaining new skills.

3) More people being able to enjoy the natural environment through investment in access to natural places and networks between sites.

4) Richer, more sustainable, natural places, meeting the needs of local communities.

5) An increase in communities' sense of ownership of local natural places, by establishing strong partnerships between communities, voluntary organisations, local authorities and others.

For more information on this programme, please visit the Access to Nature website: www.naturalengland.org.uk/leisure/grants-funding.

Contact for all Changing Spaces programmes:
Call the Changing Spaces Advice Line helpline on 0845 3 671 671 (opening hours 8am to 7pm Monday to Friday) for further details of any of the Changing Spaces programmes.

Heroes Return
World War 2 veterans from the UK, Channel Islands and Republic of Ireland can apply for travel and accommodation costs to visit the places where they saw active service. They can also receive funding to take part in an official commemoration in the UK.

Eligibility
Veterans who fought with or alongside British forces in World War 2 and who are resident in the UK and the Republic of Ireland. War widows and widowers of veterans are also eligible for funding, and carers and spouses can receive funding to travel with veterans.

Applications
Applicants can apply for a fixed amount grant of between £150 and £5,500 depending on the number of people taking part and the destination. BIG is focusing on supporting each eligible application and meeting the demand as and when it occurs between 1 April 2009 and the deadline for applications, which is 31 January 2011.

Grants will be given towards the costs of commemorative visits. A fixed amount of money will be available for each veteran and their spouse and/or carer towards the cost of their visit. There will five levels of funding according to the destination. These fixed amounts have been set so that there is enough money to cover the cost of travel and insurance.

Contact
If you have any general questions about the scheme and whether you are eligible, ring the application helpline – 0845 0000 121.

Fair Share Trust
Some parts of the UK have missed out on Lottery funding in the past. The Fair Share Programme aims to help provide a better balance in funding. Fair Share received £50 million of Lottery money, which was put into a trust – the first Lottery model of its kind. The funding is secure and any interest earned on the original sum covers the management costs, which means that the total £50 million will be spent as grants in the Fair Share Trust areas. Since launching in 2003, the Fair Share Trust has established itself in 80 neighbourhoods across the UK through the work of local delivery partners – 'local agents'. The programme in England runs until 2013.

The trust is entirely managed by Community Foundation Network (CFN), the UK's largest independent community charitable grantmaker, which has set up partnerships with its members – community foundations – and other local grant-making bodies to manage the programme locally. These local agents work with the trust communities to prioritise and agree spend, in line with the guidance for delivery.

Selected neighbourhoods in each area are receiving targeted support from these agents in order that local people have the opportunity to make decisions on where the funding goes.

The Fair Share Trust programme aims to:

- build capacity and sustainability – by involving local communities in decision making about Lottery funding
- build social capital – by building links within and between communities to promote trust and participation
- improve liveability – by improving the living environment for communities.

Each local agent sets up a local advisory panel, involving people from the communities receiving the funding, to agree local priorities, drawn from neighbourhood assessment documents, based on local strategic partnership data highlighting local community needs and issues. Once the local priorities were identified, the local agents and local panels began identifying potential funding recipients. Each local agent would vary in their approach of

identifying projects for funding, tailoring the approach in line with local circumstances. The initial setting up phase has been completed, grants have been made and now the outcomes are being gathered through monitoring and results evaluated. By the end of October 2009, £29.9 million had been spent through the programme in local neighbourhoods.

For more information on the Fair Share Trust, please visit the CFN website – www.communityfoundations.org.uk.

Reaching Communities
The budget for Reaching Communities is £130 million. This programme has been extended and will run until at least 2010. Reaching Communities will fund projects with grants of between £10,000 and £500,000, that help people and communities who are most in need, particularly those people or groups that are hard to reach. Projects can be new or existing activities, or be the core work of an organisation.

This programme is designed to achieve changes in communities as a result of funding. For example:

- people having better chances in life, including being able to get better access to training and development to improve their life skills
- strong communities, with more active citizens, working together to tackle their problems
- improved rural and urban environments, which communities are better able to access and enjoy
- healthier and more active people and communities.

Eligibility
You can apply to Reaching Communities if you are:

- a registered charity
- a voluntary or community group
- a statutory body, (including schools)
- a charitable or not-for-profit company
- a social enterprise – a business that is chiefly run for social objectives, whose profits are reinvested in the business rather than going to shareholders and owners.

In the light of current economic circumstances BIG has relaxed the eligibility criteria for this programme. Please refer to the 'updated signposting guide' on BIG's website.

Applications
There have been high levels of interest in this programme and BIG states that it has had to turn down some very good projects. You should consider contacting BIG before embarking on work for this programme to discuss whether there is

another programme to which your project might be better suited. This programme is under regular review to ensure it is meeting those communities most in need.

Contact
National helpline for advice on 0845 410 20 30.
Email – general.enquiries@biglottery fund.org.uk.
Lottery Funding Helpline on 0845 275 00 00 or go to www.lotteryfunding.org.uk.

Research programme
The following information has been taken directly from BIG's website:

The Research Programme is now closed. All applications for funds and the subsequent assessments have been completed. No further applications can be accepted to this programme.

Summary of the programme
The programme funded projects related to social, medical and socio-medical research. The original £25 million budget was increased to £29.5 million in view of demand. The programme's aim was to enable VCS organisations to produce and disseminate evidence-based knowledge, to influence local and national policy and practice and, in the longer term, develop better services and interventions for beneficiaries. In doing so the programme would develop VCS capacity to engage with, use and do research.

Grants for up to five years of between £10,000 and £500,000 were available to charities and voluntary sector organisations, with up to £1 million for exceptional projects. In round one, we awarded 28 development grants with a total value of £222,300 and 24 Research grants with a total value of £7.74 million.

Applicants can email the team at researchprogramme@aeat.co.uk.
[Check BIG's website for the current status of this programme.]

The People's Millions
In 2005 ITV teamed up with BIG to launch The People's Millions, allowing people across the UK to vote for projects in their community to win cash from the Lottery. Since then a total of 229 awards and £13.6 million has been given out to projects around the UK – including skate parks, sensory play areas, woodlands regeneration and even audio sculptures. The People's Millions is a partnership between the Big Lottery Fund and ITV where the public can vote for awards of up to £50,000 for projects in their ITV region.

BIG wants to fund projects that help communities to transform or enjoy their environment. That means buildings, amenities, public and green spaces and the natural environment. Priority is also given to local environment projects that get more people involved in the local community and help people in the community who are most in need and are original and innovative. Films are shown on ITV regional news programmes and viewers are asked to vote for the project they want to see be awarded a grant. If your group would like to be put forward as a beneficiary of this scheme you should visit BIG's website on www.biglotteryfund.org.uk or www.peoplesmillions.org.uk.

The Secret Millionaire Fund

BIG has joined with Channel 4 to create the Secret Millionaire Fund website which will allow applicants to:

- nominate a community project they think would benefit from funding, or
- apply directly themselves.

Successful applicants to the fund may then be selected for filming by Channel 4 and appear on the website or on the TV programme itself.

The partnership is based on one of Channel 4's most popular TV programmes – The Secret Millionaire – with 4.5 million viewers. Each week a millionaire leaves their luxury life behind, takes on a secret identity and for 10 days lives undercover in a deprived area of the UK. On their final day, the millionaires come clean and donate thousands of pounds to projects they feel will most benefit.

Eligibility
In order to be eligible for application applicants must:

- be a voluntary or community organisation, school, parish or town council, or health body
- have a UK-based bank or building society account in the name of their organisation that requires at least two people to sign cheques or make a withdrawal.

To successfully apply to the Secret Millionaire Fund, the same eligibility criteria as Big Lottery Fund Awards for All programme apply. This varies according to which country you are in so visit www.channel4.com/programmes/ the-secret-millionaire and take the simple eligibility test.

Applications
For further information on how to apply, visit secretmillionaire.channel4.com.

People and Places

This programme will fund capital and revenue projects that encourage

coordinated action by people who want to make their communities better places to live. It will support local and regional projects throughout Wales that focus on:

- revitalising communities
- improving community relationships, or
- enhancing local environments, community services and buildings.

The main aim is to bring people together to create significant improvements to communities and the lives of people most in need. Projects should be community led; helping people to develop the skills and confidence to become more involved in their community is an integral aspect to this programme.

BIG will encourage organisations to work together, and will accept applications from organisations based anywhere in the UK. However, projects must mainly benefit people in Wales. Organisations not currently working in Wales should be able to demonstrate that they are aware of social and policy issues relevant to the local area and the project.

Eligibility
Grants will only be awarded to voluntary, community or public sector organisations either working separately or together.

The recession
In recognition of the effects the recession has had on communities in Wales, an extra £2 million has been set aside to be allocated in two rounds during the financial years ending 31 March 2010 and 31 March 2011. You can apply for this through the existing People and Places programme for a limited period. For further details visit: www.biglotteryfund.org.uk/ prog_people_places. A new programme will be opened in 2011.

Community Assets

The Community Assets programme is not funded by the Lottery, the funding is provided by the Office of the Third Sector. However, the programme is delivered by BIG, because it was considered to have the necessary expertise. The aim of the programme is community empowerment. It offers capital grants for third sector organisations and local authorities to refurbish local authority buildings in England for third sector ownership.

Community Assets aims to empower communities by facilitating the transfer of genuine assets from local authorities to third sector ownership for the benefit of the community. Genuine assets will

generate operational, financial and other benefits for third sector organisations without significant liabilities, over a long-term period.

myplace

The Big Lottery Fund is delivering myplace on behalf of the Department for Children, Schools and Families (DCSF). This is not Lottery funding. myplace aims to deliver world class youth facilities driven by the active participation of young people and their views and needs. So far, the programme has funded 62 projects across England worth £240 million. myplace offers a significant opportunity to those with the vision, ambition and drive to deliver world class places for young people to go. It will reward those who:

- are developing plans for ambitious, world class places that will offer young people the widest possible range of high quality activities and co-located support services
- are putting young people in the lead to plan and deliver dedicated youth projects driven by their views and needs
- are working in partnership across sectors to develop robust, financially sustainable co-funded projects that respond to local needs and priorities
- require between £1 million and £5 million of capital investment to deliver an outstanding building project.

For more information on myplace, please visit: www.biglotteryfund.org.uk/ prog_myplace.

Current programmes for Northern Ireland only

Building Change Trust

In November 2008 BIG announced details of the Building Change Trust – a multi-million pound investment to help develop and shape the future of Northern Ireland's community and voluntary sector. The Building Change Trust will invest £10 million over the next 10 years to help community groups and larger voluntary organisations adapt and develop new ways of working. It will not make grants in a traditional way, but will look at what resources already exist in communities and identify ways to support communities to develop and change.

The following organisations are responsible for the delivery and operation of the Building Change Trust:

- Community Foundation for NI
- Community Evaluation NI
- Rural Community Network

- Volunteer Development Agency
- Business in the Community NI.

The trust will identify detailed programmes that promote volunteering and develop the local community infrastructure and leadership skills in rural and urban communities. Part of the money will be invested to offer loans and advice to community and voluntary organisations. The Community Foundation has responsibility for the day-to-day running of the Trust. For further information visit: www.buildingchangetrust.org.

The Big Deal
The aim of The Big Deal is to encourage children and young people up to the age of 25 to become involved in activities that enhance their personal and social development. We also want to encourage young people to acquire the skills, knowledge and opportunities that can help them contribute to family and community life. An individual child or young person can apply for an award of £500 and a group can apply for an award of between £500 and £2,500.

Eligibility
Individuals and groups of children and young people can apply for small grants.

Contact
Website: www.thebigdealni.com
Email: info@thebigdealni.com
Tel: 028 9033 1880.

Current programmes for Scotland only

2014 Communities
2014 Communities is focused on building a 'legacy of wellbeing before and beyond the Commonwealth Games [which are being held in Glasgow in 2014]'. This is a micro grant programme aimed at grassroots sports and community organisations. Through the programme BIG hopes to encourage more people to take part in sport or physical activity, increase the numbers of those volunteering in sport or physical activity, and bring communities together through sport and volunteering.

The programme offers local sports clubs, voluntary and community organisations, community councils and schools grants of £300 to £1,000 to support and stimulate grassroots involvement in sport and physical activity. In year one of the programme (2008/09), BIG has £500,000 to award in grants. The programme will continue up to the Glasgow Commonwealth Games in 2014, but the funding focus and delivery may change, based on learning leading up to 2014.

For this programme projects should achieve one or more of the following outcomes:

- more people take part in sport or physical activity
- more people volunteer in sport or physical activity
- more people and communities are brought together through taking part or volunteering in sport or physical activity.

Priorities
Groups such as women and girls, people with disabilities, people over 50 years of age or under 25 years of age and people from black and minority ethnic communities are more likely to receive funding. These priorities may change in the future and will be updated on the 2014 webpage.

Grants
Grants of between £300 to £1,000 will be offered, based on a process similar to the Awards for All model (see separate entry on page 16). However, supporting documentation such as constitutions or other governing documents and bank statements will only be requested once a conditional offer has been made. If the documents are satisfactory the grant will be paid directly into the organisation's bank account.

Eligibility
Grants may be offered to sports clubs, voluntary and community organisations, community councils and schools. Branches of a larger organisation may be eligible to apply, but BIG will ask the larger organisation for written support in the event of an offer. Independent branches may apply in their own right. Groups can only apply for one grant in a 12 month period; decisions will be made within 15 working days. For further information on how to apply visit: www.biglotteryfund.org.uk/2014_guidance_notes.pdf.

Investing in Ideas
Investing in Ideas can award grants of £500 to £10,000 to test and develop ideas that could eventually become fully-fledged projects. Investing in Ideas could pay for the preparation and planning that can turn a basic idea into a well-planned project including:

- market research
- feasibility studies
- business planning
- committee training
- exchange visits in the UK to see how other projects work
- community consultation
- professional advice
- technical reports and scheme design studies.

It is important that the idea has the potential to fit with one of four areas of investment:

- growing community assets
- dynamic inclusive communities
- life transitions
- supporting 21st century life.

For further information see the Investing in Communities section of BIG's website.

Current programmes for Wales only

Life Skills Project
The Life Skills project has approximately £14 million available to deliver services throughout Wales that will support targeted groups of economically inactive people (see below) to engage or re-engage with education, learning, volunteering and employment. The target groups are:

- care leavers
- carers and former carers returning to work
- economically inactive families.

This is the first time that National Lottery money has been matched with European Social Fund (ESF) at source. The ESF funding is being distributed via the Welsh European Funding Office.

The aims of the Life Skills project are to:

- enable participants from the target groups to develop their life skills, increase their confidence and re-engage with, and continue to access, education, learning, volunteering or employment
- develop individual long-term support plans to enable beneficiaries to continue to access and remain in education, learning or employment opportunities, in collaboration with other agencies.

Please note: The Life Skills project is not a grant-making programme. The project will follow a strict competitive tender process (the Restricted Procedure Process) in accordance with EU Directives and UK Regulations. For detailed information, including Q&A, visit: www.biglotteryfund.org.uk/prog_life_skills_project. The pre-information notice and the bidder information pack are available from www.sell2wales.co.uk/notices. Type 'life skills project for Wales' in the search field. Queries relating to the Life Skills project should be logged via www.biglotteryfund.bravosolution.co.uk.

Big Thinking – strategic framework to 2015

The Big Thinking consultation process for funding in 2009–2015 was the largest consultation ever carried out by a lottery distributor. The process, feedback and evaluation, 'What you told us', was published in June 2009, with BIG's Strategic Framework to 2015.

BIG wants its funding to be flexible, responsive and more personalised for applicants. It promises to 'minimise unnecessary effort on behalf of applicants, making decisions as early as possible and communicating them clearly'. We will have to wait and see whether these promises translate to the grant applicant.

BIG's aim is to become a more effective and efficient funder – an intelligent funder – securing greater impact and influence from its work. It describes an intelligent funder as one that:

- offers support (apart from financial) to the organisations it funds
- works with other funders to develop and share leading practice
- promotes the analysis of the impact of its funding to policymakers.

This means being more than just a distributor of money – it means engaging and supporting organisations that apply for funding, building and using evidence of need to inform the development of programmes, sharing this evidence more widely, and learning, developing and sharing good grant-making practice with other funders.

Outcomes
The framework confirms the proposal in the consultation that, to contribute most effectively to successful outcomes, BIG's funding is best placed in three areas:

- reducing isolation
- helping people through certain key transitions (for example leaving care, redundancy)
- assisting more people in communities to feel empowered.

These areas will characterise all of BIG's funding for the next six years. The framework provides the reasoning behind these hoped-for outcomes and in a general way how they might be achieved. However, it is not clear from the framework document how these areas will be applied to the development of future funding programmes. BIG states that it wants 'to continue discussing our priorities and our direction of travel with you', and hopefully this is what will inform the next set of programmes.

Risk takers
The framework states that 'BIG will be unashamedly assertive in taking risks to address unpopular or challenging issues that have been neglected by other funders, where this fits with our mission'. This will not be easy to achieve as BIG also states that it wants its funding to be 'supported and inspired by the communities we are looking to help' and that public involvement in the Lottery's work is positive and will be expanded. It might be difficult to meet both ideals when the public is often against supporting unpopular issues. However, on the bright side, there was significant support in the consultation feedback for 'local decision-making panels' and little support for armchair voting on TV. Much will depend on how these proposals are developed.

Additionality and the commitment to fund the voluntary sector
The framework offers a renewed commitment to additionality: BIG will 'complement and add value to others' work at a local level, not duplicate or replace it'. This will need to be monitored against practice, as the pressure on public finances and more outsourcing of public services will create even less distinct boundaries between what is 'additional' and what is not.

The framework states that the voluntary and community sector is BIG's 'major partner' and that it will receive at least 80% of its funding. This is an improvement on the previous percentage, even if it will mean less funding in total, because of the contribution to the Olympics. However, given that the remaining 20% will predominantly be provided through partnerships involving voluntary sector organisations, (where the local authority facilitates bids with local groups, for example) this is encouraging.

Partnerships
BIG 'will not force partnerships' but will 'encourage links between organisations working to deliver the same ends'. If BIG can use its position to act as a helpful broker between groups this has the potential to be a positive measure.

Types of funding
The framework states that BIG will deliver a 'mixed portfolio of funding' but that grants will continue to be its main business. It will not deliver loans directly but may explore doing this with partners if stakeholders support it.

In line with its intelligent funder concept BIG is currently focused on delivering existing programmes in a way that responds to the needs of the sector and

communities during the recession. The open programmes Reaching Communities and Awards for All are continuing, with Reaching Communities receiving an extra £20 million.

BIG also has also found an extra £43 million, to be invested throughout the UK, which will go towards a recession-related programme, which has yet to be launched. For further information please visit: www.biglotteryfund.org.uk. Future programmes are still being developed; the new funding portfolio will begin in 2010.

What's Next?
UK and overseas
BIG has confirmed that the International programme, which funds UK-based organisations working overseas, will continue. At the time of writing this had been subject to recent consultation and details were due to be announced 'in due course'. Other UK-wide programmes will be considered by BIG's UK Board in the coming months and will be rolled out from 2010.

England
During 2009/10, the open programmes Reaching Communities and Awards For All will continue. BIG also plans to announce smaller scale initiatives during the year, including some aimed at helping communities cope with the effects of the recession.

BIG will continue to develop open, community and targeted funding programmes for the period up to 2015. This will be done by working with partners at national level and through BIG's regional offices.

BIG's new funding portfolio will be launched in 2010.

Northern Ireland
BIG will consult further with stakeholders during autumn 2009, as the next round of programmes is developed. Plans for the first phase of funding programmes for 2009–2015 will be published in early 2010. In the current financial year (2009/10) BIG has promised to commit funding to a number of projects with aims that reflect the current socio-economic climate. BIG Awards for All and the Big Deal programmes are open for applications.

Scotland
BIG will build on Investing in Communities, hoping to improve and refocus it where necessary to take account of the needs and priorities of Scottish communities. This will be done in dialogue with stakeholders and customers, reflecting the policy

directions of Scottish ministers. The aim is to open for applications by June 2010. In the meantime, funding is available through Awards for All, which provides funding of up to £10,000 for a wide range of community and voluntary activity.

Investing in Ideas, the ideas development fund, will continue to support the exploration and testing of new ideas, with grants of up to £10,000.

The 2014 Communities programme will continue to offer grants of up to £1,000 for grassroots projects that promote physical activity or sports related volunteering in local communities in the run up to the 2014 Commonwealth Games.

Wales
Working within the overall UK Strategic Framework, BIG will:

- embark on a new portfolio with a Community Asset Transfer programme from late 2009, which will be launched in partnership with the Welsh Assembly Government
- follow this with a programme aimed at reducing poverty and isolation amongst older people
- launch programmes to promote the citizen's voice and reduce the impact of climate change.

A new demand-led programme will be launched in 2010, responding to the needs of Welsh communities. Whilst very similar to the current People and Places programme, BIG will gather intelligence on the projects and areas funded and work closely with stakeholders to ensure that the programme is promoted successfully to those most in need. Working with stakeholders, experts and policymakers, an Innovation Fund will be set up to support social innovation that will complement the support provided at a UK level and specifically address the Welsh social and cultural context.

BIG will continue to welcome applications for funding while developing new programmes, through the small grants scheme, Awards for All (see separate entry on page 16), with grants of up to £5,000, and the People and Places programme for larger grants for projects that support a wide range of co-ordinated action by people to make their communities better places in which to live.

Useful contacts

Regional offices

England Regional Offices
North East
2 St James Gate
Newcastle upon Tyne
NE1 4BE
Tel: 0191 376 1600
Textphone: 0191 376 1776
Fax: 0191 376 1661
Email:
enquiries.ne@biglotteryfund.org.uk

North West
10th Floor
York House
York Street
Manchester
M2 3BB
Tel: 0161 261 4600
Textphone: 0161 261 4647
Fax: 0161 261 4646
Email:
enquiries.nw@biglotteryfund.org.uk

Yorkshire and the Humber
3rd floor
Carlton Tower
34 St Pauls Street
Leeds
LS1 2AT
Tel: 0113 224 5300
Textphone: 0113 245 4104
Fax: 0113 244 0363
Email:
enquiries.yh@biglotteryfund.org.uk

East Midlands
4th Floor
Pearl Assurance House
Friar Lane
Nottingham
NG1 6BT
Tel: 0115 872 2950
Fax: 0115 872 2990
Email:
enquiries.em@biglotteryfund.org.uk

West Midlands
Apex House
3 Embassy Drive
Edgbaston
Birmingham
B15 1TR
Tel: 0121 345 7700
Textphone: 0121 345 7666
Fax: 0121 345 8888
Email:
enquiries.wm@biglotteryfund.org.uk

Eastern
2nd Floor
Elizabeth House
1 High Street
Chesterton
Cambridge
CB4 1YW
Tel: 01223 449000
Textphone: 01223 352041
Fax: 01223 312628
Email:
enquiries.ea@biglotteryfund.org.uk

London
5th Floor
1 Plough Place
London
EC4A 1DE
Tel: 020 7842 4000
Textphone: 0845 039 0204
Fax: 020 7842 4010
Email:
enquiries.lon@biglotteryfund.org.uk

South East
Chancery House
2nd Floor
11–17 Leas Road
Guildford
GU1 4QW
Tel: 01483 462900
Textphone: 01483 568764
Fax: 01483 462915
Email:
enquiries.se@biglotteryfund.org.uk

South West
Beaufort House
51 New North Road
Exeter
EX4 4EQ
Tel: 01392 849700
Textphone: 01392 490633
Fax: 01392 491134
Email:
enquiries.sw@biglotteryfund.org.uk

Strategic Grants Office – England
1st Floor
Chiltern House
St Nicholas Court
25 – 27 Castlegate
Nottingham
NG1 7AR
Tel: 0115 934 2950
Textphone: 0115 934 2951
Fax: 0115 934 2952
Email:
strategicgrants@biglotteryfund.org.uk

Northern Ireland
1 Cromac Quay
Cromac Wood
Belfast
BT7 2LB
Tel: 028 9055 1455
Textphone: 028 9055 1431
Fax: 028 9055 1444
Email:
enquiries.ni@biglotteryfund.org.uk

Scotland Office
1 Atlantic Quay
1 Robertson Way
Glasgow
G2 8JB
Tel: 0141 242 1400
Textphone: 0141 242 1500
Fax: 0141 242 1401

Email:
enquiries.scotland@biglotteryfund.org.uk

Wales Offices
2nd Floor
Ladywell House
Newtown
Powys
SY16 1JB
Tel: 01686 611700
Textphone: 01686 610205
Fax: 01686 621534
Email:
enquiries.wales@biglotteryfund.org.uk

6th Floor
1 Kingsway
Cardiff
CF10 3JN
Tel: 029 2067 8200
Textphone: 0845 602 1659
Fax: 029 2066 7275

Applications All application forms and guidance are available via the website or by calling 08454 102030.

The Percy Bilton Charity

Disabled, disadvantaged young people and older people

£448,000 to organisations
(2007/08)
Beneficial area UK.

Bilton House, 7 Culmington Road, Ealing, London W13 9NB

Tel. 020 8579 2829 **Fax** 020 8579 3650

Website www.percybiltoncharity.org.uk

Correspondent Wendy Fuller, Charity Administrator

Trustees *Miles A Bilton, Chair; James R Lee; Stefan J Paciorek; Kim Lansdown.*

CC Number 1094720

Information available Accounts were available from the Charity Commission. The charity has a clear and concise website.

The Percy Bilton Charity was founded on 9th July 1962 by the late Percy Bilton for exclusively charitable purposes. Percy Bilton was an entrepreneur who in the 1920s and 1930s built up a group of successful property companies which in the 1970s was listed on the London Stock Exchange. He endowed the charity with a substantial parcel of shares in Percy Bilton Limited, which later became Bilton plc.

Although the companies were legally separate, the charity shared in the success of Bilton plc for many years receiving a steadily increasing dividend income. The investments in both Bilton plc and in the unquoted company were sold in 1998 and the total proceeds are now invested in a diversified investment portfolio.

During his lifetime, Percy Bilton took a keen personal interest in the activities of the charity retaining his involvement until his death in 1982. The directors of the charity, who are its trustees, have continued the charity's activities in accordance with the charitable objects set out by the founder.

Summary

Funding is available to registered charities in the UK whose primary objectives are to assist one or more of the following groups:

- disadvantaged / underprivileged young people (under 25)
- people with disabilities (physical or learning disabilities or mental health problems)
- older people (aged over 60).

There are two types of grant available to organisations:

Large grants – normally for building projects or for items of capital expenditure. They range from about £2,000 up to a usual maximum of £5,000. Please note: no grants are made for running costs.

Small grants – funding of up to £500 for small charities working with people who are disabled, older people and young people for furniture and equipment.

Guidelines

The charity provides the following information on its website:

Amount of grant
The amount offered will usually depend on the number of applications received in relation to the funds available for distribution. You may therefore not receive the full amount requested.

Major appeals
In the case of major appeals and minibuses please apply after 75% of the funding has been secured, as offers are conditional upon the balance being raised and the project completed within one year. We also require grants to be taken up within 12 months of the offer and it is essential to ascertain that your project is likely to be completed within this time scale before applying.

Who the charity will fund
The charity will consider capital funding for the following projects and schemes:

- *Disadvantaged/underprivileged young people (under 25)*
  Supported housing schemes and educational and training projects to encourage disadvantaged young people who may be homeless and/or unemployed away from crime, substance/alcohol misuse and homelessness. Facilities for recreational activities and outdoor pursuits specifically for young people who are educationally or socially underprivileged or disadvantaged.

- *People with disabilities (physical or learning disabilities or mental health problems)*
  Residential, respite care, occupational and recreational establishments for children, young people and adults with physical or learning disabilities or enduring mental health problems.

- *Older people (aged over 60)*
  Day centres, nursing and residential homes, sheltered accommodation and respite care for the frail or sufferers from dementia or age related disorders. Projects to encourage older people to maintain their independence.

General

In 2007/08 the charity had assets of £17.6 million and an income of £724,000. Grants were made totalling £600,500, of which £448,000 was given to organisations, £112,000 was donated to individuals and £41,000 was given in food parcels to older people.

Grants to organisations were categorised as follows:

Large grants
Disability	£146,000
Young people with a disability	£114,000
Older people	£71,000
Disadvantaged young people	£66,000

Small grants
Disability/older people	£26,000
Disadvantaged young people	£24,000

Grants in 2007/08
Beneficiaries receiving larger grants included:

Disadvantaged/at risk young people
Friends of Longridge – Marlow (£6,000), for the purchase of the freehold of Longridge Boating Centre in order to secure the site which is used for water sports training and activities for youth groups; A690 Youth Initiative – Sunderland (£5,200), for the provision of a mobile cage structure to provide a safe environment for street based sports activities for young people who are not interested in engaging with traditional

centre based youth provision; Caldecott Foundation – Kent (£4,000), towards the construction of 'Willow Trees', a 6-bedded residential home for children with severe behavioural problems who receive care, therapy and education at the foundation; Avon Tyrrell UK – Hampshire (£3,000), towards the construction of a six-berth log cabin to provide upgraded accommodation at their outdoor residential centre for young people of all backgrounds and abilities; and, EC Roberts Centre – Portsmouth (£1,800), towards the purchase of an interactive tactile panel for use by children attending the Centre which offers support and assistance to families facing homelessness and relationship breakdown.

Children and young people with disabilities

Children's Hospice South West – North Somerset (£17,000), for the purchase of a wheelchair accessible multi-people vehicle to transport families to and from the hospice and on day trips; Haven House Foundation – Essex (£5,000), to purchase washable flooring to replace unhygienic carpeting at the children's hospice; Children's Adventure Farm Trust, Cheshire (£4,000), for the installation of a 'spider's web' climbing frame for the adventure playground at the activity centre which is accessible to children with a wide range of physical, learning and sensory disabilities; Blaen Wern Farm Charitable Trust – Wales (£3,000), for external building works at the residential centre for children with disabilities and their families/carers. Works include providing a tarmac surface to the car park, erecting fencing and installing a new cattle grid; and, Norman Laud Association – West Midlands (£1,800), for the purchase of a plasma flat screen television for the lounge at the respite care home for children with disabilities.

Disability – general

4SIGHT – West Sussex (£5,000), for the installation and equipping of a training kitchen as part of the refurbishment of the Bradbury Resource Centre for people with a visual impairment; Thames Hospicecare – Windsor (£4,500), for the purchase of furnishings and equipment for the refurbished out-patient clinic at Thames Valley Hospice; Carlisle Mencap (£4,000), towards the refurbishment of California House, a residential and respite home for people with a learning disability; Sanctuary Care – Worcestershire (£3,500), for the purchase of a wheelchair accessible minibus for Shaftesbury Place residential home for adults with physical

disabilities; Northampton Mencap (£3,000), for the construction of a purpose-built headquarters and social centre for adults with a learning disability; Phoenix Group Homes – Essex (£2,700), for the installation of a new fitted kitchen at the residential and day project at 6 Oxford Road for adults with alcohol misuse and mental health problems; and, United Response – Sheffield (£1,800), for the purchase of IT equipment for use by 43 residents of their supported housing in Sheffield who have learning disabilities and a range of communication needs.

Older people

Northwood Day Centre – Stoke-on-Trent (£6,500), for the purchase of a Parker bath with spa and booster pump to be used by District Nurses for their patients as well as older people in the local community who have difficulty using a bath at home owing to health issues and poor mobility; Age Concern St Helen's (£5,300), to purchase computer equipment for IT classes for older people with special needs to be held at venues in the community such as sheltered housing complexes; Voluntary Action Rutland (£4,000), for the construction of an extension to the Rutland Volunteer Centre to provide a resource centre facility for older/disabled people; Extra Care Charitable Trust – Telford (£3,600), to purchase exercise equipment as part of the health programme for their sheltered housing scheme for older people in Telford; The Hand Partnership – Norfolk (£2,400), for the purchase of three electric scooters for loan to older people with mobility problems; and, Furzedown Project – London (£2,000), for the purchase of a wheelchair accessible minibus for the day centre which provides activities for older people, many of whom are housebound or disabled.

Exclusions

The charity will not consider the following (the list is not exhaustive):

- running expenses for the organisation or individual projects
- salaries, training costs or office equipment/furniture
- consumables (e.g. stationery, craft materials)
- publication costs (e.g. printing/distributing promotional information leaflets)
- projects for general community use even if facilities for the disabled are included
- projects that have been completed
- items that have already been purchased

- provision of disabled facilities in schemes mainly for the able-bodied
- general funding/circular appeals
- play schemes/summer schemes
- holidays or expeditions for individuals or groups
- trips, activities or events
- community centres or village halls for wider community use
- community sports/play area facilities
- pre-schools or playgroups (other than predominantly for disabled children)
- refurbishment or repair of places of worship/church halls
- research projects
- mainstream pre-schools, schools, colleges and universities (other than special schools)
- welfare funds for individuals
- hospital/medical equipment
- works to premises not used primarily by the eligible groups.

Applications

If in doubt regarding the suitability of an appeal, contact the charity either in writing, giving a brief outline, or by telephone. If you have already received a grant, please allow at least one year from the date of payment before re-applying. Please note: terms and conditions apply to all grant offers. Copies are available on application.

Large grants (£2,000 and over)

Please apply on your organisation's headed notepaper giving or attaching the following information. 1–6 must be provided in all cases and 7 as applicable to your appeal:

1) A brief history of your charity, its objectives and work
2) Description of the project and what you intend to achieve
3) A copy of your most recent annual report and audited accounts
4) Details of funds already raised and other sources that you have approached
5) Proposals to monitor and evaluate the project
6) Any other relevant information that will help to explain your application
7) The following additional information that applies to your appeal

Building/Refurbishment appeals

- A statement of all costs involved. Please itemise major items and professional fees.
- Confirmation that the project has on-going revenue funding.
- Confirmation that all planning and other consents and building regulations approvals have been obtained.
- Details of ownership of the premises and if leased, the length of the unexpired term.

• Timetable of construction/ refurbishment and anticipated date of completion.

Equipment appeals
• An itemised list of all equipment with estimate of costs. Please obtain at least two competitive estimates except where this is not practicable, for example, specialised equipment.

Contribution towards purchase of minibuses

Please note that minibuses can only be considered if used to transport older and disabled people with mobility problems.

Please give details of provision made for insurance, tax and maintenance etc. We require confirmation that your organisation can meet future running costs.

Small grants (up to £500)

Please apply on your organisation's headed notepaper with the following information:

1) Brief details about your organisation and its work
2) A copy of your most recent annual accounts
3) Outline of the project and its principal aims
4) Breakdown of the cost of item/s required
5) If your organisation is not a registered charity, please supply a reference from a registered charity with whom you work or from the Voluntary Service Council.

The Birmingham Community Foundation

General

£3.7 million (2007/08)

Beneficial area Greater Birmingham.

Nechells Baths, Nechells Park Road, Nechells, Birmingham B7 5PD

Tel. 0121 322 5560 **Fax** 0121 322 5579

Email team@bhamfoundation.co.uk

Website www.bhamfoundation.co.uk

Correspondent Karen Argyle, Grants Officer

Trustees *David Bucknall, Chair; Ian Warwick-Moore McArdle; John Andrews; Cllr Mahmood Hussain; John Kimberley; Kay Cadman; Dorian Chan; Angela Henry;*

Miss S Ahmed; R Harris; Dr J W Higgins; D R Scard; Mrs A Sheldon.

CC Number 1048162

Information available Annual report and accounts were available from the Charity Commission. Full details on the foundation's website.

Summary

The Birmingham Community Foundation was established in 1995 to help local people 'create, encourage and resource initiatives that would alleviate poverty and deprivation, and also promote employment within our community'.

The general objects of the foundation are:

• to help local people, provide local solutions through an effective grant making programme in areas of poverty and deprivation
• to stimulate new initiatives and partnerships within the community and to link these with the major regeneration initiatives in the city
• to build a long-term endowment fund for the sustainability of the communities within Greater Birmingham; providing support for many years to come
• to provide people and businesses with the opportunity to maximise their charitable contribution in ways which bring genuine benefit to their local community.

The foundation aims to build up an endowment fund by encouraging local individuals, businesses and other organisations to give donations and consequently invest in the long-term future of their local community.

Like many community foundations, it administers individual funds which enable donors to direct their contributions to specific locations and/or target groups. The foundation also distributes money from statutory sources. Small grants are generally given to community based groups involved in activities that regenerate and build communities, however priority is given to those projects which:

• encourage community responsibility
• develop community capacity
• are unable to access other forms of funding
• do not duplicate other work being done within the area.

Grantmaking

The Birmingham Community Foundation manages a number of funds,

which are summarised below. Much of the information has been taken from the foundation's highly useful and up-to-date website.

Charles Henry Foyle Trust

This fund is open to voluntary and community organisations working within Birmingham, with a preference for the south west area. Grants usually range from £2,500 to £5,000 but can be up to £10,000. Projects should benefit the local community and in doing so meet at least one of the objectives listed below:

• enhance the education and skills of local people, particularly the young – including the use of theatrical arts and music
• assist communities in local regeneration programmes
• protect and improve the local environment
• support the improvement of sports and leisure facilities
• celebrate and promote the cultural diversity of the City of Birmingham.

Charles Henry Foyle Trust Primary School Fund

This is a new fund aimed at supporting primary schools in Birmingham, for activities, events or materials/equipment that are not usually provided through the LEA as part of the National Curriculum. The maximum grant available is £2,500.

The trustees are keen to receive applications from primary schools that are able to demonstrate their project will bring benefit to their children and in doing so meet at least one of the objectives listed below:

• enhance the education and skills of children in the arts, including music, dance and drama
• provide additional (non text book) reading material for children to access for pleasure
• support the improvement of sports and leisure facilities, both indoor and outdoor
• promote activities that reflects the cultural diversity of the local population
• support the inclusion of children with additional needs in extra-curricular activities
• cover transportation and entrance costs to Non Curriculum events
• provide support/and or recreational, pre or after school activities, including breakfast clubs.

ESF Community Grants

The European Social Fund (ESF) is a European Community programme. It aims to increase employment and reduce inactivity by helping to tackle the barriers to work faced by disadvantaged groups.

ESF Community Grants is the ESF's small grants arm, made available through the Birmingham Community Foundation. Local groups can apply for funding for new projects which improve access to mainstream provision for disadvantaged or excluded people. Groups should be based in Birmingham and must be independent. Those that are branches of larger national voluntary organisations may be eligible if they can show that they have a separate management committee and accounts which are not consolidated.

Fairshare
The Fair Share Fund is a ten-year project, which targets those areas that suffer considerable disadvantage and have previously received less than their fair share of National Lottery funding. The places in Greater Birmingham eligible for funding are: Dudley – St Andrews, Sandwell – Great Bridge, Walsall – Alumwell and North Solihull.

More information on the local priorities and how to apply is available on the foundation's website.

Grassroots Grants
Grassroots Grants is a key element of the Government's strategy for building stronger and more active communities. Applications are welcome from voluntary and community organisations that are able to demonstrate their project will build their capacity and bring benefit to the local community. Priority is given to groups which are unable to access other forms of funding. Projects should not duplicate other work being done within the area.

The grassroots grants programme is open to community groups with an annual income of less than £30,000.

Letisha and Charlene Educational Awards
This fund was established in memory of Charlene Ellis and Letisha Shakespeare, who were innocent victims of a drive-by shooting in January 2003. The organisation consists of the families of the two girls and representatives from Aston Pride New Deal for Communities, the Birmingham Mail and Birmingham Community Foundation.

Each award offers support for one year for people living in north-west Birmingham who are aged 16 or over and who need financial help to continue with their education. Awards are up to £2,000.

Sports Relief
This programme aims to empower local people and enable them to create lasting change in their communities. Projects should be run by people directly affected by the issues they are dealing with. Priority will be given to small, locally based groups or organisations in areas of disadvantage that have a clear understanding of the needs of their community. Grants range from £1,000 – £10,000. For more information please go

to 'Sports Relief' page on the foundation's website.

Urban Living Community Cohesion Chest
This is a 'Housing Market Renewal Pathfinder' focused on improving places and supporting communities. The Pathfinders have been set up to deal with the wide range of problems that affect local homes, including: overcrowding, lack of housing choice, empty properties and run down neighbourhoods. The objective of the community cohesion grant is to give organisations the support to make a difference in their area. The programme is focused in eight priority areas: Aston, Handsworth, Lozells, Newtown, Winson Green, Smethwick, West Bromwich and Greets Green.

Organisations must meet the following criteria in order to apply:

- be based and/or provide your services in the Pathfinder area
- be from the voluntary and community sector and have a constitution in place
- have a child protection and/or vulnerable people policy if you intend to work with children, vulnerable groups or young people
- have a bank account with a minimum of two other members of the group as authorised signatories.

Grants range from £1,000 to £10,000 and priority will be given to groups working in partnership with other organisations in the area and to those who have not previously received an Urban Living Community Cohesion grant.

Please note: if none of the above funds are applicable to you, you can complete a general application form and the foundation will try to identify a suitable funding stream for you. General application forms are available directly from the foundation or to download from the website, where further information on any of the above can be found.

Exclusions No funding is available for:

- projects operating outside the Greater Birmingham area
- general appeals or large national charities (except for local branches working specifically for local people)
- individuals, for whatever purpose
- organisations and individuals in the promotion of political or religious ideology.

Applications Applicants should complete the appropriate form, depending on whether they are applying for a specific fund or making a general application. Forms are available from the foundation or can be downloaded from its website (follow the links to the relevant fund page).

Grants are allocated on a rolling programme and there are no deadlines for the receipt of applications. The foundation aims to make a decision within 12 weeks.

The Bluston Charitable Settlement

Jewish and general
£1.4 million (2007/08)
Beneficial area Mostly UK.

20 Seymour Mews, London W1H 6BQ
Tel. 020 7486 7760
Correspondent Martin Paisner
Trustees *Daniel Dover; Martin Paisner.*
CC Number 256691
Information available Accounts were available from the Charity Commission.

The trust has general charitable purposes, although in practice most grants are given to Jewish organisations. The level of grantmaking has been increasing over recent years, and the trust states that it intends to maintain the current level in the near future.

It is the trust's policy to support the following:

- the education of children
- capital expenditure projects for schools and other educational establishments
- the welfare of the underprivileged
- hospitals and medical institutions
- universities for specific research projects.

In 2007/08 the trust had assets of £10 million and an income of £1 million, mainly derived from the estate of a late member of the Bluston family. Grants were made during the year to organisations totalling £1.4 million.

Beneficiaries included: Jewish Care (£200,000); Gateshead Talmudical College and Jewish Museum (£100,000 each); Ohel Torah Beth David (£60,000); Dalaid (£50,000); London Academy of Jewish Studies (£40,000); Meir Medical Centre (£38,000); Chai Cancer Care and Prisoners Abroad (£25,000); Common Denominator (£12,000); Hammerson Home Charitable Trust (£10,000); Friends of the Sick (£6,300); and Camp Simcha (£5,000). The trust appears to have a list of regular beneficiaries.

Exclusions No grants to individuals.

Applications In writing to the correspondent. The trustees meet annually in the spring.

The Booth Charities

Welfare, health and education

£755,000 to organisations
(2007/08)

Beneficial area Salford.

The William Jones Building, 1 Eccles Old Road, Salford, Manchester M6 7DE

Tel. 0161 736 2989 **Fax** 0161 737 4775

Email boothcharities@waitrose.com

Correspondent Mrs L J Needham, Chief Executive

Trustees *William T Whittle, Chair; Richard J Christmas; Angela D Ginger; Edward W Hunt; Michael J Prior; Edward S Tudor-Evans; David J Tully; Roger J Weston; Richard P Kershaw; Philip E Webb; John C Willis.*

CC Number 221800

Information available Accounts were available from the Charity Commission.

The Booth Charities are two charities supporting disadvantaged people in Salford. Together they provide a wide range of support including pension payments to individuals and grants to local charities and facilities. A large number of grants go to organisations which have a direct connection with the charities and a substantial number of these institutions bear the Booth name.

Humphrey Booth the Elder's Charity is for the benefit of the inhabitants of Salford and is established 'for the relief of the aged, impotent or poor' with a preference for people over sixty years of age; the relief of distress and sickness; the provision and support of facilities for recreation and other leisure time occupation; the provision and support of educational facilities; and any other charitable purpose.

Humphrey Booth the Grandson's Charity is established for the income to be applied in or towards the repair and maintenance of the Church of Sacred Trinity, Salford, and in augmenting the stipend of the rector of the Church. The remaining income is then applied in furtherance of the same objects as apply to the Humphrey Booth the Elder Charity.

In 2007/08 the trust had assets of just under £27.3 million and an income of £1.1 million. Grants were made to organisations during the year totalling £755,000, and were categorised as follows:

Category	No. of grants	Amount
Relief of distress and sickness	12	£255,000
Provision and support of educational facilities	9	£144,000
Relief of aged, impotent and poor	12	£132,000
Provision and support of recreation and leisure facilities	9	£114,000
Other charitable purposes	16	£75,000

Beneficiaries included: The Booth Centre (£90,000); Salford Children's Holiday Camp (£30,000); Salford Methodist Centre (£18,600); Waterside Resource Centre (£15,500); St John's Bridge Project (£10,000); Barnardo's and the Heritage Learning Centre and Museum (£5,000 each); Listening Books (£3,000); Age Concern (£2,000); and the People's Dispensary for Sick Animals (£1,000).

Grants were made to individuals totalling £4,600.

Applications In writing to the correspondent.

The Bowland Charitable Trust

Young people, education and general

£2 million (2007)

Beneficial area North-west England.

Activhouse, Philips Road, Blackburn BB1 5TH

Tel. 01254 290433

Correspondent Mrs Carol Fahy, Trustee

Trustees *H A Cann; R A Cann; C Fahy; H D Turner.*

CC Number 292027

Information available Accounts were available from the Charity Commission.

Although the trust's beneficial area covers the whole of the UK, in practice grants are mainly made in north-west England.

'Projects may be funded over varying periods of time, but the majority are made as one off payments.'

In 2007 the trust had an income of £8.8 million and grants paid totalled almost £2 million. By far the largest

grant went to National Maths Case Studies Project (£1.3 million).

Other beneficiaries included: University of Wolverhampton Reveal Project (£225,000); Lord David Puttnam (£125,000); Ron Clark Academy (£100,000); Young Foundation (£80,000); Centre for Crime and Justice Studies (£25,000); Emmaus Preston and Lancashire County Council Education Conference (£20,000 each); St Albans Cathedral Music Trust (£15,000); Nazareth Unitarian Chapel (£14,000); Grindleton Recreation Ground Charity (£5,000); Christ Church Trust – Bridgewater Unitarians (£2,700); Stoneyholme Park Bowling Club (£2,000); and Friends of Blackburn Cathedral Music (£1,000).

Applications The charity invites applications for funding of projects from individuals, charities and other charitable organisations. The applications are made directly to the trustees, who meet regularly to assess the applications.

British Record Industry Trust

Performing arts, music therapy and general

£758,000 (2007)

Beneficial area Worldwide, in practice UK.

Riverside Building, County Hall, Westminster Bridge Road, London SE1 7JA

Email louise.smith@bpi.co.uk

Website www.brittrust.co.uk

Correspondent Louise Smith

Trustees *Paul Burger; Andrew Cleary; John Craig; Rob Dickins; David Kassner; Jonathan Morrish; Tony Wadsworth; Derek Green; Geoff Taylor; David Bryant; Ged Doherty.*

CC Number 1000413

Information available Accounts were available from the Charity Commission.

The BRIT Trust was established in 1989 and is entirely funded by the music industry. Its mission is to give young people a chance to express their musical creativity regardless of race, class, gender or ability and to encourage them in the exploration and pursuit of educational, cultural and therapeutic benefits emanating from music. This includes the

BRIT School in Croydon – the only non-fee paying performing arts school in the UK. Since its inception, over £13 million has been donated by the trust to various charities.

The trust's main source of funding is the BRIT Awards and all profits from the awards go to the trust. To date over £7 million has been received from this source. The income of the trust is primarily distributed between the BRIT School for Performing Arts and Technology in Croydon and Nordoff-Robbins Music Therapy, although smaller donations are also made to a number of other good causes.

The trustees have no direct control over the funding received from the BRIT Awards and as a result of this uncertainty in their long-term funding, have established a policy to hold back a proportion of otherwise distributable income to ensure a reasonable and realistic level of reserves. This will be the subject of regular review.

In 2007 the trust had assets of £6.5 million and an income of £1.9 million. Grants were made to 12 organisations totalling £758,000.

Beneficiaries of by far the largest grants were the BRIT School for the Performing Arts & Technology (£325,000) and Nordoff-Robbins Music Therapy (£275,000).

The other ten grants went to: Music 4 Good and EMI Music Sound Foundation (£50,000 each); Drugscope (£20,000); Young Persons Concert Foundation (£11,000); National Youth Music Theatre (£10,000); Teaching Awards Trust, Julies Bicycle and Release (£5,000 each); and Radio 2 Annual Guitar Prize and LIPA – Make It, Break It (£1,000 each).

Exclusions No scholarships or grants to individuals. No capital funding projects are considered. Only registered charities in the UK are supported.

Applications The trust considers all applications that meet its criteria within the mission statement 'to encourage young people in the exploration and pursuit of educational, cultural or therapeutic benefits emanating from music'. The trust has a long standing relationship with a number of organisations that receive funding each year and consequently is limited to the amount of resources it can offer. Applicants should visit the trust's website and complete the online form or contact the correspondent for further information.

Please note: the trust states that applications where the organisation or project is known to the UK music industry have an advantage. There is space to include an industry contact on the application form.

The Bromley Trust

Human rights, prison reform and conservation

£854,000 (2007/08)
Beneficial area Worldwide.

Studio 7, 2 Pinchin Street, Whitechapel, London E1 1SA

Tel. 020 7481 4899

Email info@thebromleytrust.org.uk

Website www.thebromleytrust.org.uk

Correspondent Teresa Elwes, Grants Executive

Trustees *Anne Lady Prance, Chair; Peter Edwards; Anthony Roberts; Bryan Blamey; Jean Ritchie.*

CC Number 801875

Information available Accounts were available from the Charity Commission.

General

In 1989 Keith Bromley set up the Bromley Trust which he termed 'the most important work of my life' committed to 'offset man's inhumanity to man'; he endowed the trust with much of his fortune. The trust supports charities concerned with human rights, prison reform and conservation and sustainability. This well organised and focused trust also offers other organisations with similar interests and objectives the chance to participate in a network of like-minded groups.

In later years, the settlor had been particularly concerned with the plight of prisoners in overcrowded prisons and the waste of public resources spent building more and more prisons. He understood the cycle of re-offending and saw the value of supporting offenders to learn a trade that would enable them to gain employment after release.

In 2004 the Bromley Trust set up three awards in memory of Keith Bromley. Three charities involved with prison reform were chosen for this additional support. They were the Butler Trust, the

Hardman Trust and the Prison Reform Trust.

Additionally, the Koestler Award Trust, which encourages and rewards a variety of creative endeavours culminating in an annual exhibition of work from prison, probation and secure psychiatric hospitals, has named a prize after Keith Bromley as he had been such a support to their work over the years. The Bromley Trust chose nature photography as this had been a great interest of the settlor's throughout his life. The Keith Bromley Award for Outstanding Nature Photography was presented for the first time at the Koestler exhibition in 2004.

The aims of the trust are given as follows:

Human rights

To combat violations of human rights and help victims of torture, refugees from oppression and those who have been falsely imprisoned; to help those who have suffered severe bodily or mental hurt through no fault of their own and if need be help their dependants; and to try in some way to offset man's inhumanity to man.

The trust supports charities campaigning for human rights under the Universal Declaration for Human Rights and those working to abate the consequence of the acute violation of these rights. These include charities working with individuals and communities that have experienced genocide, torture, rape, false imprisonment, oppression and abuse.

Prison reform

To promote prison reform within the United Kingdom with particular emphasis on the reduction of re-offending.

The trust is committed to the reduction of overcrowding in UK prisons through the reduction of re-offending. Campaigning charities and service providers are supported, particularly charities that aim to reduce the cycle of re-offending by the furtherance of education and skill training thereby helping the offender to engage more successfully in society on release. The trust is particularly interested in supporting the offenders working in the environment.

Conservation and sustainability

To oppose the extinction of the world's fauna & flora and the destruction of the environment for wildlife and for mankind worldwide.

The trust makes grants to charities involved in conservation with a particular focus on the preservation of the rainforests. It supports charities that work in tandem with the rights of indigenous people whose way of life the trust seeks to protect. The trust has chosen the Mata Atlantica (Atlantic Rainforest) as a particular area of interest. The trust also supports charities in the UK that promote sustainability and help develop responsible knowledge and use of the world's resources.

Guidelines

The trust's criteria for awarding grants is as follows:

- grants are made only to UK registered charities that fall within the aims of the trust
- both campaigning organisations and service providers are supported
- support is given to charities that have merit even if they are unproven
- advice is taken from specialists in the trust's fields of interest
- the trust likes to support smaller charities engaged in innovative work and filling a gap identified through experience in the field
- the trust tends to give unrestricted grants though occasionally the grant may be restricted to a particular area of work or a project
- the trust will join with other grant making foundations to support a particular initiative
- grants are made bi-annually
- there is a tendency to make a grant for a period of two or three years but very occasionally a one-off grant may be made
- the expedient use of funds is an important criterion in assessing all applications
- charities are encouraged to network with others working in the same field in order to complement their work, rather than see them as competitors for funds.

The trust's website contains full information on recent grants to organisations, many of which are supported on a regular basis. One-off grants are occasionally made, but are infrequent. The trust prefers to give larger amounts to fewer charities rather than spread its income over a large number of small grants.

Grants in 2007/08

In 2007/08 the trust had assets of £17 million and an income of £772,000. Grants were made totalling £854,000 and were distributed as follows:

Human rights – 33 grants totalling £374,000

Beneficiaries included: Global Dialogue and Redress Trust (£20,000 each); Writers and Scholars Educational Trust (£18,000); Anti-Slavery International (£15,000); Amera, Southall Black Sisters Trust and Inquest (£10,000 each); and

London Detainee Support Group (£5,000).

Prison reform – 21 grants totalling £270,000

Grants included those to: Prison Reform Trust (£20,000); Start-up, Hardman Trust and Shannon Trust (£15,000 each); Action for Prisoner's Families and Prison Video Trust (£10,000 each); and Prison Phoenix Trust (£5,000).

Conservation and sustainability – 18 grants totalling £210,000

Beneficiaries included: Ashden Awards (£25,000); Cape Farewell and Survival International (£15,000 each); Birdlife International (£13,000); Rio Atlantic Forest Trust (£10,000); Marine Conservation and A Rocha Lebanon (£5,000 each).

Exclusions Grants are only given to UK registered charities. The following are not supported:

- individuals
- expeditions
- scholarships, although in certain cases the trust supports research that falls within its aims (but always through a registered charity)
- statutory authorities, or charities whose main source of funding is via statutory agencies
- overseas development, healthcare or education per se. The trust only supports these areas in conjunction with the violation of human rights and where discrimination has accounted for deprivation
- local conservation projects or charities that work with single species.

Applications New applicants are directed, where possible, to the website where the trust's criteria, guidelines and application process are posted. An initial questionnaire can be accessed from the website for charities that fit the trust's remit, and should be completed and returned via email to: applicant@thebromleytrust.org.uk. All charities are visited before a grant is made.

A grant is made for one year and in most cases renewed automatically for two further years. Although most grants are unrestricted, the trust monitors each charity annually and requires certain conditions to be fulfilled before further funding is made available. Grants are always made subject to the availability of funds. The trustees meet twice a year in April and October and applications should be received the previous month. *Urgent appeals may be dealt with at any time.*

Please note: the trust asks that organisations who have previously submitted an application do not submit any further requests for funding. Applicant details are held on the trust's database and if any assistance can be provided in the future, they will make contact.

Brushmill Ltd

Jewish causes, education and social welfare

£324,000 (2007/08)
Beneficial area Worldwide.

76 Fairholt Road, London N16 5HN
Correspondent C Getter, Trustee
Trustees C Getter, Chair; J Weinberger; Mrs E Weinberger.
CC Number 285420
Information available Accounts were on file at the Charity Commission, without a list of grants.

Established in 1982, the trust gives grants for education, the relief of poverty and to Jewish causes.

In 2007/08 the trust had an income of £386,000, mainly from donations. Grants were made totalling £324,000, although a list of beneficiaries was not available.

Previous beneficiaries have included Bais Rochel, Friends of Yeshivas Shaar Hashomaim and Holmleigh Trust.

Applications In writing to the correspondent.

The Burdett Trust for Nursing

Healthcare

£1.9 million to organisations (2008)
Beneficial area Mostly UK.

SG Hambros Trust Company, SG House, 41 Tower Hill, London EC3N 4SG
Tel. 020 7597 3000 **Fax** 020 7702 9263
Email administrator@burdettnursingtrust.org.uk
Website www.burdettnursingtrust.org.uk

Correspondent Shirley Baines, Administrator

Trustees *Alan Gibbs, Chair; Sue Norman; Prof Eileen Sills; Victor West; Ray Greenwood; Andrew Smith; Dr Soek Khim Horton; Lady Henrietta St George; Joanna Webber; Jack Gibbs; William Gordon.*

CC Number 1089849

Information available Accounts were available from the Charity Commission and the trust has a helpful website.

The Burdett Trust for Nursing is an independent charitable trust named after Sir Henry Burdett KCB, the founder of the Royal National Pension Fund for Nurses. The trust was set up in 2001.

The following is taken from the trust's 2008 accounts and its website and explains the new grant making policy.

The trustees aim to target their grants at projects that are nurse-led and focused on supporting the nursing contribution to healthcare. The trust aims to use its funds to empower nurses and through this to make significant improvements to the patient care environment.

In 2008 the trustees carried out a comprehensive review of their grant-making policies and procedures. As a result of the review, the trustees decided that they would introduce four new grant funding programmes for 2009:

- Building Nursing Research Capacity – to support clinical nursing research and research addressing policy, leadership development and delivery of nursing care.
- Building Nurse Leadership Capacity – supporting nurses in their professional development to create a cadre of excellent nursing and allied health professionals who will become leaders of the future and foster excellence and capacity-building in advancing the nursing profession.
- Supporting Local Nurse-led Initiatives – to support nurse-led initiatives that make a difference at local level and are focussed explicitly on improving care for patients and users of services.
- Proactive grants.

It was agreed that the trust would invite charitable organisations to operate as its 'funding partners' to manage the first three of these programmes. After a rigorous selection process the trustees appointed the following four organisations to become their initial funding partners:

- Help the Hospices
- Florence Nightingale Foundation
- Foundation of Nursing Studies
- Queen's Nursing Institute

All of the organisations are well placed to deliver grants programmes on behalf of the trust, to achieve positive outcomes for patients, nursing and healthcare practice. For more information on each of the partner organisations, go to the relevant website or contact the trust.

Help the Hospices

This three-year programme of nurse-led projects targets issues around widening access to hospice care. Through the innovation, knowledge and leadership of hospice nurses, the programme seeks to facilitate sustainable improvements in hospice practice and services, which will ensure fairer access to palliative care for under-represented patient groups. Grants will be available to fund both pilot and more substantial initiatives which will bring new ideas, benefits and improved practice to local communities, the national hospice movement, the wider nursing profession and, most importantly, to patients. All projects will be supported by a practice facilitator at Help the Hospices, and findings will be disseminated throughout the hospice nursing sector.

Florence Nightingale Foundation

The Burdett Trust for Nursing has appointed the Florence Nightingale Foundation as a funding partner to build the leadership capacity in health services. The purpose of the funding is to manage a programme to develop leadership qualities that will endow potential future leaders, in nursing, midwifery and the allied health professionals, with the skills and self-confidence to contribute forcefully to the rapidly changing world of healthcare. The foundation, a living memorial to Florence Nightingale, is a charity that advances the study of nursing and promotes excellence in practice. It has an impressive record in successfully awarding scholarships for research, travel and leadership.

Foundation of Nursing Studies

This programme will provide support and facilitation for clinically based nurses to enable them to lead innovative local projects that will develop nurses, nursing and healthcare practice to improve the patients' experience of care in any healthcare setting across the UK. Central to the innovations will be the focus on patient needs/experiences and the use of processes that lead to sustainable practice change. Over a period of 12 months, FoNS will offer ongoing support and facilitation to project teams to help them to develop, implement and evaluate locally focused innovations that improve care. Funding of up to £3,000 will also be available to support each project team.

Queen's Nursing Institute

This three year programme of nurse-led local projects aims to improve the care of patients in their own homes and communities, and to enhance the leadership skills of the nurses involved. Each year, up to eight innovative projects, led by community nurses, midwives or health visitors, will set up new services or improved ways of working for the benefit of patients. All project leads will benefit from the QNI's support including a unique and highly-rated programme of developmental workshops during their project year. The programme will aim to achieve sustainable innovation in services, and a new cohort of confident nurse leaders for the future.

In addition to working with its funding partners, over the next five years the trust will make a series of proactive grants. Since the trust's inception proactive initiatives, i.e. grants for projects initiated by the trust, have formed an important part of its grant portfolio. The trust's main proactive grant has been to the 'Who Cares, Wins – Leadership and the Business of Caring' initiative. Associated University of Plymouth studies and the subsequent King's Fund 'Ward to Board' project have helped this initiative to punch above its weight in terms of uptake and impact. This has set the gold standard for the type of proactive work that the trust will now take forward. The trust will focus on serious, credible initiatives addressing contemporary patient care and professional issues.

Grants in 2008

In 2008 the trust had assets of £57 million and a consolidated income of £1.5 million. Grants were made totalling nearly £2 million, of which £1.9 million was given to institutions and the remaining £148,000 to individuals.

Beneficiaries during the year included: University of Sterling – Cancer Care Research Centre (£250,000); Florence Nightingale Foundation (£150,000); Sue Ryder Care (£129,000); Junius S Morgan Benevolent Fund (£100,000); University of Nottingham (£97,000); University of Glasgow (£57,000); Air Balloon Surgery – Research Unit (£22,000); and World Orthopaedic Concern UK (£15,000).

Exclusions Please contact the relevant funding partner for information on the programme criteria.

Applications The successful funding partners are listed below. Please visit their websites for information about how to apply to these joint programmes.

- Help the Hospices – www.helpthehospices.org.uk
- Florence Nightingale Foundation – www.florence-nightingale-foundation.orguk
- Foundation of Nursing Studies – www.fons.org
- Queen's Nursing Institute - www.qni.org.uk

The Clara E Burgess Charity

Children and young people

£429,000 (2007/08)

Beneficial area UK and worldwide.

RBS Trust Services, Eden, Lakeside, Chester Business Park, Wrexham Road, Chester CH4 9QT

Correspondent The Trust Section Manager

Trustee *The Royal Bank of Scotland plc.*

CC Number 1072546

Information available Accounts were available from the Charity Commission.

Registered in 1998, this trust makes grants to registered charities where children are the principal beneficiaries of the work. Grants are towards 'the provision of facilities and assistance to enhance the education, health and physical well-being of children particularly (but not exclusively) those under the age of 10 years who have lost one or both parents'. Within these boundaries grants can be made to the following causes:

- education/training
- overseas projects
- disability
- social welfare
- hospitals/hospices
- medical/health
- medical research.

In 2007/08 the trust had assets of £8.4 million and an income of £349,000. Grants were made to 28 organisations totalling £429,000.

Large grants were made to: Save the Children (£100,000); St Kentigern Hospice (£52,000); Woodlands Hospice (£37,500); Winnies Castle of Love (£28,000); and Rainbow Centre for Children and PSS (£20,000 each).

Other beneficiaries included: Positive Action on Cancer (£17,500); Sefton Children's Trust (£15,000); Treetops Hospice (£10,000); Macmillan Cancer Support (£9,000); Chernobyl Children in Need (£6,000); Sand Rose Project (£5,000); and Home Start (£1,000).

Exclusions No grants to non-registered charities.

Applications In writing to the correspondent.

The Audrey and Stanley Burton 1960 Charitable Trust

Charities supporting education and the arts, Jewish people/Israel, social welfare, health, and overseas and developing countries

£1.8 million (2007/08)

Beneficial area Worldwide. In practice UK with a preference for Yorkshire.

Trustee Management Ltd, 19 Cookridge Street, Leeds LS2 3AG

Tel. 0113 243 6466

Email trustee.mgmt@btconnect.com

Correspondent Keith Pailing, Trustee Management Limited

Trustees *Amanda Burton; Raymond Burton; Jeremy Burton.*

CC Number 1028430

Information available Accounts were available from the Charity Commission.

The trust was established for general charitable purposes at the discretion of the trustees by an initial gift from S H Burton who died in 1991.

In 2007/08 the trust had assets of £1.2 million and an income of almost £1.7 million, including a donation of £1.2 million from Audrey Burton. Grants were made during the year totalling over £1.8 million, which included an exceptional grant from restricted funds of more than £1.5 million to the University of Leeds for the refurbishment of the Art Gallery.

There were 153 general grants made totalling £296,500 and were categorised as follows:

Social welfare – 51 grants totalling £91,000

Beneficiaries receiving £1,000 or more included: Henshaws College and the Medical Foundation for the Care of Victims of Torture (£10,000 each); Bat-I About Kidz (£5,000); Rainbow Trust (£3,000); CISV International and REACT (£2,000 each); and Children's Adventure Farm and Yorkshire Air Ambulance (£1,000 each).

Overseas and developing countries – 17 grants totalling £85,000

Beneficiaries included: OXFAM (£35,000 in total); UNICEF (£15,000 in total); Save the Children (£10,000 in total); Concern Worldwide (£2,000); and Anti-Slavery International (£1,000).

Health – 24 grants totalling £42,000

Beneficiaries included: Alzheimer's Research Trust (£10,000); MND Association (£3,000); Cookridge Cancer Centre (£2,500); and Changing Faces and Spinal Injuries Association (£1,000 each).

Education and the arts – 18 grants totalling £40,000 (excluding the substantial donation to the University of Leeds)

Beneficiaries included: Royal Hall Restoration Trust (£10,000); Live Music Now (£4,000); Harrogate International Festival (£3,000); Leeds Grand Theatre Trust (£2,000); and Dyslexia Action (£1,000).

Jewish/Israel – 35 grants totalling £39,000

Beneficiaries included: Hebrew University (£5,000); Holocaust Educational Trust (£3,000); British Technion Society (£2,500); and Donisthorpe Hall and Weizmann UK (£1,000).

Exclusions No grants to individuals.

Applications In writing to the correspondent. Unsuccessful applicants are not always notified.

The Derek Butler Trust

Medical, health, arts (particularly music) and general

£537,000 (2007/08)

Beneficial area Worldwide, in practice UK.

Underwood Solicitors, 40 Welbeck Street, London W1G 8LN

Tel. 020 7526 6000

Email hguest@underwoodco.com

Correspondent Miss Hilary A E Guest, Trustee

Trustees *Bernard W Dawson; Donald F Freeman; Revd Michael Fuller; Miss Hilary A E Guest.*

CC Number 1081995

Information available Accounts were available from the Charity Commission.

The trust was established in 2000 for general charitable purposes, with an interest in medical research, health and the arts.

In 2007/08 it had assets of £11.7 million and an income of almost £462,000. Grants were made during the year totalling £537,000, which included £50,000 in awards through the Derek Butler London Prize.

There were 29 grants made to organisations, with beneficiaries including: Core (formerly Digestive Disorders Foundation) (£108,000); Trinity College of Music Bursaries (£72,000 in total); Crusaid (£65,000); The Food Chain UK (£30,000); St Christopher's Hospice (£21,000); Holidays for Carers and Bampton Classical Opera (£10,000 each); Animal Health Trust (£5,500); GMFT Charity (£3,000); and Pimlico Opera (£2,000).

Applications In writing to the correspondent. 'The trustees continue to seek new charities to which they can make suitable donations.'

Edward Cadbury Charitable Trust

General

£789,000 (2007/08)

Beneficial area Worldwide, in practice mainly UK with a preference for the Midlands region.

Rokesley, University of Birmingham Selly Oak, Bristol Road, Selly Oak, Birmingham B29 6QF

Tel. 0121 472 1838 **Fax** 0121 472 7013

Email ecadburytrust@fsmail.net

Correspondent Sue Anderson, Trust Manager

Trustees *Dr Charles E Gillett, Chair; William Southall; Charles R Gillett; Andrew Littleboy; Nigel Cadbury; Hugh Marriott.*

CC Number 227384

Information available Accounts were available from the Charity Commission.

The trust was established in 1945 for general charitable purposes. The main areas of grantgiving are education, Christian missions, the ecumenical movement and interfaith relations, the oppressed and disadvantaged, the arts and the environment.

Up to 100 grants are made each year, many of them small – between £500 and £5,000. As well as its usual grantmaking, the trustees occasionally seek projects where a significant grant can make a real impact. These grants can be very large, for example, in 2006 a grant of £1 million was made to the Special Collections Centre at the University of Birmingham. A few grants are awarded to UK groups working overseas and to overseas charities. Grants are rarely made to local charities outside the Midlands region.

The trust describes its grantmaking policy for the future as follows:

The main aims and objectives of the trustees in the forthcoming year are to build on and enhance the successful programme of grant giving undertaken within the year ended 5 April 2008 and to continue to support charities, principally within the Midlands region, which encourage community development and inclusiveness, provide compassionate support to those in need and promote educational, cultural and environmental projects.

In 2007/08 the trust had assets of £28 million and an income of £896,000. There were 80 grants made totalling £789,000. Grants were distributed as follows:

Category	Value
Conservation and environment	£371,000
Community projects and integration	£118,000
Ecumenical mission and interfaith relations	£103,000
Compassionate support	£91,000
Education and training	£90,000
Arts and culture	£17,000

Beneficiaries included: Ironbridge Gorge Museum Trust (£250,000); Centre for Studies in Security & Diplomacy, University of Birmingham (£88,000); Responding to Conflict (£50,000); South Birmingham Young Homeless Project (£45,000); Northfield Eco Centre – Birmingham (£38,000); Beacon Centre for the Blind – Wolverhampton (£25,000); St John of Jerusalem Eye Hospital (£10,000); Farming and Countryside Education (£5,000); Community Service Volunteers (£2,000); and Deafblind UK (£1,000).

Exclusions Grants to registered charities only. No student grants or support for individuals.

Applications In writing to the correspondent at any time and allowing three months for a response. Appeals should clearly and concisely give relevant information concerning the project and its benefits, an outline budget and how the project is to be funded initially and in the future. Up-to-date accounts and the organisation's latest annual report are also required.

Applications that do not come within the trust's policy may not be considered or acknowledged.

The William A Cadbury Charitable Trust

Local welfare and disability charities, penal reform, Quaker charities and overseas

£685,000 (2007/08)

Beneficial area West Midlands, especially Birmingham and, to a lesser extent, UK, Ireland and overseas.

Rokesley, University of Birmingham Selly Oak, Bristol Road, Selly Oak, Birmingham B29 6QF

Tel. 0121 472 1464 (am only)

Email info@wa-cadbury.org.uk

Website www.wa-cadbury.org.uk

Correspondent Carolyn Bettis, Trust Administrator

Trustees *James Taylor; Rupert Cadbury; Katherine van Hagen Cadbury; Margaret Salmon; Sarah Stafford; Adrian Thomas; John Penny; Sophy Blandy; Janine Cobain.*

CC Number 213629

Information available Accounts were available from the Charity Commission.

This trust was established in 1923 for general charitable purposes and is described by the trust as follows:

William was the second son of Richard Cadbury, who, with his younger brother George, started the manufacture of chocolate under the Cadbury name. He came from a family with strong Quaker traditions which influenced his whole life. It was this Quaker ethos which underpinned his commitment to the advancement of social welfare schemes in the city of Birmingham.

William Cadbury established the trust soon after his two years as lord mayor of Birmingham from 1919 to 1921, wishing to give more help to the causes in which he was interested. One such was the building of the Queen Elizabeth Hospital, a medical centre with the space and facilities to bring together the small specialised hospitals scattered throughout Birmingham … He did much.to encourage the city library and art gallery and a wide circle of Midlands artists who became his personal friends. Through this charity, William Cadbury also secured several properties for the National Trust.

As time went on, members of his family were brought in as trustees and this practice has continued with representatives of the next two generations becoming trustees in their turn, so that all the present trustees are his direct descendants.

The trust gives grants in the following fields:

Birmingham and the West Midlands
- social welfare – community and self-help groups working with the disadvantaged (including younger and older people, ethnic and religious minorities, women, homeless people and people with disabilities) and counselling and mediation agencies
- medical – medical and healthcare projects including medical research
- education and training – for schools and universities, adult literacy schemes, training for employment
- the Religious Society of Friends (Quakers)
- places of religious worship and associated social projects
- conservation of the environment – including the preservation of listed buildings and monuments
- the arts – including music, drama and the visual arts, museums and art galleries
- penal affairs – including work with offenders and ex-offenders, penal reform and police projects.

International
- social welfare, healthcare and environmental projects
- sustainable development.

Please note: The international grants programme has recently been refocused on a small number of organisations with which the trust has close and well established links. Ad hoc applications for this programme are unlikely to be successful.

Ireland
- cross-community initiatives promoting peace and reconciliation.

United Kingdom
- the Religious Society of Friends (Quakers)
- penal reform.

Grantmaking

In 2007/08 the trust had assets of £21 million and an income of £787,000. Grants were made totalling £685,000.

Grants were broken down in the accounts by category, with details of grants of over £1,000, as follows:

International – grants totalling £164,000
Beneficiaries included: Concern Universal (£120,000 – 2 grants); British Red Cross, Welfare Association and Campaign for Female Education (£10,000 each); and Cerebral Palsy Africa (£5,000).

Penal affairs – grants totalling £90,000
Beneficiaries included: Birmingham Citizens Advice Bureau (£48,000); St Giles Trust (£15,000); Female Prisoners Welfare Project (£11,000); and Howard Legal for Penal Reform and Four Square (£2,000 each).

Medical and health care – grants totalling £49,000
Beneficiaries included: Birmingham St Mary's Hospice (£15,000); and Aston University, Action for M.E. and Worcester Acute Hospitals NHS Trust (£10,000 each).

Community – grants totalling £44,000
Beneficiaries included: ARCH – Domestic Violence Outreach Project (£15,000); Cares Sandwell (£10,000); Birmingham Tribunal Unit (£5,000); and Pathway Project (£1,500).

Young people – grants totalling £43,000
Beneficiaries included: Dorothy Parkes Centre (£12,000); Perdiswell Young Peoples Leisure Club (£10,000); and Warstock and Billesley Detached Youth Work Project (£6,000).

Society of Friends – grants totalling £43,000
Beneficiaries included: Quaker Peace and Social Witness (£25,000); Worcester Quaker Meeting (£10,000); and Woodbrooke Quaker Study Centre (£3,000).

Mediation and Counselling – grants totalling £38,000
Beneficiaries included: Family Mediation Worcestershire and Guild of Psychotherapists (£15,000 each); and Relate – Birmingham (£5,000).

Disability – grants totalling £38,000
Beneficiaries included: Motor Neurone Disease Association (£15,000); Friends of Victoria (£12,000); and Sunfield (£8,000).

Church (social) – grants totalling £36,000
Beneficiaries included: Cascob Church, Litchfield Cathedral and Friends of St Michael Disoed (£10,000 each).

Children – grants totalling £29,000
Beneficiaries included: PCC of St Mary and St Ambrose Edgbaston (£15,000);

and NCH – Coseley Health & Family Centre (£7,000).

Arts – grants totalling £27,000
Beneficiaries included: Orchestra of St John's and Albatross Arts Project (£10,000 each).

Environment and conservation – grants totalling £27,000
Beneficiaries included: Avoncroft Museum of Historic Buildings (£10,000); Elenydd Wilderness Hostels (£8,000); and Shropshire Wildlife Trust (£2,000).

Homelessness – grants totalling £26,000
Beneficiaries included: Church Housing Trust (£15,000); and St Basil's (£10,000).

Ireland – grants totalling £13,000
Beneficiaries included: Amnesty International UK (£8,000); and Corner House Cross Community Family Centre (£3,000).

Education and training – grants totalling £12,000
Beneficiaries included: George Bell Institute and Speaks Volumes (£5,000 each).

Care for older people – grants totalling £5,000
No beneficiaries listed in the accounts; grants awarded were under £1,000 each.

Exclusions The trust does not fund:
- individuals (whether for research, expeditions or educational purposes)
- projects concerned with travel, adventure, sports or recreation
- organisations which do not have UK charity registration (except those legally exempt)
- overseas charities not registered in the UK.

Applications In writing to the correspondent, including the following information:
- charity registration number
- a description of the charity's aims and achievements
- a copy of the latest set of accounts
- an outline and budget for the project for which funding is sought
- details of funds raised and the current shortfall.

Applications can also be submitted on the trust's online application form. Please also forward a copy of the organisation's latest set of accounts.

Applications are considered on a continuing basis throughout the year. Small grants (amounts not exceeding £2,000) are assessed each month. Major grants are awarded at the trustees' meetings held twice annually, normally in May and November. Applicants whose appeals are to be considered at one of the meetings will be notified in advance.

The trust receives many more applications than can be supported. Even if your project meets our requirements we may not be able to help, particularly if you are located outside the West Midlands.

The Barrow Cadbury Trust and the Barrow Cadbury Fund

Young, adult and criminal justice, migration and poverty and exclusion

£2.4 million (2007/08)

Beneficial area Unrestricted, with a preference for Birmingham and the Black Country (Wolverhampton, Dudley, West Bromwich, Smethwick and Sandwell).

Kean House, 6 Kean Street, London WC2B 4AS

Tel. 020 7632 9060 **Fax** 020 7632 9061

Email general@barrowcadbury.org.uk

Website www.barrowcadbury.org.uk

Correspondent Jackie Collins, Grants and Outreach Manager

Trustees Ruth Cadbury, Chair; Anna C Southall; Anna Hickinbotham; Erica R Cadbury; Nicola Cadbury; Tim Compton; Tamsin Rupprechter; Gordon Mitchell; Harry Searle; Richard Brennan.

CC Number 1115476

Information available Accounts were on file at the Charity Commission. The trust has an excellent, informative website.

The Barrow Cadbury Trust was set up in 1920 as the Barrow & Geraldine S Cadbury Trust and merged with the Paul S Cadbury Trust in 1994. Barrow Cadbury was the eldest son of Richard Cadbury, one of the two brothers who established the Cadbury chocolate factory. His main interests lay in the Quakers, peacetime reconstruction and the relief of war victims after the First World War. He believed that the profits from industry should be diverted into social causes that would safeguard the true welfare of people. In later life, he

took a great personal interest in the administration of his trust fund, personally overseeing accounts, writing cheques himself, and addressing envelopes in his own hand.

Barrow's wife, Geraldine Southall, was a thinker and innovator, descended from a family of inventors and entrepreneurs. She campaigned for reform of the penal system, and the treatment of children and young adults in the criminal justice system. Geraldine was an early believer in working with the policy-makers and opinion-formers of her day to achieve social change.

The trust aims to encourage a fair, equal, peaceful and democratic society. The income generated from the endowment left by Barrow Cadbury and his wife Geraldine is used to make grants to support groups, (usually registered charities) that are working to achieve the trust's objectives. Grants are made to enable groups to act as catalysts of social change.

The trust was incorporated as a company limited by guarantee in June 2006. In August 2006, the trustees of the unincorporated separate charity, the Barrow Cadbury Trust (registered charity number: 226331) transferred the assets, subject to their liabilities, and activities of that charity to this trust.

The company, the Barrow Cadbury Fund, administered and managed by the trustees of the trust, is not a registered charity and supports non-charitable activity where this meets the trust's priorities. Please note: it is not possible to apply to the fund.

The trust aims to work in partnership with groups it funds in order to:

- build bridges between policy makers and grassroots activity
- find ways of identifying best practice from projects to help social change
- encourage new solutions to old problems.

Grantmaking

In 2007/08 the trust had assets of £69 million and an income of £3.1 million. Grants were made totalling £2.4 million.

The following information is taken from material provided by the trust.

The trust promotes social justice through grantmaking, research, influencing public policy and supporting local communities. The following themes are prominent across the trust's work:

- supporting the independence and diversity of the voluntary sector
- addressing gender-based disadvantage
- addressing disadvantage based on race and ethnicity
- funding groups, projects and programmes in Birmingham and the West Midlands.

The trust seeks to develop partnerships with the many projects it supports. The trust's main priority is to fund grassroots, user-led projects, usually operating at national level. Projects that are likely to have a high impact on social change at a policy or practice level are favoured. The trust looks for visionary projects, often those that are considered radical or risky and great emphasis is placed on projects that are backed by strong leadership. Detailed examples of previously funded projects are available on the trust's website.

There are three main types of grant:

- small grants – up to £3,000
- minor grants – up to £10,000
- major grants – over £10,000.

The average grant for grassroots projects is between £25,000 and £30,000 per year. The maximum grant is £50,000 per year for three years, though this size of award is only made to groups which have been funded previously. Grants are rarely made for more than two years to groups that are not already known to the trust. Equally, applications for core costs will only be accepted from organisations the trust is already aware of. The trust expects to make around 80 grants a year, of which around 50 will be major grants.

The trust is willing to provide match funding for projects. Organisations should make it clear in their initial proposal if they require match funding or a contribution to a large project and state whether or not they have secured other funding already. If not, the trust may still consider the application but the final award may depend on securing all of the funding.

The availability of funds generally dictates what grants the trust is able to make but it does try to ensure a fair geographic spread. The primary focus is on Birmingham and the West Midlands but applications from elsewhere are considered under some programmes. Please refer to the specific grant programme criteria below to see which geographic areas are covered.

The trust always receives more applications than it is able to fund. Even if your organisation is eligible and the project meets the criteria, your application may not be successful. Assessments are based on the grant criteria but decisions will be influenced by the finance available and the overall profile of our grant making through the year.

Programme priorities

The programme priorities are based on social objectives that are of particular concern to the trust. These are based on the existing strengths of work previously funded and current or possible areas of policy development. Projects will be chosen that the trust believes will help to achieve tangible shifts in policy and practice.

The trust aims to develop clusters of activity around each social objective. This means identifying complementary projects, that is, those that add value to the efforts of other groups supported by the trust. It also aims to find ways of connecting them across community sectors and with people involved at different levels of decision-making (including policy officials, practitioners and leaders of statutory and mainstream organisations). This approach means that it is unlikely that the trust will support more than one of the same type of project in any cluster.

The trust aims to stay flexible and respond to current circumstances and will monitor and regularly review its objectives. Any amendments will be highlighted on the trust's website and published each year but this should not affect any projects that it is already considering.

Organisations should meet the following eligibility criteria before applying:

- preferably be a grassroots, user-led project
- have a formal structure and governing documents (you do not have to be a registered charity or incorporated charitable company)
- have a bank account in your own name.

If at the time of the application you do not have these in place the trust can support you to develop them and allow you time to meet these requirements.

The trust's work is divided into three main programme areas:

- criminal justice
- migration
- poverty and inclusion.

The following summary guidelines are drawn largely from the trust's website. For further details and the latest information on any of the funding programmes below, go to the website or contact the trust directly.

Criminal Justice

This programme aims to support people who are within or at risk of entering the criminal justice system, to improve their life chances – with a particular focus on young adults. The trust's current criminal justice work includes:

- Transition to Adulthood (T2A) Alliance
- T2A pilots

- Supporting women offenders
- Young adults and criminal justice grassroots.

Funding is available under the grassroots programme for projects based in Birmingham or the Black Country (Wolverhampton, Dudley, West Bromwich, Smethwick and Sandwell). The trust is looking to fund grassroots groups working with disadvantaged young people (16–25) who are at risk of or involved in criminal activity.

We want to support groups that take a long-term view about working with disadvantaged young people, recognising that change may take time and that improving life chances can take many forms. We expect that young people will play an active role in projects we fund.

Your project might address one or more of these but we are willing to consider other ideas that will reduce the risk of disadvantaged young people being involved in criminal activity.

- Supporting young people in preparing to access formal education or employment.
- Supporting young people through peer mentoring or access to positive role models.
- Working with young people to change their perspectives and behaviours.
- Projects that use conflict resolution models.
- Projects that use restorative justice models.
- We will consider funding diversionary activities, but only as part of a wider project that leads to attitudinal or behavioural change.

Migration

The trust's interest in migration derives from urgent and emerging needs identified by the local voluntary and community organisations it supports. The impact of recent large-scale immigration and unprecedented population mobility upon both migrants and established disadvantaged communities in the UK has not been fully explored or understood.

A core aspect of the trust's work in this area involves supporting grassroots organisations working with the most vulnerable groups of refugees, asylum seekers and migrants. Grant funding in this area is available through the *Migration Grassroots Funding Stream.*

Under this stream the trust looks to fund, 'grassroots groups working with refugees, asylum seekers, undocumented migrants and other marginalised migrants. We seek to enable grassroots groups to support the most vulnerable migrants. We also seek to empower migrants and

ensure they are not excluded from the public debate on migration'.

Please find below some guidance on the types of projects and/or organisations we are likely to support:

- those which help ensure that migrant, refugee and asylum seeker voices contribute to the public debate on migration
- those which seek to improve the lives of undocumented migrants or other groups facing extreme hardship
- those which promote a more balanced public debate on migration and asylum
- those which focus on addressing injustice or unequal treatment faced by some migrants
- those which address specific issues experienced by undocumented migrants, asylum seekers and refugees, such as the restriction of access to health care and education.

You may apply for this programme from anywhere in the UK but most awards will be made in the West Midlands.

Poverty and Inclusion

Traditionally, the Barrow Cadbury Trust has had a strong focus on funding grassroots groups that are working to combat poverty and inequality. The new 'Poverty and Inclusion' funding programme continues this and encourages groups to be creative and responsive in tackling these issues. As well as supporting grassroots projects we want to use this learning to help shift the focus of debate on to ways in which inequality and poverty can be tackled productively and collaboratively.

There are three grant programmes under 'Poverty and Inclusion':

Bridging communities

The trust recognises that cities in the West Midlands are becoming super diverse, which many welcome and embrace. However, for some it can feel like a battle for resources and lead to inter-community tensions. We believe that many of these tensions have their roots in poverty and inequality rather than as a consequence of people from different ethnic and religious groups living in the same space. We will fund local groups that bring communities together around issues of common cause, that tackle a problem that affects all, or that aim to reduce tensions by getting people together to actively address them.

The types of project we will fund will very much depend on the local context but we want to support projects that can show:

- specific scenarios where an inter-community response will produce practical outcomes to particular problems

- how they will bring people together and for what reason – we will expect any social activity to be part of a broader plan
- how solidarity can be built in their community and why it is needed
- how bringing people together will result in an improvement for all.

Tackling poverty

Tackling poverty and deprivation is fundamental to the mission of the trust. We believe that many communities have the resources, skills and creativity, if given the chance, to find solutions to poverty and ways to generate and keep money within the local community. We are also concerned that in a time of economic decline many are forced to find short-term solutions that will result in long-term debt and exploitation.

We are open to new ideas of community responses to tackling poverty but we will also consider projects that focus on:

- supporting people to find ways out of poverty that build skills, confidence and opportunities
- enabling people to access safe finance
- supporting people to generate and keep wealth within communities.

Inequalities

We want to fund grassroots groups that address gender and/or race and ethnic based disadvantage. Groups will need to identify the inequality and state how it will be addressed.

We are interested in supporting projects that:

- lead to empowerment
- create examples that others can learn from
- engage excluded individuals and communities in the involvement in community life and/or political processes
- bring people together to tackle inequality.

Your project may fit under one or more of these themes. You can only apply for this programme if your project is based in the West Midlands.

Please note: the trust is currently reviewing its previous work around gender issues, specifically supporting a range of women's projects. Please go to the website or contact the trust for the latest information.

Exclusions The trust does not fund:

- activities for which central or local government are responsible
- animal welfare
- arts and cultural projects
- capital costs for building, refurbishment and outfitting
- endowment funds
- fundraising events or activities
- general appeals
- general health
- debt counselling

- individuals
- housing
- learning disability
- medical research or equipment
- mental health
- older people
- physical disability
- promoting religion or belief systems
- schools
- sponsorship or marketing appeals.

The following areas of work are also unlikely to receive funding:

- *counselling* – unless it forms part of a wider project within one of the programme areas
- *colleges and universities* – only under the research funding of the trust
- *drug and alcohol users* – this remains as a possible area of funding under the criminal justice programme only as part of a broader project
- *environmental projects* – this would only be considered under the poverty and inclusion programme as part of a broader project
- *homelessness and destitution* – only for those leaving the criminal justice system or in relation to the migration programme
- *IT training* – only if it forms part of a wider project
- *sporting activities* – only if it forms part of a wider project.

Applications In writing to the correspondent. The trust does not have an application form but asks that organisations submit an outline proposal which covers the following key points.

- The organisation and what it does – this should include a brief background of the organisation, its aims, activities and contact details. If you have been funded previously for the same project you should describe the successes to date.
- The programme area and grant programme being applied for – projects cannot cover more than one programme area but under the poverty and inclusion programme, proposals may cover more than one grant criteria (bridging communities, poverty, inequality).
- Where the project will take place – applicants should provide as much detail as possible about the specific area in which the project will take place.
- A description of the specific project for which funding is sought – explain what is intended and how it will be done.
- Who will benefit from the project – identify the individuals or organisations that will benefit from the project.

- The size of grant needed – how much money you are requesting, for what and over what period?
- What success will look like – applicants should explain what they hope will change as a result of this project and how they will know that it has been successful.

Proposals should be no more than two to three sides of A4 and no further information need be submitted at this stage.

The grants team will assess the application and contact you. The trust aims to make initial contact within one month of receiving a proposal. If it decides to proceed further, it will work with the applicant to develop the proposal.

If you would like to speak to a member of the grants team prior to submitting your proposal please contact Asma Aroui on 020 7632 9068 or email a.aroui@barrowcadbury.org.uk.

The Cadogan Charity

General charitable purposes, social welfare, medical research, services charities, animal welfare, education and conservation and the environment

£1.4 million (2007/08)

Beneficial area Worldwide. In practice, UK with a preference for London and Scotland.

18 Cadogan Gardens, London SW3 2RP

Tel. 020 7730 4567 **Fax** 0207 881 2300

Correspondent P M Loutit, Secretary

Trustees *Earl Cadogan; Countess Cadogan; Viscount Chelsea; Lady Anna Thomson.*

CC Number 247773

Information available Accounts were available from the Charity Commission.

The trust was established in 1966 for general charitable purposes and operates two funds: the general fund and the rectors' fund. The rectors' fund was created with a gift from Cadogan Holdings Company in 1985 to pay an annual amount to one or any of the rectors of Holy Trinity Church – Sloane Street, St Luke's Church and Chelsea Old Church. The general fund provides support for registered charities in a wide range of areas (see below).

In 2007/08 the trust had assets of £32 million and an income of £1.4 million. 71 grants were made totalling £1.4 million and were categorised as follows:

Social welfare in the community – 41 grants totalling £896,000
The largest grants went to the Natural History Museum and St Paul's Cathedral Foundation (£250,000 each) and Children's Trust – Tadworth and Christchurch Chelsea (£100,000 each).

Other beneficiaries included: London Playing Fields Foundation (£20,000); Dockland Settlements (£15,000); St Mary's Church – Birnam (£13,000); Guild of Air Pilots and Navigators (£8,000); Leonard Cheshire Foundation (£6,000); Lifelites (£5,000); and Addaction (£1,000).

Education – 2 grants totalling £260,000
Beneficiaries were the Royal Veterinary College (£250,000) and Oatridge Agricultural College (£10,000).

Military charities – 8 grants totalling £161,000
Beneficiaries included: In-Pensioners' Mobility Fund (£100,000); Help for Heroes (£35,000); Army Benevolent Fund and Royal British Legion (£5,000 each); SSAFA Forces Help and Battle of Britain Memorial Trust (£3,000 each).

Medical research – 12 grants totalling £32,000
Beneficiaries included: Alzheimer's Research Trust (£5,000); Corda, Marie Curie Cancer Care, Progressive Supranuclear Palsy and Tommy's, the Baby Charity (£2,000 each); and Epilepsy Research Foundation (£1,000).

Conservation and the environment – 2 grants totalling £20,000
Beneficiaries were the Scottish Countryside Alliance Educational Trust and Game and Wildlife Conservation Trust (£10,000 each).

Animal welfare – 3 grants totalling £12,000
Beneficiaries were: Animals Health Trust and World Wildlife Fund (£5,000 each); and Moorcroft Racehorse Welfare Centre (£2,000).

Rectors' fund – 3 grants totalling £4,500
Beneficiaries were the rectors of Holy Trinity Church – Sloane Street, St Luke's Church and Chelsea Old Church (£1,500 each).

Exclusions No grants to individuals.

Applications In writing to the correspondent.

CAF (Charities Aid Foundation)

Capacity building for small and medium sized charities

Around £1.5 million

Beneficial area Worldwide, in practice mainly UK.

25 Kings Hill Avenue, Kings Hill, West Malling ME19 4TA

Tel. 01732 520000 **Fax** 01732 520001

Email enquiries@cafonline.org

Website www.cafonline.org (follow the link 'for charities')

Correspondent Grants Team

Trustees *David Weymouth; Kim Lavely; Lord Cairns; Adele Blakeborough; Sir Graham Melmoth; David Locke; Dominic Casserley; Connie Jackson; Philip Hardaker; Peter Wolton; John Lorimer; Iain Mackinnon; Jenny Watson.*

CC Number 268369

Information available Accounts were available from the Charity Commission.

In 1924, The National Council of Social Service (now the NCVO) set up a charities department to encourage more efficient giving to charity. In 1958 the charities department began administering deeds of covenant – the first ever means of charities receiving untaxed donations. The following year, the department was re-named the charities aid fund, the purpose of which was to distribute large sums of money for charitable purposes. In 1968, the fund published the first Directory of Grant Making Trusts – a pioneering effort to find new donors and new funding sources, (now produced by the Directory of Social Change).

The fund, under the new title, Charities Aid Foundation became an independent registered charity in 1974 and its objectives are to benefit any charitable organisation anywhere in the world. In practice, it works to raise the profile of charitable giving, lobby for tax breaks and provide an increasingly broad suite of services to charities and their supporters. The foundation helps both individual and company donors as well as charities.

CAF provides banking and investment services to charities, as well as a fundraising support service to help organisations process and manage donations. It also supports the growth and development of small and medium-sized charities through its grant programme by offering expertise and funding in flexible ways.

Guidelines

Main grant programme
At the time of writing, the foundation's main grant programme was closed and under review. A new programme is due to be launched soon.
The foundation offers the following overview of the future programme in its 2008/09 accounts:

Our grants programme has been under review throughout the year. A small number of top-up grants have been awarded to complete the work with existing grant-holders. For our 2009/10 programme we will focus on supporting initiatives that aim to make positive changes in the way people give to charity and the way that charities work with donors. We will engage and seek the views of key stakeholders to determine the focus. A proportion of each grant will support research, analysis and dissemination and we will seek to use approaches and learning to underpin the further development of our broader activities.The programme will be funded by our donor clients. Awards that meet our funding priorities will be made by CAF employees with responsibilities delegated by the Board of Trustees with the support of a newly formed Advisory Committee.

For the latest information please go to the website or contact the grants team on Tel: 03000 123 334.

Previously around £1.5 million has been available through this programme.

Venturesome
Venturesome, a social enterprise initiative, operates where a charity needs finance but its requirements may be too risky for a bank loan or outside the criteria of a grantmaker. It offers loans and investment support to charities and other social enterprises, to suit the needs of individual organisations. This support might take the form of underwriting, unsecured loans or equity type investments and it is anticipated that the money loaned will be repaid over time. The programme will only invest in social purpose organisations that:

- are registered in the UK
- can clearly state their charitable purpose and social impact (organisations do not have to be registered charities but do need to be of charitable purpose)
- have a history of trading and/or income
- are looking for between £20,000 and £350,000
- have a legal structure which allows them to take on debt/equity funding.

Venturesome manages a fund of £10 million on behalf of CAF and 12 external investors, including individual philanthropists, foundations and banks. It is also a partner in the Community Land Trust Fund where it manages the Investment Fund element. In 2008/09 Venturesome helped over 40 organisations and had loan commitments totalling £2.2 million.

Technically, CAF made grants worth £372 million in 2008/09, but almost all of these are 'donor directed' payments where the foundation administers the funds of other donors who are using its financial services. These include separate trusts set up within CAF by donors seeking to use the administrative and grant payment services of CAF while keeping for themselves the decisions about where those grants should go.

Exclusions Grants will not usually be given for:

- capital items, buildings, vehicles, maintenance costs
- start-up costs of a new charitable organisation
- funding that should properly be the responsibility of statutory agencies
- schools, universities or NHS trusts
- work already completed.

Please note: full eligibility criteria will be available on the foundation's website when the new grants programme is launched.

Applications All applications must be submitted on an application form. There are several ways to view the guidelines and request an application form:

- visit the website
- in writing to the correspondent
- email enquiries@cafonline.org
- telephone 01732 520 000.

Please note: at the time of writing, the foundation's main grant programme was closed and under review. The Venturesome programme remains open.

Community Foundation for Calderdale

General

£874,000 (2007/08)

Beneficial area Calderdale, with ability to manage funds outside of this area.

Community Foundation House, 162a King Cross Road, Halifax HX1 3LN

Tel. 01422 349 700 **Fax** 01422 350 017

Email enquiries@cffc.co.uk

Website www.cffc.co.uk

Correspondent Megan Vickery, Grants Manager

Trustees *Dr Rose Wheeler; Leigh-Anne Stradeski; Brenda Hodgson; Mike Payne; Alison Roberts; Kate Hinks; Susan Fisher; Rod Hodgson; Russell Earnshaw; Juliet Chambers; Jennifer Feather; Roger Moore; Anne Clare Townley.*

CC Number 1002722

Information available Accounts were on file at the Charity Commission. Additional information is taken from the foundation's website.

The foundation, as a registered charity, was established for the support or promotion of any charitable purposes, the relief of poverty, the advancement of education (including training for employment or work), the advancement of religion or any other charitable purpose for the benefit of the community in the area of the Metropolitan Borough of Calderdale and its immediate neighbourhood and other charitable purposes in the United Kingdom with a preference for those which are in the opinion of the executive committee beneficial to the community in the area of benefit.

By raising money, through its network of supporting 'members' and donors, and holding a long-term investment fund, the Community Foundation for Calderdale is able to address local need indefinitely – the interest gained on the invested money is given out in grants. This gives local people the opportunity to give to local causes, see where their money has gone and be able to contribute to a permanent pot of cash to benefit the community forever. The foundation also manages several external programmes, such as Grassroots Grants.

Grants have been given to support causes as varied as social clubs for older people, community recycling schemes,

children's after-school clubs, community bands, sports clubs, refugee centres, and individuals in crisis. Grants of up to £5,000 are available and, in exceptional circumstances, up to £10,000.

In 2007/08 the foundation had assets of £6 million and an income of £843,000. Grants were made totalling £874,000, of which £852,000 was given to 212 organisations and £21,000 awarded to 238 individuals.

Funds available
The foundation has a range of different funds designed for small community and voluntary groups working to help local people across Calderdale.

Grant schemes change frequently. Please consult the foundation's website for details of current programmes and their deadlines.

Each scheme tends to have a different application procedure and size of award. A selection of current programmes is listed below.

General programme – This is the foundation's main grants programme and is open to constituted voluntary, community and faith groups, run for and by local people and registered charities working in Calderdale. Grants of up to £5,000 are available (in exceptional circumstances up to £10,000) and priority is given to projects which: achieve outstanding community impact; help people living in communities identified as being particularly disadvantaged; benefit people from black and minority ethnic communities; help people with special needs; benefit older people; and/or benefit young people under the age of 19. Organisations can apply through a single application process – and the foundation will direct the application to the appropriate fund. Some schemes may have additional requirements, which applicants will be made aware of during the application process.

Grassroots grants – This is a £130 million programme that aims to invest in a thriving community sector across the whole of the UK. It is funded by Office of the Third Sector. The programme is designed to run from 2008–2011 and is divided into two parts: an £80 million small grants fund for community organisations; and a £50 million endowments programme to enable local funders to generate additional donations on a matched basis and invest them in endowments. The foundation is the 'local funder' for Calderdale and Kirklees providing small grants for community and voluntary groups and raising money to build the Grassroots Endowment Fund for Calderdale and for Kirklees.

4Health 4Fun 4Life – This programme invites voluntary and community foundations to tender for projects that will meet the aims of the Health Halifax Programme. The idea is to find exciting new ways of encouraging families to be healthier and stay healthier.

Grants for health – This programme is managed by the foundation on behalf of NHS Calderdale. It is specifically interested in projects that will make a real and sustained difference to local people's health. The programme aims to give local organisations the opportunity to be a part of the national drive to improve people's health through one of the following themes: cancer and end of life care; care closer to home; drugs and alcohol; learning disability; long-term conditions (stroke, respiratory, COPD, heart conditions); maternity and children; mental health; planned care (i.e. eye care); sexual health; and urgent care.

Further information on any of the programmes can be found on the website or by contacting the foundation directly.

Exclusions The foundation will not fund any of the following:

- general appeals
- projects which have already taken place or for retrospective funding
- projects which would normally be funded from statutory sources, such as Calderdale MBC, the Local Education Authority, Social Services or Central Government
- projects for the advancement of religion
- projects where the main beneficiaries are animals
- projects that do not directly benefit people living in Calderdale
- political activities
- applications made up entirely of core and/or running costs (exceptions may be made in extraordinary circumstances).

Applications The foundation's website has details of the grant schemes currently being administered. Application packs for all of the programmes are available to download from the website. Alternatively, contact the foundation directly and they will send a pack by post.

If you wish to discuss your project before applying, the grants team are always happy to answer any queries (Tel: 01422 438738). The foundation also runs a monthly drop-in, where groups can go for advice and support on their applications.

The Campden Charities

Welfare and education (particularly the under-25s)

£511,000 to organisations
(2008/09)

Beneficial area The former parish of Kensington, London; a north-south corridor, roughly from north of the Fulham Road to the north of Ladbroke Grove (a map can be viewed on the website).

27a Pembridge Villas, London W11 3EP

Tel. 020 7243 0551 **Fax** 020 7229 4920

Website www.cctrustee.org.uk

Correspondent Chris Stannard, Clerk to the Trustees

Trustees *Revd Gillean Craig, Chair; David Banks; Elisabeth Brockmann; Chris Calman; Dr Kit Davis; Steve Hoier; Susan Lockhart; Tim Martin; Terry Myers; Ben Pilling; Victoria Stark; Richard Walker-Arnott.*

CC Number 1003641

Information available Accounts were on file at the Charity Commission and there is a good website.

Summary

During the course of the financial year to 31 March 2006 the management of the assets of the Campden Charities was transferred to the Campden Charities Trustee. The Uniting Order granted by the Charity Commissioners in a letter dated 25 January 2005 came into effect on 1 April 2005. This order united the Campden Charities Trustee and the Campden Charities under the former's charity number. Since then there has been aggregated accounts and reporting.

The Charities is focused on supporting relief in need and education in the former parish of Kensington and the former Royal Borough of Kensington. It must spend at least half of its income available for grantgiving on relief in need and up to half on the advancement of education.

During the year the charities had assets of £71 million and an income of £2.8 million. Grants to organisations totalled £551,000, with a further £1.5 million going to individuals.

Grantmaking

The following extract from the Charities 2008/09 accounts describes the current grantmaking policy:

The trustees have developed an innovative approach to grantgiving over the last three years. Their objective is to help financially disadvantaged individuals and families towards financial independence. They seek to do this by identifying the needs of individuals and tailoring packages of support to help them overcome the obstacles they face in improving their circumstances. This help is not restricted to a single payment, trustees want to continue to help people until their circumstances change; this may mean making a number of grants, sometimes over a period of years.

The trustees make incentive payments to non-statutory not for profit organisations that refer and support individuals. After twelve months of receiving such referrals trustees may enter into partnership arrangements to fund work delivered by these organisations to enhance the support offered to individuals. The trustees do not accept unsolicited applications from organisations.

The trustees are guided in their grantgiving by two fundamental principles:

i) Independence
Grants will not be made to support statutory services; neither are the trustees party to local or central Government initiatives or political priorities. The trustees value their position as an independent local grant maker.

ii) Fairness
Trustees seek to make the application process fair to all potential beneficiaries. All grant applications are made and considered in the same manner. There are no privileged applicants and individual trustees are required to declare an interest where appropriate.

Distribution of grants
The scheme governing the Charities directs the trustees to apply one half of the Charities' income to the relief of need and the other half to the advancement of education save that if in so far as income in any one year is not required for application for the advancement of education, it may be applied to the relief of need.

The young people whom the trustees wish to assist with educational support are those from impoverished backgrounds. Often those young people in greatest need have at some stage become disenfranchised from formal education and they find it difficult to re-engage without extensive professional advice and support. Independent applications made by these young people to the Charities are often inappropriate or ill advised. Whilst it is relatively straightforward to make substantial grants to academically able scholars, it is more challenging to provide appropriate financial support directly to those individuals who may need it most.

Similarly adults who have experienced long periods of unemployment often become demoralised; occasionally they find themselves in a 'benefits trap' where they would be financially worse off in low paid employment. Lone parents often cannot finance childcare that would enable them to train. Many of the poorest people have also accumulated significant debt. In recognition of these and many other issues, the trustees employ an unusually large Grants Officer team so that instead of funding individuals at arms length, Grants Officers can build up a relationship with families in need and work with them to tailor individual packages of assistance. Grants Officers also actively seek ways to work with other not-for-profit partners to support the Charities' beneficiaries.

The trustees believe that the resources of the Charities' are well deployed not only in making grants but also in funding a team of Grants Officers that can bring 'added value' to the grants made.

Direct grants to individuals

Grants are made in response to direct applications from individuals responding to the Charities' publicity and referrals are also welcomed and encouraged from all not-for-profit organisations and statutory agencies. This year 289 Grants totalling £256,000 were made in support of vocational education. 200 individuals and families of working age also received grants totalling £98,000 for child-care, fares, goods and services to assist them towards financial independence. In addition 58 grants totalling £214,000 were awarded to encourage academically able young people from disadvantaged backgrounds to attend university.

£375,000 was awarded to 291 pension age beneficiaries in a programme to assist the financially worst off. Many of them had transferred from the Campden Pensioners scheme which ended the year with 549 beneficiaries who received a total of £563,000. Trustees have also continued the experimental programme of support for those individuals over 55 with little prospect of obtaining work before they reach retirement age, to encourage them to remain active and to participate in the community.

Grants to Organisations

The aim of funding not-for-profit organisations has been to direct funding to those that are supporting individuals receiving direct grants. The focus is on outcomes for individual beneficiaries rather than responding to organisation requests. In 2008/09 Grants Officers negotiated and renewed individual partnership agreements to support and train individuals with 13 organisations, £512,000 was awarded in this way. Trustees have also continued to award £1,000 to other organisations for each successful referral of an individual; £57,000 was awarded for such referrals during the year. This referral funding is intended to help organisations working within the Charities' objects with individual beneficiaries. Such funding may lead to partnerships in the future.

Grantmaking 2008/09

Beneficiaries of partnership funding included: NOVA (£119,000); Westway Community Transport (£91,000); My Generation (£66,000); Earls Court YMCA (£60,000); Nucleus Legal Advice Centre (£42,000); and Staying Put (£18,000).

Beneficiaries of referral funding included: Servite Houses (£6,000); Sixty Plus (£4,000); London Cyrenians (£3,000); Streetlytes (£2,000); and Ethiopia Woman's Group (£1,000).

Exclusions No grants for:

- UK charities or charities outside Kensington, unless they are of significant benefit to Kensington residents
- schemes or activities which are generally regarded as the responsibility of the statutory authorities
- UK fundraising appeals
- environmental projects unless connected with education or social need
- medical research or equipment
- animal welfare
- advancement of religion or religious groups, unless they offer non-religious services to the community
- commercial and business activities
- endowment appeals
- projects of a political nature
- retrospective capital grants.

Applications The Charities are trying to target its resources where they can be of the most direct benefit to financially disadvantaged individuals. The Charities therefore **do not** receive unsolicited applications for funding from organisations. However the Charities' officers are eager to meet with colleagues from other not-for-profit organisations to explore ways in which we can work together to help individuals to end dependency on benefits or improve a low wage.

If you have contact with individuals whom you would like to refer, [...] telephone 020 7313 3797.

Capital Community Foundation

Community activities

£2.7 million (2007/08)

Beneficial area The London boroughs including the City of London.

357 Kennington Lane, London SE11 5QY

Tel. 020 7582 5117 **Fax** 020 7582 4020

Email enquiries@capitalcf.org.uk

Website www.capitalcf.org.uk

Correspondent Victoria Warne, Head of Grants

Trustees *Carole Souter, Chair; Gordon Williamson; Ade Sawyerr; Clive Cutbill; Michael Brophy; Kathy Seligman; Nicholas Hammond; Richard Battesby.*

CC Number 1091263

Information available Accounts were available from the Charity Commission. Full details of the foundation's current programmes are available from its website.

Capital Community Foundation provides grants to non-profit groups (you do not need to be a registered charity) that are for community benefit. The foundation manages and distributes funds on behalf of several donors, including companies, individuals and government programmes and is able to offer a number of grant programmes which cover different areas and type of activity. Contact the foundation directly or visit its website for up-to-date information on current programmes.

During 2007/08 the foundation had assets of £1.5 million and an income of £3.5 million. Grants were made to 470 organisations totalling £2.7 million. This was broken down by programme as follows:

Programme	Value
Local Network Fund	£1,300,000
Columbia Foundation	£259,000
Deptford Challenge Trust	£257,000
Lambeth First Community Chest	£205,000
Neighbourhood Renewal Community Chest – Southwark	£176,000
Land Securities	£147,000
New Cross Gate	£138,000
'Londonations'	£100,000
Other small grants awarded	£161,000

Grants in 2007/08

Local Network Fund – 222 grants

To support projects working with children and young people aged 0–19 years.

Beneficiaries included: Bethwin Road Playground and Zoom In Ltd (£7,000 each); Ebony Horse Club (£6,600); Friends of Greenwich Pennisula Ecology Park (£5,400); Refocus Project (£5,000); BESA Albanian Community Group (£4,700); and Barnfield Project (£1,900).

Columbia Foundation – 14 grants

To enhance the quality of life through the arts and a range of other projects, primarily in London.

Beneficiaries included: Royal Shakespeare Company and Southbank Centre (£50,000 each); Chickenshed (£25,000); and Ice and Fire Theatre Company and Battersea Arts Centre (£12,000 each).

Deptford Challenge Trust – 15 grants

To improve the quality of life for people who live in Deptford, by supporting a variety of community groups responding to local need, and in particular projects building a shared sense of community.

Beneficiaries included: AbleOne and Second Wave (£30,000 each); Lewisham Vietnamese Woman and Children's Association (£25,000); Art in Perpetuity Trust (£5,000); Noah's Ark Childrens Venture (£4,200); Stone Crabs (£3,600); and Create Arts (£3,200).

Lambeth First Community Chest – 53 grants

To provide resources to community, voluntary and faith organisations to develop and run their own activities, in particular activities promoting community wellbeing.

Beneficiaries included: South Central Youth (£5,000); Westbury Estate TRA (£4,400); Ethiopian Social Centre and Friends of Kennington Park (£3,000 each); United Families Working Together (£2,500); and Renton Close Community Centre (£1,900).

Neighbourhood Renewal Community Chest – Southwark – 46 grants

To support projects that bring people together to improve their local neighbourhood and community relations.

Beneficiaries included: Deaf Parenting UK, Collective Artistes and Pioneer African Caribbean Over 50's Group (£5,000 each); Aylesbury Everywoman's Centre (£4,700); Friends of Mini Mints (£3,800); Rotherhithe Under 5's (£1,400); and Lightening Ensemble Theatre Company (£1,000).

Land Securities Capital Commitment Fund – 33 grants

To support a range of local community projects, in particular groups working with children, young people and education.

Grants included those to: In-Deep Community Taskforce (£7,000); Westminster Society, Pimlico Toy Library and Domestic Violence Intervention Project (£5,000 each); Southwark Mysteries (£4,800); Your Story (£3,600); and Southwark Sea Cadets (£1,500).

New Cross Gate – 10 grants

Supports projects helping to improve the experience and life chances of residents in New Cross.

The largest grants were made to 170 Community Project and Lewisham Muslim Women's Group (£35,000 each). Other grants included: Aging Well Fun Club and Recycled Juveniles Forum (£5,000 each); and Holiday Activities Provision Initiative (£4,900).

'Londonations' – 50 grants

To support projects reaching Londoners with particular needs, projects tackling social issues and those bringing people of different backgrounds together.

Grants were made totalling £2,000 each. Beneficiaries included: Deafroots Association, Me Too and Co, Street Talk, Tideway Sailability, Puddenecks Club and Friends of Greenmead.

Other small grants were made from Sport Relief, Deutsch Bank, Coutts Bank Fund, CP Russel Fund, Markit Fund Top Corner Fund and Bristol and West Fund. Information on the beneficiaries from these funds was not available.

For further information on the foundation's current funds and guidance on how to apply, go to the foundation's website.

Exclusions Generally, no grants for individuals, political groups or activities which promote religion.

Applications In order to qualify for a grant from the foundation your organisation must have:

- a management committee of at least three people who are not related and are not paid wages by your group
- a governing document (e.g. constitution or Memorandum and Articles of Association)
- a bank account with at least two unrelated signatories for transactions (Pass Book accounts or those which permit only cash withdrawals are not accepted)
- a child protection policy and procedures if the project will be working with children.

As the foundation offers funds on behalf of different donors, you may apply to each and every programme for which your group is eligible. However, the criteria do vary for each grant programme, so be sure to read the guidance carefully. If you are unsure about your eligibility, please call the grants team on Tel: 020 7582 5117 before making an application.

Application forms and guidance notes specific to each programme are available from the foundation and/or the website.

Each programme has its own set of closing dates. All applications must reach Capital Community Foundation by 5pm on that date.

The Carpenters' Company Charitable Trust

Education and general

£812,000 to organisations
(2007/08)

Beneficial area UK.

Carpenters' Hall, 1 Throgmorton Avenue, London EC2N 2JJ

Tel. 020 7588 7001

Email info@carpentersco.com

Website www.carpentersco.com

Correspondent The Clerk

Trustees *Peter A Luton; Malcolm R Francis; Michael I Montague-Smith; Guy Morton-Smith.*

CC Number 276996

Information available Accounts were available from the Charity Commission.

The trust's income is derived from a capital sum gifted by the company's corporate fund, supplemented when warranted by further grants from the corporate fund. Charitable causes benefiting from grants include organisations supporting older people, disabled people, homeless people, young people and children, education, medical and museums. Craft causes receive a high priority when awards are considered.

Educational grants are also awarded to individuals, only for wood related courses undertaken in the UK.

In 2007/08 the trust had assets of £19.7 million and an income of an income of over £2.7 million. Grants were made totalling £830,000, which included £18,000 to individuals.

Grants were broken down as follows:

Category	Value
Craft activities	£476,500
Young people's and children's organisations	£88,000
Welfare	£54,000
Medical, hospitals and hospices	£41,000
Homeless and older people	£32,000
City of London	£27,000
Disabled people	£25,000
Religious organisations	£24,000
Museums	£3,000
Miscellaneous	£66,500

The Building Crafts College received a grant of £357,000.

Exclusions Grants are not normally made to individual churches or cathedrals, or to educational establishments having no association to the Carpenters' Company. No grants (except educational grants) are made to individual applicants. Funds are usually only available to charities registered with the charity commission or exempt from registration.

Applications In writing to the correspondent.

Cash for Kids – Radio Clyde

Children

£1.2 million (2008/09)

Beneficial area Radio Clyde transmission area, i.e. west central Scotland.

Radio Clyde, 3 South Avenue, Clydebank Business Park, Glasgow G81 2RX

Tel. 0141 204 1025 **Fax** 0141 565 2370

Email cashforkids@radioclyde.com

Website www.clyde1.com/cashforkids

Correspondent Trust Administrator

Trustees *Paul Cooney; Ewan Hunter; Ian Grabiner; Sir Tom Hunter.*

SC Number SCO03334

Information available Information was taken from the charity's website.

This is a Christmas appeal established by the radio station and CSV, a charity supporting media involvement in volunteering and in community support generally. Since 1981 it has helped to support children under 16 who are facing financial, emotional, physical or educational challenges.

The trust states:

Every single penny donated to the charity goes towards helping disadvantaged children and young people in the west of Scotland. We are able to make this promise because the charity uses an annual donation from the Hunter Foundation combined with its sponsorship income to cover all operational costs.

The trust funds individuals and community organisations in Inverclyde, Argyll and Bute, Dumfries and Galloway, East Ayrshire, South Ayrshire, North Ayrshire, East Dumbartonshire, West Dumbartonshire, Renfrewshire, East Renfrewshire, Glasgow City Council, North Lanarkshire and South Lanarkshire.

In 2008/09 the appeal raised £1.2 million. No other recent financial information was provided by the trust.

Cash for Kids awards grants in four different ways:

1) sustainable grants – small grants for children at Christmas
2) special grants – these are given to organisations throughout the year
3) family grants – these are dispensed to local authority social work departments that nominate children in need on their caseloads
4) group grants – donations are also dispersed to a wide variety of deserving children's groups and support agencies across west and south-west Scotland. The grant application process opens in October. All grant applications must be submitted by the beginning of November.

Grants to organisations

The trust supports projects delivered by organisations working with disadvantaged children and young people, who are aged 16 years and under.

Disadvantages experienced by children and young people include:

- illness, distress, abuse or neglect
- any kind of disability
- behavioural or psychological difficulties
- living in poverty or situations of deprivation.

Any application should focus on the children that the project will work with and how the project will change their lives for the better.

Projects must be able to demonstrate that they are community based, volunteer led and representative of the client group they seek to serve. They must demonstrate meaningful engagement and consultation with young people. They should also provide a cost-effective approach to interventions and demonstrate good quality data collection systems that provide information on the tangible difference their project makes.

For further information, please contact the trust directly or go to the website.

Exclusions The trust does not fund:

- trips or projects abroad
- medical treatment/research
- unspecified expenditure
- deficit funding or repayment of loans
- retrospective funding (projects taking place before the grant award date)
- projects unable to start within six months of the grant award date
- distribution to another/other organisation/s
- general appeals or endowment funds
- relief of statutory responsibility
- the promotion of religion.

No funding for capital expenditure except in very special circumstances which must be made clear at the time of applying. Organisations whose administration costs exceed 15% of total expenditure will not be supported.

Applications Application forms and guidelines are available from the trust's website.

Sir John Cass's Foundation

Education in inner London

£1.7 million to organisations (2007/08)

Beneficial area The inner London boroughs – Camden, Greenwich, Hackney, Hammersmith and Fulham, Islington, Kensington and Chelsea, Lambeth, Lewisham, Newham, Southwark, Tower Hamlets, Wandsworth, Westminster and the City of London.

31 Jewry Street, London EC3N 2EY

Tel. 020 7480 5884 **Fax** 020 7488 2519

Email contactus@sirjohncass.org

Website www.sirjohncass.org

Correspondent Richard Foley, Grants Manager

CC Number 312425

Information available Accounts were available at the Charity Commission and guidelines for applicants were provided by the trust. Information is also available via the foundation's website.

The Sir John Cass Foundation dates formally from 1748. The foundation takes its name from its founder who was born in the City of London in 1661 and, during his lifetime, served as both Alderman and Sheriff. He was also MP for the City and knighted in 1713. In 1710 Cass set up a school for 50 boys and 40 girls in buildings in the churchyard of St Botolph-without-Aldgate. Intending to leave all his property to the school, when he died in 1718 of a brain haemorrhage, Cass had only initialled three pages of his will. The incomplete will was contested, but was finally upheld by the Court of Chancery 30 years after his death. The school, which by this time had been forced to close, was re-opened, and the foundation established.

The history of the foundation touches upon education in and around the City of London at almost every level, ranging from primary education to postgraduate study and representing an historical microcosm of the development of English education over more than three centuries. Today, the foundation has links in the primary, secondary and tertiary sectors of education. It provides support to its primary school in the City of London and its secondary school in Tower Hamlets, as well as the Sir John Cass Department of Art, Media and Design (part of London Metropolitan University) and the Cass Business School (part of City University).

The foundation also funds schools and organisations benefiting young people from inner London and provides support with education costs to young residents of inner London who are under the age of 25 and from disadvantaged backgrounds. In addition, the foundation supports three academies; St. Mary Magdalene and the City of London Academies in Islington, and St. Michael and All Angels Academy in Camberwell.

Grantmaking

Grants, usually for amounts between £1,500 and £65,000, are made to organisations for educational work with children and young people in inner London. The majority of grants are revenue funding for projects, though capital grants are occasionally made. The foundation has also supported a number of inner London schools in their bids for specialist school status.

There is also a substantial programme of support for individual students with priority to those aged 19–24. (see *The Educational Grants Directory* published by the Directory of Social Change).

In 2007/08 the foundation had assets of £50 million and an income of £2.2 million. Grants were made totalling £1.9 million, of which £1.7 million was given to organisations and schools and £229,000 was awarded in grants to individuals.

In May 2006 the foundation issued new guidelines for schools and organisations as follows (these remain current as at October 2009):

Duration and size of grants
Many of the grants are for one year, but grants can also cover activities lasting two or three years. In such cases, we may taper the grant in the second and third years. Our budget for grants to schools and organisations in 2007/08 is £750,000. Most grants we make are for sums between £10,000 and £30,000. There is no minimum or maximum grant size. The amount you request should be the amount you need for your project.

Criteria
The foundation will only consider proposals from schools and organisations that benefit children or young people under the age of 25, who are permanent residents of named *inner* London boroughs (Camden, Greenwich, Hackney, Hammersmith and Fulham, Islington, Kensington & Chelsea, Lambeth, Lewisham, Newham, Southwark, Tower Hamlets, Wandsworth, Westminster and the City of London) and from disadvantaged backgrounds or areas of high deprivation.

Priorities
The foundation has four areas of focus for grantgiving, which are as follows:

- widening participation in further and higher education
- truancy, exclusion and behaviour management
- prisoner education
- new initiatives.

There are one or more priorities for each area of focus. Details of the priorities and our aims and objectives for each area of focus are as follows.

Widening Participation in Further and Higher Education
Aim

To promote access to further and higher education for disadvantaged young people in inner London.

Objective

To increase the number of inner London students from disadvantaged backgrounds successfully participating in further and higher education.

Priorities

Work with communities currently under-represented in further and higher education and/or hard to reach learners (e.g. care leavers or young people with learning difficulties). Applications could involve work with secondary school pupils as well as those in further education and universities.

Truancy, Exclusion and Behaviour Management
Aim

To encourage and support children and young people's attainment through initiatives that help them engage with, and stay in, education.

Objectives
- to reduce truancy levels amongst pupils attending primary and secondary schools
- to reduce levels of exclusions and expulsions
- to improve pupil motivation, behaviour and achievement through initiatives that promote children and young people's emotional well being and social development.

Priority

Work with primary and secondary schools in challenging circumstances and/or those with higher than average truancy, exclusion or expulsion rates. Challenging circumstances could include, for example, schools in areas of high social deprivation or in special measures, as well as schools that have higher than average rates of truancy, exclusion or expulsion.

Prisoner Education
Aim

To reduce re-offending through education and initiatives that promote employability.

Objectives
- to improve the literacy and numeracy skills of prisoners and ex-offenders
- to help prisoners and ex-offenders gain skills and education qualifications that will help them into employment.

Priority

Work with prisoners and ex-offenders that helps secure employment and prevent re-offending.

New Initiatives
Aim
To influence and improve education policy and practice, both within the foundation's area of benefit and more widely.

Objectives
i) To test new and ground breaking approaches to learning that have the potential to enhance and influence education policy and practice.

ii) To support work that focuses on identified needs and gaps in statutory provision.

Priorities
- projects that are pioneering and original in their approach to teaching or learning and are strategic (relates to objective i)
- projects addressing an identified need within a geographical area or learning establishment that are new and innovative in context i.e. must be a new initiative for the school or borough, but need not be a completely new approach to education (relates to objective ii)
- projects that focus on addressing under-achievement in literacy and numeracy in primary and secondary schools (relates to objectives i and ii)
- projects seeking to attract greater numbers of young people into the teaching profession (relates to objectives i and ii).

Applicants should say which priority their project addresses as well as describing how their project meets that priority. Applications need not meet more than one priority but, for those that do, applicants are welcome to describe how their application meets each of the priorities.

Grants in 2007/08

The foundation distributes over £1 million annually in grants. Since 1998, the foundation has been a major sponsor of inner London secondary schools seeking to become specialist schools and its grants have helped to unlocked several million pounds of additional government support. During 2007/08, in order to reduce the accumulated unrestricted reserves, the foundation awarded £1.6 million towards the Government's Academy Programme and £1 million towards the Sir John Cass School of Education, University of East London, over a five year period.

There is no such thing as a typical project, however, examples of projects funded recently include:

- £58,000 over two years to London Action Trust towards the Dyspel project at Wandsworth prison

- £50,000 to Youth at Risk towards a behaviour management programme for nine inner London schools
- £29,000 to Aimhigher Central London Partnership towards a project that encourages looked after children to enter higher education
- £20,000 to Elmgreen School towards their bid to be a designated specialist school.

Grant making in 2007/08 was categorised as follows:

Category	Value
Academy programme – from reserves	£900,000
Schools and organisations	£726,000
Individuals	£229,000
Foundation schools	£59,000
Diocesan boards	£30,000

Schools and organisations
Beneficiaries included: Spitalfields Festival – for musical projects in Tower Hamlets schools (£50,000); St Giles Trust – for NVQ 3 training for prisoners (£35,000); Parliament Hill School – for a project with disaffected white girls in Camden (£30,000); Bud Umbrella – for complementary treatment for children with behavioural disorders (£14,000); National Literacy Trust – for a literacy programme with The Science Museum (£6,000); and Prisoner's Education Trust – for bursaries for ex-prisoners (£4,500).

Diocesan boards and institutions
Beneficiaries were: Southwark Diocesan Board of Education – academy programme (£500,000); London Diocesan Board for Schools – academy programme (£430,000); Diocese of London – chaplaincy at London Metropolitan University (£25,000); City University – Sir John Cass Lecture (£10,000); and St Botolph's Church – Founder's Day and other activities (£5,000).

Foundation's schools
Beneficiaries were Sir John Cass's Foundation and Redcoats Church of England Secondary School (£47,000) and Sir John Cass's Foundation Primary School (£12,000).

Individuals
Grants to individuals totalled £229,000.

Exclusions
There are many activities and costs that the foundation will not fund. The following list gives a sample of the type of activities the foundation does not support:

- projects that do not meet a foundation priority
- conferences, seminars and academic research
- holiday projects, school journeys, trips abroad or exchange visits
- supplementary schools or mother tongue teaching

- independent schools
- youth and community groups, or projects taking place in these settings
- pre-school and nursery education
- general fund-raising campaigns or appeals
- costs for equipment or salaries that are the statutory responsibility of education authorities
- costs to substitute for the withdrawal or reduction of statutory funding
- costs for work or activities that have already taken place prior to the grant application
- costs already covered by core funding or other grants
- capital costs, that are exclusively for the purchase, repair or furnishing of buildings, purchase of vehicles, computers, sports equipment or improvements to school grounds.

Applications The foundation operates a two stage application process – an initial enquiry and a full application stage.

The following information has been taken from the foundation's website:

Stage 1
Complete and submit the initial enquiry form which is available from the foundation's website and on request from the correspondent. The form asks for:

- outline information about your proposed project
- information about how the project meets the foundation's priorities
- a summary of the project that includes the following information: the aims of the project including outputs and outcomes, how the project will be delivered; the duration of the project, including when and where it will take place; and a budget covering project costs.

We will consider your enquiry and inform you, within three weeks, whether or not you may proceed to Stage 2. If we have any queries we may contact you during this time to discuss details of your project submitted in the initial enquiry form. We receive a large number of applications. Unfortunately, this means that good projects sometimes have to be refused even if they meet a priority. If we invite you to proceed to Stage 2 and submit a full application, we will send you a copy of our Stage 2 application guidelines for schools and organisations.

Stage 2
Complete your detailed application and send it to us with copies of your memorandum and articles of association (or constitution) and your organisation's latest annual report and accounts.

Assessment and decision making process

On receipt of your application our staff may meet with you as part of our assessment process. After we have received responses to any queries and any further information requested, a report on your application will be considered by the foundation's grants committee, whose decision is final. The grants committee meets in March, June and November each year. It normally takes between two and four months from receipt of a full application until a decision is made.

Notification of the decision

All applicants will be sent formal notification of the outcome of their applications within two weeks of the committee decision.

Successful applicants

Those who are offered a grant will be sent a formal offer letter and copies of our standard terms and conditions of grant. Copies of our standard terms and conditions of grant are available on our website. Additional conditions are sometimes included depending on the nature of the grant.

Monitoring and evaluation

Staff will contact you to clarify and agree how the outputs and outcomes for your project will be monitored and evaluated. Your project will be visited at least once during the lifetime of the grant. If your grant covers more than one year you will be asked to submit a progress report for each year. Continuation of multi-year grants is dependent upon satisfactory progress towards agreed outputs and outcomes. At the end of the grant you will be asked to provide a final report. The foundation provides guidance on the structure and content of these reports.

Unsuccessful applicants

Applying for funding is a competitive process and the foundation's grants budget is limited. Because of the high volume of applications received, good projects sometimes have to be refused, even if they meet a priority. All applications are assessed on merit. If your application is refused you can apply again twelve months after the date you submitted your last application.

CfBT Education Trust

Organisations involved in education; particularly those concerned with the development and management of schools, managing and delivering effective learning and teaching, overcoming barriers to learning, and projects involving communication, language and multi-lingualism

£1.5 million (2007/08)
Beneficial area Worldwide.

60 Queens Road, Reading RG1 4BS
Tel. 0118 902 1000 **Fax** 0118 902 1434
Email research@cfbt.com
Website www.cfbt.com
Correspondent Karen Whitby, Research Manager

Trustees *Tim Walsh; John Webb; John Harwood; Philip Wood; Sara Hodson; Graham Colls; Marion Headicar; Sir Jim Rose; Stuart Laing; Sue Hunt; Margaret Platts.*

CC Number 270901

Information available Accounts were available from the Charity Commission.

The principal object of CfBT Education Trust is to advance education for the public benefit and this is achieved in part through the following aims:

- to promote and assist teaching in educational or training establishments or other organisations throughout the world
- to carry out or commission educational research
- to provide counselling and guidance
- to provide advice and consultancy services on education matters
- to provide training and other support for educators, which enables them to improve the quality of education.

Each year the trust invests around £1 million in practice-based educational research projects that help to inform education policy and practice in the UK and overseas. This funding comes under the Evidence for Education programme. Components of the programme include

intervention studies, guidance materials for practitioners as well as literature reviews and perspectives or think-pieces on key educational issues. The programme is currently focused on eight key funding themes:

- governance and organisation of schools
- voice of young people and parental participation
- professional learning of people in education
- the motivation and engagement of learners
- integrating education with other services
- personalised learning
- school improvement
- language and communication.

Investment is likely to take the form of:

- commissioned research and development projects
- research awards by competition/tender
- funding for projects in response to applications and invitation.

More information on the Evidence for Education programme is available on the CfBT website and in the 'Guide to Applicants' document.

In 2007/08 the trust had assets of £33 million and an income of £119 million. Please note: this is total trading income from teaching, consultancy, counselling and support for educators and does not reflect the amount available for grants. Grants awarded totalled £1.5 million and were distributed under four categories.

Organisation and improvement of schools (incorporating *governance and organisation of schools, school improvement* and *professional learning of people in education*).

Beneficiaries included: Education in Conflict, Emergencies, Reconstruction and Fragile States (£302,000); Public Private Partnerships in Basic Education: An International Review (£234,000); Student Integration in the United World College, Bosnia and Herzegovina (£55,000); Level Playing Field? The implications of school funding in England (£48,000); Role of Video – Teacher Education – Ghana Case Study (£30,000); and Adult Skills and Higher Education: Separation or Union? (£12,000).

Learner Perspective (incorporating *voice of young people and parental participation, motivation and engagement of learners* and *personalised learning*).

Beneficiaries included: Designing Educational Technologies for Social Justice (£52,000); Gifted and Talented

Education (£45,000); How Effective are Bullying Prevention Programmes for Children with Special Educational Needs? (£31,000); and Update report on Raising the Statutory Leaving age to 18? (£11,000).

Language and Communication
Grants went to: National Writing Project for Teachers and English Language Teaching – Bridging Programmes for Further Education (£20,000 each).

Other
Grants went to: UK Strategic Forum for Educational Research (£20,000) and Programme scoping: Start-up phase for Gifted and Talented and Learning and Skills Programmes (£16,000).

A total of £107,000 was given for smaller grants under £10,000 each.

Exclusions The trust will generally not consider funding for:

- business development
- funding an extension or expansion of current service delivery
- funding an extension of existing R&D projects which are funded by other sources
- projects which are only innovative because they are being carried out at a local rather than a national level
- buildings, equipment or capital costs
- staff salaries (apart from researcher/ consultant fees)
- day-to-day running costs
- general appeals
- grants to replace statutory funding
- funding for individuals to undertake professional development, including those undertaking masters degrees or doctorates
- expeditions, travel, adventure/holiday projects
- gap year projects
- arts, religion, sports and recreation
- conservation, heritage or environmental projects
- animal rights or welfare
- educational exchanges between institutions.

Applications Applicants should first submit an outline proposal to the research manager, Karen Whitby who will advise whether the proposal meets the agreed criteria and also how to proceed. The outline should be no more than three sides of A4 and include the following information:

- the issue or problem to be addressed
- the reasons for addressing it
- the expected outcome(s)
- what happens in the course of the project
- the amount of funding required and how long it will be needed.

Full applications are considered at the meetings of trustees in March, July, September and December.

Further application information and upcoming deadline dates are available on the trust's website and in the 'Guide to Applicants' document.

The Charities Advisory Trust

General
£676,000 (2007/08)
Beneficial area UK and overseas.

Radius Works, Back Lane, London NW3 1HL
Tel. 020 7794 9835 **Fax** 020 7431 3739
Email people@charitiesadvisorytrust.org.uk
Website www.charitiesadvisorytrust.org.uk
Correspondent Dame Hilary Blume, Director
Trustees Dr Cornelia Navari; Dr Carolyne Dennis; Brij Bhasin; Ms Dawn Penso.
CC Number 1040487
Information available Accounts were available from the Charity Commission.

The Charities Advisory Trust is a registered charity, with an eclectic portfolio of interests. It generates income for its projects through initiatives such as Card Aid, the Good Gifts Catalogue, the Green Hotel, Medical Student Electives and Peace Oil.

The trust is an innovative organisation, concerned with redressing inequalities and injustice in a practical way. It believes the method of generating funds should reflect the ethical concerns of the organisation.

The trust is self-financing. It earns its income through its activities. As a matter of policy, at the outset of any initiative, the sustainability of the venture is considered, and a plan put in place to ensure viability. Some activities are subsidised by others. The trust not only earns its income, it also gives around £500,000 a year in charitable donations.

In 2007/08 the trust had assets of £2.6 million and an income of almost £2.9 million. Grants were made during the year totalling £676,000.

The main beneficiaries listed in the accounts were: Survivors Fund – Rwanda (£114,500); Mozaik Foundation – Bosnia and Herzegovina (£100,000); Africa Education Trust (£92,000); Rainforest

Concern (£81,500); Sight Savers International (£62,000); Chira Fund (£54,000); ORBIS UK (£47,000); Sahabhagi Vikash Abhiyan (£41,500); Ashwini (£34,000); Accord (£24,500); VETAID (£23,000); Kings College Hospital (£2,700).

Smaller grants were made to a wide range of institutions through the Card Aid and Good Gifts schemes.

As mentioned above, grantmaking is only part of the trust's work. The trust's annual report describes some its other interesting and diverse activities:

We do not measure our success by our finances. Much of our work is about helping others to generate funds, by providing practical help – e.g. selling their cards, and by encouraging new, innovative ways of generating funds which can be copied.

The large amount of funds raised through Good Gifts has enabled us to develop more ambitious projects, in partnership with the delivering charities. We always do 'what it says on the tin', but for example, the demand for Goats for Peace enabled us to set up a model farm in Rwanda: creating jobs and supplying better quality goats. Similarly, the chicken banks in India led to the establishment of village egg committees, and a marketing operation for the eggs and chickens.

Our work is shifting towards mentoring projects – drawing on our experience – and encouraging people to believe they can change things for the better.

Good Gifts Catalogue interest continued to be high. At Tesco's request we developed a Good Gifts range for sale in Tesco. This worked well. This possibly marked the zenith of alternative gifts, and the novelty factor of this type of giving, pioneered by the Charities Advisory Trust, may have passed.

There is scarcely a major charity in the UK that has not developed an alternative gift scheme, many of them backed by lavish advertising campaigns. This is bound to impact on the future income of our Good Gifts Catalogue.

Card Aid held its own surprisingly well. Sales to companies continue to fall, in part because we set a minimum order level so lost many customers who placed small orders. The changes in the printing industry necessitated a change in the service we could offer. Our annual Scrooge Award which campaigns to increase the amount going to charity from cards sold on the high street, is so well regarded that is was used by Which?, the consumer magazine, as the basis of a large-scale feature. The Scrooge Awards have had a major impact on retailers. The John Lewis Partnership brought out a range giving 25% to charity, as a direct result of our campaign, and many retailers were using 10% as a guideline.

Visits to projects supported by the trust, together with the reports from the delivering charities, showed how well the money had been spent, and how many lives had been helped. It is not often that one can honestly say that £20 has made a long-lasting change for the better for a whole family, but this is exactly what we see with Good Gifts beneficiaries of say chickens or goats.

Peace and reconciliation work continue to be a central part of the Trust's work. 'Slim Peace', a film we supported, which showed co-operation between Arabs and Jews, from Israel and the West Bank, was selected by Queen Noor of Jordan, to launch the King Hussein Foundation in the USA. Peace Oil sales continue to be strong, and we are considering developing other 'Peace' products. Slim Peace groups were set up as a project in Israel, and provide a neutral meeting point for people from all communities.

A major activity in 2008 was recycling Chelsea Flower Show. We sponsored a Good Gifts Garden, as a way of promoting the Good Gifts Catalogue. We won a gold medal for our small garden. We became aware that the gardens built for the show were simply dismantled and thrown away. We intervened to set up a recycling programme – and invited schools and community projects to come and help themselves to a bit of Chelsea! The project received excellent publicity. Joan Ruddock, the minister for climate change, recycling and waste, came and visited the site, and Sky News came and filmed it! Altogether over £200,000 worth of plants, paving, fencing etc was salvaged. And the Good Gifts Garden was re-planted at the Mayow Park in Lewisham.

In November, the director was invited to Slovenia, to launch a Slovenian Good Gifts Catalogue, and train local charities on fundraising.

A substantial grant was made to the Mozaik Foundation in Sarajevo to enable them to purchase a building, thus saving a historic building in the old town, and providing, in effect, an endowment for the organisation. We are developing joint projects with the Sarajevo organisation as part of our peace and reconciliation work.

The medical student electives programme goes from strength to strength. 30 students went to ASHWINI and 8 to SVYM in South India, and 7 dental students went to CIDS in Coorg. Plans to extend the medical student electives to Rwanda are underway.

The Green Hotel increased its profits available for distribution, yet again. Apart from preserving a historic palace and its historic garden (which wins the prize for the best garden in Mysore year after year) the hotel provides stable employment for its large staff.

One sad event: our canal boat, March Hare, which had given much happiness to many families and disadvantaged people, sank! Fortunately the boat was insured. We have hopes of purchasing another canal boat in the future, so we can continue to offer breaks to those who would otherwise not get the chance. March Hare was particularly used by homelessness projects and those dealing with addicts, helped by a change of environment.

Exclusions No grants to individuals in need, or gap year trips to the developing world, large fundraising charities or missionary work

Unsolicited applications for projects of which the trust know nothing are rarely responded to. In such cases where support is given, the amounts are usually £200 or less.

Applications The trust's website gives the following advice.

We are willing to consider applications for any charitable purpose.

To apply, simply send us details of your proposal (no more than two pages in length) in the form of a letter. You might try to include the following information:

- the aims and objectives of your organisation
- the project for which you need money
- who benefits from the project and how
- breakdown of the costs and total estimated costs
- how much money you need from us
- other funding secured for the project
- a summary of your latest annual accounts.

If we refuse you it is not because your project is not worthwhile – it is because we do not have sufficient funds, or it is simply outside our current area of interest.

Charitworth Limited

Religious, educational and charitable purposes In practice, mainly Jewish causes

£913,000 (2007/08)
Beneficial area Worldwide.

Cohen Arnold and Co., New Burlington House, 1075 Finchley Road, London NW11 0PU

Tel. 020 8731 0777 **Fax** 020 8731 0778
Correspondent David Halpern, Trustee
Trustees *David Halpern; Reilly Halpern; Sidney Halpern; Samuel J Halpern.*
CC Number 286908

Information available Accounts were available from the Charity Commission.

This trust was set up in 1983 and its objects are the advancement of the Jewish religion, relief of poverty and general charitable purposes. It is particularly interested in supporting Jewish charities.

In 2007/08 the trust had assets of £29 million and an income of £5.9 million. 20 grants were made totalling £913,000 and sundry donations (of under £6,000) totalling £42,000.

As in previous years, almost all beneficiaries were Jewish organisations. Beneficiaries of the largest grants were Zichron Nahum (£185,000); British Friends of Tchernobil (£165,000); and Cosmon Belz (£130,000).

Other beneficiaries included: Chevras Maoz Ladal (£90,000); Dushinsky Trust (£39,000); Centre for Torah Education Trust (£25,000); Finchley Road Synagogue (£13,000); Friends of Viznitz (£10,000); Beer Yaakov (£8,500); and Beis Soroh Schneirer (£6,000).

Applications In writing to the correspondent.

The Childs Charitable Trust

Christian
£352,000 (2007/08)
Beneficial area Worldwide.

3 Cornfield Terrace, Eastbourne BN21 4NN

Email info@childstrust.org
Correspondent Melanie Churchyard
Trustees *D N Martin; R H Williams; A B Griffiths; S Puttock.*
CC Number 234618

Information available Accounts were available from the Charity Commission.

The objects of the trust are the furtherance of Christian Gospel, education, the relief of poverty and other charitable causes. The principal object is the furtherance of the Christian Gospel and the trustees are actively involved in supporting and encouraging Christian charities to achieve this goal. There is a preference for large-scale projects in the UK and abroad and ongoing support is given to some long-established Christian organisations.

In 2007/08 the trust had assets of £8.9 million and an income of £552,000. Grants were made totalling £352,000. No grants list was available from the latest accounts.

Previous beneficiaries include: Home Evangelism, ICC Mission Reserve, Latin Link, Mission Aviation Fellowship, Counties Evangelistic Work, Echoes of Service and Mustard Seed Relief, Scripture Union, Orphaids, LAMA Ministries, ELAM Ministries, Hour of Revival and University of Bristol.

Applications In writing to the correspondent. The trust has previously stated that its funds are fully committed and further applications are not welcomed.

The Childwick Trust

Health, people with disabilities and older people, welfare and research in connection with the bloodstock industry and Jewish charities in the UK and education in South Africa

£2.8 million (2007/08)

Beneficial area UK, South Africa.

9 The Green, Childwick Bury, St Albans AL3 6JJ

Tel. 01727 844666

Email karen@childwicktrust.org

Website www.childwicktrust.org

Correspondent Karen Groom, Trust Secretary

Trustees John Wood, Chair; Anthony Cane; Peter Glossop; Sarah Frost; Peter Anwyl-Harris.

CC Number 326853

Information available Accounts were available from the Charity Commission.

The trust was established in 1985 by the settlement of assets of the late founder, Mr H J Joel. The principal objects of the trust under which grants are awarded are as follows:

- to assist older people in need including the former employees of the settlor and of companies associated with the settlor and the families of such former employees
- to make payments to charities or for charitable objects connected with horse racing or breeding within the United Kingdom or people involved with horse racing or horse breeding who shall be in need
- to make payments to Jewish charities within the United Kingdom or support Jewish people in need within the United Kingdom
- to support charities and charitable objects for the education and benefit of people and the families of people who intend to work, are working, or have worked in the mining industry in the Republic of South Africa
- to support the education of people resident in the Republic of South Africa
- to make payments for the benefit of charities for the promotion of health and relief of people with disabilities within the United Kingdom.

A summary of the main grant categories is given below, alongside the percentage analysis of grants made per object in 2007/08. (Summaries are taken from the trust's website.)

Health – 44% of grant expenditure
Around half of the funds distributed by The Childwick Trust are within this area and cover a wide range of charities supporting children and adults with disabilities plus care of older people. This includes hospices and those in the Services, Mr Joel himself served in the First World War with the 15th Hussars. A small number of research grants are also considered.

The majority of grants given are typically between £2,000 and £10,000 with a handful of more sizeable amounts for larger projects. The trust is pleased to help both small local charities within Hertfordshire as well as larger national organisations throughout the United Kingdom.

Education in South Africa – 32% of grant expenditure
This area of the trust's activity reflects the Joel family's long involvement in the mining industry in South Africa. The trust's grants are channelled through The Jim Joel Education and Training Fund based in Johannesburg. This fund which receives around a third of the funds distributed each year has achieved considerable success in funding Early

Childhood Development projects in the poorer areas of South Africa. Applications should be made to Mrs G. Bland (Fund Director) at jimjoel@iafrica.com.

The Racing World – 19% of grant expenditure
This reflects Mr Joel's long standing connection with the racing industry and his huge success within the sport over many years. A major portion of the donations are for the welfare of those in need within the Newmarket area.

Jewish Charities – 5% of grant expenditure
Mr Joel was Jewish and the trust continues his lifetime support for charities that promote the Jewish faith and care for Jewish people of all ages who are in need. Grants are made within the United Kingdom only.

Grants in 2007/08

In 2007/08 the trust had assets of £69 million and an income of £2.9 million. Over 200 grants were made totalling £2.8 million. Most grants were for under £10,000.

UK
Beneficiaries of the largest grants included: Racing Welfare – Suffolk (£200,000); British Racing School – Suffolk (£174,000); Animal Health Trust – Suffolk (£75,000); and RAFT – Middlesex (£50,000).

Other beneficiaries included: Leonard Cheshire Homes – Oxfordshire (£30,000); Jessie May Trust – Wiltshire (£20,000); Disability Trust – West Sussex (£11,000); Chase Hospice – Surrey (£10,000); Brain Research Trust – London (£8,000); Regain – Oxfordshire (£7,000); and Jewish Child's Day – London and Women's Counselling Centre – Hertfordshire (£5,000 each).

A further 54 grants of less than £5,000 were made totalling £130,000.

South Africa
Beneficiaries included: Ntataise Rural Pre-school Development Trust (£91,000); ASHA Training and Development Trust (£54,000); Sekhukhune Educare Project (£25,000); Thusanang Association (£14,000); NECTA (£6,600); and Jim Joel Music Scholarship – the Orchestra Company (£4,300).

Exclusions Grants to registered charities only. No funding for:

- general appeals
- animal welfare charities
- students' individual education or gap year costs
- drug or alcohol related causes or HIV/ Aids related charities

- organisations outside of the UK, apart from pre-school education in South Africa.

Applications In writing to the correspondent. Please note: the trust welcomes initial enquiries by email or telephone, but asks that formal applications are sent by post.

There is no official application form but the trust does provide the following guidelines for potential applicants:

- applications should be made to Karen Groom (Trust Administrator) on the charity's official headed paper and include the email address of the writer
- letters should be no longer than two sides of A4 and describe 'fully, clearly and concisely' the project for which funding is being sought and who the beneficiaries will be
- detailed costing or a project budget should be included and, if possible, a copy of the latest annual report (accounts will be viewed via the Charity Commission website)
- details of other sources of funding and any funding applications currently being made are also helpful to include.

The trustees meet in May and December to consider applications. Applications are assessed before each meeting to check that they meet the trust's objectives. Applicants will be informed of the outcome within six weeks following the meeting.

Please note: Applications for funding in South Africa should be made to Mrs G. Bland (Fund Director) at jimjoel@iafrica.com.

CHK Charities Limited

General charitable purposes

£2.3 million (2007/08)

Beneficial area Worldwide, mainly UK, with a special interest in national charities and the West Midlands.

c/o Kleinwort Benson Trustees Limited, 30 Gresham Street, London EC2V 7PG

Tel. 020 3207 7338 **Fax** 020 3207 7665

Website www.chkcharities.co.uk

Correspondent Nick R Kerr-Sheppard, Administrator

Trustees David Peake; Charlotte Percy; David Acland; Joanna Prest; Katharine Loyd; Lucy Morris; Rupert Prest; Serena Acland; Susanna Peake.

CC Number 1050900

Information available Accounts were available from the Charity Commission.

CHK Charities Limited was established in 1995. The origin of the charity derives from the wish of Sir Cyril Kleinwort and his descendants, who constitute the members of the company, to devote some of their time and resources to charitable activities. The company's objectives are very wide and it is an exclusively grantmaking trust with no direct operating activity of its own.

Grantmaking

The trust's set meetings are held twice a year. Consideration of appeals received is undertaken by small groups of trustees who have the authority to make grants in specific fields up to individual amounts of £25,000. These groups meet roughly bi-monthly, so appeals can be dealt with quickly and their decisions are reviewed and ratified at the next trustee meeting.

Impromptu meetings of the trustees are convened as and when applications exceeding £25,000 have to be considered between regular meetings. The trust seeks to provide support to a significant number of charitable organisations working in the fields on which it concentrates its activities. Included in this are national or West Midlands based charities working in countryside matters, drug prevention, education, job creation, population control, culture, conservation, deafness, blindness, and the provision of treatment and care for people with disabilities. The trust's current policy is to consider all written appeals received within these broad guidelines.

In approved cases, the trustees will provide assistance towards start-up or capital costs and ongoing expenses. This may take the form of a conditionally renewable grant for, say, three to five years following which support may be withdrawn to enable the resources to be devoted to other projects. Such grants are subject to annual progress reports and only released at the trustees' discretion.

The majority of grants fall between £3,000 and £5,000, reflecting the trustees' policy of contributing to a large number of causes that fall within its target area. Small one-off grants are available for things like building/ refurbishment projects, purchase of specialist equipment or other similar capital expenditure, or assistance with running costs. Larger grants are the result of close knowledge of specific charities by one or more of the trustees, often extending over many years. Medium sized grants are usually continuing programmes that have been developed over time.

'The trust aims to 'make a difference'; it does not support individuals or very small and narrowly specialised activities but, on the other hand, it tries to avoid 'bottomless pits' and unfocussed causes.' Further information on the trust's funding guidelines is available on its website.

In 2007/08 the trust had assets of £71 million and an income of £2.5 million. There were 221 grants made totalling £2.3 million, categorised as follows:

Youth care – 45 donations (£341,000)
Grants included those made to: St Clement & St James' Community Development Project (£100,000); Reed's School (£20,000); Federation of London Youth Clubs and Fields in Trust (£10,000 each); Active Ten 20 and Honeypot Charity (£5,000 each); Kazzum (£3,000); and Life Cycle UK (£2,000).

Education – 21 donations (£319,000)
Grants included those made to: Life Education Centres UK (£200,000); Plunkett Foundation (£15,000); Wynstones (£7,000); Cricket Foundation (£5,000); Reading Quest (£4,000); and City University London (£1,600).

General welfare and social problems – 15 donations (£254,000)
Beneficiaries included: Home Start UK (£200,000); Comex (Walsall) Limited and Family Holiday Association (£5,000 each); and Association for Post-Natal Illness (£3,000).

Conservation and preservation – 16 donations (£249,000)
Grants included those made to: Northleach Church Restoration Fund (£100,000); SS Great Britain (£5,000); Gordon Russell Trust (£4,000); and St Peter's Church – Cornwell (£1,000).

Disabled and handicapped treatment and care – 37 Donations (£241,000)
Beneficiaries included: Home Farm Trust (£50,000); Thomas Morley Trust (£12,000); Wellchild (£10,000); Demand and Disabled Online (£5,000 each); Arthritis Care (£4,000); and Inspire Foundation (£3,000).

Reproductive healthcare control – 3 donations (£220,000)
Beneficiaries were: Margaret Pyke Memorial Trust (£110,000); University

of Cape Town Trust (£100,000); and Interact Worldwide – Formerly Population Concern (£10,000).

Miscellaneous – 8 donations (£131,000)

Grants included those made to: Charities Aid Foundation (£88,000); War Memorials Trust (£10,000); Oxford Citizens Advice Bureau (£5,000); and Samaritans (£3,000).

Artistic causes – 17 donations (£98,000)

Beneficiaries included: Ashmolean Museum (£10,000); Midlands Art Centre (£7,500); Corn Exchange Wallingford (£5,000); Cotswold Players (£3,000); and Rehearsal Orchestra (£1,500).

Medical care and research – 7 donations (£71,000)

Grants were given to: Specal (£38,000); Alzheimer's Research Trust (£10,000); MS Research (£6,000); and Asthma Relief (£2,000).

Employment and job creation – 6 donations (£69,000)

Grant recipients included: Prince's Youth Business Trust (£27,000); Employment Opportunities for People with Disabilities (£6,000); Quaker Social Action (£5,000); and St Loye's Foundation (£2,500).

Countryside matters and animal welfare and disease – 9 donations (£67,000)

Grants included those made to: Langford Trust (£20,000); European Squirrel Initiative (£10,000); British & Irish Hardwoods Trust (£5,000); and Garden Organic (£3,000).

Blindness – 8 donations (£46,000)

Grants included those made to: Sense (£10,000); Eyeless Trust and Forge (£5,000 each); and British Council for Prevention of Blindness (£3,000).

Care of older people – 9 donations (£43,000)

Grant recipients included: Notsey Trust (£14,000); Carers UK and Combat Stress (£5,000 each); and Charity Search (£1,000).

Hospital and nursing home building and equipment – 3 donations (£28,000)

Beneficiaries were: Maggies Centre (£20,000); King Edward VIIs Hospital Sister Agnes (£5,000); and St Luke's Hospital for the Clergy (£3,000).

Homeless and housing – 7 donations (£25,000)

Grants included those made to: Nehemiah Project (£5,000); Church Housing Trust (£4,000); Porch Steppin' Stone Centre Project (£3,000); and Nightstop UK (£2,000).

Crime prevention – 3 donations (£20,000)

Grant went to: Gloucestershire Crimestoppers (£10,000) and Scarman Trust and Sofa Project (£5,000 each).

Drug prevention and treatment – 3 donations (£13,000)

Beneficiaries were: Nelson Trust and Phoenix Futures (£5,000 each); and FinishFree (£3,000).

Hospices – 2 donations (£13,000)

Grants went to: St Christopher's Hospice (£7,500) and Helen and Douglas House (£5,000).

Deafness – 3 donations (£12,000)

Grant recipients were: National Deaf Children's Society (£5,000); Vitalise (£4,000); and Ear Foundation (£3,000).

Exclusions The following will not normally be considered for funding:

- organisations not registered as charities or those that have been registered for less than a year
- pre-school groups
- out of school play schemes including pre-school and holiday schemes
- projects which promote a particular religion
- 'bottomless pits' and unfocussed causes
- very small and narrowly specialised activities
- community centres
- appeals for places of worship
- local authorities
- umbrella or grant-making organisations
- universities and colleges and grant maintained private or local education authority schools or their Parent Teachers Associations, except if these schools are for students with special needs
- individuals or charities applying on behalf of individuals
- general requests for donations
- professional associations and training of professionals
- projects which are abroad even though the charity is based in the UK
- expeditions or overseas travel
- 'campaigning organisations' or citizens advice projects providing legal advice
- community transport projects
- general counselling projects, except those in areas of considerable deprivation and with a clearly defined client group.

Applications The trust does not have an application form, but suggests that the following guidelines be used when making an application:

- applications should be no longer than four A4 sides
- include a short summary of the organisation and its status, for example, registered charity
- confirm the organisation has a Child Protection Policy and carries out CRB checks (if appropriate)
- provide a summary of the project and why a grant is needed
- explain how it will be monitored and evaluated
- state any funds that have already been raised/applied for
- explain where on-going funding (if required) will be obtained when the grant has been used
- state the amount needed if the request is for revenue funding for a specific item
- enclose a job description if the request is for a salary
- include the most recent audited accounts.

Applications can be submitted at any time during the year. Trustees usually meet every two months. Both successful and unsuccessful applicants are expected to wait at least one year before reapplying.

Additional information on the application process can be found on the trust's website.

The Church and Community Fund

Church of England and social welfare

£956,000 (2008)

Beneficial area England and Wales.

Church House, 27 Great Smith Street, London SW1P 3AZ

Tel. 020 7898 1541

Email kevin.norris@c-of-e.org.uk

Website www.centralchurchfund.org.uk

Correspondent Kevin Norris, Secretary

Trustee *The Archbishops' Council.*

CC Number 1074857

Information available An annual review was available from the fund's website, which also includes guidance.

The Church and Community Fund is an excepted charity but its trustee, the Archbishops' Council, is registered under the above number. The main objects of the fund are described, as follows, on its website:

- to enhance the Church's mission by:
  - promoting spiritual and numerical growth
  - enabling and supporting the worshipping Church and encouraging and promoting new ways of being Church, and
  - engaging with issues of social justice and environmental stewardship
- to sustain and advance the Church's work in education, life long learning and discipleship
- to encourage the maintenance and development of the inherited fabric of church buildings for worship and service to the community.

Typical projects supported by the CCF might include employing a youth worker, renovating an old church hall for use as a community centre, providing hot meals for the homeless in a church room and much more. The CCF is a very flexible fund and there is plenty of scope for imagination. We can support both capital and revenue projects as well as some preliminary costs such as feasibility studies or professional fees.

In brief, all projects should seek to strengthen the relationship between the church and the local community, should benefit the Church locally and as a whole, and should manifest a sense of vision in responding to need(s).

In 2008 the fund had assets of £15 million and an income of £759,000. Grants were made totalling £956,000.

The fund's chair, the Ven. George Howe, offers the following interesting perspective on the fund's work in 2008 and beyond in the annual review:

2008 saw a significant increase in the number of applications received by the Fund. We were delighted to be able once again to award a record amount in grants to projects, together with a modest increase in grants to the central Church. However, our capacity to deal with a fast growing number of applications, together with the inevitable impact of the recession on our income, has led us to re-examine our criteria, which will lead to a more focussed approach in 2009.

We continue to give priority to more deprived parishes, and have been successful in supporting projects to help the victims of poverty in both urban and rural communities. Once again we have given a significant proportion of our funds to enable youth and children's work, through funding the employment of specialist workers.

We have taken the need for better evaluation seriously, and as a result have gained encouraging evidence of our success in enabling projects to unlock funds from other sources. The first year of our Small Grants Partnership with two dioceses (Ripon & Leeds and Truro in 2008) bore fruit in using local knowledge to make a real difference to small, harder to reach projects.

As we all face challenging times, the Church's engagement with the local community will become all the more vital, not least in ensuring that the needs of those already relatively deprived or isolated are not forgotten. Both staff and trustees are thoroughly committed to contribute to that active engagement, and thus bring new hope and vitality to our communities.

The fund's 2008 annual review also gives some examples of projects that have received funding during the year:

St. Michael's, Sutton (£9,000), towards the running costs of a church-based community project, providing youth work, employment-related support and community activities; Doncaster Minster – Sheffield (£5,000), towards the salary of a Heritage Access Worker, who is responsible for improving the opportunities for the wider community to access the church and its grounds; St. David's, Tudhoe, Durham (£4,500), to help employ a Youth Leader, running a weekly youth club for children and young people across three parishes. Invitations have been sent to other churches, the local school, and housing estates in the area, with the result that a group of 14 has now grown to 29; St. Michael's, Handsworth – Birmingham (£3,000), to help in the creation of a community garden on the site of the derelict church hall; and GAP Community Project – Canterbury (£1,000), to help run a recreational group for young people and adults with special needs across Thanet. This includes craft, drama and music activities, as well as outings and camping trips.

Exclusions The fund will not support:

- projects that are essentially insular and inward looking
- the routine maintenance of or extraordinary repairs to the fabric of buildings, including churches, church halls, parsonage houses etc.
- projects which are primarily about maintaining the nation's architectural heritage
- projects which are primarily about liturgical reordering
- restoration works to bells or organs
- research projects or personal grants
- the repayment of debts or overdrafts
- projects which are not directly connected with the Church of England, ecumenical or other faith partnerships in which the Church of England element is small and projects which are predominantly secular in nature
- anything for which the Church Commissioners' funds or diocesan core funding are normally available, including stipend support
- feasibility studies (the fund is able to offer limited support towards the preliminary costs of projects, for example professional fees, but where a grant is awarded at this stage, no further funding will be available for the main body of the work).

Applications The committee meets four times a year to consider eligible applications. An application form is available from the fund's website or from the secretary.

Church Burgesses Trust

Ecclesiastical purposes, education and other charitable purposes

£1.5 million (2008)

Beneficial area Sheffield.

c/o Wrigleys Solicitors LLP, 3rd Floor, Fountain Precinct, Balm Green, Sheffield S1 2JA

Tel. 0114 267 5594 **Fax** 0114 267 5630

Email godfrey.smallman@wrigleys.co.uk

Correspondent Godfrey J Smallman, Clerk

Trustees D F Booker; Revd S A P Hunter; Nicholas J A Hutton; Julie Banham; Peter W Lee; J F W Peters; Prof. G D Sims; Ian G Walker; Mike R Woffenden; D Stanley; B R Hickman; Mrs S Bain.

CC Number 221284

Information available Accounts were available from the Charity Commission.

The Sheffield Church Burgesses Trust is governed by the Charter of Queen Mary of 8 June 1554 as varied by a Scheme of the Charity Commission sealed on 23 August 1999 and a supplemental Royal Charter granted on 8 May 2003. The trust's income is divided 71.5% for ecclesiastical purposes, which includes Cathedral maintenance and the building and adaptation of churches and halls and the furthering of ministry in the four Sheffield Anglican deaneries; 10.7% for general charitable purposes in the city; and, the remaining 17.8% for educational purposes administered by a separate charity, the Church Burgesses Educational Foundation.

It is the policy of the trust in its grant making to support charitable causes in Sheffield, Sheffield Cathedral and the Sheffield City Anglican parishes to the maximum possible extent that its income allows. The trust favours pump priming grants and is keen to be an enabler, rather than a long-term funder, of new projects.

In 2008 the trust had assets of £34.9 million and an income of £2.6 million. Grants were made totalling £1.5 million, allocated as follows:

Category	Value
Cathedral expenditure	£485,300
Ecclesiastical grants to institutions	£402,600
Church Burgesses Educational Foundation	£365,000
General grants to organisations	£258,000
Ecclesiastical grants to clergy	£14,000

Applications In writing to the correspondent. The trustees meet in January, April, July and October and at other times during the year through its various committees. At these meetings decisions are made about the work of the trust, which are then implemented through its officers and advisors. The day to day administration of the trust, work in connection with its assets, liaison with outside bodies such as the Diocese of Sheffield, the administration of its grant programmes and the processing and handling of applications prior to their consideration by relevant committees is delegated to the Law Clerk and applications should be made to him/her.

The trust invites applications from Anglican parishes, from individuals involved in Christian work of a wide variety of types and from charities both national and local, involved in general charitable work within the trust's geographical area of remit.

The trust makes it a condition of most grants that follow up reports are made to the trust so that the impact of its grant making can be assessed.

The Church Urban Fund

Welfare and Christian outreach in deprived communities in England

£1.9 million (2008)

Beneficial area The most deprived areas of England.

Church House, 27 Great Smith Street, London SW1P 3AZ

Tel. 020 7898 1647

Email enquiries@cuf.org.uk

Website www.cuf.org.uk

Correspondent Lucy Palfreyman, Director of Finance and Resources

Trustees *Bishop Peter Broadbent; Patrick Coldstream; Michael Eastwood; Ven Paul Hackwood; Andrew Hunter Johnston; Rev Denise Poole; Derek Twine; Betty Thayer; Rev David Walker; Brian Carroll.*

CC Number 297483

Information available Accounts were available from the Charity Commission.

The Church Urban Fund was set up in 1988 in response to the Church of England's Faith in the City report which drew attention to the increasing levels of poverty in urban areas and to the widening gap between rich and poor. The report suggested that the church should 'set up a fund to help churches work more closely with their local communities to help people tackle poor housing, poor education, unemployment and poverty'. An initial capital sum was raised from what was presented at the time as a one-off appeal.

This original capital sum has now been virtually exhausted and the trust is looking to change the way it operates. At present, it is in the process of moving from being an endowment fund to what it is describing as a 'faith-based foundation model' (similar to the community foundation model). The move from fund to foundation is a significant cultural shift for the trust and will mean two things:

- greater emphasis will be put on fundraising activities – a Marketing Communications and Fundraising Board sub-committee, who will take responsibility for coordinating the approach, has been formed to deal with this
- the trust will be operating on a 'money in, money out' basis – this should create a closer relationship

between fundraising and support for local people in poor communities.

Community foundations in the UK have a particular focus on a geographical area and it is there that they raise and spend their funds. The trust has a national remit, serving faith communities throughout the UK and this will be the basis for the new foundation. It is difficult to say for certain how the changes will affect the trust's grant-making but it is likely that the fund will not be able to guarantee the same level of stability in its grantmaking, meaning that the dioceses may be more limited in their ability to develop long-term strategic plans.

The trust was set up to support faith-based groups working in the poorest communities in England. Grants are allocated through the Church of England diocesan areas delivering essential support to the places of greatest local need. The poorest areas are targeted using a measure known as the multiple indices of deprivation. The trust offers support to groups working in both urban and rural areas, the priority being the most deprived and marginalised communities. In carrying out these objectives, consideration is given to initiatives or projects that involve ecumenical co-operation with other Christian bodies or co-operation with people of other faiths. The vision of the trust is to bring about lasting and positive change in the lives of people most on the margins of society.

The trust supports projects which:

- tackle major problems in the local area, such as poverty, unemployment, disaffected young people, lack of community facilities, loneliness and isolation, inadequate housing and homelessness
- equip communities to address local needs and issues and encourage people to take control of their lives
- empower the church to take an active role in wider community development, particularly through inter-faith and ecumenical developments
- are innovative, will make a practical impact and can develop partnerships with other agencies.

The trust encourages the dioceses of the Church of England to become more involved in the process of grantmaking. The aim here is to streamline and speed up the grant-making process, use local knowledge and experience and to be more responsive to the needs and aspirations of local community groups and churches. Dioceses are at different stages of engagement with this.

Each diocese will have established and developed a set of key strategies, objectives and priorities for tackling poverty and disadvantage in their area. Each will also have been advised of an indicative sum that could be awarded to work within the diocese.

In 2008 the trust had assets of £2.8 million and an income of over £2.7 million. There were 229 grants made totalling £1.9 million.

The trust currently offers two grant programmes described as follows:

Church urban fund grant – the main programme

This offers grants of up to £30,000 over a three year period and covers both revenue and capital grants (although the majority are for revenue). This maximum sum is reserved for those projects with the highest priority and in general awards are about £15,000.

The trust particularly assists churches in deprived areas in their outreach to their local community and aims to support the mission of the church. The following criteria are applied by the trust when awarding grants:

- the project needs to be based in the local community and to have local community involvement in identifying needs, initiating responses and running the project
- the project must be open to all regardless of faith, ethnic origin, disability, gender or sexual orientation
- projects do not have to be Anglican but there needs to be a strong link between the project and a faith group
- the project must have charitable purposes
- the project must be able to raise part of the required money from other sources
- the project needs to be directly tackling the effects of profound poverty and should be working in the most deprived 10% of areas in England. The trust uses the most up-to-date and appropriate government issued indices of multiple deprivation (IMD) as a guide and measure to determine the local areas (super output areas – SOAs) to be prioritised.

Exceptions
- The following is an explanation of exceptions to the criteria given by the trust, applicants are advised to also refer to the grants policy and procedure manual available from the trust's website:

The area IMD score is made up of seven component domains, these being, barriers to housing and services, crime and education,

employment, health, income and living environment deprivation. As with the SOA score, each domain is also scored 1 to 32,482 (the total number of SOAs). If the project is not within one of the priority SOAs, but is directly addressing one of the above domains that has a score of 1 to 3,248, an application can be submitted for consideration if the organisation or project is serving a target group that is deemed to be intrinsically disadvantaged and not covered by the geographic IMD scores or domains, for example, homeless people, people with drug and alcohol problems, refugees and asylum seekers, prostitutes/people working in the sex industry.

Priorities
Priority will be given to:

- projects based within areas where there are the greatest levels of deprivation in England
- projects identified by dioceses as being key to the reduction of deprivation in their area
- projects which, by their nature, are limited in the funds they can access and therefore are in particular need of trust support
- projects where the trust's support will make the greatest impact.

Continuation funding
All projects seeking continued funding from the fund are required to undergo an evaluation process. This takes the form of a continuation funding workshop, which brings together people who have been involved with the project.

Mustard seed programme

This is a rolling programme where there are no deadline dates and requests of up to £5,000 will be considered. The programme aims to provide grants to enable churches and faith-based organisations to engage in social action through supporting them to initiate, develop and formulate ideas and opportunities in preparation for undertaking larger pieces of work or improving existing provision.

The trust provides the following information on the mustard seed programme:

- grants can be given for specific activities but not for on-going revenue expenditure, deficit funding, or retrospective spending
- the grant requested should represent at least a third of the funding required
- grants are made for one year only with the expectation that the money will be spent within twelve months from the date of the award
- applications for a further mustard seed grant in the following year from

the same organisation will not normally be considered
- among other things, grants are provided for training, pilot projects, start-up equipment, social audits and community consultation exercises and needs assessments.

Grants in 2008

Grants awarded were categorised in the following areas:

Category	No.	Value
Community based activities	40	£541,000
Young people and children's work	21	£315,000
Social welfare	24	£296,000
Mustard seed grants	77	£265,000
Opening up churches and other buildings	18	£215,000
Homelessness and housing	7	£84,000
National development work	13	£58,000
Flood disaster relief grants	8	£41,000
Employment and training	2	£25,000
Other	19	£81,000

Beneficiaries included: Holy Trinity Church – Walton Breck (£33,000); Nightstop Teesside (£24,000); A Rocha UK (£20,000); Allens Croft Project (£18,000); Strood Community Project, the Rock – Carlisle (£15,000); South Brent Deanery (£5,000); and Northampton Hope Centre (£2,000).

Exclusions Grants are not made for:

- projects outside England
- individuals
- projects not directly tackling profound poverty or specific issues caused by poverty
- direct support for other grant giving bodies
- publications, research and campaigning activities
- revenue and capital funding for regional and national voluntary/ community organisations and public and private sector organisations
- replacement of statutory funding
- projects without church or faith links
- work that has already been funded by CUF for six years
- activities open only to church members and evangelistic activity not part of a response to poverty
- clergy stipends including church army posts
- internal re-ordering of churches for worship, church maintenance and repairs
- work that does not increase the capacity of the organisation, for example Disability Discrimination Act (DDA) compliance, unless as part of a wider scheme
- organisations with an annual turnover of over £150,000 or with significant reserves
- ongoing costs of credit unions

- general appeals
- 100% of funding.

The trust will not make retrospective grants or help pay off deficits or loans.

Applications The trust has produced a detailed and helpful grants policy and procedure manual and applicants are advised to read this before making an application. The manual is available from the trust's website.

The following guidance is taken from the manual:

Church Urban Fund grant – the main programme:
To help ensure that projects are rooted in their communities, the fund has developed a two-stage application process in which proposals are considered by the local diocese before being forwarded to the national office. The first step is to contact the CUF link officer in your diocese. A list of all link officers can be found on the trust's website or obtained by email to resources@cuf.org.uk. Applicants should state clearly the location of their project. As an integral element of the process all applicants must liaise and work closely with the link officer in the development of their ideas and bid. All applications must be submitted to the respective link officer in the first instance (any applications sent directly to the trust will be forwarded to the diocese for consideration and validation).

The officer will help you to determine whether your project meets the fund's criteria. They will also guide you through the process of securing a recommendation from the diocesan bishop, who prioritises all requests against the overall urban strategy for the diocese and forwards them to the fund.

When the application reaches the trust's offices, a member of the grants unit will contact the project to arrange an assessment visit. The application and the recommendation of the grants officer who has visited the project are then carefully considered by the grants committee, whose award decisions are ratified by the trustees.

The fund always receives more applications than it has resources to support. Therefore, even if a project fits the criteria, it may not be possible to make a grant.

The trust's funding committee meets four times a year, in the first week of March, June, September and December. Deadlines for applications vary between dioceses as each has its own assessment process prior to submission to the trust.

Mustard seed grant
The trust welcomes applications from churches and faith-based groups that 'want to turn their ideas into action.' There is a simple application form to fill in, available

from the relevant link officer. Alternatively, a form of application tailored to the individual project can be used (for example DVD, letter). For the latter, please ensure that the questions asked in the form are answered in this alternative format.

The trust will undertake the assessment of applications. It will want to talk to those setting up the project; this may be face to face or by telephone. The aim of these conversations is to assist in effectively describing the project and to help ensure that the issues involved have been thought through. It is expected that work supported under this programme will grow into more substantive and established activities.

The City Bridge Trust (formerly known as Bridge House Trust)

Social welfare in Greater London

£15.5 million (2008/09)

Beneficial area Greater London.

PO Box 270, Guildhall, London EC2P 2EJ

Tel. 020 7332 3710 **Fax** 020 7332 3127

Minicom 020 7332 3151

Email citybridgetrust@cityoflondon.gov.uk

Website www.citybridgetrust.org.uk

Correspondent Clare Thomas, Chief Grants Officer

Trustees *The Corporation of the City of London. Membership of the grants committee: Joyce Nash, Chair; William Fraser; Kenneth Ayers; John Barker; John Bird; Raymond Catt; William Dove; Revd Dr Martin Dudley; Gordon Haines; Michael Henderson-Begg; Barbara Newman; Rt Hon the Lord Mayor Ian Luder; Simon Walsh.*

CC Number 1035628

Information available Detailed annual report, accounts and guidelines are available from the trust or from its website.

The purpose of the charity was, for many years, to maintain the bridges connecting the City of London to Southwark. It now puts its surplus

revenue to charitable purposes for the benefit of Greater London, which it has chosen to do so far by making grants to charitable organisations. It has done so in an unusually open way, with detailed grants schemes and in meetings that are open to the public. In all cases priority is given to projects which tackle deprivation or disadvantage.

In 2008/09 the trust made 264 grants grants totalling £15.5 million.

Main Grants Programme

Type of grants
Grants are given for either running costs or capital costs. Grants for running costs can be from one to three years. Projects of an 'exceptional or strategic nature' may then make an application for a further two years, a maximum total of five years in all. The trust will also consider supporting core costs incurred in providing services which meet the funding criteria.

Grants may be awarded for feasibility studies or disability access audits (up to £5,000 per grant) to help organisations obtain the best advice to develop their proposed projects.

The following guidelines are taken from the trust's extensive website. The trust frequently reviews its guidelines so please see its website for up-to-date details.

There are five themes under the main grants programme, each with its own specific aims and objectives.

- Access for disabled people
- London's environment
- Children and young people (those aged up to 25 years)
- Older people in the community (those aged 60 and over)
- Strengthening the voluntary and community sectors.

In all cases priority is given to projects which tackle the greatest deprivation or disadvantage. The trust's current programmes are:

- Accessible London
- Bridging Communities
- Improving Londoners' Mental Health
- London's Environment
- Older Londoners
- Positive Transitions to Independent Living
- Strengthening the Third Sector.

Accessible London
Aims
To reduce disadvantage experienced by disabled people by removing those barriers that prevent full participation in society. Particular emphasis is given to artistic and sporting activities and

improving the accessibility of transport and community buildings. The trust's definition of disability is that contained in the Disability Discrimination Act 2005.

Objectives
- To make third sector buildings and services more accessible.
- Ensure buildings are better designed, constructed and equipped to meet the needs of disabled people.
- Improve access to transport services.
- Support community transport schemes that can demonstrate they are more sustainable and financially independent.
- Increase access to new opportunities or report improved well-being as a result of participation in arts or sporting activities.

Funding Priorities
Your application must address one of the following priorities:

1) Accessible transport
- Offers up to 50% of the capital cost of new accessible vehicles.
- Supports work which looks to generate new business and develop new income streams for community transport schemes, improving their longer-term financial sustainability.

Please note: organisations applying for funding for an accessible vehicle need to demonstrate how many people will benefit and must take out membership of the Community Transport Association (for the life of the vehicle).

2) Accessible buildings
- Supports work which improves access to buildings in the voluntary and community sector (including capital and related project management costs).
- Offers funding for access audits, disability equalities training and related consultancy up to a maximum of £5,000.

Applicants must show that an independent access audit has been undertaken.

Please note: the trust produces a useful publication, 'Opening Doors across London', for those interested in this area.

3) Accessible Arts and Sports
- Projects which increase participation in arts and sports.

Applicants should specify which of these themes they are applying under.

Grants in 2009
Beneficiaries included: Bradians Trust and St Patricks Community Outreach (£50,000 each); Hampstead Theatre

(£19,000); Archway Project (£16,000); Theatre Peckham (£5,000); PCC of The Ascension Hanger Hill with West Twyford St Mary (£3,800); House of Illustration (£3,000); and Twickenham United Reformed Church (£850).

Bridging Communities
Aims
This programme aims to strengthen links between communities by building on commonalities and encouraging groups to come together. It also supports improving access to services and increasing the confidence of minority groups to participate fully.

Objectives
- To increase the number of leaders from different communities with better leadership skills, understanding and respect for each other.
- To have more people from different backgrounds working together on projects which have benefited the whole community and improved community relations.
- To raise the number of adults learning English and using it to increase their participation in the wider community/access services.
- More large, established mainstream and minority community organisations working together to deliver improved services.

Funding Priorities
- Leadership initiatives which bring people together two or more different communities (geographical, faith-based, cultural, ethnic or communities of interest).
- Work involving different communities working together on volunteering or active citizenship projects.
- English Language skills for adults who are not accessing mainstream courses.
- New partnership work between mainstream and minority community organisations on specific issues.

Grants in 2009
Beneficiaries included: London Citizens (£81,000); Changemakers Foundation (£75,000); Southwark Muslim Women's Association (£69,000); and Pan Intercultural Arts and Women's Centre Sutton (£25,000 each).

London's Environment
Aims
This programme is designed to improve the quality of London's environment and its sustainable development.

Objectives
- To increase Londoners' knowledge of environmental issues and the principles of sustainable development.
- To enhance London's biodiversity.

- To reduce London's environmental footprint, (the excessive use of natural or non-renewable resources).

Funding Priorities
Your application must address one of the following priorities:
- projects to promote environmental education
- work to maintain and enhance London's biodiversity.

Please note: the trust also manages a 'Greening the Third Sector' programme which aims to share experience and best practice with regard to improving environmental performance. Grants are available to cover the costs of an eco-audit, training or consultancy provided by approved consultants. More information on this scheme is available on the trust's website.

Grants in 2009
Beneficiaries included: Green Thing – Green Thing Trust for Green Thing Limited (£25,000); Camden and Westminster Refugee Training Partnership (£24,000); and Long Lane Pasture Trust (£17,000).

Improving Londoners' Mental Health
Aims
To support work which meets a wide range of mental health needs and ensures that services are reaching marginalised communities.

Objectives
- To have fewer older people with depression and more people reporting improvements in well-being.
- To increase the number of children and young people receiving specialist help.
- To have more homeless, transient people and rough sleepers in touch with mental health services.
- To increase the number of offenders receiving help and reduce the amount of prisoners with mental health problems inappropriately imprisoned.
- Improve access to mental health services for refugees and asylum seekers.
- Raise the number of people successfully managing to live independently or in supported accommodation.

Funding Priorities
- Projects combating depression amongst older people.
- Specialist services for children and young people (and families and carers).
- Helping homeless people, transient people and rough sleepers.

- Supporting prisoners, ex-prisoners and others in contact with the Criminal Justice System.
- Work amongst refugee and asylum seekers (particularly around trauma).
- Supporting resettlement for people with mental health issues living independently or in supported accommodation.

Grants in 2009
Grants were made to: Hillingdon Mind Enterprises (£105,000 – 3 years); Waterloo Community Counselling (£102,000 – 3 years); and Stuart Low Trust (£30,000 – 3 years).

Older Londoners
Aims
To contribute to a London where people can enjoy active, independent and healthy lives in their old age.

Objectives
- Have a greater number of older people over 75 years living healthier and more active lives.
- To have more older people actively contributing in their communities through volunteering.
- Improving the quality of life for those with dementia and Alzheimer's.
- To have fewer older people with depression and more people reporting improved well-being.

Funding Priorities
Your application should address one of the following priorities:
- work with older people (75 years old and above) including social, cultural, educational, volunteering activities and projects encouraging healthy lifestyles
- projects which encourage healthy lifestyles with older people (65 and above)
- non-medical services that support older people of any age living with dementia and Alzheimer's.

Grants in 2009
Grants were made to: Age Concern Sutton (£126,000 – 3 years); Queens Crescent Community Association – QCCA (£64,000 – 3 years); Age Concern Hackney (£50,000 – 2 years); Farsophone Association in Britain and Kilburn Older Voices Exchange – KOVE (both £20,000 over 2 years); and Association of Eritrean Jeberti in the UK (£19,000 – 2 years).

Positive Transitions to Independent Living
Aims
To improve the range of services for people who are going through difficult transitions and challenges.

Objectives
- To have more disabled people reporting increased choice and control in their lives and living independently.
- Raise the number of young disabled people taking up educational or employment opportunities.
- Help disabled parents manage their parental responsibilities successfully.
- To have more care-leavers living independently and taking educational opportunities or employment.
- Increase the number of ex-offenders successfully resettled within the community and reduce re-offending.

Funding Priorities
- Services for people with a newly acquired disability.
- Projects assisting young disabled people, such as managing the move from residential care to independent living or supporting disabled school leavers into employment/college.
- Support for disabled people and young care leavers in managing independent living.
- Projects supporting disabled parents.
- Work with ex-offenders leaving custody.

Grants in 2009
Beneficiaries included: Advocacy Project – Camden & Westminster Citizen Advocacy (£120,000 – 3 years); Prisoners Abroad (£90,000 – 3 years); Ethiopian Community in Britain (£63,000 – 3 years); National Rheumatoid Arthritis Society (£54,000 – 3 years); and Spitalfields Music (£22,000).

Strengthening the Third Sector
Aims
To strengthen the voluntary and community sector so that it can deliver effective, efficient and sustainable services helping reduce disadvantage.

Objectives
- To have more people undertake volunteering and volunteering standards are raised.
- To help minority ethnic and/or refugee community organisations become more sustainable and work more collaboratively.
- To encourage more strategic approaches to Information and Communication Technology (ICT) development in the sector.
- Increase the number of organisations with improved financial management, financial skills and evaluation systems.

Funding Priorities
Your application must address one of the following priorities and please note this programme is for second-tier and membership organisations only.

- Increase and improve volunteering.
- Strengthening minority ethnic and refugee community organisations and encourages collaboration between them.
- New and strategic approaches to the use of ICT.
- Improving financial management and skills services.
- Improving evaluation quality.

Grants in 2009
Grants were made to: Voluntary Action Camden and London Advice Services Alliance – LASA (both £100,000 over 2 years); Interlink Foundation (£80,000 – 2 years); and Life Education Centres (£22,000).

Exceptional grants
The trust occasionally makes grants outside its priority areas. Consideration may be given to applications from organisations which demonstrate that they are:

- responding to new needs and circumstances which may have arisen since the trust fixed its priorities (for example a major catastrophe impacting upon London)
- projects that require short-term assistance to cope with unforeseen circumstances enabling them to adapt to change and move forward (need arising from poor planning will not be considered).

Please note: the trust states that only a small number of grants are likely to be made in this category.

Strategic work
The trust is also working alongside other partners in several strategic initiatives including:

- reducing knife crime among young people
- improving the quality of impact measurement in the third sector
- improving communications skills in the third sector
- improving access advice for developing buildings
- reducing the third sector's carbon footprint.

More information on the trust's strategic work is available on its website.

Principles of good practice
The trust expects applicants to work to its principles of good practice. These include:

- involving beneficiaries in the planning, delivery and management of services
- valuing diversity
- supporting volunteers
- taking steps to reduce the organisation's carbon footprint.

Monitoring and evaluation

The trust requires all grants to be monitored and evaluated. Details of the trust's monitoring and evaluation policy can be found on the website.

Exclusions The trust cannot fund:

- political parties
- political lobbying
- non-charitable activities
- work which does not benefit the inhabitants of Greater London.

The trust does not fund:

- individuals
- grant-making bodies to make grants on its behalf
- schools, PTAs, universities or other educational establishments (except where they are undertaking ancillary charitable activities specifically directed towards one of the agreed priority areas)
- medical or academic research
- churches or other religious bodies where the monies will be used for religious purposes
- hospitals
- projects which have already taken place or building work which has already been completed
- statutory bodies
- profit making organisations (except social enterprises)
- charities established outside the UK.

Grants will not usually be given to:

- work where there is statutory responsibility to provide funding
- organisations seeking funding to replace cuts by statutory authorities, except where that funding was explicitly time-limited and for a discretionary (non-statutory) purpose
- organisations seeking funding to top up on under-priced contracts
- work where there is significant public funding available (including funding from sports governing bodies).

Applications Application forms are available from the trust or downloadable from its website, along with full and up-to-date guidelines. Please note: the trust will not consider applications sent by fax or conventional email.

The City Parochial Foundation

Social welfare

£11.5 million (2008)
Beneficial area Greater London.

6 Middle Street, London EC1A 7PH
Tel. 020 7606 6145 **Fax** 020 7600 1866
Email info@cityparochial.org.uk
Website www.cityparochial.org.uk
Correspondent Bharat Mehta, Chief Executive to the Trustees
Trustees *Nigel Pantling, Chair; Miles Barber; Maggie Baxter; Tzeggai Yohannes Deres; Revd Dr Martin Dudley; The Archdeacon of London, The Ven. Peter Delaney; Archie Galloway; Roger Evans; Deborah Finkler; Cllr Lynne Hillan; Robert Hughes-Penney; Robert Laurence; Elahe Panahi; Ingrid Posen; Wilfred Weeks; Peter Williams.*
CC Number 205629
Information available Accounts were available from the Charity Commission. Full information is also available on the foundation's excellent website.

Summary

The City Parochial Foundation (CPF) describes its formation and work as follows:

Our assets derive from the philanthropy of the people of London. Around 1,400 separate charitable gifts and bequests, some of them 400 years old, were held by the 112 parishes within the City of London, their income to be used for the benefit of the churches or, more often, the poor of those parishes. A scheme [was] declared in 1891 which brought all the endowments together into two funds – a City Church Fund and a Central Fund. Together these constituted the City Parochial Foundation.

We achieve our aims by funding charitable work. We make grants through our open programme and we also fund special initiatives. We aim to develop supportive relationships with the community and voluntary organisations that we fund and to encourage the sharing of learning and skills. Where it is relevant and appropriate we use this knowledge to influence and promote change and we work with the organisations we fund to achieve this.

As an independent funder we are particularly interested in work which is viewed as challenging and we are willing to take risks. One of our longstanding principles is to support activities which government agencies will not or are unlikely to fund. We also want to make sure that we are able to respond to new issues as they arise and find creative ways of tackling deep-rooted problems relating to poverty. We use our knowledge, reputation and other resources to achieve this. We update our priorities every five years to ensure we are responding to the changing nature of poverty.

Funding available

We are one of the largest independent charitable foundations in London. Each year we expect to make funds of approximately £6 million available, of which more than £4 million will be allocated to our open programme, and the remainder to our special initiatives and commissioning other work. We expect to make between 90 and 100 grants each year through the open programme.

There is no minimum or maximum size of grant and the amount you request should be the amount you need. However, the average grant is likely to be about £45,000 in total, although a significant number of grants will be smaller (between £5,000 to £30,000) while a few will be larger (more than £70,000).

Who and what we will fund

We fund registered charities, industrial and provident societies and friendly societies. In exceptional cases we will fund other types of organisations undertaking charitable activities. The majority of our funding is for revenue costs, though we can also fund small capital items.

We want to make sure that our funds reach the people who need them most, especially those who are excluded and are particularly disadvantaged and discriminated against. Some of our work benefits all those living in poverty, while other work targets particular groups. These may include women, black and minority ethnic communities, asylum seekers and refugees, lesbians and gay men, disabled people (including those with mental health issues), young men and poor white communities. We therefore welcome applications from these groups and others who can demonstrate that they are particularly affected by poverty.

Trust for London – We work closely with our sister fund, Trust for London, which supports small, new and emerging voluntary organisations. The trust is operated by the same staff and trustees but has separate funding guidelines. [Please refer to the separate entry on page 355 for this trust for further details.]

Guidelines 2007–11

The foundation's guidelines are summarised below. The full document is available from the foundation's website.

Our funding guidelines provide information about us, what we will and will not fund, and how you can apply to us. We update our priorities every five years to ensure we are responding to the changing nature of poverty.

Open programme

Our open programme has four priority areas. We aim:

- to improve employment opportunities for disadvantaged people
- to promote the inclusion of recent arrivals to the UK
- to promote social justice
- to strengthen the voluntary and community sector.

We will also fund exceptional work to tackle poverty which falls outside our open programme.

Please read our funding guidelines to gain a better understanding of our priorities before making an application to us. [see the 'Applications' section to find out how to obtain a copy.]

Special Initiatives

In addition to the open programme, we also fund special initiatives where we want to make a more strategic impact and, where appropriate, influence the work of others. Often the special initiatives arise from work which we are funding in our open programme which identifies gaps in a particular area of work.

These initiatives are larger in scale than our open programme and we expect to commit more than £1 million each year to this work. We are actively involved in these initiatives and work closely with the organisations we have funded. We have already identified a number of areas we want to investigate and support and we will publicise these in due course, both on our website and through relevant voluntary and community sector networks, as they develop.

We will also develop some of these initiatives with other funders as we believe that there are many benefits in pooling our resources to gain greater insight and impact on a particular issue.

Research

We occasionally fund research when it increases knowledge of the areas of work outlined in our open programme or of other aspects of poverty in London. In particular we are interested in work which has a clear application to policy and practice. We generally commission such work and make the research available on our website and through other means.

Grantmaking in 2008

In 2008 the foundation had assets of £171.1 million and an income of £9.1 million. Grants were made totalling £11.5 million.

The following analysis of grantmaking within the Open Programme during the year is taken from the foundation's excellent annual report [including grants awarded]. It provides an interesting insight into the aspirations and achievements of an organisation which is dynamic, proactive and not afraid to tackle challenging issues:

Improving employment opportunities – 36 grants totalling £1.94 million

When we developed our new funding priorities in 2006 our expectation was that the economy would continue to grow and there would be an expansion in jobs in the capital. Unfortunately, this situation has changed significantly because of the sharpest downturn the global economy has experienced for decades.

Our focus however remains on those who are most disadvantaged and vulnerable in the labour market as they will be most adversely affected by the recession. Key to this is the Government's 'welfare to work' reform agenda, which aims to encourage long-term unemployed and economically inactive people into work.

While this in itself may be a good thing, it is very difficult to achieve in the current climate – as the success of this strategy relies on the availability of reasonably paid jobs, which would move people off benefits. There also needs to be access to good quality support provided by organisations with knowledge and sensitivity to the needs of long-term unemployed people. We are concerned that the increasing move by Government to award large-scale contracts to fewer providers (to deliver employment support services) hinders this approach.

During 2008, we supported a range of organisations, many piloting new approaches. One third of our funding under this aim went towards employment support for disabled people. This included funding DeafPlus [£51,000], towards the cost of developing an employability project for deaf people in east London, the Organisation of Blind Africans and Caribbeans [£30,000], to help reduce the barriers to employment faced by its members and Heart 'n Soul [£80,000 in 2 grants], which is working to improve the employment opportunities of people with learning disabilities.

We continue to support organisations to learn from their work and to share their learning more widely, particularly with policy makers. During the year we organised two seminars on employment support – one

focused on people with mental health problems and another on people with learning difficulties. Representatives of the Department for Work and Pensions (DWP) attended along with ten organisations involved in this work. The latter were able to make recommendations directly to the DWP as part of its consultation on how specialist employment support services for disabled people could be improved.

We welcomed the report of the TUC's Commission on Vulnerable Employment, to which we had made a submission, and responded to some of its recommendations. These included the need for more legal employment rights advice, as result of which we funded two specific projects in west London. This continues to be a priority area for us in the coming year along with work to support women (especially lone parents and black and minority ethnic women), job retention schemes, and work with employers to encourage and enable the employment of disadvantaged Londoners.

Promoting social justice – 26 grants totalling £1.67 million

Empowering people to speak out about inequality and poverty, particularly those who are most affected, and campaigning for changes to policy and practice, are essential to meeting our mission. This is because we recognise that influencing those with significantly more resources than us, such as the Government, can have a greater impact on tackling poverty and its root causes.

During 2008 we supported a broad range of organisations. This included funding Liberty [£35,000], towards a campaign to promote and defend the fundamental rights and freedoms currently protected by the Human Rights Act; Galop [£57,000], to provide guidance and resources to help organisations make their policies and practices more inclusive of transgender people; and End Child Poverty [£70,000], towards its work in London.

Our funding from the previous year contributed to a number of significant achievements in 2008. These included the following causes.

- Homeless Link, among others, successfully persuading the Government and the Mayor of London to commit to ending rough sleeping by 2012.
- Fawcett's Sexism and the City campaign successfully calling on the Government to introduce legislation to tighten controls on lap dancing clubs.
- Launch of the Independent Asylum Commission's final report *Deserving Dignity*, which made 180 recommendations as to how the UK's role as a safe haven for those fleeing persecution could be upheld and improved.

• Publication of a participatory peer research report by ATD Fourth World, *Voices for a Change – Finding solutions to the problem of poverty in London*.

We were also involved in discussing with other funders the value of this work by jointly organising an event with the Baring Foundation – *Funding campaigning and policy work – the philanthropy of changing minds*. Speakers included Shami Chakrabarti, Director of Liberty, who gave a passionate account of why support from charitable trusts is so critical for campaigning organisations. She argued that funding campaigning is crucial to democracy, because without independent voices it is undermined.

Caroline Cooke, Head of Policy Engagement & Foresight at the Charity Commission, also spoke at the event, and sought to dispel the persistent myth that charities could not or should not campaign, and that funders should not fund campaigning. She stressed that charities can campaign and carry out (non-party) political activity, indeed, the Charity Commission sees both as key ways in which charities can make a difference – and we fully endorse this approach. Across our funding aims, 43% of our funding was spent on policy change and campaigning work in 2008, and a further 17% on projects which included a significant element of this.

Promoting the inclusion of recent arrivals to the UK – 22 grants totalling £1.12 million

Early data, as well as historical trends, reveal that the economic downturn is leading to a slowing down of migration to the UK. Nevertheless, London remains home to many migrants from around the world, many working in key areas of the economy. While the majority are able to navigate the complexities of the capital, there are some who are disadvantaged and living in poverty, particularly asylum seekers and undocumented migrants. Unlike other new arrivals, those who are undocumented do not have any 'legal' status and are therefore highly vulnerable to exploitation.

The different outcomes experienced by new communities was highlighted in recent research by IPPR (Institute for Public Policy Research), funded by us and launched in November 2008. The report, Moving Up Together focused on four communities – from Bangladesh, Iran, Nigeria and Somalia – and examined their labour market participation, their own perceptions of their integration, and how their fortunes might change over generations.

During the year we funded a range of work under this aim. One particular area relates to promoting mental health, especially among those individuals who have experienced trauma or torture. This is vital work in helping

them rebuild their lives. We supported five organisations working in this field including: Off the Record [£48,000], towards a dedicated mental health project for young refugees and asylum seekers; Maya Centre [£60,000], to provide counselling and group therapy support to newly arrived refugee women; and Refugee Therapy Centre [£27,000], towards the costs of its Introductory Counselling course on refugees.

Another priority area for us is work which counters the negative images of recent arrivals to the UK. As a result we funded the Migrants Resource Centre [£90,000], to empower migrants to challenge their portrayal in the media by improving their writing, research, public-speaking and campaigning skills; the Refugee Council to improve the campaigning and PR skills of refugees and asylum seekers, particularly around the issue of destitution; and Ice and Fire [£19,000], to develop a documentary play comprised of first-hand accounts of undocumented migrants living and working in London.

Related to this was Photovoice's new photographic work New Londoners: Reflections on Home, which we funded, and was launched by Ed Balls, the Secretary of State for Children, Schools and Families. Through the project, 15 young separated refugees were mentored by 15 emerging and established London photographers to create personalised photo stories about their views and experiences of living in the capital.

We made a detailed consultation response to the Mayor of London's draft strategy for refugee integration in London. This highlighted a range of issues including the role of the media, access to social welfare advice, employment and training opportunities and funding of refugee community organisations. We hope the valuable work undertaken by the Greater London Authority in relation to refugees and migrants continues and we look forward to working with the Authority on this and other relevant issues.

Strengthening the voluntary & community sector – 7 grants totalling £410,000

We recognise the voluntary and community sector needs other forms of support in addition to grants. We are currently focusing on three areas where there seem to be particular skills gaps: campaigning and policy change; research; and evaluation and learning.

We made seven grants under this aim in 2008, including three to CVSs (Councils for Voluntary Service) to deliver capacity-building to small groups in these specific areas of interest [£168,000 in total]. We also funded Akina Mama wa Afrika [£55,000], to

strengthen African women's organisations in London.

Alongside grants, we continued to provide 'funding plus' support to groups, especially through training. This included a pilot four-day Influencing Public Policy course, delivered by the Sheila McKechnie Foundation at our offices, which had extremely positive feedback and will run again in 2009.

In addition, 86 people from 67 groups funded by the Foundation and Trust for London attended one of eight free training days we funded Charities Evaluation Service (CES) to deliver. This year, for the first time, we offered training on data collection, and CES also piloted two new courses focussing on evaluating the effectiveness of campaigning and using evaluation findings to influence change.

During the year we ran a number of learning seminars, bringing together groups working in common fields. One seminar focussed on the infrastructure support needs of Somali community organisations and how joint work between Somali organisations (particularly those working in the same geographical area) can be developed and encouraged. This has led to further meetings by those who attended the event to take forward this issue.

Another learning seminar related to research by the National Children's Bureau, which we had funded. The focus of this was the needs of young lesbian, gay and bisexual people from black and minority ethnic communities. Little is known about this population and the aim of the event was to share the findings of the research and to examine what support could be provided to these young people.

We also continued to provide individual consultancies to organisations, particularly relating to governance and management issues and strategic planning.

Special initiatives

The foundation also funds special initiatives over several years. In 2008 funding for these initiatives totalled £1.15 million, the largest of which is described below:

London Citizens – London Living Wage 2008–12 (£685,000 in 2008)

Although work is the most important route out of poverty, more and more poor households in the capital include someone who is working. Fifteen per cent of all full-time and 45 per cent of all part-time workers in the capital are low-paid (one in five of London's workers).

To counter this, a Living Wage campaign was initiated by London Citizens in 2001. This stipulates an hourly pay rate set above the National Minimum Wage (currently set by the GLA at £7.45 an hour) and includes entitlements such as annual leave and sick leave, to ensure a decent standard of living. It is not mandatory, like the National Minimum Wage, but more than 100 employers in the capital are now paying it, including Barclays, Westfield, the London School of Economics and Transport for London.

The campaign is strongly supported by both the previous and current Mayor of London Mayor Johnson stated: 'Paying the London Living Wage is not only morally right, but makes good business sense too. What may appear to be an unaffordable cost in a highly competitive market should more often be viewed as a sound investment decision. I believe that paying decent wages reduces staff turnover and produces a more motivated and productive workforce.

We agree. Not only are we a Living Wage employer – and encourage the groups we fund to pay a Living Wage – but we have also funded work related to this campaign since its inception. The campaign has achieved a great deal to date – it is estimated by researchers at Queen Mary College, University of London that since the campaign began, it has provided an additional £20 million into the pockets of low-paid workers across London.

However, we feel that with a major injection of funds, more significant and rapid change could be achieved. We therefore awarded £850,000 over four years towards this initiative, which was our major new development in 2008.

Exclusions The foundation will not support proposals:

- which do not have a direct benefit to Londoners
- that directly replace or subsidise statutory funding (including contracts)
- that are the primary responsibility of statutory funders such as local and central government and health authorities
- from individuals, or which are for the benefit of one individual
- for mainstream educational activity including schools
- for medical purposes including hospitals and hospices
- for the promotion of religion
- for holidays and respite care
- for endowment funds or to grant-making bodies seeking to distribute grants on our behalf
- for work that has already taken place
- for general appeals
- for animal welfare
- for children's work including pre-school groups and after school clubs
- for general youth work

- for festivals, sports and leisure activities
- for large capital appeals (including buildings and minibuses)
- from applicants who have been rejected by us in the last six months
- from organisations currently receiving funding from our sister fund Trust for London, unless this is coming to an end.

The foundation is unlikely to support proposals:

- from organisations based outside London
- from large national charities which enjoy widespread support
- for work that takes place in schools during school hours
- where organisations have significant unrestricted reserves (including those that are designated). Generally up to six months expenditure is normally acceptable
- where organisations are in serious financial deficit.

Applications The foundation's funding guidelines for 2007–11 are available to download from its website. Alternatively contact the foundation's office for hard copies. It is strongly recommended that potential applicants read the guidelines before making an application.

There is a two-stage application process:

Stage one
An initial proposal to be submitted by post. There are three closing dates for proposals to be submitted by – you may submit your proposal at any time but it will only be assessed once the next closing date has passed. Closing dates are:

- 7 February for the June Grants Committee
- 30 May for the October Grants Committee
- 25 October for the March Grants Committee.

Stage two
All organisations whose initial proposals are shortlisted will be visited by the foundation to assess their suitability for funding.

The Clore Duffield Foundation

Arts/museums, Jewish charities, education, older people and disadvantaged people
£4.3 million (2008)
Beneficial area UK, the larger grants go to London-based institutions.

Studio 3, Chelsea Manor Studios, Flood Street, London SW3 5SR
Tel. 020 7351 6061 **Fax** 020 7351 5308
Email info@cloreduffield.org.uk
Website www.cloreduffield.org.uk
Correspondent Sally Bacon, Executive Director
Trustees *Dame Vivien Duffield, Chair; Caroline Deletra; David Harrel; Michael Trask; Sir Mark Weinberg.*
CC Number 1084412
Information available Excellent annual report available from the Charity Commission. The foundation also has a helpful website.

The foundation makes a small number of main programme grants, though they can sometimes be very large, mainly in the fields of:

- museums, galleries and heritage sites (particularly for learning spaces)
- the arts
- education
- health, social care and disability
- Jewish charities with interests in any of the above areas.

In 2008 the foundation had assets of £76.8 million and an income of £3.6 million. Grants were made totalling £4.3 million, and were broken down as follows:

Category	Value
Arts, heritage and education	£2,600,000
Jewish support	£611,000
Health and social care	£592,000
Leadership training	£517,000

The foundation's 2008 annual report highlights key projects and achievements during the year:

Performing arts
2008 was the fourth full year of operation of the Core Duffield Performing Arts Awards, designed to encourage direct and memorable participation in the arts by children and young people, particularly by those living in areas where high-quality provision in the performing arts is more

difficult to access. A £1 million donation is supporting around 150 projects over the period 2005 to 2009, through grants ranging from £1,000 to £10,000, awarded in two funding rounds per year. These span all art forms, and a wide range of organisations – from schools, to community groups and performing arts organisations – in England, Scotland, Wales and Northern Ireland.

The foundation has seen extensive evidence of the importance of making small grants available to organisations which lack the resources of larger institutions, and was immensely gratified by the diverse range of projects funded through 2008, which included 31 projects spanning dance, drama, theatre, music, storytelling, puppetry and poetry. The beneficiaries of the successful initiatives of the seventh and eighth round of these awards included: young people from the Salford Lad's and Girl's Club [£10,000], who were preparing an interpretation of Swedish Drill classes from the early 1900s; the National Youth Theatre [£9,000], with an innovative script writing venture, focussed on the life of Razia al-Din, an 11th Century female Sultan; a group from Devon creating a sound art opportunity for preschool children to be broadcast on local radio; a 'zombie' musical devised, written and produced by young people from the North West; and a project to revive the native Lancashire dialect via a series of theatre performances involving 7–18 year olds from Hands-On drama group [£9,000], who performed at the Citadel Arts Centre. Funded projects included young storytellers working on an intergenerational local history project with Age Concern in Wigton, Cumbria; boys from north-west Rotherham were given an insight into employment opportunities through poetry and creative writing; pupils in Sheffield translating pieces of fictional text into dance; young musicians in Hertfordshire writing original compositions; and 50 primary students participating in a performing arts summer school to aid their transition to secondary school.

Beyond the Clore Performing Arts Awards, new donations included funding for a new studio space at the Place [£19,000] (located in the heart of London, the Place unites dance training, creation and performance in a purpose-built centre), and Aldeburgh Music [£100,000] (a performance centre of energy and inspiration for music and the arts) and continued funding for the Southbank Centre's major completed refurbishment [£1 million].

Museums, galleries and heritage

2008 saw a continued emphasis on supporting museum, gallery and heritage education, with continued support towards a Clore Creative Studio within a major new development for the Whitechapel Art Gallery [£60,000], and continued support for the long-awaited Clore Education Centre within the redeveloped Museum of London [£300,000 in 2007].

During 2008 the foundation made its final donation for the refurbishment of London Zoo [£200,000] in the form of funding for the new Clore Rainforest Lookout (formerly the Clore Centre for Small Mammals). The foundation also continued support for the education and family learning programmes of the Wordsworth Trust in Cumbria [£25,000], and the Harnham Water Meadow Trust near Salisbury [£25,000].

Visual arts education

During 2008 the foundation's support for Engage [£19,000], the National Association for Gallery Education, enabled it to continue running Children's Art Day. A legacy of the foundation's Artworks programme (2000 to 2004), the day encourages schools to be inspired by galleries and artists and the donation supported events at over 100 galleries across the UK.

Also during the year, the foundation completed its three-year funding for the work of the Art Room [£20,000 in 2007]. The Art Room is a pioneering charity based at Oxford Community School, aimed at 7–15 year olds who are experiencing difficulties at school. The Art Room works with children to raise their self-esteem, self-confidence and independence through art. There are many reasons why children might attend the Art Room. They have all been identified by their teachers as finding it hard to engage with mainstream education and require special time away from their school. They may also have special learning difficulties or have an interrupted education; some are disruptive or withdrawn; others have been bullied or may be at risk of exclusion; some are asylum seekers, refugees or victims of war. All children have different needs, but all of them benefit from being at the Art Room when they need it most.

Social care

Children and young people remained high on the foundation's agenda beyond the sphere of the arts. This was reflected in donations to Community Links, Save the Children, Evelina Children's Hospital, Camp Simcha and the NSPCC. The trustees were also pleased to be supporting a number of health and social care projects including the Alzheimer's Society, Marie Curie Cancer Care, and the National Hospital for Neurology and Neurosurgery.

Exclusions
Potential applicants should note that their organisation must be a registered charity to be eligible. Unfortunately, the foundation does not fund projects retrospectively and will not support applications from the following:

- individuals
- general appeals and circulars.

It should also be noted that the following are funded only very rarely:

- projects outside the UK
- staff posts
- local branches of national charities
- academic or project research
- conference costs.

Applications
There is no application form for your initial approach to the foundation. If your project falls within the foundation's funding criteria, please send a letter of application. This letter should be no longer than two sides of A4 paper, and should include the following information:

- a brief overview of the work of your organisation
- a concise account of the project you are seeking funding for
- a clear statement of the sum you are seeking from the foundation and the total cost of the project.

You should enclose a standard-sized (DL), stamped, self-addressed envelope – if this is not included, the foundation will not be able to respond to your application. No annual accounts or additional information should be included at this stage, and all applications should be on your organisation's headed paper with your contact details and charity number clearly displayed.

Timing and procedures
- There is no deadline for the Main Grants Programme and applications are accepted on a rolling basis. You should receive a response from the foundation within four weeks of contacting them if you have included a self-addressed envelope.
- All letters of application will reviewed by the foundation's staff in the first instance, and then by the trustees.
- If the foundation decides to progress your application to the next stage (a meeting of the trustees), you will be contacted within six weeks and asked to submit a full proposal, for which guidance will be provided.
- Trustees meetings are typically held twice a year. Successful and unsuccessful applicants are usually contacted in writing within two weeks of the meeting.
- Please do not send applications by recorded delivery as the foundation is not able to guarantee that a member of staff will be on site to receive them.
- Email applications will not be accepted.

Closehelm Ltd

Jewish and welfare

£538,000 (2007/08)

Beneficial area UK.

30 Armitage Road, London NW11 8RD

Tel. 020 8201 8688

Correspondent Henrietta W Van Praagh, Secretary

Trustees *A Van Praagh; Henrietta W Van Praagh; Hannah R Van Praagh.*

CC Number 291296

Information available Accounts were available from the Charity Commission, without a list of beneficiaries.

The trust supports the advancement of religion in accordance with the Jewish faith; the relief of poverty; and general charitable purposes.

In 2007/08 the trust had assets of £7 million and an income of £4.5 million, which included profits on the disposal of assets. Grants were made totalling £538,000. No further information was available.

Applications In writing to the correspondent.

The Clothworkers' Foundation

General charitable purposes, in particular social inclusion, young people, older people, disability, visual impairment and textiles

£5 million (2008)

Beneficial area UK.

Clothworkers' Hall, Dunster Court, Mincing Lane, London EC3R 7AH

Tel. 020 7623 7041 **Fax** 020 7397 0107

Email foundation@clothworkers.co.uk

Website www.clothworkers.co.uk

Correspondent Sam Grimmett, Grants Assistant

Trustees *John Stoddart-Scott, Chair; Carolyn Boulter; Neil Foster; J A H West; Oliver Howard; Michael Howell; Michael Jarvis; Anthony Harding Jones; Richard Jonas; Michael Malyon; Christopher McLean May; Robin Booth; John Wake; Henry Arundel McDougal.*

CC Number 274100

Information available Accounts were available at the Charity Commission. The foundation has a good website with detailed annual report.

The Clothworkers' Company is an ancient City of London livery company, founded in 1528 and the twelfth of the 'Great Twelve' companies. One of the functions of livery companies was to support their members in times of need. As they grew wealthier, they were also able to benefit outsiders. The Clothworkers' Company acquired a number of trusts, established by individual benefactors for specific charitable ends. These totalled over 100 by the Twentieth Century. In addition, the company has always made payments to good causes from its own funds.

The Clothworkers' Foundation was set up in 1977 by the company as the independent arm for the whole of its charitable work.

The foundation's early income came from a leasehold interest in a City of London property, 1 Angel Court. Subsequent funding from the company, together with the sale of the long leasehold interest in Angel Court in 1994, represents the assets of the foundation which are substantially invested in stocks and shares. Income from these investments, together with unrestricted donations from the company, is given away each year to a wide range of charities. During its first 30 years, the foundation has made grants totalling around £73 million.

The objects of the foundation are for general charitable purposes and the foundation seeks to improve quality of life, particularly for people and communities that face disadvantage.

Grant programmes

The foundation has two programmes that are open to unsolicited applications: the Main Grants Programme and the Small Grants Programme.

Main Grants Programme is open to UK registered charities:

- with an annual turnover of under £10 million
- applying for a grant of over £1,000 for capital costs.

Small Grants Programme is open to UK registered charities:

- with an annual turnover under £250,000

- applying for a grant of between £500 and £10,000 for capital costs.

Applications to the Main Grants Programme and Small Grants Programme must fall under one of the following areas:

Encouragement of Young People
Preference will be given to organisations working with economically disadvantaged young people in deprived areas.

Social Inclusion
Support for organisations which seek to tackle such problems as substance abuse, homelessness, offending and family breakdown.

Older people
Priority will be given to projects focusing on those in need or at risk of social exclusion.

Disability
Support for organisations tackling the needs of the physically and/or mentally disabled, but not work purely to meet the requirements of the Disability Discrimination Act.

Visual impairment
Support for organisations addressing the needs of blind or visually impaired people.

Textiles
UK academic institutions involved in textiles, technical textiles and colour science. Heritage projects involving textiles collections, particularly those of national importance.

Grantmaking policy

We fund one-off grants for capital costs for UK registered charities with an annual turnover of under £10 million.

Capital costs include:

- building purchase and renovation
- equipment (including IT hardware)
- vehicles
- training costs and professional fees relating to capital projects being funded by us.

We do not fund revenue costs including:

- running costs∗ for your charity/project
- events
- training costs (unless they are included as part of a larger capital appeal).

∗Ineligible costs include: salaries, expenses, administration, hire of space/premises, marketing and publicity, utility bills.

For charities which, by their nature, have no capital requirements, we will consider funding one-off projects such as production of publications (not regular newsletters etc.) or setting up a new website.

Textile Heritage Projects

- our primary interest is in supporting the cataloguing, indexing, storing, conserving,

- display and access to important UK textile collections and archives
- we wish to encourage access to past history in order to stimulate scholarly research and future design
- we are more interested in cloth and its manufacture than costumes
- our priority is British textiles
- we will not fund the purchase of art textiles.

Grantmaking in 2008

In 2008 the foundation and associated trusts had assets of £89.2 million and an income of £6.3 million. There were 280 grants made during the year by the foundation and associated trusts, to an impressive range of charities and organisations working across the UK, totalling £5 million.

The foundation's annual review provides an interesting analysis of grantmaking during the year, including the effect of the economic downturn:

Reflecting the turmoil in financial markets, the value of the foundation's investments at the end of 2008 reduced to £89 million from £111 million in 2007. Income dropped from £8.7 million to £6.3 million, as a result of the company making a lower donation than in the prior year.

The trustees are adopting a prudent approach to grantmaking in 2009 in the expectation that an extended downturn will have a significant impact on income over the next two years.

Unfortunately, the economic crisis has hit many charities, and as a result we have seen some projects abandoned or downscaled. Sadly, a number of charities have failed, although to date we have had little direct exposure to such closures. However, we are being yet more rigorous in assessing applicants' financial circumstances and monitoring their progress during the life of a project. We are also being somewhat circumspect in supporting ambitious appeals which are at an early stage, given our lower income, the tight market for fundraising generally and a reluctance to tie up our grant-making capacity for an extended period.

Grantmaking activity

We made 280 grants in 2008, of which 53% were for £10,000 or less. Our approval rate was 33%, broadly similar to 2007 and considerably higher than earlier years.

Distribution by grants programme	Value
Main grant programme	£3,440,000
Small grant programme	£540,000
Regular grants	£495,000
Proactive	£472,000

Reactive giving

The bulk of our giving in 2008 was from our Main Grants Programme, under which

commitments of £3.5 million were made. These were for capital projects at charities in one of six categories: encouragement of young people, social inclusion, disability, older people, visual impairment and textiles.

This was the second year of our Small Grants Programme, to which we allocate 10% of the total grants budget. Open to smaller charities, it seeks to provide a quick turnaround to requests for grants of up to £10,000. With 89 grants disbursed totalling £540,000 in 2008, we believe it is achieving its objective of helping small organisations proceed with capital projects in a timely manner.

We accept applications for these two programmes from any eligible charity with a project which meets our guidelines. Although we do not have set targets on what type of capital we wish to fund and most grants relate to buildings and equipment, we do receive a lot of appeals for minibuses, IT equipment and community halls, and support a number of these. For community projects, we focus our giving on areas suffering deprivation.

We do not have predetermined allocations to our six categories, and the proportions change from year to year. In 2008, over 70% of the total grant commitments were in the areas of young people, disability and social inclusion.

Our Regular Grants Programme does not accept applications, and comprises a small number of charities selected by the foundation to receive a grant each year, subject to annual review. In 2008, this accounted for £495,000, the majority of which went to charities which distribute grants to individuals in need, and to provide educational bursaries.

Proactive grants programme

Following a strategic review in 2006, the trustees established a Proactive Grants Programme, under which three areas would be allocated £1.25 million each over a five-year period. The areas are autism, mathematics and conservation, reflecting the foundation's longstanding interest in disability, education and arts and heritage. The intention is that we should make a significant impact on each area during the life of the programme. In 2008, £472,000 was committed under this programme, and a further £550,000 allocated to be awarded in subsequent years. The foundation selects potential beneficiaries under the programme, and unsolicited applications are not accepted.

Examples of beneficiaries in each category during the year, including the purpose for which grants were made, include:

Disability – 70 grants totalling £1.5 million

Royal Star and Garter Home for Disabled Sailors Soldiers and Airmen (£150,000), for en-suite shower rooms at the new nursing care home in Solihull; Core Arts (£50,000), for the purchase of freehold for arts organisation in east London providing activities for people with mental health issues; Julia Perks Foundation (£30,000), towards the purchase of a building in Dorset to provide therapy and counselling for life-limited children and families; Southview School Fund (£20,000), for the installation of therapy pool for use by children with disabilities in Kent; and Mind in Tower Hamlets (£12,000), for improvements to drop-in centre kitchen and alarm system.

Encouragement of Young People – 73 grants totalling £1 million

Halton YMCA (£75,000), for the redevelopment of facilities for homeless young people in Cheshire; Family Action in Rogerfield and Easterhouse (£60,000), towards the construction of multi-purpose community facility for residents of Greater Easterhouse, Glasgow; London Community Cricket Association (£30,000), towards flooring, a website and marketing materials of the indoor centre for this charity which uses cricket to engage disadvantaged young people; Jobs Education and Training (£20,000), towards equipping this youth resource in a deprived area of Derby; and Spitalfields Farm Association (£15,000), for a new van to provide a mobile farm service to east London communities.

Social Inclusion – 73 grants totalling £988,000

F N Charrington Tower Hamlets Mission (£75,000), towards the provision of self-contained flats in London's East End for homeless men in alcohol/drug recovery and rehabilitation; Wirral Churches' Ark Project (£50,000), for an extension to a hostel for the homeless; St Paul's Parish Church (£40,000), for a major upgrade of a community hall in Durham; Space Counselling Service (£20,000), towards the renovation of the building and a security upgrade for a charity providing counselling and therapy to disadvantaged people in Berkshire; and Cardinal Hume Centre (£11,000), for an IT server and hardware at a centre for homeless young people in London.

Conservation – 5 grants totalling £431,000

Institute of Conservation (£180,000), for the chief executive's salary over three years; Historic Royal Palaces (£140,000), for postgraduate textile conservation internships; Textile Conservation Centre

Foundation (£46,000), for a research paper on the cultural value of conservation, and MA scholarships; National Museum of Labour History (£40,000), for a textile conservation studio in Manchester; and City and Guilds of London Institute (£25,000), for bursaries in stone and wood conservation at City and Guilds of London Art School.

Older people – 26 grants totalling £387,000

St John's Home, Northampton (£75,000), towards construction of a stand-alone dementia unit at a residential care home; Edward Mayes Trust (£25,000), towards the construction of four new properties for older people in Manchester; Burma Star Association (£17,000), for grants for needy older UK veterans and their dependents; All Hallows Centre (£15,000), towards disabled and upgraded toilet facilities at a community centre for older people in Liverpool; and Age Activity Centre (£12,000), for a minibus for a centre in Tooting.

Mathematics Education – 3 grants totalling £202,000

Maths Inspiration (£202,000 over 3 years), for UK-wide interactive lectures to engage and inspire young people in maths education; Exicoe (£50,000), for a mathematics bursaries for A-Level students from deprived backgrounds; and New Philanthropy Capital (£20,000), for a research project on numeracy.

Autism – 6 grants totalling £163,000

Wirral Autistic Society (£50,000), towards the building costs of a respite unit for people with autism; Rowdeford Charity Trust (£40,000), performance studio providing psychotherapy for children with complex and profound learning difficulties including autism; Autism Cymru (£25,000), for the development of online technology to provide web-based autism training opportunities across the UK; Sussex Autistic Society (£20,000), for a vehicle to facilitate programme of community activities for young people with autism; Hope for Autism (£18,000), for office equipment; and Resources for Autism (£10,000), for a minibus for the day centre.

Visual Impairment – 6 grants totalling £99,000

Metropolitan Society for the Blind (£34,000), grants and pensions for needy visually-impaired individuals; St John of Jerusalem Eye Hospital (£25,000), towards general funds; and Advisory Council for Alcohol and Drug Addiction (£15,000), towards health education resources for visually-impaired young people.

Other – 2 grants totalling £90,000

Medical Emergency Relief International Charitable Trust (£80,000), towards rapid response assistance in emergencies and crisis situations; and Advisory Council for Alcohol and Drug Addiction (£10,000), towards health education resources for visually-impaired young people.

Exclusions The foundation does not make grants to:

- non UK-registered charities
- organisations with an annual turnover of over £10 million (charities working in textiles with an annual turnover of over £10 million wishing to make an application are requested to contact the foundation)
- non-capital costs, such as running costs, salary costs
- organisations that have received a grant from the foundation in the last five years
- heritage projects (other than textiles)
- environment projects
- arts and education projects are unlikely to be funded unless they are predominantly focused on disadvantaged young people, older people or disabled people
- projects that do not fit in with one of our programme areas
- individuals
- general or marketing appeals
- educational establishments
- grant-makers
- overseas work/projects
- medical research or equipment
- political, industrial, or commercial appeals
- relief of state aid or reduction of support from public funds
- events
- appeals from any organisation where the money will be used for religious purposes, or projects which promote a particular religion.

Applications There are separate application forms for the main and small grants programmes available from the foundation's website, which also gives full details of the application process and criteria for funding. Both programmes require the following information:

- completed application form
- full project budget
- latest accounts for the organisation as submitted to the Charity Commission
- copy of the correspondence confirming Northern Ireland charitable status if registered in NI.

The foundation does not accept draft applications or applications by email,

please post your finished application. Applications are accepted at any time, there are no deadlines. Decisions normally take six weeks for the small grants programme and six months for the main grants programme.

Any applicants who have specific queries after reading the foundation's guidelines should contact the grants assistant on 020 7623 7041. The foundation does not however, provide advice on matters which are covered on its website.

If your application is not successful, you must wait six months before re-applying.

Richard Cloudesley's Charity

Churches, medical and welfare

£683,000 to organisations (2007/08)

Beneficial area North Islington, London.

Reed Smith LLP, 26th Floor, Broadgate Tower, 20 Primrose Street, London EC2A 2RS

Tel. 020 3116 3624

Email kwallace@reedsmith.com

Correspondent Keith Wallace, Clerk

Trustees *Kevin A Streater, Chair; Kathleen Frenchman; Roger Goodman; Revd Canon Graham Kings; Brian H March; Michael Simmonds; David R Stephens; Cllr Terry Stacy; Martin Black; Christopher Moss; Rupert Perry; Miranda Coates; Dorothy Newton; Courtney Bailey.*

CC Number 205959

Information available Accounts were available from the Charity Commission.

Summary

The charity was founded in 1518 by the will of Richard Cloudesley. He left the rent from a 14 acre field in Islington, London, to be used for the benefit of residents of Islington parish. The field was in Barnsbury and its centre was what is now Cloudesley Square. The charity's 2007/08 annual report and accounts state that property owned by the charity in the area was being redeveloped to be sold, although this process was taking longer than expected – it is likely that the 2008/09 accounts will show a significant increase in income and a reduction in assets when they become available.

Grants ranging from £100 to around £40,000 are given to Church of England churches and to charities supporting a range of beneficiaries, for the 'sick poor in the ancient parish of Islington'. As part of its help to the 'sick poor' the trust operates a welfare fund making quick and modest grants to needy individuals.

The trust can only assist in activities in the ancient parish of Islington which is now the northern part of the modern London Borough of Islington – roughly everything north of Chapel Market and City Road. 'It is clear that there are few bodies that confine their work to such a small area and the trust does help charities in Islington as a whole, or Islington and nearby London boroughs.' The trust requires applicants to provide an assessment of the proportion of what they do that can be said to be related to people living in the ancient parish. This limited geographical scope makes for difficulties in granting funds to nationally organised charities. Some of these have locally accounted branches – and others have locally identifiable projects – but without some restriction like this, the trust will be unable to assist.

The trust's policy tends to be to make grants that are free of conditions. Feedback from grantees suggest that this gives much needed flexibility in helping to fill gaps caused by the more rigid terms that other funders are constrained to adopt. However, the trust is aware of the need for accountability and is able to exercise some monitoring through accounts, information, trustee contact and the occasional visit.

Most grants are given to charities previously supported, though the amounts are clearly reassessed each year as they frequently vary.

Grantmaking in 2007/08

In 2007/08 the charity had assets of over £24.7 million and an income of £999,000. Grants were made to organisations totalling £683,000 and were categorised as follows:

Churches – 19 grants totalling £350,000
Beneficiaries included: St. Mary, Ashley Road (£40,000); St. John's District Church (£31,000); St. David's, Lough Road (£24,000); Emmanuel, Hornsey Road (£16,000); St. Jude with St. Paul,

Mildmay Park (£10,000); Christchurch, Highbury Grove (£8,000); and St. Saviour, Hanley Road (£5,000).

Medical and welfare – 73 grants were made totalling £333,000
Beneficiaries included: CARIS (Islington) Churches Bereavement Service (£23,000); Islington MIND (£18,000); Choices Confidential Pregnancy Advice (£11,000); Union Chapel Homelessness Project (£10,000); Sunnyside Community Gardens Association (£6,000); Medical Foundation for Care of Victims of Torture (£5,000); Factory Community Mental Health Drop in Group (£3,000); Equinox Care (£2,000); and Islington Pensioners Forum (£1,000).

The above figure includes a grant of £160,000 to the charity's own Welfare Fund for further distribution to individuals in need in the Islington area. Grants made from the Welfare Fund totalled £187,000. [See *A Guide to Grants for Individuals in Need* published by Directory of Social Change.]

Applications Applicants should write to the correspondent requesting an application form.

Applications should be in time for the trustees' meetings in April and November and should be accompanied by the organisation's accounts. The following information should be supplied:

- details of the work your organisation undertakes
- how it falls within the geographical area of the trust
- details of what the grant will fund.

If you would like acknowledgement of receipt of your application please send a stamped, addressed envelope.

Block grants are considered twice a year, in late April, and early November, at a grants committee meeting. Recommendations are made by the grants committee at these meetings and are reviewed and authorised by the trustees two weeks later. The trust will give brief reasons with any application that is not successful.

Clydpride Ltd

Relief of poverty, Jewish charities and general charitable purposes

£2.6 million (2008)

Beneficial area Unrestricted.

144 Bridge Lane, London NW11 9JS
Tel. 020 8731 7744 **Fax** 020 8731 8373
Correspondent L Faust, Secretary
Trustees *L Faust; M H Linton; A Faust.*
CC Number 295393

Information available Accounts were on file at the Charity Commission; without a list of grants.

The objects of this trust are to advance religion in accordance with the Jewish orthodox faith, the relief of poverty and general charitable purposes. The main focus is to support the 'renaissance of religious study and to alleviate the plight of poor scholars'. For example, the trust has recently made grants to an institution for advanced Talmudical study and research.

In 2008 the trust had assets of £9.4 million and an income of £3.5 million. Grants were made totalling £2.6 million. No further information was available.

Previous beneficiaries include: Achiezer; Achisomoch Aid Company; Beis Chinuch Lebonos; Beis Soroh Scheneirer Seminary; Bnei Brak Hospital; Comet Charities Limited; EM Shasha Foundation; Friends of Mir; Gevurath Ari Torah Academy Trust; Mosdos Tchernobil; Notzar Chesed; Seed; Society of Friends of Torah; and Telz Talmudical Academy Trust.

Applications The trust states that unsolicited applications are not considered.

The Coalfields Regeneration Trust

General, health, welfare, community regeneration, education, young people and older people

£11.5 million (2007/08)

Beneficial area Coalfield and former coalfield communities in England (North West and North East, Yorkshire, West Midlands and East Midlands, Kent), Scotland (West and East) and Wales.

Silkstone House, Pioneer Close, Manvers Way, Wath Upon Dearne, Rotherham S63 7JZ

Tel. 01709 760272 **Fax** 01709 765599

Email info@coalfields-regen.org.uk

Website www.coalfields-regen.org.uk

Correspondent Janet Bibby, Chief Executive

Trustees *Peter McNestry, Chair; Ken Greenfield; Jim Crewdson; Prof. Anthony Crook; Dawn Davies; John Edwards; Peter Fanning; Vernon Jones; Peter Rowley; Joe Thomas; Wayne Thomas; Fran Walker; Sylvia Wileman; Nicholas Wilson; Shaun Wright.*

CC Number 1074930

Information available Accounts were available at the Charity Commission. The trust's website is informative and helpful to applicants.

Summary

Set up in 1999, the Coalfields Regeneration Trust is an independent charity dedicated to the social and economic regeneration of coalfield communities in England, Scotland and Wales. It was set up in response to a recommendation by the government's Coalfields Task Force Report. The report highlighted the dramatic effects that mine closures had, and continue to have, on communities in coalfield areas.

The trust provides advice, support and financial assistance to community and voluntary organisations which are working to tackle problems at grassroots level within coalfield communities. It is closely connected with the areas it serves, operating through a network of staff based at offices located within coalfield regions themselves.

The trust's mission is: 'Working closely with partners, the trust is a key agency promoting and achieving social and economic regeneration in the coalfields of England, Scotland and Wales.' The aim is to make coalfields sustainable, and to work towards the point where they can be prosperous, viable and cohesive without support.

In addition to grantmaking, the trust has invested and acted strategically where a more structured intervention is necessary. In areas where mines have just closed or are under threat, such as in Selby, the trust has demonstrated that with government support it can act swiftly to ensure that the worst effects do not happen.

Many coalfields' wards continue to be the most deprived in the country. The trust works with people at a very grassroots level in order to build confidence and encourage them to actively participate in taking their communities forward. The trust believes in giving people aspirations for the long-term sustainability of their communities and is committed to standing by them to achieve their goals. This is illustrated in the collaboration with English Partnerships in establishing Initiate, a roving team to ensure that local people are connected to the major site developments on former coalfield sites and the trust intends to continue to build on this work to ensure that it makes a contribution towards making that happen.

General

In 2007/08 the trust had assets of £902,000 and an income of £12.6 million mainly from grants and donations received. Grants were made during the year totalling £11.5 million.

The trust has offices in the coalfield areas of England, Scotland and Wales. Each office has at least one regeneration manager and one administrative worker. These teams continue to provide essential support, application forms, advice and guidance to help applicants with their project and represent the trust's ongoing commitment to grass-roots regeneration of coalfield communities.

The following information is taken from the trust's website.

Programmes

One of the major strengths of the Coalfields Regeneration Trust is the flexibility of our funding programmes. They're there to help people, not make them jump through hoops.

At the one end of the spectrum we give grants from our 'community chest' to small organisations to help them develop, and at the other end we give large grants of up to £100,000 to bigger voluntary, community and statutory organisations.

Our grants programme is about helping groups who respond to local need. But we're also proactive in developing ideas and projects that address key issues such as worklessness, isolation, skills, sector development and sustainability.

In short, the trust is always interested in working with partners to deliver projects and programmes that will contribute to the regeneration of coalfields communities.

We try to keep our application form as simple as possible. However, as we are using public money we will need quite a bit of information from you, for we must manage our funds in a proper way.

It is important that we can judge how effective our funding decisions are in contributing to the regeneration of the coalfields. It is also important that the activities we support fit in well with our own priorities and those of other regeneration programmes.

Social investment (funding) themes (2008 – 2011)

The trust has identified four key funding themes that respond to the needs of coalfield communities. A project must address one or more of the themes and for guidance on the suitability of your project please contact your regional office.

Access to Employment

This theme aims to connect people living in deprived neighbourhoods to mainstream opportunities. We will be seeking forward-thinking and locally designed approaches that offer a route for people to get back into work. These approaches include:

- engagement programmes that concentrate on pre-employment support provide information, advice and guidance and which prepare people for work

- work experience programmes that develop valuable skills, experiences and which respond to labour market demands

- employment programmes such as transitional labour market and wage subsidy schemes.

Education and Skills

This theme aims to support people in accessing learning opportunities and developing their skills through added value activity (not statutory mainstream provision). These approaches include:

- projects that raise aspirations and encourage a return to learning

- projects that engage people in formal and informal education
- projects that improve educational attainment and provide accredited training
- targeted work with young people promoting further education
- out of school hours' activity.

Health and Well Being
This theme aims to improve the health and lifestyles of people living in coalfield communities through community based approaches and preventative projects that are additional to statutory provision:

- projects that encourage healthier lifestyles, prevent ill health, promote self help or support groups and improve an individual's quality of life
- projects that develop opportunities for people to participate in active leisure pursuits
- the development of extra curricular activity programmes for children and young people
- preventative or awareness raising projects tackling issues such as poor diet, teenage pregnancy, substance misuse and mental health.

Access to Opportunities
This theme aims to improve access to services in coalfield communities recognising that limited community infrastructure and geographical isolation can prevent people from taking up opportunities. These approaches include:

- projects that create new facilities, improve existing facilities or acquire community owned assets to deliver services responsive to gaps in provision, evidenced community need and which demonstrate ongoing sustainability
- the development of transport solutions such as community transport or wheels to work initiatives
- improved access to services that tackle poverty and debt
- the development of new childcare provision
- the provision of support services or facilities to enable the development of new social enterprise initiatives
- the provision of support for the third sector to build capacity, improve service delivery and equip itself to take up procurement or commissioning opportunities.

Main Grants Programme
The trust can make grants from £10,001 to £100,000 in England, £10,001 to £50,000 in Scotland and £10,001 to £100,000 in Wales, to voluntary, community and statutory organisations (Please note, Statutory organisations can only apply for grants over £30,000). Awards can be for capital or revenue for up to three years or to the end of the funding programme. Different timescales apply in different countries and our regional offices can give you details. The application and assessment process involves a telephone interview or site visit and we aim to get a decision within 23 weeks of a complete application being received. All awards are reviewed annually and continued funding is subject to the terms and conditions of the grants being met. Applicants are expected to plan and prepare for the continuation of the project beyond the period of the grant.

The trust has a policy booklet to accompany this programme which is available from its website.

Bridging the Gap (BtG)
This is the trust's programme offering grants from £500 to £5,000 in England and Scotland (£500 to £10,000 in Wales), to voluntary and community groups for projects that can be completed within 12 months. A group can have one grant in any 12-month period and each application must be for a different activity. The application process is simple and we aim to get a decision within 12 weeks of receiving a completed application.

A detailed information booklet is available from the trust's website.

Strategic Interventions/Special Projects
In addition to making grants that help groups respond to local need, we are also proactive in developing ideas and projects that address key issues. These might focus on worklessness, isolation, skills, sector development and sustainability. The trust is always interested in working with partners to deliver projects and programmes that will contribute to the regeneration of coalfields communities. If you wish to discuss your ideas please get in touch with us.

Grantmaking in 2007/08

Grants paid during the year totalled £11.5 million – this included £9.8 million of new grants approved during the year, broken down as follows:

Exclusions The following are not eligible to apply for the Main Grants programme:

- individuals
- private businesses
- organisations that we believe are in a poor financial position or whose financial management systems are not in good order. We will base our opinion on an organisation's financial position and management systems, an analysis of their accounts, other management information and interviews with the organisation itself
- voluntary and community organisations and groups who hold 'free reserves' that total more than 12 months' operating costs and who are not contributing enough funds to the project. We will assess how much money the organisation has available in free reserves using information from their accounts. (Free reserves are the amounts of money an organisation hold that are not restricted by any other funder for any other purpose and do not include fixed assets such as the value of buildings)
- organisations whose purpose is to raise funds for a specific project
- 'friends of groups' where the end beneficiary will clearly be a statutory body
- organisations not established in the UK
- pigeon (flying) clubs.

The following are not eligible to receive support from the Bridging the Gap programme:

- individuals
- private businesses
- statutory bodies
- national organisations
- parish, town and community councils
- organisations with total income (from all sources) above £100,000
- organisations that we believe are in a poor financial position or whose financial management systems are not in good order
- organisations whose purpose is to raise funds for a specific project
- 'friends of groups' where the end beneficiary will clearly be a statutory body

Grants value	England		Scotland		Wales	
	Amount	Number	Amount	Number	Amount	Number
under £10,000	£1,070,000	168	£481,000	95	£372,000	50
£10,000 – £30,000	£512,000	22	£15,000	1	£91,000	5
£30,000 – £60,000	£775,000	19	£89,000	2	£188,000	4
£60,000 – £300,000	£5,150,000	55	£170,000	2	£587,000	7
over £300,000	£345,000	1	–	–	–	–
Total	**£7,850,000**	**249**	**£755,000**	**100**	**£1,240,000**	**66**

- organisations not established in the UK
- pigeon (flying) clubs.

Applications The following is taken from the trust's website.

Main Grants Programme
Voluntary and community organisations and groups

Most voluntary and community organisations and groups working to regenerate coalfield communities are eligible to apply to us for funding; this includes statutory bodies such as local authorities. Please note that we process applications from Parish, Town and Community Councils in the same way as we process applications from voluntary organisations and community groups. We may make grants to voluntary and community organisations and groups including Community Interest Companies and Social Enterprises, providing business plans are in place and the activity will not result in personal/private benefit and delivers a recognised social benefit, if they have the following:

- a constitution or a set of rules to show that the group is legally eligible to receive a grant and entitled to run the planned project. The constitution must also have an acceptable 'dissolution' clause, which guarantees that any assets purchased with a grant from the trust are kept for the benefit of the community
- have a bank or building society account in the organisation's name, with the signatures of at least two members of the group needed for each cheque or payment. (Please note that it is good financial practice to make sure that these people are not related)
- have up-to-date annual accounts (for groups that have been established for more than 12 months), or a 12-month cash-flow forecast for new organisations (less than 12 months old), which are presented and audited/approved in line with Charity Commission guidelines and/ or their constitution.

Branches of voluntary and community organisations

We can accept applications from branches of larger organisations, including national bodies, as long as the branch has:

- its own independent constitution and separate company registration number from the national body (where applicable)
- a bank or building society account in the name of the branch
- independent accounts in the name of the branch
- a management board or committee which can operate independently of the national body
- independent policies and procedures

- no financial dependence on the national body.

Statutory organisations
Statutory organisations include:

- local authorities
- health authorities, including health trusts
- schools and further-education colleges
- other organisations that receive public funds.

Statutory organisations will only be supported when it is clear that there is no other organisation within the community with the capacity to manage and deliver the project effectively in the target area.

Ineligible applications
Applications are not eligible for consideration by the trust if:

- they do not meet our funding themes or charitable objectives
- the project beneficiaries are located outside our recognised coalfield communities
- they are entirely or mainly set up to promote religious or political beliefs
- the activity is a statutory responsibility, or a replacement for statutory provision
- funding is to be used to exclusively draw down landfill tax credits
- the activity shows a conflict of interest with the applicant group
- it will result in individuals' personal gain or benefit
- previous grants have been unsatisfactorily managed
- an organisation/group has previously received 6 years funding for the same activity or more than one capital grant within a CRT funding period.

Bridging the Gap Grants Programme
Voluntary and community organisations and groups

Most voluntary and community organisations and groups working to regenerate coalfield communities are eligible to apply to us for funding. We may make grants to voluntary and community organisations and groups if they have the following (this includes community interest companies and social enterprises providing the activity will not result in personal/private gain and delivers a recognised social benefit):

- constitution or a set of rules to show that the group is legally eligible to receive a grant and is entitled to run the planned project. The constitution must also have an acceptable 'dissolution' clause, which guarantees that any assets purchased with a grant from the trust are kept for the benefit of the community even if the group comes to an end or is 'dissolved'
- bank or building society account in the organisation's name, with the signatures of at least two members of the group needed for each cheque or payment.

(Please note that it is good financial practice to make sure that these people are not related)
- annual accounts (for groups that have been established for more than 12-months), or a 12-month cash-flow forecast for new organisations (less than 12 months old), which are presented and audited/approved in line with Charity Commission guidelines and/or their constitution.

Branches of voluntary and community organisations

We can accept applications from branches of larger organisations, as long as the branch has:

- its own independent constitution and separate company registration number from the national body (where applicable)
- bank or building society account in the name of the branch
- independent accounts in the name of the branch
- a management board or committee which can operate independently of the national body
- independent policies and procedures
- no financial dependence on the national body.

Ineligible applications
Applications are not eligible for consideration by the trust if:

- they do not meet our funding themes or charitable objectives
- the project beneficiaries are located outside our recognised coalfield communities
- they are entirely or mainly set up to promote religious or political beliefs
- the activity is a statutory responsibility, or a replacement for statutory provision
- funding is to be used to exclusively draw down landfill tax credits
- the activity conflicts with the interest of the applicant group
- it will result in individuals' personal gain or benefit
- previous grants have been unsatisfactorily managed
- the project will take more than twelve months to complete
- the grant request is for a contribution towards a larger project with costs in excess of £100,000.

How to apply

For advice on how to apply for any of the trust's funding programmes please contact your nearest regional office. They will supply the appropriate application forms and provide advice and support to help you submit your application.

If you have any problems using our services or if you need extra support with the grant application and assessment process, please let us know how we can do more to help and we will make every effort to meet your needs. For example, we may be able to offer you documents in large print, face-to-face contact or an assessment interview involving more than one member of your group.

Regional offices

Head Office – Yorkshire
Silkstone House
Pioneer Close
Manvers Way
Wath Upon Dearne
Rotherham
S63 7JZ

Tel: 01709 760272
Fax: 01709 765599

East Midlands Office
Unit 4
Markham Vale Environment Centre
Markham Lane
Markham Vale
Chesterfield
S44 5HY

Tel: 01246 820970
Fax: 01246 827808

North East Office
The Eco Centre
Room 7b
Windmill Way
Hebburn
Tyne & Wear
NE31 1SR

Tel: 0191 428 5550
Fax: 0191 428 5005

North West Office
Unit 39
Bold Business Centre
Bold Lane
Sutton
St Helens
WA9 4TX

Tel: 01925 222066
Fax: 01925 222047

West Midlands Office
Lymedale Business Centre
Lymedale Business Park
Hooters Hall Road
Newcastle under Lyme
ST5 9QF

Tel: 01782 563112
Fax: 01782 296541

Scotland Office
2/6 The e-Centre
Cooperage Way Business Centre
Cooperage Way
Alloa
FK10 3LP

Tel: 01259 272127
Fax: 01259 272138

Wales Office
Part Unit 7
Maritime Office
Woodland Terrace
Maes-y-coed
Pontypridd
Rhondda Cynon Taff
CF37 1DZ

Tel: 01443 404455
Fax: 01443 408804

The R and S Cohen Foundation

Education, relief in need and the arts

£1.5 million (2007/08)
Beneficial area Worldwide.

42 Portland Place, London W1B 1NB
Email mel@nottinghillfilms.com
Correspondent Mel Holland
Trustees *Lady Sharon Harel-Cohen; Sir Ronald Cohen; Tamara Harel-Cohen; David Marks; Jonathan Harel-Cohen.*
CC Number 1078225
Information available Accounts were available from the Charity Commission.

The foundation was established in 1999 by Sir Ronald Cohen, chair of Bridges Ventures investment company, for general charitable purposes.

In 2007/08 the foundation had assets of £6.4 million and an income of £99,600. Grants were made totalling £1.5 million.

The beneficiaries of the largest grants during the year were the Bridges Charitable Trust (£500,000), a charity connected to Bridges Ventures, and the Portland Trust (£265,000), of which Sir Ronald Cohen is also a trustee.

Other beneficiaries included: The Prince's Foundation for Children/Art (£62,500); Refuge (£45,000); Responsible Action (£30,000); Chief Rabbinate Trust (£25,000); Jewish Leadership Council (£20,000); National Portrait Gallery (£10,000); Jewish Book Council (£5,000); Down Syndrome Education International (£3,000); and Trickle Up (£2,500).

Applications In writing to the correspondent.

The John S Cohen Foundation

General, in particular music and the arts, education and environment

£393,000 (2007/08)
Beneficial area Worldwide, in practice mainly UK.

PO Box 21277, London W9 2YH
Tel. 020 7286 6921
Correspondent Mrs Diana Helme, Foundation Administrator
Trustees *Dr David Cohen, Chair; Ms Imogen Cohen; Ms Olivia Cohen; Ms Veronica Cohen.*
CC Number 241598
Information available Accounts were available from the Charity Commission.

The objectives of the foundation are general charitable purposes in the UK or elsewhere and it is particularly active in supporting education, music and the arts and the environment, both built and natural.

In 2007/08 the foundation had assets of £8.4 million and an income of £508,500. Grants were made to 122 organisations totalling £393,000. Grants are generally for £5,000 or less.

Larger grants were made to: Southbank Centre (£48,000); Royal National Theatre (£20,000); Glyndebourne Festival and the National Gallery (£15,000 each); Royal Parks Foundation, Natural History Museum and Cambridge University Library (£10,000 each); RVW Trust (£9,000); Scottish Opera (£7,500); and Public Catalogue Foundation (£7,000).

More typical grants included those to: British School at Rome, English National Opera and Jewish Literary Trust (£5,000); Royal College of Music (£4,500); Edinburgh International Book Festival (£3,500); English Pen, INDEX on Censorship and Volunteer Reading Help (£3,000 each); British Museum, National Life Story Collection and Shelter (£2,000 each); Community of the Holy Fire – Herefordshire, Music of Life, Scottish Seabird Centre and Wildfowl and Wetlands Trust (£1,000 each).

Grants of less than £1,000 each included those to: AJEX Charitable Foundation; Cancerkin; Liberal Jewish Synagogue;

Royal Society for the Protection of Birds; Shooting Star Trust; York Late Music Festival; and Zoological Society of London.

Applications In writing to the correspondent. 'Grants are awarded after the submission of applications to the trustees. The trustees review the application to judge if the grant falls within the charity's objectives and whether the application meets its requirements in terms of the benefits it gives. Each application is discussed, reviewed and decided upon by the trustees at their regular meetings.'

The Colt Foundation

Occupational and environmental health research

£711,500 to organisations (2008)
Beneficial area UK.

New Lane, Havant, Hampshire PO9 2LY
Tel. 023 9249 1400 **Fax** 023 9249 1363
Email jackie.douglas@uk.coltgroup.com
Website www.coltfoundation.org.uk
Correspondent Mrs Jacqueline Douglas, Director
Trustees *Prof. David Coggon; Clare Gilchrist; Prof. A J Newman Taylor; Juliette O'Hea; Peter O'Hea; Alan O'Hea; Jerome O'Hea; Natasha Lebus; Patricia Lebus.*
CC Number 277189
Information available Accounts were provided by the foundation.

This foundation was established in 1978 and its primary aim is to promote and encourage research into social, medical and environmental problems created by commerce and industry.

The foundation considers applications for funding high quality research projects in the field of occupational and environmental health, particularly those aimed at discovering the cause of illnesses arising from conditions at the place of work. The work is monitored by the foundation's scientific advisers and external assessors to achieve the maximum impact with available funds. The trustees prefer to be the sole source of finance for a project.

The foundation also makes grants through selected universities and colleges to enable students to take higher degrees in subjects related to occupational and environmental health. PhD Fellowships are awarded each year, and the foundation is committed to support the MSc course in Human & Applied Physiology at King's College, London. More than 80 students have been supported since the inception of the foundation and grants to students account for over one-quarter of the foundation's annual grants.

Donations to organisations vary from a few thousand pounds to over £100,000 and may be repeated over two to five years. Beneficiaries are well-established research institutes (awards to individuals are made through these). The foundation takes a continuing interest in its research projects and holds annual review meetings.

In 2008 the foundation had assets of £17.9 million and an income of £821,500. Grants were made during the year totalling £802,000, which included £711,500 to 20 organisations and £89,000 to students.

Some institutions received more than one grant during the year. Beneficiaries included: National Heart and Lung Institute (£124,500); University of Aberdeen (£87,000); University of Central London (£38,000); University of Edinburgh (£22,000); and ELEGI – Poland (£8,400).

Exclusions Grants are not made for the general funds of another charity, directly to individuals or projects overseas.

Applications In writing to the correspondent. Initial applications should contain sufficient information for the scientific advisers to be able to comment, and include a lay summary for the trustees' first appraisal. This lay summary is regarded as important, as the majority of trustees do not have a medical or scientific background and this helps them with their decision making.

The trustees meet twice each year, normally in May and November. Applications should reach the correspondent by 23rd March and 1st October in time for these meetings so that advice can be obtained from external assessors beforehand. However, applicants can submit a single sheet 'lay summary' at any time during the year, so that advice can be given on whether the work is likely to fall within the remit of the foundation, prior to working on a full application.

The foundation does not have application forms. Applicants are asked to read the following guidelines carefully and follow them when preparing an application:

- what is the work you would like to do?
- why does the work need doing?
- who is doing or has done similar work, and how will your work add to it?
- how do you intend to carry out the work, and why do you think this is the right approach?
- what resources will you need to do the work, and are these resources available?
- who will do the work, and how much time will each of the people involved devote to it?
- how long will the work take?
- how much money do you need to complete the work?
- when do you plan to start?

Applicants are advised to visit the foundation's helpful website.

Colyer-Fergusson Charitable Trust

Social isolation, exclusion or poverty, community activity (often through churches), church maintenance, environment and the arts

£601,500 (2008/09)
Beneficial area Kent.

Hogarth House, 34 Paradise Road, Richmond TW9 1SE
Tel. 020 8948 3388
Email grantadmin@cfct.org.uk
Website www.cfct.org.uk
Correspondent Jacqueline Rae, Director
Trustees *Jonathan Monckton, Chair; Nicholas Fisher; Robert North; Ruth Murphy.*
CC Number 258958
Information available Accounts and information on new priority areas were provided by the trust.

In 1969 Sir James Herbert Hamilton Colyer-Fergusson created the Colyer-

Fergusson Charitable Trust with an initial settlement of £50,000. The trust aims to make grants to charities and churches in Kent to improve quality of life, tackle poverty, social isolation or exclusion and protect the natural resources and heritage of the local areas for their inhabitants. It also supports the sustainability of local churches.

Extra consideration is given to projects that encourage self help, involve users in their management, have built in evaluation procedures and will use funds to lever funding from other sources.

The trust requires all grant recipients to submit monitoring reports online to keep the trustees informed about the progress of the work supported by the grant.

In 2008/09 the trust had assets of £26.9 million and an income of £831,500. Grants were made totalling £601,500 under the previous priority areas of:

- projects that are innovative or developmental and aim to tackle social isolation, exclusion or poverty as they affect the community
- projects that involve the utilisation of church buildings or other church resources by the wider community and can demonstrate a practical need
- projects that involve the preservation of the natural environment or heritage and promote community access to these resources
- projects that will use the arts to provide the community with a new creative experience or increase access to the arts in locations where access is limited.

Beneficiaries included: Minster Abbey (£75,000); Deal Town Football Club (£40,000); St Giles Trust (£30,000); Alkham Valley Community Project (£21,000); Capel-le-Fern Village Hall (£15,000); Thanington Neighbourhood Community Centre (£12,500); Betteshanger Social Club & Community Centre (£10,000); and Volunteer Reading Help (£5,000).

New priority areas announced at the end of November 2009 are:

Supporting Communities in Kent

Kent is a large and diverse county characterised by areas of affluence and pockets of deprivation. The trustees keep local needs under regular review and consider the work of other Kent funders to ensure that their grants are targeted where they can have the greatest impact. With this in mind the trustees have decided to focus their grants on the following six programme areas:

- safer communities
- protecting and supporting older vulnerable people
- refugees and asylum seekers
- caring for carers
- transition to independence for young people leaving care
- encouraging active living

Supporting Churches in Kent

The trust has supported churches in Kent for over thirty years. The trustees are aware that churches in Kent are not only important local landmarks but also essential community resources at the heart of many villages. Dwindling congregation numbers means that it is increasingly difficult for parishes to raise the funds to maintain church buildings. This programme will make grants to support the fabric and maintenance of churches in Kent, improve and re-order church buildings and where possible encourage their sustainability.

Full details of the new priority areas are available from the trust's website.

Exclusions No grants are considered for the following:

- animal welfare charities
- individuals directly
- research (except practical research designed to benefit the local community directly)
- hospitals or schools
- political activities
- commercial ventures or publications
- the purchase of vehicles including minibuses
- overseas travel or holidays
- retrospective grants or loans
- direct replacement of statutory funding or activities that are primarily the responsibility of central or local government
- large capital, endowment or widely distributed appeals
- applications from churches or charities outside Kent.

Applications All applicants must complete the online application form. There is no deadline for applications and they will all be acknowledged. Trustees meet regularly during the year and decisions are usually processed within six months. All applicants will be notified in writing. The trust requests applicants, where possible, to submit any supporting material by email as scanned documents or files.

Comic Relief

Social welfare
£12 million in the UK (2007/08)
Beneficial area UK and overseas.

5th Floor, 89 Albert Embankment, London SE1 7TP

Tel. 020 7820 5555

Minicom 020 7820 5500

Email ukgrants@comicrelief.com

Website www.comicrelief.com

Correspondent Gilly Green, Head of UK Grants

CC Number 326568

Information available Annual report and accounts are available from the Charity Commission. Full information is also available from the charity's excellent website.

Since 1985 Comic Relief has raised around £500 million to tackle poverty and social injustice in the UK, Africa, and more recently in some of the poorest countries in other parts of the world. This entry is primarily concerned with grantmaking in the UK.

In 2002, Comic Relief started a second initiative, Sport Relief. Half of its income goes to the International Children and Young People's programme, the other half to projects in the UK that are using sport to increase social cohesion and inclusion.

The charity also administers Robbie Williams' Give It Sum Fund for community-based projects in his home area of north Staffordshire.

The charity principally receives its income through the generosity of the public via its Red Nose Day fundraising event. This is held every two years in partnership with the BBC, and the extent of the grantmaking depends entirely on the success of the preceding event.

In 2007/08 grants across all programmes totalled almost £47 million (£71.3 million in 2006/07) – this includes £12 million of grants made in the UK. Red Nose Day 2009 raised over £78 million. The following summarised press release describes the charity's new strategy (detailed below) for spending this money:

The new grants strategy builds on Comic Relief's experience as a grant maker, as well as the changing needs and priorities of the most disadvantaged communities in the UK and internationally.

Key highlights are:

New commitments to small grants in partnership with local organisations – As a result of the global recession more communities and individuals are affected by poverty. Comic Relief has made more money available to fund local solutions with local people and grantmakers. Comic Relief will be funding £6.1 million through the Community Foundation Network in support of disadvantaged local communities across the UK. Also, building on international partnerships, the African Women's Development Fund and the Nelson Mandela Children's Fund, will be making Comic Relief funded grants to smaller organisations focusing on women, children and young people in Africa.

New Special initiatives – As part of Comic Relief's ongoing commitment to create systemic, sustainable change in the lives of poor and disadvantaged people the charity has new areas of focus internationally and has now formed strategic partnerships in the areas of health and education. Since Red Nose Day, Comic Relief has already invested £6.3 million to tackle malaria in Africa (in Uganda and Zambia). Education is an issue Comic Relief has funded for many years; it is now strengthening its commitment and investing more money in long-term special initiatives, with £10 million to help get children into and achieving in school in Africa. In addition to the new areas of focus, in the UK Comic Relief can announce an additional £2 million over two years for Time to Change – the anti-stigma campaign which is working to change public attitudes towards mental health, which it first funded in 2008.

New focus on impact and learning – Comic Relief is setting out the difference it aims to make through its grant giving and explicitly states what outcomes it wants to achieve through each of its grants programmes, in partnership with the organisations it supports. It aims to really understand the difference its money is making through the changes in people's lives (in ways that are in keeping with the size and ambitions of the grant). It is committed to sharing this learning with the sector, other funders, policy makers, with communities who are involved and the public who donate so generously.

New open programmes – Comic Relief now has a 'Sport for Change' programme which is open in the UK and in development internationally. For the first time organisations will be able to apply for funding to bring about social change through sport. The Nelson Mandela Children's Fund have also recently been awarded £500,000 to make grants to smaller organisations in Southern Africa who are using sport as a tool for change in the lives of disadvantaged children and young people.

Comic Relief Grants Director, Judith McNeill, said: 'This new grants strategy is informed by more than 20 years of grant making, across the UK and internationally, mostly in Africa, working with thousands of fantastic organisations. We want to continue to work in partnership, to share our stories and successes, including with the public, and crucially share our challenges and failures with each other. In the midst of a recession we have a responsibility to use our resources well and make every penny count.

Grantmaking principles

The charity describes its UK grant making principles as follows:

We aim to treat all organisations applying to us fairly and efficiently. We try to make applying for a grant as simple as possible, while making sure that the money the public works so hard to raise is well spent.

What we look for in applications

We always get many more applications than we can fund, so we have to make some difficult choices. We want to make sure that our funding is spread around the UK and that we support some large-scale initiatives as well as smaller, community-based groups. We also want to see that your organisation is well managed, your project is well planned and that you have the skills and experience to carry out the work.

We will undertake various checks to establish the authenticity of your organisation.

When we come to consider your application in detail we will look at the extent to which you work within the following principles as we believe that working in this way will help deliver the best possible outcomes.

We have designed our application form to help us understand the extent to which you take account of these principles in the way you work. You may find it helpful to consider the information below as you complete your application.

Understanding the context

Organisations need to demonstrate their understanding of the local or national context in which they are working, and the root causes of the issues they wish to tackle. This should include local decision making structures and the role of other relevant players.

Consulting with key players

We want to see that organisations are informed by the views of relevant stakeholders and where possible ensure that people who will benefit from projects are consulted at the outset and their views incorporated in project design.

Building on good practice and considering new ideas and approaches

We want to see how organisations are drawing on 'good practice' and knowledge of 'what works' to inform the work they do. But we also welcome projects that wish to experiment with new ideas and approaches to familiar problems.

Involving users

Where possible, we want to see how people benefiting from the projects we fund actively participate in those projects – from membership of advisory groups and trustee boards to feeding back on the value of the services – to help inform future plans.

Valuing diversity and working with others

We expect organisations to demonstrate a commitment to diversity and show how this runs through their governance, service delivery and policy development. We recognise that some organisations will need help to develop their approach to diversity.

Evaluating and learning

Organisations will need to show how they have learnt from past experience, how they capture the learning from the work they do, and how they will use the evidence they have built up to inform their future plans.

UK Grant Programmes

For the period 2009–2012 the charity's UK grants programmes are focusing on the following areas:

Mental Health
Background
- mental health problems affect one in four people at some point in their lives.
- as well as dealing with the impact of living with mental ill-health, many people also have to cope with stigma, discrimination and social exclusion, and can find it hard to get their voices heard in the decisions which affect their lives.

Too many people continue to have little say in their treatment or the services they need. Comic Relief has had a long history of helping people get their voices heard and promote a fairer society, and since 2005 mental health has become a key focus of our work.

Aim of the programme

This programme aims to promote the rights and support the recovery of people who have mental health problems, and to help them feel more included in society. It also aims to reduce the stigma and discrimination faced by people with mental health problems.

We believe that change will be most effective and sustainable if organisations working in this field are led by those with direct experience of mental ill-health. We recognise that some groups may not currently be user led, but we will want to see organisations moving towards this over the lifetime of their grant.

Within this user-led ethos, we want to support work which helps people get the services they need and their voices heard. This might be through individual or collective advocacy, user groups, peer support or campaigning for example. We also want to support work which aims to reduce stigma and discrimination.

Outcomes
The organisations we fund will need to show how their work will help deliver one or more of the following outcomes:

- greater involvement of people who have mental health problems in decisions that affect their lives
- a reduction in stigma and discrimination, and a positive change in people's attitudes towards mental health
- more inclusive and accessible mental health services and organisations, in particular for people from black and minority ethnic communities

Who will we fund?
This programme has a strong user-led ethos. By this, we mean that projects will need to show how people with direct experience of mental ill-health are actively and meaningfully involved in and leading the work. In most cases, we will look for a majority of people with direct experience to make up the trustee board or governing body. Where this is not the case, we will seek a firm commitment to involving users in the running of the project and where appropriate, want to see a move towards becoming a user-led organisation.

We encourage applications using a variety of approaches including advocacy, the development of social enterprises, user or peer support groups and campaigning activities – although these are examples only and we will consider any work which meets the aims and outcomes above.

We are especially keen to support work which addresses the needs and rights of people from communities who are often overlooked, such as those from black and minority ethnic communities or older people.

Other important information
The focus of this programme is to ensure people get access to the services they need, their rights are recognised and their voices heard. It also aims to reduce stigma and discrimination. We will therefore not usually fund core service delivery, such as therapeutic interventions. In addition, we will only fund other types of projects such as employment initiatives if they are run by people with direct experience of mental health problems.

Domestic and Sexual Abuse (Young People)
Background
- The impact of domestic and sexual abuse on young people is widespread: more than 750,000 children and young people witness violence in the home.
- Young women are almost four times more likely to experience sexual violence than older women.

Since the early 1990s, Comic Relief has worked to tackle domestic violence at a local and national level. Over the last four years we have focused our grantmaking on young survivors: young people who have experienced abuse themselves or have witnessed family violence. This work has given us a clear insight into the critical and often hidden needs faced by this group, and we know that services remain patchy and underfunded. This year we have widened our focus to include sexual abuse.

Aim of the programme
This programme aims to provide support for young people aged 11–25 who have witnessed or directly experienced domestic and sexual abuse and meets one or more of the outcomes listed below.

How we define 'domestic and sexual abuse':

Our criteria includes: young people who have grown up in homes where they witness violence and harm. It also includes young people directly affected by abuse caused by a family member, by an outsider such as a stranger or family friend, or as a result of their own dating experiences.

Work will be funded to meet both immediate and longer-term needs. There is no one solution for young people who have grown up in the shadow of abuse; we want to hear from you about what works.

There are two strands to the open programme:

- Crisis Support:
We will fund support services with the aim of helping young survivors to cope with the physical, emotional and mental harm that they have experienced. This could include services such as counselling, advocacy and group work.

Applications should demonstrate how your support services will build a safer future for young survivors. This could include activities that help young people cope better or increasing their understanding of abuse.

- Young Voices:
We will fund work that helps young people to heal through having a voice. This could include setting up a new survivors group or support for an existing group.

This fund will also cover work which aims to build networks of young survivors who can speak out to policy makers, planners and the sector, so that their views and voices are heard directly.

Outcomes
The organisations we fund will need to show how their work will help deliver one or more of the following outcomes:

- Crisis Support:
Young survivors aged 11–25 feel that support services have helped them to cope and improve their mental and emotional wellbeing, or helped to keep them safe and increase their resilience against future harm.

- Young Voices:
Young survivors aged 11–25 feel that having a voice and hearing from fellow survivors has helped to progress their healing process. Policy makers and planners are more aware of the needs of young survivors.

Who will we fund?
We welcome applications from a range of agencies who reach young survivors; we will give priority to applications from groups who can demonstrate a track record around domestic and sexual abuse, or work with young survivors.

This is a funding programme focusing on the needs of survivors aged 11–25; we do not fund work with younger children. We are particularly keen to explore work with young women aged 16–25 in relation to our 'Young Voices' initiative, and in order to bridge the gap between adult and children services.

We welcome applications for work with young boys and young men as well as girls and young women. We recognise the gendered nature of domestic and sexual abuse and would like ALL work to be grounded in an understanding about the dynamics of power and control.

We are especially keen to encourage applications for work with young people from black and minority ethnic communities as well as hard to reach groups of survivors such as young people excluded from school and young people at risk of homelessness.

Other important information
Defining domestic and sexual abuse in relation to young people is often complicated, with agencies working to different criteria (for example the government only defines domestic abuse survivors from the age of 16). If you would like to talk to us about whether your work meets our criteria please ring us for a chat.

Refugee and Asylum Seeking Women

Background

- According to the UN, refugee and asylum seeking women are more likely to be affected by violence than any other group of women
- As a result they are often forced to flee their homes and seek sanctuary elsewhere in the world.

Comic Relief has a long commitment to supporting refugees and asylum seekers and over the last four years, we have paid special attention to the needs of women who have experienced rape, torture and other forms of violence in their home countries.

For those who arrive here in the UK, even with the source of persecution behind them, many women are often too frightened or ashamed to tell their stories. Without the support to disclose their traumatic experiences, they are not able to present the full stories behind their claims for asylum, and as a result many women are denied the right to stay. They can then end up living in poverty, becoming destitute and feeling so desperate that they are exploited again in the UK or returned to dangerous situations in their home countries.

Aim of the programme

This programme aims to provide support for refugee and asylum seeking women who have experienced rape, torture and other forms of violence in their home countries and meets one or more of the outcomes listed below. We are especially keen to make sure that women get the help they need in making their claims for asylum, and also get access to emotional and practical services they need to help rebuild their lives.

There are two strands to the open programme:

- **Direct support to women**

We will fund support services with the aim of helping women cope better with the trauma they have experienced. This could include services such as counselling, group work or self-help support. We will also fund services that help women access legal support, health care and housing for example.

- **Training**

We are also interested in supporting organisations to develop training for people working both in refugee and mainstream organisations to increase their skills, knowledge and practice in working with this vulnerable group. We hope that some of this work may be accredited and will have the potential to be adopted more widely by other organisations.

Outcomes

The organisations we fund will need to show how their work will help deliver one or more of the following outcomes:

- refugee and asylum seeking women will feel more able to cope with the trauma they have experienced
- women will get the specialist support they need to make successful applications for asylum around rape, violence and torture
- organisations will have increased knowledge of the needs of vulnerable refugee and asylum seeking women and be able to meet their needs more effectively.

Who will we fund?

We welcome applications from a range of agencies who can reach this vulnerable group of women. We will give priority to organisations with a strong track record of working with this group or who can demonstrate a broad understanding of services that are needed.

We will generally fund work targeting women aged 18 and over, but may consider work with younger women so long as it does not replace services that would be considered a statutory responsibility.

Other important information

If you would like to talk to us about whether your work meets our criteria, please ring us.

Sport for Change

Background

- Over recent years there has been a growth in the number of agencies thinking about the positive role sport can play in our lives.
- As well as the more obvious health and participation benefits, there has been growing awareness of the broader social, emotional and cohesion opportunities that sport can bring.
- The 2012 Olympics and increased measures around sport in schools have also helped put 'sport for good' onto the public agenda.

Since 2002, we have funded a range of sports-based projects exploring how sport can be used to bring about positive change. Work has included looking at how sport can help to tackle conflict in communities, as well as bringing improvements to the lives of people who are isolated or excluded. While sport alone will never be the solution to poverty, it can work in conjunction with broader community programmes to bring about changes such as increased engagement and a reduction in isolation.

We have developed this new programme to support a range of innovative projects that are using sport as a tool for making a real difference in the communities in which they are based.

Aim of the programme

The aim of this programme is to understand more about how sport can play a part in delivering positive change within the lives of individuals and communities, and to meet one or more of the outcomes listed below.

We will fund organisations that are using sport to address a social issue or community concern such as substance use, crime related problems, integration, exclusion of older people, community cohesion, gangs or knife crime, mental health, and young people at risk. These are examples only and we welcome applications for work tackling any social issue so long as the need for the work is clearly explained.

Outcomes

The organisations we fund will need to show how their work will help deliver one or more of the following outcomes:

- increased sense of inclusion and well-being by marginalised and disadvantaged people
- greater community involvement
- an increased understanding of how sport can help bring about positive changes in the lives of individuals and communities
- greater knowledge across the community and sports sectors about effective work which uses sport as a tool for social change.

Who will we fund?

We welcome applications from community groups and organisations using sport as part of a broader programme of work to bring about change at an individual and/or community level. We will fund across all age ranges and within a broad range of communities.

We are happy to receive applications from consortia of agencies as long as there is a lead community-based organisation. Applicants will also need to:

- demonstrate how they are using sport as part of a broader programme to achieve a measurable social change or impact
- show how the work is based in community development principles
- have monitoring and evaluation systems in place to track the impact of the work.

Other important information

This programme aims to fund projects that are using sport as a tool for social change. We therefore cannot fund:

- projects which aim only to increase participation in sport
- projects aiming to develop sporting excellence
- individual athletes or sports teams
- one-off sporting events

The maximum grant size in this programme is £100,000 in total.

If you would like to talk to us about whether your work meets our criteria please ring us for a chat.

How to Apply

An application to Sport for Change begins with an initial 'Letter of Interest' and then, if invited, a full proposal. The Letter of Interest should be no more than 2 sides of A4 (minimum font size Arial, 11pt) and should cover:

- a clear analysis of the issue or concern to be addressed in the area
- a description of the organisation and an indication of competence in the area of the proposal
- a description of the project including:
  – who it will benefit
  – a description of the activities you will run (and their fit into a broader programme of work)
  – an outline of the positive changes you want to bring about for the people you are working with
- how the project will lead to new ways of thinking and acting
- a brief overview of your budget, income sources and costings for the project.

Deadlines: Letters of Interest may be submitted at any time and may take up to eight weeks to be reviewed.

Full Proposal: If an application is chosen for further consideration, you will be invited to submit a full proposal. Invited organisations have up to four months to submit a full proposal and need to allow at least 12 weeks for a funding decision once the proposal has been submitted.

Sexually Exploited and Trafficked Young People (aged 11 to 25)
Background

- Young people are at risk of sexual exploitation. 75% of women working in prostitution started before they were 18; the majority want to get out.
- Trafficking is a growing problem, with the UK recognised as a significant transit and destination country for trafficked children and young adults, and the internet continues to be used as a means of sexually exploiting young people.
- Those trafficked for other reasons such as for domestic servitude, benefit fraud or growing cannabis are at also at high risk of sexual exploitation.
- This exploitation has very harmful effects; trafficking and sexual exploitation puts young people at risk and damages the wellbeing of those affected, often pushing vulnerable young people further into poverty.

Comic Relief has been funding work in this area for several years. Despite a welcome increase in the attention given to this issue by statutory and voluntary services, there is still a lack of accurate information, young people's circumstances often go unrecognised by professionals and services on the ground remain patchy. For this reason, we continue to fund in this area.

Aim of the programme

This programme aims to reduce harm to young people who have been sexually exploited or trafficked.

We will fund work which addresses the above aim and one or more of the outcomes below. We are especially keen to help young people find routes out of prostitution or other forms of sexual exploitation, but we know for some this is difficult and will take time. We will therefore fund work which meets both immediate and longer term needs.

We recognise that this remains a growing field of work, so if you have an innovative project that you feel addresses the overall aim rather than one of the outcomes below, please contact us for discussion as we may be interested in supporting your work.

Outcomes

The organisations we fund will need to show how their work will help deliver one or more of the following outcomes:

- fewer young people will be sexually exploited or trafficked
- more sexually exploited and/or trafficked young people and those at risk will know their rights, understand their situation and/or have access to the help and support they need
- more sexually exploited and/or trafficked young people will have increased choice to make positive decisions about their futures.

Who will we fund?

We welcome applications from a range of organisations supporting young people aged 11–25 – some set up specifically to support sexually exploited young people and those at risk; others with a wider young people's brief who want to target this group. We will also support other organisations working around sexual exploitation or trafficking who want to address young people's needs; or projects in other fields whose work includes these young people at risk, such as housing.

We recognise we need to be flexible around the age range of people supported. Some young people, for example, young men and some trafficked young people, may not come to the attention of professionals or realise their situation themselves until they are 'older'. Therefore, although we expect that most of the services we fund will be aimed at younger people we will consider supporting projects working with those over the age of 25 where the case for need is made.

Young People and Alcohol (aged 11 to 25)
Background

- The proportion of young people drinking has decreased in recent years; but the amount of 'frequent' teenage drinkers has risen sharply. This increase is widely acknowledged to contribute to social problems such as poor health, violence and anti-social behaviour.
- Some young people, such as those living in deprived areas or leaving care, are seen as especially vulnerable to drink related problems, and alcohol use at this age is a significant factor in school exclusion, teenage pregnancy, and youth offending.
- Services for young people who have got into difficulty with drinking are patchy; and despite the huge cost to society, this sector is poorly funded. So we continue to run a dedicated alcohol programme with a focus on young people.

Aim of the programme

This programme aims to provide support for young people aged 11–25 who are drinking excessively and meets one or more of the outcomes listed below.

We will fund services that aim to reduce the levels of young people's drinking, create greater awareness of the dangers of harmful drinking and provide direct support to young drinkers at the greatest risk – those drinking excessively and dangerously. This could include individual or group work sessions, or both.

Outcomes

The organisations we fund will need to show how their work will help deliver one or more of the following outcomes:

- a reduction in alcohol consumption by young people
- a reduction in harm and increased access to help for young people who have alcohol problems
- closer working relationships between alcohol and young people's services
- an increase in relevant skills to deliver services targeted at young people who have alcohol problems.

Who will we fund?

We welcome applications from voluntary and community organisations working with young people with alcohol problems aged between 11 and 25.

We particularly welcome applications from agencies working with those who are vulnerable and at high risk of heavy drinking. We are also interested in funding services that target particular groups such as those from black and minority ethnic communities and young women, as these groups find it especially hard to access services. We also welcome applications for work supporting training that equips staff with specialist skills in working with young people with alcohol problems.

We particularly want to encourage joint applications from young people's agencies and alcohol agencies where expertise can be shared, innovative approaches developed and where the added value of working together can be shown.

We also recognise that some organisations will work with people around a variety of substances. In these circumstances we specifically want to support the alcohol element of the work and our funding is likely to reflect this.

Other important information
This programme targets young people who are drinking excessively and need help. We are also interested in how we can help prevent high levels of drinking amongst young people. We will work with others to establish a funding programme led by young people using their personal experience to create innovative education, prevention, and awareness resources.

Young People with Mental Health Problems (aged 11 to 25)
Background
- For many young people adolescence is a confusing time of change; for those who experience additional difficulties with their mental health, this can be a frightening and isolating time.
- Over the last twenty-five years rates of anxiety and depression amongst young people have increased by 70%.

Young people are often reluctant to seek help from mental health services for fear of being stigmatised, and despite the greater focus on children's and young people's well-being, the availability of support both within and outside mental health settings is still patchy. If left unsupported, the impact of ill health and stigma can be devastating, but with the right help at the right time, young people with mental health problems can make great improvements to their well being. We have a long history of supporting young people with mental health problems and we are committed to continuing to grow this area.

Aim of the programme
This programme aims to provide support to young people with mental health problems aged 11–25. We will fund work which meets the aim above and one or both of the outcomes below.

There are two strands to the programme:

- Services for young people
We are keen to fund a range of services and approaches to help young people experiencing mental health problems to make positive changes in their lives. This could include individual counselling, group work or peer support. We especially

welcome applications where support is provided in settings in which young people feel comfortable, and do not fear being labelled or stigmatised.

- Training
We will also fund work that ensures those working with young people with mental health problems, especially in general youth work settings, have access to good quality training to improve their skill base and confidence levels.

Outcomes
The organisations we fund will need to show how their work will help deliver one or more of the following outcomes:

- increased access to appropriate services for young people with mental health problems, resulting in improved mental health
- a greater understanding and specialist skill base amongst practitioners working with young people with mental health needs.

Who will we fund?
We encourage applications from organisations working with young people aged 11–25 providing general counselling and therapeutic interventions, as well as specialist projects focused on particular issues such as eating disorders or bi-polar conditions.

We also welcome applications from organisations targeting particular sections of the community such as young homeless people or asylum seekers. We are keen to look at innovative ways of supporting young people with mental health problems such as peer support and other young people-led approaches.

We are happy to support work taking place in general youth work settings as well as within specialist services. All work however must target young people with mental health problems. We will also fund specialist mental health training for staff working with this group of young people.

Other important information
We recognise the importance of strong local partnerships between voluntary and statutory agencies in delivering effective services to young people with mental health problems. We know that, in practice, this means that agencies from these different sectors may be sharing resources and working together on specific projects. We are interested in hearing how you work within the local strategies on young people and mental health and how our funds can help you achieve the best possible outcomes in this complex funding environment.

Please note, we cannot support work seeking to improve young people's general well-being in this programme, as we target our funds towards those with recognised mental

health problems with a need for specialist support.

Older People
Background
The numbers of older people are set to rise significantly (there are now more people aged 65+ than children under 16) and many will continue to enjoy healthier, happier lives for longer. But as the numbers grow, there will be increasing demands on services. This, together with the impact of age discrimination, poverty and isolation, will mean that the needs of many older people may go unmet. Many will find they will have little say in decisions which affect their lives and little opportunity to participate in the communities in which they live.

We believe that older people themselves are uniquely placed to help tackle these challenges. With firsthand knowledge of the issues affecting them, older people can be supported to develop and deliver projects to bring about real change at the local, regional and national level. Whilst we recognise that older people are a diverse group and have different lifestyles, abilities and needs, we believe that the one thing they have in common is a wealth of experience that can enrich the communities in which they live.

Comic Relief has a long standing commitment to working with older people. Our focus has been on ensuring the needs of older people are met, their rights upheld and their views respected.

Aim of the programme
This programme aims to support older people to bring positive change to their communities. The programme also aims to help older people feel less isolated, especially those who are most excluded.

We believe that change will be most effective and sustainable if it is led by older people, as they are best placed to identify their own needs and propose solutions to address those needs.

Projects must therefore be able to demonstrate the active engagement of older people in the development and delivery of the work.

What we will fund
We welcome a wide range of applications from community groups and organisations where older people are developing ideas for action and change. We encourage applications using a variety of approaches including the development of social enterprises, forums for older people, local community activities and campaigning; although we will consider any work which meets the aims and outcomes of the programme.

Examples of the types of projects we will fund include:

- bringing the generations together to learn from each other through, for example, the creative arts or IT
- older people acting as a resource to other older people and supporting those who may be less physically and mentally able
- projects that are engaging hard to reach groups such as Black and minority ethnic elders
- activities which generate profits to further social or environmental goals, such as community cafes run by older people.

Outcomes
The organisations we fund will need to show how their work will help deliver one or more of the following outcomes:

- an increase in the participation of older people to effect positive change
- an increase in the involvement of older people who are the most excluded
- a decrease in older people's feelings of isolation.

Who will we fund?
We will fund projects targeted at the 65+ age group and particularly welcome applications from older people which address the needs of those who experience the greatest levels of isolation and exclusion such as Black and minority ethnic elders, frail older people, older people with mental health needs, older carers and those on lower incomes.

Other important information
The programme is intended to support older people becoming a force for change. The extent to which this is demonstrated will be considered when we assess an application.

We cannot make grants to:

- individual older people or
- for services which statutory bodies have a duty to provide.

We expect most awards to be between £15,000 and £40,000 per year depending on the size and nature of the project for which you are applying. Grants may be for up to three years. If you have an idea which meets the criteria but costs more than £40,000, then please call us to discuss your proposal before you submit your application.

If you would like to talk to us about whether your work meets our criteria, please email us at: ukgrants@comicrelief.com or call us on 020 7820 555.

Local communities
Background
One in five people in the UK live in poverty.

Poverty in the UK today is much more complex than simply being a measure of homelessness or unemployment; it can affect old and young, families and single people, and many whole communities face deprivation. People living in disadvantaged communities face a range of issues such as poor employment opportunities and reduced levels of physical and mental health.

Comic Relief has made a longstanding pledge to place funding into disadvantaged communities. We believe that local people should have a say in the decisions that are made about where they live, and are often best placed to know what is needed to bring about change.

We want to enable groups to create strong, thriving communities; this could involve helping people of all ages to feel more included in their community, provide more accessible services, or supporting people to build new skills. We also want to make sure that communities are equipped to respond to challenging economic, social and cultural trends. Whether it is unemployment or older people living in isolation, many individuals need help coping with challenging times.

How to apply
The funding for our communities programme is devolved to the Community Foundation Network. [Contact your local community foundation to find out if they are administering this programme in your area – further information can be found on the Community Foundation Network's website: www.communityfoundations.org.uk]

Comic Relief's full UK Grant Making Strategy is available from its website.

Exclusions There are certain types of work and organisations that Comic Relief does not fund. Please do not apply if your proposal falls into one of these categories:

- grants to individuals
- medical research or hospitals
- churches or other religious bodies where the monies will be used for religious purposes
- work where there is statutory responsibility to provide funding
- projects where the work has already taken place
- statutory bodies, such as local authorities or Primary Care Trusts or organisations seeking funding to replace cuts by statutory bodies
- profit-making organisations, except social enterprises
- funding for minibuses.

Applications We receive many more applications than we are able to fund and we usually only support work which fits our current priorities, so before you apply for funding, please read through all of the following carefully.

Essential Information for Applicants

Who can apply?
We accept applications from the voluntary and community sector throughout the UK including: constituted voluntary and community groups, charities, social enterprises, co-operatives, faith organisations, and community interest companies.

What we fund
We make grants in the programme areas outlined. You can make only one application to one programme at a time.

Where we fund
We fund work in England, Scotland, Wales and Northern Ireland – and are very keen to make sure that we reach all parts of the UK, especially areas which often miss out, such as rural communities.

How long we fund for
We usually make grants for between one and three years.

The type of grants we give
We can give grants for running costs and capital costs.

However, we give building costs a very low priority, and only fund these in exceptional circumstances. We do not fund capital costs where they are part of a much larger appeal.

We usually make grants to cover project costs, but we recognise that you may wish to include a contribution towards your organisational costs so that it reflects the true cost of running your project. This is sometimes known as full cost recovery. We are happy for you to do this, but you will need to show us how you have worked out these additional organisational costs.

How much we give
We can pay for all or some of your project costs, but we encourage you to get some of your funding from other sources if you can. There is no minimum or maximum grant in most of our programmes, but where there are limits, these are clearly stated in the programme guidelines. Our grants on average vary between £25,000 and £40,000 per year, and rarely exceed this upper limit.

We are unlikely to make large grants to very small organisations, and we will not usually fund all the costs of an application made by charities with an annual income over £10 million. These charities will be expected to make a contribution themselves or secure other income towards the costs of the project.

If your work is regional, national or provides a model that could be widely replicated, we may be able to fund at a higher level. Please call us to discuss this before you submit an application.

Reserves

Any well-run organisation should have some money set aside, to cope with changes in funding and to be able to meet their commitments. However, where your 'free' (unrestricted or designated) reserves are significant (more than one year's running costs), we will ask you to set out your reserves policy and to explain why you really need these funds. In these cases, we may not fund the full amount you ask for or may not fund at all if we feel you have enough money to pay for the work yourself.

The number of applications you can make

You can make only one application at a time. If your application is unsuccessful, we are happy to provide feedback on the reasons for this. However, you cannot reapply for the same or a different project for another 12 months.

If you currently hold a grant with us, you can apply again, for the same or a different piece of work, within the last nine months of your existing grant. We do not give automatic priority to work we have funded in the past.

The number of grants you can hold at any one time

You can usually only hold one grant at any one time. Sometimes, however, large, national organisations may hold more than one grant with us where they can demonstrate they are the only organisation able to deliver work in a specific location or the work is particularly groundbreaking. In this situation, please contact us before submitting your application.

Please ensure that you have read the charity's Grant Making Principles and Essential Information for applicants. An application form is available via the charity's website.

The Ernest Cook Trust

Educational grants focusing on children and young people for the environment, rural conservation, arts and crafts, literary and numeracy and research

£1.6 million (2007/08)
Beneficial area UK.

Fairford Park, Fairford GL7 4JH

Tel. 01285 712492 **Fax** 01285 713417
Email grants@ernestcooktrust.org.uk
Website www.ernestcooktrust.org.uk
Correspondent Mrs Ros Leigh, Grants administrator
Trustees *Anthony Bosanquet, Chair; Harry Henderson; Andrew Christie-Miller; Patrick Maclure; Miles C Tuely; Victoria Edwards.*

CC Number 313497

Information available Accounts were available from the Charity Commission. Information is also available via the trust's website.

Ernest Edward Cook was a grandson and joint heir to the fortune of Thomas Cook, the famous travel agent. He presided over the banking and foreign exchange business of the firm, and was probably responsible for the successful development of the traveller's cheque. When the travel agency was sold in 1928, Ernest Cook devoted the remainder of his life to the preservation of English country houses, the estates to which they belonged, the paintings and furniture which they contained and also to the well-being of the communities of those estates.

Before his death, Mr Cook had made arrangements for the continuing care of his estates by either The Ernest Cook Trust or The National Trust, of which he was for a long time by far the greatest benefactor. He left his extensive collection of paintings to the National Art Collections Fund, for the benefit of provincial galleries.

The Ernest Cook Trust was established in 1952 and is its purposes are to maintain the estates given to it by Ernest Cook and to give grants to support educational and research projects. Many of the schemes it supports relate to the countryside and environmental and architectural conservation, and all are educational in emphasis.

The trust's grants policy is influenced by Ernest Cook's two great passions, namely art and country estates. Grants, which must always be for clearly educational purposes, aim principally to focus upon the needs of children and young people. To that end the trustees are keen to support applications from the UK which educate young people about the environment and the countryside. Projects which introduce pupils to the wide spectrum of the arts are also encouraged.

All applications are expected to link in with either the national curriculum or recognised qualifications and particular weight is given to projects which improve levels of literacy and numeracy.

It is appreciated that sometimes a contribution will be required towards the salary of an education officer, but the trust always expects to be a part funder and does not usually commit funds for more than one year; successful applicants are normally asked to wait two years before applying for further help.

A few research grants are awarded if the work links in to the trust's purposes.

Grants range from £100 to £4,000 in the small grants category, of which modest amounts for educational resources for small groups form a large part. At the two main meetings grants are mostly in the range of between £5,000 – £15,000, with only a few larger awards for projects closely connected with the trust's educational interests. One award of £50,000 is made annually; application for this is by invitation only.

In 2007/08 the trust had assets of £82.2 million and an income of £4.7 million. Grants were made totalling £1.6 million, categorised as follows:

Arts, crafts and architecture – 184 grants totalling £848,000
Beneficiaries included: Edward Barnsley Trust (£25,000), to cover the cost of an apprentice; Chetham's School of Music (£21,000), towards an early years music project; English National Ballet (£12,700), for the spring education programme; Artsway (£10,600), towards a project to encourage artists to work in schools; Foundation for Young Musicians (£10,000), towards bursaries for young musicians; Liverpool Cathedral (£9,000), to cover the cost of instrument tuition for members of Girl's Voices; Scottish Ensemble (£7,500), to help with the school based element of the Lifelong Learning Programme; Withywood Community School (£6,800), towards the cost of ten music lessons for 60 pupils; Children's Music Workshops (£5,000), to help with the Bess of Hardwick project for schools; and Langham Arts Trust (£4,000), towards the cost of Proms Praise for Schools. Small grants of £3,000 or less included those to: Canterbury Festival, Scottish Schools Orchestra Trust, Victoria Baths Trust, Same Sky, Lifeforce, Bishopsland Educational Trust and Donagh Weefolk Playgroup.

Environment – 139 grants totalling £512,500
Beneficiaries included: Oxford University Botanic Garden (£25,000), towards the Oxfordshire 2010 Challenge for schools; Year of Food and Farming (£20,000), towards educational work in the North

East and South West; Good Gardeners' Association (£10,000), towards the cost of an education officer; Royal Entomological Society (£9,600), to cover the cost of the school and farm wildlife programme; Rockingham Forest Trust (£8,000), towards the People in the Forest project; Groundwork London (£7,500), towards the cost of an education officer for the Eco Schools project; Yorkshire Agricultural Society (£7,000), towards the cost of the information boards, education adviser and information packs; Arable Group Ltd (£6,000), for bursaries for students taking part in the TAG Asset programme; and Scottish Seabird Centre (£5,000), towards educational resources for the website. Small grants of £3,000 or less included those to: Marine Connection, Gordon Infant School, Footprint Trust Limited, University of London, Conservation Volunteers Northern Ireland and a range of primary schools across the UK towards educational projects.

Literacy and numeracy – 42 grants totalling £109,000

Beneficiaries included: National Library of Wales (£10,000), towards the cost of 2,000 education packs; Volunteer Reading Help (£8,400), to recruit, train and support ten volunteer reading helpers; and, Independent Photography (£3,800), towards an art/literacy project. Small grants included those to: Bethnal Green Bengali Women's Group, Arab Cultural Community, Rowandale Integrated Primary School, Manor High School, Barbican Centre, Get Hooked on Fishing and Ramsden Hall School.

Other – 39 grants totalling £88,500

Beneficiaries included: Engineering Education Scheme in Wales (£10,500), towards bursaries for the scheme; RNLI (£7,000), towards the salary of a learning officer; Farmor's School Bursaries (£5,100), 17 awards of £300 were made to pupils at Farmor's School on the ECT's Fairford Estate. The awards were for the purchase of resources for the pupils' continuing education; Down's Syndrome Association (£2,000), towards web-based resources for teachers; Wavertree Trust (£1,200), towards an interactive whiteboard for NVQ courses; and Chimneytots Pre-School (£500), towards the cost of a wobble board.

Exclusions Applicants must represent either registered charities or not-for-profit organisations. Grants are normally awarded on an annual basis and will not be awarded retrospectively.

Grants are not made to:

- individuals
- agricultural colleges
- education work which is part of social support, therapy or medical treatment
- building and restoration work
- sports and recreational activities
- work overseas.

Support for wildlife trusts and for farming and wildlife advisory groups is largely restricted to those based in counties in which the trust owns land (Gloucestershire, Buckinghamshire, Leicestershire, Dorset and Oxfordshire).

Applications There is no application form. Applicants are asked to send a covering letter addressed to the grants administrator as well as describing their educational project clearly on no more than two additional sheets of A4, specifying how any grant will be spent. A simple budget for that project should be included, noting any other funding applications. The latest annual report and accounts for the organisation should also be provided. Please do not send further supporting material or email applications.

Successful applicants will be asked to complete an Agreement which includes the ability to pay the grant by BACS. The Agreement also requires the applicant to submit a report on the funded project; failure to do so will ensure the rejection of any further application and may result in a request to repay the award.

The full board of Trustees meets twice a year, in April and October, to consider grants in excess of £4,000; applications for these meetings should be submitted by 31 January and 31 August respectively. Meetings to consider grants of £4,000 or less are normally held in February, May, July, September and December. Notification about the date of payment of grants is given when the offer is made.

If necessary, please contact the Grants Office to discuss a potential application: staff will be pleased to assist you.

The Alice Ellen Cooper Dean Charitable Foundation

General

£790,500 (2007/08)

Beneficial area Worldwide, in practice, mainly UK, with a preference for Dorset and west Hampshire.

Edwards and Keeping, Unity Chambers, 34 High East Street, Dorchester DT1 1HA

Tel. 01305 251333 **Fax** 01305 251465

Email office@edwardsandkeeping.co.uk

Correspondent Rupert J A Edwards, Trustee

Trustees *John R B Bowditch; Mrs Linda J Bowditch; Rupert J A Edwards; Douglas J E Neville-Jones; Emma Blackburn.*

CC Number 273298

Information available Accounts were available from the Charity Commission.

The foundation was established for general charitable purposes in 1977 with an initial gift by Ellen Cooper Dean and supplemented by a legacy on her death in 1984. Donations are only made to registered charities with a preference for local organisations in Dorset and west Hampshire. Grants usually range from £1,000 to £10,000 each.

In 2007/08 the foundation had assets of £16.25 million and an income of £917,500. There were 128 grants made totalling £790,500.

In addition to supporting local and national charities in the areas of health, social disadvantage, education, religion, community, arts and culture, amateur sport and disability, mainly on a regular basis, the foundation has made overseas grants to advance education, relieve poverty, sickness, and suffering caused by conflict and disasters.

Larger grants were made to: Cherry Tree Nursery – Sheltered Work Opportunities Project (£50,000); West of England School & College (£36,000); Piers Simon Appeal and the Wessex Autistic Society (£25,000 each); East Holton Church and the Royal British Legion – Dorset (£20,000 each); and Water Aid (£15,000).

Other beneficiaries included: Action for Kids, Dorset & Somerset Air Ambulance Trust and the Spinal Injuries Association (£10,000 each); Child Aid (£8,000);

Dorset Blind Association (£7,500); Beaminster School, Coping with Chaos, Huntington's Disease Association and SOS Children's Villages UK (£5,000 each); Jubilee Sailing Trust and Dorset Action on Abuse (£3,000 each); The Seeing Ear and Special Toys Educational Postal Service (£2,000 each); and Foundation for the Study of Infant Deaths and the War Memorial Trust (£1,000 each).

Exclusions No grants to individuals. Grants to registered charities only.

Applications In writing to the correspondent. Applications are considered from both local and national charitable organisations.

Each application should include:

- name and address of the organisation
- charity registration number
- details of the project
- details of the community, including area covered and numbers who will benefit from the project
- details of fundraising activities and other anticipated sources of grants
- a copy of the latest financial accounts.

County Durham Foundation

Tackling social disadvantage and poverty and general charitable purposes

£1.8 million (2007/08)

Beneficial area County Durham, Darlington and surrounding areas.

Jordan House, Forster Business Centre, Finchale Road, Durham DH1 5HL

Tel. 0191 383 0055 **Fax** 0191 383 2969

Email info@countydurhamfoundation. co.uk

Website www.countydurhamfoundation. co.uk

Correspondent Barbara Gubbins, Chief Executive

Trustees *Andrew Martell; David Watson; Lady Sarah Nicholson; Katherine Welch; John Hamilton; Mark I'anson; Michele Armstrong; David Martin; Christopher Lendrum; Richard Tonks; Ada Burns; Prof. Tim Blackman; Alex Worrall; Gerald Osborne; George Garlick.*

CC Number 1047625

Information available Accounts were available at the Charity Commission. The foundation's website is user-friendly and informative for those seeking grants.

The aim of the County Durham Foundation is to build up endowment funds so as to provide long-term income that is used to provide grants to approved projects within County Durham and Darlington (and in specified circumstances across the North East). The foundation supports and promotes charitable purposes in these areas and has focussed on combating social disadvantage and poverty in its grant distribution. It receives donations and manages funds for individuals, companies, trusts and government departments who want to support the local community.

Grantmaking

The foundation currently holds over 85 different funds all of which have their own policy and criteria. The majority of endowment-based funds are now donor advised, where the foundation works with the fund holder to determine potential recipients. Programmes delivered during the year include:

- **Community Action** This fund is for the support of local, voluntary and community activity at a grassroots level in County Durham and Darlington, funded by contributions from various private endowment and revenue fund holders.
- **The Banks Group Community Fund** This fund provides capital support for the purchase of specific items funded through landfill tax credit in conjunction with local developers, the Banks Group.
- **Grassroots Grants** Grants are available to support small, informal voluntary and community groups with an annual turnover of less than £20,000 per annum. Grants are available between £250 and £5,000 and can be used for capital items, revenue or a combination of both.

Grant schemes change frequently. Please consult the foundation's website for details of current programmes and their deadlines.

In 2007/08 the foundation had assets of £5 million and an income of £2.3 million. Grants made totalled £1.8 million. The foundation categorised its grantmaking as follows:

- buildings or refurbishment of premises (£388,000)
- purchase and repair of equipment (£333,000)

- funding of core activities (£296,000)
- education and training (£275,000)
- environmental projects (£177,000)
- travel and transport (£68,000)
- events (£64,000)
- sporting activities (£57,000)
- holidays and respite care (£50,000)
- art, craft and drama activities (£40,000)
- welfare (£39,000)
- social activities (£3,000).

Full details of grants distributed throughout the year can be found on the foundation's website.

Exclusions The foundation will not fund:

- projects outside County Durham and Darlington
- national or regional charities with no independent office in County Durham or Darlington
- groups that have more than one year's running costs held as free reserves
- projects which should be funded by a statutory body
- sponsored events
- improvements to land that is not open to the general public at convenient hours
- projects promoting political activities
- deficit or retrospective funding
- faith groups promoting religious, non-community based activities.

Funding is not normally given for:

- medical research and equipment
- grants for more than one year
- school projects
- general contributions to large appeals (but specific items can be funded)
- building or buying premises and freehold or leasehold land rights
- minibuses or other vehicles
- overseas travel
- animal welfare.

Some of the programmes have other exclusions. If your project is at all unusual please contact the foundation to discuss your application before submitting it.

Applications An expression of interest form should be completed in the first instance instead of a full application form. This can be downloaded, completed online or requested from the foundation by post or telephone.

If the foundation feels that the project meets the criteria for one of its funds, applicants will then be asked to complete a full application form. This system is designed to save organisations time in completing a detailed application for a project that may not be supported. There are exceptions to this procedure and applicants should view the website or contact the correspondent for further information.

The foundation has a variety of grant programmes running, with new ones being added all the time. It supports groups, projects and individuals mainly in County Durham and Darlington, and in some circumstances, across the North East. Organisations which are not registered charities are considered but must be a not-for-profit organisation that is benevolent, charitable or philanthropic and established to alleviate disadvantage in the community.

The most successful applications are from user-led, self-help projects that can show real community support and demonstrable benefits. The foundation encourages applications from groups working in the following areas:

- children and young people – groups and projects that help children and young people access activities and services where they play a key role in the decision making
- vulnerable people – groups and projects working with disadvantaged people, in particular providing increased access to services and facilities for people with disabilities, the homeless and older people
- community regeneration – local partnerships plus residents and tenants' associations that aim to improve health, education, reduce crime levels (and improve community safety) and to regenerate employment, housing and the physical environment with the support of their local community
- self-help groups – community based, small self-help groups who deliver basic services
- environmental improvements – small-scale environmental projects particularly improvements to community held land
- education, capacity and skills development – group and community-based training and education programmes, particularly for those who have had no previous access to training opportunities
- health – groups and community based projects providing access to healthy eating, increased physical activity and self-help services, which aim to improve the health and well being of communities; and in particular
- applications from groups working in rural areas.

Cripplegate Foundation

General

£1.4 million to organisations
(2008)

Beneficial area London borough of Islington and part of the City of London.

76 Central Street, London EC1V 8AG

Tel. 020 7549 8183 **Fax** 020 7549 8180

Email grants@cripplegate.org.uk

Website www.cripplegate.org

Correspondent Kristina Glenn, Director

Trustees *John Tomlinson; Stella Currie; Barbara Riddell; Paula Kahn; Judith Moran; Revd Katharine Rumens; Tom Jupp; Joe Trotter; John Gilbert; Lucy Watt; David Sulkin; Heather Lamont; Rob Hull; Mark Yeadon; Anne-Marie Ellis; Rob Abercrombie.*

CC Number 207499

Information available Accounts were available at the Charity Commission. The foundation has an excellent website.

Summary

The first recorded gift to the Church of St Giles without Cripplegate was by the Will of John Sworder dated 2nd April 1500. Cripplegate Foundation was established in 1891 by a Charity Commission scheme which amalgamated all the non-ecclesiastical charitable donations previously administered as separate trusts. The early governors of the foundation built an institute on Golden Lane, containing reading and reference libraries, news and magazine rooms, classrooms, a theatre and even a rifle range. The institute was run until 1973, when it was closed and the foundation became a grant-giving trust.

The original beneficial area of the foundation was the ancient parish of St Giles, Cripplegate, to which was added in 1974 the ancient parish of St Luke's, Old Street. On 1 April 2008, the Charity Commission agreed a scheme which extended the foundation's area of benefit. This now covers the Parish of St Giles, Cripplegate in the City of London and the former parish of St Luke, Old Street (both as constituted by the Act of Parliament of the year 1732–3), and the London Borough of Islington.

Please note: although the foundation's area of benefit has been extended to cover the whole of Islington, Governors have agreed that the foundation will

need to develop partnerships and significantly increase its income before it can fully fund new initiatives in north Islington.

The foundation's website gives the following synopsis of the area of benefit:

Islington is changing rapidly. As the older population is moving out of the area, new communities, notably refugee and asylum seekers, are moving in. The polarisation between the rich and poor is marked. For the foundation this can mean that older communities often need additional support as their families no longer live locally. Newer residents, such as those from Somali, Kurdish and Bengali communities, are developing their own organisations. Local schools report that up to 100 languages are spoken by pupils.

The funding environment changes constantly as central government provides funding through programmes such as EC1 New Deal. Many of these sources of funding for local Islington groups are for purposes laid down by government. The money has to be spent to achieve specific targets and requires detailed reporting.

The foundation's grantmaking is informed by a knowledge of available funding streams, its links with other funders and a knowledge of and long-term relationship with the local area. If necessary, the foundation is able to advise organisations of more appropriate funding or provide match funding. The foundation ensures it is not replacing or duplicating statutory funding.

In November 2008 the foundation successfully launched its report, 'Invisible Islington: Poverty in Inner London', which will shape its priorities and work over the next five years. This has also helped to make the foundation more visible and encouraged new partnerships with both statutory and voluntary sector organisations.

Overall, the foundation gives around £1 million a year to a wide range of organisations including projects for young people, community groups, health and mental health projects.

Programmes

The foundation currently administers six grants programmes which are:

- main grants programme
- schools programme
- pro-activity programme
- grants to individuals programme
- Islington Community Chest
- Finsbury Educational Foundation Fund.

The following programme information is drawn largely from the foundation's detailed website.

Main Grants Programme
Current priorities
Three themes capture the foundation's priorities:

1) Reducing poverty: applications which work with the poorest sections of the community to help to reduce poverty are encouraged.
2) Increasing access to opportunities and making connections: this addresses access to opportunities by the most deprived residents such as those on low income and black and minority ethnic residents. It includes access to cultural and arts facilities as well as education and employment.
3) Social cohesion: applications are encouraged which promote integration of communities and active participation in society.

All applicants must show how their work will address one of these themes.

The foundation funds:

- core costs for key Islington organisations
- project funding
- salary costs
- capital costs.

Schools Programme
The schools programme aims to:

- raise achievement
- enrich the curriculum
- improve opportunities for young people and their families.

Each primary school in south Islington can apply for up to £10,000 over three years. Each secondary school and special school in south Islington can apply for funding for specific projects which meet the foundation's criteria.

The foundation works closely with schools and voluntary organisations to develop new programmes of work.

Pro-Active Programme
The foundation has a history of proactively identifying and targeting important local needs that may not be reflected in applications. More than 30% of the foundation's funding is currently allocated in this way and is central to the foundation's approach to funding. Over recent years the foundation has been involved in:

- supporting the establishment of 'Xaawaley', a new domestic violence service for Somali women in 2007, run in partnership with three Somali organisations
- setting up the Canonbury Community Development Group in 2005 to help

improve the quality of life for Canonbury residents
- setting up a 'TEXT' writers in schools project in 2003
- developing Drum Counselling mental health service for young people aged 16 -25 in south Islington
- setting up South Islington Advice Project welfare rights service in Kings Cross in 2005
- setting up Essex Road Advice Project welfare and legal rights service in Essex Road in 2007
- launching Invisible Islington in 2008.

How the foundation develops its pro-activity programme
The foundation identifies gaps in services through an analysis of information available on the area, local networks and its grant giving programmes.

We call meetings and hold small conferences to discuss issues and problems. We introduce people to new contacts in their field of work. We set up a steering group to take the issue forward – through foundation funding or links to other organisations or funders.

Grants to Individuals Programme
The foundation provides financial help to individuals to relieve hardship and distress.

The foundation takes a holistic approach to its individual grant giving. In addition to providing financial assistance, our Grants Officer, an experienced welfare rights adviser, ensures that applicants receive all state benefits and services to which they may be entitled. All applicants are visited at their homes. Referrals are made to local services such as playgroups, training projects, counselling services or advice services.

All applications are dealt with in strict confidence and all applicants are treated fairly, equally and in a non-judgmental manner.

What kind of grants are made
Grants of up to £500 can be made for a wide variety of needs such as:

- clothing
- essential household items and furniture
- basic electrical goods such as cookers, fridges and washing machines
- aids and adaptations for people with disabilities
- start-up packages for newly housed homeless people
- respite breaks (but only for those who have not had a respite break in the previous five years).

Islington Community Chest
This provides small grants to voluntary and community groups based in

Islington. The foundation administers the programme on behalf of the Islington Strategic Partnership.

Islington Community Chest aims to:

- support small and new local groups based in Islington with an income of less than £100,000 a year
- promote a vibrant cohesive community
- contribute to local regeneration
- empower people to take an active part in their communities
- develop trust between people and build confidence.

Additional priorities in 2009/10 are:

- improvement of local residents' mental and physical health and independence and choice for older and vulnerable people
- improving the environment and tackling climate change
- raising educational achievement
- improving skills, encouraging volunteering and helping local residents find work
- contributing to safer communities; reducing antisocial behaviour and crime through drugs and alcohol.

Funding is provided by the Islington Strategic Partnership for organisations with a turnover of less than £100,000. Grants of up to £5,000 are available for smaller projects. Grants of up to £10,000 are available for larger partnership projects such as environmental projects. Over £400,000 is available in 2009/10.

Grassroots Grants funding provided by the Office of the Third Sector is also administered through the foundation for organisations with a turnover of less than £30,000. Over £100,000 is available in 2009/10.

There is one application form for both Community Chest and Grassroots Grants. The panel will make decisions on the source of funding so it is not necessary to submit separate applications for each fund.

What kind of grants are made from the Islington Community Chest fund?
The fund supports:

- parent and toddler groups
- sports activities
- social clubs
- youth clubs and other young peoples' organisations
- tenants' and residents' associations
- black and minority ethnic (BME) community groups
- new refugee communities
- supplementary schools

95

- women's groups and victim support groups including victims of racial harassment or domestic violence
- activity-based clubs
- events
- arts projects
- specialist training courses for staff, management committee and volunteers
- publications or exhibitions of work.

Finsbury Educational Foundation Fund

Finsbury Educational Foundation provides funding of £40,000 a year to promote education in a small area of south Islington. The foundation has decided to allocate its funding to a sports and music programme with London Symphony Orchestra in 2008/09.

Grantmaking in 2008

In 2008 the foundation had assets of £26 million and an income of £2.5 million. Grants were made to organisations during the year totalling almost £1.4 million (grants were also made to individuals totalling £136,000). Grants to organisations were categorised as follows:

Category	Value
Disabilities	£35,000
Work with older people	£18,000
Education and training	£95,000
Schools and work with schools	£93,000
Arts, leisure and environment	£84,000
Community groups and infrastructure	£92,000
Social welfare and advice	£404,000
Health and mental health	£58,000

Grant programmes administered by the foundation on behalf of others included:

Category	Value
Islington Community Chest	£412,000
Grassroots grants	£69,000
Islington drug and alcohol action team	£15,000
Neighbourhood management	£3,000
Newlon Fusion	£5,000

Beneficiaries across all themes included: Mary Ward Legal Centre (£169,000); Islington Voluntary Action Council (£65,000); Urban Hope (£45,000); Writers in Schools Project (£32,000); Industrial Trust (£16,000); Clod Ensemble (£11,000); Step Together Dance Project and the Garden Classroom (£5,000 each); Inner City Films (£4,000); Golden Lane Campus (£2,700); and Islington Cyclists Action Group (£280).

Exclusions In the main grants programme no funding is given for:

- national charities or organisations outside the area of benefit
- schemes or activities which would relieve central or local government of their statutory responsibilities

- grants to replace cuts in funding made by the local authority or others
- medical research or equipment
- national fundraising appeals
- advancement of religion unless the applicant also offers non-religious services to the community
- animal welfare
- retrospective grants
- commercial or business activities
- grants for events held in the church of St Giles without Cripplegate
- grants to organisations recruiting volunteers in south Islington for work overseas.

In the individuals programme the following will not be funded:

- funeral costs
- the purchase of computers
- child care costs
- money that has been stolen
- items already bought or ordered
- housing costs or council tax
- repayment of debts
- education needs (apart from school uniforms)
- wheelchairs or disability vehicles and scooters
- grants for students not normally resident in the area of benefit.

The Islington community chest will not fund:

- political activities
- promotion of religion
- construction or acquisition of buildings
- general appeals
- debts
- events which have already taken place
- expenses already incurred
- national organisations with local branches in Islington
- statutory organisations.

Applications Each programme has a different application form and deadline dates. Applicants are encouraged to telephone or email the foundation to discuss their project before making a full application.

Full details of the application process are available on the foundation's website.

The Cross Trust

Christian work

£726,000 (2007/08)

Beneficial area UK and overseas.

Cansdales, Bourbon Court, Nightingales Corner, Little Chalfont HP7 9QS

Tel. 01494 765428

Email davids@cansdales.co.uk

Correspondent David Stephenson

Trustees Michael S Farmer; Mrs Jenny D Farmer; Douglas J Olsen.

CC Number 298472

Information available Accounts were available from the Charity Commission.

The trust's objects are:

- work for the furtherance of religious and secular education
- advancement of the Christian faith in the UK and overseas
- relief of Christian workers, their dependants, and other people who are poor, sick, older or otherwise in need
- support for any religious or charitable institution.

In 2007/08 the trust had assets of £316,000 and an income of £239,500 (these figures are considerably reduced from previous years). Grants were made during the year totalling £726,000.

A list of beneficiaries was not included in the trust's accounts, although there is a reference to two grants which were made to organisations with which a trustee is connected. These were: The Areopagus Trust (£100,000); and the Kingham Hill Trust (£7,600).

Previous beneficiaries included: Oakhill College, Friends of St Ebbe's Trust, Proclamation Trust, Friends International, Rock Foundation, Agape Missionaries, OMF Asia Interactive and St Andrews Partnership.

Applications The trust has previously stated that no unsolicited applications are considered, and that funds are fully committed.

The Peter Cruddas Foundation

Children and young people

£3.9 million (2007/08)

Beneficial area UK, with a particular interest in London.

66 Prescot Street, London E1 8HG

Tel. 020 3003 8360 **Fax** 020 3003 8580

Email s.cox@pcfoundation.org.uk

Website www.petercruddasfoundation.org.uk

Correspondent Stephen D Cox, Administrator

Trustees *Lord David Young, Chair; Peter Cruddas; Martin Paisner.*

CC Number 1117323

Information available Accounts were available from the Charity Commission. The foundation also has a clear and simple website.

Established in December 2006, this is the charitable foundation of Peter Cruddas, founder of City financial trading group CMC Markets, who has pledged to donate at least £100 million to good causes during his lifetime. It was incorrectly reported in the general press that the foundation would be building up an endowment, however this is not the case and there are no plans to do so in the foreseeable future.

The foundation provides the following information about its funding priorities:

The foundation gives priority to programmes calculated to help disadvantaged and disengaged young people in the UK towards pathways into education, training and employment. Preference will be given to the support of projects undertaken by charitable organisations.

Priority Funding Programmes of the Peter Cruddas Foundation will change from time to time and you are advised that applications meeting the criteria will receive priority. Details of the Priority Funding Programmes can be found on the foundation's website: www.petercruddasfoundation.org.uk.

Priorities in 2009 were:

- pathways/support for young disadvantaged or disengaged young people into education, training or employment
- crime diversion schemes
- work experience/skills projects for young people
- mentoring of young people in London
- general youth work in London.

These priorities will remain in place for the foreseeable future.

There is also a small grants scheme to help small and medium-sized organisations with the general theme of 'helping young people achieve more'. The foundation looks to make grants of around £500 to £2,000. An amount is allocated each month to this scheme and applications are not carried over.

In 2007/08 the foundation had an income of almost £3.1 million, mainly in the form of a donation from CMC Markets. Grants were made during the year totalling £3.9 million, categorised as follows:

Support of disadvantaged young people – £1.43 million
The beneficiaries were: The Princes Trust (£500,000); Duke of Edinburgh Awards (£499,500); Harris Manchester College (£224,000); Coram (£100,000); Tick Tock Club – Great Ormond Street Children's Hospital (£75,000); and the Willow Foundation (£2,000).

Other – £2.45 million
The beneficiaries were: The Dean and Canons of Windsor – College of St George (£1.49 million); The National Osteoporosis Society (£375,000); Royal Opera House Foundation (£241,000); Policy Exchange Limited (£140,000); The Royal Hospital Chelsea (£100,000); The Chichester Festival Theatre (£50,000); Young Adult Trust (£20,000); Heart Cells Foundation (£12,000); and Dementia (£10,000). Small grants were made totalling £15,000.

The foundation has supported more than 60 charities in its first 3 years and this number grows each month.

Applications On an application form available to download from the foundation's website.

The foundation provides guidance on how to complete the application form, also available on the website.

Please note: the foundation states that it is currently receiving a very high number of appropriate applications.

Cullum Family Trust

Social welfare, education and general charitable purposes

£406,000 (2007/08)
Beneficial area UK.

Wealden Hall, Parkfield, Sevenoaks TN15 0HX

Correspondent Peter Geoffrey Cullum, Trustee

Trustees *Peter Geoffrey Cullum; Ann Cullum; Claire Louise Cullum; Simon Timothy Cullum.*

CC Number 1117056

Information available Accounts were available from the Charity Commission.

Established towards the end of 2006, this trust is the vehicle for the philanthropy of Peter Cullum, executive chairman of the Towergate insurance group. Mr Cullum was voted Entrepreneur of the Year by Ernst & Young in 2006.

The trust's accounts state its objects as:

- the relief of poverty and the advancement of education and religion
- any other charitable purposes.

In 2007/08 the foundation had assets of £17.9 million and an income of £11.1 million, which included a donation of almost £10.7 million from the founder. Grants were made during this, the first year of grantmaking, totalling £406,000.

The main beneficiaries were: Kids Company (£166,000); City of Norwich School (£105,000); Sussex Community Foundation (£75,000); and the Born Free Foundation (£50,000). Small grants were made totalling £10,000.

Applications In writing to the correspondent.

Cumbria Community Foundation

General charitable purposes in Cumbria, in particular grantmaking to children and young people, older people and their carers, people with disabilities, the unemployed and people on low incomes

£1 million (2007/08)
Beneficial area Cumbria.

Dovenby Hall, Dovenby, Cockermouth CA13 0PN

Tel. 01900 825 760 **Fax** 01900 826 527

Email enquiries@cumbriafoundation.org

Website www.cumbriafoundation.org

Correspondent Andrew Beeforth, Director

Trustees *Peter Hensman; Ian Brown; Derek Lyon; Eric Apperley; June Chapman; Susan Aglionby; David Brown; James Carr; Chris Coombes; Rob Cairns;*

Elaine Woodburn; Trevor Hebdon; Bob Mather; Robin Burgess; Heike Horsburgh; Sarah Dunning; Shirley Williams; Dick Raaz; Stewart Young; Peter Stybelski; Catherine Alexander; Christine Hughes; Mike Casson.

CC Number 1075120

Information available Accounts were on file at the Charity Commission and further information was available from the foundation's website.

Established in 1999, with the funding support of the local authorities and a founding donation of £1 million from British Nuclear Fuels Ltd., the foundation focuses on improving the community life of people in Cumbria, and in particular those in need by reason of disability, age, financial or other disadvantage.

These wide charitable objects allow the foundation to support most local charities. The foundation also responds to local disasters, such as floods, storms and Foot and Mouth to help those people affected. Grant levels differ from programme to programme but awards are mostly under £10,000.

In 2006/07 the objects of the charity were extended to enable the foundation to make limited grants immediately outside the principal area of benefit (Cumbria), subject to the majority of funds being spent in Cumbria.

In 2007/08 the foundation had assets of £3.4 million and an income of £1.7 million. Grants are normally made to small, local charities and voluntary groups but have also been made to individuals in response to community need. During the year grants were made to 513 organisations totalling just over £1 million. 64 grants were made to individuals totalling £66,000.

The foundation manages more than 30 separate funds, each with different criteria and geographical interests, and distributes around £1 million each year. Distribution of grant awards reflects the money available through the different funds.

Total grants distributed through the funds operated by the foundation were as follows:

Fund	Value
Local Network Fund	£569,000
Allerdale Community Fund	£68,000
Coalfields 'Bridging the Gap' Community Chest	£65,000
Community Champion	£63,000
Cumbria Key Fund	£53,000
Sellafield Site Fund	£51,000
Cumbria Communities Fund	£45,000
Allerdale Invest!	£37,000
Fluor Cumbria Fund	£29,000
Sport Relief Fund	£22,000
Alston Moor Community Chest	£20,000

CN Group Fund	£14,000
Cumbria Community Foundation Trust	£13,000
Youth Work Aid Fund	£10,000
Allerdale Youth Bank	£5,800
Roselands Trust	£5,300
Barrow Community Trust	£3,700
Rockcliffe and Westlinton CWM Trust Fund	£2,900
Kipling Fund for younger people	£2,300
High Sheriffs Crimebeat Fund	£2,100
Dora Beeforth Memorial Fund	£2,100
Kipling Fund for older people	£1,800
HSBC Fund	£1,500
Russell Armer Fund	£1,300
Cumberland and Westmorland Herald Fund	£1,200
Cumbria Cultural Fund	£1,000
DAT Community Chest	£510
Janetta Topsy Laidlaw Fund	£300

In addition the foundation also provides administrative and assessment support services for another six funds and grants awarded from these were as follows:

Fund	Value
Mary Grave Trust	£93,000
Joyce Wilkinson Trust	£41,000
Holehird Trust	£38,000
Cumberland Educational Foundation	£18,000
Edmund Castle Educational Trust	£8,400
Allerdale Sport Action Zone	£1,800

The foundation is currently targeting its grants to meet the following strategic aims:

- rural community regeneration
- urban deprivation
- children and young people
- mental health
- hidden and emerging need
- other aims.

Grants are categorised under these aims as follows:

Children and young people – 376 grants totalling £805,000
Beneficiaries included: Allerdale YouthBank and Cumbria Federation of Young Farmers' Clubs (£7,000 each); Kendal School of Gymnastics (£6,300); Lakeland Orienteering Club (£6,000); Belle Vue Church – Carlisle (£5,600); and Pitstop Project Barrow and Workington Sea Cadets (£5,000 each).

Rural community regeneration – 105 grants totalling £132,000
Beneficiaries included: Works 4 You Ltd Cleator Moor (£8,000); Phoenix Enterprise Centre – Cleator Moor (£6,200); and South Tynedale Railway Preservation Society, Alston Producers' Markets and Fit 4 Life West Cumbria (£5,000 each).

Hidden and emerging need – 18 grants totalling £27,000
Beneficiaries included: West Cumbria Carers (£5,000); Fit 4 Life West Cumbria (£1,000) and Rising Sun Trust – Workington (£500).

Urban deprivation – 33 grants totalling £66,000
Grants went to: Salterbeck Alliance for Community Enterprise Ltd – 2 grants

(£13,000); Cumbria Alcohol and Drug Advisory Service and Interchoc Co-operative Society Ltd (£10,000 each); and West Cumbria Domestic Violence Support (£5,000).

Mental health – 10 grants totalling £19,000
Beneficiaries included: Allerdale Disability Association (£5,000); Alzheimer's Society – Furness (£1,000); and Eden Mind Ltd (£490).

Other aims – 35 grants totalling £42,000
Unfortunately no grants list was available for this category.

Exclusions The following are not supported:

- animal welfare
- deficit funding
- general large appeals
- boxing clubs
- medical research and equipment
- non-Cumbrian projects
- sponsored events
- replacement of statutory funding
- projects that have already happened
- applications where a grant from that fund has been received within the last year (except Grassroots Grants)
- individuals (except for specific funds).

Please contact the foundation for further information on individual restrictions on any of the grant programmes.

Applications Applications should include the following supporting information:

- a copy of the organisation's governing document (not required for registered charities)
- a copy of the latest accounts (or bank statements covering the last quarter, if the organisation has been operating for less than a year)
- details of an independent referee
- a copy of the organisation's child protection or safeguarding policy (if the project will involve working with children and/or young people).

The foundation prefers to receive applications via email, even if the supporting documents have to be sent by post.

Applicants are encouraged to contact the foundation prior to making an application in order to confirm their eligibility.

Applications are accepted throughout the year and decisions are usually taken within two months. Some programmes offer a faster process for small urgent projects.

Itzchok Meyer Cymerman Trust Ltd

Advancement of the orthodox Jewish faith; education; social welfare; relief of sickness; medical research and general charitable purposes

£856,000 (2007/08)
Beneficial area Worldwide.

15 Riverside Drive, Golders Green Road, London NW11 9PU
Tel. 020 7272 2255
Correspondent I M Cymerman
Trustees *Mrs H F Bondi; I M Cymerman; M D Cymerman; Mrs R Cymerman; Mrs S Heitner.*
CC Number 265090
Information available Accounts were available from the Charity Commission.

The trust was established in 1972 and its objectives are the advancement of the orthodox Jewish faith and general charitable purposes. Almost all the trust's grants are to Jewish charitable organisations although occasional grants to individuals in need are made. Many grants are made to the same organisations each year.

In 2007/08 the trust had assets of £2.2 million and an income of £851,000. 96 grants were made totalling £856,000. Grants were categorised as follows:

Category	Value
Advancement of education	£744,000
Advancement of religion	£50,000
Relief of poverty	£36,000
Medical care and research	£27,000

Beneficiaries included: Centre for Torah Education (£100,000); Friends of Ohr Akiva Institute (£90,000); Telz Talmudical Academy Trust (£50,000); Kolel Breslaw (£43,000); Beth Hamedrash Gur (£38,000); Beis Aaron Trust (£25,000); Pardes Chana Institutions (£15,000); Yeshivat Kollel Breslov (£10,000); and TAT Family Relief Fund (£5,000).

Applications In writing to the correspondent.

The D'Oyly Carte Charitable Trust

Arts, medical welfare, environment

£1.1 million (2007/08)
Beneficial area UK.

1 Savoy Hill, London WC2R 0BP
Tel. 020 7420 2600
Correspondent Jane Thorne, Secretary
Trustees *Jeremy Leigh Pemberton, Chair; Francesca Radcliffe; Julia Sibley; Henry Freeland; Andrew Jackson; Michael O'Brien.*
CC Number 1112457
Information available Accounts were available from the Charity Commission.

The trust was founded in 1972 by Dame Bridget D'Oyly Carte, granddaughter of the founder of both the Savoy Theatre and the Savoy Hotel. Its distributable income increased significantly on her death in 1985, when it inherited her shareholding in The Savoy Hotel plc, and again in 1998 following the company's sale.

The trust supports general charitable causes connected with the arts, medical welfare and the environment. Certain charities in which the founder took a special interest continue to be supported on a regular basis.

Grants start at around £500. The majority are for amounts under £5,000 although some can be for larger amounts. Most funding goes to the arts and medical welfare.

The majority of grants made by the trust are on a one-off basis although term grants are also agreed from time to time for a maximum period of three years, particularly in respect of bursary funding for educational establishments, mainly in the arts sector, and to help newly created charities become established. Recipients of these grants are required to report regularly to the trust for monitoring purposes.

The trustees have continued their commitment to make grants to charities that do not enjoy a high profile in order to create significant impact on the work of the charity concerned, and, recognising the day-to-day funding needs of charities, the trustees continue to consider applications for core costs.

Grantmaking in 2007/08

During the year the trust made 273 grants totalling £1.1 million. The trust's annual report includes the following description of its grantmaking activities during the year:

The distribution of grants between the sectors continues to favour charities in the arts and medical welfare sectors, with a smaller proportion going to environmental charities. However, whatever the cause, the trustees always try to direct their funds to where they can make a material difference, and this aim steers them away from significant appeals. The trustees realise the vital impact their funding can make, and the encouragement it can give, particularly to smaller charities seeking to provide desperately needed services in the community.

This year again, the arts took the largest proportion of the trust's spending at £529,000 compared to £416,000 in the previous year, whilst spending on the medical welfare sector amounted to £411,000 compared to £346,000 in the previous year. In the third sector, the environment, £120,000 was distributed compared to £122,000 in the previous year.

Distribution of grants
Arts – 135 grants totalling £549,000
The average grant in this sector was £4,064 compared to £3,947 the previous year.

During the year, the Royal Academy of Dramatic Art once again received the largest grant in this sector of £20,000 towards bursaries. Other above average grants included those to: Samling Foundation (£10,000); Academy of Ancient Music Trust and London Handel Society (£5,000 each); and Nash Concert Society (£4,500).

Medical/Welfare – 103 grants totalling £401,000
The average grant in this sector was £3,892 compared with ££3,874 in the previous year.

Above average grants in this sector included those to: Help the Hospices (£15,000); Children's Hospice South West (£6,300); Children's Trust, Brainwave Centre Ltd and Challenging Behaviour Foundation (£5,000 each); and East Anglia Children's Hospices (£4,500).

The Environment – 35 grants totalling £145,000
The average grant in this sector was £4,138 compared to £4,143 in the previous year.

Above average grants in this sector included those to: Trees for Life

(£6,500); Scottish Native Woods (£5,900); and Gazen Salts Nature Reserve, Painshill Park Trust and Marine Conservation Society (£5,000 each).

Guidelines for applicants

The following information is taken from the 'Grantmaking Policy' section of the trust's annual report and accounts.

Notwithstanding the trust's overall charitable objectives, the trustees regularly review their policies, objectives and guidelines, and, following a detailed review in December 2005, determined that their priorities for support [...] would continue to focus on:

The arts

- promotion of access, education and excellence in the arts for young people to increase their opportunities to become involved outside school and to build future audiences
- access to the arts for people who least have access to them
- performance development of graduates in the performing arts in the early stages of their careers and to encourage their involvement in the community through performances and workshops for the benefit of those with special needs and those who would otherwise have no opportunity to hear or participate in a live performance.

Medical and welfare

- promotion and provision of music and art therapy to improve the quality of life for older people and the disabled, and in the palliative care of children
- support for charities concerned with alleviating the suffering of adults and children with medical conditions who have difficulty finding support through traditional sources
- support and respite for carers with emphasis on the provision of holidays for those carers who wouldn't normally have a break from their responsibilities – and with special emphasis on projects and schemes that allow young carers to enjoy being children.

The environment

- preservation of the countryside and its woodlands – with emphasis on the encouragement of voluntary work and active involvement in hands-on activities
- protection of species within the United Kingdom and their habitats under threat or in decline
- conservation of the marine environment and sustainable fisheries
- heritage conservation within the United Kingdom based on value to, and use by, the local community – the trust favours projects that seek to create a new use for fine buildings of architectural and historic

merit to encourage the widest possible cross-section of use. (The trust does not normally support major restorations unless a specific element of the work can be identified as appropriate to the aims of the trust.)

Exclusions The trust is unlikely to support the following:

- animal welfare
- applications from individuals, or for the benefit of one individual
- charities requiring funding for statutory requirements
- charities operating outside the UK
- conferences or seminars
- exhibitions
- expeditions and overseas travel
- general appeals
- large national charities which enjoy widespread support
- maintenance of religious buildings
- medical research
- NHS Trust hospitals for operational or building costs
- recordings and commissioning of new works
- religious activities
- schools, nurseries and playgroups (other than those for children with special needs)
- support and rehabilitation from drug or alcohol abuse.

Due to the volume of appeals received, the trustees have decided not to consider requests from charities that have had an application turned down until two years have elapsed after the date of rejection.

Applications Potential applicants should write to the correspondent with an outline proposal of no more than two A4 pages. This should cover the work of the charity, its beneficiaries and the need for funding. Applicants qualifying for consideration will then be required to complete the trust's application form.

The form should be returned with a copy of the latest annual report and accounts. Applications for specific projects should also include clear details of the need the intended project is designed to meet and an outline budget.

The majority of applications are considered in March, July and November. The trust states that it is happy to discuss potential applications on the telephone.

The Roald Dahl Foundation

Haematology and neurology conditions affecting children and young people up to the age of 25

£409,600 (2007/08)

Beneficial area UK.

81a High Street, Great Missenden, Buckinghamshire HP16 0AL

Tel. 01494 890465 **Fax** 01494 890459

Email enquiries@roalddahlfoundation. org

Website www.roalddahlfoundation.org

Correspondent The Grants Director

Trustees *Felicity Dahl, Chair; Martin Goodwin; Roger Hills.*

CC Number 1004230

Information available Annual report and accounts are detailed, clear and helpful and were available at the Charity Commission. The foundation has an informative website.

This foundation was set up by Roald Dahl's widow, Felicity Dahl, to continue to support causes important to Roald Dahl during his lifetime. The aims of the foundation are to provide help with problems for which he felt a particular concern, including neurology and haematology. Following a review of the foundation and its aims and objectives, the trustees decided to cease funding literacy projects at the end of 2008. Each year the foundation will raise an amount of money for chosen projects in these two fields. The projects will be chosen by the trustees with the help of an advisory board, either from outside applications or internal ideas.

Guidelines

The foundation makes grants to benefit children and young people up to the age of 25 years who are living with the following conditions:

Neurology

- epilepsy

acquired brain injury as the result of:

- benign brain tumour
- encephalitis
- head injury
- hydrocephalus
- meningitis
- stroke

- neuro degenerative conditions, defined as conditions in which there is progressive intellectual and/or neurological deterioration.

Haematology

- any chronic debilitating blood disease of childhood, excluding leukaemia and related disorders

conditions include:

- sickle cell anaemia
- thalassaemia
- haemolytic anaemia
- bone marrow failure syndrome
- haemophilia
- Von Willebrand's disease.

Specifically applications from organisations will be considered for:

- establishing specialist paediatric nursing posts where there is an emphasis on community care for a maximum of 2 years. We require information about the source of permanent funding at the end of the pump priming period
- the provision of information and/or support to children and young people, and their families
- specific projects within residential and day centres to benefit children and young people within the above-mentioned criteria
- small items of medical equipment, not available from statutory sources, to enable children to be cared for in their own homes
- other projects which specifically benefit children and young people within the above mentioned medical criteria may be considered.

Grants to individuals

Small grants of up to £500 are available to children and young adults up to 25 years who meet the above mentioned medical criteria and whose families are dependent on state benefits or have a similarly low income. Grants are made to meet specific needs including household items, clothing, fuel bills, toys, stimulation equipment etc. No retrospective grants are made. Only in very exceptional circumstances will grants be made for holidays and then only in the UK.

All applications must be submitted on the family's behalf by a social worker or health care professional on the form available from the foundation.

Further information about applying for grants for individuals is given on the relevant application form which can be downloaded from the foundation's website or which can be sent by post on request.

During 2009 the foundation is undertaking a review of its grantmaking priorities and processes. Any changes are due to be implemented by the autumn of 2009 and details will be publicised on the foundation's website.

In 2007/08 the foundation had assets of £1.8 million and an income of £814,000 including £297,200 in general donations and £415,600 from the proceeds of the annual Readathon, (the proceeds of which are shared with CLIC Sargent, a leading cancer care charity for children and their families). Grants were made totalling £409,600 and included commitments from previous years. Grants were categorised as follows:

Neurology – 12 grants to organisations totalling £124,000

Beneficiaries included: King's College Hospital Charity (£30,000), to provide a portable EEG system for the paediatric unit of the hospital; NHS Greater Glasgow and Clyde (£18,400), towards establishing a new nursing post; Brain and Spine Foundation (£12,500), for a pilot project on how to support pupils with ABI; National Society for Epilepsy (£6,500), towards an awareness project in Buckinghamshire and Hertfordshire; and Children's Hospice South West (£3,400), for two special beds for children with epilepsy.

There were 11 grants totalling £5,200 made to individuals for computers and 8 grants nurse training grants totalling £1,400.

180 small grants of under £500 totalling £54,100 were made to individual children and their families.

Haematology – 3 grants to organisations totalling £78,400

The beneficiaries were: Whittington Hospital, London (£42,500), towards establishing a specialist nurse position; Bradford Teaching Hospitals NHS Foundation Trust (£32,000), towards establishing a specialist nurse position; and Royal Belfast Hospital (£4,000), for books and toys for the children's haematology outpatients department.

There were 3 small grants made for nurses' training totalling £500 and 63 grants made totalling £17,700 to individual children and their families.

Literacy grants were also made during the year totalling £52,700.

The Quentin Blake Award

Quentin Blake is one of Britain's best-loved and most successful illustrators and children's authors. His first drawings were published in Punch when he was 16. He has illustrated nearly 300 books with writers such as Russell Hoban, Joan Aiken, Michael Rosen, John Yeoman and, most famously of all, Roald Dahl. He has also illustrated classic books for adults, and created his own characters such as Mister Magnolia and Mrs Armitage. He is the president of the Roald Dahl Foundation.

The Quentin Blake Award is an annual award made to a charity supported by the foundation during the previous calendar year, which Quentin Blake feels touches the lives of children in a special way. The award is made to an organisation selected by Quentin Blake which he feels has special merit and would benefit from additional support for a new project.

During the year the award was made to ClearVision.

Exclusions The foundation does not consider applications:

- for general appeals from large, well-established charities
- from any organisation which does not have charitable status or exclusively charitable aims
- for national appeals for large building projects
- from statutory bodies (apart from our Specialist Nurses programme)
- for research in any field
- from outside the UK
- for arts projects
- for school or higher education fees
- for core funding
- from organisations for people with blood disorders which are cancer related due to the relatively large number of charities helping in the oncological field.

Applications The following guidelines can be downloaded in full from the foundation's website.

First, make sure that your project or application falls within the criteria listed. Then request (or download) and complete the application form providing all the required information and, if you feel that any other information is relevant, a covering letter. All applicants are strongly encouraged to telephone to discuss their ideas for an application before completing and returning the form. Organisations considering applying for funding for a specialist nurse post must contact the foundation before submitting an application as additional information about the longterm funding of the post will be required.

Application forms should be sent, together with a copy of the organisation's accounts and annual report for each of the last two years, to the Grants Director. Applications for posts should include a copy of the proposed job description and person specification.

When completing the form you should clearly demonstrate how your project fits our eligibility criteria and funding priorities. You should also clearly tell us what activities you would undertake with the funding, who will benefit (including the number of beneficiaries, their age ranges and whether they are from a specific area or community), how they will benefit (for example what the project will do to help, support or empower them) and how you will measure the outcomes of the project.

We endeavour to visit as many organisations applying for funds as possible, but we may simply telephone for more information.

The Daiwa Anglo-Japanese Foundation

Anglo-Japanese relations
£457,000 to organisations
(2007/08)
Beneficial area UK, Japan.

Daiwa Foundation, Japan House, 13/14 Cornwall Terrace, London NW1 4QP

Tel. 020 7486 4348 **Fax** 020 7486 2914

Email marie.conte-helm@dajf.org.uk

Website www.dajf.org.uk

Correspondent Prof. Marie Conte-Helm, Director General

Trustees *Sir Michael Perry; Hiroaki Fujii; Lady Lucy Adrian; Nicholas Clegg; Sir John Whitehead; Mr Dozen; Mr Hara; Mr Everett; Merryn Somerset Webb; Sir David Brewer; Lord Brittan; Sir Peter Williams; Andrew Smithers; Akira Kyota.*

CC Number 299955

Information available Accounts were on file at the Charity Commission and the foundation has a detailed website

The Daiwa Anglo-Japanese Foundation is a UK charity, established in 1988 with a benefaction from Daiwa Securities Co Ltd. The foundation's purpose is to support closer links between Britain and Japan. It does this by:

- making grants available to individuals, institutions and organisations to promote links between the UK and Japan in all fields of activity
- enabling British and Japanese students and academics to further their education through exchanges and other bilateral initiatives

- awarding of Daiwa Scholarships for British graduates to study and undertake work placements in Japan
- organising a year-round programme of events to increase understanding of Japan in the UK.

In 2003 the foundation introduced its restructured grants policy to bring a greater focus to its funding activities and to give encouragement to collaborations between British and Japanese partners.

The foundation awards grants to individuals and institutions in the UK and Japan in all areas of the visual and performing arts, the humanities, the social sciences, science and engineering, mathematics, business studies and education, including schools and universities, and grassroots and professional groups.

In 2007/08 the foundation had assets of nearly £36 million and an income of nearly £1.8 million. Charitable expenditure totalled £1.5 million, including £328,000 given in scholarships and £616,000 given in grants, awards and prizes (£457,000 of which was awarded to organisations).

Grants were awarded as follows:

- UK – Daiwa Foundation Small Grants – £230,000
- Japan – Daiwa Foundation Small Grants – £85,000
- Daiwa Foundation Awards – £146,000
- Special Project Grants – £15,000
- Royal Society Joint Project Grants – £35,000
- UK – Japan 2008 Grant(s) – £25,000
- Daiwa Adrian Prizes – £65,000

The foundation's annual accounts provide a useful summary of its grant-making programmes:

Daiwa Foundation Small Grants
Daiwa Foundation Small Grants are available from £1,000–£5,000 to individuals, societies, associations or other bodies in the UK or Japan to promote and support interaction between the two countries. They can cover all fields of activity, including educational and grassroots exchanges, research travel, the organisation of conferences, exhibitions, and other projects and events that fulfil this broad objective. New initiatives are especially encouraged.

Daiwa Foundation Awards
Daiwa Foundation Awards are available from £5,000–£15,000 for collaborative projects that enable British and Japanese partners to work together, preferably within the context of an institutional relationship. Daiwa Foundation Awards can cover projects in most academic, professional, arts, cultural and educational fields. (Support for scientific collaborations is separately provided through

the Royal Society-Daiwa Anglo-Japanese Foundation Joint Project Grants scheme).

The Royal Society Daiwa Anglo-Japanese Foundation Joint Project Grants
These grants support travel, subsistence and research for collaborative projects between British and Japanese researchers in the field of science. They are funded by the Foundation and administered by The Royal Society.

Special projects
The foundation wishes to be receptive to new initiatives and therefore endeavours to respond flexibly to proposals that meet its general objectives but may fall outside of the criteria for our Small Grants and Awards programmes.

Daiwa Adrian Prizes
Named to commemorate the late Lord Adrian, [Daiwa Adrian Prizes] are awarded every three years in recognition of significant scientific collaboration between Japanese and British research teams.

Exclusions Daiwa Foundation Small Grants cannot be used for:

- general appeals
- capital expenditure (for example, building refurbishment, equipment acquisition, etc.)
- consumables (for example, stationery, scientific supplies, etc.)
- school, college or university fees
- research or study by an individual school/college/university student
- salary costs or professional fees
- commissions for works of art
- retrospective grants
- replacement of statutory funding
- commercial activities.

Daiwa Foundation Awards cannot be used for:

- any project that does not involve both a British and a Japanese partner
- general appeals
- capital expenditure (for example, building refurbishment, equipment acquisition, etc.)
- salary costs or professional fees
- commissions for works of art
- retrospective grants
- replacement of statutory funding
- commercial activities.

Applications Application forms are available to download at: www.dajf.org.uk. Applicants should submit three completed forms. Japanese applications for the Small Grants fund should be sent to the Tokyo office. All other applications should be sent to the address listed here.

There are two application deadlines each year: 31 March (for a decision by 31

May) and 30 September (for a decision by 30 November). The foundation encourages applicants to submit their application as early as possible.

Baron Davenport's Charity

Almshouses, hospices, residential homes for older people, children and young people under the age of 25

£1.15 million to organisations and individuals (2008)

Beneficial area Warwickshire, Worcestershire, Staffordshire, Shropshire and West Midlands.

Portman House, 5–7 Temple Row West, Birmingham B2 5NY

Tel. 0121 236 8004 **Fax** 0121 233 2500

Email enquiries@barondavenportscharity.org

Website www.barondavenportscharity.org

Correspondent Mrs Marlene Keenan, Administrator

Trustees *Christopher Hordern, Chair; Sue M Ayres; William M Colacicchi; Paul Dransfield; Philip A Gough; Rob Prichard.*

CC Number 217307

Information available Accounts were available from the Charity Commission. The charity also has a simple website.

Established in 1930 by Mr Baron Davenport, the charity is now governed by a Charity Commission Scheme dated 16th April 1998.

Of the income, 40% goes in grants for individuals, specifically for widows, single and divorced women (of 60 years and over) and women deserted by their partners together with their children, who are under 25 and in financial need.

The remaining 60% of the income is distributed, in Birmingham and the counties of the West Midlands, equally to:

- almshouses, residential homes for older people and hospices
- charities that assist children and young people under 25.

Grants are made to a large number of organisations each year – some organisations are funded in consecutive years, but every grant must be separately applied for each year; there is no automatic renewal.

In 2008 the charity had an income of £1.15 million, almost all of which was distributed in grants to organisations and individuals.

Unfortunately, although submitted to the Charity Commission, the charity's 2008 accounts were not yet available to view at the time of writing (November 2009). Previous beneficiaries included: Birmingham St Mary's Hospice; Donna Louise Trust; Acorns Children's Hospice; Almshouse Charity Birmingham; Beacon Centre for the Blind; Compton Hospice; Job's Close Residential Home for the Elderly; Trinity Hospital; Primrose Hospice; Cancer Help Centre; Berrow Cottage Homes; Coventry and District Free Church Homes for the Elderly; Gracewell Homes Foster Trust.

Exclusions There are no exclusions, providing the applications come within the charity's objects and the applying organisation is based within the charity's beneficial area, or the organisation's project lies within, or benefits people who live in, the beneficial area.

Applications In writing to the correspondent, accompanied by the latest accounts and any project costs. Distributions take place twice a year at the end of May and November and applications should be received at the charity's office by 15 March or 15 September. All applications are acknowledged and those not within the charity's objects are advised.

Peter De Haan Charitable Trust

Social welfare, the environment and the arts

£2.6 million (2007/08)

Beneficial area UK.

1 China Wharf, 29 Mill Street, London SE1 2BQ

Tel. 020 7232 5471

Email stusontaylor@pdhct.org.uk

Website www.pdhct.org.uk

Correspondent Mrs Sam Tuson Taylor

Trustees *Peter Charles De Haan; David Peter Davies; Janette McKay; Paul Vaight; Opus Corporate Trustees Limited.*

CC Number 1077005

Information available Accounts were available from the Charity Commission.

Background

The objects of the charity are wide-ranging and allow [it] to operate as a generalist grant-making charity.

The charity will not exist in perpetuity and the reserves will gradually be spent over a 20 year period from the date of constitution. It is this policy which governs the annual level of donations and this year we expect to make grants of between £2 million and £3 million.

General

In 2007/08 it had assets of £23.3 million and an income of £417,000. Grants were made to 169 organisations during the year totalling over £2.6 million.

The charity's grantmaking currently focuses on three areas:

- social welfare
- environment
- arts.

In all areas, the trustees will consider funding up for to a maximum of three years.

Grants during the year included the following:

Category	Value	No of grants
Social welfare	£985,000	139
Environment	£736,000	6
The arts	£263,000	24

Guidelines

Social Welfare

Our current social welfare programme is directed towards the following:

- disadvantaged children and young people – their health, education and well-being
- support for older people
- early intervention and community support projects which target social change through promoting enterprise and education
- special needs, counselling and therapy.

Charitable appeals should be able to demonstrate:

- tangible benefits on a significant scale to disadvantaged or vulnerable people
- encouragement of and motivation towards self-help and self-sufficiency
- practical improvement in the day to day quality of life of the beneficiaries.

We are unlikely to support the following social welfare projects:

- mainstream activities of local organisations which are part of a wider network of others doing similar work
- information and advice services
- enterprises where the primary focus is not the needs of those at greatest disadvantage
- childcare, nurseries, pre-school and after-school clubs
- community transport
- vocational training
- general capacity building
- prisoner resettlement
- work which is primarily the responsibility of central government or health authorities.

Environment

We are interested in applications which endeavour to enhance understanding of nature and wildlife and which inspire and attract the public interest, thereby investing in the future of the environment.

Charitable appeals should be able to demonstrate the following:

- practical and sustainable benefits of a significant scale
- effective operation with, or alongside, local communities and cultures
- recruitment, training and employment of a broad base of volunteers.

We are unlikely to support the following environmental projects:

- non-UK projects
- conservation of well-supported or non-native species
- enhancement of habitat for sporting purposes where there are no wider conservation benefits
- expeditions or fieldwork outside the UK
- recycling projects
- individual energy efficiency or waste reduction schemes
- local green space projects
- horticultural training or therapy
- playground or school ground improvements
- zoos, captive breeding and animal rescue centres
- work that is routine or low impact.

Arts

Our current Arts programme focuses on initiatives in any medium, which

- are available to a large audience
- increase learning
- attempt to address issues of community and social deprivation.

We are particularly interested in charities which support the provision of opportunities to participate in the arts in educational and community settings, especially for individuals or groups whose access to the arts is limited.

We are unlikely to support the following arts projects:

- individual artists – we accept applications only from organisations
- projects whose audience is likely to be restricted
- festivals
- broadcasting
- websites and publications in any medium.

Grants in 2007/08

Beneficiaries during the year included:

Social welfare

Missing People (£250,000); YouthNet (£200,000); New Horizon Centre (£80,000); Rainbow Trust (£100,000); Bede Home Association and Cardinal Hume Centre (£30,000 each); Dandelion Trust for Children, Noah's Ark Community Café and Twelves Company (£23,000 each); Walsall Street Teams (£20,000); Accept, Exodus Project and Perthes Association (£15,000 each); Big Buzz, Community Equality Disability Action, the Foresight Project, James Hopkins Trust, Leicestershire and Rutland Crimebeat Ltd, Raven House Trust Ltd, ReachOut Youth, Refugees into Jobs, Women Acting in Today's Society, Women's Aid Leeway Norwich and Women's Centre for Blackburn & District (£10,000 each); Broomhouse Centre Representative Council (£7,500); Donacaster Housing for Young People (£5,000); Parity (£3,000); CAN, Changing Faces, Off The Fence Trust, Spadework and Willow Burn Hospice (£2,000 each); and Adelaide House, ASHA Centre, British Blind Sport, Listening Ear, Migrants Resource Centre, Project Caleb, Special Toys Educational Postal Service, Winston's Wish and YMCA England (£1,000 each).

Environment

London Wildlife Trust (£400,000); Leicestershire & Rutland Wildlife Trust (£275,000); Kent Wildlife Trust (£116,000); and John Muir (£90,000).

Arts

L'Ouverture (£60,000); Scene and Heard (£45,000); Blue Elephant Theatre (£43,000); Pembroke House Youth Centre (£33,000); Southwark Playhouse (£23,000); King's Christian Centre (£19,000); Theatre in Education (£5,000); Sarum Orchestra (£4,000); Full Body and the Voice, Ice and Fire Theatre Company and the Whitechapel Art Gallery (£2,000 each); and Ascendance Repertory Company Ltd, Children's Discovery Centre and Sudden Productions (£1,000 each).

Exclusions The trust will not accept applications for grants:

- that directly replace or subsidise statutory funding
- from individuals or for the benefit of one individual
- for work that has already taken place
- which do not have a direct benefit to the UK
- for medical research
- for adventure and residential courses, expeditions or overseas travel
- for holidays and respite care
- for endowment funds
- for the promotion of a specific religion
- that are part of general appeals or circulars
- from applicants who have applied to the trust within the last 12 months.

In addition to the above, the trust is unlikely to support:

- large national charities which enjoy widespread support
- local organisations which are part of a wider network of others doing similar work
- individual pre-schools, schools. Out-of-school clubs, supplementary schools, colleges, universities or youth clubs
- websites, publications, conferences or seminars.

Applications In writing or via email to the correspondent.

Grants may be for project-based applications or to subsidise core costs.

The following information should be included:

- a statement that you have made reference to the website
- a description of the charity's aims and achievements
- charity registration number
- an outline and budget for the project for which funding is sought
- a copy of the latest financial statements
- details of funds raised and the current shortfall.

Applications are considered on a continuing basis throughout the year. Major grants are awarded at the trustee meetings held quarterly in March, June, September and December.

Notification of the outcome of applications will be by email. Where an email address is not available, no notification will be possible.

The charity states that it is not seeking applications from wildlife trusts.

The Debmar Benevolent Trust

Jewish

£813,000 (2007/08)

Beneficial area UK and Israel.

3rd Floor, Manchester House, 86 Princess Street, Manchester M1 6NP

Tel. 0161 236 4107

Correspondent Martin Weisz, Trustee

Trustees *Martin Weisz; Gella Klein; Hilary Olsberg; Rosalind Halpern; Vivienne Lewin.*

CC Number 283065

Information available Accounts were available from the Charity Commission, without a list of grants.

Grants are given towards the advancement of the orthodox Jewish faith and the relief of poverty.

In 2007/08 the trust had assets of over £9.1 million and an income of £3.8 million, mainly from donations. Grants were made during the year totalling £813,000.

Unfortunately, unlike previous years, a list of beneficiaries was not provided by the trust in its 2007/08 accounts. Previous beneficiaries included: Beis Hamedrash Hachodosh, Chasdei Belz, Chevras Mauous Lador, Gevurath Ari, Telz Talmudical Academy, Friends of Assos Chesed, Pardes Chana, ATLIB, Bobov Institutions, Ohr Akiva Institute, Tomchei Shaarei Zion, Ponivitch Institutions, Yeshiva Shaarei Zion, Beis Yoel High School, Format Charity Trust and Manchester Kollel.

Applications In writing to the correspondent.

Derbyshire Community Foundation

Social welfare

£1.5 million (2007/08)

Beneficial area Derbyshire and the city of Derby.

Foundation House, Unicorn Business Park, Wellington Street, Ripley, Derbyshire DE5 3EH

Tel. 01773 514 850 **Fax** 01773 741 410

Email info@derbyshirecommunityfoundation.co.uk

Website www.derbyshirecommunityfoundation.co.uk

Correspondent The Grants Team

Trustees *Helen Bishop; Arthur Blackwood; David Coleman; Kjell Karlsen; Nick Mirfin; Matthew Montague; Clive Moesby; David Moss; Lucy Palmer; Rt Rev. Alastair Redfern; Pat Taylor; David Walker; Robin Wood.*

CC Number 1039485

Information available Accounts were on file at the Charity Commission. Further information is available from the foundation's website.

As stated in the foundation's 2007/08 accounts:

Derbyshire Community Foundation's vision is to revitalise local life by means of a fund for Derbyshire, provided for the good of the community by people with the commitment and means to give. By meeting visible needs today, and anticipated and unexpected future needs, we hope to make a difference to Derbyshire forever.

Our objectives are:

- to build an endowment fund for the people of Derbyshire, to provide a growing sum for grants to tackle disadvantage and to enhance the quality of life in our county
- by making grants creatively on behalf of our donors and other funders, to create the bridge between people who care about the local community and the wide range of groups and individuals that need their help.

To support these objectives, we have Local Decision Making Panels across the county, comprising over 50 volunteers who live in their panel area and are involved in (and have a strong understanding of) the voluntary and community sector and what running an organisation involves. This helps us to ensure that funding is directed where it is most needed and that all bids are considered in accordance with both the foundation's constitutional objectives and the criteria of our funders and donors. In addition to our four core panels (covering North East, North West and South Derbyshire and Derby City), the foundation also manages a number of fund specific panels.

Current grants programmes

The foundation distributes funds on behalf of companies, individuals and local, regional and national government agencies, through a variety of grantmaking programmes. There are 14 main grant programmes:

Comic Relief Fund

Comic Relief has partnered the foundation to help distribute some of its funds into the City and County. The funds available have been split into two distinct themes, one related to sports and the other one for general community groups carrying out certain types of work.

Groups can apply for up to £10,000, however given the limited sums available this means the foundation is only likely to fund around three groups per financial year should all applicants apply for the full amount.

Derbyshire Building Society Fund

This fund is currently looking to support community and voluntary organisations helping with financial education and sport in the community. The maximum grant is £1,000.

Derbyshire Community Foundation General Fund

The foundation is building up a long-term fund with contributions from local companies and individuals. It will support applications for awards of up to £1,000. However, due to limitations of resources, applications of up to £500 are favoured.

The fund aims to support as wide a range of voluntary groups as possible, both in terms of where they are based and the work that they do. The overarching purpose of each grant made is to enhance the quality of life for people living in Derbyshire communities and to tackle disadvantages and inequalities they face.

Fair Share Sinfin & Austin Fund

This funding stream is administered by the foundation on behalf of the National Fair Share program and was devised to tackle issues within the Sinfin & Austin wards of Derby City creating a stronger community and to improve opportunities for residents. The fund consists of three main strands: community and voluntary group support, children and young people and training and education. The maximum grant per stream is currently £10,000.

Firm Foundations Fund

Firm Foundations is a broad funding stream aiming to improve the quality of life for Derbyshire residents by supporting a thriving community and voluntary sector that offers a wide range of services and facilities to local communities. The maximum grant is currently £5,000 (preference is given to bids of around £2,000).

Grassroots Grants

This fund supports a broad range of community and voluntary groups with a variety of different costs. As with all of the foundation's funds, the overarching purpose of each grant made is to enhance the quality of life for people living in Derbyshire communities and to tackle disadvantages and inequalities faced by people living in the county and city today. Groups can apply for a minimum of £250 and a maximum of £5,000.

The Hutchinson Music Award

Grants of up to £250 each are made to talented young musicians from Derby and Derbyshire, to help with the cost of their music education.

Jefford Weller Fund

This fund provides financial assistance to any community and voluntary organisation tackling homelessness issues and/or addressing housing problems. The maximum grant is £2,000.

John Weston Fund

This fund was set up by local benefactor John Weston in 2002 and has two strands.

- Strand one: support to individual young people with personal development.
- Strand two: financial assistance to community and voluntary groups tackling issues related to health and well-being or supporting young people within the community.

Community groups can apply for up to £2,500.

RBS Derbyshire Charitable Fund

Its aim is to benefit the wide diversity of community and voluntary groups who are working hard to address the many needs within the local area. There are three main themes: health, young people and community life. The grant range is currently £50 to £1,000.

Southern Derbyshire Learning Fund

This fund was designed to support community and voluntary groups offering opportunities for people to gain new skills, which will ultimately allow people to enter or re-enter employment. The maximum grant is currently £2,000.

Targeted Support Fund

This is one strand of the government's 'Real Help for Communities' programme. It has been designed to relieve the pressure on charities brought

on by the effects of the current recession – mainly an increase in demand for services in the past 12 months. Grants of £10,000 to £40,000 will be available for organisations in Derby city only.

Tom Carey Fund

This fund has been set up to support new and existing community activity in the Abbey ward of Derby City. Its main purpose is to improve the quality of life for residents in this area. The maximum grant is currently £10,000 although preference will be given to applications of up to £5,000.

Vickers Art Award

The Jonathan Vickers Charitable Settlement have set up a named fund to allow a biennial Art Award to support rising artists to produce new work in response to the heritage, landscape and people of Derbyshire. The aim is to enrich the cultural life of the County of Derbyshire with new art of national importance, accessible to and informed by local people. More information is available on the website: www.vickersartaward.co.uk.

More information on all of the fund's listed above including, grant priorities, types of project costs funded, application documents and deadlines, can be found on the foundation's website.

Grants in 2007/08

In 2007/08 the trust had assets of £6.1 million and an income of £2 million. Grants totalled £1.5 million.

During the year 25 grants were payable to community groups and voluntary organisations in excess of £7,001 amounting to £602,000, 95 grants were paid between £4,000 and £7,000 amounting to £564,000, and 305 grants of up to £3,999 amounting to £316,000.

Grants of £7,001 or more included those made to: Derbyshire Rural Community Centre (£147,000); Derby CVS (£84,000); South Normanton and Pinxton Development Project (£63,000); LINKS Chesterfield and North East Derbyshire Council for Voluntary Service (£32,000); SCILLS – Sherwater Community for Independent Living (£15,000); Viva Chamber Orchestra and SAIL – Sexual Abuse and Incest Line (£10,000 each); Hollingwood After School Club (£9,900); Shipley Hall Cricket Club (£8,700); and Woodville Parish Council (£7,200).

Exclusions The foundation's general exclusions are:

- profit making organisations where individual members benefit financially (legitimate social enterprises and community interest companies can

receive funding but the foundation asks that you read the additional guidelines related to this type of group structure)
- medical equipment
- animal charities
- any project which promotes faith or involves the refurbishment/building of a place of worship
- statutory bodies including schools, hospitals, police etc.
- any project which directly replaces statutory obligations
- any project which promotes a political party
- projects which benefit people outside of Derbyshire
- retrospective funding (grants for activities which have already taken place)
- sponsored events.

Applications The foundation offers several different funds, each offering funding for a maximum of twelve months and each with a specific focus or set of criteria. Please visit the foundation's website for full details of the current grant programmes and the relevant application documents. If you require any further help in deciding which fund to apply for contact the grants team on 01773 514850.

Applicants should download and complete the appropriate application form from the website and send it to the correspondent with the following supporting documents:

- annual accounts
- bank statements
- group constitution
- management committee form (please download this from the website)
- minutes from the last management committee meeting.

Applications are passed to a member of the grants team for assessment and to prepare all of the information ready to present to the award making panel. During this time, applicants are likely to be contacted by the grants team for an informal chat about their application and their group, which helps the foundation to understand the background of the project and gives the best chance of a successful bid.

The decision on whether to award a grant is made by, either a panel of independent people from the local community, who meet every eight weeks, or by a panel set up by the fund-holder, who will usually meet once every three months. Please note: the grants team are entirely independent and will not make any funding recommendations to the panels.

Applicants will be informed of the decision date for their application and are invited to call the grants team or check the website to find out the decision two days after the panel date. You will also receive the panel decision in writing within one week of the panel date.

The foundation states that it is willing to provide full, honest feedback on all decisions and is happy to discuss any outcome with applicants.

Devon Community Foundation

General

£1.2 million (2007/08)
Beneficial area County of Devon.

The Factory, Leat Street, Tiverton EX16 5LL

Tel. 01884 235887 **Fax** 01884 243824

Email grants@devoncf.com

Website www.devoncf.com

Correspondent Kathy Beechen, Deputy Chief Executive

Trustees *David Stevens; Michael Gee; Dr Katherine Gurney; Steve Hindley; Mike Bull; Tim Legood; Anthony Melville; Mark Haskell; Dr Anne Mildmay White; Michael Hockin; Chris Hill; Arthur Ainslie; Martin Lamb; David Searle; Peter Keech; Paul Ellis; Jane McCloskey.*

CC Number 1057923

Information available Accounts were available from the Charity Commission.

Devon Community Foundation is an independent local charity that aims to promote and support local charitable and community organisations throughout Devon to tackle disadvantage. This is achieved by channelling funds to grass roots organisations within the community to support a wide variety of causes. We act as a conduit for a variety of funds, including those from the statutory, voluntary and corporate sectors, and for donations and income from our own endowed funds.

The foundation always has a variety of grant programmes running and new ones are regularly added. It supports groups and projects throughout Devon. Organisations can hold more than one grant at a time from the different funds available. It is not necessary to be a registered charity to receive a grant from

the foundation, but you must be a not-for-profit organisation that is benevolent, charitable or educational and established to alleviate disadvantage in your local community.

In 2007/08 the foundation had an income of £1.5 million and made grants totalling £1.2 million.

Funds Available

The foundation has a range of different funds designed for small community and voluntary groups working to help local people across Devon.

Grant schemes change frequently. Please consult the foundation's website for details of current programmes and their deadlines.

Each scheme tends to have a different application procedure and size of award.

Grassroots Grants

This programme is funded by the Office of the Third Sector and delivered by the Community Development Foundation. Grants of £250 to £5,000 are available to voluntary and community groups in Devon (including Torbay and Plymouth).

Small grants/Rural fund

Grants of up to £500 are available for community projects and groups which are not eligible for other grant-making programmes. This now incorporates the Wales and West Utilities General Fund, Rural Fund, North Devon Relief Fund and the Clare Milne Trust Fund which provides small grants for groups working with people with disabilities.

Friends Provident Exeter Positive Steps Fund

Grants of up to £5,000 are given for community projects helping vulnerable unemployed people in Exeter to build the skills and self-confidence they need to help them back on the road to work.

Comic Relief Fund

This fund supports a range of activities, particularly those which are sports based. Projects should make a lasting change to the local community. Grants of between £1,000 and £10,000 are available.

Exclusions The foundation does not fund:

- statutory organisation's including schools
- regional or local offices of national organisations
- projects promoting political activities
- commercial ventures
- individuals
- projects for the sole benefit of animals or plants
- other grant-making organisations
- churches.

Individual programmes may have further eligibility criteria. Please check the foundation's website or contact the foundation directly to confirm that your organisation is eligible to apply.

Applications The foundation's website has details of the grant schemes currently being administered.

The Diana, Princess of Wales Memorial Fund

Humanitarian causes, refugees and asylum seekers and penal affairs in the UK; post-conflict and palliative care overseas

£3.8 million (2008)
Beneficial area Unrestricted, mainly the UK and Africa.

The County Hall, Westminster Bridge Road, London SE1 7PB

Tel. 020 7902 5500 **Fax** 020 7902 5511

Email memorial.fund@memfund.org.uk

Website www.theworkcontinues.org

Correspondent Helen Jones, Office Manager

Trustee *The Diana, Princess of Wales Memorial Fund Trustee Company.*

CC Number 1064238

Information available Accounts were available from the Charity Commission.

The Diana, Princess of Wales Memorial Fund is an independent grant-giving trust established in September 1997 for general charitable purposes and seeks to continue Diana's humanitarian work in the United Kingdom and overseas. Humanitarian work played an important part in the Princess's life, both at home and abroad. Her interests were reflected in the organisations of which she was patron or president. In the UK these included the Great Ormond Street Hospital for Sick Children in London and the Royal Marsden Hospital, which specialises in the treatment of cancer. Her patronages also included Centrepoint, the National Aids Trust and the English National Ballet. Overseas she made many visits to Angola,

Australia, Bosnia, Egypt, India, Pakistan, North America and many European countries. She spoke out on a wide range of issues and used her high profile to raise awareness as well as funds for charitable causes.

The trust was established with donations given in memory of Diana by people around the world in the days and months following her death in 1997 which totalled about £20 million. In addition, a further £80 million was generated through commercial activities. In the first nine years of its existence, the trust pledged some £76 million in grants to over 350 organisations around the world. Charities with which the Princess had a close connection in her lifetime were invited to submit proposals for funding, and more than 90 such organisations received money from the trust in the first year. Since then, the trust has focused on disadvantaged and marginalised people, providing them with support, a voice and an opportunity to realise their full potential. The trust seeks to respond to emerging issues of the day and speak out on behalf of causes that are not widely recognised or popular and to support those that would otherwise find it difficult to gain funding.

The trust works to secure sustainable improvements in the lives of the most disadvantaged people in the UK and around the world by giving grants to organisations, championing charitable causes, advocacy and campaigning, raising awareness, enabling marginalised people to have their voices heard, bringing representatives of disadvantaged people together with decision makers and offering other non-financial support including use of the fund's meeting rooms (see page 108). The trust has confirmed its belief that it can make a greater and more sustainable impact for those who need it most by a carefully targeted portfolio of work over a limited number of years. **As such, the trust plans to substantially spend out its existing capital over the period to the end of 2013.**

In November 2004, a $25 million joint grants scheme between the Diana, Princess of Wales Memorial Fund and the Franklin Mint was announced as part of their out-of-court settlement of a legal dispute. Under the joint grants scheme, some £13.5 million of grants have been made to a jointly agreed list of excellent charitable causes that resonate with the memory of the late Diana, Princess of Wales.

Funding guidelines

The trust's website states:

From 2007 to 2012, the fund's grant-making activities will be grouped under three initiatives, each of which has a desired outcome and a set of strategic objectives to be achieved over five years. The three initiatives are:

- *Palliative Care* – under which the trust is committed to spending up to £10 million over five years to promote the scale-up of palliative care in Ethiopia, Malawi, Kenya, Rwanda, South Africa, Tanzania, Uganda, Zambia and Zimbabwe, and its integration into their governments' health policies;
- *Refugee and Asylum Seekers* – under which the trust is committed to spending up to £10 million over five years to raise awareness and highlight the needs and issues of young refugees and asylum seekers;
- *Partnership* – under which the trust is committed to spending up to £5 million over five years to follow-up and add leverage to its previous investments into penal affairs in the UK, and internationally into its programme on eradicating explosive remnants of war.

Palliative Care

The desired outcome of this initiative is that palliative care is accepted as an essential part of, and integrated into, the care and treatment of people with HIV/AIDS, cancer and other life-limiting illnesses.

In working to achieve this outcome the initiative will operate at an international, regional and national level, in partnership with other donors and national and international organisations. It will use the fund's unique name and associations to promote palliative care.

It is focused on nine countries in sub-Saharan Africa; Ethiopia, Kenya, Malawi, Rwanda, South Africa, Tanzania, Uganda, Zambia and Zimbabwe.

The initiative has six objectives.

- Objective 1: an HIV/AIDS community and donors that has integrated palliative care in the continuum of care for people with HIV/AIDS and their families.
- Objective 2: a strong palliative care sector capable of scaling up delivery and influencing health policy.
- Objective 3: a workforce, from medical professionals to informal carers, that is trained to ensure the delivery of high quality palliative care.
- Objective 4: an increase in long-term donor funding for palliative care that makes it a sustainable intervention.
- Objective 5: a strong, effective and sustainable regional organisation that

effectively promotes and supports palliative care in Africa.
- Objective 6: an increased evidence base to demonstrate the effectiveness and impact of palliative care in Africa.

Refugee and Asylum Seekers

The desired outcome of the initiative is that the rights of refugees and people seeking asylum in the UK are upheld.

The initiative has three objectives.

- Objective 1: change immigration legislation to meet international standards on children's rights and ensure the priority of the best interests of the child.
- Objective 2: encourage the fair and humane treatment of refugees and people seeking asylum.
- Objective 3: disseminate good practice.

Partnership

The desired outcome of the Partnership Initiative is that systemic change takes place in the UK and internationally in areas in which the fund has already made significant investments.

The initiative currently has two strategic objectives:

- Penal Affairs: the objective is to secure a sustained reduction in child and youth imprisonment in the UK
- Lethal Litter: the objective is to increase the protection of civilians from the effects of cluster munitions and other explosive remnants of war internationally.

Please note: each strategic objective has planned activities and specific approaches. For further information on each of the objectives, go to the website or contact the trust directly.

Voluntary sector rooms

From its inception, the fund has sought to promote and support the voluntary sector in whatever ways it can. In addition to its grant-making programmes the fund lets out meeting rooms at its offices in County Hall, free of charge, to other voluntary sector organisations that meet our criteria. Voluntary sector organisations that are eligible to use the rooms are those working with:

- displaced people – this includes children and adults made homeless or deprived of rights for other reasons
- people at the margins – this includes those who are jobless, homeless or excluded through public prejudice or through mental and physical disability, addiction and disease
- survivors of conflict and those requiring conflict mediation
- the dying and bereaved
- second tier organisations supporting the above work.

Grantmaking in 2008

In 2008 the trust had assets of £22 million and an income of £2.3 million. Grants totalled £3.8 million and were distributed in the following areas:

Palliative Care – 26 grants totalling £1.1 million

Beneficiaries included: Hereford Muheza Link Society (£231,000); Island Hospice and Bereavement Service (£155,000); PASADA (£95,000); Kenya Hospices and Palliative Care Association (£61,000); Wits Health Consortium (£45,000); Catholic Diocese of Mansa Home Based Care (£20,000); Zambia Ministry of Health (£5,000); and University of Dundee (£2,000).

Refugee and Asylum Seekers – 9 grants totalling £2.4 million

Beneficiaries included: Church of England Children's Society (£907,000); Bail for Immigration Detainees (£345,000); British Refugee Council (£205,000); Scottish Refugee Council (£182,000); Rayne Foundation (£100,000); and Refugee Action (£25,000).

Partnership – 1 grant of £266,000

The sole beneficiary was Landmine Action – Cluster Munitions Coalition.

Exclusions The trust will not fund individuals or projects outside its funding priorities.

Applications Grants are provided on an 'invitation-to-bid' basis or through negotiated partnerships with selected organisations that have the capacity to deliver the initiatives' desired outcomes. Projects will be rigorously assessed against the initiatives' strategic objectives, and to maximise impact grants are awarded for up to five years with a mid-term review.

As the fund is engaged in proactive grant-making, providing grants on 'invitation to bid' basis, the fund is unable to accept general requests for funding from either organisations or individuals. The demand for funds is always greater than the money available, and the fund is of the belief that we can help more people by distributing grants to organisations that have the capacity to deliver the desired outcomes of our three initiatives.

The Djanogly Foundation

General, medicine, education and social welfare

£1.2 million (2007/08)
Beneficial area UK and overseas.

3 Angel Court, London SW1Y 6QF
Tel. 020 7930 9845
Correspondent Christopher Sills, Secretary
Trustees *Sir Harry Djanogly; Michael S Djanogly; Lady Djanogly.*
CC Number 280500
Information available Accounts were available from the Charity Commission.

The foundation was established in 1980 and supports developments in medicine, education, social welfare, the arts, Jewish charities and welfare of older and younger people. The foundation is particularly concerned with funding projects that are new and may require a number of years to become established. In such cases the grant making activity will be related to the development phases of these projects.

In 2007/08 the foundation had assets of £15 million and an income of £1.4 million. There were 51 grants made totalling £1.2 million.

Beneficiaries of the largest grants were: Great Ormond Street Children's Hospital and British Museum Development Trust (£200,000 each); Weizmann Institute Foundation (£175,000); Jerusalem Foundation (£161,000); University of Nottingham (£100,000); National Gallery Trust (£83,000); and Nottingham Playhouse (£50,000).

Smaller grants included those to: Royal Anglican Benevolent Fund (£30,000); Jewish Care (£12,000); St Nicholas School (£8,000); Norwood (£5,000); Imperial War Museum (£2,000); and WIZO (£500).

Applications In writing to the correspondent.

The DM Charitable Trust

General

£2.4 million (2007/08)
Beneficial area England and Wales and Israel.

Ground Floor, Sutherland House, 70–78 West Hendon Broadway, London NW9 7BT
Correspondent S J Goldberg, Trustee
Trustees *S J Goldberg, Chair; D Cohen; P Klein.*
CC Number 1110419
Information available Accounts were available from the Charity Commission.

The trust was set up in 2005 for the relief of poverty and sickness, educational purposes and the support of Jewish organisations.

In 2007/08 the trust had assets of £1.5 million and an income of £1.9 million. Grants totalled £2.4 million, however a list of beneficiaries was unavailable in this year's accounts. The accounts state that: 'Charitable donations are detailed in a separate publication entitled *The DM Charitable Trust Schedule of Charitable Donations*, which can be obtained by writing to the trustees at the charity's principal office'. Despite putting a request in writing enclosing an SAE, no reply was received.

Applications In writing to the correspondent.

The Dollond Charitable Trust

Jewish and general

£1 million (2007/08)
Beneficial area UK and Israel.

c/o FMCB, Hathaway House, Popes Drive, Finchley, London N3 1QF
Tel. 020 8346 6446
Email gwz@fmcb.co.uk
Correspondent Jeffery Milston, Trustee
Trustees *Arthur Leslie Dolland; Adrian Dollond; Jeffery Milston; Melissa Dollond; Brian Dollond; Rina Dollond.*
CC Number 293459
Information available Accounts were available from the Charity Commission.

Although the constitution of the charity is broadly based, the trustees have adopted a policy of principally assisting the Jewish communities in Britain and Israel. The trustees have been following a policy of accumulating income and building up the fund with the intention of the charity making its mark with a major project, through the establishment of an Anglo-Israel Institute in Britain to provide a focus for cultural and educational activities.

In 2007/08 the trust had assets of £26.8 million and an income of £2 million, including a donation of £1.3 million from the settlor, Arthur Dollond. There were 60 grants made totalling £1 million (£458,500 in 2006/07).

A substantial donation of £400,000 was made during the year to Yavneh College, Borehamwood. Other larger grants were made to: British Friends of Shuvu/ Return (£135,000 in total); Jerusalem College of Technology (£56,000); and Yeshivas Ateret Shlomo (£20,000).

More typical grants included those to: Beis Sorah Schneiver School, Great Ormond Street Hospital, Kol Torah College Jerusalem, Norwood Ravenswood, Side by Side and WST Charity Limited (£10,000 each); and British Friends of Ariel, Cancer Research UK, Jewish Deaf Association, Menorah Foundation, Torah Vodaas Ltd and Yeshiva Brisk (£5,000 each).

Applications In writing to the correspondent.

The Drapers' Charitable Fund

General charitable purposes including education, heritage, the arts, prisoner support and textile conservation

£1 million (2007/08)

Beneficial area UK, with a special interest in the City and adjacent parts of London and Moneymore and Draperstown in Northern Ireland.

The Drapers' Company, Drapers' Hall, Throgmorton Avenue, London EC2N 2DQ

Tel. 020 7588 5001 **Fax** 020 7628 1988
Email charities@thedrapers.co.uk

Website www.thedrapers.co.uk
Correspondent Andy Mellows, Head of Charities
Trustee *The Drapers' Company.*
CC Number 251403
Information available Detailed accounts were available at the Charity Commission. The company has a helpful and informative website giving full details of the trust.

The Drapers' Company is a City livery company, one of those descended from the guilds of London, and the trust has a trail of historical connections, the most important of which are with Queen Mary College, University of London and Bancroft's School in Essex, but which also includes Adam's Maintained Comprehensive School in Wem, Shropshire and various Oxford and London university colleges.

The trust aims to improve the quality of life and expectations of people and their communities within the UK, particularly those disadvantaged or socially excluded, through the award of grants in the fields of education and relief of need. It also aims to support organisations and institutions, particularly those with historic links to the Drapers' Company and the City of London, within the fields of education, heritage, the arts, prisoner support, and in Northern Ireland, to promote the company's textile heritage through support for technical textiles and textile conservation.

In directing its grant making, the trust applies criteria such as geographical area, particular types of project, beneficiary group or specific areas of charitable activity.

The trust is a flexible grantmaker, responding to a broad range of appeals from a wide variety of organisations. It supports many initiatives and projects which are traditionally outside the mainstream of grant making. The main themes for support are reviewed tri-annually and the annual objectives within the three year period remain the same, to distribute net income within the themes chosen for support in an efficient and effective manner.

There is no minimum or maximum grant size, but the majority of grants awarded are normally for sums under £10,000. Awards are seldom made for sums in excess of £20,000. Funding may be given towards capital costs such as buildings and equipment provided that the overall scale of the project does not make the trust's grant seem insignificant. Appeals for the provision of core costs, which may include running costs such as staff salaries and overheads, are also accepted. Applicants will be expected to demonstrate that plans are in place to meet future funding requirements of these core costs.

In 2007/08 the trust had assets of over £26 million and an income of £1.7 million. 245 grants were made totalling £1 million.

The trust's current priorities for funding are:

Education and training
- affiliated schools, colleges and universities
- outreach programmes
- leadership and volunteering
- promotion of the learning of science.

Relief of need
- homelessness
- the causes and effects of social exclusion – in this category beneficiaries must be young people under 25 years old, projects should be based in deprived inner city areas and preference will be given to such projects in inner city London and to returning young people to education, employment or training
- prisoners – preference is given to young offenders
- ex-servicemen and women
- welfare – this includes the provision of care or support services and preference will be given to projects for older people, vulnerable people or those disadvantaged due to poverty and carers, particularly young carers
- disability – in this category, projects to ease the lives and reduce the suffering of those with disabilities or those suffering long-term disability or ill health. Preference will be given to charities which improve the quality of life for adults with less visible disabilities such as hearing impairment, dyslexia, mental health problems or chronic fatigue syndrome.

Textiles
- technical textiles
- textile conservation.

Heritage and arts
- support for the preservation of the nation's heritage and the provision of public access to the arts and heritage, particularly in Greater London – the City of London and the Mayoralty
- museums, memorials and monuments, especially those related to former exploits of the armed forces, the history of London or the textile trade.

Northern Ireland
- projects falling under the company's other themes for support in the area

of historic involvement for the Drapers' Company, particularly in and around Draperstown and Moneymore.

Grantmaking in 2007/08

Beneficiaries of the largest grants included: Bancroft's School (£85,000); Help for Heroes (£51,000); Queen Mary – University of London (£50,000); Hertford College – Oxford (£34,000); and Project Trust (£20,000).

Other beneficiaries included: Hanover Foundation (£15,000); Zimbabwe Farmers Trust Fund (£11,000); Women's Aid – Orkney (£10,000); Butler Trust (£7,500); Blundell's School (£6,000); and Beatbullying (£5,000).

Exclusions Grants are not usually made for:

- individuals
- schools, colleges and universities (except in North Wales and Greenwich and Lewisham through the Thomas Howell's Education Fund for North Wales and Sir William Boreman's Foundation)
- churches
- almshouses
- animal welfare
- counselling or advocacy
- medical research/relief, hospitals or medical centres
- children's disabilities, physical disabilities or medical conditions
- holidays or general respite care
- organisations solely assisting refugees, asylum seekers or specific cultural or ethnic groups within the UK
- organisations that are not registered charities, unless exempt from registration
- funds that replace or subsidise statutory funding
- local branches of national charities, associations or movements
- work that has already taken place
- general appeals or circulars
- loans or business finance.

Applications Applications can be made at any time during the year. The charities committee meets four times a year (October, January, April and July). Applicants should complete the 'application summary sheet' (available to download from the website) and submit it together with a document on proposed funding. This should include detailed information about the organisation and the project/activity to be funded; full costings and project budget for the proposed work for which the grant is requested, or the organisation's income and expenditure budget for the current year (whichever is appropriate); and the most recent audited financial statements and trustees report. Applications should be submitted by post only.

For full details of the application process and the trust's current priorities, applicants are advised to refer to the trust's website.

The Dulverton Trust

Young people and education, conservation, welfare and general

£3 million (2008/09)

Beneficial area Unrestricted. Mainly UK in practice. An interest in the Cotswolds. Limited support to parts of Africa. Few grants for work in London or Northern Ireland.

5 St James's Place, London SW1A 1NP

Tel. 020 7629 9121 **Fax** 020 7495 6201

Email trust@dulverton.org

Website www.dulverton.org

Correspondent Col. Christopher Bates, Director

Trustees *Christopher Wills, Chair; Sir John Kemp-Welch; Tara Douglas-Home; Lord Dulverton; Lord Gowrie; Dr Catherine Wills; Richard Fitzalan Howard; Sir Malcolm Rifkind; Dame Mary Richardson.*

CC Number 206426

Information available Accounts were available from the Charity Commission. The trust also has a clear and concise website.

This is one of the trusts deriving from the tobacco-generated fortune of the Wills family. It has an endowment worth £79.6 million and a body of trustees which combines family members with others who have achieved distinction in public life.

The Dulverton Trust is unusual in saying that an application, outside its guidelines, may be accepted if it is supported by an individual trustee – most trusts say that their trustees decide their grantmaking intentions and policies first, and then stick to them.

There is a clear, reported family connection with the Cotswold area (though no longer apparently with Bristol, where many of the Wills factories were located). Sir John Kemp-Welch is a former Chairman of the London Stock Exchange; Sir Malcolm Rifkind is a former foreign secretary; and Lord Gowrie is best known for his interests in the arts (although the trust excludes the arts entirely from its grantmaking).

General

Apart from a few special programmes described below, the trust makes one-off grants and will not normally consider further applications until a period of at least two years has passed.

The trust supports national, regional and local charities operating in England, Scotland and Wales, especially in areas where there is a significant amount of deprivation, and particularly where a grant would make a real difference to the recipients. Grants are also made overseas, particularly in eastern and southern Africa.

The trust makes two types of grant:

- *Major* – for charities that operate nationally or across the geographical regions of the UK. Support will normally be restricted to charities whose annual income is below £50 million.
- *Minor* – for smaller charities usually working at local or county level. Support will normally be restricted to charities whose annual income is below £400,000. A fixed sum of money is earmarked each year for these awards and the maximum grant is £3,500. Priority will be given to charities working in areas of severe deprivation or rural isolation.

Grants in 2008/09

In 2008/09 the trust had assets of £59 million and an income of £1.4 million. During the year the trust received 1,261 appeals for funding, 252 of which received a grant, making the success rate around one in five. Though there are wide areas of 'exclusion' these can be funded if an application is recommended by a trustee. Grants paid during the year totalled £3 million and were distributed amongst the following categories:

Category	%	Value
Young people and education	34%	£1,000,000
General welfare	22%	£664,000
Africa	11%	£320,000
Minor Appeals	9%	£275,000
Conservation	7%	£208,000
Preservation	7%	£196,000
Miscellaneous	5%	£147,000
Peace and security/humanitarian support	3%	£97,000
Religion	1%	£35,000
Local appeals (Cotswolds)	1%	£25,000

The following analysis of the trust's areas of interest and achievements during the year is provided by the trust in its excellent annual report (with grant figures added where necessary):

Young people and Education

Young people and Education continues to be the largest single category supported by the trust, accounting this year for a little over one third of the grants by value; the largest number of perennial grants also falls within this category. This reflects the priority placed by trustees on assisting the development of young people, particularly those suffering from disadvantage. In May 2008, trustees renewed for another four years the Dulverton and Michael Wills Scholarships awarded at Oxford University for Eastern European students, which represent by far the largest annual recurring grant awarded by the trust. Following the deliberations of the Scholarships Sub-Committee, trustees agreed, inter alia, that full scholarships are preferable to partial awards and that the Michael Wills Scholarships should be more closely aligned with the original purpose of these awards; namely, reconciliation. In addition, the Dulverton Scholarships will in future be restricted to non-arts subjects, and the list of eligible nationalities will be reviewed. Further discussions took place with the University to agree how these changes will be implemented. Trustees had earlier renewed scholarships at Atlantic College, although these were switched to benefit two African students, starting in 2009.

The final payment was made in 2008/09 of the two-year funding awarded for two African students at Pestalozzi International Village. Trustees agreed in February 2009 that the Pestalozzi scholarships would not be renewed and the Atlantic College Scholarships would not be further extended. Instead, consideration would be given to helping African students in Africa.

Many of the projects supported under the Youth and Education category help disadvantaged young people in different ways, including those run by Fairbridge (£32,000); Right Track Scotland (£30,000); Independent Panel for Special Education Advice (£25,000); Place2Be and YWCA Scotland (£20,000 each); Keyfund Federation (£15,000); and Endeavour Training (£9,000). Unfortunately, the perennial grant awarded to Weston Spirit was nullified when this charity ceased operating. And the conditional grant awarded to Clubs for Young People had to be rescinded after the plan to merge with UK Youth was suspended at a late stage.

The trustees continue to believe that introducing young people to challenging experiences in the 'great outdoors' is important, hence the exceptional grant for bursaries, in addition to the perennial grant,

for the Outward Bound Trust (£15,000) and support for Jubilee Sailing Trust (£36,000); Marine Society and Sea Cadets (£30,000); Venture Trust (£25,000); Raleigh International (£15,000); Island Trust (£10,000); YMCA England (£7,000); and Ocean Youth Trust South (£5,000). The importance placed on the introduction of inner-city primary school children to the countryside was underlined by the grants to the Country Trust (£12,000) and Farms for City Children (£30,000).

The trustees place emphasis on the encouragement of young people to consider a career in science and engineering, hence the grants to Brightside Trust (£24,000); Generating Genius (£20,000); Industrial Trust (£15,000); the Arkwright Scholarship Trust (£14,000); and the Centre for the Advancement of Science and Technology Education (£7,500).

The grants to Prisoners' Education Trust and Shannon Trust (£30,000 each) – (and also Caring for Ex-Offenders and NACRO under the General Welfare Category) reflect trustees' concerns about the unacceptably high rates of recidivism amongst ex-prisoners. Teach First's innovative work to recruit inspiring young teachers for inner city secondary schools was recognised by the award of a three-year grant. Finally, a grant paid to FOCUS Charity in 2007/08 was rescinded and refunded because the charity was unable to fulfil the conditions.

General Welfare

General Welfare is the next largest category, accounting this year for 22.1% of grant expenditure. As always, a very wide range of charitable activity falls under this heading. Trustees' concern for the welfare of former members of the Armed Forces was recognised by grants to Veterans Aid (£36,000) and St Oswald Stoll Foundation (£22,000) – and also Combat Stress in the Miscellaneous Category.

Support was provided for families through grants to the British Association for Adoption and Fostering and Trussell Trust (£25,000 each); Army Families Federation (£22,000); Circle Supporting Families in Scotland, Gingerbread and Families Need Fathers (£20,000 each); Twins and Multiple Births Association (£18,000); Families for Children (£15,000); and Lilias Graham Trust and One Plus One (£10,000 each).

The problems of homelessness persist, and help was provided for Crisis UK (£30,000); Shelter (£30,000); and Emmaus UK (£15,000). Hard-pressed carers were assisted through awards to Carers UK (£30,000); Princess Royal Trust for Carers (£22,000); and Kiloran Trust (£5,000). Trustees were only too well aware of the likely increase in problems of indebtedness, and were happy to support the excellent

work of Christians Against Poverty with a three-year grant.

The RNLI received a further exceptional perennial grant (£25,000) towards a course to train inshore lifeboat crews; the chairman and finance director visited this course at the Lifeboat College and were impressed by the quality of the volunteers. As a result of the quinquennial review, the guidelines were amended to indicate that in future the trust would not normally provide support for people with disabilities; this change was made in order to clarify the trust's policy, and also in recognition that this area is well covered by other grantmakers. In consequence, a number of charities for disabled people which have previously received Dulverton support will in future be ineligible.

Africa

Grants amounting to 10.6% of the awards went to projects in Africa, reflecting the quality of appeals received and the fact that more can often be achieved for relatively modest sums in Africa than in the UK. The largest grant was the perennial award for Book Aid International (£36,000), for its much-needed work in delivering books to east Africa.

The Kariandusi School Trust (£35,000) was commended for its remarkably cost-effective work in rebuilding primary schools in the Rift Valley in Kenya; these schools were put under greater pressure in 2008 by the influx of families displaced by inter-communal violence. Also in Kenya, a supplementary grant was awarded to the Starehe Girls' Centre (£13,000) to cover the increase in costs of building materials caused by the violence.

The perennial grant to Voluntary Service Overseas (£27,000) continued, for the sponsorship of eight placements in east Africa. The excellent international work of the Duke of Edinburgh's Award (£26,000) was supported with a grant towards establishing Open Award Centres in Kenya and Uganda for youngsters not in formal education. The third of three grants was made to Hope and Homes for Children (£25,000) for its innovative work with orphans in South Africa. School-Aid UK (£25,000) received further support for its good work in shipping superseded text books and other equipment donated by UK schools to needy schools in Africa. Tusk Trust (£25,000) received support for another excellent project, the Koiyaki Guide School in the Maasai Mara.

The grants to Tools for Self Reliance (£23,000); International Rescue Committee UK (£22,000); Students Partnership Worldwide (£20,000); TreeAid (£17,000); and Farm Africa (£15,000) were all for projects designed to assist local communities in east Africa to help them to improve self-sufficiency. An unusually large number of grants were awarded for projects in Uganda, reflecting the generally more peaceful conditions in that country.

Minor Appeals

The sum available for minor appeals from small charities was increased at the quinquennial review, and maximum individual grants were increased from £3,000 to £3,500. Trustees continued to be encouraged by the worthiness and variety of the appeals considered, and the ability of a modest grant to make a significant difference to a small charity. A total of 120 grants were awarded to organisations such as Scout Groups, Youth Clubs and community groups, with priority as always given to the more disadvantaged regions of the UK. An exceptional grant made to the Chelsea Festival was rescinded after the event was cancelled.

Conservation

After a lean year in 2007/08, the conservation category attracted 6.9% of the grants made in 2008/09. The marine environment was supported with grants to the Marine Conservation Trust (£30,000); the Marine Stewardship Council (£25,000); and the Fair Isle Bird Observatory Trust (£10,000); the latter reflected long-term trust support to Fair Isle, with the first grant having been made in 1954. Earthwatch Institute – Europe (£25,000) received a grant towards encouraging disadvantaged young people to get involved in environmental projects. The perennial grant to UK CEED (£23,000) was continued, to support their important work in demonstrating how environmental protection and economic development priorities can be reconciled. Wildscreen (£25,000) was commended for its excellent work in preserving and collating film footage and photographs of endangered species. Projects to encourage children to take an interest in wildlife and the environment were supported at Naturedays (£19,000); Sir Harold Hillier Gardens and Arboretum (£15,000); and Westcountry Rivers Trust (£11,000).

Preservation

The Preservation category was awarded 6.5% of the grants made. The trustees continued their policy of making one significant grant each year to a major ecclesiastical building, and this was awarded to St George's Chapel at Windsor Castle (£40,000). The perennial grant to the National Churches Trust (£45,000) was further enhanced in recognition of the steadily increasing preservation problems faced by parish churches. Trustees commended the important and unique projects at the Knockando Woolmill Trust (£25,000) and the Great Dixter Charitable Trust (£20,000) which were supported with conditional grants, dependent on the

outcome of Heritage Lottery applications, both of which were confirmed before the year end. The grant to the United Kingdom Antarctic Heritage Trust (£25,000) for the preservation of Scott's Hut, though outside the trust's normal geographical area of interest, was awarded in recognition of the long association between Sir Peter Scott and 2nd Lord Dulverton.

Miscellaneous

This category accounted this year for 4.9% of the grants, well below the 10% ceiling set by trustees. It embraces charities which trustees consider to be worthy of support, despite being at the margins of the trust's guidelines, and also some which provide services for the benefit of the charitable sector as a whole. The largest grant was the continuation of the three-year grant to Combat Stress (£40,000), and this was augmented by a grant to Gardening Leave (£20,000), a new charity which offers horticultural therapy for veterans suffering from Post Traumatic Stress. An exceptional grant was awarded to the National Gallery (£30,000) towards the Titian Appeal. REACH Volunteering (£12,000) continued to receive a perennial grant for its excellent work in support of the whole charitable sector, by matching skilled volunteers to the needs of individual charities.

Peace and Humanitarian Support

As a result of the quinquennial review, this category was changed to Peace and Humanitarian Support, and will in future concentrate on work connected with peace intervention and infrastructure for disaster relief. Some 3.6% of the grants went towards this category. The largest grant was the perennial award to the Royal United Services Institute (£30,000), and this was supplemented towards the end of the year by a further urgent grant towards a study of the attitude of the Zimbabwean Army. The outstanding work of Encompass (£32,000) in bringing together young people from Israel, Palestine, Indonesia, UK and US through participation in outward bound activities was supported with a further grant. St Ethelburga's (£25,000) received support towards new reconciliation initiatives. A conditional grant was made to the Oxford Research Group towards a high-level international conference, but this was deferred beyond the year end.

Religion

This category was discontinued as a result of the quinquennial review. Three grants had previously been awarded, the largest of which was for the Awareness Foundation – formerly known as the Trinity Foundation for Christianity & Culture (£20,000), towards providing a course to assist with inter-faith understanding. In future, religious education may be considered under the Youth and

Education Category, and inter-faith work under General Welfare.

Local Appeals

Within the allocation of £25,000 for Local Appeals in the Cotswolds, Lord Dulverton approved a total of eight small grants, which were subsequently ratified by trustees.

Exclusions The trust will not usually give grants for the following:

- individuals (the trust gives grants only to registered charities)
- museums, galleries, libraries, exhibition centres and heritage attractions
- individual churches, cathedrals and other historic buildings (except for limited support under the preservation category)
- individual schools, colleges, universities or other educational establishments
- hospices, hospitals, nursing or residential care homes
- expeditions or research projects
- activities outside the stated geographical scope.

Support is rarely given to charities whose main beneficiaries live within Greater London or Northern Ireland.

Grants are not normally available in the following areas of activity:

- health and medicine, including drug and alcohol addiction, therapy and counselling
- support for people with disabilities
- the arts, including theatre, music and drama
- sport, including sports centres and individual playing field projects
- animal welfare or projects concerning the protection of single species
- expeditions and research projects
- individuals volunteering overseas
- conferences, cultural festivals, exhibitions and events
- salaries for specific posts
- major building projects, including the purchase of property or land
- endowments
- work that has already taken place (retrospective funding)
- appeals which seek to replace statutory funding.

Applications

How to apply

Please read the guidelines carefully, making sure that none of the exclusions apply to your charity or project. If you believe that your appeal falls within the funding policy of the trust, apply as follows:

1) Send your application by post to the Director. The trust reserves the right

not to respond to appeals by email from unfamiliar sources.

2) There is no set application form, but you should restrict your application to two pages.

3) Make sure you include your organisation's full contact details, together with an email address and telephone number. Also please confirm your charitable status, giving the registered charity number.

4) Include a brief description of the background, aims and objectives of the charity; details of the specific purpose for which funding is sought together with the funding target; and the balance of funding outstanding at the time of the application.

5) Finally, please enclose a copy of your most recent annual report and accounts if they are not available on the Charity Commission's website.

If you wish to make initial enquiries, establish eligibility, discuss time scales or need to seek further guidance about an application, please telephone the trust's office and ask to speak to one of the Directors.

When to apply

The trustees meet four times a year to consider major appeals: in February, May, July and October. Minor appeals are considered four times a year at variable times between the main agenda meetings. There are no deadlines or closing dates.

The selection procedure can take between three to six months so it is advisable to apply in plenty of time, especially if funding is required by a certain date.

Assessment process

Each application is considered on its merits and all will receive a reply as soon as possible, although research and consultation may delay a response from time to time. The trust will usually acknowledge receipt of your application by email, so remember to include a current email address. If you do not have one, the trust will send you an acknowledgement by post. All rejected applications will receive notification and an outline explanation for the rejection will usually be given.

Applications that are listed for consideration for a Major Grant will normally receive a visit from one of the trust's directors who will subsequently report to the trustees.

Following the trustees' meeting, successful applicants will be notified of their award in writing. The trustees' decisions are final.

Dunard Fund

Classical music, the visual arts, environment and humanitarian causes

£2 million (2007/08)

Beneficial area UK with a particular interest in Scotland.

4 Royal Terrace, Edinburgh EH7 5AB

Tel. 0131 556 4043 **Fax** 0131 556 3969

Correspondent Mrs Carol Colburn Høgel, Trustee

Trustees *Carol Colburn Høgel; Elisabeth Høgel; Catherine Høgel; Erik Høgel; Colin Liddell.*

CC Number 295790

Information available Accounts were available from the Charity Commission.

The charity, established in 1986, is funded annually by Marlowe Holdings Limited, of which the correspondent is both a director and a shareholder. The funds are committed principally to the training for and performance of classical music at the highest standard and to education in and display of the visual arts, also at international standard. A small percentage of the fund is dedicated to environmental and humanitarian projects.

In 2007/08 the fund had assets totalling £4.6 million, an income of £1.3 million (including a donation of £1 million from its benefactor), and made 45 grants totalling £2 million. Grants were categorised as follows:

Culture and the Arts – 12 grants totalling £944,000
Beneficiaries included: Edinburgh Festival Society (£286,000); Festival City Theatres Trust (£250,000); Oxford University Development Trust and Edinburgh Sculpture Workshop (£150,000 each); Sir John Soane's Museum (£130,000); Glyndebourne (£25,000); Perth Festival of the Arts (£6,000); Appeal of the Arts/Stewart's Melville College and the Art Fund (£5,000 each); The Cockburn Association (£1,000); and Deeside Suzuki Piano Festival and Innerpeffray Library (£500 each).

Music – 24 grants totalling £829,000
Beneficiaries included: The Royal Scottish Academy of Music and Drama (£150,000); Scottish Opera (£125,000); Scottish Chamber Orchestra (£101,000); Welsh National Opera (£75,000); The English Concert (£60,000); Royal Scottish National Orchestra and English National Opera (£50,000 each); The

Handel House Trust (£25,000); Royal Opera House and Aldeburgh Music (£20,000 each); Royal Northern College of Music and Wigmore Hall (£10,000 each); Royal Hospital Chelsea Concerts and Southbank Sinfonia (£2,000 each); and European Union Youth Orchestra (£1,000).

Humanitarian and Environmental – 9 grants totalling £187,000
Beneficiaries were The Prince's Charities Foundation (£100,000); Napier University (£40,000); Maritime Rescue and The Royal Botanical Gardens (£20,000 each); Sherborne Abbey and Paisley Abbey (£2,000 each); and The Salvation Army, John Muir Trust and British Red Cross (£1,000 each).

Exclusions Grants are only given to charities recognised in Scotland or charities registered in England and Wales. Applications from individuals are not considered.

Applications We have been informed that the fund is not currently accepting applications and will not be doing so for the foreseeable future.

The Dunhill Medical Trust

Medical research and older people

£3 million (2007/08)

Beneficial area UK.

3rd Floor, 16–18 Marshalsea Road, London SE1 1HL

Tel. 020 7403 3299 **Fax** 020 7403 3277

Email info@dunhillmedical.org.uk

Website www.dunhillmedical.org.uk

Correspondent Claire Large, Administrative Director

Trustees *Ronald E Perry; Timothy Sanderson; Prof. Roger Boyle; The Rt Revd Christopher Chessun; Prof. Martin Severs; Kay Glendinning; Prof. James McEwen; Prof. Roderick Hay; Richard Nunneley.*

CC Number 294286

Information available Detailed annual report and accounts and guidelines available on the trust's website.

The Dunhill Medical Trust originated in a will trust left by Herbert Dunhill in 1950 to support medical research. The trust was formally registered as a charity in the 1980s was established in 1950 with charitable objects focused on medical research, care and facilities and specifically the research into the provision of accommodation and care for older people.

The trust's current charitable priorities are:

- care of older people
- research into diseases and issues of ageing
- projects related to disabilities and rehabilitation in respect of older people.

These priorities are reviewed every three years (or more often if deemed appropriate by the trustees), and may be changed in accordance to the trustees' view of the most effective application of available funds.

The trustees wish to encourage approaches by charities and institutions that have not previously applied for funding which fall into the above priority areas. They particularly welcome proposals that demonstrate original thinking and where the potential outcomes have a prospect of wide application within the community of older people generally.

The trust continues to support projects that are less likely to attract funding from mainstream sources. Priority is also given to pilot studies which could establish whether major funding is justified and to the development of research capacity within the medical, clinical and scientific community. Wherever possible the trust will support organisations directly rather than through third parties.

Applications can only be considered from organisations or groups which are charitable as defined by UK charity law. This includes UK registered charities and relevant exempt charities such as universities. Where deemed appropriate, applications from other not-for-profit organisations such as the NHS may be considered. To achieve a better balance in its distribution of funds the trust may occasionally actively seek out projects for support.

Grantmaking

During 2007/08 the trust had assets of £86 million and an income of £3.3 million. Grants were made to 49 organisations totalling £3 million.

The distribution of grants by category was broken down as follows:

- medical knowledge and research – 55%
- major initiatives – 22%

- provision of accommodation for older people – 14%
- services relating to medical care or care for older people – 9%.

During the year the trust received approximately 280 grant applications of which 73% met the basic criteria for funding. Of these, 55% were either within the priority areas designated by the trustees, or were applications for Serendipity Awards (which may be in any area of medicine/medical science/health).

Grants are made through four main programmes. The following information is taken largely from the trust's very useful website.

Research grants

These grants take four forms:

- programme and project grants
- research related infrastructure costs (such as buildings or equipment for specific purposes)
- DMT Research Fellowships, which are awarded in partnership with Royal Colleges and other professional bodies
- Serendipity Awards.

Applications in the following areas are of particular interest to the trust:

- diseases and issues of ageing
- the care and environment of older people
- disabilities that predominantly affect older people
- rehabilitation of older people
- initiatives aimed at evaluating and improving patient care or public health
- areas where it is difficult to attract funding (for example incontinence, end of life research)
- pilot studies which could establish whether major studies are justified.

The trust is keen to support applied research projects on a smaller scale than are normally considered by major funders such as the Research Councils and the Wellcome Trust. Research grants are normally within the range £10,000 to £500,000 and awarded for a maximum of three years.

Priority will be given to the following types of work:

- clinical research rather than basic science
- research which has the potential to be translatable into effective practice within a reasonable time frame
- research carried out on a multidisciplinary basis
- health services research and public health research
- activities that will expand the research capacity in the above areas.

The trust will also consider applications related to the more qualitative end of the research spectrum, such as research related

to modifiable risk factors for well-being and health (for example environmental factors, diet, stress, exercise, social participation, recreation etc.)

The trust will consider applications for direct costs such as staffing, consumables, buildings or equipment for specific purposes related to research. Travel or conference fees will only be supported where these are an integral part of a research project. Exceptionally, the trust may endow innovative academic posts within the priority areas. Although the trust does not award grants to cover the revenue or capital costs of hospices, research undertaken within a hospice setting is eligible for consideration.

Previous beneficiaries of research grants include: Royal College of Physicians, University of East Anglia, University of Leeds, the Stroke Association and St Georges Hospital Medical School.

More information on DMT research grants can be found on the trust's website.

Serendipity awards

Announced in spring 2007 DMT Serendipity Awards are intended to fund the testing of an idea which comes from an unexpected clinical or laboratory observation, or from well-grounded practice, to obtain proof of concept.

They are not awarded as a form of pump priming. Unlike other research funding Serendipity Awards need not of necessity involve work around ageing and associated issues. These awards may therefore include activity that may fall outside the main focus of the Dunhill Medical Trust's work but which has the potential to convince other funding bodies to take the idea forward.

General grants

General grants are to fund work that is not research, or research-related.

There are four categories of award.

- building grants
- equipment grants
- core costs/staffing grants
- small grants, usually under £10,000.

A key aim is that the trust's funding should encourage and support innovative applications. As a rule to qualify for consideration, grant applications must be for an activity with a focus on older people.

Applications that address the following are of particular interest to the trust:

- the care and environment of older people
- solutions that address disabilities that predominantly affect older people or initiatives that aid their rehabilitation
- areas that have difficulty attracting funding, such as incontinence.

The trust will consider applications for direct costs such as staffing, buildings or equipment for specific purposes related to the above.

Although there is no lower limit for a grant, in practice no awards are for less than £1,000. Whilst there is no upper limit, grants in excess of £1 million are awarded only in the most exceptional circumstances. Grants are normally awarded for a maximum of three years. Special rules apply to small grants under £10,000 and to major initiatives.

Previous beneficiaries of general grants include: Age Concern Kirklees, Alzheimer's Support, Deafway, Age Care, Schonfeld Square Foundation, Yemeni Elderly Small Health and Sparkbrook and Sixty Plus.

More information on the general grants programme is available on the trust's website.

Reasearch Training Fellowships

This programme was launched in Autumn 2009 and aims to provide training opportunities for talented clinicians, health professionals and scientists who wish to pursue a research career in the fields of ageing, rehabilitation or palliative care.

At the time of writing there was no further information available, but details should be published on the trust's website in due course.

Please note: all requests for funding are first appraised against criteria set out within DMT's Grant Making Policy, available to download from the website. The Dunhill Medical trust is a member of the Association of Medical Research Charities.

Exclusions The trust will not fund:

- organisations based outside the UK, or whose work primarily benefits people outside the UK
- large national charities, with an income in excess of £10 million, or assets exceeding £100 million
- issues that are already well-funded in the UK, such as heart disease, cancer or HIV/AIDS
- sponsorship of individuals
- sponsorship of conferences or charitable events
- services or equipment that would be more appropriately provided by the NHS
- charities representing specific professions or trade associations
- grants to cover the revenue or capital costs of hospices*
- travel or conference fees (except where these items are an integral part of a project)

- new or replacement vehicles (unless an integral part of a community-based development)
- general maintenance
- institutional overheads associated with research activity (i.e. the trust will not pay the full economic cost of research activities).

*Although the trust does not award grants to cover the revenue or capital costs of hospices, research undertaken within a hospice setting is eligible for consideration.

Applications By post or email to the Secretary of the Trustees. All applicants for general or research grants are asked to provide an initial outline, including a brief description of the organisation and of the project/work or research to be carried out.

Once the initial application has been assessed, eligible applicants will be sent a formal grant application form which will request additional and supporting information.

As the application procedure differs depending upon whether you are apply for a general or research grant, you are strongly advised to visit the trust's website before making an application to ensure that you have all the relevant information. Once you have done so, if you still require any specific advice regarding your application, please contact the trust's office.

Full applications are considered by the Grants and Research Committee which meets quarterly (normally in February, May, July and November). The committee makes recommendations on whether applications should be supported and decisions are then referred to the board of trustees for approval at their quarterly meetings (normally held in March, June, September and December). Applications approved are normally notified within one week of the meeting. Generally, decisions are made within about three months, although research applications may take longer, due to the requirements of the peer review process.

The Charles Dunstone Charitable Trust

General
£2 million (2007/08)
Beneficial area UK and overseas.

H W Fisher and Company, 11–15 William Road, London NW1 3ER

Tel. 020 7388 7000

Correspondent The Trustees

Trustees *Denis Dunstone; Adrian Bott; Nicholas Folland.*

CC Number 1085955

Information available Accounts were available from the Charity Commission.

Registered with the Charity Commission in March 2001, in 2007/08 the trust had an income of £141,000, with assets standing at £3.9 million at year end.

Grants were made to 100 organisations totalling approximately £2 million and were broken down into the following categories:

Category	Value
Arts and culture	£54,000
Children and young people	£479,000
Community care	£538,000
Education and training	£206,000
Ethnic organisations	£24,000
General	£1,000
Medical and disability	£131,000
Social Welfare	£237,000
Sport	£300,000

Exclusions The trustees do not normally make grants to individuals.

Applications 'Proposals are usually requested by the trustees and unsolicited applications are not likely to be successful.'

The James Dyson Foundation

Science, engineering, medicine and education
£2.5 million (2007/08)
Beneficial area UK, local community around the Dyson company's UK headquarters, in Malmesbury, Wiltshire.

Tetbury Hill, Malmesbury, Wiltshire
SN16 0RP

Tel. 01666 827 205

Email jamesdysonfoundation@dyson.
com

Website www.jamesdysonfoundation.
com

Correspondent The Dyson Press Office

Trustees *Sir James Dyson; Lady Deirdre
Dyson; Valerie West; Prof. Sir Christopher
Frayling.*

CC Number 1099709

Information available Accounts were
available from the Charity Commission.

This company foundation was set up in
2002 to promote charitable giving,
especially to charities working in the
fields of science, engineering, medicine
and education.

The following information has
previously been provided by the
foundation.

As a company, Dyson has always been
passionate about charitable giving and
educational work, but the foundation
enables this altruistic work to be more
structured, considered and democratic. With
a committee to manage giving, and
registered charity status, it is intended that
the James Dyson Foundation will assist
educational institutions working in the field
of design, technology and engineering, as
well as charities carrying out medical or
scientific research, and projects which aid the
local community around Dyson, in
Malmesbury, Wiltshire.

Each year, we donate a number of Dyson
vacuum cleaners to charitable causes within
the James Dyson Foundation's objectives.
We occasionally donate small grants to
charitable projects that share our
philosophies and objectives.

In 2007 the foundation hoped to start
work on the Dyson School for Design
Innovation but due to a series of
problems and mounting costs the project
was discontinued in 2008. However, the
funds will continue to be set aside for
future projects. As a result, the
foundation is not currently donating
large grants.

In 2007/08 the trust had assets of
£7.3 million and an income of
£3 million. Grants totalled £2.5 million
and were distributed in three categories
as follows:

Education and Training – £1.8 million
Education is an important focus for the
James Dyson Foundation. James Dyson is
particularly passionate about Design and
Technology – a subject which challenges the
young people of the UK to be creative, by
using their hands and brains to create things
that work.

The foundation supports educational projects
by means of bursaries and awards, such as
awards to the Royal College of Art's Industrial
Design Engineering students. However the
Foundation's support extends beyond
monetary support: design engineers from
Dyson host workshops at schools and
universities throughout the country and the
foundation provides free resources to Design
and Technology teachers throughout the UK.

The largest grants in this category went
to Bath Technology Centre
(£1.3 million) and the Dyson Design
Awards (£246,000).

Grants of less than £50,000 included
those to: James Dyson Award (£44,000);
Pompidou Project (£24,000); D and T
Show (£17,000); Royal College of Art
(£12,000); the Prince's Trust (£5,000);
and Design and Engineering Lectures
and Workshops (£3,800).

Other grants of less than £1,000 each
totalled £14,000.

Science and medical research –
£608,000
The foundation has previously partnered
with several medical charities, including
CLIC and the Meningitis Research
Foundation, and donated the sales of
various limited edition vacuum cleaners
to them. Grants are also made to general
medical and scientific research
organisations at the trustees discretion.

Grants were made to: Target Pink
(£552,000); Bath Royal United Hospital
– Opera Night (£50,000); CLIC (£3,000);
and Starlight Children's Foundation
(£2,000).

Social and community welfare – £7,000
The James Dyson Foundation seeks to
support charitable projects local to
Malmesbury, the town where Dyson is
based. In particular, the trustees of the
foundation are especially keen to support
organisations that work within the fields of
design and engineering education and
medical and scientific research.

Under this category all grants totalled
less than £1,000 and were not listed in
the accounts.

Applications Applications in writing
on headed paper to the correspondent.
Organisations can also apply via email or
through the foundation's website.

The Sir John Eastwood Foundation

Social welfare, education and health

£377,000 (2007/08)

Beneficial area UK, but mainly
Nottinghamshire in practice.

PO Box 9803, Mansfield NG18 9FT

Fax 01623 847955

Correspondent David Marriott,
Secretary

Trustees *Gordon G Raymond, Chair;
Diana M Cottingham; Valerie
A Hardingham; Constance B Mudford;
Peter M Spencer.*

CC Number 235389

Information available Accounts were
available from the Charity Commission.

The trust makes grants to registered
charities benefiting Nottinghamshire,
although other applications are
considered. Priority is given towards
people with disabilities, older people and
children with special needs.

In 2007/08 the trust had assets of just
under £9 million and an income of
£4.7 million, mainly from Adam
Eastwood & Sons Limited, a company
which is wholly owned by the
foundation. (In 2008 the trustees made
the decision to wind the company up
and cease trading – it appears that the
charitable activities of the foundation
will continue for the foreseeable future.)
Grants were made during the year
totalling £377,000. Most grants were for
less than £3,000, with some
organisations recieving more than one
grant during the year.

Larger grants included those to: Meden
Charitable Trust (£20,000); Newark and
Notts Agricultural Society, Nottingham
University and Bilsthorpe Miners
Welfare Scheme (£10,000 each); and
Bluebell Wood Children's Hospice and
Bridge St Methodist Church (£5,000
each).

Other grants of less than £5,000 each
included those made to: RNID (£4,000);
Warsop United Charities and
Alzheimer's Society (£3,000 each);
Nottingham Hospice Limited, Army
Benevolent Fund and Literacy
Volunteers (£2,000 each); and National
Talking Newspaper, No Panic, Aspley
Methodist Church and Balderton
Resource Centre (£1,000 each).

Exclusions No grants to individuals.

Applications In writing to the correspondent.

The EBM Charitable Trust

Children and young people, animal welfare, relief of poverty and general

£1.2 million (2007/08)

Beneficial area UK.

Moore Stephens, St Paul's House, 8–12 Warwick Lane, London EC4M 7BP

Tel. 020 7334 9191 **Fax** 020 7651 1953

Email keith.lawrence@moorestephens.com

Correspondent Keith Lawrence, Secretary

Trustees *Richard Moore; Michael Macfadyen; Stephen Hogg.*

CC Number 326186

Information available Accounts were available from the Charity Commission.

The trustees report, as has been the case in previous years, stated simply that 'beneficiaries included charities involved in animal welfare and research, the relief of poverty and youth development'. Furthermore, that resources would be maintained at a reasonable level in order continue funding general charitable purposes.

The trust manages two funds, the general fund and the Fitz' fund. The Fitz' fund was established following the death of Cyril Fitzgerald, one of the original trustees of the charity who left the residue of his estate to the trust. The money is held as a designated fund for animal charities and gave £10,000 during the year.

The trust gives around 30 grants a year for amounts between £2,500 and £250,000. Most grants are for between £10,000 and £50,000.

In 2007/08 the trust had assets of £38 million, which generated an income of £898,000. Grants were made to 28 organisations totalling £1.2 million.

The largest grants were made to: Home of Horseracing Trust (£250,000); British Racing School (£125,000); Injured Jockey's Fund (£100,000); Royal Veterinary College (£75,000); and Animal Health Trust (£70,000).

Other grants included: Cardinal Hume Centre (£40,000); Macmillan Cancer Support (£30,000); Treloar Trust (£20,000); Brain Research Trust (£10,000); Dogs for the Disabled (£8,500); RNIB (£5,000); and New Astley Club (£3,500).

Applications The following is taken from the annual report and accounts:

Unsolicited applications are not requested as the trustees prefer to support donations to charities whose work they have researched and which is in accordance with the wishes of the settlor. The trustees do not tend to support research projects as research is not a core priority but there are exceptions. The trustees' funds are fully committed. The trustees receive a very high number of grant applications which are mostly unsuccessful.

The Maud Elkington Charitable Trust

Social welfare and general charitable purposes

£468,000 (2007/08)

Beneficial area Mainly Desborough, Northamptonshire and Leicestershire.

c/o Harvey Ingram Owston, 20 New Walk, Leicester LE1 6TX

Tel. 0116 257 6129 **Fax** 0116 255 3318

Email paula.fowle@harveyingram.co.uk

Correspondent Mrs Paula Fowle, Administrator

Trustees *Roger Bowder, Chair; Allan A Veasey; Caroline A Macpherson.*

CC Number 263929

Information available Accounts were available from the Charity Commission.

The principle aim of the trust is to distribute grants, particularly, but not exclusively, in Desborough and Northamptonshire; grants are also made in Leicestershire. Grants are made to rather small projects, where they will make a quantifiable difference to the recipients, rather than favouring large national charities whose income is in millions rather than thousands. It is the usual practice to make grants for the benefit of individuals through referring agencies such as social services, NHS Trusts or similar responsible bodies.

In 2007/08 the trust had assets of £20 million and an income of £697,000. Grants were made to 285 organisations totalling £468,000.

Beneficiaries included: Northamptonshire County Council Social Services (£33,000, comprising 91 individual payments); Leicester Charity Link (£21,000, comprising 17 individual payments); Leicester Grammar School – bursaries (£8,800); Age Concern – Wigston and Oadby (£7,500); Mayday Trust (£5,000); SSAFA Forces Help (£3,300); Charnwood 20–20 and National Autistic Society – Leicester (£2,000 each); Carers Centre – Leicestershire and Rutland (£1,500); and MENCAP (£1,300).

193 grants below £1,000 were made totalling £140,000; these were not individually listed.

Exclusions No grants to individuals.

Applications In writing to the correspondent. There is no application form or guidelines. The trustees meet every seven or eight weeks.

The John Ellerman Foundation

National UK charities supporting health, disability, social welfare, arts and conservation and overseas projects

£4.3 million (2008/09)

Beneficial area Mainly UK.

Aria House, 23 Craven Street, London WC2N 5NS

Tel. 020 7930 8566 (general) 020 7451 1471 (direct) **Fax** 020 7839 3654

Email enquiries@ellerman.org.uk

Website www.ellerman.org.uk

Correspondent Eileen Terry, Appeals Manager

Trustees *Richard Edmunds; Dr John Hemming; Sue MacGregor; David Martin-Jenkins; Surgeon Vice-Admiral Anthony Revell; Lady Sarah Riddell; Beverley Stott; Dominic Caldecott.*

CC Number 263207

Information available Accounts were available at the Charity Commission. The foundation has a helpful and informative website.

The foundation was established on the death of Sir John Ellerman in 1970 as a generalist grant-making trust. John Ellerman had inherited his substantial wealth from the business interests set up by his father, especially in shipping – the family business was called Ellerman Lines. Sir John and his wife Esther had throughout their lives developed a profound interest in philanthropy.

Today the foundation uses Sir John's legacy to make grants totalling around £4 million a year to about 150 different charities, mostly in the United Kingdom; The foundation makes grants to UK registered charities which work nationally, not locally. For historical reasons it continues to support a few charities operating in southern and east Africa.

The foundation's mission is 'to be and be seen as a model grantmaker to the charitable sector.' It aims to achieve its mission by managing its funds in such a way that it can both maintain its grant-making capacity and operate in perpetuity, funding nationally-registered charities so as to encourage and support those which make a real difference to people, communities and the environment.

Guidelines

The foundation gives significant grants which it is hoped will enable charities to make a difference to the cause they serve. The minimum grant is £10,000 and the foundation aims to develop relationships with funded charities. Requests for a contribution to large capital appeals are not encouraged. The foundation is especially open to receiving applications for core funding. Charities which receive core funding will be expected to account for expenditure and identify what it has enabled them to do.

The foundation will only consider applications from registered charities with a UK office. Under the Health and Disability, Social Welfare and Arts programmes, support will only be given to charities working throughout the UK or England. Applications from individuals, local/regional charities or those just operating in Wales, Scotland or Northern Ireland will not be considered.

The foundation inclines towards supporting charities which:

- offer direct practical benefits rather than work mainly on policy or campaigning
- involve and attract large numbers of volunteers
- co-operate closely with others working in similar or related fields
- do innovatory work
- are small or medium sized (annual income of less than £25 million).

The foundation receives many more applications than it can fund. On average, only 1 in 5 of all appeals within the guidelines is successful. The foundation states that it recognises that preparing good applications places heavy demands on the time and resources of charities, and diverts energies from their ultimate purpose; it therefore has a two-stage application process.

Stage 1
Applicants are advised to read the Guidelines for Applicants and Category Guidelines, available on the foundation's website. Please ensure that you are eligible to apply, and do not appear in the list of exclusions. Send your latest annual report and audited accounts to the correspondent, together with a letter – no more than one or two sides of A4. This should include the following information:

- about your charity – when registered, what you do, who your beneficiaries are and where you work
- about your need for funding – your turnover, reserves, main sources of income, why you need funds now, and, if you are requesting funds for a particular project, rough costings.

All letters are studied by the appeals manager and at least one trustee who recommend whether your proposal should be brought to the attention of the full board. If your application is not to go forward, the foundation will tell you at this stage, rather than ask you to complete an application form. Please note that circulars are not responded to.

Stage 2
If a proposal is of sufficient interest to the board, you will be sent an application form. You should return this within one month. There are no specific deadlines for applications, as the board meets regularly throughout the year. (The application form is also available on request in electronic format; however applicants are requested to post a printed version when applying.)

Applicants may be asked for additional information and, as a matter of routine, staff and/or trustees try to visit as many organisations as possible. Your application will then be considered at the next available board meeting. These take place every two months and you will be informed shortly thereafter.

Applications and correspondence should be sent to the correspondent and appeals manager, Eileen Terry.

Foundation staff are always happy to discuss potential applications by telephone. Before calling, please ensure that you have read the 'Guidelines for Applicants' and are eligible to apply.

Grants in 2008/09

In 2008/09 the foundation had assets of £93 million and an income of £1.9 million. Grants were made totalling £4.3 million. This amounted to 86% of total expenditure for the year. The foundation plans to reduce the spending rate slightly in 2009/10 so total grants are expected to be marginally lower (around £4.1 million).

The foundation makes grants in the following five categories (shown here with details of funds generally allocated):

- health and disability (30%)
- social welfare (30%)
- arts (20%)
- conservation (10%)
- overseas (10%).

Health and disability – 55 grants totalling £1.3 million
At present the focus of the foundation's funding in this area is directed towards the following:

- organisations, including self-help groups, for the relief and support of those with serious medical conditions
- severe physical disabilities, including deaf and blind people
- mental illness and learning disabilities
- carers, including nurses and the families of sufferers, and hospices (currently funding for hospices is given solely through Help the Hospices).

The foundation is particularly interested in charities which can demonstrate all or most of the following:

- real benefits to patients/sufferers and the quality of their lives
- a particular commitment to the young and/or to older people
- self help programmes, including the provision of acknowledged expert information and advice
- promotion of all aspects of healthy living.

Please note: the foundation does not support medical research or NHS Hospital Trusts.

Beneficiaries included: Diabetes UK (£35,000); Asthma UK (£33,000); Haemophilia Society (£28,000); Papworth Trust (£25,000); Action for ME and Lost Chord (£20,000 each); and Jennifer Trust and Wheelyboat Trust (£10,000 each).

Social welfare – 46 grants totalling £1.3 million

Social welfare reflects the founder's personal commitment to the seriously disadvantaged and needy. At present the focus of funding is directed towards the following:

- disadvantaged children and young people
- needy parents and families
- older people.

The special focus of interest for the foundation for 2008 and perhaps for the next few years is support for charities working with older people, especially those over 75 and suffering poverty and isolation. They may be living independently or in residential care and from either rural or urban communities. The foundation welcomes applications from national charities working with and for older people in practical ways and which aim specifically to:

- reduce isolation and combat poverty
- promote health and well-being
- encourage family and inter-generational contact
- improve the quality of housing, security and residential care.

The foundation is particularly interested in charities which can demonstrate all or most of the following:

- tangible benefits on a significant scale to disadvantaged/vulnerable people
- sharing of good ideas and collaborative work with other charities
- encouragement of and motivation towards self-help and self-sufficiency
- employment and training of a broad base of volunteers
- practical improvement in the day to day quality of life of beneficiaries.

Beneficiaries included: Volunteer Reading Help (£51,000); Place2Be (£50,000); Counsel and Care (£45,000); Dementia Advocacy Network (£39,000); STOP – Trafficking UK (£30,000); Grandparent's Association (£25,000); Papyrus (£20,000); and Clubs for Young People (£15,000).

Arts – 40 grants totalling £1 million

The third largest category, this reflects Sir John Ellerman's passion for opera and theatre. At present the focus of funding is directed towards the following:

- music and opera
- museums and galleries
- theatre and dance.

The foundation is particularly interested in charities which can demonstrate all or most of the following:

- excellence within the field
- commitment to attracting new audiences and wider public access
- youth participation and motivation
- originality and creativity in design, production and/or presentation
- lasting impact.

Generally the foundation does not support educational projects, festivals, productions or tours. Exceptionally on occasions it may support cathedral restoration.

Beneficiaries included: Bletchley Park Trust, English National Opera and Music for Youth (£50,000 each); Pallant House Gallery (£30,000); Aldeburgh Music (£25,000); National Children's Orchestra and Unicorn Theatre (£15,000 each); and York Minster Fund (£10,000).

Conservation – 16 grants totalling £388,000

Conservation of the environment and natural world is a category reflecting the fact that Sir John Ellerman was a distinguished zoologist and expert on small mammals. This is one of the two smallest categories.

At present the focus of funding is UK-based charities working throughout the UK and/or internationally in at least one of the following areas:

- protection of threatened animals, plants and habitats
- promotion of better understanding of and solutions to major environmental issues like climate change and biodiversity (applications for good research by an institute whose primary purpose is research even though its charitable status may come from association with a university are considered)
- development and extension of conservation facilities/sites
- promotion of sustainable ways of living, including renewable energy technologies.

The foundation is particularly interested in charities which can demonstrate all or most of the following:

- practical and sustainable benefits of significant scale
- collaborative work with others and the open sharing of ideas
- effective operation with or alongside local communities and cultures

- recruitment, training and employment of a broad base of volunteers.

Beneficiaries included: University of Cape Town Trust (£50,000); Woodland Trust (£40,000); Scott Polar Research Institute (£30,000); Association of Rivers (£25,000); Buglife (£20,000); and Elephant Family (£12,000).

Overseas – 19 grants totalling £322,000

In 2006/07 the foundation moved to making grants overseas either within the joint collaboration with the Baring Foundation or by invitation only. Along with conservation this is one of the two smallest categories, and reflects the fact that Sir John Ellerman lived partly in South Africa and based much of his philanthropic work there

Please note: In early 2009, unsolicited applications were not being accepted in this category.

At present the funding has two elements:

- Joint International Programme with the Baring Foundation: almost all overseas funding allocation now goes towards a joint programme in Africa administered by the Baring Foundation – visit: www.baringfoundation.org.uk. This programme seeks to help refugees and displaced peoples
- Charities in South Africa: where support is confined to charities set up by, or closely connected with, the founder in and around Cape Town, which the foundation has helped to fund for many years and with which there are long established relationships.

Exclusions Grants are made only to registered charities, and are not made for the following purposes:

- medical research
- for or on behalf of individuals
- individual hospices
- local branches of national organisations
- 'Friends of' groups
- education or educational establishments
- religious causes
- conferences and seminars
- sports and leisure facilities
- purchase of vehicles
- the direct replacement of public funding
- deficit funding
- domestic animal welfare
- drug or alcohol abuse
- prisons and offenders.

Because of the volume of appeals which are received, the trustees do not consider further requests from charities which have had an application turned down until at least two years have elapsed since the letter of rejection. Similarly, funded charities can expect to wait two years from the last grant payment before a further application will be considered. Circulars will not receive a reply.

Applications In writing to the correspondent following the foundation's guidelines available from its website.

The Englefield Charitable Trust

General charitable purposes with a preference for local charities in Berkshire

£405,000 (2007/08)

Beneficial area Worldwide. In practice, UK with a special interest in Berkshire.

Englefield Estate Office, Englefield Road, Theale, Reading RG7 5DU

Tel. 0118 930 2504 **Fax** 0118 932 3748

Email sandyreid@englefield.co.uk

Correspondent Alexander S Reid, Secretary to the Trustees

Trustees *Sir William Benyon; James Shelley; Lady Elizabeth Benyon; Richard H R Benyon; Mrs Catherine Haig; Zoe Benyon.*

CC Number 258123

Information available Accounts were available from the Charity Commission.

The trust was established in 1968 for general charitable purposes by the settlor Sir William Benyon. The trustees consider each application on its own merit and give preference to local causes in Berkshire.

In 2007/08 the trust had assets of £10.9 million and an income of £326,500. There were 129 general grants made totalling £360,000. Grants were also made for affordable housing totalling £45,000. The trust had previously stated its intention to increase its charitable donations, which it has done during this financial year. This policy is again stated in the 2007/08 annual report, although the current economic climate may impact on this.

Grants were made ranging from £100 to £96,000 during the year, although most were for £5,000 or less.

Beneficiaries included: St Mary the Virgin Church, Reading (£96,000); Englefield PCC (£18,200); Ufton Court Education Trust (£12,500); Newbury & District Agricultural Society (£10,500); Reading YMCA (£6,000); Policy Exchange (£5,000); Multiple Sclerosis Therapy Centre (£4,700); Friends of Victoria Park (£4,000); Swings and Smiles (£3,000); Thatcham Relief in Need Charity and St Matthew's Church, Midgham (£2,000 each); and ARC Addington Fund, Christian Solidarity Worldwide, Miriam Dean Fund and Thatcham & District Rotary Club (£1,000 each).

Exclusions Individual applications for study or travel are not considered.

Applications In writing to the correspondent enclosing the latest accounts, stating the charity's registered number and the purpose for which the money is to be used. Applications are considered in March and September. Only applications going before the trustees will be acknowledged.

Entindale Ltd

Orthodox Jewish charities

£1.3 million (2007/08)

Beneficial area Unrestricted.

8 Highfield Gardens, London NW11 9HB

Tel. 020 8458 9266 **Fax** 020 8458 8529

Correspondent Barbara Bridgeman, Secretary

Trustees *Allan Becker; Barbara Bridgeman; Stephen Goldberg.*

CC Number 277052

Information available Annual report and accounts were available from the Charity Commission, with limited analysis of grants made.

This trust aims 'to advance religion in accordance with the orthodox Jewish faith'. In 2007/08 it had an income of £1.5 million derived mainly from rent on its properties worth £14 million. Grants were made to organisations totalling £1.3 million.

During the year, 151 grants of over £100 were made, with many grants probably going to previous beneficiaries. There were 41 grants of £10,000 or over, including those to: Jewish Learning Exchange (£80,000); Yesodey HaTorah Schools (£70,000); Chevras Machzikei

Mesivta (£60,000); Chevras Maoz LaDol (£48,000); Vaad Ho Rabbonim Leinyonei Tzodokoh (£35,000); Notzar Chesed (£27,000); and Boinei Olom (£12,000).

Beneficiaries of smaller grants included: Chasdel Cohen (£9,000); Achieve Trust (£5,000); Ihud Mosdos Gur (£1,000); Finchley Central Synagogue (£750); and Friends of Yeshivas Brisk (£500).

Applications In writing to the correspondent.

The Equitable Charitable Trust

Education of disabled or disadvantaged children and young people

£892,000 (2008)

Beneficial area Mainly UK: overseas projects can sometimes be supported.

Sixth Floor, 65 Leadenhall Street, London EC3A 2AD

Tel. 020 7264 4995 **Fax** 020 7488 9097

Email jlong@equitablecharitabletrust. org.uk

Website www.equitablecharitabletrust. org.uk

Correspondent Jennie Long, Grants Officer

Trustees *Brian McGeough; Roy Ranson; Peter Goddard.*

CC Number 289548

Information available Accounts were on file at the Charity Commission. The trust also has a very good website.

The trust has recently updated its funding guidelines. The following summary has been taken from its informative website:

The Equitable Charitable Trust is an education charity. It makes grants of around £1 million each year towards projects for children and young people under the age of 25 who are from disadvantaged backgrounds or disabled.

Its funds are highly oversubscribed and the trustees have therefore identified three specific priorities for the types of projects they wish to support:

- education projects or services that support the learning and development of disabled children and young people in the UK
- formal education projects for disadvantaged children and young people

121

in the UK that support delivery of the National Curriculum (curriculum enrichment projects) or that deliver accredited vocational learning that will increase employability
- education projects that will help increase participation in, or improve the quality of, education for disadvantaged or disabled children and young people in developing countries.

Types of grant
Grants can be made for project costs, capital expenditure, equipment and/or the salary costs of a post.

Area of benefit
The majority of projects funded by the trust take place within the UK at local or regional level, though national projects and those benefiting children or young people overseas (in developing countries only) are also supported.

Please note: grants for overseas projects are only made through UK registered charities.

Types of organisations funded
We support a broad range of organisations; from small and medium sized not-for-profit organisations to large charities. However, priority is normally given to organisations and charities with annual incomes of under £5 million. You do not need to be a UK registered charity to apply unless you are applying for a grant towards a project or work that will take place outside the UK.

Length of Grants
The length of funding can range from one to three years. Grants of more than one year are paid in annual instalments, with instalments beyond the first year dependent on receipt of progress reports that are satisfactory to the trustees.

Size of Grants
The size of grants ranges from £2,500 to £30,000. Most are for sums between £5,000 and £20,000. It is rare for a multi-year grant to exceed £10,000 per year and most multi-year grants will be for sums between £5,000 and £7,500 per year.

Grants in 2008

In 2008 the trust had assets of £6.8 million and an income of £725,000. Grants were made totalling £892,000. 40 grant beneficiaries (51%) received funding for projects benefiting disadvantaged children and young people and 39 beneficiaries (49%) were given funding towards projects benefiting disabled children and young people. 64% of grants were given for project funding, while salary costs and capital grants represented 21% and 15% of funding awards respectively.

The trust provides a comprehensive list of the grants made during the year in its

accounts, and also describes the purposes for which they were made. Examples are as follows:

- Voluntary Services Overseas: £55,000 – for year three of a three year grant towards a volunteer education project in Eritrea
- Sunfield: £50,000 – a capital grant towards building costs of an independent residential school in Worcestershire for profoundly disabled children and young people
- Prior's Court Foundation: £30,000 – a capital grant towards the cost of improving facilities at an independent special school providing early intervention for children with severe autism
- Afghan Connection: £27,000 – a capital grant towards the cost of building and equipping a new girls' school in Afghanistan
- Birmingham Focus on Blindness: £20,000 – a one year grant towards specialist ICT equipment for blind and partially sighted school children in Birmingham
- Drake Music Project: £15,000 – a one year grant towards an Assistive Music Technology project for disabled young people in Manchester and the North West
- Lambourne End: £10,000 – for year one of a two year grant towards the salary of a Farm and Environment Education Worker at a centre in Essex
- FARA: £5,000 – a capital grant towards a new specialist residential education centre for young people with learning disabilities in Romania
- Hampstead Theatre: £1,200 – a one year grant towards a scriptwriting project for young people with disabilities from the Royal Free Hospital School in London.

Exclusions
The trust does not make grants towards the following:

- general appeals or mail shot requests for donations
- informal education projects and those that are only loosely educational
- projects felt to be more akin to social work than education
- therapeutic treatments
- supplementary schooling and homework clubs
- mother tongue language classes
- state maintained or voluntary aided schools, colleges or universities, either directly or via another charity (for example Friends, PTAs)
- local authorities
- public schools or independent schools that are not specifically for children and young people with disabilities or special educational needs

- sports education, facilities or activities (for example playing fields, sports clubs, or projects that are delivered through the medium of sport)
- projects or work related to the Olympic Games or Cultural Olympiad
- salaries for posts that are not directly related to service delivery (we would not make a grant towards the salary of a fundraiser or book-keeper, for instance)
- minibuses
- pre-school education projects (unless these are solely for the benefit of children with disabilities or special needs)
- individuals
- bursary schemes
- projects that promote religious belief or practice
- holidays, recreational activities or overseas trips
- capital applications for equipment or facilities that will be only partly used for education or by under 25s from disadvantaged or disabled backgrounds (for example outdoor education centres that also deliver recreational activities, or that are not exclusively for the use of disadvantaged or disabled children and young people).

Applications
The trust offers the following application guidance on its website:

Applications can be submitted at any time and are considered monthly by the trustees. The trust does not have an application form, but recommends that organisations follow the guidelines outlined below when applying for a grant.

Applications should be no longer than four A4 sides, in font size no smaller than 11 point and should begin with a short (half page) summary. Your budget and accounts are additional to this.

Applications should:

- describe your organisation clearly, its background and track record, what it does and who it seeks to benefit or help;
- provide details of your organisation's status (for example registered charity, company limited by guarantee) and its trustees;
- state the name of the project you are asking us to fund, and clearly and succinctly describe it; explain what the structure of the project will be; why it is needed; the number of people who will benefit from it; their ages; how you will ensure it is cost effective; provide details of any partners (other organisations, statutory bodies etc.), and say what stage the project has so far reached. If young people are involved in the development or monitoring of the project please provide details;

- explain which of our priorities your project addresses and how it meets the priority;
- say what the aims of the project are and what outcomes (practical results, changes and/or improvements) it hopes to achieve. If you are seeking funding to continue an existing project or a pilot, it is important that you are able to demonstrate the effectiveness of the work and what the outcomes have been to date;
- describe how the aims, progress and outcomes of the project will be monitored and evaluated and, where appropriate, how you will disseminate good practice to others;
- describe how the project will be managed and name the people who will be in charge of it and their relevant experience or qualifications. If the application is for a salary, please include a copy of the job description for the post;
- ask for a specific amount;
- enclose a detailed budget for the full duration of the project (if it is a three year project don't just send us a one year budget!), together with a full copy of your organisation's most recent audited or independently inspected accounts. It is important that if the accounts show a significant surplus or deficit of income, you explain the reason for this;
- state what funds have already been raised for the project and list any other funding you have applied for;
- explain where on-going funding (if required) will be obtained when the trust's grant ends;
- provide the names and addresses of two independent referees that know your organisation's work. Tell us who these individuals are and how they/their organisations are connected to yours. Trustees, current volunteers or beneficiaries are not suitable referees.

Please keep your application as simple as possible and avoid the use of technical terms and jargon.

Applications should be addressed to Brian McGeough and Peter Goddard, the Joint Managing Trustees.

The trust receives a large number of applications each year and application numbers have increased significantly in the past year. Regrettably, this means we have to decline many good applications.

The trust is normally able to provide a decision within eight weeks of receipt of an application.

In some cases an in-principle decision is made by trustees pending receipt of references, further information or a visit being arranged. All grants are subject to the trust's terms and conditions of grant. [A copy of these can be downloaded from the trust's website].

Applicants who are unsuccessful will be notified in writing and cannot re-apply for at least six months from the date of notification.

The Eranda Foundation

Research into education and medicine, the arts and social welfare

£5.7 million (2007/08)
Beneficial area UK.

PO Box 6226, Wing, Leighton Buzzard LU7 0XF

Tel. 01296 689 157

Email eranda@btconnect.com

Correspondent Gail Devlin-Jones, Secretary

Trustees *Sir Evelyn de Rothschild; Renée Robeson; Leopold de Rothschild; Miss Jessica de Rothschild; Anthony de Rothschild; Sir Graham Hearne; Lady Lynn de Rothschild.*

CC Number 255650

Information available Accounts were available from the Charity Commission.

Established in 1967, this is one of the foundations of the de Rothschild finance and banking family. The foundation supports the promotion of original research, and the continuation of existing research into medicine and education, fostering of the arts and promotion of social welfare.

In 2007/08 it had assets of £87 million and an income of £5.1 million. Grants were made to 95 organisations totalling £5.7 million and were distributed in the following categories:

Education – 40 grants totalling £3 million

Beneficiaries included: Cambridge Business School (£1.9 million); Outward Bound Trust (£250,000); Trinity College Cambridge (£128,000); British Technion Society (£100,000); Index on Censorship (£60,000); Liberal Jewish Synagogue (£36,000); American Wild Horse Conservancy (£15,000); Cumberland Lodge (£10,000); and Israel-Dispora Trust (£5,000).

Health, welfare and medical research – 28 grants totalling £1.7 million

Beneficiaries included: Cystic Fibrosis Trust (£350,000); Royal Hospital Chelsea (£252,000); Multiple Sclerosis Society (£150,000); RD Crusaders Foundation (£100,000); Integrated Rural Development Centre (£76,000); Alzheimer's Society (£30,000); Cancer Bacup (£10,000); and Wellbeing of Women (£5,000).

Arts – 27 grants totalling £832,000

Beneficiaries included: Royal Academy of Dramatic Art (£271,000); Tate Gallery (£65,000); London Philharmonic Orchestra (£37,000); Masterclass Media foundation (£20,000); Jewish Music Institute (£15,000); Battersea Arts Centre (£11,000); and Gate Theatre (£7,600).

Exclusions No grants to individuals.

Applications In writing to the correspondent. Trustees usually meet in March, July and November and applications should be received two months in advance.

Essex Community Foundation

Social welfare and general

£1.2 million (2007/08)
Beneficial area Essex, Southend and Thurrock

121 New London Road, Chelmsford, Essex CM2 0QT

Tel. 01245 355 947 **Fax** 01245 246 391

Email general@essexcf.org.uk

Website www. essexcommunityfoundation.org.uk

Correspondent Grants Team

Trustees *John Spence; Charles Clark; Christopher Holmes; John Stanger; David Boyle; Margaret Hyde; Stephen Packham; Carol Golbourn; Rhiannedd Pratley; Martin Hopkins; John Barnes; Jason Bartella.*

CC Number 1052061

Information available Accounts were on file with the Charity Commission.

The foundation was set up in 1996 and manages funds on behalf of individuals, companies, charitable trusts and public agencies in order to give grants to voluntary and community organisations working to improve the quality of life for people living in Essex, Southend and Thurrock. Support generally falls under the broad heading of social welfare and can cover core costs/revenue costs, new or continuing projects, one-off initiatives and capital costs. The foundation is particularly interested in small grass-roots groups.

Applications should meet the following criteria:

- have clear project aims and objectives
- demonstrate that the grant will make a real difference to people in the community
- involve local participation and support self-help wherever possible

Grantmaking

In 2007/08 the foundation had assets of £8.9 million and an income of £2.8 million. 378 grants totalling £1.2 million were distributed from various funds to support all aspects of social welfare. Grants ranged from £50 to over £50,000 each, with the average being around £3,100. 42% of applications awarded were to first time applicants. Of the total amount awarded in grants, £633,000 was distributed through Local Network Fund for Children and Young People.

The foundation manages over 40 different named funds. In 2009 these included:

- Acorn Fund – supports social and community activities, encouraging community involvement and self-help and innovative charitable activity within Essex, Southend-on-Sea and Thurrock
- Baker Tilly Charitable Fund – support some of the smaller, less well known charities in the community
- Bartella Charitable Fund – to support charitable activity helping disadvantaged children/young people living in the Chelmsford district
- Belinda Starling Memorial Fund – to help young people in Essex, whose literary drama or music ambitions and talents cannot take root without help and encouragement, and money
- Jerome Booth Charitable Fund – general charitable purposes in the community
- Britvic Community Fund – supporting charities and voluntary groups in Essex, initially with a particular focus on those working with families in the Chelmsford area
- Chiron Fund – to support new and existing methods of social and community activities, encourage community involvement and self-help

within Essex, Southend-on-Sea and Thurrock
- Coombewood Amenity Fund – to support people suffering with mental health problems in south Essex
- Marion Ruth Courtauld Education Fund – supports educational and cultural opportunities for young people from Braintree
- William Julien Courtauld Medical Fund – help for those in need of medical support in Braintree.
- e2v Foundation – long-term support for local charities
- Essex & Suffolk Water Community Fund – grants for environment, health and well-being or community support
- Essex & Suffolk Water Abberton Scheme Community Fund – set up specifically to engage with communities affected by the Abberton Scheme. Charities and organisations in the area affected by the scheme will be able to apply for grants which meet the criteria of protecting the environment, promoting health and well-being, education or community support
- Essex County Council Chairman's Fund – supports voluntary and community organisations and charitable activities that enrich the lives of young people by increasing their awareness and participation in activities exploring culture and heritage
- Essex County Council Millenium Fund (excludes Southend and Thurrock) – as a way of celebrating the millennium, Essex County Council took the decision to establish an endowed fund to support the people of Essex for generations to come in the key areas of carers, community support, enhancing the environment and young people
- Essex County Council Tree Initiative Project – involves planting 250,000 trees, shrubs and hedgerows to improve the ecology of Essex and beauty of the countryside. The foundation is one of several partners delivering this project for Essex county Council and it has funding for 25,000 trees, shrubs and hedgerows available to voluntary and community groups who want to enhance their local communities
- Essex County Fire and Rescue Service Charitable Fund – supporting the less well-known, smaller charities, which, through their own activities, are complimenting the work of the Fire Service
- Essex Rural Fund – support for charitable groups and projects in rural Essex

- Fair Share Trust Basildon and Tendring – one of the areas across the UK identified to receive their share of £50 million over 10 years, with the aim of making a lasting impact on the lives of disadvantaged people
- FMW Community Fund – established to give long-term support to local charities
- Grassroots Grants and Endowment Challenge (Essex, Southend and Thurrock) – part of a £130 million nationwide drive by the Government's Office of the Third Sector to support thousands of voluntary and community groups throughout England. Through the foundation, voluntary groups in Essex will benefit from a grants programme which will see £2 million distributed
- Greenfields Community Fund – support charitable activity in the Braintree district. Groups can apply for grants to support projects, which could be anything from new play equipment, to improving wildlife areas or renovating community halls
- Harlow Education Trust – to advance the educational skills of young people in the district.
- Roger and Jean Heath Charitable Fund – distributes grants to support a diverse range of voluntary and community activity in Essex
- High Sheriffs' Fund (inc. Essex Crimebeat) – each year the High Sheriff of Essex makes awards to voluntary groups and gives recognition to individuals who are tackling local problems. Essex Crimebeat was launched in 2001 to target 8 to 25 year olds encouraging them to take a greater involvement in their own communities and address issues that affect them
- Hutton Charity – support to medical care and research within hospitals across Essex.
- Margaretting Fund – gives grants to voluntary and community groups, working in the Chelmsford and Margaretting areas, which are offering support to people who are in need, hardship or distress
- Ian and Angela Marks Charitable Fund – support voluntary and community groups in Essex
- Milsom Charitable Fund – in memory of Gerald Milsom, a well known figure in Stour Valley
- PB Charitable Fund – makes grants at the discretion of the foundation's trustees to voluntary and community groups in Essex
- Searle Trust – to support community activity in the parish of Debden

- Skills Investment Fund – aims to provide an opportunity for business leaders to become champions, take ownership of issues, and therefore create a vehicle to make a real difference to the skills base throughout the county.
- Southend Fund – offer voluntary organisations working in Southend a unique resource to help them fund their charitable activities, now and in the long term
- Alastair and Patricia Stewart Charitable Fund – in appreciation of what Essex has given them, Alastair and Patricia chose to support Essex Community Foundation, who they felt are the professionals who will know which Essex charity needs helping now and far into the future
- Hew Watt Family Charitable Fund – to support charitable activity in Thurrock
- WOMAC Fund – set up by a group of women working in the motor industry who have an annual fundraising event to help cancer related causes.

Further information on the different funds that are available and the foundation's grant guideline can be found on the website.

The foundation's accounts list the 50 highest grants made during the year. The three largest grants by far were those made to the Beacon Project (£70,000); Inclusion Ventures (£65,000); and Basildon, Billericay and Wickford CVS (£52,000).

Other grants included: Prince's Trust (£16,000); Chelmsford Agency for Volunteering (£12,000); Kemp-Welch Partnership Project (£10,000); Mistley Cricket Club (£7,000); Whatever Youth Club (£6,500); Theatre Resource (£5,500); and Maldon Carers Centre (£5,200).

Exclusions The foundation does not support the following:

- political activities
- statutory bodies undertaking their statutory obligations (including schools)
- general appeals
- activities which support animal welfare
- projects that operate outside of Essex, or benefit non-Essex residents
- retrospective funding.

Applications Essex Community Foundation manages a number of funds, many of which are tailored to the individual wishes of the donors. However, with the exception of the four funds listed below, all you have to do is complete a general application form and the foundation will find the right fund for you.

Application forms are available from the foundation's office or can be downloaded from the website. Deadlines are usually twice a year on 9 January and 9 September; please contact the foundation for exact dates. Grants are awarded within three months of the deadlines.

If in doubt about the suitability of your project for funding, call the foundation's grants team on 01245 356018, or email: grants@essexcf.org.uk

The four funds which use a specific application form are: Grassroots Grants, Crimebeat, High Sheriff's Award and Marion Ruth Courtauld Educational Fund. They may also have different application deadlines. Further information about each of these funds is available from the foundation's website, or by contacting the grants team, as above.

Euro Charity Trust

Education and relief of poverty

£4.4 million (2007)

Beneficial area Worldwide, mainly India, Africa, Bangladesh and the UK.

51a Church Road, Edgbaston, Birmingham B15 3SJ

Correspondent Ahmed Omer, Trustee

Trustees *Ahmed Omer; Nasir Awan; Abdul Malik; Abdul Alimahomed; Afzal Alimahomed.*

CC Number 1058460

Information available Accounts were available from the Charity Commission.

The objects of this trust are listed as 'the relief of poverty, to assist the vulnerable and to assist in the advancement of education in the UK and the rest of the world'. The trust receives all its income from Europackaging Holdings Limited. Donations are made to both organisations and individuals worldwide.

Europackaging has grown from a small paper bag merchants into a large diversified packaging group. Paper bag production commenced in 1984 and today the firm is the UK's largest manufacturer. It has its own facilities for polythene bag manufacture, and also recycles both plastic and paper products.

In 2007 the trust had assets of £3.5 million and an income of £422,500. Grants were made worldwide totalling £4.4 million. Over two thirds of the charity's grantmaking is concentrated in India. It is also likely grants are made to organisations in the local area around Europackaging sites (in the UK in Birmingham and in Malaysia) and Malawi, where the settlor is originally from.

In 2008 the charity had an income of £708,000 and a total expenditure of £3 million. Unfortunately, although submitted, the 2008 accounts were not available from the Charity Commission at the time of writing (November 2009).

The charity's priorities for 2009 were:

- education
- providing housing and accommodation for the poor
- providing health and water facilities
- caring for orphans and children in need.

Applications In writing to the correspondent.

The Eveson Charitable Trust

People with physical disabilities, (including those who are blind or deaf), people with mental disabilities, hospitals and hospices, children who are in need, older people, homeless people and medical research into problems associated with any of these conditions

£2.5 million (2007/08)

Beneficial area Herefordshire, Worcestershire and the county of West Midlands (covering Birmingham, Coventry, Dudley, Sandwell, Solihull, Walsall and Wolverhampton).

45 Park Road, Gloucester GL1 1LP

Tel. 01452 501352 **Fax** 01452 302195

125

Correspondent Alex D Gay, Administrator

Trustees *David Pearson, Chair; Bruce Maughfling; Rt. Revd Anthony Priddis, Bishop of Hereford; Martin Davies; Louise Woodhead; Bill Wiggin; Richard Mainwaring.*

CC Number 1032204

Information available Accounts were available from the Charity Commission.

The trust was established in 1994 by a legacy of £49 million from Mrs Violet Eveson to support the following causes:

- people with physical disabilities (including those who are blind or deaf)
- people with mental disabilities
- hospitals and hospices
- children in need, whether disadvantaged or have mental or physical disabilities
- older people
- people who are homeless
- medical research in any of these categories
- general charitable purposes.

It is the policy of the trust to support many charities on an annual basis provided such beneficiaries satisfy the need for continued support. Many capital and specific projects are also supported.

Grants are currently restricted to the geographical areas of Herefordshire, Worcestershire and the county of West Midlands, as a policy decision of the trustees. The trust does not instigate programmes of its own, but responds to the applications which it receives. Grants vary in amount but the average size of grants is around £7,000 to £8,000.

In 2007/08 the trust had assets of £72 million and an income of £822,000. Grants were made to 278 organisations totalling £2.5 million and were categorised as follows:

Social care and development – 189 grants totalling £1.2 million
The focus of grantmaking in this category is on organisations that provide human and social services to a community or target population, including services for children, young people, physically and mentally disabled, older people and homeless people. Beneficiaries included (shown top):

Health care – 59 grants totalling £1 million
Grants focused on the prevention or treatment of specific diseases, the prevention or treatment of diseases generally and/or health problems, the rehabilitation of disabled individuals, residential nursing homes for the frail, severely disabled, older people and those

offering terminal care. Beneficiaries included (shown middle):

Accommodation – 30 grants totalling £251,000
Most grants under this category went to organisations providing non-health related accommodation and respite/ holiday accommodation. Beneficiaries included (shown bottom):

There were also 74 grants of £3,000 or less. These included grants to small local charities within the trust's remit and geographical area.

Exclusions Grants are not made to individuals, even if such a request is submitted by a charitable organisation.

Applications The trustees meet quarterly, usually at the end of March

Social care and development

Name	Purpose	£
Megan Baker House – Leominster	Towards running costs of a charity benefiting children with motor disabilities	60,000
Age Concern – Hereford	Two grants benefiting older people – for a mobile day centre and towards the costs of moving premises	30,000
Maggs Day Centre – Worcester	Two grants for day centre services and a rough sleepers project	25,000
Herefordshire Voluntary Action	'Wheels2Work' – a transport scheme benefiting disadvantaged young people in isolated rural areas	20,000
Birmingham Settlement	Towards services benefiting disadvantaged children	15,000
Big issue Foundation	Towards a support service for homeless magazine vendors in Birmingham	7,500
Birmingham City FC Football in the Community	Towards activities benefiting disadvantaged and disabled children during camp in Ross-on-Wye	5,000
City of Birmingham Orchestra	Towards a project specifically benefiting children in special schools	3,800

Health care

Name	Purpose	£
Macmillan Cancer Relief	Towards a major appeal to provide a new cancer unit at Hereford County Hospital	150,000
Autism – West Midlands	Towards capital improvements to Coddington Court School, which provides residential and educational facilities for children with autistic spectrum disorders	50,000
Acorns Children's Hospice Trust	General grant towards the costs of their hospices in Birmingham, Walsall and Worcester	35,000
Medical Research Institute – Coventry	Towards equipment for Warwick University to be used during research into aspects of hospital acquired infection	28,000
Salters Hill Charity Limited	Towards building improvements at their home near Ledbury that provides accommodation and activities for people with learning disabilities	15,000
Living Painting Trust	Towards a library service benefiting people in our area who are blind or partially sighted	6,000

Accommodation

Name	Purpose	£
St. Basil's Centre – Birmingham	For refurbishment of accommodation	50,000
West Mercia Womens Aid	Two grants towards childcare benefiting disadvantaged children living with their mothers in temporary accommodation in Hereford and Worcester / Kidderminster	20,000
Depaul Trust	Towards running costs of a hostel in Birmingham that benefits young homeless people	10,000
Dodford Children's Holiday Farm – Bromsgrove	Towards refurbishment of a kitchen at holiday farm benefiting disadvantaged children	6,000
Haven – Wolverhampton	Towards a resettlement service benefiting homeless women and their children	4,000

and June and the beginning of October and January.

Applications can only be considered if they are on the trust's standard, but very simple, 'application for support' form which can be obtained from the administrator at the offices of the trust in Gloucester. The form must be completed and returned (together with a copy of the latest accounts and annual report of the organisation) to the trust's offices at least six weeks before the meeting of trustees at which the application is to be considered, in order to give time for necessary assessment procedures, often including visits to applicants.

Before providing support to statutory bodies (such as hospitals and schools for people with learning difficulties), the trust requires written confirmation that no statutory funds are available to meet the need for which funds are being requested. In the case of larger grants to hospitals, the trust asks the district health authority to confirm that no statutory funding is available.

Where applications are submitted that clearly fall outside the grantmaking parameters of the trust, the applicant is advised that the application cannot be considered and reasons are given. All applications that are going to be considered by the trustees are acknowledged in writing. Applicants are advised of the reference number of their application and of the quarterly meeting at which their application is going to be considered. The decisions are advised to applicants in writing soon after these meetings. Funded projects are monitored.

The Execution Charitable Trust

Mainly local multi-purpose community projects supporting social welfare

£1.5 million (2008)
Beneficial area Worldwide, in practice mainly UK.

Block D, The Old Truman Building, 91 Brick Lane, London E1 6QL
Tel. 020 7375 2007
Email info@executionlimited.com

Website www.executioncharitabletrust. org
Correspondent Cheryl Mustapha-Whyte, Trustee
Trustees *Jacky Joy; John R Moore; Cheryl Mustapha-Whyte; Damien Devine; Peter Ward; Neil Strong.*
CC Number 1099097
Information available Accounts were available from the Charity Commission.

This trust funds local multi-purpose community projects in deprived areas in the UK that tackle the root causes, as well as the symptoms, of poverty and isolation. It was established in 2003 by stockbrokers Execution Ltd as a means of distributing funds raised from their 'charity days', when all commission revenues generated on the day are donated to charity. In 2008 the trust raised £1.1 million from this annual event.

From the outset the trust established a relationship with New Philanthropy Capital (NPC), itself a registered charity, set up in 2001 by a team of ex-City financiers which provides research based advice to donors on where and how their philanthropic funds can be targeted most effectively. Since then a partnership has grown out of a mutual commitment to tackling deprivation, disadvantage and degradation in the UK and beyond. NPC also provides evaluation of results to monitor the effectiveness of grants.

The criteria by which NPC selects charities are determined by the trust. These criteria ensure that the trust is able to locate projects for funding that are:

- in deprived communities – mainly in the UK
- run by local people wherever possible
- meeting local needs, respecting race and gender issues individual to those communities.

The trust looks to fund locally driven, successful, community projects which struggle to raise private funds due to a lack of a wider profile. The trust distributes its funds to organisations in all parts of the UK and is willing to consider funding organisations in disadvantaged communities for almost any purpose, from core funding and salaries, to project costs.

In 2008 the trust had assets of £928,000 and an income of £1.2 million. 67 grants were made totalling £1.5 million.

Grants are categorised as follows:

- General – 66 grants totalling £1.1 million

- Absolute Return for Kids, for local and international projects – £401,000.

Along with Absolute Return for Kids, the largest grant beneficiaries included: Trinity Community Centre – London; London Citizens, LondonFARE – Glasgow; ULW – Manchester; the Warren – Kingston upon Hull; Peace One Day – London; Windsor Women's Centre – Belfast; and the Strategy – Mid Glamorgan.

Applications The trust does not consider unsolicited applications for grants.

The trust has appointed New Philanthropy Capital (NPC) to proactively identify effective organisations on its behalf. If you believe your organisation matches the funding criteria listed here and you want to provide basic contact details and a short outline of your project, go to the Execution Charitable Trust's website and fill in the online form.

Esmée Fairbairn Foundation

Social welfare, education, environment, arts and heritage

£21.5 million (2008)
Beneficial area UK.

Kings Place, 90 York Way, London N1 9AG
Tel. 020 7812 3700 **Fax** 020 7812 3701
Email info@esmeefairbairn.org.uk
Website www.esmeefairbairn.org.uk
Correspondent Dawn Austwick, Chief Executive
Trustees *Tom Chandos, Chair; Felicity Fairbairn; Beatrice Hollond; James Hughes-Hallett; Thomas Hughes-Hallett; Kate Lampard; Baroness Linklater; William Sieghart.*
CC Number 200051
Information available Detailed guidelines for applicants and excellent annual report and accounts, all available on the clear and helpful website.

Ian Fairbairn established the foundation in 1961 (renamed Esmée Fairbairn Foundation in 2000). He was a leading city figure and his company, M&G, was the pioneer of the unit trust industry. Ian Fairbairn endowed the foundation with the greater part of his own holding in M&G, and in the early years the majority of grants were for economic and financial education.

His interest in financial education stemmed from his concern that most people had no access to stock exchange investment, and were therefore precluded from investing their savings in equities and sharing in the country's economic growth. It was precisely this concern that had led him into the embryonic unit trust business in the early 1930s.

The foundation was set up as a memorial to Ian Fairbairn's wife Esmée, who had played a prominent role in developing the Women's Royal Voluntary Service and the Citizens Advice Bureaux before being killed during an air raid towards the end of the Second World War. Her sons Paul and Oliver Stobart contributed generously to the original trust fund, as co-founders.

Summary

In January 2008 the foundation adopted a new, more general funding approach. From the foundation's press release:

Esmée Fairbairn Foundation has launched a new funding approach.

The majority of our funding will now be channelled through the Main Fund which will be an open, less prescriptive way of working, through which we will listen to ideas. We expect to fund a wider range of work than before, although our core interests remain in the fields of culture, education, environment and social development.

As part of our new funding approach we are also running a number of smaller, more focused funding strands. These will be in areas where we think a more direct intervention may have a greater impact.

General

In 2008 the foundation had assets of £725 million (£938 million in 2007) and an income of £32 million, mostly from investments. Grants were made during the year totalling £21.5 million.

Guidelines

The Esmée Fairbairn Foundation aims to improve the quality of life throughout the UK. We do this by funding the charitable activities of organisations that have the ideas and ability to achieve change for the better. We take pride in supporting work that might otherwise be considered difficult to fund.

Funding is channelled through two routes.

1) Main Fund

The Main Fund distributes about two-thirds of funding. Responsive to shifts in demand, it supports work that focuses on the UK's cultural life, education, the natural environment and enabling people who are disadvantaged to participate more fully in society.

What areas do we support?

Our primary interests are in the UK's cultural life, education, the natural environment and enabling people who are disadvantaged to participate more fully in society.

We welcome your suggestions about how we can help your organisation. We are particularly interested in hearing about how the work you are proposing:

- addresses a significant gap in provision
- develops or strengthens good practice
- challenges convention or takes a risk in order to address a difficult issue
- tests out new ideas or practices
- takes an enterprising approach to achieving your aims
- sets out to influence policy or change behaviour more widely.

We can only fund work that is legally charitable. You do not have to be a registered charity to apply, but your constitution must allow you to carry out the work you propose.

What type of funding do we offer?

At Esmée Fairbairn we are happy to consider requests to fund core costs or project costs. These may include running costs such as staff salaries and overheads but generally not equipment costs.

New and emerging organisations may apply and we are willing to help finance the early stages of developing a convincing new idea in order to test its feasibility and give it the best possible chance of success.

We occasionally fund research where we consider it is likely to have a practical impact.

If you ask for our assistance, you should tell us how much you need. The average Esmée Fairbairn grant is worth about £50,000, but we are happy to consider requests for less or more money.

2) Strands

The following four topics are identified for more detailed attention. These will develop over time, and allow the foundation to make a more focused contribution in an area of interest. Others may come on stream in due course. Check the foundation's website for up-to-date information.

Biodiversity – Supporting practical conservation action and the science which underpins it. The strand will focus on species and habitats that are uncharismatic or hard to fund and aims to support the development of effective conservation approaches. Linking science and practical action, it will prioritise partnership applications involving research organisations, practical conservation charities and voluntary nature societies.

Food – The aim of the Food Strand is to promote an understanding of the role of food in enhancing quality of life. It will prioritise the enjoyment and experience of food rather than its production and we seek to enable as many people in the UK as possible to access, prepare and eat nutritious, sustainable food. We are interested in work that influences policy and practice across a range of food-related areas. We expect to support a mix of practical projects that have wide significance, and some research and policy based work.

Museum & Heritage Collections – This strand will focus on time-limited collections work including research, documentation and conservation that is outside the scope of an organisation's core resources. We will prioritise proposals that are at an early stage of development where it may be difficult to guarantee tangible outcomes. We will also prioritise proposals that have the potential to share knowledge with other organisations through partnership working or dissemination.

New approaches to learning – Devising, testing and disseminating new approaches to teaching and learning that address current and future challenges in state schools and pre-schools.

Grants in 2008

The Main Fund

Category	Value	No. of projects
Arts, culture and heritage	£4,360,000	70
Environment	£3,820,000	45
Citizenship or community development	£3,020,000	61
Education	£1,820,000	34
Human rights and conflict resolution	£1,620,000	21
Prevention or relief of poverty	£1,020,000	21
Other charitable purposes	£1,570,000	15
Total	**£17,230,000**	**267**

The average grant size from the Main Fund was £64,500; there were a total of 4,824 applications made to the Main Fund, which means that just over 5.5% of applicants were successful. The following is a sample of beneficiaries from the Main Fund and the purposes for which grants were given:

Lloyds TSB Foundation for Scotland (£750,000), towards a new £10 million fund over three years for vulnerable 14–19 years olds; The Soil Association (£398,000), towards developing membership over three years to increase unrestricted core income; ADFAM

National (£384,000), towards the salaries of a stakeholder involvement co-ordinator, administrator and running costs of the new membership support project over five years, to develop ADFAM into a national umbrella organisation for self-help/peer support groups and services, and professionals working with families affected by drugs and alcohol; Forum for the Future (£240,000), towards core staff and overhead costs of the sustainable Bristol region project; Shelter (£237,000), towards the costs over three years of the pilot Knowsley Child Support Service aimed at meeting the needs of homeless children and thereby breaking the cycle of inter-generational homelessness; British Trust for Ornithology (£180,000), towards the salary and travel costs of the co-ordinator over five years for the 'Bird Atlas 2007–11'. An estimated 50,000 volunteers will assess changes in distribution and numbers of the UK's birds; Muslim Youth Helpline (£178,500), towards the salary of the helpline supervisor and contribution to core costs over four years; Children in Scotland (£103,000), towards the salary of an early years' policy officer over three years to make a lasting impact on Scottish early years policy, provision and practice; North Highland Forest Trust (£88,000), towards the salaries of the biodiversity forester and part time support staff over three years, promoting sustainable management of biodiversity-rich woodland; Positive Action for Refugees and Asylum Seekers (£53,000), towards core costs over three years of intensive support and emergency provision to destitute asylum seekers in Leeds; Sahara in Preston (£30,000), towards the salary of a project worker over two years to support a range of support services to BME women who are victims of domestic violence and forced marriage; The Oil Depletion Analysis Centre (£20,000), towards costs over two years of establishing a network to spread awareness among local authorities of peak oil and to stimulate policies to protect communities against its worst impacts; and Westminster Befriend A Family (£10,000), towards core costs to provide befriending, mentoring and family support to families with children aged 0–8 years.

Strands

Category	Value	No. of projects
New Approaches to Learning	£1,120,000	19
Food	£642,000	9
Biodiversity	£615,000	7
Museum & Heritage Collections	£583,000	13
Total	**£2,960,000**	**48**

The following is a sample of beneficiaries from the four Strands and the purposes for which grants were given:

Sustain (£204,000), towards the costs of a campaign over three years to introduce legislation requiring public bodies to purchase food supplies from sustainable sources; Marine Biological Association (£195,000), towards research costs over three years to improve the design of artificial urban coastal habitats to maximise biodiversity; LIFT for Learning (£124,000), towards the salary over three years for the communications and strategy director of DigiSmart, a pioneering ICT and literacy project; Community Food Initiatives North East (£90,000), towards the costs over three years of the expansion of community based food initiatives into rural Aberdeenshire and Moray; The Dartington Hall Trust (£50,000), towards the salaries of a conservation co-ordinator and conservation officer, plus a contribution towards specialist materials; Institute of Education (£36,000), towards developing new teaching and learning strategies for classical instrumental tuition, in order to increase motivation, achievement and inclusion amongst children; Caroline Walker Trust (£20,000), towards the cost of learning resources for staff who support children and adults with learning disabilities to encourage eating well and improve nutritional health; Almond Valley Heritage Trust (£12,000), towards the salary of a collection development officer to work on the shale oil collection; and The Edge Foundation (£7,500), towards research costs of projects offering hands on learning opportunities designed to engage and motivate young people of all abilities, linking schools, communities and employers.

Development Fund – £360,000

The foundation made two grants from its Development Fund. These were made to: The Henry Smith Charity (£354,000), towards supporting a strong and resilient voluntary sector in Northern Ireland, jointly funding six organisations through a partnership with The Henry Smith Charity; Archbishops' Council of the Church of England (£6,000), towards Welfare Futures and the Church – a study on the potential implications of the church's involvement with welfare provision.

Finance Fund – £400,000

The foundation made three grants from its Finance Fund. These were made to: Battersea Arts Centre (£200,000), towards the organisation's five year business plan leading to enhanced

financial sustainability by 2013; Community Finance Solutions (£125,000), towards business advice for Community Land Trusts, providing affordable housing in rural areas; and New Economics Foundation (£75,000), towards the salary of the head of business and finance researcher.

TASK Fund

The foundation also makes grants from its TASK (Trustees' Areas of Special Knowledge) Fund to support organisations known to individual trustees. There were 107 awards made totalling £990,000.

Exclusions The foundation does not support applications for:

- individuals or causes that will benefit only one person, including student grants or bursaries;
- support for a general appeal or circular;
- work that does not have a direct benefit in the UK, including expeditions and overseas travel;
- the promotion of religion;
- capital costs – meaning construction or refurbishment costs or items of equipment (other than those essential to a project we are supporting);
- work that is routine or well-proven elsewhere or with a low impact;
- healthcare or related work such as medical research, complementary medicine, counselling and therapy, education and treatment for substance misuse;
- work that is primarily the responsibility of central or local government, health trusts or health authorities, or which benefits from their funding. This includes residential and day care, housing and homelessness, individual schools, nurseries and colleges, supplementary schools and vocational training;
- projects that primarily benefit the independent education sector;
- environmental projects related to animal welfare, zoos, captive breeding and animal rescue centres;
- individual energy efficiency or waste reduction schemes;
- retrospective funding, meaning support for work that has already taken place.

Applications
Applying for a grant from the Main Fund
Please follow these three steps:

1) Read through the guidance notes, paying careful attention to the sort of work we support – and what we do not.
2) If you think your organisation's activities could attract Esmée Fairbairn funding, go through the self-assessment checklist for eligibility [available from the foundation's website].

3) If you can answer 'yes' to each of the self-assessment checklist questions, submit a first stage application [available from the foundation's website].

What happens next

We will then get back to you, aiming to acknowledge your first stage application within a week of receiving it. Within a month we will either suggest taking it to the second stage or decline to support it.

If you are invited to proceed to the second stage, we will ask you for some additional information that will depend on what you have already told us and the size and complexity of the work you would like us to support.

How will we evaluate your application?

We receive many more applications than we can support. Therefore, we have to be selective.

As part of our selection process, we look to support work that has the best chance of achieving its objectives or will leave behind knowledge and experience that could benefit others.

Every application for support is different and we examine each according to the likelihood of it making a difference in the applicant organisation's area of work. Depending on the nature of your application, these are some of the criteria we will apply:

- How strong are your ideas and how well equipped are your people to carry them out?
- How well do you understand the issues you are addressing and what is your track record?
- Do you have a clear plan or idea and the capacity to deliver it?
- What difference would help from us make to your work?
- Does your work have the potential to be applied more widely or can it influence the work of others?
- Would receiving our support make you more likely to attract help and engagement from others?
- How would your organisation be stronger by the end of the grant and how developed are your long-term plans for sustainability?

There is a different application process for the funding strands. To learn more about the strands and how to apply, visit the foundation's website.

The February Foundation

Education, heritage, community-based charities, environment, animals and medical/ welfare

£2.25 million (2008/09)

Beneficial area UK and overseas

Chantala, Wilby Road, Stradbroke, Eye IP21 5JN

Email rps@thefebruaryfoundation.org

Website www.thefebruaryfoundation.org

Correspondent Richard Pierce-Saunderson, Trustee

Trustees *Richard Pierce-Saunderson; James Carleton; The February Foundation (Cayman).*

CC Number 1113064

Information available Accounts were on file at the Charity Commission, without a list of grants.

The foundation was established in 2006 for general charitable purposes and has a broad range of interests. The following grant-making policy is taken from the foundation's accounts.

The foundation will consider the following organisations for the receipt of grants, equity investment or loans:

- charities for the benefit of persons who are making an effort to improve their lives
- charities for the benefit of persons no longer physically or mentally able to help themselves
- charities which protect the environment
- charities offering formal education resulting in recognised qualifications
- small or minority charities where small grants will have a significant impact
- companies where the acquisition of equity would be in line with the foundation's investment policy.

In 2008/09 the foundation had assets of £10.3 million and an income of £546,500. Grants were made totalling £2.25 million and were broken down as follows:

Category	No. of grants	Amount
Education	2	£1,500,000
Life skills development	2	£450,000*
Heritage	5	£448,000
End-of-life care	12	£65,000
Healthcare and medicine – treatment and patient support	9	£40,000

Although no individual beneficiaries are listed in the accounts, the foundation does offer some insight into its grant-making objectives:

General

Given the foundation's stated objective of structuring its giving in an informed manner, the foundation conducted evaluations of almost 300 charities which either had applied to the foundation for funding, or which were selected by the foundation as potential candidates for funding.

Education

The foundation's objective in its education grant strategy is to enable universal access. Managing its existing grant commitments in this area will be a strong feature of the foundation's future giving strategy.

Life skills development

The foundation believes that supporting disadvantaged young persons in their determination to better themselves must begin with equipping those persons with life skills through formal or informal education. Only through the acquisition of life skills such as financial literacy, self-respect and dietary knowledge can this constituency be empowered to escape their disadvantaged circumstances. The foundation will continue to manage its existing commitments in this area. *£250,000 of the total is the payment of a grant awarded and recognised in the prior year accounts.

Heritage

The foundation is committed to preserving the legacy of British heritage in the UK and overseas. Furthermore, it is determined, through managing its existing commitments in this area, to enable children to learn about unique aspects of British history, and thus to encourage them to develop and hold values of courage, dignity, respect and endeavour.

End-of-life care

The foundation is committed to supporting end-of-life care provision in the UK. Following a review of its end-of-life care strategy, the foundation will focus on grass-roots giving, and will continue to monitor the implementation of the government's End-of-Life Care strategy.

Healthcare and medicine

The foundation's giving in this area has been varied, with one major focus on supporting the provision of outdoor sports training and competitions for disabled persons.

Applications Email applications are preferred, and such applications will be processed in advance of hardcopy applications. Due to a high volume of applications, the foundation expects response times to be around 12 weeks from the date of the original application.

Please ensure that the subject field of any communication you send contains the name of your organisation or cause. **Emails with empty subject fields will**

be automatically deleted, whilst those with incomplete subject fields will experience a delay in processing.

All applications should be accompanied by full accounts for your most recent completed financial year (audited or unaudited). **This is essential.**

The Allan and Nesta Ferguson Charitable Settlement

Peace, education and overseas development

£3.6 million to organisations (2008)

Beneficial area Unrestricted, with a local interest in Birmingham and Bishop's Stortford.

Stanley Tee Solicitors, High Street, Bishop's Stortford CM23 2LU

Tel. 01279 755200

Email jrt@stanleytee.co.uk

Website www.fergusontrust.co.uk

Correspondent Richard Tee, Trustee

Trustees *Elizabeth Banister; David Banister; Lesley Roff; Richard Tee.*

CC Number 275487

Information available Annual report and accounts were on file at the Charity Commission. The trust also has a clear and simple website.

The Allan & Nesta Ferguson Charitable Trust was set up in memory of two generations of the Ferguson family to promote their particular interests in education, international friendship and understanding, and the promotion of world peace and development.

Grants are given to charitable organisations involved in projects supporting the interests of the trust, and also to individual students who are undertaking a gap year or studying for a PhD.

The trust gives the following information for organisations on its website:

Charitable organisations can be situated either in the UK or overseas but must be registered as a charity with the Charity Commission and will principally be educational bodies or aid organisations involved in projects supporting educational and development initiatives, including the promotion of world peace and development. All grants made by the trust are project based and must have an educational aim, element or content. In general the trustees will not consider applications for core funding or the construction of buildings in the UK. Overseas, however, the trustees will consider funding aid projects for example water treatment, food and medical supplies or the provision of basic facilities that are the pre-requisite of an educational or development initiative.

Grants made to charities during the year will vary both in size and amount, and will probably total between £5 million and £6 million. The amount of the grant is entirely at the discretion of the trustees and no reason for giving, withholding or offering a partial grant will be made.

In 2008 the trust had assets of £23.2 million and an income of £1.4 million. Grants were made to organisations totalling over £3.6 million.

Grants were categorised as follows, shown here with examples of beneficiaries receiving £15,000 or more:

Educational bodies – £2.3 million
Large grants were awarded to: The Open University and the Cambridge Foundation (£500,000 each); and Coventry University (£468,000). Other beneficiaries included: Royal Academy of Music (£45,000); Cranfield University (£35,000); University College London (£30,000); Foundation for Young Musicians (£25,000); London Business School (£20,000); and Child Soldiers Coalition Education & Research Trust (£15,000). Smaller grants totalled £354,000.

Overseas development – £1.2 million
Beneficiaries included: Microloan Foundation (£35,000); Christian Aid and Soteria Trust (£30,000 each); Garden Africa (£25,000); New Vision Development Organisation Kenya (£20,000); and Interact Worldwide and the Resource Alliance (£15,000 each). Smaller grants totalled £584,000.

Educational projects encompassing the promotion of world peace – £174,500
Beneficiaries included: CHIPS and Justice Africa (£30,000 each); Institute for Law & Peace (£20,000); and Concordis International Trust and Fellowship of Reconciliation (£15,000 each). Smaller grants totalled £64,500.

Applications Applications by charities for small to medium grants (up to a maximum of £50,000) may be submitted at any time and will be considered on a regular basis. Applications for larger grants will be considered at biannual meetings held in March and October and applications should be submitted at the very latest in the previous months (February or September).

Grants to charities will be on a matching funding basis only so that if the applicant has raised 50% of their budget the trustees will consider awarding matching funding up to a maximum of 50%. However, if the applicant has raised less than 50% of their budget the trustees will only consider awarding a maximum of 30% funding. Evidence of actively seeking funds from other sources is seen by the trustees as being a beneficial addition to any application. No repeat applications will be considered within three years of the conclusion of the grant term.

The trust prefers applications to be submitted online. Alternatively, forms can be downloaded and sent by post. Please do not extend the length of the forms, or add any attachments. Applications must not exceed three pages. Please use text size 12. If you are applying for more than one project, please use a separate form for each project.

All applications by email will be acknowledged and a decision will usually be given within three months of the application. No progress reports will be given and no correspondence will be entered into in the meantime.

The Fidelity UK Foundation

General, primarily in the fields of arts and culture, community development, education and health

£4.4 million (2008)

Beneficial area Particular preference is given to projects in Kent, Surrey, London and continental Europe.

Oakhill House, 130 Tonbridge Road, Hildenborough, Tonbridge TN11 9DZ

Tel. 01732 777364 **Fax** 01732 834143

Email foundation@fil.com

Website www.fidelityukfoundation.org

Correspondent Susan Platts-Martin, Chief Executive

Trustees *Edward C Johnson; Barry Bateman; Anthony Bolton; Robert Milotte; Richard Millar; John Owen.*

CC Number 327899

Information available Accounts were available at the Charity Commission. The foundation also has a clear and simple website.

This foundation was established in 1988 to strengthen not-for-profit organisations primarily in regions surrounding Fidelity International's major corporate locations. Particular preference is given to projects in Kent, Surrey, London and continental Europe. Grants from the foundation are made only for charitable purposes and are designed to encourage the highest standards of management and long-term self-reliance in non-profit organisations. Taking an investment approach to grant making, it funds organisations where it can add lasting, measurable value. Their aim is to support major initiatives that charitable organisations undertake to reach new levels of achievement.

The foundation's charitable giving is mainly in the areas of:

- arts and culture
- community development
- education
- health.

The following additional information is provided by the foundation on its website:

Types of projects
Because our goal is to help strengthen charitable organisations, we seek to support the types of projects that such organisations undertake to achieve their goals and reach long-term self-sufficiency. We have found that our resources can be most productive with charitable organisations taking significant measures to reach greater levels of proficiency. Most often, this entails major projects such as:

- capital improvements
- technology upgrades
- organisational development
- planning initiatives.

Assessment of the organisation
Beyond our basic guidelines, we review an organisation to determine whether our collaboration and investment can add value. Among the factors we consider are:

- the organisation's financial health
- the strength of its management team and board
- evidence of an overall strategic plan.

We also look at the size and scope of an organisation, evaluating its position within the context of its market and the needs of the constituents it serves. This analysis helps us evaluate if a grant has the realistic potential to measurably improve a charitable organisation's impact in its sector.

Potential for success
Like an investor, we ultimately seek to understand the potential returns of a project: Will it work? What will it achieve? In evaluating its potential for success, we seek evidence of:

- institutional commitment to the project on behalf of the organisation's board
- a realistic project budget
- a thorough implementation plan, including a plan for performance measurement
- net value to the organisation and the community it serves
- significant support from other funders, among other criteria.

Grantmaking in 2008

In 2008 the foundation had assets of £82.6 million and an income of £7 million. Grants were made totalling £4.4 million, and were broken down as follows:

Education – 15 grants totalling £1.5 million
Beneficiaries included: Royal Shakespeare Company, the Treehouse Trust and National Museums Scotland (£250,000 each); Royal Opera House Foundation and the Federation of London Youth Clubs (£200,000 each); Chatham Historic Dockyard Trust (£162,000); and Prior's Court Foundation (£100,000). Other grants were made totalling £97,000.

Health – 12 grants totalling £1.05 million
Beneficiaries included: Max Delbrueck Centre for Molecular Medicine (£281,000); Hubrecht Institute (£194,500); University of Cambridge – Institute of Education (£170,000); Trinity Hospice (£100,000); Breakthrough Breast Cancer (£93,000); Muscular Dystrophy Campaign (£80,000); Albert Ludwig's Universtat Frieburg (£79,000); and Tommy's, the Baby Charity (£25,000). Small grants were made totalling £33,000.

Arts and culture – 11 grants totalling £1.04 million
Beneficiaries included: The Mary Rose Trust (£300,000); Great Dixter Charitable Trust (£250,000); Watts Gallery (£200,000); Scottish Ballet (£100,000); and Historic Royal Palaces (£81,000). Other grants totalled £114,000.

Community – 19 grants totalling £516,500
Beneficiaries included: The Meath Epilepsy Trust (£100,000); Broadway Homelessness and Support (£64,000); and Latitude Global Volunteering (£25,000). Small grants totalled £108,000.

Exclusions Grants are not generally made to:

- start-up, sectarian, or political organisations
- private schools, and colleges or universities
- individuals.

Grants are not made for:

- sponsorships or benefit events
- scholarships
- corporate memberships
- advertising and promotional projects
- exhibitions.

Generally grants are not made for running costs, but may be considered on an individual basis through the foundation's small grants scheme. Grants will not normally cover the entire cost of a project. Grants will not normally be awarded to an organisation in successive years.

The foundation receives many more applications for grants than it is able to fund so not all applications that fall within the guidelines will receive grants.

Applications To the correspondent in writing. Applicants should enclose the following:

- Fidelity UK Foundation summary form (form can be downloaded from the foundation's website)
- organisation history and objectives
- description of request and rationale, addressing the following questions:
  - how the project fits into the larger strategic plan of your organisation
  - what a grant will allow your organisation to achieve
  - how a grant will change or improve the long-term potential of your organisation
  - what the implementation plan and timeline for the project will be
  - how the project will be evaluated.
- itemised project budget
- list of other funders and status of each request
- list of directors and trustees with their backgrounds
- current management accounts
- most recently audited financial statements.

There are no deadlines for submitting grant proposals. All applications will normally receive an initial response within three months. The volume of requests as well as the review process require a three to six month period, which should be factored into the applicant's funding plan.

The Sir John Fisher Foundation

General charitable purposes with a preference for the shipping industry, medicine, the navy or military and music and theatre

£723,000 (2007/08)

Beneficial area UK, with a preference for charities in the Furness peninsula and adjacent area and local branches of national charities.

Heaning Wood, Ulverston LA12 7NZ

Tel. 01229 580349

Email info@sirjohnfisherfoundation.org.uk

Website www.sirjohnfisherfoundation.org.uk

Correspondent Dr David Hart Jackson, Trust Secretary

Trustees *Diane S Meacock; Sir David Hardy; Daniel Purser Tindall; Rowland Frederick Hart Jackson.*

CC Number 277844

Information available Accounts were available at the Charity Commission. The foundation also has a clear and simple website.

The foundation was established by a deed of settlement made in 1979 by the founders, Sir John and Lady Maria Fisher. The foundation states that it gives grants to charities concerned with the Furness peninsula and local branches of UK charities.

It supports charitable causes and projects in six main categories; these are:

- maritime
- medical and disability
- education
- music
- arts
- community projects in and around Barrow-in-Furness.

The foundation gives priority to applying its income to projects and causes based in Barrow-in-Furness and in the surrounding Furness area. Exceptionally, occasional community projects from the remainder of Cumbria and north Lancashire will be considered. Some projects are supported nationally, particularly maritime projects and some music and art projects. The foundation also supports nationally a limited amount of high quality medical research.

In 2007/08 the foundation had assets of £47.1 million and an income of £925,000. During the year there were 123 grants were totalling £723,000. Grants were broken down as follows:

Local organisations – £366,500
Beneficiaries included: Barrow Sea Cadet Corps (£32,000); Lancaster University (£30,000); Barrow & District Society for the Blind (£25,000); The Wordsworth Trust (£20,000); Barrow Dads' Group (£10,000); Citizens Advice Bureau South Lakeland (£8,000); Ulverston International Music Festival (£7,000); Home Start South Cumbria (£5,000); Ulverston Victoria High School Orienteering Club (£4,000); Lake District Summer Music School (£3,500); Barrow Amateur Swimming Club (£2,000); West Lakeland Orchestra Society (£1,000); and Kendal South Choir (£500).

National organisations – £318,000
Beneficiaries included: National Maritime Museum – Cornwall (£70,000 in total); University of Dundee and RNLI Crew Training (£20,000 each); Cancer Research UK (£15,000); Anglo-Austrian Music Society and London Handel Society Ltd (£10,000 each); The Prostate Cancer Research Foundation (£7,000); Tall Ships Youth Trust and NSPCC (£5,000 each); Mission to Seafarers and the Fire Services National Benevolent Fund (£1,000 each); and John Rylands University Library (£500).

Exclusions The trustees will generally not fund:

- individuals
- sponsorship
- expeditions
- promotion of religion
- places of worship
- animal welfare
- retrospective funding
- pressure groups
- community projects outside Barrow-in-Furness and surrounding area (except occasional projects in Cumbria or north Lancashire or if they fall within one of the other categories supported by the foundation).

Applications The foundation's trustees fund projects requiring either capital or revenue support. There is no general limit to the grant which can be awarded to any one project. Most grants given are for less than £10,000. In the past the trustees have given larger grants to major one-off projects or for research projects over defined periods.

The trustees are in appropriate cases willing to express an intention to commit funds for up to three years, if it can be shown that substantial benefit will result from an extended period of funding. An intention to commit funds for future years is always subject to funds being available at the time.

Urgent grants for small (less than £4,000) amounts can be considered between meetings, but the trustees would expect an explanation as to why the application could not be considered at a normal meeting.

Applications should be made by submitting a completed application form, either by email or post, together with all relevant information (set out on the application form) to the secretary at least six weeks in advance of the trustees' meeting. The trustees meet at the beginning of May and the beginning of November each year.

You are always welcome to contact the Secretary for an informal discussion before submitting an application for funding.

The trustees expect to receive feedback from the organisations they support, to help in their decision making process. Organisations are asked to provide a brief one page report about nine months after receipt of a grant (or when the specific project assisted has been completed). A feedback form is available from the foundation's website.

Fisherbeck Charitable Trust

Christian, homelessness, welfare, education and heritage

£451,600 to organisations (2007/08)

Beneficial area Worldwide.

Home Farm House, 63 Ferringham Lane, Ferring, Worthing BN12 5LL

Tel. 01903 241027

Email ian@roffeyhomes.com

Correspondent The Trustees

Trustees *Ian R Cheal; Mrs Jane Cheal; Matthew Cheal.*

CC Number 1107287

Information available Accounts were available from the Charity Commission.

This trust was registered with the Charity Commission in December 2004, and it is the vehicle for the charitable activities of the Cheal family, owners of Roffey Homes developers.

The charity's objects are to encourage charitable giving from the extended Cheal family and to apply these funds to the making of grants for the following charitable objects:

- the advancement of the Christian religion
- support the provision of accommodation for the homeless and meeting their ongoing needs
- the relief of poverty
- the advancement of education
- to encourage conservation of the environment and the preservation of our heritage
- such other charitable objects in such manner as the trustees shall from time to time decide.

In 2007/08 the trust had assets of £176,400 and an income of £484,000, mostly from donations and gifts. Grants were made totalling £456,000, most of which went to organisations.

There were 21 grants of £5,000 or more listed in the accounts, with most beneficiaries appearing to receive support each year. Beneficiaries included: Tear Fund (£48,000); Urban Saints (£44,500); Bible Society (£28,000); Release International (£24,000); National Trust (£19,000); Hope for Lugazi (£12,000); Scripture Union (£9,000); and Sustrans (£6,000).

Other grants to organisations of £5,000 and under totalled £52,000. Grants were also given to two individuals totalling £4,500.

Exclusions Grants are only made to individuals known to the trust or in exceptional circumstances.

Applications Grants are given in accordance with the wishes of the Cheal family.

The Fishmongers' Company's Charitable Trust

General, in particular education, relief of poverty and disability

£585,000 to organisations (2008)

Beneficial area UK, however this refers to charities whose objects extend throughout England. Special interest in the City of London and its adjacent boroughs.

The Fishmongers' Company, Fishmongers' Hall, London Bridge, London EC4R 9EL

Tel. 020 7626 3531 **Fax** 020 7929 1389

Email clerk@fishhall.co.uk

Correspondent Peter Woodward, Clerk

Trustee *The Worshipful Company of Fishmongers.*

CC Number 263690

Information available Accounts were available from the Charity Commission.

The trust was established in 1972 for general charitable purposes and its focus is in the areas of education, relief of poverty and disability, almshouses, fishery related organisations, the environment and heritage.

In March 2009, the trust merged with the Billingsgate Christian Mission Charitable Trust and will administer it as a designated fund. For further information, please contact the trust directly.

Grantmaking

In 2008 the trust had assets of £12 million and an income of £875,000. Grants were made totalling £661,000, of which £585,000 was given to organisations and £76,000 to individuals. Organisational grants range from £1,500 to £350,000 but the majority are for under £5,000. As in previous years, two of the largest grants went to Gresham's School, for scholarships, (£331,000); and Jesus Hospital Almshouses (£28,000).

Grants were categorised as follows:

Category	Value
Education	£446,000
Hardship	£68,000
Fishery	£45,000
Disability and medical	£17,000
Heritage	£8,700
Environment	£1,000

Beneficiaries included: Marion Richardson School (£30,000); City and Guilds of London Art School (£25,000); Lord Mayor's Appeal (£9,000); Atlantic Salmon Trust (£8,800); Billingsgate Seafood Training School (£5,000); Harrietsham Almshouse (£4,900); Help for Heroes (£3,000); St Magnus the Martyr (£1,500); and Nancy Oldfield Trust, Broadway and Airbourne Forces Museum (£1,000 each).

Exclusions No grants to individuals except for educational purposes. Ad hoc educational grants are not awarded to applicants who are over 19 years old.

Applications In writing to the correspondent. Meetings take place three times a year in March, June/July and October/November, and applications should be received a month in advance. No applications are considered within three years of a previous grant application being successful. Unsuccessful applications are not acknowledged.

The Football Association Youth Trust

Sports

£612,000 (2007/08)

Beneficial area UK.

Football Association Ltd, 25 Soho Square, London W1D 4FA

Tel. 020 7745 4589 **Fax** 020 7745 5589

Email mike.appleby@thefa.com

Correspondent Mike Appleby, Secretary

Trustees *Raymond G Berridge; Barry W Bright; Geoff Thompson; Jack Perks.*

CC Number 265131

Information available Accounts were available from the Charity Commission.

The principal activity of the trust continues to be the organisation or provision of facilities which will enable pupils of schools and universities and young people under the age of 21 in the UK to play association football or other games and sports including the provision of equipment, lectures, training colleges, playing fields or indoor accommodation.

In 2007/08 the trust had assets of £4.3 million and an income of £216,000. Grants were made during the year totalling £612,000. Grants were broken down as follows:

Category	Amount	No. of grants
Schools and Universities	£433,000	7
English Schools FA	£100,000	2
County Football Associations	£76,000	92
County FA Fairplay Medals	£6,200	–
FA School Club Link Programme	£5,000	–
Youth Referees Programme	£4,300	–
Other	£2,600	2

The trust will also be providing £747,000 to Girls' Centres of Excellence around the country for the 2009/10 season.

Applications In writing to the correspondent. Grants are made throughout the year. There are no application forms, but a copy of the most recent accounts should be sent.

The Football Foundation

Grassroots football, community and education

£82.1 million (2007/08)
Beneficial area England.

30 Gloucester Place, London W1U 8FF
Tel. 08453 454 555 **Fax** 08453 457 057
Email enquiries@footballfoundation.org.uk
Website www.footballfoundation.org.uk
Correspondent Robert Booker, Director of Finance
Trustees *Richard Scudamore; Roger Burden; Peter McCormick; Philip Smith.*
CC Number 1079309
Information available Annual report and accounts were available from the Charity Commission. The foundation also has a clear and informative website.

The Football Foundation is the UK's largest sports charity funded by the Premier League, The FA, Sport England and the Government.

Our mission is to improve facilities, create opportunities and build communities throughout England.

As the country's largest funder of grassroots football, the foundation has delivered thousands of facility and community projects,

as well as free kit and safe goalposts, since its launch in July 2000.

Our unique partnership with the Premier League, The FA, Sport England and the Government, each of whom invest £15 million every year, ensures we are well placed to deliver funding at grassroots level.

In 2007/08 the foundation had a total income of £67.7 million, which included unrestricted income of: £24.5 million from the government, £9.5 million of which came from Sport England; £12.2 million from the Football Association; £12.2 million from the Premier League; and £2 million from Barclays Spaces for Sport. Restricted income for various programmes included: £6.9 million from the Premier League/Professional Footballers' Association; a further £4.2 million from Sport England; and £3.6 million from Kickz. Grants were made across all programmes totalling £82.1 million (2006/07: £56.2 million).

Achievements and performance in 2007/08

The following review of activities and achievements during the year is provided in the foundation's informative annual report:

In meeting our objectives, 4,096 grants were awarded during the year compared with 5,438 grants in the previous year. The reduction in grant number is as a direct result of the closure during the year of the coaching pack scheme, which has resulted in excess of £1,300 grants per annum in the past. The reduction in the number of grants awarded has not, however, resulted in a reduction in the total amount granted. On the contrary, the value of grants awarded in this financial year has significantly exceeded the last financial year.

Modernising facilities
The provision of new or refurbished facilities continues to be the foundation's key contribution to the increase in stock of quality sport sites. For example, Wallsend Boys Club operates over 20 teams around North Tyneside. Due to a lack of quality facilities the teams had to play in various locations around the area. With the help of an £850,000 foundation grant towards a £1.2 million project the club were able to improve the drainage of the existing pitches and provide a six changing room pavilion.

Increasing participation
The foundation's most important measure of performance is increased participation. For example, Longhill Ward Community Association was awarded £444,000 towards a new changing room and pitch drainage project back in 2004. The development work

has had a dramatic impact on participation on the site. Matches are no longer called off due to water-logging and more players are able to play regularly as they can now change in comfort and safety. Since completion, participation at the site has increase by 192% overall, with female participation increasing by 345%.

Strengthening links
The foundation uses the power of football to engage with socially excluded young people. For example, working with Her Majesty's Prison and Youth Offending Institute Ashfield, the foundation is providing a grant of £282,000 towards a £455,000 project that will offer a comprehensive package of sport for young people aged 15 to 18 at the prison. The aim is to focus on trying to support young offenders so that they do not re-offend once they are released.

Barclays Spaces for Sports
The programme has delivered 200 multi-use sports facilities in the most deprived areas of the country. All sites are now fully operational and offering opportunities for over 25 different sports, including football, basketball, tennis, BMX and skateboarding. On average, over 69,000 users are attracted each week. 4,045 coaching packs have been awarded benefiting over 141,365 people.

The majority of the £30 million budget has now been spent on the capital build for the 200 sites, both flagship and local. Of the budget, £5 million has been set aside to provide a revenue fund to sustain and develop the sites through to 2010. The foundation will administer this revenue development through providing grants from the fund (£50,000 each for flagship projects and £20,000 each for local sites). This commitment runs until at least September 2010. Two people, a Programme Manager and Programme Officer, are employed by the foundation for this period to manage and administer this ongoing commitment. They will also have the responsibility of supporting the projects by creating an exit strategy once the current funding runs out. These posts and sustainability requirement had always been factored into the overall programme budget by Barclays.

Kickz
Following a successful pilot programme in London, it was agreed to extend the programme from September 2008, to be funded by:

- £4.7 million from the foundation
- £3 million from the Metropolitan Police – toward 2 projects in each of the 32 London boroughs, and
- £1 million through the Department of Culture, Media and Sport from the Premier League's Good Causes fund to add projects through clubs outside London.

The foundation's funding would be split, match-funding the £3 million provided by the Met police for the London projects, with the remaining £1.7 million for projects outside London. This year has seen a significant growth in the number of individual projects being delivered in separate locations, with the number of projects rising from 25 to 90. There are now 31 professional clubs delivering the programme, including all 2007/08 Premier League clubs. One third of Year 1 Kickz projects are based in the top 5% most deprived areas in the country, with over three quarters based in the top 20% most deprived areas, and 90% in the top 30%.

All 14 professional football clubs in London now deliver Kickz, following the recent introduction of Barnet and Dagenham & Redbridge. Those London clubs with the relevant expertise and capacity are delivering up to seven individual projects in multiple London boroughs. 62 projects are currently being delivered in London. This is only two projects short of achieving two in each of the 32 London boroughs.

Premier League/Professional Footballers' Association Community Fund

Since September 2007, the foundation has been managing and administering the PL/PFA Community Fund, a three-year programme, funded by the Premier League and the Professional Footballers' Association (PFA). This money is ring-fenced for community work delivered entirely through the community schemes at Premier League clubs. The funding seeks to build on the excellent and varied nature of the work already being delivered by Premier League club community schemes whilst also ensuring some standardisation across all schemes by supporting clubs to improve their standards of delivery and monitoring of impact. Premier League clubs' community schemes are the only beneficiaries of this funding, enabling them to deliver projects which will genuinely benefit and meet the needs of their local community.

Since the programme began, all 20 club community schemes have been assessed and have passed the Fit for Purpose standard of the 2007/08 season.

All 20 clubs claimed a £20,000 Central Initiatives grants for this initial season, which they use towards the costs of delivering a range of extra activities on behalf of the Premier League, PFA and the foundation, including the Premier League schools tournament, the Prince's Trust Football Initiative, Sports Relief, Creating Chances, Playing for Success, Premier League Reading Stars, Your Game, Kick it Out, Level Playing Field and Annual Audit.

15 clubs received transitional assistance support, totalling £124,200 for last season, using the funding for items and services such as acquiring charitable status, purchasing laptops or office equipment, IT support and software installation, monitoring systems, employing bid writers to assist in application writing and refurbishing their community offices.

Two rounds of project assessment have already taken place with [just over] £6.4 million in grant-aid committed to 11 education and life-long learning projects, 9 health and wellbeing projects, 7 social inclusion projects and 5 equalities projects. A total of £3.7 million of partnership funding has already been secured by the PL/PFA Community Fund. Sources of this partnership funding include Primary Care Trusts, Local Authorities and Housing Associations.

Grant programmes

The following funding streams are available from the foundation – check the foundation's website for up-to-date information on programmes closing or re-opening. The foundation also has several programmes which it operates in partnership with other organisations and ones which offer vouchers such as the Junior Kit Scheme. Full details of these are also available on the foundation's website.

Facilities Programme

The facilities scheme gives grants for projects that:

- improve facilities for football and other sport in local communities
- sustain or increase participation amongst children and adults, regardless of background age, or ability
- help children and adults to develop their physical, mental, social and moral capacities through regular participation in sport.

The types of facilities we give money for include:

- grass pitches drainage/improvements
- pavilions, clubhouses and changing rooms
- artificial turf pitches and multi-use games areas
- fixed floodlights for artificial pitches.

We also provide development (revenue) grants to deliver football development associated with the new facility for example coaching, football development officer etc.

The maximum grant available from the foundation for each facilities project is £1 million. However, applicants must show they have tried hard to get other funding for the project and that there is no further money available.

The most we can pay is 90% of the project costs, but we will only award as much as this in exceptional circumstances. For example, applications where there is an outstanding need for a facility and where the project will have a major effect on under-represented groups in football (such as women and girls, people on low incomes, black and ethnic-minority groups and disabled people).

We also provide (revenue) funding to deliver football development associated with the new facility for example coaching, football development officer etc. The maximum development funding that can be included with a facilities grant is 20% of the total grant awarded.

We have a fast track system for facilities grants of up to and including £20,000.

Community Large Grants Scheme

The Community Large Grant scheme aims to create opportunities and build communities by funding projects that use football and sport to contribute to one of the following Community Programme Objectives.

- Preventing and reducing offending.
- Promoting respect amongst communities and bringing people together through football.
- Improving educational attainment and lifelong learning.
- Encouraging personal development from participation in football and sport through to volunteering, training and employment.
- Tackling the rise of obesity in children and adults.
- Improving the mental health and wellbeing of children and adults.
- Tackling regional health inequalities in life expectancy and chronic illness.

The Community Large Grant scheme aims to create opportunities and build communities by funding projects that use football and sport as a force for social change. We fund projects that address social exclusion and inequalities in education and health.

Can you apply?

New Stage One submissions will be accepted from October 2009

We only fund organisations that are 'not for profit'. We do not fund individuals.

Applications from clubs will only be accepted from those based in England and/or affiliated to The Football Association. Applications from Wales will only be accepted if they are made through the Community Scheme attached to the club playing in the English Football League.

Applications that include partnership funding from the Football Pools Investment Committee will not be considered nor will applications for contributions to support Kickz projects.

What do we give money for?
We aim to support projects that:

- generate new activity
- use football and where appropriate other sports to focus on one of the following Foundation's Community Programme Strategy objectives:
  - preventing and reducing offending
  - promoting respect amongst communities and bringing people together through football
  - improving educational attainment and lifelong learning
  - encouraging personal development from participation in football and sport through to volunteering, training and employment
  - tackling the rise of obesity in children and adults
  - improving the mental health and wellbeing of children and adults
  - tackling regional health inequalities in life expectancy and chronic illness.

The Community Programme Strategy can be viewed by visiting the publications page of the foundation's website.

We do not fund:

- statutory core business, although applications for Special Educational Needs (SEN) curriculum time activity are eligible
- capital costs
- one off events
- retrospective costs or expenses
- stand alone educational materials
- projects with a total project cost of less than £10,000.

How much money can we give you?
The maximum grant available is £150,000 for projects that last between one and three years.

The foundation is only able to support a percentage of the total project cost. Percentage support is determined by need and will, therefore, vary. However, it will not exceed 90% of the total project costs.

Please note we can contribute to management costs but this contribution will not exceed 12.5 % of the total project cost.

Community Small Grants Scheme
The Football Foundation is **not** accepting any applications to the Community Small Grant scheme.

Full applications already submitted, received and acknowledged will be processed as normal.

A new Community Small Grant scheme will be lunched in July.

What will the scheme be?
The scheme will provide funding for projects that use football to:

- increase participation by both players and volunteers.

This will be done by supporting the costs associated with providing **new** activity.

Applications Application forms and guidance notes are available on request directly from the foundation or downloadable from the website. See the general section for details of each scheme.

You can also apply for a grant online.

Gwyneth Forrester Trust

General
£450,000 (2008/09)
Beneficial area England and Wales.

Lancaster House, 7 Elmfield Road, Bromley BR1 1LT
Tel. 020 8461 8014
Correspondent Christopher Perkins, Trustee
Trustees *Wendy J Forrester; Anthony J Smee; Michael B Jones; Christopher Perkins.*
CC Number 1080921
Information available Accounts were available from the Charity Commission.

Established in May 2000, the trustees support a specific charitable sector each year.

In 2008/09 the trust had assets of £17 million and an income of £467,500. Grants were made during the year totalling £450,000.

During the year the trust focused on organisations involved with research into strokes and heart disease and charities helping sufferers of those conditions. Due to the current global financial situation the trustees have decided to maintain this current policy into 2009/10.

Beneficiaries in 2008/09 were: The Stroke Association and the British Heart Foundation (£100,000 each); and Cardiac Risk in the Young, CORDA, Different Strokes, Heart Research UK and Speakability (£50,000 each).

Exclusions No grants to individuals.

Applications The trust has previously stated that 'applications for aid cannot be considered'.

The Donald Forrester Trust

Children and young people, older people's welfare, hospitals and hospices, physical disability, blind and deaf people, community care and social welfare, medical research, overseas relief, animal welfare, services and ex-services, religious organisations, maritime, mental health, the homeless, arts, culture and sport, environmental heritage, trades and professions, education and general charitable purposes
£980,000 (2007/08)
Beneficial area UK and overseas.

Lancaster House, 7 Elmfield Road, Bromley BR1 1LT
Tel. 020 8461 8014
Correspondent Christopher A Perkins, Trustee
Trustees *Wendy J Forrester, Anthony J Smee; Michael B Jones; Hilary J Porter; Christopher A Perkins.*
CC Number 295833
Information available Annual report and accounts available from the Charity Commission.

When Donald Forrester, a successful London businessman and company director, died in 1985, his widow Gwyneth set up the Donald Forrester Charitable Trust which was established in 1986. The trust's grantmaking now covers a wide range of categories. Most grants go to well known (and often, though not exclusively, national) charities.

The trust is, for the most part, reliant on income from Films & Equipments Limited and the increased gift aid and the maintained dividend from the company has allowed the trust to continue to increase total charitable giving. During 2007/08 the trustees reviewed grant making policies and agreed that the existing method of selecting charitable causes for support should broadly continue but the trust should apply some of its resources to longer term funding projects.

In 2007/08 the trust had an income of £831,000 and £980,000 was distributed to 125 charities. Assets stood at £7.8 million.

Most grants were for £5,000 with the exception of 1 grant of £20,000, 6 grants of £15,000 and 21 grants of £10,000. Administration costs for the trust are very low.

Category	£	No. of grants
Animals and birds	£20,000	4
Art, culture and sport	£5,000	1
Blind and deaf	£35,000	5
Children and young people	£95,000	15
Community care and social welfare	£70,000	12
Education	£25,000	2
Environmental heritage	£45,000	2
Homeless	£10,000	2
Hospices and hospital	£80,000	10
Medical relief and welfare	£70,000	10
Maritime	£20,000	3
Medical research	£230,000 *	10
Mental health	£20,000	3
Older people's welfare	£60,000	13
Overseas	£70,000	12
Physically disabled	£75,000	11
Religious organisation	£15,000	3
Services and ex-services	£30,000	5
Trades and professions	Nil	–

* In March 2008 the trustees awarded a grant to Cambridge Foundation to finance a Research Fellowship in the Department of Clinical Neurosciences, Cambridge University, for three years at £60,000 per annum, payable in March 2008, March 2009 and March 2010.

Examples of beneficiaries in the various categories included:

Animals and birds
Animal Defence Trust, Cats Protection League and David Sheldrick Wildlife Trust (£5,000 each).

Art, culture and sport
Wheel Power (£5,000).

Blind and deaf
Guide Dogs for the Blind and Sight Savers International (£10,000 each); and National Deaf Children's Society and SENSE (£5,000 each).

Children and young people
Barnardo's and Children's Society (£10,000 each); and Children with Leukaemia, Cystic Fibrosis Trust, Great Ormond Street Children's Charity, ICAN, Over the Wall, Pestolozzi International Village and the Sick Children's Trust (£5,000 each).

Community care and social welfare
Camphill Village Trust and Kenward Trust (£10,000 each); and the Attlee Foundation, Carers UK, Citizens Advice Bureaux Bromley, National Association of Citizen Advice Bureaux, Samaritans and Women's Royal Voluntary Service Trust (£5,000 each).

Education
Churcher's College 1722 Society (£15,000); and Royal Masonic School for Girls (£10,000).

Environmental heritage
British Red Cross Flood Appeal (£20,000); EIA Charitable Trust (£10,000); and Friends of Conservation (£5,000).

Homeless
Epic Trust and the Passage (£5,000 each).

Hospices and hospitals
Rowans Hospice (£15,000); Demelza Hospice, Mildmay Mission Hospital and St Kentigern Hospice and Palliative Care Centre (£10,000 each); and Friends of University College London Hospitals and Hospice of St Francis Berkhampsted (£5,000 each).

Medical relief and welfare
Cancer Backup (£15,000); Macmillan Cancer Relief and Stroke Association (£10,000 each); and Action for Dysphasic Adults, Haemophilia Society, Lymphoma Association, Multiple Sclerosis Luton and Dunstable (£5,000 each).

Maritime
RNLI (£10,000); and British & International Sailors Society (£5,000).

Medical research
Royal College of Surgeons (£10,000); and Asthma UK, Dimbleby Cancer Fund, Leukaemia Research Fund, Prostate Research Campaign UK and RAFT (£5,000 each).

Mental health
MENCAP (£10,000); and Guideposts Trust (£5,000).

Older people's welfare
Abbeyfield Bishop's Stortford Society, Age Concern Birmingham, Age Concern Hillingdon, Aid for the Aged in Distress, Anchor Trust, Elizabeth Finn Care and Methodist Homes for the Aged (£5,000 each).

Overseas
Agents of Change (£15,000); and African Children's Educational Trust, Build Africa, Nyumbani UK, Practical Action, Water Aid and ZANE: Zimbabwe (£5,000 each).

Physically disabled
Canine Partners (£15,000); Parkinson's Disease Society and Scope (£10,000 each); and Disabled Living Foundation, Jubilee Sailing Trust, Limbless Association and Vitalise (£5,000 each).

Religious organisations
Friends of Friendless Churches and West London Mission (£5,000 each).

Services and ex-services
Help for Heroes (£10,000); and British Limbless Ex-Service Men's Association and the Not Forgotten Association (£5,000 each).

Exclusions No grants to individuals.

Applications The trust supports a substantial number of charities on a regular basis. We are informed that regrettably, detailed applications, which place 'an intolerable strain' on administrative resources, cannot be considered. It is suggested that very brief details of an application should be submitted to the correspondent on one side of A4.

The trustees normally meet twice a year to consider and agree on the grants which are paid half yearly. There are no specific requirements under the trust deed and over the years the trustees have supported a wide range of national and international charities and endeavoured to achieve a balance between the large institutions and the smaller charities that experience greater difficulty in fund-raising. The trustees have developed a fairly substantial list of charities that are supported on a regular basis, but new proposals, both regular and 'one-off' are considered at each meeting.

Four Acre Trust

Youth work, respite breaks, mentoring schemes and health related work overseas

£2.3 million (2007/08)
Beneficial area Worldwide.

Treferanon, St Weonards, Hereford HR2 8QF

Tel. 01981 580 002

Email info@fouracretrust.org.uk

Website www.fouracretrust.org.uk

Correspondent June Horton, Trust Administrator

CC Number 1053884

Information available Accounts were available from the Charity Commission.

The trust was established in 1996 to advance education, relieve sickness and poverty and for general charitable purposes. The trust supports charities that help people to make the most of their lives and prefers to prevent problems occurring rather than trying to cure them. The trust is keen to support local, district or small national organisations that have low reserves and a significant volunteer element. The trust prefers to support young people more often than older people and revenue expenses rather than capital. Core costs will be financed if necessary. The main areas of support are:

- respite breaks and holidays
- school holiday activity schemes
- mentoring schemes
- youth work in local communities.

The trust is looking to build long-term relationships with grant beneficiaries and is happy to continue funding beyond one year as long as there is still sufficient need.

Please note: around 25% of the trust's grant aid is given to charities that are registered in the UK but which operate abroad. Support in this area is currently focused on water and sanitation projects and eye care services.

In 2007/08 the trust had assets of £9.7 million and an income of £986,000. Grants were made to 240 institutions totalling £2.3 million. The trust provides grants ranging from £3,000 to £75,000. The 50 largest grants were listed in the trust's accounts.

Beneficiaries included: Room to Read (£105,000); Visions for the Future (£77,000); International Childcare Trust (£71,000); Essex Assn of Boys Club (£60,000); Tarabai Hospital (£53,000); Sight Savers (£48,000); Fostering Network (£33,000); Centre 63 Church of England Youth (£29,000); Whitehaven Harbour Project (£25,000); Let Us Play schemes (19,000); John Fawcett Foundation (£10,000); and Belfast Activity Centre (£7,500).

Exclusions The trust does not support the following:

- advice services
- advocacy
- alcohol projects
- animal welfare
- applications from charities/ organisations based abroad
- arts
- basic services (as opposed to imaginative new projects) for disabled or older people
- branches of national charities
- commercial publications
- conferences or seminars
- counselling
- direct replacement of statutory funding
- drop-ins
- drugs, HIV/AIDS projects
- establishing funds for scholarships or loans
- general appeals
- heritage
- individuals
- IT training/projects
- individual parish churches
- large UK-charities which enjoy wide support, including local branches of UK-charities
- medical (including research), general healthcare or costs of individual applicants
- mental health care
- overseas projects other than eye care and water provision
- overseas travel, conference attendance or exchanges
- performances, exhibitions or festivals
- prisoner and offender projects
- refugee projects
- religious activities
- research projects
- school related projects
- science
- sports
- stage, film or television production costs
- university or similar research.

The trust does not pay off deficits or loans, replace withdrawn or reduced statutory funding or give grants retrospectively. Grants are not given towards any large capital, endowment or widely distributed appeal.

Applications Application forms are available from the trust's website and should be submitted by email. Telephone calls prior to application are welcomed. The trustees meet in February, April, June, August, October and December. All applications are replied to, and are usually processed within three months. All applicants are visited by one of the trust's field officers to discuss how the trust may best offer support. A brief but full report is required on the outcome of the funding.

Rejected lottery bids will be considered, but organisations are asked to telephone the trust to discuss the project before making an application.

Please note: the trust always receives more applications than it has funds to support and even if a project fits the trust's policy priorities, it may not be possible to make a grant.

The Foyle Foundation

Arts and learning

£5.1 million (2007/08)

Beneficial area UK.

Rugby Chambers, 2 Rugby Street, London WC1N 3QU

Tel. 020 7430 9119 **Fax** 020 7430 9830

Email info@foylefoundation.org.uk

Website www.foylefoundation.org.uk

Correspondent David Hall, Chief Executive

CC Number 1081766

Information available Annual report and accounts were available from the foundation's website.

Summary

The foundation was formed under the will of the late Christina Foyle. She was the daughter of William Foyle who, with his brother, founded the family owned bookshop Foyles in Charing Cross Road, London, which she managed after her father's death. The foundation is an independent charity and there is no connection with Foyle's Bookshop.

The foundation makes around 200 grants each year, most of which are for between £10,000 and £50,000, in the fields of arts and learning.

The number of grant applications from the English regions, Scotland, Wales and Northern Ireland continued to increase and consequently the amount in grants to these areas has also increased. The total of grants made to London organisations declined from the previous year. Most regions of England saw an increase in the value of grants with the exception of the North East and South West regions. Wales and Northern Ireland both registered an increase in grants (by value) for the second year in a row.

General

In 2007/08 the foundation had assets of £68.5 million and an income of £3.8 million. There were 168 grants made during the year totalling over £5.1 million, including:

Category	Value	No.
Arts	£2,320,000	70
Learning	£1,920,000	64
Health*	£991,000	33
Other	£100,000	1

*The foundation no longer makes health-related grants.

Guidelines

The following information is provided by the foundation:

1. Objectives

The foundation will support charities registered in the United Kingdom, the dominant purpose of which is to benefit either the Arts or Learning. Please note that we do not support applications from individuals.

1.1 Arts

The foundation seeks applications that make a strong artistic case for support in either the performing or visual arts. Our Arts programme has a twofold purpose to help sustain the arts and to support projects that particularly help to deliver artistic vision. Typical areas of support include:

- helping to make the arts more accessible by developing new audiences, supporting tours, festivals and arts educational projects;
- encouraging new work and supporting young and emerging artists; and
- building and infrastructure projects to construct new arts facilities or improve or re-equip existing arts venues.

Generally, we make grants for specific projects. We will consider applications for core funding (but generally only from smaller organisations or from those not receiving recurrent revenue funding from the Arts Council or local authorities).

Please note that community arts activity will not generally be supported.

1.2 Learning

The foundation will support projects which facilitate the acquisition of knowledge and which have a long-term strategic impact. Key areas for support are:

- libraries, museums and archives; and
- special educational needs and learning difficulties.

State funded schools and special schools may be supported (see special guidance notes). Private schools will not generally be supported.

Citizenship, esteem-building, training, skills acquisition to aid employment, independent living, early learning projects or playgroups will not generally be considered.

2. General

Applications should be for the benefit of people in the United Kingdom. Applications from individuals or organisations without charitable status will be ineligible.

The foundation will consider both revenue and capital projects.

Organisations and projects that provide direct benefits and services to the public, rather than special interest groups will be favoured.

Applications for grants because funding is difficult to obtain will be of particular interest.

Applicants should demonstrate how the project or funding request will be sustainable, if this is an ongoing activity, beyond the end of any grant.

As part of the project appraisal process the level and purpose of the applicant's reserves will be taken into account.

Social and community welfare organisations, whose dominant purpose is not Arts or Learning, will not normally be supported. For example, a community centre would not be eligible whereas an arts centre would be.

Retrospective funding will not be considered, nor will funding for projects that have already started (except for capital projects still underway and which will not be completed for some time).

An organisation may only apply for one grant per year. Where an applicant that is part of a wider national organisation is supported, no other affiliated or regional branches of that organisation will be supported in that year.

3. Size of Grants

The majority of grants will be in the range of £10,000 to £50,000. Applications for less than £10,000 per annum will generally not be accepted.

The maximum amount of a large grant will not normally exceed £500,000 and may be payable over several years. In exceptional circumstances, larger grants over this amount may be considered where, for example an overriding factor is that the project might not occur without the foundation grant or where the project is of national importance.

Where a grant of over £50,000 per annum has been awarded, the foundation will not normally accept any further applications from the same charity within three years from the date of the award or final instalment.

Any grant should be able to be drawn down within two years of being awarded, otherwise the foundation may withdraw the grant.

Grantmaking in 2007/08

Arts

Beneficiaries included: Opera North and Leeds Grand Theatre Development Trust (£125,000); Chichester Festival Theatre (£100,000); the Cambridge Foundation (£75,000); Grizedale Arts (£50,000); Yorkshire Sculpture Park (£40,000); Brentwood Theatre Trust and Music Theatre Wales (£25,000 each); National Student Drama Festival (£24,000); City of London Sinfonia (£20,000); Cheltenham Festivals (£16,000); Welsh Chamber Orchestra (£15,000); and Northern Actors Centre and Scottish Borders Community Orchestra (£10,000 each).

Learning

Beneficiaries included: Royal National Theatre (£250,000); National Museums and Galleries of Northern Ireland (£150,000); World Monuments Fund in Britain (£100,000); Royal Aeronautical Society (£50,000); Worcester Cathedral Development and Restoration Trust (£30,000); Friends of Colnbrook School and the Manchester Museum (£25,000 each); North of England Institute of Mining and Mechanical Engineers (£20,000); Children's Discovery Centre (£15,000); Oxford Centre for Hebrew and Jewish Studies (£14,000); and Swaffham Museum Limited (£12,000).

Exclusions No grants to individuals, organisations which are not registered charities or for international work. No retrospective funding.

Applications The following is taken from the foundation's guidelines for applicants, which is available on their website.

All applicants should complete and return the Main Grants Scheme application form, together with supporting information. Applicants should provide additional information, where relevant, as detailed in the Supplementary Information and Building Project Checklists which follow. The application form and documentation is to be sent to the correspondent. Applications are accepted all year round. We have no deadlines. Except for capital projects, it may take up to four months, occasionally longer, to receive a decision from the trustees, so apply well in advance. Please note that competition is intense; we receive many more applications than we are able to fund.

Capital Projects
Please note for capital projects seeking more than £50,000 the foundation will now only consider these twice a year in the spring and autumn. Therefore it could be up to six months before we take a decision on your project.

It is expected that all applications will be acknowledged within two weeks including applications which do not qualify for consideration which will be rejected.

The Chief Executive may wish to discuss the application, request further information and visit the applicant, in order to appraise the application before it is presented to trustees. The Chief Executive will report to the trustees at the first available meeting and will notify the applicant of the trustees' decision.

Supplementary Information – *checklist of supplementary information where an application is submitted for a specific project (including building projects). To be provided in addition to the Main Grants Scheme application form.*
Applicants should submit a summary covering the following points:

- name of project
- description of the project or funding request
- why the project is needed
- when the project will start?
- how long the project will take?
- how many people will benefit from/ participate in the project?
- total cost of project (please provide a project budget)
- amount of grant sought
- when the funding is required
- amount to be raised from other sources (if applicable) and how will this be raised?
- will the project proceed without funding from the foundation?
- how will the project/service be sustainable in the future (if ongoing)?
- who will manage the project from within the organisation?
- how will the project be monitored and evaluated and how and when would progress reports be provided to the foundation (if required).

Additional Information – Building Projects
The following issues should be addressed and summarised:

- If your project is one phase of a larger project then please provide a summary of the cost, aims and timescales of the entire project, as part of the context for your application
- To what level of the RIBA design stages has the project progressed? Please note that usually we will not accept an application if the design has not reached RIBA Stage D
- Has the project obtained outline, or full, planning permission and listed building consent (if relevant)?
- Please detail the indicative project timescale from start to completion
- Has a robust project budget including contingency been allowed for? (please provide details). Please demonstrate why you consider that your contingency budget is sufficient
- What risk factors have been considered and how will these be minimised?

- Has a realistic strategy/timescale for raising the project funding been devised?
- Please describe your project management structure and state why this is considered adequate
- Has a professional technical team been recruited? How were they chosen? Were EU procurement regulations followed? If not, why not?
- Who are or will be *(if known)*:
  – the architects and technical team
  – the project managers
  – the main contractors
- New building projects should also provide an outline business plan, including income/expenditure projections.

The Hugh Fraser Foundation

General

£814,000 (2007/08)

Beneficial area UK, especially western or deprived areas of Scotland.

Turcan Connell WS, Princes Exchange, 1 Earl Grey Street, Edinburgh EH3 9EE

Tel. 0131 228 8111

Correspondent Katrina Muir, Trust Administrator

Trustees *Dr Kenneth Chrystie; Belinda Ann Hanson; Patricia Fraser; Blair Smith.*

SC Number SC009303

Information available Accounts were provided by the trust.

This foundation was established in 1960 with general charitable purposes. Its annual accounts give the following guidance on the general grant-making policy:

The trustees' policy is to support a broad range of charitable projects particularly in Scotland but also elsewhere at the discretion of the trustees.

The trustees consider that grants to large, highly publicised national appeals are not likely to be as effective a use of funds as grants to smaller and more focused charitable appeals.

The trustees also consider that better use of the funds can be made by making grants to charitable bodies to assist them with their work, than by making a large number of grants to individuals.

The trustees are prepared to enter into commitments over a period of time by making grants in successive years, often to

assist in new initiatives which can maintain their own momentum once they have been established for a few years.

The foundation makes donations to charities working in many different sectors principally hospitals, schools and universities, arts organisations and organisations working with the handicapped, the underprivileged and the aged.

Please note: the Hugh Fraser Foundation has recently merged with the Emily Fraser Trust, a related charity. As a result, the trustees will, in exceptional circumstances, help individuals and the dependents of individuals who were or are engaged in the drapery and allied trades and the printing, publishing, books and stationary, newspaper and allied trades in the UK.

In 2007/08 the foundation had assets of £52 million and an income of £4.9 million. Grants paid during the year totalled £814,000. This included £42,000 paid to 18 individuals.

The foundation provided the following analysis of grants to institutions which includes future commitments and pledges:

Category	No.	Value
Disadvantaged and handicapped	107	£396,000
Education and training	31	£228,000
Music, theatrical and visual arts	66	£138,000
Medical research facilities	28	£112,000
Older people, homeless and hospices	26	£89,000
Youth organisations	26	£71,000
Conservation and environment	15	£49,000
Religion	9	£18,000
Miscellaneous	54	£202,000

Exclusions Grants are not usually awarded to individuals.

Applications In writing to the correspondent. The trustees meet on a quarterly basis to consider applications.

The Joseph Strong Frazer Trust

General, with broad interests in the fields of social welfare, education, religion and wildlife

£583,000 (2007/08)

Beneficial area Unrestricted, in practice, England and Wales only.

Floor A, Milburn House, Dean Street, Newcastle upon Tyne NE1 1LE

Tel. 0191 232 8065 **Fax** 0191 222 1554

Correspondent The Trustees

Trustees *Sir William A Reardon Smith, Chair; David A Cook; R M H Read; William N H Reardon Smith; William I Waites.*

CC Number 235311

Information available Accounts were available from the Charity Commission.

Established in 1939, the trust has general charitable purposes and gives to a wide range of causes, with broad interests in the fields of medical and other research, social welfare, people with disabilities, children, hospitals, education, maritime, young people, religion and wildlife. Recipients are based throughout England and Wales.

In 2007/08 the trust had assets of £11.6 million and an income of £507,000. There were 423 grants made totalling £583,000, categorised in the accounts as follows:

Category	No. of grants	Amount
Medical and other research	72	£108,000
Caring organisations	62	£82,500
Other trusts, funds and voluntary organisations	57	£73,000
Children	44	£54,000
Deaf and blind people	27	£44,000
Hospitals and home	28	£39,500
Young people	31	£34,500
Disabled people	19	£28,000
Maritime	19	£26,500
Leisure activities, animals and wildlife	20	£26,000
Religious bodies	19	£22,500
Armed forces	11	£14,000
Older people	5	£9,000
Schools and colleges	4	£8,500
Mental health	5	£8,000

All beneficiaries received £5,500 or less, and most organisations received more than one grant during the year. Beneficiaries of £3,000 or more were listed in the accounts, and included: Alzheimer's Society and Royal National Institute for the Deaf (£5,500 each); Cancer Research – Wales and Covent Garden Cancer Research Trust (£5,000 each); Barnet Bereavement Project and the Prisoners' Education Trust (£4,000 each); and Arthritis Research Campaign and St Mungo Association (£3,000 each). There were 313 organisations which received smaller grants.

Exclusions No grants to individuals.

Applications In writing to the correspondent. Trustees meet twice a year, usually in March and September. Application forms are not necessary. It is helpful if applicants are concise in their appeal letters, which must include a stamped, addressed envelope if acknowledgement is required.

The Freemasons' Grand Charity

Social welfare, medical research, hospices and overseas emergency aid

£3.9 million in non-Masonic grants (2007/08)

Beneficial area England, Wales and overseas.

60 Great Queen Street, London WC2B 5AZ

Tel. 020 7395 9261 **Fax** 020 7395 9295

Email info@the-grand-charity.org

Website www.grandcharity.org

Correspondent Ms Laura Chapman, Chief Executive

Trustee *The council, consisting of the president, deputy president, vice president, and 30 council members, listed in the annual reports.*

CC Number 281942

Information available Accounts were available at the Charity Commission. The trust also has a clear website.

This trust is the central charity of all freemasons in England and Wales. It provides grants for four purposes:

- the relief of 'poor and distressed freemasons' and their dependants
- the support of other Masonic charities
- emergency relief work worldwide
- the support of non-Masonic charities in England and Wales.

Guidelines

The following guidance on is provided by the charity:

The Freemasons' Grand Charity gives grants principally in the following areas:

- vulnerable people (for example, people with disabilities or healthcare needs, older people and babies)
- medical Research
- opportunities for young people
- hospices.

Minor Grants

Core funding grants of between £500 and £5,000 are given to smaller charities whose annual income does not exceed about £1 million.

Major Grants

Grants of between £5,000 and £50,000 are made only for a designated purpose and generally to larger charities. Funding may be granted for up to three-year periods in certain circumstances where there is evidence of an on-going need for charitable grant funding.

- the average grant size is likely to be between £10,000 and £25,000
- a very few major grants of over £50,000 may be approved each year
- the purpose might be to fund a salary or to deliver a specific project
- grants may be made for capital projects provided the application is for an identifiable element of the project.

Hospice Grants

The hospice grants are made as part of a nationwide project and total approximately £500,000 each year. Hospice grant applications should be made on a separate form which is available from either the appropriate Provincial Grand Lodge, the Freemasons' Grand Charity office or is available to download from the charity's website.

Medical Research Grants

Preference is given to medical research applications from charities that are members of the Association of Medical Research Charities (AMRC). If a charity is not a member of the AMRC its research project should have been peer reviewed in accordance with the guidelines of the AMRC. We recommend that charities applying for a grant to fund medical research should read the AMRC guidance prior to submitting an application.

Grants for Religious Buildings

A small number of grants are awarded annually to religious buildings of national importance. Typically the grant will be for no more than £5,000. Please note that The Freemasons' Grand Charity does not accept direct approaches from applicants in this category. Applications are only considered following the recommendation of the Provincial Grand Lodge, which must also be supporting the appeal.

Grantmaking in 2007/08

In 2007/08 the trust had assets of £57.5 million and an income of £15.8 million. Grants were made to 102 non-Masonic charities totalling £3.9 million, and were broken down as follows:

Category	Amount
Medical research	£1,200,000
Vulnerable people	£1,100,000
Opportunities for young people	£803,000
Hospices	£600,000
Other small grants less than £10,000	£117,500
Emergency grants	£62,500

The annual report highlight key grants awarded during the year:

Medical Research

A grant of £1 million, payable over five years, was awarded to Ovarian Cancer Action to fund research. £83,000, payable in two instalments, was granted to Deafness Research UK to fund research into age-related hearing loss. A grant of £25,000 was made to Epilepsy Research UK for research into epilepsy in children.

Vulnerable People

The National Autistic Society received £50,000 to fund the education advisory service. SSAFA was awarded £100,000 to fund facilities for visiting families at Selly Oak and Headley Court. A payment of £25,000 was made to Vitalise to fund specialist breaks for people with Alzheimer's disease and their carers. [£180,000 was also awarded to Air Ambulances.]

Opportunities for young people

£500,000, to be paid over five years, was approved for The Scout Association. Outward Bound received £40,000 to pay for courses for children from disadvantaged areas. A grant of £72,000, payable in three instalments, was made to the RNLI to fund an introductory crew training course for young people.

Hospices

A total of 194 adult hospice services and 33 children's hospice services received grants.

Emergency grants

The British Red Cross received a grant of £20,000 to assist relief efforts following the earthquake in China.

Exclusions Local charities (ones serving an individual city or region) should apply to the provincial grand lodge of the region in which they operate, (these are listed in telephone directories, usually under 'freemasons' or 'masons').

Those not eligible for a grant are:

- individuals (other than for the relief of 'poor and distressed freemasons and their poor and distressed dependants')
- charities that serve an individual region or city, for example, a regional hospital, local church, day centre or primary school
- organisations not registered with the Charity Commission, except some exempt charities
- activities that are primarily the responsibility of central or local government or some other responsible body
- organisations or projects outside of England and Wales
- charities that are deemed to hold funds in excess of their requirements.

Grants are not normally given to:

- activities that are primarily the responsibility of central or local government
- animal welfare
- arts
- capital building costs
- environment
- organisations with political objectives.

Applications Application forms are available from the charity's office or from its website. This form must be completed in full accompanied by a copy of the latest annual report and full audited accounts; these must be less than 18 months old.

Hospice grant applications are made on a separate form, available from either the appropriate provincial grand lodge or the charity's office.

Applications may be submitted at any time throughout the year.

Applications are not accepted for 'emergency grants' which are made as 'the need arises' and at the trustees' discretion.

The Freshfield Foundation

Environment and healthcare

£438,000 (2007/08)
Beneficial area UK.

2nd Floor, MacFarlane and Co., Cunard Building, Water Street, Liverpool L3 1DS
Tel. 0151 236 6161 **Fax** 0151 236 1095
Email paulk@macca.co.uk
Correspondent Paul Kurthausen, Trustee
Trustees Paul Kurthausen; Patrick A Moores; Mrs Elizabeth J Potter.
CC Number 1003316
Information available Accounts were available from the Charity Commission.

The foundation was established in 1991, and aims to support organisations involved in sustainable development, and increasingly, climate change mitigation. In previous years the foundation had a preference for organisations in Merseyside – it would appear that this is no longer the case as the foundation moves to tackle broader issues.

In 2007/08 the foundation had assets of £6.2 million and an income of £205,000.

Grants were made during the year totalling £438,000.

During the year grants were made to 11 organisations involved in sustainable development. They were: Friends of the Earth (£80,000); Sustrans (£70,000); New Economics Foundation (£55,000); Forestry Stewardship Council (£50,000); Centre for Tomorrow's Company (£35,000); Transport 2000 Trust and Cambridge University (£30,000 each); Soil Association (£20,000); Cree Valley Community Woodland Trust (£15,000); Global Canopy Foundation (£10,000); and the Ecology Trust (£3,000).

A grant of £40,000 was also made to the Osteopathic Centre for Children under 'healthcare'.

Towards the end of 2008 the foundation made grants of £500,000 and £200,000 to New Economics Foundation and Friends of the Earth respectively which reflect its increasing ambitions to mitigate climate change.

Applications In writing to the correspondent, although the trust states that 'the process of grantmaking starts with the trustees analysing an area of interest, consistent with the charity's aims and objectives, and then proactively looking for charities that they think can make the greatest contribution'. With this in mind, a letter of introduction to your organisation's work may be more appropriate than a formal application for funding.

The Patrick Frost Foundation

General

£310,000 (2007/08)
Beneficial area Worldwide, but only through UK charities.

c/o Trowers and Hamlins LLP, Sceptre Court, 40 Tower Hill, London EC3N 4DX
Tel. 020 7423 8000 **Fax** 020 7423 8001
Correspondent Mrs Helena Frost, Trustee
Trustees Mrs Helena Frost; Donald Jones; Luke Valner; Dominic Tayler.
CC Number 1005505
Information available Accounts were available from the Charity Commission.

The foundation makes general welfare grants to organisations and grants to help small charities that rely on a considerable amount of self-help and voluntary effort.

In 2007/08 the foundation had assets of £5.4 million and an income of £335,500. Grants were made to 36 organisations totalling £310,000.

Beneficiaries included: Dogs for the Disabled, London Narrow Boat Project and Humberside Police Authority (£20,000 each); Action on Addiction, Motivation Charitable Trust and Opportunity International (£10,000 each); and Family Holiday Association, Chance for Children Trust, Medical Foundation for the Care of Victims of Torture, Naomi House Children's Hospice and Contact the Elderly (£5,000 each).

Exclusions No grants to individuals or non-UK charities.

Applications In writing to the correspondent, accompanied by the last set of audited accounts. The trustees regret that due to the large number of applications they receive, they are unable to acknowledge unsuccessful applications.

The Gannochy Trust

General

£1.6 million (2007/08)

Beneficial area Scotland, with a preference for the Perth and Kinross area.

Kincarrathie House Drive, Pitcullen Crescent, Perth PH2 7HX

Tel. 01738 620653 **Fax** 01738 440827

Email admin@gannochytrust.org.uk

Website www.gannochytrust.org.uk

Correspondent Fiona Russell, Secretary

Trustees *Dr Russell Leather, Chair; Mark Webster; Dr James H F Kynaston; Ian W McMillan; Stewart N Macleod.*

SC Number SC003133

Information available Accounts were provided by the trust.

The Gannochy Trust was founded in 1937 by Arthur Kinmond Bell, known as A K Bell, for charitable and public purposes for the benefit of the community of Perth and its immediate environs as a direct result of his family's successful whisky distilling business.

A K Bell's philanthropy has been developed into one of the more substantial grant-making trusts in Scotland. Originally, the trust contributed to worthy charitable causes solely within Perth and its immediate environs. In 1967 a Scheme of Alterations was approved by the Court of Session to expand its grant-making footprint to the whole of Scotland, but with a preference for Perth and its environs. The trust has made significant contributions to a wide variety of projects across Scotland over many years, ranging from major national flagship projects to smaller, but nonetheless important, community projects.

The trust has four grant-making themes:

1) Inspiring young people.
2) Improving the quality of life of the disadvantaged and vulnerable.
3) Supporting and developing community amenities.
4) Care for the natural and man-made environment.

Please note: Themes 3 and 4 are restricted to Perth and Kinross.

In 2007/08 the trust had assets of £132 million and an income of £5.9 million. Grants totalled £1.6 million.

Beneficiaries included: University of Dundee – Diabetes Clinical Research (£500,000); Perth and Kinross Leisure – Bell's Sports Centre (£360,000); Riverside Museum Appeal Trust (£350,000); University of Dundee – Ninewells (£200,000); Greenock Arts Guild Limited and Perth and Kinross Heritage Trust (£100,000 each); Scottish Veteran's Garden City Association – Scone House Project (£80,000); and Glenfarg Public Hall Association (£60,000).

Exclusions

- General applications for funds will not be considered – applications must be specific, and preferably for a project with a defined outcome, not general running costs.
- Donations will not be made to individuals.
- Donations will only be made to organisations which meet the OSCR Charity Test.
- Projects where the benefit of a donation will be realised outside Scotland.
- Donations will rarely be made to projects that do not demonstrate an element of self or other funding.
- Donations will not be made that contribute to an organisation's healthy reserves or endowments.
- Applications will seldom be considered for more than a three-year commitment.

- Applications will not be considered for holidays, with the exception of those for the disabled and disadvantaged living in Perth & Kinross where the project has a tangible recreational or educational theme.
- Applications will not be considered for animal welfare projects, with the exception of wildlife projects within Perth & Kinross that meet the sub-themes within theme 4.
- Applications will not be considered from schools for recreational facilities unless there will be a demonstrable and sustained community involvement, preferably for the disadvantaged or vulnerable.
- Applications from pre-school groups, play schemes, after school clubs and parent-teacher associations.
- Applications will not be considered from cancer and other health-related charities unless they demonstrate that their project directly provides tangible relief from suffering and direct patient benefit.
- Applications from places of worship will not be considered unless there is a distinct community benefit through use as a community centre or village hall, and where there is not a similar facility nearby.
- Applications will not be considered from charities re-applying within a year of their previous appeal or award, or instalment thereof.
- Applications will not be considered where funding would normally be provided by central or local government.
- Waste disposal/landfill, pollution control and renewable energy projects will not be considered if they are the sole purpose of the project, and unless they meet the criteria within theme 4.
- Applications will not be considered for political or lobbying purposes.

Applications On a form which can be downloaded from the trust's website. Full guidelines are available.

The Gatsby Charitable Foundation

General

£40.9 million (2007/08)

Beneficial area Unrestricted.

Allington House, 1st Floor, 150 Victoria Street, London SW1E 5AE

Tel. 020 7410 0330 **Fax** 020 7410 0332

Email contact@gatsby.org.uk

Website www.gatsby.org.uk

Correspondent Peter Hesketh, Director

Trustees *Bernard Willis; Sir Andrew Cahn; Miss Judith Portrait.*

CC Number 251988

Information available Excellent annual report and accounts are available from the trust's website.

This is one of the Sainsbury Family Charitable Trusts, which share a joint administration. It supports organisations that aim to advance policy and practice within its selected areas.

The foundation is proactive and seldom responds to conventional short-term applications – 'trustees generally do not make grants in response to unsolicited appeals' – but it does expect organisations to respond to its published long-term priorities: 'the trustees identify first the areas where they sense that something needs to be done. They hope organisations will respond to these priorities and propose projects.'

Specific areas of support, which are set out later in this entry, come under the headings shown in this table (with payments made during 2007/08):

Category	Value
Plant Science	£10,750,000
The Arts	£9,100,000
Science and Engineering Education	£7,080,000
Africa	£5,130,000
Neuroscience	£2,720,000
Mental Health	£1,200,000
Institute for Government	£78,000
General	£4,800,000

There are big annual fluctuations in the size of its new awards each year to different categories of work because of the large multi-year funding commitments decided by the foundation.

Background

This is one of the largest and most interesting grant-making trusts in the UK, with an income of £198.7 million in 2007/08 (£89.1 million in 2006/07). This income included substantial donations totalling £181 million from the settlor, Lord Sainsbury of Turville, comprising of £115 million in cash, a further £35 million from Innotech Advisers (a company owned by him) and shares in J Sainsbury worth £28.5 million and another investment worth £2.5 million. It allocates large sums to long-term programmes and so the figure for yearly grant approvals fluctuates considerably.

In 2007/08 grants were made totalling £40.9 million (£117.2 million in 2006/07). In 2008/09 it is expected that the figure for grants payable will be £61.8 million.

The foundation was set up in 1967 by David Sainsbury, created life peer and Lord Sainsbury of Turville in 1997. He was a Labour minister with the Department of Trade and Industry until November 2006. He himself has never been a trustee of Gatsby but is still contributing massively to the endowment of the trust, and it is generally supposed that the trustees pay close attention to the settlor's wishes. Since leaving his ministerial office, Lord Sainsbury has been able to re-engage with the foundation. A substantial part of the foundation's investments are in the form of shares in the Sainsbury company. In over 40 years of grant-making the Gatsby Charitable Foundation has distributed a sum approaching £700 million; Lord Sainsbury has stated his intention to give away £1 billion in his lifetime.

General

Some of the foundation's activities and achievements are described by Lord Sainsbury in his foreword to the foundation's 2007/08 annual report:

I am delighted that the past year has seen excellent progress in the main areas of the foundation's activity.

Two fields of scientific research remain my leading priorities: plant science and neuroscience. It has always been the policy of Gatsby to fund basic research in exciting and rapidly developing areas of science where technological developments are creating new research possibilities, and this year our ambitious plans to create two new world-class institutions have taken definite shape.

It was over 20 years ago that Gatsby established the Sainsbury Laboratory in Norwich. At the time, the world of molecular plant pathology was one of the new, fast-developing areas of plant science. It was with a sense of adventure, timeliness and opportunity that the foundation created the Sainsbury Laboratory and I am delighted that the laboratory has made a huge contribution to our understanding of how plants and microbes interact.

In the past two decades, enormous progress has been made in understanding how genes control the way organisms develop. I believe that these advances have set the stage for a new synthesis that will draw on molecular, cellular, whole organism and population biology to elucidate how organisms are

constructed. In addition, this synthesis will shed light on the evolution and significance of biological diversity.

So now, with a similar sense of timeliness and opportunity, the foundation is establishing a new laboratory, to be called Sainsbury Laboratory – Cambridge, which will focus on the world of plant diversity. Construction is now underway for the new centre, which will bring together many leading plant scientists. Completion is due at the end of 2010 and the foundation is consulting an advisory panel of eminent scientists to guide the laboratory's scientific focus and to help identify those who are the rising stars of tomorrow.

Gatsby has supported fundamental research in neuroscience for more than 12 years, most notably through the creation of the Gatsby Computational Neuroscience Unit at University College London. I am therefore delighted that the foundation has moved forward with its initiative to establish a new neuroscience centre in the UK. Understanding how the brain works is probably the last great scientific frontier and for me is one of the most exciting areas of scientific endeavour today. I am delighted that the Wellcome Trust has joined Gatsby to collaborate on the creation of what will become the Sainsbury-Wellcome Centre for Neural Circuits and Behaviour. Negotiations for hosting the new centre are currently underway with University College London.

The primary goal of the new centre will be to support research that focuses on elucidating exactly how neural circuits of the brain carry out information-processing that directly underlies behaviour. Over the past decade research in this area has been transformed by sophisticated technologies, improved data management tools, and computationally sophisticated approaches to modelling and analysis. The prospect now exists to create a wiring diagram of entire circuits that generate behaviour, and ultimately entire brains. While the classic types of research grants generally support individual exploration, a new centre will allow the opportunity to build new space, add new technology and bring world-class researchers together geographically.

Of course, centres of excellence such as these could not succeed without a steady flow of inspired scientists coming through the education system, and so Gatsby remains committed to nurturing science and engineering teaching in secondary schools and further education colleges. Our projects in this area seek to ensure that physical science and engineering in particular are taught by qualified and motivated teachers, with the right resources and support at their disposal.

Excellence of a different kind is the goal of the foundation's newly established Institute for Government, based in London and devoted to developing the highest standards of management and policy-making in the civil service. Working with politicians from all the main parties and senior civil servants, the Institute's seminars and research studies will help stimulate deeper thinking and stronger skills in both management and the formulation and implementation of policy.

Another new step comes in our work in Africa. In addition to Gatsby's longstanding involvement with small-scale farmers and entrepreneurs, we are seeking to act as a catalyst in the growth of whole economic sectors. It is here we believe the potential is greatest to bring about lasting change and benefit large numbers of people. The first such area is the cotton and textiles sector in Tanzania.

Choosing to prioritise in some areas inevitably means withdrawing from others. I have been immensely proud of the achievements made over many years by the organisations we have supported in their work on behalf of disadvantaged children. Having helped draw attention to impressive projects in this area, we are confident that other funders will come forward to offer support.

Objectives

The trustees' objectives within their current fields of interest include:

- **Plant Science**, to develop basic research in fundamental processes of plant growth and development and molecular plant pathology, to encourage young researchers in the field of plant science in the UK;
- **Neuroscience**, to support world-class research in the area of neural circuits and behaviour, and in the area of theoretical neuroscience; and to support activities which enhance our understanding in this field;
- **Science and Engineering Education**, to support improvement in educational opportunity in the UK for a workforce that can better apply technology for wealth creation by incubating innovative programmes in the field of science and engineering education and promoting excellence in teaching and learning;
- **Africa**, to promote economic development and income generation through selected programmes supporting small scale manufacturing and enterprise and market sector development in selected African countries;
- **Institute for Government**, an independent centre available to politicians and the civil service, focused on making government more effective;
- **Arts**, to support the fabric and programming of institutions with which

Gatsby's founding family has long connections;
- **Mental Health**, to improve the quality of life for people with long-term problems by improved delivery of services.

The trustees occasionally support other charitable work which falls outside their main fields of interest [such projects and organisations are classified under 'general', and a sample of those supported in 2007/08 are listed at the end of this section].

Within these categories the trustees make grants for projects which they judge to have particular merit. Many of their grants are for projects which the foundation has helped to initiate. It is the policy of the trustees rigorously to evaluate programmes and projects and carefully to assess when the evaluations should most usefully take place.

Grantmaking in 2007/08

The following analysis of grantmaking during the year is largely reprinted from the foundation's excellent annual report and accounts, with the inclusion of additional figures where appropriate.

Plant Science
Sainsbury Laboratory – Norwich [£3.65 million]
The Sainsbury Laboratory at Norwich had another very successful year.

The laboratory sees immense opportunities in combining pathogen genomics with effector functional assays, and took delivery of a Solexa/Illumina sequencing instrument that unleashed a data flood that required the strengthening of the laboratory's bioinformatics capacity. As a result of the recent recruitment programme, the laboratory is now fully staffed with a new generation of outstanding group leaders who have significantly diversified and re-invigorated the laboratory's existing research portfolio. The Kamoun Group is investigating the molecular mechanisms that enable pathogens, such as potato late blight, to suppress plant defences. Work in the Lipka Laboratory is focused on the cell biology of non-host resistance and the Zipfel Group is researching how plants activate defence upon perception of conserved pathogen molecules. The laboratory also welcomed new Council members Jeff Dangl and Joe Ecker, who perpetuate the excellent contributions of their predecessors Steve Kay and Jim Carrington.

An assessment of the laboratory's impact was commissioned in a report from Evidence Ltd, which confirmed the laboratory's position as a world leader in plant sciences. This report can be downloaded in full from www.tsl.ac.uk.

Sophien Kamoun has already made a significant leadership contribution to the

Sainsbury Laboratory in his position as Senior Research Scientist alongside Jonathan Jones, and the laboratory is well placed to make further ground-breaking contributions to plant and pathogen science during the next research cycle, 2009–14.

Sainsbury Laboratory – Cambridge
Work continues on the creation of the new Sainsbury Laboratory at Cambridge University [£5.27 million in total]. The new laboratory will have a scientific focus on plant development. It will be approximately twice the size of the Norwich laboratory, supporting the research of around 120 scientists together with ancillary staff. The laboratory building, which will also house the Darwin Herbarium, is to be located on an outstanding site in the private part of the Cambridge Botanic Garden. Overall design work is essentially complete, formal planning approval was granted in late 2007, ground works commenced mid-year and trustees anticipate that the building will be complete and ready for use by the start of 2011.

An international group of leading plant scientists, chaired by Elliot Meyerowitz, has been established to advise the foundation and to assist in the recruitment of the laboratory's principle investigators. This group [had] its fourth meeting in Telluride, Colorado in June 2009, when Gatsby hosted a meeting to look at plant molecular biology in the 21st century.

In a connected parallel initiative earlier this year, the foundation supported the move of Professor David Baulcombe and his research group to the Cambridge Department of Plant Science, and has provided additional funding for the creation of new research posts in the department. Dr Ian Henderson has recently been appointed to the first of these positions.

Trustees are delighted to report that, in the past year, David Baulcombe's research has been recognised in the joint award with Victor Ambros and Gary Ruffkin of both the Franklin Medal in Life Science and The Lasker Award in Basic Biomedical Science.

Plant Science Network
The trustees continue to recognise the need to encourage the highest quality undergraduates to consider taking courses in plant sciences, leading to increased quality of plant science graduates. As in previous years, support is provided to students of the highest calibre to develop and sustain an interest in plant science research, through the Sainsbury undergraduate and postgraduate studentship programmes [£228,000 in total].

Gatsby funding has created a network of excellence in plant science that has been very successful in maintaining a high profile for plant science research in the UK. The network consists of Gatsby funded undergraduates, postgraduates and their supervisors and Gatsby alumni. The network meets annually, for presentations, talks and discussions, and provides an important forum for undergraduate and graduate students to meet influential members of the UK plant science community.

The Gatsby Plants Summer School has proved to be highly successful, and this year, trustees agreed to a further three years of support [£217,000]. The Summer School provides excellent international speakers and hands-on experience of plant science to encourage students to take second-year plant-related courses at their universities. Feedback from students, tutors and practical leaders indicates that the Summer School is a resounding success and extremely worthwhile in steering students towards plant science courses.

Trustees have previously offered two separate fellowship schemes over the past few years and also provided modest ad-hoc support across the UK plant science community generally. However, they have decided not to continue these activities, wishing instead to focus resources elsewhere.

Science and Plants for Schools (SAPS)
SAPS continued to develop new educational resources and worked to promote exciting teaching of plant science and molecular biology. There has been some success with those involved in curriculum development. The SAPS team ran a series of successful workshops for both GCSE and A-level examiners of the three major awarding bodies in England. The Welsh Joint Education Committee, as part of its A-level practical examination, utilised a SAPS protocol and specially designed kits were prepared and supplied to 119 examination centres. SAPS involvement in curriculum development in Scotland was maintained with representation on the Biology Subject Advisory Group of the Scottish Qualifications Authority.

SAPS is now set to enter a new and exciting phase. Over the summer of 2008 Gatsby trustees decided the time was right to shift the focus of SAPS for the future. They now wish to build on the success of SAPS and leverage its record of achievement and reputation in the school science community. The aim will be to focus on greater interaction with the awarding bodies, QCA and other key stakeholders to help shape and define the plant science content of the various curriculum specifications. This shift in emphasis will, in turn, require increased interaction and collaboration with the UK plant science researcher community so that new and emerging advances can be made available for integration into post-16 curricula.

To deliver a more focused programme, the trustees have decided to wind down the SAPS Charity and channel future funding for SAPS through the University of Cambridge. The SAPS Programme will now be located in the Botanic Garden at Cambridge in close proximity to the new Sainsbury Laboratory.

Trustees wish to thank the former SAPS Trustees, Professor John Gray, Professor John Parker, Mr Stephen Tomkins and Miss Judith Portrait, for the many years of outstanding contribution to the programme and also to the outgoing director Paul Beaumont for his leadership of SAPS over the past five years.

Trustees are delighted that Ginny Page, former Senior Education Manager at the Royal Society, [took] over as director of the SAPS programme, effective 1st January 2009. Further information on the work of SAPS can be found at www.saps.org.uk.

Neuroscience
Trustees are delighted to confirm their intention substantially to increase their support to UK neuroscience via the establishment of a new institute. They are further delighted that the Wellcome Trust wishes to collaborate on this initiative in bringing about a new research centre to be called the Sainsbury-Wellcome Centre for Neural Circuits and Behaviour.

Gatsby and Wellcome are currently in discussion with UCL as the host university and for the appointment of the inaugural director. Gatsby will take the lead responsibility for the creation, oversight and long-term support of the centre.

The remit of the new centre will be to use state-of-the-art molecular and cellular biology, imaging, electrophysiology and behavioural techniques, supported by relevant computational modelling, to identify the determinants of information processing in the brain. There will be international level scientists working within the centre, a sharp focus to its scientific goals, and novel types of infrastructure support to enable them to stay abreast of an exciting and fast-moving field. The primary goal will be to support research that focuses on elucidating exactly how neural circuits of the brain carry out information-processing that directly underlies behaviour.

Gatsby Computational Neuroscience Unit (GCNU)
Trustees continue to provide core support for the Gatsby Computational Neuroscience Unit at University College London [UCL received funding totalling £1.7 million]. Additional funds were provided for the support of a series of workshops run by faculty in the Unit in 2007/08.

Highlights of the annual review conducted by the International Scientific Advisory Board,

chaired by Professor Jon Driver, included praise for the expanding efforts to engage in collaborations with experimental scientists at, and beyond UCL, and the high quality of the students and post-doctorate students in the unit.

The Unit reported on a very active year, with substantial collaborations across UCL and beyond, including Columbia University. Research highlights include Maneesh Sahani's collaboration with Jennifer Linden on understanding the complexities of the brain's coding of auditory input; Peter Latham's study of memory storage and retrieval in spiking neural networks; Yee Whye Teh's development of a class of models for the statistical structure in text; Risi Kondor's use of mathematically sophisticated tools from group theory to elucidate fundamental aspects of the representation of stimuli that enjoy particular mathematical properties such as symmetry; and Peter Dayan's work on the interaction between learnt and pre-specified behavioural choices, and the potential role of this in anomalies of decision-making.

Six of the Unit's current and former students and post-doctorate students were awarded faculty positions this year at the Universities of California, Cambridge, Edinburgh, Princeton, Texas and UCL.

Häusser Laboratory: Neural Computation Group
Trustees continue to support the work of Professor Michael Häusser at University College London. Additional funds were provided to the London Centre for Nanotechnology at UCL in 2008 to host and ensure successful operation and development of a new state-of-the-art electron microscope, recently purchased by the Häusser Laboratory. Dr Arnd Roth has initiated a collaboration with Professor Gabriel Aeppli, Director of the LCN, and colleagues to develop a new approach for neural circuit reconstruction using high-volume electron microscopy.

Over the past year, the laboratory has embarked on several exciting new lines of work, and continued its highly fruitful collaborations and interactions with other groups at UCL, in particular with members of GCNU. The links were further strengthened by its active participation in workshops sponsored by Gatsby at UCL and Columbia University. The laboratory held a successful group retreat in February featuring informal presentations and brainstorming sessions to develop the scientific direction of the group. Research highlights include Tiago Branco's exciting discovery of directional selectivity in cortical pyramidal neuron dendrites; Lisa Beeren and Mickey London's combination of patch-clamp recording and multi-unit recordings using silicon probes in barrel cortex in vivo (in collaboration with Peter

Latham from the Gatsby Unit); Benjamin Judkewitz's development of targeted in vivo single-cell electroporation, which he has used to engineer channelrhodopsin expression in defined networks of neurons, enabling their activation with light; and Taro Ishikawa's success in making patch-clamp recordings from single cerebellar neurons in awake animals processing multi-sensory inputs.

Columbia University: Gatsby Initiative in Brain Circuitry

The Gatsby Initiative in Brain Circuitry at Columbia University in New York provides small, highly innovative research grants, new faculty and graduate research. Collaborative efforts are in place between the GCNU in London and the Columbia Centre for Theoretical Neuroscience. To date, 34 Gatsby pilot project grants have been awarded, covering a wide variety of topics. The pilot project grant programme allows researchers to explore and initiate highly innovative research projects prior to obtaining funding from conventional sources.

Highlights from projects supported by Gatsby pilot grants include the development of a novel nonlinear optical technique that can be used to image selectively the plasma membrane of neurons, paving the way for future imaging of the activity of neuronal networks in vitro or in vivo; a non-optical approach to recording from large numbers of neurons using novel nanofibre array technology for dissecting neural circuit function; development of ways of bypassing spinal cord injuries to restore function using a robotic rehabilitation technique to explore the engineering of a functioning motor system circuit; and investigations to uncover the functional significance of adult neural stem cells and how they contribute to the plasticity of neural circuits.

With the support of the Gatsby Initiative, the centre for Theoretical Neuroscience is expanding its space to make room for a new faculty candidate and during the coming year they will initiate the new Gatsby studentship programme which will support the top Columbia students during the later stages of their graduate work. [Columbia University received £760,000 in total.]

Connectomics: Centre for Brain Science at Harvard University, MIT and Stanford

Trustees have awarded a four-year $4.88 million multi-lab grant to explore and refine specific types of technology that will permit scientists to construct wiring diagrams of whole regions of the nervous system ('connectomes'). The goal is to establish a high-throughput, high-resolution method for automatically constructing neural wiring diagrams more quickly and more accurately than previously possible. This technology will be readily transferred to scientists around the world with 'no strings attached', enabling a collective effort at multiple institutions that will generate wiring diagrams of multiple parts of brains of various animals. Connectomic analyses of the brain will provide a structural foundation for modelling and interpreting functional brain data, and for elucidation of how cognitive function stems from underlying neural circuit architecture.

Science and Engineering Education

Following a review of activities in this category during 2006–07, trustees have agreed to focus Gatsby's work on three key aims:

- to support teachers of 11–19 physical science, by piloting new approaches to science teacher recruitment and professional development and by supporting curriculum resources which encourage innovation in the classroom;
- to support the teaching of engineering and science in the Further Education (FE) sector, by developing a range of professional development opportunities for lecturers in FE and supporting the teaching of the 14–19 engineering diploma; and
- to support the current national drive for greater rationalisation and coordination of UK science, technology, engineering and mathematics (STEM) education.

Gatsby Technical Education Projects (GTEP) (www.gtep.co.uk) was established as a separate charity in 1996 to develop and manage a range of innovative projects [£3 million in total]. The Trustees of GTEP are Mr Christopher Stone (resigned 9 April 2008), Miss Judith Portrait and Mr Bernard Willis (appointed 9 April 2008). Mr Peter Hesketh and Mr Nigel Thomas lead the staff team.

Trustees continue to explore ways in which Gatsby, working independently or with other institutions, can make a difference in the field of science and engineering education. What follows is a brief account of Gatsby's main education programmes.

Support of physical science teachers

Trustees continue to pilot new approaches to science teacher recruitment and professional development and the development of curriculum resources which encourage innovation in the classroom.

The flagship programme in this category is the Science Enhancement Programme (SEP) (www.sep.org.uk). SEP supports physical science teachers by introducing exciting and contemporary science into secondary schools. To this end, SEP develops novel classroom resources and supports professional development for science teachers. Curriculum topics addressed by SEP this year have included polymers, visible and infra-red imaging, and advanced building materials.

SEP resources are used in most UK secondary schools, and more than 10,000 science teachers have become SEP associates. Strategic partnerships with organisations such as the Royal Society of Chemistry (RSC), Institute of Physics (IOP) and the Science Learning Centres ensure that SEP's reach continues to widen.

The Physics Enhancement Programme (PEP) is a joint initiative with the Training and Development Agency for Schools (TDA) and the IOP. PEP began as a pilot scheme in 2004 with the aim of increasing the number of specialist physics teachers by enabling recruitment to physics teaching from a wider range of degree subjects. PEP provides an intensive six-month course in physics prior to entering traditional Initial Teacher Training (ITT) and offers additional support during ITT and the first two years of teaching. In 2007, more than 140 PEP participants started their teacher training. This represented nearly a quarter of all the new specialist physics trainees beginning courses in England in 2007.

Since 2005, Trustees have supported a programme at Oxford University to raise awareness of materials science in schools and to inspire more people to study materials, engineering and the physical sciences at degree level (outreach.materials.ox.ac.uk). The programme supports teachers and pupils via a variety of means, including residential courses, master classes and curriculum resources. The programme has proved popular, with more than 2,500 teachers and pupils directly involved to date.

In partnership with the IOP and RSC, Trustees are providing additional support for teachers involved in the pilot of the TDA's Science as an Additional Specialism Programme (SASP). The SASP programme is aimed at existing teachers who wish to teach physics or chemistry but who lack a specialist degree in these subjects. It provides training of up to 40 days in the relevant subject area and associated pedagogy. Trustees believe that, for many teachers, this formal training alone will be insufficient to facilitate confident teaching of physics and chemistry. Gatsby is therefore working with the IOP and RSC to offer additional subject-specific support to SASP teachers for up to two years after completion of the training course. Trustees hope that, if it is demonstrated that this additional mentoring-style support brings benefits, the government will decide to fund similar provision for all future SASP participants.

Support of engineering and science in Further Education

The New Engineering Foundation (NEF) (www.neweng.org.uk) continues to be a key partner for Gatsby's work in Further Education (FE) and in 2007 trustees supported the expansion of NEF's highly successful Industrial Fellowship programme [£447,000]. The programme now enables both engineering and science lecturers in FE colleges to engage in technical professional development activities by providing them with industrial placements. Annually, the programme supports three lecturers from each of 20 colleges, with good practice shared across the network of participants.

Work is also in hand to develop a national Knowledge and Technology Transfer (KTT) framework for FE. It is hoped this framework will enable more FE colleges to play a full part in the provision of innovative KTT solutions with business and industry, thereby strengthening the colleges' educational provision and underpinning the overall economic development at local and regional levels.

The Technology Enhancement Programme (TEP) (www.tep.org.uk), based at Middlesex University, is a unique programme that supports the engineering curriculum by developing innovative classroom resources [£252,000]. Working closely with a wide range of educational and industrial partners, TEP acquired its reputation for excellence through its support for Design & Technology at Key Stages 3 and 4 over the past 15 years. TEP has now been refocused towards supporting teachers of the new engineering diploma, especially at Level 3. In related support, trustees also made a grant to the Royal Academy of Engineering for their work on the new engineering diploma. This was in addition to Gatsby's continuing support for the Academy's Best programme (www.raengbest.org.uk) and the Sainsbury Management Fellowships (www.smf.org.uk) [£617,000 in total].

Support of greater coordination of UK STEM education

Trustees are supporting an initiative to help bring about greater coordination in science education: the Science Community Representing Education (SCORE). SCORE is a partnership between the Association for Science Education (ASE), the Biosciences Federation, the Institute of Biology, the IOP, the Royal Society, the RSC and the Science Council. It aims to improve science education by harnessing the expertise and resources of these key organisations to support the development of effective education policy and projects. A three year grant towards the core costs of SCORE began in April 2008.

Trustees are also supporting the creation and running costs of a National Science, Technology, Engineering and Mathematics (STEM) Centre. The centre will be co-located with the National Science Learning Centre (NSLC) in York and will house a National STEM Resource Centre which will, for the first time, assemble in one place a definitive collection of government, learned society, charitable foundation and commercial STEM curriculum support resources. It will also facilitate the use of the NSLC building by mathematics and engineering teachers and lecturers (in addition to the existing use by science teachers) and seek more widely to improve the national coordination of STEM enhancement and enrichment activities. The new centre will open in late 2009.

The Advisory Committee for Mathematics Education (ACME) was established in 2002 to act as a single voice for the mathematical community, seeking to improve the quality of education in schools and colleges. ACME advises policy-makers on issues such as the curriculum, assessment and the supply and training of mathematics teachers and now receives just under half its funding from government sources.

Trustees are also helping to support the national roll-out of after-school science and engineering clubs with a grant to STEMNET towards the costs of disseminating good practice from the initial 250 pilot clubs [£67,300].

Support of national education policy

In addition to supporting programmes such as those described above, trustees fund a small number of research projects which seek to inform and influence national education policy. Projects have included: how secondary schools are choosing to deploy their specialist science teachers; work relating to the 14–19 diploma qualifications and the supply and retention of physics teachers.

In addition, trustees provided £1 million to support the establishment of the Royal Society's education policy unit. The first of its kind in the UK, the unit will support and build on the work of ACME and SCORE and will seek to establish and disseminate a reliable evidence base relating to education policy.

Other support for schools and colleges

The Teacher Effectiveness Enhancement Programme (TEEP) offers teachers professional development in classroom pedagogy. TEEP has developed a framework for effective teaching and learning, drawn from existing research evidence on the characteristics and behaviours of effective teachers and learners. The framework includes a generic lesson-planning tool which can be used in any subject area and develops the specific behaviours that effective teachers demonstrate.

Three independent evaluations of the programme all conclude that TEEP has a positive impact on teachers' practice and on student outcomes.

TEEP is increasingly mentioned in Ofsted reports as supporting the improvement of teaching and learning and student attainment. The programme continues to be heavily over-subscribed and, in order to meet this demand, a whole-school model of TEEP training is currently being piloted.

Support in the university sector

In addition to the school and FE-based programmes which form the core mission of Gatsby in this category, trustees have also approved funding for a few projects in universities, predominantly focused on knowledge and technology transfer initiatives. Trustees' continuing support for the Institute for Manufacturing (IfM) at the University of Cambridge has been described extensively in previous annual reports. Other institutions currently receiving support are the Science and Technology Policy Research Unit at the University of Sussex [£156,000], Loughborough University's Sports Technology Institute [£98,000] and the University of Manchester's Proof-of-Principle Programme [£45,000].

Africa
Overview

Gatsby has been funding and implementing programmes in Africa since the 1980s with an overall objective of stimulating job creation and improved incomes for the poor. During this period grants have mostly focused on two areas: the dissemination of agricultural research to small-holder farmers and providing assistance to small and medium enterprises (SMEs). Over the past year, the agricultural programmes have mostly been administered by the Kilimo Trust and African Agricultural Capital, both based in Uganda. The funding for SME development has been through the four Gatsby trusts based in Cameroon, Kenya, Tanzania and Uganda. In addition to these core areas, Gatsby has also started a major new sector development programme in Tanzania looking to improve the performance of the cotton and textile sector.

Also support has been given towards a new programme in Rwanda providing capacity-building to government.

Importantly, the political and social context has been volatile over the past year in the countries in which Gatsby operates: in Cameroon there has been a short period of riots; in Tanzania the President dismissed his cabinet over corruption scandals; and in Kenya the elections resulted in a prolonged period of major unrest and tribal violence unseen in east Africa since the atrocities in

Rwanda. Although these events have not had a major long-term impact on the programmes, they have highlighted the fragile operating environment in which the foundation is working.

Agriculture Programmes
Kilimo Trust [£2.1 million in total]

The Kilimo Trust has had an important year. Since its launch in 2005, it has been managing and implementing the majority of Gatsby's agriculture related programmes in east Africa. These have included a set of legacy programmes that Gatsby supported prior to Kilimo's existence, in addition to new programmes initiated by Kilimo staff and board of trustees. Over the past year, Kilimo has appointed a new CEO and has developed a new strategy which is more focused: based on understanding and catalysing markets rather than purely disseminating research. Kilimo is now looking to prioritise and scale-up successful programmes.

The major programmes operated by Kilimo over the past year include:

- the 'push-pull' programme, which is based on novel strategies that combine a tactic for institute suppression and elimination of striga, on the one hand, and controlling stemborers, on the other, in cereals production systems. The governments of Uganda, Kenya and Tanzania have committed themselves to full deployment of the available package and Kilimo is leading efforts to establish a regional consortium for implementing a comprehensive programme known as 'Programme to unlock the production potential of cereals in east Africa by eliminating the striga threat'.

- tree projects operating in Uganda, Tanzania and Kenya which aim to introduce, propagate and distribute new varieties of trees that are fast growing and will help reduce deforestation, while offering income-earning opportunities to smallholders. Kilimo aims to build business capacity of thriving smallholder nurseries in east Africa to use cloning techniques for the production of tree-planting materials.

- the Maendeleo Agricultural Technology Fund (MATF), which is managed through FARM Africa and seeks to promote adoption of innovative viable agricultural technologies by farming communities in Kenya, Uganda and Tanzania, while promoting socially and economically profitable agricultural models that can be replicated in other areas for wider impact. An in-depth assessment of lessons, outcomes and impacts of MATF was conducted during the year.

During the year, Kilimo also initiated projects focused on creating favourable market conditions.

These include:

- development of value chains between supermarkets and producers of African indigenous vegetables and sweet potatoes; and

- support to the development of wholesale markets for fresh produce in east Africa, as a critical value chain linkage.

Further information on Kilimo can be found at www.thekilimotrust.org.

African Agricultural Capital (AAC)

Gatsby partnered with the Rockefeller Foundation and Incofin to set up AAC in 2005. AAC is a unique investment company providing loan, equity and quasi-equity finance to agricultural SMEs across east Africa. AAC focuses on supporting SMEs that buy from or sell to large numbers of small-holder farmers. Like Kilimo, AAC is based in Kampala, Uganda. Over the past year, AAC has continued to operate well and has now fully invested the initial capital of $7 million in 15 investments. In January 2008, Gatsby agreed to provide up to a further $3 million of funding and AAC is actively raising further funds from other donors. Over the past year, AAC has also started to develop a new system for measuring the social and broader economic impact of these investments. This monitoring system will also be used during due-diligence to inform initial investment decisions.

West Africa

In February 2008, Gatsby disbursed the final payment to the International Institute of Tropical Agriculture (IITA) for the agricultural programme in Nigeria and Niger [£327,600]. This programme is disseminating improved cowpea varieties to small-holder farmers as an inter-crop with sorghum to improve soil quality and provide fodder for livestock. This is important for the Sahelian Zone in west Africa where soil fertility and crop yields are a major problem.

Building expertise and back-up research

Trustees continued their support for the Rothamsted International African Fellowship Programme during 2007–08 [£263,500]. This programme enables African agricultural scientists to address a specific problem identified in their own environment which can be assisted by advanced technologies available in Europe. In 2007–08, eight scientists took advantage of this opportunity.

Trustees also continued to support Rothamsted's Nematode Initiative in east and southern Africa (NIESA) during 2007–08. This programme aims to develop a network of competent nematologists in east and southern Africa by funding three PhD students to undertake studies in this area, while also developing an interactive network of nematologists and agricultural professionals with an interest in nematology

in the region. Over the past year, this programme has made good headway: students progressed well on their PhDs and several training events were held in Africa.

SME programmes

Our support to SME development has continued over the past year through continued core funding to the four country trusts in Cameroon, Uganda, Kenya and Tanzania. Each of these trusts has continued to evolve separately in its own environment.

Cameroon Gatsby Foundation (CGF) [£335,500] is almost entirely focused on a microfinance programme for women; it has more than 5,000 borrowers, many of whose businesses have grown considerably over the past 13 years. CGF is now looking to scale up and become fully sustainable from loan interest. Uganda Gatsby Trust (UGT) is managed from Makerere University and serves approximately 1,500 larger-scale SMEs with a focus on technology development, the development of workspace, provision of loan finance and improved business practices.

Kenya Gatsby Trust (KGT) [£192,000] as a particular emphasis on access to both local and international markets, and improvements in quality and improved financial management which SMEs need in order to be able to compete in these markets. KGT has also successfully piloted factoring finance which it wants to scale further. It has also initiated, and is continuing to help facilitate, the development of a national wholesale market for fruit and vegetables in Nairobi.

Tanzania Gatsby Trust (TGT) [£405,500] is predominantly focused on provision of finance, through wholesale finance to Microfinance Institutes (MFIs), community banks and retail microfinance through group lending to women, and through small business finance to agro-processing companies. TGT also supports some SMEs' access to markets technologies through a partnership with the College of Engineering and Technology. More recently, TGT has assisted the development of a major programme in the cotton and textiles sector in Tanzania.

Each of these trusts has an annual programme of about £750,000 divided between grants and recycling microfinance loans. For the last 15 years, trustees have also actively supported a programme in South Africa. The key focus has been the improvement of the teaching of science and mathematics, linked to the professional development of a cadre of industrial managers. The overall programme was completed over the past year and, looking forward, trustees have decided to focus their support in east Africa.

New Programmes

Tanzania cotton and textile programme

In September 2007, trustees began supporting a major long-term programme focused on developing the cotton and textile sectors in Tanzania. Gatsby has committed an initial sum of £1.1 million for the first phase. Based on a comprehensive feasibility study, the programme is focused on addressing constraints in the supply chain in both the cotton and textile sectors. Over the past year, the institutional structures and steering committee have been established, and activity plans and budgets are in place. Field trials in growing cotton through minimum-tillage conservation agriculture have proved to be successful and plans are in place to pilot contract farming with the ginners. A tender has been set up to contract a seed company in order to multiply cotton seed. Within textiles, plans have been developed to set up the necessary postschool and graduate training, and a preliminary study of foreign direct investment has been completed. Depending on performance, this programme is likely to continue over the medium-term.

Rwanda government capacity-building

This year, trustees also agreed to fund a new 15- month programme providing technical assistance and capacity-building support to the government in Rwanda. This will help the government develop the internal capacity and processes needed to support the programme.

Future directions

In summer 2008, Gatsby reviewed the Africa portfolio and the overall strategic focus of the programmes. Trustees decided to concentrate on fewer geographical areas and to reduce the areas which they support. The trustees wish to assist the six local institutions to develop and become more effective and, in addition, to focus on a small number of large sector development programmes across east Africa, similar to the cotton and textile programme in Tanzania.

Institute for Government

This year, the Gatsby Trustees funded the inception of a new Institute for Government.

Good government is central to a fair and prosperous society. But until now there has been no single institution in the UK which is independent of government or any single political party to develop the highest standards of management and policymaking in the civil service.

The new Institute for Government is independent and cross-party. It will work at the highest level, with political leaders from all parties and senior civil servants. It will draw on expertise and research from all sectors including business and academe, but it will be independent of academic institutions. Its mission is focused on the UK, but it will draw significantly on expertise and experience from abroad. Its initial focus will be on central government, but it will inevitably have an interest in local government and the devolved national administrations as well as the wider international context.

The Institute will have three core activities:

- supporting the development of the skills and capabilities of senior policymakers in the UK;

- conducting and supporting practical research into key questions of public administration and governance; the research will be intended both to have direct and immediate positive effects and to provide a deeper understanding of the underlying issues;

- publishing and promoting thought leadership on effective government and public administration.

In practice, the three activities will overlap. Work and engagement with policy-makers will help to identify key questions of structure which may become the focus of research; the conclusions of hands on research and organisational development with government will feed directly into the Institute's work in promoting the skills and thinking of policymakers. The Institute's publications can draw on both these activities to share its conclusions more widely, while providing a valuable source of institutional memory for Whitehall.

The Institute's initial core of staff was headed by Dr David Halpern, the Director of Research, who has led the Institute's initial planning and first projects. He was joined in September 2008 by the Institute's first Executive Director, Sir Michael Bichard. Sir Michael will be accountable to an all-party governing body, chaired by Lord Sainsbury of Turville.

The Arts

Trustees continue to provide core support for organisations with which Gatsby has a longstanding history, in particular, for those initiated by earlier generations of the Sainsbury family, in Norwich, in partnership with the University of East Anglia (UEA) [£1.8 million], and, more recently, the Royal Shakespeare Company [£5.25 million towards redevelopment costs and the Artists' Development Programme].

Mental Health

The focus of trustees' support is the Sainsbury Centre for Mental Health (SCMH) [£1.1 million]. SCMH has been at the forefront of innovation and reform in mental health policy and practice since it was founded in 1985.

The Trustees are: Mr Christopher Foy and Miss Judith Portrait. SCMH Trustees are advised by: Baroness Neuberger and Lord Ramsbotham.

SCMH's work is focused on two much-neglected areas: the mental health of people in contact with the criminal justice system; and mental health and work.

SCMH believes that the mental health of prisoners needs urgent and radical action. There is now a mass of clear evidence that prisoners are getting inadequate mental health care. Despite recent advances in the creation of 'inreach' teams, there are unacceptable gaps in care, especially for those with depression and anxiety.

SCMH's other priority is employment and mental health. People who have mental health problems are at double the risk of losing their jobs than those who do not. SCMH worked with employers to see how they could support employees with mental health problems and develop workplaces where all of their staff can feel at ease.

Talking therapies such as cognitive behavioural therapy (CBT) can play a role in helping people to remain in work. SCMH is working with other leading charities to bring this onto the national agenda and continues to support the Department of Health's Improving Access to Psychological Therapies Programme.

General

Beneficiaries during the year included: National Children's Bureau (£1 million), for the Children's Residential Care Unit, Research Department and related programmes on children's personal health and social development; Centre for Cities (£809,000), towards core costs; London Borough of Greenwich (£475,000), towards a collaborative project to develop a new model of care for families where a parent has a long-term mental health problem; I CAN (£330,000), towards core costs and towards extending the Early Years accreditation programme and to start up more Early Years nurseries for children with speech disorders; Manchester College of Arts & Technology (£142,400), towards the development of the enterprise support programme; National Centre for Social Research (£90,300), towards continued funding of the annual British Social Attitudes Survey; University of Oxford (£60,000), towards the 'Options for Britain' public policy research project; Association of Young People with ME (£25,000); and Auditory Verbal UK (£17,500).

Exclusions No grants to individuals.

Applications See the entry for the Sainsbury Family Charitable Trusts. Generally, the trustees do not make grants in response to unsolicited applications, although a single application will be considered for support by all the trusts in the group.

The Robert Gavron Charitable Trust

The arts, policy research and general

£863,000 (2007/08)

Beneficial area Mainly UK.

44 Eagle Street, London WC1R 4FS

Tel. 020 7400 4300 **Fax** 020 7400 4245

Correspondent Mrs Dilys Ogilvie-Ward, Secretary

Trustees *Lord Robert Gavron; Charles Corman; Lady Katharine Gavron; Jessica Gavron; Sarah Gavron.*

CC Number 268535

Information available Annual report and accounts, with 2002/03 grants list.

This is a personal and family trust, with no full-time paid staff, whose grants go mainly, though not exclusively, to charities already known to the trustees.

The trust concentrates its funding on health and welfare (including charities for people with disabilities), prisons and prison reform, arts and arts education, social policy and research and education.

In many cases the trustees prefer to make grants to organisations whose work they personally know and admire. This does not, however, mean that charities unknown to the trustees personally do not receive grants. One freelance adviser visits and reports on new applicants to the trust and his reports are taken into account by the trustees when they make their decisions. This leads to a number of grants to new organisations during each financial year. These include small charities working in areas which cannot easily raise funds and which are without the resources themselves for professional fund-raising. Small charities supported during the year include those working in prisons and with ex-offenders, and those working with adults and children with disabilities. The trust has also continued to help previously funded small charities which come into these categories.

In 2007/08 the trust had assets of £8.9 million and an income of £1 million. Grants were made totalling £863,000 and ranged from £25 up to £100,000.

Major beneficiaries during the year were: King Alfred School (£100,000); St Peter's College Foundation, Arab Israel Children's Tennis and Young Foundation (£50,000 each); University of York (£40,000); and Barbados Cricket Association (£31,000).

Smaller grants included those to: Friends of Highgate Cemetery (£15,000); One World Action (£12,000); Sadler's Wells Development Trust (£10,000); Rainbow Drama Group (£5,000); University of the Arts – London (£2,500); Youth at Risk (£1,000); and ZSV Trust (£100).

Exclusions The trust does not give donations to individuals or to large national charities.

Applications Although the trust indicates that its funds are fully committed and that it would have difficulty in considering further appeals, particularly due to the current financial climate, new projects may be supported.

In writing only to the correspondent. Please enclose a stamped addressed envelope and latest accounts. There are no regular dates for trustees' meetings, but they take place about five times a year.

J Paul Getty Jr Charitable Trust

Social welfare, arts, conservation and the environment

£3 million (2008)

Beneficial area UK.

1 Park Square West, London NW1 4LJ

Tel. 020 7486 1859

Website www.jpgettytrust.org.uk

Correspondent Elizabeth Rantzen, Director

Trustees *Christopher Gibbs, Chair; Lady Getty; Vanni Treves; Christopher Purvis.*

CC Number 292360

Information available Accounts were available from the Charity Commission. The trust also has a useful website.

The trust funds projects to do with poverty and misery in the UK, and unpopular causes in particular. Its main aim is to fund well managed projects which will 'help to relieve poverty, support disadvantaged people, and effect long-term change where help is not readily available from the public or private purse'. The trust also provides some funding for the arts, and towards the conservation of the natural and built environment.

Grants, usually for revenue or capital costs, are often for three-year periods and can be up to a maximum of £250,000. There are also a large number of small grants of £5,000 or less.

The trust has continued to increase its level of grantmaking, taking the view that it should start assuming a long-term level of total return on its investments that will ignore short-term fluctuations, especially in gains or losses of capital. Nevertheless the trust remains heavily oversubscribed, with a success rate of less than 10%, no doubt the result of its own accessibility to those working in fields few others are interested in funding.

Background

The J Paul Getty Jr Charitable Trust began distributing funds in 1986. Since then nearly £38 million has been given to over 3,000 worthwhile causes all over the UK.

The trust was funded entirely by Sir Paul Getty KBE, who died in April 2003 in London, where he had lived since the 1980s. He took a close interest in the trust, but also continued to make major personal gifts to the arts and other causes in England. For example, he gave £50 million to the National Gallery, £3 million to Lord's Cricket Ground, £17 million to the British Film Institute, £1 million towards the Canova Three Graces and £5 million towards the restoration of St. Paul's Cathedral. These were personal gifts and had no connection with this trust.

It is important to note that this trust does not have any connection with the Getty Trust in the USA, to which J. Paul Getty Senior left his money, and which finances the J. Paul Getty Museum in California.

In 2008 the trust had assets of £44 million and an income of £2 million. Grants were made totalling £3 million, with 118 new awards being made.

Guidelines for applicants

The following guidelines have been taken from the trust's very useful website. For more information on any of the points, contact the trust directly.

The trust can award grants towards both revenue and capital costs. However, the trustees will not normally approve grants to cover more than 20% of a charity's entire annual running costs, as we feel it is important for organisations to develop a range of income sources and not become dependent on any single funder.

Main grants can be between £10,000 and £250,000 over a period of 1 to 3 years. Multi-year grants will often be paid as a single instalment. On average it takes us between 3 and 6 months to award a main grant, so please allow plenty of time when making your application.

Small grants of up to £5,000 are also available for smaller charities. Applications are made in exactly the same way as for our main grants programme. However, if you are successful, your grant may be awarded in as little as 2 to 3 months.

If you are a faith-based community group planning to apply for a grant of £5,000 or less, assistance may be available through the Church Urban Fund Mustard Seed Programme, to which the J Paul Getty Jnr Charitable Trust makes a contribution. We recommend that you look at www.cuf.org.uk for further guidance, or contact Nick Waters at the Church Urban Fund (020 7898 1647).

Eligibility

At present, our grant making is largely focused on supporting registered charities in England, although applications may sometimes be considered from other parts of the United Kingdom if the project is likely to be of nationwide significance.

Occasionally, we will fund organisations of comparable charitable status, such as Industrial Provident Societies or Community Interest Companies, but only where there is a very strong connection with one or more of our current funding priorities.

Please note that we are unable to fund individuals, or charities based outside the UK.

Areas of interest

We are currently inviting applications from registered charities in the following areas:

- *Reducing Re-offending*: projects aiming to improve the lot of people in prison and smooth the transition for those leaving prison, maximising their chances of successful resettlement
- *Improving Prospects*: projects providing meaningful occupation for young people aged 14–19 to improve their employability and diminish the risk of social exclusion; work to improve the treatment of refugees and asylum seekers
- *Repairing Communities*: projects led from within the community with the aim

of integrating different social and ethnic groups in pursuit of worthwhile goals
- *Repairing Lives*: projects making a lasting impact on the lives of people with substance misuse problems; projects helping people who are homeless or at risk of homelessness
- *Preserving Heritage*: conserving or restoring buildings and landscapes which are of national value and accessible to the public; saving from export art and manuscripts of national importance; developing conservation skills, especially among disadvantaged groups
- *Sustaining the Arts:* nurturing and developing artistic endeavour of the highest quality.

Further details on the type of work the trust funds in each category can be found on the website.

We aim to ensure that our grants are made to charities which do not discriminate on the grounds of age, gender, disability, marital status, sexual orientation, religion, race, colour or nationality, and therefore we support organisations with a clear commitment to equal opportunities. However, we recognise that the sensitive nature of some of the work we fund means that appropriate restrictions on staff or participants may sometimes need to be applied.

Grantmaking in 2008

The level of narrative reporting on the trust's activities has reduced in recent years, however the following breakdown of grants by category is provided:

Category	Amount	Percentage
Heritage and conservation	£494,000	16%
Children and young people	£489,000	15%
Offenders	£466,000	15%
Homelessness	£364,000	12%
Mental health	£261,000	8%
Arts (not related to social welfare)	£237,000	8%
Disadvantaged communities	£220,000	7%
Drugs and alcohol	£213,000	7%
Environment and landscape	£159,000	5%
Ethnic minorities/refugees	£117,000	4%
Women	£47,000	2%
Other social welfare	£16,000	1%
Other	£11,000	0%
Families	£4,000	0%

Beneficiaries during the year, which were uncategorised, included: Church Urban Fund and Emmaus UK (£150,000 each); Local Solutions – Liverpool (£111,000); Trail Blazers – Aylesbury (£90,000); Prison Reform Trust (£50,000); Barnstaple Poverty Action Group (£38,000); the Green Team – Edinburgh (£30,000); Asian Advisory Service – Derby (£14,000); Stepney Bank Stables – Newcastle Upon Tyne (£10,000); and Moor Trees – Devon (£8,100).

Exclusions Grants are not given for:

- individuals
- organisations based outside of the UK
- schools, universities or public sector organisations
- routine maintenance, repairs, refurbishment or modernisation costs, or large-scale development projects, such as church restoration work or the construction of new village halls and local community centres
- medical care or general health and wellbeing programmes
- one-off events, residential or adventure trips.

Priority is likely to be given to projects in the less prosperous parts of the country, particularly outside London and the South East, and to those which cover more than one beneficial area.

Please remember this trust has no connection with the Getty Foundation in the USA.

Applications Applications must be submitted using the online form accessible through the trust's website. There are no closing dates, and all applicants should receive an initial response within six weeks. The form will ask you to provide:

- information on the work of the organisation
- details of the organisation's size and income
- an overview of the project/work for which funding is required
- the daytime contact details of someone with whom the trust can discuss the application.

When starting an application for the first time applicants will be asked to complete a short eligibility quiz to check that their project falls within the trust's criteria. If successful you will be able to begin the full application (guidance on completing the form is given within the form itself).

If the project is short-listed for a grant of over £5,000, the trust will request more detailed information about the charity and the specific project.

The trustees meet quarterly to consider applications, usually in April, July, September and December. It usually takes between three and six months for larger grants to be awarded. For requests of £5,000 or less it may be possible for the trustees to award a grant between meetings.

The G C Gibson Charitable Trust

Art, music and education, health, hospices and medical research, community and other social projects and religion

£556,000 (2007/08)

Beneficial area UK, with interests in Suffolk, Wales and Scotland.

c/o Deloitte and Touche, Blenheim House, Fitzalan Court, Newport Road, Cardiff CF24 0TS

Tel. 029 2048 1111

Correspondent Karen Griffin

Trustees *Simon Gibson; Jane M Gibson; Robert D Taylor; Martin Gibson; Lucy Kelly.*

CC Number 258710

Information available Accounts were available from the Charity Commission.

The trust was established in 1969 by G C Gibson, now deceased, for general charitable purposes. Grants are given mainly for art, music and education; health, hospices and medical research; community and other social projects and religious causes.

Whilst the trust will consider donations for capital projects, the average donation of £5,000 is more suited for meeting the revenue commitments of an organisation. Applications are considered from charities working throughout the United Kingdom and preference is given to applications from charities who have already received donations from the trust as the trust recognises the importance of providing recurring donations wherever possible.

In 2005/06 the trust had assets totalling £13.35 million and an income of £635,000. Grants were made to 151 organisations totalling £556,000, categorised under the following headings shown here with examples of beneficiaries :

Community and other social projects – 66 grants totalling £226,000

Botanic Garden Conservation and International and Help for Heroes (£10,000 each); Weston Spirit (£8,000); New Astley Club – Newmarket (£6,000); Action for the River Kennet, Chelsea Pensioners Appeal and Suffolk Foundation (£5,000 each); Amelia Trust

and Crown Court Witness Service (£4,000 each); Appledore Lifeboat Crew Account and Toynbee Hall (£3,000 each); Army Benevolent Fund and Peter Blundell Society (£2,000 each); and Campaign to Protect Rural Hampshire and Worshipful Company of Pattern Makers Educational Fund (£1,000 each).

Health, hospices and medical research – 41 grants totalling £165,000

Breast Cancer Haven – London and St Nicholas Hospice – Bury St Edmunds (£10,000 each); King Edward VII Hospital (£8,000); Marie Curie Cancer Care (£6,000); Addenbrooks Hospital, Dorset Health Wish Trust and Medical Foundation (£5,000 each); Bury St Edmunds Nuffield Hospice and Cystic Fibrosis Research Trust (£4,000 each); Guideposts Trust and Starlight Children's Foundation (£3,000 each); Arthritis Research Campaign and Telephones for the Blind Fund (£2,000 each); and RNIB (£1,000).

Arts, music and education – 24 grants totalling £90,000

Royal Welsh College of Music & Drama (£10,000); Cheltenham Ladies College – Performing Arts Centre and National Museum of Wales (£5,000 each); British Youth Opera and Royal National College for the Blind – Hereford (£4,000 each); Arts Active Trust and Wales Millennium Centre (£3,000 each); and Council for Music in Hospitals and Welsh National Opera (£2,000 each).

Religion – 20 grants totalling £75,000

Friends of Llandaff and St David's Cathedral (£5,000 each); Parish Church of All Saints – Slawston (£4,000); Everychild (£3,000); and Scripture Union and St Mary Burwell Preservation Trust (£2,000 each).

Exclusions No grants to individuals.

Applications In writing to the correspondent by October each year. Trustees meet in November/December. Successful applicants will receive their cheques during January.

Organisations that have already received a grant should re-apply describing how the previous year's grant was spent and setting out how a further grant would be used. In general, less detailed information is required from national charities with a known track record than from small local charities that are not known to the trustees.

Please note: 'Due to the volume of applications, it is not possible to acknowledge each application, nor is it possible to inform unsuccessful applicants.'

Simon Gibson Charitable Trust

General

£488,000 (2007/08)

Beneficial area UK, with a preference for East Anglia and south Wales.

Wild Rose House, Llancarfan, Vale of Glamorgan CF62 3AD

Tel. 01446 781459

Email marsh575@btinternet.com

Correspondent Bryan Marsh, Trustee

Trustees *Bryan Marsh; Angela Homfray; George Gibson; Deborah Connor.*

CC Number 269501

Information available Accounts were available from the Charity Commission.

The Simon Gibson Charitable Trust was set up by a settlement in 1975 by George Simon Cecil Gibson of Exning, near Newmarket, Suffolk. The trust is a general grant-making charity and therefore makes grants to the full range of charitable causes, including religious and educational causes. Local charities applying are restricted to East Anglia and south Wales. Grants can vary from £1,000 to £10,000 but most grants fall in the range £3,000 to £5,000.

In 2007/08 the trust had assets of £12.5 million and an income of £589,000. Grants were made to 121 organisations totalling £488,000.

The largest grants were made to: Ely Cathedral Appeal Fund, Prostate Cancer Charity and the Prince's Trust (£10,000 each). Other beneficiaries included: Action on Addiction, Barnardo's, Breast Cancer Campaign Wales, Jubilee Sailing Trust, Save the Rhino, The Suffolk Foundation and the Welsh Livery Guild Charitable Trust (£5,000 each); RNLI and Welsh National Opera (£4,000 each); Air Training Corp, Barry YMCA, Gurkha Welfare Trust, National Eye Research Centre, Welsh School in London and Wildlife Trust of South and West Wales (£3,000 each); Amelia Trust Farm and Brecon International Festival of Jazz (£2,000 each); and Exning Methodist Church Trustees (£1,000).

Exclusions No grants or sponsorships for individuals or non-charitable bodies.

Applications 'There are no application forms. Charities applying to the trust should make their application in writing in whatever way they think best presents their cause.' The trust acknowledges all applications but does not enter into correspondence with applicants unless they are awarded a grant. The trustees meet in May and applications should be received by March.

The Girdlers' Company Charitable Trust

Medicine and health, education, welfare, welfare of young people, heritage, environment, humanities and Christian religion

£590,500 (2007/08)

Beneficial area UK, with a preference for City and East End of London, and Hammersmith and Peckham.

Girdlers' Hall, Basinghall Avenue, London EC2V 5DD

Tel. 020 7448 4851 **Fax** 020 7628 4030

Email clerk@girdlers.co.uk

Correspondent John Gahan, Charities Manager

Trustee *Court of the Company of Girdlers.*

CC Number 328026

Information available Accounts were available from the Charity Commission.

Established in 1988, the trust's main areas of interest are: medicine and health, education, welfare, welfare of young people, heritage, environment, humanities and Christian religion throughout the UK, with a preference for the City and East End of London, Hammersmith and Peckham.

In 2007/08 the trust had assets of £3.6 million and an income of £356,000. Grants were made totalling £590,500, and were broken down in the following categories (with some organisations receiving grants in more than one category):

Welfare: young people – 29 grants totalling £181,000
Beneficiaries included: London Youth (£48,000); Leyton Orient Community Sports Programme (£28,600); Westminster House Youth Club (£15,000); Arbour Youth Centre (£11,000); Sports Aid London (£10,000);

The Salmon Youth Centre (£6,000); Chelsea Youth Club (£5,000); Sir Francis Chichester Trust (£2,000); and Southwark Sea Cadet Unit (£1,000).

Education – 22 grants totalling £177,000
Beneficiaries included: Gordon's School (£14,000); Royal School of Needlework (£11,000); Guildhall School of Music and Drama (£10,000); The Oval Trust (£9,000); The Country Trust (£6,000); Cafe Africa Trust (£5,000); London College of Fashion (£3,500); and Young Actors' Theatre (£1,000). Scholarships to students from New Zealand totalled £77,000.

Welfare: other – 28 grants totalling £106,000
Beneficiaries included: Resource Information Service (£16,000); Irish Guards (£12,500); Habitat for Humanity (£10,000); Royal Star & Garter Homes (£9,000); The AHOY Centre (£5,000); The Army Benevolent Fund (£4,000); Relationships Foundation (£2,000); and Notting Hill Churches Homeless Concern (£1,000).

Medicine and health – 17 grants totalling £103,000
Beneficiaries included: Royal Surgical Aid Society (£12,500); Florence Nightingale Foundation (£10,000); Queen Elizabeth's Foundation for the Disabled (£7,500); The Cancer Treatment and Research Trust (£6,000); Haven House Foundation (£5,000); and The Food Chain (£1,000). New Zealand Fellowships totalled £25,000.

Heritage, environment, humanities and religion – 13 grants totalling £24,000
Beneficiaries included: St Paul's Cathedral School Foundation (£6,000); Lord Mayor's Charity (£5,000); The Museum of Leathercraft (£3,000); Hackney Youth Orchestra Trust (£1,000); and Southwark Arts Forum (£900).

Exclusions Applications will only be considered from registered charities. Whilst it is extremely rare for grants to be made to individuals, the trustees will consider applications from, or on behalf of, a person who is disabled or disadvantaged needing financial support to enable their participation in a course of training or study leading to employment.

Applications Applicants should write to the correspondent. To be considered for a donation please cover each of the following points:

- the beneficial area under which a grant is sought

- a brief summary of the organisation's background and aims
- the specific nature of the request, highlighting the change you wish to bring about
- how you will know if you have achieved these changes
- your charity registration number.

Applications from charities whose beneficiaries reside in Hammersmith or Peckham are considered annually. Donations are in the order of £1,000.

Each April and November the trustee considers general applications with 10 donations of approximately £1,000 being made on each occasion. The closing dates are the last Friday in January and August. Successful applicants are unlikely to be awarded a further donation within the following 5 years.

Successful applicants will be informed in May and December.

The Glass-House Trust

Social housing and the urban environment, art and child development

£358,000 (2007/08)

Beneficial area Unrestricted, but UK in practice.

Allington House, 1st Floor, 150 Victoria Street, London SW1E 5AE

Tel. 020 7410 0330 **Fax** 020 7410 0332

Website www.sfct.org.uk

Correspondent Alan Bookbinder, Director

Trustees *Alexander Sainsbury; Timothy Sainsbury; Jessica Sainsbury; Elinor Sainsbury; Miss Judith Portrait.*

CC Number 1017426

Information available Annual report and accounts were available from the Charity Commission. Brief information is also available from the Sainsbury Family Charitable Trusts' website.

This is one of the Sainsbury Family Charitable Trusts, which share a joint administration. They have in common an approach to grantmaking which is described in the entry for the group as a whole.

It is the trust of Alexander Sainsbury and three of the four other trustees are his

155

brother and sisters, who each have trusts of their own.

In 2007/08 the trust had assets of almost £12.2 million and income of £600,500. Grants were paid during the year totalling £358,000.

Grantmaking in 2007/08

The trust's main areas of interest are (with the number and value of grants made):

Category	No. of grants	Amount
Built environment	1	£176,000
Child development	2	£80,000
Art	5	£62,500
Social policy	2	£24,000
Overseas	1	£15,000
General	1	£1,200

Within each of these categories the recipients were as follows:

Built environment

Glass-House Community-led Design, for a further grant towards this project's core costs. This project was established by trustees in 2000 and provides design advice to residents participating in the regeneration of social housing.

Child development

A Space (£70,000), towards the director's salary for A Space in the London Borough of Hackney, an innovative project providing emotional support for children within a number of the Borough's primary and secondary schools; and Families, Children & Childcare Project (£10,000), towards further research on how demographic factors and individual mother or child characteristics are related to the use of non-maternal care.

Art

London Musicians Collective (£40,000), towards the costs of Resonance FM; Tate Millbank (£10,000), towards the major retrospective of the paintings of Peter Doig; Arts Educational School Trust, Tring Park School (£5,000), towards the Robert Cohan project, a collaboration with the Rambert School of Ballet and Contemporary Dance to document Cohan's dance and choreographic methods in association; Intoart Projects (£5,000), towards provision of a free studio space and materials for a learning disability arts project; and Paintings in Hospitals (£2,500), towards running costs.

Social policy

Transform Drug Policy Foundation (£20,000), towards core costs; and London School of Economics & Political Science (£4,000), towards a second community-led seminar on the alternatives to demolition of low demand housing stock.

Overseas

Akany Avoko, Madagascar, towards the salary of a development manager.

General

The Sainsbury Archive, towards running costs.

Exclusions Grants are not normally made to individuals.

Applications See the guidance for applicants in the entry for the Sainsbury Family Charitable Trusts. A single application will be considered for support by all the trusts in the group. However, in the case of this trust, 'trustees initiate proposals to be considered and do not encourage unsolicited approaches'.

Global Charities (formally GCap Charities)

Children, young people and disadvantaged adults

£2 million (2008/09)

Beneficial area UK (Classic FM), London (Capital Radio), Cardiff (Red Dragon FM), Crawley (Mercury FM), London (Choice FM) and Peterborough, Colchester, Suffolk, Norwich, Cambridgeshire, Berkshire and north Hampshire, Bristol, Wiltshire, Oxfordshire, Gloucestershire, Exeter and East Devon, Plymouth, Somerset, Sussex, Hampshire and West Sussex, Dorset and New Forest, Essex and Kent (Heart Network).

30 Leicester Square, London WC2H 7LA

Tel. 020 7054 8389

Email charities@thisisglobal.com

Website www.thisisglobal.com/charities

Correspondent Simon Knapp, Head of Operations and Finance

Trustees *Martin George, Chair; Nigel Atkinson; David Briggs; Moira Swinbank; Paul Soames; Peter Williams.*

CC Number 1091657

Information available Accounts were available from the Charity Commission.

Capital Charities Limited was incorporated on 23 January 2002 and began trading on 29 June 2002. On May 2006 the charity changed its name to GCap Charities Limited. The Charity changed its name again to Global Charities Limited on 16 October 2008 following the acquisition of GCap Media plc by Global Radio Limited in June 2008.

Global Charities is the grant-giving charity of Global Radio, the UK's largest commercial radio company. Its mission is to improve the lives of the people in the communities in which its radio stations broadcast.

The group now includes the following stations: Heart (Peterborough, Colchester, Suffolk, Norwich, Cambridgeshire, Berkshire and north Hampshire, Bristol, Wiltshire, Oxfordshire, Gloucestershire, Exeter and East Devon, Plymouth, Somerset, Sussex, Hampshire and West Sussex, Dorset and New Forest, Essex and Kent); 95.8 Capital FM; Hit Music Network; Classic FM; and Gold.

On a general note, whilst Global Charities may effectively be a collective of local funders, the size and scope of funds available in the potential beneficial area is greater than the actual giving of many UK-wide funders. Furthermore, the charity is committed to awarding grants in the locality that the money is raised so that once reasonable management and administration expenses have been met it is able to confirm to donors that money raised locally is spent locally.

Guidelines

The objects of the charity are to relieve poverty, hardship or distress, and to promote the physical and mental welfare of children in need of care and attention, and any other such object or purpose as is charitable under UK law.

The charity aims to achieve its objectives through the distribution of grants to charities running projects that help to make a real difference to the lives of children, young people and adults, who:

- experience poverty and disadvantage
- have/are experiencing abuse, neglect, homelessness, violence or crime
- have an illness or disability.

In accordance with the objectives of the charity the grant-giving strategy has been to focus on awarding small amounts to a large number of small grassroots children's projects all over the relevant radio station's transmission areas. The charity's various individual funds invite applications for grants through application forms which are regularly reviewed and updated by the grants panel to ensure applications comply with the funding criteria.

The trustees have in each area of operations delegated to a panel of experts from the voluntary sector, local community and radio station representatives the task of assessing application forms and making recommendations on what grants the charity should make. They are guided in their recommendations by a list of conditions as to what the charity will fund to ensure that the money is used in the best interests of the intended beneficiaries. Groups that are successful with their applications are required to complete a project report form and provide receipts to show how the grant money has been spent.

Generally, the charity's appeals funds have one or two rounds of small grant giving in the year in order to improve accessibility of funding and cash management of the charity. Operationally, in order to reduce the pressure on the volunteer grant panel, Global Charities staff have and will continue to undertake more sifting of applications prior to panel consideration. These revisions will form the basis of policy and procedure outside London, although the charity will remain flexible to respond to particular local needs.

The charity's funding categories are:

- community, playgroups and toy libraries
- young people
- social and leisure
- disability, health, illness and counselling
- refuge and homeless projects
- language and literacy.

It also occasionally awards large grants to fund specific applications from registered charities with vision and creativity, with which they can work to achieve a joint goal. In general, specific charities are targeted for these programmes as they are strategic and may last for more than one year.

In addition, one of the charity's key achievements is the development of the v programme, a three year partnership with v, the volunteering charity, to create new volunteering opportunities for 16 to 25 year olds. The charity's radio stations have donated air-time worth £3–4 million over three years to v, who will match this amount in a grant to the charity to give out as grants to volunteering projects. So far, the charity has given out over £1.6 million of grants to such projects, generating over 8,000 new volunteering opportunities.

Grantmaking 2008/09

During the year the charities had assets of £1.4 million and an income of £3.4 million. Grants were made across the charities' geographical areas of benefit totalling £2 million and were categorised as follows:

Category	No.	Value
Disability, health, illness and counselling	256	£550,000
Young people	131	£532,000
Social and leisure	109	£492,000
Community, playgroups and toy libraries	171	£271,000
Refuge and homeless projects	28	£137,000
Language and literacy	27	£57,000

Beneficiaries included: Sixth Sense Theatre (£7,500); Cambourne Youth Partnership (£5,000); Havens Hospices – Essex (£3,000); Bangladeshi Parents Association (£2,100); Howbury Friends (£1,800); and Centrepoint – Hammersmith and Fulham (£1,600).

Beneficiaries of the large grants programme included: Prince's Foundation for Children and the Arts (£100,000); Missing People (£61,000); and Impact Initiatives (£25,000).

The charity has also distributed 66 grants totalling £401,000 to eligible groups in the year as part of its v project to develop volunteering activities for young people.

Exclusions Each individual branch has specific exclusions, generally however the charities will not fund:

- individual children or families
- retrospective funding
- statutory funding, such as schools and hospitals
- salaried posts
- deficit funding
- medical research
- purchase of minibuses
- trips abroad
- distribution to other organisations
- distribution to individuals
- religious activities
- political groups
- general structural changes to buildings
- projects which are part of a larger charity organisation and not separately constituted
- core funding for a national or regional charity.

Applications The charity provides the following guidance on its website:

If you have a general enquiry regarding how to apply for funds please contact us (Tel: 020 7054 8391). We are always glad to answer questions from any organisation, charity or group on our grants process. Each station has at least one round of grant awards in the year. We attempt to fund as many eligible applications as possible,

although this is always limited to the funds raised in the year. Details are given on each of our stations' websites [...] as well as how to apply for application forms. These forms are reviewed and updated by local grants panel in conjunction with the overall board to ensure the application process is as accessible as possible and to ensure applicants are guided though our funding criteria.

The Golden Bottle Trust

General with a preference for the environment, health, education, religion, the arts and developing countries

£943,000 (2007/08)

Beneficial area Worldwide.

Messrs Hoare Trustees, 37 Fleet Street, London EC4P 4DQ

Tel. 020 7353 4522 **Fax** 020 7353 4521

Email enquiries@hoaresbank.co.uk

Correspondent Miss J Moore

Trustees *Messrs Hoare Trustees (H C Hoare; D J Hoare; R Q Hoare; A S Hoare; V E Hoare; S M Hoare; A S Hopewell.)*

CC Number 327026

Information available Accounts were available from the Charity Commission.

The trust was established in 1985 for general charitable purposes, by C Hoare and Co. bankers, the oldest remaining private bank in the UK. The trust is managed by the company, Messrs Hoare Trustees, and continues to receive most of its income from C Hoare and Co.

In 2007/08 the trust had assets of £7.1 million and an income of almost £1.2 million, including £1 million from the Hoare family. Grants were made totalling £943,000, categorised as follows:

Category	Value
Health and Education	£364,000
Related charities*	£271,500
Religion	£74,000
Environment	£72,000
Staff match funding	£56,000
Children	£43,700
Arts	£34,300
Other	£27,300

*Related charities included: the Bulldog Trust (£230,000); the Henry C Hoare

Charitable Trust (£30,000); Training for Lfe (£8,000); West Country Rivers (£2,000); and the Heythrope Hunt Charitable Trust (£1,500).

Other beneficiaries, receiving £5,000 or more, were: China Oxford Scholarship Fund (£100,000); Eton College (£50,000); Jesus College Cambridge (£20,000); Trinity Hospice (£14,000); Migratory Salmon Fund, Theatre of Memory Trust, Ahoy Centre, Royal Academy and Wells Cathedral Girl Choristers' Trust (£10,000 each); RIDA Drawings and Archives (£7,500); Royal College of Surgeons (£7,000); and Flora & Fauna International (£5,200).

Exclusions No grants for individuals or organisations that are not registered charities.

Applications In writing to the correspondent. Applications are considered from bank staff and external registered charities. The trust may, in certain circumstances, also undertake fundraising events to sponsor a specific cause.

The Goldsmiths' Company Charity

General, London charities and the precious metals craft

£3 million (2007/08)

Beneficial area UK, with a special interest in London charities.

Goldsmiths' Hall, Foster Lane, London EC2V 6BN

Tel. 020 7606 7010 **Fax** 020 7606 1511

Email charity@thegoldsmiths.co.uk

Website www.thegoldsmiths.co. uk/charities

Correspondent Miss H Erskine, Charity Administrator

Trustees *The Court of Assistants of the Goldsmiths' Company. The Charity Advisory Committee consists of: D A E R Peake, Chair; S A Shepherd; A M J Galsworthy; Hon. Mark Bridges; Revd D Paton; W H C Montgomery; Dr C Mackworth-Young; Mrs S Hamilton; J R Polk; Mrs V R Beverley; R O'Hara.*

CC Number 1088699

Information available Exemplary annual report and accounts with a

narrative exploration of grantmaking and a comprehensive grants list covering the amount awarded and the purpose of the grant. There is also a good website.

Summary

Each year the charity gives over 300 small grants of between £500 and £5,000. Most of these are in response to applications received, and can be for almost any purpose, including supporting core costs. A dozen or so large grants are also given annually, generally up to a maximum of £100,000. These are usually to organisations proactively sought out by the charity rather than as a result of applying for a grant.

The charity's grant making policies fall into three main areas:

- general charitable support
- support of the Goldsmith's craft
- education.

Grants to individuals in need are only provided through the social services departments of named London boroughs. The charity selects new named boroughs on a regular basis. Please contact the charity directly for further information.

General charitable support
This category is split into six sub-sections: general welfare, medical welfare, young people, heritage, church and arts. Grants are usually one off but can occasionally be given for up to three years. Recurring grants are assessed annually on their own merits. The charity's policy is to give small grants, averaging around £3,000.

Grants are made to London-based or national charities, but not to local provincial charities. Where charities are members, branches or affiliates of an association, appeals are accepted from the governing body or head office of that association only. In the case of church restoration, block grants are made to the Historic Churches Preservation Trust and therefore appeals from individual churches will not normally be considered.

Goldsmith's craft
The charity is committed to supporting a range of training opportunities that reflect the issues and opportunities facing the industry and the people working within it.

These include the sponsorship and management of the last formal indentured apprenticeship scheme for young people (aged 16–21) wishing to enter the industry as trainees in London

and the South East. The charity also supports the 'Getting Started' programme – an annual one-week introductory business course for recent jewellery and silversmithing graduates from across the UK. A programme of masterclasses and seminars to underpin the professional development of individuals working within the trade is also supported.

Education
The charity has long history of support for education. The current Education Committee was formed in 1944 to ensure the continuance of the charity's traditional role as an innovator and supporter of less recognised, but important needs.

The committee works within the following policy guidelines:

- to foster aspects of education considered to be in most need of encouragement
- to fill gaps in educational provision
- to help in situations where the charity's limited finances can have most impact through the multiplier effect.

The charity currently funds four major proactive projects: development grants for teachers; Science for Society courses for teachers; primary school projects in literacy and numeracy; and, second degree postgraduate medical students.

Grants in 2007/08

During the year the charity had assets of £81 million and an income of £3.8 million, mainly from investments. Grants were made totalling £3 million. The total amounts granted within each of the three main areas mentioned above were:

Category	Value
General charitable work	£1,200,000
Support of the craft	£1,400,000
Education	£395,000

Grants for general charitable work in 2007/08 were further categorised as follows:

Category	Value
General welfare	£502,000
Medical welfare and disabled	£223,000
Young people	£173,000
Arts	£150,000
Heritage	£60,000
Church	£53,000

Beneficiaries across all categories included: 7th Rifles Welfare Fund – to provide combined mess facilities at Dalton barracks (£100,000); Somerset Community Foundation – for the rural deprivation project (£60,000); National Churches Trust – for general funds (£30,000); City Music Society – for sponsorship of a series of concerts

(£19,000); Federation of London Youth Clubs (London Youth) – for general funds and Chemistry Olympiad – to provide medals for the 2009 event (£10,000 each); Strawberry Hill Trust – towards regilding the state rooms (£6,000); Council for Music in Hospitals – for work in Northern Ireland (£5,000); Core Arts – for the poetry tutor's costs (£3,000); and CMO Productions – for the 2008 summer school holiday project (£1,000).

Exclusions Applications are not normally considered on behalf of:

- medical research
- animal welfare
- memorials to individuals
- overseas projects
- individual housing associations
- endowment schemes
- charities with a turnover of more than £10 million.

Applications Applications should be made by letter, no more than two sides of A4 in length, highlighting the case for the company to give its support.

The letter should be accompanied by:

- the completed application form, which can be downloaded from the company's website. The form may be re-typed, but should follow the same format and length (three sides of A4). All questions should be answered. Do not cut and paste information on the form. Legible handwritten applications are acceptable.
- the charity's most recent annual report and audited accounts (or financial report required by the Charities Act).

Applications are considered monthly, except in August and September, and there is usually a three to four month delay between receipt of an appeal and a decision being made. Applications from any organisation, whether successful or not, are not normally considered more frequently than every three years.

Any enquiries should be addressed to the correspondent.

Mike Gooley Trailfinders Charity

Medical research and general

£439,500 (2007/08)

Beneficial area UK.

Trailfinders Ltd, 9 Abingdon Road, London W8 6AH

Tel. 020 7938 3143 **Fax** 020 7937 6059

Correspondent Louise Breton, Trustee

Trustees *Mark Bannister; Michael D W Gooley; Bernadette M Gooley; Tristan P Gooley; Fiona Gooley; Louise Breton.*

CC Number 1048993

Information available Accounts were on file at the Charity Commission, without a list of grants.

The charity supports medical research, community projects which encourage young people in outdoor activities and armed forces veteran organisations particularly the Soldiers, Sailors, Airmen and Families Association – Forces Help.

In 2007/08 the charity had assets of £9.8 million and an income of £1.1 million, which included a £1 million from Trailfinders. Grants were made during the year totalling £439,500.

No beneficiaries were listed in the charity's accounts. Previous donations have included: £400,000 to Alzheimer's Society; £100,000 to Prostate Cancer Charity; and £40,000 to Second World War Experience Centre.

Exclusions Grants are not made to overseas charities or to individuals.

Applications In writing to the correspondent.

The Gosling Foundation Limited

Relief of poverty, education, religion, naval and service charities and general charitable purposes beneficial to the community

£1.9 million (2007/08)

Beneficial area Worldwide. In practice UK.

21 Bryanston Street, Marble Arch, London W1H 7PR

Tel. 020 7495 5599

Correspondent Miss Anne Yusof, Secretary

Trustees *Sir Donald Gosling; Sir Ronald F Hobson; R J Knight; A P Gosling.*

CC Number 326840

Information available Accounts were available from the Charity Commission.

The foundation was established in 1985 by Sir Donald Gosling, co-founder of NCP car parks and former seafarer. The foundation's endowment derives from his personal fortune and its objects are the relief of poverty, education, religion and general charitable purposes beneficial to the community. About 200 grants are given each year to a wide range of charities, with naval and other service related charities receiving substantial support.

In 2007/08 the foundation had assets of almost £92 million and an income of £4.3 million. There were 200 grants made totalling £1.9 million. Grants were categorised as follows:

Purposes beneficial to the community – 109 grant totalling £894,000
Beneficiaries included: Armed Forces Memorial Trust (2 grants totalling £350,000); Greater London Fund for the Blind (£100,000); Maritime Reserve Centenary Fund (2 grants totalling £60,000); Special Boat Service Association (£50,000); HMS Ark Royal (Central Fund) (2 grants totalling (£35,000); Royal Marine Band (£30,000); SAMA (£20,000); Naomi House (2 grants totalling (£12,000); Shooting Star Trust Children's Hospice (£10,000); Portsmouth Field Gun Association (2 grants totalling £7,000); Blue Cross, Canine Partners for Independence, Changing Faces and Prostate Research

Campaign (£5,000 each); Sparks (2 grants totalling £3,500); Fight for Sight, Cancer Research UK, Bobby Moore Fund and Spinal Injuries Association (£3,000 each); Action for ME, Cancer Research UK, Integrated Neurological Services, St John Ambulance (£2,000 each); DebRA, Help for Heroes, Labrador Rescue Trust, Rotary Club of London Charitable Trust, Paul Strickland Scanner Centre, Riding for the Disabled Association, Royal Star and Garter Homes and Wooden Spoon Society (£1,000 each); St Margaret's Somerset Hospice (£500); and Royal Hospital Cornwall – Children's Ward (£250).

Advancement of education – 47 grants totalling £582,000

Beneficiaries included: Prince's Foundation (2 grants totalling £102,000); Prince's Teaching Institute and Royal Marines Museum (£100,000 each); Outward Bound Trust and Prince of Wales Charitable Foundation (£50,000 each); Tennis Foundation (2 grants totalling £25,000); Seafarers UK (£21,000); Twickenham Sea Cadets (2 grants totalling £20,000); Maritime Foundation (£7,000); Beacon Foundation, Costal Forces Heritage Trust, Old Vic Theatre Trust, Purcell School of Music and Royal Welsh College of Music and Drama (£5,000 each); Charles Dickens Primary School and Prince's Trust – Hampton Estates (£3,000 each); 64th Birkenhead Sea Scout Group and Sacred Heart Primary School (£2,000 each); George Thomas Education Trust, Pace Centre Limited, Southbourne Sea Scout Group and Whizz Kids (£1,000 each).

Relief of poverty – 35 grants totalling £404,000

Beneficiaries included: White Ensign Association (3 grants totalling 205,000); SSAFA Forces Help (3 grants totalling £61,000); Britannia Association and STOP – Trafficking UK (£25,000 each); Royal Navy Benevolent Fund (2 grants totalling £12,000); GEAR and HMS Ocean Welfare Fund (£10,000 each); British Forces Foundation, Sandy Gall's Afghanistan Appeal and St Lazarus Charitable Trust (£5,000 each); Royal British Legion (2 grants totalling £3,000); HMS Dumbarton Castle Welfare Fund and Toynbee Hall (£2,000 each); Entertainment Artistes' Benevolent Fund (£1,000); British Red Cross Society (£500); and City of Westminster Charitable Trust (£200).

Advancement of religion – 9 grants totalling £51,000

Beneficiaries were: Annual National Service for Seafarers, Holy Trinity Parish Church and Portsmouth Cathedral Development Trust (£10,000 each); HMS Heron CAF – Church Fund (2 grants totalling £8,000); Darlmouth Baptist Church and St Paul's Trust Centre (£5,000 each); Hands Around the World (£2,000); and St Paul's Church Knightsbridge (£500).

Applications In writing to the correspondent. The grant-making policies of the foundation are 'regularly reviewed' and currently are:

- applications should fall within the objects of the foundation
- there is no minimum limit for any grant
- all grants will be approved unanimously
- the charity will only make grants to individuals in exceptional circumstances.

GrantScape

Environmental and community-based projects

£2.5 million (2008/09)
Beneficial area UK.

Office E, Whitsundoles, Broughton Road, Salford, Milton Keynes MK17 8BU
Tel. 01908 545780 **Fax** 01908 545799
Email helpdesk@grantscape.org.uk
Website www.grantscape.org.uk
Correspondent Mr S Hargreaves, Contact
Trustees *Dave Bramley; Doug De Freitas; Jacqueline Rae; Alan Loynes; Alastair Singleton; Steven Henry.*
CC Number 1102249
Information available Information was available on the charity's website.

GrantScape is a company limited by guarantee and is enrolled with ENTRUST as a Distributive Environmental Body. Its vision is 'to improve the environment and communities by the channelling and management of charitable funding towards deserving and quality projects.'

Its generic grant-making policy is as follows.

- GrantScape will only make grants in line with its charitable objectives.
- Grants will be made on a justifiable and fair basis to projects which provide best value.
- Grants will be made to projects that improve the life of communities and the environment.
- GrantScape will make available specific criteria for each of the grant programmes that it manages.
- All grants are subject to meeting the generic grant-making criteria as well as the specific grant programme criteria.

In 2008/09 it had assets of £2.9 million and an income of £999,000. Grants were committed across the following programmes, some of which have now closed. Grants were made totalling £2.5 million.

In addition to the programmes listed, the charity has continued to administer Landfill Communities Fund grants from earlier programmes.

Current programmes

Grants are available in specific geographical areas from the following programmes:

Caird Bardon Community Programme
Grant amount:
- the Caird Bardon Community Programme has approximately £300,000 available per annum
- grants are awarded between £5,000 and £60,000
- match Funding is not required.

Contributing Third Party Donation:
A CTP Donation of 10% of any grant award made will be required.

(If you require further information, please refer to the separate document 'Contributing Third Party (CTP) Guidance', which can be downloaded in the application pack from the charity's website. Alternatively, contact the Grant Support Team on 01908 545780)

Project location:
Projects must be located in West Yorkshire, specifically within 10 miles of the Caird Bardon Limited Peckfield landfill site (LS25 4DW).

Project purpose:
Grants will be available for community and environmental projects.

Projects must comply with the requirements of the Landfill Communites Fund (LCF). Details of the LCF can be found on ENTRUST's website: www.entrust.org.uk.

Public access requirements:
Projects must be available and open to the general public – as a minimum, for four evenings a week, or two days a week, or 104 days a year.

Ineligible applicants:
- Individuals
- Commercial organisations

Project exclusions:
Grants will not be available for:

- single user sports facilities (for example bowls, golf clubs)
- projects that are considered statutory requirements
- projects that are solely aimed to meet the requirements of the Disability Discrimination Act
- revenue funding and core cost funding
- Retrospective funding (projects that have already been completed)
- projects at schools
- bus services, minibus services, or vehicles
- projects at hospitals, or hospices, or day care centres
- any works to public highways
- Staff posts and costs where they are not based, or specifically undertaking works, at the actual project site
- projects to deliver visual enhancements (such as 'a view'), as this does not improve, maintain or provide a general public amenity
- village or town centre enhancements, such as walkways, street works or signage
- CD's, websites or remote interpretation about a site
- public car parks, unless they are specific to the general public amenity
- public conveniences
- allotments, or fruit growing projects
- charity buildings, offices of charities, Citizens' Advice Bureau and advice centres
- large scale perimeter/security fencing programmes that do not directly enhance the public amenity.

Judging criteria:
The main criteria used when assessing applications received will be:

- the level of community support for and involvement in the project
- the local community benefit and enjoyment which will result from the project.

Other factors will also be considered which must be demonstrated in the application:

- the ability of the applicant to deliver the project
- how the work will be continued after the project has been completed, i.e. its sustainability and legacy
- value for money.

CWM Community and Environmental Fund

Grant amount:
- the CWM Community and Environmental Fund has approximately £200,000 available per annum
- grants are awarded between £5,000 and £50,000
- match funding is not required.

Contributing Third Party Donation:
A CTP Donation of 10% of any grant award made will be required

(If you require further information, please refer to the separate document 'Contributing Third Party (CTP) Guidance', which can be downloaded in the application pack from the charity's website. Alternatively, contact the Grant Support Team on 01908 545780)

Project location:
Projects must be located in Carmarthenshire and be within 10 miles of a licensed landfill site.

Project purpose:
Grants are available for community and environmental projects, particularly those which can demonstrate the enhancement of biodiversity.

Grants will be available for capital improvement works to public amenity projects, for example:

- village halls
- village greens
- public playgrounds *(see note below)*
- sports fields and facilities
- nature reserves
- community centres
- cycle paths
- country parks.

(Applications involving playgrounds on Council owned land will only be funded if applicants can demonstrate significant community fundraising efforts to help financially support the project.)

Management, administration and professional costs will only be considered for funding if they form part of a wider application for a capital project and can only constitute a maximum of 10% in total of the amount applied for.

Projects must comply with the requirements of the Landfill Communites Fund (LCF). Details of the LCF can be found on ENTRUST's website: www.entrust.org.uk.

Priority:
Priority will be given to applicants that clearly understand and can demonstrate the social, economic and environmental benefits the project will provide.

Public access requirements:
Projects must be available and open to the general public – as a minimum, for four evenings a week, or two days a week, or 104 days a year.

Ineligible applicants:
- organisations operating for the purpose of making and distributing profit
- schools
- individuals
- single user sports facilities.

Project exclusions:
Grants will not be available for:

- projects that have already been completed (retrospective funding)
- projects that are considered statutory requirements
- projects that are solely aimed to meet the requirements of the Disability Discrimination Act
- projects that are located on private land
- revenue costs will not normally be funded.

Judging criteria:
The main criteria used when assessing applications received will be:

- the level of community support for and involvement in the project
- the local community benefit and enjoyment which will result from the project.

Other factors will also be considered which must be demonstrated in the application:

- the ability of the applicant to deliver the project
- how the work will be continued after the project has been completed, i.e. its sustainability and legacy
- value for money.

Programme	Applications closed	Value (approx)
Caird Bardon Community Programme	Ongoing	£300,000 pa
CWM Community and Environmental Fund	Ongoing	£248,000 pa
Waste Recycling Group – Local Nature Conservation Challenge for Bedfordshire & Luton	September 08	£100,000
Waste Recycling Group – Joint with Church Urban Fund	March 09	£15,000
Waste Recycling Group – Inner London Nature Conservation Fund	March 09	£100,000
Waste Recycling Group – Working with Nature	April 09	£1,300,000

New grant programmes are introduced from time to time – check the charity's website for up-to-date information.

Exclusions Specific exclusions apply to each programme – see Current programmes for details.

Applications Applications are made online via the charity's website.

The Great Britain Sasakawa Foundation

Links between Great Britain and Japan

£665,000 (2007)

Beneficial area UK, Japan.

Dilke House, 1 Malet Street, London WC1E 7JN

Tel. 020 7436 9042 **Fax** 020 7355 2230

Email grants@gbsf.org.uk

Website www.gbsf.org.uk

Correspondent Stephen McEnally, Chief Executive

Trustees *Earl of St Andrew, Chair; Hiroaki Fujii; Prof Nozomu Hayashi; Michael French; Jeremy Brown; Prof. Harumi Kimura; Yohei Sasakawa; Prof. Shoichi Watanabe; Sir John Boyd; Prof. Peter Mathias; Prof. David Cope; Taysuya Tanami.*

CC Number 290766

Information available Accounts were available at the Charity Commission. Their annual report is available at the foundation's website.

The foundation was established as a result of a visit to London in 1983 by the late Ryoichi Sasakawa during which he met a number of senior British figures to discuss the international situation and, in particular, UK-Japanese relations. It was agreed at these discussions to enhance mutual appreciation and understanding of each other's culture, society and achievements by the setting up of a non-governmental, non-profit making body for this purpose. A donation of almost £10 million was subsequently made by The Sasakawa Foundation (now called The Nippon Foundation), and the Great Britain Sasakawa Foundation was inaugurated in May 1985, in parallel with similar

initiatives in Scandinavia, France and the United States.

The foundation aims to promote relations between the UK and Japan by advancing the education of British and Japanese citizens in each other's culture, society and achievements. Grants are intended to provide 'pump-priming' for projects, **not** core funding, and can be for up to three years.

Support is given for projects in the following fields:

- arts and culture
- science, technology and the environment
- humanities and social issues
- Japanese language
- medicine and health
- schools, education and youth exchanges
- sport.

At present the foundation is particularly interested in helping projects in the areas of science, medicine, the environment and modern society.

During the year the main activities supported by the foundation included:

- visits between Japan and Britain by artists, teachers, academics, and young people
- exhibitions of fine and applied art, and the performance of drama, music and dance
- research and study, seminars, workshops, lectures and publications
- teaching and development of Japanese language and cultural studies.

In 2007 the foundation had assets of £24 million and an income of £690,000. 234 awards were made totalling £665,000. This included eight Butterfield Awards in medicine totalling £65,000 and 27 awards totalling £88,000 which were awarded in Japan. Other expenditure, including staff costs, investment advisory fees and other support costs, was quite high, totalling £244,000.

Beneficiaries during the year included:

Young people and Education
Japan Experience Study Tour 2007: Allerton Grange High School – Leeds (£22,000); Community Links, GLOBE/ NCY Trust (£6,000); Clifton Scientific Trust (£5,000); President Kennedy Youth Club – Coventry (£3,000); Project Trust (£1,200); and Gatton Park Education Trust (£1,000).

Japanese Language
British Association for Teaching Japanese as a Foreign Language – 2 grants (£7,000); SOAS Language Centre

(£3,300); and Nihongo Club – Cambridge (£1,000).

Arts & Culture
University College for the Creative Arts (£8,000); British Museum (£7,500); Ichiza Theatre Company (£6,000); Raindance Film Festival and Alnwick Garden Trust (£4,000 each); Pecha Kucha London (£3,500); Northern Gallery for Contemporary Art (£1,500); and Parasol Unit Foundation for Contemporary Art (£1,000).

Humanities and Social Issues
National Institute for Japanese Studies – 2 grants (£30,000); Asia Pacific Technology Network (£10,000); Global Oriental Ltd (£5,000); Japan Society (£2,000); Leeds University – Dept of East Asian Studies (£1,600); and University College London – Dept of Philosophy (£1,000).

Science, Technology & Environment
Queens University Belfast – School of Biological Sciences (£5,000); Open University – Dept of Physics & Astronomy (£4,500); Tango Eco-Future Park (£2,000); and Royal Botanic Gardens – Kew (1,500).

Medicine and Health
Institute of Reflective Practice (£6,000); Pathological Society of Great Britain and Ireland (£5,000); Bristol University – Dept of Physiology & Pharmacology (£2,600); and Glasgow University – Institute of Biomedical & Life Sciences (£1,400).

Sport
Glasgow University Shorinji Kempo Club (£4,000); North Lakes Jujitsu Association (£3,000); Aikido Union England (£2,700); and Tomari Budokai (£2,000).

Butterfield Awards
The Butterfield Awards were established in 2001 to commemorate the achievements of Lord Butterfield, a medical researcher, clinician and academic administrator, and former chair of the foundation. The awards aim to 'encourage exchanges and collaborations between researchers and practitioners in medicine and health'.

Eight awards were made in 2007 and beneficiaries included: Dr T Ogi, Sussex University with Professor Y Miki and Dr K Takenaka, Tokyo Medical and Dental University (£12,000); Dr K Chalkidou, National Institute for Health and Clinical Excellence with Dr S Ono, Tokyo University (£10,000); Dr J Fossey, Bath University with Dr K Morigaki, National Institute of Advanced Industrial Science & Technology (£5,000); and Dr M Miyashita, University of Tsukuba with

Dr D Stensel, Loughborough University (£3,500).

Exclusions Grants are not made to individuals applying on their own behalf. The foundation will consider proposals from organisations that support the activities of individuals, provided they are citizens of the UK or Japan.

No grants are awarded for the construction, conservation or maintenance of land and buildings, student fees or travel in connection with study for a qualification.

Applications The foundation expresses a strong preference for emailed applications. A form will be emailed on request, and is also available from the foundation's website, where detailed information is given about the foundation's grantgiving and application procedures. Application forms are also available from both the London headquarters or from the Tokyo office at: The Nippon Foundation Bldg 4F, 1–2–2 Akasaka Minato-ku, Tokyo 107–0052.

The application form requires the following information:

- a summary of the proposed project and its aims, including dates, its likely impact and long-term sustainability
- the total cost of the project and the amount of the desired grant, together with a note of other expected sources of funds
- a description of what elements of the project grant funding has been requested for (the foundation prefers to support identifiable activities rather than general overheads).

Organisations should be registered charities, recognised educational institutions, local or regional authorities, churches, media companies, publishers or other bodies that the foundation may approve.

Telephone enquiries or personal visits are welcomed by the foundation's staff to discuss eligibility in advance of any formal application. The awards committee meets in London in February, May and October. Applications should be received by December, March and August. Awards meetings in Tokyo are held in April and October, with applications to be submitted by February and September.

School applicants are requested to first file an application with Connect Youth International, Japan Exchange Programme, 10 Spring Gardens, London SW1A 2BN (which is part of the British Council), to which the foundation grants external finance, aimed at encouraging

exchanges (both ways) for schools in Great Britain and Japan, (their website is: www.connectyouthinternational.com).

All applicants are notified shortly after each awards committee meeting of the decisions of the trustees. Those offered grants are asked to sign and return an acceptance form and are given the opportunity to say when they would like to receive their grant.

Please note: the foundation receives requests for two to three times the amount of money it actually has available for grants and many applicants receive much less than they asked for.

The Community Foundation for Greater Manchester

General

£4.3 million (2007/08)

Beneficial area Greater Manchester.

1st Floor, Beswick House, Beswick Row, Manchester M4 4LA

Tel. 0161 214 0940 **Fax** 0161 214 0941

Email enquiries@communityfoundation.co.uk

Website www.communityfoundation.co.uk

Correspondent Julie Langford, Deputy Chief Executive

Trustees *Dr Tom Manion, Chair; John Sandford; Chris Hirst; Richard Hogben; Tony Burns; Gary Newborough; David Dickman; Simon Webber; Jo Farrell; Han-Son Lee; Sandra Lindsay; Natalie Qureshi; Laura Harper.*

CC Number 1017504

Information available Accounts were on file at the Charity Commission. Full information is available on the foundation's website.

The Community Foundation is a community of donors committed to improving the quality of life and helping to build stronger communities across Greater Manchester. Since the foundation began in 1989, over £20 million has been distributed to over 8,000 community groups and projects, changing the lives of many people in the area. The foundation represents a new generation of social business, accountable, transparent, creative and active in engaging committed donors and matching them with

areas of genuine concern. This is done in a manner that improves, develops and supports Greater Manchester's many diverse voluntary and community organisations.

The foundation's income, comes, as with many community foundations, from a range of mostly statutory sources and each fund has its own criteria and conditions. With over 60 funding streams the foundation distributes grants to community groups, projects and social entrepreneurs across Greater Manchester. Many of the groups supported by the foundation have never applied for funding before and are run by volunteers. For easy accessibility to the process, a dedicated grants team has been established. The team gives advice, processes applications and monitors the impact the foundation's grants have in the local community to ensure real needs are met and lives improved.

The foundation serves the metropolitan borough areas of Bury, Bolton, Manchester, Oldham, Rochdale, Salford, Stockport, Tameside, Trafford, and Wigan. This adds up to a total population of over 2.6 million and an estimated 20,000 voluntary and community groups operating throughout the area.

The foundation gives priority to projects which:

- are run by local volunteers who wish to improve the circumstances of individuals and communities in economically/socially excluded and/or deprived areas of Greater Manchester
- have no access to a professional fundraiser and experience difficulty in attracting funding from other sources
- encourage involvement of local residents in improving, designing, identifying and implementing community activities
- promote voluntary participation and social inclusion as well as community involvement and self-help
- meet and demonstrate an emerging or immediate need and serve to build the community's awareness
- do not duplicate an existing provision or service (if the project resembles an existing provision, you will be expected to explain why your services are needed in addition to existing provision or clarify how they are different).

Grantmaking in 2007/08

In 2007/08 the foundation had assets of £3.4 million and an income of £6.1 million. Grants were made to 902 organisations totalling £4.3 million. 57% of these beneficiaries had recieved no previous grant funding. The average grant for the year was £4,800.

The following information on the current grant funds for groups and organisations has been taken from the foundation's website:

Ask Community Action Fund

Manchester-based property developers Ask Development use this fund to support communities in areas where their projects are under development or future schemes planned. The company's staff are involved in the decision-making panel, considering applications referred to them by the foundation's grants team.

Applications up to £1,000 can be supported and should be made through the foundation's Small Grants Programme.

Bank of New York Fund

Having opened their first UK office outside London in Manchester city centre in late 2005, the Bank of New York set up a fund with the foundation in order to provide investment into the local communities surrounding the company and from which they recruit their employees. The bank encourages its employees to become involved in this fund by fundraising and participating in decision-making panels.

Grants of up to £2,000 are available to small community groups and projects. Applications are referred to the Bank of New York from the foundation's Small Grants programme. Further fund criteria can be found in the Small Grants Programme application guidelines which are available on the website along with the appropriate application and monitoring forms.

Bardsley Fund

Bardsley Community Fund was set up in 1998 by Roland Bardsley, founder of Bardsley Homes and Construction. Bardsley encourages its employees to get involved in fundraising and payroll giving to add to the company's contributions. Employees also sit on the grants panel which makes decisions on where the funding should go.

The fund was originally aimed at supporting disadvantaged children and young people and their families from the Tameside area. Recently, however, the criteria were expanded making the fund available to community and voluntary groups from all over Greater Manchester with a focus on those neighbourhoods in which the company works.

Applications of up to £2,000 can be submitted by groups and organisations which fit the Small Grants programme criteria.

Burnt to the Ground Fund

The Burnt to the Ground Fund was established in May 2007 after a fire on Dale Street in the Northern Quarter destroyed two buildings, rendering homeless a substantial number of small businesses.

Grants from this fund will support the following causes:

- small emergency grants of up to £500 for businesses and enterprises who have lost equipment/business
- donations to organisations involved in the rescue operation during the fire
- critical intervention grants of up to £500 to community based groups and organisations.

Please note: priority will be given to requests for support from businesses and organisations directly affected by the Dale Street fire. If you are interested in applying, please contact Alke Horn on 0161 214 0958.

Borough of Rochdale Small Grants Fund

This fund aims to support local community groups, projects or individuals throughout the borough, under the eight priority themes listed below:

- safety, including crime and disorder
- sustainable neighbourhoods, including the environment and housing
- prosperity, skills and jobs
- lifelong learning, including early years and schools
- transport
- health and well being
- culture, sports and arts
- community cohesion, including issues of race and disability.

Grants between £100 and £5,000 are available to applicants.

Bury MBC Community Fund

The fund's current funding priority is to encourage and support grassroot community activity. This means small, community-based and locally controlled groups that manage themselves, encourage active participation from volunteers, have minimal cash reserves and limited access to funding support. Grants of up to £7,000 are available.

Organisations applying for funding should be running projects which address at least one of Bury MBC's Community Strategy Delivery Themes:

- safe, strong and confident communities
- children and young people
- sustainable communities and transport
- healthier communities and vulnerable people
- quality services.

Please note: the fund does not support larger, more sophisticated organisations that have a track record of attracting funding, particularly when such groups have a turnover of more than £50,000 a year.

Dedicated Micros Community Action Fund

Set up in 2004, this fund distributes funds raised by employees, which are matched by the company. Employee involvement continues at grants panel level, where applications are reviewed against the criteria and approved by a selection of staff who have been trained for this role. By the end of 2006 more than £70,000 worth of funding had been distributed by this fund.

Applications to this fund are made through the Small Grants Programme.

Fair Share Trust Programmes

These programmes operate in Abram, Alt, Barton, Droylsden, Great Lever, Lostock, Micklehurst, Middleton, Sale Moor and St James. The Fair Share Trust Programme is a fund set up by the Big Lottery to benefit those areas in England, Scotland and Northern Ireland which had not received their fair share of lottery funding. It is a thirteen year programme aimed at strategically addressing local issues, as identified by a panel of individuals who live and work in the area. The individual programmes have identified their own priorities for the distribution of funds and applicants are advised to visit the foundation's website for guidelines, available funding and appropriate forms.

Grassroots Grants

The purpose of this fund is to encourage and support small local informal voluntary and community groups and organisations, many of whom are dependent on volunteers. This may be the first grant for many of the groups that apply to the grassroots fund.

The programme will be available for local organisations for a period of three years from summer 2008 to March 2011. Grants are available for community groups and organisations aiming to improve circumstances for people in communities within one of the following boroughs: Bury, Manchester, Oldham, Rochdale Salford, Stockport, Tameside, Trafford and Wigan.

Organisations must:

- be a not-for-profit, third sector voluntary or community group, active in their local community for not less than 12 months, prior to 31 December 2007 (groups and organisations do not have to be registered charities to apply)
- have an evidenced income of less than £30,000 per annum, taken as an average turnover for the last three financial years (or over the life of the group if it is less than three years old), and net of any grants received through the Grassroots Grants programme
- be volunteer led (i.e. with largely volunteer based input)
- be connected with and/or meeting the needs of the local community

- have a governing document that has as a minimum the name, aim/purpose, objects, a dissolution clause for the organisation, a list of trustees/committee members, and trustees/committee member signatures.

The maximum grant request that will be considered is £5,000 and the minimum is £250. For maximum flexibility groups or organisations can apply for either a one-off grant payment or a grant spread over a maximum of the three year period (2008–2011), but with no portion of that spread being less than the minimum grant amount. Please note: the maximum amount of funding that individual groups or organisations can receive during the lifetime of this programme is £5,000.

Applicants can either download an application form or follow the online application process for Grassroots Grants available through the foundation's website.

Irwell Valley Housing Association Fund
At the time of writing, no details were available for this fund and applicants should contact the foundation for up-to-date information.

Manchester Fund
This fund was launched on 1 March 2007 with the transfer of 70 previously dormant funds held by Manchester City Council.

The key aim of the fund is to encourage and support education and grassroot community activity in Manchester. To remain as true to the individual funds' original purposes as possible the fund now has a number of key priorities:

- support for young people and youth projects
- early years projects
- school based projects including health and healthy living
- support for young families and parents
- educational attainment projects including lifelong learning
- educational inclusion projects.

There are two categories of grants available:

- up to £250 for informal unconstituted groups
- up to £1,500 for groups with constitutions or rules of association.

The fund can support applications from either schools or small, community-based and locally controlled groups that manage themselves, encourage active participation from volunteers, have minimal cash reserves and limited access to funding support.

Sage Community Fund
Sage, a leading supplier of business management software, with an office in Salford Quays, gives an annual allocation for grantmaking in line with the Community Foundation's Small Grants Programme. The

company also engages their own employees in the fund, making decisions on applications as part of a grants panel. Grants of up to £2,500 are available to community groups and organisations from Greater Manchester. The fund has a focus on projects related to local employment, children and young people and ICT skills development.

Salford Community Fund
The Salford Community Fund has been created from 14 funds held in trust by Salford City Council which have, over time, become dormant. It aims to improve the lives of local Salford people and at the same time continue to meet the wider aim of the original donors, which is to benefit young people.

The fund's priorities relate to projects and activities that fall outside of statutory provision but encourage, support and promote education and meet one or more of the following priorities:

- support for young people and youth projects
- early years projects
- school based projects including health and healthy living
- support for young families and parents
- educational attainment projects including lifelong learning
- educational inclusion projects.

Priority will be given to projects that benefit individuals up to 25 years of age. There are two categories of grants available:

- up to £250 for informal unconstituted groups
- up to £1,500 for groups with constitutions or rules of association.

Small Grants Programme
The Community Foundation's Small Grants Programme invites applications from small, local grassroot community groups and projects working across Greater Manchester to improve the lives of people in their local communities. A great variety of projects ranging from small-scale events to longer-term activities can be supported as long as there is a clearly defined benefit for the local community. Funding is available for groups/projects benefiting communities within the ten boroughs of Greater Manchester.

Small community groups/projects are asked to provide a copy of their constitution or set of rules (if available), financial statements (if available) and a description of the project/activity they wish to run along with a thorough breakdown of costs. Applications from informal groups that do not have a constitution will also be considered.

Requests for grants up to £500 for genuine emergencies or time critical projects can be processed within 20 working days. This fast track process is in place to react swiftly to short term and time critical emergency

requests only. Applications up to £2,000 are submitted to a panel of independent panel members who make decisions on applications based on criteria of the Small Grants Programme.

Stockport Fund
The Stockport Fund aims to support the activities of local community or voluntary groups, projects or individuals that contribute positively to the quality of life and wellbeing of people and communities in the borough. Stockport metropolitan borough council and its partners have a vision for the borough, the community strategy, which forms the basis of the priority criteria for this funding.

Organisations, groups or individuals who would like to run projects, deliver services or activities which address any or all of the priorities listed below may be eligible to apply for funding:

- older people
- children and young people
- safer, stronger communities
- sustainable environment
- physical and economic regeneration.

Grants of up to £3,000 will be available to:

- pay for one off projects or events
- local or borough wide projects
- pay for minor start-up costs
- purchase equipment.

Applications for annual running costs for an organisation or service will be considered but please note that this does not include staff costs.

Trafford MBC Small Grants Fund
This fund aims to support local community groups, projects or individuals throughout the borough. Priority is given to applications whose projects/activities address the following themes:

- community cohesion including issues of race and disability
- lifelong learning including activities which improve access to employment
- health and well-being
- improving access to community and voluntary sports, arts and cultural activities
- sustainable neighbourhoods including environmental issues
- safety including crime and disorder
- improving transport to community facilities in cases of special enablement.

Grants of up to £2000 are available to applicants. Fast-track grants may be available if your application is up to £500 and of a time critical nature.
Further information on all of the above funds, and application forms, are available from the foundation's website.

Exclusions The foundation will not support the following:

- organisations and projects outside the Greater Manchester area
- organisations trading for profit or intending to redistribute grant awards
- major capital requests, such as building and construction work
- requests that will replace or enhance statutory provision
- academic or medical research and equipment
- overseas travel
- promotion of religious or political beliefs
- retrospective grants
- projects that fall within statutory sector responsibility
- sponsorship or fundraising events
- contributions to large/major appeals (where the application sum would not cover at least 75% of the total project cost)
- holidays and social outings (except in cases of specific disablement or proven benefit to a community or group of people)
- local branches of national charities unless locally managed, financially autonomous and not beneficiaries of national marketing or promotion
- more than one application at a time for the same project.

Applications The foundation's website provides full guidelines for each of the programmes for which organisations can apply. It also provides application and monitoring forms for each programme.

If you are applying for a grant for the first time, or if you would like advice before making an application, call the foundation on 0161 214 0940. Applications will only be accepted if submitted on the foundation's application form. All sections of the form must be completed even if the information is supplied in the form of a report, leaflet and so on. The foundation prefers not to receive applications by fax; completed forms should be returned by post. The decision of the foundation's trustees is final and no discussion will be entered into. The foundation will, however, try to provide helpful feedback to both successful and unsuccessful applicants.

Applicants are requested to provide copies of the organisation's constitution, and a copy of the latest, relevant annual accounts and the last two bank statements with their applications. Decisions are almost always given within three months but the exact time will often depend on a number of factors and not just when the appropriate committee next meets.

One of our grants administrators may contact you for further information or to discuss your application with you. The foundation operates a 24-hour grant line where application forms can be obtained at any time. The grant line telephone number is 0161 214 0951. Contact the foundation directly for up-to-date information on deadlines for programmes and the dates of panel meetings.

The Grocers' Charity

General

£1.2 million (2007/08)
Beneficial area UK.

Grocers' Hall, Princes Street, London EC2R 8AD

Tel. 020 7606 3113 **Fax** 020 7600 3082

Email anne@grocershall.co.uk

Website www.grocershall.co.uk

Correspondent Anne Blanchard, Charity Administrator

Trustee *Directors of The Grocers' Trust Company Ltd (about 30).*

CC Number 255230

Information available Annual accounts and an annual report with list of grants (for £1,000 or more), detailed narrative breakdown of grants/grantmaking and guidelines for applicants.

The Grocers' Charity was established in 1968, and has general charitable aims. It describes its work as follows in its 2007/08 accounts:

The charity has wide charitable aims, with education continuing to be a high priority. A significant proportion of the charity's expenditure is committed to this category in the form of internal scholarships and bursaries at schools and colleges with which the Grocers' Company has historic links.

The balance is spread across several areas of interest, namely medicine, relief of poverty (including youth), heritage, disability, the arts, churches, and older people.

Each year, the charity sets a budget that establishes expected income for the period and sets a target for the distribution of income and reserves through grants to charities. There is a broad categorisation of the nature of the budgeted grants, but this is advisory, and does not restrict the types of grant allocated. Once the overall financial parameters have been set, the policy on awarding grants is flexible, allowing due consideration of the worthiness of applications received from charities during the year. Over a period of time, this may result in different categories of need attracting a greater level of support, although there are certain charities to which the charity contributes on a regular basis. Amongst these, education continues to be a high priority and a significant proportion of the charity's expenditure is committed to this category in the form of scholarships and bursaries at schools and colleges with which the Grocers' Company has historic links. Donations to churches under the patronage of the Grocers' Company and payments to their respective Parochial Church Councils also feature annually.

The amounts awarded per grant vary considerably. Excluding the grants provided to institutions with which there is an historic connection, 175 grants were awarded in 2007/08 from a total of 977 applications received. Of these, thirty-six were for £1,000 or less and the remainder, with the exception of major grants, ranged between £1,500 and £30,500.

Major grants are awarded each year. This year the maximum budgeted amount was increased from £100,000 to £250,000. Each year a different area of charitable activity is chosen for major grant support, and every member of the company has the opportunity to nominate a charity. The nominations are then reviewed and a short-list produced. Charities on the short-list are invited to give a presentation to the Education and Charities Committee, after which the awards are decided. This year, the chosen areas were the Arts, Heritage and Medicine, including medical research. Five major grants were awarded, totalling £250,000; three to charities specialising in medicine, one to the Holburne Museum, for the development of its existing facilities, and one to St. Paul's Cathedral Foundation in support of the 300th Anniversary Restoration Campaign. This year the charity introduced a new initiative by providing £88,000 of matched funding to enable it to donate amounts equal to the sums raised for suitable charities by members of the company. The scheme was hugely successful with more than fifty charities benefiting.

Grantmaking in 2007/08

During the year the charity had assets of £11.4 million and an income of £1.6 million of which £1.3 million came as a gift from the Grocers' Company. Grants totalled £1.2 million and were summarised as follows:

Category	Value
Education	£313,000
Medicine	£258,000
Relief of poverty (including youth)	£178,000
Heritage	£134,000
Disability	£130,000
The arts	£83,000
Churches	£52,000
Older people and other	£38,000

Beneficiaries of grants of £1,000 or more are listed in the annual report and annual review. Some examples of recipients within each of the above categories are given below.

Education
A total of 27 donations were made in this category, including those to: Oundle School for bursaries (£83,000) and scholarships (£49,000); Ewell Castle School (£60,000); Mossbourne Community Academy (£15,000); the Elms – Colwall (£12,000); Reed's School (£6,500); City of London School for Boys (£6,000); the mansion House Scholarship Scheme and the Frank Longford Charitable Trust (£5,000 each); City of London School for Girls (£4,000); Royal College of Art (£3,000); and St Paul's Cathedral School (£2,000).

Medicine
There were 29 donations made in this category, including those to: Rheumatology Discretionary Fund UCL (£78,000); St Peter's Trust (£59,000); Breast Cancer Haven (£35,000); the Arena Trust, Cancer Vaccine Institute, Food for the Brain, LEPRA, Rockinghorse Appeal – Brighton and St Nicholas' Hospice – Bury St Edmunds (£5,000 each); Institute of Cancer Research (£4,000); Walk the Walk Worldwide (£2,300) and the Multiple Sclerosis Resource Centre (£1,500).

Relief of poverty (including youth)
There were 37 grants in this category, including those to: Trinity Sailing Trust (£31,000); Veterans Aid (£26,000); SSAFA (£10,000); VSO (£7,500); Childhood First, Children's Country Hospital Funds, Emmaus Hampshire, Quaker Social Action, St Mungo Community Housing Association, Tower Hamlets Mission, Training for Life and Youth Sport Trust (£5,000 each); Special Boat Service Association (£4,000); Bishop Creighton House Settlement (£3,000); and Toynbee Hall – Young Peoples and Families Project (£2,000).

Heritage
There were 19 donations made in this category, including those to: St Paul's Cathedral Foundation – major grant (£75,000) and fabric fund (£5,000); Canterbury Cathedral Development Ltd (£10,000); Fulham Palace Trust and Royal Artillery Museums (£5,000 each); Airborne Forces Museum (£3,000); the ADEPT Foundation, City of London Archaeological Trust and Stowe House Preservation Trust (£2,000 each).

Disability
There were 31 donations made in this category, including those to: Combat Stress and Help for Heroes (£11,000 each); Bedfordshire Garden Carers, Canine Partners for Independence, HemiHelp, Living Paintings Trust, the Meath Epilepsy Trust and the Royal Star and Garter Home (£5,000 each); the Elizabeth Foundation and Share Community Ltd (£4,000 each); Bromley by Bow Centre, City and Hackney Mind, Deafness Research UK, Disability Challengers, Queen Elizabeth's Foundation and Tower Hamlets Opportunity Group (£3,000 each); and the Cairn Trust and Whizz-Kidz (£2,500 each).

The arts
There were 18 donations made in this category, including those to: the Holburne Museum (£24,000); English National Ballet School, English National Opera and Polka Theatre – Wimbledon (£5,000 each); Arts for All (£3,500), City of London Choir and the Voices Foundation (£2,500 each); the Young Vic (£2,000); and Camberwell Choir School (£1,500).

Churches
There were 21 donations listed in this category, including those to: St Peter's – Ugborough (£7,000); St Mary-le-Bow – London (£5,000); All Hallows – Bromley by Bow (£3,000); All Saints – Crowborough (£2,500); and St Mary's – Bucknell, St Peter's – Dumbleton and St Stephen Walbrook – London (£2,000 each).

Older people and general
There were 12 grants made in this category, including those to: Cleanup UK and Hospital of the Blessed Trinity – Guildford (£5,000 each); Contact the Elderly (£4,500); Women's Institutes (£4,250); West London Centre for Counselling (£3,500); Charity Search (£2,000); and St Mary-le-Bow Churchwardens (£1,500).

Grant guidelines

- the charity will consider requests to support both capital and revenue projects
- it is usual practice for successful applicants to be advised that a further request for support will not be entertained until at least two years have elapsed from the date of the successful application
- unsuccessful applicants are advised that a further request will not be considered until at least one year has elapsed from the date of the relevant application
- donations are made by way of a single payment and are of a non-recurring nature (although occasionally a commitment to fund a project for a limited period will be agreed)
- public acknowledgement of the Charity's support is allowed, although it is preferred that it is undertaken in an unobtrusive manner.

Exclusions Only UK registered charities are supported. Individuals cannot receive grants directly, although grants can be given to organisations on their behalf. Support is rarely given to the following unless there is a specific or long-standing connection with the Grocers' Company:

- cathedrals, churches and other ecclesiastical bodies
- hospices
- schools and other educational establishments.

Applications Applications for grants can be considered from UK registered charities only and must comply with current guidelines, including restrictions, as detailed in the Grocers' Charity Annual Review and on the Grocers' Company website: www.grocershall.co.uk

- Applications should be made on a form available from the correspondent.
- The latest audited accounts of the applicant, together with its annual report should accompany the application.
- Applications, which may be submitted at any time of the year, are not acknowledged, but all receive notification of the outcome in due course. (This may take several months depending on the time of year when the application is submitted).
- The charity's financial year runs from 1 August to 31 July, and applications are considered at meetings held four times during that period – November (September), January (November), April (February) and June (May).

Please note: Applications for consideration in a given period must be received by the beginning of the month shown in brackets, for example applications for the November meeting must be received at latest by the beginning of September.

The M and R Gross Charities Limited

Jewish causes

£3.1 million (2007/08)

Beneficial area UK and overseas.

Cohen Arnold and Co., New Burlington House, 1075 Finchley Road, London NW11 0PU

Tel. 020 8731 0777 **Fax** 020 8731 0778

Correspondent Mrs Rivka Gross, Secretary

Trustees *Mrs Rifka Gross; Mrs Sarah Padwa; Michael Saberski.*

CC Number 251888

Information available Accounts were available from the Charity Commission.

This trust makes grants to educational and religious organisations within the orthodox Jewish community in the UK and overseas.

In 2007/08 the trust had assets of £26 million and an income of £9.1 million. Grants were made totalling £3.1 million. A list of recent beneficiaries was not included in the latest accounts.

Previous beneficiaries, many of whom are likely to be supported each year, include: Atlas Memorial Limited (£3 million); United Talmudical Associates Limited, a grant-making organisation which distributes smaller grants made by the trust (£1.3 million); Chevras Tsedokoh Limited (£530,000); Kolel Shomrei Hachomoth (£75,000); Telz Talmudical Academy & Talmud Torah Trust (£50,000 each); Gevurah Ari Torah Academy Trust (£40,000); Friends of Yeshivas Brisk (£30,000); Beis Ruchel Building Fund (£25,000); Beth Hamedresh Satmar Trust (£26,000); Kehal Chareidim Trust (£12,000); Daas Sholem (£10,000); Craven Walk Beis Hamedrash and Union of Orthodox Hebrew Congregations (£5,000 each); and Yetev Lev Jerusalem (£2,400).

Applications In writing to the organisation. Applications are assessed on a weekly basis and many of the smaller grants are dealt with through a grant-making agency, United Talmudical Associates Limited.

The Gulbenkian Foundation

Education, arts and welfare

£1.9 million (2007)

Beneficial area UK and the Republic of Ireland.

50 Hoxton Square, London N1 6PB

Tel. 020 7012 1400 **Fax** 020 7739 1961

Email info@gulbenkian.org.uk

Website www.gulbenkian.org.uk

Correspondent Andrew Barnett, Director

Trustee *The foundation's Board of Administration in Lisbon. UK resident trustee: Martin Essayan.*

Information available Comprehensive annual reports with full details of the foundation's thinking, policies and grants. The foundation also has an excellent website. As the foundation is not a charity registered in the UK there are no files at the Charity Commission.

Summary

The foundation is organised around programmes in four areas:

- cultural understanding
- fulfilling potential
- environment
- innovation.

In 2009 it undertook a strategic review of its activities which resulted in its Strategic Plan.

The foundation develops its own work, initiatives and partnerships, and is not generally open to applications, with the exception of its Innovation Fund.

Background

This is described as follows by the foundation:

Calouste Sarkis Gulbenkian was an Armenian born in 1869. He became a British citizen, conducted much of his work in Britain, and finally settled in Portugal. The Calouste Gulbenkian Foundation was established in 1956, a year after his death.

The headquarters of the foundation are in Lisbon and consist of the administration, which deals with grant-giving throughout the world, together with a museum housing the founder's art collections, a research library, a centre for scientific research, concert halls, indoor and open-air theatres, exhibition galleries and conference halls, a centre for modern art, a children's pavilion, an

orchestra, a choir and a ballet company. The foundation also maintains a Portuguese Cultural Centre in Paris, and a grant-giving branch in London for the United Kingdom and the Republic of Ireland [with which this entry is concerned.].

There is one resident trustee in London, but the UK branch operates with wide local discretion. However grants for more than £15,000 have to be referred back to Lisbon, a necessarily more complicated and time-consuming process.

General

In 2007 the UK branch of the foundation made 140 grants totalling almost £1.9 million, broken down as follows:

Category	Value
Arts	£683,000
Social Welfare	£573,000
Education	£498,000
Anglo-Portuguese Cultural Relations	£141,000
Total	**£1,890,000**

The foundation is well known for the comprehensive accounts of its grantmaking in its excellent annual reports. Reproduced here is part of the director, Andrew Barnett's first preface to the foundation's accounts, which describe the foundation's attitude and approach.

There's scarcely an organisation I can think of that doesn't have to manage their accounts – whether the organisation is in the private sector, providing products and generating sales income, in the public sector, delivering services and raising taxes, or in the voluntary sector, raising funds through donations or grants to achieve the beneficial goals they set themselves.

Though, of course, we have to operate within our means, we are in a privileged position in having access to funds that we do not need to generate. This affords us immense freedom of action but carries with it a responsibility to make the most of our legacy and to work in a genuine spirit of collaboration with our partners and grantees. Our independence and the involving way in which we work are just two aspects of the ethos that distinguishes the Gulbenkian story.

It's a privilege to get to tell that story, and to help shape future accounts. However, the credit for the past year's achievements is owed to my predecessor, Paula Ridley, and the expert staff she nurtured during her eight years as director, as well as to our 'overseeing' Trustee, Martin Essayan, to whom our Lisbon-based board has delegated much of the governance of the UK Branch. All have played a part in ensuring the vitality and continued reputation of an organisation said by many 'to punch above its weight'.

The Challenge Ahead

The quality of the people – their passion, their skills and experience – is just one of the ingredients of that success. The critical work is that done by our grantees and partners, diligently working on the front line to produce some of the excellent outcomes [...].

But I do not see our role purely as one of grantmaking. Rather, I see it as having a wider purpose: working with others to enrich and broaden the lives of individuals through exploration and experimentation, through exchanging ideas, and by explaining them to those who can make a difference. A focus on improving life experiences allows us to bring together our potentially disparate cultural, educational and social change interests; and renewed clarity of purpose is essential in an environment with more challenges, though at the same time more opportunities, than perhaps we have faced in our previous 53 years of existence.

We experience a more involved government, who have invested significantly in the arts and education; and there is a genuine interest across the political spectrum in addressing social ills and providing wider access to the fruits of economic success. We benefit too, as a society, from a more competitive environment for ideas than in the past, with more think-tanks, policy institutes, and many more charitable foundations dispersing increasingly large sums of money.

The issues also change: with increasing numbers of older people; more widespread substance abuse and mental health problems; a plateauing of educational attainment accompanied sometimes by poor behaviour in schools; unprecedented levels of migration; and a fracturing of the bonds that traditionally held families and communities together. These are all problems that are prevalent across Europe and in other countries from which we should be prepared to learn.

That provides a unique opportunity for a charitable foundation with such strong European roots. Our founder, Calouste Gulbenkian, spent much of his life in London, Paris and Lisbon, and was rightly proud of his Armenian heritage. So, it is no coincidence that the foundation finds its operations spread across Portugal, France and the UK, and with interests in many other parts of the world which make it one of the few truly international foundations.

Open Programme

The foundation now has just one programme which is open to applications.

Innovation Fund

In 2009 we are introducing a new fund to support genuinely innovative ideas and unusual partnerships across our cultural, educational and social interests. **This is now the only funding stream open to applications.**

Guidelines

- Not-for-profit organisations can apply for R&D funding to scope a new idea which enables them to work together with other organisations or experts **outside their usual practice**, or to enable them to undertake active research into areas they would not normally have the time or money to explore. This fund is not open to individuals.
- We particularly welcome ideas that take the perspective of people at the receiving end of activities or services, whether as audiences, participants or clients.
- We are also looking for ideas that demonstrate a cross-sectoral approach.
- If projects are specifically local they must be of a kind that have not been implemented elsewhere and which can set a precedent for emulation in other places, or serve as a national pilot.
- Although the host applicant and prime beneficiaries should be resident in the UK or Republic of Ireland, we are also interested in proposals that may involve European partners or that emulate good practice in other countries.
- Although we may occasionally give funding for projects that are developed as a result of an Innovation grant, we stress that we do not guarantee continued support.
- The funds available for Innovation Grants are modest in scale and **competition is likely to be strong**.
- As a guide, it is expected that grants will average between £10,000 and £25,000.

Exclusions The UK Branch of the foundation gives grants only for proposals of a charitable kind, from registered charities or similar not-for-profit organisations. It does not fund individuals. It deals only with grant applications from organisations in the UK and the Republic of Ireland and only with projects which benefit people in these countries.

Please note we do not give grants for:

- housing or the purchase, construction, repair or furnishing of buildings
- equipment, including vehicles, IT, or musical instruments

- student grants or the education, training fees, maintenance or medical costs of individual applicants
- establishing funds for scholarships or loans
- teaching or research posts or visiting fellowships
- support for gap year activities
- commercial publications
- festivals
- UK cultural or other work in Portugal
- scientific research
- medicine or related therapies
- religious activities
- sports
- holidays of any sort
- animal welfare.

We never make loans or retrospective grants, nor help to pay off deficits or loans, nor can we remedy the withdrawal or reduction of statutory funding.

We do not give grants in response to any large capital, endowment or widely distributed appeal.

Applications
Innovation Fund *only*
How and when to apply
Outline ideas should be submitted by email using the Initial Enquiry Form, available from the foundation's website. Initial Enquiries can be sent in at any time of the year, but you should allow at least three months between this and the proposed starting date of your research period. Initial Enquiries will be assessed in the context of other applications and, if short-listed, fuller information will be requested and applicants invited to discuss their project with us. We will specify the additional information we need and the date we require it by. After completion of this stage, final applications will be considered at one of our three annual Trustee Meetings.

Please email the completed Initial Enquiry Form to: info@gulbenkian.org.uk

H C D Memorial Fund

Health, education, environment and community action

£436,000 to organisations in the UK (2007/08)

Beneficial area Worldwide.

Knowlands Farm Granary, Barcombe, Lewes BN8 5EF

Correspondent Harriet Lear, Secretary

CC Number 1044956

Information available Accounts were available from the Charity Commission.

The trust was established in 1995 for general charitable purposes and principally makes grants to organisations in the UK and abroad engaged in the fields of health, education, environment and community action.

The grants policy is to make grants as determined by the trustees at twice-yearly meetings. The policy is flexible as regards to donees, but currently:

- maintains a balance between home and overseas grants
- directs grants mainly towards
  - the relief of human need, whether due to poverty, ill-health, disability, want of education, or other causes
  - projects which aim to mitigate the effects of climate change
- prefers projects which are small or medium-sized
- permits the taking of risks in an appropriate case.

During 2007/08 the trust made grants to a variety of charitable organisations. The organisations concerned support medical work, poverty relief work and education in Africa, Central and South America, India, Pakistan and Laos; and help for refugees and prisoners and other social and educational work in the United Kingdom and Republic of Ireland. Environmental projects, particularly in relation to climate change, have also received considerable support.

In this financial year the trust had assets of £707,000 and an income of £959,000. Grants were made to 34 organisations totalling £754,000. Grants ranged from £3,000 to £70,000; most are for amounts between £10,000 and £20,000.

Organisations operating overseas – 15 grants totalling £318,000
Beneficiaries included: San Carlos Hospital – Mexico, for health purposes (£66,000); Impact Foundation – Asia and Africa, for health (£40,000); Practical Action – Peru and Nepal, for development (£30,000); Angels International – Malawi, for health (£23,000); CAFOD – Ethiopia, for health (£20,000); Tanzania Development Trust – Tanzania, for education (£16,000); and Mpora Orphanage Fund – Uganda, for education (£3,000).

Organisations operating in the UK – 19 grants totalling £436,000
Beneficiaries included: St Nicholas Church – Bristol, for community

purposes (£70,000); Woodland Trust, for environmental purposes (£50,000); Operation Noah, for climate change (£40,000); Newhaven Community Development Association, for people with disabilities (£30,000); Refugee Support Group Devon, for refugees (£20,000); Turntable Furniture, for community purposes (£15,000); Country Trust, for environment and education (£10,000); and Meath Epilepsy Trust, for health (£5,000).

Exclusions The following are unlikely to be supported:

- evangelism or missionary work
- individuals
- nationwide emergency appeals
- animal charities.

Applications In writing to the correspondent, although please note that the trust has a preference for seeking out its own projects and only very rarely responds to general appeals.

'Unsolicited applications are not encouraged. They are acknowledged, but extremely rarely receive a positive response. No telephone enquiries, please.'

The Hadley Trust

Social welfare

£2.3 million (2007/08)
Beneficial area UK, especially London.

Gladsmuir, Hadley Common, Barnet EN5 5QE

Tel. 020 8447 4577 **Fax** 020 8447 4571

Email carol@hadleytrust.org

Correspondent Carol Biggs, Trust Administrator

CC Number 1064823

Information available Annual report and accounts were available from the Charity Commission, without a full grants list.

The trust was established in 1997 for welfare purposes. In 2007/08 it had assets worth £69 million and an income of £4 million. Grants were made to 64 organisations totalling £2.3 million.

The trustees' approach is to further the trust's objects by engaging with and making grants to other registered charities. In general, the trustees prefer to work with

small to medium-sized charities and establish the trust as a reliable, long-term funding partner.

Over the last few years the trust has become increasingly focused on some core areas of activity where the trustees feel the trust is able to have the greatest impact. Consequently the trust has tended to establish more in-depth relationships with a smaller number of selected partners.

The result of this policy is that the trust does not take on many new funding commitments. Nevertheless the trustees will always consider and respond to proposals which might enhance the effectiveness of the trust.

Grantmaking in 2007/08

Grants were broken down in the following categories during the year. The trust also provides further information about grantmaking within several categories, and a brief analysis of its relationship with the five largest recipients of grants during the year, although how much each received is not stated.

Category	%	Value
Social investment	31.3	£711,000
Young people	18.7	£425,000
Crime and justice	15.2	£345,000
Medical	12.6	£286,000
International	11	£250,000
Disability	5.8	£132,000
Hospices	3.7	£84,000
Other	1.7	£39,000

The social investment category includes a substantial amount of research and policy work carried out with partner organisations. The trust's involvement with charities working with young people is focused on adoption and fostering policy and practice, looked-after children and young people at risk. Crime and justice related activities include research and policy work together with funding of support for prisoners including advice and information, education and rehabilitation services. The proportion of funds devoted to medical charities was larger than in prior years due to one unusually large investment (see below). In the international arena, the trust supported several large international aid agencies and also funded research into transferable technology here in the UK.

New Economics Foundation
The trust has been engaged with New Economics Foundation (NEF) for a number of years on a programme of work on Social Return on Investment. The early phases of this work, which emphasised the application of SROI to social enterprises, were well received and gained a momentum of their own. In the last three years the trust and NEF have pressed ahead to use the ideas to inform other areas of policy. The programme is called 'Measuring what Matters' and addresses four main policy areas. These are:

Enterprise-led Regeneration; Community Development Finance; Alternatives to Imprisonment for Women; and Residential Care for Children.

Second Chance

Second Chance works with disadvantaged young people in the Portsmouth area. The charity exposes the youngsters to various stimulating outdoor experiences. The Hadley Trust has provided modest levels of support to the charity over a number of years. However, each year the trust is typically able to make a more substantial contribution to assist one of our partner organisations with infrastructure/capacity-building projects. In the last financial year one of the recipients was Second Chance who were able to purchase their own land and fishing lakes close to Portsmouth.

Prison Reform Trust

The Hadley Trust has been a long-term funder of the Prison Reform Trust's advice and information service. Besides providing an invaluable service to prisoners and their families the work provides important input to PRT's policy and lobbying activity.

Policy Exchange

The trust has continued to increase its involvement in policy work and its developing relationship with the think-tank Policy Exchange is part of this. Recent policy projects have included work on regeneration, mental health in prisons, gun crime and the welfare system.

British Urological Foundation

This funding is focused on training surgeons in the latest robotic techniques so that they are able to use new robotic equipment for surgical procedures. The trust has also continued its support for BUF's medical research programme through the 'Hadley Fellowships'.

Applications In writing to the correspondent.

Paul Hamlyn Foundation

Arts, education and learning in the UK and local organisations supporting vulnerable groups of people, especially children, in India and social justice

£13.4 million (2008/09)
Beneficial area UK and India.

18 Queen Anne's Gate, London SW1H 9AA

Tel. 020 7227 3500 **Fax** 020 7222 0601

Email information@phf.org.uk

Website www.phf.org.uk

Correspondent Tony Davey, Information and Resources Officer

Trustees *Jane Hamlyn, Chair; Michael Hamlyn; Robert Boas; James Lingwood; Baroness Estelle Morris; Claus Moser; Anthony Salz; Peter Wilson-Smith; Tom Wylie.*

CC Number 1102927

Information available Accounts were available at the Charity Commission. Detailed information is also available on the foundation's helpful website.

Paul Hamlyn was a publisher and philanthropist. He established the Paul Hamlyn Foundation in 1987 for general charitable purposes and on his death in 2001 he bequeathed the majority of his estate to the foundation so that it became one of the UK's largest independent grant-giving organisations. He was committed to opening new opportunities and experiences for the less fortunate members of society.

The following is taken from the foundation's website:

The foundation is one of the larger independent grant-making foundations in the UK. Grants are made to organisations which aim to maximise opportunities for individuals to experience a full quality of life, both now and in the future. In particular it is concerned with children and young people, and others who are disadvantaged. Preference is given to supporting work which others may find hard to fund, perhaps because it breaks new ground, is too risky or is unpopular. Initiatives are established by the foundation where new thinking is required or where it is believed there are important unexplored opportunities.

Below are the values that underpin the Paul Hamlyn Foundation in how it operates as an independent grant-making foundation. They very much mirror the values of the founder. He believed there was a 'better way', that way being 'a society that is fair, allows people to realise their potential, fights prejudice, encourages and assists participation in and enjoyment of the arts and learning, and understands the importance of the quality of life for all communities'.

- strategic – wanting to make changes to policy and opinion
- enabling – giving opportunities and realising potential
- courageous – fighting prejudice and taking risks

- focussed and flexible – through targeted and open grants schemes
- supportive – giving advice to applicants who need help
- fair – clear application processes, equality of opportunity
- value for money – controlling costs and expecting money to be well used.

The foundation states that it will: continue to support organisations which have a constructive influence on the law and public policy affecting grant-making charities, argue for proportionate regulation and accountability of charities, share our experiences with other grantmakers, learn from other grant makers and organisations with similar values, and encourage philanthropy. We will, where possible, influence policy, legislation and change public opinion in our desire to find a better way. We will also support charitable organisations by developing and sharing knowledge about the most effective way of helping people and communities reach their potential and have a better quality of life.

The funding programmes are: arts; education and learning; and social justice. The foundation also works in India supporting vulnerable groups of people, especially children.

The foundation's strategic aims up to 2012 are:

1) Enabling people to experience and enjoy the arts.
2) Developing people's education and learning.
3) Integrating marginalised young people who are at times of transition.

In addition, we have three related aims:

- Advancing through research into the understanding of the relationships between the arts, education and learning and social change.
- Developing the capacity of organisations and people who facilitate our strategic aims.
- Developing the foundation itself to be an exemplar foundation, existing in perpetuity.

Grantmaking in 2008/09

In 2008/09 the foundation had assets of £466.3 million and an income of £17.4 million. Grants were made totalling £13.4 million, broken down in each area of interest as follows:

Category	Value
Arts	£4,420,000
Education and learning	£3,410,000
Social justice	£3,040,000
India	£453,000
Other grants	£2,100,000

The annual report gives an insight into the foundation's objectives in each area, summarised here along with a selection of beneficiaries.

Arts programme

This programme is primarily aimed at increasing people's experience, enjoyment and involvement in the arts, with a particular focus on young people.

We support organisations and groups through our open grants scheme, concentrating on work that is transformational at three levels: for the participants, for the funded organisations themselves and, more generally, for the sector in which they operate. We also give grants to talented individuals through our Special Initiatives: the Awards for Artists, JADE Fellowships and Breakthrough Fund.

This year has enabled the Arts programme to consolidate both the Breakthrough Fund and the extension of our Awards for Artists to composers. We also strengthened the analysis of our Open Grants in terms of public outcomes and impact, while continuing to research new possible Special Initiatives.

Beneficiaries included: Unicorn Theatre (£295,000 over three years), to underpin the creation of an ensemble of actors for young audiences; Sistema Scotland (£234,000), core support over two years to grow children's orchestras in Raploch, on the outskirts of Stirling; B arts (£160,000), towards a three-year programme of workshops and training for individuals within culturally isolated communities in north Staffordshire, empowering these 'Barefoot Doctors' to deliver arts projects in their local communities; Synergy Theatre Project (£130,000), for funding towards Synergy's new writing programme to develop prisoners' and ex-offenders' playwriting skills to raise awareness about issues surrounding criminal justice; Sing London (£74,000 over three years), for organisational development; People United (£30,000), core support to underpin the salary of the founder and director; Tête-à-Tête Productions Ltd (£5,000), for series of initiatives to support the artists taking part in the 2008 Tête-à-Tête summer festival at Riverside Studios, enabling them to share feedback and attend each other's performances and events.

Education and Learning programme

This programme has a strong focus on supporting innovation and aims to achieve significant impact, ideally at a national level, across a range of education themes. Our work fosters the development and sharing of new practice, experiences and learning between and within schools, local authorities and voluntary organisations.

This year has seen significant developments across the Education and Learning programme as a number of new ideas for Special Initiatives have crystallised and moved from research and scoping work into implementation phases.

Beneficiaries included: I CAN (£300,000), to support the development phase of a national initiative; Mobex Network Limited (£165,000), for a year-long alternative education programme delivered in four UK locations in close partnership with schools, that aims to turn 'cycles of failure into cycles of success'; Amana (£141,000), towards a programme that aims to improve the quality of educational support and provision for Black and Minority Ethnic (BME) young people, particularly those from the Somali community; Learning Futures (£128,000), towards developing new teaching and learning practices in schools; Brook Street Childcare (£80,000), funding for teacher and assistant to scale-up a successful pilot of a Nurture Group at Brook Street Primary School; South Warwickshire Carers Support Service (£39,000), for the Educational Support Project to work with young carers in education whose caring responsibilities at home lead to educational underachievement, truancy and exclusion; and Learning Away (£34,000), towards school residentials.

Social Justice programme

This programme is concerned about social justice for young people living in the margins of society, particularly those groups who are most disadvantaged and making critical transitions in their lives.

These young people include groups such as, asylum seekers, refugees and migrants facing multiple barriers to integration, young offenders leaving prison, young people at risk of offending, those struggling with mental ill-health, victims of violence and abuse, and those with complex needs, including disability. For many, social injustice means they are not regarded as equal citizens and struggle to access resources to meet basic needs. Often their views are not fully taken into account in decision making that affects their lives, and public perceptions of them lead to stigma and caricature. At this time of economic recession, our concern is with those who are most vulnerable who suffer the most, and our commitment is to support work that helps those who may have no-one to turn to for help – even when that work is risky.

Beneficiaries included: Dance United (£200,000), for support for the Artistic Management Team in order for it to focus on new areas of work. This will include creating new work through partnerships with organisations in the social exclusion sector; Levenmouth YMCA (£150,000), for an initiative tackling anti-social behaviour, delivering changes of behaviour and attitude through positive young person centred activities; Citizenship Foundation (£120,000), to bring together local young asylum seekers/refugee groups and youth groups involving established residents, in order to empower them to jointly engage in positive community action; National Children's Bureau (£89,000), to explore and record the views of children and young people in Northern Ireland, especially marginalised children, to ensure these are heard and taken seriously; and Shetland Arts Development Agency (£7,500), for a restorative arts project with marginalised young people who have been referred to the Community Mediation Team due to interpersonal difficulties.

Exclusions In the UK the foundation does not support:

- individuals or proposals for the benefit of one individual
- funding for work that has already started
- general circulars/appeals
- proposals about property or which are mainly about equipment or other capital items
- overseas travel, expeditions, adventure and residential courses
- promotion of religion
- animal welfare
- medical/health/residential or day care
- proposals from organisations outside the UK, except under our India programme
- proposals that benefit people living outside the UK, except under our India programme.

The foundation is unlikely to support:

- endowments
- organisations to use their funding to make grants
- websites, publications or seminars unless part of a wider proposal.

In India, the foundation does not support:

- individuals or proposals for the benefit of one individual
- retrospective funding (for work that has already started)
- general circulars/appeals
- proposals that solely concentrate on the purchasing of property, equipment or other capital items
- overseas activities, including travel, expeditions, adventure and residential courses.

Applications The foundation's guidance on its application procedure is particularly detailed and helpful:

Applicants should submit an application using the outline application form which can be completed online. It will be acknowledged automatically by email.

You will hear from us within four weeks whether or not we accept your outline application and wish to take it forward.

If we accept your outline application, a member of our staff will contact you to progress your proposal.

You will normally be asked to send further details about the proposed work which should include the following information – in this order and up to a maximum of eight pages in total:

- what do you aim to achieve? (please describe in approx 50 words)
- how will you achieve your aim(s)? (please describe in approx 50 words)
- how your specific objectives link with the aims of the scheme to which you are applying
- job description (if you are applying for funding for a post)
- anticipated problems and how you will address them
- start date and length of work
- who will undertake the work?
- number of beneficiaries
- total budget for this work
- exact breakdown of how PHF money would be spent
- other funders/fundraising
- monitoring and evaluation plans
- dissemination strategy
- sustainability/future funding
- independent referee
- appropriate letters of support.

Please ensure that the above information reaches us by email. You can send any additional supporting information by post if necessary.

In addition to the details requested above, we would also like you to send us:

- an annual report and audited financial statements or equivalent (ideally electronically)
- name of your organisation's Chief Executive or equivalent.

We will then assess your application. This may involve correspondence and meetings between our staff and your representatives, and may also include consultation with our trustees, advisers and independent referees.

We will normally complete the assessment within two to three months of receiving the further details as listed above. The assessed proposal will then go to a decision making meeting.

Applications for up to £10,000 are normally considered by staff.

Applications over £10,000 and up to £150,000 are normally considered by the relevant programme committee.

Applications for over £150,000, or applications which are novel or potentially contentious, are considered first by the relevant programme committee and then by the full board of trustees.

The programme committees and the full board of trustees meet four times a year. We do not publish meeting dates.

Please allow six months between making an outline application and the start date for the work you propose to carry out with our funding, or longer if the proposal is particularly large or complex.

We will not consider applications from organisations outside the UK, or applications to help people who live outside the UK. This does not apply to our India programme.

The Helen Hamlyn Trust

Medical, the arts and culture, education and welfare, heritage and conservation in India, international humanitarian affairs and 'healthy ageing'

£4.1 million (2008/09)

Beneficial area Worldwide.

129 Old Church Street, London SW3 6EB

Tel. 020 7351 5057 **Fax** 020 7352 3284

Email andrew.gray@helenhamlyntrust.org

Correspondent Andrew P Gray, Trust Administrator and Secretary

Trustees Lady Hamlyn; Dr Kate Gavron; Dr Shobita Punja; Brendan Cahill; Margaret O'Rorke; Anthony Edwards; Dr Deborah Swallow; Mark Bolland.

CC Number 1084839

Information available Accounts were available from the Charity Commission.

Registered with the Charity Commission in January 2001, in April 2002 the assets and activities of the Helen Hamlyn 1989 Foundation were transferred into this trust.

The trust has wide powers to make grants. The trustees bring forward recommendations for projects to support and these recommendations are subject to approval by the board.

The current strategy for grantmaking is concentrated on the following areas of activity: medical, the arts and culture, education and welfare, heritage and conservation in India, international humanitarian affairs and healthy ageing. Within these areas of activity the trust also supports a number of projects with a design focus which are undertaken by the Helen Hamlyn Research Centre at the Royal College of Art, London.

Additionally, small grants of up to £10,000 are made to a wide variety of small charities in the fields of education and welfare, the arts and culture and, especially, healthy ageing.

The trust's core aim is to initiate and support innovative medium to long-term projects, which will effect lasting change and improve quality of life.

Individual projects aim to:

- encourage innovation in the medical arena
- increase access to the arts and support the professional development of artists from the fields of music and the performing arts
- increase intercultural understanding, provide opportunities for young people to develop new interests and practical skills which will contribute to their education and their future lives and to create opportunities for young offenders to acquire practical skills which will support their personal development for their future lives
- conserve heritage in India
- improve international relations
- provide practical support to enable older people to maintain their independence for as long as possible.

In 2008/09 it had assets of £4.26 million and an income of £3.16 million, mainly from donations. Grants were made totalling almost £4.1 million. Grants were broken down into the following categories, shown here with examples of beneficiaries:

Education and welfare – £2.6 million
The largest grant during the year was £2 million over 5 years to the Helen Hamlyn Centre at the Royal College of Art for the Chair of Design:

The focus of the Chair is to provide intellectual leadership in the delivery of research-based programmes in order to advance the Centre's activities in three core research areas: inclusive design, design for patient safety and workplace design. The key

173

objective is to manage the 'bridge' between academic enquiry and knowledge transfer to business and industry to ensure that research leads to practical outcomes to enhance quality of life. The Chair is designed to build upon the achievements of the Centre over the past nine years in transforming design into practical innovation across a broad spectrum of applications for the benefit of a wide cross-section of the public both in the UK and internationally. The Helen Hamlyn Centre was endowed by the Trust's predecessor, The Helen Hamlyn Foundation, with an award of £3 million in 2002.

Other beneficiaries included: Design Dimension Educational Trust (£210,500); Royal Horticultural Society (£196,000 in total); The Butler Trust (£40,600); DEMOS – Capabilities Programme (£15,000); and Barton Training Trust (£5,600).

Arts and culture – £815,500
Beneficiaries included: The Royal Opera House (£594,000 in total); London Symphony Orchestra (£131,000); Southbank Centre – Royal Festival Hall (£35,000); Sanskriti Pratishthan – India (£2,600).

International humanitarian affairs – £380,000
The beneficiary in the category was the Institute of International Humanitarian Affairs, Fordham University, New York, which received grants for the Senior Fellow (£330,000) and negotiation training (£50,000).

Medical – £250,000
The beneficiaries were: Fight for Sight (£240,000); Association Le Sothiou – West Africa (£5,000); DEMAND (£4,300); and World Cancer Research Fund (£1,000).

Heritage and conservation in India – £27,000
The beneficiaries were: Indian National Trust for Conservation and Heritage (£11,000 in total); Mehrangarh Museum Trust (£10,600); and Shanu Exports (£5,400).

Healthy ageing – £24,500
The beneficiaries were: Volunteer Reading Help (£9,600); Herriot Hospice Homecare (£8,000); St Wilfred's Care Home (£6,000); and Oakley Rural Day Care Centre (£1,000).

Applications
'The trustees bring forward recommendations for projects to support.'

Hampton Fuel Allotment Charity

Relief in need, health, education of children and young people and social welfare
£1.1 million awarded to organisations (2007/08)

Beneficial area Hampton, the former borough of Twickenham, and the borough of Richmond (in that order).

15 High Street, Hampton, Middlesex TW12 2SA

Tel. 020 8941 7866 **Fax** 020 8979 5555

Email info@hamptonfuelcharity.co.uk

Website www.hfac.co.uk

Correspondent M J Ryder, Clerk

Trustees *Reverend D N Winterburn, Chair; R Ellis; G Hunter; Mrs M T Martin; J Mortimer; Dr J Young; Reverend G Clarkson; S Leamy; J Cardy; D Cornwell; D Parish.*

CC Number 211756

Information available Accounts were available at the Charity Commission. The trust also has a useful website.

The trust was created following the 1811 Enclosure Act by the granting of 10.14 acres of land for producing a supply of fuel for the poor of the ancient parish of Hampton. Subsequently the land was rented out for nurseries. In 1988 the land was sold for development and the sale proceeds formed the financial base for the current work of the trust.

Historically, the trust's area of benefit was the ancient town of Hampton, now the area covered by the parishes of St Mary's Hampton, All Saints Hampton and St James's Hampton Hill. In 1989 the area was widened so that where the trust's income was not required in the ancient town of Hampton, help could be provided elsewhere in the London borough of Richmond upon Thames. The current priority area after the ancient town of Hampton, is the remainder of the former borough of Twickenham and then the remainder of the present Richmond upon Thames. Grants to individuals are restricted to the first two areas.

As the name of the trust suggests, its original purpose was to make grants of fuel to those in poverty. The trust has continued to fulfil its original purpose, while assuming many other roles and tasks.

The objects of the trust are:

- the relief of need, hardship or distress of those within the area of benefit
- support for those who are sick, convalescent, have disabilities or who are infirm
- promoting the education of children and young people
- provision and support for recreation and other leisure-time occupations in order to improve the conditions of life in the interests of social welfare.

In 2007/08 the trust had assets of around £39 million and an income of £2 million. Grants were made totalling nearly £1.8 million, of which £1.1 million was given to organisations and the remaining £662,000 was awarded to individuals.

Grantmaking

The trust's income is allocated within the broad headings of:

- general medical support which will benefit those in the area of benefit
- organisations assisting people with disabilities
- organisations which support social or medical welfare needs
- organisations engaged in social welfare including older people, young people, recreation and leisure
- organisations providing housing for those in need
- organisations providing additional educational support
- organisations engaged in community activities.

The trust funds the following:

- individuals, their social welfare and individual support
- young people, through youth training organisations and clubs
- education, through nurseries, play groups, schools and colleges
- the community, through community based organisations
- people with disabilities, as individuals and through disability organisations
- older people, through older people's welfare organisations and clubs
- housing, through housing associations and trusts
- caring for the sick, through hospitals and hospices
- recreation and leisure, through social and sporting clubs.

Grants were broken down as follows (including a description of the charity's objectives within each category, taken from its website):

People with disabilities – grants totalling £313,000

A central aim of the trust is to support people with disabilities, either physical or mental. In order to meet this aim, the trust gives both direct help to individuals and support to a wide range of organisations. These organisations usually focus on a particular disability or in some cases provide specialist homes for their clients. The type of help also varies enormously, from providing transport or creating an art exhibition to arranging holidays and offering translation services.

Beneficiaries included: Richmond Fellowship Foundation International (£60,000); St John Ambulance – Teddington, Hampton and Parkfields Division (£50,000); Richmond Borough Association for Mental Health (£25,000); Alzheimer's Society South West London Branch (£15,000); Whitton Network (£9,000); Kingston Advocacy Group (£6,000); Cancer Resource Centre (£4,000); and Richmond Macular Disease Support Group (£300).

Community – grants totalling £231,000

The trust acknowledges the importance of communities and community groups which it supports. The trust recognises a real lack of good quality facilities from which they can operate effectively. The trust is addressing this by funding the construction of the White House Community Association and refurbishing a variety of church halls. To ensure a maximum use of these venues it has helped improve kitchen facilities to meet changes in health and safety regulations.

Beneficiaries included: Richmond Citizens Advice Bureaux Service (£55,000); White House Community Association (£35,000); Duke Street Church – Richmond (£20,000); Linden Hall Day Centre (£15,000); Online Communities Limited (£10,000); Richmond and Kingston Accessible Transport (£7,700); Environment Trust for Richmond upon Thames (£5,500); and Vietnamese Community Association in South West London (£1,800).

Education – grants totalling £128,000

One of the trust's primary aims is to advance the education of young people in need of financial assistance, however, they are aware that funding must not replace statutory funding. During the last ten years, every state school in Hampton, Twickenham and Teddington has received support from the trust. Back when computers were rare and expensive, some schools were assisted with their purchase. More recently, a number of grants have been given for environmental improvements to school grounds and play areas.

Beneficiaries included: London Borough Richmond upon Thames, Early Years and Childcare (£45,000); London Borough Richmond upon Thames, Schools Targeted Assistance (£35,000); Richmond Music Trust (£20,000); Museum of Richmond (£6,500); Richmond Avicenna Supplementary School (£3,000); and Young Scientists Event – Richmond (£1,000).

Young people – grants totalling £101,000

Youth organisations play a vital role in developing the social skills, character and self-esteem of our young people. Mindful of this fact, our trustees have endeavoured to support a wide range of youth organisations across the borough. These include everything from the traditional scout and guide movements to various community groups and skills training projects.

Beneficiaries included: Richmond Youth Partnership (£40,000); Hearts of Teddlothian Football Club and Crossway Pregnancy Crisis Centre (£10,000 each); Richmond Junior Chess Club (£3,500); 2 x 2 Opera (£1,400); Thames Explorer Trust (£840); Artfelt Theatre Company (£600).

Recreation and leisure – grants totalling £85,000

The trust has been able to support a wide range of activities, often with modest sums so that people can come together and enjoy common interests. Grants have been used to either attract and train people in a particular activity, or to provide better equipment to improve the quality of an activity.

Beneficiaries included: Twickenham Cricket Club (£20,000); Twickenham and Thames Valley Bee-Keepers' Association (£15,000); Orange Tree Theatre (£10,000); Briar Road Allotment Holders Association (£5,000); and Richmond upon Thames Art Council (£1,000).

Older people – grants totalling £73,000

The trust supports a wide variety of organisations and has tried to ensure that older people living on limited means or suffering from infirmity have been able to get out and about, socialise and have as active a life as possible.

Beneficiaries included: Age Concern – Richmond upon Thames (£49,000); Elleray Hall Day Centre – Teddington Old People's Welfare Association (£11,000); WRVS Hampton Darby and Joan Club (£7,300); Tangley Hall Intensive Day Care Centre (£1,900); and Churches Together in Teddington (£450).

Hospitals and hospices – grants totalling £70,000

Helping to care for the sick, convalescent or infirm has been a principal role of the trust since its inception in 1811. Over the past ten years it has provided a number of grants to hospitals and hospices, some of which are outside our benefit area but treat patients from within it.

Beneficiaries were: Shooting Star Children's Hospice (£35,000); Mulberry Centre – West Middlesex Hospital (£20,000); and Princess Alice Hospice (£15,000).

Housing – grant totalling £18,000

In many ways a natural extension of work already undertaken, the trust has contributed to various housing schemes for people with special needs, working with housing specialists, such as Central and Cecil Housing Trust and Richmond Upon Thames Churches Housing Trust. Although the need for specialist housing is far greater than can be met by the trust, a positive contribution is being made, improving the quality of life for occupants and, in some cases, offering peace of mind to carers.

The sole beneficiary during the year was the Hampton War Memorial Charity (£18,000).

Other – grants totalling £79,000

Beneficiaries included: SPEAR (£30,000); Addiction Support and Care Agency (£11,000); Home-Start Richmond upon Thames (£8,000); Cruse Bereavement Care (£3,000); and Mediation in Divorce (£2,000).

Exclusions The charity is unlikely to support:

- grants to individuals for private and post-compulsory education
- adaptations or building alterations for individuals
- holidays, except in cases of severe medical need
- decoration, carpeting or central heating
- anything which is the responsibility of a statutory body
- national general charitable appeals
- animal welfare
- advancement of religion or religious groups, unless offering a non-religious service to the community
- commercial and business activities
- endowment appeals
- projects of a political nature
- retrospective capital grants.

For the present grants for major 'one-off' projects are limited, generally to £30,000. Applicants are advised to contact the clerk prior to formally submitting such applications.

The trustees are reluctant to support ongoing revenue costs of organisations unless they can show clearly that within the trust's area of benefit a substantial number of people are being charitably assisted. They also expect organisations to show that other support will be forthcoming and that the organisation will become self-reliant over an identified period of years.

Applications In writing to the clerk on the application form available from the trust or its website. Please do not send requests by email. On receipt of your application form the clerk will review it and may wish to ask further questions before submitting it to the trustees for consideration. All eligible applications will be considered.

The general grants panel meets every two months, considers all project grants and for over £25,000 and makes a recommendation to the quarterly meeting of the trustees. The clerk will be pleased to inform organisations about the dates of meetings when their application is to be considered. Organisations are advised to put in their applications well in advance of meeting dates.

In the case of major capital or other large projects, it may be, that on occasions, a small group of trustees are asked to discuss the scheme with the organisation and its advisors. It may also involve a site visit or an independent evaluation by an assessor.

Conditions may be attached to any grant and the trust should be kept regularly informed as to the progress and effectiveness of a project. In certain cases, where conditions have been attached to the grant, written confirmation of acceptance of these by the organisation will be required prior to the grant being paid.

The trustees accept no liability for any commitment by an applicant to expenditure for which a grant is requested until the applicant has been informed in writing that the trustees have approved a grant.

Major capital projects on a 'once and for all' basis are paid in instalments as work progresses. Applicants may like to discuss their project with the clerk prior to completion of an application form.

Due to the volume of applications received it is not always possible to fund organisations even though they may fall within the trust's criteria.

The Kathleen Hannay Memorial Charity

Health, welfare, Christian and general

£222,000 (2007/08)

Beneficial area UK.

15 Suffolk Street, London SW1Y 4HG

Tel. 020 7036 5685

Correspondent G Fincham, Administrator

Trustees *Jonathan F Weil; Simon P Weil; Christian Alison K Ward.*

CC Number 299600

Information available Accounts were available from the Charity Commission.

The trust supports a wide variety of UK and overseas charitable causes. In furtherance of its objectives, the trust continues to make a substantial number of grants to charitable organisations both on a one off and recurring basis.

In 2007/08 the trust had assets of almost £15 million and an income of £292,000. Only four grants were made during the year totalling £222,000. The trustees were unable to meet before the end of the financial year so the majority of the donations agreed were not made until early in the following financial year. At a meeting held in May 2008 the trustees sanctioned further donations totalling £206,000, for which provision has not been made in these accounts.

Beneficiaries in 2007/08 were: Monkton Combe School – to establish a bursary fund at the pre-Prep School (£150,000); Children's Fire and Burn Trust – towards work with children affected by scalds and burns (£40,000); St Mary Magdalene, Hullavington PCC – towards the renewal and renovation of the church (£30,000); and the Reverend JPR Saunt – towards sponsoring the education of 'Lilian Lwanga' in Uganda (£4,000).

Exclusions No grants to individuals or non-registered charities.

Applications In writing to the correspondent. The trustees usually meet in March (applications should be submitted in February).

The Haramead Trust

Children, social welfare, education, people with disabilities, homeless people, medical assistance, victims and oppressed people and religious activities

£1.2 million (2007/08)

Beneficial area Worldwide, in practice developing countries, UK and Ireland, locally in the East Midlands.

Park House, Park Hill, Gaddesby LE7 4WH

Correspondent Michael J Linnett, Trustee

Trustees *Simon P Astill; Mrs Winifred M Linnett; Michael J Linnett; Robert H Smith; David L Tams; Revd Joseph A Mullen.*

CC Number 1047416

Information available Accounts were available from the Charity Commission.

The Haramead Trust was established in 1995 for general charitable purposes. The trust focuses its grant giving on the relief of those suffering hardship or distress, children's welfare, the relief of suffering animals and education in relation to the advancement of health.

The trustees may visit funded projects, both in the UK and overseas, for monitoring purposes or to assess projects/organisations for future grants. Travel and administration costs are borne by the settlor; only audit costs are met by the trust.

In 2007/08 the trust had assets of £1.1 million and an income of £1.3 million. There were 169 grants made totalling over £1.2 million, which were split geographically as follows:

Region	Value
UK and Ireland	£500,000
Developing countries	£474,000
East Midlands	£252,500

Grants of £10,000 or more included those to: CAFOD (£120,000); British Red Cross (£100,000); Shelter (£60,000); Leicestershire and Rutland Organisation for the Relief of Suffering (£25,000); Love & Share (£20,000); Intercare and Menphys (£15,000 each); and Dove Cottage Day Hospice, Leicester Charity Link, Phoenix Futures and Streetwise (£10,000 each).

Grants between £5,000 and £9,999 totalled £578,000; grants of less than £5,000 totalled £73,000.

Applications In writing to the correspondent. The trustees meet every two months.

The Peter Harrison Foundation

Sports for people in the UK who have disabilities or are disadvantaged; support for children and young people in the south east of England who are terminally ill, have disabilities, or are disadvantaged; and educational initiatives for children, primarily in the south east of England

£2.1 million (2007/08)

Beneficial area UK, south east of England.

Foundation House, 42–48 London Road, Reigate RH2 9QQ

Tel. 01737 228 000 **Fax** 01737 228 001

Email enquiries@ peterharrisonfoundation.org

Website www.peterharrisonfoundation. org

Correspondent John Ledlie, Director

Trustees *Peter Harrison, Chair; Joy Harrison; Julia Harrison-Lee; Peter Lee.*

CC Number 1076579

Information available Accounts were available at the Charity Commission. The foundation's website is informative and gives clear guidelines for applicants for grants.

The foundation was established for general charitable purposes by Peter Harrison in April 1999. The aims of the foundation are to provide sports for people who have disabilities or who are disadvantaged in the UK; support for children and young people who are terminally ill, have disabilities, or are disadvantaged in the south east of

England; and educational initiatives for children, primarily in the south east of England.

Peter Harrison is a keen and active sportsman and believes that education and sport provide the key stepping-stones to self-development, creation of choice, confidence building and self reliance. A pioneering and successful businessman, entrepreneur and sportsman he wishes to share his success by making these stepping stones more readily available to those who have disabilities or who are disadvantaged and who may not otherwise have the opportunity to develop their self potential.

In the first few years since its formation, the foundation has distributed over £10 million and has made grants to over two hundred and fifty charities. This has been achieved through the foundation's grants programmes.

In 2007/08 the foundation had assets of £30 million and an income of £2.3 million. Grants committed during the year totalled £3.1 million and grants were paid totalling £2.1 million through the following programmes.

Grant programmes

Opportunities through sport

This programme is nationwide and applications are accepted from charities throughout the United Kingdom. Sporting activities or projects which provide opportunities for people who have disabilities or who are otherwise disadvantaged are supported in order to fulfil their potential and to develop other personal and life skills.

Grants will often be one-off grants for capital projects. The foundation will, however, also consider revenue funding for a new project or if funding is key to the continuing success or survival of an established project. Applications are welcomed for projects that:

- provide a focus for skills development and confidence building through the medium of sport
- have a strong training and/or educational theme within the sporting activity
- provide sporting equipment or facilities for people with disabilities or disadvantaged people
- have a high degree of community involvement
- help to engage children or young people at risk of crime, truancy or addiction.

Special needs and care for children and young people

This programme is for charities in the south east of England and applications are accepted only from charities in: Berkshire;

Buckinghamshire; Hampshire; Isle of Wight; Kent; Oxfordshire; Surrey; East Sussex; and West Sussex. Applications from charities based in or operating in London are not accepted, but the foundation may consider funding charities based in London for a specific project taking place in the South East that meets its criteria. Applications are welcomed for projects that:

- work with or benefit children with disabilities, chronically or terminally ill children or provide support for their parents and carers;
- help to engage children or young people at risk of crime, truancy or addiction;
- are organised for young people at risk of homelessness or that provide new opportunities for homeless young people.

Opportunities through education

This programme supports education initiatives, primarily in the south east of England, which are of particular interest to the trustees. Through this programme the specialist schools programme and bursary places for children from the Reigate and Redhill areas in Surrey are funded.

Applications are not invited for this programme.

Trustees' discretion

This programme supports projects that are of particular interest to the trustees and external applications are not invited.

Guidelines for applicants

The foundation accepts applications from registered charities, community amateur sports clubs, friendly societies or industrial provident societies and organisations in Scotland and Northern Ireland recognised by the Inland Revenue. The foundation also accepts applications from local branches of national charities but only if they are either a separate legal entity or have the endorsement of their national head office.

The foundation wishes to support those charitable activities that demonstrate an existing high level of voluntary commitment, together with well planned and thought out projects.

Grantmaking in 2007/08

Grants committed in 2007/08 and for which applications were invited were as follows:

Opportunities through sport – 21 grants totalling £714,000

Beneficiaries included: Loughborough University (£150,000); United Kingdom Sailing Academy (£118,000); Spinal Injuries Association (£70,000); Ahoy Centre (£53,000); Prince's Trust and

Cricket Foundation (£50,000 each); Panathlon Foundation Limited (£30,000); British Polio Fellowship (£15,000); Thomley Hall Centre Ltd (£9,700); and Erb's Palsy Group (£5,000).

Special needs and care for children and young people – 14 grants totalling £617,000

Beneficiaries included: Children's Trust (£250,000); Elizabeth Foundation (£50,000); Medical Engineering Resource Unit – MERU (£45,000); Lifelites (£36,000); Karers 4 Kidz (£30,000); Walton Firs Foundation (£25,000); Burned Children's Club (£23,000); Children's Hope Foundation (£13,000); and Yvonne Arnaud Theatre Management (£11,000).

Grants awarded at the trustees' discretion and for which external applications are not invited were as follows:

Trustees' discretion – 18 grants totalling £1.1 million

Beneficiaries included: Old Reigatians Rugby Football Club (£850,000); Royal Ballet School (£75,000); Reigate Methodist Church (£50,000); Almeida Theatre Company Limited (£28,000); Stockport Canal Boat Trust for Disabled People (£11,000); Chase Children's Hospice Care for Children (£5,000); Right to Play Limited (£500); and Marie Curie Cancer Care (£100).

Opportunities through education – 13 grants totalling £201,000

Grants went to: Harrison Scholars – 6 awards (£101,000); Hamond's High School (£20,000); St Bede's School, Werneth School and Hayward School (£15,000 each); Charles Burrell High School and Rosemary Muskar High School (£13,000 each); and Rumworth School (£10,000).

Exclusions The foundation does not fund:

- general fundraising appeals
- retrospective funding
- other grant-making bodies to make grants on the foundation's behalf
- projects that directly replace statutory funding or activities that are primarily the responsibility of central or local government
- individuals
- holidays or expeditions in the UK or abroad
- outdoor activity projects such as camping and outward-bound expeditions
- overseas projects
- projects that are solely for the promotion of religion.

Applications The foundation has a two stage application process.

Step 1: Initial enquiry
Potential applicants are asked to first read the information on eligibility and grant programmes available on the foundation's website. If your project meets the criteria for one of the open programmes (such as Opportunities through Sport or Special Needs and Care for Children and Young People), then complete the online initial enquiry form. This can be found in the 'application process' section of the foundation's website.

Applications are processed as quickly as possible, but please be aware that the foundation receives a large number of applications and it may sometimes take up to two months for an initial enquiry form to be considered.

Applications are first assessed by the foundation's staff. If it is felt the project will be of interest, they will arrange either to visit the project or to conduct a telephone discussion with the applicant about it. Depending on the outcome of these discussions, you may then be invited to submit a full application.

If your initial enquiry is not successful you will be notified by email. The foundation receives many more applications than it is able to support and unfortunately have turn down many good proposals, even though they meet the criteria. No feedback is given on unsuccessful applications.

Step 2: Full application
Applicants should only submit a full application form if their initial enquiry has been successful. Completed forms should be sent by post to the correspondent.

If an application is successful the applicant will normally be contacted by telephone followed by a grant offer letter. The letter will explain the conditions which apply to all grant awards and also set out any special conditions which apply to your organisation. It will also confirm details of how and when you will receive the grant and how payment is made.

If an application is unsuccessful the applicant will be informed by letter. The main reason for not funding projects is the volume of applications received.

Organisations supported by the foundation are required to show how they have used the grant and, depending on the grant amount and the nature of the project, may be asked to undertake a review and evaluation of the project being funded. This will normally be on completion of the project, but for charities receiving their grant in several instalments, interim reports may be requested. Full details of the monitoring information required are given in the foundation's grant offer letter.

The foundation aims to ensure that all grant applications that are eligible for consideration within the foundation's grants criteria are given equal consideration, irrespective of gender, sexual orientation, race, colour, ethnic or national origin, or disability.

The Maurice Hatter Foundation

Jewish causes and general

£392,000 (2007/08)
Beneficial area Unrestricted.

Ivan Sopher & Co, Unit 5, Elstree Gate, Elstree Way, Borehamwood WD6 1JD

Tel. 020 8207 0602

Correspondent Jeremy S Newman, Trustee

Trustees *Sir Maurice Hatter; Ivor Connick; Jeremy S Newman; Richard Hatter.*

CC Number 298119

Information available Accounts were available from the Charity Commission.

The foundation was established in 1987 for general charitable purposes, mainly for Jewish causes.

In 2007/08 it had assets of £8.6 million and an income of over £2.6 million, including £2 million in donations. Grants were made during the year totalling £392,000 (£1 million in 2006/07).

Grants were categorised as follows:

Category	Value
Education	£178,300
Medical research	£134,400
Social welfare	£45,000
Religion	£30,000
Culture and environment	£5,000

Beneficiaries included: University College Hospital Charity Fund (£50,000); Ray Tye Medical Aid Foundation (£48,000); Civitas Limited (£25,000); British Friends of Haifa University (£21,000); British ORT (£10,000); and the Reform Foundation Trust (£5,000).

Applications Unsolicited applications will not be considered.

The Charles Hayward Foundation

Heritage and conservation, criminal justice, hospices, older people, overseas and young people at risk

£1.9 million (2007)

Beneficial area Unrestricted, in practice mainly UK with some overseas funding.

Hayward House, 45 Harrington Gardens, London SW7 4JU

Tel. 020 7370 7063/7067

Website www. charleshaywardfoundation.org.uk

Correspondent David Brown, Administrator

Trustees *A D Owen, Chair; I F Donald; Mrs J M Chamberlain; Sir Jack Hayward; Mrs S J Heath; B D Insch; J N van Leuven; Miss A T Rogers; Ms J Streather.*

CC Number 1078969

Information available Accounts were available from the Charity Commission.

Sir Charles Hayward was born in 1893 in Wolverhampton, Staffordshire. In 1911 he started his own business making wooden patterns for the developing engineering trade. His early involvement in the motor industry proved to be a springboard for his later success culminating in the formation of Firth Cleveland Ltd. He was Chairman from its inception in 1953 until 1973 when he retired.

Sir Charles used his personal fortune to establish and endow two charitable trusts, the Hayward Foundation and the Charles Hayward Trust. The two charities were combined on 1st January 2000, to become the Charles Hayward Foundation.

In 2007 the foundation had assets of £53 million and an income of £2.3 million. Grants were made totalling £1.9 million. During the year the foundation reviewed its grant-making policy in order to focus on a narrower range of activities, as reprinted here:

Current categories:
- Heritage and conservation
- Criminal justice
- Hospices
- Older people
- Overseas
- Young people at risk.

There is also a small grants scheme for grants up to £5,000.

Following a review the following categories have been discontinued:
- community facilities (except for small grants in the north west of England only)
- people with disabilities
- medical research
- early intervention and under fives.

Activities to which funds may be allocated

We predominantly fund capital costs. Occasionally, project funding may be offered for start-up or development activities where these are not part of the on-going revenue requirement of the organisation.

We place great emphasis on funding projects that are developmental or innovative. We would like to enable things to happen that would not otherwise happen. We prefer funding a project in its early stages rather than finishing off an already well supported appeal.

We also value projects that are preventive or provide early intervention. Our preferred area of impact is at the community and neighbourhood level.

We also wish to promote good practice. We would like to help with the development of solutions to society's problems and help to expand the take-up of these solutions where they are most needed.

Organisations eligible to apply

We will normally make grants to UK registered and exempt charities only. New charities that are yet to be registered may be considered for start-up funding if they are able to demonstrate good governance and sound financial management.

Geographical targeting

Our area of operation for our main grants programmes is the United Kingdom. Except in our community facilities small grant scheme we do not target particular regions. We consider the quality of projects more important than their geographical location. Nevertheless, we also recognise that London organisations in particular are well served by charitable trusts.

We also have an overseas grants programme which makes grants to UK registered charities which undertake projects in the Commonwealth Countries of Africa, India and Pakistan.

Socio-economic targeting

Although we consider levels of socio-economic deprivation in an area are an important factor in determining the value of a project, more important criteria for our grantmaking are innovation, excellence and the development of new services and activities.

Size and scope of grants

The small grant scheme makes grants up to £5,000 only to charities with an annual turnover of less than £250,000.

In our other programmes, grant sizes are typically from £10,000 to £25,000 one-off grant. Where agreed, project funding may be granted for a maximum of three years in duration, and will be tapered downwards if appropriate. Project funding may be up to £15,000 per year over three years.

Heritage and conservation

We would like to concentrate our grant making on the following:
- Industrial heritage
- Conservation and preservation of pictures, manuscripts, books and artefacts
- Purchase of land or reclamation of recently purchased land to be used for nature reserves or inner-city gardens, parks etc., where these will be maintained in perpetuity.

Exclusions are:
- Community arts troupes
- Community arts centres
- Endangered species
- Conservation of gardens
- Environmental conservation
- Animal rescue
- Art and history workshops
- Fellowships and academic education
- Opera and ballet
- Artistic productions
- Heritage railways.

Criminal justice

We would like to support:
- Alternatives to custody
- Victim support services
- Schemes to help prisoners maintain links with their families and be better parents
- Accommodation and support for offenders on release
- Rehabilitation of offenders
- Help for families suffering from domestic violence.

We will continue to occasionally fund prison reform activities.

The following is excluded:
- Welfare of prisoners and their families.

Hospices

We would like to support:
- Capital expenditure for day care and home care
- Start-up funding for domiciliary services

179

- Capital expenditure for organisations which provide care for people with terminal illness.

The following are excluded:

- Equipment and computers
- Training facilities and costs.

Older people

In this policy area we wish to fund preventative and early intervention programmes allowing older people to stay in their own homes and remain independent. We are particularly interested in seeking out programmes which show some creativity in improving the quality of life of older people. We wish to focus on the following.

- Programmes aiming to alleviate isolation and depression in older people.
- Capital costs for informal day care or social and recreational activities – except those contracted by government.
- Setting up schemes which mainly use volunteers to give practical help, assistance and support for older people living in their own homes.
- Expansion or improvements to older persons' care homes, sheltered and supported accommodation.

The following areas are excluded:

- Almshouses
- Meals on wheels
- Lifelong learning
- Workshops, events and productions for older people.

Overseas

We will accept applications for projects in India, Pakistan and the Commonwealth countries of Africa. We favour high impact projects that have immediate results. We will only fund overseas projects through UK registered charities, which must be able to provide an adequate local monitoring function for the grant. We will consider the following areas:

- Clean water and sanitation
- Basic health education programmes
- Cure and rehabilitation from disease and disability
- Young people at risk, orphans, street children
- Basic training in farming skills and income generation.

The following are exclusions:

- Overseas disability awareness
- HIV and AIDS
- Victims of famine, war and disaster
- Basic education
- Gap years, electives, project visits overseas.

Young people at risk

Trustees will, until further notice, not accept unsolicited applications for Young people at Risk projects but will continue their support through internally researched programmes.

Other areas

We may wish to consider projects outside our main areas of interest when such projects develop novel interventions into society's ills or address causes which are rare or unpopular.

Small grant scheme

We have a small grant scheme which makes more rapid grants to smaller organisations. The grants are valued up to £5,000 and are only available to organisations with a turnover of less than £250,000. Applications for small grants will be accepted for activities fitting any of our UK funding categories above, except young people at risk.

In addition, small grants valued up to £5,000 will be made towards community facilities in the north west of England. We will contribute up to £5,000 towards capital projects to accommodate community activities, where the project is a capital build or extension costing less than £250,000. The new facilities must accommodate new activities, which are at a demonstrably advanced stage in their planning. The activities must be designed to meet the basic needs of new clients and users.

- Capital costs of community centres and village halls
- Capital costs of community facilities provided by churches and faith groups
- Capital costs for CABx
- Capital costs for rescue organisations.

The following areas are excluded:

- Existing parks, playgrounds and recreation grounds
- Sports clubs and sports facilities
- Community transport
- Refugees and asylum seekers.

Grants are only offered towards expenditure not yet incurred. Grants are paid on evidence of expenditure such as receipts or invoices. For project grants, budgets and management accounts will be required. The grant offer may be withdrawn after 12 months if it is not taken up. We do not seek publicity for our grants.

Exclusions The following types of recipients will be excluded:

- large national organisations, with substantial fundraising or income generating capacity
- organisations that have large reserves or endowment funds
- individuals
- voluntary sector development and support organisations
- organisations that restrict their benefit to one section of society
- other grant-making organisations.

We will not fund:

- academic chairs
- animal charities
- bursaries
- church restoration
- computers
- education
- endowment funds
- environmental and animal sciences
- fundraising activities
- general repairs
- academic research
- paying off loans
- revenue funding of core costs, general funding, continuing funding and replacement funding
- replacement of government or lottery funding or activities primarily the responsibility of central or local government or some other responsible body
- travel, outings, holidays and gap schemes
- expenditure that has already been incurred or will have been incurred by the time the application can be considered by our trustees.

Applications There is no application form. Your initial application should be made in writing to the Administrator, David Brown. It should provide the details listed below. You may add any enclosures that help to describe your organisation or the project. The foundation will advise you whether more information is required.

All applications will receive an acknowledgement. However, as there is often a waiting list, and the trustees meet only four times a year to consider applications, you may have a wait of several months before you receive a decision. Please note that there are always many more applications than the foundation are able to fund out of their limited resources. On average, the trustees approve one in twenty applications. You are advised to read these guidelines very carefully, as inappropriate applications waste time.

Details required in your application:

Name and location of organisation – The official name of your organisation and its location

Contact details – Give your name and position within the organisation, contact telephone number and address.

Description of organisation – Provide a description of your present work and the priorities you are addressing. Quantify the scale of your operation – how many people do you help and how?

Description of proposed project – Describe the project you are undertaking, detailing the number of people and groups who will benefit and how. Specify how life will be improved for the target group.

Project cost – For larger projects give a breakdown of the costs. Capital and revenue costs should be kept separate. For a capital project, include only information on the capital costs.

Funds raised and pledged – Give a breakdown of the funds raised to date towards your target, separating capital and revenue, where applicable. Include the amount of any of your own funds or reserves going into the project, and any money you intend to borrow.

Outstanding shortfall – Specify the amount of money you still need for capital and revenue separately.

Timetable – State the timetable for the project; when it will start and be finished.

Accounts – Include one set of your latest audited accounts.

The Headley Trust

Arts, heritage, welfare, overseas development

£2.2 million (2007)
Beneficial area Unrestricted.

Allington House, 1st Floor, 150 Victoria Street, London SW1E 5AE
Tel. 020 7410 0330 **Fax** 020 7410 0332
Website www.sfct.org.uk
Correspondent Alan Bookbinder, Director
Trustees *Sir Timothy Sainsbury; Lady Susan Sainsbury; Timothy James Sainsbury; J R Benson; Judith Portrait.*
CC Number 266620
Information available Excellent annual report and accounts were available from the Charity Commission.

This is one of the Sainsbury Family Charitable Trusts which share a joint administration. Like the others, it is primarily proactive, aiming to choose its own grantees, and its annual reports state that 'proposals are generally invited by the trustees or initiated at their request'. The extent to which readers should in general be deterred by this is

discussed in the separate entry, under the Sainsbury name, for the group as a whole.

In this particular case, the statement and the general sentiment that unsolicited applications are unlikely to be successful seems to be contradicted in the same document where, under the 'health and social welfare' heading the trust notes that '[the trustees] will consider applications which deal with educational and psychological support for pre-school families [and] homelessness projects [...]'

The trust has a particular interest in the arts and in artistic and architectural heritage and has made large grants to museums, galleries, libraries and theatres.

There are ongoing programmes for the repair of cathedrals and medieval churches and other conservation projects in the UK and overseas. The trust also supports a range of social welfare issues. Its support for activities in developing countries is focused on sub-Saharan Anglophone countries and Ethiopia. There is also a small Aids for Disabled Fund. Like many of the others in the Sainsbury group, the Headley Trust prefers to support 'innovative schemes that can be successfully replicated or become self-sustaining'.

General

The settlor of this trust is Sir Timothy Sainsbury. His co-trustees include his wife, eldest son and legal adviser. The trust's staff includes the director of the Sainsbury family's charitable trusts, Alan Bookbinder.

In 2007 the trust had assets totalling £79 million and an income of just over £2.6 million. Grants were made during the year totalling £2.2 million.

Grants approved in 2007 were categorised with the number of grants and their value, as seen in the table below.

Grantmaking in 2007

The following grant examples are prefaced by the trust's description of its

interests in that area, mainly drawn from its annual report. The grant totals are the amounts paid during the year, and include grants approved in previous years.

Arts and Heritage – UK – £876,000
The trustees respond to a wide and eclectic variety of building conservation or heritage projects in the UK. They also support regional museums with revenue costs or the purchase of unusual or exceptional artefacts, aim to promote educational access to museums and galleries for both the disabled and disadvantaged, and wish to encourage arts outreach and musical opportunities for young people. They continue to be interested in notable archaeological projects in the UK. They wish to encourage both the revival of rural crafts and the continuing richness of the English Crafts movement. The trustees have made a major commitment to the Victoria & Albert Museum's new Ceramics Gallery which will be one of the most important in the world.

Grants included those to: Hove Museum (£70,000); Common Ground (£60,000); Wildscreen Trust and Durham County Council (£40,000 each); National Trust for Scotland (£30,000); Bowes Museum Trust (£25,000); Christ Church – Spitalfields (£20,000); and University of Manchester (£10,000).

From the Cathedrals Programme
The trustees also allocate a substantial sum each year for repair work to the fabric of cathedrals and large ecclesiastical buildings of exceptional architectural merit (pre-18th century). Modern amenities, organ repair/restoration and choral scholarships are not normally eligible.

Five grants were made to: Boston Stump Restoration Appeal (£50,000); Ely Cathedral Trust (£39,000); Southwell Minster (£30,000); and Howden Minster and Selby Abbey Appeal (£15,000 each).

From the Museums' Treasure Acquisition Scheme
This scheme was designed to help local and regional museums purchase archaeological artefacts. It runs alongside and in collaboration with the Museums, Libraries and Archives Council/Victoria and Albert Museum Purchase Grant Fund. 15 grants of less than £5,000 were

Category	Grants approved	Amount	Average grant
Arts and heritage (UK)	27	£568,000	£21,000
- Cathedrals Programme	5	£149,000	£30,000
- Parish Churches Programme	60	£137,000	£2,300
- Museums' Treasure Acquisition Scheme	15	£21,000	£1,400
Arts and heritage (overseas)	8	£209,000	£26,000
Developing countries	13	£264,000	£20,000
Education	10	£182,000	£18,000
Health and social welfare	36	£630,000	£18,000
- Aids for Disabled	48	£26,000	£540
Total	**222**	**£2,187,000**	**£9,900**

awarded during the year, totalling £21,000.

Beneficiaries included: Barbican House Museum – Lewes, Saffron Walden Museum, Northampton Museum & Art Gallery, Derby Museums and Art Gallery and Wiltshire Heritage Museum – Devizes.

Please note: this scheme has its own application form, available from the Headley Museums Archaeological Acquisition Fund website, www.headley-archaeology.org.uk.

From the Parish Churches Programme
Funding for fabric repair and restoration is considered for medieval parish churches (or pre-16th century churches of exceptional architectural merit) in rural, sparsely populated, less prosperous villages, through a process of review, diocese by diocese. Urban churches are not eligible, and funding is available for fabric only (including windows), not refurbishment nor construction of church halls nor other modern amenities.

Grants of £5,000 or less were made to 60 churches throughout the diocese of Winchester, Guildford, Hereford, Chester, St David's, Ely, and St Edmundsbury and Ipswich.

Arts and Heritage – Overseas – £209,000

Trustees support conservation projects of outstanding artistic or architectural importance; particularly the restoration of buildings, statuary or paintings, primarily in the countries of Central and Eastern Europe. They seek out reputable local non-governmental organisations as partners in these countries. They are also willing to consider archaeological projects in the region.

There were seven grants made in this category. The beneficiaries were: Transylvania Trust – Romania (£70,000); Holley Martlew Archaeological Foundation (£60,000); Friends of Cerveny Dvur – Czech Republic (£28,000); National Museum – Moldova (£23,000); National Trust – Slovakia (£18,000); St Georges Anglican Church – Venice (£10,000); and Diocese in Europe (£500).

Health & Social Welfare – £656,000

Trustees give priority to charities helping carers of an ill or disabled relative, and those that support older people of limited means. They are interested in tackling the causes and effects of social exclusion. They will consider applications which deal with educational (for example literacy) and psychological support for pre-school children and their families. They continue to see parenting education and support

programmes as a priority, and to promote the wellbeing of the family. The trustees will consider homelessness projects, particularly for older people, and are interested in care and support for families with autistic children.

Larger grants included those to: Brighton & Sussex Medical School (£150,000); the Passage – Victoria (£120,000); HACT– Housing Association Charitable Trust (£90,000); PSS (£70,000); Acorn Christian Foundation (£30,000); and Relationships Foundation UK (£21,000).

Grants of less than £5,000 were made to 26 organisations totalling £34,000. Beneficiaries included: Ataxia UK, Crisis, Fine Cell Work and Samaritans.

Developing Countries – £264,000

The trustees' primary geographical areas of interest are sub-Saharan Anglophone Africa and Ethiopia. Priority project areas are:

- water/sanitation, for example providing access to safe, potable water for disadvantaged communities, preserving areas of culturally or ecologically important swampland or marshland, improving urban or rural sanitary condition and promoting the better use of water.
- environment, for example preserving natural woodland, promoting better use of wood stocks for fuel or construction.
- education and literacy, for example improving the quality of education and levels of literacy for underprivileged adults or children through training support, materials, construction.
- healthcare, for example improving standards of health (particularly reproductive) and assisting people with disabilities to lead a more fulfilled life.
- community and voluntary sector development, for example projects which provide training, support and information to assist the development of community groups and local charities.

Trustees will also consider emergency appeals and projects.

Beneficiaries included: Café Africa Trust – UK (£54,000); Law Society of Zimbabwe (£50,000); Convention on Business Integrity (£30,000); Foundation for Reconciliation in the Middle East (£20,000); and Tear Fund (£10,000).

Grants of less than £5,000 were made to four organisations totalling £8,000.

Education – £182,000

The trustees' main area of interest is in providing bursary support, primarily for UK students, particularly for artistic or technical skills training. The bursaries are intended for postgraduate study, except in exceptional circumstances. They also aim to provide performing opportunities for talented young artists, as well as opportunities to participate

in the performing and creative arts for young people who are disadvantaged or disabled.

Beneficiaries included: National Youth Orchestra of Great Britain and Cutty Sark Trust (£40,000 each); Carousel (£30,000); English Pocket Opera Company (£15,000); and Bishopsland Educational Trust (£10,000).

Grants of less than £5,000 were made to three organisations totalling £6,800.

Aids for Disabled Fund

The trustees make a number of small grants to appropriate charities, agencies and local authorities to provide aids for disabled individuals. These are awarded for a range of aids and equipment, including, but not limited to, the following:

- specially adapted computer systems for the partially blind
- voice-activated computers for sufferers of spinal injuries
- stair-lifts and wheelchairs for people with restricted mobility.

Grants totalling £26,000 were made for these purposes during the year.

Exclusions Grants are not normally made to individuals.

Applications The Museums' Treasure Acquisition Scheme has its own application form, available from the Headley Museums Archaeological Acquisition Fund website: www.headley-archaeology.org.uk. For information on the small Aids for Disabled Fund, call the trust on 020 7410 0330.

Otherwise, see the guidance for applicants in the entry for the Sainsbury Family Charitable Trusts. A single application will be considered for support by all the trusts in the group. However, for this as for many of the trusts, 'proposals are generally invited by the trustees or initiated at their request. Unsolicited applications are discouraged and are unlikely to be successful, even if they fall within an area in which the trustees are interested'.

The Heart of England Community Foundation

General

£1 million (2007/08)

Beneficial area The city of Coventry and Warwickshire.

Pinley House, Sunbeam Way, PO BOX 227, Coventry CV3 1ND

Tel. 024 7688 4386 **Fax** 024 7688 4640

Email info@heartofenglandcf.co.uk

Website www.heartofenglandcf.co.uk

Correspondent Ms Kate Mulkern, Director

Trustees *John Atkinson, Chair; Peter Deeley; Mrs Margaret Backhouse; Mrs Sally Carrick; Andrew Corner; Stewart Fergusson; David Green; Brian Holt; Donald Hunter; Zamurad Hussain; Lady Jane Liggins; Susan Ong; Ven. Michael Paget-Wilkes; Peter Shearing; John Taylor*

CC Number 1117345

Information available Accounts were available from the Charity Commission.

In general, the foundation seeks to promote any charitable purposes for the benefit of the community in the city of Coventry, the county of Warwickshire and, in particular, the advancement of education, the protection of good health, both mental and physical, and the relief of poverty and sickness.

The Heart of England Community Foundation has a portfolio of around 20 grant making programmes (see below) for use by local community and voluntary groups. This enables benefactors to support community projects according to their own geographical or thematic criteria, and to have as much or as little involvement as they like in the awarding process. This portfolio often changes, so it is worth checking the community foundation's website when applying for funding, to keep informed of which funds are available at any time.

Funds are held on behalf of individuals, families, trusts, companies and statutory bodies, investing them to get maximum returns. The foundation can engage with groups on behalf of the funders – promoting their criteria, making awards and collecting feedback.

Grantmaking in 2007/08

In 2007/08 the trust had assets of £1.8 million and an income of £1.4 million. Grants totalled £1 million and were made to 245 projects across the beneficial area averaging around £4,086 each. Grants are broken down by subject and geographical area:

Grants by subject area	%
Community	33
Health and sport	17.4
Cultural	16.6
Disability	10.2
Employment	8.3
Environment	6.8
Crime and safety	5.3
Addiction	2.3

Grants by location	%
Coventry	40
Nuneaton and Bedworth	24
Stratford upon Avon	13
Warwick	9
Rugby	8
North Warwickshire	6

Funds and beneficiaries

The foundation manages the following list of funds, which includes a grants summary and some examples of beneficiaries:

Local Network Fund *(109 grants: £545,000) – A fund set up by the Children and Young People's unit of the Department for Education and Skills to tackle poverty and disadvantage amongst young people.*
All grants given were for £7,000 or less, with beneficiaries including: Blackwell Youth Club, Nic Nac Pre School, Coventry Tamil Welfare Association and Rugby Sea Cadets (£7,000 each); Somali Cultural and Resource Centre Coventry (£6,300); West Indian Community Association – Coventry (£4,300); Perform Your Arts Out (£2,500); Atherstone Theatre Workshop (£2,200); Friendship Project (£2,100); Griff and Coton Cricket Club and Coventry International Skating Club (£1,300); Hatton Park Youth Club (£700); and Pastels Day Centre Limited (£500).

Coventry Neighbourhoods Involvement Fund *(24 grants: £92,000) – A fund to encourage local residents to work with service providers to improve the areas in which they live, funded through the Neighbourhood Renewal Fund.*
Beneficiaries included: WATCH (£8,000); Willenhall Community Forum, Minorities of Europe and Heels and Toes Parents Association (£5,000 each); Angels Residents Group (£4,200); Eritrean Community Network Coventry (£2,700); Spon End And Chapelfield Community Forum (£2,000); and Shree Mandhata Samaj Coventry (£1,700).

Coalfields Regeneration Trust – Bridging the Gap *(10 grants: £76,000) –* This fund targets the regeneration of former coal mining communities. Beneficiaries included: Newdugate Road Allotment Association, Pastoral Care Project, Keresley Family History Society and Diners Delight (£10,000 each); Nuneaton Credit Union (£9,000); Camphill Community Festival (£6,000); D.I.A.L. Nuneaton and Bedworth (£3,400); and Grove Farm Community Association (£2,100).

Youth Enterprise Fund *(7 grants: £60,000) – This fund has been established to fund work involving young people, and is currently the only fund managed by the Heart of England Community Foundation to be targeted specifically at schools*
Beneficiaries were: Coventry North East Federation (2 grants totalling £12,000); Lyng Hall School and Specialist Sports College and Hereward College (£10,000 each); City College Coventry and Youth Service (£9,700 each); and Coundon Court School (£7,800).

John F Miller Fund *(17 grants: £58,000) – A Fund established to provide support to a range of projects in the Bedworth area.*
Beneficiaries included: Sycamore Counselling Service (£5,000); South Warwickshire Retired Miners Leisure Club (£4,500); Rainbow Sunshine Company (£2,700); Poets Corner Friendship Group (£2,100); Bedworth Arts Centre (£1,500); and Nuneaton and Medworth Older Peoples Forum (£1,000).

Creative Engagement Fund *(13 grants: £54,000) – This fund was re-launched in April 2008 to replace the Engaging with Enterprise and Employment Fund.*
Beneficiaries included: Frontline Audio Visual (£5,000); Coventry Youth Offending Service (£4,800); Coventry and Warwickshire YMCA (£4,700); Willenhall Community Forum (£4,300); Kairos WWT – Women Working Together (£3,100); and Amazon Initiatives Limited (£1,900).

Heart of England Fund *(21 grants: £30,000) – A permanent fund to support grass-roots projects that involve local people.*
Beneficiaries included: Triangle Theatre Company (£3,000); Tell Woman Collective, Grapevine and Whitley Local History Group (£2,000 each); Coventry Canal Society (£1,700); Safeline (£1,500); Age Concern – Shipston on Stour and Luddington Village Hall (£1,000 each); Family Project – Coventry (£500); and West Midlands Pensioners Convention (£400).

Sport Relief *(7 grants: £23,000) – A joint fund from Comic Relief and BBC Sport to use the power and passion of sport to tackle poverty and disadvantage.*
Beneficiaries were: SCWIG – Safer Communities, Wellbeing and Intergenerational Group (£9,900); Sikh Community Centre – Leamington Spa (£5,000); Adventure Activities for All Abilities 4As (£3,000); Pegasus Group – Riding for the Disabled (£2,000); Tai Chi Friends Club (£1,800); Wellesbourne Sports Association (£1,000); and Poets Corner Friendship Group (£750).

Youell Foundation Fund *(5 grants: £23,000) – A permanent family fund which is building up endowment levels.*
Shipston Home Nursing (2 grants of £5,000); Mercia MS Therapy Centre (2 grants of £4,000); St James Church (£5,000).

Sheldon Trust *(3 grants: £8,500) – A fund offering grants of up to £5,000 to community projects and special needs projects in the Midlands area.*
Beneficiaries were: Rugby Town Junior Football Club (£5,300); Snitterfield Cricket Club (£3,200 in total).

Keepmoat PLC Fund *(6 grants: £7,100) – A fund supporting smaller, less well-resourced groups running community-led voluntary projects in Coventry, Nuneaton and Atherstone.*
Grants went to: Healthy Hearts and Stratford upon Avon Equine Facilitated Learning Group (£2,000 each); Family Project – Coventry (£1,500); Stockton Football Cricket and Netball Club (£1,000) and Alzheimer's Society Coventry (£600).

Coventry Neighbourhoods Community Fund *(4 grants: £6,600) – A fund to encourage and foster good relations amongst local residents living within Coventry, funded by through the Neighbourhood Renewal Fund.*
Beneficiaries were FolesHillfields Vision Ltd (£2,000); Positive Images Multicultural Festival (£1,900); Lentons Lane Over 50s Club (£1,600); and Ensemble 1685 (£1,000).

The High Sheriff's Warwickshire Fund *(3 grants: £4,800) – This fund supports projects that build stronger communities, prevent crime, develop social responsibility, give purpose to the young and assist disadvantaged communities.*
Grants went to: Hub 119 Ltd (£2,500); Alzheimer's Society Coventry (£1,300); and Luddington Village Hall (£1,000).

Women's Employment Initiative Fund *(1 grant: £4,700) – The main aim of this fund is to reduce barriers to employment for women in Coventry.*

St Peters Community Centre – Hillfields (£4,700)

29th May 1961 Charitable Trust Small Grants Fund *(3 grants: £4,100) – Provides small grants on behalf of the 29th May 1961 Charitable Trust.*
Grants were made to: Hub 119 Ltd (£2,500); Phantom Knights (£1,000); and Chace Centre (£700).

AXA Enterprise Fund *(6 grants: £4,000) – Also funded by AXA Sun Alliance, gives grants to educational activities for young people and children in the Coventry area.*
Beneficiaries included FolesHillfields Vision Ltd (£1,500); the Shysters (£1,000); Grangehurst After School Club (£975); and Nova Theatre Group (£500).

National Grid Fund *(2 grants: £2,500) – Permanent fund support for projects involving whole communities or neighbourhoods in areas where National Grid may be working.*
Grants went to: Rugby Town Junior Football Club (£1,500); and Holy Family Catholic Primary School (£1,000).

AXA Fund *(2 grants: £750) – An AXA Sun Alliance permanent fund for community programmes.*
Grants went to Wayfarers Gateway Club – Coventry (£500); and Coventry and Warwickshire YMCA (£250).

Kingscliffe Fund *(one grant: £500) – A permanent fund established by an anonymous individual to support young people in and around Southam and Dunchurch.*
Southam and District Childminders Association (£500)

Exclusions Grants will not usually be considered for the following:

- statutory provision
- individuals
- activities that promote religious activity
- activities that are not socially inclusive
- organisations with a turnover of over £100,000 excluding restricted funding
- grantmaking bodies
- mainstream activities of schools and colleges
- medical research
- animal welfare
- political activities
- organisations with substantial reserves
- general and major fundraising appeals
- sporting clubs except when aimed at addressing disadvantage
- continuation funding

Applications Application forms may be downloaded from the foundation's website (www.heartofenglandcf.co.uk located under 'Forms and reports') or, you can call on 024 7688 4386 and a copy will be sent it to you.

Although guidance on how to complete the application form is included within the form itself, you are encouraged to telephone the foundation to discuss your project in advance of applying. Grants Officers, who cover specific geographical areas and funds, will be pleased to assist you.

None of the above grant programmes run to deadlines, however applicants should expect an answer within 12 weeks. Applicants to the grassroots programme should expect to hear within 15 days.

Heathside Charitable Trust

General and Jewish
£373,000 (2007)
Beneficial area UK.

Hillsdown House, 32 Hampstead High Street, London NW3 1QD
Tel. 020 7431 7739
Correspondent Sir Harry Solomon, Trustee
Trustees *Sir Harry Solomon; Lady Judith Solomon; Geoffrey Jayson; Louise Jacobs; Juliet Solomon; Daniel Solomon.*
CC Number 326959
Information available Accounts for 2008 were overdue at the Charity Commission at the time of writing.

This trust has general charitable purposes, with a preference for Jewish organisations.

In 2007 it had assets of £4.3 million and an income of £947,000, of which £827,000 came from donations. Grants were made totalling £373,000; however, a list of grant beneficiaries was not available.

In 2006, the largest grant was £141,000 to Joint Jewish Charitable Trust. Large grants also went to Raft (£35,000), Jewish Education Defence Trust (£25,000), Community Security Trust (£25,000), Jewish Care (£15,000), with £10,000 each to British Friends of Jaffa Institute, GRET and Motivation.

Other beneficiaries included Holocaust Educational Trust, First Cheque 2000, Royal London Institute, Royal National Theatre, Jewish Museum, Cancerkin, King Solomon High School, Babes in Arms, Marie Curie Cancer Care and Weitzmann Institute.

Applications In writing to the correspondent, at any time.

The Hedley Foundation

Young people, health and welfare

£949,000 (2007/08)

Beneficial area UK.

1–3 College Hill, London EC4R 2RA

Tel. 020 7489 8076

Email pbarker@hedleyfoundation.org.uk

Website www.hedleyfoundation.org.uk

Correspondent Pauline Barker, Appeals Secretary

Trustees *John F Rodwell, Chair; Patrick R Holcroft; George R Broke; Lt Col. Peter G Chamberlin; Lorna B Stuttaford; Angus Fanshawe.*

CC Number 262933

Information available Accounts were on file at the Charity Commission, but without a grants list (available on request).

The Hedley Foundation was set up in 1971 and endowed from a family trust of which the principle asset was the compensation received on nationalisation of the family mining concerns.

The main objective of the trustees' grantmaking is to assist and encourage development and change. Grants are for specific projects only and are mostly one-off, though the trustees sometimes agree to help fund the introduction of new and innovative projects with a series of up to three annual grants. Few grants exceed £5,000 and most of them go to charities where they can make an impact. The foundation does not support large or national appeals or appeals from cathedrals and churches.

Currently about 70% of the foundation's budget goes towards supporting young people; specifically, their education, recreation, support, training, health and welfare. Its subsidiary objective is to support disabled people and the terminally ill through the provision of specialist equipment and support for carers.

Grants in 2007/08

During the year the foundation had assets of £28 million and an income of £1.4 million. Grants were made to 348 organisations totalling £949,000.

Beneficiaries included: Colonel's Fund (£26,000 in 2 grants); Action on Addiction (£20,000); Combat Stress (£18,000 in 3 grants); Marchant Holiday School (£15,000); Bag Books (£10,000); British Youth Opera (£5,000); Yorkhill Children's Foundation (£4,000); Butterwick Hospice (£3,000); Rochford Trust (£1,500); and Kinmos Volunteer Group Ltd (£500).

Please note: The foundation shows an unusual and intriguing combination of a very long list of small awards, and also evidence of a highly active body of trustees.

Exclusions Grants are made to UK registered charities only. No support for individuals, churches and cathedrals, core revenue costs, salary or transport funding, or for very large appeals.

Applications Application forms are downloadable from the foundation's website. Once completed in typescript, the form should be printed off and sent by post to the appeals secretary named above, accompanied by your email address, or a self-addressed envelope (not necessarily stamped).

The trustees meet six times a year. The closing date for a meeting is three weeks beforehand. All applications will be acknowledged, but, in the case of those short-listed, not until after they have been considered by the trustees. The trustees usually meet in January, March, May, July, September and November. A list of meeting dates for the current year is published on the foundation's website.

In 2007/08 the foundation received nearly 1,500 applications, of which less than two-thirds were within the stated criteria. As a result, the foundation made 348 grants and urges that applicants should not be surprised, or too disappointed, if they are unsuccessful.

Help the Aged

Welfare of older people

£5 million (2007/08)

Beneficial area UK and overseas.

York House, 207–221 Pentonville Road, London N1 9UZ

Tel. 020 7278 1114 **Fax** 020 7278 1116

Email info@helptheaged.org.uk

Website www.helptheaged.org.uk

Correspondent Grants Unit

Trustees *Dr Beverly Castleton; Henry Cathcart; Dr June Crown; Brian Fox; Rosemary Kelly; Janet Lord; Tony Rice; Michael Roberts; Len Sanderson; Prof. John Williams; Christopher Woodbridge; Angus Young; Josephine Connell; Simon Waugh; Hilary Wiseman.*

CC Number 272786

Information available Accounts were on file with the Charity Commission. The charity also has a useful website.

In April 2009 Help the Aged and Age Concern joined together to create a new charity dedicated to improving the lives of older people. Operating under the name 'Age Concern and Help the Aged', it aims to speak with one voice on behalf of all older people. From spring 2010 the new name for both merged organisations is Age UK.

One of the most important forms of support for other charities by Help the Aged is best described as 'support in kind'. For example, its staff carries out fundraising training for other UK charities which share the objectives of Help the Aged. Help is, nevertheless, also given in the more traditional form of grants.

In 2007/08 the charity had assets of £19 million and an income of £72 million. Grants totalling £5 million were broken down as follows:

Category	Value
Research	£2,900,000
Day centres, social clubs and initiatives	£1,600,000
Campaigning for older people	£298,000
Senior mobility projects	£207,000

There are also extensive grant-making programmes overseas, amounting to £9.1 million, which are not covered here.

A significant proportion of the charity's grantmaking is focused on research which aims to improve the quality of life of older people. This includes:

- biomedical research into age-related conditions
- social policy research to inform our campaigning work.

More information on research grants is available on the charity's website.

However, perhaps of most interest to readers of this entry is the money the charity gives in grants through its Community Services division. They are usually small, and go to community-based groups for projects such as building and equipping day centres, setting up lunch clubs or buying minibuses, under a range of programmes and schemes. The following information is taken from the charity's website.

Community grants

The charity provides support for older people's community groups and forums, enabling them to provide valuable services and to make older people's voices heard.

At the time of writing the grants programme was under review and further details were unavailable. For the latest information please go to the charity's website or contact the Grants Unit by emailing: grants.unit@ace.org.uk or calling 020 8765 7738.

SeniorMobility

SeniorMobility provides grants for groups and projects to buy urgently needed vehicles, scooters and mobility equipment. The SeniorMobility campaign restores independence and reduces isolation by increasing older people's access to special vehicles and local transport schemes.

Why is there a need for SeniorMobility?

In 2006, 4 per cent of over-65s agreed strongly and 8 per cent agreed slightly that they felt trapped in their own home (Help the Aged/GfK NOP 2006). By making more vehicles and equipment available, SeniorMobility helps keep people active and independent, at the same time as reducing isolation and improving quality of life.

Who can SeniorMobility help?

SeniorMobility is aimed at helping community groups and projects working with older people, including:

- day centres and luncheon clubs
- nursing homes
- dial-a-ride and other community transport schemes
- shopmobility
- gardening projects
- care and repair
- meals on wheels.

In other words, any group needing vehicles or equipment to continue their work is invited to get in touch with SeniorMobility.

What can SeniorMobility provide?

- accessible minibuses – 8, 12 or 16 seaters
- community cars
- multi-purpose vehicles
- adapted gardening vans
- mobile day-care, and information centres
- care and repair vehicles.

What else does SeniorMobility do?

A SeniorMobility transport expert can deal with all aspects of a vehicle purchase on behalf of a project – including the financial and legal paperwork – for a nominal fee. Projects that have secured enough funding for the vehicle by themselves can enjoy significant price discounts by purchasing it through SeniorMobility's bulk-buying scheme.

Where can I find out more?

Contact Graham Lale, SeniorMobility Manager on telephone: 020 7239 1825 or email grahamlale@helptheaged.org.uk

Exclusions The charity does not support:

- continuation of existing activity or replacement of other funding, including bridging funding for loans, reducing deficits incurred by projects, or to make up shortfall due to underbidding for a service contract
- commercial companies or statutory bodies, such as government agencies and health trusts
- organisations artificially created as trusts, designed to meet the needs of community care proposals or to attract European funding
- applications to provide one-off benefit to older people, such as outings, general entertainment, leisure clubs, holidays and single events
- the establishment of new services by applicants whose existing service provision does not meet required standards
- reimbursement for expenditure already incurred
- residential or nursing homes, except to support independent living of older people and where benefits extend to the wider community
- registered social landlords, except where there is a clearly defined project focussing on a vulnerable group, for example, homeless older people
- individual members of the public
- replacing spending cuts made by local or central government.

Applications For more information on how to apply for community grants contact the Grants Unit by emailing grants.unit@ace.org.uk or calling 020 8765 7738. For further information on the SeniorMobility programme contact Graham Lale, SeniorMobility Manager on: 020 7239 1825 or grahamlale@helptheaged.org.uk.

The Helping Foundation

Orthodox Jewish

£3.6 million (2008/09)

Beneficial area Greater London and Greater Manchester.

1 Allandale Court, Waterpark Road, Salford M7 4JN

Correspondent Benny Stone, Trustee

Trustees *Benny Stone; David Neuwirth; Rabbi Aubrey Weis; Mrs Rachel Weis.*

CC Number 1104484

Information available Accounts were available from the Charity Commission.

Registered with the Charity Commission in June 2004, 'the objects of the charity are the advancement of education according to the tenets of the Orthodox Jewish Faith; the advancement of the Orthodox Jewish Religion and the relief of poverty amongst older people or persons in need, hardship or distress in the Jewish Community'.

In 2008/09 the foundation had assets of £38.7 million and an income of £6.9 million, including £5.2 million from donations. Grants were made during the year to 17 organisations totalling almost £3.6 million.

The beneficiary of the largest grant, as in previous years, was the Talmud Education Trust (£1.9 million). Other beneficiaries included: Notzar Chesed (£731,000); Friends of Mir (£360,000); Asser Bishvil Foundation (£290,000); TTT (£68,000); Bourne Heights (£35,000); Jewish Rescue & Relief Committee (£26,000); Chirat Devora & Chochmat Sholom (£15,000); Talmud Torah Chinuch Norim (£2,000).

Applications In writing to the correspondent.

The Hertfordshire Community Foundation

General

£1.2 million (2007/08)

Beneficial area Hertfordshire.

Foundation House, 2–4 Forum Place, Fiddlebridge Lane, Hatfield AL10 0RN

Tel. 01707 251 351

Email grants@hertscf.org.uk

Website www.hertscf.org.uk

Correspondent David Fitzpatrick, Chief Executive

Trustees *J Stuart Lewis, Chairman; John Peters; Kate Belinis; Caroline McCaffrey; Betty Goble; William Tudor John; David Fryer; Michael Master; Richard Roberts.*

CC Number 299438

Information available Accounts were available from the Charity Commission.

Launched in 1989, the foundation is one of a growing number of community trusts in the UK, which supports and provides funds to local charities and voluntary groups that serve the local community and benefit the lives of the people they serve. The foundation is able to support a wide range of charitable activities, in and around Hertfordshire. The foundation advises, therefore, that it is always worth contacting them to discuss the project, in case they can help or direct you to someone else who can.

Grants in 2007/08

In 2007/08 the foundation had assets of £3.4 million, an income of £1.5 million and made grants totalling £1.2 million. This included 257 grants to organisations and 57 grants to individuals. The main area of the foundation's grant-making activity is in the field of social welfare. Its priority areas are as follows:

- disadvantaged children and families
- activities and opportunities for young people
- access to education, training and employment
- the quality of life of older people
- other community needs.

The majority of grants awarded from the foundation's unrestricted funds are made to local charities and voluntary groups for work within these areas. The foundation manages a growing number of funds on behalf of local donors. Each has its own remit, reflecting the donor's particular charitable interests and concerns. Please contact the foundation for up-to-date details.

Programmes – Foundation Grants

Development grants – Grants of up to £5,000 a year, annually for up to three years. Projects often need time to get established, and some assurance of funding for an agreed length of time. Where a commitment is given to support a project over a period of more than one year, grants will be payable by instalments, and subject to satisfactory progress reports and visits.

Beneficiaries included: Citizens Advice Bureau Hertfordshire (£15,000); Broxbourne and East Hertfordshire Credit Union (£8,000); Hertfordshire PASS (£6,000); and Hitchin Town Bowls Club (£2,900).

Project grants – Grants of up to £5,000 on a one-off basis. These grants are designed to help make something happen, whether on their own or

together with other income. Major purchases or specific projects may be financed under this category.

Grants included those to: Satsang Mandal (£5,000); Age Concern Hertfordshire (£2,500); Hertfordshire Area Rape Crisis and Sexual Abuse Centre (£1,500); and Dacorum Indian Society (£500).

Small grants – Grants of up to £500 on a one-off basis – usually for small groups. The foundation can provide a quick response to requests for all sorts of purposes, such as, start-up costs for a new group or project, equipment, training programmes, printed materials and so on.

Beneficiaries included: Neomari Beadcraft Training Services (£500); Grandparents' Association (£490); and Alzheimer's Disease Society (£175).

Individual Grants – for children – Grants of up to £300 on a one-off basis. These grants are only made following referral by a professional, such as a social worker or health visitor. Please note: grants are only payable to third parties, such as a shop, in order to purchase a much needed item.

Other programmes

The foundation also administers several external funds.

Grassroots Grants – Grants of between £250 and £5,000 to help build stronger and more active communities. The main aim is to support projects that meet an identified need in the local community, such as, putting on a local event, contributing to rental costs or paying for additional activities.

Sport Relief – Set up by Comic Relief and BBC Sport to use the power of sport and exercise to help tackle the exclusion and isolation experienced by some of the poorest and most disadvantaged communities, both in the UK and abroad. It will support community based projects that use sport to overcome barriers, work with excluded and isolated peoples, and draw communities together. Grants of between £250 and £5,000 are available to organisations in Hertfordshire with a turnover of less than £100,000.

More information on these programmes, including guidelines and details of the application process, can be found on the foundation's website.

Exclusions No grants are made towards:

- UK or general appeals, or those with no specific Hertfordshire focus

- statutory or public bodies, or to replace withdrawn statutory funding
- religious or political causes, medical research, holidays, overseas travel or full-time education
- individuals, except within the terms of special funds, for example The Children's Fund.

Applications Application packs are available from the foundation. An initial telephone call or email to check eligibility is welcomed.

Alan Edward Higgs Charity

Child welfare

£572,000 (2007/08)

Beneficial area Within 25 miles of the centre of Coventry only.

Ricoh Arena Ltd, Phoenix Way, Coventry CV6 6GE

Tel. 024 7622 1311

Email clerk@higgscharity.org.uk

Correspondent Peter Knatchbull-Hugessen, Clerk

Trustees *Peter J Davis; Marilyn F Knatchbull-Hugessen; Andrew Young.*

CC Number 509367

Information available Accounts were available from the Charity Commission.

Grants are made to benefit 'wholly or mainly the inhabitants of the area within 25 miles of the centre of Coventry'. The main activity supported is the promotion of child welfare, and particularly the welfare of underprivileged children.

It is the aim of the trustees to reach as wide a selection of the community as possible within the geographical limitations. They are happy to receive applications for grants from local bodies or associations and from national organisations that can show that any grant from the charity would be used to benefit people resident within the geographical area. The increasing range and diversity of donations continue to be welcomed.

In 2007/08 the trust had assets of £17.7 million and an income of £574,000. Grants totalled £572,000. This consisted of meeting the capital (£308,000) and revenue (£152,000) costs of the Alan Higgs Centre Trust and other grants to organisations amounting to £256,500.

Beneficiaries included: Coventry Institute of Creative Enterprise (£40,000); The Living Environment Trust (£28,000); Belgrade Theatre (£20,000); Family Holiday Association (£10,000); Shakespeare Hospice Appeal (£5,000); Guideposts Trust (£3,000); and the RSPB (£1,000).

Exclusions Applications from individuals are not entertained. No grants for the funding of services usually provided by statutory services, medical research, travel outside the UK or evangelical or worship activities.

Applications In writing to the clerk to the trustees, along with:

- a copy of the latest audited accounts
- charity number (if registered)
- a detailed description of the local activities for the benefit of which the grant would be applied
- the specific purpose for which the grant is sought
- a copy of the organisation's policy that ensures the protection of young or vulnerable people and a clear description of how it is implemented and monitored.

The Hilden Charitable Fund

Homelessness, minority groups and race relations, penal affairs and overseas development

£446,000 (2007/08)

Beneficial area UK and developing countries.

34 North End Road, London W14 0SH

Tel. 020 7603 1525 **Fax** 020 7603 1525

Email hildencharity@hotmail.com

Website www.hildencharitablefund.org.uk

Correspondent Rodney Hedley, Secretary

Trustees *Ms M E Baxter; A J M Rampton; Prof. D S Rampton; Prof. M B H Rampton; J R A Rampton; Ms C S L Rampton; Mrs E K Rodeck; Prof. C H Rodeck; H B Woodd; C H Younger; E J Rodeck; Miss E M C Rampton.*

CC Number 232591

Information available Accounts were available at the Charity Commission. The trust also has a helpful website.

This grant-making trust was established in 1963 by an initial gift from Anthony and Joan Rampton. Priorities in the UK are homelessness, minorities and penal affairs. For projects in developing countries, priorities are projects which focus on community development, education, and health. These priorities are reviewed on a three year cycle and may change from time to time, as dictated by circumstances. The trust has also allocated a small budget to help community groups run summer playschemes for the benefit of children from refugee and ethnic minority families. Grants from this scheme rarely exceed £1,000.

The aim of the fund is to address disadvantage, notably by supporting causes which are less likely to raise funds from public subscriptions. Both the UK and overseas funding policy is directed largely at supporting work at community level.

Whilst the trust's policy is to address needs by considering and funding specific projects costs, the trustees are sympathetic to funding general running, or core costs. In awarding these types of grants, they believe that great value can be added, as most charities find fund raising for core costs most difficult.

All grant recipients are expected to send a report on how they have made use of their grant. The trust's staff team ensure adequate grant monitoring. Feedback is given to the trustees via regular mailings as well as at the quarterly meetings. Similarly the secretary produces briefings on all aspects of grantmaking and policy development within the priority areas.

In establishing a secretariat for the trust in 1992, the trust aimed not only to effectively administer the grant making process but also to provide a helpful service to applicants on funding and good practice and applicants are encouraged to telephone the trust's offices for this service. The trustees and the staff team look to network with other funding and voluntary sector organisations, to identify new needs, improve standards and to prevent duplication.

Guidelines

UK grants
The main interests of the trustees of the Hilden Charitable Fund are:

- homelessness
- minorities and race relations
- penal affairs
- developing countries.

Grants are rarely given to well funded national charities. Fund policy is directed largely at supporting work at a community level within the categories of interest stated above.

Preference is given to charities with an income of less that £200,000 per year.

Priorities given to different types of work within the main categories may change from time to time, as dictated by circumstances. Capital or revenue grants rarely exceed £5,000.

Overseas grants
Funds are available for capital and revenue funding. The funding programme is designed to help small and medium size initiatives. Trustees will consider applications from any countries within the developing world. Trustees wish to fund community development, education and health initiatives. Trustees will particularly welcome projects that address the needs and potential of girls and women.

Trustees will be pleased to hear from UK Non Governmental Organisations/charities and hope that UK NGOs/charities will encourage their local partners, if appropriate, to apply directly to Hilden for grant aid.

Summer playscheme grants
The trust has allocated a small budget to help community groups run summer playschemes for the benefit of children from refugee and ethnic minority families.

Grantmaking

In 2007/08 the trust had assets of almost £12.3 million and income of £462.000. There were 104 grants made totalling £446,000, broken down as follows:

Category	No. of grants	Amount
Minorities	26	£136,000
Overseas	21	£106,000
Penal affairs	17	£72,000
Homelessness	16	£70,000
Scotland	1*	£33,000
Playschemes	21	£20,000
Other	2	£9,000

To the Scottish Community Foundation for onward distribution.

The trust provides the following review of its activities during the year in its annual report (with grant totals for the year included):

Minorities
The immediate legal and welfare needs of asylum seekers and refugees were met through grants to: Asylum Aid [£6,000]; Association of Visitors to Immigration Detainees [£5,000]; Cambridge Refugee

Support Group [£5,000]; Detention Advice Service [£5,000]; Dover Detainees' Visitors Group [£3,500]; Ethnic Access Link – Worcester [£5,000]; Slough Refugee Group [£5,000]; Southampton and Winchester Visitors Group [£3,000]; and the UK Lesbian and Gay Immigration Group [£5,000].

Supplementary schools were funded: Claudia Jones Organisation – Hackney [£5,000]; and Southwark Somali Refugee Council [£5,000].

Grants were made to develop services within established groups: Central Africa Refugee Link – West Midlands [£3,000], and the West Hampstead Women's Centre's Somali women's project [£5,000]. The Marsha Phoenix Memorial Trust's homework club was funded [£4,500], and the New Bolton Somali Association was funded for its community programme [£5,000]. Both the Community Integration Trust – Birmingham [£5,000], and Skilltrain – Wandsworth [££3,000] were funded for training courses for refugees.

Compass – Liverpool [£5,000], the Counselling and Prayer Trust [£6,500], and the Guild of Psychotherapists [£5,000] were all funded for their provision of therapeutic services to the black and minority ethnic community. Lena Garden Primary School – Hammersmith, was funded so that refugee children could take part in a Farms for City Children working holiday [£6,400]. Changing Faces was funded for a major campaign on facial disfigurement [£5,000].

Workshops addressing knife and gun crime in south London were funded by a grant to the Charlton Advice Centre [£5,000]. Tolerance International was funded to run workshops in secondary schools in London on racial understanding and tolerance [£5,000].

Overseas
In the year, 21 grants were made to projects in 11 countries:

- Bangladesh: Church Mission Society, Ekota Slum programme, Dhaka [£7,000]
- Kenya: International Child Care Trust, the children and women's programme at Kakamega [£5,000]
- Learning and Development Kenya, street children's hostel, Nakuru [£5,000]
- India: Amar-Lata Gramin Seva Foundation, community health programme, Ganges delta [£3,300]
- Womankind Worldwide, the Irula community development programme, Tamil Nadu [£8,000]
- Iraq: Tolerance International, Iranian refugee camp assistance, Ashraf [£5,000]
- Mali: Burley-Tereli Friendship Trust, school buildings programme, Tereli [£5,000]
- Papua New Guinea: Melanesia Educational Development Foundation, national school children sponsorship scheme [£2,000]
- Philippines: Francis-Clarissa Foundation, street children project Manila [£3,000]
- South Africa: Ons Plek, street girls' hostel, Cape Town [£5,000]
- Presidents Award for Youth Empowerment Trust, young ex-offenders and prisoner training award scheme [£5,000]
- Tanzania: Arusha Mental Health Trust, clinic costs, Arusha [£5,000]
- Community Development and Relief Agency ,water programme, Kamera [£5,000]
- Tanzania Development Trust, classrooms, Samaritan Girls Secondary School, Mbeya [£5,600]
- Uganda: The Busoga Trust, wells programme, Kidera [£5,000]
- The Mityana Charity, school and farm project, Mityana [£7,000]
- Trust for Africa's Orphans, rain water storage project, Ssembabule [£5,000]
- Zambia: Baynard Zambia Trust, Kalwa regional development programme [£7,500]

Grants affecting more than one country
The new community interest company Majority World was funded for its programme to develop 'fair trade' photography sources and to promote the employment of African photographers [£5,000]. The Jubilee Debt Campaign was given a donation towards its office costs [£2,500], and The Good Earth Trust was funded for the promotion of appropriate earth technology in brick making in Kenya and Uganda [£5,000].

Awarding grants direct to projects overseas
Hilden funds charitable projects both registered in the UK, which work with their partners overseas, and direct to charities constituted in the countries themselves.

By directly funding overseas, trustees' consider that some 'value added' may be achieved by both minimising overhead costs incurred by the UK based charities, and by building on the indigenous projects' capacity and infrastructure. In awarding grants directly overseas, the trustees ensure that the charities' objectives, legal and financial standing, and relevant 'foreign contributions' regulations are investigated. In 2007/8, the value of all grants awarded to projects direct was £30,000 amounting to 28% of the total grantmaking in the year for overseas initiatives.

Penal affairs
In the year 17 projects were funded. These programmes within prisons were funded: The Irene Taylor Trust for music workshops in a number of prisons [£5,000]; Kainos Community, at the Verne Prison – Portland [£5,000], City of Exeter YMCA, at Exeter Prison [£5,000], and Outside Chance [£3,500] at a number of young offender institutions, all provided courses and regimes preparing inmates for release. Parents in Prisons was grant aided to provide psychological counselling of pregnant women and mothers at HMP Bronzefield and HMP Holloway [£5,000]. The Prisoner's Advice Service was funded for its information and advice service for inmates [£5,000].

Three community chaplaincy re-settlement services were funded: New Hope Mentoring Programme – West Midlands [£5,000]; Opengate – Durham, for women ex-offenders [£2,500], and Restoring Broken Walls Trust – Doncaster [£5,000]. Training programmes for ex-offenders were funded: Dance United, for its young people academy in Bradford [£5,000], and Cleveland Housing Advice Service – Middlesbrough, for its volunteer placement scheme [£5,000]. The Synergy Project was funded to run a range of crime awareness courses involving ex-offenders, for school age children in south-west London [£2,000].

Families of offenders were helped with support and advice by grants to the Cedar Wood Trust – North Shields [£3,000]; SPODA (Supporting Anyone Whose Life is Affected by Someone Else's Substance Abuse) – West Midlands [£4,500]; and Prisoners' Families and Friends Service – Greater London [£5,000]. Wakefield Prison Visits Childrens Play Facility was funded as a key part of the prison's visitor centre [£5,000].

Homelessness
In the year 16 projects were funded. Day care services were funded at: Barons Court Project – London [£3,000]; Comex (Wallsall) Ltd [£3,000]; The Centre Project – Leicester [£5,000]; Deptford Churches Centre [£5,000]; Freedom Trust – Barnstaple [£5,000]; St George's House Charity – Wolverhampton [£5,000]; Daventry Contact [£3,000]; Maggs Day Centre – Worcester [£5,000]; Pitstop – Leatherhead [£5,000] and Open Door Taunton [£3,000]. In Bristol Hilden funded the One 25 Limited drop-in for female street sex workers [£5,000]. Lifeshare Limited Manchester was funded for an outreach service for male sex workers [£5,000], and Bridge Oasis Church Trust – Birmingham for a street recovery scheme [£5,000]. The needs of homeless families were recognised by the award of grants to Brighton Unemployed Centre Families Project [£4,000], and the Furniture Scheme Richmond Upon Thames [£5,000]. A winter night shelter scheme was funded: North London Action for the Homeless [£4,000].

Playschemes
In the summer of 2007, the fund allocated £20,000 for a playscheme programme. 21 projects were funded. Applications from organisations working with refugee and immigrant communities were given priority.

Most projects funded were based in Greater London.

Exclusions Grants are not normally made for well established causes or to individuals, and overseas grants concentrate on development aid in preference to disaster relief.

Applications

When making an application, grant seekers should bear in mind the points below. The fund expects all applicants to complete the application form. Your case for funds should be concise (no more than two sides of A4), but supporting documentation is essential. Please ensure your application includes enclosures of:

- your most recent independently inspected accounts
- your most recent annual report
- projected income and expenditure for the current financial year.

Please be clear in your application form about when the proposed work is to commence, and give the relevant timetable.

Your application for funds should cover the following:

- clear explanation about who is responsible for managing the project
- a coherent plan of how the work is going to be carried out together with relevant budgets. Project budgets should be presented in the context of the overall income and expenditure of the applicant NGO/Charity
- a plan of how the work is going to be maintained and developed in the future by involving relevant agencies and attracting money and resources
- an explanation of why the local project seeks the help of a UK agency
- details of local costs (for example salaries of state-employed teachers and medical personnel, cost of vehicles, petrol etc) and notes of any problems over exchange rates or inflation
- an account of the political, economic, religious and cultural situation in the country/area
- a brief comment on the extent to which the project can rely on government and local state funding in the country concerned
- details of monitoring and evaluation.

Overseas applications

Applicants applying direct from outside the UK must complete the Overseas Application Form.

Please note: Applicants from the UK applying for funds for their project partners, must complete both the UK Application Form and the Overseas Application Form.

Application forms, including one for Summer Playschemes, are available from the trust's website or offices. Please note that forms must be submitted to the secretary by post as hard copies; forms submitted by email or other electronic means are not accepted. Applicants are advised to ensure that they have read the application guidelines at the top of the form prior to completion.

Potential applicants in Scotland should contact the Scottish Community Foundation, 22 Carlton Road, Edinburgh EH8 8DP; Tel: 0131 524 0300; website: www.scottishcf.org

Lady Hind Trust

General with some preference for health and disability related charities

£328,000 (2007)

Beneficial area England with a preference for Nottinghamshire and Norfolk.

c/o Berryman Shacklock, Park House, Friar Lane, Nottingham NG1 6DN

Tel. 0115 945 3700 **Fax** 0115 948 0234

Correspondent Bill F Whysall, Trustee

Trustees *Charles W L Barratt; Tim H Farr; Nigel R Savory; Bill F Whysall.*

CC Number 208877

Information available Accounts were available from the Charity Commission.

The trust was established in 1951 for general charitable purposes. In 2007 the trust had assets of £13 million, which generated an income of £399,500. Grants were made totalling £328,000, with most being for £5,000 or less, and were broken down geographically as follows:

Nottinghamshire – £155,000

Beneficiaries included: Nottingham Almshouse Charity (£20,000); Southwell Minster (£10,000); Lincolnshire & Nottinghamshire Air Ambulance (£7,500); University of Nottingham Neonatal MRI Scanner and the Jonathan Young Memorial Trust (£5,000 each); St John the Baptist and All Saints Churches, Collingham (£3,000); Bromley House Library and Open Minds (£2,000 each); and Hucknall Nightstop, Radford Visiting Scheme and Weston Spirit, Nottingham (£1,000 each).

Norfolk – £91,500

Beneficiaries included: St Martin's Housing Trust (£25,000); Norwich Cathedral (£13,000); Norfolk Churches Trust (£7,500); True's Yard Fishing Heritage Museum (£5,000); Mancroft Advice Project (£3,000); Nancy Oldfield Trust (£2,500); Football in the Community (£1,500); and Buckingham Emergency Food Appeal, Gt Yarmouth & Waveney Contact and Norfolk Autistic Society (£1,000 each).

Elsewhere – £79,500

Beneficiaries included: Elizabeth Finn Trust (£2,500); East Anglia's Children's Hospices and the Huntington's Disease Association (£2,000 each); and the Alzheimer's Society, British Polio Fellowship, Contact the Elderly, Independence at Home, Parkinson's Disease Society, Starlight Children's Foundation and Association of Wheelchair Children (£1,000 each).

Exclusions Applications from individuals are not considered.

Applications Applications, in writing and with latest accounts, must be submitted at least one month in advance of trustee meetings held in March, July and November. Unsuccessful applicants are not notified.

The Hintze Family Charitable Foundation

Education, Christian churches, museums, libraries and galleries

£4.4 million (2008)

Beneficial area England and Wales.

5th Floor, 33 Chester Street, London SW1X 7BL

Tel. 020 7201 6862

Correspondent Oliver Hylton, Trustee

Trustees *Michael Hintze; Nick Hunt; David Swain; Steven Walters.*

CC Number 1101842

Information available Accounts were available from the Charity Commission.

Set up in 2003, the main objects of the foundation are providing support for:

- Christian churches in England and Wales, particularly the Diocese of Southwark
- relief of sickness and people with terminal illnesses
- resources and equipment for schools, colleges and universities (in particular

to enable the acquisition and retention of antiquarian books to be used as a learning resource)
- promoting access to museums, libraries and art galleries.

In 2008 the foundation had an income of £3.9 million mostly from donations and grants totalling £3.8 million. Just under £1.5 million was carried forward at year end. Grants were made to 37 institutions totalling £4.4 million and were broken down as follows:

Category	Value
Education – cultural	£2,000,000
Health	£1,000,000
Education – core	£902,000
Religion	£399,000

Commitments made in the year included £1.5 million to the Prince's Foundations over two years. Other beneficiaries included: Lockwood Charitable Foundation (£1 million); Friends of the University of Sydney (£680,000); the National Gallery (£500,000); and International Theological Institute (£119,000).

Applications The foundation offers the following application guidance in its latest accounts:

The foundation invites applications for grants or commitments from charities which serve the objects of the foundation. No specific format is required for applications. Applications, along with potential donations and commitments identified by the Chief Executive and the trustees, are considered in formal trustee meetings.

The Hobson Charity Limited

Social welfare and education

£2.7 million (2007/08)
Beneficial area UK.

21 Bryanston Street, Marble Arch, London W1H 7PR

Tel. 020 7495 5599

Correspondent Deborah Hobson, Trustee and Secretary

Trustees *Deborah Hobson; Sir Donald Gosling; Sir Ronald F Hobson; Lady Hobson; J Richardson.*

CC Number 326839

Information available Accounts were available from the Charity Commission.

Established in 1985, the Hobson Charity Limited is the charitable vehicle of Sir

Ronald Hobson, founder of Central Car Parks and later co-owner of NCP car parks with business partner, Sir Donald Gosling, also a trustee (see also the Gosling Foundation). Both charities are administered from the same address.

General

In 2007/08 the charity had assets of £591,000 and an income of £3.9 million, mainly from donations. Grant commitments were made during the year totalling £4 million, with administration costs being very low at just over £6,000. Grants paid out during 2007/08 totalled £2.7 million.

Grants were awarded in the following categories:

Category	Paid in 2007/08	No. of grants
Advancement of education	£1,550,000	27
Other purposes beneficial to the community	£878,500	50
Relief of poverty	£261,000	4
Advancement of religion	£12,000	3

Grants in 2007/08

Advancement of education
The largest single donation during the year was £1 million, given in three grants to the Woodard Corporation Limited, which runs the largest group of independent Church of England schools in England and Wales – the organisation also received £800,000 during 2008/09. Other beneficiaries included: Royal Marines Museum (£100,000); Coram Foundation (£70,000); Wells Cathedral Girl Choristers Trust (£50,000 in total); Churchill Archives Centre (£20,000 in total); Royal Philharmonic Orchestra (£15,000); Dancing for the Children and Mill Hill School Foundation (£10,000 each); and Savannah Education Trust (£2,000).

Other purposes beneficial to the community (general)
Beneficiaries included: the Armed Forces Memorial Trust (£350,000 in total); Great Ormond Street Hospital (£100,000 in total) – a further £400,000 has been committed to the hospital up to 2012; Moorfields Eye Hospital (£50,000); Opera North (£25,000); Diabetes UK (£20,000); North London Hospice (£16,000 in total); Gloucestershire Emergency Accommodation Resource and the Polar Extreme Foundation (£10,000 each); Children with Leukaemia (£5,000); Hendon Band of the Salvation Army (£2,000); and Pentland Finchley Carnival (£1,000).

Relief of poverty
The grants were made to: White Ensign Association (£120,000); Army Benevolent Fund (£80,000); SSAFA (£60,000 in total); and Fund for Refugees in Slovenia (£1,000).

Advancement of religion
The grants were made to: St Martin-in-the-Field Development Trust (£10,000); and Hendon Salvation Army and WIZO UK (£1,000 each).

Exclusions No grants to individuals, except in exceptional circumstances.

Applications In writing to the correspondent. The trustees meet quarterly.

The Jane Hodge Foundation

Medical care and research, education and religion

£1.1 million (2007/08)
Beneficial area Unrestricted, in practice UK with a preference for Wales.

Ty Gwyn, Lisvane Road, Lisvane, Cardiff CF14 0SG

Tel. 029 2076 6521

Email dianne.lydiard@ janehodgefoundation.co.uk

Correspondent Margaret Cason, Secretary

Trustees *Lady Moira Hodge; Eric Hammonds; Robert Hodge; Joyce Harrison; Derek L Jones; Ian Davies; Margaret Cason.*

CC Number 216053

Information available Accounts were available from the Charity Commission.

The foundation was established in 1962 and its objective is to apply its income in the following areas:

- the encouragement of medical and surgical studies and research, and in particular the study of and research in connection with the causes, diagnosis, treatment and cure of cancer, poliomyelitis, tuberculosis and diseases affecting children
- the general advancement of medical and surgical science
- the advancement of education
- the advancement of religion.

In 2007/08 the foundation had assets of £27 million and an income of just over £1.3 million. Grants were made totalling £1.1 million.

The following extract is taken from a review of activities given in the 2007/08 trustees' report:

Sir Julian Hodge Chair in Asset Finance Law – Swansea – The annual payment of £25,000 was made in January 2008, being the fourth instalment of the agreement reached to extend support of this Chair for a further five years (2005 – 2009).

Cardiff Business School – Julian Hodge Institute of Applied Macroeconomics – The annual payment of £100,000 to the Julian Hodge Institute of Applied Macroeconomics and the £25,000 for PhD students there was made as usual during the year, following the agreement of the trustees to extend their support for a further three years at the same level. The old arrangement terminated in August 2008, so the new agreement covers the years 2009 to 2011.

George Thomas Memorial Trust – The trustees have agreed to support the Christmas 2008 Light up a Life Appeal by way of matched funding up to a maximum of £50,000.

Wallich Clifford Community – The last payment of £26,000 agreed in support of their Task Force Project was paid during the year. This completes our commitment to the charity.

Royal Welsh College of Music and Drama – It has been agreed to allocate £100,000 to the College payable over two years to support the establishment of five International Chairs in Music at the college. The first payment was made in September 2008 and the second will be made twelve months from that date.

Archdiocese of Cardiff – St. Peter's Church – A donation of £50,000 was approved by the trustees as a contribution to the Cathedral Restoration Appeal, due to run until 2020. This was released in January 2008.

Grants are categorised as follows:

Educational
Beneficiaries included: Cardiff Business School (£139,000 in three grants); University of Wales – Swansea (£25,000); Christ College, MENCAP and Arts Active Trust (£5,000 each); Council for Education in World Citizenship (£4,500); Welsh Heritage Schools Initiative (£3,500); and Cardiff University – Centre for Journalism (£3,000).

Medical
Beneficiaries included: George Thomas Hospice Care (£58,000 in two grants); Bobath Cymru (£10,000 in two grants); Healing Foundation and Hospice of the Valleys (£5,000 each); and Children's Heart Foundation (£3,000).

Religious
Grants included those made to: Archdiocese of Cardiff (£50,000); Order of St John (£7,500); St Woolas Cathedral Appeal (£5,000); and Holy Trinity Presbyterian Church of Wales and Llanishen Methodist Church (£3,000 each).

Other
Beneficiaries included: Wallich Clifford Community (£26,000); Race Equality First (£7,000); Help the Aged (£6,000); and Vale of Glamorgan Railway, Prince's Trust Cymru and Morriston Orpheus Choir (£5,000 each).

Exclusions Applications are only considered from exempt or registered charities. No grants to individuals.

Applications In writing to the correspondent. Applications for grants are considered by the trustees at regular meetings throughout the year. Applications are acknowledged.

Sir Harold Hood's Charitable Trust

Roman Catholic charitable purposes

£461,000 (2007/08)
Beneficial area Worldwide.

Haysmacintyre, Fairfax House, 15 Fulwood Place, London WC1V 6AY

Tel. 020 7722 9088

Correspondent Margaret Hood, Trustee

Trustees *Dom James Hood; Anne-Marie True; Nicholas True; Margaret Hood; Christian Elwes.*

CC Number 225870

Information available Accounts were available from the Charity Commission.

This trust supports Roman Catholic charities. In 2007/08 it had assets of £14 million and an income of £570,000. Grants were made totalling £461,000.

The accounts for this year do not give details of individual beneficiaries but are categorised as follows:

Category	Value
Single Grants	£69,000
Aid	£6,000
Churches	£74,000
Education	£54,000
Homeless	£20,000
Hospitals	£12,000
Leprosy	£12,000
Missionary	£37,000
Nursing	£5,000
Prisoners	£25,000
Retreat Centre	£20,000
Schools	£12,000
Seminary	£7,000
Vatican	£4,000
Young people	£46,000
Special Grants	£43,000
Services	£15,000

No further information was available.

Exclusions No grants for individuals.

Applications In writing to the correspondent. The trustees meet once a year to consider applications, usually in November.

The Sir Joseph Hotung Charitable Settlement

General

£1.4 million (2007/08)
Beneficial area Worldwide.

c/o HSBC Private Bank (UK) Ltd, 78 St James' Street, London, SWIA IEJ

Correspondent Sir Joseph Hotung, Trustee

Trustees *Sir Joseph E Hotung; Sir Robert D H Boyd; Victoria F Dicks; Michael Gabriel; Joseph S Lesser.*

CC Number 1082710

Information available Accounts were available from the Charity Commission.

Set up in 2000, in 2007/08 this trust had assets of £1.6 million and an income of £1.7 million, mainly from donations from Sir Joseph Hotung. Grants totalled £1.4 million.

During the year grants were made for the following charitable purposes.

- Various grants totalling £275,000 were made to the School of Oriental and African Studies for the Sir Joseph Hotung Programme for Law, Human Rights and Peace Building in the Middle East.

- Various grants totalling £816,000 were paid to St George's Hospital Medical School to fund the Chairs in

Molecular Vaccinology, Immunology and Rheumatology.

- A donation of £250,000 was made towards the renewal of St Martin-in-the-Fields Church.
- A donation of £50,000 was made to the London Symphony Orchestra.
- A donation of £25,000 was made to the Oriental Ceramic Society.
- Grants of £1,200 were made to the International Spinal Research Trust.
- A donation of £500 was made to the Victoria & Albert Museum.

Applications In writing to the correspondent.

The Albert Hunt Trust

Welfare

£1.7 million (2007/08)
Beneficial area UK.

Coutts & Co., 440 Strand, London WC2R 0QS

Tel. 020 7663 6825 **Fax** 020 7663 6794

Correspondent Steve Harvey, Senior Trust Manager

Trustees *Coutts and Co; R J Collis; Mrs B McGuire.*

CC Number 277318

Information available Accounts were available from the Charity Commission.

The Albert Hunt Trust was established in 1979 and its mission statement is:

to promote and enhance the physical and mental welfare of individuals, or groups of individuals, excluding research or the diagnosis and treatment of specific medical conditions, by the distribution of trust funds, at the sole and absolute discretion of the trustees, principally to charities registered in England and Wales that are actively engaged in that field of work.

A very large number of modest grants are given to a wide range of organisations, both national and local, each year. Most grants are for between £1,000 and £2,000 and many seem to go to new beneficiaries. There are around 80 grants for £5,000 or slightly more each year and these tend to go to regularly supported, national charities. The grant-making capacity of the trust has increased in recent years following the death of Miss M K Coyle, a long-standing trustee, who bequeathed £17 million from her estate to the trust.

In 2007/08 the trust had assets of £44 million and an income of £1.6 million. Grants were made to 469 institutions totalling £1.7 million.

Beneficiaries of the largest grants were: Spectrum Safe Centre (£104,000); Demelza House Children's Hospice and the Home Farm Trust (£50,000 each); the Meath Epilepsy Trust and White Lodge Centre (£30,000 each); Phyllis Tuckwell Hospice and the Tree House Trust (£25,000 each); Dorward House (£20,000); SENSE (£16,000); Age Concern – Seven Oaks and District (£15,000); and the Linden Lodge Charitable Trust (£12,000).

Beneficiaries of grants of £10,000 included: Chilterns MS Centre, Cornwall Multiple Sclerosis Therapy Centre Ltd, Farleigh Hospice, the Nelson Trust, Penumbra, Rainbow Living, Rossendale Trust, St Christopher's Hospice, Treloar Trust and the Wessex Autistic Society.

Beneficiaries of grants of £5,000 included: Acorns Children's Hospice Trust, Bedfordshire and Northamptonshire Multiple Sclerosis Therapy Centre, British Limbless Ex-Servicemen's Association, ChildLine, Friends of the Elderly, Greater London Fund for the Blind, Independent Age, Leonard Cheshire Foundation, the Manna Society, MIND, the Pasque Charity, Refuge, Royal Hospital for Neuro Disability, Samaritans, Sussex Lantern, Thames Hospice Care and Wirral Autistic Society.

Beneficiaries of grants of £2,000 or less included: Action for Kids, Bootle Salvation Army, Cancer Backup, Disability Intiative, Guideposts Trust, Hearing Concern, Holidays with Help, Just 42, Manchester City Mission, National Kidney Federation, Open Sight, Prisoners Abroad, Scope, Sheffield Mencap and Gateway, U-Turn Project, Vitalise and Walsall Bereavement Support.

Exclusions No grants for medical research or overseas work.

Applications In writing to the correspondent. All appeals should be by letter containing the following:

- aims and objectives of the charity
- nature of appeal
- total target if for a specific project
- contributions received against target
- registered charity number
- any other relevant factors.

The correspondent has stated that no unsolicited correspondence will be acknowledged unless an application receives favourable consideration. Trustees meet in March, July and November although appeals are considered on an ongoing basis.

The Hunter Foundation

Education, young people, children, relief of poverty and community development

About £8 million (2007/08)
Beneficial area UK and overseas.

Marathon House, Olympic Business Park, Drybridge Road, Dundonald, Ayrshire KA2 9AE

Email info@thehunterfoundation.co.uk

Website www.thehunterfoundation.co.uk

Correspondent Sir Tom Hunter, Trustee

Trustees *Sir Tom Hunter, Chair; Lady Marion Hunter; Jim McMahon; Robert Glennie; Vartan Gregorian.*

SC Number SCO27532

Information available Despite making a written request for the accounts of this foundation (including an sae) these were not provided. The following entry is based on the details filed with the Office of the Scottish Charity Regulator and information on the foundation's website.

Summary

The following information is taken from the foundation's website:

The Hunter Foundation (THF) is committed to adventure philanthropy, investing capital and intellect into tackling the root causes of societal problems through holistic and systemic interventions.

Our focus in the developed world is to invest in national educational programmes that challenge stubborn, system wide issues that prevent children from achieving their potential.

In the developing world we largely invest in holistic developments that embed solutions within communities and countries, again with education being central to our programmes.

Our aim is to act as a catalyst for change by investing in pilot programmes with strategic partners and often alongside government that, if proven, are then adopted by government or the community for embedding nationally where possible.

To date THF has invested, or committed to invest, £35 million and last year the THF founders pledged a further £100 million for investment in Scotland and the developing world.

Principles of investment
Objective
Effect positive, long-term cultural change to deliver a 'can do' attitude initially in Scotland via major investment in, largely, educational programmes.

Why?
The more enterprising the nation, the more economically stable it becomes providing the necessary funds to deliver for all. Education is the ultimate change agent in achieving this end goal.

Investment principles
- proactive identification of investments via definitive research and analysis
- active investment management against targets
- joint ventures and partnerships dominate
- measurable ROI via definitive analysis
- exit strategies predominate – invest against target adoption of programmes by government.

Investment profile
Four distinct profiles across short, medium or long-term objective impact:

- national educational programmes or pilots therein to deliver on our objective
- policy influence to support delivery and Government investment
- advocacy to secure extended investor base and support
- support for disenfranchised or suffering children.

Investments to date
- over £35 million committed from THF to date
- this has leveraged £175 million of public and private sector additional investment (5x multiplier effect)
- 3 to 5 % of all investment funds are applied to independent research and evaluation of programme impacts
- educational investments matched funded by government with clear policy adoption a pre-requisite outcome of measured programme success.

Funding guidelines

By way of guidance to applicants some basic facts about our investments are as follows:

UK and Ireland
THF invests in programmes that embed a 'can do' spirit in children and that tackle the root causes of the problems that see children consigned to the 'Not in Education, Employment or Training' group (NEET Group).

We do not fund capital projects nor individual causes and we always look towards investing in programmes that are nationally scalable and capable of being embedded for systemic change.

Developing World
In the developing world we look towards investing in holistic programmes of intervention that support self-sustainable communities thriving. Often these combine health, education, agriculture and business creation and development interventions.

We are currently working with the Clinton Foundation on the Clinton-Hunter Development Initiative. This initiative is concentrating in Malawi & Rwanda on pilot projects that could be replicated throughout different countries. Until we have completed these pilot programmes we will are unlikely to be in a position to consider new project funding as we fundamentally believe in taking a very strategic investment approach and this will only come from testing out models of intervention.

Unlike in the UK and Ireland we do consider capital projects and often fund, for example, schools development.

On occasion we also fund humanitarian causes as we have done in both Northern Uganda and the Niger, albeit we always aim to integrate our approach and build in as much sustainability as is possible under the circumstances.

Grantmaking in 2007/08

During the year the foundation had an income of £11 million. Grants usually total around £8 million each year.

Previous beneficiaries include: Determined to Succeed, the Children's Charity, Make Poverty History, Band Aid for Village Reach Mozambique, Cash for Kids at Christmas Charitable Trust, Maggie Care Centre, Retail Trust, Variety Club, NCH Action for Children Scotland, Cancer Research, Prince's Scottish Youth Business Trust and Children in Need.

Applications The foundation offers the following application guidance on its website:

The Hunter Foundation proactively sources programmes for investment, or works with partners to develop new programmes where a gap or clear need is identified. As such it is very rare indeed for THF to fund unsolicited bids, however if you wish to apply please complete a maximum two page summary outlining how your project fits with our aims and objectives and email it to info@thehunterfoundation.co.uk. This summary should include:

- summary of project
- impact of project
- any independent evaluation undertaken of your project/programme
- if this is a local programme how it could be scaled to become a national programme
- current sources of funding
- funding sought from the Hunter Foundation.

Please note: we do not have a large staff and thus we will not consider meetings in advance of this information being provided. If your project appears to be of initial interest, we will then contact you to discuss this further.

The Huntingdon Foundation

Jewish education

£461,000 (2007/08)

Beneficial area Mainly Jewish communities in the UK. There is some grant giving in the US.

8 Goodyers Gardens, London NW4 2HD

Tel. 020 8202 2282

Correspondent Benjamin Perl

Trustees Benjamin Perl, Chair; Dr Shoshana Perl; R Jeidel (USA); Jonathan Perl; Naomi Sorotzkin; Joseph Perl.

CC Number 286504

Information available Accounts were available from the Charity Commission.

The foundation was established in 1960 for general charitable purposes. It defines its principal activity as 'the establishment and continued support of Jewish schools'. The foundation also supports other educational organisations, charities and orthodox Jewish higher education establishments in the U.S.

In 2007/08 the trust had assets of £11 million and an income of £737,000. Grants were made totalling £450,000. A further £11,000 in education start up costs was incurred in the establishment of a proposed school in Watford and the establishment of the Morasha Jewish Primary School in Finchley.

Beneficiaries of general grants included: Bais Medrash Gevoha L'Torah Ateres Yisrael, Torah Temima Primary School, Tikun, JNF, Noam Primary School, Edgware Jewish Primary School, American Friends of Hala and Bais Yaccov Primary School.

The accounts do not list the amounts given to individual recipient organisations.

Exclusions Individuals.

Applications In writing to the correspondent. The trustees meet several times a year.

Hurdale Charity Limited

Advancement of Jewish religion, relief of poverty and general charitable purposes

£1.6 million (2007/08)
Beneficial area Worldwide.

Cohen Arnold and Co., New Burlington House, 1075 Finchley Road, London NW11 0PU

Correspondent Abraham Oestreicher, Correspondent

Trustees M Oestreicher, Chair; Mrs E Oestreicher; P Oestreicher; D Oestreicher; A Oestreicher; J Oestreicher; B Oestreicher.

CC Number 276997

Information available Accounts were available from the Charity Commission.

The trust supports charitable activities mostly concerned with religion and education. Almost all of the support is given to Jewish organisations that are seen to uphold the Jewish way of life, both in the UK and overseas.

In 2007/08 the trust had assets of £18 million and an income of £2.2 million. Grants were made to organisations totalling £1.6 million, however a list of beneficiaries was unavailable with this year's accounts.

Previously, grants were made to: UTA (£240,000); Mesifta (£220,000); Chevras Moaz Ladol (£85,000); Yetev Lev Jerusalem Trust (£78,000); Vyoel Moshe Trust (£70,000); Beis Ruchel £34,000); Kollel Rabinow (£23,000); Craven Walk Beis Hamedresh Trust (£22,000); Ezras Bis Yisroel (£15,000); Mosdos Belz Bnei Brak (£11,000); Pesach Project Trust (£10,000); Shaarei Chesed (£9,000); Kehal Chasidei Bobov (£5,500); Hachzakos Torah V'chesed (£4,500); Medical Aid Trust (£3,000); Yeshiva Law of Trust (£2,000); and Zichron Yechezkal Trust (£1,000).

Applications In writing to the correspondent.

Impetus Trust

The development of charities working with people who are economically disadvantaged and general

£356,000 (2007/08)
Beneficial area Worldwide, in practice, UK.

20 Flaxman Terrace, London WC1H 9PN

Tel. 020 3384 3940

Email info@impetus.org.uk

Website www.impetus.org.uk

Correspondent Stephen Dawson, Trustee

Trustees Stephen Dawson, Chair; Nat Sloane; Andy Hinton; Ian Meakins; Chris Underhill; Amelia Howard; Stephen Lambert.

CC Number 1094681

Information available Accounts were available from the Charity Commission.

Impetus Trust was set up in 2002 and is believed to be the UK's first general venture philanthropy charitable fund.

We provide charities with strategic funding, expertise and capacity building support over a defined period of time, usually between three and five years, so that they can focus on transforming more lives. We bring our business skills, our energy and our passion to help charities at a critical stage in their development to create maximum social impact.

Impetus provides an integrated venture philanthropy package, translating venture capital and business frameworks for the not for profit sector. Throughout the relationship, we maintain a high level of engagement including monthly meetings with the chief executive, and careful monitoring to ensure progress against agreed objectives. This approach is one of our distinguishing characteristics and underpins our successful track record on impact.

Impetus provides strategic funding, capacity building and hands-on management support to charities that turn around the lives of a substantial number of disadvantaged people. We work with small to medium-sized

charities that are at a critical stage in their development. We are continually looking to increase our portfolio of charitable investments and we are always keen to hear from charities that meet our selection criteria.

The trust's founders, Stephen Dawson and Nat Sloane, wanted to enable donors and charities to maximise their effectiveness by creating an organisation and building an approach which would provide an impetus for:

- charities to make a step change in their performance
- donors to have confidence to give or give more
- people to contribute time and expertise
- combining the best of the business and non-profit worlds.

The trust's strategic objectives are:

- investment in charities – continuing to invest in new charities
- support from donors – raising funds to support a growing portfolio of charities and work towards long-term income sustainability for Impetus
- working with partners – to secure and manage high quality associates
- evaluation, communication and excellence – reviewing the trust's approach.

In 2007/08 the trust had assets of almost £1.8 million and an income of £1.85 million, mainly from donations. During the year the trust supported nine charities, and grants made to these organisations by the Impetus Trust totalled £356,000 – including additional leverage from the trust's supporters and partners, the total benefit to these organisations amounted to £1.4 million. These organisations (and the amount they received from the Impetus Trust) were: St Giles Trust and Naz Project London (£67,500 each); beat (£56,000); LEAP Confronting Conflict (£45,000); CamFed International (£40,000); Key Fund (£30,000); IntoUniversity (£25,000); and Acumen and Street League (£12,500 each).

The trust currently has a portfolio of 13 charities with which it works. As well as the charities mentioned above, the portfolio also includes: SpeakingUp, the Fairtrade Foundation; Blue Sky; and Teens and Toddlers.

Guidelines

The trust will only consider funding charities that meet the following criteria.

1) Coverage

Impetus backs charities and social enterprises that are achieving clear outcomes with significant numbers of economically disadvantaged people.

2) Ambition

We support charities and social enterprises that have the ambition to effect far reaching change for the economically disadvantaged.

3) Outcome focused

We seek charities and social enterprises that help the economically disadvantaged tackle challenging issues such as long-term unemployment, persistent offending, violence and addiction with the aim of:

- improving their levels of education, attainment or achievement and thus
- achieving higher levels of self-sufficiency and employability

4) Backing the Chief Executive

The quality of leadership – we seek Chief Executives with the vision, energy, enterprise and determination to motivate their teams and help economically disadvantaged people realise their full potential.

5) Supporting the whole organisation

We seek to back a team and their vision. We provide funding and expertise to support the development of whole organisation and not just a particular project or activity.

6) Distinctive and good prospects for sustainability

We target our support at charities and social enterprises which are distinctive and have strong prospects for success and sustainability in their sector.

Structural criteria

- turnover of at least £250,000
- operational and with audited accounts for at least 3 years
- HQ and significant portion of management in England. The majority of organisations supported by Impetus operate only in the UK, and a small number have operations internationally.

Exclusions Grants are not made to:

- organisations focusing on animals, culture or heritage rather than people
- organisations whose services are conditional upon the acceptance, profession or observance of a particular religious position
- organisations substantially/exclusively working in the areas of research or advocacy (unless impact on people's lives is demonstrable)
- umbrella organisations.

Applications

In writing to the correspondent including the following information:

- how long the charity has been running
- what you see as the charity's unique positioning in your sector
- the charity's annual income

- the charity's main achievements over the past five years (for example income generation; social impact, etc.)
- the charity's aims and goals for the next 3–5 years
- why the charity is applying for Impetus investment
- how you heard about Impetus.

Your application must also include:

- a copy of your current strategic/business plan
- the charity's latest audited accounts
- a summary of the charity's strengths, weaknesses, opportunities and threats.

We will consider the information provided and respond as soon as possible. If you fit our criteria and we believe that your charity could become one of those we hope to work with, we will invite your Chief Executive and Chair for a meeting with us. It will take a minimum of four months from that meeting for an investment to be agreed.

The decision-making process will include meetings with your trustees and management as well as site visits and analysis of your financial data. We carry out this due diligence to ensure long-term success in our partnership with you. If we decide not to form a partnership with you, we hope that you still find that you have benefited substantially from the process. We would like to stress that, throughout this process, the decision to proceed is as much for you as for us. Our approach is not right for everyone and you should only proceed if you are convinced that you need this full venture philanthropy package.

Investream Charitable Trust

Jewish

£2.6 million (2007/08)

Beneficial area In practice the UK and Israel.

38 Wigmore Street, London W1U 2RU

Tel. 020 7486 2800

Correspondent The Trustees

Trustees M Morris; M Golker; G S Morris.

CC Number 1097052

Information available Accounts were available from the Charity Commission.

The trust's income has been derived from Investream Limited and its subsidiary undertakings, and other companies under the control of Mark

Morris and Maurice Golker, two of the trustees. In 2007/08 it had an income of £4.2 million, mostly from donations and gifts and made grants totalling £2.6 million. Assets stood at £1.8 million.

The trustees intend for the foreseeable future, to continue their policy of distributing income within a short period of time from its receipt rather than accumulating reserves for future projects. They are, however, involved in and are considering various long-term projects such as educational premises located in the UK and Israel.

The trustees have adopted a policy of making regular donations to charitable causes, having regard to the level of the trust's annual income. They regularly appraise new opportunities for direct charitable expenditure and from time to time make substantial donations to support special or capital projects.

Grants in 2007/08 were broken down by the trust as follows:

Category	Value
Education	£2,100,000
Poor and needy	£451,000
Medical	£106,000
Community and older people's needs	£25,000

Beneficiaries included: Jewish Care, Cosmon Belz, Chana, Project Seed, Menorah High School for Girls, Train for Employment, Woodstock Sinclair Trust and Chai Cancer Care. Individual grant amounts were not disclosed in the accounts.

Applications In writing to the correspondent.

The Isle of Anglesey Charitable Trust

General

£377,000 (2006/07)

Beneficial area The Isle of Anglesey only.

Isle of Anglesey County Council, County Offices, Llangefni, Anglesey LL77 7TW

Tel. 01248 752607 **Fax** 01248 752696

Email gvwfi@anglesey.gov.uk

Correspondent David Elis-Williams, Treasurer

Trustee Anglesey County Council.

CC Number 1000818

Information available The latest accounts were not available at the

Charity Commission at the time of writing.

The trust, independent in law from, but administered by, the Isle of Anglesey County Council was set up with an endowment from Shell (UK) Limited when the company ceased operating an oil terminal on Anglesey, according to the terms of the 1972 private Act of Parliament which had enabled the terminal to be set up in the first place.

The objects of the trust are 'to provide amenities and facilities for the general public benefit of persons resident in the Isle of Anglesey'.

In a statement on the council's website at the end of 2008, the trust stated that the 'current economic climate has had a dramatic affect on the fund of late, with its value dropping by more than £4 million. It is now valued at around £10.5 million'.

The trust chairman, Elwyn Schofield, said that, 'projected investment income still stands at around £450,000, which allowed the trust to honour its commitments to many schemes which will benefit the communities and residents of Anglesey. Reaching our investment target has allowed us to continue to fund Oriel Ynys Môn, village halls and facilities, small works and minor grants, which are so important to many of our communities.'

Despite the financial difficulties the trust has also decided to continue to set aside £300,000 for enterprise agency, Menter Môn, for regeneration projects.

For the latest information on the funding available contact the trust directly.

Grantmaking

In 2006/07, the latest available accounts at the time of writing [August 2009], the trust made grants totalling £377,000.

By far the largest grant (£257,000) was made towards the running costs of Oriel Ynys Mon Gallery which is run by the County Council; this grant is made annually. A further 62 grants were made totalling £120,000, the majority of which were for under £6,000, and were categorised as follows:

Category	No. of grants	Amount
Village hall running costs	34	£52,000
Community and sporting facilities	13	£41,000
Minor works to churches and chapels	7	£21,000
Other grants	8	£6,300

The sum of £1.8 million has been earmarked towards 'regeneration schemes' from the trust's capital fund,

although this has not yet been allocated in full. Two large grants were made to Menter Mon Monased (£300,000) and Ymddiriedolaeth Syr Kyffin Williams (£150,000) from this fund during the year.

The trust's accounts provide information as to the distribution of its income to various organisations in Anglesey, however, it is not possible to ascertain from the accounts whether any of the grants awarded are used to subsidise the county council by providing facilities and/or services which should be provided by the local authority.

Exclusions No grants to individuals or projects based outside Anglesey.

Applications In writing to the correspondent, following advertisements in the local press in February. The trust considers applications once a year.

Isle of Dogs Community Foundation

Regeneration and general

£996,000 (2007/08)

Beneficial area The Isle of Dogs (the wards of Blackwall, Millwall, Limehouse, East India and Lansbury).

Jack Dash House, 2 Lawn House Close, Isle of Dogs, London E14 9YQ

Tel. 020 7345 4444 **Fax** 020 7538 4671

Email admin@idcf.org

Website www.idcf.org

Correspondent Tracy Betts, Director

Trustees *Sister Christine Frost; Mark Bensted; David Chesterton; Gabrielle Harrington; Mohammed Shahid Ali; Stella Bailey; Howard Dawber; Jeffrey Hennessey; Elizabeth Passey; Shiria Khatun; Timothy Archer; Adrian Greenwood; Ava Sam.*

CC Number 802942

Information available Accounts were available from the Charity Commission.

Established in 1990, the Isle of Dogs Community Foundation (IDCF) aims to establish a permanent and independent source of local charitable funds and use them to make grants to local charities and voluntary groups for the benefit of the community. Support is focused on Millwall and Blackwall, which remain

among the most deprived wards in the country. However, in January 2008, IDCF extended its area of benefit to include the wards of Limehouse, East India and Lansbury. Although funding priorities are reviewed regularly, the areas of training and employment, community development and education seem to receive regular support.

IDCF offers three main types of grants:

- *fast track grants* of up to £800 – intended for small items of equipment, social outings, events and other items of one-off expenditure
- *standard grants* of between £800 and £10,000 – for general purposes, capital items, or running costs
- *large grants* over £10,000 p.a. – for multiple years are also available to larger, well established organisations.

The foundation also manages a pilot grants programme on behalf of Poplar Harca that is open to voluntary and community groups and residents in the East India area. Further details can be found on the foundation's website.

It should be noted that grant schemes can change frequently. Please consult the foundation's website for details of current programmes and their deadlines.

Exclusions IDCF will not fund:

- individuals
- projects with primarily religious activities
- projects with primarily political activities
- projects or activities that are a statutory service
- activities that are the responsibility of the local or health authorities
- activities that have already taken place.

Applications The foundation's website has details of the grant schemes currently being administered. Please note: the foundation asks that grant seekers discuss their potential applications with the director, Tracey Betts, before the forms are submitted.

The J J Charitable Trust

Environment, literacy

£540,000 (2007/08)

Beneficial area Unrestricted.

Allington House, 1st Floor, 150 Victoria Street, London SW1E 5AE

Tel. 020 7410 0330 **Fax** 020 7410 0332

Website www.sfct.org.uk

Correspondent Alan Bookbinder, Director

Trustees *John Julian Sainsbury; Mark Sainsbury; Miss Judith Portrait; Ms Lucy Guard.*

CC Number 1015792

Information available Annual report and accounts were available from the Charity Commission. Brief information is also available from the Sainsbury Family Charitable Trusts' website.

Summary

This is one of the Sainsbury Family Charitable Trusts, which share a joint administration. They have a common approach to grantmaking which is described in the entry for the group as a whole.

A relatively small number of grants are made. Few of them are for less than £5,000 and occasional grants can be for more than £100,000. 'Proposals are generally invited by the trustees or initiated at their request. Unsolicited applications are discouraged and are unlikely to be successful, even if they fall within an area in which the trustees are interested. The trustees prefer to support innovative schemes that can be successfully replicated or become self-sustaining.'

The settlor of this trust is Julian Sainsbury and he is still building up the endowment, which included making a donation of £1.3 million in 2007/08 alone.

In 2007/08 the trust had assets of £29 million and a total income of £2.4 million, including the donation from the settlor. Grants were approved during the year totalling £540,000.

Grantmaking in 2007/08

The trust's main areas of interest are (with number and value of grants approved):

Category	No. of grants	Amount
Literacy support	5	£250,000
Environment – UK	11	£230,000
Environment – overseas	2	£50,000
General	1	£10,000

The following examples of grants approved are prefaced by the trust's description of its interests in that area, taken from its annual report.

Literacy support

The trustees aim to improve the effectiveness of literacy teaching at primary and secondary education stages for children with general or specific learning difficulties,

including Dyslexia, and to do the same through agencies working with ex-offenders or those at risk of offending. They also seek to target help at those who have become disaffected from education and who now find themselves homeless, in prison or without access to training and employment.

Their selection of projects to support takes account of relevant government initiatives and ongoing developments within prison education. The trustees seek projects that pilot new ideas for teaching and supporting people with specific learning difficulties, or that provide demonstrations that are likely to be of wider interest. Given budget constraints within the education and criminal justice sectors, the trustees seek to support projects aiming to deliver cost-effective solutions.

The beneficiaries were: London Libraries Development Agency (£80,000), towards Opening the Doors, a partnership between libraries and homelessness charities to encourage people at risk to benefit from library and educational services; KPMG Foundation (£70,000), towards the voluntary sector monitoring of the government-funded roll out phase of Every Child a Reader; Shannon Trust (£60,000), towards the employment costs of a volunteer development manager; British Dyslexia Association (£30,000), towards the consolidation of the rescue plan; and Dyslexia Association of Staffordshire (£10.000), a final grant towards core costs in 2008/09.

Environment – UK

Grants are made for environmental education, particularly supporting projects displaying practical ways of involving children and young adults. The trustees do not support new educational resources in isolation from the actual process of learning and discovery. They are more interested in programmes which help pupils and teachers to develop a theme over time, perhaps combining IT resources with the exchange of information and ideas between schools.

The trustees are particularly interested in projects that progressively enable children and young people to develop a sense of ownership of the project over time, and that provide direct support to teachers to deliver exciting and high quality education in the classroom.

The trustees have begun to support projects outside the schools sector which focus on sustainable agriculture and bio-diversity. This involvement is likely to grow in future years. The trustees are also interested in the potential for sustainable transport, energy efficiency and renewable energy in wider society. In some cases the trustees will consider funding research, but only where there is a clear practical application.

Proposals are more likely to be considered when they are testing an idea, model or strategy in practice.

Beneficiaries included: Small Woods Association (£60,000), towards a woodland regeneration and social enterprise programme involving young offenders at Tick Wood, Shropshire; The Ashden Awards (£50,000), towards the 2008 awards; Hampshire Development Education Centre (£18,000), towards the second and third years of the pilot project for a model of sustainable development in nine Hampshire schools; Council for Environmental Education (£10,000), towards research on the requirements of teachers in delivering environmental education; and Devon Wildlife Trust (£3,000), towards the third development year of the Garden Centre Approval Scheme.

Environment – Overseas

The trustees continue to support community-based agriculture projects, which aim to help people to help themselves in an environmentally sustainable way.

The beneficiaries were: FARM Africa (£30,000), to retain the Ethiopian forestry team while major longer term funding is secured; and SOS Sahel (£20,000), towards a study on support to pastoralist communities to take advantage of future challenges and then affect policy-making processes in Kenya and Mali.

General

The beneficiary was the Future Trust, towards Mayhern Theatre's drama project to explore teenage pregnancy, parenthood and sexual health.

Applications See the guidance for applicants in the entry for the Sainsbury Family Charitable Trusts. A single application will be considered for support by all the trusts in the group.

However, for this as for many of the trusts, 'the trustees take an active role in their grantmaking, employing a range of specialist staff and advisers to research their areas of interest and bring forward suitable proposals. Many of the trusts work closely with their chosen beneficiaries over a long period to achieve particular objectives. It should therefore be understood that the majority of unsolicited proposals we receive will be unsuccessful'.

John James Bristol Foundation

Education, health, older people and general

£1.1 million (2007/08)

Beneficial area Worldwide, in practice Bristol.

7 Clyde Road, Redland, Bristol BS6 6RG

Tel. 0117 923 9444 **Fax** 0117 923 9470

Email info@johnjames.org.uk

Website www.johnjames.org.uk

Correspondent Julia Norton, Chief Executive

Trustees *Joan Johnson; David Johnson; Elizabeth Chambers; John Evans; Andrew Jardine; Andrew Webley; John Haworth.*

CC Number 288417

Information available Accounts were available from the Charity Commission.

The foundation was established in 1983 and its objects are the relief of poverty or sickness, the advancement of education or other charitable purposes amongst the inhabitants of Bristol, and other charitable purposes with no defined beneficial area. The foundation's main aim is to benefit as many residents of the city of Bristol as possible by granting money as diversely as they can within the foundation's key focus areas of education, health and older people. This may include making grants to organisations carrying out the following work:

- encouraging young people, through grants to schools, youth organisations and other charities, to make the most of their educational opportunities
- improving health care through grants for medical research, equipment in hospitals, specialist equipment and holidays and care at home for individuals whose health needs are recognised by a registered charity
- assistance, through organisations, to older residents of Bristol in ways which will encourage them and help improve their quality of life.

In 2007/08 the foundation had assets of £44 million and an income of £2 million. Grants totalling £1.1 million were categorised as follows:

Health – 44 grants totalling £515,000
Beneficiaries included: Penny Brohn Cancer Care (£200,000); FareShare Community Food Network (£36,000); Barnardo's – Bristol Base (£23,000); Bristol Area Stroke Foundation (£20,000); Marie Curie Cancer Care (£14,000); Hammer Out (£10,000); Caring at Christmas (£5,000); and Bristol and District Tranquiliser Project (£2,200).

Education – 38 grants totalling £488,000
Beneficiaries included: Barton Hill Settlement (£28,000); Re:Work (£20,000); AT – Bristol (£17,000); Fairfield High School (£10,000); Wheels Project Ltd (£7,500); the Grove @ Bedminster Down (£4,000); Gay Elms Primary School (£2,900); and Computers for Life (£1,000).

Bristol Independent Schools (Bursary Fund) – 9 grants totalling £240,000
Beneficiaries were: Bristol Grammar School, Clifton College, Clifton High School, Queen Elizabeth Hospital, Red Maids' School and Redland High School (£30,000 each); and Badminton School, Colston's Collegiate School and St. Ursula's School (£20,000 each).

Older People – 207 grants totalling £112,000
Beneficiaries included: Motability (£10,000); Age Concern – Bristol (£8,000); Southville Community Development Association (£4,000); Shire Advice Service (£3,000); and Concorde Wheelchair Dancers, Pensioners Voice and Dolphin Society (£1,000 each).

Bristol Schools (prizes and awards) – 30 grants totalling £88,000
Beneficiaries included: Bristol Cathedral Choir School (£4,500); Hartcliffe Engineering Community College; Merchants' Academy, City Academy – Bristol and Oasis Academy – Brightstowe (£3,000 each); and Colston's Collegiate School (£1,000).

General – 7 grants totalling £7,900
Beneficiaries of grants over £1,000 were: Relate Avon (£3,000); and Friends of Hartcliffe Millennium Green, Canynges Society and Caring at Christmas – Bristol Nightstop (£1,000 each).

Exclusions No grants to individuals.

Applications The trustees meet quarterly in February, May, August and November to consider appeals received by the end of January, April, July and October. There is no application form and appeals should be submitted by post, to the chief executive on no more than two sides of A4.

Applications **must be submitted by post**, email applications will not be considered.

If further information is required it will be requested and a visit to the applicant may be made by a representative of the foundation. Grants are normally only given to charitable bodies who can clearly show that they are benefiting Bristol residents, and working within the foundation's key focus areas of education, health and older people. The grant-making policy is reviewed annually.

Jay Education Trust

Jewish

£1.9 million (2007/08)

Beneficial area Worldwide.

37 Filey Avenue, London N16 6JL

Correspondent Rabbi A Schechter, Trustee

Trustees *Rabbi A Schechter; G Gluck; S Z Stauber.*

CC Number 1116458

Information available Accounts were available from the Charity Commission.

The objects of the charity are: the relief of poverty in the Jewish Community worldwide; the advancement of religious education according to the beliefs and values of the Jewish Faith worldwide and any charitable purpose at the discretion of the trustees for the benefit of the community.

In 2007/08 the trust had assets of almost £3 million, an income of £2 million and made 76 grants totalling £1.9 million.

Beneficiaries included: Mifalei Tzedoko Vochesed (£200,000); United Talmudical Associates (£82,000); British Friends Of Igud Hakolelim B'Yerushalayim (£70,000); Lolev Charitable Trust and Toldos Aharon Israel (£50,000 each); Edupoor Ltd (£35,000); Chachmei Tzorfat Trust (£34,000); Heichel Aharon (£25,000); Friends of Sanz Institutions (£16,000); Yad Vochessed (£14,000); Zedokoh Bechol Eis (£2,700); Belz Yeshiva London (£2,500); Jewish Seminary For Girls (£2,000); and Comet Charities Ltd (£1,250).

Applications In writing to the correspondent.

The Jerusalem Trust

Promotion of Christianity

£2.3 million (2008)
Beneficial area Unrestricted.

Allington House, 1st Floor, 150 Victoria Street, London SW1E 5AE

Tel. 020 7410 0330 **Fax** 020 7410 0332

Email jerusalemtrust@sfct.org.uk

Website www.sfct.org.uk

Correspondent Alan Bookbinder, Director

Trustees *Rt Hon. Sir Timothy Sainsbury; Lady Susan Sainsbury; Dr V E Hartley Booth; Phillida Goad; Dr Peter Frankopan.*

CC Number 285696

Information available Accounts were available from the Charity Commission.

This is one of the Sainsbury Family Charitable Trusts, which share a joint administration. Their approaches to grantmaking have aspects in common which are described in the entry for the group as a whole. The trust is primarily proactive, aiming to choose its own grantees, and it discourages unsolicited applications.

The trust supports a wide range of evangelical organisations, across a broad though usually moderate spectrum of Christian activity. The number and value of grant approvals in 2008 were categorised as follows:

Category	No. of grants	Amount
Christian education	17	£871,400
Evangelism and mission work (UK)	58	£724,000
Christian evangelism and relief work overseas	24	£480,000
Christian media	9	£423,400
Christian art	6	£21,500

Grantmaking in 2008

In 2008 the trust had assets of almost £67.1 million and an income of £3.2 million. Grants were paid during the year totalling £2.3 million, which included grants approved during previous years.

The following are examples of grants that were approved during the year, including a description of the trust's interests in each category taken from the accounts.

Christian education

Trustees are particularly interested in the development of Christian curriculum resource materials for schools in RE and other subjects; the support, training and retention of Christian teachers in all subjects; and lay training.

Transforming Lives (£220,000), towards core costs; St John's College – Nottingham (£135,000), towards costs of the Story of the Church of England; Stapleford Centre (£110,000), towards core costs; Christian Education Movement (£50,000), towards Christian resources aimed at Key Stage 2 on sex and relationships; and the Right to Life Charitable Trust (£20,000), towards costs of DVD and resource packs on abortion.

Evangelism and mission work (UK)

Trustees are particularly interested in Christian projects that develop new ways of working with children and young people; in church planting and evangelistic projects and those that undertake Christian work with prisoners, ex-prisoners and their families.

Youth for Christ in Britain (£80,000), towards the cost of a staff development programme; Global Day of Prayer London (£50,000), towards the Global Day of Prayer 2008; London Institute for Contemporary Christianity (£37,500), towards the costs of a regional development worker for the Imagine project; St James the Less (£22,500), towards the costs of a project manager's salary; and Alliance of Religions and Conservation (£10,000), towards the Green Gospels.

Christian evangelism and relief work overseas

Trustees are particularly interested in proposals for indigenous Christian training centres, the provision of Christian literature in Central and Eastern Europe and Anglophone Sub-Saharan Africa.

Tearfund (£70,000), towards the costs of their work in Burma following Cyclone Nargis and the Kale Heywet community development training programme in Ethiopia; Advantage Africa (£60,000), towards the salary costs of a programme manager; Carlile College (£35,000), towards the salary costs of the head of training, specifically to work with smaller organisations in Nairobi's informal settlements; Matheteuo (£22,500), towards the costs of a programme of Theological Education by Extension in the Anglican Province of Uganda; and Intercontinental Church Society (£9,000), towards the support costs for the first Area Bishop for North Africa.

Christian media

Trustees are interested in supporting media projects that promote Christianity. They are also interested in supporting training and networking projects for Christians working professionally in all areas of the media and for those considering media careers.

Jerusalem Productions Ltd (£250,000), for disbursement by Jerusalem Productions during the calendar year of 2008; Churches' Media Council (£80,000), towards the salary costs of the director; World Share (£25,000), towards the costs of ECTV in Turkey; Evangelical Alliance (£20,000), towards the costs of setting up two media hubs; and YMCA (£6,000), towards the Winchester Passion.

Christian art

Trustees focus mainly on a small number of commissions of works of art for places of worship.

The main beneficiary was: St Alban's Cathedral Music Trust (£10,000), towards the costs of the community opera, Alban. Small grants were also made to: Art & Christianity Enquiry, Art & Sacred Places; St Clement's Church, Notting Dale & St James' Church, Norlands; Sanctus 1; and the Parish of St Andrew Fulham Fields.

Exclusions Trustees do not normally make grants towards building or repair work for churches. Grants are not normally made to individuals.

Applications See the guidance for applicants in the entry for the Sainsbury Family Charitable Trusts. A single application will be considered for support by all the trusts in the group.

However, for this as for many of the trusts, 'proposals are generally invited by the trustees or initiated at their request'.

Jerwood Charitable Foundation

The arts, education, design, science, engineering and other areas of human endeavour

£1.6 million (2007)
Beneficial area UK.

171 Union Street, Bankside, London SE1 0LN

Tel. 020 7261 0279

Email shonagh.manson@jerwood.org

Website www.jerwoodcharitablefoundation.org

Correspondent Shonagh Manson, Director

CC Number 1074036

Information available Accounts were available from the Charity Commission.

The Jerwood Charitable Foundation (the foundation) was established in 1998 with general charitable purposes. In 1999 it took over the administration of a number of initiatives of the Jerwood Foundation (the parent company), including the Jerwood Applied Arts Prize, Jerwood Choreography Award and Jerwood Painting Prize.

In 2005 the charitable foundation became completely independent after receiving the final endowment donation from the Jerwood Foundation. However, as the foundation has previously stated, it retains close ties with all of the Jerwood family. 'We continue to see ourselves as closely linked with, and will continue to seek guidance from, the Jerwood Foundation on our activities and of course, as ever, will work closely with other Jerwood family members especially the Jerwood Space.' (The Jerwood Space is a major initiative of the company, offering affordable rehearsal spaces for dance and theatre companies to develop their work).

The aims of the foundation are the distribution of funds to individuals and organisations for the promotion of visual and performing arts and education in the widest sense. It has four main objectives:

- to support artists in the early stages of their careers
- to support the wider infrastructure of arts organisations
- to respond positively to those taking artistic risks
- to explore the opportunity of identifying small programme related investment opportunities.

Funding policy
The foundation is a major sponsor of all areas of the performing and visual arts, particularly projects which involve rewards for excellence and the encouragement and recognition of outstanding talent and high standards, or which enable an organisation to become viable and self financing. It rarely sponsors single performances or arts events, such as festivals, nor does it make grants towards the running or core costs of established arts organisations.

The following information is taken from the foundation's website:

In every case the Jerwood Charitable Foundation (JCF) seeks to secure tangible and visible results from its grants and sponsorships. Influence and effect beyond the immediate recipient of a grant is encouraged. The JCF aims to be active in identifying and creating new projects for sponsorship. We aim to monitor chosen projects closely and sympathetically, and are keen to seek recognition of the JCF's support. Our strategy is to support outstanding national institutions while at the same time being prepared to provide seed corn finance and financial support at the early stages of an initiative when other grant-making bodies might not be able or willing to act.

The JCF may wish to be sole sponsor (subject to financial considerations) or to provide partnership funding. In particular the JCF seeks to develop, support and reward young people who have demonstrated achievement and excellence, and who will benefit from a final lift to launch their careers. This special role is intended to open the way for young achievers and give them the opportunity to flourish.

The JCF has the benefit of association with capital projects of the Jerwood Foundation. These include the Jerwood Space, the Jerwood Theatres at the Royal Court Theatre, the Jerwood Gallery at the Natural History Museum and the Jerwood Sculpture Park at Ragley Hall, Warwickshire. The support for these initiatives by the Jerwood Foundation will be a factor when considering any applications.

The JCF normally only funds projects based within the United Kingdom. It no longer considers applications from organisations operating overseas. The JCF will not merely be a passive recipient of requests for grants but will also identify areas to support and develop projects with potential beneficiaries.

Types of Grants
The foundation will rarely commit to repeat funding over a number of years, preferring to make revenue donations on a one-off basis. However, it is prepared, in many cases, to maintain support if the partnership has been successful and consistency will help to secure better results.

The JCF also provides 'challenge funding', whereby the foundation will make a grant provided the recipient or other interested party can match the remaining shortfall.

Grant levels vary between the lower range of up to £10,000 (often plus or minus £5,000) and more substantial grants in excess of £10,000. The

foundation states that there should be no expectation of grant level as all applications will be assessed on merit and need.

Projects and awards
The foundation actively pursues and develops initiatives in the arts world as well as receiving unsolicited applications for funding. Projects and awards cover a wide range of arts activities currently in the following areas:

- music
- dance
- theatre
- literature
- visual arts
- film
- multi disciplinary
- Mission Models Money (action research programme).

Jerwood prizes/awards
The foundation continues to fund and monitor established awards such as the Jerwood Drawing Prize, the Jerwood Applied Arts Awards with the Crafts Council, the season of New Playwrights at the Royal Court Theatre and Jerwood Jazz Generation. The foundation also develops new schemes to reflect its objective of supporting talent and excellence in its areas of interest.

In 2007 the foundation had assets of £28.2 million and an income of £1.1 million. 44 grants were made totalling £1.6 million.

Beneficiaries included: Jerwood Moving Images (£125,000); Jerwood Creative Studio at Sadlers Wells (£120,000); Artangel (£100,000); Glyndebourne Young Singers (£70,000); Music Theatre Wales (£37,000); Royal Society of Literature (£28,000); Manchester International Festival (£20,000); Aldeburgh Poetry Festival (£13,000); Sequences and Repetitions (£5,000); and Liederkreis (£1,000).

More information on the projects, initiatives and awards supported by the foundation can be found on the website.

Exclusions The Jerwood charitable Foundation will not consider applications on behalf of:

- individuals
- building or capital costs (including purchase of equipment)
- projects in the fields of religion or sport
- animal rights or welfare
- study fees or course fees
- general fundraising appeals which are likely to have wide public appeal
- appeals to establish endowment funds for other charities

- appeals for matching funding for National Lottery applications
- grants for the running and core costs of voluntary bodies
- projects which are of mainly local appeal or identified with a locality
- medical or mental health projects
- social welfare, particularly where it may be considered a government or local authority responsibility
- retrospective awards
- projects outside Great Britain
- schools which are trying to attain Special Schools Status
- touring or production costs
- environmental or conservation projects.

The foundation may, where there are very exceptional circumstances, decide to waive an exclusion.

Applications Applications should be by letter to the director, outlining the aims and objectives of the organisation and the aims and objectives of the specific project or scheme for which assistance is sought. The following supporting documents should be sent with the application:

- a detailed budget for the project, identifying administrative, management and central costs
- details of funding already in place for the project, including any other trusts or sources which are being or have been approached for funds. If funding is not in place, details of how the applicant plans to secure the remaining funding
- details of the management and staffing structure, including trustees
- the most recent annual report and audited accounts of the organisation, together with current management accounts if relevant to the project.

The foundation may wish to enter into discussions and/or correspondence with the applicant which may result in modification and/or development of the project or scheme. Any such discussion or correspondence will not commit the foundation to funding that application.

Successful applicants will be invited to report to the foundation at the completion of their project and to provide photographs of the work or project supported.

As the foundation receives a large number of applications, it is not possible to have preliminary meetings to discuss possible support before a written application is made.

Jewish Child's Day

Charitable purposes of direct benefit to Jewish children who are disadvantaged, suffering or in need of special care

£717,000 (2007/08)

Beneficial area Worldwide. In practice, mainly Israel and UK.

5th Floor, 707 High Road, North Finchley, London N12 0BT

Tel. 020 8446 8804 **Fax** 020 8446 7370

Email info@jcd.uk.com

Website www.jcd.uk.com

Correspondent Jackie Persoff, PA to the Executive Director

Trustees Joy Moss, Chair; June Jacobs; Stephen Moss; Virginia Campus; David Clayton; Francine Epstein; Rhonda Marcus; Susie Olins; Suellen Winer; Amanda Ingram; Gaby Lazarus.

CC Number 209266

Information available Accounts were available at the Charity Commission. The trust also has an informative website.

The trust was established in 1947 to encourage Jewish children in the UK to help less fortunate Jewish children who were survivors of the Nazi holocaust. The trust exists to improve the lives of Jewish children, in the UK, Israel or elsewhere overseas, who for any reason are suffering, disadvantaged or in need of special care.

In 2007/08 the trust had assets of £649,500 and an income of just over £1 million. Grants were made to 121 organisations totalling £717,000.

Beneficiaries included: Children of Chernobyl (£151,000); Micha Haifa (£101,000); Manchester Jewish Federation (£37,500); Eilya (£14,000); Alyn Hospital (£9,000); Step by Step (£8,400); Gan Hayeled (£7,000); Shema and Roots for Generations (£5,000 each); Kfar Hayarok Youth Village (£4,500); Cystic Fibrosis Foundation of Israel (£3,500); Ezra Youth Movement (£3,000); Shilo Israel Children's Fund; and Schneider (£500).

Exclusions Individuals are not supported. Grants are not given towards general services, building or maintenance of property or staff salaries.

Applications If your organisation meets JCD's criteria, you could apply for a grant ranging from £500 to £5,000 towards the cost of small or medium size items of equipment or a project that will directly benefit children.

The committee considers applications in February, June and September each year. Completed application forms should be sent together with a set of audited accounts by 31 December, 30 April and 31 July accordingly.

To apply for a grant from JCD please contact Jackie Persoff on 020 8446 8804 or jackie.persoff@jcd.uk.com.

The Joffe Charitable Trust

Alleviation of poverty and protection/ advancement of human rights

£431,000 (2007/08)

Beneficial area Mainly developing countries.

Liddington Manor, The Street, Liddington, Swindon SN4 0HD

Tel. 01793 790203

Email joffetrust@mail.com

Correspondent Lord Joffe, Trustee

Trustees Lord Joel Joffe; Lady Vanetta Joffe; Deborah Mila Joffe.

CC Number 270299

Information available Annual report and accounts were available at the Charity Commission.

The Joffe Charitable Trust was established in 1968 by the settlor, Lord Joffe and Vanetta Joffe. The objectives of the trust are widely drawn but in reality most grants are made for the relief of poverty and the advancement of human rights in the developing world.

The trust conducts its activities through grantmaking and the trustees have an ongoing relationship with a large number of charities, (the settlor is a former chair of Oxfam and the Giving Campaign). The decisions made as to which organisations/projects to support are based on the trustees' assessment of the quality of leadership within an organisation and the impact that the initiatives which they support are likely to have. Grants usually range from

£1,000 to £50,000. The trust also provides interest free loans.

Guidelines

The trust has previously offered the following information on its grant-making aims and objectives:

The trust's primary focus is the alleviation of poverty and protection/advancement of human rights in the developing world. Its secondary purpose is the support of individuals in the voluntary sector anywhere in the world who the trustees judge are likely to make a real difference in alleviating poverty, advancing human rights and increasing the efficiency and effectiveness of the voluntary sector.

Essential criteria when agreeing grants are:

- leadership
- clear and narrow focus
- clear objectives
- value for money
- effective financial controls
- sustainability
- replicability/scaling up
- campaigning potential.

Grants must aim to make a significant difference to the organisation and cause. The trust will consider core costs which fit into the criteria.

Grants in 2007/08

In 2007/08 the trust had assets of £14 million and an income of £513,000. Grants were made totalling £431,000.

The largest grants went to: Acid Survivors Trust International (£50,000); War on Want (£38,000); and Microloan Foundation (£35,000).

Other beneficiaries included: Africa Now (£30,000); Global Witness and Charities Aid Foundation (£25,000 each); New Economics Foundation (£20,000); Alive and Kicking (£15,000); International Commission of Jurists (£10,000); and David Astor Trust (£7,500). Smaller grants of less than £5,000 totalled £66,000.

Exclusions Likely exclusions are humanitarian assistance; large charities, except perhaps for important projects which might not otherwise happen; the arts; and charities likely to exclusively benefit causes in the developed world.

Applications In writing to the correspondent. It should be noted that funds are often committed to charities of special interest to the trustees. The trust does not acknowledge unsuccessful applications due to a lack of resources, nor will reasons for the application being turned down be given.

The Elton John Aids Foundation

HIV/AIDS welfare and prevention

£830,000 in the UK (2008)
Beneficial area Unrestricted.

1 Blythe Road, London W14 0HG
Tel. 020 7603 9996 **Fax** 020 7348 4848
Email admin@ejaf.com
Website www.ejaf.com
Correspondent Robert Key, Executive Director
Trustees *Sir Elton John, Chair; David Furnish; Lynette Jackson; Frank Presland; Anne Aslett; Marguerite Littman; Johnny Bergius; James Locke; Rafi Manoukian; Scott Campbell.*
CC Number 1017336
Information available Accounts were available from the Charity Commission.

This foundation was established in 1993 by Sir Elton John to empower people infected, affected and at risk of HIV/AIDS and to alleviate their physical, emotional and financial hardship, enabling them to improve their quality of life, live with dignity and exercise self-determination.

The foundation is the largest independent funder of HIV/AIDS projects in the UK and one of the 20 largest international AIDS charities. It has worked across 17 countries and supported over 1,200 projects with grants totalling more than £43 million.

A sister organisation with an office in Los Angeles was established in 1992 to fund programmes in the Americas and the Caribbean.

The foundation believes and values that:

- everyone is entitled to dignity and respect
- everyone has the right to access the best medicine
- everyone has the right to information, opportunities and choices as part of the empowerment process
- those most directly affected by the epidemic are central to finding effective solutions
- care and concern for each and every person, respect for their human and legal rights – particularly of the most vulnerable and marginalised – is central to any caring community.

The foundation continues to fund a broad range of services for those living with or affected by HIV/AIDS, including education, peer support, medical care, income generation, counselling and testing. The foundation funds operational research but does not support pure medical research.

Particular emphasis is given to the most disadvantaged or high risk groups, both nationally and internationally and to community driven programmes that place people living with HIV/AIDS at the centre of service provision.

The foundation's vision for the future is to help programmes:

- expand the provision of life saving medical treatment for people living with HIV/AIDS
- enable pregnant women to protect their unborn children from acquiring the disease
- mitigate the impact of HIV/AIDS on children by funding medical care, food, education and emotional support so that they can grow to adulthood and thrive
- strengthen national and regional networks of HIV positive people so they can advocate for their own needs and play a central role in shaping services
- champion the rights of HIV positive people living on the margins of society.

In 2008 the foundation had assets of £23 million and a consolidated income of £16 million. Grants were made totalling £6.9 million. This included grants to 11 projects in the UK totalling £830,000.

Grantmaking

In pursuing its objectives the foundation's grant making activities fall in to three programmes: UK projects; international projects (in Russia, Ukraine, India, Bangladesh, Cambodia, Kenya, Uganda, Tanzania, Zambia, Malawi, South Africa, Lesotho, Nepal and Ireland); and small grants.

The foundation's work is specifically targeted in each country based on strategy documents that identify who, what, where and how funding can make the most difference. Grants are currently focused on five key themes:

- women and children
- positive lives
- livelihoods
- vulnerable groups
- innovation.

This entry will focus on the foundation's UK activities. Further information on the foundation's international grantmaking, including country specific policy guidelines and examples of previous projects, can be found on the foundation's website.

Grantmaking in the UK

The following information on the foundation's UK policy taken from the website:

EJAF has been awarding grants across the UK since its inception in 1993. Initially our funding was aimed at easing the suffering of those that were dying of AIDS, including: improving hospital environments and meals; providing respite care and complementary therapies. Since then, our funding has responded to the changing face of the epidemic in the UK, especially the increased efficacy and availability of antiretroviral therapy (ART).

Whilst we continue to support people living with HIV/AIDS, including regional support groups across the UK, we have particularly focused our work on more marginalised populations. These communities, although vulnerable to HIV/AIDS, often find it harder to access mainstream services. They include prison populations, refugees and asylum seekers, male sex workers, black and minority ethnic groups and lesbian, gay and bisexual young people.

For the past 14 years we have supported hardship and nutritional support programmes reaching over 36,000 people. HIV/AIDS still causes immense poverty in the UK. We support an adult and a children's UK wide hardship fund that provide emergency grants to people in need, as well as projects which provide and deliver nutritious food for those who are not able to get out or cook for themselves.

We have also worked to influence government and sector policy in a number of areas including commissioning reports into prison HIV/AIDS services, homophobia in schools and a survey of young people living with haemophilia.

During the next strategic cycle, EJAF seeks to support programmes that demonstrate value for money and fully involve people living with HIV.

Gay and bisexual men living with HIV (MSM) – We are seeking UK wide collaborative programmes that enable MSM to manage their mental, physical and emotional health, be confident about disclosing their HIV status and reduce the risk of onward transmission of HIV. Programmes should make use of new technologies and demonstrate how they aim to measure the impact of their interventions, particularly in relation to increases in self esteem and disclosure to sexual partners and reductions in risk taking behaviour and unsafe sex.

Long-term survivors and older people – We are seeking UK wide collaborative programmes that address the impact and social isolation of HIV on those who have been living with HIV for over 10 years and/or those aged over 50. Programmes should demonstrate how they would reach those in rural and low prevalence areas and how they aim to measure the impact of their interventions, especially in relation to reduction in social isolation and increases in HIV disclosure and use of non HIV statutory and voluntary social care services.

Employment and training – We are seeking UK wide collaborative programmes that enable people living with HIV to access training and support in order to gain employment, remain in employment and increase their income levels. Programmes should demonstrate how they aim to measure the impact of their interventions in relation to qualifications gained, reduction in unemployment levels, increases in income levels of people living with HIV and use of non HIV employment and training services.

Children affected by HIV – We are seeking UK wide collaborative programmes that address the needs of children infected and affected by HIV, their parents and carers. Programmes for children need to demonstrate a child centred approach. All programmes should demonstrate how they aim to measure the impact of their interventions in relation to benefits on the child, their families/carers and use of non HIV statutory and voluntary social care services.

Poverty and nutrition – We are seeking UK wide collaborative programmes that address the impact of poverty on people living with HIV in the UK. Programmes should demonstrate how they aim to measure the impact of their interventions in relation to improvements in living conditions, access to culturally appropriate nutrition and increased income levels.

Regional Grants Fund – EJAF also operates a regional grants programme open to collaborative regional HIV programmes addressing the above issues, particularly those operating in Brighton, the east of England, the Midlands, London, the North West, South Central, Yorkshire and the Humber areas. Programmes should demonstrate how they aim to measure the impact of their interventions.

Exclusions For both UK and international grants the foundation will not fund:

- academic or medical research
- conferences
- grants to individuals
- repatriation costs
- retrospective funding.

Applications The foundation's website has an interactive map which you can use to select a country you are interested in. This will take you to a page containing an overview of the country and the foundation's work within it, some examples of previous projects, details of the current grant strategy for that country and the application procedure.

Organisations interested in applying should complete a 'concept note' (available to download from the relevant country page) and email it to: grants@ejaf.com

The Jones 1986 Charitable Trust

People with disabilities, welfare of older people, welfare of younger people, education and purposes beneficial to the community

£769,000 (2007/08)

Beneficial area UK, mostly Nottinghamshire.

Smith Cooper, Haydn House, 309–329 Haydn Road, Sherwood, Nottingham NG5 1HG

Tel. 0115 960 7111 **Fax** 0115 969 1313

Correspondent David Lindley

Trustees *Robert Heason; Richard Stringfellow; John David Pears.*

CC Number 327176

Information available Accounts were available from the Charity Commission.

The charity was established in 1986 with very wide charitable purposes. The trust primarily supports causes in the Nottingham area and much of its grant-giving goes to charities assisting people with disabilities or for medical research into disabilities and the welfare of older people. The trust also supports charities supporting the welfare of the young, education and purposes beneficial to the community. The trust prefers to develop a relationship with the organisations funded over an extended period of time.

In 2007/08 the trust had assets of £19 million and an income of £4.4 million. 56 grants were made totalling £769,000 and were categorised as follows:

Medical research – 8 grants totalling £280,000

Beneficiaries included: Queen's Medical Centre – Nottingham University Hospital NHS Trust (£193,000); Nottingham University Hospitals Charity (£25,000); Prostate Cancer Research (£20,000); Fight for Sight (£13,000); and Myasthenia Gravis Association (£3,000).

Relief of sickness or disability – 25 grants totalling £248,000

Beneficiaries included: Prince of Paste Anglers (£30,000); Riding for the Disabled – Highland Group (£25,000); Southwell Care Project (£18,000); Long Eaton Society for Mentally Handicapped Children and Adults (£10,000); Emmanuel House (£5,000); Dystonia Society (£3,000); and Meningitis Trust (£1,000).

Purposes beneficial to the community – 13 grants totalling £122,000

Beneficiaries included: Ruddington Framework Knitters Museum (£22,000); Nottingham Arts Theatre (£20,000); Beeston Parish Church (£10,000); Nottingham Historic Churches Trust (£6,500); and Derbyshire Housing Aid (£4,000).

Welfare of older people – 3 grants totalling £44,000

Beneficiaries were: Age Concern – Nottingham and Nottinghamshire (£25,000); Radford Care Group (£15,000); and St John's Day Care Centre for the Elderly (£4,000).

Relief of sickness or disability for young people – 1 grant of £40,000

The sole beneficiary was Cope Children's Trust.

Education – 4 grants totalling £26,000

Beneficiaries were: Place2be (£10,000); Rutland House School for Parents (£7,500); Fun Days – Shepherd School (£5,000); and Aspley Wood School (£3,000).

Welfare of the young – 2 grants totalling £9,000

Beneficiaries were Boy's Brigade – Nottinghamshire Battalion (£5,000) and Nottinghamshire Scouts (£4,000).

Exclusions No grants to individuals.

Applications In writing to the correspondent. The trust invites applications for grants by advertising in specialist press. Applications are considered for both capital and/or revenue projects as long as each project appears viable.

The Jordan Charitable Foundation

General charitable purposes

£602,500 (2008)

Beneficial area UK national charities, Herefordshire and Sutherland, Scotland.

8th Floor, 6 New Street Square, New Fetter Land, London EC4A 3AQ

Tel. 020 7842 2000

Email jordan@rawlinson-hunter.com

Correspondent Ralph Stockwell, Trustee

Trustees *Sir Ronald Miller; Sir George Russell; Ralph Stockwell; Christopher Jan Andrew Bliss; Simon Paul Jennings; David Geoffrey Barker.*

CC Number 1051507

Information available Accounts were available from the Charity Commission.

The Jordan Charitable Foundation was established in 1995. The grant-making policies are guided by the original intentions of the founders. Grants are made to UK national charities and also to charities that are local to the county of Herefordshire, and in particular, charities operating within the city of Hereford and to a much lesser extent, charities in Sutherland, Scotland, as there is a connection between the founders and this area. The trustees assist towards funding of a capital nature and towards defraying revenue costs.

In 2008 the foundation had assets of £35.7 million and an income of £1.2 million. Administration and the cost of generating funds amounted to £230,000. Grants were made totalling £602,500 and were given in three geographical areas: UK charities received the largest share of £291,000, with Hereford receiving £266,000 and Sutherland receiving £26,500.

The largest grants were made to: Hereford Cathedral Perpetual Trust (£215,000); Herefordshire MIND (£26,000); Blue Cross (£25,000); and CLD Youth Counselling Trust and County Air Ambulance Trust (£15,000 each).

Other grants of £10,000 or less each included those made to: Brooke Hospital for Animals, the Samaritans and the Stroke Association (£10,000 each); Sutherland Schools Pipe Band (£6,000); Age Concern, British Heart Foundation, Injured Jockeys' Fund and Herefordshire Nature Trust (£5,000 each); Children's Hospital Association – Scotland (£2,000); and Prostate Cancer Charity (£1,000).

The accounts contained no information regarding what aspects of the beneficiaries' work was being supported.

Applications In writing to the correspondent.

The Joron Charitable Trust

Jewish, education, medical research and general

£1.86 million (2007/08)

Beneficial area UK.

115 Wembley Commercial Centre, East Lane, North Wembley HA9 7UR

Correspondent Bruce D G Jarvis, Chair

Trustees *Bruce D G Jarvis; Mrs Sandra C Jarvis; Joseph R Jarvis.*

CC Number 1062547

Information available Accounts were available from the Charity Commission.

The trust's policy is to make grants to registered charities in the fields of education, medical research and other charities who can demonstrate that the grants will be used effectively.

In 2007/08 the trust had assets of £835,000 and an income of over £1.9 million, largely in donations from Ravensale Ltd. Grants to 25 organisations totalled £1.86 million.

A grant of £1 million was made to the Roan Charitable Trust, apparently for the onward distribution in further grants to other organisations. Other beneficiaries included: A & E Bunker Charitable Settlement (£200,000); Jewish Care (£100,000); the Wilderness Foundation (£60,000); Child's Dream Foundation (£51,000); Theodora Children's Trust (£25,000); Scleroderma Society (£20,000); Rainbow Trust Children's Charity (£15,000); the Ian Rennie Hospice at Home (£10,000); and Hope and Homes for Children (£1,500).

Applications 'There is no formal grants application procedure. The trustees retain the services of a charitable grants advisor and take account of the advice when deciding on grants.'

The Anton Jurgens Charitable Trust

Welfare and general

£380,000 (2007/08)

Beneficial area UK with a preference for the south east of England.

Saffrey Champness, Lion House, 72–75 Red Lion Street, London WC1R 4GB

Tel. 020 7841 4000 **Fax** 020 7841 4100

Correspondent Mrs Maria E Edge-Jurgens, Trustee

Trustees *Eric M C Deckers; R Jurgens; Frans A V Jurgens; John F M Jurgens; Maria E Edge-Jurgens; M A J Jurgens.*

CC Number 259885

Information available Accounts were available from the Charity Commission.

This trust has general charitable purposes, although welfare and children's groups feature prominently in the grants, as do organisations based in the south east of England. The trust states its main aim as 'alleviating suffering by making grants to charitable organisations that try to help those who are vulnerable in our society.'

In 2007/08 the trust had assets of £6.9 million and an income of £299,000. Grants to 90 organisations were made totalling £380,000.

Beneficiaries included: Silcester Parochial Council (£25,000); Highland Hospice (£15,000); Ability Net, Kid's Company and Royal School for Deaf Children – Margate (£10,000 each); Childlink Adoption Society (£8,000); the Fifth Trust (£6,000); Bucks Disability Information Network and Queen Alexandra Hospital Home (£5,000 each); Hope House (£4,000); Haemophilia Society (£3,000); Barnabas Adventure Centres and Vitalise (£2,000 each); and Bury Shopmobility (£1,000).

Applications In writing to the correspondent. The trustees meet twice a year in June and October. The trustees do not enter into correspondence concerning grant applications beyond notifying successful applicants.

The Kay Kendall Leukaemia Fund

Research into leukaemia

£2 million (2007/08)

Beneficial area Unrestricted.

Allington House, 1st Floor, 150 Victoria Street, London SW1E 5AE

Tel. 020 7410 0330 **Fax** 020 7410 0332

Email info@kklf.org.uk

Website www.kklf.org.uk

Correspondent Alan Bookbinder, Director

Trustees *Judith Portrait; Timothy J Sainsbury; Christopher Stone.*

CC Number 290772

Information available Annual report and accounts were available from the Charity Commission. The trust also has a clear and helpful website.

This is one of the Sainsbury Family Charitable Trusts, which share a joint administration. They have a common approach to grantmaking which is described in the entry for the group as a whole.

This trust is solely concerned with funding research into the causes and treatment of leukaemia, which is done on the advice of an expert advisory panel.

The trust's website offers a clear and simple summary of its grantmaking:

Programme/Project Grants

Research grants are normally awarded for programmes/projects of 3–5 years' duration. Support may be awarded for 3 years in the first instance with a final 2 years being dependent upon a review of progress over the first 3 years. Programme grants may be renewed once for a period of up to 5 years. The maximum period of funding for a particular programme will be 10 years. It is intended that the KKLF funding should not be the 'core' funding of any research group. Applicants should state clearly how their proposal relates to their core funding.

What will be funded

Grants will be awarded for research on aspects of leukaemia and for relevant studies on related haematological malignancies. Requests for support for basic science programmes may be considered.

Grants will also be awarded for the support of programmes associated with the care of patients with leukaemia. Phase 3 Clinical trials will not normally be supported but applications for phase 1 or 2 studies may be considered.

Proposals which are closely related to the care of leukaemia patients or to the prevention of leukaemia and related diseases are particularly encouraged.

Grants are usually awarded to give additional support to programmes already underway, the aim being to further strengthen activities which are already of high quality. It follows that the KKLF will accept proposals from groups which already have support from other agencies.

The trustees will consider proposals from both UK and non-UK based organisations where the work to be funded is based primarily within the UK.

A preliminary letter or telephone call to the administration offices of the Kay Kendall Leukaemia Fund, or to one of its scientific advisers, may be helpful to determine whether or not a proposal is likely to be eligible.

Other Awards
Capital funding

Requests for capital grants for leukaemia research laboratories or for clinical facilities for leukaemia will be considered either alone or in conjunction with proposals for the support of research and/or patient management. Capital requests must give a budget estimate of costs, together with a full justification.

Equipment grants

Requests for single large items of equipment will be considered. Requests must give detailed cost estimates and a full scientific justification.

Clinical care

Requests for clinical support must give full costing and a detailed explanation of how this support will enhance the existing service and/or research activities.

Fellowships

The KKLF Fellowship Programme offers support for highly-motivated first-class clinicians and scientists who wish to pursue a career in haematological research into leukaemia and associated malignancies. There are 3 levels of Fellowships, Junior, Intermediate and Senior and they are designed according to the level of research experience already obtained. Details are available on the trust's website.

The trust also describes future plans as follows:

The trustees have agreed to a spend-out of the charity's capital which is expected to be completed by about 2027. They would wish to maintain the current budget for scientific research and are proposing to add a new £1 million p.a. programme on patient care and patient-centred projects associated with leukaemia. As a result, trustees are planning to spend an annual budget of £3.4 million, an increase of approximately £1 million per annum.

Funding from the patient care budget will, in the first instance, be made for capital grants, grants to hospitals within selected Strategic Health Authorities, small grants to individuals, and finance and welfare benefit advice to individuals within the selected Strategic Health Authority areas.

Grantmaking in 2007/08

In 2007/08 it had assets of £50.1 million and an income of £2.1 million. Grants were paid during the year totalling over £2 million.

Beneficiaries included: Institute of Cancer Research (£410,000 in total); University of Cambridge (£385,000 in total); Imperial College School of Medicine (£287,000 in total); and University of Manchester (£214,000 in total).

Exclusions Circular appeals for general support are not funded.

Applications A preliminary letter or telephone call to the administration offices of the Kay Kendall Leukaemia Fund may be helpful to determine whether or not a proposal is likely to be eligible. Application forms are available by contacting the trust's office.

Research Proposal
Applicants should complete the approved Application Form and include a research proposal (aims, background, plan of investigation, justification for budget). The research proposal should be 3–5 single-spaced pages for project grants (excluding references, costings and CV) and up to 10 single-spaced pages for programme grants. Applications should be submitted by electronic mail in addition to the provision of a hard copy with original signature. The trustees will take account of annual inflation and of salary increases related to nationally negotiated pay scales and these should not be built into the application.

Salaries should generally be on nationally agreed scales.

Tenured or non time-limited appointments will not be supported.

The trustees may, from time to time, set special conditions for the award of a grant.

Final decision on the award of a grant is made by the trustees, having taken into account advice from their scientific advisers.

The trustees consider proposals twice each year, normally May and October. To allow for the refereeing process, new full proposals for the May meeting should be received by 28 February and for the October/November meeting by

15 July. Late applications may be deferred for six months.

The Kennedy Charitable Foundation

Roman Catholic ministries and general, especially in the west of Ireland

£468,500 (2007/08)

Beneficial area Unrestricted, but mainly Ireland with a preference for County Mayo and County Sligo.

12th Floor, Bank House, Charlotte Street, Manchester M1 4ET

Tel. 0161 236 8191 **Fax** 0161 236 4814

Email kcf@pye158.freeserve.co.uk

Correspondent Alan Pye

Trustees *Patrick James Kennedy; Kathleen Kennedy; John Gerard Kennedy; Patrick Joseph Francis Kennedy; Anna Maria Kelly.*

CC Number 1052001

Information available Accounts were on file at the Charity Commission, without an analysis of grantmaking.

Established in 1995, the foundation has no permanent endowment and is funded by donations. Grants are predominantly made to organisations connected with the Roman Catholic faith, mainly in Ireland.

In 2007/08 the foundation had an income of £595,000 and made 65 grants totalling £468,500.

Beneficiaries included: Short Strand Community Forum (£41,000); Pontifical Irish College Trust (£34,000); Ireland Health Foundation (£23,500); Little Sisters of the Poor (£20,000); Diocese of Hexham & Newcastle (£15,000); Trafford New Diabetes Unit (£11,000); Society of African Missions (£10,000); Cornerstone (£3,500); Bridge Project (£2,500); Children with Leukaemia (£2,000); and Cancer Research UK (£1,000).

Grants of less than £1,000 included those to: Society of St Columban for Foreign Missions, Children's Liver Disease Foundation and Diocese of Birmingham.

Applications The foundation says that 'unsolicited applications are not accepted'.

Keren Association

Jewish, education and general

£6.5 million (2007/08)

Beneficial area UK.

136 Clapton Common, London E5 9AG

Correspondent Mrs S Englander, Trustee

Trustees *E Englander, Chair; Mrs S Englander; P N Englander; S Z Englander; B Englander; J S Englander; Mrs H Z Weiss; Mrs N Weiss.*

CC Number 313119

Information available Accounts were on file at the Charity Commission, without a list of grants.

The trust has general charitable purposes, supporting the advancement of education and the provision of religious instruction and training in traditional Judaism. Support is also given to needy Jewish people.

In 2007/08 the trust had assets of £19 million and an income of £8.5 million. Grants were made totalling £6.5 million. A list of grant recipients was not included in the accounts.

Previous beneficiaries include: Beis Aharon Trust, Yeshivah Belz Machnovke, U T A, Yetev Lev Jerulalem, Lomdei Tom h Belz Machnovke, Friends of Beis Yaakov, Yeshlvat Lom dei Torah, Friends of Arad, Kupat Gmach Vezer Nlsuin, Clwk Yaakov and British Heart Foundation.

Applications In writing to the correspondent.

The King's Fund

Health and health care, especially in London

£1.2 million (2008)

Beneficial area London.

11–13 Cavendish Square, London W1G 0AN

Tel. 020 7307 2400 **Fax** 020 7307 2809

Email grants@kingsfund.org.uk

Website www.kingsfund.org.uk

Correspondent Kate Batlin, The Funding and Development Department

Trustees *Sir Cyril Chantler; Strone Macpherson; Jude Goffe; David Wootton; Dr Penelope Dash; Simon Stevens; Jacqueline Docherty; Prof Julian Le Grand.*

CC Number 1126980

Information available Accounts were on file at the Charity Commission and the fund has a good website.

The King's Fund is a leading independent health care charity, originally set up in 1897 by the Prince of Wales, later King Edward VII, to support the improvement of the health of Londoners and health care in London.

In 2007 the trustees of King Edward's Hospital Fund for London (registration number 207401) as it was then known, petitioned the Privy Council to establish a new body by Royal Charter. This was granted and the King's Fund was registered with the Charity Commission. The King's Fund took over the operations of the King Edward's Hospital Fund for London on 1 January 2009.

In 2008 the fund had assets of £114 million and a consolidated income of £13 million. Grants were made totalling £1.2 million.

The fund seeks to understand how the health system in England can be improved. Today it fulfils this mission through a range of activities, including research and policy analysis as well as grantmaking.

The fund categorises its activities into three broad areas:

1) Developing people and organisations
The fund looks to understand how the health system can be improved and, using that insight, it helps to shape policy, transform services and bring about behaviour change. Its work in this area includes research, analysis, leadership development and service improvement. It also offers a wide range of resources to help everyone working in health to share knowledge, learning and ideas.

2) Developing policies and ideas
The fund aims to influence health and social care policy and generate informed debate.

The overall goal in this area is to have a growing and measurable impact on both policy makers and service providers. The fund works independently and with partners to deliver a range of outputs, based on a mix of primary research, analysis, commentary, facilitated debate and discussion.

3) Developing services
Under this category the fund aims to build upon, and inform, its policy work by testing ideas out in practice and supporting innovation to generate learning.

The key activities underlying the development of services include the Partners for Health in London funding and development programme, focusing initially on four areas:

- end-of-life care, sexual health, mental health advocacy and integrated health care
- delivering, on behalf of the Department of Health, the current Enhancing the Healing Environment programmes and developing new areas of application
- delivering a national awards scheme to identify and promote best practice in community organisations working to improve health
- developing analytical tools to be used throughout the National Health Service.

In 2008 the fund awarded £608,000 through the Partners for Health awards and £575,000 through the Enhancing the Healing Environment national programme. Both programmes are now closed but despite attempts to contact the fund, it has not been possible to confirm whether or not they, or similar programmes, will be opening again in the future. Potential applicants are therefore advised to check the fund's website or contact them directly for the latest information.

The fund also manages the GlaxoSmithKline IMPACT Awards. The awards have been running since 1997 and are designed to recognise and reward charities that are doing excellent work to improve people's health. They are funded by GlaxoSmithKline and managed in partnership with the King's Fund. The awards are open to registered charities that are at least three years old, working in a health-related field in the UK, with a total annual income between £10,000 and £1 million. For further information go to the website or contact the fund directly.

Applications Applicants are advised to check the fund's website or contact them directly for the latest information on current funding programmes.

The Mary Kinross Charitable Trust

Relief of poverty, medical research, community development, young people and penal affairs

£868,000 (2008/09)
Beneficial area UK.

36 Grove Avenue, Moseley, Birmingham B13 9RY

Correspondent Fiona Adams, Trustee

Trustees *Elizabeth Shields, Chair; Fiona Adams; Neil Cross; Jonathan Haw; Robert McDougall.*

CC Number 212206

Information available Accounts were available from the Charity Commission.

This trust makes grants in the areas of medical research, community development, young people, penal affairs, health and mental health. Grants made under the heading 'young people' tend to be made with crime prevention in mind.

The trust prefers to work mainly with a group of charities with which it develops a close connection, led by at least one of the trustees. It describes its grant policy as follows:

Trustees wish to continue the policy of the founder which was to use the trust income to support a few carefully researched projects, rather than to make many small grants. The fields of work chosen reflect the particular interests and knowledge of trustees and at least one trustee takes responsibility for ensuring the trust's close involvement with organisations to which major grants are made.

When the trust makes a major grant core office costs are often included, which may enable the recipients to apply for other sources of funding. Unfortunately, the trust has to disappoint the great majority of applicants who make unsolicited appeals.

In 2008/09 the trust had assets of £21 million and an income of £737,000. Grants were made totalling £868,000 and were distributed as follows:

Category	Value
Medical research	£357,000
Community development	£211,000
Young people	£99,000
Penal affairs	£78,000
Health	£59,000
Mental health	£38,000
Miscellaneous	£26,000

Beneficiaries included: Moseley Community Development Trust (£190,000); Juvenile Diabetes Research Foundation (£97,000); Queen's Medical Research Institute – University of Edinburgh (£50,000); Hepatitis C Trust (£30,000); Peninsula Medical School Foundation (£25,000); Prospex (£20,000); Bendrigg Trust (£11,000); Prison Radio Association (£5,000); Skye and Lochalsh Mental Health Association (£2,000); and West Midlands Charity Trusts Group (£900).

Exclusions No grants to individuals.

Applications 'Because the trustees have no office staff and work from home, they prefer dealing with written correspondence rather than telephone calls from applicants soliciting funds.' Please note: unsolicited applications to this trust are very unlikely to be successful.

Ernest Kleinwort Charitable Trust

General purposes, in practice, mainly to wildlife and environmental conservation both nationally and overseas, disability, medical research and welfare of older and young people

£952,000 (2007/08)

Beneficial area UK, in particular Sussex; overseas.

Kleinwort Benson, 30 Gresham Street, London EC2V 7PG

Tel. 020 3207 7338

Correspondent Nick Kerr-Sheppard, Secretary

Trustees *Kleinwort Benson Trustees Ltd; Madeleine, Lady Kleinwort; Richard Ewing; Simon Robertson; Sir Christopher Lever; Sir Richard Kleinwort; Marina Kleinwort; Alexander Kleinwort.*

CC Number 229665

Information available Accounts were available from the Charity Commission.

The trust is an entirely grant-making organisation and makes between 150 and 250 grants a year, the majority of which fall between £100 and £2,000. More than half of the money goes to Sussex based charities.

Support is principally given to charities working in the fields of wildlife and environmental conservation (national and international) and charities operating in the county of Sussex. In approved cases, the trustees will provide assistance towards start-up or capital costs and ongoing expenses. This may take the form of a grant for say, three years, following which support may be withdrawn to enable the resources to be devoted to other projects. The trustees do not normally respond favourably to appeals from individuals, nor to those from small local charities for example individual churches, village halls, etc. where there is no specific connection.

In 2007/08 the trust had assets of just over £51 million and an income of £1.5 million. 184 grants were made totalling £952,000 – these figures include 129 grants made to Sussex charities totalling £615,000. Many of the beneficiaries had been supported in previous years. Grants were categorised as follows:

Wildlife and conservation – 31 grants totalling £220,000
Beneficiaries included: Tusk Trust and WWF – UK (£50,000 each); Herpetological Conservation Trust (£15,000); Birdlife International and the Environmental Investigation Agency (£10,000 each); Froglife (£6,500); RSPB Northern Ireland (£5,000); World Pheasant Association (£3,000); Folly Wildlife Rescue Trust (£1,000); and Weald and Downland Open Air Museum (£450).

People with disabilities – 50 grants totalling £197,000
Beneficiaries included: Disabilities Trust (£28,000); Mark Davies Injured Riders' Fund (£15,000); Mill Hall School (£8,000); Talking Newspaper Association (£6,000); Farrell Trust (£4,500); Sussex Autistic Society (£3,000); Amaze (£2,000); and Blind in Business (£500).

Medical research – 15 grants totalling £134,000
Beneficiaries included: St Richard's Hospital Charitable Trust (£25,000); International Spinal Research Trust (£20,000); Macmillan Nurse Appeal (£15,000); Sussex Multiple Sclerosis Treatment Centre (£10,000); Pathways to Health (£2,000); Foundation for the Study of Infant Deaths (£1,500);

Leukaemia Research Fund (£750); and Prostate Cancer Research Fund (£200).

Miscellaneous – 12 donations totalling £94,000
Beneficiaries included: River Trust (£70,000); Antarctic Heritage Trust (£5,000); Sussex Heritage Trust (£2,000); Cuckfield Society (£1,500); Royal National Mission to Deep Sea Fishermen (£1,000); and Sussex Police Choir (£750).

Care of young people – 23 grants totalling £79,000
Beneficiaries included: Prince's Trust (£21,000); Lodge Hill Trust (£15,000); Amberly Working Museum (£5,000); Fields in Trust (£2,500); Bognor Fun Bus Company Limited (£1,000); Sussex Clubs for Young People (£750); Sussex Supreme Twirlers (£300); and Radley College (£100).

Reproductive health care – 3 grants totalling £73,000
Beneficiaries were: Interact Worldwide (£40,000); Marie Stopes International (£30,000); and Jamaica Family Planning Association (£2,900).

General welfare and social problems – 15 grants totalling £60,000
Beneficiaries included: Impact Foundation (£15,000); Sussex Community Foundation (£12,000); Lorica Trust Ltd (£10,000); Chichester Diocesan Association for Family Support Work (£5,000); Family Holiday Association (£2,000); Miracles (£1,000); and Royal Air Force Benevolent Fund (£600).

Hospices for the benefit of Sussex – 4 grants totalling £54,000
Beneficiaries were: St Barnabas Hospice (£40,000); St Catherine's Hospice (£7,700); Heatherley Cheshire Home (£4,500); and St Peter and St James' Hospice and Continuing Care Centre (£1,500).

Care of older people – 12 grants totalling £30,000
Beneficiaries included: Brendoncare Foundation Development Trust (£15,000); Little Black Bag Housing Association (£4,500); Contact the Elderly (£2,000); Sussex Housing and Care (£750); Independent Age (£450); and Rowan's Hospice (£50).

Exclusions Individuals and local charities outside Sussex are normally excluded. Very small, narrowly specialised activities and unfocussed causes are also avoided.

Applications In writing to the correspondent, enclosing a copy of the most recent annual report and financial statements. Trustees meet in March and

October, but applications are considered throughout the year, normally within two to three months of receipt. Consideration of appeals received is undertaken by small groups of trustees to whom authority has been delegated to make individual grants of up to £10,000 each. These groups meet quarterly so applications for smaller grants can be dealt with quickly. Only successful applicants are notified of the trustees' decision.

The Sir James Knott Trust

General charitable purposes, in practice, support for people who are disadvantaged, young people, older people, the disabled, education and training, medical care, historic buildings, the environment, music and the arts and seafarers' and services' charities

£1.1 million (2008/09)

Beneficial area Tyne and Wear, Northumberland, County Durham inclusive of Hartlepool but exclusive of Darlington, Stockton-on-Tees, Middlesbrough, Redcar and Cleveland.

16–18 Hood Street, Newcastle upon Tyne NE1 6JQ

Tel. 0191 230 4016 **Fax** 0191 230 2817

Email info@knott-trust.co.uk

Website www.knott-trust.co.uk

Correspondent Vivien Stapeley, Secretary

Trustees *Prof. Oliver James; Charles Baker-Cresswell; Sarah Riddell; Ben Speke.*

CC Number 1001363

Information available Accounts were available from the Charity Commission.

This trust is established for general charitable purposes; in practice its primary objective is to help improve the conditions of people living and working in the north east of England.

Background

James Knott was one of the merchant giants of the nineteenth century. The Prince Line Ltd was a major shipping company that was held in the highest regard by all who sailed in their ships and by passengers voyaging on the round the world service. The Prince Line gave Knott enormous wealth and over the years he and his wife became well-known on Tyneside for their philanthropy. In 1920 and in order that his charitable giving could continue after his death he provided funds for the James Knott Settlement. The focus of his charitable interest was to support charitable bodies and organisations mainly connected with the north east of England.

The Sir James Knott Trust aims to help improve the conditions of people living and working in the north east of England allocating grants to charities working for the benefit of the population and environment of Tyne and Wear, Northumberland and County Durham, including Hartlepool. The main donations are in the fields of community issues and events, service charities, historic buildings and heritage, education, arts and culture, health, environment, public services and housing.

General

Grants are normally only made to registered charities specifically operating in or for the benefit of the north east of England (Tyne and Wear, Northumberland, County Durham inclusive of Hartlepool but exclusive of Darlington, Stockton-on-Tees, Middlesbrough, Redcar and Cleveland).

The trustees have wide discretion on the distribution of funds and meet to consider grant applications three times a year. Grants totalling about £1 million a year are made, funded out of income. The trustees try to follow the wishes and interests of the trust's founder where this is compatible with the present day needs of the North East. Charitable works known to have been of particular interest to Sir James are given special consideration, for example, Army Benevolent Fund, Northumberland Playing Fields Association, Mission to Seafarers, Royal British Legion, the YMCA and YWCA, Barnardo's, RUKBA, Historic Churches Trust, schools and universities.

In recent years, grants have been given in support of the welfare of people who are disadvantaged, young people, older people, people with disabilities, education and training, medical care, historic buildings, the environment, music and the arts and seafarers' and services' charities. Detailed examples of recent grants can be found on the trust's website.

In 2008/09 the trust had assets of £30 million and an income of £1.3 million. Grants were made to 394 organisations totalling £1.1 million and were distributed as follows:

Category	Value
Community issues/events	£329,000
Education and training	£167,000
Service charities	£159,000
Arts and culture	£139,000
Health, sport and human services	£122,000
Historic buildings/heritage	£85,000
Public services	£64,000
Conservation/horticultural/biodiversity/ environmental	£44,000
Homeless/housing	£7,000

By far the largest grants went to Academy School – Ashington and TS Northumbria (£50,000 each).

Beneficiaries of smaller grants included: Northumbria Historic Churches Trust (£18,000); Diocese of Durham and Diocese of Newcastle (£15,000 each); Scout Association – Durham County (£11,000); Sage Gateshead (£10,000); YMCA – North East (£8,000); NSPCC and Greggs Trust (£5,000 each); Southwick Neighbourhood Youth Project (£3,000); Sea Cadets – Jarrow (£2,500); Tomorrow's People (£2,000); and Simonburn Village Hall (£1,500).

Exclusions Individuals, the replacement of funding withdrawn by local authorities or organisations that do not have an identifiable project within the beneficial area.

Applications In writing to the correspondent, giving a brief description of the need, with relevant consideration to the following points:

- the type of organisation you are and how you benefit the community
- how you are organised and managed
- how many staff/volunteers you have
- if a registered charity, your registered number, if not you will need to submit the name and registered number of a charity which is prepared to administer funds on your behalf
- your relationship, if any, with similar or umbrella organisations
- your main funding source
- the project you are currently fundraising for, including the cost, the amount required and when the funds are needed
- please give details of who else you have approached and what response have you had

- please confirm whether you have you applied to the Big Lottery Fund (if not, state why not)
- please enclose a copy of your latest trustees' report and accounts (if you are a new organisation then provide a copy of your latest bank statement).

Not all of these points may apply to you, but they give an idea of what the trustees may ask when considering applications. Applicants may be contacted for further information.

Trustees normally meet in spring, summer and autumn. Applications need to be submitted at least three months before a grant is required. However, if your application is for a grant of less than £1,000, this can usually be processed outside meetings and usually within one month.

The Neil Kreitman Foundation

Arts and culture, education, health and social welfare and Jewish charities

£540,000 (2007/08)

Beneficial area Worldwide, in practice UK, USA and Israel.

Citroen Wells & Partners, Devonshire House, 1 Devonshire Street, London W1W 5DR

Tel. 020 7304 2000 **Fax** 020 7304 2020

Email gordon.smith@citreonwells.co.uk

Correspondent Gordon C Smith, Trustee

Trustees *Neil R Kreitman; Gordon C Smith.*

CC Number 267171

Information available Accounts were available from the Charity Commission.

The foundation was established in 1974 and makes grants to registered or exempt charities for the arts and culture, education, health and social welfare and Jewish charities.

In 2005/06 the foundation received £15 million from the Kreitman Foundation when it ceased operating, however a predicted increase in grantmaking as a result of this has not happened.

In 2007/08 the foundation had assets of £20.7 million and an income of £846,500. Grants were made to 19 organisations totalling £540,000, which were categorised as follows:

Arts and culture – 13 grants totalling £452,000
Beneficiaries included: the British Museum (£120,000); Crocker Art Museum (£66,500); Ancient India and Iran Trust (£28,000); Royal National Theatre (£15,500 – during the previous year a grant of £476,000 was made); Hindu Kush Conservation Association (£7,000); and Cambridge University (£5,000).

Education – 2 grants totalling £10,500
Beneficiaries were: Yale University (£10,000); and the School of Oriental and African Studies (£500).

Health and welfare – 4 grants totalling £77,200
Beneficiaries were: Sierra Club Foundation (£35,200); Release (£20,000); International PEN (£12,000); and KIDS (£10,000).

Exclusions No grants to individuals.

Applications In writing to the correspondent.

Maurice and Hilda Laing Charitable Trust

Promotion of Christianity and relief of need

£2.2 million (2008)

Beneficial area UK and overseas.

33 Bunns Lane, Mill Hill, London NW7 2DX

Tel. 020 8238 8890 **Fax** 020 8238 8897

Correspondent Elizabeth Harley, Secretary

Trustees *Andrea Currie; Peter Harper; Robert Harley; Ewan Harper; Charles Laing; Stephen Ludlow.*

CC Number 1058109

Information available Accounts were available from the Charity Commission.

This trust was established in 1996 and is mainly concerned with the advancement of the Christian religion and relieving poverty, both in the UK and overseas. The trust is administered alongside the Beatrice Laing Trust, the Martin Laing Foundation and the Kirby Laing

Foundation with which it shares members of staff and office space; collectively they are known as the Laing Family Trusts.

In practice grants awarded fall into three main categories:

- to organisations seeking to promote Christian faith and values through evangelistic, educational and media activities at home and overseas
- to organisations seeking to express Christian faith through practical action to help people in need, for example, those with disabilities, the homeless, the sick, young people, prisoners and ex-offenders
- to organisations working to relieve poverty overseas, with a particular emphasis on helping children who are vulnerable or at risk. In most cases these grants to overseas projects are made through UK registered charities who are expected to monitor and evaluate the projects on behalf of the trust, providing progress reports at agreed intervals.

The trust offers the following analysis of its future grant-making plans:

Grant expenditure totalled £2.2 million, a rise of 31.7% on the previous year. This reflects the decision made by the trustees in 2006, after consultation with the settlor, to work towards winding up the trust over a 10–15 year period. Since then the trustees have planned for a controlled increase in the level of their grant expenditure, a pattern which is likely to continue despite the anticipated drop in income rising from the economic recession. This year's excess of charitable expenditure over income was drawn from reserves of unexpended income from previous years. The depletion of these reserves, which now stand at £33,000, means that it is likely that capital will be expended on the grant-making programme in future years.

In 2008 the trust had assets of £32 million and an income of £1.6 million. 91 grants were made totalling £2.2 million. Grants were categorised as follows:

Category	No.	Value
Religion	29	£995,000
Children and young people	8	£365,000
Overseas aid	27	£336,000
Social welfare	15	£238,000
Health and medicine	3	£51,000
Miscellaneous	9	£170,000

Beneficiaries included: Lambeth Fund (£185,000); Ethiopian Graduate School of Theology (£175,000); Charities Aid Foundation (£170,000); SAT-7 Trust Ltd (£150,000); St Martin-in-the-Fields (£100,000); Workaid (£50,000); YMCA UK National Trust (£25,000); Hope UK (£10,000); and Children in Crisis,

Cutting Edge Ministries and Jesus Army Charitable Trust (£5,000 each).

Exclusions No grants to groups or individuals for the purpose of education, travel, attendance at conferences or participation in overseas exchange programmes. No grants towards church restoration or repair.

Applications In writing to the correspondent. One application only is needed to apply to this or the Kirby Laing Foundation, Martin Laing Foundation or Beatrice Laing Charitable Trust. Multiple applications will still only elicit a single reply, even then applicants are asked to accept non-response as a negative reply on behalf of all these trusts, unless a stamped addressed envelope is enclosed. After the initial sifting process, the Maurice and Hilda Laing Trust follows its own administrative procedures.

These trusts make strenuous efforts to keep their overhead costs to a minimum. As they also make a very large number of grants each year, in proportion to their income, the staff must rely almost entirely on the written applications submitted in selecting appeals to go forward to the trustees. Each application should contain all the information needed to allow such a decision to be reached, in as short and straightforward a way as possible.

Specifically, each application should say:

- what the money is for
- how much is needed
- how much has already been found
- where the rest of the money is to come from.

The trustees meet quarterly to consider applications for grants above £10,000. In most cases the trust's administrators will have met with applicants and prepared reports and recommendations for the trustees.

Applications for smaller amounts are considered on an ongoing basis throughout the year. The administrators are authorised to make such grants without prior consent up to a maximum of £100,000 in each quarter, the grants to be reported to the trustees and approved retrospectively at the following quarterly meeting.

All recipients of grants over £5,000 are asked to report on how the money has been spent and what has been achieved.

The Laing Family Foundations

General

£11 million (2007/08)

Beneficial area UK and overseas.

33 Bunns Lane, Mill Hill, London NW7 2DX

Tel. 020 8238 8890 **Fax** 020 8238 8897

Correspondent Miss Elizabeth Harley

Information available Excellent information available on the individual trusts.

The following trusts (except the Rufford Maurice Laing Foundation) are administered from a common office in north London and an application to one is seen as an application to all. However, they have different funding patterns and each has its own entry.

They are:

- The Kirby Laing Foundation
- The Rufford Maurice Laing Foundation
- The Beatrice Laing Trust
- The Maurice and Hilda Laing Charitable Trust.

There is an evangelical Christian background to the group, but collectively the grants lists cover most fields of welfare and health as well as the promotion of Christianity, at home and overseas. Support for medical research, of the scientific sort is limited, and there is no general support for the arts (though one trust has a limited interest in this field).

Over 1,000 grants a year are made. Though many of them are small, very large grants can also be made.

Most of the grants are for national organisations, big or small, with only limited support for local organisations or local branches of the larger networks.

Two of the trusts have strong specialist interests:

- advancement of Christianity: the Maurice and Hilda Laing Charitable Trust
- small local grants for welfare and disability: the Beatrice Laing Trust.

Trustees, even those who are older, are much involved in the grant-making process, and take a personal interest in many of the larger projects supported.

The trusts do not normally act collectively.

The general application requirements are set out in the 'applications' section – these will suffice for all except specialist applications, the details for which are found in the 'applications' section of the relevant entries.

Exclusions No grants to groups or individuals for the purpose of education, travel, attendance at conferences or participation in overseas exchange programmes.

In general the trusts rarely make grants towards the running costs of local organisations, which they feel have to be raised from within the local community.

Applications None of the trusts issue application forms and an application to one is seen as an application to all.

An application for a grant towards a specific capital project should be in the form of a short letter giving details of the project, its total cost, the amount raised and some indication of how it is to be financed.

A copy of the organisation's latest annual report and accounts, together with a stamped addressed envelope, should be enclosed. Unless an sae is enclosed applicants are asked to accept non-response as a negative reply. Applications for small amounts are considered on an ongoing basis.

The Kirby Laing Foundation

Health, welfare, Christian religion, young people and general

£2.8 million (2007)

Beneficial area Unrestricted, but mainly UK.

33 Bunns Lane, Mill Hill, London NW7 2DX

Tel. 020 8238 8890 **Fax** 020 8238 8897

Correspondent Elizabeth Harley

Trustees *Lady Isobel Laing; David E Laing; Simon Webley; Rev Charles Burch.*

CC Number 264299

Information available Accounts were available from the Charity Commission.

Along with the other Laing family trusts, this is a general grantmaker, with a Christian orientation and awarding almost all kinds of grants, few of them very large. It is unusual in the group for having a small number of artistic and cultural grants.

General

The foundation is administered alongside, and shares its three staff with, the Beatrice Laing Trust, the Martin Laing Foundation and the Maurice and Hilda Laing Charitable Trust. An application to any one of these four trusts, collectively known as the Laing Family Trusts, is treated as an application to all although, after the initial 'sorting' process, applications considered suitable for further consideration by the Kirby Laing Foundation follow the foundation's own administrative and decision making process.

The trust states that it intends to wind up its activities within the next 10–15 years and as a result, anticipates a significant increase in the level of charitable expenditure.

In 2007 the foundation had assets amounting to £55 million and an income of £1.8 million. Grants were made totalling £2.8 million.

Grantmaking

Grants over £5,000 each were categorised as follows:

Religion – 20 grants totalling £1.6 million
Beneficiaries included: Cambridge Foundation (£1.2 million); Tyndale House – 4 grants (£187,000); SAT 7 Trust Ltd (£50,000); Wells Cathedral (£25,000); Youth for Christ (£20,000); Bible Society (£10,000); Church Mission Society (£6,000); and Urban Saints (£5,000).

Children and young people (including education) – 8 grants totalling £461,000
Beneficiaries included: Royal Academy of Engineering (£250,000); United Learning Trust (£150,000); Monkton Combe School (£25,000); and Youth Sport Trust (£10,000).

Health and Medicine – 15 grants totalling £243,000
Beneficiaries included: Oxford Radcliffe Hospitals NHS Trust Charitable Funds (£75,000); Restoration of Appearance and Function Trust (£45,000); Royal College of Surgeons of England (£20,000); and Autism Speaks (£5,000).

Social Welfare – 7 grants totalling £163,000
Grants included those to: Royal Hospital Chelsea (£100,000); Abbeyfield UK (£25,000); Church Housing Trust (£8,000); and Justice First (£5,000).

Cultural and Environmental – 17 grants totalling £116,000
Beneficiaries included: Norwich Theatre Royal (£20,000); Contemporary Dance Trust (£10,000); and Royal Watercolour Society (£5,000).

Overseas Aid – 12 grants totalling £105,000
Beneficiaries included: Dhaka Ahsania Mission (£20,000); Mines Advisory Group (£15,000); British Red Cross UK/Int (£10,000); and FARM Africa (£5,000).

Exclusions No grants to individuals, no travel grants and no educational grants. The foundation rarely gives grants for the running costs of local organisations.

Applications One application only is needed to apply to this or the Beatrice Laing Trust or Maurice and Hilda Laing Charitable Trust. Multiple applications will still only elicit a single reply.

These trusts make strenuous efforts to keep their overhead costs to a minimum. As they also make a very large number of grants each year, in proportion to their income, the staff must rely almost entirely on the written applications submitted in selecting appeals to go forward to the trustees.

Each application should contain all the information needed to allow such a decision to be reached, in as short and straightforward a way as possible. Specifically, each application should say:

- what the money is for
- how much is needed
- how much has already been found
- where the rest is to come from.

Unless there is reasonable assurance on the last point the grant is unlikely to be recommended. The trustees meet four times a year to consider the award of grants of over £20,000. Decisions on smaller grants are made on an ongoing basis.

For all grants above £5,000 the foundation asks for a report from the charity one year after the grant has been made, describing briefly how the grant has been spent and what has been achieved. For larger and multi-year grants more detailed reports may be required. Where a grant is paid in instalments the usual practice is not to release the second and subsequent instalments until a review of progress has been satisfactorily completed.

The Beatrice Laing Trust

Relief of poverty and advancement of the evangelical Christian faith

£1 million (2007/08)
Beneficial area UK and overseas.

c/o Laing Family Trusts, 33 Bunns Lane, Mill Hill, London NW7 2DX

Tel. 020 8238 8890

Correspondent Elizabeth Harley, Secretary

Trustees *Sir Martin Laing; David E Laing; Christopher M Laing; John H Laing; Charles Laing; Paula Blacker; Alexandra Gregory.*

CC Number 211884

Information available Accounts were available at the Charity Commission. See the entry on the Laing Family Foundations for the work of the group as a whole.

This trust was established in 1952 by Sir John Laing and his wife, Beatrice, both now deceased. The trust's objects are the relief of poverty and the advancement of the evangelical Christian faith in the UK and abroad and these are achieved through the trust's grant-making programme, which is its only charitable activity.

The Beatrice Laing Trust is administered alongside the Maurice and Hilda Laing Charitable Trust, the Martin Laing Foundation and the Kirby Laing Foundation with which it shares members of staff and office space; collectively they are known as the Laing Family Trusts. The Beatrice Laing Trust concentrates mainly on small grants for the relief of poverty in its broadest sense, both throughout the UK and overseas.

In the UK grant recipients include organisations working with children, young people and older people, the homeless and those with physical, mental or learning difficulties. Grants to projects overseas are concentrated on building the capacity to provide long-term solutions to the problems faced by countries in the developing world rather than providing emergency aid.

In addition to the trust's own funds, the trustees are invited to make nominations to the grants committee of the J W Laing Trust, for donations totalling 20% of that trust's income up to a maximum of

£550,000 per annum. The trustees use these funds to support the advancement of the evangelical Christian faith through projects of new church building or extension or church mission activities.

Grants are usually only made to UK registered charities. A very small number of individuals are supported, mostly for retired missionaries who were known to the founders and who receive an annual grant.

The trust notes in its latest accounts that:

the grant-making process is largely reactive rather than proactive and it should be noted that any fluctuation in the level of grants funded across the categories shown is therefore, a reflection of the applications received rather than a change in the trustees' priorities. This is also true of the geographical spread of grants made.

The vast majority of grants fall into the £1,000 to £5,000 range. Most of these represent either modest annual grants towards the core costs of selected national organisations working with the trust's priority groups, or small capital grants to local organisations working to relieve poverty in their local communities.

For all grants above £5,000 the trust asks for a report from the charity 12 months after the grant has been paid, describing briefly how the grant has been spent and commenting as appropriate on what has been achieved. For larger and multi-year grants more detailed reporting may be required. Most of the larger grants are only paid following the fulfilment of certain conditions, and some grants are paid in instalments, usually over three years. Where a grant is payable in instalments it is the trust's usual practice not to release payment of the second and subsequent instalments until a review of progress has been satisfactorily completed.

Grants of over £5,000 are awarded by the trustees at meetings held twice a year. Grants of under £5,000 are made on a monthly basis by the trust director and are ratified at the trustees' annual meeting.

In 2007/08 the trust had assets of £41 million and an income of £1.6 million. 205 grants totalling over £1 million which were categorised as follows:

Health and medicine – 67 grants totalling £316,000
Beneficiaries of the largest grants included: Children's Trust and North London Hospice (£25,000 each); Beacon Centre for the Blind and the Meath Epilepsy Trust (£20,000 each); and Help the Hospices, Northampton Society for Autism and SENSE (£10,000 each).

Beneficiaries of smaller grants included: Camphill Village Trust (£7,500); Arthritis Care, the Cedar Foundation, Deafblind UK, Garden House Hospice, Medical Foundation for the Care of Victims of Torture, Rainbow Living, Iain Rennie Hospice at Home, Springboard Opportunity Group and Wings South West (£5,000 each); Guildford and Waverley Crossroads Care (£4,000); Kingwood Trust (£3,500); Echo Disability Resource Centre (£3,000); the Aidis Trust, Medical Engineering Resource Unit and Scottish Spina Bifida Association, (£2,500 each); Downs Syndrome Scotland and Preston Carers Centre (£2,000); ACT, Ipswich MENCAP, Sheffield MIND, Spadework and Where Next Association (£1,000 each).

Overseas aid – 43 grants totalling £295,000
Beneficiaries of the largest grants were: Impact Foundation (£40,000 in three grants); Echoes of Service (£30,000); VSO (£25,000 in two grants); Médecins Sans Frontières UK and SENSE International (£20,000 each); and Africa Now, International Centre for Eye Health, Merlin, Oxfam and Workaid (£10,000 each).

Beneficiaries of smaller grants included: Book Aid International (£7,500); Footsteps Inernational, LEPRA, Motivation, Royal Commonwealth Society for the Blind, Tools for Self Reliance and Water Aid (£5,000 each); Africa Educational Trust (£2,500); Operation Youth Quake and Skillshare International (£2,000 each); and the British-Nepal Medical Trust (£1,500).

Social welfare – 61 grants totalling £236,000
Beneficiaries of the largest grants included: SSAFA and Trinity Centre Winchester (£25,000 each); and Church Housing Trust, Corton House, Methodist Homes for the Aged and Queen Alexandra Hospital Home (£10,000 each).

Beneficiaries of smaller grants included: Crisis, In Kind Direct, Notting Hill Housing Trust, Portman House Trust, Prisoners Abroad, St Giles Trust and Women's Link (£5,000 each); Ipswich Housing Action Group (£3,500); Asylum Welcome and Counsel and Care for the Elderly (£3,000 each); Apex Charitable Trust, Enfield CAB, Inside Out Trust, Pact, Prisoners' Education Trust, Refugee Council and Wirral Churches Ark Project (£2,500 each); Brighton Unemployed Centre Families Project, Derbyshire Housing Aid and Plymouth Guild of Voluntary Service (£2,000 each); Not Forgotten Association (£1,500); and Age Concern Norfolk, the Camden Society, Housing the Homeless Central Fund, Open Door Centre – Exmouth and Splitz Support Service (£1,000 each).

Children and young people (including education) – 21 grants totalling £130,000
Beneficiaries of the largest grants were: East Park School and the TreeHouse Trust (£25,000 each); and the Garwood Foundation and MacIntyre Care (£20,000 each).

Beneficiaries of smaller grants included: Hendon Sea Training Corps and Red Balloon Learner Centre Group (£5,000 each); Family Holiday Association and Ormiston Children and Families Trust (£3,000 each); After Adoption and Sandwell Young Carers Project (£2,500 each); Baby Equipment Loan Service, SeeSaw and Westminster Children's Society (£1,000 each); and Sensory and Physical Support Children's Fund (£250).

Religion – 13 grants totalling £37,000 including £4,900 to individuals
Beneficiary of the largest grant was Echoes of Service (£30,000 in four grants).

Beneficiaries of smaller grants were: International Gospel Church and People International Worldwide (£1,000 each); and Woodcroft Women's Fellowship (£150).

Exclusions No grants to individuals; no travel grants; no educational grants.

Applications In writing to the correspondent. One application only is needed to apply to this or the Kirby Laing Foundation, Martin Laing Foundation or Maurice and Hilda Laing Charitable Trust. Multiple applications will still only elicit a single reply; even then applicants are asked to accept non-response as a negative reply on behalf of all these trusts, unless a stamped addressed envelope is enclosed. Applications are considered monthly.

These trusts make strenuous efforts to keep their overhead costs to a minimum. As they also make a very large number of grants each year, in proportion to their income, the staff must rely almost entirely on the written applications submitted in selecting appeals to go forward to the trustees. Each application should contain all the information needed to allow such a decision to be reached, in as short and straightforward a way as possible.

Specifically, each application should say:

- what the money is for
- how much is needed
- how much has already been found
- where the rest of the money is to come from.

Unless there is reasonable assurance on the last point the grant is unlikely to be recommended.

Where larger grants are contemplated, meetings and visits are often undertaken by the trust's staff.

The Lancaster Foundation

Christian causes

£4.2 million (2007/08)

Beneficial area UK and overseas, with a local interest in Clitheroe.

c/o Text House, 152 Bawdlands, Clitheroe, Lancashire BB7 2LA

Tel. 01200 444404

Correspondent Rosemary Lancaster, Trustee

Trustees *Rosemary Lancaster; John Lancaster; Steven Lancaster; Julie Broadhurst.*

CC Number 1066850

Information available Annual report and accounts on file at the Charity Commission.

The object of the charity is to financially support Christian based registered charities across the world. Grants are awarded at the absolute discretion of the trustees. Although many applications are received, the administrative structure of the charity does not allow for the consideration of unsolicited requests for grant funding.

In 2007/08 the trust had assets of £51 million and an income of £2.8 million. 30 grants were made totalling £4.2 million.

By far the largest grant was made to the Grand at Clitheroe (£2.6 million). Other beneficiaries included: Oasis Charitable Trust – the Grand (£275,000); New Generation Music and Mission (£224,000); Open Arms International (£173,000); Love and joy Ministries (£74,000); MIC South Africa (£33,000); Cornerstone Film Trust (£22,000); Christians Against Poverty (£12,000);

Open Doors UK (£2,000); and Windermere Education (£1,000).

Applications The trust has previously stated: 'We do not consider applications made to us from organisations or people unconnected with us. All our donations are instigated because of personal associations. Unsolicited mail is, sadly, a waste of the organisation's resources.'

The Lancaster-Taylor Charitable Trust

'Educational excellence'

£3 million (2007/08)

Beneficial area UK and overseas.

Macfarlanes Solicitors, 10 Norwich Street, London EC4A 1BD

Correspondent The Trustees

Trustees *Steven Lloyd Edwards; Rosalind Anita Jane Smith; Lindsay Diane Dodsworth.*

CC Number 1106035

Information available Accounts were on file at the Charity Commission, without a list of grants.

Established in 2004, the 'primary focus of the trust is currently on making grants to education organisations for the furtherance of educational excellence'.

In 2007/08 the trust had assets of £12 million and an income of almost £6 million, mostly from donations. Grants to four organisations totalled £3 million. A list of beneficiaries was unavailable: 'full details of grants have been given to the commission, but were not included within the accounts as disclosure would prejudice the purpose of these grants'.

Applications 'The trustees meet regularly and decisions are made at trustees' meetings.'

The Allen Lane Foundation

Charities benefiting asylum-seekers and refugees, gypsies and travellers, lesbian, gay, bisexual or transgender people, offenders and ex-offenders, older people, people experiencing mental health problems and people experiencing violence or abuse

£756,000 (2008/09)

Beneficial area UK

90 The Mount, York YO24 1AR

Tel. 01904 613223 **Fax** 01904 613133

Email info@allenlane.org.uk

Website www.allenlane.org.uk

Correspondent Tim Cutts, Executive Secretary

Trustees *Clare Morpurgo; Lea Morpurgo; John Hughes; Christine Teale; Zoe Teale; Guy Dehn; Juliet Walker; Jane Walsh; Fredrica Teale.*

CC Number 248031

Information available Accounts were available at the Charity Commission. The foundation has a helpful and informative website with detailed information on grant giving.

The Allen Lane Foundation is a grant-making trust set up in 1966 by the late Sir Allen Lane, founder of Penguin Books, to support general charitable causes. The foundation has no connection now with the publishing company, but five of the trustees are members of the founder's family.

The foundation wishes to fund work which will make a lasting difference to people's lives rather than simply alleviating the symptoms or current problems, is aimed at reducing isolation, stigma and discrimination and which encourages or enables unpopular groups to share in the life of the whole community.

As the foundation's resources are modest, it prefers to fund smaller organisations where small grants can have more impact. Organisations should be not-for-profit, but need not be registered charities (provided their activities are charitable) and work to benefit groups of people who are unpopular in UK society today. The foundation makes grants in the UK but does not make grants for work in London.

In 2008/09 the foundation had assets of £12 million and an income of £666,000. Grants were made totalling £756,000, of which 131 were committed new grants with a total value of £777,000.

Allen Lane Lecture
Each year the foundation hosts a lecture in memory of Sir Allen Lane. Past lecturers have included Mary Robinson, former President of the Irish Republic, The Bishop of Oxford the Rt. Rev Richard Harries and The Rt. Hon. Frank Field MP. In 2009, Kathleen Duncan OBE was the guest lecturer with the title 'Hard Times, but Great Expectations' at the Ismaili Centre in London. Since 1999 the text of each lecture each year has been published on the foundation's website.

The Allen Lane Foundation is interested in funding work which benefits people in the following groups, or generalist work which includes significant numbers from more than one such group:

- asylum-seekers and refugees (but not groups working with a single nationality)
- gay, lesbian, bisexual or transgender people
- gypsies and travellers
- offenders and ex-offenders
- older people
- people experiencing mental health problems
- people experiencing violence or abuse.

If the beneficiaries of your work do not include a significant proportion of people from one or more of these groups it is very unlikely that your application will be successful.

The foundation's policy remains broadly unchanged from last year, although a recent review has concluded that people from black and minority ethnic communities have been removed as a separate priority. Groups and organisations working with BME communities are still encouraged to apply within the other priorities. The trustees are keen to make the foundation's criteria as clear as possible to save applicants from wasted effort and disappointment, although this does mean that the guidelines list an ever increasing list of exclusions.

Guidelines

The following summary has been taken largely from the foundation's website.

The foundation will make grants for start-up, core or project costs. The grants are relatively small and are likely therefore to be appropriate for costs such as:

- volunteers or participants expenses
- venue hire
- part-time or sessional staffing costs
- work aimed at strengthening the organisation such as trustee or staff training.

Examples of the kind of activities which might be suitable for funding are:

- advocacy
- arts activities where the primary purpose is therapeutic or social
- befriending or mentoring
- mediation or conflict resolution
- practical work, such as gardening or recycling, which benefits both the provider and the recipient
- provision of advice or information
- self-help groups
- social activities or drop-in centres
- strengthening the rights of particular groups and enabling their views and experiences to be heard by policy-makers
- work aimed at combating stigma or discrimination
- work developing practical alternatives to violence
- research and education aimed at changing public attitudes or policy.

These lists are not exhaustive and there will be many other appropriate items/activities which could be funded.

While recognising (and being willing to support) on-going, tried and tested projects, the foundation is particularly interested in unusual, imaginative or pioneering projects which have perhaps not yet caught the public imagination.

Making an application

An application should be no more than four sides of A4 but the project budget may be on extra pages. It should be accompanied by your organisation's last annual report and accounts if you produce such documents and the budget for the whole organisation (and the project budget if they are different) for the current year.

The application should include the following information:

- the aims of your organisation as a whole;
- how these aims are achieved;
- numbers of paid staff or volunteers working for your organisation;
- how your proposals make a lasting difference to people's lives rather than simply alleviating the symptoms or current problems;

- how the proposals reduce isolation, stigma and discrimination or encourage or enable unpopular groups to share in the life of the whole community;
- why your cause or beneficiary group is an unpopular one;
- what you want the grant to pay for;
- what difference a grant would make to your work;
- the cost of the work;
- whether you are asking the foundation to meet the whole cost of the work;
- details of any other sources of funding you are approaching;
- details of how you know if the work has been successful;
- details of how the work, and the way it is done, promotes equal opportunities. If you do not think equal opportunities are relevant to your work please say why.

If further information is needed this will be requested and a visit may be arranged when the application can be discussed in more detail.

All applications should be made to the Foundation's office and ***not*** sent to individual Trustees. If you have any queries about making an application you are encouraged to phone the staff for clarification.

Where grants are given

The foundation makes grants for work all over the United Kingdom but not where the beneficiaries of the work all live in London. Organisations which have their offices in London are eligible provided the people who benefit from their work are not only in London. The foundation does not make any grants overseas and has ceased its grant programme in the Republic of Ireland.

Size and length of grants

The grants are relatively modest. The foundation has no maximum grant, but most awards are for less than £10,000, with the average grant in 2008/09 being around £6,000. Grants repeated for more than one year vary from about £500 per annum up to £5,000 per annum, for a maximum of three years.

The foundation will make single grants, or grants for two or three years. It is unlikely to make a second grant immediately after one has finished and if an application is refused, we ask applicants to wait a year before applying again.

Organisations who can apply

Registered charities and other organisations which are not charities but which seek funding for a charitable project.

To be eligible for a grant you should be able to answer yes to the following questions:

- Does your work benefit people from one or more of our priority groups?

- Are you confident that your application is not subject to any of the exclusions listed?
- If your work relates to a relatively local area – for example a town, village or local community, was your income last year less than about £100,000? or
- If your work covers a wider area – for example a county, region or nation, was your income last year less than about £250,000?
- Is it more than a year since you last applied?
- Does your work take place in the UK?
- Does your work take place outside London?

Grants in 2008/09

People experiencing violence or abuse – 21 grants totalling £158,000
Beneficiaries included: STOP (Trafficking UK) – towards general costs of this national project to support trafficked people (£15,000); West Cumbria Domestic Violence Support – towards salary costs relating to the perpetrator programme (£11,000); Jericho Road Project – for salary costs of the volunteer manager at this Project in Nottingham which supports women in prostitution (£10,000); Survivors Helping Each Other – for core costs of this group in Newark which supports survivors of childhood abuse (£9,000); South Cheshire CLASP – towards the Walking Tall Project which helps people affected by domestic violence and Cornwall Rape and Sexual Abuse Centre – for the cost of group work with survivors of rape and sexual abuse (£8,300 each); Rape and Abuse Line – towards core costs of this organisation working in the Highlands (£8,000); Advocacy After Fatal Domestic Abuse – towards the core costs of this new national support organisation (£5,000); Restore – towards the salary of the part-time project manager working with women involved in prostitution in Derby (£4,000); Hull Lighthouse Project – towards outreach work for women in prostitution in Hull and Homoeopathy for All – towards costs of therapeutic services for women suffering domestic abuse in Herefordshire (£3,000 each); and Survivors of Domestic Abuse – for core costs of this organisation based in Neath (£2,800).

Beneficiaries from more than one unpopular group – 24 grants totalling £148,000
Beneficiaries included: Bristol Crisis Service For Women – for volunteer training and expenses for this project which primarily supports women who self injure (£15,000); Caroline Walker Trust – towards a practical guide for eating well for vulnerable older people, including those with mental health problems and learning disabilities (£10,000); Birmingham Ex-Offenders Service Team – for core and training costs of this project which works with ex-offenders from BME communities, offenders and people whilst in prison (£7,500); Hull Asylum Seeker Support Group Ltd – towards the costs of a new prison support project working with foreign nationals in Hull Prison (£7,200); One Voice 4 Travellers Limited – contribution to the STAR project working with older women in the Gypsy and Travelling communities in East Anglia (£6,000); and Polish Veterans' Association – for core costs of social activities for older people from the Polish community in Bradford (£1,000).

Asylum seekers and refugees – 21 grants totalling £148,000
Grants included those to: Integrating Toryglen Community – for venue costs relating to the Integration and Orientation Programme for refugees and asylum seekers across Scotland (£15,000); Northern Ireland Committee for Refugees and Asylum Seekers (NICRAS) – towards staffing and running costs of an organisation supporting refugees and asylum seekers (£11,000); Churches Together with Refugees in Coventry – for the salary of a co-ordinator's post (£10,000); City of Sanctuary Leicester – towards core costs of this new organisation which aims to build a culture of hospitality for refugees and asylum seekers (£9,000); Refugee Voice Wales – for training scheme for refugee community organisations across Wales (£6,000); Kent Refugee Help – for a support worker for bail applications for people detained in Dover Immigration Removal Centre (£5,000); Oasis Cardiff – towards the running costs of a drop-in facility (£2,000); South Tyneside Asylum Seekers and Refugee Church Help – for rent and refreshments for drop-in sessions in South Shields (£1,500).

Older people – 25 grants totalling £113,000
Beneficiaries included: Kincardine and Deeside Befriending – towards volunteer expenses and core costs of befriending older people (£9,000); Age Concern – Sir Gar – for volunteer travel expenses in Llanelli (£6,700); Friendship at Home Scheme – towards the salary of an assistant manager at this scheme based in Cleethorpes supporting older people (£6,500); Bream Voluntary Car Service – for core costs of this service based in Gloucestershire (£6,000); Ainsdale Community Care Programme – towards core costs of an older persons day care scheme in Southport (£5,500); Come Alive at Fifty Five – to cover venue hire and tutor costs relating to this Liverpool-based organisation's Grow your Own project (£5,300); Mind Active – towards core costs of providing activities for older people in residential care homes in South East Northumberland (£5,000); Govan Care Project – for this Glasgow-based organisation promoting the care of older people (£2,000 each); Moelfre Over 50s Club – towards core costs of an over 50's club on the Isle of Anglesey (£1,600); Activity Friends Selston – towards the cost of activities for older people in rural Nottinghamshire (£1,500); and Temple Club – towards costs of social activities for older people in Keady, Co. Armagh (£1,100).

People experiencing mental health problems – 18 grants totalling £81,000
Grants included those made to: Norfolk Eating Disorders Association – for costs relating to a volunteer co-ordinator at this association based in Norwich (£8,500); Umbrella Centre of Herne Bay – for costs of therapeutic activities at this centre in Kent (£6,000); Green Project – towards the core costs of this horticultural Project in the East Riding of Yorkshire (£4,000); Cascade Theatre Co Ltd – for the Theatre of Opportunities project in Poole (£3,700); Strides! – for a part-time development worker for this organisation in Leicester (£2,700); Survivors of Depression in Transition – a contribution towards core costs and the cost of setting up a new group in North Sheffield (£2,000); Moving On – towards core costs of a social club in Bridport supporting people with mental health issues (£1,000).

Offenders and Ex-offenders – 5 grants totalling £37,000
Beneficiaries were: Make Justice Work – for core costs of this national organisation running a media campaign to raise public awareness of the costliness of locking up low level offenders and the futility of short-term sentences (£15,000); Fair Share Gloucestershire – for a project working with prisoners and their families at HMP Gloucester (£10,000); Friends and Families of Prisoners – towards the core costs of this project in Swansea (£6,000); String of Pearls Project – towards the cost of training programmes for ex-offenders to develop as mentors in the South West (£5,000); and Yorkshire and Humberside Circles of Support and Accountability – towards costs of a regional conference for this organisation

working in the community with sex offenders (£500).

BME and Migrant workers – 9 grants totalling £34,000
Beneficiaries included: Homeplus – towards the cost of rent for emergency accommodation for destitute migrant workers in Belfast (£9,000); Multi Ethnic Aberdeen – towards the Including Me Project which will support existing and new BME groups (£7,500); Dalit Solidarity Network UK – towards the core costs of raising awareness of caste discrimination (£5,000); Ballymoney Community Resource Centre – for the Ethnic Minorities and Migrant Workers Support Project for this organisation in Northern Ireland (£4,500); Long Sutton Migrant Workers' Forum – a contribution towards costs of conversational classes at this group in Lincolnshire (£3,000); and Strood Community Project – towards activities for older Punjabi women at this project in Kent (£2,000).

Gypsies and Travellers – 5 grants totalling £23,000
Beneficiaries included: National Federation of Gypsy Liaison Groups – towards costs relating to Gypsy and Traveller Law Reform meetings (£6,000); Clearwater Gypsies – towards core costs of this group in Chichester (£4,500); Irish Traveller Movement in Britain – towards core costs of this organisation working to raise the capacity and social inclusion of the traveller communities (£3,000); and Kushti Bok – contribution towards core costs of this gypsy and traveller-led group in Dorset (£1,000).

Everyone/open to all – 1 grant of £2,800
The sole beneficiary was the Maitri Project who received a contribution towards the core costs of the running of a drop-in centre in Leicester.

Lesbian, Gay, Bisexual and Transgender – 1 grant of £1,000
The sole grant went to Parents Enquiry North East for core costs.

Exclusions The foundation does not currently make grants for:

- academic research
- addiction, alcohol or drug abuse
- animal welfare or animal rights
- arts or cultural or language projects or festivals
- children and young people or families
- endowments or contributions to other grant-making bodies
- health and healthcare
- holidays or holiday playschemes, day trips or outings
- housing
- hospices and medical research

- individuals
- museums or galleries
- overseas travel
- particular medical conditions or disorders
- physical or learning disabilities
- private and/or mainstream education
- promotion of sectarian religion
- publications
- purchase costs of property, building or refurbishment
- refugee community groups working with single nationalities
- restoration or conservation of historic buildings or sites
- sports and recreation
- therapy, such as counselling
- vehicle purchase
- work which the trustees believe is rightly the responsibility of the state
- work outside the United Kingdom
- work which will already have taken place before a grant is agreed
- work by local organisations with an income of more than £100,000 per annum or those working over a wider area with an income of more than £250,000.

The foundation will not normally make grants to organisations which receive funding (directly or indirectly) from commercial sources where conflicts of interest for the organisation and its work are likely to arise.

Applications There is no formal application form, but when sending in an application the foundation asks that you complete the registration form (available on the foundation's website) and return it with your application. Applications should be no more than four sides of A4 but the budget may be on extra pages. It should be accompanied by your last annual report and accounts (if applicable) and the budget for the whole organisation (and the project budget if they are different) for the current year.

The foundation now no longer has application deadlines. Applications are now processed continually. When the foundation has received your application they will usually be in touch within two weeks either to:

- ask for any further information
- to tell you whether the application will be going forward to the next stage of assessment and what the timetable for a final decision will be
- to inform you that they are unable to help.

The time it takes to process an application and make a grant is usually between two and six months.

The LankellyChase Foundation

Social welfare, community development, arts, heritage, penal affairs, mental health and prevention of abuse

£5.4 million (2008/09)
Beneficial area UK.

1 The Court, High Street, Harwell, Didcot OX11 0EY
Tel. 01235 820044 **Fax** 01235 432720
Email enquiries@lankellychase.org.uk
Website www.lankellychase.org.uk
Correspondent Peter Kilgarriff, Chief Executive
Trustees *Nicholas Tatman (Chair); Ann Stannard; Dodie Carter; Paul Cotterill; Leo Fraser-Mackenzie; Victoria Hoskins; Marion Janner; Andrew Robinson; Kanwaljit Singh; Clive Martin.*
CC Number 1107583
Information available Accounts were available at the Charity Commission. The foundation has an excellent website.

The Chase Charity and the Lankelly Foundation were established through the generosity of two separate entrepreneurs who successively developed a complex of property companies which operated in and around London. The Chase Charity was founded in 1962 and the Lankelly Foundation six years later and both reaching out to the most isolated in our society.

As time went by the two trusts adopted similar grant-making policies and whilst recognising that their differences of scale and emphasis were positive qualities; they reflected, particularly in the case of the Chase Charity, the founders' love of England's heritage and the arts, and these differences caught the attention of different needy groups, enabling the trusts to be more effective together than if they operated separately.

After so many years of working together, jointly employing the staff team, in 2005 the two trusts resolved to take the next natural step and amalgamate to form the LankellyChase Foundation. The foundation is established for general charitable purposes and its mission is 'to promote change which will improve the quality of people's lives ... particularly on areas of social need to help the most disadvantaged in our society to fulfil their potential.'

In 2008/09 the foundation had assets of £90 million and an income of £6.4 million. Grants were made totalling £5.4 million.

The foundation offers detailed guidelines for its programmes for 2009–2014. These are largely reprinted below.

Guidelines

The foundation concentrates on smaller charities, many of which will have only a local or regional remit. Applications from large national charities will be considered but support will be rare and limited. The foundation looks for user involvement as well as the proper use and support of volunteers and applicants will have to provide evidence of sound management and a commitment to equal opportunities.

It is recognised that the black voluntary sector and minority ethnic groups have particular needs and applications are welcomed from such organisations working within the priority areas. Grants should be effective, achieve something which otherwise would not happen, or sustain something which otherwise might fail.

The foundation does not generally support organisations or work based in London or Northern Ireland, although there are exceptions to this. Throughout the rest of the UK the aim is to treat different geographical areas fairly and applications are welcomed from groups who feel isolated by their location.

Programmes in 2009–2014

- *Arts* – promoting excellence and exploring the power of the arts
- *Breaking cycles of abuse* – promoting safe and protective behaviours
- *Custody and community* – promoting alternatives
- *Free and quiet minds* – seeking to restore troubled minds and lives
- *Local people, local places* – strengthening local communities and organisations

Each of these programmes contains a number of elements which are described below. Please note that although most of the programmes are open, there are elements which are closed to unsolicited applications.

The arts

The foundation values the contribution made by the arts to people's mental, physical and economic health. For this Arts Programme the trustees are focussing on three specific areas: promoting the use of the arts by people with severe mental ill health, encouraging vulnerable young people to participate in arts activities and, through a closed programme, helping young artists to pursue a career in the arts. In all three of these areas, we place excellence in the arts as a core goal.

What we want to achieve

Unlocking creativity – arts and severe mental ill health – We are exploring the use of the arts in promoting the recovery of patients detained due to severe psychiatric illness. The projects funded so far have shown that patients and the staff who care for them, benefit from artists bringing arts activities into secure settings. However, more work is needed to establish the nature of the impact of the arts on psychiatric patients and to persuade some medical practitioners that this is more than an optional extra in their work with the severely mentally ill. Men and women entering the secure psychiatric system lose not only their liberty but also ready access to things which people otherwise take for granted – friends, family and choice. Patients in medium or high security hospitals will rarely see a play, hear a concert, play an instrument or write a song, even though there is a growing body of evidence to show that participation in such activities has a beneficial effect on the mental health of an individual. We therefore welcome applications from arts based charities wishing to offer the best possible standard of arts activities to those who are in medium and high security psychiatric hospitals.

Young people and the arts – We know from past experience that the arts are a powerful medium for reaching troubled young people, changing their vision and improving their life chances. We have therefore decided to fund organisations offering excellent art experiences to vulnerable 11 to 21 year olds; for example young carers, those excluded from school, those leaving care, those at risk of offending and young people struggling with addiction, mental illness and the limitations imposed by poverty. We expect the organisations carrying out this work to be arts based and they must offer young people the best participatory experience possible aiming to move the participants from a negative to a positive world view; from hopelessness to a realisation that they have something to offer society.

Excellence in the arts – This part of the programme is closed to external applications. Over the years of our support for the arts, we have encouraged young talented people, who seek to develop their ability and pursue a career in this field. We fund the Kirckman Concert Society Ltd to give concert platform experience to promising young musicians. We also provide an award for work in glass, through Central Saint Martins College of Art and Design. In an extension of this programme, we are developing partnerships with other centres of artistic excellence around the country which are in a position to help young people further their artistic abilities and ultimately gain employment in the arts.

Eligibility

We will only work with registered charities, industrial and provident societies, exempt charities and community interest companies or organisations applying for charitable status. Only arts based organisations fall within this programme; art therapy organisations are not eligible to apply. We will not consider applications from schools, further education colleges or organisations based in Greater London or Northern Ireland.

Guideline amounts

Our grants are generally in the region of £10,000 – £15,000 a year for up to three years. In exceptional cases we will consider larger grants.

Breaking cycles of abuse

The foundation is committed to a society where all children, young people and adults should be able to live free from fear of physical, emotional or sexual abuse in personal relationships or by strangers. With this programme we wish to support projects working to break cycles of abuse and promote safe and protective behaviours.

The LankellyChase Foundation accepts the following within its definitions of abuse: physical abuse, emotional abuse or mental cruelty, neglect, sexual abuse and sexual exploitation.

What we want to achieve

Domestic abuse – To promote increased safety for adults and children in the community we welcome applications from organisations providing services with the following focus:

Domestic violence prevention work in black, Asian, minority ethnic and refugee communities – We would like to support work which is culturally sensitive, while ensuring that it improves the safety of women and children and regards reducing domestic violence as its main focus.

Programmes for perpetrators of domestic abuse – Support to help local organisations develop domestic violence perpetrator programmes for non-convicted men. (These must be run in accordance with Respect's Accreditation Standards and receive a similar level of statutory funding support.)

Rape and sexual violence – We wish to support projects that assist male and female victims to recover and make informed life choices. We will consider applications for work in the following areas:

- rape crisis and survivors of sexual abuse – in partnership with Rape Crisis and the Survivors Trust, a specific programme is being created for organisations wishing to apply under this area of work. Please contact the foundation for further information.
- sexual exploitation – projects aimed at children and young people who are being, or are at risk of being, sexually exploited by criminal practices that threaten their physical and mental wellbeing.
- women in prostitution – projects that provide a dedicated service to women involved in, or at risk of being involved in, prostitution and affected by related issues (including drugs, homelessness, pregnancy, children in care etc.) to ensure they are able to access services appropriate to their needs, supporting them to make informed choices about their life circumstances and, where appropriate, to implement change.

Young people – We will consider projects aiming to encourage positive attitudes and behaviours in personal relationships. We will focus particularly on projects working with alienated young people living in deprived environments or who have experienced domestic violence or abuse.

Child protection – We will consider applications for work promoting, supporting and developing child protection practice in community and voluntary sector organisations.

Summer activities small grants programme – Each year the trustees set aside funds to support summer activities for children and young people between the ages of 5–17 years. Each grant will be for £500 and will be available to qualifying organisations in England, Wales, Scotland and Northern Ireland. The guidelines and application form are published on the foundation's website from February to April each year, with a closing date early in May.

Eligibility
Organisations must be registered charities, industrial and provident societies, exempt charities or community interest companies. Applications will need to show targeted work providing opportunities for real and measurable change for people whose lives are affected by, or are at risk of, abuse or exploitation. All organisations will be expected to be affiliated to a relevant nationally recognised body and adhere to national standards of practice. You will need to have policies and procedures that show an awareness of safety issues for staff and clients.

You will also need a strategic plan for the work you are asking us to fund, showing how the proposed work enhances and complements services already being provided, either within your own organisation or in partnership with other agencies, and what will be achieved in terms of benefits to the organisation and/or to individuals.

Guideline amounts
Grants will be available for 1–3 years and are generally up to a maximum of £45,000 in total, although a limited number of larger grants may be considered. Capital items will only be considered if they are necessary for the work being funded but not for building costs or for disabled access.

Exclusions
In addition to the general exclusions imposed by the foundation, in this area of work the foundation will not support:

- capital expenditure
- supplementary education
- organisations or work based in the Greater London area
- projects working exclusively with: substance misuse/drug rehabilitation services, drug education, mediation or bereavement services
- generic counselling services
- mainstream activities of local organisations which are part of a wider network of others doing similar work for example Crossroads or Homestart
- childcare, nurseries, pre-school and after-school clubs.

Custody and community

The Custody and Community programme includes within its remit those affected by, or at risk of, incarceration of different kinds. The backdrop to the programme is the trustees' deep concern at the rising prison population and their belief that the increase reflects, at least in part, the numbers of chronically excluded people 'falling through the net' of mainstream health and social care services.

In addition, we view with disquiet the detention of asylum seekers without judicial oversight and without having committed any offence.

What we want to achieve
The programme reflects our assessment of the areas where we consider there is serious unmet need, where there are gaps or systemic weaknesses in statutory provision and where the opportunity is ripe for policy change.

Applications should fall within one of the following categories:

Women offenders – The foundation strongly supports the conclusions of the 2007 Corston Report on women in the criminal justice system. We would like to fund models of service delivery that fit into the blueprint set out in the report as well as campaigning and advocacy. We take a broad view of who may be considered to be an 'offender' in the context of this part of the programme. We will include work with women with extreme vulnerabilities that are likely to lead them to become entangled in the criminal justice system, for example, projects for women sex-workers. We will expect organisations applying under this heading to have significant expertise in work with women with multiple vulnerabilities.

Short-term or remand prisoners with multiple complex needs (including young offenders) – We will fund work with prisoners who are likely to be in and out of prison frequently. They may have multiple problems including mental health issues and often do not engage with, or are excluded from, services inside or outside custody.

Immigration detainees – We echo the concerns of HM Inspectorate of Prisons about the anxiety, frustration and stress suffered by detainees and the difficulties they face in accessing information about the progress of their cases, legal advice and bail. We are concerned about the treatment of vulnerable detainees including those with mental health problems, torture victims, those who have been trafficked and children.

Eligibility
Across all three areas we are interested in funding service delivery as well as work that strengthens the voice, self-confidence and sustainability of the voluntary sector in the field (for example campaigning, development of social enterprise ideas, establishment of networks or consortia, strategic partnerships on particular issues, collaboration with high profile organisations outside the immediate field and research).

We welcome applications from local community-based projects whose usual field of work is not necessarily criminal justice. We have seen some excellent practical work done by such organisations when they reach out to offenders in their communities or to those returning from custody. More than 25% of prisoners are from BME communities. We aim to make 1 in 4 grants to BME-led organisations or to work targeting BME service users. All applicants for work in the criminal justice system should demonstrate that they reach a proportionate cross-section of their local prison or offender population. We will report on progress towards the target each year in our annual report.

Where we work
The programme works across the United Kingdom, including London, though special conditions apply to work in the south west of England and Northern Ireland. We are funding some work in Northern Ireland but we do not accept unsolicited applications for work in the province.

The TLC Partnership in the South West – The Tudor Trust and the LankellyChase Foundation are working together to support voluntary organisations working within the criminal justice field in the South West. This collaboration will continue until 2010. All applications for work in the South West should be submitted under this part of the programme. The guidelines are published separately on the LankellyChase and Tudor Trust websites and applications should be made initially to Karen Flippance at LankellyChase.

Guideline amounts
Our grants are generally in the region of £10,000-£15,000 a year for up to three years. In exceptional cases we will consider larger grants.

Free and quiet minds

The Free and Quiet Minds programme focuses on the needs of the most rejected and ignored people in society; specifically, those who have been detained in psychiatric hospitals, people from black and minority ethnic communities with mental health problems and destitute asylum seekers.

What we want to achieve
Secure psychiatric care – When people commit terrible acts, either against themselves or others and are subsequently detained in secure psychiatric accommodation, we, the public, are usually relieved. However, the aim of the professionals who care for them is to help them recover their mental health and eventually return to society, whether via prison or not. We wish to promote that process of recovery and return and we will support charities working with patients and staff in medium secure and high security hospitals which share these same aims.

Black and minority ethnic groups – We seek applications from all charities (although BME led charities will be given preference) that wish to provide mental health services to people in BME communities and to those who care for them. In relation to this, the trustees welcome the Department of Health's Delivering Race Equality (DRE) initiative, whose aims we share. The trustees have agreed that information about the Free and Quiet Minds Programme should be included on the DRE website (www.actiondre.org.uk or www.mentalhealthequalities.org.uk/dre) to encourage applications from registered charities striving to tackle mental health problems in BME communities.

Asylum seekers - achieving a fair and just asylum system – We recognise that over the last decade or so, the UK has seen fluctuating numbers of people applying for safe haven in the country. Unfortunately, the public has not received a balanced and accurate message about asylum seekers and this has hindered attempts to develop a fair and just system for dealing with them. We

therefore welcome applications from organisations endeavouring to promote a true representation of the circumstances in which asylum seekers find themselves. We would also be interested in looking at requests offering alternative ways of addressing the problems which arise in this field.

Destitute asylum seekers – This part of the programme is closed to external applications. For the next five years the trustees will continue to fund organisations working with destitute asylum seekers; the programme will focus on the provision of their most urgent basic needs, such as accommodation, legal help and advice and food and clothing.

Eligibility
Organisations which apply must be registered charities, industrial and provident societies, exempt charities and community interest companies or organisations applying for charitable status. We will not support large national charities or organisations based in Northern Ireland. We will not support organisations based in London except where the work will have national significance.

Guideline amounts
Our grants are generally in the region of £10,000 – £15,000 a year for up to three years. In exceptional cases we will consider larger grants.

Local people, local places

The foundation is committed to helping local organisations to find long-term solutions to local issues and engaging the skills and talents of individuals to transform communities for the benefit of all. The trustees acknowledge that some areas have suffered from lengthy periods of economic decline and that multi-purpose organisations can play a vital role in community renewal.

What we want to achieve
We want to engage with organisations by providing strategic support which may involve the funding of key posts or underpinning core costs and therefore invite applications from organisations that are:

- community controlled and managed
- responsive to the needs of all sections of their community
- developing funding strategies which move towards greater sustainability.

We aim to:

- support local organisations to achieve lasting positive social change and to set clear outcomes to measure the impact on communities
- encourage new and sustained investment to ensure that local people do not remain on the margins of society and have every opportunity to participate in decisions that affect their lives

- enable organisations to have their voices heard and influence the development of policies that have an impact on communities
- develop the strengths and abilities of the people working within local organisations and to encourage partnership working with other voluntary and statutory agencies.

Support for Historic Churches – This programme is not open to unsolicited applications but will work with churches identified through the new partnership. We have agreed a new partnership with the Churches Conservation Trust to support local communities to manage and improve the community use of Grade 1 and Grade 2* Listed Buildings. It replaces the foundation's small grants scheme for Grade 1 Listed Buildings in rural areas. The programme will demonstrate new ways of working with congregations and communities in disadvantaged areas to prevent the loss of historic churches and show how the regeneration of a historic church building can be a catalyst for community renewal.

Guideline amounts
Organisations approaching the foundation under this programme will need to have a clear business/development/strategic plan in place.

Revenue grants: It is likely that any initial grant will be restricted to three years with a review to consider extending support dependent upon the progress made to achieve the agreed outcomes established in the initial application. On average revenue grants of up to £50,000 over three years are available.

Capital grants: Up to £50,000 to help organisations acquire an asset, adapt an existing building or to purchase equipment that supports the long-term sustainable development of the organisation. Priority for capital grants will be given to organisations working in the more remote rural areas of the UK where access to community facilities is severely restricted.

Exclusions
In addition to the general exclusions imposed by the foundation, in this area of work the foundation will not support:

- fundraising posts
- organisations or work based in the Greater London area.

Loan fund
In addition to the revenue and capital grants the trustees have developed a loan fund that may have particular relevance for this programme. A separate application form and details of the loan fund are available on the foundation's website.

Grants in 2008/09

Grants for the year 2008/09 were detailed in the respective grants programmes as follows:

Category	Value
Developing communities	£1,400,000
Breaking the cycle of abuse	£1,300,000
Offenders and society	£1,200,000
Arts	£449,000
Refugees and asylum seekers	£389,000
Annual grants	£224,000
Heritage	£79,000

Beneficiaries across all programmes included: Family Welfare Association – London (£135,000); Rape Crisis England and Wales – Essex (£75,000); Arts and Minds – Essex (£60,000); Diversity Hub – Leicester (£45,000); the Forgiveness Project – London (£30,000); Fairshares – Gloucester (£21,000); Malt Cross Trust Company – Nottingham (£17,000); Villages in Action – Crediton, Devon (£10,000); and MAAN – Liverpool (£7,000).

Exclusions The foundation receives many more applications from worthwhile projects than it can hope to fund and as a consequence it does not support the following areas of work which are in addition to those specifically mentioned in the guidelines to the current programmes:

- access to buildings
- advancement of religion
- after school and homework clubs
- animal charities
- breakfast clubs
- bursaries and scholarships
- child befriending schemes
- circular appeals
- expeditions/overseas travel
- festivals
- formal education including schools, colleges and universities
- general counselling
- holidays/holiday centres
- hospitals and hospices
- individual youth clubs
- individuals – including students
- medical care and medical research
- mother and toddler groups/playgroups
- museums/galleries
- organisations working with particular medical conditions
- other grant-making organisations
- research
- sport
- transport, vehicles
- work that has already taken place
- work which is primarily the responsibility of central or local government, education or health authorities.

Applications Application forms are available from the foundation's office or its website. Please send with your application an itemised income and expenditure budget for the work for which funding is requested, a supporting letter (no more than two sides of A4) and the organisation's most recent annual report.

Applicants are encouraged to contact the foundation for advice if necessary.

Largsmount Ltd

Jewish

£540,000 (2008)

Beneficial area UK and Israel.

50 Keswick Street, Gateshead NE8 1TQ

Tel. 0191 490 0140

Correspondent Simon Kaufman, Trustee

Trustees *Z M Kaufman; Naomi Kaufman; Simon Kaufman.*

CC Number 280509

Information available Accounts were on file at the Charity Commission, without a list of grants.

Registered in 1980, this trust supports Orthodox Jewish charities for the advancement of religion and education.

In 2008 it had assets of £3.2 million and an income of just over £1 million, including donations. Grants were made during the year totalling £540,000. Details of beneficiaries during the year were not available, although the accounts note that a grant of £235,000 was given to the M Y A Charitable Trust, a connected charity. This charity has also been the largest beneficary in previous years.

Applications In writing to the correspondent.

The Leathersellers' Company Charitable Fund

General

£1.1 million to organisations (2007/08)

Beneficial area UK, particularly London.

15 St Helen's Place, London EC3A 6DQ

Tel. 020 7330 1451 **Fax** 020 7330 1445

Email grussell-jones @leathersellers.co.uk

Website www.leathersellers.co.uk

Correspondent Geoffrey Russell-Jones, Administrator

Trustee *The Leathersellers Company.*

CC Number 278072

Information available Accounts were available from the Charity Commission.

Summary

The following information is taken from the company's website:

The Leathersellers' Company is one of the ancient livery companies of the City of London, ranked fifteenth in the order of precedence. It was founded by royal charter in 1444 with authority to control the sale of leather within the City. The company no longer has this regulatory role, and instead devotes its energies to support for charity, education and the British leather trade.

The policy of the trustees is to provide support to a broad range of registered charities or educational establishments in the fields of education and sciences, relief of those in need, the disabled, children and young people, medicine and health, the arts, the church and environment. At the same time support is provided to registered charities associated with the Leathersellers' Company, the leather and hide trades, education in leather technology and for the welfare of former workers in the industry and their dependants. Of grants awarded in 2008, 86% were to registered charities or educational establishments and 14% were to individuals.

Charitable grants are made to registered charities and individuals and are one of two types; a single grant or a multi-year grant. All multi-year grants are subject to annual review.

The trustees receive appeals from a wide range of registered charities and its policy is based upon the principle of making sure the money goes to those areas most in genuine need and those decisions are based on thorough investigations, including visits to individual charities, coupled with common sense.

Grants in 2007/08

During the year the trust had assets of £39 million and an income of £1.5 million. Grants were made totalling £1.3 million of which £184,000 was paid to 120 individuals for education and science purposes.

Grants to organisations were broken down as follows:

Category	No.	Grant total
Education and sciences	27	£337,000
Relief of those in need	52	£233,000
Arts, church and environment	39	£199,000
Disabled	18	£95,000
Medicine and Health	14	£79,000
Other	25	£42,000

Grants to charities analysed by type were as follows:

- single – 103 grants totalling £260,000
- multi-year – 105 grants totalling £884,000

The largest grants were made to: University of Northampton (£63,000); Colfe's School Ltd (a related trust) (£60,000); Prendergast School (£50,000); Reach out Projects – Chellington (£25,000); Pelican Cancer Foundation (£20,000); Kid's Cookery School, Prison Advise and Care Trust, Missing People and Michael Palin Centre for Stammering Children (£15,000 each).

Other aggregate grants under £15,000 totalled £483,000.

Applications
In writing to the correspondent.

Appeals must be from registered charities operating within the UK. Priority will be given to charities connected with leather, the leather trade, and the London area due to the company's long associations there. We will also consider charities that are based throughout the United Kingdom.

Please send no more than two sides of A4 in the first instance describing the charity and giving an idea of its financial situation and what you need. Do not send sets of audited accounts as these will be sought later if we require them.

Please note: the trust states that it willl soon only be accepting online applications. See the trust's website for further details.

The William Leech Charity

Health and welfare in the north east of England and overseas aid

£371,000 (2007/08)

Beneficial area Northumberland, Tyne and Wear, Durham and overseas.

Saville Chambers, 5 North Street, Newcastle upon Tyne NE1 8DF

Tel. 0191 243 3300 **Fax** 0191 243 3309

Email enquiries@williamleechcharity.org.uk

Website www.williamleechcharity.org.uk

Correspondent Mrs Kathleen M Smith, Secretary

Trustees *Prof. Peter H Baylis; Cyril Davies; Adrian Gifford; Roy Leech; Richard Leech; N Sherlock; David Stabler; Barry Wallace; Prof. Chris Day.*

CC Number 265491

Information available Accounts were available from the Charity Commission. The charity also has an informative website.

In 1972 Sir William Leech set up The William Leech Property Trust (now The William Leech Charity) and donated to it some 300 tenanted properties, the income from which was to be distributed in accordance with his guidelines.

The purpose of charity is to make grants for charitable purposes in line with the guidelines of the founder. The main fund remains unrestricted and continues to make grants and interest free loans to registered charities in the north east of England at the discretion of the trustees.

In 2007/08 the charity had assets of nearly £16.2 million and an income of £471,000. During the year there were 149 grants made totalling £371,000. Grants ranged from £100 to £50,000, with some organisations receiving more than one grant during the year, and were allocated as follows:

The Main Fund – 128 grants totalling £279,500
The trustees are concerned with community welfare and medical care which accounts for more than 53% of the grants awarded, with a further significant amount distributed to projects for young people, initiatives for older people and the maintenance of churches.

Beneficiaries included: Peals (£50,000); Macmillan Nurses (£30,000); Central Palz (£20,000 in total); Northern Institute for Cancer Research and the People's Kitchen (£10,000 each); Bible Reading Fellowship and the Children's Foundation (£5,000 each); Newcastle City Centre Chaplaincy (£4,000); Primary Immunodeficiency Association (£3,000); Allendale Preschool Playgroup and Seaham Youth Initiative (£2,000 each); RNIB and Sunderland Youth Orchestra Music for All (£1,000 each); and Safety Crackers (£500).

The Lady Leech Fund – 21 grants totalling £70,400
The Lady Leech Fund is used to make grants to overseas projects focussing primarily on the medical, educational and environmental needs of children in underdeveloped countries, and also emergency aid in response to natural disasters.

Beneficiaries included: St John of Jerusalem Eye Hospital (£7,000); Newcastle West Methodist Circuit (£6,000); Children's Vision International and the Microloan Foundation (£5,000 each); Northumbrian Healthcare (£4,000); Durham University – Sri Lanka in Focus Project (£3,000); Haller Foundation (£2,000); and King Edward VI School – Morpeth (£1,000).

The Men's Health Fund
Some years ago the trustees designated a fund to award grants to the Community Foundation for approved Men's Health initiatives, promoting fitness, well being and medical check ups for men in an effort to reduce the incidence of late diagnosis of prostate and other cancers. During the year the trustees awarded the Community Foundation a further £21,000.

Exclusions The following will not generally receive grants. The chairman and secretary are instructed to reject them without reference to the trustees, unless there are special circumstances:

- community care centres and similar (exceptionally, those in remote country areas may be supported)
- running expenses for youth clubs (as opposed to capital projects)
- running expenses of churches – this includes normal repairs, but churches engaged in social work, or using their buildings largely for 'outside' purposes may be supported
- sport
- the arts
- applications from individuals
- organisations which have been supported in the last 12 months. It would be exceptional to support an organisation in two successive years, unless we had promised such support in advance
- holidays, travel, outings
- minibuses (unless over 10,000 miles per annum is expected)
- schools
- housing associations.

Applications

The Main Fund
As it is the intention of the trustees to favour support for those charities who help others by utilising the generous time and skills of volunteers, they accept applications in the

short form of a letter, rather than expecting the completion of a complicated application form, which may seem daunting to some applicants.

In order to safe-guard our charity status, it is important that we are accountable for how funds are distributed. As such, the following protocols exist for making and investigating applications.

Please note we only accept applications from registered charities, and the registered charity address must be included in the application process. For large grants and multiple grants, trustees would like to see as much supporting information as possible, and in rare cases, they may wish to interview the applicant.

Your applications must include:

- a description of the project that the charity is undertaking, who it hopes to help, and any evidence which will support the need for this particular project
- how much the project will cost, capital and revenue, with an indication of the amounts involved
- how much the charity has raised so far, and where it expects to find the balance
- the type of support sought; such as small grant, multiple grant, loan, etc.
- how much does it cost to run the charity each year, including how much of the revenue is spent on salaries and employees. Where does the revenue come from? How many paid workers are there? How many volunteers are there?

The Lady Leech Fund
Applications to this fund should be submitted in a letter containing:

- the name, address and registration number of the charity
- the name and contact details of the person who is authorised by the charity to apply for funding
- a description of the project that the charity is undertaking, who it hopes to help, and any evidence which will support the need for this particular project
- how much the project will cost, capital and revenue, with an indication of the amounts involved
- how much the charity has raised so far, and where it expects to find the balance
- a description of the connection between the Developing World Project, and the people in the north east of England
- how much does it cost to run the charity each year, including how much of the revenue is spent on salaries and employees. Where does the revenue come from? How many paid workers are there? How many volunteers are there?

Application letters can be written and submitted via the charity's website.

The Kennedy Leigh Charitable Trust

Jewish charities and general
£688,000 (2007/08)
Beneficial area Israel and UK.

Ort House, 126 Albert Street, London NW1 7NE
Tel. 020 7267 6500
Email naomi@klct.org
Correspondent Naomi Shoffman, Administrator
Trustees *Geoffrey Goldkorn; Lesley D Berman; Carole Berman Sujo; Angela Sorkin; Michele Foux; Alexander Sorkin.*
CC Number 288293
Information available Annual report and accounts on file at the Charity Commission.

The trust's objects require three-quarters of its grant-making funds to be distributed to charitable institutions within Israel, with the remainder being distributed in the UK and elsewhere. The trust's mission statement reads as follows:

The trust will support projects and causes which will improve and enrich the lives of all parts of society, not least those of the young, the needy, the disadvantaged and the underprivileged. In meeting its objectives the trust expects to become involved in a wide range of activities. The trust is able to provide several forms of support and will consider the funding of capital projects and running costs. The trust is non-political and non-religious in nature.

In 2007/08 the trust had assets of £19 million and an income of £681,000. Grants were made totalling £688,000.

Listed UK beneficiaries included: University of Cambridge Kennedy Leigh Fund (£150,000 to fund the shortfall in the fund to allow the Kennedy Leigh Lectureship in Modern Hebrew to continue); St John Ophthalmic Eye Hospital (£27,000 a year for three years); CHAI Lifeline (£25,000 a year for three years); Oxford Centre for Hebrew Studies (£25,000 a year for three years to fund a programme for visiting Israeli academics and writers); and North London Hospice (£10,000).

The beneficiaries of new and continuing donations in Israel included: Haznek, Jerusalem Print Workshop, Haifa

University, Yad Vashem, Elem, MILO Centre, Hospice of the Upper Galilee and Association for Children at Risk.
Exclusions No grants for individuals.
Applications The trust stated in its 2007/08 accounts:

The funds available for distribution outside of Israel are all but committed for the foreseeable future to several UK charities. The trustees are therefore unable to consider applications for funding from charitable organisations outside of Israel at this time.

The Lennox and Wyfold Foundation

General
£1.1 million (2007/08)
Beneficial area Worldwide.

c/o RF Trustee Co. Limited, Ely House, 37 Dover Street, London W1S 4NJ
Correspondent G Fincham, Secretary
Trustees *R J Fleming; A R Fleming; W L Hannay; C M Fleming; Mrs C F Wilmot-Sitwell.*
CC Number 1080198
Information available Accounts were available from the Charity Commission.

This foundation was established in 2000 for general charitable purposes and was formerly known as the Wyfold Foundation. In September 2005, the foundation received all the assets of the Lennox Hannay Charitable Trust which has now been wound up.

In 2007/08 the Lennox and Wyfold Foundation had assets of £36 million and an income of £475,000. Grants to 110 organisations totalled £1.1 million.

Grants were made to a wide variety of UK registered charities ranging from medical research to welfare of the young and the old, from the arts to animal welfare and in some cases whilst the donations have been made to a relevant UK organisation, some of the ultimate beneficiaries are overseas.

In previous years a guideline of distributing 5% of the total fund annually has been followed but in all years, due to the volume of applications from worthy causes, this figure has been exceeded and from time to time capital has been distributed in certain special cases. It is expected that the foundation will continue this policy in the next financial period.

The trustees met twice during the financial period to consider the applications for assistance made and each application is considered on its own merit.

Grants awarded were categorised as follows:

Category	No. of grants	Amount
Health	31	£493,000
Relief in need	16	£207,000
Education	10	£167,000
Arts, culture, heritage, science	18	£89,000
Citizenship/community development	8	£50,000
Poverty	7	£41,000
Animal welfare	3	£25,000
Armed forces/ emergency services	6	£24,000
Environment	5	£18,000
Amateur sport	3	£15,000
Human rights, conflict resolution	1	£2,000
Religion	2	£1,500

By far the largest grants were to: Breakthrough Breast Cancer, towards the Generations Study (£250,000); and Eton College endowment fund (£100,000).

Beneficiaries of other grants included: Absolute Return for Kids (£45,000); RNIB (£40,000); DeafBlind UK and Royal Marsden Cancer Campaign (£30,000 each); Amber Foundation, the Ditchley Foundation and Fight for Sight (£20,000 each); Tusk Trust (£11,000); Elephant Family and St George's Chapel – Windsor (£10,000 each); Bucklebury Memorial Hall (£6,000); and Chipping Norton Theatre and Friends Trust, Gloucestershire Air Ambulance, Mary Hare Foundation and Reform Research Trust (£5,000 each).

Applications In writing to the correspondent.

The Mark Leonard Trust

Environmental education, young people and general

£340,000 (2007/08)

Beneficial area Worldwide, but mainly UK.

Allington House, 1st Floor, 150 Victoria Street, London SW1E 5AE

Tel. 020 7410 0330 **Fax** 020 7410 0332

Website www.sfct.org.uk

Correspondent Alan Bookbinder, Director

Trustees *Zivi Sainsbury; Judith Portrait; John Julian Sainsbury; Mark Sainsbury.*

CC Number 1040323

Information available Accounts were on file at the Charity Commission.

This is one of the Sainsbury Family Charitable Trusts, and it mostly supports environmental causes and work for young people, although it also gives towards general charitable purposes. Grants are made to support innovative schemes through seed-funding with the aim of helping projects to achieve sustainability and successful replication. The following descriptions of its more specific work are taken from its 2007/08 annual report:

Environment

Grants are made for environmental education, particularly to support projects displaying practical walls of involving children and young adults. The trustees do not support new educational resources in isolation from the actual process of learning and discovery. They are more interested in programmes which help pupils and teachers to develop a theme over time, perhaps combining IT resources with the networks for exchanging information and ideas between schools.

The trustees are particularly interested in projects that progressively enable children and young people to develop a sense of ownership of a project, and that provide direct support to teachers to deliver exciting and high quality education in the classroom.

The trustees are also interested in the potential for sustainable transport, energy efficiency and renewable energy in wider society. In some cases the trustees will consider funding research, but only where there is a clear practical application. Proposals are more likely to be considered when they are testing an idea, model or strategy in practice.

Youth Work

Grants are made for projects that support the rehabilitation of young people who have become marginalised and involved in anti-social or criminal activities. Trustees wish to apply their grants to overcome social exclusion. They are also interested in extending and adding value to the existing use of school buildings, enhancing links between schools and the community, and encouraging greater involvement of parents, school leavers and volunteers in extra-curricular activities.

An essential part of the youth work which the trustees wish to support will be a sense of realising the personal choice and responsibility of young people, building

identity through taking their views and plans seriously and offering the tools to translate their aspirations and talents into practice. Above all, grants will be made towards work which gives young people, with the support and guidance they need, the autonomy and permission to be themselves and to be creative and enterprising. The trustees believe that creating this culture in young people in contemporary Britain will be essential for the future health of society.

In 2007/08 the trust had assets of £11 million and an income of £643,000. The management and administration charges included payments totalling £3,300 to a firm of solicitors in which one of the trustees is a partner. Whilst wholly legal, these editors always regret such payments unless, in the words of the Charity Commission, 'there is no realistic alternative'. Grants were approved totalling £340,000, broken down as follows:

Environment – 12 grants totalling £139,000
The largest grants went to the Ashden Awards and the Small Woods Association (£30,000 each). Other grants included: Envision (£12,000); Plumpton College and Transport 2000 Trust (£10,000 each); Council for Environmental Education (£5,000); and Devon Wildlife Trust (£2,000).

Youth work – 6 grants totalling £188,000
The largest grant was made to Kikass TV (£50,000). Other beneficiaries were: Just for Kids Law (£38,000); New Learning Centre (£30,000); and Uniting Britain Trust (£20,000).

General – 2 grants totalling £13,000
These were £10,000 to St Stevens Church – Lympne and £3,300 to Save the Rhino International.

Exclusions Grants are not normally made to individuals.

Applications 'Proposals are generally invited by the trustees or initiated at their request. Unsolicited applications are discouraged and are unlikely to be successful, unless they are closely aligned to the trust's areas of interest.' A single application will be considered for support by all the trusts in the Sainsbury family group.

The Leverhulme Trust

Scholarships for education and research

£48.5 million (2008)
Beneficial area Unrestricted.

1 Pemberton Row, London EC4A 3BG
Tel. 020 7042 9881 **Fax** 020 7822 5084
Email enquiries@leverhulme.org.uk
Website www.leverhulme.org.uk
Correspondent Paul Read
Trustees *Sir Michael Perry, Chair; Patrick J P Cescau; Niall W A Fitzgerald; Dr Ashok S Ganguly; Paul Polman.*
CC Number 288371

Information available Accounts were available at the Charity Commission. Detailed annual 'Guide to Applicants', and an annual report, available from the trust. Excellent website with very detailed grants information.

This trust derives from the will of William Hesketh Lever, the first Viscount Leverhulme. A businessman, entrepreneur and philanthropist who supported a variety of educational, religious, civic, community and medical causes. On his death in 1925, Lord Leverhulme left a proportion of his interest in the company he had founded, Lever Brothers, in trust for specific beneficiaries: to include firstly certain trade charities and secondly the provision of 'scholarships for the purposes of research and education', thus the Leverhulme Trust was established. In November 1983 a redefinition of the trust's objectives was brought about and subsequently, the Leverhulme Trust has concentrated its attention solely on research and education.

The trust continues to combine the direct initiatives of the trustees made in the light of specialist peer review advice with a portfolio of awards made by a research awards advisory committee, itself comprising eminent research colleagues drawn predominantly from the academic world.

The awarding of scholarships for research and education continues to be represented by awards for the conduct of research and awards and bursaries for educational purposes. In terms of support, there are five main patterns of award, namely:

- research grants
- fellowships
- academic collaboration
- prizes
- fine and performing arts.

Awards for education are predominantly bursaries for students in fine and performing arts although there is a small involvement with innovative educational approaches in these disciplines.

Programmes

1) Research grants

(i) Research project grants

The aim of these awards is to provide financial support for innovative and original research projects of high quality and potential, the choice of theme and the design of the research lying entirely with the applicant (the Principal Investigator). The grants provide support for the salaries of research staff engaged on the project, plus associated costs directly related to the research proposed.

Proposals are favoured which:

- reflect the personal vision of the applicant
- demonstrate compelling competence in the research design
- surmount traditional disciplinary academic boundaries
- involve a degree of challenge and evidence of the applicant's ability to assess risk.

(ii) Research programme grants

In the one major departure from its policy of operating in the responsive mode, the trust selects on an annual basis two themes of research for which bids are invited. Normally one grant is awarded for each theme. The grants provide funds to research teams for up to five years to enable them to explore significant issues in the social sciences, in the humanities and, to a lesser extent, in the sciences. The scale of the awards (each one at a sum of up to £1.75 million) is set at a level where it is possible for a research team to study a significant theme in depth by conducting a group of interlinked research projects which taken together can lead to new understanding. The themes are selected not to exclude particular disciplines from the competition but rather to encourage research teams to look upon their established research interests from a set of refreshing viewpoints. Themes in recent years have included Security and Liberty and Ceremony and Ritual.

[The themes for the 2009/10 cycle are: Beauty and The Impact of Diasporas.]

2) Fellowships

Full details on the range of fellowships available to individuals can be found in the trust's 'Guide for Applicants'.

3) Academic collaborations

(i) International Networks

These collaborations enable a Principal Investigator based in the UK to lead a research project where its successful completion is dependant on the participation of relevant overseas institutions. A significant research theme must be identified at the outset which requires for its successful treatment international collaboration between one or more UK universities, and two or more overseas institutions (normally up to a maximum of seven institutions in total). Networks should be newly constituted collaborations. Full justification should be given for the involvement of all participants, with each participant bringing specific – and stated – expertise which can directly contribute to the success of the project. Details of the proposed methodology for the research project should be provided at the outset, as well as a clear indication of the anticipated outcomes (publications, websites), and of the dissemination strategy to be adopted.

Value and duration

The value of an award is normally up to £125,000, the activities involved lasting for up to three years.

Topics

Applications for research on any topic within the entire array of academic disciplines are eligible for support. However, an exception is made for areas of research supported by specialist funding agencies and in particular for medicine. In such cases, applicants should consider an application to these alternative funding bodies as being more appropriate. Specific attention is paid to the reasons given by applicants in justifying their choice of the trust as the most appropriate agency for the support of their project.

Institutions

The Principal Investigator should be employed at a university or other institution of higher or further education in the UK. The award is made to that institution, which must agree to administer the grant, for allocation among the participating institutions.

(ii) Visiting Professorships

The objective of these awards is to enable distinguished academics based overseas to spend between three and ten months inclusive at a UK university, primarily in order to enhance the skills of academic staff or the student body within the host institution. It is recognised that Visiting Professors may also wish to use the opportunity to further their own academic interests. The over-riding criteria for selection are first the academic standing and achievements of the visitor in terms of research and teaching, and secondly the ability of the receiving institution to benefit from the imported skills and expertise. Priority will be given to new or recent collaborative ventures.

Applications:

- must be made by a member of academic staff, based in a UK university or other higher education institution, who will be responsible for co-ordinating the visit. The host academic's employing institution must also agree to administer the grant, if awarded, and to provide appropriate facilities for the Visiting Professor. Applications may not be submitted by the visitor.

Value

The sum requested should reflect the individual circumstances of the visitor and the nature and duration of the proposed activities. A maintenance grant up to a level commensurate with the salary of a professor in the relevant field at the receiving institution may be requested. Economy travel costs to and from the UK will also be met. Requests for associated costs, if justified by the programme, may include, for example, travel within the UK, consumables, and essential technical assistance.

4) Philip Leverhulme Prizes

Philip Leverhulme Prizes are awarded to outstanding scholars (normally under the age of 36) who have made a substantial and recognised contribution to their particular field of study, recognised at an international level, and whose future contributions are held to be of correspondingly high promise. Approximately 25 Prizes are available each year across the five topics which are offered.

The Prizes commemorate the contribution to the work of the trust made by Philip Leverhulme, the Third Viscount Leverhulme and grandson of the Founder.

Topics

For the 2010 competition the selected disciplines are:

- Earth, Ocean and Atmospheric Sciences
- History of Art
- Law
- Mathematics and Statistics
- Medieval, Early Modern and Modern History.

The disciplines selected are intentionally broad, and nominations will be considered irrespective of a nominee's departmental affiliation.

Value

Each Prize has a value of £70,000; use should be made of the award over a two or three year period. Prizes can be used for any purpose which can advance the Prize holder's research, with the exception of enhancing the Prize holder's salary.

Nominees

Nominees must hold a post (irrespective of the source of funding) in a UK institution of higher education or research and should normally be under age 36. However, nominations are accepted for those aged 36 to 39 inclusive if they have had a distinct career change or break.

5) Fine and Performing Arts
(i) Training and Professional Development

(a) Bursaries and Scholarships

These awards provide bursaries or scholarships for highly talented students who are receiving training in the fine and performing arts. Grants are made in the form of support for maintenance, training and professional development. The selection and nomination of students is the responsibility of the arts training organisation concerned, and their nomination should be based upon a combination of outstanding talent, potential and their financial need.

Applications for the above awards must come from the arts training institution concerned, clearly indicating the envisaged programme of training, as well as the number of students being nominated for support. Applications from individual students are not eligible for these awards.

(b) Innovative Teaching Activity

In exceptional circumstances, the trust supports innovative and distinctive teaching activities in the fine and performing arts.

(ii) Artists in Residence

These awards are intended to support the residency of an artist of any kind or nationality in a UK institution in order to foster a creative collaboration between the artist and the staff and/or students of that institution. The term 'artist' encompasses visual artists, creative writers, musicians, poets and other producers of original creative work. The resident artist should work in an interactive way with their surroundings, and contribute recognisably to the life and work of the host department or centre. Applications should come jointly signed from the artist and a representative of the proposed host group, as Principal Applicant. Individual artists seeking a residency may not apply directly to the trust.

The scheme is intended to bring artists into research and study environments where creative art is not part of the normal curriculum or activities of the host department. It is not the objective of the scheme to provide additional teaching strength to the host institution. Priority will be given to new or recent collaborative ventures.

Institutions

All institutions of higher education in the UK (including museums) are eligible to host an artist in residence. The institution undertakes to provide a sympathetic environment for the visiting artist, and will take responsibility for all administrative aspects of the residency.

Value

The award covers a stipend for the resident artist, plus up to £2,500 for costs associated with the artist's activity, for example consumables or materials. The maximum total cost can be up to £12,500 overall for a typical residency.

Full and detailed guidelines for applicants are available from the trust's website.

Grantmaking in 2008

In 2008 the trust had assets of £1.25 million and an income of £51.2 million from investment income, which included £37.5 million in dividends from Unilever plc. Grants were made totalling £48.5 million and were awarded as detailed in the following categories:

Category	Value
Responsive Mode Projects	£23,660,000
Research Awards Advisory Committee	£7,900,000
Africa Awards	£5,800,000
Designated Programmes	£3,800,000
Major Research Fellowships	£3,400,000
Leverhulme Prizes	£1,950,000
Visiting Fellows and Professors	£1,920,000

Beneficiaries included the following institutions, most of which received multiple awards: Royal Society (£3.6 million); Mandela Rhodes Foundation (£2.5 million); Cambridge University (£2.3 million); Imperial College London (£1 million); Newcastle University (£857,000); Liverpool University (£691,000); Aberdeen Univèrsity (£615,000); Durham University (£525,000); TATE (£481,000); Cardiff University (£375,000); Trinity Laban (£333,000); Royal Academy of Engineering (£300,000); and Sunderland University (£250,000). Grants totalling less than £250,000 each were made to 124 institutions.

Exclusions When submitting an application to the trust, applicants are advised that the trust does not offer funding for the following costs, and hence none of these items may be included in any budget submitted to the trust:

- core funding or overheads for institutions
- individual items of equipment over £1,000
- sites, buildings or other capital expenditure
- support for the organisation of conferences or workshops, which are not directly associated with International Networks, Early Career Fellowships or Philip Leverhulme Prizes
- exhibitions
- contributions to appeals
- endowments

- a shortfall resulting from a withdrawal of or deficiency in public finance
- UK student fees where these are not associated with a Research Project Grant bid or with Fine and Performing Arts schemes detailed in the Guidelines for Applicants.

Applications Each programme, scholarship and award has its own individual application deadline and procedure. Full guidelines and application procedures for each award scheme are available from the trust directly or via its website.

Lord Leverhulme's Charitable Trust

Welfare, education, arts and young people

£760,000 (2007/08)

Beneficial area UK especially, Cheshire, Merseyside and surrounding areas.

Leverhulme Estate Office, Manor Road, Thornton Hough, Wirral CH63 1JD

Tel. 0151 336 4828 **Fax** 0151 353 0265

Correspondent Mrs S Edwards, Administrator

Trustees A E H Heber-Percy; A H S Hannay.

CC Number 212431

Information available Accounts were available from the Charity Commission, without a full list of grants.

There are two restricted funds within the trust. One generates income which is paid to National Museums and Galleries in Liverpool for the trustees of the Lady Lever Art Gallery. The second is Lord Leverhulme's Youth Enterprise Scheme; the income from this sponsors young people in the Wirral and Cheshire areas who receive support from the Prince's Youth Business Trust.

In 2007/08 the trust had assets of £22 million and an income of £552,000. Grants were made totalling £760,000 and were categorised as follows:

Category	Value
Education	£250,000
Community	£201,000
Religious establishments	£145,000
Health	£107,000
Arts	£34,000
Environmental	£19,000
Animal welfare	£4,000

Only grants of over £20,000 were listed in the accounts. Beneficiaries of these larger grants were: University of Liverpool (£200,000); Foundation of the College of St George and RNLI (£100,000 each); Royal College of Surgeons (£50,000); Royal Horticulture Society and the Lady Lever Art Gallery (£30,000 each); Prince's Youth Business Trust (£27,000); and All Saints Trust (£26,000).

Exclusions No grants to non-charitable organisations.

Applications The trust states:

Priority is given to applications from Cheshire, Merseyside and south Lancashire and the charities supported by the settlor in his lifetime. Others who do not meet those criteria should not apply without prior invitation but should, on a single sheet, state briefly their aims and apply fully only on being asked to do so. The trustees are concerned at the continuing volume of applications which they receive despite the forgoing warning.

The Joseph Levy Charitable Foundation

Young people, older people, health and medical research

£132,000 (2008/09)

Beneficial area UK and Israel.

1st Floor, 1 Bell Street, London NW1 5BY

Email info@jlf.org.uk

Website www.jlf.org.uk

Correspondent Sue Nyfield, Director

Trustees Mrs Jane Jason; Peter L Levy; Melanie Levy; Claudia Giat; James Jason.

CC Number 245592

Information available Accounts were provided by the trust.

The foundation was established in 1965 by the late Joseph Levy, property developer and philanthropist, who helped to rebuild post-war London in the 1950s and 60s.

He worked tirelessly all his life for many charitable causes and in particular had a deep concern for the welfare of young people. His longstanding interest in youth began as a member and manager at Brady

Boys' Club. He subsequently became a Vice-President of the London Federation of Boys' Clubs, now London Youth. In 1963 he became a Founder Trustee of the Cystic Fibrosis Research Trust, now the Cystic Fibrosis Trust, acting as Chairman for almost twenty years till his retirement in 1984. He was awarded the MBE in 1976 and the CBE eight years later for his dedication to charitable causes.

As noted below, the amount committed each year varies considerably, however due to its grant-making capacity the foundation retains an entry here.

In 2008/09 the foundation had assets of £13 million and an income of £842,000. Grants were committed during the year totalling £132,000 (2007/08: £4 million; 2006/07: £869,000). A multi-year commitment to For Dementia was accounted for as payable during 2007/08 and the charity will receive just over £1 million each year in the three years up to 2010/11.

The foundation carried out a review of its activities in 2006/07:

The review was completed and it was agreed to continue to limit funding to charities with which the foundation already has a long-term commitment or which is already known by the trustees. Therefore the trustees agreed to continue to keep the foundation closed to all unsolicited applications.

Exclusions No grants to individuals, under any circumstances.

Applications No grants to unsolicited applications.

The Linbury Trust

Arts, heritage, social welfare, humanitarian aid and general

£5.5 million (2007/08)

Beneficial area Unrestricted.

Allington House, 1st Floor, 150 Victoria Street, London SW1E 5AE

Tel. 020 7410 0330 **Fax** 020 7410 0332

Website www.linburytrust.org.uk

Correspondent Alan Bookbinder, Director

Trustees Lord Sainsbury of Preston Candover; Lady Sainsbury; Sir Martin Jacomb; Sir James Spooner.

CC Number 287077

Information available Accounts were available from the Charity Commission.

This is one of the Sainsbury Family Charitable Trusts, which share a joint administration. They have a common approach to grantmaking which is described in the entry for the group as a whole, and which is generally discouraging to organisations not already in contact with the trust concerned, but some appear to be increasingly open to unsolicited approaches.

Over time, much of the trust's money has gone in major capital projects. It also funds numerous revenue projects in the following fields:

- arts
- education
- environment and heritage
- medical
- social welfare
- developing countries and humanitarian aid.

Under each of these categories, the trust makes grants very selectively; it gives priority to charitable causes where it has particular knowledge and experience. In past years the trust has supported major capital projects such as the National Gallery and the Royal Opera House, as well as other museums and galleries. It also has a special interest in dance and dance education; Lady Sainsbury being the well known ballerina Anya Linden. However, while the trust is particularly associated with supporting the arts, it is worth noting that some 65 per cent of the value of grants made over the last ten years (1998–2008) has been to other causes.

General

The trust takes a proactive approach towards grantmaking and, consequently, unsolicited applications are not usually successful. However, the trust will consider proposals which fall within its guidelines and gives grants to a wide range of charities. The sums awarded may be small or may amount to many millions, either on a once-only basis or as a commitment over a number of years.

Within the UK, priority is given to causes that are either national in scope, or that are based in regions of which trustees have a particular knowledge or interest. Preferred causes are as follows (not in order of priority).

- Disadvantaged young people, including those who are homeless or are in danger of becoming so, or who are drug abusers.

- Specific medical causes which the trustees have adopted and where, in the trustees' opinion, inadequate research is currently undertaken, or inadequate treatment and understanding exists; for example, Chronic Fatigue Syndrome. Medical causes to which these criteria do not apply are generally not supported. The trustees usually take specialist advice before making decisions.

- Although general educational causes are not supported unless they cover the particular needs of disadvantaged young people or specific medical causes, limited exceptions are made when the trustees have particular knowledge concerning specific educational appeals.

- Appeals for the benefit of older people will be considered if the results can be shown to improve their quality of life directly and in a cost effective way, and particularly when the goal is to help people to continue living in their own homes.

- National heritage appeals will be considered and, in particular, appeals for historic buildings and major arts institutions. Trustees occasionally make grants for initiatives to safeguard the natural environment.

- Grants for the visual arts, the performing arts and for education in the arts will be favourably considered where, in the opinion of the trustees, the aim is to produce work of the highest standard, and where long-term benefits will result. Arts festivals are generally not supported.

- Grants for capital projects or 'one-off' grants for specific purposes will not normally be repeated or supplemented within four years of the original grant, and then only in exceptional circumstances.

Grantmaking in 2007/08

In 2007/08 the trust had assets of £159 million and an income of £9.3 million. The trustees paid grants totalling £5.5 million and approved 81 grants amounting to £6.2 million.

The trust gives the following review of grantmaking during the year:

Arts – £2.7 million
The Linbury Trust has supported excellence in the visual and performing arts for many years. This support has included a series of major grants made to a select number of the UK's most important cultural institutions, usually towards major capital projects. The trustees are currently supporting a major redevelopment project being undertaken by

the Ashmolean Museum [£2.4 million], part of the University of Oxford, which will comprehensively modernise this nationally important museum. The Linbury Trust is the lead private benefactor to the project.

The trustees continued their sponsorship of the Linbury Biennial Prize for Stage Design [£177,000]. This unique award gives the most talented recent graduates in stage design the chance to work with leading British companies on opera, theatre or dance productions. The trustees are delighted that the National Theatre, which for many years has hosted the awards ceremony and exhibition for the Prize, will increase its involvement with the Prize in future.

Smaller grants were also made to: Blackpool Grand Theatre, Serpentine Gallery, Birmingham Royal Ballet, Federation of British Artists and Royal Opera House Foundation.

Education – £1.1 million
Trustees have over many years been stalwart supporters of dance education in the UK. Most recently, they gave a grant of £1 million towards the refurbishment of White Lodge, the Royal Ballet School's junior department, situated in Richmond Park.

They made a one-off grant of £100,000 to the University of Liverpool towards the restoration of the Victoria Building, an iconic, red-brick late Victorian structure at the heart of the University campus (and which gave rise to the phrase 'redbrick university'). The University has created the Victoria Gallery and Museum, which will house its art and heritage collections.

The City & Guilds of London Art School is in the early stages of a major project that will substantially upgrade its premises in south London. Trustees gave a grant towards the feasibility study [£63,000]. The Hampshire Museums Trust is in the process of modernising the Willis Museum, in Basingstoke. In the re-opened Museum, temporary exhibitions will be shown in the Sainsbury Gallery.

Trustees made an important contribution [£50,000] to the newly-established fund, administered by RIBA, that will endow the Giles Worsley Travel Fellowship. Created in memory of the distinguished architectural historian and critic Giles Worsley, the Fellowship will allow one architect or architectural historian per annum to study for three months at the British School at Rome.

Smaller grants were also made to ten other organisations, including: Arts Educational School Trust, British Dyslexia Association, British School at Rome and Volunteer Reading Help.

Social welfare – £742,000
The Linbury trustees have had a long-standing interest in the welfare of ex-

servicemen and women. Accordingly they share the widespread concern as to whether the Ministry of Defence is fulfilling its responsibilities in this field, in view of the numbers of badly injured members of the forces returning from Iraq and Afghanistan in particular. SSAFA is seeking to provide adequate accommodation for the families of injured servicemen and women, so that they can be near their injured relative during the period following evacuation to either Headley Court (in Surrey) or Selly Oak (in the Midlands); the trustees gave £250,000 to this appeal.

The trustees gave a first-time grant to Action for Prisoners' Families, a national organisation that supports families of whom a member is imprisoned, and which are therefore unusually vulnerable [£50,000]. Trustees also accept the related proposition that a reasonably stable family environment reduces the risk of re-offending. They renewed support for Safe Ground, which uses this principle in its work with serving prisoners.

The trustees also take particular interest in charities working with severely disadvantaged and under-achieving young people. They continue to support programmes designed to help young people to break free from the nexus of low aspirations, anti-social behaviour, substance abuse, crime and, in all too many cases, re-offending, which are so often the product of long-term economic deprivation, failure to benefit from the opportunities provided by education, and family breakdown. Their grants to Circomedia, Depaul Trust [£50,000], and Foundation Training Company [£50,000] fall into this category.

The trustees also support organisations that use the arts to work with disadvantaged people. The trustees renewed their support for Dance United's Academy in Bradford [£50,000], and the Firebird Trust, and initiated a multi-year grant to fund Greenhouse Schools Project's dance work in a number of schools in disadvantaged areas of south-east London.

Environment and heritage – £454,000
Further sums were paid under existing grants to St George's Chapel, Windsor [£150,000], and to Strawberry Hill [£50,000], the gothic villa in Twickenham built by Horace Walpole.

The trustees renewed their support for the Ashden Awards for Sustainable Energy [£100,000]. The Ashden Awards, which were initiated in 2001, annually reward outstanding and innovative projects in the UK and overseas which promote the use of sustainable sources of energy at a local level, and thereby improve the quality of life. The trustees also maintained their support for the Sainsbury Archive, situated at the Docklands site of the Museum of London; this is an

important resource for the study of British commercial and social history over the last 150 years.

Grants were also made to Fauna and Flora International and St Giles in the Fields Church – London.

Developing countries and humanitarian aid – £375,000
The trustees maintained their interest in supporting organisations that work in the medical field in Palestine including Al Quds University Medical School Foundation and St John of Jerusalem Eye Hospital [£100,000 each].

They made a one-off grant to Interhealth [£50,000], a charity that provides medical services, primarily to those working in the charitable aid and overseas development sectors, towards the cost of relocating its London premises.

Grants were also made to: Butrint Foundation, Calabash International Literary Festival Trust – Jamaica and Save the Rhino International.

Medical – £75,000
The trustees' primary area of interest in the Medical category is in research into CFS/ME. During the 1990's Linbury was perhaps the most important source of funding for research into these conditions, and thereby contributed significantly to the level of awareness of them that exists today among both the medical profession and the general public. Although trustees no longer actively solicit research proposals, they did initiate support for a major study into paediatric issues in CFS/ME under the aegis of the University of Bristol.

Exclusions
No grants to individuals.

Applications
See the guidance for applicants in the entry for the Sainsbury Family Charitable Trusts. A single application will be considered for support by all the trusts in the group.

Please note: 'the trustees take a proactive approach towards grantmaking; accordingly, unsolicited applications to the trust are not usually successful'.

The Enid Linder Foundation

Health, welfare and general
£765,500 (2007/08)
Beneficial area Unrestricted.

Moore Stephens, St Paul's House, 8–12 Warwick Lane, London EC4M 7BP
Tel. 020 7334 9191 **Fax** 020 7651 1953
Email martin.pollock@moorestephens.com
Correspondent Martin Pollock, Secretary
Trustees *Jack Ladeveze; Audrey Ladeveze; M Butler; C Cook; Jonathan Fountain.*
CC Number 267509
Information available Accounts were available from the Charity Commission.

There are often no more than ten new grants each year, with most money going to a mixed group of regularly supported beneficiaries, mainly in the fields of health and social welfare, particularly of children and disabled people, medical education and research. Local (normally London and the south), national and international charities are supported.

The aims of the foundation are:

- to fund research and teaching related to all areas of medicine by way of medical electives and general support costs to students and chosen medical universities
- to assist in the funding of chosen research fellowship schemes which are of particular interest to the trustees
- to distribute in full, in accordance with the governing Trust Deed, all the income available each year
- to maintain resources at a reasonable level in order to continue to provide general charitable assistance in the foreseeable future.

The main objectives for the year are shaped by these strategic aims with a view to maintaining both a stable medical electives scheme at universities, to support the research fellowship schemes and to continue funding chosen general charitable causes.

General

In 2007/08 the foundation had assets totalling almost £12.5 million and an income of £546,500. Grants were made totalling £765,500, which included £629,000 for 'general charitable causes' and £132,500 to nine teaching hospitals and universities, all of which were supported in the previous year.

The largest beneficiary during the year was the Royal College of Surgeons, which recieved £347,000 in total under the 'general charitable causes' heading. Other beneficiaries included: National Children's Orchestra (£40,000); Medicins Sans Frontieres and Victoria & Albert Museum (£25,000 each); Practical Action and Bath University (£15,000 each); Bath

Intensive Care Baby Unit, Kidscape, Music in Hospitals and St Christopher's Hospice (£10,000 each). Just four of these were not supported in the previous year.

Grants were also made to two individuals totalling £4,000.

Applications In writing to the correspondent. Although unsolicited applications are accepted, the trust states that it prefers to support organisations whose work it has researched.

The George John and Sheilah Livanos Charitable Trust

Health, maritime charities and general

£632,000 (2008)
Beneficial area UK.

Jeffrey Green Russell, Waverley House, 7–12 Noel Street, London W1F 8GQ
Tel. 020 7339 7000
Correspondent Philip N Harris, Trustee
Trustees *Philip N Harris; Timothy T Cripps; Anthony S Holmes.*
CC Number 1002279
Information available Accounts were available from the Charity Commission.

The trust gives grants from its income of about £200,000 a year but has also been making substantial awards from capital. Grants are widely spread and the previously reported interest in maritime causes, while still existing, is not as prominent as it was.

The trust says that 'funds are fully committed and unsolicited applications are not requested'.

In 2008 the trust had assets of £3.4 million and an income of £209,000. Grants were made to 58 organisations totalling £632,000.

The largest donation of £200,000 went to St Mary's Hospital in London, which also received the same amount in 2009 to complete a £1 million commitment over five years towards a research programme into meningitis, septicaemia and shock.

Other beneficiaries of larger grants were: The Watts Gallery (£100,000);

Parkinson's Disease Society (£50,000); Fight for Sight (£47,000); University of Dundee – Child Health Studentship (£27,000); Ekklesia Project Fakenham (£18,000); Caius House – Wandsworth (£17,500); Naomi House (£15,000); and the Cancer Resource Centre, Headway and London Youth (£10,000 each).

Other beneficiaries included: City University London and Listening Books (£5,000 each); Coram Family and Kidscape (£3,000 each); Colchester Furniture Project (£2,000); and Chiswick House and Gardens Project and Phab Kids (£1,000 each).

Exclusions No grants to individuals or non-registered charities.

Applications Unsolicited applications are not requested.

Lloyds TSB Foundation for England and Wales

Social and community needs

£23.7 million (2008)
Beneficial area England and Wales.

Pentagon House, 52–54 Southwark Street, London SE1 1UN
Tel. 0870 411 1223 **Fax** 0870 411 1224
Email enquiries@lloydstsbfoundations.org.uk
Website www.lloydstsbfoundations.org.uk
Correspondent Mrs Linda Kelly, Chief Executive
Trustees *Prof. Ian Diamond, Chair; Janet Bibby; Prof. Clair Chilvers; Sarah Cooke; Pavita Cooper; Irene Evison; Mike Fairey; John Hughes; Alan Leaman; Anne Parker; Rosemary Stevenson.*
CC Number 327114
Information available The foundation provides comprehensive information on its activities and achievements, all of which is available on its excellent website.

Recent developments

At the end of 2009, together with the foundations for Northern Ireland and the Channel Islands, the foundation for

England and Wales was still in discussions with the Lloyds Banking Group over future funding arrangements. It is likely that the deal will involve a reduction in income for the foundations, falling from 1% to 0.5% of the group's pre-tax profits. The Lloyds TSB Foundation for Scotland has refused to accept this arrangement and has suspended its grant-making activities for the foreseeable future.

Inevitably, this new arrangement will have an impact on the level of funding available from the foundation in the future.

The foundation provides comprehensive information on its activities and achievements, much of which is reproduced here.

We support and work in partnership with recognised charitable organisations which help disadvantaged people to play a fuller role in communities throughout England and Wales.

The Lloyds TSB Foundation for England and Wales is one of the UK's leading grant makers and supports local, regional and national charities working at the heart of communities to tackle disadvantage across England and Wales.

The foundation is keen to fund small and medium charities with less than twelve months' reserves and the majority of charities that we support have an annual income of under £1 million.

Our extensive network across England and Wales means our funding is always driven by local needs. We pride ourselves on our local and national presence and knowledge, strong links with the voluntary sector and our close personal contact with charities.

Our grants managers visit all charities applying for a grant of over £5,000 to ensure that we understand applicants' needs and can give a high level of guidance and support.

An accessible funder, we aim to be:

- accessible to all
- approachable and supportive
- responsive and customer-focused
- straightforward
- timely and transparent.

What do we fund?
In support of our mission statement, the foundation adopts the following grant-making approach:

- we fund work that helps disadvantaged people to play a fuller role in the community
- we support both well established and new work across the voluntary sector

- we provide 'second stage funding' to support charities' development – we fund organisations that are looking to innovate, expand, improve or maintain their capacity, effectiveness or services
- we fund running costs, including salaries, to ensure that charities can continue to operate their core services
- we provide grants of up to three years appropriate to the charity's size.

Core costs

The foundation is also one of the few grant makers who fund core costs – day-to-day running expenses such as salaries and other overheads. Without this kind of help many smaller charities, offering vital support in their communities, would struggle to survive. And that's why we encourage applicants to include running costs in their applications where relevant.

Programmes

Community Programme

The Community programme focuses on funding core work that helps disadvantaged people to play a fuller role in the community.

To be eligible:

- you must be an underfunded charity (12 months of reserves or less)
- if you work locally or in a region you must have an income of £1 million or less
- if you work nationally you must have an income of £5 million or less
- your work must enable disadvantaged people to play a fuller role in the community in one (or more) of the following ways – through:
  - improved social and community involvement
  - improved life choices and chances
  - helping people to be heard
- you will need to be clear on the specific changes and benefits that your work will provide for your users/beneficiaries to help them to play a fuller role in the community.

What type of funding do we provide?

We fund charities to continue and develop existing community-based work, or to develop the organisation or its services. We can support charities in a range of ways – examples include funding to:

- maintain and or improve their capacity and or effectiveness
- encourage learning and best practice
- enable the continued provision of services
- support the expansion of services
- help improve the quality of services
- lobby or campaign at a local, regional or national level.

We make grants of one to three years that are appropriate to the size and needs of each charity.

The foundation also introduces new programmes from time to time – potential applicants should check the foundation's website for up-to-date details of current programmes.

In 2008 the foundation had assets of £9.24 million and an income of £28.5 million. There were 665 grants made during the year totalling £23.7 million.

Grantmaking in 2008

During the year, grants made through the Community programme and the Ex-prisoners Continuation Funding programme (the latter of which is no-longer running), were broken down geographically as follows:

Region	No. of grants	Value
North East & Cumbria	70	£2,900,000
Lancashire & north Manchester	64	£2,100,000
Lincolnshire & Nottinghamshire	51	£2,000,000
Yorkshire	46	£2,000,000
Wales	59	£1,800,000
Cheshire & south Manchester	41	£1,800,000
West Midlands	40	£1,800,000
Essex & north-east London	64	£1,600,000
Kent & south-east London	41	£1,400,000
Hertfordshire & north-west London	30	£1,300,000
Devon & Cornwall	46	£1,200,000
South central & south-west London	36	£1,100,000
East	34	£900,000
South West Central	19	£800,000

The following summary analysis of grantmaking is taken from the foundation's 2008 Annual Report, the full version of which is available from the foundation's website.

Tackling local & national disadvantage

The foundation's focus is on supporting charities that tackle one or more of the pressing problems faced by people living on the margins of society. We fund charities' core work to help their users and beneficiaries to play a fuller role in the community and champion their needs.

In 2008, we made grants of £19.2 million through our main Community programme to support the core work of 636 small and medium charities working to tackle issues in over twenty 'areas' of disadvantage.

Top 5 funding areas	Value
Children and young people	£3,000,000
People with disabilities	£2,700,000
Advice, advocacy and outreach	£2,000,000
Geographic-based support	£1,600,000
Health, including mental health	£1,300,000

Funding local & national solutions

The foundation's extensive geographical presence and knowledge ensures that our funding has both local relevance and national impact. Our portfolio of grant making programmes operates locally and nationally – we provide funding to address a range of issues that affect individuals as well as multiple communities. We are also able to target specific areas of geographical deprivation.

Delivering lasting changes & benefits

We aim to help charities to deliver lasting benefits for their individual users and beneficiaries and we use our size and reputation to support sustainable change in communities across England and Wales. In particular, we support charities that can achieve this through:

- improved social and community involvement
- improved life choices and chances
- helping disadvantaged people to be heard.

Supporting charities' running costs

Through our feedback process, we have identified the need to support charities' core running costs over a longer time period – multi-year grants of an appropriate size are essential to ensure that charities have both the time and resources to deliver their objectives. This is particularly true of funding for posts/salaries where effective recruitment, training and delivery require a minimum of two-year funding.

Funding type	Value
Core – salary costs	£9,600,000
Project costs	£5,200,000
Core – salary and operational costs	£3,000,000
Core – operational costs	£1,400,000

In 2008, 73% of all funding for the Community Programme was for core running costs (50% salaries). The average Community programme grant size in 2008 was £30,000 and 94% of grants were for more than one year (42% for three years).

Helping small & medium 'underfunded' charities be sustainable

To ensure that the work of small and medium charities is sustainable, we focus our funding on helping charities to continue and develop their existing community-based work, or to develop the organisation or services.

Income per annum	No. of charities supported
Up to £100,000	219
£100,001 to £250,000	224
£250,001 to £500,000	125
Over £500,001	68

The Community programme specifically supports smaller local, regional and national charities – charities that work tirelessly to deliver essential services to local communities, often with limited resources and staff/volunteers. During 2008 we targeted 49% of funding to charities with an annual income of under £100,000 and 70% to those with income of under £250,000.

Facilitating smaller charities' voice
We aim to facilitate the 'voice' of smaller groups within their local, regional and national networks, through effective communications and facilitating contacts.

Case Studies
The following are some of the organisations that received a grant during 2007/08 through the Community Programme:

Wolverhampton Elder Asians and Disabled Group (£60,000 over 3 years)
The foundation gave a grant of £60,000 towards the costs of a project co-ordinator. The charity helps 80 Asian elders each week, providing them with opportunities to interact with other members and improve their health and well-being through a range of sessions including benefits advice.

Centre Place – Worksop (£59,600 over 3 years towards the manager's salary)
Centre Place in Worksop's grant will support their work providing housing advice and support for over 160 young people leaving home for the first time as well as teenage single parents, most of whom are not in school.

CIL De Gwynedd (£39,000 over 2 years towards the salary of the Development Officer and vehicle costs)
The Centre for Independent Living provides a range of support, advice and outreach services to disabled people living in the country of rural Gwynedd.

Public transport does not meet their needs and so the charity runs a bus service to bring clients to the centre, ensuring that they do not become socially isolated. The centre also functions as the main education and training hub for disabled people in Gwynedd.

Hop, Skip and Jump (£30,000 over 3 years towards the salary of the team leader)
Hop, Skip and Jump is a play and support centre for children with special needs and their families. The charity welcomes families from across the south west of England, providing free facilities including adventure playgrounds, sensory rooms and musical instruments to children of all ages. Hop, Skip and Jump also understands the pressures that parents, carers and siblings of special needs children face, particularly for those on a low income or in single parent families. The Team Leader will co-ordinate the work of staff members and the centre's many volunteers, providing more children and their families with the opportunity to be part of a supportive community.

Rev and Go (£22,500 over 3 years towards the core costs)
Rev and Go works with young people, some of whom have been excluded from school or are at risk of not being in education, employment or training. Based in Cotgrave, one of the most deprived areas of south Nottinghamshire, the project uses motorcycling as a reward and learning tool to develop skills and behaviours which will help them through their transition into work and adulthood. The voices of the young people involved are key to managing the project and experience shows that the charity's clients take their responsibilities seriously and respond with respect for the trust they have been shown.

Speaking Up Groups – County Durham
Speaking Up received £10,000 over 1 year to help people with learning disabilities to plan self advocacy meetings and workshops, as well as day centre activities.

Advocacy Matters – Wales (£7,700 towards the costs of the Taking Part project)
Advocacy Matters (Wales) provides advice and advocacy for people with learning disabilities across south Wales. The Taking Part group is a team of disabled volunteers that works with the charity to help improve the quality of their services. Supporting disabled people to contribute to the development of the charity is an important part of how Advocacy Matters (Wales) helps its clients to become active participants in the community.

Grants in 2009 (likely to be awarded over several years) included those to:

A National Voice – Nottingham (£70,000), towards the salary and on costs of the East Midlands Regional Officer and running costs; Trust Links Limited – Southend-on-Sea (£30,000), towards the Growing Together Project; BF Adventure – North Cornwall (£25,000), towards the salary and on costs of the project manager; East Lancashire Women's Refuge Association (£20,000), towards the salary of the Children's Community Support Worker; Lincoln MIND (£18,000), towards the staffing costs of the Befriending Scheme; Swansea Bay Asylum Seekers' Group (£15,000), towards the Welcome2Play Project and drop-in costs; Home Start Ceredigion (£10,000), towards the cost of travel and training for volunteers; and the Dyslexia Association Preston & District (£5,000), towards running costs and volunteer expenses.

Exclusions
The foundation does not fund the following types of organisations and work:

Organisations
- organisations that are **not** registered charities
- second or third tier organisations (unless there is evidence of direct benefit to disadvantaged people)
- charities that mainly work overseas
- charities that mainly give funds to other charities, individuals or other organisations
- hospitals, hospices or medical centres
- rescue services
- schools, colleges and universities.

Types of work
- activities for which a statutory body is responsible
- capital projects, appeals, refurbishments
- environmental work, expeditions and overseas travel
- funding to promote religion
- holidays or trips
- loans or business finance
- medical research, funding for medical equipment or medical treatments
- sponsorship or funding towards a marketing appeal or fundraising activities
- work with animals or to promote animal welfare.

Applications
We aim to be accessible and supportive to charities that request funding from us.

Step 1 – Read our guidelines
Please check our guidelines and individual criteria for the programme you are interested in so that you are clear what is and is not funded.

Step 2 – Check if your charity is eligible
Before you apply you need to complete our short charity eligibility questionnaire which you can find on our website. If you don't have access to the internet or would prefer to talk to us first, please call 0870 411 1223.

Please note: charity eligibility does not mean that your work meets the criteria for all of our programmes.

Step 3 – We will contact you to discuss whether your work is eligible
If your charity is eligible, one of our team will contact you to discuss whether the work you are seeking funding for fits within our guidelines – and if it does to discuss the next steps.

Step 4 – Assessment
If your work is eligible for consideration and you are applying for a grant of over £5,000, your local Grant Manager will visit you to discuss your funding requirements. If you are applying for a grant of under £5,000, the Grant Manager will carry out a telephone assessment.

Assessment visits take one to two hours, and your local Grant Manager will discuss a range of issues relevant to your potential application, including: your governance; your finances; your evidence of need; your work;

and the difference it will make to your users/ beneficiaries.

The Grant Manager will tell you whether or not to proceed with an application. If you are advised to apply, they will help you to make the best application.

Step 5 – Complete the application form

If your local Grant Manager recommends that you complete an application form, they will give you a copy of the form. You will need to read the accompanying guidance notes and include:

- a copy of your most recent annual report and full signed accounts. These should be signed as approved on behalf of your Management Committee or equivalent. You must make sure your charity annual returns are up to date and registered with the Charity Commission – we will check this when we assess your application. (If your records are not up to date this could delay your application being processed)
- a copy of your charity's most recent bank statement so that we can verify the account details
- the relevant job description if you are applying for funding towards the cost of a post, a copy of your equal opportunities policy or if you do not have one, information about your commitment to equal opportunities. We will also need to know about the other governance policies that you have in place that are relevant to your work.

Step 6 – Return your application form to us

You will need to submit a signed copy of the form together with the supporting documents to us.

Step 7 – The decision on your application

We respond to all applications that we receive and it takes from three to six months for a decision to be made on your

application. Your local Grant Manager will tell you when you are likely to hear the decision.

Common reasons for unsuccessful applications

The foundation cannot fund all eligible applications even if they are of a high quality because each year the total amount requested by charities exceeds the money that we have available. Other reasons for the foundation not being able to make a grant include:

- charities' core work not being sufficiently focused on our mission
- applications not falling within our guidelines
- charities not filling in the application form properly
- charities not having up-to-date annual returns or accounts filed with the Charities Commission or other relevant regulatory bodies.

When can I reapply?

If you receive a grant, you will not be eligible to apply for another grant from the Community Programme for another two years from receipt of the grant (or from receipt of the final payment if it has been two or three-year funding). If your application is unsuccessful, you must wait for a year before you apply again.

Lloyds TSB Foundation for Northern Ireland

Social and community need, education and training

£1.9 million (2008)

Beneficial area Northern Ireland.

2nd Floor, 14 Cromac Place, Gasworks, Belfast BT7 2JB

Tel. 028 9032 3000 **Fax** 028 9032 3200

Email info@lloydstsbfoundationni.org

Website www.lloydstsbfoundationni.org

Correspondent Sandara Kelso-Robb, Executive Director

Trustees *Gary Mills, Chair; Paddy Bailie; Angela Colhoun; James Grant; David Patton; Tony Reynolds; Robert Agnew; Janet Lecky; Brian Scott.*

IR Number XN72216

Information available Full information on the foundation's helpful website, including the latest annual review.

Recent developments

The four Lloyds TSB Foundations, covering England and Wales, Scotland, Northern Ireland and the Channel Islands are shareholders in Lloyds TSB Group and together receive a percentage of the Group's pre-tax profits.

Due to the current economic climate there has been a reduction in the Group's profits, wiping out much of the income for the foundations.

The Foundation for Scotland has decided to suspend its grantmaking pending negotiations with the Group on a more acceptable funding arrangement.

The Lloyds TSB Foundation for Northern Ireland will continue its grant-making programme but has issued the following statement:

Fortunately, the foundation in Northern Ireland operates prudently and has a low cost base. Our rolling grant programmes focusing on Social and Community Welfare and Education and Training are ongoing, with quarterly closing dates, and continue to provide grants to underfunded local charities. However, two changes have been made to the programme, namely that the maximum amount that can be applied for is £5,000 and that to be eligible, organisations must

---

LLOYDS TSB FOUNDATION FOR ENGLAND AND WALES
Regional contact details

	Tel.
Cheshire & South Manchester: cheshire&southmanchester@lloydstsbfoundations.org.uk	07500 787747
Devon & Cornwall: devon&cornwall@lloydstsbfoundations.org.uk	07770 925946
East	07912 798053
Essex & North East London: essex&nelondon@lloydstsbfoundations.org.uk	07770 925943
Hertfordshire & North West London: herts&nwlondon@lloydstsbfoundations.org.uk	0870 411 1223
South East London & Kent: selondon&kent@lloydstsbfoundations.org.uk	07872 031792
Lancashire & North Manchester: lancashire&northmanchester@lloydstsbfoundations.org.uk	07734 973464
Lincolnshire & Nottinghamshire	07734 973060
Mid & South Wales: mid&southwales@lloydstsbfoundations.org.uk	07802 540793
North East & Cumbria: northeast&cumbria@lloydstsbfoundations.org.uk	07802 337481
North Wales: northwales@lloydstsbfoundations.org.uk	07500 787749
North West Midlands	07500 787751
South Central & South West London: southcentral&swlondon@lloydstsbfoundations.org.uk	07872 031793
South West Central: southwestcentral@lloydstsbfoundations.org.uk	07500 787750
West Midlands: westmidlands@lloydstsbfoundations.org.uk	07500 787746
Yorkshire	07500 787745

have had an income of under £250,000 within the previous twelve months. The trustees and executive team will continue to review the parameters of this programme as, unfortunately, the funding situation could worsen in the medium term. However, we are still in receipt of very significant funding that will be allocated wisely to many voluntary and community sector organisations throughout Northern Ireland.

Summary

The foundation allocates its funds in support of the Northern Ireland community, to enable people, primarily those in need, to be active members of society and to improve their quality of life.

Most donations are said to be one-off, with a small number of commitments made over two or more years. The trustees say that they prefer to make donations towards specific items rather than contributions to large appeals, though the trust will consider core funding for small local charities. Applications which help to develop voluntary sector infrastructure are encouraged. Donations are generally between £2,500 and £5,000.

Programmes

The foundation's main grant programme, the Standard Grant Programme, makes one year grants of up to £5,000 to underfunded, grassroots organisations with a total income of less than £250,000. Donations are generally in the region of £2,500 to £5,000 but there is no minimum amount set by the trustees.

The foundation also manages other short-running, ad-hoc programmes. In 2007, for example, the foundation ran a Creating Change pilot programme and in 2008, it announced a one year International Grant Programme. A Special Initiatives Programme was also established in 2008 to recognise the funding requirements of those organisations undertaking work of a strategic or Northern Ireland-wide nature. Consequently, potential applicants are advised to visit the foundation's website or contact them directly to ensure that they keep up to date with the latest programme information.

Guidelines for applicants

The guidelines for applicants, detailed on the foundation's website, read as follows:

The overall policy of the charity is to support underfunded charities which enable people, especially disadvantaged or disabled people, to play a fuller role in the community.

The trustees are keen to encourage the infrastructure of the voluntary sector and welcome applications for operational costs. This may include a contribution toward salary costs, and training and education for managers and staff, with the exception of the pre-school sector. The trustees are also keen to support sector self-rationalisation.

The foundation has two main target areas to which it seeks to allocate funds:

- social and community needs
- education and training.

Social and Community Needs

A wide range of activities are supported and the following are meant as a guide only.

Community services

Family centres, youth and older people's clubs, after school clubs; play schemes (not salaries), help groups, childcare provision.

Advice services

Homelessness, addictions, bereavement, family guidance, money advice, helplines.

Disabled people

Residences, day centres, transport, carers, information and advice, advocacy.

Promotion of health

Information and advice, mental health, hospices, day care, home nursing, independent living for older people.

Civic responsibility

Juveniles at risk, crime prevention, promotion of volunteering, victim support, mediation, rehabilitation of offenders.

Cultural enrichment

Improving participation in and access to the arts and national heritage for disadvantaged and disabled people.

Education and Training

The objective is to enhance educational opportunities for disadvantaged people and those with special needs:

Towards employment

Projects which help socially excluded people develop their potential and secure employment. Employment Training (for disadvantaged people and those with special needs).

Life skills

Promotion of life skills, independent living skills for people with special needs.

Early years

Enhancing education for pre-school children and young people (where no other support is available).

Grantmaking in 2008

In 2008 the foundation had an income of £2.1 million. Grants were made to 333

organisations totalling £1.9 million. Most of the grants made were for social welfare purposes.

Grants were distributed across four programmes:

Programme	No.	Value
Standard grant programme	299	£1,400,000
Creating change programme	19	£378,000
International grant programme	11	£100,000
Special initiatives programme	4	£60,000

They were broken down geographically as follows:

Region	No. of grants
Belfast	122
County Antrim	40
County Down	56
County Tyrone	32
Derry	29
County Londonderry	18
County Fermanagh	12
County Armagh	17
Great Britain	7

Grants approved by programme area in the Standard Grants Programme were as follows:

Category	No. of grants
Community services	133
Disability	19
Education and training	61
Advice services	24
Cultural enrichment	21
Civic responsibility	12
Promotion of health	29

Beneficiaries of the standard grant programme included: CAB Fermanagh – towards the Disability Advocacy (Tribunal Representation) Project (£10,000); Ardoyne Association – to support the Outreach and Detached Advice Service (£8,500); Gingerbread Northern Ireland – towards the salary and core costs of the Lone Parent Centre (£7,000); Adapt Eating Distress Association – towards administrative support to maintain and enhance the existing service (£5,000); Ballee and District Community Group – towards the cookery school (£3,000); Women Making Waves – to provide courses and workshops for disabled and able bodied women in the group (£2,500); Churches Voluntary Work Bureau – towards awards, certificates and volunteer costs (£2,000); Carrick Preschool – towards new play equipment (£1,000); Ballybay Community Association – for community activities (£970); and GLM Silver Threads Group – towards the Ten Years On celebration event (£200).

Exclusions Grants are not usually given for:

- organisations that are not recognised as a charity by HM Revenue and Customs
- individuals, including students
- animal welfare
- environmental projects including those that deal with geographic and scenic issues – however, the trustees

may consider projects that improve the living conditions of disadvantaged individuals and groups

- activities that are normally the responsibility of central or local government or some other responsible body
- schools, universities and colleges (except for projects specifically to benefit students with special needs)
- hospitals and medical centres
- sponsorship or marketing appeals
- fabric appeals for places of worship
- promotion of religion
- activities that collect funds for subsequent redistribution to others
- endowment funds
- fundraising events or activities
- corporate affiliation or membership of a charity
- loans or business finance
- expeditions or overseas travel
- construction of and extension to buildings
- salary or training costs for the pre-school sector.

Please note: organisations must have a total income of less than £250,000 to be eligible to apply to the Standard Grant Programme.

Applications The foundation offers the following advice on applying to the Standard Grant Programme on its website:

Who can apply?
The Standard Grant Programme is open to any organisation that is registered as a charity with HM Revenue and Customs. Constituted groups with charitable purpose, but not registered as a charity and have an annual income of less than £2,000, may apply for a grant of up to £1,000.

How to apply?
The application pack should be downloaded from the foundation website. The downloaded application form is in Microsoft Word format to enable it to be completed on screen before printing off a hard copy. The application form should then be signed and dated by the three required signatories, before attaching copies of the required supporting documents.

When to apply?
The closing dates for applications are normally the second Friday of January, April, July and October. Always check the website for the latest closing dates, as they may change due to statutory holidays. Applications will be accepted until 5pm on each closing date.

- Applicants are required to leave one year between applications whether they are successful or unsuccessful.

- Organisations who have received three years consecutive funding must leave two years before reapplying.
- All applicants will be informed in writing of the decision approximately ten weeks from the closing date for applications.

Unfortunately, demands made on the foundation always out-strip the funds available, and this means that many good applications, whilst meeting the criteria, will still be unsuccessful.

Please note: the application process for other programmes may differ. Organisations are advised to contact the foundation for details (as appropriate).

Lloyds TSB Foundation for the Channel Islands

General

£1.4 million (2008)

Beneficial area The Channel Islands.

PO Box 160, 25 New Street, St Helier, Jersey JE4 8RG

Tel. 01534 845889

Email john.hutchins@lloydstsbfoundations.org.uk

Website www.ltsbfoundationci.org

Correspondent John Hutchins, Executive Director

Trustees *Andrew Ozanne, Chair; David Christopher; Wendy Hurford; Peter Mourant; Sir Rocky Goodall; Advocate Susan Pearmain; Pauline Torode.*

CC Number 327113

Information available Accounts were available from the Charity Commission.

Recent developments

The four Lloyds TSB Foundations, covering England and Wales, Scotland, Northern Ireland and the Channel Islands are shareholders in Lloyds TSB Group and together receive a percentage of the Group's pre-tax profits.

Due to the current economic climate, there has been a reduction in the group's profits, wiping out much of the income for the foundations.

The Foundation for Scotland has decided to suspend its grantmaking

pending negotiations with the Group on a more acceptable funding arrangement.

The Lloyds TSB Foundation for the Channel Islands will continue its grant-making programme but has issued the following statement on the matter:

The foundation's operations have been affected by the current economic downturn, a result of the deed of covenant with the Lloyds Banking Group being based on a three year average of the group's profits. I expect the foundation's income to reduce in the coming years, with a need to return our reserves to a positive position. This will impact the foundation's ability to provide the volume of grants that were provided in previous years. The foundation has been working with those charities it supports on the islands, communicating this message and supporting them in seeking alternative funding, wherever possible. We will continue our commitment to Channel Island charities, enabling them to help change peoples lives for the better. The commitment to the International Grant Giving will be retained in principle but due to reduced income levels it is unlikely that previous levels will be maintained.

Summary

The foundation's mission is to 'support charitable organisations which help people, especially those who are disadvantaged or disabled, to play a fuller role in communities throughout the Channel Islands'.

In 2008 it had an income of £1.2 million and made donations to 42 charities totalling £1.4 million. Of these, 19 donations were made in Jersey in the sum of £589,000, and 20 in the Bailiwick of Guernsey in the sum of £694,000. One donation was made to Channel Island-wide for an amount of £10,000 and two donations to international charities totalling £65,000. In addition, 73 donations totalling £25,000 were paid through the Staff Matched Giving Scheme.

At the end of 2008 the foundation had a deficit on reserves of £438,000 due to a change in its accounting policy, whereby the full cost of multi-year grants will now be recognised in the year that they are approved.

Guidelines for applicants

The overall policy of the trustees is to support underfunded charities which enable people, especially disadvantaged or disabled people, to play a fuller role in the community. The trustees are keen to support organisations which contribute to local community life at the grassroots level. The trustees are also keen to encourage the infrastructure of the voluntary sector and encourage applications for operational costs. This includes salary costs, which may be funded over two or three years, and training and education for managers and staff.

Donations for one-off projects are generally in the region of £2,500 to £25,000, but there is no minimum amount set by the trustees. Applications for larger amounts will be considered where there is a wider benefit. The trustees generally make donations towards specific items rather than making contributions to large appeals, for example, building costs. The majority of donations are made on a one off basis. Successful applicants are advised to leave at least one year before reapplying.

The foundation has two main objectives to which it allocates funds:

Social and community and needs
A wide range of activities are supported, and the following examples are meant as a guide only:

Advice services – Addictions (particularly substance misuse rehabilitation), bereavement, counselling, emergency and rescue services, family support, helplines, homelessness, housing, parenting.

Community relations – Crime prevention (particularly activities involving young people), mediation, promotion of volunteering, rehabilitation of offenders, victim support, vulnerable young people.

Community facilities and services – After school clubs, community centres, family centres, older people's clubs, playschemes, transport, youth organisations.

Cultural enrichment – Improving participation in and access to the arts and national heritage; activities with an educational focus for all ages; improvements to buildings of historic or architectural value which increase their benefit to the community; projects which have a strong focus on benefit to people and the social environment.

Disabled people – Advocacy, carers, day centres, information and advice, sheltered accommodation, transport.

Promotion of health – Day care, information and advice, mental health, holistic medicine, home nursing, hospices. The trustees will, on an exceptional basis, also fund research projects in health related areas.

Education and training
The objective is to enhance learning opportunities for disabled and disadvantaged people of all ages. The following examples are meant as a guide only:

- lifelong learning
- literacy skills
- pre-school education
- promotion of life skills and independent living skills (particularly creating positive opportunities for disabled people)
- skills training for disabled people, including pre-vocational training
- skills training for disadvantaged people, to enhance their potential to secure employment.

Areas of Special Interest
The trustees review their areas of special interest from time to time, so contact the foundation directly for up-to-date information. Current priorities are:

- *Creating Positive Opportunities for Disabled People* – enabling people with either learning or physical disabilities to live independently.
- *Family Support* – including the development of relationship skills for young people, and encouraging good relationships between generations.
- *Homelessness* – in particular helping homeless people back into mainstream society, including support after temporary or permanent accommodation has been secured.
- *Promoting Effectiveness in the Voluntary Sector* – supporting the training of trustees, management, staff and volunteers, and encouraging the sector to communicate and work together.
- *Prevention of Substance Misuse* – including both education and rehabilitation.
- *The Needs of Carers* – for example, information and support services, and the provision of respite care.
- *Challenging Disadvantage and Discrimination* – promoting understanding and encouraging solutions which address disadvantage, discrimination or stigma.

Social Partnership Initiative
In addition to the above objectives there is a Social Partnership Initiative which is designed to encourage real working partnerships to be set up between the voluntary sector and the relevant state departments, to stimulate the voluntary sector into seeking out opportunities to develop new services and increase knowledge and key skills. For more information on this programme please contact the foundation.

Grantmaking in 2008
Grants were distributed as per the following examples:

Donations in Jersey
Beneficiaries included: Jersey Mencap (£140,000); Brighter Futures (£84,000); Band of the Island for Jersey (£52,000); Centre Point Trust (£40,000); St Andrews Church First and Victim Support Jersey (£20,000 each); Jersey Kidney Patients (£11,000); Holidays for Heroes (£10,000); and Ace of Clubs – Jersey (£2,500).

Donations in Guernsey and Sark
Beneficiaries included: Guernsey Cheshire Home (£180,000); Mind – Guernsey (£90,000); Guernsey Youth LBG (£75,000); Dyslexia Day Centre (£35,000); Victim Support and Witness Service (£21,000); Guernsey Scout Association (£14,000); Friends of Le Murier (£10,000); Samaritans Guernsey (£7,000); and Sark School and Community Centre Trust (£1,000).

Two international grants were made to the Jubilee Sailing Trust (£40,000) and Christian Aid (£25,000). The sole general Channel Island grant went to the Council for Music in Hospitals (£10,000).

Exclusions No grants for:

- organisations which are not recognised charities
- activities which are primarily the responsibility of the Insular authorities in the Islands or some other responsible body
- activities which collect funds to give to other charities, individuals or other organisations
- animal welfare
- corporate subscription or membership of a charity
- endowment funds
- environment – conserving and protecting plants and animals, geography and scenery
- expeditions or overseas travel
- fabric appeals for places of worship
- fundraising events or activities
- hospitals and medical centres (except for projects which are clearly additional to statutory responsibilities)
- individuals, including students
- loans or business finance
- promotion of religion
- schools and colleges (except for projects that will benefit disabled students and are clearly additional to statutory responsibilities)
- sponsorship or marketing appeals
- international appeals – trustees may from time to time consider a limited number of applications from UK registered charities working abroad.

Applications Applications are only accepted on the foundation's own form. These, along with guidelines, are available from its website or from the foundation's office in Jersey and can be returned at any time. They must be returned by post as the foundation does not accept forms that have been emailed or faxed.

All applications are reviewed on a continual basis. The trustees meet three times a year to approve donations. Decision-making processes can therefore take up to four months. Applications up to £5,000 are normally assessed within one month and all applicants are informed of the outcome of their application.

Applicants are encouraged to discuss their project with one of the foundation's staff before completing an application form. This will help ensure that your project is within its criteria and that you are applying for an appropriate amount. You will also be informed of when you should hear a decision.

The London Marathon Charitable Trust

Sport, recreation and leisure

£1.4 million (2007/08)

Beneficial area London and any area where London Marathon stages an event (South Northamptonshire).

Kestrel House, 111 Heath Road, Twickenham TW1 4AH

Tel. 020 8892 6646 **Fax** 020 8892 6478

Email lmct@ffleach.co.uk

Correspondent David Golton, Secretary

Trustees Bernard Atha; Simon Cooper; Eileen Gray; Dame Mary Peters; Joyce Smith; John Graves; James Dudley Henderson Clarke; John Austin; John Disley; Sir Rodney Walker; John Bryant.

CC Number 283813

Information available Accounts were available from the Charity Commission.

The trust was formed to distribute the surplus income donated to the charity by its subsidiary, the London Marathon Limited, which organises the annual London Marathon and other such events

each year. Funds are given for much-needed recreational facilities across the city, as well as in areas where London Marathon Limited stages an event. This currently includes South Northamptonshire – Silverstone.

Projects once again include the provision of MUGAs (Multi Use Games Areas); improvements to existing children's play areas and the development of new ones; the refurbishment and expansion of existing sports and community facilities both indoor and outdoor; assistance to rowing by contributions to various organisations to provide new accommodation and boats; and the trustees have also set aside a further sum towards their commitment to the maintenance of the legacy remaining after the London 2012 Olympics. As in previous years, the grants they have made will benefit both the able bodied and the disabled and include the sports of athletics, cricket, tennis, gymnastics, sailing, football, boxing, and climbing.

Please note: the trust has no connection to the fundraising efforts of the individuals involved in the race, who raise over £40 million each year for their chosen good causes.

In 2007/08 the trust had assets of £12 million and an income of £4.7 million. Grants were made to 34 organisations totalling just under £1.4 million.

Most of the grants made during the year were in Greater London, with around half being made through borough councils. Other grants included those to: Charlton Athletic Community Trust and Downside Youth Club (£100,000 each); Royal Canoe Club (£80,000); Corbets Tey School (£60,000); Royal Albert Dock Trust (£41,000); Friends of Chestnuts Park (£20,000); Bexley Cricket Club (£15,000); Dockland Settlement (£11,000); and Charlton Park Riding for the Disabled (£6,000).

Exclusions Grants cannot be made to 'closed' clubs or schools, unless the facility is available for regular public use. No grants are made for recurring or revenue costs. Individuals are not supported.

Applications On a form available from the correspondent. Applications are welcomed from London Boroughs and independent organisations, clubs and charities. The trustees meet once a year; the closing date is usually the end of August.

The Lord's Taverners

Youth cricket, minibuses for organisations supporting young people with disabilities and sports and recreational equipment for young people with special needs

£2.4 million (2008)

Beneficial area Unrestricted, in practice, UK.

10 Buckingham Place, London SW1E 6HX

Tel. 020 7821 2828 **Fax** 020 7821 2829

Email contact@lordstaverners.org

Website www.lordstaverners.org

Correspondent Nicky Pemberton, Head of Foundation

Trustees John Ayling; John Barnes; Leo Callow; Mike Gatting; Richard Groom; John Hooper; Peter Johnson; Christopher Laing; Roger Oakley; Jonathan Rice; Martin Smith; Richard Stilgoe; Anthony Wreford; Simon Cleobury; Denise Horne; Nicholas Stewart; Robert Powell; Sally Surridge; Bob Bevan.

CC Number 306054

Information available Accounts were available at the Charity Commission. The foundation has a helpful and informative website.

The Lord's Taverners started life as a club founded in 1950 by a group of actors who used to enjoy a pint watching the cricket from the old Tavern pub at Lord's. In the early days, the money raised each year was given to the National Playing Fields Association (now the Fields in Trust), whom the Taverners still support, to fund artificial cricket pitches. Since then the Taverners has developed into both a club and a charity. There are now three fundraising groups – Lord's Taverners, Lady Taverners and Young Lord's Taverners. The trust has 28 regional groupings (all volunteer) throughout the UK and Northern Ireland. The Lady Taverners has 24 Regions.

The principal activities and charitable mission continue to be 'to give young people, particularly those with special needs, a sporting chance'.

Around 50% of the funds awarded by the trust are given to cricket projects for equipment and competitions for those young people playing the game at grass-roots level in schools and clubs. The remaining 50% is given to special needs schools or organisations, supporting their work to encourage youngsters to participate in recreational activities and a wide range of disabled sports.

The trust's mission is carried out by:

- encouraging participation in youth cricket, particularly in disadvantaged areas
- supporting recreational and sporting activities for youngsters with special needs.

The Lord's Taverners is recognised by the England and Wales Cricket Board (ECB) as the official national charity for recreational cricket. Most cricket grants are distributed in association with the ECB. An annual grant is also made to the English Schools Cricket Association.

Grantmaking

In 2008 the trust had assets of £3.1 million and an income of £5.3 million, including over £3.4 million generated through fundraising activities. Grants totalled around £2.4 million from restricted and unrestricted funds. Please note: the trust has taken the decision to change its financial year to solve long running budgeting difficulties. Consequently, the figures provided here are for the nine months from December 2007 to September 2008, not the full 12 months. The trust's new financial year wil now run from 1 October to 30 September.

The trust's charitable giving is channelled through five key funds:

- youth cricket at grassroots level
- the supply of specially adapted minibuses
- sports wheelchair sponsorship scheme
- sports and recreation facilities for young people with special needs (SRSN)
- the Brian Johnston Memorial Trust.

Youth cricket – grants totalling £808,000

Each year the trust provides grants of more than £750,000 to encourage participation in cricket by young people.

Cricket equipment bags – the trust provides hard ball equipment bags with enough items to equip a full team (at u16, u13 and u11 levels and girls 15–18) at a cost of £25. Kwik Cricket bags are provided free of charge. 926 cricket bags were distributed in the period under review.

Applications are considered from cricket clubs affiliated to a National Governing Body, individual schools or other organisations directly involved in the organisation of youth cricket and which have a genuine need for assistance. Application forms are available on the trust's website and should be submitted to your local ECB Development Manager to be countersigned. Completed applications are processed in batches approximately every 4–6 weeks, although the whole process may take around 3–4 months.

Chance to shine – the trust's aim is to give as many young people as possible a sporting chance and, therefore, it tries to distribute its limited resources as widely and as fairly as possible. In 2008, the trust made grants totalling £150,000 to the programme. Over 200,000 boys and girls were involved in schools cricket programmes across 2,000 primary and secondary schools through the Chance to shine scheme.

Please note: after lengthy discussions between the trust and Chance to shine, it has been agreed that any clubs and schools taking part in the Chance to shine programme will not be eligible to apply to either the Lord's Taverners Cricket Equipment Scheme or the Grant Aid Scheme for non-turf pitches/batting ends/nets.

Non-turf pitch grants – grants are made towards the installation of non-turf pitches, practice ends and nets. Applications will be considered from cricket clubs affiliated to a National Governing Body, individual schools or other organisations directly involved in the organisation of youth cricket and which have a genuine need for assistance. Applications will not be accepted from clubs or schools involved in the Chance to shine programme.

Awards do not normally exceed the following levels:

- non-turf match pitch – £3,000
- non-turf practice – £2,000
- outdoor nets – £1,000.

Application forms are available on the trust's websitewww.lordstaverners.org or by ringing Janine Holt on 0161 877 6643.

Citicricket – this was initially set up by Channel 4 in 2000 under the name of Street Cricket with the objective of giving children in deprived city areas the opportunity to experience the benefits of playing cricket. The Lord's Taverners began its support of the project in 2002 and the following year took over the funding of the programme. In the

summer of 2008 the project was re-launched under the name of CitiCricket to reflect the initiatives' core objectives.

The programme is now present in eight counties including Berkshire, Gloucestershire, Nottinghamshire, Warwickshire, Yorkshire, Lancashire, Leicestershire & Rutland and Oxfordshire. During 2008, 11 new clubs were formed, 56 junior sections added and 93 new coaches qualified.

Funding for other cricket projects – exceptionally, one-off grants are steered towards major projects designed primarily to assist in the furtherance of youth cricket. For further details please contact the Cricket Administrator Richard Anstey on 020 7821 2828 on either a Tuesday or Thursday.

Applications will be considered for grants toward the cost of youth cricket festivals, tournaments, regional competitions and for youth special coaching schemes. Grants towards refreshments, trophies, overseas tours, clothing or individual/team sponsorship are not available. Application forms are available on the trust's website.

The trust also funds the National Table Cricket Competition; a game which provides young people who have severe physical disabilities with an opportunity to compete in a competitive game of cricket. For further information about Table Cricket and how your school can get involved, please call 020 7821 2828.

Minibuses – 36 minibuses awarded totalling £1.2 million

The minibus scheme provides vital transport and mobility for youngsters with special needs, that is to say, those with physical, sensory or learning disabilities. Since 1975 the trust has provided over 900 minibuses.

Each minibus costs around £44,000 (depending on specifications). The trust asks that organisations make a minimum contribution of £8,000 to their minibus (dependent on specifications). This is done for the following reasons:

- it demonstrates that the organisation is able to raise funds to maintain the vehicle once it has been received it (each minibus costs about £4,000 a year in running costs)
- it is hoped that if the organisation has invested in the vehicle, it will be treated with respect
- once the minibus has been received it belongs to the organisation, provided the vehicle's use falls within the trust's guidelines.

The trust states that there is currently a waiting list of two years for all applications on new minibuses. However, there is a fast track (6-month waiting list) option for organisations able to make a contribution of £16,000 or more.

The trust provides very detailed information regarding applications for minibuses including waiting lists, self help contributions, eligibility and terms and conditions. Application forms and guidelines are available to download from the trust's website.

Sport wheelchair sponsorship scheme – 60 grants totalling £60,000
The trust assists with the purchase of manual chairs for those between 8 and 25 years of age. It will generally award funds of up to 50% of the cost of the wheelchair to those who apply through their sports club, association or school and whose application complies with the scheme guidelines. The grant will be paid directly to the wheelchair supplier. There is also a multi-sports wheelchair scheme which enables applicants to obtain a chair at a subsidised cost of £350.

Application forms are available on the trust's website.

Sport and recreation for young people with special needs – grants totalling £200,000
Since 1988 the trust has given grants towards sports & recreational equipment under a programme known as SRSN (Sport & Recreation for young people with Special Needs). Over 2,000 organisations have received help with many types of equipment from sports wheelchairs to special pool hoists, multi-sensory equipment to play ground equipment. We look to encourage those youngsters with special needs, particularly those with mobility, sensory and mental disabilities, to participate in sporting and recreational activities within a group environment. In 2008, 33 grants were made under this programme.

Grants do not normally exceed £5,000. Examples of equipment which has been funded are specially adapted sports equipment, outdoor play equipment, soft play and multi-sensory equipment, riding equipment, pool hoists, water ski equipment and sports wheelchairs.

Application forms are available to download from the trust's website.

Brian Johnston Memorial Trust – grants totalling £40,000
The Lord's Taverners is the sole corporate trustee of the Brian Johnston Memorial Trust, which raises funds to enable financial support to be given to young cricketers with potential to succeed in the game, as well as to cricket

for blind people. More information is available on the trust's website.

Exclusions
Youth cricket
The following is not normally grant aided:

- building or renovation of pavilions
- sight screens
- bowling machines
- mowers/rollers
- overseas tours
- clothing
- refreshments
- trophies.

Sport for young people with special needs
The following will not normally be considered for a grant:

- capital costs
- general grants
- running costs including salaries
- individuals (although applications will be considered for equipment to enable an individual to participate in a team/group recreational activity)
- holidays/overseas tours.

Minibuses
Homes, schools and organisations catering for young people with special needs under the age of 25 years are entitled to only one minibus per location, although applications are accepted for a replacement.

Applications The trust committee meets regularly to review applications for grant aid. All applications must be presented on the appropriate application forms and should be submitted to the secretary. Please see the 'Grantmaking' section for further information on individual programmes.

Application forms with detailed application instructions are available from the secretary or on the charity's website.

John Lyon's Charity

Children and young people in north and west London

£4.9 million (2008/09)

Beneficial area The London boroughs of Barnet, Brent, Camden, Ealing, Kensington and Chelsea, Hammersmith and Fulham, Harrow

and the Cities of London and Westminster.

45 Pont Street, London SW1X 0BX
Tel. 020 7591 3330 **Fax** 020 7589 0807
Email info@johnlyonscharity.org.uk
Website www.johnlyonscharity.org.uk
Correspondent The Grants Office
Trustee *The Governors of Harrow School.*
CC Number 237725

Information available Accounts were available from the Charity Commission. The charity also has a clear and helpful website.

This is one of the largest local educational charities in the country, supporting both formal and informal educational activities of every sort. Its budgets vary greatly from year to year for historical reasons, and from one part of its beneficial area to another. There are, however, significant cross-borough grants.

The charity began in the late 16th century when John Lyon donated his 48 acre Maida Vale farm as an endowment for the upkeep of two roads from London to Harrow and Kenton. In 1991, the charity was given discretion to use the revenue from the endowment to benefit the inhabitants of the London boroughs through which these roads passed.

The charity is an independent branch of the larger Harrow Foundation which also governs Harrow and the John Lyon schools. The charity makes over 60 substantial new grants a year, for amounts normally between £2,000 and £50,000 and there are a further 50 or so for amounts of £2,000 or less under its small grants programme. Larger awards may be for periods of up to three years.

Guidelines

The following guidelines are offered by the charity:

John Lyon's Charity gives grants to groups and organisations for the benefit of children and young adults who are resident in the London boroughs [of Harrow, Barnet, Brent, Ealing, Camden, City of London, City of Westminster, Hammersmith & Fulham and Kensington & Chelsea].

Grants from the charity are restricted to these areas and are made in accordance with certain rules covering allocation and consultation with these local authorities.

In general the charity only gives grants to groups and organisations which are registered charities or who have automatic charitable status. The charity does not give grants to individuals. In exceptional circumstances applications will be considered from organisations with charitable status pending.

We give grants to:

- support education and training, particularly for young adults
- broaden horizons and encourage an appreciation of the value of cultural diversity through activities such as dance, drama, music, creative-writing and the visual arts
- provide child-care, support for parents, help where parental support is lacking
- enhance recreation through sport, youth clubs and playschemes
- help young people achieve their full potential
- develop new opportunities for young people.

What we fund

- capital costs (for example equipment, furniture etc.)
- revenue costs (for example salaries, running costs).

Main Grants Programme

There are no strict limits on the amount of grant that may be awarded. Grants can be agreed in principle for up to three years but are subject to monitoring conditions and the release of each tranche is dependent on the specific approval of the trustee.

In exceptional circumstances some fixed-term grants may be eligible for renewal depending on records of achievements, and the availability of funds.

Small Grants Programme

The Small Grants Programme welcomes 'one off' grant requests of up to £5,000 with no repeat funding. Requests for over £2,000 will be subject to the completion of a short application form. Small grants are considered up to six times a year.

The John Lyon Access to the Arts Fund

The John Lyon Access to the Arts Fund is open to all state primary schools in the charity's nine boroughs: Barnet, Brent, Camden, Ealing, Hammersmith & Fulham, Harrow, Kensington & Chelsea, Westminster and the City of London.

Grants awarded under this programme are available to assist primary schools in accessing and taking part in arts activities at the many high class institutions in London. Activities could include visits to the theatre, a musical experience or to a museum or art gallery. To be eligible the school must provide a clear rationale for the activity, explain how it will add value to the school experience and demonstrate an existing commitment to the arts.

There is no restriction on which institution you can visit, but the activity must enhance the current activities of the class or year group and be the kind of experience that the children do not normally have access to. Suggestions for suitable requests include:

- travel costs (including coach costs) to venues within London
- match funding for ticket prices (if the school is paying for one class to participate in an activity the charity could be asked to support the costs of enabling a second class to also take part
- a contribution towards the costs of participating in a venue-based education programme.

Successful applications must include the following:

- evidence that this activity is in addition to, and not a replacement of, existing annual arts activities
- a clear rationale for taking part in the activity
- details of how it will add value to the children's school experience.

Grantmaking in 2008/09

In 2008/09 the charity had assets of £169.9 million and an income of £5.9 million. Grants were made during the year totalling £4.9 million, which included grants committed in previous years. Grants were broken down by programme area as follows:

Category	Value
Schools, Education & Training	£1,730,000
Arts in Education	£1,170,000
Youth Clubs & Youth Initiatives	£681,000
Child Care & Support for Families	£557,500
Special Needs	£314,000
Sport	£279,000
Counselling	£152,500
Other	£5,000

The charity also gives a helpful breakdown of its grants by the purpose for which they were made:

Purpose	Value
Project support	£1,960,000
Running costs	£1,300,000
Salaries	£598,000
Buildings and refurbishment	£513,000
Bursaries and scholarships	£490,000
Equipment	£19,000
Other	£5,000

The charity's website lists the beneficiaries of the largest 20 grants during the year. They were: London Diocesan Board for Schools (£250,000); Harrow School Bursaries (£181,600); The John Lyon School Bursaries (£162,000); National Theatre (£100,000); Brent Play Association (£90,000); Excellence in Teaching & Learning and Phoenix Cinema (£70,000 each); Harrow Club W10 (£54,000); West London Sports Trust, NIACE, Godolphin & Latymer School, IntoUniversity, Royal Court Young Writers Programme, Tavistock & Portman NHS Foundation Trust, H&F Partnership Against Crime, Tate Britain and Endeavour Training (£50,000 each); Harrow School Apprenticeships Programme (£48,000); Church Street Neighbourhood Management (£42,500); and English Chamber Orchestra Charitable Trust (£40,000).

Exclusions Grants are restricted to the London boroughs of Harrow, Barnet, Brent, Ealing, Camden, City of London, City of Westminster, Hammersmith & Fulham and Kensington & Chelsea.

Grants are not made:

- to individuals
- for research, unless it is action research designed to lead directly to the advancement of practical activities in the community
- for feasibility studies
- for medical care and resources
- in response to general charitable appeals, unless they can be shown to be of specific benefit to children and young people in one or more of the geographical areas listed
- as direct replacements for the withdrawal of funds by statutory authorities for activities which are primarily the responsibility of central or local government
- to umbrella organisations to distribute to projects which are already in receipt of funds from the charity
- for the promotion of religion or politics
- for telephone helplines
- as core funding for national charities
- for advice and information services
- to housing associations.

Applications The charity's main and small grants programmes have a two stage application process:

Stage One – Initial Proposal
Please write to the Grants Office with the following information:

- a summary of the main purpose of the project
- details of the overall amount requested
- the timescale of your project
- some indication of how funds from the charity would be allocated.

Stage Two – Application Form
If your Initial Proposal is assessed positively, you will be advised whether you will need to complete an application form. Forms are required for all applications to the Main Grants Programme and for requests of over £2,000 to the Small Grants Programme.

If you qualify for Stage Two you will be advised by your Grants Officer when your application form must be returned.

Applications by fax or email will not be accepted.

Further details and a guide to writing a good proposal letter are available via the charity's website.

The John Lyon's Access to the Arts Fund

The John Lyon Access to the Arts Fund has a **single stage** application process and requests are made by application form. Applications can be made at any time.

An application form is available via the charity's website.

The M K Charitable Trust (formerly the Mendel Kaufman Charitable Trust)

Orthodox Jewish charities

£589,000 (2007/08)

Beneficial area Unrestricted, in practice mainly UK.

c/o Cohen Arnold and Co., 1075 Finchley Road, London NW11 0PU

Tel. 020 8731 0777

Correspondent Simon Kaufman, Trustee

Trustees *Z M Kaufman; S Kaufman; A Piller; D Katz.*

CC Number 260439

Information available Accounts were available at the Charity Commission but without a list of grants.

This trust was established in 1966 for general charitable purposes and applies its income for the provision and distribution of grants and donations to Orthodox Jewish charities. The trust's income is derived from investments and from donations from the trustees and associates.

In 2007/08 it had assets of £5.9 million and an income of £776,000. Grants were made totalling £589,000. 'Grants totalling £211,000 were made during the

year to six charities with which this charity has some trustees in common.'

Unfortunately, no further information was available regarding the trust's grant-making activities.

Applications In writing to the correspondent. The trust accepts applications for grants from representatives of Orthodox Jewish charities, which are reviewed by the trustees on a regular basis.

The Madeline Mabey Trust

Medical research, children's welfare and education

£452,000 (2007/08)

Beneficial area UK and overseas.

Mabey House, Floral Mile, Twyford, Reading RG10 9SQ

Tel. 0118 940 3921 **Fax** 0118 940 3675

Correspondent Joanna Singeisen, Trustee

Trustees *Alan G Daliday; Bridget A Nelson; Joanna L Singeisen.*

CC Number 326450

Information available Accounts were on file at the Charity Commission, but without a list of grants.

The 2007/08 trustees report states:

The principal areas of benefit continue to be the education and welfare of children both in the UK and overseas, and medical research into the causes of and cures for life threatening illnesses. The trust favours identifying organisations itself, although it is willing to consider applications for grants. The intention is to fund organisations rather than individuals directly.

During the year the trust had assets of nearly £570,000 and an income of £877,000 (up following the previous year's fall). Grants totalling £452,000 were made to 99 organisations. Regrettably, as in previous years, a list of beneficiaries was not included with the accounts.

Exclusions No grants to individuals.

Applications In writing to the correspondent. Please note: unsuccessful applications are not acknowledged.

The R S Macdonald Charitable Trust

Visual impairment, cerebral palsy, children and animal welfare

£716,500 (2008/09)

Beneficial area Scotland.

21 Rutland Square, Edinburgh EH1 2BB

Tel. 0131 228 4681

Email secretary@rsmacdonald.com

Website www.rsmacdonald.com

Correspondent Richard K Austin, Secretary

Trustees *Richard Sweetman, Chair; Richard K Austin; Donald Bain; Fiona Patrick; John Rafferty.*

SC Number SC012710

Information available Annual report and accounts were provided by the trust. Information was also taken from the trust's website.

Established in 1978, this is the trust of the late R S MacDonald, whose family founded the famous whisky distiller Glenmorangie plc in 1893. The value of the trust has increased substantially due to the realisation of shares in the company, which were sold in 2005/06 to LVMH (Moët Hennessy Louis Vuitton), the proceeds of which have now been reinvested.

General

The trust supports charities concerned with the following:

- neurological conditions
- visual impairment
- child welfare
- animal welfare.

Six organisations are mentioned in the trust deed and these are often, but not always, supported. The trust is prepared to give very large grants to enable organisations to carry out major projects or develop ideas.

In 2008/09 the trust had assets of £41.9 million and an income of almost £1.8 million. Grants were made during the year totalling £716,500.

Beneficiaries included: Capability Scotland (£120,000 in total), for various projects, with further commitments up to 2010/11; Children 1st (£100,000 in total), for work supporting survivors of abuse at various locations across

Scotland; Rotary Residential & Care Centres (£50,000), towards refurbishing accommodation; Sense Scotland (£30,000); Tommy's, the Baby Charity (£25,000); RNIB Scotland (£20,000); Scottish Adoption Association (£15,000); Garvald (£8,000); and the Royal Blind Society (£2,000).

Exclusions Grants are not given to non-registered charities or individuals, or for projects which have already started or been completed.

Applications In writing to the correspondent, including a copy of the latest audited accounts and constituting documents. Applications will normally be considered by the trustees at meetings in May and November and need to be received no later than 31 March and 30 September, respectively, to be considered at these meetings.

The level of award made will vary according to the nature of the project for which funding is sought, but will not normally exceed £40,000. The average award granted is likely to be less than £20,000.

The trustees will consider applications for funding over periods of up to three years. They will also consider applications both for revenue and capital funding.

Applicants will be informed of the trustees' decision with regard to their application within three weeks of the trustees' meeting at which their application has been considered.

The Mackintosh Foundation

Mainly theatre and the performing arts, also children and education, medicine, homelessness, community projects, the environment, refugees and other charitable purposes

£411,000 (2008/09)
Beneficial area Worldwide. In practice, mainly UK.

1 Bedford Square, London WC1B 3RB
Tel. 020 7637 8866 **Fax** 020 7436 2683
Email info@camack.co.uk

Correspondent Nicholas Mackintosh, Appeals Director
Trustees *Sir Cameron Mackintosh, Chair; Nicholas Mackintosh; Nicholas Allott; D Michael Rose; Patricia Macnaughton; Alain Boublil; Robert Noble.*
CC Number 327751
Information available Accounts were available from the Charity Commission.

The foundation was established in 1998 by the settlor, Sir Cameron Mackintosh, to advance education in the arts, particularly the performing arts of music and drama; to establish and maintain scholarships, bursaries and awards for proficiency in drama, music or ancillary performing arts; and to relieve poverty, hardship and distress.

The foundation has endowed Oxford University at a cost of well over £1 million with a fund known as *The Cameron Mackintosh Fund for Contemporary Theatre*, part of which has been used to set up a Visiting Professorship of Contemporary Theatre at the university. It also provided a fund of £1 million over a period of 10 years, to the Royal National Theatre, for revivals of classical stage musical productions under the auspices of the RNT.

Partnership funding of £500,000 over five years, has been provided by the foundation in respect of theatres and other organisations under the Art Council's *Arts for Everyone* scheme.

The foundation has also provided financial support to a number of projects in the United States including a major grant of $1.5 million over 5 years to The Alliance of New American Musicals to support the creation and production of new plays by American writers and artists.

In 2008/09 the foundation had assets of £10.3 million and an income of around £100,000. Grants were made totalling £411,000.

The foundation classifies its grants in the following way:

- children and education
- community projects
- environment
- homelessness
- medical
- theatre and performing arts
  - theatre buildings
  - theatre company development
  - promotion of new theatrical and musical works
  - theatre related pastoral care
  - theatrical training and education.

The main beneficiaries during the year were: Great Ormond Street Hospital (£45,000); Highland Council (£26,000); Royal Marsden Cancer Campaign (£20,000); Theatre Investment Fund (£15,000); Royal & Derngate Theatre (£12,000); Macmillan Cancer Support (£10,500); Disasters Emergency Committee (£10,000); Tricycle Theatre Company (£7,500); Maggies' Centres (£6,300); and Motivation (£5,800).

Exclusions Religious or political activities are not supported. Apart from the foundation's drama award and some exceptions, applications from individuals are discouraged.

Applications In writing to the correspondent outlining details of the organisation, details of the project for which funding is required and a breakdown of the costs involved. Supporting documentation should be kept to a minimum and a stamped, addressed envelope enclosed if materials are to be returned. The trustees meet in May and October in plenary session, but a grants committee meets weekly to consider grants of up to £10,000. The foundation responds to all applications in writing and the process normally takes between 4–6 weeks.

The MacRobert Trust

General

£735,000 (2007/08)
Beneficial area UK, mainly Scotland.

Cromar, Tarland, Aboyne, Aberdeenshire AB34 4UD
Tel. 01339 881444
Website www.themacroberttrust.org.uk
Correspondent Air Comm. R W Joseph, Administrator
Trustees *W G Morrison, Chair; Mrs C J Cuthbert;; Group Capt. D A Needham; J Swan; H Woodd; C Crole; Keith Davis; C W Pagan; J D Fowlie; H B Woodd.*
SC Number SC031346
Information available Annual report and accounts were available from the trust's website.

Originally several trusts established by Lady MacRobert in memory of her three sons who were all killed as aviators, the eldest in a civil air accident in 1938 and the middle and youngest as officer pilots

243

in the Royal Air Force on operational sorties in 1941.

This trust was established on 6 April 2001 when the assets of the no longer operating MacRobert Trusts, a collection of four charitable trusts and two holding companies were merged into the new, single MacRobert Trust. The merging of these trusts has led to a decrease in management and administration cost and a general increase in grantmaking.

The trust has assets comprising of Douneside House (a holiday country house for serving and retired officers of the armed forces and their families) and an estate of 1,700 acres of woodland and 5,300 acres of farmland and associated residential properties let by the trust. The surplus income generated from these assets, following management and administration costs, is donated in grants.

Guidelines

The following guidelines are taken from the trust's website:

Lady MacRobert recognised that new occasions teach new duties and therefore the new trust deed gives wide discretionary powers to the trustees. The trust is reactive so, with very few exceptions, grants are made only in response to applications made through the correct channels.

The trustees reconsider their policy and practice of grant giving every five years. The beneficial area is United Kingdom-wide but preference is given to organisations in Scotland. Grants are normally made only to a recognised Scottish Charity or a recognised charity outside Scotland.

Trust's Categories of Interest
Currently, the major categories under which the trustees consider support are:

- science and technology
- young people
- services and sea
- ex-servicemen's and ex-servicewomen's hospitals and homes
- education
- disability
- community welfare.

The minor categories are:

- agriculture and horticulture
- arts and music
- medical care
- Tarland and Deeside.

The trustees look for clear, realistic and attainable aims. Grants vary but most lie between £5,000 and £10,000. Occasionally the trustees make a recurring grant of up to three years.

The trustees recognise the need to assist voluntary organisations which need funds to complement those already received from central government and local authority sources. However, this is not to say that the trust makes a grant where statutory bodies fail to provide.

The trustees are prepared to make core/ revenue grants where appropriate but favour projects.

The trustees recognise that, at present, experiment and innovation are much more difficult to fund and the trust's role in funding them is, therefore, the more significant.

Grantmaking in 2007/08

In 2007/08 the trust had assets of £56.8 million and an income of £2.5 million. During the year the trust made grants totalling £735,000, broken down as follows:

Category	No. of grants	Amount
Education	10	£159,500
Disability	17	£106,300
Young people	18	£92,000
Science and technology	6	£79,500
Services and sea	8	£80,300
Community welfare	12	£68,000
Arts and music	10	£46,000
Medical care	4	£42,000
Agriculture and horticulture	6	£30,000
Tarland and Deeside	12	£22,000

Beneficiaries across all categories included: National Library of Scotland (£100,000); Robert Gordon University (£47,000); Poppyscotland (£35,000); Marie Curie Cancer Care (£25,500); Association for Children's Palliative Care (£20,000); Scottish Ballet (£14,000); Centre for Science Outreach University of Durham (£10,000); Abernethy Trust (£8,000); Art in Healthcare and HIV Support Centre (£5,000 each); Caring for Life (£4,000); and Scottish Education & Action for Development (£2,000).

Exclusions Grants are not normally provided for:

- religious organisations (but attention will be given to youth/community services provided by them, or projects of general benefit to the whole community)
- organisations based outside the United Kingdom
- individuals
- endowment or memorial funds
- general appeals or mailshots
- conservation
- work with animals
- political organisations
- student bodies as opposed to universities
- fee-paying schools, apart from an Educational Grants Scheme for children who are at, or who need to attend, a Scottish independent

secondary school and for which a grant application is made through the Head Teacher.

- expeditions, except those made under the auspices of recognised bodies such as the British Schools Exploring Society (BSES)
- community and village halls other than those local to Tarland and Deeside
- retrospective grants
- departments within a university, unless the appeal gains the support of, and is channelled through, the principal.

Applications The application form and full guidelines can be downloaded from the trust's website, although applications must be posted.

The trustees meet to consider applications twice a year, in March and October. To be considered, applications must be received for the March meeting by 31 October previously and for the October meeting by 31 May previously.

Applicants are informed of the trustees' decision, and if successful, payments are made immediately after each meeting.

The Manifold Charitable Trust

Education, historic buildings, environmental conservation and general

£1.6 million (2007)

Beneficial area UK.

Studio Cottage, Windsor Great Park, Windsor SL4 2HP

Email helen.niven@cumberlandlodge.ac. uk

Correspondent Helen Niven

Trustee *Manifold Trustee Company Limited.*

CC Number 229501

Information available Accounts were available from the Charity Commission.

This trust was established in 1962 for general charitable purposes. It had previously focused much attention on the preservation of churches, however following the death in 2007 of its founder, Sir John Smith, the trust is now allocating most of its grants for educational purposes. The trust still makes grants to the Historic Churches Preservation Trust for onward distribution to churches; however it would seem that the amount has been reduced on previous years.

As noted in the past, the trust continues to make grants in excess of its income, preferring to 'meet the present needs of other charities rather than reserve money for the future'.

In 2007 the trust had assets of £11.7 million and an income of £707,000. During the year there were 124 grants made totalling over £1.6 million, which included an exceptional donation of £1 million to New College Oxford.

Grants were apportioned roughly as follows:

Category	%
Education, research and the arts	70
Repairs to churches and their contents	23
Other causes	7

Almost half of these grants made were of £1,000 or less, and only 11% were for £10,000 by number.

Beneficiaries included: Historic Churches Preservation Trust (£140,000 in total); Eton College (£78,000); Thames Hospice Care (£50,000); Imperial College (£15,000); Berkeley Castle Charitable Trust and Maidenhead Heritage Trust (£10,000 each); Berkshire Medical Heritage Centre (£7,500); Gislingham PCC (£6,000); Household Cavalry Museum Trust (£5,000); Brompton Ralph PCC (£4,500); Morrab Library (£2,500); and Richmond Building Preservation Society, Askham PCC and Westray Heritage Trust (£1,000 each).

Exclusions Applications are not considered for improvements to churches as this is covered by a block grant to the Historic Churches Preservation Trust. The trust regrets that it does not give grants to individuals for any purpose.

Applications The trust has no full-time staff, therefore general enquiries and applications for grants should be made in writing only, by post or by fax and not by telephone. The trust does not issue application forms. Applications should be made to the correspondent in writing and should:

- state how much money it is hoped to raise
- if the appeal is for a specific project state also (a) how much it will cost (b) how much of this cost will come from the applicant charity's existing funds (c) how much has already been received or promised from other sources and (d) how much is therefore still being sought
- list sources of funds to which application has been or is intended to

be made (for example local authorities, or quasi-governmental sources, such as the national lottery)
- if the project involves conservation of a building, send a photograph of it and a note (or pamphlet) about its history
- send a copy of the charity's latest income and expenditure account and balance sheet.

Applications are considered twice a month, and a reply is sent to most applicants (whether successful or not) who have written a letter rather than sent a circular.

The Manoukian Charitable Foundation

Social welfare, education, medical, the arts and 'Armenian matters'

£1.6 million (2008)
Beneficial area Worldwide.

c/o Berwin Leighton Paisners, Adelaide House, London Bridge, London EC4R 9HA

Correspondent The Trustees

Trustees *Mrs Tamar Manoukian; Anthony Bunker; Steven Press; Dr Armen Sarkissian.*

CC Number 1084065

Information available Accounts were available from the Charity Commission.

Set up in 2000, the foundation has received donations from sources associated with the Manoukian family.

The objects of the charity are the promotion of general charitable purposes; the trustees give particular emphasis to projects with medical, educational or cultural aspects and those that relate to Armenian matters, although they consider applications for other charitable purposes.

Applications are considered on the basis of whether they meet the general aims of the foundation and the nature of the project concerned. The foundation will consider providing assistance to projects that may be partly funded by others if this will enable the project to proceed. The trustees have tended to give greater consideration to educational and cultural projects as well as those which

are intended to relieve poverty, illness and suffering.

In 2008 the foundation had an income of £2.4 million almost entirely from donations. Grants totalled £1.6 million. The sum of £990,000 was carried forward at year end. Donations were broken down into the following categories:

Category	Value
Medical research	£881,000
Social services and relief	£515,000
Education and training	£124,000
Culture and the arts	£10,000
Other	£11,000

Beneficiaries included:

Medical research and care (3 grants)
Elton John AIDS Foundation (£815,000); Chronic Care Centre (£59,000); and CLIC Sargent Cancer care (£7,500).

Social services and relief (8 grants)
Human Rights Watch (£103,000); Mission Enfance (£46,000); Give a Child a Toy – Lebanon (£35,000); NSPCC (£10,000); Chain of Hope – Mozambique (£5,000); Havens Christian Hospice (£2,000); and Westminster PHAB (£500).

Education and training (3 grants)
Eurasia Program – Cambridge University (£108,000); Harvard College – Armenia educational programme (£13,000); and Prince's Foundation for Children and the Arts (£2,500).

Culture and the arts (1 grant)
English National Ballet School (£10,000).

Religion (1 grant)
Out Lady of Lebanon Church (£3,000).

Applications 'Requests for grants are received from the general public and charitable and other organisations through their knowledge of the activities of the foundation and through personal contacts of the settlor and the trustees.' The trustees meet at least once per year.

Marshall's Charity

Parsonage and church improvements

£1 million (2008)
Beneficial area England and Wales with preference for Kent, Surrey, Lincolnshire and Southwark.

Marshall House, 66 Newcomen Street, London SE1 1YT

Tel. 020 7407 2979 **Fax** 020 7403 3969

Email grantoffice@marshalls.org.uk

Website www.marshalls.org.uk

Correspondent Richard Goatcher, Clerk to the Trustees

Trustees *Anthea Nicholson; Colin Bird; David Lang; Michael Dudding; Colin Stenning; Stephen Clark; Gina Isaac; Bill Eason; Jeremy Hammant; John Heawood; Surbhi Malhotra; Revd Jonathan Rust; Ven Christine Hardman; Tony Guthrie; Lesley Bosman; John Murray.*

CC Number 206780

Information available Accounts were on file at the Charity Commission. The trust has a useful and up-to-date website.

The charity supports parsonage buildings throughout England and Wales, helps with the upkeep of Anglican churches in Kent, Surrey and Lincolnshire (as the counties were defined in 1855), supports the parish of Christ Church, Southwark and makes grants for education to Marshall's Educational Foundation. Special consideration is given to parishes in urban priority areas. Further information on the types of grant available can be found on the charity's website.

Grants to churches are usually between £3,000 and £5,000, though they can be higher. The majority of grants to parsonages range from £1,000 to £4,000.

In 2008 the charity had assets of £16 million which produced an income of £1.4 million. Grants were made totalling £1 million, broken down as follows:

- support for parsonages – £680,000
- repair of churches – £254,000
- Christ Church, Southwark – £64,000
- Marshall's Educational Foundation – £38,000.

Beneficiaries of church restoration grants included: Lincolnshire Old Churches Trust and Christ Church – Camberwell (£6,000 each); All Saints – Maidstone, Holy Trinity – Raithby and St Paul – Spalding (£5,000 each); All Saints – Bigby (£4,500); St Mary – Hainton (£3,500); Holy Trinity – Beckenham (£2,500); St Peter – Streatham (£1,000); and Friends of Kent Churches (£550).

Exclusions No grants to churches outside the counties of Kent, Surrey and Lincolnshire, as defined in 1855. No church funding for the following:

- cost of church halls and meeting rooms
- kitchens
- decorations, unless they form part of qualifying repair or improvement work

- furniture and fittings
- work to bells, brasses or clocks
- private chapels or monuments
- stained glass, although work to repair ferraments can be supported
- grounds, boundary walls and fences
- external lighting.

Applications Applicants should write a letter or send an email to the correspondent, giving the name and location of the Church and a brief (30 – 40 words maximum) description of the proposed work. If appropriate the charity will then send out an application form. Applications for parsonage grants should be made by the relevant Diocesan Parsonage Board. Trustees usually meet in January, April, July and October.

Mayfair Charities Ltd

Orthodox Judaism

£7.8 million (2007/08)

Beneficial area UK and overseas.

Freshwater House, 158–162 Shaftesbury Avenue, London WC2H 8HR

Tel. 020 7836 1555

Email mark.jenner@highdorn.co.uk

Correspondent Mark Jenner, Secretary

Trustees *B S E Freshwater, Chair; D Davis; S I Freshwater.*

CC Number 255281

Information available Accounts were available from the Charity Commission.

Established in 1968, the trust makes grants to Orthodox Jewish colleges and institutions for the advancement of religion and education and to other organisations for the relief of poverty, in the UK and Israel. It largely appears to be a vehicle for the philanthropic activities of property investor B S E Freshwater, who is closely connected with the management of some of the major beneficiary organisations.

In recent years, the trustees have decided to support certain major projects which, during the year under review and subsequently, have received substantial financial grants from the company. At the present time the trustees have entered into commitments for the financial support of colleges and institutions which would absorb approximately £7 million over the next five years.

This statement has been in the trust's accounts for several years, presumably

indicating that major commitments are made each year on a rolling basis.

In 2007/08 the trust had assets of £69.2 million and an income of £4.4 million. Grants were made to over 600 organisations totalling £7.8 million, which included £4.8 million for the advancement of religion and education and £3 million for the relief of poverty.

There are no set amounts for sizes of grants – several substantial donations were made during the year and many organisations received small grants for a little as a few hundred pounds.

The major beneficiaries during the year, some of whom probably represent the major commitments made by the trust for future years, were: SOFT (£1.18 million); Beth Jacob Grammar School For Girls Ltd (£870,000); Merkaz Lechinuch Torani (£683,000); Ohr Akiva Institute (£251,000); Kollel Chibas Yerushalayim (£248,000); Mesivta Letzeirim (£200,000); Chevras Maoz Ladal (£198,000); Congregation Ichud Chasidim (£159,500); Chaye Olam Institute (£129,000); United Talmudical Association (£110,000); and Talmud Torah Zichron Gavriel (£100,000).

Other beneficiaries included: Friends of Bobov (£75,000); Regent Charities Ltd (£50,000); Comet Charities Ltd (£42,500); Woodstock Sinclair Trust (£24,000); Yesodei Hatorah School (£20,000); Beis Aharon Trust (£15,000); Ezer Mikodesh Foundation (£12,000); Gateshead Jewish Teachers Training College (£8,000); Edgware Foundation (£6,000); Heritage House (£5,000); Kiryat Sanz Jerusalem (£2,500); and PAL Charitable Trust (£1,000).

Applications In writing to the correspondent.

The Medlock Charitable Trust

Education, health and welfare

£1.7 million (2007/08)

Beneficial area Overwhelmingly the City of Bath, and Boston in Lincolnshire.

St George's Lodge, 33 Oldfield Road, Bath BA2 3ND

Tel. 01225 428221 **Fax** 01225 789262

Correspondent Leonard Medlock, Trustee

Trustees *Leonard Medlock; Jacqueline Medlock; David Medlock; Peter Carr.*

CC Number 326927

Information available Accounts were available from the Charity Commission.

The trust describes its grantmaking policy as follows:

The trustees have identified the City of Bath and the borough of Boston as the principal but not exclusive areas in which the charity is and will be proactive. These areas have been specifically chosen as the founder of the charity has strong connections with the City of Bath, the home of the charity, and has family connections of long standing with the borough of Boston.

To date, the charity has supported and funded a number of projects in these areas by making substantial grants. These grants have been made to fund projects in the areas of education, medicine, research and social services all for the benefit of the local community. During the year, the trustees also receive many applications for assistance from many diverse areas in the United Kingdom. These are all considered sympathetically.

In 2007/08 the trust had assets of £27 million and an income of £1.3 million. Grants were made to 196 organisations totalling £1.7 million.

The largest grant during the year was made to the Boshier-Hinton Foundation, which received £312,000. Other major grants went to the Quartet Community Foundation (£75,000) and the Butterfly Hospice Trust (£70,000).

Beneficiaries of smaller grants included: Covidien UK Ltd (£52,000); Holbourne Museum (£50,000); Beach Cliff School (£30,000); Somerset 500 Club (£25,000); Karnataka Parents Association (£20,000); Wiltshire Music Centre Trust (£10,000); Off the Record (£7,000); Yorkshire Eye Research (£2,000); NSPCC (£1,000); and Banes Credit Union (£500).

Exclusions No grants to individuals or students.

Applications In writing to the correspondent.

Mercaz Torah Vechesed Limited

Orthodox Jewish

£1.3 million to organisations and individuals (2007/08)

Beneficial area Worldwide.

28 Braydon Road, London N16 6QB

Tel. 020 8880 5366

Correspondent Joseph Ostreicher, Secretary

Trustees *Jacob Moishe Grosskopf; Joseph Ostreicher; Mordche David Rand.*

CC Number 1109212

Information available Accounts were on file on the Charity Commission, without a list of grants.

The charity was formed for the advancement of the orthodox Jewish faith, orthodox Jewish religious education, and the relief of poverty and infirmity amongst members of the orthodox Jewish community.

Set up in 2005, in 2007/08 the charity had an income of £1.3 million from donations and made grants also totalling £1.3 million. Assets stood at £42,000. Grants are made to organisations and individuals. There were no details of donations included with the accounts filed at the Charity Commission.

Applications In writing to the correspondent.

The Mercers' Charitable Foundation

General welfare, older people, conservation, arts, Christian faith activities and educational institutions

£5 million (2008/09)

Beneficial area UK; strong preference for London and the West Midlands. The foundation is keen to stress that it currently has geographical restrictions on its welfare and educational grant making. Please see individual programme information for details.

Mercers' Hall, Ironmonger Lane, London EC2V 8HE

Tel. 020 7726 4991 **Fax** 020 7600 1158

Email mail@mercers.co.uk

Website www.mercers.co.uk

Correspondent The Clerk

Trustees *First Mercer Trustee Limited; Second Mercer Trustee Limited*

CC Number 326340

Information available Accounts were available from the Charity Commission.

The Mercers' Company has several trusts, the main one being the Mercers' Charitable Foundation. The foundation was established in 1983 to make grants and donations for the benefit of a wide range of charitable purposes including welfare, education, the arts, heritage and religion. Its primary source of income is gift aid donations from the Mercers' Company. On 1st August 2008 the Mercers' Company Educational Trust Fund transferred all of its assets and liabilities to the foundation.

The foundation seeks to support a range of organisations with the common theme of providing effective services and facilities to those in need and to strengthen communities. Whist continuing to support small grassroots organisations, the foundation has developed relationships with some much larger organisations, complementing work that is funded by statutory bodies.

The foundation runs a number of responsive grant-making programmes, each with agreed guidelines and each year identifies a small number of organisations working within the key programme areas who are then invited to submit proposals for the larger grants. In most cases the work takes place in London or the West Midlands. These proposals are subject to detailed scrutiny by the specialist committees and the executive staff. The grant-making committees each meet a minimum of four times a year to discuss applications and recommend grants to the trustees.

The company has several categories of grantmaking. The following descriptions of funding categories are taken from guidance available on the foundation's website. The principle areas of support are:

General Welfare

The company seeks to support disadvantaged and marginalised individuals, particularly those living in Greater London and known areas of deprivation in the south east of England.

247

The company does this by awarding grants to organisations that work in the following fields:

- reducing offending
- social welfare
- special needs
- youth work
- care for older people.

Education

The company seeks to improve the availability and quality of educational opportunities for children and young adults, especially in London and in particular areas of the West Midlands – Walsall, Sandwell and Telford – where the Company has established City Academies in recent years. The company's funding policy includes a strong emphasis on the State maintained sector, by the provision of:

- Advice and guidance
- Dissemination of good practice
- Financial help.

Support for the Christian faith

We encourage appeals within the following category from a wide variety of sources under the general heading 'advancement of religion'. These are not exclusively from Anglican organisations, but we discourage appeals from overseas unless there is a UK charitable arm. Appeals may be broadly grouped into those relating to buildings and those connected with people; we look particularly sympathetically on the latter.

Buildings

We aim to help keep churches alive, but consider only appeals from the following areas.

- Churches in the City of London.
- Churches with a Mercer connection – historic or a present Mercer closely involved.
- Cathedrals, as their funding sources are often limited.
- Grade I and Grade II* churches outside these criteria and high-profile historic memorabilia may be considered by the Heritage and Arts Committee if of particular importance.

People

We aim to contribute to deepening understanding and acceptance of the Christian religion, and to developing its relationships between its denominations and with other world faiths. We seek appeals that:

- develop understanding and tolerance between denominations and faiths
- help young people to learn about the Christian faith and develop their spiritual lives
- support clergy and help them to develop their outreach work
- provide spiritual training for clergy and lay people

- provide respite, recuperation and spiritual nourishment for clergy and their families
- improve the effectiveness of parish administration through support for core costs for key people.

Heritage and the arts

Heritage appeals are considered within the following categories:

- material or fabric conservation and refurbishment
- library/archive conservation
- wildlife/environment conservation.

In 2008/09 the foundation had assets of £8 million and an income of £6.5 million. Grants listed in the accounts totalled £5 million and were broken down as follows:

Education – £1.8 million

Beneficiaries included: Teach First (£130,000); Royal Ballet School (£100,000); Thomas Telford School (£38,000); Barbican Centre (£33,000); British Association for the Advancement of Science (£15,000); and London Symphony Orchestra, Open House and Volunteer Reading Help (£10,000 each).

Social, medical, young people and community welfare – £1.2 million

Beneficiaries included: Federation of London Youth Clubs (£100,000); Shelter (£50,000); Autism Speaks, Body and Soul, Children's Trust and Treehouse Trust (£25,000); and YMCA – England, Canonbury Community Baptist Church, Connection at St Marin's and Family Welfare Association (£10,000 each).

Care for older people – £927,000

Beneficiaries included: Earl of Northampton's Charity (£880,000); and Almshouse Association and Field Lane Foundation (£10,000 each).

Heritage and the arts – £400,000

Beneficiaries included: Victoria and Albert Museum (£20,000); Watts Gallery (£19,000); the Pilgrim Trust (£15,000); and Aldeburgh Productions, British Museum, Royal College of Art, the Royal Philharmonic Society and Wilton's Music Hall (£10,000).

Church – £360,000

Beneficiaries included: Christianity and Culture (St John's College) (£36,000); Hexham Abbey (£20,000); Mildmay Mission Hospital and Village Church for Village Life £10,000 each).

Other – £316,000

Beneficiaries included Gresham College (£291,000).

Exclusions These should be read alongside the specific exclusions for the particular category into which an application falls.

- animal welfare charities
- endowment appeals
- work overseas (unless there is a significant relationship with the organisation)
- projects that are primarily political
- activities that are the responsibility of the local, health or education authority or other similar body
- activities that have already taken place
- other grant-making trusts
- sponsorship or marketing appeals
- fundraising events
- loans or business finance
- running costs such as rent and service charges.

The foundation also states:

We can not support capital projects that are submitted by public health or education authorities. Whilst we normally consider a range of capital projects from charities, in the current economic climate we have decided to concentrate our support on maintaining service delivery. Our capital support is restricted to appeals that are within the **last 20% of their target** and for which support in the region of £5,000-£20,000 will make a difference, are **not awaiting an outstanding lottery decision** and include a **realistic business plan** showing how the building will be used and future revenue predictions.

Applications Applications can be made online via the foundation's website. Grants officers are happy to give advice by telephone or email.

Community Foundation for Merseyside

Community development, regeneration and general

£3.5 million (2008/09)

Beneficial area Merseyside, Halton and Lancashire.

c/o Alliance and Leicester, Bridle Road, Bootle, Merseyside, GIR OAA

Tel. 0151 966 4604 **Fax** 0151 966 3384

Email info@cfmerseyside.org.uk

Website www.cfmerseyside.org.uk

Correspondent Cathy Elliott, Chief Executive

CC Number 1068887

Information available Accounts were available at the Charity Commission, without a list of beneficiaries.

The Community Foundation for Merseyside connects donors with local causes in Merseyside. By providing grants to local communities, the foundation helps them focus on building a better stronger Merseyside for future generations.

At present the foundation's main function of distributing grants to local communities is supported by distinct funds, confined to specific objectives within time-limited periods. However, its long-term vision is to be sustainable; to be the biggest funder of the voluntary sector on Merseyside and to have substantial endowment – enabling the foundation to utilise unrestricted funds in creative grantmaking.

Their aim over the coming years is to address long-term sustainability by engaging with high-value donors to build endowment, while developing and cementing their position as a community leader within the voluntary sector.

By increasing public awareness of their work, they will work with and advise donors who are passionate about their communities to establish endowment funds that will make a lasting impact on local lives.

In 2008/09 the foundation had assets of £2 million and an income of £4.2 million. During the year grants were made to 797 organisations totalling over £3.5 million.

Grant Programmes 2009/10

The foundation delivers a range of grant-making programmes across Merseyside, Halton and Lancashire. The number and type of grants available from the foundation can vary considerably over time.

As the end 2009, the following funds were available for applications – as with other community foundations, funds may close and new ones open, so check the foundation's website for up-to-date information (smaller, unpublicised funds may also be open – see table below):

Grassroots Grants

The Grassroots Grants programme is funded by the Office of the Third Sector and administered by The Community Foundation for Merseyside.

Please ensure you meet the following eligibility criteria before applying:

- your group must be a not for profit, third sector voluntary or community group living and operating locally in Sefton, St Helens, Knowsley, or Wirral for at least 12 months prior to the round closing date [for organisations in Lancashire, this fund is administered by the Community Foundation for Lancashire – further details are available from their website: www.lancsfoundation.org.uk]
- your group must have a total annual income of less than £30,000 (or a £30,000 average over the last 3 years) net of any funding received through the Grassroots Grants programme.

The programme was designed to respond to local issues, improve organisational capacity and help support the diverse needs of communities. Grant applications should show how funding will help groups support activities and services with regard to the following:

- The programme aims to enable groups to: flourish, continue or expand their work; build their capacity and provide support for provisions for local people, advocacy, and to help strengthen community voice; it also aims to complement each area's Local Area Agreement (LAAs simplify some central funding, help join up public services more effectively and allow greater flexibility for local solutions to local circumstances. LAAs set out the priorities agreed between central government, your local authority, Local Strategic Partnership and other local partners). They focus on the following areas:
  - children and young people
  - healthier communities and older people
  - employment, learning and skills, education or training
  - urban renewal, safer stronger communities or environment.

Liverpool ONE Foundation

The Liverpool ONE Foundation aims to help the lives of local people in Merseyside, especially Liverpool, by providing support for good causes in and around the city.

Projects should meet one or more of the following themes:

- the prevention or relief of poverty
- education and skills – especially for young people
- social and community advancement
- health.

Funding is available from three different fund programmes. Grants range from £500 to over £5,000 in some circumstances. The programmes are:

Programme 1

£500 to £5,000 in any 12 month period may be offered for applications which

address one or more of the four 'themes' but are for more general activities.

Programme 2

Over £5,000 may be awarded in any 12 month period for projects which are clearly strategic in their delivery (for example any links or partnerships are identified, and the proposed activity will compliment other services in the community), and will create a sustainable service within the community.

Programme 3

Over £5,000 may be awarded over a 3 year period for groups who require a long-term funding commitment for a clearly strategic activity or service.

Merseyside Police and High Sheriff's Charitable Fund

The Merseyside Police and High Sheriff's Charitable Fund provides grants to voluntary bodies and community groups in Merseyside to support community safety, crime prevention and security initiatives in their locality.

Grants are available in the boroughs of Knowsley, Liverpool, Sefton, St. Helens and Wirral conforming to the objects of the fund.

Every application must conform to the objects of the fund which are:

- to promote for the public benefit in and around Merseyside a safer and increased quality of life through the prevention of crime and the protection of people and property from criminal acts
- to secure the advancement of education for the public benefit in all matters relating to community safety.

Successful funding will depend on the ability to meet both of these objectives.

Groups will be encouraged to obtain complementary grant-aid or funding. Applicants should state in their application who else they have applied to, or have secured money from, or who else they intend to apply to, indicating the amount involved. Typical grants will normally range from £500 to £2,500 and may be less than the figure applied for. In exceptional circumstances, grants of higher value may be considered.

Mersey Docks & Harbour Company 500 Fund

The Mersey Docks and Harbour Company 500 Fund provides funding of between £50 and £500 to registered charities, voluntary and community groups working in Sefton, Liverpool or Wirral, that can show local community involvement in the decision making of the organisation.

To be eligible for a grant your project must demonstrate a local community need and meet with your group's aims and objectives. Your project must:

- build the capacity of the community to help itself
- be based on real need
- show value for money.

Priorities:

- groups who have unrestricted funds of less than £5,000
- innovative projects
- projects connected with the river/sea.

Examples of what may be funded:

- new equipment
- training costs
- hiring of venues for specific meetings
- printing of new publicity material and events.

Employable Communities Fund

The Employable Communities Fund supports groups within the community, voluntary and faith sectors to target worklessness and progress individuals towards employment through learning, and educational opportunities.

Grants of up to £12,000 per year are available to eligible groups working in Sefton, Liverpool, Knowsley, St Helens and Wirral.

For more information please download the criteria and application forms from our fund partners Merseyside Expanding Horizons (0151 330 0552; www.expandinghorizons.co.uk) or Merseyside Disability Federation (0151 291 9570; www.merseydisability.org.uk).

Mando Group Foundation

Grants of up to £2,000 are available to aid the education and employability of young people of school leaving age across Merseyside.

Who can apply?

- voluntary or community groups based on Merseyside
- voluntary or community groups that are delivering activities which will enhance education or employability for young people.

To be eligible for a grant your group must:

- have a constitution, bank account, and independently examined accounts for grants of £250 or more
- have a constitution or set of rules, bank account, and some form of income/ expenditure records for grants of under £250
- be able to demonstrate that your group has the capacity to deliver your proposed project, while reflecting good value for money
- be able to spend any money awarded within 6 months of the offer
- be working with people of school leaving age or above.

Examples of what may be funded include educational courses, educational materials, CV writing/interview techniques.

Please note: on-going revenue costs, including salaries, will not be considered.

Grantmaking in 2008/09

The following is a breakdown of the foundation's grant distributions by fund during the year:

Programme	No. of grants	Amount
Wirral Third Sector Health Innovation	34	£1,040,000
Grassroots Grants	443	£988,500
Fairshare Trust	13	£614,000
Employable Communities	60	£294,000
Knowsley Voluntary and Community Fund	57	£194,200
Sport Relief	32	£91,000
Change Up	11	£82,000
Mark McQueen Foundation	2	£45,000
Sefton Council	10	£42,000
Arts & Culture	11	£38,000
Camelot Foundation	2	£29,000
Barclays Wealth	2	£27,000
Merseyside Young Transformers	12	£15,400
Mersey Docks and Harbour Company	31	£14,700
Green Machine	27	£13,500
Merseyside Police	9	£13,500
Keepmoat Fund	8	£12,000
John Goore Trust	27	£8,200
Alliance & Leicester	15	£6,500
X Fund	8	£2,100
Community Safety	4	£2,000
Joseph Harley Trust	6	£1,700
Community Champions	1	£1,400
Jim Hosker Memorial Fund	1	£100

Applications The policy of the foundation is to award grants to organisations that have made a formal application for a grant, that fulfil the requirements of the relevant grant fund and that have the necessary systems to administer a grant. All grant applications are subject to a formal appraisal by the foundation's staff before being presented to the local grant panel for a decision when a scoring system is used to guide decisions.

Full guidelines and application forms for individual funds are available from the foundation's website.

Milton Keynes Community Foundation

Welfare and the arts

£734,000 (2008/09)

Beneficial area Milton Keynes Unitary Authority.

Acorn House, 381 Midsummer Boulevard, Central Milton Keynes MK9 3HP

Tel. 01908 690276 **Fax** 01908 233635

Email information@ mkcommunityfoundation.co.uk

Website www.mkcommunityfoundation. co.uk

Correspondent Bart Gamber, Grants Director

Trustees *Judith Hooper; Fola Komolafe; Francesca Skelton; Jane Matthews; Michael Murray; Peter Kara; Peter Selvey; Richard Brown; Roger Kitchen; Ruth Stone; Stephen Norrish.*

CC Number 295107

Information available Accounts were available from the Charity Commission.

Established in 1986, the foundation is a local grant-making charity that helps to improve the quality of life for people living within the unitary authority area of Milton Keynes. It awards around 150 grants each year to local voluntary organisations and charities, supporting projects that benefit the whole community, including; public health, the needs of children and young people, older people, people with special needs, arts and culture and projects providing services to the community.

The foundation helps to build stronger communities by encouraging local giving and raises a large part of its funds through a membership scheme, supported by local people and companies who make an annual donation.

In 2008/09 the foundation had assets of £6.9 million and an income of £1.8 million. Grants were made from various funds totalling £734,000.

Funds Available
The foundation has a range of different funds designed for small community and voluntary groups working to help local people across Milton Keynes.

The foundation has three main grant programmes.

- *Small Grants* – up to £1,500. These grants are considered monthly.
- *Community Grants* – up to £5,000 for groups with an annual turnover of less than £20,000.
- *Development Grants* – for established groups looking at the next stage of their development. Funding for one, two or three years is available for innovative projects and the maximum awarded is £25,000 per year. Please note: due to the economic climate the foundation is currently not accepting new applications for this type of grant. However, it will endeavour to have the programme running again as soon as possible.

The foundation also manages the *Grassroots Grants* programme on behalf of the Office for the Third Sector. This provides grants of up to £5,000 for small community organisations with an annual turnover of less than £20,000.

It is important to note that grant schemes can change frequently. For full details of the foundation's current grant programmes and their deadlines please consult the foundation's website.

Exclusions No grants are made to the following types of organisation:

- statutory organisations – including schools, hospitals and borough councils (applications from parish councils for community projects are accepted)
- political parties or groups affiliated to a political party
- individuals.

Grants are normally not given for:

- sponsorship and fundraising events
- contributions to major appeals
- projects outside the beneficial area
- political groups
- projects connected with promoting a religious message of any kind
- work which should be funded by health and local authorities or government grants aid
- retrospective grants, nor grants to pay off deficits.

Applications Application forms and guidelines are available on the foundation's website or can be requested by calling the office. The grants staff can be contacted to assist with any queries or help with applications.

The Brian Mitchell Charitable Settlement

General
£345,000 (2007/08)
Beneficial area UK.

Round Oak, Old Station Road, Wadhurst TN5 6TZ

Tel. 01892 782072

Email mitchell@inweb.co.uk

Correspondent The Trustees

Trustees *Brian Mitchell; Hon. Michael Devonshire; Duncan Oakley; Andrew Buss; John Andrews.*

CC Number 1003817

Information available Accounts were available from the Charity Commission.

The objects of the charity are to support or promote such charitable purposes as the trustees may in their absolute discretion determine.

In 2007/08 the settlement had an income of £281,000 and made grants totalling £345,000. Assets stood at £579,000.

A total of 15 awards were approved by the trustees during the year covering a wide range of charitable activities including education, music and the arts and also sporting activities. During the year the trustees identified four charities where projects have been given assurance of continuing annual support during the lifetime of the settlor.

Beneficiaries in 2007/08 included: the Skinners School (£207,000); Glyndebourne (£50,000); Canterbury Cathedral (£15,000); Hospice on the Weald (£11,000); St Barnabas Project (£10,000); the Temple Church (£8,000); Sailability (£7,000); British Blind Sport and Vision Aid Overseas (£5,000 each); Oasis Trust (£1,500); and Shelter Box (£490).

Applications In writing to the correspondent.

The Monument Trust

Arts, health and welfare (especially AIDS), environment and general
£16.3 million (2007/08)
Beneficial area Unrestricted, but UK in practice.

Allington House, 1st Floor, 150 Victoria Street, London SW1E 5AE

Tel. 020 7410 0330 **Fax** 020 7410 0332

Website www.sfct.org.uk

Correspondent Alan Bookbinder, Director

Trustees *Stewart Grimshaw; Linda Heathcoat-Amory; Sir Anthony Tennant.*

CC Number 242575

Information available Accounts were available from the Charity Commission.

This is one of the Sainsbury Family Charitable Trusts, which share a joint administration, but are otherwise independent of each other. They have a common approach to grantmaking which is described in the entry for the group as a whole. In this case the trust notes that: 'proposals are generally invited by the trustees or initiated at their request. Unsolicited applications are not generally encouraged and are unlikely to succeed, unless they closely match the areas in which the trustees are interested'.

In 2007/08 the trust had assets of £215.1 million (£113.8 million in 2006/07) and an income of £112.2 million (£6.1 million in 2006/07). This substantial increase in funds is due to the trust being the major beneficiary of the settlor, the late Simon Sainsbury's estate. As a result the trust's grantmaking increased from £2.5 million in 2006/07 to over £16.3 million in 2007/08. The trust anticipates continuing to make substantial grants over the coming years.

The trust's main areas of interest are (with number and the value of grant approvals during the year, including support costs):

Category	Grants approved	Value
Arts and Heritage	34	£14,200,000
Social Development	25	£3,350,000
Health and Community Care	25	£2,320,000
General	2	£102,000

The following is the only indication of the policies of the trust, beyond what can be deduced from the grants approved: 'The trustees continue to support a number of arts and environmental projects of national or regional importance. In other areas they prefer to help prove new ideas or methods that can be replicated widely and where possible become self-sustaining.

Grants in 2007/08

Arts and Heritage
There were 25 grants for more than £10,000 in this category, including a large capital donation of £9 million to the Art Fund towards the purchase of Dumfries House, its estates and contents and associated costs. For more information on Dumfries House, see the entries for the Garfield Weston Foundation and the Prince's Charities Foundation, both of whom also made substantial donations.

Other beneficiaries included: Victoria & Albert Museum (£2 million over three years), towards the Medieval and Renaissance Galleries; Bowes Museum Trust (£500,000), towards the renovation of the Bowes Museum; Wells Cathedral (£250,000 over two years), towards the final phases of the redevelopment project; Ulster Museum (£150,000), towards the refurbishment appeal; Christ Church – Spitalfields (£100,000), towards the organ restoration; Whitechapel Art Gallery (£50,000), towards expansion of the gallery; Heritage Works Buildings Preservation Trust Ltd (£37,500), towards core costs; Yorkshire Ballet Seminars (£20,000), towards running costs; and City of London Corporation (£8,000), towards a historic planting scheme for Keats House, Hampstead.

A further nine grants of £10,000 or under were made in this category.

Social Development
There were 22 grants made for £10,000 or more. Beneficiaries included: Lloyds TSB Foundation for Scotland (£1 million over three years) towards Inspiring Scotland, a programme which will provide long-term support for charities using a 'venture philanthropy' model; Judge Business School, University of Cambridge (£300,000 over three years), towards bursaries for MBA scholars from the not-for-profit sector; The Prince's Trust (£174,000 over three years), towards the costs of a coordinator and direct support to ex-offender supporters in the south east of England; London Youth Support Trust (£124,000 over two years), towards the charity's offender resettlement and accommodation programme; Penal Affairs Consortium

(£72,000 over three years), towards a campaign director and a network co-ordinator; Matrix Research (£30,000), towards developing a toolkit on the costs and effects of reoffending; and Stonewall (£20,000), towards core costs.

Two further grants were made of £10,000 or less.

Health and Community Care
There were 14 grants of more than £10,000 made, with beneficiaries including: Help the Hospices (£800,000 over four years), for a national programme to develop modern hospice leadership for up to 150 senior hospice staff; Aidspan (£500,000 over three years), towards provision of technical support for recipients of grants from the Global Fund to Fight AIDS, Tuberculosis and Malaria; Crusaid (£200,000 in 3 grants): £150,000 over three years towards the National Hardship Fund for disbursement to HIV-positive people in poverty, £40,000 towards developing the remit and reach of this fund to meet the needs of people in rural areas and £10,000 towards the cost of the 2008 HIV and Poverty conference; Revolving Doors Agency (£120,000 over two years), towards exploring new ways to help people with a personality disorder and drug or alcohol problems achieve settled lives; Keystone Development Trust (£40,000), a final grant for Imagine, an initiative based on using local museums and the arts to foster a sense of discovery and imagination in children; and Waverley Care (£25,000), for support services provided at SOLAS.

Nine grants of £10,000 or less were also made.

General
The main grant was made to the Ashden Awards for Sustainable Energy (£99,000), towards the costs of commissioning short documentaries, with a further grant of £3,000 being made to another organisation.

Exclusions Grants are not normally made to individuals.

Applications See the guidance for applicants in the entry for the Sainsbury Family Charitable Trusts. A single application will be considered for support by all the trusts in the group.

Proposals are generally invited by the trustees or initiated at their request. Unsolicited applications are not generally encouraged and are unlikely to succeed, unless they closely match the areas in which the trustees are interested.

The Henry Moore Foundation

Fine arts, in particular sculpture, drawing and printmaking
£1.2 million (2007/08)
Beneficial area UK and overseas.

Henry Moore Foundation, Dane Tree House, Perry Green, Much Hadham SG10 6EE

Tel. 01279 843 333 **Fax** 01279 843 647

Email admin@henry-moore-fdn.co.uk

Website www.henry-moore-fdn.co.uk

Correspondent Alice O'Connor, Grant Contact

Trustees Prof. Dawn Ades; David Ansbro; Prof. Malcolm Baker; Marianne Brouwer; Prof. Andrew Causey; James Joll; Simon Keswick; Greville Worthington; Laure Genillard; Duncan Robinson.

CC Number 271370

Information available Information was available from the foundation's website and accounts were on file at the Charity Commission.

The foundation was established in 1977 to promote the public's appreciation of the fine arts and in particular the works of Henry Moore. It concentrates most of its support on sculpture. The aims of the foundation are achieved through specific projects initiated within the foundation both at Perry Green and in Leeds, particularly exhibitions and publications, and by giving grant aid to other suitable enterprises.

The foundation's grant-making programme has been revised to provide additional financial resources to support the work of living artists and contemporary art practice. Special consideration is given to projects outside London and to venues with limited opportunities to show contemporary art. The foundation is willing to support projects in the UK which involve artists from another country but overseas projects must include a British component.

Grantmaking

In 2007/08 the foundation had assets of £101 million. Its income was over £1 million and £5.2 million was spent on funding the Moore institutions and their exhibitions, publications, library, the

Perry Green estate, research and works of art acquisitions.

Grants were made totalling £1.2 million, full details of which can be found in the foundation's annual review.

In 2008 the foundation reduced the number of grant categories from nine to five. Funding is now available under the following areas:

New projects
This includes exhibitions, exhibition catalogues and new commissions. The foundation expects to award a very small number of grants as follows: exhibition (£40,000), catalogue (£15,000) and commission (£60,000). Please note: most awards are likely to be substantially less than this.

Beneficiaries include: Liverpool Biennial, 'Made Up': new commissions by: Annette Messager, David Altmejd, Sarah Sze, U Ram Choe, Tue Greenfort and Ai Wei Wei; Brighton, Fabrica: an exhibition, Thomas Hirschhorn; and Manchester, Whitworth Art Gallery for 'kinderzimmer' by Gregor Schneider.

Collections
This is designed to provide minor capital grants help public institutions acquire, display and conserve sculpture. The maximum grants available will be around £15,000 for acquisition, £20,000 for display and £20,000 for conservation.

Grants have been made to: Massachusetts, Cambridge – MIT List Visual Arts Center – towards conservation and re-installation of Henry Moore 'Three-Piece Reclining Figure, Draped' (1976) and Guildford, Watts Gallery – towards conservation of the sculpture collection and conservation and display of 'Physical Energy'.

Research and development
For sculptural projects whether creative (for example, contemporary commissions), academic (for example, permanent collection catalogues of sculpture) and practical (for example, a long-term conservation project) that require funding for more than one year. Maximum grants are likely to be in the region of £20,000 per annum.

Fellowships
For artists: grants of up to £6,000 each are available to artists, who are supported by host institutions, for fellowships or residences of 2–6 months.

Previous beneficiaries include: Aldeburgh ArtOffice for Christian Marclay and Cove Park for Abraham Cruzvillegas. *For post-doctoral research*: one year funding of up to £21,000 is available to scholars who have recently finished their PhD to allow them to develop

publications. Three or four fellowships will usually be awarded in the spring. Applications must be supported by an appropriate UK university department.

Dr Rachel Wells of the Courtauld Institute of Art previously received a grant for her project: 'Scale in Contemporary Sculpture: The Enlargement, the Life-size, the Miniaturisation'.

Conferences, lectures and publications
Grants of up to £5,000 are available. Please note: a publication can be a book or a journal but not an exhibition catalogue or a permanent collection catalogue.

Beneficiaries include: Ashmolean Museum, Oxford – for a 3-volume catalogue of the Ashmolean's holdings of Medieval and Renaissance sculpture, by Jeremy Warren; University of Glasgow – for a conference on Bernini's 'paragoni'; and Public Monuments and Sculpture Association – for 'Sculpture Journal'.

Exclusions The foundation does not give grants to individual applicants or for revenue expenditure. No grant (or any part of grant) may be used to pay any fee or to provide any other benefit to any individual who is a trustee of the foundation.

Applications In writing to the correspondent. The guidelines state that the foundation does not issue application forms but that all applicants should cover the following points:

- the category under which the application is being made i.e. new projects, collections etc.
- the aims and functions of the organisation
- the precise purpose for which a grant is sought
- the amount required and details of how that figure is arrived at
- details of efforts made to find other sources of income, whether any firm commitments have been received, and what others are hoped for
- details of the budget for the scheme and how the scheme will be monitored.

Applicants should also advise the foundation whether it is envisaged that any trustee will have an interest in the project for which a grant is sought.

Organisations may include supporting material with their application and this will be returned if requested. Applications are usually considered at quarterly meetings and should not be made by telephone or in person.

John Moores Foundation

Social welfare in Merseyside and Northern Ireland; and emergency relief overseas

£682,000 (2007/08)

Beneficial area Primarily Merseyside (plus Skelmersdale, Ellesmere Port and Halton); Northern Ireland; and overseas.

7th Floor, Gostins Building, 32–36 Hanover Street, Liverpool L1 4LN
Tel. 0151 707 6077 **Fax** 0151 707 6066
Email info@johnmooresfoundation.com
Website www.jmf.org.uk
Correspondent Phil Godfrey, Grants Director
Trustees *Barnaby Moores; Jane Moores; Kevin Moores.*
CC Number 253481
Information available Accounts were on file at the Charity Commission.

The foundation was established in 1964 with aims and objectives which were widely drawn at the beginning to allow for changing patterns of need. During the last twenty years the foundation has confined giving to four main categories:

- Merseyside – this is the priority area and receives 60–80% of the annual grant total
- Northern Ireland – usually receives around 15% of annual grants
- World crises – including man-made or natural disasters such as famine, flood or earthquake, which by definition require large one-off grants to prevent loss of life. These donations are usually made to major relief agencies
- One-off exceptional grants to causes that interest the trustees.

Please note: the foundation does not respond to unsolicited applications in the last two categories.

The foundation aims to enable people who are marginalised, as a result of social, educational, physical, economic, cultural, geographical or other disadvantage, to improve their social conditions and quality of life by way of making grants. It prefers to assist small, grassroots and volunteer driven organisations and new rather than long-established groups, particularly those groups that find it more than usually difficult to raise money.

In line with the foundation's commitment to equal opportunities, it supports projects which aim to counter racism, sexism or discrimination of any kind. Projects which particularly focus on such anti-discrimination would be expected to have substantial input from the discriminated groups concerned.

Consideration is given to organisations working in the foundation's target areas for giving, which are:

- grassroots community groups
- black and minority ethnic organisations
- women including girls
- second chance learning
- advice and information to alleviate poverty
- support and training for voluntary organisations.

And, in Merseyside only:

- people with disabilities
- carers
- refugees
- homeless people
- child care
- complementary therapies.

The foundation is an enabling funder and would like to help groups achieve their targets and outcomes in their own way. Groups can be given advice with setting up monitoring and evaluation systems that best meet their needs and capacity.

Guidelines

The guidelines for applicants, detailed on the foundation's website, read as follows

We make grants towards:

- start up and running costs
- volunteer and programme costs
- education and training costs
- one-off project costs
- equipment
- salaries.

We will consider funding:

Local community groups

Local community groups/projects in disadvantaged areas, run by and for local people, including support and self-help groups, tenants' associations, and community action. Where there are unmet needs in the community we would support fresh approaches and new ideas for tackling them. We also encourage networking with groups doing similar work either locally or in other regions.

Black and minority ethnic organisations

Projects run by and for people from black and minority ethnic communities, including travellers and migrant workers, especially those which work towards redressing the disadvantage faced by such groups. Projects may be broad-based or concentrate on a particular group, for example, women, older people, etc. We also support non-black community groups who are developing and implementing culturally sensitive policies, and cross-community trust-building initiatives.

Refugees

Projects working towards emergency support to incoming refugees (including legal advice) and helping their integration into community life including basic education, literacy, training, health and general social welfare. Schemes that target excluded people within the refugee community and initiatives that enable them to meet their own needs are also supported.

Women including girls

Projects which work towards redressing the disadvantages faced by women in society, including women's health and support groups, literacy and second chance learning.

Young people

Local groups running projects in disadvantaged areas which provide facilities or opportunities for children and young people (up to the age of 21), for example, play-schemes, youth clubs, and detached youth work. We would particularly encourage projects which are, or which are working towards being, user-led.

Family support

Projects giving support to families to allow parents to access learning/employment. This would also include parenting skills, mutual support/self help, families in crisis, and childcare. After school clubs and playgroups etc. might only be funded where there is a family support element.

Second chance learning

Projects run by non-statutory organisations which enable people who have little or no education to return to learning. Grants may be given to organisations towards the cost of courses (including tutors), childcare, advice and information services etc.

Homeless people

Projects to provide services for homeless people or to furnish accommodation including: provision of emergency food, shelter and clothing; support, advice and advocacy; and training and second chance learning.

Advice and information to alleviate poverty

Projects providing welfare rights, or other advice and information services, to alleviate poverty. Priority will be given to funding local independent advice projects, and we will not normally fund those which are part of a national network. Groups would be encouraged to hold or to be working towards a nationally-recognised quality standard in advice-giving.

Grassroots social health initiatives

Projects run by local non-statutory organisations which aim to improve people's physical and/or mental health. Priority will be given to projects in disadvantaged areas where health problems arise from social and environmental factors, and which work with vulnerable groups. Issues might include stress, HIV/AIDS, self-harm, substance misuse etc.

Support and training for voluntary organisations

Training for voluntary and community organisations to enhance the skills particularly of management committee members, but also of staff, to enable them to operate more effectively and improve the quality of the service they offer. Funding is also available for the recruitment and training of volunteers. We will consider applications from Credit Unions for the training of management committee members or the development of a new business plan.

People with disabilities

Projects for adults with disabilities, which would be expected to have substantial input from people with disabilities in the running of the project.

Carers

Projects which benefit carers by the provision of support services, advice, information or non-medical respite care.

Grants in 2007/08

In 2007/08 the foundation had assets of £22 million and an income of £834,000. 110 grants were made totalling £682,000. Of these, 42 were made for revenue costs for more than one year. Around 60% of the grants made in Merseyside were for £5,000 or less and of these about 6% were for £1,000 or less. All grants made in Northern Ireland were for less than £5,500, with the average being around £3,400. The foundation aims to maintain its annual grantmaking at around £700,000.

Grants in Merseyside were categorised as follows:

Category	No.	Value
Advice	5	£44,000
Alternative therapy	3	£15,000
Black and minority ethnic organisations	7	£32,000
Carers	4	£17,000
Child care	3	£17,000
Community organisations	14	£68,000
People with disabilities	9	£50,000
Family support	4	£29,000
HIV/AIDS	1	£10,000
Homeless people	1	£2,500
Refugees and asylum seekers	4	£12,000
Second chance learning	5	£39,000
Social welfare	7	£25,000
Training for community groups	3	£21,000
Women	8	£45,000

Grants in Northern Ireland were distributed as follows:

Category	No.	Value
Advice	1	£5,000
Carers	1	£3,600
Child care	8	£27,000
Community organisations	6	£13,000
People with disabilities	3	£11,000
Homeless people	1	£5,000
Second chance learning	2	£7,600
Social welfare	4	£15,000
Women	3	£11,000

International grants were given to two organisations totalling £158,000.

Beneficiaries across all categories included: British Red Cross (£150,000 in two grants); Liverpool 8 Law Centre (£22,000); Newton-le-Willows Family and Community Centre (£11,000); Somali Umbrella Group (£10,000); Sightline Vision North West Ltd (£7,500); Inner City South Belfast Surestart (£5,000); Cloney Rural Development Association (£2,500); Ballymena and District Disability Forum (£1,800); and Brookvale Residents Association (£100).

Exclusions Generally the foundation does not fund:

- individuals
- national organisations or groups based outside Merseyside even where some of the service users come from the area
- statutory bodies or work previously done by them
- mainstream education (schools, colleges, universities)
- faith-based projects exclusively for members of that faith, or for the promotion of religion
- capital building costs – except to improve access for disabled people
- festivals, carnivals and fêtes
- medicine and health – except under the headings listed above
- holidays, expeditions and outings
- gifts, parties etc.
- sport
- vehicles
- animal charities
- arts, crafts, heritage, or local history projects
- conservation and environmental projects
- employment and enterprise schemes
- victims – except rape crisis and domestic violence projects
- academic or medical research
- uniformed groups (for example scouts, cadets, majorettes)
- sponsorship, advertising or fund-raising events.

Applications may be refused where the foundation considers that the organisation concerned is already well funded or has excessive reserves.

Unsolicited applications which fall outside the policy criteria are not considered. Unsolicited applications for the categories World Crises and One-off exceptional grants are not responded to.

Applications Please refer to the foundation's website and make sure your project falls within the criteria. If you are unsure, or if you would like to discuss your application before submitting it, please telephone the foundation staff who will be happy to advise you.

Applications should be made by letter (no more than four sides of A4) accompanied by a completed application form. Application forms and guidance notes can be obtained by letter, phone or email, or from the foundation's website.

Decisions about which projects to fund are made by the trustees who meet five to six times a year to consider Merseyside applications and four times a year to consider Northern Ireland applications. As a general rule, Merseyside applicants should allow three to four months for a decision to be made, and applicants from Northern Ireland should allow four to five months. Applicants are welcome to telephone the foundation to find out at which meeting their application will be considered.

The Peter Moores Foundation

The arts, particularly opera and social welfare

£3.6 million (2007/08)

Beneficial area UK and Barbados.

c/o Wallwork, Nelson and Johnson, Chandler House, 7 Ferry Road, Riversway, Preston PR2 2YH

Tel. 01772 430000 **Fax** 01772 430012

Email moores@pmf.org.uk

Website www.pmf.org.uk

Correspondent Peter Saunders, Administrator

Trustees *Michael Johnson, Chair; Eileen Ainscough; Ludmilla Andrew; Nicholas Payne; Kirsten Suenson-Taylor; Joanna Laing.*

CC Number 258224

Information available Accounts were available from the Charity Commission.

The foundation concentrates on supporting opera and other forms of music, and the opera-connected Compton Verney House project which receives up to one-third of the available funds. Peter Moores himself worked professionally in opera.

General

Grants are made in the fields of fine art (including Compton Verney House), music (performance and recording), training, health, young people, race relations, heritage, social welfare and the environment. The foundation also focuses its work in Barbados through the Peter Moores Barbados Trust.

In 2007/08 the foundation had an income of just under £5.3 million, almost all of which came from a donation from the related Peter Moores Charitable Trust. (The sole purpose of the charitable trust is to make donations to the foundation and, to a lesser extent, the Compton Verney Collection Settlement, and therefore does not merit an entry here.) During the year the foundation made grants totalling over £3.6 million, including £1.8 million to Compton Verney House, broken down as follows:

Category	Value
Fine art	£1,820,000*
Musical performance	£964,000
Music	£212,000
Health	£207,000
Heritage	£119,000
Social	£167,000
Young people and education	£144,000

*including the donation to Compton Verney House

Beneficiaries across all categories included: 'HIV/AIDS charites' (£126,000); English Pocket Opera (£100,000); Buxton Festival (£90,000); Childline (£72,000); Worshipful Company of Barbers (£50,000); Game and Wildlife Conservation Trust and Welsh National Opera (£40,000 each); Rossini in Wilbad (£35,000); Georgian Theatre Richmond (£23,000); Royal College of Music Main Scholarship (£19,000); Woodhouse Grove School (£10,000); and Textile Conservation Foundation (£8,000). Small grants were also made in each category.

Applications In writing to the correspondent, but applicants should be aware that the foundation has previously stated that it 'will normally support projects which come to the attention of its patron or trustees through their interests or special knowledge. General applications for sponsorship are not encouraged and are unlikely to succeed.'

The J P Morgan Foundations

Education, community, young people, women and the arts

£1.2 million (2006/07)

Beneficial area UK, with a special interest in London (south and east), Bournemouth, Edinburgh and Glasgow.

10 Aldermanbury, Floor 8, London EC2V 7RF

Tel. 020 7325 1308 **Fax** 020 7325 8195

Correspondent Ketisha Kinnbrew, Secretary

Trustees *Carol Lake; Campbell Fleming; Swantje Conrad; Jakob Stott; Eva Lindholm; J P Morgan Asset Management Marketing Limited.*

CC Number 291617

Information available Accounts for 2007/08 were overdue at the Charity Commission at the time of writing.

Summary

The JPMorgan Foundations are two independent [but, connected] grantmaking charities that comprise of the JPMorgan Educational Trust (Charity Commission no. 325103) and the JPMorgan Foundation (Charity Commission no. 291617). Through these charities JPMorgan seeks to support and strengthen the communities that it works in. Funding is given for community development, education of young people and community life.

Please note: the foundation is currently winding up its activities.

The following description in the foundation's 2006/07 accounts gives a fuller explanation of it's future plans:

The increase in grant numbers and donations reflected the trustee policy decision taken in 2006 that all awards would be made by the foundation and no awards would be made from JPMorgan Educational Trust (the connected charity) for 2007. It also reflected the decision to move the foundation towards an orderly closure within a target period of three and a half years (as at 1 January 2007) and to that end to spend out the funds in equal portions. It was further agreed that all new awards would be of a significant amount in order to make a real difference.

The JPMorgan Foundations has previously stated that the JPMorgan

Educational Trust will be wound up by 2011. It is not clear whether or not this is still the case in the light of the decision to wind up the JPMorgan Foundation. Despite attempts to contact the foundation, it has not been possible to confirm the future plans for the Educational Trust.

In 2006/07 the foundation had assets of £2.7 million and an income of £292,000. 54 grants were made totalling £1.2 million. They were broken down by area as follows:

Area	Value
London	£750,000
Bournemouth	£85,000
Edinburgh and Glasgow	£100,000
UK-wide projects	£150,000

Exclusions Projects not usually supported include:

- open appeals from national charities
- direct appeals by individuals
- charity gala nights and similar events
- medical charities.

Applications The foundation is due to wind up its activities 2010. The future of the JPMorgan Educational Trust remains unclear.

Please contact the foundation for further information.

The Mulberry Trust

General

£399,000 (2007/08)

Beneficial area UK, with an interest in Harlow, Essex and surrounding areas, including London.

Farrer and Co, 66 Lincoln's Inn Fields, London WC2A 3LH

Tel. 020 7242 2022

Correspondent Ms Cheryl Boyce

Trustees *John G Marks; Mrs Ann M Marks; Charles F Woodhouse; Timothy J Marks; Chris Marks; Rupert Marks; William Marks.*

CC Number 263296

Information available Accounts were available from the Charity Commission.

Around 70 grants are made each year, most being for amounts of £5,000 or less. Grants go to a wide range of causes, with both local institutions, including hospices and universities, and national charities receiving funding. Around half the grants seem to go to regularly supported recipients.

In 2007/08 the trust had assets of £6.8 million and an income of £187,000. Grants were made totalling £399,000, broken down as follows:

Category	No. of grants	Amount
Education and research	16	£163,000
Christian church and leadership	17	£83,000
Community and environment	7	£38,500
Disadvantaged	14	£30,000
Parenting, family and children's work	6	£27,000
Housing	3	£17,000
'Over indebtedness'	1	£15,000
Health	5	£11,000
Other material grants	8	£7,500
Emergency relief	1	£2,000

Applications The trust has stated that it 'will not, as a matter of policy, consider applications which are unsolicited'.

The Edith Murphy Foundation

General, individual hardship, animals, children and the disabled

£1 million (2007/08)

Beneficial area UK with some preference for Leicestershire.

C/o Crane and Walton, 113–117 London Road, Leicester LE2 0RG

Tel. 0116 2551901

Correspondent David L Tams, Trustee

Trustees *David L Tams; Pamela M Breakwell; Christopher P Blakesley; Richard F Adkinson.*

CC Number 1026062

Information available Accounts were available from the Charity Commission.

The foundation was set up in 1993 by the late Mrs Murphy in memory of her late husband, Mr Hugh Murphy, with the following objectives:

- to assist those who by reason of their age, youth, infirmity, disablement, poverty or social and economic circumstances are suffering hardship or distress or are otherwise in need
- to provide relief of suffering of animals of any species who are in need of care and attention and the provision and maintenance of facilities of any description for the reception

and care of unwanted animals and the treatment of sick or ill-treated animals
- to make donations for general charitable purposes.

Following the death of Mrs Murphy in 2005, her will provided for the foundation to receive certain benefits including a proportion of the residue of her estate. The value of the benefits received following the then year end amounted to £28.2 million. A further £1.8 million was added in 2007. This has resulted in the level of grant giving increasing substantially in recent years.

In 2007/08 the foundation had assets of £31 million and an income of £1.2 million. Grants to organisations totalled just over £1 million and were broken down as follows:

Category	Value
Welfare	£627,000
Children's charities	£150,000
Help for the disabled	£141,000
Education	£51,000
Animal charities	£45,000

Major beneficiaries were: Rainbows Children's Hospice (£80,000); Vitalise (£75,000); The Benjamin Foundation (£70,000); Headway (£65,000); De Montfort University, Help the Aged, The Islamic Foundation and University of East Anglia (£50,000 each); Holy Rosary Parish – Ghana and LOROS Hospice (£35,000 each); and All Saints' Church Thurcaston with Cropston, Leicester Cathedral and Teenage Cancer Trust (£25,000 each).

Other grants included those to: The Stroke Association (£20,000); Combat Stress (£15,000); and Big C Local Cancer, Changing Faces, Horse's Voice Rescue & Rehabilitation Centre, Konnect 9, Leicester and Leicestershire Animal Aid Association, Motor Neurone Disease Association, PDSA and Southrepps Village Hall (£10,000 each).

Grants of less than £10,000 each totalled £139,000.

Applications In writing to the correspondent.

The John R Murray Charitable Trust

Arts and literature

£734,000 (2007/08)
Beneficial area UK.

50 Albemarle Street, London W1S 4BD
Correspondent The Trustees

Trustees John R Murray; Virginia G Murray; Hallam J R G Murray; John O G Murray; Charles J G Murray.

CC Number 1100199

Information available Accounts were available from the Charity Commission.

The trustees will normally only make grants or loans to other registered charities in area in which the trustees have an interest in the arts and literature (although not strictly limited to such areas) and where the award of a grant will have an immediate and tangible benefit to the recipient in question.

In the medium term the trustees' principal aim will be the continued support of the National Library of Scotland (as the ownership of the John Murray Archive) and its curatorial and preservation responsibilities for the archive as well as developing its support of the arts and in particular literature.

Set up in 2003, in 2007/08 the trust had assets of £25.4 million and an income of £547,000. Grants to 20 organisations totalled £734,000. A further £10,000 went to an individual.

Beneficiaries included: National Library of Scotland (£259,000); Strawberry Hill Trust (£80,000); Wordsworth Trust (£70,000); Bodleian Library (£45,000); Koestler Trust (£35,000); the British Library (£32,000); Keats Shelley Memorial Association (£31,000); and British School at Rome, Carmarthenshire Heritage Regeneration Trust and Charles Darwin Trust (£30,000 each).

Applications The trustees will not consider applications for grants.

The National Art Collections Fund

Acquisition of works of art by museums and galleries

Around £6 million (2008)
Beneficial area UK.

Millais House, 7 Cromwell Place, London SW7 2JN
Tel. 020 7225 4800 **Fax** 020 7225 4848
Email grants@artfund.org
Website www.artfund.org
Correspondent Johnathan Guy Cubitt
Trustees David Verey; Paul Zuckerman; David Barrie; Dr Wendy Barron; Prof.

Michael Craig-Martin; Christopher Lloyd; Dr David Landau; Prof. Lord Renfrew of Kaimsthorn; Jonathan Marsden; Charles Sebag-Montefiore; Antony Snow; Timothy Stevens; Dr Deborah Swallow; Prof. William Vaughan; The Hon. Felicity Waley-Cohen; Sally Osman; James Lingwood; Richard Calvocoressi.

CC Number 209174

Information available Annual report and accounts were available from the Charity Commission. An annual review, with accounts, which gives a full illustrated record of all works assisted is also available. The fund has an informative website.

Known simply as The Art Fund, this fundraising and membership charity believes that everyone should have the opportunity to experience great art at first hand, and it works to achieve this by:

- enriching museums and galleries throughout the UK with works of art of all kinds
- campaigning for the widest possible access to art
- promoting the enjoyment of art through its membership scheme.

The Art Fund's grant-giving policy is to support applications for financial assistance towards acquisitions by fully or provisionally accredited museums, galleries and historic houses of works of art of all kinds, dating from antiquity to the present day. It also receives gifts and bequests of works of art for presentation to public collections and helps to secure works of national and international importance, and good quality works of great local interest.

Grantmaking in 2008

The fund gives the following review of its activities in 2008:

2008 was another record-breaking year for The Art Fund, marked at its start and finish by two extraordinary grants. In January, we gave £1 million from reserves towards the acquisition of ARTIST ROOMS, Anthony D'Offay's collection of 731 works of post-war and contemporary art, for Tate and the National Galleries of Scotland. And at the end, we offered our largest-ever grant for a single work of art – another £1 million, so that Titian's Diana and Actaeon could be bought for The National Gallery and the National Galleries of Scotland. Contemporary and historic – our commitment to both is as strong as ever. In between we offered a further 172 grants, worth a total of £5.6 million, to 87 museums all over the UK. In common with every other charity, The Art Fund is feeling the effects of the financial crisis; however, our careful stewardship of resources in past years has paid off, enabling us to support some important acquisitions and initiatives and to use our reserves as they should be used: to offer exceptional grants for exceptional works as the need arises.

We have continued our efforts to encourage more focused collecting, joining forces with the Crafts Council to launch Art Fund Collect, a £50,000 scheme to encourage acquisitions of contemporary craft. Meanwhile, the five partnerships in Art Fund International have begun making their first acquisitions, and now have a real opportunity to exploit a falling contemporary art market.

As an independent charity with no government or lottery funding, we need to raise money before we can spend it, so we have continued to try to increase our profile and support. The overwhelming majority of museums are keen to help, and now display our logo alongside the works we have helped them acquire, and we are working hard with them to improve our overall levels of visibility. Internally, we launched a new Patrons scheme, enabling members to make an additional monthly donation to add to the value of their membership for our cause.

Towards the end of the year, we were approached by Tate and National Galleries of Scotland to see if we would help fulfil the vision behind the ARTIST ROOMS acquisition – that the works should be seen at venues across the UK, not just in London and Edinburgh. Although we have only done it infrequently, supporting exhibitions is in fact specifically allowed for in our Charter. We have entered an agreement to support the tours for two years with the possibility of a third, starting in 2009, and believe it will do much to raise our profile and bring our core purpose – enabling the public to see great works of art – to life.

In 2008 the fund had assets of 30 million, an income of £10 million and during the year paid out grants to institutions totalling almost £6 million. Grants paid in 2008 included those to: London Tate (£1.1 million); National Galleries of Scotland (£625,000); National Portrait Gallery (£445,000); National Trust (£130,000); Mercer Art Gallery (£74,000); Falmouth Art Gallery (£45,500); Captain Cook Memorial Museum (£25,000); Museum of the University of St Andrews and Towner Art Gallery (£16,000 each); British Architectural Library Drawings & Archives Collection (£10,000); Sheffield Galleries and Museums (£7,000); and Bradford National Media Museum, Chepstow Museum and York Museum (£5,000 each).

Exclusions Grants for works of art are restricted to institutions which have a permanent exhibition space, are open to the public and accredited with the Museums, Libraries and Archives Council.

Applications

The Art Fund actively encourages strong applications from national and designated museums for objects which will enrich their collections and supports their efforts to expand into new collecting areas when appropriate. The Art Fund considers applications for whatever amount is needed. Applicants are expected also to apply for any public funding for which they might be eligible, and to raise funds from other sources if they can. The Grants Office requires all applications to be made online. Please see our website for full details and contact the Grants team to discuss any potential application.

The National Churches Trust (formerly the Historic Churches Preservation Trust with the Incorporated Church Building Society)

Preservation of historic churches

£2 million (2008)
Beneficial area UK.

31 Newbury Street, London EC1A 7HU
Tel. 020 7600 6090 **Fax** 020 7796 2442
Email info@nationalchurchestrust.org
Website www.nationalchurchestrust.org
Correspondent Alison Pollard, Grants Manager
Trustees *Michael Hoare, Chair; Graham Brown; Diana Hunt; Lottie Cole; Revd Dr Nicholas Holtam; Peter Readman; Antony Wedgwood; Jennie Page.*
CC Number 1119845

Information available Accounts were available at the Charity Commission. The trust has a new website which is both informative and helpful.

The National Churches Trust was launched in 2007 as a national, non-profit organisation dedicated to supporting and promoting places of worship used by Christian denominations in the UK. The trust promotes the use of these buildings by congregations and the wider community. It also advocates the conservation of places of worship of historic value for the use and enjoyment of future generations.

The trust was formed to act as a catalyst within the sector and to consolidate and expand the role played by its two predecessor charities, the Historic Churches Preservation Trust and the Incorporated Church Building Society.

Its key roles are to:

- encourage good management practices and regular maintenance by providing advice on access to funding, support and training and by developing and implementing practical solutions to the needs of the sector
- provide an annual grants programme of £2 million that allocates funds for both building restoration and modernisation
- encourage projects that benefit communities, integrate places of worship fully into their local areas and enable buildings to be open to the wider public
- work to enhance the public and governmental perception of and support for Christian places of worship.

General

In 2008 the Charity Commission appointed the National Churches Trust (NCT) as the sole trustee of the Historic Churches Preservation Trust (HCPT) and also granted a 'uniting direction'. Consequently, the NCT and HCPT are treated as a single charity for administrative, accounting and regulatory purposes. They will however, remain legally distinct so that the HCPT will operate as restricted funds within the NCT. A similar process is envisaged for the Incorporated Church Building Society (ICBS), which has been managed by the HCPT since 1983.

Founded in 1953, the HCPT, now the National Churches Trust (NCT), is the leading fundraising body involved in the restoration of architecturally and historically significant parish churches.

Over the decades, work that was originally begun to reverse the neglect brought about by the socio-economic changes of the late 19th and early 20th centuries and to repair the damage of World War II, has become increasingly important and far-reaching.

The trust has helped virtually every church named in Simon Jenkins' 'England's Thousand Best Churches'. Whichever way the grants are analysed – by architectural style or importance, historical interest or significance, by geographical area, by rural or urban community, by denomination – the trust's net has been spread wide. Wales is the newcomer to the grants system, as the trust's remit was only extended to the Principality in 1987. With the support of the Esme Mitchell Trust, since 1984 a small number of churches in Northern Ireland have also been helped. Over £27 million in grants and loans to churches of all denominations has been awarded in the UK.

Spreading awareness of the needs of churches and encouraging participation in their restoration and revival at both national and local level is also an important part of the trust's remit. Six local county trusts – in Cheshire, Essex, Kent, Lincolnshire, Staffordshire and Wiltshire were active when the trust was established. Since then, most of England has been covered.

The trust has often helped with the first essential tranche of money to get things under way, but the county trusts are all individual and independent. Representatives from the local trusts have always been members of the trust's grants committee and their ground level knowledge is considered essential in understanding the situation and pressures facing the local area. At the time of writing, only Wales, Lancashire, Cumbria and the metropolitan districts of London, Birmingham and Merseyside have no local trust.

The NCT receives no government funding, other than via the Gift Aid scheme and relies entirely on voluntary giving. The majority of income comes from legacies and grant-making trusts and foundations, with the remaining balance made up from donations from places of worship, members of the public, subscriptions from 'Friends' and investment income.

During 2008 the trust adopted a strategy which aims to move the trust from its historical role as a grantmaker to an organisation providing a much wider range of services. The trustees recognise the need to strengthen the trust's

understanding and knowledge of the sector within which it operates. This has prompted three key organisational changes:

- a new policy unit has been established
- a national advice-line has been set up to provide support and advice
- the adoption of a well structured communications programme.

Guidelines

To help those applying for grants, the trust has developed straightforward application packs. These can be downloaded from the website along with detailed guidelines.

The trust advises that before applicants complete an application pack, it is important for them to make sure that their project will be eligible by checking it meets the following criteria:

- the building must be open for regular public worship – the trust does not currently have grants available for cathedrals, but any other Christian places of worship can apply if they meet the eligibility criteria
- it must be sited in England, Northern Ireland, the Isle of Man, Scotland or Wales
- the congregation must belong to a denomination that is a member or associated member of Churches Together in Britain and Ireland
- all projects must be overseen by an architect who is either ARB, RIBA or AABC accredited, or by a chartered surveyor who is RICS accredited.

In 2008 to 2010 the trust will be managing four main grant programmes. A summary of each, detailed on the trust's website, reads as follows:

Cornerstone grants – Grants of £40,000 and above for structural repair projects that will cost more than £50,000. A structural repair means essential work to the fabric of the building.

Foundation grants – Grants of £2,500 to £35,000 for structural repair projects.

Community grants – Grants from £2,500 for providing facilities that will benefit your place of worship and local community, for example, accessible toilets, kitchens and meeting rooms. Grants will usually be up to £25,000 and will not exceed 50% of the project cost.

WREN (Waste Recycling Environmental Ltd) – The National Churches Trust are pleased to be working with WREN (www.wren.org.uk) to administer a number of grants on their behalf. If your place of worship is sited within a 10 mile radius of a landfill site operated by Waste Recycling

Group (WRG Ltd) you may qualify for one of these grants.

If you belong to an Anglican congregation that is planning to build a new church or to enlarge the worship area of an existing church, the trust may be able to assist with a grant towards the cost through the Incorporated Church Building Society. Please contact the National Churches Trust office by email at grants@nationalchurchestrust.org with basic information on the new building and cost.

Grantmaking in 2008

In 2008 the trust had assets of £4.5 million and an income of £1.9 million. 186 grants were made totalling £2 million.

Category	No.	Value
Foundation grants	161	£1,400,000
Cornerstone grants	8	£390,000
Community grants	14	£275,000
Waste recycling environmental limited (WREN)	3	£30,000

A total of £425,000 was also committed through restricted and designated funds.

Grants in 2008 awarded by denomination:

Denomination	No.
Anglican	170
Methodist	8
Baptist	2
United Reformed	2
Society of Friends	1
Other	3

The following are examples of recent beneficiaries of grants for repairs and are reproduced from the trust's website:

St Peter, Lenton, Lincolnshire – grant of £40,000

Architecturally, this Grade I listed church consists of three periods: Early English, Decorated and Perpendicular. The last major restoration was carried out in 1879. Pevsner mentions it in his 'Buildings of England', with particular reference to the Armyne Monument in the chancel. St Peter is important to the community, who have no village hall and are enthusiastic about maintaining their church for future generations.

St Peter, Darwen, Lancashire – £20,000

St Peter is a Grade II* listed church built in 1827–29 and is the work of Thomas Rickman who was also architect of New Court, St John's College, Cambridge. The Church is correctly orientated in accordance with ecclesiastical convention: the tower is situated at the west end, the nave is of a good size and flanked by aisles either side. There are galleries supported off cast iron columns with seating to three sides. The meeting space, formed some time ago after a re-ordering of the west end, is used regularly throughout the week for groups from the local community.

All Saints, Stanton, Suffolk – £7,000

All Saints is Grade II* listed and was built between 1320 and about 1370. Major restoration in 1870 retained all the original features. The south aisle is particularly fine with ball-flower decoration outside and within a fine piscina and tomb recess. The chancel arch is very high and slender and the south porch forms the base of a 14th century tower originally standing alone. Standing in the centre of the village, All Saints is used by the local primary school and also houses a monthly Sunday School. There is a good working relationship with Stanton Methodist Church.

St Michael and All Angels, Brinkworth, Wiltshire – £5,000

This Grade I building of the Perpendicular Style (1360–1500) has evolved through several additions and rebuilding. The tower and chancel were probably rebuilt in 14th century, and nave and south aisle in the early 15th, when the north aisle and porch were also added. There is a fine medieval wagon roof, good stained glass and examples of wall paintings dating from medieval to the 18th century. An imposing 20th century organ has been recently refurbished.

St Andrew, Alwington, Devon – £4,500

The origins of this Grade I church are unknown, but there is evidence that a church was on the site in the 13th century. At the corner of the tower there is still the base of a 13th century preaching cross which is a National Scheduled Monument. The south aisle is associated with the Pine-Coffin family, formerly of Portledge House, and records show an unbroken line of Patrons of the church from the male line of the family. The church is acknowledged to be one of the most beautiful in North Devon, set in a rural and relatively isolated location. There are no shops or public houses at Alwington, so the church has become the natural 'community centre' for a small local population.

St Mabli, Llanvapley, Monmouthshire – £2,500

The Book of Llandaff records the church being given by a local ruler Brithigon Hael to the Bishop of Llandaff in 860AD. The oldest parts of the fabric date from 1250 with much of it 15th century. It is of rubble stone with sandstone dressings and stone tiled roofs, with some original tracery and a fine tower with two 17th century bells. The nave has a 16th century wagon vaulted roof and Norman font, and the chancel has an unusual 13th century double bowl piscina and carved 17th and 18th century memorial floor slabs. The south porch has a medieval holy water stoup and in the churchyard is the base of a medieval preaching cross listed Grade II*. Llanvapley is a village of about 35 houses with surrounding farms. It has no

shop, and the pub is among 5 in the immediate area which have closed in the last few years. The church closed in late 2004 when the roof became dangerous. Immediate repairs, supported by CADW and local funding meant the church could re-open in April 2006. The PCC runs social events throughout the year.

Holy Trinity, Hartshill, Warwickshire – £1,500

Holy Trinity was built between 1841 and 1848 and is of unusual design. The west doorway is massively imposing with a Norman-style arch over 6 orders of columns and a large spoked window above. The parish serves former colliery and agricultural dwellings with a more recent infill of modern housing. The church has a policy of being open to the community and there is much activity on the premises during the week, including a thriving carer/toddler group and an over 50s club with 30 plus members. Holy Trinity also sponsors youth workers as mentors in the local High School.

Exclusions Please be aware that the trust cannot make grants for certain purposes including:

- non-church buildings (such as church halls and vicarages)
- bell repairs
- organ repairs
- repairs to internal furnishings
- redecoration, other than after structural repairs
- clock repairs
- monument repairs.

Applications Application packs can be downloaded from the trust's website. The grants committee meets quarterly to consider applications.

Please note the following statement from the trust: Demand for our grants has risen considerably over recent months and this means that new applicants will not hear from us immediately. You will receive an acknowledgement of receipt as soon as your application arrives, but it is likely that the grants department will not contact you again until at least three months after receipt. We aim to send decisions to applicants within six months where possible. Please ensure that your application is complete when you send it to us. If you are awaiting the outcome of an English Heritage/CADW/Historic Scotland/Heritage Lottery Fund application, please do not apply to us until you know the outcome of any such application.

The Nationwide Foundation

Social welfare

£1.7 million (2007/08)

Beneficial area UK.

Nationwide House, Pipers Way, Swindon SN38 2SN

Tel. 01793 655113 **Fax** 01793 652409

Email enquiries@nationwidefoundation.org.uk

Website www.nationwidefoundation.org.uk

Correspondent P Vinall, Secretary

Trustees *Richard Davies; Lucy Gampell; John Kingston; Simon Law; Karen McArthur; Dr Michael McCarthy; Jen McKevitt; Tony Prestedge; Benedict Stimson; Maxine Taylor.*

CC Number 1065552

Information available Accounts were on file at the Charity Commission. Full information and guidelines are available from the foundation's website.

This foundation is funded principally from contributions from Nationwide Building Society.

It makes grants to registered UK charities (including those in Northern Ireland) which offer financial and/or housing related support to:

1) Survivors of domestic abuse
2) Older people who are one of the following:
   - aged 70 years and over
   - aged 50 years and over who have dementia
   - aged 50 years and over from Black and Minority Ethnic (BME) groups
   - aged 50 years and over who are carers for family members or partners who are also 50 years or older
   - aged 50 years and over who have experienced or are experiencing financial abuse
   - aged 50 years and over who are rurally isolated.

Further information on the foundation's funding priorities is available on its website.

There are two grants programmes under which funding is provided to registered charities:

- Small Grants Programme – this offers one-off grants of up to £5,000 to registered charities with an income of under £500,000.

- Investor Programme – this offers three year grants of up to £300,000 to organisations with incomes not exceeding £10 million. The foundation also accepts joint bids from such charities working with other organisations (not necessarily charities).

Please note: at the time of writing the Investor Programme was closed to new applications and a replacement scheme had yet to be announced. For further information please contact the foundation directly.

In 2007/08 the foundation had assets of £3.9 million, an income of £1.2 million and made grants totalling £1.7 million. A total of £630,000 was paid to 138 charities under the small grants programme and £1.1 million to 18 charities under the Investor Programme.

Only the recipients of Investor Programme grants were listed in the accounts. Beneficiaries included: Domestic Violence Partnership (£81,000); Refuge (£72,000); Broken Rainbow (£69,000); Public Sector Broadcasting Trust (£60,000); Kurdistan Women's Refugee Organisation (£51,000); Safer Wales (£45,000); Addaction (£42,000); PFFS (£40,000); Storybook Dad (£29,000); Castle Gate Family Trust (£28,000); and Young Offenders Partnership (£6,800).

Exclusions The trust will not fund the following:

- applications which do not fit the funding guidelines or comply with the information on the website
- charities which are not registered with either the Charity Commission for England and Wales; the Office of the Scottish Charity Regulator; HM Revenue & Customs (for charities in Northern Ireland); or HM Revenue & Customs (for those charities with a turnover of under £5,000)
- individuals
- charities with incomes exceeding £500,000 in respect of the Small Grants Programme
- charities with 'unrestricted reserves' which exceed 50% of annual expenditure, as shown their accounts
- charities which are in significant debt as shown in their accounts
- promotion of religion or politics
- overseas travel and work outside of the UK
- charities which have received a grant or donation from the foundation or Nationwide Building Society within the past 12 months

- charities which have been declined by the foundation under the same grant programme within the past 12 months.

Applications Application forms are only accessible via the foundation's website. Applicants should expect to wait up to three months for a final decision.

Nemoral Ltd

Orthodox Jewish causes

£437,000 (2007)

Beneficial area Worldwide.

Cohen Arnold and Co., New Burlington House, 1075 Finchley Road, London NW11 0PU

Tel. 020 8731 0777

Correspondent Rifka Gross, Secretary

Trustees *Ellis Moore; Rifka Gross; Michael Saberski.*

CC Number 262270

Information available Accounts for 2008 were overdue at the Charity Commission at the time of writing.

The trust supports the promotion of the Jewish religion, Jewish education and the relief of poverty in the Jewish community in the UK and abroad. In 2007 it had assets of £3.6 million and an income of £931,000. Grants were made totalling £437,000. A list of grant beneficiaries was not included in the trust's accounts.

Applications In writing to the correspondent.

Network for Social Change

Third world debt, environment, human rights, peace, arts and education

£756,000 (2007/08)

Beneficial area UK and overseas.

BM 2063, London WC1N 3XX

Tel. 01647 61106

Email thenetwork@gn.apc.org

Website thenetworkforsocialchange.org.uk

Correspondent Tish McCrory, Administrator

Trustees *Sue Gillie; Bevis Gillett; Sam Clarke; Monica Marian Sanders; Sara Robin; Tom Bragg; Anthony Stoll; Cathy Debenham.*

CC Number 295237

Information available Accounts were available from the Charity Commission.

Network for Social Change, formerly the Network Foundation, is a group of philanthropic individuals who have come together to support progressive social and ecological change. Grants, mainly for up to £15,000, typically go to organisations addressing such issues as environmental sustainability and economic and social justice.

Funding is given in the UK and overseas to projects which are likely to affect social change, either through research, public education, innovatory services or other charitable activities. The network tends to favour structural change, rather than relief work, but there is no set policy on the specific types of organisations it will fund.

In each year a new major and longer-term project may also be initiated.

Organisation

The network is unusual in its organisation and offers the following information about how it operates:

Network members are each personally active in sponsoring, assessing, selecting and commending projects to fellow members. Our funding processes are designed to encourage members to find worthwhile projects, assess their potential and evaluate their achievements. Those without previous experience of such an undertaking work alongside more experienced members.

Most network members are members of one of the six Funding Pools: Arts and Education for Change, Economic Justice, Green Planet, Health and Wholeness, Human Rights and Peace. They meet two or three times a year between the biannual conferences to assess the projects that have been submitted to that pool. Two pool members are appointed as assessors to examine each project in detail, and to obtain written references from external referees. Where possible the projects are visited by the assessors. In the case of overseas projects, Network can obtain advice from well-established charitable trusts: Ashoka, Right Livelihood, Gaia Foundation, and Practical Action (formerly Intermediate Technology Development Group). Funds are raised mainly at the network conferences in February and October each year. At the

February conference, the pools present the projects that they have selected, invite questions from other members, and ask for funding.

While all members participate in the process, it is clearly understood that the legal responsibility for the distribution of funds raised at the Pools meeting remains with the trustees, and that the charitable monies are given for the general purposes of Network for Social Change. On the pledging forms, members can express a preference for certain pools, but they recognise that the trustees have the final responsibility for the allocation of funds.

Matters relating to the running of network are discussed at the biannual business meetings. All members are encouraged to contribute to the running of the organisation: as conference organisers, coordinators, convenors, links with specialist sub-groups, or as directors/trustees. The trustees have final responsibility for all decisions.

Grantmaking in 2007/08

In 2007/08 the network had assets of £84,000, an income of £789,000 and made grants totalling £756,000. Only grants of £10,000 or more were listed in the accounts.

Beneficiaries included: Peace Direct (£69.000); Climate Movement (£44,000); Prison Reform Trust (£32,000); MEDACT (£26,000); Poverty and Environment Trust (£21,000); INTERIGHTS – International Centre for The Legal Protection of Human Rights (£14,000); Wilton's Music Hall Trust and Asylum Welcome (£12,000 each); and University of Sussex, Community Arts North West and Project 21 (£10,000 each).

Further information on recent grant beneficiaries can also be found on the website.

Applications The network chooses the projects it wishes to support and does not solicit applications. Unsolicited applications cannot expect to receive a reply.

However, the network is conscious that the policy of only accepting applications brought by its members could limit the range of worthwhile projects it could fund. To address this, the network has set up an online 'Project Noticeboard', accessible via its website, to allow outside organisations to post a summary of a project for which they are seeking funding. Members of the network can then access the noticeboard and, if interested, contact the organisation for further information with a view to future sponsorship. The network states

that any posts will be available on the website for six to nine months.

The Frances and Augustus Newman Foundation

Medical research and equipment

£404,000 (2007/08)

Beneficial area UK and overseas.

c/o Baker Tilly, Chartered Accountants, Hartwell House, 55–61 Victoria Street, Bristol BS1 6AD

Tel. 0117 945 2000 **Fax** 0117 945 2001

Email hazel.palfreyman@bakertilly.co.uk

Correspondent Hazel Palfreyman, Correspondent

Trustees *Sir Rodney Sweetnam, Chair; Lord Rathcavan; John L Williams.*

CC Number 277964

Information available Accounts were available from the Charity Commission.

The foundation aims to advance the work of medical professionals working in teaching hospitals and academic units, mostly (but not exclusively) funding medical research projects and equipment, including fellowships of the Royal College of Surgeons. Grants range from £1,000 to £100,000 a year and can be given for up to three years.

In 2007/08 the trust had assets of £11 million and an income of £354,000. 15 grants were made totalling £404,000.

Grants are usually distributed in the following categories:

- UK ongoing research
- Research fellowships awarded through the Royal College of Surgeons
- UK 'one off'.

During the year, grants were only made through the UK 'one off' category for medical research or medically related purposes. Beneficiaries included: Peterhouse and Eagle Project – Phase 2 (£100,000 each); University College Cambridge – New Generation Fellowship (£50,000); Meningitis UK (£40,000); Royal College Surgeons – Dupuytrens Disease (£25,000); Age Care – Bradbury Centre (£10,000); and Eastwood Nursery School (£1,000).

Exclusions Applications are not normally accepted from overseas. Requests from other charities seeking funds to supplement their own general funds to support medical research in a particular field are seldom supported.

Applications Applications should include a detailed protocol and costing and be sent to the secretary. They may then be peer-reviewed. The trustees meet in June and December each year and applications must be received at the latest by the end of April or October respectively. The foundation awards for surgical research fellowships should be addressed to the Royal College of Surgeons of England at 35–43 Lincoln's Inn Fields, London WC2A 3PE, which evaluates each application.

The North British Hotel Trust

Health and social welfare

£532,500 (2007/08)

Beneficial area Scotland.

Samuelston Mill House, Haddington, East Lothian EH41 4HG

Email nbht@samuelston.com

Correspondent Claire Smith, Clerk

Trustees *Ian C Fraser; Jonathan R M MacQueen; Patrick Crerar; Graham Brown; Mrs Jeanette Crerar; Mike Still; James Barrack; John Williams.*

CC Number 221335

Information available Accounts were available at the Charity Commission, without a list of grants.

The trust was established with shares from the North British Hotels Trust Company for general charitable purposes. Giving is concentrated in areas where the company operates, namely, mainly Scotland. There are also four hotels in England, with grants being made close to those in Scarborough, Harrogate and Barnby Moor in Yorkshire.

The trust's only source of income is from its investment in North British Trust Hotels Limited and the trust holds 50% of the voting rights in this company.

The trust has a non-trading subsidiary trust, the North British Hotel Cancer and Leukaemia in Childhood Edinburgh Trust.

In 2007/08 the trust had assets of £9.6 million and an income of £358,000. Grants were made during the year totalling £532,500.

The only beneficiaries listed in the trust's accounts are organisations which had yet to receive their grants at year end. These were: National Library of Scotland (£40,000); and Glenurquhart Care Project, Isobel Fraser Residential Home and Roses Charitable Trust (£10,000 each).

Previous beneficiaries include: Dunedin School; Duke of Edinburgh New Start Programme; Hospitality Industry Trust – Scotland; Family Mediation – Argyll & Bute; Craigmillar Childline Services; and Westhill Senior Citizens' Club.

Exclusions No grants to individuals.

Applications On an application form available from the correspondent.

North West London Community Foundation

General

£550,000 (2007/08)

Beneficial area London boroughs of Barnet, Brent, Ealing, Enfield, Haringey, Harrow and Hillingdon.

Room 1, The Wealdstone Centre, 38–40 High Street, Harrow HA3 7AE

Tel. 020 8427 3823 **Fax** 020 8427 2104

Email info@nwlcommunityfoundation. org.uk

Website www. nwlcommunityfoundation.org.uk

Correspondent Kath Sullivan, Grants Officer

Trustees *Natalie Forbes, Chair; Kanti Nagda; David Wood; Tajinder Nijjar; Howard Bluston; Allan Conway; Malcolm Churchill.*

CC Number 1097648

Information available Accounts were available from the Charity Commission, without a list of grants; information was also taken from the foundation's website.

Established in 2001, this community foundation makes grants from various

funds to local organisations in the London boroughs of Barnet, Brent, Ealing, Enfield, Haringey, Harrow and Hillingdon.

The fields of interest are:

- children and young people who are disadvantaged or living in poverty
- community development
- social exclusion and isolation
- bringing communities together
- health
- learning disabilities.

In 2007/08 the trust had assets of £225,000 and an income of £755,000. Grants were made totalling £550,000. As with all community foundations, grants are made from funds and programmes that can open and close depending on the availability of external funding. The following funds were open at the time of writing, although potential applicants should contact the foundation or go to its website for current information.

Grassroots grants

This scheme is part of a £130 million drive by the government to support thousands of groups and projects, working to improve their local communities. Small grants of £250 to £5,000 are available to local community and voluntary organisations operating in Brent, Barnet, Harrow and Hillingdon. Organisations must have a turnover of less than £30,000 to be eligible.

Veolia Water Three Valleys Fund

Priority will be given to environmental projects which improve community awareness of the environment in the boroughs of Barnet, Brent Harrow and Ealing. Applicants must be a voluntary organisation or be able to provide evidence that an organising committee exists, holding a dedicated bank account with accessible, auditable income and expenditure records. Grants are usually in the range of £250 to £500.

Business Objects Foundation

Business Objects values the capacity of people. The mission of our foundation is to broaden access to education so each member of our local community can acquire the education required to lead a dignified life.

Funding Priorities

The scheme has established an employee driven corporate giving program that focuses on providing access to education for vulnerable children and young people. Specifically, it funds projects related to:

- core curriculum subjects – literacy, English language, maths and science
- technology skills.

Preference is given to applicants who:

- are collaborating with other community players to maximize impact
- impact on more than one population through the delivery of their services for example, children and their families.

Comic Relief

This fund gives to small, locally based groups or organisations in disadvantaged areas. Groups should have a clear understanding of the needs of their community and be taking action designed to address those needs.

Around 50% of the available funds will be given to sports projects that:

- increase access to sport and exercise for people who face social exclusion and isolation
- help people who are experiencing difficulties in their lives.

The remaining funding will support community groups running projects that:

- increase local services
- build the skills of local people
- increase community cohesion
- respond to local economic needs.

Exclusions No grants to individuals or to organisations outside the foundation's beneficial area.

Applications Application forms and further details are available from the correspondent or from the foundation's website.

The Community Foundation for Northern Ireland

Community, peace building, social exclusion, poverty and social injustice

£3.3 million (2007/08)

Beneficial area Northern Ireland and the six border counties of the Republic of Ireland.

Community House, Citylink Business Park, 6a Albert Street, Belfast BT12 4HQ

Tel. 028 9024 5927 **Fax** 028 9032 9839

Email info@communityfoundationni.org

Website www.communityfoundationni.org

Correspondent Avila Kilmurray, Director

Trustees *Tony McCusker, Chair; Les Allamby; Mike Bamber; Barbary Cook; Sammy Douglas; Dr Jeremy Harbison; Noreen Kearney; Julie Knight; Dr Mike Morrissey; Dr Duncan Morrow; Stephanie Morrow; Conal McFeely; Tayra McKee; Anne McReynolds; Hilary Sidwell; Colin Stutt.*

IR Number XN45242

Information available Annual report and accounts were available from the foundation. The foundation also has a helpful and informative website.

The Community Foundation for Northern Ireland, formerly the Northern Ireland Voluntary Trust, was established in 1979 with a grant of £500,000 from government. It is an independent grant-making organisation that manages a broad portfolio of funds and programmes that aim to tackle social exclusion, poverty and social injustice, as well as developing communities and promoting peace and reconciliation.

In 2007/08 the foundation had assets of £17.4 million and an income of £4.4 million. There were 391 grants made during the year across all programmes totalling £3.3 million, broken down as follows:

Category	Amount
Peace building	£1,400,000
Building community infrastructure	£1,000,000
Active citizenship	£454,500
Social justice	£228,000
Social inclusion	£165,000

Grant programmes 2009/10

The foundation's open programmes are:

The Turkington Fund

The Turkington Fund is being established in recognition and celebration of the contribution of older people to our society. It aims to offer funding for locally based community projects that are run by, and for, older people.

Amount of funding available

Grants will generally range between £200 – £3,000 maximum. The fund will allocate some £60,000 each year in a range of small grants.

What the fund will support

- the promotion of interaction between older people and other sections of the community
- activities to address shared concerns amongst groups of older people
- activities that focus on the positive contribution of older people within the community
- projects that enhance the active participation of older people in decision-making and policy influence
- encouragement of older people to engage with a range of social, educational, health and cultural activities.

As these are guidelines only, please contact the Community Foundation for Northern Ireland if you wish to discuss any idea in more detail.

Who can apply?

Priority will be given to those applications that show a clear involvement of older people in the design and delivery of a project. The project does not need to be new or particularly innovative in nature, but its programme must be realistic and clearly thought through. An emphasis will be placed on locally-based self-help groups that are working in disadvantaged areas.

What the fund cannot support

The Turkington Fund will not normally fund the following:

- salaried posts
- trips abroad
- individuals
- vehicles
- major capital building programmes
- running costs of large organisations
- holiday schemes
- the promotion of religion
- statutory organisations.

How to Apply

Please plan your project and then download and complete the application form and return it to the Community Foundation for Northern Ireland.

See the foundation's website for up-to-date information on closing dates for this fund.

Community Arts Small Grants

The Community Foundation for Northern Ireland is offering Small Grants ranging from £500 to £1,000 for community arts projects.

The aims of the funding are:

- to support grassroots arts initiatives that foster 'a shared future' and that promote the inclusion of the new immigrants, asylum-seekers and their families as well as travellers
- to encourage communities that experience difficulties with cultural and ethnic diversity to use community arts as a way to take up the challenge of social inclusion
- to give community and arts organisations the opportunity to develop small scale, new or innovative inclusive projects that will make a difference at local level.

Guidelines

- projects should involve or target ethnic minority groups to encourage integration of communities
- participants should be involved in planning the project
- only small scale projects will be considered. This grant is not intended to form a small part of a large project
- applicant organisations should have a constitution or be linked to a constituted organisation
- applicants must complete a Community Foundation Small Grants Application form in full
- applicants should state clearly what they propose to do, who will be involved, the cost and how much they need from this Community Arts Fund
- applications should state a timetable for delivering the project
- the project must be carried through within one year of being offered funding.

What we will not fund

- projects that do not involve or target ethnic minority groups
- projects for individuals or for private companies
- projects that do not have a high level of user participation
- statutory organisations
- general appeals
- projects promoting party politics or a particular religion
- retrospective applications where the project is complete
- projects fully funded from other sources
- capital costs
- running costs
- continuation of salaried positions
- overseas travel.

Decision Making

Applications will be assessed using a formal process, and priority will be given to projects involving or targeting ethnic minority groups. Preference will be given to projects that involve more disadvantaged communities and proposals that evidence high levels of participation will score higher. There are no set deadlines – applications will be considered on a rolling basis. Please note: Grant applications should be made at least **ten weeks** before project start date.

Telecommunity Programme

The Telecommunity Programme is an 'own name' fund set up with capital from BT, management and unions and matched by Community Foundation funds.

Purpose

The programme targets work with young people (teenagers) and people with disabilities in community based organisations in areas of disadvantage.

How to Apply?

There is no formal application form for Telecommunity, hence groups are asked to write to Telecommunity [at the foundation's address] and include the following information:

- a description of your group – its aims and activities
- a description of the proposed project, its origins, purpose and cost
- an outline of how the group plans to evaluate its work
- a copy of your group's constitution and latest annual report, if available
- a recent statement of accounts
- a list of your committee members
- a contact address and daytime telephone number.

Groups will be expected to provide a report on the progress of the project.

Please allow plenty of time for your application to be processed. The Committee meets in January, May and September each year. Applications should be received at least a month before the Committee meeting.

Local Community Fund

The foundation has been tasked to continue to administer this programme for 2009/10 – check the foundation's website for up-to-date information after the current round.

The Programme Criteria are as follows:

- develop community capacity and leadership
- promote partnership working, within and between communities
- help communities improve their local environments
- develop intervention programmes with young people
- encourage more active participation by previously excluded groups in local community services.

Priority Areas

Grants will only be made within the Super Output Areas listed below:

Andersonstown 2 & 3	Highfield 2
Ballysillan 1	Island
Bloomfield 1	Ladybrook 2 & 3
Chichester Park 1	Legoniel 2
Cliftonville 1	Sydenham 1
Falls Park 1 & 3	Upper Malone 2

Applications

Please note that applications will only be accepted if consultation on local priorities has been undertaken with neighbouring community groups and with the Community Foundation for Northern Ireland.

Application forms and guidelines are available on request from the Community Foundation for Northern Ireland. For further information please contact Sharon Killen at: skillen@communityfoundationni.org

One Small Step Grant Fund

What's the aim of the One Small Step Grant Fund?

The One Small Step grant fund encourages initiatives that stimulate people into action to build a peaceful future. It is about spreading the message that we are all responsible for developing a peaceful society in Northern Ireland. The fund will support small local projects organised by individuals – these projects should encourage people into action. The context is one of peace being an issue for each of us as individuals, for all of our organisations and for our communities. For more information on the One Small Step campaign please see the website: www.onesmallstepcampaign.org.

Who can apply?

Individuals who wish to do something specific to further the concept and principles of One Small Step. Applicants should have the support and backing of a community-based organisation or group through which they can develop their work and manage any grant monies. The project should however be the applicant's personal idea; the work must be carried out voluntarily and should be distinct from and additional to the organisation's planned annual schedule of activities. Applicants must also be able to nominate two independent referees (see application form) who are familiar with their previous work and confident of their ability to see through the proposed project.

What sort of initiative will be eligible?

- activities that advocate the One Small Step principles aimed at making a positive difference to the applicant's own life and that of his/her community (geographic or community of interest) in working towards a 'shared future'
- projects designed to get more people involved in building a peaceful society and simultaneously acting as a catalyst for further action
- projects should have demonstrable community impact, spreading the One Small Step message
- proposals need to involve people locally and be clear and specific
- proposals should be well planned, deliverable and costed realistically.

Examples of eligible activities may include events, training, seminars or publications that promote cross-community activities and understanding. All projects should give something back to the individual's community. Grants may, for example, cover eligible costs for transport, training, speakers and, occasionally, small equipment purchases where the link to the One Small Step concept, and the need, are clearly evident.

What size of grant will be available?

Grants will range from £500 to £1,500. Partnership funding is encouraged.

What will not be funded?

- proposals in which One Small Step funding would be a small part of a large project
- proposals that do not show how they will have an impact in the community
- projects that have already started
- established annual events
- projects that exist as part of an organisation's scheduled annual activities
- core running costs
- capital purchases and vehicles
- holidays and day trips
- promotion of religion
- statutory organisations or replacement of statutory funding.

When to apply?

Applications will be accepted on an ongoing basis by the Community Foundation.

Application Process

- applicants should complete the application form available from the Community Foundation. An original signed copy of the application is required
- two non-related referees will be required. These should be people who are familiar with the applicant's work
- all applications should be received at least 12 weeks before the start date of the project.

Comic Relief and Sport Relief

The foundation also administers grant programmes on behalf of Comic Relief and Sport Relief. Guidelines and an application form can be found on the foundation's website, and also the separate entry for Comic Relief.

Exclusions Specific exclusions apply to individual programmes – see each specific section for details.

Applications See the specific sections for details of the application procedures for individual programmes.

The Northern Rock Foundation

Disadvantaged people

£10.5 million (2007/08)

Beneficial area Cumbria, Northumberland, Tyne and Wear, County Durham and the Tees Valley.

The Old Chapel, Woodbine Road, Gosforth, Newcastle upon Tyne NE3 1DD

Tel. 0191 284 8412 **Fax** 0191 284 8413

Minicom 0191 284 5411
Email generaloffice@nr-foundation.org.uk
Website www.nr-foundation.org.uk
Correspondent Penny Wilkinson, Chief Executive

Trustees *Alastair Balls, Chair; David Chapman; David Faulkner; Jackie Fisher; Tony Henfrey; Chris Jobe; Lorna Moran; Frank Nicholson; Mo O'Toole; Julie Shipley.*

CC Number 1063906

Information available Excellent report, accounts, newsletter, guidelines and application forms, all available on the foundation's website.

An important message from Northern Rock Foundation about grant programmes:

In response to changing regional circumstances, including the impact of the recession, trustees have agreed to a changed focus in their grant giving. From 2010 there will be increasing investment in homelessness projects and a new focus on developing initiatives specifically for those who are financially excluded to address growing need in the region. Trustees further agreed, from 2010, to re-focus culture and heritage grants towards projects which also tackle disadvantage as a principal objective.

The foundation will develop these plans over the remainder of this year [2009] and information on these will be available early in 2010 [check the foundation's website for up-to-date information].

Applications to the Culture and Heritage Programme stopped being accepted on the 7th August 2009.

We are currently accepting applications under our three grant programmes.

- **Independence and Choice** – services for people with mental health problems, people with learning disabilities, older people and carers
- **Building Positive Lives** – one-to-one help for young people at risk, homeless people, substance misusers and groups that face prejudice and discrimination
- **Safety and Justice** – reducing the incidence and impact of domestic and sexual violence, abuse and hate crimes.

As part of our support for older people's projects in Independence and Choice, we are accepting applications from organisations providing welfare benefits advice and targeted benefit take-up campaigns.

Overall, we are continuing our policy of funding fewer, better grants, and engaging with applicants and grant-holders to help them maximise their effectiveness. We are also making grants for work across the North East and Cumbria. If your work fits within one of these three programmes, you can apply **now** in the normal way.

In February 2008, the Chancellor announced that the foundation would receive a minimum of £15 million a year in 2008, 2009 and 2010 from Northern Rock, as part of the arrangement under which the bank was taken into temporary public ownership. The foundation's trustees intend to spend up to £11 million through their grant programmes this year.

The aim of the foundation is to help those who are disadvantaged and to improve quality of life in the north east of England (Northumberland, Tyne and Wear, County Durham and the Tees Valley) and Cumbria.

When talking specifically about disadvantage, the foundation means the problems people face because of:

- age – for example, young people and older people
- disability
- displacement – for example, refugees and asylum seekers
- a lack of employment opportunities
- geography – where people live may affect their ability to get basic services, to work together for mutual benefit or to enjoy a healthy and fulfilled life
- crime – for example, victims of domestic abuse
- prejudice and discrimination – for example, against lesbians and gay men or black and minority ethnic communities.

As described above, the foundation is also increasing its emphasis on projects which focus on homelessness from 2010 onwards in response to the current economic situation.

Grant programmes for 2010

Independence and Choice

Giving people with mental health problems, people with learning disabilities, older people and carers a choice of excellent services that help them to become or remain independent.

Everyone has a right to lead a rich and fulfilling life and to have choices about how they live. With the right support, advice and information, vulnerable people can live more independently and participate more fully in society. This programme is designed to improve the amount and range of services for people that, we think, receive the least support from other sources. They are:

- people with mental health problems
- people with learning disabilities
- older people
- carers.

We will fund a wide range of organisations providing different types of services and support – it is up to you to tell us how your work will address the needs of the groups we want to help. For older people, however, as well as other support, we also have a special objective to invest in welfare benefits advice and targeted benefit take-up campaigns.

In the programme as a whole, we want to help organisations that deliver support over and above what statutory authorities provide. This means that we will not fund services that should be the responsibility of statutory organisations or those which were previously funded by local authorities or the NHS. However, we recognise that the state does not meet the comprehensive range of vulnerable people's needs, and that the quality and choice of services is patchy. In this programme we want to address these gaps in provision.

You will need to have some track record of work in the relevant field and be able to show us that you will run high-quality services that meet the widest range of people's needs. We will prioritise work in places where there is little or no provision. We will also seek to link organisations together to share good practice. Innovation is not a requirement, but we are happy to consider proposals that the statutory sector would find too difficult or risky to fund, or which take a new approach to providing services where it is sensible to do so. In this programme we are also especially concerned to see that the people who use your services are involved in their development and delivery.

Building Positive Lives

Helping people who lack self-confidence or motivation, or who face discrimination, to have the individual support they need to lead more positive and fulfilling lives.

Some people find it very difficult to do well in life, to feel good about themselves, to make connections with others or to build positive relationships. They may be facing a crisis, experiencing prejudice or discrimination, or they may be living in disadvantaged communities where there are low aspirations and expectations of what people can achieve. In such circumstances people are unlikely to benefit from wider opportunities to become involved in their communities, to take part in education or training or to get a job.

In this programme we will invest in organisations providing one-to-one services that help people to overcome barriers, explore their ambitions and achieve their goals.

The groups we want to target are:

- people who misuse substances such as drugs, alcohol and solvents
- homeless people
- people who face prejudice and discrimination because of their identity, including refugees and asylum seekers, black and minority ethnic groups and lesbian and gay communities
- disadvantaged young people aged 11–25.

The kinds of services we will fund include:

- crisis support
- schemes that help people find and keep a home
- conflict mediation
- mentoring and befriending
- personal development programmes, including life skills and those that use arts as a tool to engage people
- advice projects.

The activities may take place in a range of settings, and we will also support detached and outreach work. In all cases you will need to show us how you will measure the progress people make as a result of your work.

We won't fund the provision of supported accommodation, the teaching of literacy and numeracy, or teaching English to speakers of other languages.

Safety and Justice

Reducing the incidence and impact of domestic abuse, sexual violence, prostitution, child abuse and hate crimes, by investing in better support for victims.

People affected by these crimes experience long-term social, emotional, psychological and economic impacts. The crimes share low reporting levels, high rates of cases 'dropping out' of the criminal justice system, and high levels of repeat victimisation. Many victims do not report a case for fear of further abuse, or because they think they will not be believed or taken seriously. They may also be prevented from getting the help they need because of the myths and misunderstanding that surround the issues. Some victims will experience abuse in several ways – for example women forced into prostitution by abusive partners.

We want to invest in organisations that can help:

- reduce the incidence of these crimes
- reduce their impact on victims and their families
- reduce repeat victimisation
- increase the number of cases going through the criminal justice system.

These are ambitious goals, and our investments will always be part of a much bigger picture. Our contribution will be to increase the availability of services to victims, to improve the quality and impact of organisations' work, to improve communication and sharing of good practice in the field and to lever in other statutory and charitable resources.

Examples of the kinds of work in which we might invest include:

- advocacy and support
- crisis services
- schemes that encourage reporting of crimes
- prevention and education programmes with children and young people
- projects that encourage survivors to get involved in policy and practice development
- research that has a clear application to policy and practice.

We will provide funding to expand the work of existing organisations where it is effective, to develop new services and to help organisations come together to learn from each other and work together on a problem. We are interested in organisations whose work responds to the needs of victims where the crimes overlap, as well as those concentrating on one area. If your proposal is for joint work by a consortium that includes statutory organisations we can consider it, but we will not support individual applications from public sector bodies for their own work.

Please note: choose the programme whose description best fits the intended results of your work. Do not tick more than one box on the application form. Most importantly please do not apply if your plan does not really fit anywhere within our programmes.

Grantmaking in 2008

During the year the foundation had assets of £30.1 million and an income of almost £16.7 million. Grants were paid totalling £10.5 million (£23.9 million in 2006/07), and were categorised as shown in the first table below (including the previous category of Culture and Heritage).

The foundation also provides further useful analysis of its grantmaking during the year:

In 2008, the foundation received 439 new requests for grants and there were 42 pending applications at the end of 2007. Of these 481 requests, 142 were ineligible for funding or were withdrawn by applicants. Of the eligible requests, 148 were successful, 91 were rejected by trustees and 100 were pending at the end of the year.

£9.5 million was awarded under the foundation's main grant programmes. As the table below identifies, 27% of the amount awarded was to projects within Tyne and Wear and 25% to projects benefiting the whole of the North East and Cumbria.

Geographically, grants were distributed as shown in the second table below.

Beneficiaries during the year included:

Building Positive Lives
Keyfund Federation Limited (£210,000 over 3 years), to fund a development programme for young people in the North East and Cumbria; Fairbridge in Tyne and Wear (£142,000 over 3 years), to provide personal development programmes to disadvantaged young people aged between 18 and 25; The People's Kitchen (£105,000 over 3 years), towards volunteer training and recruitment, core costs, and towards work with the Cyrenians to support homeless people in crisis in Newcastle; Hexham and Newcastle Diocesan Trust (£90,000 over 3 years), to continue to employ a project worker to run an asylum seeker and refugee project in

Category	Grant total	% of amount awarded	Success rate of eligible applications %
Building Positive Lives	£3,000,000	30	47
Independence and Choice	£2,760,000	27	60
Culture and Heritage	£2,000,000	20	53
Safety and Justice	£1,800,000	17	89
Policy grants	£337,000	3	n/a
Other awards	£175,000	2	n/a
Training and Development grants	£79,000	1	n/a
Exceptional	£30,000	–	n/a

Area	No. of grants	Amount approved	Success rate of eligible applications %
Tyne and Wear	32	£2,690,000	53
North East and Cumbria	25	£2,330,000	57
Cumbria	23	£1,860,000	55
Tees Valley	17	£1,180,000	46
Durham	15	£757,000	33
Northumberland	11	£732,000	46
Total	**132**	**£9,550,000**	**55**

four locations in Newcastle and Stockton; Methodist Church Cumbria District (£65,000 over 3 years), to employ a volunteer co-ordinator to recruit, train and manage volunteers to provide help two projects trying to reduce rates of reoffending among young people; Blue Sky Trust (£45,000 over 3 years), to improve the self-confidence and well-being of women with HIV in north-east England by providing a weekly drop-in with planned activities; Media 19 (£35,000), to work with young parents in the North East through a digital self-portrait project; and Women 4 Women (£9,000 over 3 years), to develop befriending support for isolated lesbians and bisexual women across the North East.

Independence and Choice

Contact a Family Incorporated (£233,000 over 3 years), towards the salaries of two posts to support parent carers of children with disabilities in the North East and Cumbria; North Tyneside Carers Centre (£123,000 over 3 years), to employ one full-time carer support worker and one part-time information worker; Washington Mind (£102,000), for a full-time development worker and towards the core costs of the organisation, which supports people with mental health problems in Washington, Tyne and Wear; Newcastle and Gateshead Arts Studio Ltd (£90,000 over 3 years), towards the core costs of the organisation, which runs an arts studio for people with mental health problems; Tees Valley Asian Welfare Forum Limited (£60,000 over 3 years), towards supporting Asian older people; The Botanic Centre Middlesbrough Limited (£55,000 over 3 years), to enable an environmental charity to provide a programme of personalised support, basic skills training and work experience for volunteers with mental health problems and learning disabilities; Learning Library (£17,500 over 3 years), towards the costs of an outreach worker for the Learning Library in Wheatley Hill, Easington, County Durham, which loans toys and specialist equipment to adults and children with learning disabilities; and Haig Colliery Mining Museum (£8,000), to develop a reminiscence project for older people in Cumbria about mining and its associated heritage and culture.

Culture and Heritage*

Kendal Brewery Arts Centre (£200,000 over 3 years), towards the costs of employing staff to develop the Women's Arts International festival in Kendal, Cumbria; The Wordsworth Trust (£150,000 over 3 years), towards the costs of a three-year exhibition programme at the Wordsworth Trust, Grasmere, Cumbria; Kendal Arts International (£100,000 over 3 years), towards the core costs of the organisation, developing a programme of Cumbria-wide outdoor events; Durham County Council (£60,000 over 3 years), to develop an enhanced visual arts programme, which will attract wider audiences, at the DLI Museum and Durham Art Gallery; European Players (£20,000), to develop and produce a theatre project at the Literary and Philosophical Society, Newcastle to celebrate the 90th anniversary of the end of the First World War; and Sunderland Museums (£10,000), towards an exhibition exploring the significance of the and Winter Gardens Victorian period in the history of Sunderland.

Safety and Justice

Women's Support Network (£148,000 over 3 years), towards the manager's salary and related costs of this project in Middlesbrough supporting victims of sexual violence; My Sister's Place (£126,000 over 3 years), to provide a support service for victims of domestic violence in Middlesbrough; Impact Family Services (£109,000 over 3 years), to support mothers who are victims of domestic violence and whose children attend a child contact centre in Sunderland or South Tyneside; Show Racism the Red Card (£61,000 over 3 years), to create and deliver a film and teachers' pack on Islamophobia for use with young people aged 10+ across the North East; Open Clasp Theatre Company (£40,000), towards the Herstory Told project which will use drama to look at the impact of sexual exploitation and losing or giving up children on young women in the North East; and Survivors of Domestic Abuse (£5,000), to enable this survivor-led group to support victims of domestic abuse in Redcar.

(* Please note that the Culture and Heritage programme is no longer running.)

Exclusions

There are certain organisations, projects and proposals that we will **not** consider for grants. You should be aware that it costs the equivalent of several small grants to administer ineligible applications each year. If your organisation or your project falls into one of the categories below please **do not apply** to us for a grant:

- activities which are not recognised as charitable in law
- applications for under £1,000
- charities which appear to us to have excessive unrestricted or free reserves (up to 12 months' expenditure is normally acceptable), or are in serious deficit
- national charities which do not have a regional office or other representation in north-east England or Cumbria
- grant-making bodies seeking to distribute grants on our behalf
- open-ended funding agreements
- general appeals, sponsorship and marketing appeals
- corporate applications for founder membership of a charity
- retrospective grants
- replacement of statutory funding
- activities primarily the responsibility of central or local government or health authorities
- individuals and organisations that distribute funds to individuals
- animal welfare
- mainstream educational activity, schools and educational establishments
- medical research, hospitals, hospices and medical centres
- medical treatments and therapies including art therapy
- fabric appeals for places of worship
- promotion of religion
- expeditions or overseas travel
- minibuses, other vehicles and transport schemes except where they are a small and integral part of a larger scheme
- holidays and outings
- playgrounds and play equipment
- private clubs or those with such restricted membership as to make them not charitable
- capital bids purely towards compliance with the Disability Discrimination Act
- amateur arts organisations
- musical instruments
- sports kit and equipment.

Applications

The foundation provides comprehensive advice on making an application (see the publication entitled: *Grant Programmes – Guidance for Applicants*), of which the following is but a brief summary.

Making an application

First check this list

- Are you sure that neither your organisation nor the purpose for which you want a grant come under our list of exclusions?
- Will the activity for which you want a grant take place in our area?
- Does your proposal clearly fit within one of our programmes?

If you can answer yes to all three questions you are eligible to apply to us.

Completing an application for a grant

The foundation has different grant application processes: one for requests from £1,000 to £20,000; the other for requests over £20,000. **Make sure you complete the correct application form. [Application forms are available from the foundation's website.]**

Complete the correct application form using the notes provided below. Make sure you attach all the required materials. Failure to supply the right information will delay the processing of the application. Keep copies of all material, including the application form, for yourself.

For all grants you need to complete the following sections about the organisation that is applying.

- Contact name: this must be the person who wrote the application and can answer questions about it.
- Project name: only fill this in if your project has a separate name from your organisation's.
- Legal structure: please tell us which of the following describes your organisation, and give any registration number.
  - unincorporated association/voluntary group
  - trust
  - community interest company
  - industrial and provident society
  - company limited by guarantee
  - other (please specify).
- Previous applications: have you previously applied to the foundation for a grant? If the answer is 'yes' please quote the application number which can be found on previous correspondence from the foundation.
- Deadlines: your organisation may be working to deadlines that we need to know about. These may be, for example, deadlines from other funders, or because a project may run out of money at a known date. Please let us know what the deadline is and describe the reason for it.
- Specify which programme: choose the one that best fits the results you want to achieve, even if you think your work covers several. Do not tick more than one. Please note: the foundation is no longer running the Money and Jobs, Strong and Healthy Communities, and Better Buildings programmes.
- Amount requested: put in the total for which you are asking, for example, if you want £30,000 a year for three years write '£90,000 over 3 years' in the box.
- How soon could you start: write what you honestly believe to be the case. We understand that the date may be changed later.
- Local authority: please specify which cities, counties, districts or boroughs will most

benefit from your work. If your work will cover the whole region, say so.
- Signature: the person who signs the application must be the Chairperson or Treasurer of the organisation applying for a grant.

For *grants under £20,000* you must then complete the sections about your proposal following the guidance.

For *grants over £20,000* you must provide a brief supporting statement (no more than two A4 pages) describing:

- your organisation, its aims, its management procedures and its experience which qualifies it to take on this project
- the need your project is attempting to meet and evidence of its importance, scale and urgency
- what exactly you plan to do and how
- how that will meet the aims of the grant programme under which you have applied. For example, if you apply under Building Positive Lives you will need to explain how your idea will help people in our priority groups to overcome barriers and move on in their lives; if you apply under Independence and Choice you will need to show how your idea will improve the quality and choice of services for our priority groups
- how, if the programme requires it, you can demonstrate a level of user involvement in the design, planning, management and service delivery
- how you will evaluate the project, i.e. measure its success, learn from your experience and where appropriate share the lessons with others
- the timetable for the project
- how, if appropriate, you would continue when a Northern Rock Foundation grant expires.

What you must send to us

- Your fully completed application form.
- A copy of your current year's budget and most recent management accounts. Management accounts are the regular reports you produce, usually monthly or quarterly, to show your up-to-date income and expenditure in the current year.
- A signed copy of your most recent audited or independently examined accounts. If you do not have audited or independently examined accounts because you are a small organisation, a copy of your financial record book will suffice. If you do not have any of these because yours is a new organisation, tell us so in your accompanying letter.
- A copy of your governing document (constitution, rules, memorandum and articles of association etc.).
- An application budget showing the amount you are requesting from the

foundation, the overall cost if you are asking us to contribute to a project or to core activities, and information about applications to other funding sources. Please ensure your budget is correctly calculated and that the amount you are requesting can be justified by reference to the budget.
- For organisations seeking funding for staff salaries, a copy of the relevant job descriptions and person specifications.
- For charities awaiting registration with the Charity Commission, a copy of relevant correspondence confirming your application to register as a charity.
- If you are applying for over £20,000, your supporting statement.

Information should be accurate and comprehensive. If something essential is missing we will ask you to supply it and the processing of your application will be delayed.

You may also send a small sample of supporting or illustrative material that gives us a flavour of your organisation. Bear in mind that we will be unable to read large quantities of extra material so consider carefully what you enclose to make sure it is concise and helpful. We can only return originals if you enclose a stamped addressed envelope.

[The foundation also has an online application form.]

Please avoid telephoning to enquire about progress.

The Northwood Charitable Trust

Medical research, health, welfare and general

Around £1.5 million (2007/08)

Beneficial area Scotland, especially Dundee and Tayside.

William Thomson and Sons, 22 Meadowside, Dundee DD1 1LN

Tel. 01382 201534 **Fax** 01382 227654

Email bmckernie@wtandsons.co.uk

Correspondent Brian McKernie, Secretary

Trustees *Brian Harold Thomson; Andrew Francis Thomson; Lewis Murray Thomson.*

SC Number SC014487

Information available Brief annual report and accounts, with a list of the 50 largest donations only, available from the trust for £10.

The Northwood Trust is connected to the D C Thomson Charitable Trust, D C Thomson and Company and the Thomson family. It was established by Eric V Thomson in 1972 and has received additional funding from other members of the family.

The brief annual report notes that 'the trustees have adopted the principle of giving priority to assisting Dundee and Tayside based charities' and says 'unsolicited applications for donations are not encouraged and will not normally be acknowledged'. Other than this there is little indication of the trust's grant-making policy, beyond what can be deduced from the partial, uncategorised grants lists, and there was no review of the trust's grantmaking in previous reports.

Grants total around £1.5 million each year. No recent information was available.

Previous beneficiaries include Tenovus Medical Projects, Tayside Orthopaedic and Rehabilitation Technology Centre, Macmillan Cancer Relief Scotland, Brittle Bone Society, Dundee Repertory Theatre, Dundee Samaritans, Dundee Age Concern, Couple Counselling Tayside and Tayside Association for the Deaf.

Applications The trust has previously stated that funds are fully committed and that no applications will be considered or acknowledged.

The Norwich Town Close Estate Charity

Education in and near Norwich

£517,000 to organisations and individuals (2007/08)

Beneficial area Within a 20-mile radius of the Guildhall of the city of Norwich.

1 Woolgate Court, St Benedict's Street, Norwich NR2 4AP

Email david.walker@ norwichcharitabletrusts.org.uk

Correspondent David Walker, Clerk

Trustees *David Fullman; John Rushmer; Michael Quinton; Brenda Ferris; Geoffrey Loades; Joyce Hopwood; Philip Blanchflower; Sally Barham; Anthony Hansell; Nigel Black; Peter Colby; Richard Gurney; Jeanette Southgate; Robert Self.*

CC Number 235678

Information available Accounts were available from the Charity Commission.

The charity has the following objects:

- to provide 'relief in need' and pensions to Freemen or their widows or daughters where required
- the promotion of education of those in need of financial assistance who are Freemen or the sons or daughters of Freemen
- to make grants for an educational purpose to bodies whose beneficiaries reside within the 20-mile radius of the Norwich Guildhall.

In 2007/08 the charity had assets of £19.5 million and an income of £815,000. Grants were made to organisations and individuals totalling £517,000, broken down as follows:

Category	Value
'Other bodies'	£288,000
Pensions	£112,000
Educational	£102,000
Relief in need	£11,600
Television licences	£4,000

Beneficiaries categorised under 'other bodies' included: YMCA Norfolk (£50,000); Norfolk and Norwich Association for the Blind (£35,000); Norwich Puppet Theatre Trust (£25,000); Friends of Nightingale School (£15,000); Larkman Primary School (£10,000); University of East Anglia (£8,800); Hethersett Pre-School Playgroup (£5,000); Whitwell Hall Country Centre (£4,000); and Norfolk Country Music Festival (£2,000).

Exclusions No grants to: individuals who are not Freemen (or dependants of Freemen) of the city of Norwich; charities more than 20 miles from Norwich; or charities which are not educational. Revenue funding for educational charities is not generally given.

Applications After a preliminary enquiry, in writing to the clerk.

When submitting an application the following points should be borne in mind:

- Brevity is a virtue. If too much written material is submitted there is a risk that it may not all be assimilated.
- The trustees like to have details of any other financial support secured.
- An indication should be given of the amount that is being sought and also how that figure is arrived at.

- The trustees will not reimburse expenditure already incurred.
- Nor, generally speaking will the trustees pay running costs, salaries, for example.

The Nuffield Foundation

Education, child protection, law and justice, older people, and capacity development

£6.8 million (grants awarded to organisations in 2008)

Beneficial area UK and Commonwealth.

28 Bedford Square, London WC1B 3JS

Tel. 020 7631 0566 **Fax** 020 7232 4877

Email info@nuffieldfoundation.org

Website www.nuffieldfoundation.org

Correspondent Clerk to the Trustees

Trustees *Baroness O'Neill, Chair; Sir Tony Atkinson; Prof. Genevra Richardson; Prof. Lord Krebs; Prof. Sir David Watson; Dr Peter Doyle; Prof. David Rhind.*

CC Number 206601

Information available Excellent annual report and accounts and annual review; detailed guidelines for applicants (summarised below, but all potential applicants should see a full copy).

Summary

The Nuffield Foundation is one of the UK's best known charitable trusts which was established in 1943 by William Morris (Lord Nuffield), the founder of Morris Motors. Lord Nuffield wanted his foundation to 'advance social well being', particularly through research and practical experiment. The foundation aims to achieve this by supporting work which will bring about improvements in society, and which is founded on careful reflection and informed by objective and reliable evidence.

The foundation's income comes from the returns on its investments. It does not fundraise, or receive money from the government. The foundation's financial independence and lack of vested interests helps to ensure an impartial and even-handed approach to problems in the projects it funds. Most of the foundation's income is spent on grants some of which are for research and others support practical innovation or development, often in voluntary sector organisations. In both cases the preference is for work that has wide significance, beyond the local or routine. The foundation looks to support projects that are imaginative and innovative, take a thoughtful and rigorous approach to problems, and have the potential to influence policy or practice.

The foundation's grantmaking reflects its aim of bringing about improvements in society through research and practical experiment. The wide range of activities supported by the foundation fall into two main categories:

- support of research and innovation that will bring about beneficial social change though project grants
- development of research and professional capacity in the sciences and the social sciences, targeted at people in the early stages of their careers.

'Project grants' are made to organisations and institutions to support research, developmental or experimental projects that meet a practical or policy need.

The following is reprinted from the foundation's materials:

Research and innovation for beneficial social change

The foundation currently (2009) has three grant programmes in this field. These are as follows.

- **Law in Society** promotes access to, and understanding of, the civil justice system.
- **Children and Families** helps to ensure that the legal and institutional framework is best adapted to meet the needs of children and families.
- **Open Door** – for projects that advance social well being, but lie outside the main programme areas.

Grants are mainly for research (usually carried out in universities or independent research institutes) but are also made for practical developments or innovation, often in voluntary sector organisations. The foundation supports people with creative ideas to identify change or interventions which will have a practical impact for researchers, policy makers and practitioners.

The foundation also has an **Education Programme** which supports research and development work in specific priority areas. Unsolicited grant proposals are not accepted, but other funding opportunities arise from time to time.

Nuffield has supported innovative research and development in education for over 50 years. Current supported work builds on this tradition, prioritising areas in which influence

on policy and practice can be brought to bear.

There are four areas of priority at the moment [2009]:

- education 14–19
- speech and language difficulties
- assessment
- Curriculum Policy and Practice.

We support a range of different kinds of activities in these areas: research, intervention studies, development projects, reviews, seminars, capacity building and practical work. Recognising the presence of other, larger, funders in the field, we husband our resources carefully and target projects which can clearly have a beneficial impact on the development of learning and educational provision. We are supported by the Nuffield Foundation Education Advisory Committee, chaired by Professor Sir David Watson. The Committee advises on all aspects of the foundation's education and curriculum work.

Our focus is primarily on education 4–19 across the four countries of the UK. However, we are increasingly interested in the transitions into schooling and out of development of cross-national perspectives on education and educational research.

The foundation has a genuine interest in innovative work which is interdisciplinary in character. From time to time we may launch new areas and call for proposals – these will be posted on the front page of the website. We also want to keep the door open to high-quality proposals for work at the boundary between education and other areas of interest to the foundation; if you have a proposal which meets these criteria, please see the **Open Door** grants for details of how to take your ideas further.

As a long-term funder of education research and development, Nuffield takes seriously its responsibility to make a contribution to national measures to build capacity.

Development of research and professional capacity

In science and social science, the foundation's grants for the development of research and professional capacity are targeted mainly at people in the early stages of their career.

- Science Bursaries for Schools and Colleges enable sixth form students to take part in research.
- Undergraduate Research Bursaries in Science support summer vacation research projects.
- Social Science Small Grants offers research expenses for new and established researchers working on outstanding projects.
- Social Science New Career Development Fellowships foster partnerships between

experienced social researchers and outstanding post-doctoral social scientists at the early stages of their career.

The foundation also has a Commonwealth Programme that aims to improve services in health, education and civil justice in southern and eastern Africa through the development of the expertise and experience of practitioners and policy makers; the Oliver Bird Rheumatism Programme which makes grants to support PhD students in biosciences at five UK Collaborative Centres of Excellence in rheumatic disease control; and The Elizabeth Nuffield Education Fund which offers grants to women studying to improve their employment prospects.

In addition the foundation runs a number of grant programmes that have specific objectives. For example: science bursaries for schools and colleges; undergraduate science research bursaries; the Oliver Bird PhD Studentships in Rheumatic Disease Research; the Social Science Small Grants scheme; and the New Career Development Scheme for post-doctoral social scientists and their senior partners. Details and application forms are available from the foundation or from its website. These are for individuals and so not featured in this entry.

The foundation also sets up and runs projects of its own. The two largest are The Nuffield Council on Bioethics (which is jointly funded with the Wellcome Trust and the Medical Research Council), and The Nuffield Curriculum Centre. The most recent is The Nuffield Adolescent Mental Health Initiative – a specific programme of research on time trends in adolescent mental health, set up by The Nuffield Foundation in 2005 (see website for further details). None of these are covered in this entry. Extensive publicity and information work is also carried out directly by the foundation.

Grantmaking 2008

Project grants generally range in size from £5,000 to £150,000 although increasingly larger grants for over £250,000 are made. Some grants are for research, others support practical innovation or development, often in voluntary sector organisations. In both cases the preference is for work 'that has wide significance, beyond the local or routine. The foundation looks to support projects that are imaginative and innovative, take a thoughtful and rigorous approach to problems, and have the potential to influence policy or practice'.

There are three areas of special interest and they are described below. In addition, the Open Door programme is used to fund projects that lie outside these areas of interest – or span boundaries between them – and that address the general aims of the foundation.

During the year the foundation had assets of £192 million, an income of £8.2 million and awarded grants totalling £7.2 million to organisations and individuals. Grants were categorised/ broken down in the annual report as follows:

Category	Amount
Project (social research and innovation)	£2,791,000
Open door	£1,501,000
Education	£2,305,000
Science	£2,347,000
Other	£1,699,000

Grant beneficiaries included:

Access to Justice: Faculty of Laws, University College London – Tribunal decision making (£201,000); Release – Young people, their rights and the law (£15,000); and Fair Trials International – Investigation of trial monitoring by consular officials (£12,538).

Child Protection and Family Law: British Association for Adoption and Fostering – Comparative outcomes and predictors of adult psycho-social functioning following early adversity (£148,000); and One plus One – 2008 Edith Dominian Memorial Lecture (£14,500).

Older People and their Families: This programme is to be wound up and those grant applications will now be handled as a specific theme under the 'Open Door' programme.

Education: Department of Psychology, University of York – Can pre-school training of oral language skills improve children's response to reading instruction? (£236,000); and Department of Education, University of Oxford – A review of research into how children learn mathematics (£30,000); and Centre for Studies in Science and Mathematics Education, University of Leeds – A pilot study of an applied route through secondary school science curriculum, 14 – 19 (£15,000).

Open Door: Centre for Family Law and Policy, University of Oxford – Resilience in young people orphaned by AIDS and other causes: predictors and mechanisms (£299,000); and School of Medicine, Health and Policy Practice, University of East Anglia – The role and effectiveness of disability benefits for older people (£124,000).

Commonwealth: WHO Collaborating Centre and the Section of Mental Health Policy, King's College, London – Developing primary care of mental disorders in Kenya (£227,000); and Mildmay International – Paediatric HIV and use of ARVs for multidisciplinary health workers (£75,000).

Applying for a project grant

All information about eligibility, criteria, the application process and timetable, grant conditions etc. are contained in the Complete Guide to Research and Innovation Grants for Beneficial Social Change available from the foundation's website, where you can also view the foundation's standard grant terms and conditions.

Before applying for a grant you should check that they are acceptable to you and to the organisation that will be administering the grant. In applying for a Nuffield Foundation grant you are deemed to have accepted these terms. Some of the general guidance for project grant applications reads as follows.

- The project should aim to have an impact beyond its immediate beneficiaries. It should be of more than local or regional interest.
- We will give preference to projects with outcomes which will be of interest and use to practitioners and policy makers. We do not fund research that simply advances knowledge.
- We will look for evidence that you have identified those to whom the outcomes of the project will be most relevant, and have engaged them where possible from the early stages of the project.
- Your project should include follow-up plans to assess the success or otherwise of the project/research, how effectively results were disseminated, and whether the desired impact was achieved.

The range of possible projects is wide and could include, for example, written materials, or a physical device. Again, such developments should be of general rather than local interest and the trustees will look for evidence that applicants have carefully considered how the information can be disseminated. Some element of evaluation is also desirable.

The foundation is particularly interested in dissemination of project findings to practitioners and sees this as an important activity in its own right. It encourages grant applications to include provision for this in the planning of projects, and is willing to consider applications for supplementary grants for this purpose.

Grant programmes

The foundation currently has three grant programmes in areas of social policy. These are: Access to Justice; Child Protection and Family Justice; and, Older People and their Families. Support for these three areas is through project grants, with a uniform set of criteria. Grants range in size from £5,000 to £150,000 and upwards and support research and/or innovative projects that will inform the development of policy or practice.

Access to Justice

The foundation has long had an interest in the area of access to justice. The foundation's current objectives in this area are:

- to promote developments in the legal system that will improve its accessibility to all people
- to promote wider access to legal services and advice and a better understanding of the obstacles to access to justice
- to fund research and promote developments in alternative dispute resolution
- to help promote a greater knowledge of the rights and duties of the individual, including those of the European citizen
- to examine the implications of new human rights' obligations on civil (not criminal) justice
- to help promote a greater public understanding of the role of law in society and of the legal system.

Replacement or core funding of existing services (such as law centres) will not be considered. Projects on penal policy, drugs, policing, crime prevention, criminal or environmental law will not normally be supported under the 'Access to justice' area of special interest unless they fulfil one of the objectives set out above.

Child Protection and Family Justice

This programme supports work to help ensure that the legal and institutional framework is best adapted to meet the needs of children and families. Grants in this area are considered by a separate specialist committee, whose members include academics in law, psychiatry and social work research, and practitioners in law, social work and relevant voluntary organisations. The committee is interested in a broad range of topics that go beyond child protection in a narrow sense, and in practical developments as well as research.

Particular interests include (but are not limited to):

- interdisciplinary work in family law, including other government policies with implications for families
- children at risk or in need, including 'looked after' children but also a much

broader range of children who might benefit from support

- broader provision for children in need, for instance the education of looked after children (considered jointly with the foundation's education programme)
- placement and planning for children, including adoption (special guidelines are available in this area and can be downloaded from the foundation's website)
- contact following separation or divorce, including the movement of children and child abduction
- legal and financial aspects of divorce or separation (following marriage or cohabitation) and their aftermath
- risk management that affects children.

Where a proposal is for a research study, the committee is interested in the dispassionate examination of evidence. It notes that evidence is likely to be different in different cases, for different types of children and families, and is more likely to support work that takes this approach.

Older People and their Families

The Older People and their Families programme is to be wound up and grant applications with this theme will now be handled as a specific theme under the 'Open Door' programme which supports projects of exceptional merit lying outside these policy areas but within the foundation's general terms of reference.

The following information describes the programme as it existed but readers should visit the foundation's website for current information on this theme.

The foundation wishes to fund work that starts from the perspectives, needs and interests of the older person and his or her family, rather than those of service providers. It is interested in projects that will enhance individual autonomy and choice and that recognise variation in preferences and provision.

The foundation is keen to support work that brings an international comparative perspective to bear, and is particularly interested in fostering work that considers European as well as other countries' perspectives.

As with all its areas of grantmaking, the foundation is interested in a wide range of topics. Issues that might be of interest include:

- the financial circumstances of older people and economic planning for later life. This might include planning for long-term care, pensions and insurance, (including private as well as state provision), pension splitting on divorce, intergenerational transfers and so on. It is particularly interested in projects that

recognise the complex relationship between state, private and family provision

- family solidarity and family obligations, including projects focussing on caring responsibilities between generations; their implications for the labour market; legal and social obligations; changing relationships as a result of family change; and ways of supporting family ties
- autonomy and decision-making in later life, including socio-legal matters such as competence, powers of attorney, conflicts of interest, advance directives and so on. The foundation wishes to foster work that improves autonomy as well as social responsibilities of older people
- retirement, work and citizenship, including the diverse positions of older people in employment; retirement and employments rights; and activities that promote active citizenship for older people.

The foundation is interested in innovative schemes which support interaction between professionals, informal carers and health and social workers, and notes that there may be particular scope for European comparisons here. Projects that address the relationship between health and social care will not be considered if they are routine research projects on aspects of service provision.

The foundation will not make grants for the following:

- support for mainstream academic or medical training
- medical or biological research into ageing, disability, dementia or mental illness
- housing or transport unless there is direct bearing on one of the topics above.

Education

Nuffield has supported innovative research and development in education for over 50 years. Current supported work builds on this tradition, prioritising areas in which influence on policy and practice can be brought to bear. There are four areas of priority at the moment:

- education for ages 14–19
- speech and language difficulties
- assessment
- curriculum policy and practice.

The foundation supports a range of different kinds of activities in these areas: research, intervention studies, development projects, reviews, seminars, capacity building and practical work. Recognising the presence of other, larger, funders in the field, the foundation carefully manages its resources and targets projects which can clearly have a beneficial impact on the development of learning and educational provision.

The foundation's focus is primarily on education 4–19 across the four countries of

the UK. However, it is increasingly interested in the transitions into schooling and out of development of cross-national perspectives on education and educational research.

As part of the foundation's attempt to consolidate and target support it does NOT accept unsolicited grant applications for work on any aspect of education. The foundation has a genuine interest in innovative work which is interdisciplinary in character. From time to time it may launch new areas and call for proposals – these will be posted on the front page of the website. The foundation also want to keep the door open to high quality proposals for work at the boundary between education and other areas of interest to the foundation; if you have a proposal which meets these criteria, please see the 'Open Door' grants, below, for details of how to take your ideas further.

Open Door

The foundation keeps an 'open door' to proposals of exceptional merit for research projects or practical innovations outside its special areas of interest, or to projects that span areas of interest. These must have some bearing on the foundation's widest charitable object – 'the advancement of social well-being'.

Subjects of interest include, but are not limited to: work on poverty, disadvantage, social welfare, disability, and work that crosses boundaries between our areas of special interest (for instance, learning and social provision; law and society; science and education).

Trustees are also especially interested in work that objectively examines current or proposed statutory arrangements, as independent funding can play a key role here. Through the Open Door programme, the foundation may also identify emerging areas that justify more sustained attention.

Commonwealth

Although most of the grants made by the foundation are for work in the UK, the trustees are keen to encourage projects that have a European dimension. The foundation has a Commonwealth programme supporting initiatives that develop the provision of education, health and social welfare in southern and eastern Africa through professional capacity-building.

The Nuffield Commonwealth programme is unusual amongst sources of funding of overseas work. Firstly it directly supports the development of service delivery and secondly it actively seeks partnerships between UK-based and southern organisations, where the UK-based partner is providing more than money, monitoring and moral support. It focuses on projects that improve services through development of the expertise and experience of practitioners and policy makers, and where active involvement from the UK-based organisation will increase the initiative's effectiveness.

Change is at the heart of each project supported under the programme – at individual, community, organisational and societal level. Recognising that achieving lasting change takes a long time, the programme supports only a small number of projects, but over an extended period, usually five years.

The programme has made grants every two years for the past eight years. The scheme is now under review and no further rounds have yet been announced. However, exceptional projects with a commonwealth dimension may be considered under the Open Door programme.

Exclusions The foundation normally makes grants only to UK organisations, and support work that will be mainly based in the UK, although the trustees welcome proposals for collaborative projects involving partners in European or Commonwealth countries.

The foundation cannot respond to requests for financial help from or on behalf of individuals in distress.

The trustees will not consider the following:

- general appeals
- buildings or capital costs
- projects which are mainly of local interest
- research that is mainly of theoretical interest
- day to day running costs or accommodation needs
- the provision of health or social services
- grants to replace statutory funding
- healthcare (outside mental health)
- the arts
- religion
- museums, exhibitions, performances
- sports and recreation
- conservation, heritage or environmental projects
- animal rights or welfare
- attendance at conferences
- expeditions, travel, adventure/holiday projects
- business or job creation projects
- academic journals
- medical research (other than in rheumatism and arthritis research)
- ongoing costs of existing work or services
- research that simply advances knowledge.

Grants are not made for the following purposes except when the activity is part of a project that is otherwise acceptable:

- work for degrees or other qualifications

- production of films, videos or television programmes
- purchase of equipment, including computers.

Applications If you are thinking of making an application, you must first send a written outline proposal. A member of staff will then advise you whether the proposal comes within the trustees' terms of reference and whether there are any particular questions or issues you should consider. The outline should describe:

- the issue or problem you wish to address
- the expected outcome(s)
- what will happen in the course of the project
- (for research projects) an outline of the methods to be employed
- an outline of the budget and the timetable.

The outline must not exceed three sides of A4, but you are welcome to include additional supporting information about yourself and your organisation. If you are advised to proceed with a full application, the staff member dealing with your proposal may suggest a meeting or, if matters are straightforward, may advise you to proceed straight to a full application.

If your work straddles more than one area of interest, or if you are unsure within which area it might lie, you do not need to enquire about who to send it to or how you should label it. Simply send it to one or other of the appropriate staff and they will ensure that it is handled appropriately.

The foundation currently operates several different grant programmes. Each programme publishes a comprehensive guide on its aims, policies and process for application, together with expectations for evaluation. All applications are reviewed by independent referees.

Extensive guidance on the preparation of full applications, too long to be summarised here, is available from the foundation and is published on its excellent website where you will also find application timetables for project grants.

The Ofenheim Charitable Trust

General, mainly charities supporting health, welfare, arts and the environment

£354,000 (2007/08)

Beneficial area Worldwide, in practice UK with some preference for East Sussex.

Baker Tilly, 1st Floor, Sentinel House, 46 Clarendon Road, Watford WD17 1JJ

Tel. 01923 816400

Email geoff.wright@bakertilly.co.uk

Correspondent Geoffrey Wright, Correspondent

Trustees *Roger Jackson Clark; Rory McLeod; Alexander Clark; Fiona Byrd.*

CC Number 286525

Information available Accounts were available from the Charity Commission.

Established in 1983 by Dr Angela Ofenheim, it is the policy of the trust to 'provide regular support for a number of charities in East Sussex because of the founder's association with that area'. High-profile organisations in the fields of health, welfare, arts and the environment are supported with many of the same organisations benefiting each year.

In 2007/08 the trust had assets of over £11 million and an income of £391,000. Grants were made to 60 organisations totalling £354,000.

Beneficiaries included: Trinity College of Music (£16,000); Save The Children Fund and Barnardo's (£13,000 each); Stroke Association, National Council of YMCA and Cancer Relief Macmillan Fund (£10,000 each); PCC Cherrington (£6,000); National Trust and NSPCC (£5,500 each); Universal Beneficent Association, House of St Barnabas in Soho, Centrepoint and Greenwich, Deptford & Rotherhithe Sea Cadet Unit (£3,000 each); Help for Heroes and the New Towner Trust (£2,500 each); Friends of Eastbourne Hospitals and Barn Owl Trust (£2,000 each); and Battersea Summer Scheme (£1,500).

Exclusions No grants to individuals.

Applications In writing to the correspondent. The majority of grants are to charities supported over a number of years and the trust has previously stated that unsolicited applications will not be acknowledged. Currently the trust states that the trustees also respond to one-off appeals from 'bodies where they have some knowledge'. Trustees meet in March and applications need to be received by February.

Oglesby Charitable Trust

General charitable purposes

£693,000 (2007/08)

Beneficial area The north west of England.

PO Box 336, Altrincham, Cheshire WA14 3XD

Email oglesbycharitabletrust@ bruntwood.co.uk

Website www.oglesbycharitabletrust.co. uk

Trustees *Jean Oglesby; Michael Oglesby; Robert Kitson; Kate Vokes; Jane Oglesby; Chris Oglesby; Peter Renshaw.*

CC Number 1026669

Information available Accounts were available from the Charity Commission. The trust also has a clear and helpful website.

The Oglesby Charitable Trust was established in 1992. The funding of the trust comes from annual contributions from Bruntwood Limited, part of a group of north-west based property investment companies owned by the founding trustees that has a net worth of approximately £300 million. The trust has been established to support charitable activities across a broad spectrum, and these reflect the beliefs and interests of the founding trustee family.

The trust income is currently around £750,000 per annum and grants each year will be made of around £600,000. To date, the maximum grant to any one project has been £60,000 and, generally, grants will be between £5,000 and £20,000. Since 2000, the trust has made grants of approximately £3.5 million.

It is accepted that the trust will be relatively modest in its resources and the trustees will be looking to place funds where they can make a real and measurable impact. They acknowledge that there already exists a large number of charitable and government backed organisations operating across all fields and it is not the trustees' intention to compete with, or supplement, these.

The trustees will be looking to form associations with bodies with whom they may become involved, preferably over a period of time. This is in order to form long-term relationships that will allow the trustees to fully understand and support the activities of the organisation.

To ensure that the trustees can be confident that any donations awarded are making a real difference there is an application process that must be followed [see 'Applications']. The trustees have worked hard to put together the trust funds and, consequently, they expect the recipients to understand their value and to extend a similar level of care in their use.

Grants are made mainly in the following areas:

- artistic development, both on an individual and group level
- educational grants and building projects
- environmental improvement projects
- improving the life and welfare of the underprivileged, where possible, by the encouragement of self-help
- medical aid and research.

Seed Fund

Funds are set aside in the Seed Fund for smaller grants and donations; up to £2,000. This fund is administered by the Community Foundation for Greater Manchester and applications can be obtained from the foundation's website at: www.communityfoundation.co.uk.

In 2007/08 the trust had assets of £596,000 and an income of £819,000. Over 50 main grants given totalling over £693,000, which included a donation of £12,500 for administration to the Community Foundation for Greater Manchester for the Acorn Fund (now the Seed Fund).

Unfortunately a list of grant beneficiaries for the year was not available, however, a list of organisations previously supported taken from the trust's website include: Action for Kids, Alcohol Drug Abstinence Service, Centre for Alternative Technology, Cheadle Hulme School, Cheetham's School, Fairbridge – Family Contact Line, Halle Youth Orchestra, Manchester City Art Gallery, Manchester University Arts and Drama, Motor Neurone Disease, National Asthma Campaign, National Library For The Blind, Stroke Research, Whitworth Art Gallery.

Exclusions The trust will not support:

- non registered charities
- those whose activities are for the purpose of collecting funds for redistribution to other charities
- animal charities

- charities whose principal operation area is outside the UK
- church and all building fabric appeals
- conferences
- continuing running costs of an organisation
- costs of employing fundraisers
- expeditions
- general sports, unless strongly associated with a disadvantaged group
- holidays
- individuals
- loans or business finance
- religion
- routine staff training
- sectarian religions
- sponsorship and marketing appeals.

Applications To enable the trustees to assess all applications from a similar basis, they ask that every applicant complete the online 'Stage 1 Application Form'. The trustees undertake to respond to this in six weeks. If this response is positive, then applicants will be required to complete a more detailed form under Stage 2.

By Stage 2, wherever possible, the trustees will require a proper Financial Plan prepared by the applicant. This should contain clear and measurable goals, which will be reviewed at regular intervals by the parties. In cases where the applicant does not possess either the skills or the resources to prepare such a plan, the trust may be prepared to assist.

Finally, the trustees will want to interview the applicant(s) at their place of operation or project site, both prior to the granting of funds and during the lifetime of the project, to monitor its progress. In addition the trustees will expect regular communication from the applicant, either verbal or by letter, to keep them informed of how the project is moving forward.

The P F Charitable Trust

General charitable purposes

£2.6 million (2007/08)

Beneficial area Unrestricted, with local interests in Oxfordshire and Scotland.

15 Suffolk Street, London SW1Y 4HG

Tel. 020 7036 5685

Correspondent The Secretary to the Trustees

275

CC Number 220124

Information available Accounts were available from the Charity Commission.

The trust was established in 1951 to assist religious and educational charities and for general charitable purposes. The trust makes grants to a wide range of causes and states that its policy is to continue to make a substantial number of small grants to charitable organisations both on a one-off and recurring basis.

In 2007/08 the trust had assets of £100 million and an income of £1.8 million. Grants were made totalling £2.6 million.

Grants were categorised as follows (with amounts including support costs):

Category/purpose	No. of grants	Amount
Health/saving of lives	111	£1,000,000
Relief in need	99	£647,000
Arts, culture, heritage or science	56	£321,000
Education	42	£209,000
Citizenship/community development	31	£124,000
Religion	10	£88,000
Amateur sport	7	£37,000
Armed forces	5	£57,000
Relief of poverty	10	£36,000
Environmental protection or improvement	14	£28,000
Human rights, conflict resolution or reconciliation, or the promotion of religious or racial harmony or equality or diversity	5	£13,000
Animal welfare	3	£2,500
Other	3	£161,000

Beneficiaries of the largest grants of £50,000 or more included: National Star Centre for Disabled Youth (£250,000), towards a development providing new facilities for the students; Great Ormond Street Hospital Children's Charity, towards building a new heart and lung centre and Royal Marsden Cancer Campaign, towards the continuing costs of medical research (£100,000 each); Charities Aid Foundation (£94,000) as a general donation; Scottish Community Foundation (£58,000), as a general donation; and the British Heart Foundation, towards the continuing costs of medical research, the Institute of Cancer Research, towards the continuing costs of medical research and Liverpool Cathedral, towards the integrated visitor centre project (£50,000 each).

Other beneficiaries included: Neuropathy Trust (£29,000); St Dunstan's (£27,000); Bloxham School Development Trust, Cumberland Lodge, Historic Churches Preservation Trust, Imperial War Museum, Leonard Ingrams Foundation, MacLaren Foundation, Royal Scots Dragoon Guards Museum Trust, and Trinity Hospice (£25,000 each); Seven Springs Foundation (£20,000); Oxford Brookes University (£18,000); City and Guilds of London Art School and NSPCC (£15,000 each); Citizens Advice – Banbury (£12,000); and Friends of Chelsea and Westminster Hospital, Friends of the Elderly, Memorial Arts Trust, Purcell School, RAFT and Tommy's (£10,000 each).

Exclusions No grants to individuals or non-registered charities.

Applications Applications to the correspondent in writing. Trustees usually meet monthly to consider applications and approve grants.

The Parthenon Trust

International aid, medical research, assistance to the disadvantaged including people with disabilities, culture and heritage, medical treatment and care, education, promotion of civil society and research on current affairs

£4 million (2007)

Beneficial area Unrestricted.

Saint-Nicolas 9 2000 Neuchatel, Switzerland

Tel. 00 41 32 724 8130

Correspondent J E E Whittaker, The Secretary

CC Number 1051467

Information available Although submitted on time, 2008 accounts were not available to view at the Charity Commission.

This trust was established in 1995 for general charitable purposes. The giving is international, with the organisations, as well as the activities, being based in a number of countries. Although geographically distant for UK charities, the trust is not unapproachable but applicants are urged to contact the secretary informally before submitting their applications. The trust is based in Switzerland, the home of the chair, Geraldine Whittaker and the secretary, her husband John Whittaker and is a UK registered charity.

The areas which the trust focuses on are:

- international aid organisations
- medical research
- assistance to the disadvantaged including people with disabilities
- cultural and heritage purposes
- medical treatment and care including supporting services, preventative medicine and assistance to those with disabilities
- education
- promotion of civil society and research on current affairs.

In 2007 the trust had an income of £5.3 million, mostly from donations and gifts and assets stood at £1.6 million. Grants totalled £4 million, broken down as follows:

Category	Value
Medical research	£1,500,000
Assistance to the disadvantaged	£695,000
Cultural and heritage purposes	£650,000
International aid organisations	£600,000
Medical treatment and care	£485,000
Education	£103,000
Promotion of civil society and research on current affairs	£15,000

There were 44 grants made in the year. Beneficiaries included: Cancer Research UK (£775,000 over four years); International Committee of the Red Cross (£600,000); José Carreras International Leukaemia Foundation (£275,000); Friends of Diva Opera, SMA Trust, St George's Chapel – Windsor Castle and Youth Business International (£250,000 each); Mont Blanc Foundation (£200,000); Ungureni Trust (£160,000); Royal Ballet School (£150,000); Society for the Relief of Disabled Children (£100,000); Bath University (£75,000); Winds of Hope Foundation (£50,000); Action Against Hunger UK (£25,000); Haven of Hope Christian Service (£20,000); West London Churches Homeless Concern (£19,000); Civitas: Institute for the Study of Civil Society (£15,000); Learning Challenge Foundation (£12,000); and United Aid for Azerbaijan (£10,000).

Exclusions No grants for individuals, scientific/geographical expeditions or projects which promote religious beliefs.

Applications In writing to the correspondent. Anyone proposing to submit an application should telephone the secretary beforehand. Unsolicited written applications are not normally acknowledged. Most grants are awarded at a trustees' meeting held early in the new year, although grants can be awarded at any time.

The Peacock Charitable Trust

Medical research, disability and general

£1.7 million (2007/08)

Beneficial area UK with a possible preference for London and the south of England.

c/o Charities Aid Foundation, Kings Hill, West Malling ME19 4TA

Tel. 01732 520081 **Fax** 01732 520001

Correspondent The Administrator

Trustees *Susan Peacock; Charles Peacock; Kenneth Burgin; Bettine Bond; Dr Clare Sellors.*

CC Number 257655

Information available Annual report and accounts, including a full list of grants, but without a narrative report.

This family trust was administered personally by Mr and Mrs Peacock for almost 35 years, with the assistance of Mr D Wallace who prepared reports on the majority of applicants to the trust for presentation to the trustees. Following the retirement of Mr Wallace the administration has been taken over by the Charities Aid Foundation (CAF). No changes to grant-making policy or practice have occurred with the main aims and objects being to advance the education of poor and deserving young people, and the relief of poverty, hardship, suffering and distress.

The trust has stated in the past that, in line with the founder's lifelong enthusiasm for sailing, it has an interest in supporting charities which involve disabled people in sailing activities.

The trust has also previously commented that many of the repeated grants go towards the running costs of organisations, in recognition of the fact that charities need, and sometimes lack, continuity. It says its newer grants are often for capital purposes. Some of its recent grants have also helped organisations to pay off their debts.

The trustees rely on CAF to present charities requiring grants to them; although we note the majority of present benefactors are recipients of recurrent grants. As such, the opportunity for new applicants to be successful appears limited.

Grantmaking

In 2007/08 the trust had assets of £39 million and an income of £2 million. Grants were made to over 100 organisations totalling £1.7 million. Grants ranged from £1,000 to £105,000, although the majority were for £10,000 or less. All but £133,000 of the grant total in 2007/08 went to organisations also supported in the previous year.

The largest grants were made to: Cancer Research UK (£105,000); Fairbridge (£100,000); Marie Curie Cancer Care (£82,000); Neuro Disability Research Trust (£70,000) and Chichester Harbour Trust, Macmillan Cancer Support and St Richard's Hospital Charity Trust (£50,000 each).

Other beneficiaries included: Jubilee Sailing Trust (£45,000); British Heart Foundation (£40,000); Epsom Medical Research (£30,000); Action for ME (£25,000); St John Ambulance (£12,000); Alzheimer's Society (£10,000); Woodland Trust (£8,000); Royal College of Surgeons of England (£7,000); REACH Volunteering (£6,000); League of Ventures – Search and Rescue (£5,000); and Trinity College Centre (£1,200).

Exclusions No donations are made to individuals and only in rare cases are additions made to the list of charities already being supported.

Applications In writing to the correspondent.

The Dowager Countess Eleanor Peel Trust

Medical research, older people, socially disadvantaged people and general

£599,000 (2007/08)

Beneficial area Worldwide, in practice UK, with a preference for Lancashire (especially Lancaster and District), Cumbria, Greater Manchester, Cheshire and Merseyside.

Trowers & Hamlins LLP, Sceptre Court, 40 Tower Hill, London EC3N 4DX

Tel. 020 7423 8000 **Fax** 020 7423 8001

Email secretary@peeltrust.com

Website www.peeltrust.com

Correspondent Allan J Twitchett, Secretary

Trustees *Sir Robert Boyd; Richard L Rothwell Jackson; John W Parkinson; Michael Parkinson.*

CC Number 214684

Information available Accounts were available at the Charity Commission. The foundation also has a new, helpful website.

The Dowager Countess Eleanor Peel Trust was established by trust deed in 1951 in accordance with the terms of her will. The objects of the trust are for general charitable purposes but with a preference for medical charities, charities for older people and those who are disadvantaged. There is a schedule to the trust deed listing 'scheduled charities' the trust may also support.

The trust makes significant annual grants to the Peel Medical Research Trust and the Peel Studentship Trust. These two trusts are legally distinct from the Dowager Countess Eleanor Peel Trust, having separately established trustee boards.

Grants are made to:

- medical charities including medical research
- charities in connection with older people
- charities assisting people who have fallen upon hard times through no fault of their own, and
- various charitable bodies specified in the Trust Deed

The trustees have a clear preference for supporting charities and projects in the north west of England, from where the trust fund monies originally emanated.

In each category, trustees will consider the following areas:

- medical charities – research and care specifically aimed at benefitting older people, to include Alzheimer's, macular disease, prostate cancer and Parkinson's Disease
- charities in connection with older people – old age, homes, carers
- charities for people fallen upon hard times – those helping people with a disability, hospitals, hospices, ex services charities, relief after natural or man-made disasters, mental health charities (including drug and alcohol addiction) and homelessness.

In 2007/08 the trust had assets of £14.6 million and an income of

277

£630,500. There were 53 grants made totalling £599,000, and were categorised as follows:

Category	Amount
Medical charities (including medical research)	£250,000
Other charitable purposes	£162,000
Charities assisting people facing hardship	£120,000
Charities in connection with older people	£56,000
Charities listed in the trust deed	£11,000

Larger grants included those to: University of Liverpool (£150,000); Peel Medical Research Trust (£85,000); Nottingham Trent University (£75,000); Peel Studentship Trust (£40,000). Other beneficiaries included: Cancer Care North Lancs and South Lakeland (£20,000); British Red Cross (£10,000); Age Concern England (£12,000); Deafway (£6,000); Hospital of the Blessed Trinity and Karen Hilltribes Trust (£5,000 each); Touchstones 12 (£3,000); and West Cumbria Society for the Blind (£2,500).

Exclusions Grants are not made to charities substantially under the control of central or local government or charities primarily devoted to children. Due to the number of applications received, the trust is usually unable to support small local charities with a gross annual income of less than £50,000, or those with substantial surpluses. Applications from individuals are not considered.

Applications The trustees apply the following criteria in making grants:

1) There is no geographical limitation on applications; however applications from charities in the 'preferred Locations' of Lancashire (especially Lancaster and District), Cumbria, Greater Manchester, Cheshire and Merseyside will receive preference over applications from other geographical areas.

2) The trustees focus on small to medium sized charities where grants will make a difference. Applications from large well-funded charities (with income in excess of £2.5 million per annum) will normally be rejected, unless the project is a capital project.

3) The trustees aim to support fewer charities with larger average grants (£5,000 or more).

4) The trustees' preference is to support capital projects or project driven applications and not running costs, although the trustees are flexible to take account of the needs of smaller charities.

5) The trustees do make grants to disaster appeals which are considered on a case by case basis.

Awareness
The trustees feel it is important to know the charities to which grants are or may be awarded. They will therefore from time to time arrange to visit the charity and/or arrange for the charity to make a presentation to a trustees meeting.

Applications
Applications for grants along with the required supporting information, should be forwarded by post:

Mr A J Twitchett
The Dowager Countess Eleanor Peel Trust
Sceptre Court
40 Tower Hill
London EC3N 4DX

Applications must arrive no later than four weeks before the date of a scheduled meeting. [Check the trust's website for details.]

The following information is required:

1) A general outline of the reasons for the application.
2) The amount of grant applied for.
3) The latest Annual report and Audited accounts.
4) If the application is for a major capital project, details of the cost of the project together with information regarding funds already in hand or pledged.

A grant application form can be downloaded from the trust's website.

Print it out before filling it in and enclosing it with any other information that you may feel is relevant.

Applications for Medical Research Grants
Applications for medical research grants will be categorised as appropriate for a 'minor grant' (£10,000 or less) or a 'major grant' (greater than £10,000 per annum for a defined research project for one–three years). Applications to be considered for a major grant will be assessed en-block annually at the trustee's March meeting. Applications will be competitive and will be met from funds set aside for this purpose. The following additional information is required:

- aims, objectives and direction of the research project
- the institution where the research will be carried out and by whom (principal researchers)
- An outline of costs and of funding required for the project and details of any funds already in hand.

A brief (but not too technical) annual report on the progress of projects receiving major grants will be requested from the research team.

The Performing Right Society Foundation

New music of any genre

£1.4 million (2008)
Beneficial area UK.

29–33 Berners Street, London W1T 3AB
Tel. 020 7306 4044 **Fax** 020 7306 4814
Email info@prsfoundation.co.uk
Website www.prsfoundation.co.uk
Correspondent James Hannam, Applications Manager
Trustees Sally Taylor; Nigel Elderton; Mick Leeson; Paulette Long; Anthony Mackintosh; Estelle Morris; Michael Noonan; Stephen McNeff; Edward Gregson.

CC Number 1080837

Information available Accounts were on file at the Charity Commission. Further information is available on the foundation's detailed and helpful website.

The PRS Foundation for New Music (PRSF) is the UK's largest independent funder purely for new music of any genre. Its main aims are to support, sustain and further the creation and performance of new music in the UK and increase the public's appreciation of, and education in, new music.

The foundation supports music creators, performers and promoters who are involved in creatively adventurous or pioneering musical activity. In particular, support is focused on music creators (composers/song-writers/producers) who live and work in the UK and on not-for-profit performers, festivals and promoters who are based in the UK. The foundation supports a huge range of new music activity – everything from unsigned band showcases to residencies for composers, from ground breaking commissions to live electronica, from the training of music producers to cross art form commissioning.

The foundation has a range of funding schemes and often works in partnership with other organisations to develop pioneering new programmes. In 2008 it was involved in the following activities:

- grant-giving schemes to provide core support for new music
- project grants to stimulate the creation and performance of new music
- partnership programmes with other organisations to develop long-term support for new music and stimulate significant change, for example, in professional development, international showcasing and collaboration
- the New Music Award, to create a pioneering new work and raise the profile of new music.

Full details of the foundation's activities are available on its website, including grant-making policies, priorities for each scheme and application forms.

In 2008 the foundation had assets of £276,000 and an income of £1.7 million. 404 grants were made totalling £1.4 million. The foundation offers the following analysis of its grantmaking during the year:

Approximately 19% of grants were made to new applicants and more than 789 applications were received during the year. Of the total grant expenditure:

- 67% of these funds supported new work and infrastructure across all genres
- 33% was awarded to professional development for emerging talent (for example, British Music Abroad, Aftershock, Composer in the House, Take Five, scholarships and bursaries) and collaboration (for example, Steps to New Music, Joint Commissioning Scheme, international creative exchanges). These programmes were developed in partnership with other funders.

New music across the UK has been supported, with 9% of funding to Scotland, 4% to Wales, 1% to Northern Ireland and 86% to England or UK-wide.

Unrestricted grants were categorised as follows:

Category	Value
Festivals	£238,000
Organisations	£206,000
New works	£162,000
Performance groups	£161,000
Promoters	£104,000
Partnerships	£78,000
New music award	£68,000
Special projects	£38,000
Live connections	£24,000
Jazz promoters	£15,000

Restricted grants developed with strategic partners were distributed in the following programmes:

Programme	Value
British music abroad	£198,000
Joint commissioning scheme	£62,000
Alan Hawkshaw/PRSF scholarships for NFTS	£10,000
Composer in the house	£10,000
New music plus	£5,400

A list of grant recipients was not included in the accounts. However, details of previously funded projects are available on the foundation's website, though without information on the individual grant awards.

Beneficiaries included: Supersonic Festival; Punch Records; Birmingham Jazz; Music Theatre Wales; Cambria Arts Association; Bruised Fruit; Paragon Ensemble; Cambridge Folk Festival; and Drake Music Project Scotland.

Exclusions The foundation will not offer funding for:

- individuals
- recordings/demos
- college fees
- musical equipment or instruments
- activity taking place outside of the UK.

Applications On an application form available to download from the foundation's website, or by telephoning the foundation. The application forms for each programme also include full guidelines for applicants. Only one scheme per calendar year can be applied for. Deadlines for applications vary from programme to programme. Contact the foundation or go to the website for further information. The foundation stresses that it funds **new** music.

Please note: the foundation will be rolling out an online application system across all its programmes during 2010.

The Jack Petchey Foundation

Young people aged 11 – 25 in the London boroughs, Essex and the Algarve, Portugal

£14.5 million (2008)

Beneficial area London, Essex and the Algarve, Portugal.

Exchange House, 13–14 Clements Court, Clements Lane, Ilford IG1 2QY

Tel. 020 8252 8000 **Fax** 020 8477 1088

Email mail@jackpetcheyfoundation.org.uk

Website www.jackpetcheyfoundation.org.uk

Correspondent Andrew Billington, Director

Trustee *Jack Petchey Foundation Company*

CC Number 1076886

Information available Accounts were available at the Charity Commission. The foundation's website includes guidelines, specific areas of benefit, application forms and good general information.

This foundation was established in 1999 by Jack Petchey and gives grants to programmes and projects that benefit young people aged 11 – 25. Jack Petchey was born in July 1925 in the East End of London. From a background with very few advantages he became a prominent entrepreneur and businessman. The foundation is a rapidly expanding trust that is eager to help young people take advantage of opportunities and play a full part in society by broadening their horizons and strengthening their positive skills to grow into healthy and considerate citizens.

In the UK the foundation benefits all London boroughs and Essex. In 2004, the foundation introduced a programme in the Algarve, Portugal. It focused initially on the Albufeira District. In July 2005 the Loulé District was included and in January 2006, Silves District. The objectives of the work in Portugal are the same as those established in the UK

In 2008 the foundation had an income of £8.2 million. Grants were made totalling £14.5 million.

Achievement Award Scheme

The Jack Petchey Achievement Award Scheme is run in almost 2,000 schools, colleges and clubs throughout London and Essex, contributing millions of pounds to youth organisations. The scheme is a reward and recognition initiative which enables schools and clubs to celebrate the achievements of young people and receive additional funding for the organisation.

Over £1.5 million is allocated to this scheme each year. The benefits of these awards are that they:

- enable schools/colleges/youth clubs etc., to recognise the effort, endeavour and achievement of young people in a practical and positive way
- provide additional funds for schools/colleges and youth clubs worth £3,000 – £4,000 a year, including the leader award
- enable schools/colleges and youth organisations to nominate an adult to win a leader award (for a youth worker, volunteer, teacher, non-teaching member of staff and so on).

Each month participating youth clubs, schools, colleges etc. select one young person to receive an achievement award. The month's winner receives a framed certificate and a cheque (payable to the school/college/club) to be spent on a school, club or community project of the recipient's choice.

There are two categories, one for youth or sports clubs or programmes operated outside schools and one for educational establishments.

Leader awards

Leader awards are linked to the Jack Petchey Achievement Award scheme. Awards of £1,000 are given to adults who have demonstrated, in an outstanding way, an ability to encourage and motivate young people aged 11–25 in London or Essex. The scheme is open to youth leaders, school teachers, community leaders, volunteer leaders, sports coaches and any other adults who have regular contact with young people.

Any school or club participating in the achievement award scheme can nominate a leader; 'it works best when young people, leaders, teachers or volunteers are involved in choosing an adult for this award.' The foundation can supply a nomination box and internal school/club nomination forms. To nominate a leader award winner, applicants should complete and send a nomination award form which is available from the website.

Project grants

The value of these awards is normally between £100 and £50,000. Projects must benefit young people. Registered charities or groups with charitable purposes in operation for at least 12 months can apply. The foundation is likely to support:

- organisations and charities that promote involvement and personal responsibility within society
- clubs & youth groups that demonstrate that they are enabling individuals to achieve their potential take control of their lives and contribute to society as a whole
- the training of youth leaders
- projects that assist young people to overcome problems that prevent them from reaching their potential. These may include addiction, homelessness and ill health
- projects that help develop self-esteem through involving young people in sport and other worth while activities
- youth organisations, scouts, sea cadets, police cadets, guides, army cadets, and so on
- schools and other training establishments with grants so that they can provide a better service to young people (care is taken not to give grants where statutory funding is available)

- volunteer projects
- schemes that tackle the problems faced by young people from ethnic minority groups
- projects where there is 'match funding' or demonstrable support from those involved with the organisation.

Sponsorship

The foundation will consider sponsoring young people (usually 11–25 years old) living in specified areas of London and Essex who are undertaking projects, or participating in events, that will benefit other young people or specific charities. The normal support from the foundation will be £300 (maximum of ten participants for a single event).

A sponsorship form is available from the foundation's website. Applicants should check the following points:

- do you live in the foundation's area?
- does the project benefit other young people (charity/school/community project)?
- will each applicant raise at least half of the total amount?
- brief details and, where appropriate, a budget for the project should be attached to the sponsorship form
- the form should be carefully completed by the young person concerned (not the adult leader or parent) and endorsed by the adult leader for the relevant organisation, club, school
- if a group is applying for sponsorship, their forms should be submitted together with a covering note from the leader or teacher.

London Marathon runners who meet the above criteria and complete the course, will usually be entitled to apply for £500 (maximum of two participants per organisation).

The following are considered for sponsorship funding:

- organisations and charities that promote involvement and personal responsibility within society
- clubs and youth groups that demonstrate that they are enabling individuals to achieve their potential, take control of their lives and contribute to society as a whole
- training of youth leaders
- projects that assist young people to overcome problems that prevent them reaching their potential. These may include addiction, homelessness and ill health
- projects that help develop self-esteem through involving young people in sport and other worth while activities
- youth organisations such as, scouts, sea cadets, police cadets, guides, army cadets

- schools and other training establishments so that they can provide a better service to young people (care is taken not to give grants where statutory funding is available)
- volunteer projects
- schemes that tackle the problems faced by young people from ethnic minority groups
- projects where there is match funding or demonstrable support from those involved with the organisation.

Note to youth leaders and teachers: If your club is associated with London Youth, Community Links or Essex Association of Boys' Clubs, please contact them before submitting an application to the foundation.

Petchey Academy

The Petchey Academy is a school in Hackney, which opened in September 2007. The Jack Petchey Foundation sponsors the Academy and made a £2 million contribution to the construction of the school. The state of the art building was completed on time and on budget. The school can accommodate 1,200 students. The specialism is 'Health, Care & Medical Sciences'.

The school is heavily oversubscribed with over 1,000 students chasing 180 places each year. The school does not select by ability but focuses on the local community. All the students come from within two kilometres of the school. For more information visit: www.petcheyacademy.org.uk

Jack Petchey's Speak Out Challenge!

The foundation sponsors the 'Jack Petchey's Speak Out Challenge!' a public speaking competition run by SpeakersBank in schools throughout London and Essex. 'Jack Petchey's Speak Out Challenge!' is the largest speaking competition for young people in the world. In 2008 almost 20,000 year 10 students from 32 boroughs in London and 14 districts in Essex participated in the challenge.

The students have the opportunity to talk openly and honestly on any subject they feel strongly about. Every student receives up to six hours of training in the skills of public speaking and effective communication from professional trainers. For more information visit: www.speakoutchallenge.com

Step Into Dance

Step into Dance is a fully inclusive, open access dance programme funded by The Jack Petchey Foundation and led by the Royal Academy of Dance. The programme offers weekly, extra-curricular dance classes to secondary schools in selected London boroughs. The programme aims to widen participation in dance for secondary school students aged between 11 and 16 years old.

The programme aims are as follows.

- To provide a fully inclusive and sustainable dance programme.
- To engage both students and in-school teachers in the benefits of dance and guide them to further training opportunities.

Aimed at 11–16 year olds, the programme runs over at least two terms, with dance teaching offered in ten week blocks. Participation in the programme is free for schools and dance classes are offered as two hour sessions per school, per week, on an extra-curricular basis, unless otherwise requested. For more information visit: www.stepintodance.org

Panathlon Challenge

The Panathlon Challenge seeks to inspire young people with disabilities to use competitive sport and fair play as a means of social and personal development.

Since 1996, Panathlon has provided training courses, coaching grants, free equipment and mini Paralympic type competitions to young people with disabilities in London, Kent, Essex and Merseyside. The organisation continues to expand in 2009/10.

Panathlon is the only organisation in England to offer young people with severe special needs the chance to compete in sport at both local and regional level. It is a unique social opportunity as well as a sporting one, allowing young people to meet outside of the school community, and providing opportunities both for friendship and heightened competition. The Jack Petchey Foundation has donated over £120,000 to Panathlon's activities across London and Essex since 2004. For more information visit www.panathlon.com

TS Jack Petchey

The Jack Petchey Foundation donated £1 million to enable The Marine Society and Sea Cadets to build a new power-training ship for young people. She will be named 'TS Jack Petchey'. The ship will have 16 berths and will train 16,000 young people over an anticipated lifespan of 25 years. Construction is underway and the TS Jack Petchey is expected to come into service in autumn 2009. For more information visit: www.ms-sc.org

Grants for 2008 were broken down as follows:

Category	Value
Schools	£4,200,000
Youth clubs/projects	£2,500,000
Training	£2,100,000
Uniformed organisations	£1,300,000
Sports clubs	£1,700,000
Volunteering	£1,000,000
Advice/support/counselling/mentoring	£519,000
Medical/hospice/hospital	£525,000
Disability	£362,000
General	£105,000
Olympics	£20,000
Housing/homelessness	£5,000

Beneficiaries of the largest grants included: SpeakersBank Limited (£550,000); Royal Academy of Dance (£298,000); Young Enterprise London (£270,000); Mercy Ships (£250,000); CBM (£223,000); Summer Uni London (£200,000); Newham Out of School Hours Learning (£193,000); Essex Association of Boys Clubs (£80,000); Sightsavers International (£50,000); YMCA George Williams College (£35,000); City Gateway, Knights Youth Centre and Newham Music Trust (£30,000 each); New Horizon Youth Centre (£25,000); Barbara Melunsky Refugee Youth Agency Limited (£22,000); and Alford House Club, Common Purpose, In-Volve, Kith & Kids, London International Festival of Theatre and Thames Gateway Youth Football Project (£20,000 each).

Exclusions The foundation will not accept applications:

- from applicants who have applied within the previous 12 months
- that directly replace statutory funding
- from individuals or for the benefit of one individual (unless under a sponsorship scheme)
- for work that has already taken place
- which do not directly benefit people in the UK
- for medical research
- for animal welfare
- for endowment funds
- that are part of general appeals or circulars.

The foundation is also unlikely to support:

- building or major refurbishment projects
- conferences and seminars
- projects where the main purpose is to promote religious beliefs.

The foundation only contributes to building or major refurbishment projects in exceptional circumstances.

Applications Application forms for each of the grant schemes can be downloaded from the foundation's website. There are no deadlines for applications but they should be made in 'good time' before the money is needed. The foundation holds monthly management meetings and aims to give a decision within six weeks.

The Pilgrim Trust

Social welfare and the preservation of buildings and heritage

£1.9 million (2008)

Beneficial area UK, but not the Channel Islands and the Isle of Man.

Clutha House, 10 Storeys Gate, London SW1P 3AY

Tel. 020 7222 4723 **Fax** 020 7976 0461

Email georgina.nayler@thepilgrimtrust. org.uk

Website www.thepilgrimtrust.org.uk

Correspondent Miss Georgina Nayler, Director

Trustees *Lady Jay of Ewelme, Chair; Lord David Cobbold; Dame Ruth Runciman; Tim Knox; Paul Richards; Mark Jones; Sir Alan Moses; John Podmore; James Fergusson; David Verey; Lord Crisp.*

CC Number 206602

Information available Annual report and accounts were available at the Charity Commission. The trust also has an excellent website.

The Pilgrim Trust was founded in 1930 by the wealthy American philanthropist Edward Stephen Harkness. Inspired by his admiration and affection for Great Britain, Harkness endowed the trust with just over £2 million. Harkness did not want the charity named after him, so the decision was taken to name the charity The Pilgrim Trust to signify its link with the land of the Pilgrim Fathers. It was Harkness's wish that his gift be given in grants for some of Britain's 'more urgent needs' and to 'promote her future well-being'. The first trustees decided that the trust should assist with social welfare projects, preservation (of buildings and countryside) and the promotion of art and learning. This has remained the focus of The Pilgrim Trust and the current Board of Trustees follows Harkness's guidelines by giving grants to projects in the fields of Preservation and Scholarship and of Social Welfare. Trustees review these objectives every three years.

General

In 2008 the trust had assets of almost £47.5 million and an income of £1.6 million. Grants were made across both of the trust's programme areas totalling almost £1.9 million, broken down as follows:

Field	Value
Preservation and scholarship	£1,200,000
Social welfare	£673,000

The trust provides an excellent overview of its current areas of interest and its activities during 2008 in the latest annual report, selected information from which is reproduced below.

Programmes

Preservation and scholarship

- Preservation of historic buildings and architectural features, especially projects giving a new use to buildings of outstanding architectural or historic importance; the conservation of monuments or structures important in their surroundings, including buildings designed for public performance. Trustees will consider supporting core costs and the cost of initial exploratory works for organisations seeking to rescue important buildings.
- Conservation of works of art, books, manuscripts, photographs and documents, and museum objects, where normal facilities for such work are not available, including records associated with archaeology, historic buildings and the landscape.
- The promotion of knowledge through academic research and its dissemination, for which public funds are not available, including cataloguing within museums, galleries, libraries and archives, and institutions where historic, scientific or archaeological records are preserved. Applications for the costs of preparing such work for publication will be considered, but not the publication itself.

Social welfare

- Projects to support people who misuse drugs and alcohol, particularly where those projects are seeking to reduce social exclusion through training, education, volunteering or employment. Trustees are especially interested in projects aimed at young people, black and ethnic minority groups and women.
- Projects in prisons and projects providing alternatives to custody. Trustees have a particular interest in projects that assist prisoners to acquire new skills or give support to their families.
- Trustees will consider projects that seek to inform and develop policy and practice in the priority areas outlined above.

The Trustees' objectives for 2008 were:

1) To commit £1.37 million in grants for spending in 2008 and up to £600,000 for spending in 2009 and 2010.
2) To allocate 60% of their funding to Preservation and Scholarship and 40% to Social Welfare.
3) To support projects in all parts of the United Kingdom.

4) To continue developing long-term relationships with organisations and to support these organisations with larger grants over several years.
5) To establish a new website and online application procedure.

Grantmaking

Trustees committed £1.4 million for spending in 2008 plus £494,000 for spending in 2009 and £97,000 for 2010. They awarded 89 grants with the main grants averaging just over £23,500.
The following table shows how the Pilgrim trustees committed the trust's funds during 2008. Although trustees aim to spend 60% of their grant giving on preservation and scholarship and 40% on social welfare, their commitments must reflect the quality of the applications they receive. They are not bound by these percentages; they are an aim and trustees are free to vary the allocations.

Review of the year

Partnerships

As reported last year, the Pilgrim Trust is keen to work with others so that it can both draw on their expertise and maximise the impact of its grants. The trustees are delighted by the continued collaboration with The National Archives on the National Cataloguing Scheme and the Association of Independent Museums with its Conservation Grants Scheme. The first National Cataloguing Scheme was launched in the spring covering the whole of the UK. Ten grants totalling £331,000 were awarded and these grants will enable collections that have hitherto been hidden, to become accessible to researchers, students and the general public. The Pilgrim Trust continues to be grateful to The National Archives and the funding partners for the Cataloguing Scheme.

The collaboration with Shelter to support men leaving HMP Leeds has continued with further discussions about how best to evaluate the project, which the Pilgrim trustees believe is crucial to demonstrate whether the project is aiding successful

resettlement and so reducing recidivism. The Pilgrim Trust is delighted that the LankellyChase Foundation has agreed to contribute financially towards the evaluation. Trustees hope to work more closely with other trusts and foundations in the future, particularly in these difficult economic times.

Preservation and scholarship
Preservation of secular buildings

During the year the trust has supported a number of projects that celebrate and preserve the history of lost or dying industries. Two were in the north east of Scotland. The Salmon House in Banff is listed Grade B and on the Buildings at Risk register. It is one of the last salmon bothies still intact in Scotland. It was the coastal net fishing industry was an important employer in Scotland. The Salmon House was used to prepare the salmon caught off the coast and it would be pickled or packed fresh in ice for transport either by ship or rail to market. It was also used to store and repair the nets and had a workshop to repair the boats, with sleeping and cooking space for the workmen. The interior of the building features three large brick lined vaulted chambers – two stored the ice and the third being the fish preparation area. The intention is to retain as much as possible of the interior but use it as an interpretative centre for this important but now defunct Scottish industry. It will also provide a permanent home for the Scottish Traditional Boat Festival. This Festival is now in its 14th year and is held around Portsoy's 17th century harbour. The Festival drew 18,600 visitors in 2006. Trustees were delighted to help with a grant of £10,000 towards essential repairs and were particularly pleased that the building's new use will give it a sustainable future.

Trustees awarded a grant of £20,000 to the Knockando Woolmill Trust towards the conservation of original textile machinery. The Knockando Woolmill on Speyside has been producing textiles since at least 1784. The buildings, A-Group listed and cited as 'internationally significant' by Historic Scotland, contain original textile machinery acquired over the centuries. It has always been at the heart of the local community; listed as the 'Wauk Mill' in parish records

THE PILGRIM TRUST
Grants committed by region and subject area (2008)

	Preservation and scholarship	Social welfare	Total	Percentage split by region
National organisation	£310,000	£194,500	£504,500	25.27%
Scotland	£168,600	£52,000	£220,600	11.05%
Wales	£75,100	£0	£75,100	3.76%
Northern Ireland	£45,000	£36,000	£81,000	4.06%
London	£258,000	£92,000	£350,000	17.54%
Home counties	£69,100	£0	£69,100	3.46%
Rest of England	£333,200	£362,600	£695,800	34.85%
Total by subject area	**£1,260,000**	**£737,100**	**£2,000,000**	**100%**

from 1784, the mill has since maintained its traditions of spinning and weaving through generations of families.

Knockando Woolmill grew gradually as the mechanisation of textile production developed elsewhere in the UK. This is not the large industrial mill of Yorkshire or the Scottish Borders but 18th and 19th-century farm diversification. When times were good, the Woolmill tenant would buy a new (usually second hand) piece of machinery. He would extend the mill building just enough to keep the weather off the machine; being a thrifty farmer, he re-used doors and windows from elsewhere. This has resulted in the surviving tiny, ramshackle building stuffed full of historic machinery. Spinning and weaving went hand in hand with agriculture at Knockando. There would be little work carried on in the mill during sowing or harvest time but after shearing, local farmers would bring in their fleeces to be processed and take them away as blankets and tweed cloth. Many communities had their own local district woollen mill, but the majority of these disappeared between the two World Wars. Somehow, Knockando survived. The present weaver, Hugh Jones, learnt the craft from his predecessor, Duncan Stewart, and for 30 years has continued to produce tweed, rugs and blankets on the old looms. Using expertise passed down through generations, he has managed single-handedly to sustain the traditions of the UK's oldest surviving district woollen mill.

The Knockando Woolmill Trust was set up in 2000 to rescue the Woolmill. The aim of the trust is to ensure the Woolmill survives for the next 200 years by restoring the buildings and machinery, continue to produce cloth, train a new generation of people to card, spin and weave and to share the Woolmill experience with as many people as possible. However, the philosophy is to restore the site by doing as much as is necessary but changing as little as possible.

Llanelly House is a grand house, in the centre of Llanelli, which has fallen on hard times. The original house dates from 1605 and from then until 1690s it was the home of the wealthy Vaughn family. After this the estate was acquired by the Stepney family and the house itself was radically re-modelled between 1706 and 1714. In the latter half of the 18th century the house was let and began to fall into decline. In the 19th century the property was divided up and the surrounding gardens were sold for development. Now the house is entirely enclosed by roads and buildings on all sides. By the end of the 20th century neglect and misuse had reduced it to a state of appalling disrepair and sadly the building continued to be badly affected by its current position next to the town gyratory system. However, it is

Grade 1 listed and one of only two Grade 1 houses in Carmarthenshire. According to CADW (the Assembly Government's historic environment division) it is the most outstanding domestic building to survive in south Wales.

Its significance had led the County Council to make the road in front pedestrians only and also to re-design other roads to route them away from the house. Despite over a century of abuse and neglect the CADW listing described the house as 'retaining extensive areas of original panelling' and 'to a remarkable extent the original fittings of an 18th-century house'.

Llanelli Town Council plans to restore the appearance and use of the house by working with the Carmarthenshire Heritage Regeneration Trust, which has acquired a 99 year lease from the council. Once fully restored the house will re-open as Llanelly House Community and Heritage Centre and will be run by a newly created trust. The project aims to save and restore the house as far as possible to its 18th-century form and create a sustainable centre for visitors and local people. It is hoped that it will offer this deprived area a much needed boost both to the community and to the regeneration of Llanelli town centre. The Pilgrim Trust grant was £20,000.

Trustees have also funded projects to preserve Northern Ireland's historic buildings. The Belfast Buildings Preservation Trust is a cross-community charitable organisation dedicated to the re-use of historic city buildings for which no viable or commercial use can be found. The trust was founded in 1996 and has won several awards for its work. It is constituted as a revolving fund with surplus money from completed projects being 'revolved' to the next building project. It was founded following arson attacks on two of Belfast's most important historic buildings. St Patrick's National School was the last remaining neo-gothic building in Belfast, while Christ Church was one of the few remaining remnants of the Georgian City. Applications were lodged to demolish both buildings following the fires. At the time the regeneration of Belfast's historic buildings did not feature on the political agenda. The Belfast Building Preservation Trust fought to have the significance of the built heritage recognised and was successful in restoring the school while the Diocese restored the Church. The school is now occupied by the offices of the Catholic school authorities and a Diocesan Resource Centre and bookshop. The trust retains one of the old schoolrooms, which it has restored to 19th century specification and uses as an educational resource. In addition to these two buildings, the trust has been involved with approximately 20 other historic buildings in Belfast and elsewhere.

The Pilgrim Trust was asked to support the employment of a member of staff for the trust. Until now, the work of the trust has depended upon the pro bono work carried out by its trustee and patron, Fionnuala Jay-O'Boyle. It is important that work is undertaken between projects, particularly in terms of education and lobbying. Regeneration of historic buildings and the preservation of the architectural heritage of Northern Ireland are far less developed than in the rest of the UK. For the trust it is important that the message is spread and that it works with communities to establish the critical role that heritage can play in regeneration. The most successful building preservation trust projects are those where the community is involved and is prepared to take ownership of the building in the long term. The role of the staff member would be to engage with these communities, as well as to develop new projects. The Pilgrim Trust grant was £35,000 over two years.

Although the Pilgrim Trust is not allowed, by its Trust Deed, to fund projects outside the United Kingdom, it was pleased to receive an application from The Irish Landmark Trust. As well as working in the Irish Republic the trust is registered as a charity in Northern Ireland and therefore is eligible to apply. The trust saves heritage buildings that are abandoned or at risk throughout the whole of Ireland. The trust undertakes their conservation, restoration and maintenance by converting them to domestic use suitable for short-term holiday lettings. Its buildings are varied, from lighthouses, to gate lodges, to tower houses, to school houses, to mews. All of them are individual and even eccentric and are therefore unsuitable as permanent residences. They are often in remote and delightful parts of the country and are ideal retreats for those seeking a short stay in fascinating and sensitively restored buildings.

To date it has restored 15 interesting and architecturally important buildings across Ireland; north and south. The Pilgrim Trust gave a grant of £10,000 to support the repair of the Magherintemple Gatelodge, Ballycastle, Co Antrim. Magherintemple is the seat of the Casement family and a descendant of the family still lives there. The Gate Lodge was built in the Scottish Baronial Style in 1874, possibly by the architect S P Close. It is in the same style as the extended main house. It is an attractive building with a steeply pitched roof and crow steps. It has been unoccupied and has a major damp problem, crumbling brickwork and rampant vegetation. The restoration will respect the layout of the building, but will provide two double bedrooms and living room. The yard walls will conceal the bathroom and kitchen.

Preservation of religious buildings

The Pilgrim Trust has long championed the cause of encouraging the regular maintenance of historic buildings rather than waiting to act until water is running down walls! Regular maintenance is of particular importance for parish churches and other religious buildings. Trustees have given a grant of £25,000 to The Society for the Protection of Ancient Buildings (SPAB) to assist it with training of those responsible for the care of parish churches in the importance of maintenance. The Society was founded by William Morris in 1877 to care for and preserve the UK's architectural heritage. Since its foundation, SPAB has been committed to maintenance matters, in line with William Morris' exhortation to: Stave off decay by daily care.

Faith in Maintenance is a unique project that aims to provide training and support for the thousands of volunteers in England and Wales who help to maintain our historic places of worship. It will provide 30 training courses each year helping over 6,000 volunteers to look after a variety of faith buildings across the country. Along with protecting significant historic structures, the project also encourages more people to become involved in their local community's heritage. One of the key aspects of the scheme is that the training courses are free and are available to any faith group using a historic building for its worship.

Preservation and scholarship in museums, libraries and archives

Although trustees are endeavouring to give fewer larger grants they recognised that small grants are valuable and can achieve welcome results. One such small grant in 2008 was £5,000 to the Runnymede Trust. The trust developed in the 1960s partly as a response to the growth of racist politics, especially those of Enoch Powell, which looked at the time to be turning into a mass movement, and also as an attempt to create an equivalent to the American Anti-Defamation League in Britain. Since its inception, the trust has worked to challenge racial discrimination and promote a successful multi-ethnic Britain. Its principal function in the early years was to provide briefs, background papers and research data for MPs, civil servants, local government and others concerned with policy.

One of the larger grants given by trustees in 2008 was to the Bowes Museum in County Durham. They promised £80,500 over three years towards the employment of a specialist tapestry conservator. This is a continuation of a project that began in 2003 with the employment of a textile conservator and was supported with £60,000 from the Pilgrim Trust. The Bowes Museum holds the greatest collection of European fine and decorative arts in the north of England. It also houses one of the most comprehensive textile collections in the UK. It represents the history of European textiles from the 15th to

the 19th centuries and is of international significance. It includes tapestries, carpets furnishing textiles, embroideries, lace, ecclesiastical vestments as well as printed and woven textiles.

In the 1980s a conservation studio was created in the museum and a qualified free-lance conservator was engaged to work two days per month to conserve textiles and to train a textiles assistant to continue the work. However, since the textiles assistant retired in 2000, the conservation facilities had not been used.

The Textiles Conservator who has been employed for the last three years, funded by the Pilgrim Trust, had helped the museum to achieve conservation and cleaning of three major collections, but the impact of the post was more far-reaching than this alone. In particular, the museum was able to put textiles in new displays in the museum properly cleaned, conserved and mounted.

The Bowes Museum then sought a further grant from the Pilgrim Trust to build on the progress that had been made in textiles conservation. The museum wished to employ a conservator to focus on a major part of the museums textile collection, the tapestries. The conservator is undertaking work on tapestries in particular need or of importance so that they can return to display. Some of this work is taking place within the gallery so that visitors may witness the conservation; the remainder is being executed in the museum's Textile Conservation Studio. A further part of the role will be to organise an appropriate programme of events to raise awareness of this part of the collection; for example, lectures and commentated demonstrations.

Social welfare
Projects in prison and rehabilitation of offenders

Trustees are keen to support the resettlement of offenders by funding projects that assist with the transition from custody to the community. This transition can be particular difficult for women leaving custody as they often have the added responsibility of children. The Family Service Unit in Scotland, otherwise known as Circle, has a long history of providing family support services to vulnerable children and their families. Currently it provides services across Edinburgh, West Lothian, North and South Lanarkshire and east Glasgow. The service has four main strands of operation: work with families with children where parents have substance use disorders; work with families with children where parents are in prison or post release; work with schools and children at risk and education of trainee social workers and other professionals. Family workers are for the most part, highly qualified social workers with additional training in substance use disorders and

family based interventions. The Pilgrim Trustees supported the Meet at the Gate Project that involves placing a community social worker in Cornton Vale Prison for women. The worker is responsible for identifying individuals who may be eligible for the service and doing initial assessments for risk, need and suitability. The project worker can support five individuals and their families at any one time, with a further 14 community social workers able to take on one case post-release, dependent on where the service user lives. Once released, the women can rely on the family worker for weekly meetings and support in housing, benefits, healthcare, education and employment. The workers will also assist with parenting skills, mediation within the family and provide specialist feedback and therapeutic family assistance. Trustees have agreed to provide an initial grant of £10,000 towards the service, with the possibility of further support if the project is proving to be successful.

Although trustees are keen to support prisoners on release, they also see the benefit of broadening their horizons and engaging them in the creative arts while they are in prison. During the year they were impressed by the expansion of the Koestler Trust's annual art competition for people within the criminal justice system. In 2008 there were over 5,000 entries from all over the country in categories that included photography, painting, script writing and life autobiography. In September young people from Lambeth Youth Offending Service rose to the challenge of curating the Koestler Exhibition at the Royal Festival Hall and the Koestler Trust held the biggest exhibition of adult and young offenders' art at the Royal Festival Hall. This was the first time in the Trust's 47-year history that people who have offended have selected the work displayed. The Pilgrim Trust was asked to offer financial assistance to enable the Koestler Trust to improve the way it receives the art works and to bring curatorial skills to the unpacking, storing and hanging of the exhibits. It also wished to offer the artists and writers feedback on their entries. The Pilgrim Trust's grant was £25,000.

Projects to support people who misuse drugs or alcohol

For 2008, trustees amended their priorities in the drug and alcohol field to cover projects that seek to reduce social exclusion through training, education, volunteering or employment. Therefore, trustees were pleased to receive an application from Broadreach House for a volunteering scheme at its day centre, Ocean Quay. Broadreach has been providing residential and non-residential treatment for people with drug and alcohol problems for 25 years. Trustees have supported its work in the past and have watched it develop and grow over the past few years. In 2006 Broadreach's Day Service, with funding from Futurebuilders, moved into converted industrial premises. The Service team (which includes both staff and service users) have over the past year-and-a-half developed and piloted several, separately funded strands of services and have worked to integrate the services into what is now known as the Ocean Quay project. Ocean Quay provides a range of activities that include in-house services such as support groups, group therapy, life skills training, debt management, resettlement and parenting programmes; they also include for service users, social activities such as volunteering, mentoring, facilitation, cookery, photography and woodwork. Ocean Quay is open to people prior to, during and following either residential, prison or community treatment. Users of the service can either be abstinent, on prescribed medication or dealing with ongoing substance use.

Ocean Quay's volunteering programme involves service users being trained as peer mentors and then supported to offer 1 to 1 support to drink or drug users. The volunteers are involved in all aspects of Ocean Quay's work and are in demand by local homelessness projects as mentors. They have also developed a maintenance and decorating project for householders; a breakfast café; gym and recording studio. In additions they support 'Friends on the Outside' (FOTO), which works with recently released prolific offenders affected by substance misuse. The Pilgrim Trust contributed £25,000 towards covering the salary costs of additional volunteer project workers.

Trustees are keen to support projects for people from ethnic minorities who are misusing drugs or alcohol. In the past they have supported community refugee groups working with Somali people involved in khat use. Last year, Trustees agreed a grant of £25,000 to Adfam to support the families of young Somali men. Adfam was founded in 1984 by the mother of a heroin user and, today, continues with its original aims to provide support, training and consultancy to families affected by someone else's substance misuse. It particularly seeks to support the families of drug users from Black and Minority Ethnic communities. Through its work Adfam became aware that young Somali men were over represented at every stage of the criminal justice system and that their families were doubly discriminated against. It secured three year funding to develop specialist, culturally sensitive services for this community and has employed a Somali Development Worker who is delivering family led support services in Acton, Hillingdon and Hackney working with Somali groups. It wished to expand this

project to five more areas and the Pilgrim Trust offered £25,000 to support the appointment of a further, part time worker.

Exclusions Grants are not made to:

- individuals
- non UK registered charities or charities registered in the Channel Islands or the Isle of Man
- projects based outside the United Kingdom
- projects where the work has already been completed or where contracts have already been awarded
- organisations that have had a grant awarded by us within the past two years. Please note: this does not refer to payments made within that timeframe
- projects with a capital cost of over £1 million pounds where partnership funding is required
- projects where the activities are considered to be primarily the responsibility of central or local government
- general appeals or circulars
- projects for the commissioning of new works of art
- organisations seeking publishing production costs
- projects seeking to develop new facilities within a church or the re-ordering of churches or places of worship for wider community use
- any social welfare project that falls outside the trustees' current priorities
- arts and drama projects – unless they can demonstrate that they are linked to clear educational goals for prisoners or those with drug or alcohol problems
- drop in centres – unless the specific work within the centre falls within one of the trustees' current priority areas
- youth or sports clubs, travel or adventure projects, community centres or children's play groups
- organisations seeking funding for trips abroad
- organisations seeking educational funding, for example assistance to individuals for degree or post-degree work or school, university or college development programmes
- one-off events such as exhibitions, festivals, seminars, conferences or theatrical and musical productions.

Applications
Main Grant Fund
As our primary grant outlet, this fund distributes approximately 90% of our annual grant budget. If the project fits our programme criteria, organisations can apply under this scheme for sums above £5,000.

Small Grant Fund
This fund is reserved for requests of £5,000 or less. Applications to this fund normally require less detailed assessment (though a visit or meeting may be required) but applicants should include the names of two referees from organisations with whom they work.

Full funding guidelines are available from the trust's website. Applications can also be made online, or a form can be requested from the correspondent. The trustees meet quarterly.

The Pilkington Charities Fund

General, health, social welfare, people with disabilities, older people and victims of natural disaster or war

£386,000 (2007/08)

Beneficial area Worldwide, in practice mainly UK with a preference for Merseyside.

Rathbones, Port of Liverpool Building, Pier Head, Liverpool L3 1NW

Tel. 0151 236 6666 **Fax** 0151 243 7003

Email sarah.nicklin@rathbones.com

Correspondent Sarah Nicklin, Trust Administrator

Trustees *Neil Pilkington Jones; Mrs Jennifer Jones; Arnold Philip Pilkington.*

CC Number 225911

Information available Accounts were available from the Charity Commission.

The trust was established in 1950 to assist employees or former employees of Pilkington's or any associated companies. It now mainly supports registered charities in the areas of social welfare, disability, health, medical research and overseas aid. A small proportion is reserved for the benefit of present or former employees of the Pilkington Glass Company.

Grants are awarded twice a year, in October and April. Most range from £1,000 to £8,000, though larger grants for up to £100,000 are sometimes made, and typically go to national or international charities.

In 2007/08 the trust had assets of £17.5 million and an income of £590,000. Grants were made to 88 organisations totalling £386,000, with the largest grants being awarded to the C & A Pilkington Trust Fund (£77,000). The more general distributions were for less than £8,000 each with the exception of Arthritis Research Campaign, Cancer Research UK, Help the Aged, Willowbrook Hospice – St Helens and YWCA (£10,000 each).

Other beneficiaries included: BiPolar Organisation (£8,000); Cystic Fibrosis Trust, Children at Risk Foundation and the Samaritans (£5,000 each); Leukaemia Research and St Cleopas 468 Community Centre (£4,000 each); Autism Initiative, St Michael's and Lark Lane Community Association and the Salvation Army – Liverpool Walton Corps (£3,000 each); Riverside Credit Union and Women Supporting Women (£2,000 each); and Listening Books and Warrington Wolves Foundation (£1,000 each).

Exclusions Grants are only made to registered charities. No grants to individuals.

Applications In writing to the correspondent. Applications should include the charity registration number, a copy of the latest accounts and details of the project for which support is sought.

Polden-Puckham Charitable Foundation

Peace and security, ecological issues and social change

£476,000 (2007/08)

Beneficial area UK and overseas.

BM PPCF, London WC1N 3XX

Email ppcf@polden-puckham.org.uk

Website www.polden-puckham.org.uk

Correspondent Bryn Higgs, Secretary

Trustees *Harriet Gillett; Jenepher Gordon; Linda Patten; Daniel Barlow; Bevis Gillett; Val Ferguson; Gerardo Fragoso; Ben Gillett; Suzy Gillett.*

CC Number 1003024

Information available Full accounts and information for applicants were provided by the trust.

This foundation supports 'projects that seek to influence values and attitudes, promote equity and social justice, and develop radical alternatives to current economic and social structures'.

In 2007/08 it had assets of £13 million and an income of £465,000. Grants were made to 60 organisations totalling £476,000.

Grants are made in the following categories:

Peace and security
Development of ways of resolving international and internal conflicts peacefully, and of removing the causes of conflict.

Ecological sustainability
Work which tackles the underlying pressures and conditions leading towards global environmental breakdown; particularly initiatives which promote sustainable living.

Other issues
PPCF also supports corporate responsibility, ethical investment, trade, human rights and women's issues, especially where it involves policy change work related to peace and ecological issues. PPCF also has a long-standing link with the Society of Friends and has supported the work of Quaker groups.

The foundation prefers to make grants to small, pioneering organisations that are working to influence policy, values and attitudes at a national or international level. Grants usually range from £5,000 to £15,000 per year for up to three years. Practical projects are only supported when they are of a pioneering nature and will potentially influence UK policy.

Grants in 2007/08

During the year there were 23 grants for £10,000 or more. Beneficiaries included: Quaker Peace and Social Witness (£20,000); Oxford Research Group (£18,000); New Economics Foundation and Responding to Conflict (£15,000 each); British American Security Information Council (£12,000); Climate Action Groups – Climate Outreach Information Network (£11,000); and Campaign for Better Transport and Anti-Apathy (£10,000 each).

Other beneficiaries included: Platform (£9,000); Corporate Watch Cooperative – Climate Outreach Information Network (£8,000); Living Witness Project (£6,000); Ecological Land Cooperative (£5,000); Mines and Communities Network – Missionary Society of St Columban (£4,000); Women's International League for Peace

and Freedom – Womankind Worldwide (£3,000); and Cooperation for Peace and Unity – Peace Direct (£2,000).

Exclusions The foundation does not support:

- individuals
- travel bursaries (including overseas placements and expeditions)
- study
- academic research
- capital projects (for example, building projects or purchase of nature reserves)
- community or local projects (except innovative prototypes for widespread application)
- general appeals
- organisations based overseas (unless they have a well established relationship with a UK charitable organisation).

Applications The trustees meet twice a year in spring and autumn. Application forms and guidance notes can be downloaded from the foundation's website and must be submitted via email. Applicants are also asked to submit their latest set of audited accounts and an annual report, preferably via email.

Application deadlines are usually in February/March and September but exact dates can be found on the website. Trustee meetings are generally held in April and October/November.

Please note: the foundation is happy to provide brief feedback on applications one week after the trustees have made a decision.

Porticus UK

Social welfare, education and religion

See below

Beneficial area UK.

4th Floor, Eagle House, 108–110 Jermyn Street, London SW1Y 6EE

Tel. 020 7024 3503 **Fax** 020 7024 3501

Email n.koblintz@porticus.com

Website www.porticusuk.com

Correspondent Nathan Koblintz

Trustees *L A Adams; M C L Brenninkmeyer; S R M Brenninkmeyer.*

CC Number 1069245

Information available Accounts were available from the Charity Commission.

Further information was taken from the charity's website.

The charity was previously called Derwent Charitable Consultancy, which administered the Waterside Trust, whose grantmaking has now been succeeded by other sources in the Netherlands advised by Porticus UK.

It is believed to be one expression of the philanthropy of the Brenninkmeyer family, founders of the C&A clothing stores in Europe. Long-term fundraisers will remember organisations such as the Marble Arch Trust. The family always sought the minimum of publicity for their energetic and much admired work.

Though the family's Catholic interests were always apparent, the range of their philanthropic interests have been wide and enterprising over the years.

Porticus UK is not in itself a grantmaker – it advises and assesses grants on behalf of several foundations in the Netherlands, including Stichting Porticus.

Porticus UK has four areas of interest and recommends in the region of 170 grants each year. Grants are normally in the range of £10,000 to £25,000, but occasionally larger projects are funded. Total funds available amount to around £4 million each year.

The following information on the charity's programmes and guidelines is taken from its website:

Porticus UK's mission is to have solidarity with the poor and the marginalised, reflecting our Christian responsibility and support for the social teaching of the Roman Catholic Church. We do this through the provision of high quality charity advice, grant assessment and administration, and services to our donors and partners that promote organisational effectiveness.

We aim to offer a dynamic service, providing both effectiveness and initiative whilst remaining an organisation in touch with people's needs.

The success of our work is judged, ultimately, by how much long-lasting and tangible impact is made on people's lives; whilst producing changes which ensure the respect of our network partners, beneficiaries and donors.

We do occasionally fund small grants of less than £10,000, but most of our grants are between £10,000 and £25,000. We occasionally fund larger projects.

Although our values are based in the Catholic faith, we welcome applications from all organisations, whether or not they have a faith basis.

We understand that a charity's funding priorities are not always specific project costs, and so welcome applications for developing policy, advocacy and research.

We put particular emphasis on organisations which have a proven model and wish to expand.

We define our priorities based on the interests of the trustees and identified areas of need within these interests:

Strengthening Family Relationships

Encouraging and cherishing the family relationship that is so often central to people's lives, is at the centre of what we do. The support we offer aims to strengthen those family relationships that are most vulnerable and strained. We, therefore, look for applications which are focused on:

- building networks and connections that tackle family isolation, especially where there is disability or illness
- offering respite for families with a member who is terminally ill or disabled
- encouraging family cohesion through drop-in centres and intensive family support, particularly among families who have been under considerable stress from issues of violence and abuse
- tackling isolation of older people, especially through intergenerational work.

Enriching Education

We recognise that a well-rounded, holistic education is crucial in allowing a person to shape their future. Our funding, therefore, is aimed at educational projects which deal with the disadvantaged and vulnerable, with a particular interest in Catholic schools and education based on Catholic social teaching. We are particularly interested in projects which focus on:

- pastoral care in education focused on projects which deal with character building, conflict resolution and values
- educational opportunities for groups who have missed out on traditional learning, especially prisoners and ex-offenders
- the professional development of teachers.

Transformation through Faith

As the roots of our philanthropy are in the Catholic faith, we are keen to support projects which nourish and develop that faith in a complex world. We look to fund the following particular areas:

- the development of Church and lay leadership capacities
- projects which encourage ecumenical collaboration
- organisations and projects which focus on inclusion
- the promotion of exploration and discussion around difficult issues, both within the Christian family and in dialogue with other faiths.

Ethics in Practice

Porticus UK sees moral formation and ethical decision making as crucially important in today's complex societies. We, therefore, support work guided by Catholic Social principles and directed at the development of the values and virtues of professionals and leaders. Since ethics cannot be considered in isolation, we are particularly interested in interdisciplinary and applied approaches. We will consider applications for:

- developing courses, case studies and training
- facilitating constructive public or private debates
- research projects on the ethical problems encountered in specific professions
- business ethics and medical ethics
- initiatives that enhance understandings of Catholic social teaching.

In 2007/08 the charity had an income of £445,000; 'charitable activities' were listed in the accounts as 'consultancy to charities' and totalled £438,000, although a further breakdown of this figure includes expenditure such as 'administration charges', 'travel costs', 'entertainment' and 'salaries'.

Exclusions No grants to non-registered charities.

Applications for the following will not be considered:

- high profile appeals
- major capital projects or restoration of buildings
- grants to individuals
- endowment appeals
- overseas projects (including travel).

Applications On an application form available from the charity's website. Applications can be submitted at any time.

The charity also says that: 'if you are unsure whether your project/organisation fits in with our guidelines, you are welcome to submit an initial brief outline of your organisation and funding requirements'.

The Prince's Charities Foundation

Culture, the environment, medical welfare, education, children and young people and overseas aid

£21.9 million (2007/08)

Beneficial area Unrestricted.

The Prince of Wales's Office, Clarence House, St James's, London SW1A 1BA

Tel. 020 7930 4832 ext 4788
Fax 020 7930 0119

Website princeofwales.gov.uk

Correspondent David Hutson

Trustees *Sir Michael Peat; Philip Reid; Hon. Lord Rothschild; Leslie Jane Ferrar.*

CC Number 1127255

Information available Accounts were available from the Charity Commission.

The Prince's Charities Foundation was established by trust deed in 1979 for general charitable purposes. The foundation principally continues to support charitable bodies and purposes in which the founder has a particular interest, including culture, the environment, medical welfare, education, children and young people and overseas aid.

In 2007/08 the foundation had assets of £1.2 million and an income of £5.9 million from donations and investments. During the year the foundation made grants to 186 organisations totalling £21.9 million (£4 million in 2006/07), including over £20 million to charities in which the Prince of Wales has a particular interest. One of the main beneficiaries during the year was Dumfries House, with the foundation's contribution facilitated by a £20 million loan obtained by the foundation for onward distribution:

[Dumfries House] was saved from sale and certain break-up by the intervention of His Royal Highness The Prince Charles, The Duke of Rothesay. His Royal Highness organised a group of organisations and individuals to buy the house at a total cost of £45 million. The foundation contributed £18.3 million, and with £25 million contributed by the Scottish Government and heritage organisations and trusts, the house, its wonderful collection of furniture and estate were saved for the nation only hours

before the expiry of the deadline for sale at auction. Once purchased, the house and its contents were donated to The Great Stewardship of Scotland's Dumfries House Trust, a UK registered Charity.

Grants, made from both restricted and unrestricted funds, were broken down as follows:

Category	Value
Culture	£19,300,000
Environment	£1,600,000
Medical welfare	£706,000
Education	£554,000
Children and young people	£80,000
Oversees aid	£19,300
Other	£3,100,000

There were 30 grants made over £10,000 each listed in the accounts. Many of the larger grants were awarded to other Prince of Wales charities.

Beneficiaries included: The National Art Collections Fund (£13.8 million in connection with the purchase of Dumfries House); The Great Steward of Scotland's Dumfries House Trust (£5 million); The Prince of Wales's Foundation for Integrated Health (£400,000); The Prince's Foundation for the Built Environment (£277,000); The Rainforest Project (£228,000); Northumberland Wildlife Trust (£87,000); Turquoise Mountain Foundation (£71,000); North Highlands Initiative (£65,000); The Soil Association (£35,000); Music in Country Churches (£30,000); Arts Council of Wales (£20,000); and The National Trust (£13,000).

Exclusions No grants to individuals.

Applications In writing to the correspondent, with full details of the project including financial data. The Prince's Charities Foundation receives an ever-increasing number of requests for assistance, which are considered on a regular basis by The Prince of Wales and the trustees.

The Privy Purse Charitable Trust

General

£328,000 (2007/08)

Beneficial area UK.

Buckingham Palace, London SW1A 1AA
Tel. 020 7930 4832

Email ian.mcgregor@royal.gsx.gov.uk

Correspondent Ian McGregor, Trustee

Trustees *Ian McGregor; Sir Alan Reid; Christopher Geidt.*

CC Number 296079

Information available Accounts were available from the Charity Commission.

This trust supports a wide range of causes, giving grants to UK-wide and local charities. 'The main aims of the trustees are to make grants to charities of which The Queen is patron and to support ecclesiastical establishments associated with The Queen.'

In 2007/08 it had assets of £2.2 million and an income of £432,000. Grants were made totalling £328,000 (with support costs amounting to just £456), and were broken down as follows:

Category	No. of grants	Amount
Ecclesiastical	49	£221,000
Other	310	£105,000
Education	2	£1,900

Most grants were for relatively small amounts. Larger grants were made for ecclesiastical purposes, including donations to the chapels at Hampton Court Palace (£83,000), St James's Palace (£49,000) and Windsor Great Park (£12,000). 'Sandringham Group of Parishes' also received £51,000.

Applications The trust makes donations to a wide variety of charities, but states that it does not respond to unsolicited applications.

Mr and Mrs J A Pye's Charitable Settlement

General

£588,000 (2008)

Beneficial area UK, with a special interest in the Oxford area and, to a lesser extent, in Reading, Cheltenham and Bristol.

c/o Mercer and Hole Chartered Accountants, Gloucester House, 72 London Road, St Albans, Hertfordshire AL1 1NS

Tel. 01727 869141 **Fax** 01727 869149

Correspondent David S Tallon, Trustee

Trustees *Simon Stubbings; David S Tallon.*

CC Number 242677

Information available Accounts were available from the Charity Commission.

The trust was endowed in 1965 by the Pye family of Oxford for general charitable purposes.

Guidelines

The accounts give the trust's grantmaking policy and general criteria:

In making grants the trustees seek to continue the settlors' interests while expanding them to encompass other causes. The following list is by no means exhaustive and is given for guidance only:

- environmental – this subject particularly deals with organic farming matters, conservation generally and health-related matters such as pollution research and some wildlife protection
- adult health and care – especially causes supporting the following: post-natal depression, schizophrenia, mental health generally and research into the main causes of early death
- children's health and care – for physical, mental and learning disabilities, respite breaks etc.
- youth organisations – particularly projects encouraging self-reliance or dealing with social deprivation
- education – nursery, primary, secondary or higher institutions (not individuals)
- promotion of music
- regional causes around Oxford, Reading, Cheltenham, Chichester and Bristol.

The overall policy of the trustees is to support under-funded charities in their fields of interest in order to assist those charities to play a fuller role in the community. Unfortunately, due to the demands made, it is not possible to support all applications even though they may meet the charity's criteria. However, the trustees particularly recognise the difficulty many smaller charities experience in obtaining core funding in order to operate efficiently in today's demanding environment. In addition major support is given to a limited number of causes in the fields of environment, music, education and medicine. This approach has been rewarded by significant results from beneficiaries.

In 2008 the trust had assets of £9.5 million and an income of £660,000. Grants were made totalling £588,000 to 248 organisations, many of whom received a grant in the previous year.

Beneficiaries of larger grants included: Organic Research Centre (£135,000); Music@Oxford (£77,000); University College Oxford (£50,000); Harris Manchester College (£30,000); British Trust for Conservation Volunteers (£15,000); and Oxford Literary and Debating Union Trust (£10,000).

Other beneficiaries included: Mansfield College (£6,000); Oxfordshire Community Foundation (£5,000); Marie Curie Cancer Care (£3,000); Children's with Aids Charity and the Reading Foundation for Art Charity (£2,000 each); and Bristol & District Tranquilliser Project, Dyslexia Institute and the Wildfowl & Wetlands Trust (£1,000 each).

Grants of less than £1,000 each were made to 199 organisations.

Exclusions Applications will not normally be considered in relation to:

- organisations which are not registered charities
- individuals
- activities which are primarily the responsibility of central or local government
- appeals for funds for subsequent redistribution to other charities – this would also preclude appeals from the larger national charities
- endowment funds
- fabric appeals for places of worship, other than in Oxford, Reading, Cheltenham and Bristol
- fundraising events
- hospitals and medical centres (except for projects which are clearly additional to statutory responsibilities)
- overseas appeals
- promotion of religion.

Applications There are no application forms but the following information is essential:

- registered charity number or evidence of an organisation's tax exempt status
- brief description of the activities of the charity
- the names of the trustees and chief officers (please note: more important than patrons)
- details of the purpose of the application and where funds will be put to use
- details of the funds already raised and the proposals for how remaining funds are to be raised
- the latest trustees' report and full audited or independently examined accounts (which must comply with Charity Commission guidelines and requirements).

Applications can be made at any time, with the trustees meeting quarterly to take decisions. Any decision can therefore take up to four months before it is finally taken. However, all applicants are informed of the outcome of their applications and all applications are acknowledged.

Telephone contact will usually be counterproductive, as the trust only wishes to respond to written applications.

Quartet Community Foundation (formerly the Greater Bristol Foundation)

General

£2.8 million (2007/08)

Beneficial area West England – Bristol, North Somerset, South Gloucestershire, Bath and North East Somerset.

Royal Oak House, Royal Oak Avenue, Bristol BS1 4GB

Tel. 0117 989 7700 **Fax** 0117 989 7701

Email info@quartetcf.org.uk

Website www.quartetcf.org.uk

Correspondent Helen Moss, Director

Trustees *John Kane; Alexander Hore-Ruthven; Mary Prior; Peter Rilett; Alison Reed; Tim Ross; Anna Schiff; Gail Bragg; Prof. Murray Stewart; Cedric Clapp; William Lee; Gill Stobart; Richard Hall; Lin Whitfield.*

CC Number 1080418

Information available Accounts were available from the Charity Commission.

Quartet Community Foundation supports small, community-based charities and voluntary groups in the west of England whose work benefits local people. It gives grants to a broad range of causes and welcomes applications from both new and established groups.

The foundation runs it own grants programme, the Express Programme. It also manages a range of other funds each with their own criteria, closing dates and maximum amounts. These are detailed below.

In 2007/08 the foundation had assets of £14 million and an income of £2.9 million. Grants were made totalling £2.8 million and were broken down as follows:

Category	No. of grants	Grant total
Young people	547	£1,200,000
Community	484	£627,000
Disabled people	136	£332,000
Black and minority ethnic groups	105	£296,000
Family	75	£153,000
Older People	120	£113,000
Homeless people	39	£97,000
Environmental	8	£45,000

Major beneficiaries included: Voluntary Action North Somerset (£59,000); Converging World (£40,000); Second Step Housing Association (£20,000); Re:Work (£15,000); Armstrong Hall (£12,000); Community Action (£10,000); Bradford Environmental Action Trust (£8,000); Awaz Utaoh and NESA (£7,000 each).

Grant programmes 2009

Funds for the west of England (Bristol, Bath and North East Somerset, North Somerset and South Gloucestershire)

Express Programme – Grants of up to £2,000 are awarded to small, local voluntary and community organisations where a small amount of funding can make a difference in disadvantaged areas. The work of your organisation must benefit people who are disadvantaged or isolated. People may be isolated due to poverty, disability, age, location or culture. Priority is also given to groups that:

- enable people to take opportunities that would otherwise not be available to them
- involve local people in improving their community
- reflect the concerns and priorities of people living and working in the area.

For further details contact your local office.

Bank of Ireland Charitable Fund – Grants of up to £1,000 are awarded to local voluntary and community organisations and schools that provide education, development or training opportunities to young people who are disadvantaged or isolated. The young people may be isolated due to poverty, disability, illness, location or culture. For further details contact your local office.

Grassroots Grants – This programme is funded by the Government's Office of the Third Sector and its purpose is to support small, informal voluntary and community groups and organisations, many of whom are dependent on volunteers. The programme will run from September 2008 to March 2011. Eligible groups must have been active in their local area for at least 12 months prior to applying to this fund. Groups must have evidence of income of less than £30,000 per year taken as an average over three financial years, or the life of the group.

The maximum amount awarded from this programme is £5,000 in total to any group over the period of the grant programme

(September 2008 – March 2011). You can apply for up to £5,000 which can be used all at once or over the lifetime of the funding programme. You can apply for small amounts over the period (as long as you remain eligible) provided the total amount awarded does not exceed £5,000. For further details contact your local office.

Fund for Older People – Grants of up to £2,500 for older people's groups addressing issues around health and wellbeing. Use the general application form to apply to this fund. You can apply at any time and should have a decision within 4–6 weeks of the foundation receiving the application. For further details contact your local office.

Mall's Fountain Charity Fund – Grants of up to £1,000 are awarded to small, local voluntary and community organisations which help people in need within a 25 mile radius of The Mall at Cribbs Causeway. There is one round per year for this fund and the deadline for each year is the end of January. For further details contact your local office.

Sport Relief Fund – Grants of between £250 and £5,000 are awarded to small, local voluntary and community organisations that use sport and exercise to strengthen communities and provide opportunities for people of all ages who are excluded or disadvantaged. Applications must address one or more of the following themes:

- increase access to sport and exercise for people who face social exclusion and isolation
- help people who are experiencing difficulties to regain their confidence and self esteem
- encourage people to take part in sporting activities that bring communities together.

For further details contact your local office.

Additional funds for Bristol City

Bristol City Council Development Fund – Grants of up to £5,000 are available to small, local community-based projects, either for activities, or to assist the organisation's development. Contact: Alice Meason at the Bristol office.

Bristol Children and Young People's Partnership Fund – A new fund set up by the City Council. Grants of £5000 are available to group working with young people in the city. The current theme is Transition and is targeted at young people 8–12 who are affected by issues of moving from primary to secondary education. Contact: Alice Meason at the Bristol office.

Bristol Youth Community Action (BYCA) – Grants of up to £1,000 are awarded to young people-led, community safety projects; funding for locally-based groups to provide holiday activities for young people. For further details contact the BYCA office on 0117 903 6495.

University of Bristol Students RAG Fund – Grants of up to £1,000 are awarded to local voluntary and community organisations where a small amount of money can make a difference. The work of your organisation must benefit people who are disadvantaged or isolated. People may be isolated due to poverty, disability, age, location or culture. The fund also awards grants to organisations that support people with long-term illnesses. For further details contact Ronnie Brown at the Bristol office.

Additional funds for Bath and North East Somerset

Bath Half Marathon Fund – Grants of up to £1,000 are awarded to small, local voluntary and community organisations for activities involving sport, exercise or play. All activities must have a community or charitable element. Priority is given to organisations with an annual income of less than £25,000. For further details contact Jilly Edwards at the Bath & North East Somerset office.

Additional funds for North Somerset

University of Bristol Students' RAG Fund – Grants of up to £1,000 are awarded to local voluntary and community organisations where a small amount of money can make a difference. The work of your organisation must benefit people who are disadvantaged or isolated. People may be isolated due to poverty, disability, age, location or culture. The fund also awards grants to organisations that support people with long-term illnesses. Contact: Ronnie Brown at the North Somerset office.

South Ward Neighbourhood Management Community Chest – Grants of up to £3,000 are awarded to small, local voluntary and community groups and organisations based in the South Ward of Weston-Super-Mare. Grants are awarded to support local initiatives that help reduce crime and the fear of crime, create cleaner, greener public spaces, improve the quality of life for local people or encourage local residents to get involved in community activity. Applications are accepted at any time and considered when they are received. Applicants should be notified of the decision within six weeks. Contact: Ronnie Brown at the Bristol office.

Additional funds for South Gloucestershire

Please note that, as above, funding is also available to organisations in this area through the University of Bristol Students RAG Fund. Contact: Ronnie Brown at the Bristol office.

Exclusions The foundation does not give grants to:

- individuals
- general appeals
- statutory organisations or the direct replacement of statutory funding

- political groups or activities promoting political beliefs
- religious groups promoting religious beliefs
- arts projects with no community or charitable element
- sports projects with no community or charitable element
- medical research, equipment or treatment
- animal welfare
- projects that take place before an application can be processed.

Applications Before you apply to the community foundation check that your group or project meets the following requirements:

- you must be a small charity, community group or local voluntary organisation operating in the West of England i.e. Bath and North East Somerset, Bristol, North Somerset or South Gloucestershire
- you do not need to be a registered charity but you must be able to provide a copy of your group's constitution or set of rules
- your group must be managed by a board of trustees or management committee
- you must be able to provide the foundation with up-to-date financial information for your group.

Help and advice on making an application is always available from the foundation's grant team, members of which can be contacted at the following local offices:

Bristol and South Gloucestershire: Royal Oak House, Royal Oak Avenue, Bristol BS1 4GB. Tel: 0117 989 7700; email: info@quartetcf.org.uk

Bath & North East Somerset: 12 Pierrepoint Street, Bath BA1 1LA. Tel: 01225 420 300; email: banes@quartetcf.org.uk

North Somerset: Badger Centre 3–6 Wadham Street, Weston-Super-Mare BS23 1JY. Tel: 01934 641 965; email: northsomerset@quartetcf.org.uk

Applications can be made using the online form available on the foundation's website. Alternatively you can download an application form or request one to be sent by post by contacting your local office.

Queen Mary's Roehampton Trust

Ex-service support
£497,000 (2007/08)
Beneficial area UK.

13 St George's Road, Wallington SM6 0AS

Tel. 020 8395 9980 **Fax** 020 8255 1457

Email alanbaker13@hotmail.com

Correspondent Alan Baker, Clerk to the Trustees

Trustees Col. S D Brewis, Chair; Maj. Gen. R P Craig; J J McNamara; Brig. A K Dixon; R R Holland; Dr J G Paterson; Mrs C M Walker; Mrs S Freeth; C Green; Col. K George; Col. P Cummings; Ms P Melville-Brown.

CC Number 211715

Information available Annual accounts were available at the Charity Commission.

The trust is established for the benefit of people who served in the armed forces or services established under the Civil Defence Acts 1937 and 1939 who have suffered a disability in that service and their widows/widowers or dependants.

The trust's objectives are met by making grants to any charities or organisations whose objects include the reception, accommodation, treatment or after-care of persons who come within the charity's objects. Grants are also made in aid of medical or surgical research having particular regard to the needs of people with disabilities who served in the armed forces of the crown.

In 2006, the trust conducted a strategic review of its objects and decided to simplify the categories of persons who are eligible for help, abolish the order of priority for such categories and remove the distinction between men and women beneficiaries.

In 2007/08 the trust had assets of £11 million and an income of £533,000. 38 grants were made totalling £497,000. The majority of grants were made to ex-service charities concerned with the welfare, housing and care of war disabled ex-service men and women and war widows. Grants were categorised as follows:

Care Homes – 17 grants totalling £272,000
Beneficiaries included: Broughton House (£32,000); Chelsea Pensioners Appeal

(£25,000); Haig Homes (£20,000); Scottish Veteran's Residences (£15,000); Chaseley Trust (£10,000); Royal Homes and Royal Cambridge Home for Soldiers' Widows (£5,000 each); and Community Housing and Therapy (£3,000).

Welfare grants – 15 grants totalling £172,000
Beneficiaries included: Army Benevolent Fund (£45,000); Royal Naval Benevolent Trust (£30,000); Royal Commonwealth Ex-Services League (£20,000); the 'Not Forgotten' Association (£15,000); Gurkha Welfare Trust (£12,000); British Ex-Services Wheelchair Sports Association (£10,000); Vitalise (£6,000); and Association of Jewish Ex-Service Men and Women (£2,000).

Building (new development) – one grant totalling £35,000
The sole grant was made to SSAFA Forces Help.

Other grants – 5 grants totalling £19,000
Beneficiaries were: Ex-Services Mental Welfare Society – Combat Stress (£10,000); Council of British Service and Ex-Service Organisations (£3,000); Women's Royal Naval Service Benevolent Trust (£2,500); Royal Naval Benevolent Trust (£2,000); and Spinal Injuries Association (£1,000).

Exclusions No grants to individuals.

Applications On a standard application form available from the correspondent. Representatives of the trust may visit beneficiary organisations.

The Queen's Silver Jubilee Trust

General, in practice grants to organisations supporting disadvantaged young people
£1.25 million (2007/08)
Beneficial area UK, Channel Islands, Isle of Man and the Commonwealth.

The Prince's Trust, 17–18 Park Square East, London NW1 4LH

Tel. 020 7543 1234 **Fax** 020 7543 1200

Email nicola.brentnall@princes-trust.org.uk

Website www.queenssilverjubileetrust.org.uk

Correspondent Nicola Brentnall

Trustees *Rt Hon Christopher Geidt; Sir Fred Goodwin; Stephen Hall; Sir Alan Reid; Peter Mimpriss; Sir John Riddell.*

CC Number 272373

Information available Accounts were available from the Charity Commission.

The Queen's Silver Jubilee Trust was established in 1977 and while its objects are wide, it is especially concerned with young people who are disadvantaged.

The trust gives the following summary of its grantmaking activities:

The trust gives grants to projects for young people based throughout the UK, Commonwealth, Channel Islands, and Isle of Man.

Subject to funds being available for grant-making, the trustees of The Queen's Silver Jubilee Trust will consider applications from registered charities that offer support to young people across the UK, Commonwealth, Channel Islands and the Isle of Man. The Queen's Silver Jubilee is particularly interested in those organisations that support disadvantaged young people or those that enable young people to volunteer in their local community, broadly defined.

The trustees will also consider a small number of applications from registered charities that offer general support to young people, along with applications from youth charities from the Isle of Man, the Commonwealth and the Channel Islands.

Further factors affecting eligibility:

- the age-range for those supported is 14–30
- grants can only be awarded to registered charities
- grants cannot be awarded to individuals.

The trust's annual report provides further details of its objects:

- the advancement of education
- the relief of need, hardship or distress
- the advancement of [the] physical, mental and spiritual welfare [of children and young people]
- the provision of facilities for recreation or other leisure time occupation
- other charitable purposes as the trustees see fit.

In 2007/08 the trust had assets of £34.6 million and an income of £1.1 million. Grants were made to 13 organisations during the year totalling £1.25 million. The main beneficiary, as in previous years, was the Prince's Trust, which received £1.2 million.

The other beneficiaries were: Youth Business International (£10,000); Campus Children's Holiday, Cirdan Sailing Trust, Tommy's The Baby Charity, Coaching Highland, The Arkwright Society, Florance Home Foundation, Project Trust and Liverpool Community Spirit (£5,000 each); The Malt Cross Trust (£4,000); ProjectScotland (£2,000); and the 2nd Sanquhar Boys Brigade (£1,000).

Exclusions Grants are only made to registered charities. No grants to individuals.

Applications Potential applicants are advised to email the contact before making a formal application.

Applicants must ensure that:

- their organisation is eligible
- they have read the Terms and Conditions and other guidance notes
- they enclose their most recent annual report and accounts, or financial projections and previous income expenditure charts if the organisation is less that two years old
- they enclose their most recent annual review or a brief summary of what their organisation does
- retain a photocopy of all submitted materials.

An application form is available to download from the trust's website. Deadlines for applications are also published on the trust's website.

Rachel Charitable Trust

General charitable purposes, in practice mainly Jewish organisations

£3.2 million (2007/08)

Beneficial area Unrestricted.

c/o 5 Wigmore Street, London W1U 1PB

Correspondent Robert Chalk, Secretary

Trustees *Leopold Noe; Susan Noe; Simon Kanter.*

CC Number 276441

Information available Accounts were on file at the Charity Commission without a list of grants.

This trust was established in 1978 for general charitable purposes and focuses on the relief of poverty and the advancement of religion and religious education. In practice the trust gives mainly to Jewish organisations.

In 2007/08 the trust had assets of £11 million and an income of £7.7 million which included a donation of £1 million from Leopold Noe and a further £3 million from companies in which a trustee was also a director. Grants were made totalling £3.2 million. No further information was available.

Previous beneficiaries include: British Friends of Shuut Ami, Children's Hospital Trust Fund, Cometville Limited, Encounter – Jewish Outreach Network, Chosen Mishpat Centre, Gertner Charitable Trust, Hertsmere Jewish Primary School, Jewish Learning Exchange, London Millennium Bikeathon, Manchester Jewish Grammar School, Project Seed, Shaarei Zedek Hospital, Shomrei Hachomot Jerusalem, Yeshiva Ohel Shimon Trust and Yeshiva Shaarei Torah Manchester.

Applications In writing to the correspondent.

The Rank Foundation

Christian communication, young people, education and general

£7.4 million (2008)

Beneficial area UK.

12 Warwick Square, London SW1V 2AA

Tel. 020 7834 7731

Email jan.carter@rankfoundation.co.uk

Website www.rankfoundation.com

Correspondent Jan Carter, Grants Administrator

Trustees *Earl St Aldwyn; James A Cave; Andrew E Cowan; Mark E T Davies; Lindsay G Fox; Joey R Newton; Lucinda C Onslow; Valentine A L Powell; Lord Shuttleworth; Hon. Caroline Twiston-Davies; Johanna Ropner; Rose Fitzpatrick; Daniel Simon.*

CC Number 276976

Information available Annual report and accounts were available from the Charity Commission. The foundation has an informative website.

This is a heavily proactive foundation, with offices around the country. It concentrates on:

- the promotion of Christian principles through film and other media
- encouraging and developing leadership amongst young people
- supporting disadvantaged young people and those frail or lonely through old age or disability.

Major grants are typically part of a three or five year commitment and very seldom result from an unsolicited application as the projects in this area are mainly identified by staff who have considerable experience and contacts within the field. Small grants (less than £7,500) are usually one-off. Local charities are unlikely to get recurrent funding or multi-year awards. Currently, around one in four applications result in a grant.

General

The charity was established in 1953 by the late Lord and Lady Rank (the founders). It was one of a number established by the founders at that time and to which they gifted their controlling interest in The Rank Group plc (formerly The Rank Organisation plc), best known as a film production company, though this was but one of its commercial interests. The Rank trusts and foundations all share a Christian ethos.

In 2008 the foundation had assets of £181 million and a consolidated income of £12 million. Grants were committed during the year (including multi-year awards) across various programmes totalling £7.4 million and were broken down by category as follows:

Category	Value
Community Service programme	£3,600,000
Young people (including education)	£2,000,000
Promotion of Christian Religion	£1,800,000

Grants paid during the year totalled £6.7 million.

Grantmaking in 2008

The foundation's excellent annual report provides interesting details on its areas of interest and activities during the year, details of which are reproduced here:

Promotion of the Christian religion
CTVC

The impact of religion and religious conflict worldwide is one of the defining issues of our age. Understanding the issues religion raises is central to our future as a multi-cultural society that is striving to handle living with diversity. To that end CTVC aims to stimulate and motivate people to think about moral and spiritual issues in their everyday lives and generate a greater understanding of Christianity and the other major world religions and the value systems they share.

With these objectives in mind, CTVC aspires to produce entertaining and informative programmes for TV, Radio and the Internet, thereby enabling CTVC to reach as large and as broad an audience as possible. This strategy is also supported by web-based education projects which enable young people to get their views across in the digital age and participate in constructive discussions.

2008 was a very strong year, building on the success of 2007. Continuing to deliver broadcast programmes to more viewers than at any time in the last decade, countering the trend towards smaller, more fragmented audiences across the broadcast scene. This was achieved through continuing with our diversified product range which includes the increasingly popular interactive website 'TrueTube', and through developing more co-productions with other independent production companies for broadcast. The increased success also reflects the broader subject matter of our programming that has looked at the moral and religious aspects of front-page issues such as the Environment and the Middle East situation.

Television

In the U.K. during 2008 CTVC programmes were broadcast on BBC2, BBC2 Regional (Scotland, Northern Ireland, and Wales), BBC4, ITV1, Channel 4, Five, STV and Border TV, HD Channel, Signzone, Al Jazerra English, Al Jazerra Arabic, Al Jazerra Documentary , Al Jazerra USA, and National Geographic.

CTVC programmes were broadcast a total of 85 times and this included 18 new programmes (CTVC made 16 hours of new programming in 2008), and 67 repeats. Television audiences in the UK were over 18.1 million. Two of these programmes were broadcast on Al Jazerra Arabic, America and Documentary Channels. (The reach for Al Jazerra is worldwide and is available in over 100 million households).

Programmes included 'Battle of the Bishops' for BBC This World – a profile of Archbishop Akinola at the rival conference to Lambeth, exploring the future of the Anglican Church. 'Stories of the Cross' for Five – with access to leading world experts and the latest research where new evidence revealed a whole new world of biblical history. 'Shariah TV' – a 4-part studio debate from New York with young American Muslims discussing growing up Muslim, in America. 'Islam in America' for Al Jazerra – Rageh Omaar travelled across America exploring Islam. 'Christmas Carols from Alder Hey' and 'Coleen's Christmas at Alder Hey' – inside the Liverpool Children's Hospital as everyone prepared for Christmas – included a carol service.

Radio

3.65 million listened to CTVC's programmes on BBC Radio 4, whilst an estimated 80 million more have access to programmes on the BBC World Service. Programmes included 'Suffer the Children' – John McCarthy investigated the practice of child evangelism in the USA. 'The Cult of Kidnapping' – Frank Gardiner, the BBC Security Correspondent, investigated the phenomena of kidnapping and the intermediary role, of priests. 'Countdown to the Olympics' – Gerry Northam investigated China's human rights record and its attitude to religion, which threatened to overshadow the Beijing Olympics, and 'The Oldest Bible' – Roger Bolton looked at the world's oldest bible, Codex Sinaiticus. 'Suffer the Children' was short listed for the 2008 Jerusalem Awards.

New Media – True Tube

By December 2008, there had been 6.5 million hits on the site, currently a rate of about 1 million hits every 4 to 6 weeks and there are over 500 films on the site. TrueTube has become a popular educational tool for schools both in the UK and abroad. By December 2008 2,200 educational resource packs had been downloaded on the site and, people from 141 countries had been accessing the site. TrueTube continue their partnerships with Skins and Hollyoaks and one of the actors from Hollyoaks whose character is 'Newt', presented two short documentaries for Radio 1 as part of its Mental Health Special early in 2009.

Winner of The Education Resource Award 2008, and Winner of the 2009 BETT Award for Secondary Digital Content.

Training – Videoschool

Videoschool was sub-contracted out to the CFM Trust, who had been working with CTVC to develop video-training courses for church and youth organisations over the past four years. During the course of 2007, we decided not to continue with this venture as its impact had diminished.

Community Service Programme
Community Care

Over the last year, the Community Care Programme supported over 200 registered charities (see also small appeals) with annual grants ranging in size from £250 to £170,000. During 2008 there were 28 new three-year grants awarded reserving a total of £1.8 million.

The Community Care Programme takes a proactive approach to identifying projects that will meet the key objectives to support older people, carers and people with disabilities, who are disadvantaged in the community. The programme focuses on the need for the project whether it is part of a charity's core activities or a specific area of development.

A new three year grant totalling £65,000 was awarded to Eden Mind to manage the Moving On Support Scheme. This is an innovative project that works across a number of charities in a rural setting that wish to make best and most appropriate use of volunteers. Eden Mind ensures volunteers are recruited and supported to the most suitable placement. In turn this collaborative project helps isolated older and disabled people to remain living at home with support from their wider community.

The directors are particularly interested in projects that respond to current issues. A three year grant of £85,000 was awarded to the Food Train, an award winning charity based in south-west Scotland. Through highly committed volunteers, support from statutory partners and collaboration with numerous grocery outlets, the Food Train makes sure that older people living in rurally isolated areas receive fresh food and community support on a regular basis. There is a great deal of interest in this model of community care from other areas and the grant from the Rank Foundation will help the charity to grow and modernise over a three year period.

The foundation values the work of charities that make a positive difference to the lives of people with disabilities. A new three year grant totalling £81,000 was awarded to the Megan Baker House, a charity that supports children and young people with neurological or motor disorders. The highly qualified staff import the learning style of Conductive Education to help young people learn essential life skills. The grant from the Rank Foundation helps teenagers to gain skills in order to live more independently and prepare for adulthood.

Looking to the future, the foundation will continue to seek projects that have a positive impact on the quality of life of those who are disadvantaged by age, ill health, disability or caring responsibilities. It will encourage charities to address specific problems facing people who are disadvantaged, such as access to services, opportunities for learning and participating in community life. Charities supported by the Rank Foundation must demonstrate the need for the project or activity, but equally important is the organisation's ability and capacity to manage and deliver the work.

Appeals and Special Projects
Small Appeals
230 grants were awarded from over 700 applications received, eight of which were for more than £5,000.

Special Projects
Our grant giving in the general appeals category continues to follow a broad theme covering a variety of community based projects, with programmes' addressing homelessness, poverty and crime prevention. However, the bulk of our giving remains focused on our proactive, research driven special projects category, which continues to address the ongoing challenge of reducing offending behaviour, alongside a more generic programme based on community development.

Our community development programmes in Burnley and Corby have stimulated wider interest from within the grant-making sector. These programmes seek to inspire the voluntary and community sector at a grassroots level, creating strong partnerships and addressing a wide range of social issues. Our most recent programme, in Blackpool, involves an initial investment of £500,000 and will work with five local groups, including church organisations, youth groups, local police and both a mental health and carers charity. In a town facing a significant economic challenge, we are delighted to be able to work with a variety of partners who share a common cause, to help improve the lives of local residents. The Rank Foundation appears unique in the desire to engage with local communities in a way that goes well beyond that of simple grantmaking.

With re-offending, we have continue to focus on programmes that help prepare prisoners for release, and in particular, on those who provide a 'through the gates' service. Our ongoing support of the Foundation Training Company has seen the opening of their second post prison training and resource centre, in Lambeth, a model that looks to enhance the limited opportunities offered by the Probation Service.

With the London Youth Support Trust, we hope to create a residential programme, again based in London, which will offer training and business start-up support for a number of offenders leaving Brixton Prison. With Blue Sky Development, we are helping to improve their core strategy that seeks to secure sustainable employment for ex-offenders, in spite of the increased challenges associated with an economic downturn.

We look to fund innovation, to help cement and spread best practice and to build stronger partnerships in a field where so many continue to work in isolation. One such programme is the recent effort by six major grantmakers to persuade Government to commit to the recommendations of Baroness Corston's report on the conditions of the female prison estate.

This has proved successful in that the Ministry of Justice: has continued with a dialogue that now seeks to endorse the key recommendations from the Corston Report. Our concerns were noticed because they came from voices that are rarely heard in any unified way. This important work is ongoing.

Finally, we will look at ways that serve to strengthen our relationships with other grantmakers, both in the statutory, commercial and voluntary sectors. We will also stand ready to respond to those challenges associated with increasing economic hardship, which reflects Rank's capability and leadership in the grant-making world: responsive, timely and focussed.

Youth Programme
Annually, three major business conferences take place.

- The launch conference for all new projects, usually held in the spring.
- A recall and review conference for all new workers and managers who have had our investment for 5 or 6 months, usually held in mid winter.
- Our annual business conference for the entire network, usually held in September.

For all involved, we publish in partnership with the George Williams YMCA College, an agency handbook, this will be revised on an annual basis.

The main theme for this year has been the 21st anniversary. In June we held a celebration 'Journeying Together' – 21 years of 'Youth or Adult?' The evening was in the presence of our special guest The Most Reverend and Right Honourable Dr John Sentamu, Archbishop of York and two hundred and fifty other guests. The event premiered a new publication and DVD 'Journeying Together' with at its core the spirit of our youth work.

'YARN' – the Youth or Adult? Rank Network and its website www.rankyouthwork.org were launched. Over 21 years, a considerable network has been developed which already has a wide range of achievements and ongoing involvement including the residential's mentioned above, publications, seminars, charity evenings with the Fellowship, help with the Gap Scheme, think tanks etc. We believe the prospects for the future of YARN to be extremely exciting and are looking towards developing our commitment to it.

Youth or Adult? Scheme and Youth or Adult? Apprentice Programme
This remains the flagship programme, founded in 1987, and it is the longest and largest programme of its sort in the UK. The results represent a high degree of matched funding and sustainability and 100% achievement by those that have successfully gained their professional qualification (over 90%). The foundation has supported over 230 initiatives and helped qualify over 260 full time youth workers under the auspices of Youth or Adult? and allied initiatives.

This also incorporates thousands of part timers and volunteers. Through researches for the development of YARN we estimate that there is a potential network of around 500 with an active network of 300. We are delighted to say that the full five year honours degree programme is now integral to all new projects and workers coming into 'Youth or Adult?' This will be continued through our Youth or Adult? Apprenticeship Programme.

Training and Qualifications (YMCA George Williams College, Canterbury Christchurch University):

- 25 Students have qualified and gained a Foundation Studies Diploma.
- 10 Students have gained their higher Education Diploma and Full time Professional Qualification.
- 14 Students have gained degrees (six have graduated and eight are studying for honours degrees).

Exits and Beyond
Seven projects completed our investment, five of those projects are continuing and all the workers trained and qualified have either been re-employed or promoted and employed elsewhere.

Investing in Success in South Wales – The People and Work Unit
The Build It Initiatives
All four building supervisors gained a full time youth work qualification and are now employed elsewhere. All sixteen young building apprentices achieved Industry Standard Qualifications in built environment trades.

Life Support
Fourteen of the apprentices completed their original access routes and were offered places on degree courses at the University of Glamorgan, mostly in nursing. Both these projects concerned indigenous leaders and apprentices from deprived communities. A new project in another area and estate (Glyncoch) was supported in 2008, using a similar model for regeneration and community development. At the same time sister projects in North Wales in Hoyhead (Morlo) and Caemarfon (Sylfaen) are training up youth workers and a number of apprentices specializing in building and outdoor pursuits. (In 2008 other new projects started in Wolverhampton, Greater Manchester, London and elsewhere).

Investing in Success
Many other successes from current and network projects have been recorded.

- The new Salmon Youth Centre in which we've invested for many years has opened.
- Kings Cross and Brunswick Community Association where a new 'Youth or Adult?'

project has started have just opened their refurbished Marchmont Centre.
- Jump in Lewisham completed their 'Youth or Adult? and have been re-supported under Investing in Success and are training up over 50 young leaders in their academy.
- Newquay Christian Centre has virtually doubled their youth work and are looking to double their facilities.

All in all a very successful year indeed. However, demand has risen considerably for both new projects and the Gap Scheme. We feel that the new YAP strategy helps address these demands through clearer focus and direction.

The Rank Volunteer Gap Award Scheme
Overall, the Gap Scheme has never been busier. The level of success and demand this year has posed its own problems and with the continuing development of the network we had to consider the priority in certain agencies being involved with this initiative. We have had to give priority and opportunities to newer projects coming on board. We will, of course, be reviewing these priorities from time to time but we hope that those older members of the network can continue to develop their own Gap Scheme with alternative funding. The reserve lists have lengthened but the successes on the scheme have remained at much the same level. There is a 95% success rate over our three year researches of getting those that have completed the Gap Scheme (at least 1,000 hours of voluntary work and training) into real jobs, further education or higher education. The remaining 5% represents an unknown element as often young people have moved on, quite rightly, and are out of touch with their original host agency and indeed ourselves. The Gappers have completed work with an organisation called Speakers Bank who helped to enhance levels of public speaking and confidence. A whole day was spent in contributing and creating inputs onto the website for our colleagues at CTVC TrueTube. This was a huge success and provoked a great deal of interest amongst the young leaders.

A new 'Gapper' has been taken on at CTVC for TrueTube. This alongside the new Young Carers Gap Programme and Training should add a useful fresh dimension. Add to that our new 'Gapper Facebook' Group and you have an enriched and dynamic cocktail of aspiration.

Bursaries
The Bursaries for the Jubilee Sailing Trust, the Tall Ships Youth Trust and Outward Bound Trust have continued to thrive. All add a different dimension to our leadership and community programmes.

A number of new approaches have helped.

- The challenger Yacht Fleet. The Foundation chartered its first boat and raced against others. A second Yacht was chartered for young leaders from White, Somali and African Caribbean groups in Manchester through Trinity – a 'Youth or Adult?' initiative in Rusholme, Moss Side.
- The Foundation also ran a highly successful outdoor pursuits week for supported projects in partnership with Outward Bound, Ullswater.

Both the Young Leader and 'buddying' programme continued their success on the Jubilee Sailing Trust voyages.

School Leadership Award
The chief objectives for 2008 were to continue to increase the number of good applicants for the Award, to continue to promote the idea of leadership among the award holders and to develop their understanding and experience of working with charitable causes. The field of strong applicants continued to grow.

The Fellowship held its fourth 'Leadership Day' attended by the twenty-four current Leadership Award holders. A short video was made on the topic 'Can one person change the world?' This was subsequently posted on the TrueTube website. Feedback from the award-holders praised the range and impact of the Leadership Day's programme.

The Community Action Placements programme, on which Leadership Award holders participate in one of our network projects, worked smoothly. The response from one award-holder, 'I am so grateful for the unique opportunities I have been given and can't wait for next year', provided a testament to the value of these placements.

Rank Fellowship
The Fellowship developed its contact with Fellows through the re-launch of its website, an expanded database and the establishment of a Younger Fellows group. Connections with other similar organisations were strengthened by a visit to Qatar, closer links with Fundacao Estudar and work with the Youth or Adult? Rank Network.

Charitable activity was marked by a highly successful Manchester Charities Evening in November, attended by fourteen charities and seventy five guests. A Fellowship Workshop programme was initiated, providing professional advice on marketing, legal issues and fundraising to the representatives of 25 charities.

Mentoring for younger Fellows and help with work experience continued throughout the year. The number of Fellows offering help in these areas was increased by initiatives such as the dinner in March and new additions to the Steering Committee.

Funding Policy

Major grants

The majority of the foundation's grant giving is tied to their proactive, research driven programmes and they very rarely accept unsolicited appeals for major grants.

If you are interested in a major grant (over £7,500) you should contact the respective executive director. If you would like to submit an application for a major grant, in either the Special Project or Community Care category, then you should email a one page outline to the respective executive: Caroline Broadhurst for Community Care and David Sanderson for Special Projects (see the 'Applications' section for further information).

Small grants

Small general grants are available to encourage imaginative work at local community level. Applications are only accepted from UK registered charities or recognised churches – there are no exceptions to this rule. Using another charity to bid for funds on behalf of a third party is not permitted.

In considering unsolicited appeals, the foundation prefers applications where there are relatively small, attainable targets and they place great importance on clear evidence of local support. The directors also take into account whether it is likely that any grant they make will be put to immediate use.

For further information on the foundation's funding programmes, go to the website or contact the foundation directly.

Exclusions Grants to registered charities only. Appeals from individuals or appeals from registered charities on behalf of named individuals will not be considered; neither will appeals from overseas or from UK-based organisations where the object of the appeal is overseas. In an endeavour to contain the calls made upon the foundation to a realistic level, the directors have continued with their policy of not, in general, making grants to projects involved with:

- agriculture and farming
- cathedrals and churches (except where community facilities form an integral part of the appeal)
- culture
- university/school building and bursary funds
- medical research.

Applications

Major grants

If you are interested in a major grant (over £7,500) you should contact the respective executive director. If you would like to submit an application for a

major grant, in either the Special Project or Community Care category, then you should email a one page outline to the respective executive: Caroline Broadhurst for Community Care and David Sanderson for Special Projects. This should contain the following information:

- organisation objectives, location and structure (staff numbers)
- outline of what you do and where
- what you are seeking support for – details of the specific programme including costs
- any evidence of partnership working or summary of existing evaluation.

Organisations interested in making an application for any of the youth programmes, should first contact the relevant youth office for further advice and information:

Charles Harris, Director of Youth Projects, England and Wales, The Rank Foundation Ltd, 28 Bridgegate, Hebden Bridge, West Yorkshire HX7 8EX. Email: charles.harris@rank foundation.com

Chris Dunning, Director of Youth Projects, Scotland, The Rank Foundation Ltd, 9/10 Redhills House, Redhills Lane, Penrith CA11 0DT. Email: chris.dunning@rank foundation.com

Steve Cheal, Assistant Director of Youth Projects, England, N. Ireland, Isle of Man
The Rank Foundation Ltd, PO Box 2536, Woodford Green, Essex, IG8 1JE.
Tel: 020 8500 2782;
Email: steve.cheal@rankfoundation.com

Small Grants

There is no formal application form. For administrative purposes, the foundation asks that the appeal letter be kept to one or two sides of A4 paper, which may be supported by background information. However, videos, tapes or bulky reports are not welcome and are unlikely to be returned.

The following information is required:

- charity name and registration number
- brief details about the project and the sum to be raised – please ensure you include a clear aim or list of objectives
- details of the amount raised so far towards the target and if relevant, briefly mention how you intend to raise the rest
- a copy of the last audited accounts and annual report.

The directors meet quarterly and applicants will be notified when their appeal is to be considered. Please note: due to the overwhelming number of

appeals, the foundation can only fund about 25% of current applications. If you are unsure whether your appeal is likely to succeed then please contact us for further advice.

Due to overwhelming demand, unsolicited appeals are extremely unlikely to attract a grant in connection with salaries, general running costs or major capital projects.

The Joseph Rank Trust

The Methodist Church and Christian-based social work

£2.2 million (2008)

Beneficial area Unrestricted. In practice, UK and Ireland.

Worth Corner, Turners Hill Road, Crawley RH10 7SL

Tel. 01293 873947

Email secretary@ranktrust.org

Website www.ranktrust.org

Correspondent Dr John Higgs, Secretary

Trustees *Colin Rank, Chair; Revd David Cruise; Revd Paul Hulme; Gay Moon; Sue Warner; James Rank; Michael Shortt; Tony Reddall.*

CC Number 1093844

Information available Accounts were available from the Charity Commission.

This trust was established in 2002 for the advancement of the Christian faith and represents an amalgamation of a number of charities established by the late Joseph Rank, or members of his family, during the period from 1918 to April 1942. The original trusts represented a practical expression of the strong Christian beliefs of their founder and his desire to advance the Christian faith and to help the less fortunate members of society.

The trust's three main areas of interest are:

- the adaptation of Methodist Church properties with a view to providing improved facilities for use both by the church itself and in its work in the community in which it is based
- work with young people
- projects that demonstrate a Christian approach to the practical, educational and spiritual needs of people.

The trust also offers the following information on its grant-making preferences:

In the case of work with young people, the trustees work mainly with the Children and Youth Department of the Methodist Church or with the Rank Foundation, a charity established by J. Arthur (Lord) Rank, a son of the founder. That being the case, it is seldom possible to offer support to unsolicited appeals received for that area of work.

In considering all appeals, the trustees take into account the primary objective of the trust, which is to advance the Christian faith. After earmarking funds to support their main areas of interest the trustees are prepared to consider other unsolicited appeals, although resources remaining to support such appeals are limited. Unsolicited appeals are selected for consideration by the trustees that demonstrate, in their view, a Christian approach to the practical, educational and spiritual needs of people.

In 2008 the trust had assets of £61.9 million and an income of almost £3 million. Grants were made totalling £2.2 million, broken down into categories as follows:

Category	Value
Church property schemes	£1,100,000
Youth projects	£525,000
Community service	£391,500
Religion – education	£166,000
People with disabilities	£45,000
Older people	£25,000
Education – general	£10,000
Health and healing	£10,000

The trust's also gives a geographical breakdown of its grants:

Region	Value
North West England	£315,000
North East England	£287,000
London	£269,000
Midlands	£251,000
South West England	£209,000
Ireland (North and South)	£195,000
Anglia	£184,000
South Central	£136,500
South East	£134,000
Wales	£60,000
Scotland	£25,000
National*	£25,000

*Organisations working across the UK rather than regionally.

Beneficiaries included: Ambassadors in Sport (£94,500 over 5 years), part-funding the staff costs of the London Director of Sport; PSALMS – 2nd Project (£90,000 over 5 years), towards costs of a Sports Minister to help to develop sports ministry with young adults in Gloucestershire; North East Help Link Trust – Seaham (£51,500), a one-off grant to replace a vehicle and part-funding, over 3 years, for salaries to enable the operation of a daily soup kitchen; Good News Family Care – Buxton (£45,000 over 3 years), towards

costs of a Recovery Support Coordinator, working to empower individuals to overcome dependencies; Cornerstone Church Project, Cwmbach (£30,000 over 3 years), part-funding the Centre Manager of a community project in a socially deprived ex-mining community in Wales; Yellow Wales (£30,000 over 3 years), towards the salary costs of a Training Officer to help young homeless people of Bridgend; Methodist Ministers' Pension Scheme (£25,000), towards Christmas gifts for widows and widowers of Methodist Ministers; and Gatwick Detainees Welfare Group (£15,000 over 3 years), part-funding staff costs at project working with asylum seekers and other immigrants held in detention.

Grants of less than £15,000 included those to: All Saints Community Centre – Camborne; Humber Seafarers Service; Merseyfest; and East Belfast Mission.

Exclusions No grants to individuals, for charities on behalf of individuals, or for unregistered organisations.

Applications On-going commitments, combined with the fact that the trustees are taking an increasingly active role in identifying projects to support, means that uncommitted funds are limited and it is seldom possible to make grants in response to unsolicited appeals.

If applicants consider that their work might fall within the areas of interest of the trust the following basic information is required:

- charity name and charity registration number
- an outline of the project for which funding is sought
- details of the total amount required to fund the project in its entirety
- details of the amount already raised, or irrevocably committed, towards the target
- a copy of the most recent annual report and audited accounts.

Applicants should endeavour to set out the essential details of a project on no more than two sides of A4 paper, with more detailed information being presented in the form of appendices.

In normal circumstances, papers received before the middle of February, May, August and November may be considered in March, June, September and December respectively. Visits to appeals may be made by the secretary and trustees.

All appeals are acknowledged and the applicants advised that if they do not receive a reply by a specified date it has

not been possible for the trustees to make a grant.

The Sigrid Rausing Trust

Human, women's and minority rights and social and environmental justice

£17 million (2007)

Beneficial area Unrestricted.

Eardley House, 4 Uxbridge House, London W8 7SY

Tel. 020 7908 9870 **Fax** 020 7908 9879

Email info@srtrust.org

Website www.sigrid-rausing-trust.org

Correspondent Sheetal Patel, Administrator

Trustees *Dr Sigrid Rausing; Joshua Mailman; Susan Hitch; Andrew Puddephatt; Geoff Budlender.*

CC Number 1046769

Information available Accounts were available from the Charity Commission.

The trust was set up in 1995 by Sigrid Rausing and takes as its guiding framework the United Nations' Universal Declaration of Human Rights. Its vision is 'A world where the principles of the Universal Declaration of Human Rights are implemented and respected and where all people can enjoy their rights in harmony with each other and with the environment.'

The trust made its first grants in 1996 and, from the beginning, has taken a keen interest in work that promotes international human rights. It was originally called the Ruben and Elisabeth Rausing Trust after Singrid's grandparents. In 2003 the trust was renamed the Sigrid Rausing Trust to identify its work more closely with the aims and ideals of Sigrid Rausing herself.

General

The trust has four funding categories which provide a framework for its activities:

- civil and political rights
- women's rights
- minority rights
- social and environmental justice.

Each programme has a number of sub-programmes, which can be found on the trust's website.

The trust has five main principles which guide its grantmaking:

- the essential role of core funding
- good and effective leadership
- flexibility and responsiveness to needs and opportunities
- the value of clarity and brevity in applications and reports
- long-term relationships with grantees.

The following is taken from the trust's 2007 accounts and explains the trust's grant-making policy in further detail.

The trust's defining attribute remains its commitment to support groups that work internationally, using a rights based approach. The trustees are interested in groups that address the serious global problems of our age and are aiming for long-term strategic change. There is an understanding amongst the trustees that they are trying to alter the root causes of problems rather than mitigate the effects.

They generally do not fund the provision of services, except where a group can clearly show that it has a new methodology or approach, which could bring about a substantial change in the sector in which it is used.

The trustees tend to make grants for effective and focussed advocacy and campaigning work. They also believe in getting funds as close as possible to the problem and have a strong interest in funding organisations that sub-grant onwards to small grassroots organisations in the global south.

They lay heavy emphasis on good leadership – they think it is the key to successful social change. This core belief comes out of the trustees' 'no nannying' approach. Groups that apply to the Sigrid Rausing Trust are expected to stand on their own feet. They come to the trust with ideas, it does not suggest plans to them, and it believes they are the experts and entrepreneurs best able to judge their own priorities. The trust's role is to take a decision about whether or not it wants to support what is put before it. If it does, then it tries to stand back and let the group pursue its mission.

The trust seeks to provide support in as flexible way as possible, including core funding where this is applicable to assisting a group advance their overall objectives. It is interested in long-term relationships with the groups it supports, subject to a yearly application and review process. Groups that cannot manage the trust's processes and cannot meet its deadlines without being reminded, tend not to be re-granted.

The trust gives two key types of grants:

- Main Grants – between £15,000 and £850,000 for 1–3 years
- Small Grants – up to £15,000 – for smaller organisations who find it difficult to fundraise from international funding agencies (several small grantees have also gone on to receive a Main Grant).

In exceptional circumstances the trust may also provide Emergency Funds in response to a sudden human rights crisis or in order to protect human rights defenders. Please note: grants under this programme require a recommendation by an existing grantee, another funding agency, or a contact in the field.

Existing grantees may also be eligible for an Advancement Grant, designed to support a major infrastructure step change.

A detailed breakdown of grantees under each funding stream is available on the trust's website. The funding categories are:

Civil and Political Rights
The trust funds organisations which undertake research, support and advocacy.

Beneficiaries included: International Crisis Group and Front Line – Ireland (£300,000 each); Interights (£250,000); Children's Legal Centre and International Rehabilitation Council for Torture Victims – Denmark (£200,000 each); Peace Brigades International (£150,000); Article 19 (£95,000); Commission for Looted Art (£75,000); Abdorrahman Boroumand Foundation – USA (£50,000).

Women's Rights
The trust supports organisations for social and economic participation and the implementation of rights.

Beneficiaries included: Fahamu (£405,000); CAMFED (£350,000); Urgent Action Fund – Kenya (£240,000); African Women's Development Fund – Ghana (£120,000); Domestic Violence Intervention Project (£90,000); Kings College London – International Policy Institute (£73,000); ASTRA – Poland (£45,000); and Center for Egyptian Women's Legal Assistance – Egypt (£33,000).

Minority Rights
Through this programme the trust supports marginalised, indigenous and minority people, lesbian and gay rights and refugees and migrants.

Beneficiaries included: Asylum Aid UK (£193,000); Council for Assisting Refugee Academics (£160,000); Forest Peoples Project (£125,000); International Gay and Lesbian Human Rights Commission (£75,000); Forum for the Empowerment of Women – South Africa (£55,000); and Creating Resources for Empowerment in Action (£25,000).

Social and Environmental Justice
The trust supports organisations that are involved in corporate and institutional accountability, environmental justice and labour rights.

Beneficiaries included: Global Witness (£395,000); Pesticide Action Network (£300,000); Friends of the Earth International – Netherlands (£250,000); Zero Mercury Campaign – Belgium (£200,000); Angelica Foundation – USA (£175,000); Business and Human Rights Resource Centre (£70,000); Corner House (£50,000); and Amazon Watch – USA (£40,000).

Exclusions No grants are made to individuals or faith based groups.

Applications Applications are considered only from organisations that have been invited to apply. There is, however, an open pre-application process. Applicants should check the guidelines detailed on the trust's website. If you are confident that your work falls clearly within them, and you wish to be considered for an invitation, you should complete the short two page enquiry form (for Main or Small grants, as appropriate) available on the trust's website. Completed forms should be submitted by email.

As trustees consider grant applications under each sub-programme once a year, organisations should register an enquiry as early as possible, if possible at least six months before the intended start of the project.

The trust does not give grants to individuals and only funds projects or groups that are charitable under the law of England and Wales. The vast majority of the work it funds is internationally based and it is interested in rights based advocacy and not the delivery of services.

Based on the information provided in the enquiry form, the trustees will decide which groups to invite to apply for funding. Applications pass through a careful vetting process. Even if your organisation falls within the guidelines this is not a guarantee that you will be invited to apply. The trust considers grants to cover core costs, and project work. It also considers advancement grants to help groups extend their reach and operating abilities, but only for those organisations with which it has an established relationship.

All those who receive an invitation to apply for a grant are assessed by the relevant programme officer. Applicants should be aware that the trustees take the application process and the meeting of their deadlines seriously. Sending an incomplete application can count against a group. Failing to submit reports on how the grant was spent by the requested deadline will also be taken into account.

The Rayne Foundation

Arts, education, health, medicine and social welfare

£2 million (2007/08)
Beneficial area UK.

Carlton House, 33 Robert Adam Street, London W1U 3HR
Tel. 020 7487 9650
Email info@raynefoundation.org.uk
Website www.raynefoundation.org.uk
Correspondent Morin Carew, Grants Administrator

Trustees *The Hon Robert Rayne, Chair; Lord Claus Moser; Lady Jane Rayne; Lord Bridges; Lady Hilary Browne-Wilkinson; Prof. Dame Margaret Turner-Warwick; Prof. Anthony Newman Taylor; The Hon Natasha Rayne; The Hon Nicholas Rayne.*

CC Number 216291

Information available Annual report and accounts were available from the Charity Commission. The foundation also has a helpful and informative website.

The foundation provides the following description of its activities on its excellent website.

Background

The Rayne Foundation was established in 1962 by Lord Rayne, who was Life President of London Merchant Securities plc, a diversified property and venture capital business, which he built up and of which he was chairman for forty years until 2000. Lord Rayne was also chairman, trustee or council member of numerous arts, education, medical and social welfare charities. These included Chairman of the National Theatre and St Thomas' Hospital. He remained

chairman of the Rayne Foundation until his death in 2003.

Over more than forty years at the Rayne Foundation we have given to many different causes and organisations. As well as being a traditional philanthropist, Lord Rayne took great efforts to ensure that the Rayne Foundation was actively engaged with the needs of society. Examples of the foundation's early work along these lines are the Rayne Institutes – created in London, Edinburgh and Paris in the 1960s and 1970s to build a bridge between medical research and hospitals. Lord Rayne worked with the government, universities and hospitals, drew on his property development expertise and experience and, with contributions from the foundation, he encouraged this new approach and provided buildings where medical researchers and doctors could work alongside each other. This kind of active engagement is now being revived.

Summary

Here at the Rayne Foundation our theme is bridge building. The aims and outcomes of our work are of utmost importance to us, and we measure the success of our own work, our partnerships and our investments by the degree to which they satisfy these two areas:

The 'bridge building' outcomes of our work such as:

- enlarged sympathies' – increased understanding and/or tolerance
- reduced exclusion
- reduced conflict
- new productive relationships which benefit the public.

The aims of our work:

- it can have wider than just local application or is of national importance
- it helps the most vulnerable or disadvantaged
- it provides direct benefits to people and communities
- it tackles neglected causes
- it levers other funds and encourages the involvement of other organisations
- it strives to achieve excellence.

Guidelines

We work within four sectors:

- arts
- education
- health and medicine
- social welfare and development.

Our areas of special interest

Within our four sectors we encourage applications which apply to our evolving list of areas of special interest, which are listed

below. Excellent applications outside these areas are also welcomed:

- achieving learning outcomes through the work of artists and arts organisations
- developing numeracy skills
- improved quality of life for older people.

In the last 12 months over 50% of awards have been outside these areas.

What we support

These are the specific types of costs the foundation will fund:

- salaries and all types of project costs plus a reasonable contribution to overheads (there is no fixed percentage)
- general running or core costs (normally for a maximum of three years)
- capital costs of buildings and equipment (unless specifically stated in certain sectors).

We do not specify minimum or maximum amounts [for grants]. You can apply for a specific amount or a contribution to the total cost. Please note we are rarely able to fund a project completely and urge you to approach others to part-fund alongside The Rayne Foundation.

You can apply for a grant towards a programme of any duration, although a period of greater than three years is rare.

Please check the website for full details and up-to-date information.

Grantmaking in 2007/08

In 2007/08 the foundation had assets of £39 million and an income of £2.4 million. Grants paid in the year totalled £2 million. The average award was around £15,000.

Grants were distributed as follows:

Category	Value
Arts	£394,000
Education	£436,000
Health and medicine	£164,000
Social welfare and development	£966,000

Beneficiaries included: Praxis (£250,000); the Place to Be (£200,000); Catch 22 (£50,000); Dance UK (£40,000); Cheltenham School of Music (£25,000); Sense About Science (£20,000); Refugee New Arrivals Project – Sheffield (£16,000); Missing People and Naz Project – London (£15,000 each); and Innovations in Dementia CIC and Independent Photography (£10,000 each).

The foundation made grants totalling around £1.5 million in 2009.

Exclusions Grants are not made:

- to individuals
- to organisations working outside the UK
- for work that has already taken place

- for repayment of debts
- for endowments
- to those who have applied in the last twelve months.

Please do not send 'round robin' or general appeals.

Applications Applying for a grant is a two-stage process. First you must fill in the Stage One Application Form available from the foundation's website, which you can complete and email to: applications@raynefoundation.org.uk, or print out and post. Stage One applications are accepted at any time. The foundation aims to reply with a decision within one month.

If you make it through to the second stage, the foundation will ask for a more detailed application. At this point the foundation will notify you of the date you can expect to receive a final decision. This will normally be within four months but it also depends on how long you take to complete your Stage Two application. Trustee meetings take place approximately every three months but these dates are not publicised.

Continuation funding – if you have previously received a grant from the foundation, you must complete a satisfactory monitoring report before reapplying. Organisations can only hold one grant at a time. Please use the two-stage process for all applications, even if you are asking the foundation to continue funding the same project.

Please note: the foundation states that it is 'not in a position to talk through Rayne Grants applications in detail before submission. We believe that the foundation's website contains all the information you need in order to decide whether to apply'.

The Sir James Reckitt Charity

Society of Friends (Quakers), social welfare and general

£770,000 to organisations (2008)

Beneficial area Hull and the East Riding of Yorkshire, UK and occasional support of Red Cross or Quaker work overseas.

7 Derrymore Road, Willerby, East Yorkshire HU10 6ES

Tel. 01482 655861 **Fax** 01482 655861

Email jim@derrymore.karoo.co.uk
Website www.thesirjamesreckittcharity.org.uk
Correspondent James McGlashan, Administrator
Trustees *William Upton; James Harrison Holt; Caroline Jennings; Philip James Harrison Holt; Robin James Upton; Sarah Helen Craven; Martin Dickinson; Charles Maxsted; Simon J Upton; Simon E Upton; James Marshall; Sara Fenander; Edward Upton; Becky Holt; Dr Karina Mary Upton.*
CC Number 225356
Information available Accounts were available from the Charity Commission.

The charity gives grants to a wide range of local charities in Hull and the East Riding of Yorkshire as well as to some national charities. Quaker organisations and those in line with Quaker beliefs are supported, and there is an emphasis on those concerned with current social issues. Some of the charity's grants are awarded over a period of years and many organisations are regular recipients. It has a list of regular beneficiaries which it supports on an annual basis, although the recipients are informed that the grant may end at any time at the discretion of the trustees. Most grants are for £5,000 or less.

General

In 2008 the charity had assets of £20 million and an income of £938,000. Grants were made totalling £814,000, £770,000 of which was given to organisations. The remaining £44,000 was given to 248 individuals.

Guidelines

The following grant guidelines are taken from the charity's useful website:

The trustees give support to a wide range of charitable causes. However, in accordance with the wishes of the founder, they give priority to purposes connected with the Society of Friends (Quakers) and those connected with the city of Hull and the East Riding of Yorkshire.

Beyond those two priority areas, the trustees will consider support for national and regional charities, particularly those concerned with current social issues and whose work extends to the Hull and East Yorkshire areas.

Like most other grantmakers, the trustees of the Sir James Reckitt Charity prefer to make grants to registered charities. Grants may be made to local non-registered organisations provided they are known to the local Council

for Voluntary Service through whom grants may be channelled.

Grants to individuals are very occasionally made depending on the circumstances. Appeals from individual Quakers need the support of their local Monthly Meeting. Appeals from other individuals are normally only considered from residents of Hull or the East Riding of Yorkshire.

Trustees will not normally make grants to support activities for which central or local government are responsible. Neither are they likely to support activities which collect funds to be passed on to other organisations, charities or individuals.

International causes are considered only in exceptional circumstances, such as major disasters, with support usually being channelled through the Society of Friends or the British Red Cross Society.

Grants in 2008

Grants to organisations were distributed as follows during the year:

Category	Value
Social work	£368,000
Education	£189,000
Religion	£103,000
Medical	£79,000
Children	£36,000
Young people	£25,000
Older people	£10,000
Environment	£2,300

Beneficiaries included: Bootham School Trust (£64,000); Britain Yearly Meeting (£59,000); Dove House Hospice (£30,000); Zimbabwe a National Emergency – ZANE (£20,000); Foundation Training Company Limited (£10,000); Hull Boys Club (£7,200); Hull Afro-Caribbean Association (£3,700); Humberside Scout Council (£2,900); Age Concern – East Riding (£2,200); and South Holderness Countryside Society (£650).

Exclusions Grants are normally made only to registered charities. Local organisations outside the Hull area are not supported, unless their work has regional implications. Grants are not normally made to individuals other than Quakers and residents of Hull and the East Riding of Yorkshire. Support is not given to causes of a warlike or political nature.

Applications In writing to the correspondent.

The charity provides a checklist of information on it's website which should be included in any letter of application:

- the nature of your organisation, its structure and its relationship with other agencies and networks
- the aims of your organisation and its mission statement

- the purpose of the project, the need which has been identified and evidence of the need
- exactly what the grant will be used for
- the total cost of the project and how you intend to raise any balance
- who will benefit from the project, the outcomes and how you will know if the project is successful
- whether your organisation is a registered charity or, if a small local group, is it known to a local CVS
- your bank account payee name to whom the cheque can be made payable
- a set of the latest accounts or a record of income and expenditure which has been subject to independent scrutiny
- your contact details, i.e. address, telephone number and email.

Applications are measured against the charity's guidelines and decisions are taken at a twice-yearly meeting of trustees in May and October. Applications should be submitted by mid-April and mid-September respectively.

The Reed Foundation

General, arts, education, relief of poverty and women's health

£650,000 (2007)
Beneficial area UK and Developing countries.

6 Sloane Street, London SW1X 9LE
Tel. 020 7201 9980
Email reed.foundation@reed.co.uk
Correspondent The Secretary
Trustees A E Reed; J A Reed; R A Reed; A M Chapman.
CC Number 264728
Information available Accounts were available from the Charity Commission.

This trust has general charitable purposes. There has historically been an interest in women's causes in developing countries. In 2007 the trust had assets of £15.6 million and an income of £1 million. Grants totalled £650,000.

Beneficiaries included: Academy of Enterprise (£121,000); The Royal Opera House and Womankind (£100,000 each); West London Academy (£75,000); The Big Give and Ethiopiaid – Australia

(£50,000 each); Chipping Norton Theatre (£34,000); British Humanist Association (£15,000); Haven Breast Cancer (£5,000); and Get Kids Going (£1,000).

Smaller grants totalled around £30,000.

Applications In writing to the correspondent. The trust states that it does not respond to unsolicited applications.

Reuben Brothers Foundation

Healthcare, education and general

£449,000 to organisations (2008)
Beneficial area UK and overseas.

Millbank Tower, 21–24 Millbank, London SW1P 4QP
Tel. 020 7802 5000 **Fax** 020 7802 5002
Email contact@reubenfoundation.com
Website www.reubenfoundation.com
Correspondent Patrick O'Driscoll, Trustee
Trustees Richard Stone, Chair; Simon Reuben; David Reuben; Robin Turner; Michael Gubbay; Annie Benjamin; Patrick O'Driscoll.
CC Number 1094130
Information available Accounts were available from the Charity Commission.

This relatively new trust was established in 2002 as an outlet for the charitable giving of billionaire property investors David and Simon Reuben. The foundation was endowed by the brothers with a donation of $100 million (£54.1 million), with the income generated to be given to a range of charitable causes, particularly to healthcare organisations and for educational purposes. It is likely that organisations in India and Iraq, where the brothers have their roots, may benefit as well as organisations in the UK and Israel.

In 2008 the foundation had assets of £58 million and a consolidated income of £2.3 million. 396 grants were made to organisations totalling £449,000 and 35 grants to individuals totalling £68,000. Property management costs totalled £603,000, a substantial reduction from

the £1.3 million in 2007. This was largely due to a drop in refurbishment costs.

Beneficiaries of institutional grants included: Israel Cancer Association (£143,000); Community Security Trust (£50,000); Norwood (£11,000); and Nancy Reuben Primary School, Jewish Care and Princess Royal Trust Carers (£10,000).

Applications In writing to the correspondent, although the trust has stated that applications are by invitation only.

Grant applications are processed with all requests for funds being put before the trustee meetings and the merits of each application being considered. Unsuccessful applicants are notified by post. Donations are sent out to the successful applicants having regard to the current reserves and the long-term policy of the foundation. Trustees meetings are held every month.

The Richmond Parish Lands Charity

General

£604,500 (2008/09)
Beneficial area Richmond, Kew, North Sheen, East Sheen, Ham, Petersham and Mortlake.

The Vestry House, 21 Paradise Road, Richmond TW9 1SA
Tel. 020 8948 5701 **Fax** 020 8332 6792
Website www.rplc.org.uk
Correspondent Jonathan Monckton, Director
Trustee 15 trustees all of whom live within the borough. Three of them are nominated by the borough council, five are nominated by local voluntary organisations and the remainder are co-opted from the community. The Mayor is an ex-officio member of the board of trustees.
CC Number 200069
Information available Accounts were on file at the Charity Commission. The charity also has a helpful and informative website.

Established in 1786, the charity supports a wide range of causes in specified parts of the borough of Richmond-upon-

Thames, as outlined under 'Beneficial area'.

The charity describes its objectives as:

- the relief of poverty in the London Borough of Richmond upon Thames
- the relief of sickness and distress in the borough
- the provision and support of leisure and recreational facilities in our beneficial area
- the provision educational facilities and support for people in Richmond wishing to undertake courses
- any other charitable purpose for the benefit of the inhabitants of Richmond.

In furtherance of the above, the charity's website lists its current activities as:

- general grants to charitable organisations and individuals in need within the benefit area
- grants to support the education and training of individuals and education projects within the benefit area
- winter 'Warm Campaign' of heating grants to older people in need in the benefit area
- provision of social housing to those in need from the benefit area
- hiring of the Vestry Hall as a public meeting room
- renting of the craft workshops/studios to local artists and crafts people.

In 2008/09 the charity had assets of £56.7 million and an income of £1.6 million. Grants were made to over 100 organisations totalling £604,500. Grants were also made to individuals totalling £195,000.

Beneficiaries included: Richmond MIND (£48,000); Richmond CAB (£39,000); Crossroads Care (£25,500 in total); SPEAR (£21,000); Integrated Neurological Services (£17,500); Richmond Music Trust (£15,000); Handyperson Scheme (£11,500); Care Leavers Support (£10,000); Kew Community Trust (£8,500); Central and Cecil Community Trust (£7,000); Latchmere House (£6,000); Brentford Community Football Sports (£5,000); Meadlands School Friends (£2,500); and Bold Balladiers (£1,000).

More recent information on the charity's website states that grants were made in 2009/10 totalling £350,000. The following statement is also given:

At the November 2009 RPLC AGM the Chairman Jeff Harris, warned that the RPLC's investment income is likely to fall significantly this year, however 'we are committed to maintaining our core grant support to many local charities and individuals. For the future we hope to be able to maintain this year's level of grant-giving.

Exclusions Projects and organisations located outside the benefit area, unless it can be demonstrated that a substantial number of residents from the benefit area will gain from their work. UK charities (even if based in the benefit area), except for that part of their work which caters specifically for the area.

Applications Organisations receiving core grants from the RPLC must apply by the deadlines set out in the documents [available from the charity's website] and use the new application form.

The Strategic Priority for 2009/10 is support for organisations working with people affected by family breakdown. A specific application form for applications in this category [is available from the charity's website].

If you are applying for a grant that is new or a one-off application, and it does not fall within our recent Strategic Priorities your application will not be considered until January – June 2010.

[Check the charity's website for information on current priorities.]

How to Apply
If you would like some clarification on whether your organisation would qualify for a grant, please contact the charity on 020 8948 5701 for guidance.

[There are separate application forms for larger and small grants, both available from the charity's website.]

How the charity will deal with your application
When your application is received, it will be evaluated and any queries arising from it will be followed up. You may be assured that all eligible applications will be put before the trustees.

There are currently 15 trustees, all of whom live within the benefit area. Three of them are nominated by the Borough Council, five are nominated by local voluntary organisations and the remainder are co-opted from the community. The Mayor is an ex officio member of the Board of Trustees.

Eligible applications must be received at least ten working days before the meeting at which they will be considered. All organisations receiving core grants on an annual basis now have a specified date for submission of their applications. [Deadlines are published on the charity's website.]

You will be advised by letter within fourteen days of the meeting whether or not your application has been successful. Following agreement for a grant you will be sent a Conditions of Grant form setting out the terms and conditions of the grant. Payment will be arranged on receipt of a signed agreement. A Monitoring and Evaluation Form will also be required on completion of your next application form.

Ridgesave Limited

Jewish, religion, education and general
£1.7 million (2007/08)
Beneficial area UK and overseas.

141b Upper Clapton Road, London E5 9DB
Correspondent Zelda Weiss, Trustee
Trustees Joseph Weiss; Zelda Weiss; E Englander.
CC Number 288020
Information available Accounts were available from the Charity Commission.

The trust is largely focused on supporting organisations engaged in education, the advancement of the Jewish religion and the giving of philanthropic aid.

In 2007/08 the trust had assets of £3.4 million and an income of £1.6 million. Grants were made totalling £1.7 million. No grants list was available.

Previous beneficiaries were: Keren Associates Ltd, BAT, UTA, CM L, TYY, Square Foundation Ltd, Ateres Yeshua Charitable Trust, Side by Side, My Dream Time, British Friends of Rinat Aharon, Chanoch Lenaar, and All in Together Girls.

Applications In writing to the correspondent.

The Robertson Trust

General
£9.9 million (2008/09)
Beneficial area Scotland.

85 Berkeley Street, Glasgow G3 7DX
Tel. 0141 221 3151 **Fax** 0141 221 0744
Email christine@therobertsontrust.org.uk
Website www.therobertsontrust.org.uk

Correspondent Christine Scullion, Assessment Manager

Trustees *Sir Ian Good, Chair; Richard J A Hunter; Dame Barbara M Kelly; Shonaig Macpherson; David D Stevenson; Ian B Curle.*

SC Number SC002970

Information available Detailed annual accounts were provided by the trust and it has an excellent website.

A wide range of organisations are supported each year, with grants of all sizes. There are four priority areas:

- health
- care
- education and training
- community arts and sport.

The trust also has a small grants programme for one-off donations of up to £10,000 for a particular project or activity. Outside this programme, there is no set minimum or maximum grant size.

General

The trust was established in 1961 by the Robertson sisters, who inherited a controlling interest in a couple of whisky companies (now the Edrington Group) from their father and wished to ensure the dividend income from the shares would be given to charitable purposes.

In 2008/09 the trust had an income of £9.7 million from assets of £340 million. Most of the assets are still in the form of shares in the private Edrington Group (which is controlled by the trust) and which cannot be freely sold under the terms of the trust.

Guidelines

In August 2009 the trust adopted revised guidelines for its priority areas as follows:

Health
This category includes activities which promote health, as well as those which seek to prevent or treat sickness and disease. Examples include projects which work with children who are at risk of misusing drugs or alcohol or are affected by parental substance misuse, and with people recovering from addictions to assist them to rebuild their lives.

Care
This category is broadly defined. Examples include palliative care, care for older people, people with disabilities, people with mental health issues, people who are homeless and offenders and their families. Support is given to charities working at both local and national level. The category includes sports and arts projects which have a specifically therapeutic purpose.

Education and training
This category includes support for community-based education activities, capital projects at Universities and F.E. Colleges and provision for people with special educational needs. The trust is particularly interested in supporting projects, which increase access and opportunity, develop recognised Centres of Excellence and contribute to the growth of the Scottish economy.

Community arts and sport
This category is primarily aimed at encouraging young people to participate in artistic and sporting activities within their local community. Projects should demonstrate that they provide access and opportunity and/or support emerging talent. The trust is particularly interested in supporting activities which increase the use of existing facilities; however, capital projects which seek to widen opportunity, access and participation, as well as improve provision, will also be considered.

These priority areas account for approximately two-thirds of the trust's expenditure each year. However, applications will be considered from most other areas of charitable activity, including:

- work with children, young people and families
- preservation of the environment
- the strengthening of local communities
- the development of culture, heritage and science
- animal welfare
- the saving of lives.

It should be noted that overall priority will be given to those projects and posts which relate to direct service delivery.

The Robertson Trust currently disburses around £9 million a year. There are no minimum or maximum donations. Donations are classified according to four main types, to which different guidelines apply.

Small Donations comprise revenue donations of up to £5,000 and capital donations of up to £10,000. The application process is designed to be straight-forward and this is an ideal starting points for charities who have done little fundraising before or those with one-off funding appeals.

Main Donations comprise revenue donations in excess of £5,000 and capital donations of between £10,000 and £100,000. Revenue grants rarely exceed £15,000 a year and may be for core or project funding for a maximum initial period of three years. Capital donations will be for a maximum of 10% of the total project cost.

Major Capital Donations comprise capital donations in excess of £100,000, for which the overall project costs will normally be in excess of £1 million. Major capital donations will contribute specifically to one of the trust's priority areas other than where an exceptional case is made. Applications will be considered three times a year, in January May and September, to allow the trustees to compare the merits of different applications. Organisations considering applying for a major donation are advised to telephone the trust beforehand for an informal discussion.

Development Donations are given under the trust's current special development areas, a list of which can be found in the Development section of the website.

Applications for a donation under one of these headings will only be considered after prior discussion with Christine Scullion, the Assessment Manager.

Grants in 2008/09

During the year £9.9 million was committed to 497 charities. Grants paid during the year totalled £8.3 million. Nine major capital donations totalling £2 million accounted for 20% of the donations made. The majority of donations committed during the year (68%) were to support the trust's four priority areas. These were broken down as follows:

Category	Value
Care	£2,700,000
Education and training	£1,600,000
Community arts and sports	£1,300,000
Health	£1,100,000

Just over a quarter of donations were made to organisations operating Scotland-wide (28%). The regions with the highest percentage of donations to local organisations were Glasgow (22%), Edinburgh (10%), Strathclyde excluding Glasgow (8%) and the Highlands, Islands and Argyll (8%).

Beneficiaries during the year included: the Robertson Scholarship Trust (£600,000); University of Strathclyde (£500,000); University of Edinburgh Development Trust (£300,000); Youth Scotland (£100,000); Jeely Piece Club (£70,000); East Lothian Women's Aid (£20,000); Broomhouse Centre (£10,000); Scotland's Churches Scheme (£3,500); Bobath Scotland (£740); and Lanton Village Hall (£500).

Exclusions The trust does not support:

- individuals or organisations which are not recognised as charities by the Office of the Scottish Charity Regulator (OSCR)
- general appeals or circulars, including contributions to endowment funds
- local charities whose work takes place outside Scotland
- generic employment or training projects
- community projects where the applicant is a housing association
- core revenue costs for playgroups, nurseries, after school groups etc.
- projects which are exclusively or primarily intended to promote political beliefs
- students or organisations for personal study, travel or for expeditions whether in the United Kingdom or abroad
- medical research
- organisations and projects whose primary object is to provide a counselling, advocacy, advice and/or information service.

The trust is unlikely to support:

- charities which collect funds for onward distribution to others
- umbrella groups which do not provide a direct service to individuals, for example, CVS
- feasibility studies and other research
- charities already in receipt of a current donation from the trust.

Applications Applicants are advised to read the recently revised guidelines (August 2009) before making any application. These are available to download on the trust's website.

The trust does not have an application form. Applications are invited by letter to enable applicants to express themselves in their own words without the restrictions of set questions.

However, there are certain details you should include to enable the trust to make an informed decision on whether or not to fund your organisation:

- a brief description of the organisation, including past developments and successes
- a description of the project – what you want to do, who will be involved, where will it take place and how it will be managed
- how you have identified the need for this work
- what you hope will be the outputs and outcomes of this work and the key targets you have set
- how you intend to monitor and evaluate the work so that you know

whether or not you have been successful

- the income and expenditure budget for this piece of work
- How you propose to fund the work, including details of funds already raised or applied for
- the proposed timetable.

In addition the trust will also require three supporting documents. These are:

1) A completed copy of the Organisation Information Sheet, which is available from the trust's website or the trust office.
2) A copy of your most recent annual report and accounts. These should have been independently examined or audited.
3) A job description, if you are applying for salary costs for a specified worker.

The trust requests that applicants do not send a constitution or memorandum and articles. If there is any other bulky information which you feel may be relevant, such as a feasibility study, business plan or evaluation, then you should refer to it in your application, so that the assessment team can request it if required.

Small and main donations form the bulk of the donations made by the trust and are assessed on a rolling programme with recommendations made to the trustees six times a year.

Applications for major capital donations are considered three times a year in January, May and September.

The Roddick Foundation

Arts, education, environmental, human rights, humanitarian, medical, poverty and social justice

£3 million (2007/08)

Beneficial area Worldwide.

Emerald House, East Street, Epsom KT17 1HS

Website www.theroddickfoundation.org

Correspondent J Roddick, Secretary

Trustees *J Roddick; S Roddick; T G Roddick; S C A Schlieske.*

CC Number 1061372

Information available Accounts were available from the Charity Commission.

The foundation was established in 1997 by the late Dame Anita Roddick, founder of the Body Shop. It has the following objects.

- The relief of poverty.
- The promotion, maintenance, improvement and advancement of education for the public benefit.
- The provision of facilities for recreation or other leisure time occupations in the interests of social welfare provided that such facilities are for the public benefit.
- The promotion of any other charitable purpose for the benefit of the public.

In 2007/08 the foundation received an income of £734,000. Grants given to 38 organisations totalled £3 million, with 16 grants totalling £1.2 million made in the key focus area for this year; human rights. Grants were broken down as follows:

Category	No. of grants	Total
Human Rights	12	£1,200,000
Medical	5	£784,000
Environmental	4	£460,000
Educational and Media	3	£204,000
Poverty and Social Justice	7	£198,000
Arts and Culture	3	£145,000

Examples of beneficiaries in the year included:

Human rights
The Helen Bamber Foundation (£300,000); Climate Justice Programme (£286,000); National Labour Committee (£198,000); Platform (£150,000); Concern Worldwide UK (£100,000); the Prisons Video Trust and Amnesty International (£50,000 each); Burma UK (£35,000); Guy Horton (£26,000); Adaptainer UK (£21,000); the Missing Foundation (£12,000); and Children on the Edge (£7,500).

Medical
The Hepatitis C Trust (£328,000); Children & Woman Abuse Studies Unit (£230,000); Body and Soul (£131,000); Iasis (£70,000); and West Midlands Lupus Society (£25,000).

Environmental
Soil Action (£300,000); Friends of the Earth (£100,000); UK Pesticides Campaign (£50,000); and Stakeholder Democracy Network (£10,000).

Educational and Media
Mother Jones (£150,000); Friends of Creation Spirituality (£29,000); and Red Pepper Magazine (£25,000).

Poverty/Social Justice
New Economic Foundation (£100,000); Family Therapy Institute of Santa Barbara (£40,000); Hetrich-Martin

Institute (£25,000); The Missing Foundation (£20,000); Arun Children and Families Trust (£10,000); Peepal Enterprises Ltd (£3,000); and The Body Shop Foundation (£200).

Arts and Culture

Brighton Dome and Festival Limited (£100,000); Chichester Festival Theatre (£40,000); and the Roundhouse Trust (£5,000).

Exclusions The foundation states that it is 'particularly not interested in the following.

- Funding anything related to sport
- Funding fundraising events or conferences
- Sponsorship of any kind.'

Applications The foundation does not accept or respond to unsolicited applications. 'Grants made by the foundation are at the discretion of the board of trustees. The board considers making a grant and, if approved, notifies the intended recipient'.

The Gerald Ronson Foundation

General and Jewish

£930,000 (2008/09)

Beneficial area UK and overseas.

Acre House, 11–15 William Road, London NW1 3ER

Tel. 020 7388 7000

Correspondent Jeremy Trent, Secretary

Trustees *Gerald Maurice Ronson, Chair; Dame Gail Ronson; Alan Irving Goldman; Jonathan Simon Goldstein; Lisa Debra Ronson; Nicole Julia Ronson Allalouf; Hayley Victoria Goldenberg.*

CC Number 1111728

Information available Accounts were available from the Charity Commission.

The foundation was registered with the Charity Commission in September 2005.

The trustees' grant making policy is to make donations to registered charitable organisations undertaking a wide range of charitable activities.

In 2008/09 the foundation had an income of £497,000 and assets of £12 million. Grants totalling £930,000 were made in the following areas:

Category	Value
Community and welfare	£584,000
Education	£93,000
Religion	£73,000
Arts and culture	£73,000
Medical and disability	£65,000
Overseas aid	£35,000
General	£5,000
Relief and poverty	£2,000

Beneficiaries included: Jewish Care (£401,000); Community Security Trust (£103,000); Lubavitch Foundation (£50,000); Roundhouse Trust (£35,000); Royal Opera House (£30,000); and Jewish Leadership Council and Traditional Alternatives Foundation (£25,000 each). Other grants of less than £20,000 totalled £327,000.

Applications In writing to the correspondent.

The trust generally makes donations on a quarterly basis in June, September, December and March. In the interim periods, the Chairman's Action Committee deals with urgent requests for donations which are approved by the trustees at the quarterly meetings.

Mrs L D Rope Third Charitable Settlement

Education, religion, relief of poverty and general

£381,000 to organisations (2008/09)

Beneficial area UK and overseas, with a particular interest in Suffolk.

Crag Farm, Boyton, Near Woodbridge IP12 3LH

Tel. 01473 333288

Correspondent Crispin Rope, Trustee

Trustees *Crispin Rope; Jeremy Heal; Anne Walker; Ellen Jolly; John Wilkins; Catherine Scott; Paul Jolly.*

CC Number 290533

Information available Accounts were available from the Charity Commission.

This charity is based near Ipswich, and takes a keen interest in helping people from its local area. Most of the funds are already committed to projects it has initiated itself, or to ongoing relationships. Unfortunately, only about one in ten applications to this trust can be successful.

The charity made grants in the following areas (including the amount given in grants to organisations in 2008/09):

Relief of Poverty – £163,000
Support for a number of causes and individuals where the trustees have longer term knowledge and experience, particularly those both in the UK and in the Third World who are little catered for by other charities or by grants or benefits from governments or other authorities, or are in particularly deprived areas and, for overseas work, only through established links.

General Charitable Purposes – £108,000
Public and other charitable purposes in the general region of south-east Suffolk and in particular the parish of Kesgrave and the areas surrounding it, including Ipswich.

Advancement of Education – £74,000
Support for educational projects connected with the Founder's family. Support for a proposed airship museum; support for Catholic and other schools in the general area of Ipswich; and projects relating to the interaction of mathematics and physical science with philosophy.

Advancement of Religion – £37,000
Support for the Roman Catholic religion and ecumenical work, both generally and for specific institutions connected historically with the families of William Oliver Jolly and his wife Alice and their descendants.

Guidelines

The charity offers the following distinction between projects initiated by itself and unsolicited applications:

In practice, the work of the charity may be divided into two distinct categories. Firstly it initiates, supports and pursues certain specific charitable projects selected by the founder or known to be generally in accordance with her wishes. Secondly, it approves grants to unsolicited applications that fall within the founder's stated objectives and that comply with the set of grant-making policies outlined below, specifically for this second element of its work. The trustees devote more of the charity's resources to self-initiated projects as compared to pure grantmaking to unsolicited requests. In terms of grants funded during the year, roughly £410,000 was given towards projects where the charity had either initiated the work or where a long-standing relationship over a number of years gave rise to new or continued assistance.

Successful unsolicited applications to the charity usually display a combination of the following features, as outlined in the charity's 2008/09 accounts:

Size

The trustees very much prefer to encourage charities that work at grassroots level within their community. Such charities are unlikely to have benefited greatly from grant funding from local, national (including funds from the National Lottery) or European authorities. They are also less likely to be as wealthy in comparison with other charities that attract popular support on a national basis. The charities assisted usually cannot afford to pay for the professional help other charities may use to raise funds.

Volunteers

The trustees prefer applications from charities that are able to show they have a committed and proportionately large volunteer force.

Administration

The less a charity spends on paying for its own administration, particularly as far as staff salaries are concerned, the more it is likely to be considered by the trustees.

Areas of interest

Charities with the above characteristics that work in any of the following areas:

- helping people who struggle to live on very little income, including the homeless
- helping people who live in deprived inner city and rural areas of the UK, particularly young people who lack the opportunities that may be available elsewhere
- helping charities in our immediate local area of south-east Suffolk
- helping to support family life
- helping disabled people
- helping Roman Catholic charities and ecumenical projects.

Grants made to charities outside the primary beneficial area of south-east Suffolk are usually one-off and small in scale (in the range between £100 to £1,000).

Unlike many trusts, the charity can consider helping people on a personal basis. The trustees give priority, as they do with charities, to people struggling to live on little income, within the primary beneficial area. Grants are rarely made to individuals living outside the primary beneficial area. Of the individuals assisted, most are referred by field professionals such as housing or probation officers, on whose informed advice the trustees can place some reliance [for further information, see *A Guide to Grants for Individuals in Need*, published by the Directory of Social Change].

Grantmaking in 2008/09

In 2008/09 it had assets of £39 million and an income of £1.7 million. Grants were made totalling £567,000, including £186,000 to individuals.

Beneficiaries of major grants during the year included: Science Human Dimension Project (£50,000); East Anglian Children's Hospice (£30,000); Traidcraft – project in Bangladesh (£20,000); Shelter (£15,000); Downing College – Cambridge (£10,000); Ipswich Furniture Project (£8,000); Cafod – work in Gaza (£7,000); Norfolk Venda Project (£6,500); and Mencap – Ipswich and Jacobs Hospice Homes – India (£5,000 each).

Exclusions The following categories of unsolicited applications will not be successful:

- overseas projects
- national charities
- requests for core funding
- buildings
- medical research/health care (outside of the beneficial area)
- students (a very limited amount is available for foreign students)
- schools (outside of the beneficial area)
- environmental charities and animal welfare
- the arts
- matched funding
- repayment of debts for individuals.

Applications Please send a concise letter (preferably one side of A4) explaining the main details of your request. Please always send your most recent accounts and a budgeted breakdown of the sum you are looking to raise. The trust will also need to know whether you have applied to other funding sources and whether you have been successful elsewhere. Your application should say who your trustees are and include a daytime telephone number.

The Rose Foundation

General – grants towards building projects

£1.2 million (2007/08)
Beneficial area In and around London.

28 Crawford Street, London W1H 1LN
Tel. 020 7262 1155
Website www.rosefoundation.co.uk
Correspondent Martin Rose, Trustee
Trustees *Martin Rose; Alan Rose; John Rose; Paul Rose.*
CC Number 274875

Information available Accounts were available from the Charity Commission.

Established in 1977, the foundation supports charities requiring assistance for their building projects, giving small grants to benefit as large a number of people as possible rather than large grants to small specific groups. The foundation applied to the Charity Commission to modernise its trust deed in 2002, which was to make it more applicable to how the foundation operates rather than to change how it works.

Grants are made towards small self-contained schemes (of generally less than £200,000) based in or around London and usually range from £5,000 to £10,000 each. Previously the trust has given up to £30,000, but has reduced this figure to keep to its spirit of giving a large number of smaller grants despite the decline of the stock market in recent years. Projects should commence between January and August or have started earlier but still be ongoing during that period.

The trustees' policy is to offer assistance where needed with the design and construction process, ensuring wherever possible that costs are minimised and the participation of other contributing bodies can be utilised to maximum benefit.

In 2007/08 the foundation had assets of £18 million and an income of £570,000. Grants were paid during the year to 86 organisations totalling £1.2 million.

As in previous years, the largest grant made during the year was given to St John Ambulance, which received £680,000 as part of a continuing programme of support. Other larger grants were made to the New Amsterdam Charitable Foundation (£97,000), a connected organisation based in the US; and the Fred Hollows Foundation (£32,000).

Beneficiaries of smaller grants included: Jewish Care (£20,000); Central Synagogue General Charities Fund (£12,000); Zoological Society of London (£10,000); Royal Academy of Arts (£8,000); Langdon Foundation (£4,000); Speech Language and Hearing Centre (£2,000); and Weizmann Institute Foundation (£1,000).

Exclusions The foundation can support any type of building project (decoration, construction, repairs, extensions, adaptations) but not the provision of equipment (such as computers, transportation and so on). Items connected with the finishes, such as carpets, curtains, wallpaper and so on, should ideally comprise a part of the project not financed by the foundation. Funding will not be given for the purchase of a building or a site or for the seed money needed to draw up plans.

Applications In writing to the correspondent including details of the organisation and the registered charity number, together with the nature and probable approximate cost of the scheme and its anticipated start and completion dates. Applications can be submitted anytime between 1 July and 31 March (the following year). The foundation hopes to inform applicants of its decision by the second week in July. For more information on the foundation's grant-making policies and application process, go to the foundation's website.

Rosetrees Trust

Medical research
£895,000 (2008/09)
Beneficial area UK.

140 High Street, Edgware HA8 7LW
Tel. 020 8952 1414
Email richard@rosetreestrust.co.uk
Website www.rosetreestrust.co.uk
Correspondent R Ross, Chief Executive
Trustees *R A Ross; Lee Portnoi; Clive Winkler.*
CC Number 298582

Information available Detailed accounts were on file at the Charity Commission.

The trust was established in 1987 to support medical research leading to early improved treatments or new therapies covering many medical conditions. The trust is currently supporting over 100 research projects. Its intention is to increase the amount given to medical research and to find like minded charities with which to co-fund valuable research projects.

The trust's priorities are:

- improved treatments and practical benefits for patients, for example, Royal College of Surgeons Research Fellowships where surgeons' research is based on their practical experience in treating patients; research into new imaging techniques for improves diagnosis and replacement of invasive procedures; key-hole surgery

- seed corn funding for promising researchers to carry out pilot research projects that will provide reports to submit for major grant applications, thus filling a major gap in the research funding process
- long-term support for valuable projects by leading researchers into conditions affecting large numbers of people, like dementia and arthritis where the complexity of the disease means the benefits may take a long time to be realised
- supporting young researchers with potential to become leaders in their specialised area of research
- cutting edge research into areas like tissue engineering based on stem cells, to repair the heart or build new bone.

The trust usually starts with relatively small grants, but as the reporting progresses and a good working relationship develops between the trust and the researchers, these grants are steadily increased and over a period of years can build up to substantial sums. The vast majority of grants are made through university and medical schools.

Please note: the trust is very keen to share the expertise it has developed over 20 years, which is available to co-donors at no cost. Organisations interested in sharing this knowledge should contact the trust directly.

Grants in 2008/09

During the year the trust had assets of £448,000 and an income of £877,000. Grants were made totalling £895,000 and were distributed in the following categories:

Category	Value
Cancer	£175,000
Rheumatology and tissue disorders	£164,000
Coronary and lung disease and strokes	£83,000
Immunology, transplantation and infections	£79,000
Tissue engineering and regenerative medicine	£75,000
Brain research	£72,000
Alzheimer's disease and dementia	£61,000
Eye and hearing disorders	£53,000
Digestive and urinary disorders	£44,000
Maternity and children	£42,000
Parkinson's disease	£35,000
Miscellaneous	£14,000

Beneficiaries included: University College London and Royal Free (£306,000); Hebrew University (£97,000); Kings College (£91,000); Imperial College London (£87,000); Institute of Cancer Research (£45,000); Oxford University (£27,000); Cardiff University (£26,000); Southampton University (£22,000); Manchester University (£18,000); and Newcastle University (£16,000).

Exclusions No support for individuals or for non-medical research.

Applications In writing to the correspondent. Applicants must complete a simple pro forma which sets out briefly in clear layman's terms the reason for the project, the nature of the research, its cost, its anticipated benefit and how and when people will be able to benefit. Proper reports in this form will be required at least six-monthly and continuing funding will be conditional on these being satisfactory.

The trust has previously stated:

The trustees are not medical experts and require short clear statements in plain English setting out the particular subject to be researched, the objects and likely benefits, the cost and the time-scale. Unless a charity will undertake to provide two concise progress reports each year, they should not apply as this is a vital requirement. It is essential that the trustees are able to follow the progress and effectiveness of the research they support.

The Rothschild Foundation

Arts, culture and general
£1.3 million (2007/08)
Beneficial area Unrestricted, with a special interest in Buckinghamshire.

The Dairy, Queen Street, Waddesdon, Aylesbury HP18 0JW
Tel. 01296 653235 **Fax** 01296 651142
Email f_sinclair@ritcap.co.uk
Correspondent Fiona Sinclair
Trustees *Sir Edward Cazalet; Lord Rothschild; Lady Rothschild; Hannah Rothschild; Peter Troughton.*
CC Number 230159

Information available Accounts were available from the Charity Commission.

The foundation was set up in 1956 by James Armand de Rothschild, of the Rothschild banking dynasty, for general charitable purposes. The current policy set by the trustees is to support charitable projects originated by the Rothschild family, in particular, and to make grants to other organisations at their discretion. The vast majority of awards are for £10,000 or less.

In 2000 the foundation also established a Buckinghamshire small grants programme to provide support for projects and activities within the county.

In 2007/08 assets stood at £48 million, generating a low return of £198,000. 82 grants were made totalling £1.3 million.

The level of grant-making analysis provided by the foundation has dropped significantly in the latest set of accounts compared with previous years. As such, only a brief overview can be provided here.

The largest grants by far went to: Eton College (£760,000); and the Butrint Foundation and Stoke Mandeville Hospital (£100,000 each).

Other beneficiaries included: the Royal Society and the British Association for Adopting and Fostering (£25,000 each); Watts Gallery (£20,000); Louisa Cottages Charity (£10,000); Refuge (£6,000); Lifeline Humanitarian (£2,000); and Irish Georgian Trust and Soil Association (£1,000).

Applications In writing to the correspondent. Applications are considered at half-yearly meetings.

Rowanville Ltd

Orthodox Jewish

£680,000 (2007/08)

Beneficial area UK and Israel.

8 Highfield Gardens, London NW11 9HB

Tel. 020 8458 9266

Correspondent Ruth Pearlman, Secretary

Trustees *Joseph Pearlman; Ruth Pearlman; Michael Neuberger; M D Frankel.*

CC Number 267278

Information available Accounts were available from the Charity Commission.

The objectives of the trust are 'to advance religion in accordance with the orthodox Jewish faith'. The trust provides grants to charitable institutions and free accommodation for educational use.

In 2007/08 the trust had assets of £4 million and an income of £1.2 million. Grants were made totalling £680,000.

The largest grants made included those to: Chevras Mo'oz Ladol (£44,000); Yesodey HaTorah Schools (£40,000); Gateshead Talmudical College (£28,000); Tchabe Kolel (£25,000); and Atereth Yehoshua Charity (£20,000).

Beneficiaries of smaller grants included: Beis Yaacov Institutions (£15,000); Jewish Teachers Training College (£11,000); Yad Eliezer Trust (£6,000); Kisharon (£3,200); Noam Primary School (£1,800); and Keren HaTorah (£500).

Applications The trust has previously stated that applications are unlikely to be successful unless one of the trustees has prior personal knowledge of the cause, as this charity's funds are already very heavily committed.

The Joseph Rowntree Charitable Trust

Peace, democracy, racial justice, social justice, corporate responsibility and Quaker issues

£5.9 million (2008)

Beneficial area Unrestricted, in practice mainly UK, Republic of Ireland and Europe.

The Garden House, Water End, York YO30 6WQ

Tel. 01904 627810 **Fax** 01904 651990

Email jrct@jrct.org.uk

Website www.jrct.org.uk

Correspondent Stephen Pittam, Trust Secretary

Trustees *David Shutt; Beverley Meeson; Christine Davis; Emily Miles; Margaret Bryan; Marion McNaughton; Peter Coltman; Susan Seymour; Helen Carmichael; Imran Tyabi; Paul Henderson.*

CC Number 210037

Information available Accounts were available at the Charity Commission. Detailed and up-to-date information on funding programmes is available on the trust's excellent website.

Background

The Joseph Rowntree Charitable Trust (JRCT) is established for general charitable purposes and benefits people and organisations mainly within Britain. Outside Britain, the trust makes grants for work towards peace, justice and reconciliation in both jurisdictions in the island of Ireland and, increasingly, in

relation to influencing the policies of the European Union. In 2008 the trust made its final grants in South Africa, although it will continue to make payments for these until 2012.

This is a Quaker trust and the value base of the trustees, as of the founder Joseph Rowntree (1836–1925), reflects the religious convictions of the Society of Friends. In the original founding trust deed of 1904 (from which the present deed is derived) Joseph Rowntree gave the trustees power to spend the trust fund and its income on any object which is legally charitable. In a memorandum written at the same time, which is not part of the trust deed and therefore not binding, he expressed a clear vision of how he hoped the fund would be used, while urging that 'none of the objects which I have enumerated, and which under present social conditions appear to me to be of paramount importance, should be pursued after it has ceased to be vital and pressing ... '.

There are three Rowntree trusts, each of which is independent of the others. Joseph Rowntree Foundation (JRF) is one of the largest social policy research and development charities in the UK and seeks to better understand the causes of social difficulties, and to explore ways of overcoming them. The JRF is also involved in practical housing and care work through the Joseph Rowntree Housing Trust.

Joseph Rowntree Reform Trust Limited (JRRT) promotes democratic reform, constitutional change and social justice, both in the UK and elsewhere. It is a non-charitable limited company and is therefore free to give grants for political purposes. The JRRT and JRCT have collaborated on various initiatives combating racism and encouraging democratic renewal, including research into voting behaviour in towns in the north of England, and the Power Inquiry.

Regular reviews are undertaken to reassess how it is appropriate to interpret the founder's vision in today's conditions. The trust continues to operate an ethical investment policy, aiming to ensure that, as far as possible, the trust's income is earned in ways which are compatible with its Quaker values and its grant-making policy. As Quakers, they share a belief in the equal worth of all members of the human race, together with a recognition and appreciation of diversity.

Grantmaking

The trust tries to maintain an adventurous approach to funding. Where appropriate, risks are taken and unpopular causes funded, which may not always fall neatly into one of the programme areas listed above. The trust does not usually respond to proposals which can be funded by public appeals.

The work the trust supports is about removing problems through radical solutions, and not about making the problems easier to live with. Joseph Rowntree was always very clear on one thing: for your efforts to have any lasting benefit, you must tackle the roots of a problem. If you only treat the 'superficial manifestations' of poverty, social injustice, or political inequality, then you will ease the symptoms for a time, but make no lasting difference. The trust seeks to engage in philanthropy which changes the existing power imbalances in society to effect real change.

The trust makes grants to individuals and to projects seeking the creation of a peaceful world, political equality and social justice. There should be a clear sense of objectives and details of how to achieve them. The work should be both innovative and imaginative and there should be a clear indication that the grant has a good chance of making a difference.

Though the trust has policies for all of its grant programmes, it is not prescriptive in its grantmaking. Its programme areas are widely drawn and the trustees are open to persuasion about applications which fall outside these areas. Occasionally the trust will initiate projects which it directly manages itself. The 'Visionaries for a Just and Peaceful World' project falls into this category.

The trust deliberately places itself at the cutting edge of difficult and contentious issues and believes in creating a dialogue across difference and supporting change towards a better world. It also recognises that this change can take many years to achieve and is willing to take the long view, and to take risks. In doing so, the trust tries to be flexible enough to respond quickly to the changing needs and demands of our world.

The trustees are Quakers, and decision-making and practice are based on Quaker values. Trust meetings are based on Quaker business methods. Each trust meeting starts and ends with a period of silent worship, no voting takes place and they trust that they are guided to the right decision.

Grant programmes

The trust generally funds work under one of the following six programmes:

Peace
Work that promotes the non-violent resolution of conflict, including work on the arms trade, the creation of a culture of peace, developing effective peace-building measures and supporting the right to conscientious objection to military service.

Racial justice
Work which promotes racial justice in all parts of society, including empowering black and minority ethnic people to engage in decision making and policy development, and work which monitors and challenges racism and racial injustice whether relating to colour or culture.

Power and responsibility
Work that encourages an appropriate relationship between people and the institutions that affect them; including the promotion of accountability, openness, responsiveness and a respect for human rights across the public and private sectors.

Quaker concerns
Work that helps to deepen the spiritual life of the Society of Friends or that develops Quaker responses to problems of our time.

Ireland and Northern Ireland
Work that supports the ongoing development of a just and peaceful society in both jurisdictions, through enhancing civil liberties and human rights, encouraging dialogue and co-operation across divides and promoting creative ways to handle conflict.

South Africa
The trust's programme in South Africa is **now closed to new applications**. Existing grants will be paid. The programme has supported work that promotes a just and peaceful South Africa, particularly through the reduction of rural poverty and addressing the problems of violent conflict on all levels of society

Most grants made under the first four programmes are to organisations based in Britain for work at a national level. The trust also supports a small number of organisations under these four programmes that are based elsewhere in Europe for work at a European level.

Grants policies

The following policy summaries have been largely drawn from the trust's highly informative website.

Peace grants policy
The founder hoped that his trust would 'sound a clear note with regard to the great scourges of humanity, especially with regard to war'. As part of the Quaker tradition, the trust is committed to the creation of a peaceful world, and the creation of a culture of peace. The trust recognises that complex phenomena create peace and war and that new drivers of conflict, such as climate change and access to water, are constantly emerging. The trust believes that long-term approaches to create peace are usually more effective than short-term fixes; it is idealistic, but recognises that 'pragmatism is often more effective than purity.'

Much of the work on corporate responsibility, racial justice and democracy, in Ireland (north and south) and South Africa, is already aimed at these underlying causes in order to create a culture of peace, accountability and democracy. Under the heading of 'Peace', it is anticipated that the groups funded are working to influence the behaviour and thinking of the public, and of people in powerful positions including those working in the military, national governments and international organisations. The trust supports organisations or individuals who promote values similar to its own when working towards peace and does not fund those who advocate aggressive military solutions to conflicts.

The trust wishes to fund organisations or individuals who can identify the strategic steps needed towards achieving peace and evaluates grant applications in terms of the extent to which the work proposed will ultimately advance the cause of peace and non-violence.

Areas of particular interest are organisations or individuals who are working on:

- control or elimination of specific forms of warfare and the arms trade
- influencing appropriate agencies to take or promote peaceful choices to prevent violent conflict or its recurrence
- improving, through practical measures, the effectiveness of peace building and conflict resolution
- bringing non-violent and non-military responses to conflict into the mainstream amongst NGOs, decision-makers and the wider public
- pacifism and conscientious objection to military service.

The trust will not fund:

- work on interpersonal violence, domestic violence, or violence against children
- work focused solely on specific local or regional conflicts
- work which focuses on the immediate effect of conflict on victims

- research which is more theoretical than practical, or which is not aimed at making change happen
- work focused more exclusively on other governments' policy than on that of the UK, unless the work is on pacifism or conscientious objection to military service
- work which seems only to 'preach to the converted'.

Please also note the general exclusions.

The trust is most likely to fund individuals and organisations working in the UK and (if the organisation is working on influencing an international institution such as the EU, NATO or the UN) the rest of Europe.

Grants in 2009
Beneficiaries included: Responding to Conflict – for core costs (£140,000); Conflict Casualties Monitor – for Iraq Body Count (£80,000); Acronym Institute for Disarmament Diplomacy – for worker and UK-European outreach on disarmament (£70,000); British American Security Information Council – for the facilitation of the All-Party Parliamentary Group on Global Security and Non-Proliferation (£47,000); All-Party Parliamentary Group on Conflict Issues – core and project costs (£30,000); and Christian Peacemaker Teams – for UK Christian Peacemakers Corps training (£9,500).

Racial justice grants policy
The Joseph Rowntree Charitable Trust seeks to promote racial justice and equality of opportunity as a basis for a harmonious multi-racial, multi-ethnic society in Britain. The trust seeks to work towards this aim through all its grant-making fields, but particularly through its racial justice programme. This programme area works at three levels. At local level in West Yorkshire, at a national level focusing on England, Wales, Scotland and the UK (work specific to Northern Ireland is funded through a separate programme); and at European level.

An important test of all applications to this programme area is whether they are promoting racial justice. The Racial Justice programme focuses on racial justice in its broadest sense, including black and minority ethnic communities; migration including refugee and asylum issues and Islamophobia.

The trust is keen to encourage communication and co-operation between different racial groups and welcomes applications from black and minority ethnic groups and from multi-racial groups working in these areas. The trust encourages and looks for involvement of black and minority ethnic people at all levels of the projects and organisations it supports. Any applications for work to tackle Islamophobia should describe

where the work is positioned in the context of the UK's diverse Muslim communities, and explain how it will engage with and address the needs of young people and women.

In West Yorkshire, the trust aims to promote the full participation of racially disadvantaged groups in community life. This includes members of black and minority ethnic communities and newly arrived communities and it supports local projects working for equality, social justice and civil rights.

At both national and European level, the trust is keen to support organisations developing and disseminating policy proposals, and advocating policy improvements. The emphasis is on organisations with good access to policy makers. It is also willing to make relatively small grants to some marginal and under-supported organisations doing campaign work.

At national level, JRCT supports projects working to:

- promote issues of racial justice with policy shapers, decision makers and opinion formers
- encourage black and minority ethnic people/black-led organisations to contribute to policy development on the basis of their experience in meeting needs and to participate at planning and decision making levels
- monitor and challenge racism and racial injustice whether relating to colour or culture
- tackle Islamophobia
- promote a rational and humane migration and asylum policies benefiting both migrant and settled communities
- explore and advocate ways to eliminate racial violence and harassment.

At European level, the trust expects that work undertaken on an EU-wide basis will be funded from sources in several EU member states. The priority is to fund work which has direct relevance to communities living in the UK, although the work may also impact on communities elsewhere in Europe. JRCT supports projects working to:

- promote awareness amongst policy makers and within the European institutions of the need to protect the human rights of minority communities, asylum seekers and migrants
- research and disseminate information concerning current EU policies and their impact on minority communities
- provide a forum for NGOs from all EU countries to share experiences on matters relating to race and immigration and to build alliances on shared interests
- work for a more accountable and open process for developing EU policy in relation to race and migration.

In relation to the Racial Justice programme, JRCT does not make grants for:

- local projects, except in West Yorkshire
- projects that provide services or training to members of BME communities, refugees or asylum seekers
- academic research, except as an integral part of policy and campaigning work
- work which we believe should be funded from statutory sources, or which has been in the recent past
- work which tries to make a problem easier to live with, rather than getting to the root of it.

Please also note the general exclusions.

Grants in 2009
Beneficiaries included: Immigration Law Practitioners' Association – for a simplification project (£99,000); Asylum Aid – a researcher for the Refugee Women's Resource Project (£60,000); African Caribbean Achievement Project – for the post of Strategic Client Services Manager (£55,000); East Leeds Health for All – a part-time co-ordinator to establish the peer support group and community advocates (£40,000); Church Action on Poverty – for the 'Living Ghosts' campaign (£14,000); and Institute of Race Relations – work on preventing violent extremism policies and practice (£2,800).

Power and responsibility grants policy
The responsible use of power was important to Joseph Rowntree. He saw business and politics as forms of public service to be used to promote social justice, equality and a spirit of citizenship. Whilst being fully aware that corporate and government power can be used to the detriment of individuals and communities, he recognised their potential for good and for building the kind of society he was interested in. Much has changed since 1904, but Rowntree's concern about 'the power of selfish and unscrupulous wealth' still rings true 100 years later.

The trust continues to be concerned about the way corporate and political institutions operate. Though the context is different, the trust's Quaker values remain constant and are expressed in a concern for social justice. JRCT believes that greater accountability, openness, and responsiveness within political and corporate institutions will benefit everyone.

The nature of the world today means that it is harder for people to know where, and by whom, decisions affecting their lives are taken, let alone have a chance to influence them. As such, the trust believes there is a need to strengthen the democratic process, to enhance corporate accountability, and to build confidence in the way decisions are taken. This is a newly defined area of concern for the trust, but it builds upon its experience in the corporate responsibility and democracy fields.

The trust will consider applications from organisations and individuals which:

- encourage accountability, openness and responsiveness in government, government agencies, the public services, and the private sector; or which explore an appropriate role for the media in achieving this
- foster understanding of, and respect for, human rights in government, business and civil society as a means to promote social justice
- explore appropriate relationships between people, their communities and the institutions that affect them – whether these be local and central government, quangos, or companies
- explore whether and how political participation and involvement can be increased and deepened within Britain, as a means to promote a socially just society
- promote ideas to nurture the democratic process and to counter the misuse of power
- explore how government and business might change their planning, evaluation and reward systems from their current short-term outlook to a longer-term one
- examine the relationship between government and business and ways in which they interact both for and against the public interest.

The trust wants to support initiatives which make a difference. The limited size of resources, together with its interest in influencing policy, tends to lead the trust towards supporting organisations working at the national level.

Issues of accountability, openness and responsiveness are equally relevant to the European Union and global institutions to which the UK belongs. In this programme the trust will consider applications from organisations working at a European Union level and also those aimed at increasing the accountability of the UK government and other UK bodies for the policies that they pursue within global institutions.

The ways in which business and government can be held accountable differ significantly. Applications may address either or both of these sectors.

Grants in 2009

Grants included those to: Public Interest Research Centre Ltd – core costs for programme on climate change (£139,000); Civil Liberties Trust – 'Common Values' campaign (£75,000); Media Standards Trust – core costs (£60,000); European Coalition for Corporate Justice: GARDE – to draft proposals for corporate accountability reform in Europe (€38,000); Network of European Foundations – for the Initiative for Learning

Democracy in Europe (€10,000); and Ariadne – core costs of a human rights funders network (£5,000).

Quaker grants policy

The Quaker Concerns programme supports work relating to the Religious Society of Friends. Through this programme the trust seeks to foster the development of what Joseph Rowntree, in the trust's founding memorandum, called a 'powerful Quaker ministry'. This is interpreted as widely as possible and includes practical ways to deepen the spiritual life of Friends and to develop Quaker responses to problems of our time. Trustees see the lives of individual Friends and Meetings, and their work in the wider community, as interdependent. Currently, the trust is particularly interested in:

- bringing Quaker values to the wider community, encouraging Friends to take forward innovative and practical work that brings Quaker values and beliefs to the world around them
- strengthening Quakers' shared identity. The trust supports projects which will promote Friends' understanding of Quakers' shared history, theology and spirituality, in order to strengthen Quaker faith and practice particularly through exciting initiatives and new ideas and approaches. The trust is particularly interested in this area of work as many people now come to Quakerism as adults.

Applications from Quakers in Britain and the rest of Europe (the Europe and Middle East Section) will be considered. This includes yearly meetings, local meetings, other Quaker organisations and individuals. Each application will be considered carefully, in the light of the general application requirements.

In addition, the trust will consider:

- the way in which a concern has been developed and tested
- the prospective benefit of the project to Friends and to wider society
- the relationship between the proposed project and other work within the Society of Friends
- other funds available to the applicant.

The trust will generally not make grants for core administration and management of the Society of Friends, either nationally or in local meetings or to maintain or resurrect work, where a decision has been made to 'lay it down'. No funding will also be given for an individual's personal income while they research or write a book.

Please also see the general exclusions.

Grants in 2009

Beneficiaries included: Quaker Council for European Affairs – for core costs (€120,000); the Friend Publications Ltd

– a Quaker model of investigative journalism (£30,000); Central England Area Meeting, West Midlands Quaker Peace Education Project – for a research and development project (£10,000); and Quaker Book Committee – for a book project, 'Quaker work during the 'Troubles' in Northern Ireland' (£5,000).

Ireland and Northern Ireland grants policy

JRCT aims to fund work which will contribute to the ongoing development of a just and peaceful society in the island of Ireland. It takes no position on the constitutional arrangements within the island, but recognises the strong historical, cultural and practical links between Britain, Northern Ireland, and Ireland. The trust is interested in funding work which:

- addresses the root causes of violence and injustice, rather than alleviating symptoms
- cannot be funded from other sources
- is likely to make a long-term, strategic difference.

Applications in the following areas will be considered:

- work based on international human rights standards that deals effectively and constructively with past injustice arising out of the Northern Ireland conflict
- work that facilitates the demilitarisation of paramilitary groups, and the ending of paramilitary influence in communities
- work that enables meaningful dialogue across religious, cultural or political divides in order to address common problems
- work that effectively challenges sectarianism, or discrimination arising from racism or xenophobia
- work which promotes the development of a tolerant, pluralist and multi-ethnic society
- work that promotes rational and humane migration and integration policies benefiting both migrant and settled communities
- work that encourages accountability, openness and responsiveness in all levels of government, statutory agencies and the civil service
- work that protects and enhances civil liberties and human rights
- work that promotes non-violence and creative ways to handle conflict, within specific communities or traditions, or at a national or international level
- work which strengthens civil society in order to play an appropriate role in addressing the issues listed above.

The trust is interested in supporting work in either jurisdiction, or on a cross-border basis, or at an all-Ireland level. Local work will be supported only where it is likely to have a wider impact, for example if it is testing a model which can then be replicated, or is addressing a local issue that has wider social or political implications.

In addition to the trust's general exclusions, the following types of work will not be funded:

- the delivery of basic services to people in need, including welfare advice, women's refuges, basic skills training etc.
- work with or for children and young people
- work related to health or disability
- any form of personal healing or therapeutic work, including counselling
- community relations work that does not include a clear strategy for lasting change
- historical research, documentation or archival work
- core costs of community centres, local women's groups, local voluntary sector infrastructure organisations or similar community level groups.

Please note: individuals and groups based in Ireland (the Republic) or Northern Ireland that wish to apply for funding from JRCT should apply under this programme only, rather than any of the trust's other grant programmes.

Grants in 2009
Beneficiaries included: Equality and Rights Alliance – core costs for a campaign to build an effective and resilient equality and human rights infrastructure in Ireland (€60,000); Westmeath Employment Pact – dialogue programme to explore underlying causes of intra- and inter-community conflicts affecting the Traveller community (€50,000); Border Arts 2000 – cultural dialogue initiative in Castlederg (£46,000); Cavan Community Forum – regional conference on respective roles of elected and community representatives in policy making (€10,000); and Edge Hill University – symposium to compare Irish and Muslim experiences of counter-insurgency law and policies (£6,200).

South Africa grants policy
JRCT's South Africa grants programme is now closed to new applications.

The trust has made grants in South Africa for over 40 years. Ten years after the move to democracy in 1994, the trust reviewed its grant-making policy and decided it was time to wind up the long running programme. There are four main reasons for this:

- the trust's grantmaking is most effective when there is direct engagement between applicants and grantees, trustees and staff, and it is difficult to do this from such a distance
- in the context of the enormous amount of work still needed to implement change the amount of money that JRCT has

available for funding in South Africa can only have a limited impact
- there are now many more donors operating in the country, able to commit much larger sums of money as well as having a local presence and staff
- in reviewing the programme areas and overall workload of the trust it was decided that for it to work more effectively, the overall number of programmes should be cut from seven to five.

Exclusions Generally, the trust does not make grants for:

- the personal support of individuals in need
- educational bursaries
- travel or adventure projects
- medical research
- building, buying or repairing buildings
- business development or job creation schemes
- general appeals
- providing care for older people, children, people with learning difficulties, people with physical disabilities, or people using mental health services
- work which has already been done
- work in larger, older national charities which have an established constituency of supporters
- work in mainstream education
- academic research, except as an integral part of policy and campaigning work that is central to our areas of interest
- work on housing and homelessness
- the arts, except where a project is specifically concerned with issues of interest to the trust
- work which we believe should be funded from statutory sources, or which has been, in the recent past
- work which tries to make a problem easier to live with, rather than getting to the root of it
- local work in Britain (except Racial Justice work in West Yorkshire)
- work outside the UK, Ireland and South Africa (except for groups working elsewhere within Europe at a European level).

Further specific exclusions are included for individual programmes. Within its areas of interest, the trust makes grants to a range of organisations and to individuals. It is not necessary to be a registered charity to apply to the trust. However, it can only support work which is legally charitable as defined in UK law.

Applications The trust expects all applicants to have made themselves familiar with the relevant funding

programmes, summarised here but set out in full on the trust's website and available in leaflet form.

They then require an application letter (including budget, accounts and equal opportunities policy) and a completed registration form. The details expected in the letter are set out in detail on the website and in the leaflet. Applications can be submitted either online or by post. Organisations submitting an application by post can download a registration form from the website to complete. For those submitting their applications online, the registration details are included in the initial steps.

There is a deadline for receipt of applications of around ten weeks before the meeting of trustees. It is very helpful if applications arrive well before the deadline. The period immediately after the deadline is the trust's busiest time, so it cannot normally consider applications that arrive late until the following funding round. The trust has three grant-making rounds each year. Contact the trust or go to the website for the latest information on application deadlines.

Please note: for organisations applying to the West Yorkshire Racial Justice Programme, there is a slightly different application process. Full details are available on the trust's website.

The Joseph Rowntree Foundation

Research and development in social policy and practice
£3.5 million (2008)
Beneficial area UK, with some preference for York and Bradford.

The Homestead, 40 Water End, York YO30 6WP

Tel. 01904 629241 **Fax** 01904 620072

Email info@jrf.org.uk

Website www.jrf.org.uk

Correspondent Julia Unwin, Chief Executive

Trustees *Don Brand; Debby Ounsted; Dame Dr Ann Bowtell; Susan Hartshorne; Ashok Jashapara; Bharat Mehta; Nigel*

Naish; Tony Stoller; Dame Mavis McDonald; Steven Burkeman.

CC Number 210169

Information available Accounts were available from the Charity Commission. Detailed information is available from the foundation's informative website.

This is not a conventional grant-making foundation. It supports research, of a rigorous kind, usually carried out in universities or research institutes, but also has a wide range of other activities not necessarily involving grants of any kind.

The foundation initiates, manages and pays for an extensive social research programme. It does not normally respond to unsolicited applications and many of its programmes issue formal and detailed requests for proposals. However modest proposals for minor gap-filling pieces of work in the foundation's fields of interest may sometimes be handled less formally and more rapidly.

The foundation's strategic priorities are:

- place (for example, housing, neighbourhoods)
- poverty (for example, minimum income standards, poverty and ethnicity)
- empowerment (for example, social care, independent living).

The foundation also makes some grants locally in and around York and Bradford (where the foundation has made a ten year commitment), and directly manages or initiates housing schemes.

In 2008 the foundation had assets of £202 million and an income of £9.7 million. It spent £3.5 million on grant commitments.

Grants committed include research projects by organisations and institutions including: Loughborough University (£171,000); Liverpool John Moores University (£100,000); Housing Associations Charitable Trust (£80,000); Durham University (£55,000); and Migrants' Rights Network (£37,500).

Research programmes
The foundation describes its programmes in considerable depth on its website. The following is an overview of the foundation's research. It would not be worthwhile to approach the foundation on the basis of the information in this entry on its own.

How the foundation works
The foundation does not make grants: those supported are considered partners in a common enterprise. The foundation takes a close interest in each project from the outset, often bringing together an advisory group to give guidance on a project, and taking an active role in the dissemination of the project's findings to bring about policy and practice change. Foundation staff oversee the progress of individual projects within the programme and act as a point of contact throughout.

As a general rule, the foundation aims to provide full financial support rather than being one of a number of funders. However, where the involvement of another organisation would help the project achieve its aims, joint funding may be considered.

How work gets funded
The foundation is keen to fund a variety of different kinds of projects, depending on the state of knowledge about a particular topic.

- The majority of proposals are canvassed under broad programme themes, or through specific briefs using the JRF website, email notification, direct mail, and, occasionally, advertisements.
- In addition, JRF sometimes commissions work directly.
- Occasionally JRF will consider proposals arising from an unsolicited approach.

The foundation does not have a preference for methodology but it must be appropriate for the question.

The foundation likes to be outward looking in its approach and encourages user groups and community-based groups to apply for funding where appropriate. If the proposal is for a research project the project team must include people with knowledge, experience and research skills to carry out a successful research project.

Who decides which projects are approved?
For proposals which have been received in response to a programme-based call for proposals:

1) Programme Manager and lead Assistant Director (Policy and Research) scrutinise all proposals to sift out proposals which are methodologically weak and which do not meet the foundation's brief.
2) Promising proposals are then further scrutinised by at least one independent external assessor who has relevant expertise, alongside the Programme Manager and lead Assistant Director, and the Director of Policy and Research.
3) Based on rigorous internal and external assessments, recommendations are made to the Director of Policy and Research (who makes the final decision for proposals which cost less than £100,000) and to the Trustee Board (who make the final decision for proposals which cost more than £100,000).

In some circumstances (for example when commissioning short evidence reviews or think-pieces, or commissioning pieces of work which are highly specialist and where the field is very limited), the foundation will use a 'limited competitive tender' or 'direct commission' approach.

Programmes and projects
Programmes will use different approaches to secure the advice and scrutiny they require for good governance. Programmes often have a programme advisory group or network to draw in expertise from relevant fields, to advise on priorities and progress of the programme as a whole, and on issues concerning influence and impact. Programme advisory groups and networks do not make funding decisions.

Strategic Objectives 2009–2011

The foundation's Strategic Plan outlines its objectives as follows:

What we are doing in 2009–2011
In addition to the objectives below, we will be exploring emerging issues throughout the life of this three-year plan. Most of our work centres on three themes:

Poverty
Our aim: to examine the root causes of poverty, inequality and disadvantage, and identify solutions.

Key objectives:

- to monitor child poverty and develop policy solutions to bring it to an end
- to provide authoritative annual statements on poverty and social exclusion
- to explore how poverty affects people and families in different ways at different times
- to implement an anti-poverty strategy within Joseph Rowntree Housing Trust
- to explore the nature of contemporary slavery
- to help find ways of stopping, or reversing, negative drinking cultures and patterns in the UK.

Place
Our aim: to contribute to the creation and development of strong, sustainable and inclusive communities.

Key objectives:

- to inform the debate on affordable housing
- to provide authoritative annual statements on housing and neighbourhoods
- to understand the housing needs of young people and how policy can best meet them
- to assess how community assets can contribute to a thriving civil society
- to develop a new 'model' community for the design and management of 21st century homes and neighbourhoods

● to find new and more effective ways of engaging residents in developing and managing homes and neighbourhoods

● to deliver excellent services and effective management of our land and buildings.

Empowerment
Our aim: to identify ways of enabling people and communities to have control of their own lives.

Key objectives:

● to contribute to the debate about a fairer, more transparent system of funding long-term care

● to support groups whose voices are seldom heard so they can be involved in policy, planning and practice

● to deliver excellent services that encourage people to stay healthy and lead active lives

● to develop evidence focusing on outcomes and cost-effectiveness in housing with care for older people

● to improve the experience of people who use services, live and work in different social care settings

● to help society and services move towards reflecting service users' aspirations for their lives.

Exclusions With the exception of funds for particular projects in York and the surrounding area, the foundation does not generally support:

● projects outside the topics within its current priorities

● development projects which are not innovative

● development projects from which no general lessons can be drawn

● general appeals, for example from national charities

● conferences and other events, websites or publications, unless they are linked with work which the foundation is already supporting

● grants to replace withdrawn or expired statutory funding, or to make up deficits already incurred

● educational bursaries or sponsorship for individuals for research or further education and training courses

● grants or sponsorship for individuals in need.

Applications The foundation does not respond to unsolicited applications. Instead, it issues 'calls for proposals' and invites submissions to them. Detailed information, including guidance and a proposal registration form, is available from the foundation's website.

The foundation also operates a grant funding stream called 'New Insights and Innovations' to consider proposals which reflect's its core strategic priorities but may not fall within specific programmes.

Joseph Rowntree Reform Trust Limited

Promoting political and democratic reform and defending of civil liberties

£1 million (budgeted for 2009)
Beneficial area Mainly UK.

The Garden House, Water End, York YO30 6WQ
Tel. 01904 625744 **Fax** 01904 651502
Email info@jrrt.org.uk
Website www.jrrt.org.uk
Correspondent Tina Walker, Trust Secretary
Trustees *Danny Alexander; Christine Day; Dr Christopher Greenfield; Lord (David) Shutt; Paedar Cremin; Mandy Cormack; Andrew Neal.*
Information available Helpful website for applicants but little financial information was available.

Joseph Rowntree was a Quaker businessman with a lifelong concern for the alleviation of poverty and the other great social ills of his day. He made a considerable fortune from the chocolate company which bore his name, and in 1904 transferred a large part of this wealth to three trusts, each designed to reflect and develop different aspects of his thinking about contemporary social problems. Known today as the Joseph Rowntree Foundation, the Joseph Rowntree Charitable Trust and the Joseph Rowntree Reform Trust (JRRT), all three continue to build upon the founder's original vision, applying it in their different ways to the problems of present-day society, however, they have always been separately administered and are totally independent of each other.

JRRT differs from the other Rowntree Trusts, and from almost every other trust in the UK, in that it is not a charity. Charities must not have political objectives and whilst they may engage in political activity in pursuit of their charitable aims, those aims must not in themselves be political. By contrast, this trust is a limited company which pays tax on its income. It is therefore free to give grants for political purposes; to promote political and democratic reform and defend civil liberties. It does so by

funding campaigning organisations and individuals who have reform as their objective, and since it remains one of the very few sources of funds of any significance in the UK which can do this, it reserves its support for those projects which are ineligible for charitable funding.

The trust's main aims are to:

● correct imbalances of power

● strengthen the hand of individuals, groups and organisations who are striving for reform

● foster democratic reform, civil liberties and social justice.

It rarely funds projects outside the UK, directing most of its resources towards campaigning activity in this country, and it will not fund research or any other charitable activity.

The following is taken from the trust's website:

The trust is not committed to the policies of any one political party although it has been a long-term funder of the Liberal Democrats (and predecessor parties) in order to redress the balance of financial inequality between parties and to foster political developments central to a healthy democratic process. It has also supported individual politicians or groups promoting new ideas and policies from all the major parties in the UK.

The trust has also helped a large number of non-party pressure groups needing short-term assistance: however, the trust will not normally provide long-term funding. Such groups need not be national organisations, but the national relevance of local campaigns is a crucial factor that directors will consider.

Currently, the trust has assets of around £30 million. Each year a potential grant budget of around £1 million is allocated which excludes administrative expenses and tax.

Information about grants is published on the trust's website once the grant has been ratified at a subsequent trust meeting. The list is not necessarily complete as the trust may decide that to achieve a particular grant's purpose or to protect the personal safety of those undertaking the work, it is not appropriate to make available the information.

Beneficiaries in 2009 included: Compass – to assist the campaign (£45,000); Privacy International – towards their work on privacy issues in the lead up to the General Election (£40,000); NO2ID Stopping the Database State – towards their grassroots local groups campaign (£26,000); Index on Censorship – towards their campaign against the rise of self-censorship in Britain's arts

(£12,000); Camp for Climate Action Legal Team – additional funding to assist the team to effectively protect the civil liberties of those who exercise their right to protest, responding to the media interest following the G20 protests (£5,000); and Lord Tyler – towards the preparation of a Private Member's Bill on Constitutional Renewal (£3,000).

Exclusions The trust is not a registered charity and provides grants for non-charitable political and campaigning activities. Examples of work for which the trust does not make grants are:

- the personal support of individuals in need
- educational bursaries
- travel and adventure projects
- building, buying or repairing properties
- business development or job creation
- general appeals
- academic research
- work which the trust believes should be funded from statutory sources, or which has been in the recent past
- administrative or other core costs of party organisations.

Applications Applicants should email a one page outline to the correspondent before making a formal application. If accepted, a full application can then be made.

The trust does not have a standard form, but applications should include:

- an Application Registration Form (available to download from the trust's website)
- up to four pages setting out the proposal
- a full budget for the project
- the most recent audited accounts
- a CV, if applying as an individual.

Trust staff make an initial assessment of applications and are authorised to reject those that are clearly inappropriate. All staff rejections are reported to the directors at their next meeting, when they consider all remaining applications. The meetings take place at quarterly intervals in March, July, October and December and the deadline for applications is approximately four or five weeks prior to the trust meeting. Applications for small grants of up to £5,000 can, however, be considered at any time and applicants should hear of the decision within two weeks.

Royal British Legion

Armed services
£3.4 million to organisations
(2008)

Beneficial area UK, excluding Scotland.

Haig House, 199 Borough High Street, London SE1 1AA

Tel. 08457 725 725 **Fax** 020 3207 2218

Email info@britishlegion.org.uk

Website www.britishlegion.org.uk

Correspondent Scarlet Harris, External Grants Officer

Trustees Col R R St J Barkshire; C W Carson; R E Clark; P D Cleminson; E Dixon; Brig J R Drew; J Farmer; E W Hefferman; Dr D M Henderson; G Lewis; W J H Lodge; M T McCaw; W Parkin; K F Pritchard; Ms J Rowe; D A Walker; T W Whittles; Rev M D A Williams; A Burn; J Crisford; K Draper.

CC Number 219279

Information available Accounts were available from the Charity Commission.

The Royal British Legion was formed in 1921 as a caring organisation for people in need from the Service and ex-Service community. We aim to safeguard the welfare, interests and memory of those who have served in the Armed Forces including, under certain circumstances, other support and defence organisations and the Mercantile Marine (beneficiaries).

We can also give grants to any ex-Service charity that shares this aim.

We may also give grants to non-ex-Service organisations provided that the grant will directly benefit ex-Service personnel.

We give grants to any charitable organisation in England, Wales, Ireland and the Isle of Man that shares one or more of our objects, namely:

- to relieve need and to further the education of beneficiaries and their spouses, children and dependants
- to relieve need and protect the mental and emotional health of families left by those who have died in service
- to relieve suffering, hardship and distress to spouses and dependants caused by the absence of those serving in the Royal Navy, Army and Royal Air Force on Regular, Reserve or Auxiliary engagements and, under certain circumstances, other support and defence organisations and the Mercantile Marine

- to promote and support schemes for the resettlement, rehabilitation, retraining and sheltered employment, of beneficiaries and their spouses, children and dependants.

Grants may be for:

- projects, for example, a particular time-limited activity that benefits ex-Service personnel
- services, for example, to provide a support or welfare service
- capital, for example, to build a facility or to purchase equipment.

Grants are awarded at the following levels:

- Level 1 – up to £25,000
- Level 2 – £25,000 – £500,000
- Level 3 – over £500,000.

Detailed guidelines for each funding level are available on the trust's website.

In 2007/08 the trust had assets of £199 million and an income of £104 million. Total charitable expenditure was £76 million, most of which was spent on its own services. Grants to organisations totalled £3.4 million, with a further £26 million given in grants to individuals (further information can be found in *A Guide to Grants for Individuals in Need*, also published by the Directory of Social Change).

The largest grant by far went to the Officers' Association (£1.6 million). Other beneficiaries included: Sir Oswald Stoll Foundation (£357,000); Royal British Legion Industries Ltd (£275,000); Skill Force (£186,000); E Hayes Dashwood Foundation (£120,000); Alcohol Recovery Project (£62,000); Sailors Family Centre (£50,000); Earl Haig Fund Scotland (£43,000); and Prisoners Education Trust (£25,000).

Smaller grants of £25,000 or less totalled £107,000.

Exclusions Grants are not made for:

- memorials
- commercial ventures, or any potential commercial ventures, for example clubs.

Grants are not normally given for core costs, for example, administration or running costs of an organisation that is supporting ex-Service personnel. However, there may be exceptions to this, and the Royal British Legion aims to respond flexibly to applications, and is prepared to negotiate if there are special circumstances, for example, if the withholding of grant would harm the interests of ex-Service personnel.

Applications In the first instance you should contact Scarlet Harris, External

Grants Officer (Tel. 020 3207 2138 or email: externalgrants@britishlegion.org.uk) in order to explore whether you may be eligible for a grant, and at what level, so that you can be advised further on the detailed requirements.

Following this, you will be sent an application form which will explain on it the information you need to submit depending on the size of grant you are asking for.

Successful applicants, depending on the level of grant applied for, can expect to receive an award in between two and six months of sending in a correctly completed application form.

The Rubin Foundation

Jewish charities and general

£984,000 (2007/08)

Beneficial area UK and overseas.

The Pentland Centre, Lakeside House, Squires Lane, Finchley, London N3 2QL

Tel. 020 8346 2600

Email amcmillan@pentland.com

Correspondent Allison McMillan, Secretary

Trustees *Alison Mosheim; Angela Rubin; R Stephen Rubin; Andrew Rubin; Carolyn Rubin.*

CC Number 327062

Information available Accounts were available from the Charity Commission.

This foundation is closely connected with Pentland Group Ltd (*see the Guide to UK Company Giving, published by Directory of Social Change*), with three trustees being on the board of directors of that company. The foundation's income comes from donations from the company and interest on its bank deposits. In 2007/08 it had assets of £1.1 million and an income of £143,000. Grants were made totalling £984,000.

During the year there were 18 grants for £10,000 or more, mainly going to Jewish charities. Beneficiaries included: ULIA (£405,000); Jewish Community Secondary School Trust (£250,000); Jewish Museum (£50,000); Civitas (£25,000); Peace and Sport (£14,000); and Weidenfeld Institute for Strategic Dialogue (£10,000).

There were a further 21 grants of between £1,000 and £8,000, including those to: Southbank Centre (£8,000); Board of Deputies of British Jews (£6,000); Royal Opera House Foundation (£4,200); the Roundhouse (£3,000); Cancer Backup (£1,300); and Maccabiah Football Bursaries (£1,000). Small grants of £1,000 or less were made totalling £12,000.

Applications The foundation has previously stated that 'grants are only given to people related to our business', such as charities known to members of the Rubin family and those associated with Pentland Group Ltd. Unsolicited applications are very unlikely to succeed.

The Rufford Maurice Laing Foundation

Nature conservation, sustainable development, environment and general

£5 million (2007/08)

Beneficial area Developing countries, UK.

6th Floor, 248 Tottenham Court Road, London W1T 7QZ

Tel. 020 7436 8604

Website www.rufford.org

Correspondent Simon Mickleburgh, Grants Manager

Trustees *Charles Barbour; Anthony Johnson; John Laing; Col. Iain Smailes; Robert Reilly.*

CC Number 326163

Information available Annual report and accounts, useful information on its website.

The foundation is another trust deriving from the Laing building fortune, though it does not share a common administration with the other Laing trusts. The original trust was established in 1982 by John Hedley Laing, who is also a trustee of the Whitley Laing Foundation (now the Whitley Fund for Nature) and has previously been a trustee of WWF-UK, Conservation International and the Wildlife Protection Society of India.

The trustees maintain a strong interest in nature conservation, the environment

and sustainable development projects in non-first world countries where funds are most scarce. A number of projects aimed primarily at helping young people with HIV/AIDS in the developing world are funded via the Elton John Aids Foundation. Support for other causes in the UK, including health, medicine and social welfare, is also given.

Funding policy

In April 2009 the trustees amended the foundation's grant-making priorities. The following is taken from the foundation's website and explains the changes in more detail.

In order to ensure an on-going, living legacy for the Rufford Maurice Laing Foundation and the Rufford Small Grants Foundation, the trustees made the following decisions:

- the Rufford Maurice Laing Foundation will concentrate on funding nature conservation projects in developing countries undertaken by small to medium-sized organisations
- there will be no future funding of nature conservation projects in the UK
- a small amount of funding will be made available from 2009/10 to provide grants, normally of up to £5,000, for projects that focus on either overseas development or social welfare issues in the UK.

To be considered for support by the foundation organisations should fulfil the following criteria:

- all applicants should be UK registered charities
- projects must fall within the foundation's main areas of funding
- there are only limited funds currently available due to existing commitments so only projects that meet our criteria in full are eligible, so organisations should ensure that this is the case before they apply
- the minimum grant awarded is £1,000 – there is no set maximum for nature conservation projects
- grants to projects focusing on either overseas development or social welfare issues in the UK will not normally exceed £5,000.

Grants in 2007/08

During the year the foundation had assets of £65 million and an income of £3.4 million. Grants were made to 210 organisations totalling just over £5 million.

Funding was allocated as follows:

- 61% for conservation projects primarily in the developing world

- 15% for overseas development projects, including HIV/AIDS projects in developing countries
- 15% for health and medicine projects in the UK, including scientific research into efficacy of complementary health treatments and their integration into general medicine
- 9% to social welfare initiatives in the UK.

Larger grants included those made to: Natural History Museum (£350,000); EIA Charitable Trust (£300,000); Peace Parks Foundation (£150,000); University of Southampton (£101,000); Institute of Zoology (£92,000); Impact Foundation (£60,000); Crime Concern and Wildscreen Trust (£50,000 each); and Earthwatch Institute and Ecology Trust (£30,000 each).

Grants of less than £30,000 included those to: Anti-Slavery International (£28,000); Oxford Brookes University (£25,000); British Institute for Brain Injured Children and Topsy Foundation UK (£20,000 each); St Albans High School for Girls (£16,000); Marine Conservation Society (£13,000); Changing Faces (£10,000); Children in Distress (£6,000); Woman's Trust (£3,000); and Centrepoint Soho (£1,500).

Of the grant beneficiaries listed above, many received similar support in the previous year.

In addition to the above mentioned grants, £40,000 was paid into Charities Aid Foundation (CAF) accounts to enable trustees of the Rufford Maurice Laing Foundation to issue CAF cheques to deserving causes of their choice. This further distribution included grants to wildlife, ex-service and arts charities.

The Rufford Small Grants Foundation

Due to the success of the Rufford Small Grants facility the foundation decided to establish a new grant-making trust, The Rufford Small Grants Foundation – RSGF (charity number 1117270) to award the Rufford Small Grants in perpetuity. Sufficient assets (£27 million) were transferred from the foundation to generate approximately £1.25 million in income. The new foundation started operations in 2007. More information on RSGF can be found on its website: www.ruffordsmallgrants.org/rsg.

Exclusions The foundation will not generally fund the following:

- building or construction projects
- donations to individuals or projects that directly benefit one individual

- UK projects with a local or regional focus
- loans
- endowment funds
- student/gap year conservation expeditions
- general appeals or circulars.

Applications The trust considers all applications which meet its criteria but states that 'with limited funds available it is neither possible to give detailed reasons why applications are not successful nor to enter into any dialogue or correspondence regarding projects which have been refused funding. In all cases, organisations are only able to make a single application for funding from the foundation during any one-year period.'

All applications must be received by post [addressed to the correspondent]. All new applicants must be charities registered in the UK.

There is no set form but applications must include:

- a covering letter with contact details
- a comprehensive plan outlining the project for which funding is being sought, including measurable objectives (four–six pages max)
- a full budget – with details of funding secured to date, other funding applications being made and the amount being requested from the foundation
- a copy of the charity's most recent accounts
- a copy of the latest annual report (if available).

Please note: the foundation does not accept applications for funding by email and is unable to discuss the suitability of an application by telephone.

Applications are accepted throughout the year. The foundation strives to respond to all applications within four weeks of receipt and asks that applicants do not telephone to check on their application, as they will be contacted in due course.

S F Foundation

Jewish

£2.8 million (2007/08)
Beneficial area Worldwide.

143 Upper Clapton Road, London E5 9DB

Correspondent Rivka Niederman, Secretary

Trustees *Hannah Jacob; Rivka Niederman; Miriam Schrieber.*

CC Number 1105843

Information available Accounts were on file at the Charity Commission. Charitable donations made by the foundation are detailed in a separate publication: *SF Foundation – Schedule of Charitable Donations*. The accounts stated that the publication is available by writing to the Secretary. Despite requesting this publication, including a stamped, addressed envelope, no reply was received.

Set up in 2004, this trust gives grants towards the 'advancement and furtherance of the Jewish religion and Jewish religious education and the alleviation of poverty amongst the Jewish community throughout the world.'

In 2007/08 the foundation had assets of £8.8 million, an income of £6.5 million and made grants totalling £2.8 million.

Applications 'The charity accepts applications for grants from representatives of various charities, which are reviewed by the trustees on a regular basis.'

The Saddlers' Company Charitable Fund

General

£424,500 (2008/09)
Beneficial area UK.

Saddlers' Hall, 40 Gutter Lane, London EC2V 6BR

Tel. 020 7726 8661/6 **Fax** 020 7600 0386

Email clerk@saddlersco.co.uk

Website www.saddlersco.co.uk

Correspondent Nigel Lithgow, Clerk to the Company

Trustee *The Saddlers' Company. The company is directed by the court of assistants consisting of the master, three wardens, a number of past masters and up to four junior assistants.*

CC Number 261962

Information available Accounts were available from the Charity Commission.

The Saddlers' Company Charitable Fund was formed in 1970. Over time, the objects of the fund have been refined to provide support for education, the British saddlery trade, the equestrian world, the City of London and general charitable activities. The decisions regarding the company's charities are taken by the Charities and Education Committee with regular reports back to the full trustee body.

The fund supports many of the same charities each year such as Alleyn's School and Riding for the Disabled. After making such allocations, and allowing for the agreed level of reserves, about one quarter of the remaining funds is allocated to major national charities working in all charitable sectors and the remaining three quarters are held for charitable appeals which are received throughout the year. The trustees have formulated a policy to focus on smaller charities assisting people with disabilities. To meet this policy, members of the Livery are asked to visit a charity local to them and to report on the charity's suitability to receive a grant. The Liveryman prepares a report on the charity's purpose, budgetary and financial control, administration and general viability, together with a recommendation as to whether the charity should be supported and at what level. These reports are considered by a grant committee whose recommendations are passed to the trustees.

R M Sturdy Charitable Trust

A Past Master of the Worshipful Company of Saddlers and former trustee of the fund, Mr R M Sturdy, died in 2006. By a letter of wishes, he expressed the desire that the R M Sturdy Charitable Trust, of which he was the benefactor, be administered by the Worshipful Company of Saddlers after his death. The Court of Assistants, the governing body of the Worshipful Company of Saddlers, and whose members are the trustees of the fund, concluded that the most expeditious way of fulfilling this desire would be to create a restricted fund within the Saddlers' Company Charitable Fund. In 2007/08 a transfer of £550,000 was made from the R M Sturdy Charitable Trust to the Saddlers Company Charitable Fund to establish the new fund.

Diamond Jubilee Fund

The trustees have re-affirmed their intention to make a significant charitable grant to mark the diamond jubilee of Her Majesty Queen Elizabeth II in 2012 and have determined to continue to transfer the sum of £5,000 each year into a designated fund – the Diamond Jubilee Fund – with the aim of achieving a total of £75,000 by 2012. During 2007/08 the

trust added £30,000 to enable the fund to reach its target ahead of schedule. The trustees have agreed that they should apply the income from this Designated Fund to support the British Equestrian Paralympic Teams taking part, initially, for the 2012 Paralympic Games (the year of Her Majesty's diamond jubilee) and, thereafter, for each succeeding four-yearly Games.

In 2008/09 the trust had assets of £7.1 million and a total income of £437,000. Grants were made totalling £424,500, broken down as follows:

Category	Amount
Education	£159,000
Charities for people with a disability	£123,000
General charitable activities	£69,000
The equestrian world	£49,000
Services charities	£14,000
City of London	£13,000
Saddlery trade	£3,000

The fund's accounts list all grants over £1,000, broken down into the relevant categories and examples are as follows:

Education

By far the largest grant made during the year was £130,000 to Alleyn's School for Saddlers' Scholarships, a regular beneficiary. Other beneficiaries included: City & Guilds of London Institute (£9,000); University of Liverpool (£3,900); and London Youth (£2,000).

Charities for people with disabilities

The beneficiary of the largest grant was the Riding for the Disabled Association (£27,500). Other beneficiaries included: Household Cavalry Operational Casualties Fund (£3,000); Scottish Veterans' Garden City Association and Emmaus Hampshire (£2,000 each); The Meningitis Trust (£1,500); and St Michael's Hospice (£1,000).

General charitable activities

Beneficiaries included: Help for Heroes and Rochester Cathedral Trust (£5,000 each); Leather Conservation Centre (£4,000); Salisbury Cathedral (£3,000); The Warehouse (£2,000); St Luke's Hospital for the Clergy (£1,500); and the Samaritans and Tower Hamlets Mission (£1,000 each).

The equestrian world

The main beneficiary was the British Horse Society (£37,000).

Services charities

Beneficiaries included: Army Benevolent Fund (£3,000); RAF Benevolent Fund (£2,500); Sea Cadets – London Region (£2,000); and Royal Naval Benevolent Society (£1,300).

City of London

The beneficiaries were: St. Vedast-alias-Foster (£6,000); Lord Mayor's Appeal (£5,000); City of London Police Widows'

& Orphans' Fund (£1,500); and St Paul's Cathedral (£1,000).

Saddlery trade

The beneficiaries were: Museum of Leathercraft (£2,000); and Walsall Leather Museum (£1,000).

Exclusions No grants to individuals.

Applications In writing to the correspondent. Grants are made in January and July, following trustees' meetings. Charities are asked to submit reports at the end of the following year on their continuing activities and the use of any grant received.

Erach and Roshan Sadri Foundation

Education, welfare, homelessness, Zoroastrian religion and general

£483,000 (2007/08)

Beneficial area Worldwide.

10a High Street, Pewsey SN9 5AQ

Email markcann@ersf.org.uk

Website www.ersf.org.uk

Correspondent Mark Cann, Administrator

Trustees *Margaret Lynch; Shabbir Merali; Darius Sarosh; Jehangir Sarosh; Donald Wratten.*

CC Number 1110736

Information available Accounts were on file at the Charity Commission. Detailed information is available on the foundation's website.

The main objects of the foundation are:

- providing financial assistance for education and welfare purposes
- relieving poverty by alleviating homelessness
- assisting members of the Zoroastrian religious faith.

The trustees also consider grant applications which fall outside the main criteria but have particular appeal to them. Grants are in the range of £2,000 and £100,000. 'Pump-priming' donations are offered – usually given to new organisations and areas.

In 2007/08 the foundation had income of £45,500 (£3.1 million in 2006/07).

Grants were made totalling £483,000, and were broken down as follows:

Category	Value
Education and welfare	£311,500
Zoroastrian	£80,500
Homelessness	£70,000
General	£21,500

Beneficiaries in 2008/09, as listed on the foundation's website, included: Parsi Anjuman (£48,000), towards the Indore Temple; Tyneside Cyrenians (£25,000), towards specialist equipment for the homeless hostel; Honeypot (£21,000), for the respite holiday programme; Afghan Appeal Fund (£20,000), Little Sisters of the Poor – Ireland (£15,000), towards rebuilding a nursing home; Halcrow (£10,000), for a deposit scheme for the homeless; and All Cannings (£2,000), for specialist computer equipment.

Some organisations receive more than one grant during the year.

Exclusions Applications are unlikely to be successful if they:

- involve animal welfare or heritage
- are a general appeal from large UK organisations.

Applications On a form which can be downloaded from the foundation's website, along with full and detailed guidelines. Forms can be returned by post or email. Meetings are held four times a year.

Please note: 'Unsolicited material sent in addition to the clear and concise requirements of the application form is very likely to prove detrimental to your application. The trustees insist that additional items such as annual reports, glossy brochures, Christmas cards and accounts are not sent unless specifically requested.'

The Alan and Babette Sainsbury Charitable Fund

General

£477,000 (2007/08)
Beneficial area Worldwide.

Allington House, 1st Floor, 150 Victoria Street, London SW1E 5AE

Tel. 020 7410 0330 **Fax** 020 7410 0332

Website www.sfct.org.uk

Correspondent Alan Bookbinder, Director

Trustees *The Hon. Sir Timothy Sainsbury; Miss Judith Portrait.*

CC Number 292930

Information available Accounts were available from the Charity Commission.

This is one of the Sainsbury Family Charitable Trusts, which share a joint administration and have a common approach to grantmaking.

The following information about the trust's grantmaking in 2007/08 is taken from the annual report.

The trustees concentrate their resources on a small number of programmes which build on themes in the trust's earlier grantmaking. At present these include support for ethnic minority and refugee groups, human rights and young people's participation in the arts.

In 2007/08 the trust's assets stood at £13.4 million, generating an income of £481,000. Grants totalling £477,000 were paid during the year and were distributed in the following areas shown here with examples of beneficiaries in each category:

Youth Work – 11 grants totalling £160,000
Kinder Children's Choirs of the High Peak (£35,000); Theatre Royal – Bury St Edmunds (£30,000); Southwark Playhouse (£25,000); Cooltan Arts (£12,000); and Lindsay Rural Players (£5,000).

Overseas – 6 grants totalling £116,000
British Friends of Neve Shalom and Canon Collins Educational Trust For South Africa (£28,000 each); Female Prisoners' Welfare Project Hibiscus and World Organisation for Rehabilitation Training – ORT (£20,000 each); and Kampala Music School and Anglo-Israel Association (£10,000 each).

Scientific and medical research – 1 grant of £80,000
The sole grant was made to the Multiple Sclerosis Society.

General – 5 grants totalling £67,000
Jewish Association for Business Ethics (£30,000); Holocaust Educational Trust (£20,000); Ashden Awards (£10,000); Anne Frank Trust (£5,000); and the Sainsbury Archive (£1,500).

Civil liberties – 3 grants totalling £55,000
Refugees into Jobs (£25,000); Minority Rights Group (£20,000); and Medical Foundation for the Care of Victims of Torture (£10,000).

Exclusions Grants are not normally made to individuals.

Applications The trust states that: 'proposals are likely to be invited by the trustees or initiated at their request. Unsolicited applications will only be successful if they fall precisely within an area in which the trustees are interested'. A single application will be considered for support by all the trusts in the Sainsbury family group.

The Sainsbury Family Charitable Trusts

See individual trusts

£61.05 million (2007/08)
Beneficial area See individual trusts.

Allington House, 1st Floor, 150 Victoria Street, London SW1E 5AE

Tel. 020 7410 0330 **Fax** 020 7410 0332

Website www.sfct.org.uk

Correspondent Alan Bookbinder, Director

These trusts, listed below, each have their own entries (with the exception of the Indigo Trust). However they are administered together and it is said that 'an application to one is taken as an application to all'.

Their grantmaking ranges from the largest to the smallest scale, including massive long-term support for major institutions such as the National Gallery or the Sainsbury Centre for Mental Health as well as for a range of specific issues ranging from autism to the environmental effects of aviation. There is an office with over 30 staff and a large number of specialist advisers.

However, even collectively, the trusts do not form a generalist grant-making organisation; though active in most fields of charitable activity, it is usually within particular and often quite specialised parts of each sector.

Most of the trusts use a similar formula to describe their grantmaking:

The trustees take an active role in their grant-making, employing a range of specialist staff and advisers to research their areas of interest and bring forward suitable proposals. Many of the trusts work closely with their chosen beneficiaries over a long period to achieve particular objectives. It should therefore be understood that the majority of unsolicited proposals we receive will be unsuccessful. As a rule the Gatsby, Glass-House, Linbury, Staples and Tedworth trusts do not consider unsolicited proposals.

A typical programme might have the following elements:

- support for a major, long-term research initiative, whether academic or in the form of an action research programme
- support for specialised national groups promoting good practice in the field concerned
- grants for a few service delivery organisations, often small and local, and addressing the most severe aspects of the issues involved.

In these editor's view, charities that are indeed developing new ideas and approaches would be most unwise to assume that the Sainsbury trusts will automatically get to hear of this.

'Applications' are probably not the best way forward and may perhaps be best avoided except where specifically requested. More sensible might be to write briefly and say what is being done or planned, on the assumption that, if one or more of the trusts is indeed interested in that area of work, they will want to know about what you are doing. A telephone call to do the same is fine. Staff are polite, but wary of people seeking to talk about money rather than issues.

More generally, the trusts are involved in a number of networks, with which they maintain long-term contact. Charities doing work relevant to the interests of these trusts may find that if they are not a part of these networks (which may not be inclusive and most of which are probably London-based) they may get limited Sainsbury attention.

The most inappropriate approach would often be from a fundraiser. Staff, and in many cases trustees, are knowledgeable and experienced in their fields, and expect to talk to others in the same position.

Most of the trusts do fund ongoing service delivery, but generally infrequently and usually on a modest scale. For such grants it is not clear how they choose this play scheme or that wildlife trust. To them, these may be small and relatively unimportant decisions, and they may rely on trustees or staff simply coming across something suitable, or on recommendations through what they have called their 'usual networks'.

The Sainsbury Family Trusts (with totals of grant payments or approvals for the most recent year available):

Category	Value
Gatsby Charitable Foundation	£40,900,000
Linbury Trust	£5,500,000
Monument Trust	£3,400,000
True Colours Trust	£2,500,000
Jerusalem Trust	£2,300,000
Headley Trust	£2,200,000
Kay Kendall Leukaemia Fund	£2,000,000
Ashden Trust	£799,000
Staples Trust	£596,500
J J Charitable Trust	£540,000
Alan and Babette Sainsbury Trust	£477,000
Three Guineas Trust	£469,000
Glass-House Trust	£358,000
Woodward Charitable Trust	£344,000
Mark Leonard Trust	£340,000
Tedworth Trust	£301,000
Indigo Trust	£31,000
Total	**£61,050,000**

Collective support

The trusts sometimes act collectively, with support for the same organisations from a number of the trusts. Organisations that occasionally appear in more than one grants list include the Royal Ballet School and National Portrait Gallery, and also Ashden Awards for Sustainable Energy.

It is not clear to the outsider whether such cross-trust support is the result of interaction at trustee or at officer level, or both. However it does seem that there is such a thing as being 'in' with the group of trusts as a whole – a cause of occasional resentment by those who see the Sainsbury trusts, perhaps entirely wrongly, as being something of a closed shop.

Exclusions No grants are normally given to individuals by many of the trusts (though a number of them fund bursary schemes and the like operated by other organisations). Grants are not made for educational fees or expeditions.

Applications Please do not send more than one application. It will be considered by all relevant trusts.

The trusts only fund registered charities or activities with clearly defined charitable purposes.

The trustees take an active role in their grantmaking, employing a range of specialist staff and advisers to research their areas of interest and bring forward suitable proposals. Many of the trusts work closely with their chosen beneficiaries over a long period to achieve particular objectives.

It should therefore be understood that the majority of unsolicited proposals they receive will be unsuccessful. As a rule the Gatsby, Glass-House, Linbury, Staples and Tedworth trusts do not consider unsolicited proposals.

The other trusts will consider exceptional proposals which fit closely their specific areas of interest.

There are no application forms, except in a small number of clearly defined areas:

- The Woodward Charitable Trust
- The Kay Kendall Leukaemia Fund
- The Headley Museums Archaeological Acquisition Fund.

Applications to all other trusts should be sent by post, with a description (strictly no more than two pages please, as any more is unlikely to be read) of the proposed project, covering:

- the organisation – explaining its charitable aims and objectives, and giving its most recent annual income and expenditure, and current financial position. Do not send a full set of accounts
- the project requiring funding – why it is needed, who will benefit and in what way
- the funding – breakdown of costs, any money raised so far, and how the balance will be raised.

At this stage do not send supporting books, brochures, DVDs, annual reports or accounts.

All applications will receive our standard acknowledgement letter. If your proposal is a candidate for support from one of the trusts, you will hear from us within eight weeks of the acknowledgement. Applicants who do not hear from us within this time must assume they have been unsuccessful.

Basil Samuel Charitable Trust

General charitable purposes

£498,000 (2007/08)

Beneficial area Worldwide, in practice, mainly UK.

Smith & Williamson, 25 Moorgate, London EC2R 6AY

Tel. 020 7131 4376

Correspondent Mrs Coral Samuel, Trustee

Trustees *Coral Samuel; Richard M Peskin.*

CC Number 206579

Information available Accounts were available from the Charity Commission.

The trust was established in 1959 for such charitable purposes as the trustees decide, either in the UK or elsewhere. The trust describes its activities as making grants to medical, socially supportive, educational and cultural charities plus a number of donations to other charities.

In 2007/08 it had assets of £9.8 million and an income of £478,000. Grants were made to 36 organisations totalling £498,000. Grants were categorised as follows:

Category	Value
Cultural	£263,000
Medical	£206,000
Educational	£29,000

Beneficiaries included: Royal National Theatre (£100,000); Macmillan Cancer Support (£60,000); Mary Rose Trust (£40,000); Great Ormond Street Hospital (£25,000); RNIB (£15,000); British Museum and Thomas Coram Foundation for Children (£10,000 each); Attingham Trust, Hampstead Theatre and the Police Rehabilitation Trust (£5,000 each); Commonwealth Jewish Trust (£2,000); and Countryside Foundation for Education (£1,000).

Exclusions Grants are given to registered charities only.

Applications In writing to the correspondent. The trustees meet on a formal basis annually and more frequently on an informal basis to discuss proposals for individual donations.

The Sandra Charitable Trust

Animal welfare and research, environmental protection, social welfare, health and youth development

£515,000 to organisations (2007/08)

Beneficial area UK with slight preference for south-east England.

Moore Stephens, St Paul's House, 8–12 Warwick Lane, London EC4M 7BP

Tel. 020 7334 9191 **Fax** 020 7651 1953

Email keith.lawrence@moorestephens.com

Correspondent Keith Lawrence, Secretary

Trustees *Richard Moore; Michael Macfadyen.*

CC Number 327492

Information available Accounts were available from the Charity Commission.

The trust was established in 1987 for general charitable purposes, with the main aim of the charity also being:

- to support a wide variety of beneficiaries including nurses and charities involved in animal welfare and research, environmental protection, relief of poverty and youth development.

In 2007/08 the trust has assets of almost £14.9 million and an income of £529,000. Grants were made totalling £596,000, of which £515,000 was donated to organisations and just over £81,000 to 143 individuals.

Beneficiaries of the largest grants included: Barnardo's (£75,000); Arundle Castle Cricket Foundation and the Florence Nightingale Foundation (£25,000 each); Dorchester Abbey Preservation Trust (£12,000); and Leukaemia Research and RNIB (£10,000).

More typical grants included those to: British Trust for Ornithology and Sightsavers (£5,000 each); Alone in London, Joint Educational Trust and the Woodland Trust (£3,000 each); Cure Parkinson's Trust and Music in Hospitals (£2,000 each); and Ability Net, Fine Cell Block and the Imperial War Museum (£1,000 each).

Exclusions No grants to individuals other than nurses.

Applications The trust states that 'unsolicited applications are not requested, as the trustees prefer to support charities whose work they have researched [...] the trustees receive a very high number of grant applications which are mostly unsuccessful'.

The Schreib Trust

Jewish and general

£947,000 (2007/08)

Beneficial area UK.

147 Stamford Hill, London N16 5LG

Tel. 020 8802 5492

Correspondent Mrs R Niederman, Trustee

Trustees *A Green; Mrs R Niederman; J Schreiber; Mrs I Schreiber.*

CC Number 275240

Information available Basic accounts were on file at the Charity Commission,

without a list of grants or a full narrative report.

It is difficult to glean an enormous amount of information about this trust's grant-giving policies as only brief accounts were on file at the Charity Commission. Although the trust's objects are general, it lists its particular priorities as relief of poverty and the advancement of religion and religious education. In practice, the trust only supports Jewish organisations.

In 2007/08 the trust had assets of £417,000 and an income of £313,000. Grants were made totalling £947,000.

Previous beneficiaries have included: Lolev, Yad Eliezer, Ponovitz, Craven Walk Charity Trust, Shaar Hatalmud, Beis Rochel, Beth Jacob Building Fund, Toiras Chesed and Oneg Shabbos.

Applications In writing to the correspondent.

The Schroder Foundation

General

£1.4 million (2008/09)

Beneficial area Worldwide, in practice mainly UK.

31 Gresham Street, London EC2V 7QA

Correspondent Sally Yates, Secretary

Trustees *Bruno Schroder, Chair; Edward Mallinckrodt; Nicholas Ferguson; Charmaine Mallinckrodt; Leonie Fane.*

CC Number 1107479

Information available Accounts were available from the Charity Commission.

Set up in 2005, this foundation shares a common administration with Schroder Charity Trust (Charity Commission Number 214060). It does not respond to unsolicited applications.

The foundation's grant-making policy, described in its 2008/09 accounts, reads as follows:

The objects of the foundation are to apply the income and capital for the benefit of any charitable object or purposes, in any part of the world, as the trustees think fit. The trustees have a policy of supporting a broad range of activities within the areas of the environment, education, arts, culture and heritage, social welfare, the community and international relief and development.

At their quarterly meeting the trustees consider what grants they will make and receive reports from grant recipients. The trustees travel widely in the UK and abroad and use the knowledge gained to support the work of the foundation and to inform grant-making policy. The foundation's policy is to focus on charitable causes with a previous track record or in organisations in which the foundation has a special interest. Organisations identified by the trustees for potential support are normally invited to submit a formal application outlining the project, its beneficiaries and how the funds will be applied according to the guidance for applicants to The Schroder Foundation. It is generally the trustees' policy to make only one-off grants. However, grants over a number of years are occasionally awarded.

In 2008/09 the foundation had assets of £11 million and an income of £5.3 million, due largely to a donation of £5.1 million from B L Schroder's 1969 Settlement. Grants were made to 81 organisations totalling £1.4 million.

Beneficiaries of larger grants included: Eton College (£117,000); Merlin (£80,000); Royal Geographical Society (£73,000); and University College Oxford and Campaign for Female Education – CAFED (£50,000 each).

Smaller grants included those made to: Historic Palaces Kensington (£25,000); CSV Volunteers in Child Protection (£20,000); Islay and Jura Community Enterprise Trust (£15,000); Argyllshire Gathering (£7,700); and Smaull Song (£500).

Applications 'The trustees identify projects and organisations they wish to support and the foundation does not make grants to people or organisations who apply speculatively.'

This trust does not respond to unsolicited applications.

The Francis C Scott Charitable Trust

Disadvantaged young people in Cumbria and north Lancashire

£1.3 million (2008)

Beneficial area Cumbria and north Lancashire (comprising the towns of Lancaster, Morecambe, Heysham and Carnforth).

Suite 3, Sand Aire House, New Road, Kendal LA9 4UJ

Tel. 01539 741610 **Fax** 01539 741611

Email info@fcsct.org.uk

Website www.fcsct.org.uk

Correspondent Chris Batten, Director

Trustees *Susan Bagot, Chair; Richard Boddy; Ian Pirnie; Joanna Plumptre; Alexander Scott; Madeleine Scott; Don Shore; Clare Spedding.*

CC Number 232131

Information available Accounts were on file at the Charity Commission; good website.

The trust was created in 1963 by Peter F Scott CBE, then Chairman of the Provincial Insurance Company. Peter Scott, together with his parents Francis and Frieda Scott and his sister Joan Trevelyan, endowed the trust with a significant holding of Provincial Insurance Company shares.

It supports registered charities addressing community deprivation in Cumbria and north Lancashire, and is principally concerned with meeting the needs of young people from 0–19 years. It seeks to target its funds where they can be most effective and can make a real difference to people's lives.

General

In 2008 the trust had assets of nearly £22 million and an income of £932,000. There were 121 grants paid during this period, including commitments from previous years, totalling over £1.5 million. There were 65 grants committed totalling £1.3 million, broken down as follows:

Category	No.	Value
Young people	33	£630,000
Families and children, women and men	14	£249,000
Communities and charity support	8	£186,000
Disabled, chronically ill and older people	8	£115,000
Other	2	£38,000

The trust's helpful website gives the following overview of its grantmaking policy:

What we fund

The majority of our grants are multi-year revenue grants (such as salaries and running costs), however trustees will also fund capital projects that make a tangible difference to a local community.

Whilst we prefer to fund organisations that are registered charities, we will consider offering grants to organisations who are pursuing charitable objectives providing their aims/constitution are clearly not-for-profit. We will only consider applications from national organisations where the beneficiaries and project workers are based within our beneficial area.

Please note: charities should not apply to both the Frieda Scott and Francis C Scott Charitable Trusts at the same time and we would encourage you to seek guidance from the staff if you are unsure.

Preferred Areas of Support

In broad terms, trustees are looking for projects that are responding to identified needs from a specific group or community. A project or service does not need to be new or innovative to receive funding support – the most important consideration is whether it is effective. The bulk of our grants are for revenue funding (running costs and/or salaries) over a number of years – please refer to our eight year funding model for details [see table below].

Within our overall aim of supporting charities who are addressing the needs of 0–19 year olds in the most deprived communities in Cumbria and north Lancashire, the following are our key priority areas:

- Early Years/Family Support work: The nurturing and development of 0 to 5 year olds and those who are caring for them.
- Children's work: Within the 6 to 13 age group, we are particularly keen to support projects that are assisting children with the transition from Primary to Secondary School.

Phase	Year	Focus	Objective
1	Up to 1 year	Research	Define area of need and then seek organisations to address it.
2	1–3	Core funding	Provide running costs (some or all) and actively support with staff time to ensure the project's early success.
3	4–6	Project funding	Foster a more strategic approach to funding and target project development.
4	7–8	Scale down funding	Withdraw funding over an agreed time period and attract other funders (especially statutory).
5	8+	Cease funding	Remain a background advocate for the project, but move on.

- Youth work: This trust has long supported developmental work with teenagers and will continue to fund those projects addressing the needs of the most disadvantaged within this age group.

FCSCT bursary fund for young people and community students
Trustees have recently agreed to offer local students studying on the University of Cumbria Youth and Community course a bursary of up to £750. [Contact the trust for more information].

8-year Funding Model
Following a strategic review process conducted in 2003, the trustees have adopted the following approach to revenue funding for those projects/organisations they believe require extended investment in order to become established. Appeals for capital or bursary funding are considered separately.

Please note: the trust stated in its 2008 accounts that it envisaged conducting a major review of its grant-giving policies towards the end of 2009. This was re-scheduled to take place in March 2010. The above guidelines were correct at the time of writing and are not expected to change significantly but organisations are advised to check the website or contact the trust directly for the latest information before making any application.

Grants in 2008

Young People
Beneficiaries included: Brathay Group Sponsorship Fund (£35,000); Cumbria Federation of Young Farmers (£22,000); Eden (Young) Carers (£15,000); Low Luckens Organic Resource Centre (£8,000); Maryport and Solway Sea Cadets (£6,000); Signal Film and Media (£3,000); and West Cumberland Choral Society Junior Choirs (£250).

Families and Children, Women and Men
Beneficiaries included: Living Well Trust (£30,000); Safety Net Advice and Support Centre (£20,000); Cumbria Pre-School Learning Alliance (£14,000); Barnados – Wigton (£5,000); and Slag-Bank Play Area Association (£2,000).

Communities and Charity Support
Beneficiaries receiving grants during the year included: Cumbria Community Foundation (£75,000); Marsh Community Centre (£20,000); Wigton Gathering Place (£10,000); More Music in Morecambe (£5,000); and Multiple Sclerosis Society – Furness (£500).

Disabled, Chronically Ill and Older people
Beneficiaries included: Bendrigg Trust (£21,000 in two grants); One Voice (£15,000 in two grants); Centre for Complementary Care (£10,000); Mencap – Carlisle (£5,000); and Lords House Farm (£2,500).

Other
Grants were made to: Brathay Hall Trust (£275,000); Charities Aid Foundation (£24,000 in two grants); and University of Cumbria (£18,000).

Exclusions The trust does not consider appeals:

- from individuals
- from statutory organisations
- from national charities without a local base/project
- from charities with substantial unrestricted reserves
- from medical/health establishments
- from schools/educational establishments
- from infrastructure organisations/second-tier bodies
- for projects principally benefiting people outside Cumbria/north Lancashire
- for retrospective funding
- for expeditions or overseas travel
- for the promotion of religion
- for animal welfare.

Applications The trust is always pleased to hear from charities that need help. If an organisation thinks that it may come within the trust's criteria it is encouraged to contact the director for an informal discussion before making an application.

Application forms are available to download from the trust's website or can be requested by phone, email or post. Applications should be completed and returned with the latest set of accounts (via email or post).

Grants below £5,000 are decided on a monthly basis with larger appeals going to the full trustees' meetings in March, July and November. Applications for over £5,000 should arrive at least four weeks before the meeting. Details of upcoming deadlines can also be found on the trust's website.

The Scottish Community Foundation

Community development and general
£2.7 million (2007/08)
Beneficial area Scotland.

22 Calton Road, Edinburgh EH8 8DP
Tel. 0131 524 0300 **Fax** 0131 524 0329
Website www.scottishcommunity foundation.com
Correspondent Giles Ruck, Chief Executive
Trustees *Anne Boyd, Chair; Hamish Buchan; Helen Mackie; Robert Anderson; Beth Edberg; Alan Harden; Colin Liddell; Lady Emily Stair; Bob Benson; Gillian Donald; Ian McAteer.*
SC Number SC022910

Information available Accounts were provided by the foundation. Information was also taken from the foundation's detailed website.

In common with other community foundations, the Scottish Community Foundation makes grants from various sources – both public and private – as well as having its own endowment with which it distributes money.

The foundation makes small grants, usually up to £5,000, for charities and community groups in Scotland, particularly those which are helping to build and sustain local communities.

There are two broad programmes, under which there are a range of different funds.

Scotland-wide programmes – provide awards of £250 to £5,000 for a wide range of projects. Subject to eligibility, not-for-profit groups working to benefit people in Scotland can apply to these programmes at any time, although please note that some programmes have annual deadlines.

Local grants programmes – there are a variety of programmes which benefit people in specific areas of Scotland. Each has different grant levels, deadline dates and decision making practices.

Please note that grant schemes change frequently and potential applicants should consult the foundation's website for details of current programmes and their deadlines.

Exclusions The foundation does not usually fund:

- individuals or groups which do not have a constitution
- groups other than not-for-profit groups
- groups whose grant request is for the advancement of religion or a political party (this means the foundation won't fund grant requests to support the core activities of religious or political groups)
- the purchase of second hand vehicles
- trips abroad
- the repayment of loans, payment of debts, or other retrospective funding
- payments towards areas generally understood to be the responsibility of statutory authorities
- groups who will then distribute the funds as grants or bursaries
- applications that are for the sole benefit to flora and fauna. Applicants are invited to demonstrate the direct benefit to the local community and/or service users in cases where the grant application is concerned with flora and fauna
- projects which do not benefit people in Scotland.

Please note: different grant programmes may have additional restrictions.

Applications The foundation's website has details of the grant schemes currently being administered. Organisations are welcome to contact the grants team to discuss their funding needs before making any application (Tel: 0141 341 4960).

Seafarers UK (King George's Fund for Sailors)

The welfare of seafarers

£2.55 million (2008)

Beneficial area UK and Commonwealth.

8 Hatherley Street, London SW1P 2QT

Tel. 020 7932 0000 **Fax** 020 7932 0095

Email seafarers@seafarers-uk.org

Website www.seafarers-uk.org

Correspondent Dennis Treleaven, Head of Grants

Trustees *Peter McEwen; Charles Maisey; Frank Welsh; Barry Miller; Sir John Ritblat; Capt. Duncan Glass; Rodney Hazlit; Mark Brownrigg; Anthony Lydekker; Capt. David Parsons; James Watson; Jonathan Baker; Michael Acland; Capt. Paul Du Vivier; Peter Mamelok; Timothy Warren; John Thompson; Christine Gould; Christian Marr; Commander James McClurg; Simon Rivett-Carnac.*

CC Number 226446

Information available Accounts were available from the Charity Commission. The charity also has a helpful and informative website.

The fund makes grants, often recurrent, for a wide but little-changing range of seafarer's charities. Grants range from a few hundred pounds to several hundred thousand.

General

The fund was set up in 1917 as a central fundraising organisation to support other seafarers' charities. It has a large and very costly fundraising operation, with a network of volunteer area committees backed by professional staff; but almost one third of its income comes from the interest and dividends on its investments. As reported previously, in an effort to address these high fundraising costs, the fund had a consultancy firm carry out an audit of its fundraising operation. The conclusion was that significant growth was needed in the fund's charitable income. As a result a professional fundraiser was appointed to overhaul the fundraising operation and to pursue new income streams. The strategy was part of a more general plan to modernise the fund and make it more relevant, with new activities as well as fulfilling its more traditional obligations. This new direction is reflected in the fact that the fund has now adopted the operational name of Seafarers UK.

In previous years the cost of generating funds represented around 35% of total income. The fund aimed to address this situation in future years, and in 2007 this figure had fallen to 20%. However, the fund's 2008 annual report and accounts show that the cost of generating funds had risen to 21%, mainly due to the global financial crisis which resulted in difficulties attracting anticipated revenues from fundraising events which have fixed costs.

In 2008 the fund had assets of just over £34.4 million (£42.3 million in 2007), and an income of £4.7 million. Grants were made during the year totalling

£2.55 million to organisations working with beneficiaries in the following categories:

Category	Amount
Seafarers' dependants and families	£1,150,000
Older and ex-seafarers	£1,000,000
Seafarers of working age	£280,000
Maritime youth groups	£110,000

Grantmaking in 2008

The fund's detailed annual report and accounts offer the following summary of its grantmaking in each area, starting with a general overview:

Seafarers' dependants and families

This category covers a wide variety of people and our grants are similarly diverse. Our second largest grant in this category was £150,000 to the Sailors' Families' Society, which supports over 450 seafarers' families across the UK, under its Family Support Scheme which makes monthly grants to families as well as providing annual holidays in caravans owned by the Society across the UK and special educational grants to seafarers' orphans and dependants.

This year we also made a further grant of £100,000 to the Royal Navy and Royal Marines Children's Fund. This money will be split (by the Fund) between support for special needs education, respite and childcare, clothing and equipment and special and extra lessons.

Older and ex-seafarers

The largest beneficiary charity – Shipwrecked Fishermen and Mariners' Benevolent Trust – received £277,000 for the year. This money provides help to merchant seafarers, fishermen and dependants in need. Support ranges from immediate grants to widows when a seafarer dies, regular grants to retired and older seafarers and widows and grants to those retiring early due to ill health, disability or accident. In addition, special grants are offered to meet crisis situations and beneficiaries come from across the UK.

The second largest beneficiary in this category was the Royal Naval Benevolent Trust (RNBT) who received a total of £159,000. The grant supports the Trust in their work with retired and ex-seafarers, their widows and dependants. This year the grant is split between £39,000 towards a range of capital items and improvements for their Pembroke House care and nursing home and £120,000 towards the costs of electronically propelled vehicles and stair lifts and riser/recliner chairs. Other grants of note include a total of £85,400 awarded to the Ex-Services Mental Welfare Society – Combat Stress and £50,000 awarded to Scottish Veterans' Garden City Association. Combat Stress provide specialist help and care to ex-service men and women who suffer from service-related psychological injuries ranging from clinical depression to post traumatic stress disorder. Our grant will continue to support Combat Stress in providing two key services – short-term specialist treatment at three centres in Surrey, Shropshire and Ayrshire and support services provided by 15 regional welfare officers in the veterans' homes and communities. Our grant to Scottish Veterans' will support a proposal to develop 60 units of specially adapted accommodation across Scotland providing and maintaining homes for disabled British ex-service and Merchant Navy personnel and their families.

Amongst our smaller grants we are pleased to be able to support again the Somme Nursing Homes in Belfast who needed a new roof for the kitchen annex to their nursing home and to give £2,500 to the Lord Kitchener Memorial Holiday Centre who provide respite holidays for ex-service personnel and their spouses.

Seafarers of working age

We are pleased to announce a grant of £100,000 to the Royal National Mission to Deep Sea Fishermen to continue to provide support at Mission centres located around the coast from Newlyn to Peterhead and including Northern Ireland providing welfare provision for fishermen, their families and retired fisherfolk. Of particular note is the continuing grant we have been able to make to the Seamen's Hospital Society to continue to support the development of the Seafarers Advice and Information Line (SAIL). This excellent service provides a telephone advice service via a 'local rate call' from anywhere in the UK providing information and advice, benefit checks, help completing forms and negotiating with other agencies to secure seafarers and their immediate dependants their entitlements.

Maritime youth groups

Once again our main beneficiary this year has been the Marine Society and Sea Cadets, who were awarded £100,000 as a contribution towards its Direct Grants Scheme which in turn goes to support over 360 separate Sea Cadet units throughout the UK. These grants range from providing security fencing, alarms and gates for individual sea cadet units to general building works/maintenance and equipment (boats and associated equipment). Our Charter requires us actively to promote seafaring careers to today's children and the Marine Society and Sea Cadets fulfils this role through a national programme of structured training at its separate cadet units across the country. An impressive proportion of these cadets subsequently join the Royal or Merchant Navies, where they often develop outstanding records of achievement over long careers.

While most organisations appear regularly in the grants lists from year to year, amounts can vary substantially, and the fund makes special awards to help with major capital or development programmes, in addition to its more regular grants.

Exclusions The fund does not make any grants directly to individuals but rather helps other organisations which do this. However, the fund may be able to advise in particular cases about a suitable organisation to approach. Full details of such organisations are to be found in *A Guide to Grants for Individuals in Need*, published by DSC.

Applications On an application form available from the correspondent or the charity's website. The fund also has plans to introduce an online application form – check its website for up-to-date information on any developments in this area. Trustees meet in July and November.

The Samuel Sebba Charitable Trust

General, covering a wide range of charitable purposes with a preference for Jewish organisations

£2.4 million (2007/08)

Beneficial area UK and Israel.

25–26 Enford Street, London W1H 1DW

Tel. 020 7723 6028 **Fax** 020 7724 7412

Correspondent David Lerner, Chief Executive

Trustees *Leigh Sebba; Stanley Sebba; Prof. Leslie Sebba; Victor Klein; Clive M Marks; Lady Winston; Sallie Tangir.*

CC Number 253351

Information available Accounts were available from the Charity Commission.

This trust was established in 1967 for general charitable purposes. The trust focuses on the areas of education, community, children and young people, medical, hospice and older people, arts, interfaith, medical, people with disabilities, mental health, health, asylum seekers and preventative medicine. The trust hopes to expand on its present grant giving and from time to time respond to environmental concerns and international aid.

In 2007/08 the trust had assets of £56.3 million and an income of £2 million. There were 150 grants made totalling £2.4 million, categorised as follows:

Category	Value
Education	£605,000
Community	£397,000
Disability	£321,500
Arts	£164,000
Children and young people	£140,500
Hospice and older people	£140,000
Human rights	£117,500
Medical	£112,500
Welfare	£98,500
Environment	£85,500
Refugee	£75,000
Youth at Risk	£69,000
Interfaith	£42,500
Advocacy	£21,000
Asylum Seekers and Racial Equality	£5,000
Total	**£2,400,000**

Beneficiaries across all categories included: Jewish Learning Exchange (£75,000); Tel Aviv University Trust (£60,000); Eden Association (£53,000); Hebrew University of Jerusalem (£50,000); Friends of Neve Menashe (£40,000); Kisharon (£30,000); Relatives and Residents Association (£20,000); and the American Jewish Committee (£15,000).

Exclusions No grants to individuals.

Applications Organisations applying must provide proof of need, they must forward the most recent audited accounts, a registered charity number, and most importantly a cash flow statement for the next 12 months. All applications should have a stamped addressed envelope enclosed. It is also important that the actual request for funds must be concise and preferably summarised on one side of A4. The trustees meet quarterly.

However, because of ongoing support to so many organisations already known to the trust, it is likely that unsolicited applications will, for the foreseeable future, be unsuccessful.

The Severn Trent Water Charitable Trust Fund

Relief of poverty, money advice and debt counselling

£249,000 to organisations (2007/08)

Beneficial area The area covered by Severn Trent Water Ltd, which stretches from Wales to east Leicestershire and from the Humber estuary down to the Bristol Channel.

FREEPOST RLZE-EABT-SHSA, Sutton Coldfield B72 1TJ

Tel. 0121 355 7766 or 0121 321 1324

Email office@sttf.org.uk

Website www.sttf.org.uk

Correspondent Gay Hammett, Operations Manager, Auriga Services Limited

Trustees *Dr Derek Harris, Chair; Elizabeth Pusey; Alexandra Gribben; Kim Kupfer; Sue Hayman; David Vaughan; Nachhatter Batt.*

CC Number 1108278

Information available Accounts were on file at the Charity Commission

The trust was established by Severn Trent Water Ltd in 1997 with a donation of £2 million.

The main object of the trust is to help needy individuals to pay their water bills. Assistance may also be given with other household costs if it can be demonstrated that it will help towards future financial stability or make a significant improvement to the recipient's circumstances.

Additionally, grants are made to organisations in the region to improve or expand the provision of free money advice and debt counselling services to eligible people. The organisation must be able to demonstrate that a project is likely to benefit customers of Severn Trent Water Ltd.

Organisational grants are available in three main areas:

- **revenue funding** – normally for money advice/debt counselling services
- **capital grants** – a maximum of £1,500 is available for small capital items

- **continuation funding** – organisations can apply for further funding in the final six months of the project (please note: this type of funding is not designed to continue current projects indefinitely but to enable other funding to be sourced and agreed, if appropriate).

Grants can be for up to three years. Organisations seeking revenue funding of more than one year must be able to prove that the project will be able to continue to achieve its objectives and deliver a quality service with no additional funding. The continuation of funding beyond one year will always be subject to satisfactory project performance and availability of funding. Recipients will be required to report on the progress of the project. The funding will be made quarterly in advance. Capital purchases must normally be made within three months of the grant award.

Prospective applicants should note that each year the trust decides on areas of special interest in order to target funding, for example a social group or geographical area. It is a good idea, therefore, to contact the trust to find out what these areas are before applying.

All recipient organisations will be required to provide an end of year report detailing project achievements. The trust may require the provision of further information to help publicise the work of the trust.

In 2007/08 the trust had an income of £4.6 million and made grants of £3.9 million of which £3.7 million was designated to individuals. Around £3.5 million of this was for the payment of Severn Trent water or sewage charges and £223,000 was given towards bills such as gas, electricity and 'other household needs'.

A further £249,000 was designated to organisations for money advice and debt counselling services.

In 2007 beneficiaries of revenue funding included: Bassettlaw Citizens Advice Bureau (CAB), Blakehall Community Advice Centre, Bridging the Gap, Derbyshire Housing Aid, Forest of Dean CAB, Free@last, Nottingham Unemployed Workers Centre.

ARC Addington Fund, South Leicester CAB, Melton Mowbray CAB and North West Leicestershire CAB all received capital funding.

Applications If you would like to apply for a grant on behalf of your organisation you can email the trust at:

office@sttf.org.uk. A reply within 48 hours can be expected.

Alternatively, initial interest can be lodged by posting no more that two A4 sheets outlining your proposed project to the following address: Severn Trent Trust Fund, PO Box 8778, Sutton Coldfield, B72 1TP.

Only applications from organisations within the Severn Trent Trust Fund area will be considered. A map of this area can be found on the trust's website.

ShareGift (The Orr Mackintosh Foundation)

General

£1.1 million (2007/08)

Beneficial area UK.

17 Carlton House Terrace, London SW1Y 5AH

Tel. 020 7930 3737 **Fax** 020 7839 2214

Email help@sharegift.org.uk

Website www.sharegift.org

Correspondent Rachel Addison

Trustees *Viscount Mackintosh of Halifax; Matthew Orr; Stephen Scott; Baroness Goudie.*

CC Number 1052686

Information available Accounts were available from the Charity Commission.

Creating an entirely new flow of money to charities, this unique organisation is entirely unlike other trusts included in this book. ShareGift creates its income each year by pooling and selling donations of shares, principally those which are uneconomic to sell by normal methods because they are too small or otherwise inconvenient or unwanted. The funds released from this ongoing process are used to make donations, on a regular basis, to a wide range of other UK charities each year.

The charity makes donations at its own discretion, but is guided in doing so by information gathered in the course of its work about the charities and causes which are of interest to people who donate shares or help ShareGift in other ways. Since its inception, ShareGift has generated over £12 million for 1,500 charities, from major household names to tiny local initiatives, covering a vast area of national and international work.

Grants are normally made to the general funds of the charity concerned, rather than for specific projects. ShareGift is cause neutral and there are no restrictions on the kind of charitable work it can support, or where in the world it takes place, so long as the charity receiving the donation is UK-registered. No grants are given in response to applications by charities.

General

Launched in 1996, this charity was developed by Claire Nowak, a former city investment manager, now Viscountess Mackintosh of Halifax and Chief Executive of the charity, and Matthew Orr, a stockbroker whose firm, Killik and Co., provides free of charge many of the technical and support services required to operate ShareGift.

ShareGift's success as a charity is based on the fact that many people own small parcels of shares, for a variety of reasons, such as popularly advertised flotations of companies and as the result of take-overs and mergers. In what is still largely a paper-based share registration system, small shareholdings are often a considerable nuisance, needing some know-how to handle, but being of too little value to justify paying professional fees to sell or manage. ShareGift's funds are mainly generated by working either directly with companies or with individual shareholders.

ShareGift accepts the relevant share certificates, with minimum hassle for the donor, transfers the shares into the charity's name, and, once sufficient shares in any given company have been collected by bulking together batches of similar donations from a number of donors, sells them. Donors who are UK taxpayers may also be able to claim tax relief on the gift.

Fundraising charities also work with ShareGift, primarily as a solution for donors who offer them small holdings of shares which are not viable for the charity to accept themselves. In the case of larger donations and major gifts, ShareGift generally encourages charities to accept and handle these themselves, as it is unable to act as a charitable stockbroker or as a direct conduit for donations to other charities. However, it will advise and assist charities which are having problems or are unfamiliar with dealing with a gift of shares, and, in some cases, may be able to facilitate a larger donation.

Grants in 2007/08

During the year the charity had assets of £555,000 and an income of nearly £1.5 million. 376 grants were made to 328 charities totalling £1.1 million. Individual donations ranging from £100 to £50,000 were made across the spectrum of UK charities.

Larger grants included: Oxfam – 2 grants (£60,000); Impetus Trust and British Red Cross (£50,000 each); Firefly Trust (£25,000); Mission Aviation Fellowship UK (£20,000); WaterAid – 2 grants (£15,000); and British Heart Foundation – 2 grants (£13,000).

Smaller grants of £10,000 or less included: Trees for Cities (£10,000); Art Fund – 2 grants (£7,500); PiggyBankKids (£5,000); Christian Blind Mission UK, Garden Organic and Donkey Sanctuary (£1,000 each); Columban Fathers (£750); Scoo-B-Doo (£500); and York Pregnancy Crisis Centre Service Trust (£250).

The foundation previously placed £100,000 of cash balances as a deposit with Charity Bank, so that this capital sum can be used for the wider benefit of the charity sector through Charity Bank's loan programme. Interest on this amount is waived as a donation towards Charity Bank's work. In 2007/08 this amounted to £490.

Exclusions Grants to UK registered charities only.

Applications Applications for funding are not accepted and no response will be made to charities that send inappropriate applications. ShareGift's trustees choose to support UK registered charities which reflect the broad range of charities which are of interest to the people and organisations that help to create the charity's income by donating their unwanted shares, or by supporting the charity's operation in other practical ways.

However, charities wishing to receive a donation from ShareGift's trustees can increase their chances of doing so by encouraging their supporters to donate unwanted shares to ShareGift and to make a note of their charitable interests when so doing, using the regular donation form provided by ShareGift.

In addition, ShareGift is willing to use its extensive experience of share giving philanthropically to help charities which wish to start receiving gifts of shares themselves. Charities are, therefore, welcome to contact ShareGift to discuss this further. ShareGift advises that, as basic training on share giving is now available elsewhere, charities wishing to benefit from their advice should ensure

that they have first researched share giving generally and put some thought into how their charity intends to initiate and run a share giving appeal or strategy. Further information on this and other issues is available on the charity's website.

The Sheepdrove Trust

Mainly environment and education

£831,000 (2007)

Beneficial area UK, but especially north Lambeth, London, where applicable.

Sheepdrove Organic Farm, Lambourn RG17 7UN

Tel. 01488 674726

Correspondent Juliet E Kindersley, Trustee

Trustees *Juliet E Kindersley; Peter D Kindersley; Harriet R Treuille; Barnabas G Kindersley.*

CC Number 328369

Information available Accounts were available from the Charity Commission.

The trust is endowed with money made by the Dorling Kindersley publishing enterprise, but the trust's holding of shares in the company was sold in 2000, when the endowment was valued at £18 million. The trust has general charitable purposes but has a particular interest in supporting initiatives involved in sustainability, biodiversity and organic farming. Grants are also made in other areas including educational research and spiritual care.

In 2007 the trust had assets of £21 million and an income of £1.3 million. Grants were made totalling £831,000 and were distributed in the following areas:

Arts and culture – 7 grants – £421,000
Beneficiaries included: Watermill Theatre (£300,000); University of the Arts Consortium (£60,000); Worshipful Company of Mercers (£30,000); Vauxhall City Farm (£15,000); and Newbury Fringe Food Festival (£2,000).

Education and Schools – 7 grants – £66,000
Grants went to: Kids Company (£30,000); Roots and Shoots (£20,000); Prison Phoenix Trust (£5,000); and

National Association of Farms for Schools (£250).

Farming, wildlife and preservation – 15 grants – £201,000

Beneficiaries included: Friends of the Earth (£100,000); Pesticide Action Network (£25,000); City University – David Buffin Pesticides Research (£15,000); Amics de la Terra Balears (£10,000); GM Freeze (£8,700); Women's Environmental Network (£4,500); and Wetlands Advisory Service (£510).

Medicine and Health – 9 grants – £92,000

Grants made included those to: African Water Filters – Peter Tamaloe (£50,000); Motivation (£10,000); Mother Meera Symposium (£7,600); CLIC Sargent (£5,000); and Jigsaw4U (£500).

Other – 7 grants – £51,000

Beneficiaries included: Human Rights Watch (£25,000); Corporate Watch Co-operative and Debtford Action Group for the Elderly (£5,000 each); and Lady Margaret Hall Settlement (£900).

Applications In writing to the correspondent.

The Archie Sherman Charitable Trust

Jewish charities, education, arts and general

£854,000 (2007/08)

Beneficial area UK and overseas.

27 Berkeley House, Hay Hill, London W1J 8NS

Tel. 020 7493 1904

Email trust@sherman.co.uk

Correspondent Michael Gee, Trustee

Trustees *Michael J Gee; Allan H S Morgenthau; Eric A Charles.*

CC Number 256893

Information available Accounts were available from the Charity Commission.

Most of the funds go to Jewish causes, many of which receive ongoing support of typically more than £20,000 a year each. A few arts organisations are similarly supported, although the level of donation varies year to year.

The trust states that it reviews all commitments on a forward five-year basis so that a few new projects can be undertaken and income is made available.

In 2007/08 the trust had assets of £22 million and an income of £1.5 million. Grants were made to 26 organisations totalling £854,000. Donations were divided into the following categories:

Category	No.	Value
Education and training	4	£47,000
Overseas aid	2	£84,000
General charitable purposes	14	£602,000
Health	6	£121,000

Within these categories the largest grants went to Diana and Allan Morgenthau Charitable Trust and Rosalyn and Nicholas Springer Charitable Trust (£125,000 each).

Other beneficiaries included: Jacqueline and Michael Gee Charitable Trust (£101,000); British WIZO (£71,000); Tel Aviv Foundation (£53,000); Jewish Care (£38,000); Therapeutic Riding School – Israel (£31,000); Norwood Ravenswood (£25,000); Royal National Theatre (£20,000); Yad Vashem UK Foundation (£17,000); Magen David Adorn UK (£13,000); and United Jewish Israel Appeal (£6,000).

Applications In writing to the correspondent. Trustees meet every month except August and December.

The Shetland Charitable Trust

Social welfare, art and recreation, environment and amenity

£11.7 million (2007/08)

Beneficial area Shetland only.

22–24 North Road, Lerwick, Shetland ZE1 0NQ

Tel. 01595 744994 **Fax** 01595 744999

Email mail@shetlandcharitabletrust.co.uk

Website www.shetlandcharitabletrust.co.uk

Correspondent Jeff Goddard, Acting General Manager

Trustees *Bill Manson, Chair; James Henry; Leslie Angus; Laura Baisley; James Budge; Alexander Cluness; Alastair Cooper; Adam Doull; Allison Duncan; Elizabeth Fullerton; Florence Grains; Iris Hawkins; Robert Henderson; Andrew Hughson; Caroline Miller; Richard Nickerson; Valerie Nicolson; Frank Robertson; Gary Robinson; Joseph Simpson; John Scott; Cecil Smith; Jonathon Wills; Allan Wishart.*

SC Number SC027025

Information available Accounts and annual reports were available from the trust's basic website.

The original trust was established in 1976 with 'disturbance receipts' from the operators of the Sullom Voe oil terminal. As a clause in the trust deed prevented it from accumulating income beyond 21 years from its inception, in 1997 most of its assets were transferred to a newly established Shetland Islands Council Charitable Trust, which is identical to the old trust except for the omission of the prohibition on accumulating income. This has now been renamed Shetland Charitable Trust.

The trust was run by the Shetland Islands Council until 2002. The trust is currently administered by its own separate staff.

The trust aims to provide public benefit to and improve the quality of life for the inhabitants of Shetland; ensure that people in need receive a high standard of service and care; protect and enhance Shetland's environment, heritage, culture and traditions; provide facilities that will be of long-term benefit to the inhabitants of Shetland; build on the energy and initiatives of local groups, maximise voluntary effort and input and assist them to achieve their objectives; support a balanced range of services and facilities to contribute to the overall fabric of the community; support facilities and services and jobs located in rural areas and maintain the value of the funds in the long term to ensure that future generations have access to similar resources in the post oil era.

In 2007/08 the trust had assets of £219.5 million and an income of £13.8 million. Grants were made totalling £11.7 million.

The funds are used to create and sustain a wide range of facilities for the islands, largely by funding further trusts including: Shetland Welfare Trust – day care and running costs; Shetland Recreational Trust; Isleburgh Trust; Shetland Amenity Trust; Shetland Amenity Trust; Christmas Grants to Pensioners/Disabled Households; Shetlands Arts Trust; and, Independence at Home Scheme Grants.

Exclusions Funds can only be used to benefit the inhabitants of Shetland.

Applications Applications are only accepted from Shetland-based charities. The trustees meet every two months.

SHINE (Support and Help in Education)

Education of children and young people

£2 million (2007/08)

Beneficial area Greater London and Manchester.

1 Cheam Road, Ewell Village, Epsom KT17 1SP

Tel. 020 8393 1880

Email info@shinetrust.org.uk

Website www.shinetrust.org.uk

Correspondent Stephen Shields, Chief Executive

Trustees *Jim O'Neill, Chair; David Blood; Gavin Boyle; Mark Heffernan; John Phizackerley; Richard Rothwell; Dr Caroline Whalley; Anthony Salz; Krutika Pau; Mark Ferguson.*

CC Number 1082777

Information available Accounts were on file at the Charity Commission. Good website.

The following description of the charity's work is taken from its 2007/08 annual report.

SHINE supports educational projects that work with disadvantaged, disengaged and challenged children and young people (7 – 18 years), in Greater London and Manchester. We provide grants to fund educational programmes which give these young people the extra support and attention they need to learn the basic but essential tools for life. SHINE also supports projects that help talented children from poor neighbourhoods to recognise and then realise their full potential.

SHINE projects include intensive one-to-one literacy and numeracy support, Saturday learning programmes, homework clubs and computer-assisted study projects – all specifically designed to make a meaningful difference to the children and young people who need it most. We work in partnership with primary and secondary state schools, the independent sector and world-class universities to get more from existing facilities and resources.

SHINE operates as a business, working closely with potential grant recipients to make sure their projects can be delivered. Most importantly, early monitoring and evaluation planning with those organisations which receive grants establishes the quantitative methods by which the success of these projects will be judged. When the projects are up and running, we then monitor and evaluate them rigorously to ensure they are efficient and have only the most positive effect on the young lives they help. This research means that we can prove what works, how and why. This allows us to replicate the most effective projects and help spread good practice.

The SHINE trustees take decisions on grant applications based on the recommendations of the grant-making team. Prior to each full board meeting, these recommendations are considered in detail by the grant-making trustee cluster group. We spend a significant amount of time and energy in order to find, fund and support projects which will have a measurable impact on the educational attainment of the participants.

Types of grant

SHINE funds and develops educational programmes to help disadvantaged children make the most of their time at school. These include specialist after school clubs, complementary classes on Saturdays, intensive literacy and numeracy support sessions and help for children with special educational needs, underachievers, and gifted children.

SHINE wishes to fund projects that have the following key elements:

- the main focus is on educational subjects, especially promoting literacy, numeracy and science
- content and methodology that will excite and engage participants, making creative use of IT where appropriate
- there are clear and measurable target educational outcomes. Principally this will mean linking to standardised tests (at primary level) and GCSEs or a recognised equivalent (at secondary level)
- a significant number of children/ young people will be supported
- these children/young people themselves want to improve their situation
- the project will be sufficiently long term to support sustainable improvement
- families of participants are linked to the project in a way which supports their child's learning
- there is appropriate use of volunteers
- the project budget represents value for money.

SHINE wishes to build long-term relationships and partnerships with the organisations it funds, so the majority of grants are in excess of £20,000. It funds new start-ups, pilots and development or replication of projects. It also funds core costs.

In 2009 programmes aimed at providing support were categorised under eight headings, each of which has a number of specific projects. These are described below. For more information on any of the programmes or their associated projects, please go to the charity's website.

Big Impact programmes – co-funded with other organisations to provide better literacy tuition, after-school clubs and excellent teachers to the children who need them most. These projects are often on a large scale and designed to make a substantial impact in the hope that they will then attract public funding. Projects include:

- Every Child a Reader – a £10 million partnership between charities, the business sector and government that is funding highly skilled Reading Recovery teachers in inner-city schools to provide intensive help to children with severe literacy difficulties
- Teach First – tackling the growing shortage of excellent teachers in inner London schools by recruiting, training and placing top graduates from UK universities into challenging London secondary schools for two years at a time
- Schoolfriend etc. – after-school care clubs with integrated learning opportunities using the tried and tested Schoolfriend computer programme.

SHINE on Saturdays – a core programme helping underachieving children at both primary and secondary schools by injecting 150 hours of additional and creative learning every year, accelerating and complementing their classroom achievements.

Serious Fun on Saturdays – top independent schools open their superb facilities to enrich and expand the core curriculum for local state school children unlikely to receive extra educational support at home.

Literacy – SHINE funds a variety of programmes aimed at improving literacy and communication skills. Some provide intensive, individual tuition to help struggling children get back on track; some use ICT in a fun, structured and challenging way to help failing children improve their skills and boost their confidence; others work with parents and carers to ensure they have the skills to help their children read. Current projects include: Springboard, Digismart and Every Child a Reader.

Maths – SHINE-funded maths projects provide extra support for children who have been identified as struggling in this area. Although they differ in scale and approach, they share a belief that, given some extra time, attention and support, every child can leave primary school confident in their mathematical ability. Projects include:

- Ocean maths – an intensive programme of support for 100 students and their parents in Tower Hamlets
- Every Child Counts – run by the Every Child a Chance Trust, which aims to unlock the educational potential of socially disadvantaged children through the development and promotion of evidence-based, early intervention programmes.

Science – SHINE funds programmes that give primary school children the chance to discover science for themselves. All of them aim to excite and engage children in the sciences in the hope that they will continue with these essential subjects as they progress through school. Projects include: Crest Investigators – run by the British Science Association; @ Eltham College; and @ Withington Girls.

Gifted students – programmes that challenge gifted and talented mathematicians and scientists from disadvantaged families, expanding horizons and fuelling ambitions as they see just how much they can achieve. Projects include:

- Brunel Urban Scholars – addresses the continuing low numbers of children from disadvantaged backgrounds who enter university, this project aims to find and fulfil the submerged talent of gifted teenagers from inner-city state secondary schools.
- @ City of London Girls – Serious Fun on Saturdays @ City of London School for Girls aims to develop critical thinking skills among gifted but disadvantaged students from secondary schools in Hackney, Islington and Tower Hamlets.
- Central London University Edge summer school – for 80 gifted students in year 11.

Special focus – projects that increase the educational chances of disadvantaged young people and some groups that are particularly vulnerable, such as children in care, the children of refugees and young people excluded, or at risk of exclusion, from school. There are 11 projects running in this category, including:

- Hanover Foundation – personal development coaching for teenagers from socially deprived areas of London who live with challenging personal circumstances. Coaching sessions focus on improving academic attainment, individual behaviour and personal motivation
- North Primary School – an education and family support programme providing academic and social support for refugees and newly arrived children through a weekly after-school learning club
- Rugby Portobello Trust – provides at Walmer Road School, full-time alternative education for 14–16 year olds who have withdrawn from mainstream education, have been excluded or who are at risk of this happening
- Baytree Centre – provides an effective after-school programme to support young women and their families in Brixton.

Grants in 2007/08

During the year the trust had assets of £5 million and an income of £3 million. Grants were made totalling £2 million and were distributed as follows:

Project	Value
Lift for Learning	£458,000
SHINE @ Rotherfield	£210,000
SHINE @ Southwold	£205,000
SHINE @ Sebright	£169,000
SFoS @ CLSG	£151,000
SHINE @ St Aloysius	£135,000
Every Child a Chance	£100,000
BA	£94,000
EYLA	£90,000
The Lyric	£90,000
Into University	£90,000
CLPE	£60,000
BAAF	£58,000
SFoS @ Darrick Wood	£56,000
Baytree Centre	£50,000
SHINE @ Preston Manner	£30,000
EET	£29,000
SHINE @ Archbishop Sumner	£8,600

Exclusions Shine will not fund:

- individuals
- the direct replacement of statutory funding
- schools or other educational establishments, except where funding is for activities which are clearly additional
- short-term programmes
- programmes targeted at specific subject or beneficiary groups
- parenting programmes, where the primary focus is the parent rather than the child
- activities promoting particular political or religious beliefs

- projects taking place outside Greater London, except projects that are part of SHINE's replication programme.

Applications All potential applicants must initially speak to a member of the grants team by telephoning 020 8393 1880. The trustees meet about three times a year, but not at fixed intervals.

The Shirley Foundation

Autism spectrum disorders with particular emphasis on medical research

£110,000 (2008/09)
Beneficial area UK

North Lea House, 66 Northfield End, Henley-on-Thames RG9 2BE

Tel. 01491 579004 **Fax** 01491 574995

Email steve@steveshirley.com

Website www.steveshirley.com/tsf

Correspondent Anne McCartney Menzies, Trustee

Trustees *Dame Stephanie Shirley, Chair; Prof. Eve Johnstone; Michael Robert Macfadyen; Anne McCartney Menzies.*

CC Number 1097135

Information available Accounts were available from the Charity Commission.

The foundation, (formerly known as the Shirley Foundation Charitable Trust), was established in 1996 by Dame Stephanie Shirley, a business technology pioneer and the current Chair. Dame Stephanie is a highly successful entrepreneur turned ardent philanthropist. Having arrived in Britain as an unaccompanied child refugee from Germany in 1939, she started what is now Xansa on her dining room table with £6 in 1962. In 25 years as its chief executive she developed it into a leading business technology group, pioneering new work practices and changing the position of professional women (especially in hi-tech sectors) along the way.

The foundation is established for general charitable purposes and the main areas of interest are information technology and autism (not excluding Aspergers Syndrome) which occasionally extend to learning disabilities in general. The foundation's mission is 'the facilitation and support of pioneering projects with strategic impact in the field of autism spectrum disorders, with particular emphasis on medical research'.

In 2008/09 the foundation had assets of £4 million and an income of £106,500 (£1.2 million in 2007/08). Grants were made totalling £110,000 (£1.5 million in 2007/08). The foundation continued to fund the infrastructure costs of Autism Speaks but other activities included the funding of two autism-related projects for the World Health Organisation, the first time that WHO have recognised autism in any way.

The foundation has also made a pledge of £1 million to the Balliol Archives.

Exclusions No grants to individuals, or for non autism-specific work. The foundation does not make political donations.

Applications In writing to the correspondent with an outline proposal, which must be innovative in nature with potential to be of strategic impact in the field of autism spectrum disorders. Research proposals should be aimed ultimately at determining causes of autism. It should be noted that the foundation has committed significant funding until 2012.

Shlomo Memorial Fund Limited

Jewish causes

£3.1 million (2007/08)
Beneficial area Unrestricted.

Cohen Arnold and Co., New Burlington House, 1075 Finchley Road, London NW11 0PU
Tel. 020 8731 0777 **Fax** 020 8731 0778
Correspondent I Lopian, Secretary
Trustees E Kleineman; I D Lopian; H Toporowitz; A Toporowitz; C Y Kaufman.
CC Number 278973
Information available Accounts were available from the Charity Commission.

This trust was established in 1978 to advance the orthodox Jewish religion, relief of the poor and general charitable purposes.

In 2007/08 the trust had assets of £35 million and an income of £3.9 million. Grants totalling £3.1 million were made to religious, educational and other charitable institutions. A list of grant beneficiaries was not included in the trust's accounts.

Previous beneficiaries include: Amud Haolam, Nachlat Haleviim, Torah Umesorah, Beit Hillel, ZSV Charities, Layesharim Tehilla, British Friends of Tashbar Chazon Ish, Chazon Ish, Mei Menuchos, Mor Uketsio, Shoshanat Hoamakim, Millenium Trust, and Talmud Torah Zichron Meir.

Applications In writing to the correspondent.

The Henry Smith Charity

Social welfare, older people, disability, health and medical research

£26.7 million (2008)
Beneficial area UK. Specific local programmes in East and West Sussex, Hampshire, Kent, Gloucestershire, Leicestershire, Suffolk and Surrey.

6th Floor, 65 Leadenhall Street, London EC3A 2AD
Tel. 020 7264 4970 **Fax** 020 7488 9097
Website www.henrysmithcharity.org.uk
Correspondent Richard Hopgood, Director
Trustees Rt Hon Max Egremont; Ronnie Norman; Carola Godman-Law; James Hambro; Anna McNair Scott; Merlyn Lowther; Gordon Steere; Noel Manns; Anne Allen; Rt Hon Claire Countes; Diana Barran; Marilyn Gallyer; Mark Newton; Peter Smallridge; Tristan Millington Drake; Nicholas Acland; Miko Geidroyc.
CC Number 230102
Information available Annual report and accounts available from the Charity Commission. The charity also has an excellent and informative website.

The Henry Smith Charity was founded in 1628 with the objects of relieving and where possible releasing people from need and suffering. These objects continue in the grant-making policy today. The Henry Smith Charity makes grants totalling around £25 million per

annum for a wide range of purposes across the UK, funded from investments.

Grant Programmes

The charity provides the following details on its grant programmes:

We currently offer a range of grant programmes. Each has its own guidelines to help you apply. Please read the guidelines thoroughly before making your application. [Comprehensive guidelines are available from the charity's website.]

The types of projects and services you can apply for a grant towards through our Main and Small Grants Programmes [are listed below].

Main Grants Programme

Our Main Grants Programme is for grants of £10,000 or over. There are two types of main grant:

- Capital Grants: one off grants for purchase or refurbishment of a building or purchase of specialist equipment.
- Revenue Grants: grants of up to three years for things like core costs (including salaries and overheads), or the running costs of a specific project (including staffing costs).

Please note: there are special guidelines for applications for funding for projects or services taking place wholly in Scotland. Please refer to our Guidelines for 'Work Taking Place in Scotland'.

Small Grants Programme

Our Small Grants Programme is for grants of under £10,000 per year. There are two types of small grant:

- County Grants: grants of £500 – £20,000 for small organisations working in the counties with which we have an historical association, i.e., Gloucestershire, Hampshire, Kent, Leicestershire, Surrey, East Sussex and West Sussex. To be eligible to apply for a County Grant, your annual income must be below £250,000, unless you are working county-wide, in which case your income must be below £1 million.
- Small Grants: grants of £500 – £20,000 for small UK registered charities working in any UK county not listed above. To be eligible to apply for a Small Grant, your annual income must be below £150,000.

Medical Research

Grants of up to three years for research undertaken by recognised 'Centres of Excellence'.

Priority areas of support are:

- Alzheimer's/dementia
- child health
- bowels/gastroenterology
- diseases of the lung (excluding TB)

THE HENRY SMITH CHARITY
Areas of funding

Black, Asian and Minority Ethnic (BAME)	Projects providing culturally appropriate services to Black, Asian and Minority Ethnic communities; including those that promote integration and access to mainstream services.
Carers	Projects providing advice and support; including respite services for carers and those cared for. Work can include educational opportunities for young carers.
Community Service	Projects providing support for communities in areas of high deprivation; including projects providing furniture recycling services, debt advice and community centres.
Disability	Projects providing rehabilitation, training or advocacy support to people who are disabled; this includes learning disabilities as well as physical disabilities.
Domestic and Sexual Violence	Projects providing advice, support and secure housing for families affected by domestic violence or sexual violence. Perpetrator programmes can be considered where organisations have secured, or are working towards, Respect accreditation.
Drugs, Alcohol and Substance Misuse	Projects supporting the rehabilitation of people affected by, or at risk of, drug and/or alcohol dependency, and projects supporting their families.
Ex-Service Men and Women	Projects providing services or residential care to ex-service men and women and their dependents.
Family Services	Projects providing support to families in areas of high deprivation.
Healthcare	Projects providing residential care, health care or outreach services, such as home care support. Services operated by the NHS will not normally be funded. In the case of applications from hospices, priority is given to requests for capital expenditure.
Homelessness	Projects providing housing and services for homeless people and those at risk of homelessness.
Lesbian, Gay, Bisexual and Transgender	Projects providing advice, support and counselling for people who are Lesbian, Gay, Bisexual or Transgendered.
Mental Health	Projects promoting positive mental health or providing advice and support to people experiencing mental health problems.
Older People	Projects providing residential care, health care or emotional support, such as befriending services and day care centres. Priority will be given to projects in areas of high deprivation and those where rural isolation can be demonstrated.
Prisoners and Ex-offenders	Projects that help the rehabilitation and resettlement of prisoners and/or ex-offenders; including education and training that improve employability, and projects that support prisoners' families.
Prostitution and Trafficking	Projects that provide advice and support to sex industry workers; including advice on housing support and personal health, escaping exploitation and exiting prostitution.
Refugees and Asylum Seekers	Projects providing advocacy, advice and support to refugees and asylum seekers, and those promoting integration.
Young People	Projects maximising the potential of young people who experience educational, social and economic disadvantage; including young people in, or leaving, care.

- neurology
- pancreatic disease (excluding diabetes)
- spinal conditions
- urinary and faecal incontinence
- engineering and medicine.

Further guidelines and an application form are available from the charity's website.

Holiday Grants for Children

One-off grants of up to £3,000 for organisations, schools, youth groups etc specifically for holidays or outings for children under the age of 13 who are disabled or who live in areas of high deprivation.

There are currently no Major Grants open for applications.

Through the Main Grants Programme and Small and County Grants Programmes, grants are made in the following categories (with examples of the type of work funded under each category):

Recent Grantmaking

In 2008 the charity had assets of £582 million (£772.4 million in 2007) and an income of £21.3 million. Grants were made totalling over £26.7 million, broken down as follows:

Grant expenditure	2008	2007
Main grant programme (grants above £10,000)	£22,000,000	£21,900,000
Small grants (up to £10,000)	£1,600,000	£1,600,000
Major Grant – Northern Ireland pilot	£300,000	–
Major Grant – Inspiring Scotland	£800,000	–
Grants to Poor Kindred	£500,000	£500,000
Grants to Needy Clergy	£500,000	£500,000
Grants for Christian projects	£400,000	£400,000
Grant to historic parishes (Estates Fund distributions)	£500,000	£500,000
Holiday grants	£100,000	£100,000
Total grants	**£26,700,000**	**£25,500,000**

Review of grantmaking 2008

The number of applications to our main grants programme increased by 12%, following a 9% increase last year. So far in 2009 the number of applications is 5% lower than 2008.

The number of awards made was virtually unchanged at 319, meaning we dealt with five applications for every award we made.

The average size of capital awards fell by 20%, reflecting fewer large appeals and a number of smaller awards being given. The average size of revenue grant awards increased slightly to £71,000, with most of these being three year awards.

Around 30% of the awards were given as continuation funding, following the completion of previous awards. The trustees agreed during the year that continuous funding for individual projects and posts should normally not exceed six years.

London continued to receive the highest amount of grant awards, at almost 20% of total funding. Funding in Wales increased sharply, through funding via the Community Foundation for Wales.

Northern Ireland funding was boosted in 2008 by an equivalent sum of Major Grant funding. Scotland similarly received substantial funding via Inspiring Scotland.

Recent beneficiaries

The following are a sample of organisations which received a grant in 2009:

Impetus Trust (£325,000), towards four years' support for the Reducing Re-Offending Fund, a joint venture between Impetus Trust, Indigo Trust, Esmée Fairbairn and Henry Smith Charity that will fund third sector organisations working to make a significant impact on reducing re-offending; Furzedown Project (£108,000), towards three years' running costs of a home visiting service for older people in London Borough of

Wandsworth; Amber Foundation (£90,000), towards three years' salary and on costs of a Recruitment Manager and costs associated with their work in prisons across the South West; Age Concern Warwickshire (£60,000), towards two years' salary and on costs of a part-time Counselling Co-ordinator at a support project for older people who care for grown up children with mental health problems; Chooselife Cymru (£50,000), towards two years' core costs of a centre for people with drug and alcohol dependency and their families in Cardiff; Woodhouse Close Church Community Centre (£45,000), towards three years' running costs of a lunch club for older people on an estate in a deprived part of Bishop Auckland; Skye and Lochalsh Community Care Forum (£40,000), towards three years' salary and on costs of a Deputy Manager at a community care project on the Isle of Skye; YMCA Lurgan (£35,500), towards two years' running costs of a cross sectarian youth work programme in Co. Armagh for young people at risk; Speaking Up (£32,400), towards three years' salary and on costs of the Head of Active Voices at a mentoring project in Cambridgeshire for young people with learning disabilities; Blackbird Leys Neighbourhood Support Scheme (£30,000), towards two years' core costs of the Advice Centre; University of Cambridge – Wolfson Brain Imaging Centre (£17,600), towards the development of a Brain Computer Interface to improve the quality of life of people with impaired consciousness following brain injury; Centre for African Resources Research and Development (£10,000), towards one year's running costs of the Healthittude project for people from BAME communities in Leicestershire; Relate – Brighton, Hove, Worthing & Districts (£4,000), towards running costs of a project in East Sussex that offers counselling at a reduced costs to couples experiencing financial disadvantage; Sefton Children's Trust (£2,000), towards a trip to Manor Adventure in Shropshire for a group of 72 disadvantaged young people from Liverpool; and Haverhill and District Volunteer Centre (£1,000), towards one year's running costs of a volunteering project for people in Suffolk experiencing or recovering from mental health problems.

Exclusions Grants are not made towards the following:

- local authorities and areas of work usually considered a statutory responsibility
- state maintained schools, colleges, universities and friend/parent teacher associations, or independent schools not exclusively for students with special educational needs
- organisations not providing direct services to clients such as umbrella, second tier or grant-making organisations
- youth clubs, except those in areas of high deprivation
- uniformed groups such as Scouts and Guides, except those in areas of high deprivation
- community centres, except those in areas of high deprivation
- community transport organisations or services
- professional associations or projects for the training of professionals
- start up costs or organisations unable to demonstrate a track record
- individuals, or organisations and charities applying on their behalf
- projects that promote a particular religion, or capital appeals for places of worship
- arts projects, except those which can clearly demonstrate a therapeutic or rehabilitative benefit to disabled people, prisoners or young people who experience educational, social and economic disadvantage, including young people in, or leaving, care
- education projects except those which can clearly demonstrate a rehabilitative benefit to disabled people, prisoners or young people who experience educational, social and economic disadvantage, including young people in, or leaving, care
- leisure, recreation or play activities, except those exclusively for disabled people or those which can clearly demonstrate a significant rehabilitative benefit to people with mental health problems or that significantly improve opportunities and maximise the potential of young people who experience educational, social and economic disadvantage
- overseas trips
- projects taking place or benefiting people outside the UK
- residential holidays for young people (except those that qualify under the Holiday Grants scheme)
- counselling projects, except those in areas of high deprivation and with a clearly defined client group
- environmental projects where the primary purpose is conservation of the environment
- Citizens Advice Bureau or projects solely providing legal advice
- core running costs of hospices
- feasibility studies
- social research
- campaigning or lobbying projects
- projects where website development or maintenance is the focus of the bid
- IT equipment (unless as direct support costs for a funded staff member)
- capital projects to meet the requirements of the Disability Discrimination Act
- applicants declined within the previous six months.

Applications Each of our grant programmes has a slightly different application and assessment process.

You will find information about how to make your application in the guidelines for each type of grant. Some of our grants require you to fill in an application form. For others there is no application form; instead we provide guidance about to structure your application and what supporting documents you need to send us.

Please ensure you send us all the supporting documents we ask you to include with your application. Incomplete applications will be returned unread.

We strongly recommend that you download and read the guidelines of the relevant grant programme carefully before you start your application. It is important that you follow our guidance on how to apply.

Guidelines for each programme can be downloaded from the 'Grant Programmes' section of the charity's website.

The Sobell Foundation

Jewish charities, medical care and treatment, education, community, environment, disability, older people and young people

£2.7 million (2007/08)

Beneficial area Unrestricted, in practice, UK, Israel and the Commonwealth of Independent States (CIS).

PO Box 2137, Shepton Mallet BA4 6YA

Tel. 01749 813 135 **Fax** 01749 813 136

Email enquiries@sobellfoundation.org.uk

Website www.sobellfoundation.org.uk

Correspondent Penny Newton, Administrator

Trustees *Susan Lacroix; Roger Lewis; Andrea Scouller.*

CC Number 274369

Information available Accounts were available from the Charity Commission.

The Sobell Foundation was established by the late Sir Michael Sobell in 1977 for general charitable purposes and is a grant-making trust with which he was actively involved until shortly before his death in 1993. Funding is generally restricted to small national or local charities working in the following fields:

- medical care and treatment (including respite care and hospices)
- care and education for children and adults with physical and/or mental disabilities
- homelessness
- care and support for older people
- care and support for children from disadvantaged backgrounds.

In addition, in Israel only, the foundation supports higher education, co-existence projects and projects relating to immigrant absorption.

The trustees aim to achieve a reasonable spread between Jewish charities (operating principally in the UK, Israel and the CIS) and non-Jewish charities operating in the UK, with between a third and a half generally being allocated to the former category. Grants are only made to, or through, UK registered charities.

The trustees visit Israel annually, seeing new projects and paying visits to projects which have been supported in the past. Many of the charities supported send reports of their activities to the trustees on a regular basis and, where possible, the trustees pay follow-up visits.

In 2007/08 the foundation had assets of £59 million and an income of £2.9 million. During the year grants were made to 416 organisations totalling £2.7 million, with awards ranging from £250 to £50,000.

Of these, 25 grants were made of amounts ranging from £20,000 to £50,000. The foundation renewed its support for the Royal Brompton and Harefield Trust, committing to a five year grant of £250,000. A grant of £50,000 was also given to the Jewish Museum London and the first instalment of a three year grant worth £150,000 was paid to the Rainbow Centre for Conductive Research.

Approximately 65% of grants made were to UK non-Jewish charities, 27% to

Israeli charities and charities in the CIS, 7% to UK Jewish charities and 1% to other overseas charities. This allocation is within the ranges set by the trustees for grant allocation.

Grants were categorised as follows:

United Kingdom
- medical care and treatment – 147 grants totalling £949,000
- community – 69 grants totalling £357,000
- hardship alleviation – 63 grants totalling £287,000
- education – 19 grants totalling £132,000
- medical research – 2 grants totalling £45,000
- cultural and environmental – 6 grants totalling £24,000.

United Kingdom – Jewish charities
- community – 4 grants totalling £71,000
- cultural and environmental – 2 grants totalling £70,000
- medical care and treatment – 4 grants totalling £30,000
- education – 1 grant of £10,000
- hardship alleviation – 2 grants totalling £5,200.

Israel
- education – 26 grants totalling £257,000
- medical care and treatment – 30 grants totalling £220,000
- community – 22 grants totalling £159,000
- hardship alleviation – 14 grants totalling £78,000
- cultural and environment – 2 grants totalling £15,000.

Other overseas
- community – 2 grants totalling £21,000
- hardship alleviation – 1 grant of £10,000.

Exclusions No grants to individuals. Only registered charities or organisations registered with the Inland Revenue should apply.

Applications Applications should be made in writing to the administrator using the application form obtainable from the foundation or printable from its website.

The application form should be accompanied by:

- current year's summary income and expenditure budget
- most recent annual report
- most recent full accounts
- Inland Revenue certificate of exemption (if required).

The trustees receive a large number of applications for funding from registered charities during the year and support as many as possible of those which fall within the foundation's objectives. They aim to deal with requests within three months of receipt and to respond to each application received, whether or not a grant is made.

Trustees meet every three to four months and major grants are considered at these meetings. Requests for smaller amounts may be dealt with on a more frequent basis. Most applications are dealt with on an ongoing basis, and there are no deadlines for the receipt of applications. Organisations should wait 12 months before reapplying.

The Souter Charitable Trust

Christian evangelism and welfare

About £8 million.

Beneficial area UK, but with a preference for Scotland; overseas.

PO Box 7412, Perth PH1 5YX

Tel. 01738 634745

Correspondent Andy Macfie, Secretary

Trustees *Brian Souter; Betty Souter; Ann Allen.*

SC Number SC029998

Information available Despite making a written request for the accounts of this trust (including an sae) these were not provided. The following entry is based on information filed with the Office of the Scottish Charity Regulator.

This trust is funded by donations from Scottish businessman Brian Souter, one of the founders of the Stagecoach transport company. It gives the following account of its policies:

Our stated policy is to assist 'projects engaged in the relief of human suffering in the UK or overseas, particularly those with a Christian emphasis'. We tend not to get involved with research or capital funding, but would be more likely to provide a contribution towards the revenue costs of a project. Grants are generally given to charitable organisations and not to individuals or in support of requests on behalf of individuals. Applications for building projects, personal educational requirements or personal expeditions are specifically excluded.

Most grants are one-off payments of £1,000 or less; a small number of projects receive support over three years. Previous grants indicate an interest in the support of marriage and parenting issues. There is a preference for funding revenue rather than capital costs.

In 2007/08 the trust had an income of £12 million. Grants totalled around £8 million. No further information was available.

Previous beneficiaries include: Alpha International (an Anglican evangelical movement based in London), Highland Theological College, Operation Mobilisation, Prince's Trust – Scotland, Sargent Cancer Care, Scripture Union and Turning Point Scotland.

Exclusions Building projects, individuals, personal education grants and expeditions are not supported.

Applications In writing to the correspondent. Please keep applications brief and no more than two sides of A4 paper: if appropriate, please send audited accounts, but do not send brochures, business plans, DVDs and so on. The trust states that it will request more information if necessary. The trustees meet every two months or so, and all applications will be acknowledged in due course, whether successful or not. A stamped addressed envelope would be appreciated. Subsequent applications should not be made within a year of the initial submission.

The Sovereign Health Care Charitable Trust

Health and people with disabilities

£525,000 (2008)
Beneficial area UK with a preference for Bradford.

Royal Standard House, 26 Manningham Lane, Bradford BD1 3DN
Tel. 01274 729472 **Fax** 01274 722252
Email charities@sovereignhealthcare.co.uk
Website www.sovereignhealthcare.co.uk
Correspondent The Secretary
Trustees *Mark Hudson, chair; Michael Austin; Dennis Child; Michael Bower;*

Russ Piper; Kate Robb-Webb; Robert Dugdale.
CC Number 1079024
Information available Accounts were available from the Charity Commission.

The Sovereign Health Care Charitable Trust is funded by donations received under the Gift Aid scheme from the investment income of The Hospital Fund of Bradford. Its objects are to provide amenities for hospital patients and to make grants to charitable organisations 'for the relief and assistance of needy, sick and older persons'.

In 2008 the trust had assets of £63,000 and an income of £504,000. Grants totalled £525,000 and were broken down as follows:

- grants to hospitals – £25,000
- grants to associations and institutions – £476,000
- nurses' training grant – £25,000.

Larger grants included those to: Yorkshire Air Ambulance (£35,000); Manorlands and Bradford Soup Run (£25,000 each); Airedale NHS Trust (£16,000); National Heart Research (£15,000); Bradford Teaching Hospitals (£13,000); and Macmillan Cancer Relief (£11,000).

Smaller grants of £10,000 or less included those to: AFCO (£10,000); Deafblind UK (£7,500); Heartbeat Appeal (£6,200); Christians Against Poverty (£5,000); British Red Cross (£2,500); Bradford Toy Library (£1,500); and St Georges Crypt and Help the Heroes Ball (£1,000 each).

Exclusions No grants to individuals.

Applications In writing to the correspondent.

Sparks Charity (Sport Aiding Medical Research For Kids)

Medical research

£2.3 million (2008/09)
Beneficial area UK.

Heron House, 10 Dean Farrer Street, London SW1H 0DX
Tel. 020 7799 2111 **Fax** 020 7222 2701

Email kirti@sparks.org.uk
Website www.sparks.org.uk
Correspondent Dr Kirti Patel, Medical Research Manager
Trustees *T Brooke-Taylor; Sir T Brooking; H Emeades; M Higgins; D Mills; R Uttley; S Waugh; J Wilkinson; F Benjamin; J Britton; V Glaysher; G Gregory; G Logan; D Orr; F van den Bosch.*
CC Number 1003825
Information available Accounts were on file at the Charity Commission. Information was also provided by the charity.

Sparks is one of the few charities that funds research into the wide range of conditions that can affect babies and children. It supports vital medical research that will:

- increase the life expectancy of new born babies
- reduce the health risks for babies born prematurely
- combat common conditions such as spina bifida and cerebral palsy
- develop more effective treatments for conditions affecting babies and young children.

The charity will only support research which is likely to have a clear clinical application in the near future. Therefore grant applications for routine basic research which is unlikely to have clinical application within ten years will not be considered.

Sparks funded research takes the form of project grants of up to three years in length with a clearly definable subject area and outcome, equipment grants for use within a specific research proposal as previously defined, programme grants for researchers who have a sustained track record of successful grant awards from Sparks and fellowship grants. Pilot projects of short duration to test a concept in preparation for a full application will also be considered (see website). Grants are only made to projects where the principal applicant is in a tenured position at a university or research institution.

Researchers who are making a substantial intellectual contribution to the project and require personal support from the grant may apply as co-applicants with a tenured member of staff as the principal applicant.

In 2008/09 the charity had assets of £777,000 and an income of over £3.5 million, mainly from fundraising events. 15 new research grants were made and totalled nearly £2.3 million. Major beneficiaries included: The Institute of Child Health, Programme Grant (£631,000); University of Manchester (£196,000); University of

Newcastle (£149,500 in 2 grants); University of Glasgow (£143,000); University of Liverpool (£137,000); and University College London (£132,000).

Exclusions The charity is unable to consider:

- grants for further education, for example, MSc/PhD course fees
- grants towards service provision or audit studies
- grants for work undertaken outside the UK
- grants towards 'top up' funding for work supported by other funding bodies
- grants to other charities.

Applications Sparks funds project grants up to the value of £200,000, Research Training Fellowships and Programme grants. Prior to submitting a full application, all applicants are required to complete an outline proposal form which is available for download from the charity's website in Word format. Completed outlines and any queries should be sent to: Dr Kirti Patel, Medical Research Manager, email: kirti@sparks.org.uk, direct Tel/Fax 020 7799 2111/020 7222 2701. Please refer to the Sparks website for outline closing dates. Applicants with suitable research projects will be sent an application form (by email in Word format) and a copy of the relating terms and conditions. Closing dates for full applications are generally March and October; please refer to the sparks website.

The Spring Harvest Charitable Trust

The promotion of Christianity

£693,000 (2007/08)
Beneficial area UK and overseas.

14 Horsted Square, Bellbrook Industrial Estate, Uckfield TN22 1QG
Tel. 01825 769111 **Fax** 01825 769141
Email theclerk@shct.springharvest.org
Website www.springharvest.org
Correspondent C I Macdowell, Secretary
Trustees *Revd Stephen Gaukroger; Marion White; Revd Ian Coffey; Very Revd John Richardson; Mark Smith.*
CC Number 1042041

Information available Accounts were available from the Charity Commission.

Registered as a charity in 1994, this trust seeks to 'equip the Church for action'. The main focus of the trust's grantmaking is evangelism and education, both within the UK and overseas.

In 2007/08 the trust had assets of £389,000 and an income of £546,000. Grants were made during the year totalling £693,000, and were categorised as follows (including support costs):

Category	Amount
Bible provision	£425,000
People trafficking	£256,500
Young people	£27,000
Other nominated grants	£22,000
General	£12,400
Children	£7,000

The main beneficiary was the Bible Society, which received £214,000 in total in line with the main Spring Harvest theme during the year. Other beneficiaries included: Oasis India (£110,000); The Salvation Army (£60,000); Wycliffe UK Ltd (£39,000); Clarendon Trust Ltd (£17,000); Youth for Christ (£17,000); Active Media Publishing Ltd (£5,000); Barnabus Fund (£4,000); Kingscare (£3,000); Mission Aviation Fellowship (£2,500); and the France Mission Trust (£2,000).

Exclusions Grants are not made for salaries.

Applications There is one round of funding applications per year, usually at the end of November/early December, for distribution the following year. An application form is made available on the trust's website from October.

- Spring Harvest welcomes applications on behalf of projects for the advancement of the Christian religion (such as pastoral and evangelistic work) and for educational work in the UK or elsewhere giving priority where the organisation has a Christian basis and where there is a link with the Spring Harvest theme of that year.
- Applications will only be considered if presented on our application form.
- Spring Harvest is not able to commit to on-going funding so do not usually support salary costs.
- Spring Harvest always receives many more applications for funding than they are able to meet and reluctantly have to turn down many good applications.

St James's Place Foundation

Children and young people with special needs and hospices

£2.7 million (2008)
Beneficial area UK.

1 Tetbury Road, Cirencester GL7 1FP
Tel. 01285 878 562
Email mark.longbottom@sjp.co.uk
Website www.sjp.co.uk/foundation
Correspondent Mark Longbottom
Trustees *Malcolm Cooper-Smith, Chair; David Bellamy; Ian Gascoigne; Mike Wilson; Andrew Croft; Hugh Gladman; David Lamb.*
CC Number 1031456

Information available Accounts were available at the Charity Commission. Information is also available on the company's website.

This foundation was established in 1992, when it was known as The J. Rothschild Assurance Foundation. St. James's Place is a wealth management group. Employees and Partners (members of the St. James's Place Partnership, the marketing arm of St. James's Place) contribute to the foundation throughout each year and the sums raised are matched by the company. The combined amount is distributed each year to causes determined by the contributors.

The focus of the foundation is children with learning disabilities:

The foundation will support projects that provide directly for young people (under the age of 25) within the UK who suffer from physical or mental health difficulties or conditions, or a life threatening or degenerative illness. This will include young people under the age of 25 caring for others. Where organisations include other groups, 75% of beneficiaries must fit the above parameters.

The foundation operates two programmes:

Small grants for capital items

The Small Grants Programme has a maximum of £10,000 and is only available to organisations with an annual income of less than £600,000 (this restriction does not apply to special needs schools or mainstream schools with a special needs unit).

The foundation has a policy of not granting more than £10,000 in any two year period.

Major grants for up to two years, which may be for capital or revenue

The Major Grants Programme is to a maximum of £25,000 per annum for a maximum of two years and is only available to organisations with an annual income of less than £2 million.

These grants will be few in number and will be directed at interesting or innovative projects.

Revenue applications will only be considered where they result in direct benefit to the client group.

Grantmaking in 2008

In 2008 the foundation had assets of £1.7 million and an income of £2.6 million (including the corporate donation). There were 240 grants made totalling £2.7 million.

Grants were categorised as follows:

Category	No. of grants	Amount
Major projects	6	£1,400,000
Small grants programme	106	£918,000
Partner/staff fundraising for specific charities	16	£264,000
Local office allocation	96	£91,000
Partner/staff supported projects	2	£74,500
Specific fundraising	14	£7,700

The Major Grants Programme did not run in 2008 and no payments were made.

Grants awarded to separate, major projects, included those to: The Children's Trust – Tadworth (£900,000), for the first and second tranches of a grant for a hydrotherapy pool; Hope & Homes for Children (£190,000), to support their work in Romania and Bosnia & Herzegovina; Teenage Cancer Trust (£120,000), to fund patient technology at the Teenage Cancer Trust Unit at the Royal Marsden Hospital; and Help for Heroes (£10,000), towards the Headley Court Appeal.

The foundation's annual report and accounts contains an impressive amount of detail on each one of the organisations to receive a grant through the Small Grants Programme, and the purpose for which the grant was made.

Beneficiaries included: Friends of Coln House School (£10,000), to fund two projects at this special needs school, to help young people adapt and prepare for adult life and for equipment; St Peter's Hospice (£9,600), for specialist equipment; The Bren Project (£8,800), towards the costs of the 'Moving On' project; Court Meadow School Association (£8,000), for equipment, refurbishments and maintenance; Cued Speech Association UK (£6,800), towards a Summer school based around

communication; Nordoff-Robbins Music Therapy in Scotland (£5,400), towards a project at the Berryknows Centre working with young people with special needs; St John's Hospice – Wirral (£4,000), to fund the Nurse Call System at the new Out Patient Services Unit; and Brittle Bone Society – Dundee (£2,100), to fund a youth worker at a special two day event.

Exclusions The foundation has a policy of not considering an application from any charity within two years of giving a grant.

The trust does not provide support for:

- charities with reserves of over 50% of income
- administrative costs
- activities primarily the responsibility of statutory agencies
- replacement of lost statutory funding
- research
- events
- advertising
- holidays
- sponsorship
- contributions to large capital appeals
- single faith charities
- social and economic deprivation
- charities that are raising funds on behalf of another charity.

Applications Application forms are available from the foundation office and must be returned by post. Applications will only be considered if accompanied by a signed copy of the most recent audited accounts and annual report. An initial enquiry should be made before applying for a major grant.

Applications will be assessed against a number of criteria, including user involvement, sustainability, maximum benefit and volunteer involvement. Assessment visits may be made.

Small grant applications will normally be processed within two months from date of application.

Major grant applications will be considered between July and December and successful applicants will be notified at the end of the following January.

St Katharine and Shadwell Trust

Community development

£505,000 (2008)

Beneficial area The London boroughs of Tower Hamlets, Hackney, and City of London.

PO Box 1779, London E1W 2BY

Tel. 020 7782 6962

Email enquiries@skst.org

Website www.skst.org

Correspondent The Director

Trustees *Sir Robin Mountfield; Sir David Hardy; Eric Sorensen; Lindsay Driscoll; Dan Jones; Mary Nepstad; Maj. Gen. Keith Cima; Mark Gibson; Cllr Shafiqul Haque; Cllr Denise Jones.*

CC Number 1001047

Information available Accounts were available from the Charity Commission.

We are a Community Foundation, raising funds and awarding grants to run and support a wide range of projects in East London. We have been actively working in Tower Hamlets for 18 years and in 2006 extended our work into Hackney, Newham and the City of London.

Our knowledge of the area and the relationships we have developed enable us to support and sustain positive change. Our aim is to ensure that the ideas and aspirations of local people for improving their area can be realised.

We give grants and run projects to improve the quality of life in the local area. We work in the London Boroughs of Tower Hamlets Hackney and the City of London.

We run our own grant programme called St Katharine and Shadwell that has been ongoing since the trust began as well as manage other programmes.

Grants are available to voluntary and community organisations. Some grants may be made to statutory organisations such as schools.

The grant programmes and projects may vary from year to year so please check the trust's website for up-to-date information. Grant programmes administered in 2009 included:

Comic Relief

For voluntary and community and not for profit groups in the City of London, Hackney, Newham and Tower Hamlets.

Grassroots Grants

For very small community and voluntary organisations and groups in the City of London, Hackney, Newham and Tower Hamlets.

Société Générale UK Group Charitable Trust Fund

For small social and community enterprises in the City of London, Hackney, Newham and Tower Hamlets.

St Katharine and Shadwell

The trust's own grants programme, available to benefit residents of the former wards of St Katherine or Shadwell in the London Borough of Tower Hamlets.

YouthBank Tower Hamlets

Grants are available across the whole of the London Borough of Tower Hamlets for young people aged between 14 to 24 with project ideas to benefit the community.

In 2008 the trust had assets of £7.7 million and an income of £1 million. Grants totalled £505,000.

Exclusions 'We are unable to make grants either to or for individuals.'

Applications Please see the trust's website for details of up-to-date schemes.

The Stafford Trust

Animal welfare, medical research, local community and relief in need

£696,000 (2007/08)

Beneficial area UK, with a preference for Scotland.

c/o Dickson Middleton CA, PO Box 14, 20 Barnton St, Stirling FK8 1NE

Tel. 01786 474718

Email staffordtrust@dicksonmiddleton.co.uk

Website www.staffordtrust.org.uk

Correspondent Margaret Kane or Hugh Biggans

Trustees *A Peter M Walls; Hamish N Buchan; Gordon M Wyllie; Angus Morgan.*

SC Number SC018079

Information available Information was on file at OSCR and at the trust's website.

The Stafford Trust was set up in 1991 by the late Mrs Gay Stafford of Sauchie Estate near Stirling. During her lifetime, Mrs Stafford made substantial gifts to the trust and on her death in 2005, the residue of her estate was bequeathed to the trust. Over £10 million was received in the financial year 2006/07. The trust makes grants to charities from the income generated from the trust fund.

Grants vary, but most are for between £500 and £10,000. Occasionally the trustees make a recurring grant of up to three years.

Between 1991 and 2008, grants totalling £1.2 million were made in the following areas:

Category	%
Animal welfare	27
Medical research	27
Local community projects	16
Adult welfare	11
Child welfare	10
HM Services Personnel	5
Overseas appeals	2
Environment	1
Sea Rescue	1

In 2007/08 the trust had an income of £574,000 and made grants to 28 organisations totalled £695,000.

Beneficiaries included: University of Glasgow Small Animal Hospital (£250,000); Scottish Community Foundation (£150,000); Animal Health Trust, Braveheart and Carers Forum Stirling (£30,000 each); Aberloar Childcare Trust, Community Housing Alloa, CLIC Sargent and Headway Edinburgh (£10,000 each); Central Scotland Forest Trust (£8,000); Battersea Dogs Home, Rock Trust and SSPCA (£5,000 each); Crossroads Stirling (£2,500); and Riding for the Disabled (£1,500).

Please note: Some of the grants detailed above are payable over more than one year.

Exclusions The trust does not support:

- religious organisations
- political organisations
- retrospective grants
- student travel or expeditions.

Applications The trust has a short application form which can be downloaded from its website. Applicants are invited to complete the form using their own words without the restrictions of completing set questions. Please also supply the following, where appropriate.

- A brief description of your charity.
- A copy of your most recent annual report and accounts.

- A description of the project/funding requirement – what do you want to achieve and how will it be managed. The trustees look for clear, realistic and attainable aims.
- What is the expenditure budget for the project and the anticipated timescale.
- What funds have already been raised and what other sources are being approached.
- The need for funding must be clearly demonstrated.
- What will be the benefits of the project and how do you propose to monitor and evaluate whether the project has been successful.
- If applicable, what plans do you have to fund the future running costs of the project?

The trustees usually meet twice per annum to consider applications. Applicants may be contacted for more information or to arrange an assessment visit. Successful applicants must wait at least two years from the time of receiving a grant before reapplying. In the case of a two or three year recurring grant this applies from the time of receiving the last instalment.

The Staples Trust

Development, environment and women's issues

£596,500 (2007/08)

Beneficial area Overseas, UK.

Allington House, 1st Floor, 150 Victoria Street, London SW1E 5AE

Tel. 020 7410 0330 **Fax** 020 7410 0332

Website www.sfct.org.uk

Correspondent Alan Bookbinder, Director

Trustees *Jessica Frankopan; Peter Frankopan; James Sainsbury; Alex Sainsbury; Judith Portrait.*

CC Number 1010656

Information available Excellent annual report and accounts were on file at the Charity Commission.

The Staples Trust is one of the Sainsbury Family Charitable Trusts, which share a joint administration. They have a common approach to grantmaking which is described in the entry for the group as a whole. The trust's main areas of interest are overseas development, environment, gender issues, the Frankopan Fund and general charitable purposes.

The trust is that of Jessica Frankopan (nee Sainsbury), and its trustees include her husband and her two brothers who lead the *Tedworth* and *Glass-House* trusts (see separate entries).

The trust offers the standard Sainsbury description of its grant-making practice: 'Proposals are generally invited by the trustees or initiated at their request. Unsolicited applications are discouraged and are unlikely to be successful, even if they fall within an area in which the trustees are interested. The trustees prefer to support innovative schemes that can be successfully replicated or become self-sustaining'. There is probably a special interest in Croatia, but this does not dominate grantmaking in central and Eastern Europe.

Grantmaking in 2007/08

During the year the trust had assets of £12.6 million and an income of £610,000. Grants payable totalled £596,500. This included grants payable over a period, but not accrued in the previous years accounts. In 2007/08 the trustees approved 21 grants totalling just under £1.3 million, and it is to examples of these that the rest of this entry refers.

Gender – 6 grants totalling £1.13 million

Trustees are committed to raising awareness of gender and how the diverse understanding and experiences of men and women have an impact on the structures of society. Trustees are willing to consider projects in the UK and overseas, focusing mainly on domestic violence and women's rights.

The largest commitment during the year was £1 million over a number of years to the University of Cambridge to fund the post of the Frankopan Director of Gender Studies (both Peter and Jessica Frankopan are alumni of Jesus College, Cambridge, and both have a particular interest in gender studies) – the amount paid this year was £290,500. The other grants approved in this category were to: Womenkind Worldwide (£30,000), towards the costs of an anti-sex trafficking animated film to be broadcast in source countries in continental Europe; STOP (Trafficking UK) (£20,000), towards core costs; Co-ordinated Action Against Domestic Abuse and Right of Women (£15,000 each), towards project costs and core costs respectively; and Best Beginnings (£10,000), towards core costs in

promoting the best standards of care in maternal and infant health.

Environment – 3 grants totalling £50,000

Projects are supported in developing countries, Central & Eastern Europe and the UK. Grants are approved for renewable energy technology, training and skills upgrading and, occasionally, research.

In Central & Eastern Europe, trustees are interested in providing training opportunities for community/business leaders and policy makers and in contributing to the process of skill-sharing and information exchange.

In the UK, trustees aim to help communities protect, maintain and improve areas of land and to support work aimed at informing rural conservation policy.

Grants approved were to: Latin American Mining Monitoring Programme and Tropical Forest Trust (£20,000 each), towards core costs for both organisations; and the Ashden Awards (£10,000), towards the awards in 2008.

General – 1 grant of £50,000

Grants can be awarded which do not naturally fit into other categories. The single grant of £50,000 was made to the Ashmolean Museum towards its redevelopment.

Overseas Development – 2 grants totalling £20,000

Trustees' priorities in this category are projects which contribute to the empowerment of women, the rights of indigenous people, improved shelter and housing, income-generation in disadvantaged communities and sustainable agriculture and forestry.

Trustees are particularly interested to support development projects which take account of environmental sustainability and, in many cases, the environmental and developmental benefits of the project are of equal importance.

The grants approved were to: Business & Human Rights Resource Centre (£15,000), towards the recruitment and salary costs of a new regional researcher to cover Eastern Europe and Central Asia; and INCRESE (International Centre for Reproductive Health and Sexual Rights) (£5,000), towards core costs to advocate for sexual health and the rights of Nigeria's most marginalised groups.

The Frankopan Fund – 9 grants totalling £20,000

Trustees have established a fund to assist exceptionally talented postgraduate students primarily from Croatia to further or complete their studies (in any discipline) in the UK.

Grants were made to institutions for the benefit of individuals including Central St Martin's College of Art & Design, London School of Economics & Political Science, University of Middlesex and Zagreb School of Economics & Management.

Exclusions Normally, no grants to individuals.

Applications See the guidance for applicants in the entry for the Sainsbury Family Charitable Trusts. A single application will be considered for support by all the trusts in the group.

However, for this, as for many of the family trusts, 'proposals are generally invited by the trustees or initiated at their request. Unsolicited applications are discouraged and are unlikely to be successful, even if they fall within an area in which the trustees are interested'.

The Steel Charitable Trust

Social welfare, culture, recreation, health, medical research, environment and overseas aid

£1.5 million (2008/09)

Beneficial area Mainly UK with 30% of all grants made to organisations in the Luton and Bedfordshire areas.

Holme Farm, Fore Street, Bradford, Holsworthy EX22 7AJ

Tel. 01409 281403

Email administrator@ steelcharitabletrust.org.uk

Website www.steelcharitabletrust.org.uk

Correspondent Carol Langston, Administrator

Trustees *Nicholas E W Wright; John A Childs, Chair; John A Maddox; Anthony W Hawkins; Paul Stevenson; Wendy Bailey; Mary Briggs; Philip Lawford.*

CC Number 272384

Information available Accounts were on file at the Charity Commission. The trust also has a useful website.

The trust was established in 1976 for general charitable purposes. Grants are made for social welfare, culture, recreation, health, medical research, environment, overseas aid and other general purposes. Grants are made at regular intervals during the year and the total level of grants is approximately £1 million per annum. Grants are generally made as single payments between £1,000 and £25,000. It is the trust's policy to distribute 30% of all grants in the Luton and Bedfordshire areas.

In 2008/09 the trust had assets of £18 million and an income of £1.3 million. Grants totalled £1.5 million and were broken down by the trust as follows:

Category	Value
Ill-health, disability and other disadvantage	£501,000
Health	£342,000
Arts, culture, heritage or science	£135,000
Citizenship or community development	£108,000
Education	£78,000
Poverty	£65,000
Religion	£61,000
Environmental protection or improvement	£52,000
Animal welfare	£50,000
Armed forces, police and rescue services	£42,000
International aid	£5,000
Other charitable purposes	£54,000

Beneficiaries in each category included:

Ill-health, disability and other disadvantage
Treloar Trust (£50,000); Anthony Nolan Trust (£10,000); Childhood First (£5,000); Hi Kent (£2,000); and Just 42 (£1,000).

Health
Pasque Charity (£150,000); Cancer Research UK (£25,000); Bedford Hospitals Charity (£10,000); Arrhythmia Alliance (£5,000); and Council for Music in Hospitals (£3,000).

Arts, culture, heritage or science
St Albans Cathedral Music Trust (£20,000); Cheltenham Festivals (£11,000); Scottish Kids Are Making Movies Limited (£5,000); Cambridge Handel Opera Group (£4,000); and Soundpool (£2,500).

Citizenship or community development
Salvation Army (£25,000); the Golf Foundation Limited (£10,000); Pulloxhill Parochial Church Council (£7,500); Project Scotland (£3,000); and Headingley Development Trust Limited (£500).

Education
University of Bedfordshire (£25,000); Farms for City Children (£5,000); Books Abroad (£3,000); Armonico Consort Limited (£1,500); and Teddy Bears Playgroup (£1,000).

Poverty
Bedfordshire African Community Centre Limited (£12,000); Quartet Community Foundation (£10,000); Elizabeth Finn Care (£5,000); Christians Against Poverty (£3,000); and Corby Furniture Turnaround (£2,000).

Religion
Exeter Cathedral Third Millennium Campaign (£25,000); Moggerhanger House Preservation Trust (£10,000); Lyndon Methodist Church (£5,000); the Message Trust (£3,000); and St. Margaret's Church, Owthorpe Parochial Church Council (£2,000).

Environmental protection or improvement
Friends of Luton Parish Church (£20,000); Trees for Cities and Little Ouse Headwaters Project (£5,000 each); and Moor Trees (£2,000).

Animal welfare
World Horse Welfare (£20,000) and People's Dispensary for Sick Animals and the Donkey Sanctuary (£15,000 each).

Armed forces, police and rescue services
SSAFA – Forces Help (£25,000); Royal Anglian Regiment Museum (£10,000); Northumberland National Park Mountain Rescue Team (£5,000); and Exmoor Search and Rescue Team (£2,000).

International aid
The sole beneficiary was Target Tuberculosis (£5,000).

Other charitable purposes
In Kind Direct (£8,000); Marston Vale Trust (£5,000); Llanybydder Family Centre (£4,000); and Victim Support (£2,000).

Exclusions Individuals, students and expeditions are not supported.

Applications All applicants must complete the online application form. Applications submitted by post will not be considered. There is no deadline for applications and all will be acknowledged. Trustees meet regularly during the year, usually in February, May, August and November. All successful applicants will be notified by email and will be required to provide written confirmation of the details of the project or work for which they are seeking a grant. Payment is then made in the following month.

To comply with the Data Protection Act 1998, applicants are required to consent to the use of personal data supplied by them in the processing and review of their application. This includes transfer to and use by such individuals and organisations as the trust deems appropriate. The trust requires the assurance of the applicant that personal data about any other individual is supplied to the trust with his/her consent. At the point of submitting an online application, applicants are asked to confirm this consent and assurance.

The Stewards' Company Limited (incorporating the J W Laing Trust and the J W Laing Biblical Scholarship Trust)

Christian evangelism and general
£6.1 million to organisations (2007/08)
Beneficial area Unrestricted.

124 Wells Road, Bath BA2 3AH
Tel. 01225 427236 **Fax** 01225 427278
Email stewardsco@stewards.co.uk
Correspondent Brian Chapman, Secretary
Trustees Brian Chapman; Alexander McIlhinney; Dr Alexander Scott; David Restall; Douglas Spence; James Hopewell; John McEwen; Paul Young; Robin Boles; William Brian Adams; William Wood; Andrew Street; William Rutherford Rabey; Prof Arthur Williamson; Philip Page; Denis Cooper; Alan Paterson; Philip Collett Dalling; Glyn Davies; Dr John Burness; Andrew Griffiths; Ian Childs; James Crookes; John Gamble; Philip Symons.
CC Number 234558
Information available Annual report and accounts, listing the top 50 grants, were available from the Charity Commission.

The charity supports Christian evangelism, especially but not exclusively that of Christian Brethren assemblies (different to those of the 'Exclusive' or 'Plymouth' Brethren). The work is described as follows:

The principal activities of the charity are to act as owner or as custodian trustee of various charitable properties, mainly used as places of worship and situated either in the United Kingdom or overseas, and to act as administrative trustee of a number of Christian charitable trusts, including The J W Laing Trust and The J W Laing Biblical Scholarship Trust.

The trust describes its objectives as being:

The advancement of the religion in any matter which shall be charitable, and in particular by the furtherance of the gospel of God and education in the Holy Scriptures as contained in the Old and New Testaments, and the relief of the poor.

Its grantmaking policy is described as follows:

The trust takes into account the financial resources of the benefiting charities, the efforts made by members of such charities to maximise their own funding, including where appropriate sacrificial giving by themselves and their supporters, and the assessed value of the work of such charities consistent with the objective of the main grant-making charities [i.e. Stewards Company, Laing Trust and Laing Scholarship].

In 2007/08 the trust had assets of £121 million and an income of £5.5 million. Grants were made to organisations totalling £6.1 million and were broken down as follows:

Category	Value
Overseas	£2,300,000
Home	£3,300,000
Charitable organisations and objects	£587,000

Only the largest 50 grants were listed in the accounts. Beneficiaries included: Echoes of Service (£1 million); UCCF (£852,000); Beatrice Laing Trust (£587,000); Kharis Productions (£500,000); Retired Missionary Aid Fund (£200,000); International Fellowship of Evangelical Students (£125,000); Lapido Media (£70,000); Ethiopian Graduate School of Theology (£43,000); Bible Society (£30,000); and Interhealth (£15,000).

Applications In writing to the correspondent.

The Sir Halley Stewart Trust

Medical, social, educational and religious activities

£1 million (2007/08)

Beneficial area UK and some work in Africa.

22 Earith Rd, Willingham, Cambridge CB24 5LS

Tel. 01954 260707 **Fax** 01954 260707

Email email@sirhalleystewart.org.uk

Website www.sirhalleystewart.org.uk

Correspondent Sue West, Administrator

Trustees *Lord Stewartby, President; Prof. Philip Whitfield, Chair; Prof. John Lennard Jones; Dr Duncan Stewart; William P Kirkman; George Russell; Prof. Phyllida Parsloe; Barbara Clapham; Prof. John Wyatt; Michael Ross Collins; Joanna Womack; Revd Lord Griffiths; Dr Caroline Berry; Prof. Gordon Willcock; Caroline Thomas.*

CC Number 208491

Information available Accounts were available at the Charity Commission. The trust has a helpful website for applicants.

The trust was established in 1924 by Sir Halley Stewart who endowed the charity and established its founding principles.

During the course of his life Sir Halley Stewart was a non-conformist Christian minister, an MP, a pioneering industrialist and a philanthropist. When he founded the trust he specified four objects, to advance religion and education, to relieve poverty and to promote other charitable purposes beneficial to the community. He was concerned with the prevention and removal of human misery and in the realisation of national and worldwide brotherhood. He wished the trustees to have the fullest discretion in applying the income of the trust within its objects, but not for dogmatic theological purposes. A tradition of supporting medical research into the prevention of human suffering, not its relief, was established during his lifetime. He died in 1937.

The trust has a Christian basis and is concerned with the development of body, mind and spirit, a just environment, and international goodwill. To this end it supports projects in religious, social, educational and medical fields, mainly in the UK. The trust aims

to promote and assist innovative research activities or pioneering developments with a view to making such work self-supporting.

The three principles by which the trustees are guided in administering the trust are:

- furthering for every individual such favourable opportunities of education, service and leisure as shall enable him or her most perfectly to develop the body, mind and spirit
- securing a just environment in all social life whether domestic, industrial or national
- in international relationships to fostering good will between all races, tribes, peoples and nations to secure the fulfilment of hope of 'peace on earth'.

Grants are usually in the form of salary and there is a preference to support innovative and imaginative people, often 'promising young researchers with whom the trust can develop a direct relationship.' Sometimes a contribution towards the expenses of a project is given. Grants are normally limited to two or three years but are sometimes extended. Small individual grants are sometimes given. In general, the trustees do not favour grant giving to enable the completion of a project initiated by other bodies.

The trust's website states that during the coming year the trust plans to make grants up to a budget limit of £800,000. The effectiveness of grants made in previous years will be assessed on the basis of reports by grantees, published work and personal contacts. Grants will continue to be made to further the aims of the trust in the religious, social and medical fields.

In 2007/08 the trust had assets of £24 million and an income of £1.2 million. Grants were made totalling £1 million.

Current priorities

The current priorities of the trust are in the form of three programmes, namely, medical, religious and social and educational. Details are taken from the trust's website.

Medical

Projects should be simple, not molecular, and capable of clinical application within five–ten years. They may include a social or ethical element. Non-medical trustees should be able to understand the application and appreciate the value of the work. Projects may be of a type unlikely to receive support from research councils or large research-funding charities. Projects must have ethics committee approval where needed. The trust welcomes applications direct from researchers at UK medical institutions or university departments concerned with:

- projects which aim to improve the quality of life of older people suffering from physical or psychological disorders
- the prevention of disease and disability in children
- the prevention, diagnosis and treatment of tropical infectious and parasitic diseases
- innovative projects, involving any discipline, which are likely to improve health care
- research focussing on developments in medical ethics
- innovative medical projects caring for the needs of disadvantaged groups.

Religious

The trust is committed to advancing the Christian religion and has a particular interest in innovative practical ecumenical projects in the UK. Current priorities are:

- to encourage Christian people to develop their skills in upholding and communicating their faith in the public domain
- to support and encourage the innovative teaching of Christianity within the United Kingdom
- to encourage specific groups of people to explore their experience of spirituality and their spiritual needs and strengths, and to help others to understand these
- to support innovative projects which aim to facilitate a better understanding between faiths
- theological training in cases where there is special and specific need (for example, in Africa or Eastern Europe).

Social and educational

Applications are welcomed for research, feasibility or pilot studies and development projects that are likely to improve the conditions of a particular group of people, as well as having wider implications. Trustees will normally expect that the beneficiaries of a development project will have been involved in the design of the project and its continuing governance, They will also wish to see how the work will continue after a grant from the trust has finished (sustainability plans).

In the UK the trust seeks to support innovative projects, which attempt to:

- prevent and resolve conflict, promote reconciliation and/or encourage re-connection between family members of all ages
- help people 'move beyond disadvantage' – such projects might be concerned with the social and family aspects of

unemployment, crime, imprisonment, homelessness and migration
- address the needs of older people and those of all ages who may be vulnerable or exploited
- accept responsibility for disseminating results to practitioners in a form which is likely to result in changes in their way of working.

Overseas: the trust applies the same criteria as above to proposals from UK-based charities which operate through local organisations in the poorest politically stable African countries. (Please note: for the foreseeable future the trust will fund overseas work in the field of education, water and healthcare through those organisations with which they have had previous partnerships or which trustees themselves identify. Please do not make general submissions).

Grants in 2007/08

Social and educational – grants totalling £383,000

Beneficiaries of grants over £10,000 included: Kings College (£56,000); Lambeth Trust (£40,000); Coalition for Removal of Pimping (£32,000); London Detainee Support Group (£30,000); Tools for Self Reliance and Bail for Immigration Detainees (£22,000 each); Afrikids (£20,000); and St Paul's Centre – London (£17,000).

Medical – grants totalling £304,000

Beneficiaries of grants over £10,000 included: Oxford University (£65,000); Southampton University Hospitals (£40,000); Guys Hospital (£35,000); British Orthopaedic Foundation (£24,000); the Stammering Association (£18,000); Cardiff University (£15,000); and Cerebral Palsy Africa (£12,000).

Religious – grants totalling £299,000

Beneficiaries of grants over £10,000 included: Faraday Institute – Cambridge (£56,000); Abraham Path Initiative (£50,000); Trinity Foundation (£32,000); Christianity and Culture (£30,000); and Mercian Trust (£20,000).

Exclusions

The trust will be unable to help with funding for any of the following:

- general appeals of any kind
- the purchase, erection or conversion of buildings
- capital costs
- university overhead charges
- the completion of a project initiated by other bodies.

The trust does not normally fund:

- projects put forward indirectly through other 'umbrella' or large charities

- educational or 'gap' year travel projects
- running costs of established organisations
- climate change issues
- personal education fees or fees for taught courses – unless connected with research which falls within current priority areas. Applications for such research work are normally made by a senior researcher seeking support for a student, or if coming directly from the student it should have project supervisor's written support; the trust does not favour grantmaking to enable the completion of a project or PhD.

Applications

Guidelines for applicants:

- applications will not be accepted by fax or email
- applicants should make sure that their project fits the trust's objects and falls within its current priority areas
- telephone enquiries to the trust's office are welcomed to discuss the suitability of an application. Please note: there is only one member of staff so please be patient and try again if there is no one in the office when you telephone.

The trust does not have an application form. Applicants should write to the administrator always including a one-page lay 'executive' summary of the proposed work. The proposal should state clearly:

- what the aims of the project are and why it is believed to be innovative
- what the overall budgeted cost of the project is and how much is being requested from the trust
- what the grant will be used for and how long the project will take to have practical benefits
- how the project/research results will be disseminated
- personal medical applications should be accompanied by a letter of support from a senior colleague or research supervisor
- development projects should indicate where they would hope to obtain future funding from
- where appropriate it is helpful to include a CV, job description, set of audited signed accounts and annual report.

There are no set application deadlines. When the trust has received your application they will make contact (normally within two weeks) either to ask for further information, to tell you the application will be going forward to the next stage of assessment and what the timetable for a final decision will be, or to tell you that they are unable to help.

The trust imposes terms and conditions on each award. Please note: the trust receives many applications for support, and although an application may fit the objects of the trust, it may not necessarily be able to help.

The Stobart Newlands Charitable Trust

Christian religious and missionary causes

£936,000 (2007)

Beneficial area UK.

Mill Croft, Hesket Newmarket, Wigton CA7 8HP

Correspondent Margaret Stobart, Trustee

Trustees *Richard Stobart; Margaret Stobart; Ronnie Stobart; Peter Stobart; Linda Rigg.*

CC Number 328464

Information available Accounts were available from the Charity Commission.

This family trust makes up to 50 grants a year, nearly all on a recurring basis to Christian religious and missionary bodies. Unsolicited applications are most unlikely to succeed.

The trustees are directors and shareholders of J Stobart and Sons Ltd, which is the source of almost all of the trust's income. In 2007 the trust had an income of £960,000 and made grants totalling £936,000. Its assets stood at £218,000.

As in previous years, the three beneficiaries of the largest grants were World Vision and Mission Aviation Fellowship (£200,000 each) and Operation Mobilisation (£170,000).

Other beneficiaries of larger grants of £10,000 each or more included: Tear Fund and Every Home Crusade (£35,000 each); London City Mission and Open Air Mission (£25,000 each); Way to Life (£20,000); Faith Mission (£13,000); and Trans World Radio (£10,000).

Smaller grants went to: Seamen's Christian Friends (£8,000); Trinitarian Bible Society (£6,500); Templar Trust (£4,000); and Bible Lands (£2,500).

Grants of £1,000 or less totalled £4,100.

Exclusions No grants for individuals.

Applications Unsolicited applications are most unlikely to be successful.

The Stone Family Foundation

Relief in need, social welfare and overseas aid

£422,000 (2008)

Beneficial area Worldwide.

Coutts & Co, 440 Strand, London WC2R OQS

Correspondent The Clerk

Trustees *Coutts & Co; John Kyle Stone; Vanessa Jane Stone.*

CC Number 1108207

Information available Accounts were available from the Charity Commission.

Registered with the Charity Commission in February 2005, the foundation's objects are to relieve hardship or distress worldwide, particularly where this hardship is as a result of natural disasters or war.

In 2008 the trust had an income of £7.5 million. Grants were made totalling £422,000.

Previous beneficiaries included: Hope and Homes for Children; Opportunity International; Save the Children; WaterAid; Pratham UK Ltd; Pump Aid; Rainforest Saver Foundation; Children's Fire and Burn Trust; and LSCDPA – Laos.

Loans are also available.

Exclusions No grants to individuals.

Applications 'Applicants for grants and loans must be in writing, and trustees seek the completion of formal terms and conditions.'

Stratford upon Avon Town Trust

Education, welfare and general

£1.4 million (2008)

Beneficial area Stratford upon Avon.

14 Rother Street, Stratford-upon-Avon CV37 6LU

Tel. 01789 207111 **Fax** 01789 207119

Email admin@stratfordtowntrust.co.uk

Website www.stratfordtowntrust.co.uk

Correspondent Richard Eggington, Chief Executive

Trustees *Jean Holder; Donna Barker; Jenny Fradgley; Rosemary Hyde; Juliet Short; Carole Taylor; Dr Nick Woodward; Tim Wightman; John Lancaster; Charles Michaelis; Paul Stanton.*

CC Number 1088521

Information available Accounts were on file at the Charity Commission; good website.

The Town Trust distributes the money generated by the Guild and College Estates in accordance with the Charity Commission Scheme of October 2001. The objects of the charity are:

- relief of need, hardship and distress
- relief of sickness, disability, old age and infirmity
- support of facilities for education, including the advancement of learning and knowledge
- support for facilities for recreations (with the object of improving the conditions of life for beneficiaries in the interests of social welfare) and other leisure-time occupations
- advancement of the Christian religion
- to further any other charitable purpose.

The main beneficiaries are the residents of the town of Stratford-upon-Avon, although those studying or working in the town may also benefit.

As well as being a grantmaker, the trust owns a civic hall, bandstand, chapel and a fountain which commemorates the town's 800th anniversary.

During 2008 the trust changed its financial year-end from 30 September to 31 December. Consequently all 2008 figures are for a fifteen month period, whilst 2007 comparative figures are for a twelve month period.

In 2008 the trust had assets of £3.4 million (2007: £4.1 million) and an income of £2.1 million (2007: £1.9 million), the majority of which came from donations. 225 discretionary grants were made totalling £1.2 million (2007: £866,000).

Only grants of £25,000 or more were listed in the accounts. Beneficiaries included: RSC (£100,000); Citizen's Advice Bureau (£70,000); Shakespeare's Hospice (£65,000); Stratford Upon Avon Christmas Lights Co Ltd (£50,000); World Class Stratford (£42,000); Friends of Shakespeare's Church (£30,000); Stratford in Bloom (£28,000); and Stratford High School (£25,000).

Under the trust's constitution there are two beneficiaries who have a specified entitlement to financial support:

- King Edward VI Grammar School received £706,000 out of income from the Guild Estate
- the Vicar of the Holy Trinity Church received £8,800.

Together with King Edward School and the Vicar of Holy Trinity Church, the Church Street Almshouses were also originally part of these charities but are now the property of Stratford's Municipal Charities. Though it has no strict legal obligation to do so, the trust continues to support the running costs of the 24 Almshouses by virtue of a legal agreement dated 1 April 1983. £37,000 was given towards the maintenance of the Almshouses in 2008.

Exclusions No grants to organisations outside Stratford upon Avon.

Applications Application forms can be completed online via the trust's website. Please note: there are two forms, one for those applying for less than £2,500 and one for those requesting larger grants. Awards are made on a quarterly basis. The latest application deadlines are listed on the trust's website.

The Bernard Sunley Charitable Foundation

General

£2.4 million (2007/08)

Beneficial area Unrestricted, but mainly southern England.

20 Berkeley Square, London W1J 6LH

Tel. 020 7408 2198 **Fax** 020 7499 5859

Email office@sunleyfoundation.com

Correspondent John Rimmington, Director

Trustees *John B Sunley; Joan M Tice; Bella Sunley; Sir Donald Gosling; Brian W Martin; Anabel Knight; William Tice.*

CC Number 1109099

Information available Accounts were available from the Charity Commission.

This is one of the few big trusts that will, in principle, fund any kind of charitable activity in the UK, and which offers no information on the criteria by which one application is preferred to another. No doubt as a consequence of this, the charity receives many applications, only about one in ten of which can be funded. Grants range in size from £250,000 down to less than £1,000, although most grants will be for less than £10,000. The long-noted bias towards the southern half of England continued in 2007/08, particularly amongst the larger grants.

As well as making grants for capital purposes, donations are also made for endowments, scholarship funds, research programmes and for core funding.

Background

Four trustees have held their posts since at least 1984. John B Sunley is the son of the founder Bernard Sunley and is a former chairman of Sunley Holding plc and a council member of Business for Sterling (an organisation opposed to Britain's joining the euro currency area). Joan Tice and Bella Sunley are both members of the founding family. The external trustees are Sir Donald Gosling, founder of NCP car parks and one of Britain's wealthiest men [see also the Gosling Foundation Limited], and Dr Brian Martin, former director of the foundation, who was appointed a trustee in January 2005. Two additional trustees

were appointed in October 2007 – Mrs Anabel Knight and William Tice.

In 2007/08 the trust had assets of £76 million which generated an income of £3.1 million. Grants were made totalling £2.4 million

Grants approved were classified as follows:

Category	2007/08	1960 to 2008
Children and young people	£581,000	£9,500,000
Arts	£387,000	£7,900,000
Health	£288,000	£19,000,000
Education	£288,000	£17,000,000
Community	£253,000	£15,000,000
Social welfare	£242,000	£1,100,000
Emergency and armed services	£98,000	£98,000
Religion	£67,000	£4,100,000
Amateur sport	£16,000	£16,000
Older people	£16,000	£7,300,000
Animal welfare	£5,000	£5,000
Overseas	n/a	£2,400,000
Total	**£2,200,000**	**£86,000,000**

Please note: Grants have been allocated to the relevant category for 'overseas' grants since 1999 and for 'animal welfare' since 2007 (leaving 'environment' as a stand alone category); the 'social welfare' category was created in 2002 with 'amateur sport' and 'emergency armed services' following in 2007.

Grantmaking in 2007/08

The trust gives the following review of activities during the year:

During the year, the trustees approved grants to 437 charities, totalling in value £2.3 million, which compares with 453 grants at a total value of £2 million in the previous year. Grant payments totalling £1.9 million were made. Grants to 85 charities of £5,000 or more were approved during the year.

Children and young people – 12 grants each of £5,000 or more totalled £400,000. Beneficiaries included: London Youth (£250,000); Saint Madoc Christian Youth Camp – Swansea (£50,000); Oxford-Kilburn Youth Trust (£30,000); Variety Club of GB (£20,000); Prince's Trust (£10,000); Tall Ships Youth Trust (£7,500); and Marine Society and Sea Cadets and Roundhouse Trust – London (£5,000).

A further 104 grants each of less than £5,000 totalled £183,000. Beneficiaries included: Frontier Youth Trust Birmingham and Sycamore Project – Bolton (£3,000 each); 1st Beetley Scouts – Norfolk, 2nd West Kirby Sea Scouts – Wirral, Action for Kids – London, Challenge Team UK, Farms for City Children, No Way Trust and YMCA – Reading (£2,000 each); Bolton Lads and Girls Club and Partnership for Children

(£1,500 each); and CHICKS, National Association of Clubs for Young People and Swansea Young Single Homeless Project (£1,000 each).

Arts – 7 grants each of £5,000 or more, totalling £370,000. Beneficiaries included: Historic Dockyard – Chatham, Mary Rose Trust and Royal Marines Museum (£100,000 each); Creative Foundation – Kent (£50,000); Southbank Centre (£10,000); and Music of Life Foundation (£5,000).

10 grants each of less than £5,000 totalled £17,000. Beneficiaries included: Deal Festival of Music and the Arts (£4,000); National Youth Theatre (£3,000); Watermill Theatre – Berkshire (£2,000); and Access to Art, Dulwich Picture Gallery and Pimlico Opera – London (£1,000 each).

Health – 18 grants each of £5,000 or more totalling £245,000. Beneficiaries included: Royal Marsden Hospital Cancer Campaign (£30,000); Helen and Douglas House – Oxford and Zoe's Place – Leamington Spa (£25,000 each); Head and Neck Cancer Research Trust and Vitalise (£20,000 each); Alexander Devine Children's Cancer Trust – Berkshire, Princess Alice Hospice Trust and St John of Jerusalem Eye Hospital (£10,000 each); and Home Farm Trust, Hospice in the Weald – Pembury, Juvenile Diabetes Research Foundation and Royal College of Surgeons of England (£5,000 each).

23 grants each of less than £5,000 totalling £43,000. Beneficiaries included: Royal Hospital for Children – Bristol Appeal (£3,000); Cancer Research UK and Royal Hospital for Neuro-disability – Putney (£2,000 each); Injured Jockeys Fund (£1,500); Help the Hospices, Macmillan Cancer Support and National Deaf Children's Society (£1,000 each).

Education – 9 grants each of £5,000 or more totalled £265,000. Beneficiaries included: Royal Institution of Great Britain (£100,000); Book Aid International and Convent of the Sacred Heart – Connecticut, USA (£36,000 each); Kent Association for the Blind and Spring Grover School – Kent (£20,000); London Philharmonic Orchestra (£18,000); Enterprise Education Trust (£15,000); and Royal Entomological Society (£10,000).

18 grants each of less than £5,000 totalling £24,000. Beneficiaries included: Canterbury Oast Trust, Quest School – West Malling and Vranch House School and Centre – Exeter (£2,000 each); National Literacy Trust (£1,500); and Groundwork – Dearne Valley, Kent Association for the Blind, Kipungani

Schools Trust – Kenya and Royal Institution of Great Britain (£1,000 each).

Community – 11 grants each of £5,000 or more totalled £109,000. Beneficiaries included: Calvert Trust – Exmore and Martha Trust – Deal (£25,000 each); Malt Cross Music Hall Trust – Nottingham and St Jude's Church – Southsea (£10,000 each); Princess Royal Trust for Carers (£7,500); and Crimestoppers Trust – Kent, Harlestone Association for Fitness and Fun – Northamptonshire and Kent People's Trust (£5,000 each).

92 grants each of less than £5,000 totalling £145,000. Beneficiaries included: Branscombe Village Hall – Devon and YMCA – Reigate and Redhill (£3,000 each); Bishop Cornish Education Centre – Cornwall, Byrness Village Hall – Northumberland, Dilton Memorial Hall – Wiltshire, Fifth Trust – Kent, Manton Village Hall – Rutland, Open Door Project – Lymington, Spadework – Kent, Storth Village Hall – Cumbria, Whizz-Kidz and WRVS (£2,000 each); Dogs for the Disabled (£1,200) and Concern Worldwide, Heeley City Farm – Sheffield, Queen Victoria Seamen's Rest – London and St John Ambulance – Kent (£1,000 each).

Social welfare – 17 grants each of £5,000 or more totalling £160,000. Beneficiaries included: ARC Addinton Fund (£25,000); TRAX – Oxfordshire (£20,000); DEMAND – Design and Manufacture for Disability and Nehemiah Project – London (£15,000 each); Caldecott Foundation – Ashford, Coram Family and Merlin (£10,000 each); Depaul Trust – London (£7,500); Butler Trust, English Rural Housing Association, Headway – East London, SeeAbility, Stepping Stones Trust – London, Tearfund and Unique Coffee Bar – Nottingham (£5,000 each).

54 grants each of less than £5,000 totalled £82,000. Beneficiaries included: Langley House Trust – Witney, Send a Cow and Winston's Wish (£3,000 each); Citylife – Edinburgh, Essential Needs – Harrogate, Genesis Trust – Bath, New Bridge – London, Rainbow Living – Devon and Stanmore Youth Centre – Winchester (£2,000 each); Fairbridge – Kent (£1,500); and CRISIS UK, Devon Link Up, Glasgow City Mission, Hope UK, Manchester City Mission, REACT and Samaritans (£1,000 each).

Emergency and armed services – 3 grants of £5,000 or more totalling £95,000. Beneficiaries were: SSAFA Forces Help (£50,000); White Ensign

Association (£40,000); and Army Benevolent Fund (£5,000).

A further grant was made to Ex-Services Mental Welfare Society (£3,000).

Religion – 4 grants each of £5,000 or more totalled £45,000. Beneficiaries were: St Paul's Church – Mill Hill (£20,000); Peterborough Cathedral Development and Preservation Trust and St Mary-le-Bow – Cheapside (£10,000 each); and Anglican Mainstream International (£5,000).

16 grants each of less than £5,000 totalled £22,000. Beneficiaries included: Christ Church – Selly Park and Friends of Challock Park – Kent (£3,000 each); St Leonard's Church – Colchester (£2,000); and Pier Avenue Baptist Church – Gwent, St Peter's Church – Walgrave and Tyburn Convent – London (£1,000 each).

Amateur sport – 1 grant of £5,000 or more was made to Cricket Foundation (£10,000).

Five grants each of less than £5,000 totalled £6,000. Beneficiaries included: Barmby Moor Playing Field Association – York (£2,000); South Tyneside Football Trust (£1,500); and Lakers Community Foundation – Doncaster (£1,000).

Older people – 2 grants each of £5,000 or more totalling £10,000. Beneficiaries were: Almshouse Association and Hayle Day Care Centre Trust – Cornwall (£5,000 each).

Four grants each of less than £5,000 totalled £6,000. Beneficiaries included: Age Concern – Oxford City and County (£2,000); and Anchor Society – Bristol and Holbeck Elderly Aid – Leeds (£1,000 each).

Animal welfare – 6 grants each less than £5,000 were made to beneficiaries including: Retired Greyhound Trust (£1,300); and Brooke Hospital for Animals and Tramps Fund – Gibraltar (£1,000 each).

Exclusions We would reiterate that we do not make grants to individuals; we still receive several such applications each week. This bar on individuals applies equally to those people taking part in a project sponsored by a charity such as VSO, Duke of Edinburgh Award Scheme, Trekforce, Scouts and Girl Guides, and so on, or in the case of the latter two to specific units of these youth movements.

Applications Appeals are considered regularly, but we would emphasise that we are only able to make grants to registered charities and not to individuals. There is no application form, but the covering letter to the director should give details as to the points below, and should be accompanied by the latest approved report and accounts.

The details requested are as follows:

- a description of what the charity does and what its objectives are
- an explanation of the need and purpose of the project for which the grant is required
- how much will the project cost? The costing should be itemised and supported with quotations etc. as necessary
- the size of grant requested
- how much has already been raised and from whom. How is it planned to raise the shortfall?
- if applicable, how the running costs of the project will be met, once the project is established
- any other documentation that the applicant feels will help to support or explain the appeal.

Sussex Community Foundation

Community-based projects, education, disability, health, and the relief of poverty and sickness

£860,000 (2008/09)

Beneficial area East Sussex, West Sussex or Brighton and Hove.

Suite B, Falcon Wharf, Railway Lane, Lewes BN7 2AQ

Tel. 01273 409 440

Email info@sussexgiving.org.uk

Website www.sussexgiving.org.uk

Correspondent Kevin Richmond, Administrator

Trustees *Trevor James; John Peel; Kathy Gore; Neil Hart; Jeremy Leggett; Steve Manwaring; Caroline Nicholls; Sharon Phillips; Lesley Wake; Mike Simpkin; Humphrey Price; Richard Pearson; Margaret Johnson; Michael Martin.*

CC Number 1113226

Information available Accounts were available from the Charity Commission.

The charitable objects of the foundation are:

The promotion of any charitable purposes for the benefit of the community in the counties of East Sussex, West Sussex and the City of Brighton and Hove and in particular the advancement of education, the protection of good health both mental and physical and the relief of poverty and sickness. Other exclusively charitable purposes in the United Kingdom and elsewhere which are in the opinion of the trustees beneficial to the community including those in the area of benefit.

We are particularly interested in supporting smaller community based groups where a small grant can make a really big difference.

Most of our grants are in the region of £1,000 to £5,000. In exceptional cases larger grant applications may be considered. Small applications of less than £1,000 are encouraged.

In 2008/09 the foundation had assets of £935,000 and an income of £1.7 million. During the year the foundation awarded 352 grants to community groups and charities across Sussex, totalling £860,000). This is over four times the number, and three times the value of grants awarded in 2007–08. The average grant awarded was £2,500 (approximately). The foundation has successfully reached small local organisations. 75% of the organisations funded have an annual turnover of less than £20,000, and 25% had a turnover of less than £3,000 per year.

Grants were categorised as follows:

Category	No. of grants
Animals	4
Arts and culture	49
Children and young people	73
Community buildings	15
Disability	34
Economic independence	3
Education	7
Health/medical	17
Homelessness	5
Hospices	2
Older people	43
Other	6
Social welfare	47

Funds available

Comic Relief: Check the website for closing dates for 2010 and beyond.

General awards: The foundation manages a range of funds that have their own priorities and criteria. Grants of up to £5,000 are available. Please read the criteria on the current range of funds held before you decide to apply.

Grassroots grants: Small, mainly volunteer led groups, with an income of less than £30,000 a year that have been active in their community for more than a year can apply for grants of up to £5,000.

Little Cheyne Court Wind Farm Community Fund: Funded by npower renwables this fund will support community groups (including social enterprises) based within a 7km radius of the Little Cheyne Court Wind Farm. Grants of £500 to £5,000 will be awarded.

The Rye Fund: This fund will support charitable causes in the Rye area for the benefit of the local community.

Exclusions No support for:

- individuals
- organisations that are part of central, local or regional government
- major capital appeals
- fundraising events
- sponsorship.

Applications Applicants must have a constitution or set of rules, and be able to show that they are not-for-profit, but do not always have to be a charity.

Each of the funds listed under 'Funds available' are open to applications. As the criteria and application form differs for each you are advised to refer to the foundation's website.

Please note: you may only apply to one programme at a time.

Sutton Coldfield Municipal Charities

Relief of need, arts, education, building conservation and general

£1.16 million to organisations (2007/08)

Beneficial area The former borough of Sutton Coldfield, comprising three electoral wards: New Hall, Vesey and Four Oaks.

Lingard House, Fox Hollies Road, Sutton Coldfield, West Midlands B76 2RJ

Tel. 0121 351 2262 **Fax** 0121 313 0651

Website www. suttoncoldfieldmunicipalcharities.com

Correspondent Andrew MacFarlane, Clerk to the Trustees

Trustees *Rodney Kettel, Chair; Sue Bailey; Dr Freddie Gick; John Gray; Donald Grove; Cllr Susanna McCorry; Alfred David Owen; Jane Rothwell; Cllr David Roy; Michael Waltho; Cllr James*

Whorwood; Carole Hancox; Cllr Margaret Waddington; Dr S C Martin; Cllr Malcolm Cornish; Neil Andrews.

CC Number 218627

Information available Accounts were available from the Charity Commission.

The charity, which is one of the largest and oldest local trusts in the country, dates from 1528.

The charity states that its objectives are:

- to help older people, the sick, those with disabilities and the poor
- to support facilities for recreation and leisure occupations
- to promote the arts and advance religion
- the repair of historic buildings
- the advancement of education of persons under the age of 25 through grants to schools and individuals for fees, maintenance, clothing and equipment.

Grantmaking to organisations is described as follows:

Priority is given to local organisations (large and small) that provide benefits for children and adults coping with the impact of disadvantage, sickness, older age or disability. Grants are made, for example, to local hospitals, hospices and charities. Some of these, such as St Giles Hospice, are large organisations with considerable clinical and care expertise. Others are locally organised support groups, dealing, for example, with complementary care therapies, eating disorders, prostate or breathing difficulties. Christmas lunches and summer trips are funded for local groups for older people.

Sutton's schools and colleges receive grants to purchase extra facilities and equipment that they cannot fund from their normal budgets. Charitable playgroups and nurseries are supported. SCMC does not fund independent schools and nurseries.

The charity makes awards to religious organisations, especially where these serve the wider community, for example through their centres. It also promotes art, music and drama (for example, concerts at the Town Hall and the local theatres). Recreation and leisure are supported, including some amateur sport. Where there is significant public benefit, the charity makes grants to preserve historic buildings and improve the environment.

With a few exceptions, grants are not made to groups based outside Sutton.

In 2007/08 the charity had assets of £39.4 million and an income of almost £2.1 million. Grants were made to 70 organisations totalling £1.16 million. Total grants, which includes around £40,000 to individuals, were broken down as follows:

Category	Value
Relief of those in need	£449,000
Advancement of religion	£292,000
Advancement of education	£249,000
Advancement of citizenship or community development	£71,000
Advancement of amateur sport	£58,400
Advancement of health or the saving of lives	£51,000
Advancement of environmental protection or improvement	£11,200
Advancement of the arts, culture, heritage or science	£9,000

A recent list of beneficiaries was not included in the charity's latest accounts, although due to the amount of local charities that receive support, it is likely that the list remains fairly similar each year, with Good Hope Hospital and St Giles' Hospice receiving continued support.

Exclusions No awards are given to individuals or organisations outside the area of benefit, unless the organisations are providing essential services in the area.

Applications To make a grant application:

- contact the charity, either by letter, or by telephoning: 0121 351 2262
- outline your needs and request a copy of the charity's guidelines for applicants
- if appropriate, seek a meeting with a member of staff in making your application
- ensure that all relevant documents, including estimates and accounts, reach the charity by the requested dates.

Receipt of applications is not normally acknowledged unless a stamped addressed envelope is sent with the application.

Applications may be submitted at any time. The grants committee meets at least eight times a year. The board of trustees must approve requests for grants over £30,000.

At all stages, staff at the charities will give assistance to those making applications. For example, projects and applications can be discussed, either at the charity's office or on site. Advice about deadlines for submitting applications can also be given.

There are application forms for individuals, who must obtain them from the charity.

The Sutton Trust

Education

£3.3 million (2008)

Beneficial area UK only.

111 Upper Richmond Road, Putney, London SW15 2TJ

Tel. 020 8788 3223 **Fax** 020 8788 3993

Website www.suttontrust.com

Correspondent The Trust Administrator

Trustees *Sir Peter Lampl; David Backinsell; Glyn Morris.*

CC Number 1067197

Information available Informative annual review, separate annual accounts, good website.

The Sutton Trust was established in 1997 with the aim of providing educational opportunities for children and young people from non-privileged backgrounds. It has funded a large number of access projects in early years, school and university settings, and now plans to focus primarily on research and policy work, as well as a small number of innovative pilot initiatives.

The following statement taken from the trust's 2008 accounts explains the new policy further.

During the course of the year the trustees decided to move away from large scale initiatives and refocus on research and policy work – attempting to prompt wider change in the educational system by looking into an issue, proposing and testing a solution, and advocating evidence based reform. In keeping with this model, the trust will continue to fund small scale demonstration projects which will, as before, span the early years, school and college settings and into higher education and the professions.

The trust envisages that most of these projects will be developed through existing contacts and partnerships. Please contact the trust for further information.

Grants in 2008

In 2008 the trust had assets of £1.4 million and an income of £4.8 million. Grants totalled £3.3 million and were broken down as follows:

Category	Value
University outreach	£1,500,000
School/colleges	£1,400,000
Research projects	£387,000
Early years learning	£63,000
Open access	0

Beneficiaries included: Bristol University Summer School, Oxford Access Scheme, LEAPS, Industrial Trust Schools Project, INTO University, Parents as First

Teachers, University of York, Social Mobility Summit and Durham University.

Applications The trust states that it, 'is now focusing on research and policy work, and will only be funding a select handful of small scale pilot projects. We envisage that most of these projects will be developed through existing contacts and partnerships'. As such, unsolicited applications are unlikely to be successful.

The Charles and Elsie Sykes Trust

General, social welfare and medical research

£404,000 (2007)

Beneficial area UK, with a preference for Yorkshire.

6 North Park Road, Harrogate HG1 5PA

Tel. 01423 817238 **Fax** 01423 851112

Website www.charlesandelsiesykestrust. co.uk

Correspondent Mrs Judith M Long, Secretary

Trustees *John Ward, Chair; Mrs Anne E Brownlie; Martin P Coultas; Michael G H Garnett; R Barry Kay; Dr Michael D Moore; Dr Michael W McEvoy; Peter G Rous.*

CC Number 206926

Information available Accounts were available from the Charity Commission.

Charles Sykes started his career as a twelve year old office boy, and became a successful businessman in the Yorkshire wool trade. The trust was established in 1954.

In 2007 it had assets of £12.9 million, an income of £806,000 (including £344,000 transferred from the Harrogate Good Samaritan Fund after winding up), and made 139 grants totalling £404,000.

A wide range of causes are supported, and the trust has sub-committees to consider both medical and non-medical grants.

The following is a breakdown of the total amounts awarded in each category:

Category	No. of grants	Amount
Social and moral welfare	36	£88,000
Medical research	19	£70,000
Disability	20	£55,000
Children and young people	19	£46,500
Cultural and environmental heritage	8	£34,500
Medical welfare	12	£23,000
Mental health	6	£22,000
Hospitals and hospices	3	£20,000
Sundry	4	£19,000
Blind and partially sighted	4	£13,000
Older people	5	£8,000
Deafness	2	£3,000
Overseas aid	1	£1,500

Beneficiaries receiving £5,000 or more included: Cancer Research UK (£26,000); Harrogate & District NHS Foundation Trust (£13,000); Royal Northern College of Music (£10,000); Scargill House (£7,000); and British Heart Foundation, Bowel Disease Research Foundation, Swaledale Festival, Richmond YMCA – Yorkshire and the Lighthouse Group (£5,000 each).

Exclusions Unregistered charities and overseas applications are not considered. Individuals, local organisations not in the north of England, and recently established charities are unlikely to be successful.

Applications To request funding you should download and fill in the application form, available via the trust's website. Send it to the trust along with any other relevant information, particularly enclosing a copy of your latest audited or examined accounts to the present year, together with the annual report. It is more favourable for the application if the accounts are current. If the donation is required for any particular project, please provide full details and costings.

Your request will be considered by the appropriate subcommittee, which for medical projects currently includes two doctors. The subcommittee then makes a recommendation to the next full meeting of the trustees. Please note: it is the trustees' policy only to support applications from registered charities with a preference for those in or benefiting the geographical area of Yorkshire.

Applications from schools, playgroups, cadet forces, scouts, guides, and churches must be for outreach programmes, and not for maintenance projects.

Each application will be answered by letter to state if they have been rejected, or put forward for further consideration. Those that are rejected after further consideration will be duly informed. The trustees are under no obligation to state the reasons why any particular application has been rejected, and will not enter into correspondence on the matter. Successful applications will receive a donation which may or may not be subject to conditions.

All applications are dealt with at the discretion of the trustees who meet quarterly.

The Tajtelbaum Charitable Trust

Jewish and welfare

£759,000 (2007/08)

Beneficial area Generally UK and Israel.

17 Western Avenue, London NW11 9HE

Tel. 020 8202 3464

Correspondent Ilsa Tajtelbaum

Trustees *Ilsa Tajtelbaum; Jacob Tajtelbaum; Emanuel Tajtelbaum.*

CC Number 273184

Information available Accounts were on file at the Charity Commission, without a grants list.

The trust makes grants in the UK and Israel to orthodox synagogues, Jewish educational establishments, homes for older people and hospitals.

In 2007/08 the trust had assets of £3.7 million and an income of £692,000. Grants were made totalling £759,000. A list of grant beneficiaries was not included in the trust's accounts.

Previous beneficiaries include: United Institutions Arad, Emuno Educational Centre, Ruzin Sadiger Trust, Gur Foundation, Before Trust, Beth Hassidei Gur, Comet Charities Limited, Delharville, Kupat Gemach Trust, Centre for Torah and Chesed, Friends of Nachlat David and Friends of Sanz Institute.

Applications In writing to the correspondent.

The David Tannen Charitable Trust

Jewish

£645,000 (2007/08)

Beneficial area UK.

Sutherland House, 70–78 West Hendon Broadway, London NW9 7BT

Tel. 020 8202 1066

Correspondent Jonathon Miller

Trustees *Jonathon Miller; Alan Rose; David Tannen.*

CC Number 280392

Information available Accounts were on file at the Charity Commission, without a list of grants.

The trust makes grants for the advancement of the Jewish religion. In 2007/08 it had assets of £25 million and an income of nearly £2.8 million. Grants were made totalling £645,000. A list of grant beneficiaries was not included in the trust's accounts.

Previous beneficiaries include: Cosmon Beiz Academy, Gevurath Ari Trust, Telz Academy Trust, Friends of Ohr Elchonon, Beis Ahron Trust, Wlodowa Charity, Chai Cancer Care, Kollel Skver Trust, Centre for Torah Trust, Gateshead Talmudical College, Jewish Women's Aid Trust, Torah 5759 Ltd and YTAF.

Applications In writing to the correspondent.

The Tedworth Charitable Trust

Parenting, child welfare and development and general

£301,000 (2007/08)

Beneficial area Unrestricted, but UK in practice.

Allington House, 1st Floor, 150 Victoria Street, London SW1E 5AE

Tel. 020 7410 0330 **Fax** 020 7410 0332

Website www.sfct.org.uk

Correspondent Alan Bookbinder, Director

Trustees *Alex J Sainsbury; Margaret Sainsbury; Jessica M Sainsbury; Timothy J Sainsbury; Judith S Portrait.*

CC Number 328524

Information available Accounts were available from the Charity Commission.

This is one of the Sainsbury Family Charitable Trusts, which share a joint administration and have a common approach to grantmaking.

This trust's main areas of interest are parenting, family welfare, child development, arts and the environment; the trust also makes grants for general charitable purposes.

Proposals are generally invited by the trustees or initiated at their request. Unsolicited applications are discouraged and are unlikely to be successful, even if they fall within an area in which the trustees are interested. The trustees prefer to support innovative schemes that can be successfully replicated or become self-sustaining.

In 2007/08 the trust had assets of £11.3 million and an income of £527,000. Grants were paid during the year totalling £301,000, and were broken down as follows:

Arts and the environment – 9 grants totalling £145,000

The beneficiaries during the year were: Ashden Awards for Sustainable Energy (£30,000), towards the cost of the 2007 awards; Environmental Research Association Ltd (£30,000), towards developing a sustainable income base for Resurgence, a leading environmental magazine; Navdanya International Centre for Sustainable Living (£20,000), towards the 2007 education programme; Common Ground (£20,000), towards core costs; University of Oxford (£15,000), towards the Ashmolean Museum's redevelopment appeal; Women's Environmental Network (£10,000), towards a photographic and food growing project for community groups in east London; National Byway (£10,000), towards core costs; Margate Rocks (£5,000), towards the art festivals' education programme; and Spitalfields Farm Association (£5,000), towards the healthy living project.

Parenting, family welfare and child development – 6 grants totalling £114,000

The beneficiaries were: Best Beginnings (£35,000), towards the production of an educational video for expectant and nursing mothers about breast-feeding and development of the charity's website; Centre for Attachment-based Psychoanalytic Psychotherapy (£29,000), towards fundraising and legal costs, and

the promotion of the charity's journal; University of Oxford (£14,500), towards the research programme 'Families, Children and Childcare'; Home Start (£13,500), towards core costs; University of Reading (£12,300), towards the core costs of the Winnicott Research Unit; and the Option Institute (£10,000), towards an evaluation in partnership with the University of Lancaster of the outcomes of UK families following the Son-Rise programme.

General – 4 grants totalling £42,000

The beneficiaries were: Worcester College, Oxford (£25,000), towards the endowment appeal; Open Trust (£15,000), towards the 'openDemocracy' web-based discussion forum; the Sainsbury Archive (£1,000), towards the running costs of the archive; and British Friends of the Sengwer Tribe of Kenya (£1,000), to fund the connection of the community cultural centre in Kaplolet to the mains electricity supply.

Exclusions Grants are not normally made to individuals.

Applications 'Proposals are likely to be invited by the trustees or initiated at their request. Unsolicited applications are unlikely to be successful, even if they fall within an area in which the trustees are interested.' A single application will be considered for support by all the trusts in the Sainsbury family group. See the separate entry for the Sainsbury Family Charitable Trusts.

Tees Valley Community Foundation

General

£1.8 million (2007/08)

Beneficial area The former county of Cleveland, being the local authority areas of Hartlepool, Middlesbrough, Redcar and Cleveland and Stockton-on-Tees.

Southlands Business Centre, Ormesby Road, Middlesbrough TS3 0HB

Tel. 01642 314200 **Fax** 01642 313700

Email info@teesvalleyfoundation.org

Website www.teesvalleyfoundation.org

Correspondent Hugh McGouran

Trustees *Alan Kitching; John Sparke; Keith Bayley; Christopher Hope; Jack Ord; John Bennett; Pamela Ann Taylor; Mr*

McDougall; Craig Monty; Neil Etherington; Rosemary Young; John Irwin; Jacqueline Taylor; Marjory Houseman; Keith Robinson; Brian Beaumont; Neil Kenley.

CC Number 1111222

Information available Accounts were on file at the Charity Commission. Some information was available from the foundation's website.

The foundation's main aim is the promotion of any charitable purpose for the benefit of the community in the Tees Valley and neighbouring areas. Particular focus is given to the advancement of education, arts, the environment, the protection of good health (both mental and physical) and the relief of poverty and sickness.

Support is given to local registered charities and constituted community groups run for and by local people. The foundation always has a variety of grant programmes running and new ones are regularly added.

In 2007/08 it had assets of £8.7 million and an income of £2.4 million. Grants from all funds totalled just over £1.8 million.

Funds Available
The foundation has a range of different funds designed for small community and voluntary groups working to help local people across Tees Valley.

Grant schemes change frequently. Please contact the foundation for details of current programmes and their deadlines.

Each scheme tends to have a different application procedure and size of award. A selection of some of the main programmes is listed below.

Teeside Youth Fund – This scheme makes funds available to address the needs of young people aged 8–25 that suffer from some form of disadvantage. The fund draws from a number of individual funds, which the foundation holds on behalf of businesses, individuals and trusts. Grants are made up to a maximum of £5,000.

The Teesside Power Fund – This was set up in 1994 to make grants in support of charitable projects in the nine wards in the vicinity of Teesside Power Station. Applications are welcomed from registered charities or community groups resident in the nine wards or which benefit people who live in those wards. The wards are: Eston, Dormanstown, Kirkleatham, Teesville, Newcomen, Coatham, Grangetown, South Bank and Normanby. Grants of up to £2,000 are available to enable local people to launch or run initiatives to benefit their local community.

Evening Gazette – Making a Difference Fund – This scheme aims to support the local community by awarding grants for the benefit of charitable groups and projects across the Tees Valley area. The fund's priorities are: projects that address the issues of disadvantage and/or deprivation; projects fulfilling a need not already being met; and improving the social environment.

Grassroots grants – Grassroots Grants is a £130 million programme that aims to invest in a thriving community sector across the whole of the UK. It is funded by the Office of the Third Sector. The programme is designed to run from 2008–2011. Grants are available to support small, informal voluntary and community groups.

Exclusions No grants for major fundraising appeals, sponsored events, promotion of religion, holidays or social outings. Each fund has separate exclusions; contact the foundation for further details.

Applications Contact the correspondent to discuss your project and request an application form.

The Thompson Family Charitable Trust

Medical, veterinary, education and general

£105,000 (2007/08)
Beneficial area UK.

Hillsdown Court, 15 Totteridge Common, London N20 8LR
Correspondent The Trustees
Trustees *D B Thompson; Mrs P Thompson; Mrs K P Woodward.*
CC Number 326801

Information available Accounts were available from the Charity Commission.

This trust has general charitable purposes. There appears to be preferences for educational, medical and veterinary organisations.

In 2007/08 the trust had assets of £64.5 million and an income of £2.9 million. Grants were made to 35 organisations totalling £105,000. It regularly builds up its reserves to enable it to make large donations in the future, for example towards the construction of new medical or educational facilities. 'The trustees intend to continue to reserve a proportion of the annual investment income until an appropriate project has been identified and approved'.

In view of the trustees' reserves policy, it is likely that the trust's grantmaking will increase substantially in the future.

Beneficiaries included: Racing Welfare Charities (£25,000 in two grants); North London Hospice (£11,000 in two grants); Cambridge Women's Aid, East Anglian Children's Hospices, Multiple Sclerosis Society and St Nicholas Hospice (£10,000 each); Score (£5,000); Childline and Juvenile Diabetes Research Foundation (£2,000 each); Cancer Research UK, Marie Curie Cancer Care and University of Cambridge Veterinary School Trust (£1,000 each); and Special Olympics Appeal (£500).

Exclusions No grants to individuals.

Applications In writing to the trustees.

The Sir Jules Thorn Charitable Trust

Medical research, medicine and small grants for humanitarian charities

£2.9 million (£2008)
Beneficial area UK.

24 Manchester Square, London W1U 3TH
Tel. 020 7487 5851 **Fax** 020 7224 3976
Email info@julesthorntrust.org.uk
Website www.julesthorntrust.org.uk
Correspondent David H Richings, Director

Trustees *Mrs Elizabeth S Charal, Chair; Prof Sir Ravinder N Maini; Sir Bruce McPhail; Nancy V Pearcey; Christopher Sporborg; William Sporborg; John Rhodes; Prof David Russell-Jones.*

CC Number 233838

Information available Accounts were available at the Charity Commission.

The trust also has a clear and helpful website.

The trust was established in 1964 for general charitable purposes and its primary interest is in the field of medicine. Grants are awarded to universities and hospitals in the United Kingdom to support medical research, with modest donations provided also for medically related purposes. It is a member of the Association of Medical Research Charities. Outside of medicine some funds are allocated for donations to humanitarian appeals and to special projects but on a lesser scale than the commitment for medical research.

Programmes

The trust gives the following information on its programmes:

Medical Research
The trust's main objective is to fund translational research which will bring benefit to patients through improved diagnosis or by assisting in the development of new therapies for important clinical problems. It recognises also the importance of encouraging young scientists to pursue a career in clinical research. Its two grant schemes have been designed with those objectives in mind.

1) The Sir Jules Thorn Award for Biomedical Research
One grant of up to £1.25 million is offered annually to support a five year programme of translational biomedical research selected following a competition among applicants sponsored by the leading UK medical schools and NHS organisations.

UK medical schools and NHS organisations are eligible to submit one application annually.

[Medical research guidance notes are available from the trust's website, but please note that application is by invitation only.]

2) The Sir Jules Thorn PhD Scholarship Programme
Three grants are available annually to support high quality postgraduate research training in UK medical schools under the supervision of a Senior Clinical Lecturer. A scholarship meets the cost of a stipend, tuition fees and consumables over a three year course of study leading to a PhD degree.

Scholarships are available only through medical schools invited to participate.

The Ann Rylands Special Project
This grant programme is associated with the name of Ann Rylands, daughter of Sir Jules Thorn, who chaired the trust for 24 years following the death of her father, and was responsible for introducing the concept of the Special Project in 1980.

It is the trust's major humanitarian grant scheme, offering charities the opportunity to bid for funding at a level which could have a significant beneficial impact on their work.

Funds are allocated annually to one charitable theme determined by the trustees. The total award may be for up to a maximum of £500,000, but may be spread between several projects related to the same theme.

This programme is available by invitation only from the trust. When the trustees have chosen the annual theme, they select and invite individual charities that work in the appropriate area to submit an application.

Medically-related donations
The trustees endeavour to allocate some funds each year for medicine generally, in addition to their primary commitment to medical research. They keep in mind Sir Jules Thorn's concern to alleviate the suffering of patients and to aid diagnosis.

The resources available are limited and depending on the appeals received the trustees may allocate the total fund in any one year to just one project, or divide it between several deserving appeals. Grants are awarded for a wide range of purposes. They may be linked to a very large appeal to expand important facilities for research in medical schools or to enhance patient care in hospitals. Other grants go to charities whose work is devoted to the care and comfort of patients with distressing clinical conditions. Grants under this programme are not provided for medical research.

Humanitarian
Sir Jules Thorn was a great humanitarian and whilst his endowment was provided primarily for medicine and medical research, he was content for some funds to be allocated to appeals of a humanitarian nature. Accordingly, the trustees earmark some resources each year for such purposes. The trust receives many more appeals than it can support with a grant. Each case is treated on its merits and the trustees' policy is to spread the funds as widely as possible.

The trust has two programmes:

1) Small Grants Programme
The trust receives numerous appeals from fund-raising charities. Those which are successful are awarded grants of up to £1,000. Many charities have received grants over a number of years. Requests are considered for contributions to core funding or for specific projects, but this programme does not provide substantial sums for capital appeals.

2) Larger Humanitarian Grants
Although this programme is not a major part its grant-making activities, the trust has been a consistent supporter of the humanitarian work of a limited number of charities who have received funding over a period of years.

These are restricted currently to special schemes initiated by the trust.

Grantmaking in 2008

In 2008 the trust had assets of £83.1 million and an income of over £4 million. Grants were made totalling £2.9 million, and were broken down as follows:

Category	Amount
Medically-related projects	£1,080,000
The Ann Rylands Special Project	£1,060,000
Medical research projects	£502,000
Small grants	£253,000
Non-medical projects	£25,000

Beneficiaries in the open programmes of medically-related donations and small humanitarian grants included:

Medically-related projects
Moorfields Eye Hospital Development Fund (£526,000), to fund the development of a new stem cell therapy unit to help make stem cell regeneration of the eye, and restoration of vision, a reality; Prior's Court Foundation (£250,000), to fund a training and development centre at Prior's Court School in Thatcham, for children with severe autism; and the National Hospital for Neurology and Neurosurgery Development Foundation (£105,000), towards the brain tumour unit at the hospital.

Small grants
Beneficiaries of £1,000 each, listed in the accounts, included the Anthony Nolan Trust, Changing Faces, Deafblind UK, London's Air Ambulance, SSAFA Forces Help, The Butler Trust, and West Suffolk Voluntary Association for the Blind.

Exclusions The trust does not fund:

- research which is considered unlikely to provide clinical benefit within five years
- research which could reasonably be expected to be supported by a disease specific funder, unless there is a convincing reason why the trust has been approached
- research into cancer or AIDS, for the sole reason that they are relatively well funded elsewhere
- top up grants for ongoing projects
- research which will also involve other funders
- individuals – except in the context of a project undertaken by an approved institution which is in receipt of a grant from the trust
- research or data collection overseas
- research institutions which are not registered charities

351

- third parties raising resources to fund research themselves.

Applications
Medically-related grants

Appeals are considered annually by the trustees, usually in November.

There is no specific application form. Proposals should be submitted to the trust's director and should cover:

- the background to the appeal, including any brochures and feasibility assessment
- information about the applicant, which must be an institution having charitable status. Applications from individuals cannot be considered
- details of the appeal, including the total sum being raised, donations or pledges already received, and the plans for securing the remainder. Time scales for implementation should be given
- The latest trustees' report and audited financial statements should be provided.

Potential applicants who wish to establish whether their appeal would fit the criteria should contact the trust.

Small grants

On an application form available from the trust's website or by contacting the office.

There are no specific dates for submitting applications. Appeals may be made at any time and will be considered by the trustees as soon as possible, depending on volumes.

The Three Guineas Trust

Autism and Asperger's Syndrome

£469,000 (2007/08)

Beneficial area Worldwide, in practice mainly UK.

Allington House, 1st Floor, 150 Victoria Street, London SW1E 5AE

Tel. 020 7410 0330 **Fax** 020 7410 0332

Website www.sfct.org.uk

Correspondent Alan Bookbinder, Director

Trustees *Clare Sainsbury; B Willis; Judith Portrait.*

CC Number 1059652

Information available Accounts were available from the Charity Commission.

This is one of the Sainsbury Family Charitable Trusts, which share a joint administration. They have a common approach to grantmaking which is described in the entry for the group as a whole.

Clare Sainsbury established the Three Guineas Trust in 1996 for general charitable purposes. The trust's present focus is in the area of autism and the related Asperger's Syndrome, but its grantmaking may increase and its interests widen in future years.

There is a specific fund to enable people in developing countries to hire autism practitioners from the UK to deliver practical, one-off training courses for professionals and parents in countries which have little current provision for autistic children and adults.

In 2007/08 the trust had assets of £14 million and an income of £421,000. 17 grants were made totalling £469,000.

The three largest grants went to: National Autistic Society (£94,000); Brighton and Hove Community Initiatives (£85,000); and University of Cambridge – Asperger Resource Centre (£64,000).

Other beneficiaries included: Asperger East Anglia (£50,000); Assert (£33,000); Wirral Autistic Society (£14,000); Human Appeal International (£6,000); Project Ability (£5,000); and the Sainsbury Archive (£650).

Exclusions No grants for individuals or for research (except where it has an immediate benefit).

Applications See the guidance for applicants in the entry for the Sainsbury Family Charitable Trusts. A single application will be considered for support by all the trusts in the group.

The following statement is taken from the trust's 2007/08 accounts and explains it's current application policy:

The trustees do not at present wish to invite applications, except in the field of autism and Asperger's syndrome, where they will examine unsolicited proposals alongside those that result from their own research and contacts with expert individuals and organisations working in this field. The trustees prefer to support innovative schemes that can be successfully replicated or become self-sustaining. They are also keen that, wherever possible, schemes supporting adults and teenagers on the autistic spectrum should include clients/service users in decision-making.

The Tolkien Trust

General charitable purposes

£1.3 million (2007/08)

Beneficial area UK with some preference for Oxfordshire.

9400 Garsington Road, Oxford Business Park North, Oxford OX4 2HN

Tel. 01865 722106 **Fax** 01865 201012

Email cathleen.blacburn@manches.com

Correspondent Cathleen Blackburn

Trustees *Christopher Reuel Tolkien; Priscilla Mary Anne Reuel Tolkien; Joanna Reuel Tolkien; Baillie Tolkien.*

CC Number 273615

Information available Accounts were available from the Charity Commission.

The trust's main assets are the copyrights in relation to certain works written by the late J R R Tolkien including Smith of Wootton Major, Tree and Leaf, Roverandom and Mythopoeia. Although the trust has no permanent endowment, there should always be an income from book royalties during the period of copyright. Recent film treatments of Tolkien's work, and the financial benefits that such initiatives bring, have substantially increased the income of the trust with a consequent significant increase in grant giving.

There are no specific guidelines for applicants. Past donations have been made to charities and charitable causes supporting children, young people, families, older people, homeless people, socially disadvantaged people, organisations supporting overseas aid and development, refugees, medical aid, research, education, the arts and religion.

In 2007/08 the trust had assets of £6.8 million and an income of £578,000. Grants were made to 130 organisations totalling £1.3 million.

Beneficiaries of larger grants were: Oxfam International (£220,000); Rebuilding Sri Lanka (£100,000); St Int Graalbeweging Best (£50,000); Bodleian Library – Archiving (£31,000); St Peter's Church – Eynsham (£30,000); Find Your Feet Limited (£25,000); Medecins Sans Frontieres (£20,000); Botley Alzheimer's Home (£15,000); Emmaus Oxford (£14,000); Ty Hafan Children's Hospice (£13,000); and Medical Foundation for the Care of the Victims of Torture (£10,000).

Smaller grants of less than £10,000 went to: Climate Outreach Information Network (£9,000); Trust for Research and Education on the Arms Trade (£6,000); WWF – Canada (£5,000); Horse's Voice (£3,000); and United Christian Broadcasters Ltd (£2,000).

Applications In writing to the correspondent. The majority of donations are made to charities or causes selected by the trustees. There are no guidelines for applicants and the trust does not enter into correspondence with applicants in the interests of controlling administrative costs. Grant awards are usually made in the spring.

The Tompkins Foundation

Health, education, religion, community projects and general charitable purposes

£343,500 (2007/08)
Beneficial area UK.

7 Belgrave Square, London SW1X 8PH
Tel. 020 7235 9322 **Fax** 020 7259 5129
Correspondent Richard Geoffrey Morris
Trustees *Elizabeth Tompkins; Peter Vaines.*
CC Number 281405
Information available Accounts were available from the Charity Commission.

The foundation was established in 1980 primarily for the advancement of education, learning and religion and the provision of facilities for recreation and other purposes beneficial to the community. However, most beneficiaries tend to be medical or health-related organisations. 'The trustees aim to respond to need and therefore consider that more specific plans [for the future] would be too restrictive.'

In 2007/08 the foundation had assets of £11.5 million and an income of £484,000. Grants were made to 23 organisations totalling £343,500, with 15 of the beneficiaries having received donations in the previous year.

Beneficiaries included: Royal National Orthopaedic NHS Trust and the Foundation of Nursing Studies (£50,000 each); Chicken Shed Theatre (£25,000); International Centre for Children Studies, Toynbee Hall and the Leonard

Cheshire Foundation (£20,000 each); St Edmunds School Fund (£10,000); Isabel Hospice Ball and Gayfields Home of Rest (£5,000 each); Help the Aged and St Mary's Performing Arts (£1,000 each).

Exclusions No grants to individuals.

Applications In writing to the correspondent.

The Constance Travis Charitable Trust

General

£902,500 (2008)
Beneficial area UK (national charities only); Northamptonshire (all sectors).

Quinton Rising, Quinton, Northampton NN7 2EF
Tel. 01604 862296
Correspondent Earnest R A Travis, Trustee
Trustees *Mrs Constance M Travis; Earnest R A Travis; Peta J Travis; Matthew Travis.*
CC Number 294540
Information available Accounts were available from the Charity Commission.

Established in 1986, the trust has general charitable purposes, supporting local organisations in Northamptonshire as well as organisations working UK-wide.

In 2008 the trust had assets of £27.1 million and an income of over £3.9 million from investments and donations. Grants were made during the year to 118 organisations totalling £902,500.

The largest grant was made to the Museum of Leathercraft, which received £100,000. Other larger grants included those to: Northamptonshire Community Foundation (£35,000); Cynthia Spencer Hospice Appeal (£30,000); Age Concern Northamptonshire (£20,000); Three Little Miracles Fund (£15,000); and the Royal Academy of Music (£10,000).

Other beneficiaries included: Deafness Research UK (£7,000); Action for ME, Grange Park Church, Northampton Hope Centre and RNIB (£5,000 each); Crimestoppers Trust and Prisoners Abroad (£4,000 each); Cancerbackup and St Francis' Children's Society (£3,000 each); British Liver Trust and

Volunteer Action Northamptonshire (£2,000 each); and Battersea Dogs & Cats Home and Weston Favell Ceva Primary School (£1,000 each).

Exclusions No grants to individuals or non-registered charities.

Applications In writing to the correspondent.

The Triangle Trust (1949) Fund

Social welfare, health, people with disabilities, integration and general

£574,000 to organisations (2007/08)
Beneficial area Worldwide. In practice UK.

32 Bloomsbury Street, London WC1B 3QJ
Tel. 020 7299 4245
Email lesleylilley@triangletrust.org
Website www.thetriangletrust1949fund.org.uk
Correspondent Lesley Lilley, Secretary to the Trust
Trustees *Melanie Burfitt, Chair; Dr Robert Hale; Mark Powell; Bruce Newbigging; Philip Davies; Kate Purcell; Helen Evans; Jamie Dicks.*
CC Number 222860
Information available Accounts were available from the Charity Commission.

The trust was set up by Sir Henry Jephcott in 1949 for the education and the relief of poverty of past or present employees and their dependants, of the pharmaceutical industry; the promotion of good health; and other charitable purposes.

The trustees prefer to initiate their own projects for funding, and do not normally respond to unsolicited applications. Applications will usually only be accepted from registered charities, and projects submitted must fall within one of the areas of priority funding and pass an additional test [of maintaining an open, inclusive society, or promoting the integration (or reintegration) of individuals or groups into society].

The trust supports long and short term collaborative projects and also makes grants towards the core costs of supported charities. All beneficiaries are expected to make regular reports back to the trust on their expenditure during the course of their grant. Full guidelines are available to download from the trust's website.

Grants in 2007/08

In 2007/08 the trust had assets totalling £16 million and an income of £527,000. Grants were made to 75 organisations totalling £574,000. Of these, seven awards were for grants spread over two or three years. Grants for organisations are mostly for amounts between £1,000 and £5,000 but a small number of causes are supported with larger grants. During the year, grants were distributed in the following priority areas:

Category	Value
Poverty	£140,000
Community arts and education	£133,000
Rehabilitation and integration	£126,000
Carers	£76,000
Disability	£53,000
Older people	£43,000

There were 12 beneficiaries of grants of £10,000 or more, the largest being the Family Welfare Association, which was awarded two grants totalling £55,000, one for education (£45,000) and the other for asylum seekers (£10,000). Other large grants included those made to: Leicester Charity Link (£17,000); Dundee City Council (£16,000); Somerset Community Foundation (£15,000); Seesaw (£13,000); Mobility Trust (£12,000); and Fine Cell Work (£10,000).

Beneficiaries of smaller grants included: Wonderful Beast (£7,500); Aidis Trust (£5,000); 999 Club (£4,000); the Seeing Ear (£3,000); Kennett Furniture Recycling (£2,800); Winchester Young Carers (£2,000); and Beacon of Hope (£1,000).

During the year the trust awarded ten 'block grants' to third party organisations, to be administered in grants to individuals on the trust's behalf. The trust also gives a proportion of its money to individuals in need, mostly former employees of the pharmaceutical industry or their dependants (its founder was chair of Glaxo Laboratories). In 2007/08, 56 individuals received grants totalling £43,000.

Exclusions Generally, only registered charities are funded. In addition the trust will not fund the following:

- direct applications from individuals
- overseas charities or projects outside the UK
- charities for the promotion of religion

- medical research
- environmental, wildlife or heritage appeals
- applications funded in the last two years, unless at the trustees invitation.

Applications Organisations should apply using the trust's application form, available from its website. Guidelines are also provided by the trust. Application hardcopies should be typed, and applicants should include their latest report and accounts with the application form (if submitting an online application, applicants should send their latest report and accounts separately as soon possible).

The trustees meet quarterly in February, June, October and December to award grants. Applications should be submitted in the preceding month (January, May, September and November). Please note: applicants may be asked to present their project(s) to the trustees.

The True Colours Trust

Special needs, sensory disabilities and impairments, palliative care and carers

£2.5 million (2007/08)

Beneficial area Mostly UK and Africa.

Allington House, 1st Floor, 150 Victoria Street, London SW1E 5AE

Tel. 020 7410 0330 **Fax** 020 7410 0332

Email truecolours@sfct.org.uk

Website www.truecolourstrust.org.uk

Correspondent Alan Bookbinder, Director

Trustees *Lucy A Sainsbury; Dominic B Flynn; Bernard J C Willis.*

CC Number 1089893

Information available Accounts were available from the Charity Commission.

Established in 2001, this is one of the newest of the Sainsbury family charitable trusts. It focuses its grantmaking in the following areas:

Children and young people with complex disabilities in the UK

For the foreseeable future the trustees will focus their grantmaking on programmes that will aim to have an impact on the following areas:

- improving understanding of health and safety legislation and reducing the negative impact of the application of the legislation on families and services
- improving the provision of information for families
- reducing poverty and debt in families.

Palliative care for children and young people in the UK

Grantmaking in this category will focus on:

- the establishment of the UK's first Chair in Palliative Care for Children and Young People
- the development of 24 hour support and care for children and their families
- improving the provision of information for families.

Palliative care in sub-Saharan Africa

The trust has significantly increased its support for the development of palliative care in sub-Saharan Africa and expects it to be a major focus in the future. At the time of writing the funding priorities had not yet been set for this programme, so interested groups should contact the trust for more information.

Local Causes for Disadvantaged Children

In addition to the three strategic grant programmes, the trust also makes small grants to local charities supporting disabled children, children with life-limiting conditions, their siblings and their families. The trust is especially keen to support hydrotherapy pools with public access, multi-sensory rooms and other capital improvements or equipment costs which make a significant difference to those using the services.

Please note: grants in this category tend to be small one-off contributions, not multi-year grants for on-going revenue costs. **Unsolicited applications are welcomed.**

In 2007/08 the trust had assets of £3.1 million and an income of £2.9 million. Grants made during the year totalled £2.5 million and were broken down as follows:

Category	Value	%
Children and Young People with Complex Disabilities in the UK	£976,000	38
Palliative Care for Children and Young People in the UK	£779,000	31
Palliative Care in sub-Saharan Africa	£485,000	19
Local Causes for Disadvantaged Children	£84,000	12
General	£1,600	0

Beneficiaries included: Association for Children's Palliative Care (£436,000); African Palliative Care Association (£150,000); National Deaf Children's Society (£148,000); Maua Methodist

Hospital (£90,000); Tower Hamlets Toyhouse Library (£57,000); Back-Up Trust (£25,000); Parity for Disability (£15,000); Children's Adventure Farm Trust (£10,000); and Princess Royal Trust (£6,000).

Exclusions No grants to individuals.

Applications The trust states that projects for the three strategic programmes are usually invited by the trustees or initiated at their request, and while they are keen to learn more about organisations whose work fits into these categories, unsolicited applications are not encouraged and are unlikely to be successful. **Please note: unsolicited applications for the 'Local Causes for Disadvantaged Children' programme are welcomed.**

See the guidance for applicants in the entry for the Sainsbury Family Charitable Trusts. A single application will be considered for support by all the trusts in the group. However, please see comments regarding the selection of beneficiaries.

Trust for London

Social welfare

£779,000 (2008)
Beneficial area Greater London.

6 Middle Street, London EC1A 7PH

Tel. 020 7606 6145 **Fax** 020 7600 1866

Email trustforlondon@cityparochial.org.uk

Website www.trustforlondon.org.uk

Correspondent Bharat Mehta, Clerk to the Trustees

Trustees *Nigel Pantling, Chair; Miles Barber; Maggie Baxter; Tzeggai Yohannes Deres; Revd Dr Martin Dudley; The Archdeacon of London, The Ven. Peter Delaney; Archie Galloway; Roger Evans; Deborah Finkler; Cllr Lynne Hillan; Robert Hughes-Penney; Robert Laurence; Elahe Panahi; Ingrid Posen; Wilfred Weeks; Peter Williams.*

CC Number 294710

Information available Accounts were available from the Charity Commission. Full information is also available on the trust's excellent website.

The Trust for London is an independent charitable trust set up in 1986 to support small, new and emerging voluntary organisations which have been established to improve the lives of people and communities in London. The trustees believe that local people are often in the best position to identify the problems that affect their lives and the possible solutions to those problems and aims to achieve this by funding charitable work. Most of the grants are made through the trust's funding programmes but will occasionally fund special initiatives.

The trust aims to develop supportive relationships with the community and the voluntary organisations that it funds and to provide a 'funding-plus' approach. 'Funding-plus' includes providing advice, guidance, and where appropriate, consultancy support and training to help organisations grow and develop.

The trust's funding guidelines provide information about the organisation, what it will and will not fund, and how to apply for funding. Funding priorities are reviewed every five years to ensure that they are responsive to the changing needs of London's communities.

The Trust for London works closely with its sister fund, City Parochial Foundation, which supports organisations tackling poverty in London. The foundation is operated by the same staff and trustees but has separate funding guidelines.

Guidelines 2007–2011

The trust's guidelines are summarised below. The full document is available from the trust's website.

We are not able to fund all small, new and emerging organisations that apply to us. We will therefore fund areas of work which have one (or more) of the following aims:

- to challenge discrimination faced by disabled people
- to promote the inclusion and integration of recently established communities
- to strengthen mother-tongue and supplementary schools to provide creative educational opportunities
- to address new and emerging needs

Who can apply

You will need to demonstrate that all the criteria below apply to your organisation. You must:

- benefit local people and communities in London
- be run by volunteers or have paid staff that between them work no more than 35 hours per week. This may include full-time or part-time staff but does not include tutors who work sessional hours (for example, teachers at a supplementary school)
- have a high level of user involvement, including on your management committee
- be undertaking charitable work, though you do not have to be a registered charity
- have a constitution or a set of rules which governs your activities
- be run by a group of people who may be called the trustees or the management committee
- have your own bank or building society account where two named people from the trustees or management committee have to sign all the cheques
- be able to provide annual accounts for the last year. If your organisation is very new, copies of your most recent bank or building society statements will do.

In general we will support organisations which have been established for at least a year. However, if you want to start a new organisation, or have recently been set up, you will need to tell us about the needs you are addressing, how you will do this, and provide evidence that you have a number of people involved in running your organisation.

If you are a long-established organisation, you will need to demonstrate that you are addressing new and emerging needs.

Each year we will make grants of approximately £650,000. The majority of this is spent on our open programme.

The maximum you can apply for is £15,000 per year, although the average grant will be approximately £8,000 in total. We will make grants for one, two or three years. We expect to make 50 grants each year.

In addition, we will also make a smaller number of grants to organisations that want to increase their staffing levels in order to make a step change in their development. This may include making a contribution towards the costs of a full-time post.

Grants will be made to organisations that are undertaking work in one of our priority areas. You may need to apply to other funders to fund your proposal jointly with us and we encourage you to do this, as we cannot always provide the total costs of your work.

Organisations which have previously received funding may return for support for work which is particularly effective and continues to meet our criteria and priorities. However, you should not assume we will award further funding and should apply to other funders. If you wish to apply again for the same or different work, you should contact your relevant officer at least eight months before your current funding expires. Generally we do not provide more than one grant at a time through our open programme.

What we will fund

We will support work which meets our areas of work [as outlined above]. This may be for a project or for core costs. These costs may include rent, volunteers' expenses and/or running costs. We do not fund large-scale capital projects but we can make small grants for capital items such as the purchase of equipment.

We want to make sure that our funds reach the people who need them most, especially those who are excluded and are particularly disadvantaged and discriminated against. Some of our work benefits all communities in London, whilst others target particular groups. These may include black and minority ethnic communities, asylum seekers, refugees and migrants, young people, lesbians and gay men, disabled people (including those with mental health issues) and isolated white communities. We therefore welcome applications from these groups and others who are addressing new and emerging needs in London. We also recognise that women experience discrimination in different ways and particularly encourage applications from women's organisations.

Grantmaking in 2008

In 2008 the trust had assets of £14.8 million and an income of £645,000. Grants were made to 47 organisations totalling £779,000.

The following analysis of grantmaking within the Open Programme during the year is taken from the trust's excellent annual report [including grants awarded]. It provides an interesting insight into the aspirations and achievements of an organisation which is dynamic, proactive and not afraid to tackle challenging issues:

Promoting the inclusion and integration of recently established communities – 20 grants totalling £332,000

Refugee and migrant organisations play an important role in supporting people when they arrive in the UK by providing advice and support to access mainstream public services, and by providing opportunities to celebrate culture and identity. These groups may also act as a bridge to integration by working with people from different backgrounds and promoting understanding between them.

In 2008, as in the previous year, most of the applications under this aim were for advice and information services to help recently established communities to access public services – consequently most of our funding went towards supporting this type of activity. For small groups with very limited resources, the priority is often on meeting the pressing needs of their clients, rather than for work whose main focus is on building connections across communities.

Nevertheless, we did fund such work, including providing a grant to Clapham and Stockwell Faith Forum [£8,000], to run arts-based workshops to engage women who would not normally socialise together, particularly those from new migrant communities They will be encouraged to share skills and art forms from their own cultural heritage. Ocean Women's Association [£30,000], was funded to provide a drop-in service and recreational activities for women living in east London. This includes a peer mentoring scheme, where women from different communities will be paired together to practice their English and share experiences. We also funded the Russian Community Association [£8,000], to run events to promote greater integration of Russian-speaking communities in south London.

A number of the groups we fund predominantly support people from a particular country of origin. We also fund a wide range of other groups which focus on one particular community or population – whether that is on the basis of ethnicity, gender, age, geography, sexuality, disability or faith. We were therefore very concerned when the Department for Communities and Local Government (DCLG) published draft guidance for funders, which discouraged grants to what were termed 'single groups', in the interests of community cohesion.

As the DCLG was consulting on the draft guidance we convened a meeting of funders and, together 16 independent charitable trusts made a joint representation strongly opposing it. We argued for recognition of the important role played by single groups in tackling inequality, disadvantage and discrimination. We believe that unless people's immediate needs are met, they will not be in a position to build bridges with other people and communities. We were therefore delighted when the Government eventually decided not to issue such guidance.

This approach also highlighted the value of funders working together and speaking collectively on issues on which they have authority, experience and an evidence base to comment on.

Strengthening mother-tongue and supplementary schools – 15 grants totalling £213,000

Since Trust for London was first established we have recognised the importance of supporting disadvantaged children and young people so that they can reach their full potential. Key to this is education. As a result, one of the areas of work we have funded has been community based mother-tongue and supplementary schools. Our current focus is on schools which provide creative learning. We are also keen on supporting schools which increase parental involvement in their children's education, and which strengthen links between supplementary and mainstream schools.

Our funding has enabled many parents, particularly from newly settled communities, to develop a better understanding of the UK education system and how they can best support their children's education. This included funding the Kongolese Children's Association [£16,000], to provide joint lessons in numeracy and literacy to children and their parents. The lessons will be offered in Lingala and parents will learn English so they can support their children and also learn themselves.

We have also funded a number of schools working together to develop best practice, and to highlight the specific needs of children from black and minority ethnic communities. For example, we funded the Turkish Language, Culture and Education Consortium [£20,000], to provide support to its 17 member schools. Funding will be used to improve the quality of education provided by its members, provide common teaching materials and organise seminars for parents on how they can assist their children to learn.

We strongly believe that mother-tongue and supplementary schools continue to contribute towards children and young people's attainment in mainstream schools. This provision has been invaluable for new arrivals and many migrant communities in developing a strong awareness of their culture, heritage and identity, which helps towards their integration within wider society.

Challenging discrimination faced by disabled people – 9 grants totalling £163,200

We have long been aware of the challenges faced by disabled people, particularly in being able to access the services they need. We recognise many disabled people do not have the opportunity, or feel able, to speak up about the key issues affecting them in their daily lives.

As a result, we decided to support work which gives disabled people a stronger voice and which helps them challenge the discrimination they experience.

In 2007 we received fewer than expected applications under this aim, and those we did receive were often for support services that did not necessarily empower disabled people. We also received few applications from groups that were led-by disabled people.

To address this, in 2008 we actively promoted this funding aim and broadened our eligibility criteria to include disability groups which are part of larger organisations. This approach resulted in an increase in the number of eligible applications during the year and more disability groups being funded.

This included funding Croydon People First [£15,000], for its outreach roadshow, Big Talk on the Road, which aims to improve advocacy services for people with learning disabilities, who may find it difficult to access mainstream services and consultative groups; Islington Borough User Group [£18,000], to encourage mentally ill people to voice their feelings while staying in a mental health institution, by providing volunteers who will visit them and listen to their views; and Newham Ethnic Minority Disability Alliance [£22,500], for its Speaking Out project.

As part of our commitment to making our own information accessible, we also translated our guidelines into audio files, produced an easy-read version, and paid for interpreters for deaf people attending our training courses.

Exclusions The following applications are not considered:

- from organisations which have paid staff who between them work more than 35 hours per week
- for work that is the responsibility of statutory funders such as local and central government and health authorities
- that directly replace or subsidise statutory funding
- from individuals or which are for the benefit of an individual
- for medical purposes including hospitals and hospices
- for distribution by umbrella bodies
- for general appeals
- for holiday playschemes or playgroups
- for major expenses for buying or building premises
- for research
- for trips abroad
- for the promotion of religion
- for work that has already taken place
- for animal welfare
- from applicants who have been rejected by the trust within the last six months
- from organisations which have received funding from the trust's sister fund, City Parochial Foundation.

The trust is unlikely to support proposals:

- from organisations based outside London
- for work that takes place in schools during school hours
- from organisations with significant unrestricted reserves (including those

that are designated). Generally up to six months' expenditure is normally acceptable
- from organisations in serious financial deficit.

Applications The trust's funding guidelines for 2007–11 are available to download from its website. Alternatively contact the trust's office for hard copies. It is strongly recommended that potential applicants read the guidelines before making an application.

There is a two-stage application process:

Stage one
An initial proposal to be submitted by post. There are three closing dates for proposals to be submitted by – you may submit your proposal at any time but it will only be assessed once the next closing date has passed. Closing dates are:

- 7 February for the June Grants Committee
- 30 May for the October Grants Committee
- 25 October for the March Grants Committee.

Stage two
All organisations whose initial proposals are shortlisted will be visited by the foundation to assess their suitability for funding.

The Trusthouse Charitable Foundation

General

£2.1 million (2007/08)

Beneficial area Unrestricted, but mainly UK.

6th Floor, 65 Leadenhall Street, London EC3A 2AD

Tel. 020 7264 4990

Website www. trusthousecharitablefoundation.org.uk

Correspondent Judith Leigh, Grants Manager

Trustees *Sir Richard Carew Pole, Chair; Sir Jeremy Beecham; Lord Bernstein of Craigwell; The Baroness Cox of Queensbury; The Earl of Gainsborough; The Duke of Marlborough; The Hon. Mrs Olga Polizzi; Sir Hugh Rossi; The Lady Stevenson; Baroness Hogg; Anthony Peel; Lady Janet Balfour of Burleigh.*

CC Number 1063945

Information available Accounts were available from the Charity Commission.

The Trusthouse Charitable Foundation was formed out of a trust operated by the Council of Forte plc which inherited investments in the Granada Group. Its objects are such general charitable purposes as the trustees in their discretion may from time to time determine.

The trust currently awards around 350 grants a year totalling around £2 million. The average grant is £6,000 though they can range from £1,000 to £30,000. The trust is administered on a day-to-day basis on behalf of the trustees by the Henry Smith Charity, although each charity is entirely independent.

Funding policy

In 2008, the trust completed a review of its grants criteria and has decided on a new policy, which concentrates grants on areas and charities where they can have the greatest impact. The following is taken from the trust's website and explains the new policy in more detail.

There are now two overarching themes to our grants:

Rural Issues: we accept applications from local and national charities or not-for-profit organisations which are addressing issues in needy rural areas. 'Rural' in this context means cities, towns, villages and areas with 10,000 or less inhabitants. We are interested in, for example, projects providing transport for older people, disabled or disadvantaged; contact networks for young disabled people; projects which encourage a sense of community such as community centres and village halls; employment training schemes especially those promoting local, traditional crafts; and projects addressing issues such as drug/alcohol misuse or homelessness.

Urban Deprivation: we accept applications from local or national charities or not-for-profit organisations which are working with residents of urban areas (more than 10,000 inhabitants) which are classified in the latest government Indices of Multiple Deprivation as being in the lowest 20%. We are interested in, for example, youth clubs; training schemes to help people out of unemployment; and drop in centres for the homeless.

Themed Grant: from July 2009, Trusthouse will start a three year themed grant which will fund projects addressing mental health issues for prisoners and ex-offenders. If you are working in this field, please call us for an initial discussion. We will then send you details of how to apply nearer the time.

Your application should clearly demonstrate how your project fits into one or other of these themes.

Within the trust's overarching themes, there are three broad areas of funding: community support; disability and healthcare; and arts, education and heritage.

Community Support
The trustees will consider applications in respect of:

Community – the support of carers; projects in deprived communities including community centres offering (for example) employment advice, training, debt counselling; provision of sporting facilities or equipment in deprived areas.

Drugs and Alcohol – rehabilitation of substance and alcohol mis-users.

Older people – projects addressing isolation and loneliness (for example, befriending schemes and lunch clubs); domiciliary support (for example, respite for carers), residential improvements/adaptations.

Ex-offenders – projects working with prisoners and ex-offenders to improve their life skills and reduce re-offending.

Young People – projects which build the confidence, life skills and employment skills of young people in need and holidays for deprived children and young people.

Health Care & Disability
The trustees will consider applications in respect of:

Physical and Mental Disability – projects involving rehabilitation, (including related arts and sport programmes); projects particularly for ex-service men and women (including former employees of the emergency services); projects for children (including holidays); and respite care.

Hospices & Palliative Care – the provision of domiciliary care; support for volunteers and carers; outreach services; the refurbishment of premises; the provision of equipment (excluding in all cases services or costs which are normally funded from statutory sources).

Medicine – support services (for example, specialist medical helplines) for those suffering from life limiting illnesses (medical research projects are not included).

Arts, Education and Heritage
The trustees will consider applications in respect of:

Arts – projects which enable the disabled and people living in areas of need and poverty to participate in the performance arts and to experience artistic excellence in the performing arts; projects which encourage and give opportunities to young talented people whose circumstances might otherwise deny them.

Education – projects which help children at risk of exclusion or with exceptionally challenging behaviour to realise their educational potential; projects which encourage and give opportunities to young talented people whose circumstances might otherwise deny them access to further/higher education.

Heritage: community projects (excluding large capital appeals) which restore and bring back into use heritage properties and resources, particularly in areas of need and poverty.

Please note: the trust welcomes an initial phone call to discuss whether the project fits within the guidelines.

Types of grant
The foundation offers grants under two separate programmes:

The Small Grant Programme (capital and revenue)
- offers grants under £10,000 only to organisations with annual incomes below £300,000
- grants are for one-off purposes within the priorities set out above and must be spent within six months of receipt
- grants can be for one-off capital items, such as equipment or small capital works, or towards six months running costs
- for requests of under £5,000, there is a programme to 'fast track' the appeals so that applicants will know the outcome within six to eight weeks of receipt of the application.

Applicants should complete the small grants form (Form A), which is available to download from the trust's website.

The Large Grant Programme
- is available to all organisations of any size
- normally offers grants of between £10,000 and £30,000 for capital projects only (such as equipment, building or capital works) within the priorities set out above
- capital grants will not normally be offered to very large capital projects (for example, over £1 million), but individual and discrete elements of very large projects may be considered when a significant proportion of the total appeal has already been raised.

Applicants should complete the large grants form (Form B), which is available to download from the trust's website.

Please note: the trust states that there is a high demand for larger grants and at present only one in ten applications is successful. Therefore, applicants should consider applying for a small grant if

their annual income is below £300,000 as they may stand more chance of success.

Application is by competitive process and the trustees' decisions will reflect their assessment of the relative merits of different applications and the overall balance of demand and the funds available.

Projects within the UK – The trustees will consider applications from anywhere in the UK, especially those concerned with areas of deprivation. It is not necessary to be a registered charity in order to apply however applications will only be considered from not-for-profit organisations.

Projects outside the UK – The trustees will also consider applications from charities based in the UK which undertake healthcare, health education and community projects; and projects supporting charitable work in developing countries. The foundation currently spends around 10% of its grants budget on overseas projects.

Grants in 2007/08
During the year the foundation had assets of £67 million and an income of £2.4 million. Grants were made totalling £2.1 million and were distributed as follows:

Category	No.	Value
Disabilities	65	£340,000
Young people	57	£278,000
Trustee nominations*	99	£236,000
Themed grants programme – rural older people	13	£217,000
Community service	45	£189,000
Arts	27	£115,000
Older people	23	£108,000
Medical	5	£95,000
Overseas	21	£84,000
Family support services	10	£74,000
Rehabilitation of offenders	9	£59,000
Homeless	6	£40,000
Counselling	8	£39,000
Hospices	4	£38,000
Domestic violence	5	£27,000
Education	4	£26,000
Carers	6	£26,000
Substance misuse	4	£19,000
Sport	7	£18,000
Refugees and asylum seekers	4	£17,000
Ethnic minorities	4	£15,000
Ex-service	1	£7,500
Hospice support	1	£5,000

*The trust allocates £20,000 to each trustee to make in grants at their discretion for charitable purposes outside the guidelines. Grants are released upon the approval of the grants committee.

Beneficiaries included: Age Concern – Montgomeryshire (£39,000); Arch – North Staffordshire (£23,000); Linden Lodge Charitable Trust (£20,000); Bluecoat Arts Centre Ltd (£15,000); Ravensthorpe Community Centre and LEPRA (£10,000 each); Storybook Dads

(£9,500); Mentoring Plus Ltd (£8,000); Wings – Wombourne Special Needs Support Group (£7,000); Autism Networks and Leeds Black Elders Association (£6,000 each); Home-Start Isle of Wight and Northampton Hope Centre (£4,000 each); King's Outreach (£3,000); Musical Arc (£1,500); Thorpland United Football Club (£1,100); and Merthyr Women's Aid (£800).

Exclusions The foundation will not normally consider supporting the following:

- animal welfare
- applications for revenue funding for more than one year
- capital appeals for places of worship
- grant-making organisations or umbrella groups
- grants for individuals
- feasibility studies and evaluations
- local authorities
- local education authority schools or their PTA's, except if those schools are for students with special needs
- medical research projects
- organisations that have received a grant for three consecutive years from the foundation
- projects involving the start-up or piloting of new services
- projects where the primary objective is environmental or conservation
- projects where the primary objective is the promotion of a particular religion
- revenue funding for organisations with an income of over £300,000 a year
- services operated by the NHS
- social research
- training of professionals within the UK
- renovation or alteration projects to make a building compliant with the Disability & Discrimination Act
- office IT equipment.

Applications The trustees require all applicants to complete a one page application form which summarises their appeal [...] All sections of the form must be completed fully, it is not sufficient to refer to 'see attached documents'. Applicants are also required to provide supporting information on approximately two A4 sheets in accordance with the following guidelines.

Applicants should:

- state clearly who they are, what they do and whom they seek to help
- give the applicant's status, such as registered charity (applications can also be considered from not-for-profit organisations which are not registered charities)

- describe clearly the project for which the grant is sought answering the following questions: what is the aim of the project and why is it needed; what practical results will it produce; and how many people will benefit
- state what funds have already been raised for the project, and name any other sources of funding applied for
- include a detailed budget for the project
- ask for a specific amount
- explain how the project will be monitored and evaluated
- explain where on-going funding (if required) will be obtained when the foundation's grant has been used
- include the organisation's most recent accounts agreed by an auditor or independent examiner. If these accounts show a significant surplus or deficit, please explain
- for overseas and large grants only, give the name and addresses of two independent referees i.e. people who can provide an assessment of your organisation's work but who are not directly involved with it (trustees of your organisation are not counted as being independent).

Please keep the application as simple as possible and avoid the use of technical terms, acronyms and jargon. Please do not send DVDs or CD Roms.

Application forms are available to download from the trust's website. Organisations applying for small grants should complete Form A, and those applying for large grants should complete Form B.

Applications can be submitted at any time of the year. A letter acknowledging the application will be sent within two weeks of receipt. Summaries of applications which are within the foundation's priorities and guidelines are sent to trustees with advice. If there is sufficient support, the application will be submitted to a meeting of the grants committee for a decision. Before the meeting, applicants will be asked to provide written confirmation that all staff working with the client group concerned have had appropriate checks through the Criminal Records Bureau. If a grant of more than £10,000 is under consideration, an assessment visit may be made by one of the staff or an independent assessor. If there is insufficient support, applicants will be informed, usually, within six weeks of receipt.

The grants committee meets quarterly to consider supported applications in February, May, July and November. Applications must be received at least eight weeks prior to a meeting in order to be considered at the next meeting but it cannot be guaranteed that any appeal will go to a particular meeting. Applicants whose appeals have

been considered at those meetings will be informed in writing of the trustees' decision within two weeks of the meeting. If a grant is awarded, only one grant can be supported in any 12 month period.

Applicants who are unsuccessful are required to wait a minimum of six months from the date of notification before reapplying.

Applicants whose appeals are outside the foundation's objects or current policy will be notified within four weeks of receipt

Please note: the trust states that there is a high demand for larger grants and at present only one in ten applications is successful. Therefore, applicants should consider applying for a small grant if their annual income is below £300,000 as they may stand more chance of success.

The Tubney Charitable Trust

Conservation of the natural environment and welfare of farmed animals

£7.4 million (2007/08)

Beneficial area Unrestricted, with a possible preference for the south of England.

First Floor, Front Wing, 30–31 Friar Street, Reading RG1 1DX

Tel. 0118 958 6100 **Fax** 0118 959 4400

Email info@tubney.org.uk

Website www.tubney.org.uk

Correspondent Sarah Ridley, Executive Director

Trustees *Jonathan Burchfield, Chair; Terry Collins; Jim Kennedy; René Olivieri.*

CC Number 1061480

Information available Accounts were available at the Charity Commission. The trust has an excellent website.

The Tubney Charitable Trust was created in 1997 for general charitable purposes by Miles Blackwell, retired chair of Blackwell Limited, the Oxford-based bookseller. His wife Briony was an original trustee of the trust. Miles and Briony Blackwell shared a great love of the countryside and animals, as well as a concern for the environment, and supported many charities during their lives to further their interests.

Miles and Briony died unexpectedly in 2001, at 56 and 46 respectively.

Following the subsequent bequest of their estate to the trust, it grew substantially in size. Since that time, the trustees have sought to fund areas which they believe the founders would have supported.

Please note: **the trust plans to allocate its remaining funds by 2011. For this reason it has closed its open programmes in order to focus on funding proactive work on an invitation-to-bid basis only.**

The following is taken from the trust's website and explains its position in more detail.

In accordance with the wishes of the founders, Miles and Briony Blackwell, the charity has a limited life and is spending both its income and its capital to achieve its objectives. During their strategic review at the beginning of 2008, the trustees confirmed their desire to achieve a meaningful impact on UK biodiversity and farmed animal welfare that will endure beyond the short lifespan of the trust. Importantly, the trustees made the decision that over approximately three years they will allocate most of the trust's remaining uncommitted funds (in the region of £26 million) to a small number of large, focused grants. For this reason the trustees have chosen to close the charity's open programmes and to focus on funding proactive work with grants being provided on an invitation-to-bid basis. The trust expects to allocate its funds over a period of about three years from early 2008. Its operational capacity will then be reduced and the trust will cease sometime thereafter.

The trust has established two initiatives under which grants will be awarded on an invitation-to-bid basis only:

1) Conservation of the Natural Environment Initiative
This includes:

- enhancement of UK biodiversity through work with land owners on a landscape scale
- conservation of the marine biodiversity of the UK
- conservation of uncharismatic UK species.

2) Farmed Animal Welfare Initiative
The trust supports three key areas under this programme:

a) Catalysing changes among those involved in the production, consumption and regulation of animals reared for food by:

- enabling high welfare production
- encouraging high welfare consumption
- ensuring better regulation.

b) Addressing the most pressing species-specific farmed animal welfare concerns, including:

- ending the use of cages for laying hens
- improving the welfare of broiler chickens
- ending tail docking of pigs
- reducing metabolic disease and increasing the welfare of dairy cows.

c) Strengthening the farmed animal welfare sector.

Grantmaking

In 2007/08 the trust had assets of £29 million and an income of £2.1 million. Grants were made to 27 organisations totalling £7.4 million.

Grants for 2007/08 were categorised as follows:

Conservation of the natural environment – 18 grants totalling £3.2 million
Beneficiaries included: Woodland Trust (£750,000); Devon Wildlife Trust (£500,000); National Trust (£222,000); Cumbria Wildlife Trust (£104,000); Vale Landscape Heritage Trust (£70,000); Tweed Forum Ltd. (£69,000); Yorkshire Dales Millennium Trust (£60,000); Little Ouse Headwaters Charity (£55,000); and Argyll Green Woodworkers Association (£46,000).

Welfare of farmed animals – 9 grants totalling £4.1 million
Grants were made to: Farm Animal Welfare Trust (£1.5 million); RSPCA (£1.2 million); University of Bristol – 2 grants (£965,000); Compassion in World Farming Trust – 3 grants (£243,000); World Society for the Protection of Animals (£100,000); and Soil Association (£66,000).

Applications As of June 2008 the trust no longer accepts unsolicited applications. Applications will be on an invitation-to-bid basis only.

The James Tudor Foundation

Relief of sickness, medical research, health education and palliative care

£607,500 (2007/08)
Beneficial area UK and overseas.

WestPoint, 78 Queens Road, Clifton, Bristol BS8 1QU

Tel. 0117 985 8715 **Fax** 0117 985 8716

Email admin@jamestudor.org.uk

Website www.jamestudor.org.uk

Correspondent The Secretary

Trustees *Martin G Wren, Chair; Richard R G Esler; Malcolm R Field; Roger K Jones; Cedric B Nash.*

CC Number 1105916

Information available Accounts were available from the Charity Commission. The foundation also has a helpful website.

The foundation was established in 2004. It makes grants for charitable purposes, usually in the UK, across six programme areas:

- palliative care
- medical research
- health education, awards and scholarship
- the direct relief of sickness
- the UK independent healthcare sector
- the fulfilment of the foundation's charitable objects by other means.

In line with the principal objective, the foundation seeks to help small charities stay on their feet, to significantly improve the financial position of medium to large charities and to contribute to medical research where there is a probability of positive clinical outcomes.

The following information is taken from the foundation's website.

Types of funding
Direct project support
This is the most successful area for funding requests.

Research
We will fund research where its aims match our objects and where we consider that it is likely to have a beneficial impact.

Awards and scholarships
We will occasionally fund awards and scholarships where they demonstrate that they contribute to the foundation's areas of benefit.

Building or refurbishment projects
The foundation is less likely to make grants towards capital projects (such as buildings and refurbishment costs). However, capital projects will be supported where clear benefit and good management are demonstrable.

Equipment
Items of equipment may be funded, particularly if part of a wider proposal. You should contact us first if your proposal includes requests for equipment funding.

Staffing
Staffing is occasionally supported. We would normally expect to see a proposal where self-financing is indicated within three years.

In 2007/08 the foundation had assets of £23.1 million and an income of £792,000. Grants were made totalling £607,500, broken down as follows:

Category	Value
Medical research	£181,500
Palliative care	£156,000
Health education	£101,500
Direct relief of sickness	£87,500
Other	£81,000

Beneficiaries included:

Medical Research
Tommy's, the Baby Charity (£75,000 in total); Tim Reeve Foundation/University College London (£30,000); School of Nursing and Midwifery – University of Southampton (£19,500); Islet Research (£17,500); The Raynaud's and Scleroderma Association (£16,500); CORE (£15,000); and the Meningitis Trust (£8,000).

Palliative Care
Children's Hospice South West (£45,000); St Peter's Hospice – Bristol (£35,000); CLIC (£16,000); Haven House (£10,000); and Lakelands Day Hospice (£5,000).

Direct Relief of Sickness
Barnet Care and Support Service (£12,500); World Medical Fund (£10,000); Twinkle House – Lancashire (£8,000); Sense International (£5,000); and Womankind – Bristol (£2,500).

Other
National Rheumatoid Arthritis Association (£15,000); Braveheart – Falkirk and Clackmannanshire (£10,000); Locharber Centre for Deaf People in Scotland (£4,800); National Tremor Association (£4,000); and Community Relief North London (£1,000).

Health Education
Cancer Thermal Ablation – Middlesex Hospital (£10,000); National Organisation for Foetal Alcohol Syndrome (£5,000); One25 – Bristol (£4,000); and Children Living with Inherited Metabolic Disease (£2,000).

The UK Independent Healthcare sector
No applications received in 2007/08.

Exclusions We will not accept applications for grants:

- that directly replace, or negatively affect, statutory funding
- for work that has already taken place
- for endowment funds
- for economic, community development or employment use
- for adventure or residential courses, expeditions or overseas travel
- for sport or recreation uses, including festivals
- for environmental, conservation or heritage causes
- for animal welfare
- from applicants who have applied to us within the last 12 months.

Applications On an application form available from the foundation's website. Comprehensive guidelines for applicant are also available from there.

The Tudor Trust

Welfare and general

£17.8 million (2008/09)

Beneficial area UK and sub-Saharan Africa.

7 Ladbroke Grove, London W11 3BD
Tel. 020 7727 8522 **Fax** 020 7221 8522
Website www.tudortrust.org.uk
Correspondent The Trustees
Trustees Mary Graves; Helen Dunwell; Desmond Graves; Nell Buckler; Christopher Graves; Catherine Antcliff; Louise Collins; Elizabeth Crawshaw; Matt Dunwell; James Long; Ben Dunwell; Francis Runacres; Monica Barlow; Vanessa James.
CC Number 1105580
Information available Excellent annual report and accounts are available from the trust. The trust's website also includes full, clear guidelines for applicants.

The trust meets a range of both capital and revenue needs, notably including related building costs, for voluntary and community groups. Grants can be of all sizes, very often to be paid over a period of two or three years. There is no maximum or minimum grant amount.

Much larger grants can be made, but these are more likely to be the result of proactive work by the trust.

Grants for work outside the UK are targeted and proactive, and therefore applications are not sought for this aspect of the trust's work.

In 2008/09 the trust had assets of £205 million and an income of £13.5 million.

Background

The trust was founded in 1955 by Sir Godfrey Mitchell who endowed it with shares in the Wimpey construction company (making this one of the extraordinary number of major trusts with their origins in the building industry).

The trust spends from both income and capital, and has so far maintained its levels of grantmaking despite reductions in both income and, to a greater extent, in the value of its investment portfolio.

The trustees include a substantial number of family members, including Christopher Graves who is also the director of the trust.

Grants committees meet every three weeks and are made up of both trustees and staff (though grants are the overall responsibility of the trustee committee which also itself considers some of the more substantial grants).

The staffing is modest for an organisation spending this amount of money and allocating around 350 grants a year. The 'support costs' of the grant-making activity represent around 5% of the grant total. In part this may be made possible by a substantial degree of voluntary input from trustees.

Review of Grantmaking Activities 2008/09

The following is taken from the trust's excellent annual report:

The Board set a flexible budget at the beginning of the year and agreed that, as in previous years, funds to resource this would be drawn from both income and capital. It was the trustees' intention to make no more than 350 grants: in the event we made 325 commitments (2008: 392) to a total of £17.8 million (2008: £20.4 million). The size of the average grant continues to increase, standing at £54,808 in 2009 (2008: £52,103).

Our grantmaking in 2008 was at the upper end of our budget range for that year: as noted in last year's annual report we made more grants than planned (392 against an intention of 350). The reduction in grant expenditure in 2009 therefore represents a return to more sustainable levels, with the reduction in the number of grants made allowing us to engage fully both with applicants and grant holders. The level of our grant commitments in 2009 is comparable with that of 2007 (£17.9 million).

Perhaps surprisingly, given the external economic climate and the relative openness of our guidelines, the number of applications received continued to go down, dipping below 3,000. However it is encouraging to note that the proportion of 'eligible' applications continues to increase: our hope is that clear and straightforward funding guidelines, and easy access to advice over the telephone and via our website, will continue to reduce the number of applications from groups which aren't eligible to apply for funding.

Activity	2009	2008
Number of applications	2,948	3,199
Number of eligible applications	2,619	2,801
Applications presented to committee	354	436
Number of grants made	325	392
Number of loans made	1	2
Total amount committed	£17,800,000	£20,400,000
Average grant	£54,808	£52,103

The 325 grants and one loan we made over the year addressed our ultimate aim of tackling the social, emotional and financial needs of people on the margins of society in many different ways. As we have no set funding priorities the sort of work we support is hugely varied – from an organisation supporting Gypsies and Travellers in Cornwall to a community launderette on an estate in Nottingham; from a self-help project for men in Derry to funding towards a new community building in Easterhouse, Glasgow. There is no common thread in terms of what these organisations do or who they work with – what they share is their energy, their strong foundations in their communities, a focus on inclusion, connection and integration and a clear sense of the difference they want to make.

Although we no longer fund under specific remit headings, we continue to code our grants by subject area so that we can maintain an overview of the sort of work we are supporting, and compare projects working with specific client groups or addressing similar issues. The table below gives more detail on how our grants were allocated across these various thematic areas in 2009.

As ever, the largest proportion (28%) of our funding supported work under the Community heading. As well as encompassing community development work, community centres and other community facilities such as community gardens and city farms this heading covers work ranging from local food projects to support for refugees and asylum seekers.

Tudor has always had a strong focus on supporting smaller-scale organisations, and this continued in the year under review. Our interest in smaller groups arises from our commitment to supporting groups which are firmly rooted in the communities in which they are based and our sense that our funding and support can really make a difference to smaller groups which might struggle to bring in funding from elsewhere.

Given our interest in funding groups providing direct services to marginalised people, and on work which has developed out of real community need, we also monitor the proportion of our grants going to either BME-led groups or towards specific work with BME communities: in 2009, 11% of our grants by value went towards work that was described by the funded organisation as having a specific BME focus (2008: 15%).

Tudor has a strong interest in funding capital projects, recognising that, in the right circumstance, owning a building can increase an organisation's confidence and stability and can help secure its future. We are, however, making significantly fewer capital grants than we did a few years ago: in 2001, 15% of our grants went towards capital projects while in 2009 only 6% of our grants were 'pure' capital grants. However alongside straightforward capital grants we made a

number of grants over the year connected to current or future building projects – for things like a premises search, a feasibility study, the salary of a development worker to take forward a capital project or the running costs of a self-help housing organisation. When these sorts of grants are included in the capital category we are then looking at a rather more substantial proportion of our grants – 10% – going towards some aspect of a capital project.

The capital projects Tudor has supported over the years range from voluntary sector offices and community centres to hostels, rehabilitation centres and housing. Tudor's long-term interest in the issue of affordable housing developed in a new direction during the year under review as we worked with the Esmee Fairbairn Foundation and Venturesome to establish the Community Land Trust Fund, which was launched in September 2008. Through a Community Land Trust (CLT), local people acquire co-operative ownership of land with the intention of creating affordable housing which will benefit the local area and its inhabitants in perpetuity.

Although interest in the CLT model is strong and growing, CLTs have found it difficult to access both the technical support they need to help them develop their ideas and the development finance required to bring their plans to fruition. The Community Land Trust Fund has therefore been set up with the aim of helping to establish new Community Land Trusts and to support the development of affordable housing. Tudor is acting as the administrator for the feasibility and technical assistance components of the Community Land Trust Fund and has allocated £94,000 towards this; a further £656,000 has been invested in the Community Land Trust Investment Fund, held and managed by Venturesome.

Another area of long-standing interest for Tudor is prison visitors' centres: in the past we have funded the development of new centres at HMPs Belmarsh, Edinburgh, Featherstone and Holloway. During the year under review trustees agreed to finance the construction of a new family visitors' centre at HMP Wormwood Scrubs. The planned centre for Wormwood Scrubs represents a distillation of Tudor's experience in developing the previous project and our hope is that it will prove to be an exemplar for the future. The intention is that the new family visitors' centre will be open in early 2010, managed by Prison Advice & Care Trust for the first two years.

Over the year we maintained a balance of reactive and proactive grantmaking across the UK. London continued to receive a significant proportion of our funding, although at a reducing level when compared to previous years: 23% of our grants by

THE TUDOR TRUST

	No. of grants	%	Value of grants	%
Young people	44	13%	£2,760,000	15%
Older People	11	3%	£514,000	3%
Community	97	30%	£4,970,000	28%
Relationships	33	10%	£2,030,000	11%
Housing	22	6%	£1,050,000	6%
Mental Health	40	12%	£2,100,000	12%
Substance Misuse	6	4%	£450,000	3%
Learning	8	2%	£331,750	2%
Financial Security	10	3%	£753,500	4%
Criminal Justice	29	9%	£1,820,000	10%
Overseas	25	8%	£1,010,000	6%
Total	**325**	**100%**	**£17,800,000**	**100%**

value (2008: 25%; 2007: 27%) went to organisations based in the capital. However, this figure includes grants to London-based organisations which have a national or regional focus: adjusting our figures to take this into account gives a reduced percentage of 19%.

The following table shows how our grants were allocated by region in 2009. It is good to note that an increased level of funding went to Northern Ireland – 11 grants comprising 4% of our total commitment, compared with 5 grants making up only 1% of our commitment in 2008. This reflects our efforts to revitalise contact with groups in Northern Ireland through a regular programme of visits: during the period under review Tudor grants managers visited 14 organisations across the province over two three-day visits.

Guidelines 2009–2011

The Tudor Trust is an independent grant-making charitable trust which supports organisations working across the UK. We do not focus our funding on specific themes or programmes. Instead we want to fund a wide range of people and organisations working to achieve lasting change in their communities. Our role is to support and enable their visions, trusting the groups we fund to do the work that is needed.

Tudor aims to support work which addresses the social, emotional and financial needs of people at the margins of our society. We are interested in how organisations tackle these needs, and their root causes. We want to encourage growth, progression and development, not just keeping things as they are.

Although we still make grants across our established funding areas (young people, older people, community, relationships, housing, mental health, substance misuse, learning, financial security and criminal justice) we are also open to hearing about work in areas we have not funded before. The key characteristics we look for in the organisations we support are described [in the next two sections].

We receive many more applications than we will ever be able to fund, so we have introduced a two-stage application process. This is designed to reduce the time, effort and resources organisations spend on their first approach to us. All applicants are therefore asked to complete a brief first-stage proposal for initial assessment [see Applications].

There are some types of organisation and work which we will not consider for funding [see Exclusions].

What kind of funder is Tudor?

We know that solutions to the difficulties people face are seldom straightforward or immediate. We are therefore interested in encouraging people to use their own skills and abilities as a resource for change; to find new ways of tackling deep-rooted problems or to cope with and move on from difficult situations. We recognise that this may take time so, if appropriate, we can commit funding over a sustained period.

As an independent grantmaker, an important part of our role is to support work which is untried, which has uncertain outcomes and which may be difficult to fund. However, we are not preoccupied with innovation and understand that there is a place for well-founded, practical work which seeks to bring normality and wellbeing into difficult places and situations.

We are most interested in helping smaller, under-resourced organisations which offer direct services and which involve the people they work with in their planning. The groups we fund don't have to be registered charities; we can also make grants to other groups as long as they can show us how they would use our grant for charitable purposes.

We want to fund effective people who work to high standards. We recognise that their organisations are best placed to know what the problems are and what to do about them. We trust these groups to go ahead and do the work that is needed, and want to give them the opportunity and practical tools to do so. We want to respond to ideas and energy. We don't have specific funding programmes designed to advance a particular agenda. Instead, we try to support work which is clearly needed and for which funding from Tudor can make all the difference.

Tudor aims to be a helpful and flexible funder and we want to respond imaginatively to organisations' real concerns and priorities.

Organisations dealing with complex issues are seldom themselves straightforward and so we hope to engage with the groups we support in a variety of ways, offering grants, loans, advice and development support.

Grants can take the form of core funding (including salaries and running costs), development funding, project grants or capital grants for buildings or equipment. As we want to fund work which engages with the reality and complexity of people and their problems, we look to support organisations working across sectors and boundaries (whether actual or perceived).

We usually make grants over one, two or three years, but may sometimes work alongside organisations for a longer period. However as we are keen to support a range of organisations, including those which are new to us, our funding cannot continue indefinitely.

We want to offer high levels of support and engagement when this will be helpful and appropriate. Our two-stage application process gives us more time to focus on working creatively with applicants who reach the second stage. Through constructive dialogue and increased understanding we hope to give applicants the opportunity to think about their options and develop proposals which focus on the real needs of their organisations and the people they are working with.

What are we looking for when we make grants?

Tudor's focus is on smaller groups, led by people of vision, which are committed to growth, progression and development. Some of the other characteristics we are looking for when we make grants include:

- organisations which are embedded in and have developed out of their community – whether the local area or a 'community of interest'
- organisations providing direct services to marginalised people

THE TUDOR TRUST
Grants by region: 2009

Region	No. of grants	Value of grants	Percentage	Grant per head (UK only)
East Midlands	14	£780,000	5%	£0.19
Eastern	8	£482,500	3%	£0.09
London	69	£4,070,000	23%	£0.57
North East	10	£622,250	3%	£0.25
North West	43	£2,150,000	12%	£0.32
Northern Ireland	11	£776,200	4%	£0.46
Scotland	23	£1,200,000	7%	£0.24
South East	21	£1,140,000	6%	£0.14
South West	42	£2,000,000	11%	£0.41
Wales	13	£794,500	5%	£0.27
West Midlands	13	£756,588	4%	£0.14
Yorkshire & the Humber	32	£1,970,000	11%	£0.40
Overseas	26	£1,060,000	6%	N/A
Total	**325**	**£17,800,000**	**100%**	**N/A**

- a focus on building stronger communities by overcoming isolation and fragmentation and encouraging inclusion, connection and integration
- high levels of user involvement, and an emphasis on self-help where this is appropriate
- work which addresses complex and multi-stranded, often difficult, problems in unusual or imaginative ways
- organisations which are thoughtful in their use of resources and which foster community resilience in the face of environmental, economic or social change
- organisations and people who know what difference they want to make and have the energy and vision to make it happen.

We can only consider making a capital grant for new premises or for building improvements if the organisations using the building display some of these characteristics. Good buildings which contribute positively to their environment are important, but we are most interested in what goes on inside the building and the difference building improvements would make to your work.

We are more likely to fund groups with an annual turnover of less than £1 million.

How likely are you to receive a grant from Tudor?

We aim to make around 350 grants a year but receive thousands of applications. There is no minimum or maximum grant amount that the trust will consider. It is important to understand that only a small proportion of applicants will receive a grant from Tudor, and that your proposal may be turned down even if your work falls within our guidelines. We do not want applicants to have unrealistic expectations.

This is why we have a two-stage application process. We know that putting together a full funding application places heavy demands on your time and resources, so we are asking all applicants to complete a brief first-stage proposal instead. These will be read by Tudor's trustees and staff, and those we can take forward for detailed discussion with the trustees are asked to complete a full application.

We estimate that only around one in ten applicants will go through to the second stage. Many proposals rejected at the first stage will be for valuable and interesting work; they may be rejected simply because the ideas are not ones that the trustees can take forward at that moment. Because of the numbers of applications we receive, we cannot provide individual feedback on why we are not taking your proposal through to the second stage.

If you are asked to complete a full second-stage application the chances of succeeding will be higher. But not all second-stage applications will receive funding; even at this stage the trustees have to make difficult choices about what they fund.

Recent beneficiaries

The following is a sample of beneficiaries from the 2009/10 financial year, and the purposes for which grants were made:

Family Centre Trust (£1.3 million), towards the capital costs of building a new family and visitors' centre at HMP Wormwood Scrubs; Transition Network (£240,000), over 2 years towards core costs, including salaries, for a national organisation which leads on the transition model working to help communities change how they will use energy in the future; Music in Detention (£108,000), over 3 years towards the salary of a programme manager for an organisation running music workshops with detainees in immigration removal centres; Beat (£100,000), over 3 years to fund a network support officer to support and develop eating disorder self-help groups throughout England; Longbenton Community Action Team (£80,000), over 3 years towards the salary of a community animator to continue the 'Listening Matters' process and support residents of Longbenton, Newcastle-upon-Tyne to make changes to benefit their community; Open Door – St Albans (£50,000), towards the refurbishment of a hostel for homeless people; North Glasgow Community Food Initiative (£45,000), over 3 years as continuation core funding for this healthy eating and local food growing project for marginalised communities, including refugees and asylum seekers; Mankind UK (£30,000), over 3 years towards the running costs of an organisation supporting adult male victims of rape and sexual abuse in the South East; Holbeck Elderly Aid (£20,000), towards core funding for this older people's resource centre in Leeds; and East Howden Community Association (£15,000), as continuation funding towards the salary of a development worker at a community centre on an isolated estate in North Shields.

Exclusions We want to be clear about areas in which we will not make grants, so we list here the types of proposal we will not consider for funding. Some are self-explanatory while others derive from the trust's history and experience. To save yourself time and effort please check this section carefully before starting work on your proposal.

1) We do not make grants to individuals

2) We will not consider proposals from these types of organisations:
   - statutory bodies
   - hospitals, health authorities and hospices (or towards any sort of medical care, medical equipment or medical research)
   - universities, colleges and schools (or towards academic research, bursaries or scholarships)
   - organisations working primarily with children under five
   - organisations working primarily in the fields of: physical disability; learning disability; autistic spectrum disorder; physical illness; sensory impairment
   - organisations focusing primarily on: adult learning, skills training or employment training; the restoration or conservation of buildings or habitats
   - animal charities
   - scouts, guides and other uniformed youth groups
   - voluntary rescue or first aid societies
   - museums, places of entertainment, leisure centres and clubs, social clubs or sports clubs
   - larger charities (both national and local) enjoying widespread support

3) We will not consider funding the core work of:
   - advice and information-giving bodies
   - community foundations
   - volunteer bureaux and centres
   - Councils for Voluntary Service
   - infrastructure organisations/second-tier bodies (organisations fulfilling a supporting, co-ordinating or development role within the voluntary sector)

4) Finally, we will not consider funding:
   - the promotion of religion
   - overseas projects. We run a targeted grants programme promoting sustainable agriculture in sub-Saharan Africa so we don't consider speculative proposals from overseas groups
   - one-off holidays, residentials, trips, exhibitions
   - arts and sports-based projects unless there is a particularly strong focus on developing marginalised groups
   - endowment appeals
   - work that has already taken place.

Applications The first-stage proposal

The first-stage proposal is intended to help us understand what sort of organisation you are and why you are doing the work you are doing. We do not want a detailed description or full costings of the work you are seeking funding for; we will discuss these areas with you if your application goes through to the second stage. Keeping your options open at this point allows us to work together more creatively if you are invited to send us a full application.

A first-stage proposal must include:

1) An introductory letter, of no more than one side of A4, on your organisation's letterhead.

2) A completed organisation details sheet [available from the trust's website].

3) Your answers to the following questions, on no more than two sides of A4:

- What difference do you want to make, and how will your organisation achieve this?
- Why are you the right people to do this work?
- Tell us about the people you are working with, and how you know there is a need for your work.
- How would you use funding from Tudor?

4) A copy of your most recent annual accounts, and annual report if you produce one. If your organisation is too new to have annual accounts please send a photocopy of a recent bank statement instead. Please don't send any other supporting documents.

All first-stage proposals go through an initial assessment process which involves both trustees and staff. In some cases we may phone you to discuss your proposal. We aim to let you know within a month whether or not we are inviting you to submit a second-stage application.

Address your proposal to 'The Trustees' and send it to us by post; we do not accept applications by email or fax. There are no deadlines for sending us your proposal; they are assessed as part of a rolling programme.

The second-stage application

If you are invited to put forward a full, second-stage application a member of the Grants Team will get in touch with you to discuss the next steps, to discover how best Tudor could support your organisation and its work, and to identify the information we need to move your application forward. A member of staff or a trustee may visit you so that we can gain a better understanding of your organisation and the work you do.

Although your chances of success are significantly higher at this stage, being invited to submit a second-stage application does not guarantee that a grant will be made. Not all second-stage applications get as far as committee stage, and not all applications going to committee are funded.

Tudor tries to consider all applications quickly. We aim to make a decision on most second-stage applications within three months, although in some circumstances we can act more swiftly. Complex applications can of course take longer to develop.

Trustees and staff meet every three weeks to consider applications at a Grants Committee or Trustee Committee. They will discuss your

application in detail and will usually make an immediate decision on funding, although in a few cases they may request further information or a visit if one has not already taken place.

The Douglas Turner Trust

General charitable purposes

£426,000 (2007/08)

Beneficial area Not defined. In practice, there is a preference for Birmingham and the West Midlands.

3 Poplar Piece, Inkberrow, Worcester WR7 4JD

Tel. 01386 792014

Email timpatrickson@hotmail.co.uk

Correspondent Tim J Patrickson, Trust Administrator

Trustees *J M Del Mar, Chair; J M G Fea; P J Millward; D P Pearson; S L Preedy.*

CC Number 227892

Information available Accounts were available from the Charity Commission.

The trust makes grants to registered charities, mainly in the West Midlands. Around 60% of the grant total is used to support charities on an annual basis, providing they can prove their need for continuing support. The trust administrator visits the beneficiaries every other year and makes recommendations to the trustees. Grants are made to a variety of charities, and are typically in the range of £1,000 to £5,000 but can be as high as £20,000. The largest grant this year was to Acorns Children's Hospice for £20,000.

In 2007/08 the trust had assets of £15 million, which generated an income of £526,000. Grants were made to 102 organisations totalling £426,000, broken down as follows:

Category	Value
Young people and Children	£91,000
Work in the Community	£65,000
Disabled and Health	£86,000
Hospices	£47,000
Older people	£49,000
International Aid	£25,000
Environment and Heritage	£5,000
Social Support	£4,000
The Arts	£39,000
Medical Research	£15,000

Grants awarded included the following:

Children and young people
Beneficiaries included: 870 House Youth Movement (£6,000); Scouts Association County of Birmingham (£5,000); Ackers Trust (£4,000); Children's Activity and Recreational Projects (£3,000); ER Mason Youth Centre (£2,000); HIP Kids (£1,000); and Gingerbread (£500).

Work in the community
Grant recipients included: Birmingham Settlement (£10,000); Concern Universal (£5,000); Cruse Birmingham (£4,000); Warley Woods Community Trust (£3,000); British Forces Foundation (£2,000); and Karis Neighbour Scheme (£1,000).

Health and charities for people with disabilities
Grants included those made to: Cerebral Palsy – Midlands (£10,000); Arcos (£5,000); Listening Books (£4,000); Juvenile Diabetes Research Fund (£3,000); Oesophageal Patients Association (£2,000); and Dial Walsall (£1,000).

Hospices
Grants went to: Acorns Children's Hospice (£20,000); St. Mary's Hospice (£15,000); and Compton Hospice (£12,000).

Older people
Grants included those made to: Birmingham Council for Old People (£12,000); Gracewell Homes Foster Trust (£10,000); Age Concern Birmingham (£6,000); Cotteridge Church Day Centre (£5,000); and Church Housing Trust and Independent Age (£2,000 each).

International aid
Beneficiaries included: Friends of TAFO (£7,000); Community of the Holy Fire (£5,000); and Busoga Trust (£3,000).

Environment and heritage
Grants went to: Birmingham Botanical Gardens (£4,000) and St George's Church Edgbaston (£1,000).

Social support
The sole beneficiary was the Bridge (£4,000).

The arts
Grant recipients included: City of Birmingham Symphony Orchestra (£10,000); Midlands Art Centre (£5,000); Orchestra of the Swan (£4,000); Deep Impact (£2,500) Birmingham Music Festival (£1,000); and Midlands Actors Theatre (£500).

Medical research
Grants went to: Birmingham University Cancer Research and Prostate Research Campaign (£5,000 each); Leukaemia

Research UK (£3,000); and Action Medical Research (£2,000).

Exclusions No grants to individuals or non-registered charities.

Applications In writing to the correspondent with a copy of the latest annual report and accounts. There are no application forms. The trustees usually meet in February, May, August and December to consider applications, which should be submitted in the month prior to each meeting. Telephone enquiries may be made before submitting an appeal.

Community Foundation Serving Tyne and Wear and Northumberland

Social welfare and general

£7 million (2007/08)

Beneficial area Tyne and Wear and Northumberland.

9th Floor, Cale Cross House, 156 Pilgrim Street, Newcastle upon Tyne NE1 6SU

Tel. 0191 222 0945 **Fax** 0191 230 0689

Email grants@communityfoundation. org.uk

Website www.communityfoundation. org.uk

Correspondent The Grants Team

Trustees *Hugh Welch, Chair; Jan Worters; Richard Maudslay; John Josephs; Trevor Shears; Sue Winfield; Jamie Martin; Shobha Srivastava; Lisa Charlton; Andrew Kerr; Jill Dixon; John Sands; Jo Curry; Charles Harvey; Dean T Huggins; Liz Prudhoe; Ashley Winter.*

CC Number 700510

Information available Accounts were on file at the Charity Commission. Further information was taken from the foundation's excellent website.

Established in 1988, the Community Foundation Serving Tyne and Wear and Northumberland is one of the largest community foundations in the UK. Its helpful website contains comprehensive information on all of its activities and the programmes from which grants are available.

Funds are set up by individuals, families and companies to help donors support their chosen interests. The Community Foundation manages over 200 such funds with most grants being for under £5,000 and for one off costs.

A smaller number of grants are made each year for larger amounts. For these it is suggested you talk to, or visit the foundation's website before you make an application.

Grants can be made for most types of community activity or projects. In the past support has been given to:

- projects run by and for disabled people
- community groups
- children and young peoples' groups
- projects run by and for people from minority ethnic communities
- sports groups
- older peoples' groups
- environmental projects
- arts projects
- training
- women's groups.

Grantmaking in 2007/08

In 2007/08 the foundation had assets of £44 million and an income of £10.1 million. Grants were made during the year totalling almost £7 million, broken down as follows:

Category	No. of grants	Amount
Community		
Foundation Funds	1,402	£3,450,000
Included Communities	56	£1,130,000
Local Network Fund	254	£1,020,000
Henry Smith Charity	41	£985,000
Capacity Builders	8	£207,600
Fair Share	8	£177,000

The foundation's annual report and accounts highlight some key activities during the year:

The majority of grants continued to be for amounts of under £5,000 and to provide practical support for small community groups. The Community Foundation works with outreach partners to ensure that grants are available to new and grassroots projects.

The Community Foundation provided grant-making services for One North East for their 3rd Sector Capacity Fund and 1989 Willan Charitable Trust, which awarded grants of £345,500 and £489,500 respectively in this financial year. These grants are not included in the grants-awarded figure above as the grants were made directly from the respective organisations.

During the year the David Dockray's West End Young People's Fund was established from the sale proceeds of West End Boy's Club of just under £1 million. The Adderstone Fund was also established with £250,000 gift. Ringtons celebrated their

centenary year with a donation to their fund of just over £250,000. A further eight Acorn Funds were established during the year and two acorn funds matured before the year end. There were 11 new revenue funds established including Peter and Angela Barratt, Owen Pugh Ltd and eaga plc.

The Community Foundation continued a partnership with The Greggs Trust, The Shears Foundation, Sir James Knott Trust and an anonymous donor on environmental grantmaking which awarded £148,200 grants during the year and organised a conference for voluntary organisations on environmental awareness. The Community Foundation started to monitor its own environmental footfall and appointed specialist advisors to monitor the environmental credentials of companies in the investment portfolio.

Unfortunately a list of beneficiaries was not available, although considering the range of funds available from the foundation the range of beneficiaries will be considerable.

Exclusions Grants are not normally given for:

- non charitable activities
- sponsorship and fundraising events
- small contributions to major appeals
- large capital projects
- endowments, loan repayments or for activities bought or ordered before we make a grant
- grants which will be used to make grants to a third party
- political activities
- acts of religious worship
- work which could be funded by health and local authorities or government grant aid
- work which only benefits animals.

Exceptions may be made to this at the request of the donors.

Applications With the exception of the Grassroots Grants programme, there is a single application form to complete – the foundation will allocate the application to the most appropriate fund.

The application form is available from the foundation's website, where applicants can also apply online.

Trustees of Tzedakah

Jewish charities and welfare

£426,000 (2006/07)

Beneficial area Worldwide, in practice mainly UK and Israel.

Brentmead House, Britannia Road, London N12 9RU

Tel. 020 8446 6767

Correspondent Colin Hollander, Correspondent

Trustee *Trustees of Tzedakah Ltd.*

CC Number 251897

Information available Accounts for 2007/08 were overdue at the Charity Commission at the time of writing.

The objectives of this trust are the relief of poverty; advancement of education; advancement of religion; and general charitable purposes. The trust makes over 300 grants to organisations in a year ranging from around £25 to £35,000.

In 2006/07 the trust had assets of £327,000 and an income of £478,000. Grants were made totalling £426,000.

Beneficiaries of larger grants included: Hasmonean High School Charitable Trust (£35,000); Gertner Charitable Trust (£27,000); Society of Friends of the Torah (£20,000); Hendon Adath Yisroel Synagogue (£17,000); and Medrash Shmuel Theological College (£13,000).

Other beneficiaries included: Torah Temimoh (£6,400); Willow Foundation (£4,500); Tifferes Girls School (£3,200); Sage Home for the Aged (£2,000); Wizo (£450); and Torah Movement of Great Britain (£25).

Exclusions Grants only to registered charities. No grants to individuals.

Applications This trust states that it does not respond to unsolicited applications.

The Underwood Trust

General charitable purposes, in particular, medicine and health, social welfare, education, arts, environment and wildlife

£1.2 million (2007/08)

Beneficial area Worldwide. In practice UK with a preference for Scotland and Wiltshire.

Fourth Floor South, 35 Portman Square, London W1H 6LR

Tel. 020 7486 0100

Website www.theunderwoodtrust.org.uk

Correspondent Antony P Cox, Trust Manager

Trustees *Robin Clark, Chair; Jack C Taylor; Briony Wilson.*

CC Number 266164

Information available Accounts were available from the Charity Commission.

The Underwood Trust was established in 1973. The name derives from Underwood Lane, Paisley, Scotland, which was the childhood home of one of the founders. It currently supports registered charities and other charitable organisations which benefit society nationally and locally in Scotland and Wiltshire.

The general aims of the trust are to cover a wide spectrum of activities so as to benefit as many charitable causes as possible and to make donations to organisations where its contribution really can be seen to make a difference. The trust does not wish to be the principal funder of a charity and medium sized bodies are more likely to receive grants than either very small charities or well known large national ones.

Grants are categorised under the following headings:

- medicine and health
- social welfare
- education and the arts
- environment and wildlife.

The allocation between these headings varies from year to year. Currently the specific interests are the environment and welfare, specifically, crime prevention, victim support and the re-education of offenders.

In 2007/08 the trust had assets of £35 million and an income of £1.4 million. A total of 46 grants were paid amounting to £1.2 million. Grants were categorised as follows:

Environment and wildlife – 12 grants totalling £420,000.
Beneficiaries included: Friends of the Earth (£100,000); Wiltshire Wildlife Trust (£70,000 in two grants); Thames Rivers Restoration Trust (£60,000); the Aigis Trust (£25,000); Wiltshire and Berkshire Canal Trust (£20,000); and St James Conservation Trust (£10,000).

Social welfare – 15 grants totalling £383,000.
Beneficiaries included: Restorative Solutions (£80,000); Calne Leisure Centre (£50,000); NSPCC (£40,000); Windmill Hill City Farm (£20,000); Prisoners Abroad (£15,000); and British Red Cross – National Floods Appeal (£10,000).

Medicine and health – 10 grants totalling £319,000.
Beneficiaries included: National Eye Research Centre (£100,000); Shooting Star Children's Hospice (£70,000); Speech Therapy Research Centre – Frenchay Hospital (£39,000); the Living Paintings Trust (£20,000); and Highland Hospice (£5,000).

Education and the arts – nine grants totalling £115,000.
Beneficiaries included: Industrial Trust and London Library (£50,000 each); Stage One (£25,000); Royal Overseas League Golden Jubilee Trust (£20,000); and National Youth Orchestra (£15,000).

Exclusions No grants are given to:

- individuals directly
- political activities
- commercial ventures or publications
- the purchase of vehicles including minibuses
- overseas travel, holidays or expeditions
- retrospective grants or loans
- direct replacement of statutory funding or activities that are primarily the responsibility of central or local government
- large capital, endowment or widely distributed appeals.

Applications **Please do not apply to the trust unless invited to do so.**

The trust's website clearly states that:

There has recently been a change of policy by the trustees. Recently the trust has made a number of large donations and commitments. As such there are currently no free funds in the trust and therefore the trust is unable to accept unsolicited applications. This position is expected to continue for the foreseeable future, but any changes to this will be posted on the trust's website at the time.

Please note: the trust is unable to deal with telephone or email enquiries about an application.

UnLtd (Foundation for Social Entrepreneurs)

Social enterprise

£3.5 million to social entrepreneurs (2007/08)
Beneficial area UK.

123 Whitecross Street, Islington, London EC1Y 8JJ

Tel. 020 7566 1100 **Fax** 020 7566 1101

Email info@unltd.org.uk

Website www.unltd.org.uk

Correspondent Raymond Tran

Trustees *Michael Norton; John Brown; Anthony Freeling; Norman Cumming; Alistair Wilson; Rich Benton; Rodney Stares; Martin Wyn Griffith; Richard Tyrie; Judith McNeill; Rajeeb Dey; Natalie Campbell; Andrew Croft; Dr Alison Fielding.*

CC Number 1090393

Information available Full information is on the foundation's website.

Summary

UnLtd is unique in this publication in that it exists to make grants to individuals to undertake social initiatives. In effect it makes grants for the start-up costs of new organisations and community groups to enterprising individuals who need support to implement their ideas and projects for improving their communities.

It was established in 2000 by seven partner organisations: Ashoka (since resigned), Changemakers, Comic Relief, Community Action Network, Scarman Trust, School for Social Entrepreneurs and Senscot. In 2003 the Millennium Commission invested £100 million in the organisation after a competitive process in which UnLtd was successful.

Its prime objective is to distribute Millennium Awards to social entrepreneurs. These awards are funded by the income generated from the endowment which is held by the Millennium Awards Trust of which UnLtd is the sole trustee. Award winners receive a complete, tailored package of money, training and advice at every stage of their project. Networking opportunities are also provided by UnLtd, along with intensive business support and mentoring to the most promising social entrepreneurs.

The foundation also manages several other schemes, including the UnLtd 4iP Awards and the UnLtd Sport Relief Awards. Further information on the different schemes can be found on the foundation's website.

UnLtd awards are for people:

- over the age of 16
- living in the UK
- who are applying as an individual or informal group
- who want to run projects that: benefit the public or a community in the UK, need an UnLtd award to ensure its success, offer a learning opportunity for the applicant(s), are a new initiative.

Grants in 2007/08

In 2007/08 the foundation had assets of £812,000 and an income of £9.3 million. Grants were made totalling £5.8 million, of which £3.5 million was awarded under the Millennium Awards. A further £2.3 million was given through the BIG awards.

Millenium Awards were distributed as follows:

Level	No.	Value
Level 0	48	£53,000
Level 1	847	£2,600,000
Level 2	40	£740,000
Level 3	4	£115,000

Analysis of the distribution of awards by age, gender, ethnicity and disability showed the main recipients in each category to be as follows: Age – 37 to 47 years (34%); Gender – male (52%) and female (48%); Ethnicity – white English (41%); and, Disability – no disability (94%).

A breakdown of the distribution of awards by theme and project type show that the majority of grants (23%) went to 'community and social causes', while the most popular project type was 'organising a service' (45%).

Geographically, the distribution of award winners was broken down as follows;

- London, the south east and east of England – 290
- North of England and Midlands – 338
- Northern Ireland – 76
- Wales – 74
- Scotland – 69.

Applications Applicants are advised to read the guidelines on UnLtd's website carefully to check that they meet the criteria and then contact the nearest UnLtd office (see below) to discuss their ideas.

Regional offices
Head office/London office: 123 Whitecross Street, Islington, London EC1Y 8JJ. Telephone: 020 7566 1100; Fax: 020 7566 1101/1139; Email: info@unltd.org.uk.

Birmingham office: Unit G2, The Ground Floor, The Arch, 48–52 Floodgate Street, Birmingham B5 5SL. Telephone: 0121 766 4570.

Bradford office: 15 Halfield Road, Bradford BD1 3RP. Telephone: 01274 750630.

Northern Ireland office: Room 55–57, Scottish Mutual Building, 16 Donegal Square South, Belfast BT1 5JG. Telephone: 028 9024 4007.

Scotland UnLtd office (Glasgow): 3rd Floor, Epic House, 28–32 Cadogan Street, Glasgow G2 7LP. Telephone: 0141 221 2322.

Scotland UnLtd office (Edinburgh): 54 Manor Place, Edinburgh EH3 7EH. Telephone: 0131 226 7333.

Wales office: Fourth Floor, Baltic House, Mount Stuart Square, Cardiff CF10 5FH. Telephone: 029 2048 4811.

The Michael Uren Foundation

General

£2.2 million (2007/08)
Beneficial area UK.

Haysmacintyre, Fairfax House, 15 Fulwood Place, London WC1V 6AY

Email agregory-jones@haysmacintyre.com

Correspondent Anne Gregory-Jones

Trustees *John Uren; Christopher Hill; Janis Bennett; Alastair McDonald.*

CC Number 1094102

Information available Accounts were available from the Charity Commission.

The foundation was established in 2002 with general charitable purposes following an initial gift from Michael Uren.

The trustees are particularly keen on making grants for specific large projects. This could mean that, to satisfy this objective, no significant grants are paid in one year. With the resultant reserves retained a large grant could be made in the following year.

In 2007/08 the foundation had an income of £123,000 and made 11 grants totalling £2.2 million (£606,000 in 5 grants in 2006/07). Total funds carried forward at year end totalled £56 million.

Beneficiaries during the year were: Combat Stress, the Gurkha Welfare Trust, Royal Hospital Chelsea and SSAFA Forces Help (£500,000 each); King Edward VII Hospital (£115,000); Rycote Chapel (£74,000); Parochial Church Council (£13,000); Royal London Society for the Blind (£10,000); Canterbury Cathedral (£3,000); Project Trust (£2,500); and Territorial Army (£500).

Applications In writing to the correspondent.

The Vail Foundation

Jewish

£1.4 million (2007/08)

Beneficial area UK and overseas.

5 Fitzhardinge Street, London W1H 6ED

Correspondent The Trustees

Trustees M S Bradfield; P Brett; M H Goldstein.

CC Number 1089579

Information available Accounts were available from the Charity Commission.

This foundation was set up in 2001. 'The trustees receive applications for donations from a wide variety of charitable institutions including those engaged in medical ancillary services (including medical research), education, helping the disabled and old aged, relieving poverty, providing sheltered accommodation, developing the arts etc.'

In 2007/08 the foundation had assets of £11 million, an income of £418,000 and made grants to 42 organisations totalling £1.4 million.

Organisations receiving substantial support included: KKL Charity Accounts (£400,000); Jewish Care (£150,000); and United Jewish Israel Appeal (£100,000).

Other beneficiaries included: Project Seed (£75,000); Friends of Swiss Cottage and Swiss Cottage Specialist SEN School (£50,000 each); University Jewish Chaplaincy Board (£45,000); Community Security Trust (£40,000); Jewish Learning Exchange (£35,000); Central British Fund of Jewish World Relief (£25,000); United Synagogue (£20,000); Roundabout Trust (£15,000); Yakar Educational Foundation and Simon Marks Jewish Primary School (£10,000 each); London Jewish Family Centre (£7,000); Camp Simcha, Chai Lifeline Cancer Care and Nightingale House (£5,000 each); UK Friends of the Association for the Wellbeing of Israel's Soldiers (£2,500); and Israeli Dance Institute (£1,000).

Applications 'The trustees consider all requests which they receive and make such donations as they feel appropriate.'

The Valentine Charitable Trust

Welfare, the environment and overseas aid

£814,000 (2007/08)

Beneficial area Unrestricted, but mainly Dorset, UK.

Preston Redman LLP, Hinton House, Hinton Road, Bournemouth BH1 2EN

Tel. 01202 292424 **Fax** 01202 552758

Email valentine@prestonredman.co.uk

Correspondent Douglas J E Neville-Jones, Trustee

Trustees Douglas J E Neville-Jones; Roger A Gregory; Mrs Shiela F Cox; Mrs Susan Patterson; Mrs Patricia B N Walker; Peter Leatherdale; Mrs Diana Tory.

CC Number 1001782

Information available Accounts were available from the Charity Commission.

The trust was founded by the late Miss Ann Cotton in 1990. The trust was established for general charitable purposes but in particular for the provision of amenities and facilities for the benefit of the public, the protection and safeguarding of the countryside and wildlife and the control and reduction of pollution. Miss Cotton lived most of her life in Dorset and involvement in local projects appealed to her. The present trustees do not set a limit on what they consider to be local, but when dealing

with charities with limited areas of interest, they will be likely to give preference to those which operate in Dorset.

Grantmaking

The trust offers an interesting and informative insight into its grant-making policy in its annual report, some of which is reproduced here:

Grants for one-off appeals

There are regularly one off appeals to provide funding for specific projects and the trustees have regularly made donations to such appeals where they are for local facilities. However the trustees are not keen on village halls or the fabric of church buildings.

Grants for core funding

One of the themes of comments made to the trustees by applicants concerns the problems of raising core funding. Apparently many grant-making trusts avoid providing core funding. The trustees appreciate that a one off appeal for a particular project may be much more appealing than a general request for funds just to keep a charity functioning. They therefore make regular donations to the core funding of charities. However this is always subject to review. The trustees do occasionally make it clear that such funding is only for a set period of time but in many cases they are prepared to consider such funding on an indefinite basis. They take the view that if it has been right to support a particular charity once then, unless something changes, that motive can be followed continuously.

Matched funding and pledges

The trustees regularly use the device of offering funding to a project conditional upon the applicant raising other funds before the donation will be forthcoming. Similarly offers of donations are sometimes made on the basis that they will only be made once the project actually proceeds. All such offers are subject to review up until the time they are actually made.

Social investment funding

Following Miss Cotton's death the charity's assets were invested in a very narrow range of investments. To assist with diversification the trustees developed what they term social investment funding. This involves either the purchase of premises which are then leased to an operating charity for its use, the lease is usually at a modest or nominal rent and for a relatively limited term, or the provision of a loan with an interest rate of between 0% and base rate to an operating charity to allow it to acquire property.

In 2007/08 the trust had assets of £22.7 million and an income of

£1 million. Grants were made to 127 organisations totalling £814,000.

Beneficiaries during the year included: Priest's House Museum and Wessex Autistic Society (£25,000 each); Help for Heroes and Lewis-Manning Cancer Trust (£20,000 each); The Prince's Trust and Bournemouth Symphony Orchestra (£15,000 each); Bournemouth Nightclub Outreach (£12,000); Canine Partners for Independence, Fine Cell Work and Tregonwell Alms House Trust (£10,000 each); St Phillip's Church Project (£8,000); Rainbow Trust (£6,000); Christians Against Poverty, Dorset Blind Association, Fernheath Play Association and Tree Aid (£5,000 each); Bournemouth Town Centre Detached Youth (£3,000); Cruse Bereavement Care and the Margaret Green Foundation (£2,000 each); and the Salvation Army and Traffic of the Stage (£1,000 each).

Exclusions No grants to individuals. The trust would not normally fund appeals for village halls or the fabric of church buildings.

Applications In writing to the correspondent. The trust provides the following insight into its application process in its annual report:

All applications will be acknowledged with standard letters, even those that are not appropriate for receiving a grant. This responsibility is delegated to Douglas J E Neville-Jones who then provides a report to the next trustees' meeting.

The following general comments summarise some of the considerations the trustees seek to apply when considering applications for funding.

The trustees look for value for money. While this concept is difficult to apply in a voluntary sector it can certainly be used on a comparative basis and subjectively. If the trustees have competing applications they will usually decide to support just one of them as they believe that to concentrate the charity's donations is more beneficial than to dilute them.

Regular contact with the charities to which donations are made is considered essential. Reports and accounts are also requested from charities which are supported and the trustees consider those at their meetings.

The trustees take great comfort from the fact that they employ the policy of only making donations to other charities or similar bodies. However they are not complacent about the need to review all donations made and the objects to which those have been given.

The trustees are conscious that, particularly with the smaller and local charities, the community of those working for and with the charity is an important consideration.

The trustees regularly review the classifications to which donations have been made so that they can obtain an overview of the charity's donations and assess whether their policies are being implemented in practice. They are conscious that when dealing with individual donations it is easy to lose sight of the overall picture.

John and Lucille van Geest Foundation

Medical research, healthcare and general

£872,000 (2008/09)

Beneficial area UK, with some interest in south Lincolnshire and adjoining areas; and occasionally overseas.

108 Pinchbeck Road, Spalding PE11 1QL
Tel. 01775 769501
Email trustees@ johnandlucillevangeestfoundation.org
Website johnandlucillevangeest foundation.org
Correspondent Brenda Ruysen, Clerk to the Trustees
Trustees *Hilary P Marlowe; Stuart R Coltman; Tonie Gibson.*
CC Number 1001279

Information available Accounts were available from the Charity Commission.

The foundation was founded by the late John van Geest and his wife, the late Lucille van Geest in 1990. The objects of the foundation are general charitable purposes but the grant-making policy is for grants usually to be awarded for the purpose of medical research and for welfare purposes.

In 2008/09 the foundation had assets of £29 million and an income of £1.1 million. 22 grants were made totalling £872,000.

Grants for the purpose of medical research are directed towards research into:

- brain damage for example, Alzheimer's Disease, Huntington's Disease, Parkinson's Disease and strokes
- cancer
- heart disease
- lung disease
- sight and/or hearing loss.

The trust has recently stated:

It is the trustees' intention that for the foreseeable future grants for medical research purposes shall be made in the main direct to a limited number of selected research establishments involved in one or another of such areas of research. It should be noted that the trustees already have in place a grant expenditure programme for cancer research for the years 2008 – 2012 (inclusive).

Grants for welfare purposes are directed towards people in need through illness, infirmity or social circumstances and in particular the welfare of older people and of children resident in south Lincolnshire and adjoining areas who:

- suffer from brain damage/mental illness
- suffer from cancer
- suffer from heart disease
- suffer from lung disease
- suffer from sight and/or hearing loss
- suffer from disfigurement through injury
- are physically disabled
- are bedridden
- are terminally ill
- are at risk.

Grants are also occasionally made towards victims of natural disasters and man-made disasters.

The trustees' aim is that approximately 75% of grant expenditure will be for the purpose of medical research (with grants, where possible, being made direct to the research establishment) and 25% of grant expenditure will be for welfare purposes (with the emphasis being on grants to locally based charitable institutions with minimal overheads).

Please note: The late Lucille Van Geest, who died on 3rd January 2006, bequeathed the residue of her estate to the charity. During the previous year a final payment of £606,000 was made to the trustees and the trustees subsequently recovered £35,000 income tax borne by the executors making the total value of the bequest just over £12 million.

Grants in 2008/09

Medical research – 6 grants totalling £664,000

Beneficiaries were: University of Leicester (£340,000); Foundation for the Prevention of Blindness (£130,000); University of Cambridge Brain Repair Centre (£110,000); Deafness Research UK (£40,000); Kidney Research UK (£34,000); and Cancer Research (£10,000).

Health and social welfare and facilities – 16 grants totalling £209,000

Beneficiaries included: Lincolnshire and Nottinghamshire Air Ambulance (£24,000); East Anglia Children's Hospices (£20,000); British Heart Foundation (£15,000); Age Concern – Peterborough (£12,000); Tapping House Hospice (£10,000); Blind Outdoor Leisure (£3,000); and the Dystonia Society (£1,500).

Exclusions No grants to individuals.

Applications In writing to the correspondent. Please note: only charities engaged in areas of work to which the trust's policy extends are considered (and in the case of healthcare grants, only charities providing services in south Lincolnshire and adjoining area). Telephone calls are not welcome. The trustees meet two to three times a year to consider applications, but there are no set dates. Every applicant will receive a reply.

The Vardy Foundation

Christian causes, education in the north east of England and general

£2.8 million to organisations (2007/08)

Beneficial area UK with a preference for north-east England and overseas.

Venture House, Aykley Heads, Durham DH1 5TS

Tel. 0191 374 4727

Email foundation@regvardy.com

Website vardyfoundation.com

Correspondent Jo Lavender, Foundation Executive

Trustees *Sir Peter Vardy; Lady Margaret Barr Vardy; Peter D D Vardy; Richard Vardy.*

CC Number 328415

Information available Accounts were available from the Charity Commission. The foundation also has a website.

The foundation was set up in 1989 with general charitable objectives. It makes grants and loans to organisations and individuals, and also considers the payment of vehicle leasing costs and

other expenses to third parties where these services can be obtained at better rates through the foundation than would be available to the beneficiaries themselves.

One of the major activities [of the foundation] is the establishment of secondary schools (11–18 yrs), providing an education with a distinctly Christian ethos. The Emmanuel Schools Foundation [which will receive future support from the Vardy Foundation] currently runs three schools with a fourth under construction. The goal is to have 10,000 children educated to the highest possible standards making a significant impact not only on the students, but also on the parents and the wider community.

The schools are among the top performing in the UK with children, coming from disadvantaged backgrounds, achieving outstanding success.

The foundation also supports initiatives in other countries, principally Africa. In Zambia the foundation has funded a Hydro Electric plant which was switched on in July 2007.

The foundation has helped hundreds of projects large and small both in the UK and worldwide. It looks for people who are doing tremendous and very worthwhile projects and seeks to support them. Support is invariably financial but management expertise is also called on in many instances.

In 2007/08 the foundation had assets of £20.6 million and an income of £1.7 million. Grants were made totalling almost £3 million, of which £2.8 million was distributed to 76 organisations and £137,500 to 42 individuals.

The largest grant made during the year was a donation of £1 million to the Angel Foundation, which is a TV broadcaster providing religious content.

Grants were categorised in the 2007/08 annual report and accounts as follows:

Category	No. of grants	Amount
Religion	68	£2,200,000
Relief	5	£312,000
Welfare	34	£216,300
Education	7	£160,300
Arts	4	£35,200
Total	118	£2,900,000

Other large grants included those to: Caring for Life (£250,000); Youth for Christ (£220,000); Christians Against Poverty (£175,000); and, the Message Trust (£150,000).

Current grant-making categories are described as 'education', 'international', 'music', 'social & community' and 'youth'.

Applications In writing to the correspondent.

The Variety Club Children's Charity

Children's charities

£2.3 million to organisations and individuals (2008)
Beneficial area UK.

Variety Club House, 93 Bayham Street, London NW1 0AG

Tel. 020 7428 8100

Email info@varietyclub.org.uk

Website www.varietyclub.org.uk

Correspondent Anthony Simmonds

Trustees *Kenneth R Mustoe; Paul Lawrence; Keith Andrews; Philip Austin; John E Barnett; Gary Beckwith; Anthony Blackburn; Malcolm Brenner; Laurence Davis; Alan Fraser; Anthony Henry-Lyons; Lionel Rosenblatt; John Sachs; Jonathan Shalit; Anthony Simmonds; Pamela Sinclair; Anne Wadsworth; Norman Kaphan; Russ Kane; Ronnie Nathan; Anthony Harris; Stephen Crown; Jarvis Astaire; Tony Hatch; John Ratcliff.*

CC Number 209259

Information available Accounts were available from the Charity Commission.

The charity raises money and then provides Sunshine Coaches, mobility aids or general grants to help those:

- with mental, physical or sensory disabilities
- with behavioural or psychological disturbances
- suffering through distress, abuse or neglect.

General grants are described as follows:

Applications can be made from non-profit making groups and organisations working with children under the age of 19. In general, consideration is given to funding specific items of equipment that are for the direct use of sick, disabled and disadvantaged children.

There is no upper or lower limit on the level of grant, but most grants are for less than £5,000. Many requests are for small sums under £500.

Grantmaking

In 2008 the charity had an income of £10.4 million. Grants and donations supporting the charity's activities during the year totalled almost £7.5 million.

As well as purchasing the familiar white Variety Club minibuses for schools, youth clubs, hospices etc., the charity also operates the Easy Riders Wheelchair Programme, which donates custom-designed wheelchairs, trikes and buggies to children who are contending with a wide range of disabilities, and Variety at Work, a special part of the charity which exists purely to give children wonderful experiences, rather than raise money. Its aim is simple – to bring happiness to as many youngsters as possible, so that they can look forward to magical moments. This is achieved by providing entertainment and experiences for them through all sorts of spectacular events throughout the country, all year long.

Charitable expenditure was broken down as follows:

Project	Value
Sunshine coaches	£3,500,000
Grants to individuals and organisations	£2,300,000
Variety at Work activities	£1,100,000
Electric wheelchairs	£559,000

The history of the Variety Club

The club's website has the following interesting account of the origins of the charity:

The roots of the Variety Club of Great Britain go back to 1927 when, in Pittsburgh, United States, a group of 11 men, all friends, and involved in show business, set up a social club. They rented a small room in the William Penn Hotel for their new club, which they named the Variety Club, as all its members were drawn from various branches of the show business world.

On Christmas Eve 1928 a one-month-old baby was abandoned on a seat in the Sheridan Square Theatre in Pittsburgh, Pennsylvania, with a note pinned to her dress, which read as follows:

Please take care of my baby. Her name is Catherine. I can no longer take care of her. I have eight others. My husband is out of work. She was born on Thanksgiving Day. I have always heard of the goodness of show business people and pray to God that you will look after her' (signed, 'A heartbroken mother').

When all efforts by the police and local newspapers failed to locate the parents, the theatre's 11 club members decided to underwrite the infant's support and education.

The subsequent publicity surrounding Catherine and her benefactors attracted many other show business people anxious to help. Before long Catherine had more clothes and toys than any child could possibly need. Naturally the Club members had no trouble finding other disadvantaged children to benefit from the extra gifts and while the generous show business world donated presents to Catherine, the Club continued to supply a growing number of

children with much-needed presents. As a result, by the time Catherine was adopted at the age of five, the Club that she had effectively started was well on the way to becoming a recognised children's charity.

It was not long before the Variety Club decided to actively raise funds for its adopted cause of disadvantaged children. The first fundraising event of the Club was held under a Circus Big Top, which is why the circus vernacular is used within the Club structure world-wide.

The Variety Club of Great Britain – or Tent 36 – was set up by two Americans: Robert S Wolff, chairman of RKO, who became the club's first Chief Barker, and C J Latta of ABC Cinemas/Warner Brothers. It was formed at an inaugural dinner at the Savoy in October 1949 and by the end of 1950 had already raised nearly £10,000.

From the start, Tent 36 – like the Variety Club as a whole – consisted of a group of charitable individuals and companies, the majority of whom were related to show business and were happy to give large sums of money for the cause-sometimes as straightforward cash donations and sometimes through their support for the Club's auctions and raffles with donated items. The Club numbered a formidable array of film producers, agents and celebrities within its ranks, all of whom were eager to give their time and services – free of charge – to help towards making the increasingly varied and wide ranging fundraising events as successful as possible.

Variety Club of Great Britain, along with the other members of Variety Club International, has long been characterised as 'the Heart of Show Business'. Its membership over the years is drawn in large measure from the multi-faceted world of entertainment and the leisure industries.

Exclusions For grants to organisations: trips abroad; medical treatment or research; administrative or salary costs; maintenance or ongoing costs; repayment of loans; distribution to other organisations; computers for mainstream schools or non-disabled children; basic cost of a family vehicle and non-specific appeals.

Applications There are application forms for each programme, available from the charity or through its website.

The Volant Charitable Trust

General

£3.7 million (2008/09)

Beneficial area UK, with a preference for Scotland, and overseas.

PO Box 8, 196 Rose Street, Edinburgh EH2 4AT

Website www.volanttrust.com

Correspondent Christine Collingwood, Administrator

Trustees *J K Rowling; Dr N S Murray; G C Smith; R D Fulton.*

SC Number SC030790

Information available Annual report and accounts were provided by the trust.

This trust was established in 2000 by the author J K Rowling for general charitable purposes. In recent years the trust has refined its objects and now has two broad areas of funding:

- research into the causes, treatment and possible cures of Multiple Sclerosis (the trust is currently committed to funding several long-term research projects of this type and is not considering further applications for funding in this area at the present time)
- charities and projects, whether national or community-based, at home or abroad, that alleviate social deprivation, with a particular emphasis on women's and children's issues (the trustees have already committed funds for overseas projects, and are not, therefore, considering further applications for projects outside the UK at present).

Check the trust's website for up-to-date information on any changes to the above circumstances.

The trust has simple guidelines:

- the trustees principal objective is to support charitable organisations whose purpose is to alleviate poverty and social deprivation with particular emphasis on children's and women's issues. All charities should be registered with the relevant national charity commission or equivalent body
- the trustees are prepared to support a charity by way of regular annual payments but only in exceptional circumstances would grants exceed three years. In addition, even if the activities of a charity appear to fall within the guidelines this does not automatically mean that it will receive a grant. All grants are at the discretion of the trustees

- the trustees will, as and when appropriate, support disaster appeals but will not support applications from individuals who are seeking assistance, for a specific project or charitable work which that individual may be carrying out, or to relieve a need due to illness or similar circumstances.

The trust also states that grants can be made to appropriate projects that fall outside these guidelines at the trustees' discretion.

In 2008/09 the trust had assets of £38.4 million and an income of £4.6 million, a substantial amount of which included donations from the settlor. Grants were made during the year to 47 organisations totalling £3.7 million. Grants were broken down as follows:

Category	Amount
Social Welfare	£1,100,000
International Aid	£2,550,000*
Medical Research/Relief	£30,000

*Comprises a restricted fund reserved for grants to the Disasters Emergency Committee (£2 million) and £500,000 to UNICEF.

Major grants listed in the accounts include: Motherwell and Wishaw Citizens Advice Bureau, Multi-Cultural Family Base, Pallion Action Group, Altrusa Careers Trust and Bringing East End Together (£75,000 each).

The trust anticipates that the level of grantmaking will increase further in the future.

Exclusions No grants to individuals.

Applications Applications for funding requests of £10,000 or less, for those projects based in **Scotland** only, are dealt with by our appointed agents, the Scottish Community Foundation.

All other requests for funding are dealt with via an application form available from the trust's website.

Complete and return the application form, plus any supporting materials by post. Applications should not be hand delivered. If an application is hand delivered, management at Mail Boxes are not in a position to discuss applications and will not be expected to provide any form of receipt.

Voluntary Action Fund

General

Around £2 million
Beneficial area Scotland.

Dunfermline Business Centre, Unit 14, Izatt Avenue, Dunfermline KY11 3BZ

Tel. 01383 620780 **Fax** 01383 626314

Email info@voluntaryactionfund.org.uk

Website www.voluntaryactionfund.org.uk

Correspondent Keith Wimbles, Chief Executive

Trustees Dave Milliken, Chair; Farkhanda Chaudhry, Michael Cunningham, Julie Hogg, Caron Hughes, Pam Judson, Stuart McGregor, Dorothy MacLauchlan, Abi Mordin, Helen Munro, Laurie Naumann, Jonathan Squire.

SC Number SC035037

Information available The fund has an informative website, with detailed guidance and application forms.

The Voluntary Action Fund (VAF) was constituted as a charity and registered company in December 2003. However, it is not a new organisation having formed as a development of the Unemployed Voluntary Action Fund (UVAF). UVAF was an unincorporated charity whose mission and objectives needed to be updated in order to reflect the new areas of work evolving within its portfolio. VAF has continued the legacy of grassroots grantmaking, promoting the inclusion of those most excluded within their communities.

Much of VAF's funding comes from the Scottish Government to enable it 'to support voluntary and community organisations in taking forward social change'. The fund's grant programmes are linked by the common threads of social inclusion and support for organisational development. The projects they fund are all focused on providing real solutions to identified community need. Each grant programme has its own individual criteria and priorities as well as a direct link to government policy.

The fund's website provides the following overview of its values, aims and objectives:

Mission Statement
The Voluntary Action Fund believes in the capacity of all people to make a difference in their own lives and in the lives of others. Through the effective investment of grants we will support voluntary organisations to

promote equality by tackling barriers to participation and unlocking the energies and talents in Scotland's communities.

Values
In taking forward our mission statement we adhere by the following values in all areas of our work:

- we believe in the capacity of voluntary activity in taking forward change
- we believe that barriers to participation and involvement can and should be tackled and this under pins all of our work
- we are proud of our commitment to transparency, fairness, rigour and equality across all of our practices
- we believe in learning through action and will support the promotion of enquiry and learning across all areas of our work
- we believe that strength can lie in partnership and collaboration and shall continue to develop new ways of working with key partners.

Approach
Our approach is one of:

- working alongside organisations to achieve high standards
- providing tailored training and direct support
- identifying and supporting new ways of working
- being alert to activities of wider significance and sharing information
- encouraging organisations to develop networks to share their knowledge and learn from each other
- ensuring the impact and effectiveness of our funded programmes through systematic monitoring and evaluation.

As an organisation we strive to add to our effectiveness by:

- investing in our own learning and development as Investors in People
- contributing to local and national networks and forums to influence and shape policy
- proactively building relationships with other funders.

Grant Programmes
The fund is currently managing three grantmaking programmes, summarised here from details on the website:

Volunteering Scotland Grant Scheme
The Volunteering Scotland Grant Scheme (VSGS) is funded by the Scottish Government. It is playing a key role in implementing the Volunteering Strategy for Scotland through funding the development of high quality volunteering opportunities.

VAF has recently awarded grants to 62 organisations to assist the development of high quality volunteering opportunities and volunteer support. Twenty three of the awards are for small grants of less than

£5,000, while the remaining 39 are for more substantial projects over one, two or three years.

We are not currently inviting applications to this scheme as it fully expended and we do not anticipate being able to make grants for the foreseeable future.

Equality Grants Programme
The Equality Grants Programme 2008–2011 is managed by the Voluntary Action Fund (VAF) and is funded through the Scottish Government Equality Unit. VAF provides dedicated 'investment support' including grant management, monitoring and development support for projects funded through the following streams:

- race, religion and refugee integration
- disability
- lesbian, gay, bisexual and transgender (LGBT)
- gender.

The Equalities Programme has a strong commitment to equalities and works to support organisations which combat inequality, foster integration, promote dialogue and understanding between communities.

In taking this forward, the aspiration is to work with organisations on capturing the change they are making (outcomes), and collectively as networks of funded projects – i.e. what key equality changes are being delivered across Scotland through Government funding support and where future programmes of work and funding should be prioritised to address gaps.

Community Chest
This programme is managed by VAF with funding from the Scottish Government. It has £400,000 available over the two years 2009/10 and 2010/11.

Community Chest is a small grant programme providing grants of up to £1,000 and free training to help small community groups in Scotland sustain and develop their activities.

Groups can apply for funding for a wide range of activities or operational costs. However, we are particularly keen to fund activities that will help build and develop strong organisations, for example:

- training for committee members and volunteers
- visits to other organisations or conferences
- professional support or consultancy.

We are also keen to fund groups who meet any of the following criteria:

- are based in West Dunbartonshire, South Lanarkshire or North Ayrshire
- work with disability or health related issues

- whose beneficiaries might be disadvantaged through their ethnicity, disability, gender or sexual orientation
- provide childcare.

Free training will be offered to all groups applying for a grant on topics such as charity law, making successful funding applications, and monitoring and evaluation. The training events will also provide information on where groups can go for further support and funding. Groups receiving a grant will be expected, as a condition of the grant, to attend at least one of the free training events.

Groups will be considered for a grant if they have:

- an annual income below £25,000 per year (excluding any income for capital items such as buildings or equipment)
- a signed constitution or set of rules (if you do not have a constitution you should approach your local Council for Voluntary Service (CVS) who will be happy to advise you)
- a bank account in the name of the group
- an independent referee, such as a community worker or a CVS or volunteer centre worker, who can vouch for the group and has knowledge of the plans for using the grant.

The Community Chest programme will not consider funding individuals or activities that promote a political party or religion. The Voluntary Action Fund (VAF) will also not fund groups that have had a Community Chest grant within the previous 12 month period. Parent Councils and PTA's will not be eligible to apply for a Community Chest grant as funding is likely to be used by a third party rather than the Parent Council or PTA itself and for activities that may be a statutory responsibility. Hobby groups and private clubs with a restrictive membership that do not provide a service wider than their members will be a low priority and are unlikely to receive a grant.

Applications for the Community Chest programme can be made throughout the year with deadlines on the 31 March, 30 June, 30 September and 31 December.

Grantmaking

In 2007/08 the fund had an income of £2.6 million. Grants were made totalling around £2 million. Grants usually range from £100 to £40,000. No further financial information was available.

Previous beneficiaries include: Glasgow Braendam Link, Calman Trust Ltd, Jeely Piece Club, Street League Scotland, Chinese Community Development Partnership – Glasgow, Duncholgan Playgroup, Gorbals Initiative, Sikh

Sanjog, British Red Cross, Legal Services Agency and Umoja.

Exclusions Each programme has its own set of eligibility criteria. Please contact the fund directly or go to its website for full details.

Applications Application forms and guidance notes for open programmes are available on the fund's website. The fund recommends that interested parties contact them to discuss the project before making any application.

Wales Council for Voluntary Action

Local community, volunteering, social welfare, environment and regeneration

£21 million (2007/08)

Beneficial area Wales.

Baltic House, Mount Stuart Square, Cardiff CF10 5FH

Tel. 0870 607 1666 **Fax** 029 2043 1701

Minicom 029 2043 1702

Email help@wcva.org.uk

Website www.wcva.org.uk

Correspondent Graham Benfield, Chief Executive

Trustees *Louise Bennett; Nerys Haf Biddulph; Jacquy Box; Ian Charlesworth; Maureen Davies; Walter Dickie; Eurwen E Edwards; Catrin Fletcher; Win Griffiths; Simon Harris; Margaret Jervis; John R Jones; Harri Jones; Mike Lewis; Cath Lindley; James Maiden; Marcella Maxwell; Liz Neal; Jane Pagler; Chad Patel.*

CC Number 218093

Information available Accounts were available from the Charity Commission. The charity's website does not feature all open grant programmes.

Wales Council for Voluntary Action (WCVA) represents, supports and campaigns for the voluntary sector in Wales by undertaking research on policy, providing information and training, and administering a range of grant programmes on behalf of various bodies including charitable trusts, the Millennium Commission, the National Assembly for Wales, the Big Lottery

Fund and the European Structural Funds. Although it only administers funds for other bodies and has no funds of its own, it merits inclusion here due to the diverse nature of the schemes and the amounts of money involved.

In 2007/08 WCVA had assets of £10.4 million and an income of £29 million, including £17.8 million from the Welsh Assembly and £7.3 million from European Structural Funds. Grants were made to 2,318 organisations across Wales totalling just over £21 million.

WCVA administers many and varied grant programmes (26 in 2007/08) in a similar way to a community foundation. Below is the largest (and probably most over-subscribed) fund that was open at the time of writing (November 2009) – check WCVA's website for up-to-date information on current programmes and deadlines.

Communities First Trust Fund

The Communities First Trust Fund (CFTF) aims to support any type of activity that involves local people, through small community organisations, that benefits their community. Applications are welcome from a range of community projects including music and the arts. The activities must provide some measure of economic, environmental, social or cultural benefit for people living in a Communities First area.

There are over 180 areas across Wales eligible for support from the Communities First Trust Fund. These areas have been identified in the Communities First Programme. A list of the eligible areas is available by contacting the Communities First Helpline (0800 587 8898) or email: help@wcva.org.uk

There is no minimum amount but £5,000 is the maximum you can apply for.

Applications can be submitted to the CFTF throughout the year [usually between April and January the following year] and are processed on a first come first served basis. Therefore, as there is a fixed amount of money allocated to each Communities First area, it is to your advantage to submit applications as early as possible to avoid the risk of disappointment because the ward allocation has been over-subscribed.

Grantmaking in 2007/08

The following is a breakdown of the charity's grant distributions by programme during the year:

Programme	No. of grants	Amount
Communities First	1,301	£3,580,000
Infrastructure Funding – CVCs	21	£2,960,000
Strategic Recycling – ERDF	7	£2,260,000
Mental Health	80	£2,200,000
Active Community	43	£1,340,000
Infrastructure Funding – Vol. Centres	21	£1,280,000
Social Risk – Objective 1	221	£1,110,000
Environment Wales	139	£866,000
Strategic Recycling – ESF	6	£836,500
Volunteering in Wales Fund	67	£694,000
Strategic Recycling – non Objective 1	1	£675,500
Advice Training Network	16	£671,000
Millennium Volunteers – Russell	25	£463,000
Millennium Volunteers	56	£317,000
Local Voluntary Action Capacity Building	13	£286,000
Local Regeneration	6	£280,000
Gwraidd	62	£202,000
Communities First – Music	83	£177,000
Social Risk – Objective 3	47	£171,000
Communities First – Russell	3	£162,500
Community Investment	18	£145,000
Partnership Council	29	£120,500
Russell – Youth Led	17	£100,000
Voluntary Sector Capacity Building	7	£96,000
Goldstar	23	£48,000
Russell – Youth Volunteering	6	£27,000

Exclusions Grants are made to constituted voluntary organisations only.

Applications There are separate application forms for each scheme. Contact WCVA on 0870 607 1666, or visit its website, for further information.

The Waterloo Foundation

Children, the environment, developing countries and projects in Wales

£4.3 million (2008)

Beneficial area UK and overseas.

c/o 46–48 Cardiff Road, Llandaff, Cardiff CF5 2DT

Tel. 029 2083 8980

Email info@waterloofoundation.org.uk

Website www.waterloofoundation.org.uk

Correspondent Janice Matthews, Finance Manager

Trustees *Heather Stevens; David Stevens; Janet Alexander; Caroline Oakes.*

CC Number 1117535

Information available Accounts were available from the Charity Commission. The foundation also has a helpful website.

The foundation was established in early 2007 with a substantial endowment of £100 million in shares from David and Heather Stevens, co-founders of Admiral Insurance.

Who can apply?

We welcome applications from registered charities and organisations with projects that have a recognisable charitable purpose. Your project has to be allowed within the terms of your constitution or rules and, if you are not a registered charity, you will need to send us a copy of your constitution or set of rules.

We make grants for all types of projects; start-up, initial stages and valuable ongoing funding. This can include running costs and overheads as well as posts; particularly under the World Development and Projects in Wales. We do not have any upper or lower limit on the amount of grant we offer but it is unlikely that we would offer a grant of more than £100,000.

In 2008, the foundation's second year of operation, grants were made to 196 projects totalling over £4.3 million. Grants were split as follows (the figures including grants committed for future years):

Category	No. of grants	Amount
Environment	52	£1,450,000
World development	56	£1,410,000
Child development	30	£612,000
Wales	23	£495,000
Exceptional	37	£385,000

Programmes

The foundation makes grants under four programmes:

World Development

The Waterloo Foundation aims to support projects or organisations which help the economically disadvantaged build the basis of sustainable prosperity. We have three main themes of interest, as described below.

All applicants should be able to demonstrate the impact of their programmes, and show how they meet the foundation's objectives. Where possible, evidence should be presented to prove that resources provided to developing countries will be used in a genuinely sustainable way, and not simply promote a 'hand-out' or dependency culture.

Funding priorities

1) Enterprise development

The foundation believes that development of commercial activity is at the heart of ensuring a country's prosperity and independence. The foundation is keen to support organisations which encourage economically disadvantaged individuals or communities to develop enterprise and business growth. This could be through the provision of capital and resources (where scarcity of these is a barrier to the development of sustainable economic activity), or by improving access to domestic or international markets. Support for the provision of financial services will be considered only where it is targeted at groups who are unable to access the commercial sector, and applicants should provide evidence that the proposed model is financially sustainable.

The foundation will also consider supporting projects which develop the rights of individuals and communities, and which strengthen civil society, where these can be shown to aid the growth of an enterprise culture.

2) Education

The foundation believes that educating people is key to ensuring a country's long-term development, prosperity and independence. An educated population will help bring about a more vibrant civil society, as well as increase the numbers of people available to offer their skills, knowledge and expertise to support the development of their communities.

The foundation's two key aims are:

- to increase access to education
- to increase the quality of education.

The foundation recognises that there are a large number of approaches that can be taken to meet these aims. Our priority is to fund projects or programmes which can demonstrate that they meet these aims in a highly cost-effective manner with long-term impact. Applicants are encouraged to use evidence from previous work undertaken, or other relevant research, to indicate the effectiveness of their project's approach. Relevant evidence would include:

- indicators of improved student or school performance
- data related to an increase in school enrolment, or reduction in absenteeism/ school drop-out rates
- the numbers of people who will directly benefit from the project
- any other facts or data which demonstrate the effectiveness of the project in comparison to similar programmes.

For our 2009 Funding Programme, we will prioritise projects which seek to develop secondary level education ahead of primary education. The foundation will also consider providing support for other stages of education if it can be demonstrated that these approaches are particularly effective.

3) Sanitation, hygiene and access to clean water

The foundation believes that access to sanitation, hygiene and clean water is one of the core requirements to support the sustainable development of communities. Without basic access to sanitation and safe water, an individual's ability to gain an education or undertake commercial activity is severely restricted.

The foundation is concerned about the rapid growth of urban slums, which frequently lack basic sanitation facilities. In 2009, the foundation will prioritise projects which aim to deliver improved sanitation and hygiene to these areas.

Geographical priorities

The foundation is concerned by the disparity of income which different countries within the developing world receive from international donors. Often one country appears to be favoured over another, irrespective of the actual development needs of the country itself. This is often the result of historical ties to a particular European nation. The foundation has therefore decided to select two countries which we intend to prioritise in our 2009 funding programme. These are **Benin** and the **Republic of Congo** (Congo-Brazzaville).

The foundation has also selected a number of other countries which are of specific interest to us. These are **Lesotho, Liberia, Madagascar** and **Mali**. It is anticipated that funding applications for projects relating to these countries will be prioritised ahead of others. However, applications will be accepted for projects or programmes operating in any developing country, as long as a clear need for support can be demonstrated. [Check the foundation's website for up-to-date information on funding priorities beyond 2009.]

What we will not fund

It is not our intention to provide financial support to organisations seeking to alleviate the suffering resulting from high-profile natural or man-made disasters, including the delivery of food aid or shelter.

It is also not our intention to fund projects with a principle aim to deliver increased access to improved health care.

Child Development

The foundation is keen to support research designed to give us a better understanding of the psychological and behavioural development of our children. The foundation is particularly interested in research into childhood neuro-developmental conditions and the factors that influence them. Following on from this, it is also interested in how these conditions progress as a child moves through puberty and on into adulthood, and in any links into adult mental illnesses.

Funding priorities

The neuro-developmental conditions into which the foundation is primarily interested in funding research are:

- Autistic spectrum disorders including Aspergers Syndrome
- Dyslexia
- Dyspraxia

- Certain childhood epilepsies (especially BECCTS)
- ADHD.

The foundation is also interested in research into the interaction of environmental and genetic factors in producing these conditions, particularly the areas of nutrition and diet.

Possible Funding

Occasionally, the foundation may look at supporting wide-reaching initiatives typically from organisations active in these areas, aimed at:

- improving the understanding of key professionals who deal with children who have these conditions for example, teachers, health professionals
- disseminating information to individuals/ carers/professionals.

The foundation is also interested in research into some aspects of adult mental health. Whilst it is unlikely to be able to fund research at a large scale in this area, it may be able to fund the occasional pilot project into major conditions such as OCD, Bipolar Disorder and Schizophrenia.

What we will not fund

Wider medical research into mental or physical conditions either of children or adults.

The foundation cannot at this stage fund specific individuals, either children or adults who have neuro-developmental problems and who are seeking financial help to cover medical bills, special equipment or other one–off expenses such as holidays.

Environment

For the first time in Earth's history humans are altering the natural equilibrium of the environment. We hope through this fund that we can help mitigate the damaging effects that humans are causing and contribute to a positive change both now and in the future.

Funding priorities

The foundation is keen to support initiatives aimed at reducing man-made climate change and increasing the health of the marine environment, both in the UK and worldwide. Under the Environment Fund, the foundation has two main themes:

1) Forests

The world has around four billion hectares of forests, covering 30% of the world's land area. Although tropical rainforests constitute just 5% of this land area, they play a crucial role in the maintenance of the world's environment and climate.

18–20% of global greenhouse gas emissions occur as a result of deforestation, including the burning of carbon-rich tropical peatlands (42 billion tonnes of soil carbon are stored in the forested tropical peatlands of SE Asia alone). In addition tropical forests help to generate the rainfall that stabilises local and regional weather patterns; they sustain 40% of all life on earth; and they support approximately 1 billion people who depend on them for their livelihoods.

Under our Forests programme, preference will be given to projects which seek to avoid deforestation in tropical areas, although reforestation and tree planting projects will also be considered. Projects will be considered at both strategic and local level.

Strategic initiatives could include the following.

- Lobbying for forests to be included in carbon markets, and addressing any issues which may exclude their inclusion.
- Lobbying for the increased awareness of the importance of rainforests.
- Lobbying against the drivers of tropical deforestation.

At a project level (projects should address two or more of the following).

- Localised tropical forest protection and management.
- Projects which expose and address the local drivers of tropical deforestation.
- Creating sustainable livelihoods for forest-dependent people.

2) Marine
Oceans cover more than two-thirds of the earth's surface, and the number of different species living in the oceans is estimated to be at least 178,000. Oceans are crucial to the world's economy, health and environment. Fish is an important source of food – it is estimated that 1 billion people, predominantly in developing countries, depend on fish as their primary source of protein. Also, an estimated 200 million people are directly or indirectly employed in the fish and seafood industries.

However, according to the United Nations 71–78% of the world's fisheries are either 'fully exploited', 'over exploited' or 'significantly depleted'. Some species have already been fished to commercial extinction; and many more are on the verge of collapse.

Under our Marine programme, preference will be given to projects which:

At a strategic level:

- lobby for sustainable fishing practices and techniques worldwide
- lobby for action to maintain and improve world fish stock levels, e.g. Marine Protected Areas, No Take Zones, etc.
- provide support for the marine world to stabilise climate change, in particular the uptake of greenhouse gases.

At a project level (projects should address two or more of the following):

- develop marine and fisheries protection and management
- address local drivers which cause over-exploitation of fish stocks and other seafood
- create sustainable livelihoods for coastal and seafood dependent people in developing countries.

Other interests
In addition to our forest and marine programmes foundation may occasionally support water and energy projects.

3) Water
The foundation will consider supporting projects in developing countries which promote water conservation, or increase access to water.

4) Energy
The foundation will consider offering financial support and advice for small-scale community renewable energy projects in Wales only.

What we will not support
Under the Environment Fund, foundation does not support:

- initiatives focused solely on biodiversity
- projects designed to achieve largely aesthetic environmental goals
- projects that are purely educational
- testing new renewable energy technology.

Please note: all organisations applying under the environment fund will be expected to have an environmental policy.

Projects in Wales
Although the funding priorities for the foundation are the Environment and World Development, the original founders of the foundation live and work in Wales and during the first year of the foundation's grant making, over 50% of the value of the grants across all programmes directly benefited Wales.

At a global and local level the foundation is looking for applications that have the potential to make a difference.

Following on from our review of the needs affecting the people of Wales, we would like to see applications to the Wales' fund in the areas of:

1) Working Wales
When the UK economy was expanding, Wales continued to be the least prosperous region of the UK, with economic activity lower than the UK average. The recent downturn in the global economy will undoubtedly be felt more keenly, as Wales already has a high proportion of economically inactive people. At the same time, employment levels in Wales remain stubbornly below the UK average and any cushioning effect of the high percentage of public sector employment is rapidly diminishing.

The foundation is keen to support and assist in the development of an enterprise culture in Wales and so would welcome applications from organisations and projects that will facilitate people becoming employed, whether working for others or for themselves.

Where possible, the jobs will be primarily for the beneficiary group rather than the supporting agency except, for example, where there is a need for support during the start up phase and there is a good probability of the staff position becoming self-financing within a relatively short period of time (2 to 3 years).

We are interested in promoting enterprise and employment across the board, including, but not limited to, groups with particular challenges in this area; such as people leaving care and/or institutions; those recovering from long-term sickness; older people; disabled people; ethnic minorities, etc.

The foundation will also look favourably on applications that address 'barriers to work' and will be equally receptive to both 'tried and tested' methods and those projects which are more innovative.

2) Caring Wales
It is estimated that 1 in 10 people in Wales is providing unpaid care for a family member, a total of some 340,000 people. Of these, 7,000 are likely to be children aged 5 to 15 (*source: National Office of Statistics*). There are an estimated 90,000 people providing unpaid care for family members, for more than 50 hours per week.

The foundation believes that these adults and children, who have to live and work in this way, deserve our help.

To this end, we would like to receive applications from organisations and projects providing:

- advocacy programmes for carers
- training and support for carers
- respite care.

We would also like to receive applications from organisations that are helping individual carers, particularly if those carers are working with children with the neurological problems identified in our Child Development Fund or the carers themselves are young people.

Other information and advice
- Applicants should note that the funding priorities for the foundation are World Development and the Environment.
- Applications from project/organisations in Wales that fall within the other areas of the foundation's core interests, particularly in the areas of economically disadvantaged people in poorer countries and climate-change related issues, should be made, in the first case to the World

Development fund and in the latter, to the Environment Fund.

- Although there is no upper or lower limit, awards made under the Working or Caring Wales programmes have ranged from £5,000 – £20,000.
- Applications from organisations whose primary activity is in the following areas are not eligible:
  - the arts
  - animal welfare
  - heritage
  - general health
  - groups with specific agendas (political, religious).

Exclusions The foundation will not support:

- applications for grants for work that has already taken place
- applications for grants that replace or subsidise statutory funding.

We will not consider applications for grants in the following areas:

- the arts and heritage, except in Wales
- animal welfare
- the promotion of religious or political causes
- general appeals or circulars.

We are unlikely to support projects in the following areas:

- from individuals
- for the benefit of an individual
- medical charities (except under certain aspects of our 'Child Development' programme, particularly mental health)
- festivals, sports and leisure activities
- websites, publications, conferences or seminars, except under our 'Child Development' programme.

Applications We hope to make applying for a grant fairly painless and fairly quick. However it will help us a great deal if you could follow the simple rules below when sending in an application (there are no applcation forms).

Email applications to: applications@waterloofoundation.org.uk. Include a brief description (equivalent to two sides of A4) within your email, but NOT as an attachment, of your project or the purpose for which you want the funding, detailing:

- your charity's name, address and charity number
- email, phone and name of a person to reply to
- a link to your website
- what it is for
- who it benefits
- how much you want and when
- what happens if you don't get our help
- the programme under which you are applying.

Don't write long flowery sentences – we won't read them.

Do be brief, honest, clear and direct. Use abbrevns if you like!

Don't send attachments to your email – your website will give us an introduction to you so you don't need to cover that.

Who can apply?
We welcome applications from registered charities and organisations with projects that have a recognisable charitable purpose. Your project has to be allowed within the terms of your constitution or rules and, if you are not a registered charity, you will need to send us a copy of your constitution or set of rules.

We make grants for all types of projects; start-up, initial stages and valuable ongoing funding. This can include running costs and overheads as well as posts; particularly under the World Development and Projects in Wales. We do not have any upper or lower limit on the amount of grant we offer but it is unlikely that we would offer a grant of more that £100,000.

The Wates Foundation

Assisting organisations in improving the quality of life of the deprived, disadvantaged and excluded in the community

£3 million (2008/09)

Beneficial area Berkshire, Bristol, Avon & Somerset, Buckinghamshire, Dorset, Gloucestershire, Middlesex, Nottinghamshire, Oxfordshire, Surrey, Sussex and the Greater London Metropolitan Area as defined by the M25 motorway.

Wates House, Station Approach, Leatherhead KT22 7SW

Tel. 01372 861000 **Fax** 01372 861252

Email director@watesfoundation.org.uk

Website www.watesfoundation.org.uk

Correspondent Brian Wheelwright, Director

Trustees *Revd John Wates; Jane Wates; Annabelle Elliott; James Wates; Nick Edwards; Christopher Agace.*

CC Number 247941

Information available Accounts were available at the Charity Commission.

Excellent reports and accounts, including guidance for applicants, all on the particularly clear and simple website.

In 1966, three brothers Norman, Sir Ronald and Allan Wates of the Wates building firm (now the Wates Construction Group), amalgamated their personal charitable trusts into the single entity of The Wates Foundation.

The foundation's stated mission is to 'improve the quality of life of the deprived, disadvantaged and excluded in the community in which we live.'

In 2008 the foundation widened its geographical area of benefit to include counties where members of the Wates family have a particular interest.

Guidelines

The foundation's website gives the following guidance for applicants:

The foundation aims to alleviate conditions of distress, deprivation and disadvantage that lead to social exclusion by funding charitable work across a broad range of social priorities that will bring about positive change. The foundation's current priorities are summarised in our programmes.

Organisations supported by the foundation tend to share these features:

- there is a clear sense of objectives and how to achieve them
- the work is about providing solutions to problems, not about making them more bearable
- an award has a good chance of making a difference to the organisation and to its clients and having an impact in the longer term
- the work may be a new imaginative approach, something in a new area of need, or something that is risky or sensitive
- every effort is made to comply with statutory requirements such as the Statement of Recommended Practice: Accounting and Reporting by Charities 2005
- recognised quality assurance and accreditation schemes and training for trustees and staff are used as tools to improve the organisation's effectiveness.

Grants Programmes

Foundation awards are made to work in six programmes areas. Five of these have specific aims and priorities set by the trustees. These are the criteria against which the trustees assess the relevance and potential impact of outcomes that applicants propose to achieve with the help of a foundation grant.

The sixth programme area is one in which the trustees sponsor proactively work of a strategic nature.

Foundations of Society
Objective
Under the general theme Foundations of Society, the objective of The Wates Foundation grants programmes 2008–2010 is to promote work that builds social values and responsibility and provides access to opportunities that address disadvantage.

Building Family Values
Priorities
- promoting the family unit
- social and civic responsibilities
- parenting
- opportunities for children and young people 5–25 years of age.

Community Health
Priorities
- addiction
- mental health and disabilities – the disabled
- aged and infirm
- alternative and complementary practice.

Safer Communities
Priorities
- crime in communities
- alternatives to custody
- preparing offenders for release
- resettlement of offenders after release
- female offenders.

Sustaining the Environment
Priorities
- changing life styles: education and training
- alternative and complementary practice
- conserving and sustaining the built and rural environments.

Strengthening the Charitable & Voluntary Sectors
Priorities
- capacity building of the sector
- improving the effectiveness of organisations
- quality and accreditation.

Strategic Programme
The foundation does not accept responsive applications for this programme, but will consider expressions of interest from organisations that believe that they have a proposal that meets the guidelines that follow.

Strategic aim
To initiate proactively or support jointly with partners from time to time work for the development, promotion or delivery of work that seeks to influence opinion, policy or practice in line with the foundation's Vision for a better society.

Full guidelines are available from the foundation's website.

Grantmaking in 2008/09

In 2008/09 the foundation had assets of £20.1 million and an income of £425,000. Grants were made totalling just over £3 million.

The director's report for the year, which is largely reprinted here, gives an interesting insight into the foundation's activities:

This has been a grants year of two distinct halves. Until July we were clearing our back catalogue of processed applications under the Foundation's old Programmes. Thereafter, we have been engaged in servicing the new structure and programmes that resulted from the Next Steps Review of 2008.

The broader geographical area of benefit and the personal initiative of so many of the younger generations of the Wates Families have had a leavening effect on the variety and quality of the applications going to the Family Grants Committees.

The greater personal involvement of Family members sponsoring initiatives in local communities has highlighted just how disjointed is the work of many voluntary and charitable organisations operating in a common area. We have found this to be so in Bristol, but even more so in the Oxford area. Here we have been working with organisations on the Greater Leys, the Blackbird Leys and Rose Hill estates. There are clear patterns of disadvantage and deprivation across the area with overlapping and interrelated needs being addressed by a plethora of voluntary and charitable bodies. However, it seems to us that the situation needs to be addressed not by separate awards to competing organisations, but in a more strategic approach. In consequence, we are now working with the Young Foundation to see if a greater and more sustainable impact might be achieved. This might be achieved by establishing, for example, a Community Co-ordinator on one or more of the estates.

It has been a pleasure to see a number of our beneficiaries receiving public recognition for their work. Friends of the River Crane Environment was one of ten London parks support schemes to share in the Mayor of London's Priority Parks Awards scheme. Gardening Leave, a charity that provides horticultural therapy to Ex-Service personnel suffering from mental trauma, won a Gold medal at the Ayr Flower Show.

On a broader canvas, Knowle West Media Centre in Bristol, one half of our Strategic Carbon Makeover community project, was selected in a UK-wide competition to present their work at the European Commission conference at The Hague in February on Social Fairness in Sustainable Development

– A Green and Social Europe. Straight Talking, a sexual health awareness programme which we have been supporting since its inception in 1998, was a Guardian Charity Awards winner in 2008 and also of a GlaxoSmithKline/King's Fund Impact Award.

Strategic Programme
This year we have seen a number of our strategic programmes which have a wider interest in the context of benefiting the public come to fruition.

We have funded the Restorative Justice Consortium (RJC) to draw up a nationally recognised and accredited National Occupational Standard (NOS) qualification for restorative justice practitioners. There has been close co-operation between RJC, Skills for Justice and NOS agency staff following a broad survey and regional workshops for practitioners, trainers and agencies that benefit from RJ. The aim is to agree a revised NOS standard by summer 2009 and to pilot the first accredited courses in September 2009.

In 2008 we funded an investigation into training and employment in the construction industry. The investigation sought to address concerns that links between education and training to sustainable employment in the industry are poor, with little emphasis on the civil engineering elements or crossover between building and engineering skills. Produced by Construction Youth Trust, the report Construction Careers – The Challenge to meet Employers' and Community Aspirations – reviewed the difficulties faced by young adults who are classed as NEET (not in education employment or training) in accessing vocational training, employment and careers in the construction and broader building sectors. The report has been distributed throughout the construction industry, training agencies and to the Department for Children, Families & Schools. An action plan for further dissemination and engagement of employers, learning providers, Sector Skills councils, the Mayor of London's Employment & Skills Board, local authorities, social landlords and appropriate funding agencies is now being delivered.

We have also been funding the Centre for Crime & Justice Studies (CCJS) to consider a range of topics under the general heading of What is Crime? This has generated some ground breaking research by noted academics into industrial deaths and the social harm of global insecurity and injustice. Areas that have been investigated where crime is less obviously identifiable have been the impact of the recession on health outcomes and well-being and the social impact of air pollution and the effectiveness of legislation and the different regulatory regimes. A photographic competition on the What is Crime? theme supported by an exhibition generated worldwide interest from all sections of society including schools, university students and members of the public.

Other on-going work that deserves a mention includes major funding of the work at the Croydon Family Justice Centre, – pioneering a multi-public and voluntary sector agency approach to domestic violence and sexual abuse services. The multi-faceted campaign run by the Croydon Community Against Trafficking is raising public awareness and having an impact on the issues around trafficking of people for sex and domestic servitude. Work in pupil referral units nationally by the Citizenship Foundation will come to a head in 2009 and should produce some useful models for improved effectiveness of delivery.

In line with the foundation's longstanding commitment to positive change in the criminal justice system, the trustees have been pleased to support the multi-funder alliance to promote implementation of the recommendations of the Corston Report on the management of female offenders. The foundation has made an award contributing to the costs of an independent funding sector advocate to promote the issues raised by Baroness Corston.

Finally, mention should be made of the foundation's major contribution to the Prison Radio Association's National Prison Radio Service project that is rolling out over the next two years. The foundation was a founder funder of prison radio in Feltham in the early to mid 1990s.

New Programmes
The new programmes are proving to be attractive to new applicants, not least Building Family Values that to date – and into the new reporting year – is gaining the largest number of awards. There were only three Family Grants meeting under the new scheme in 2008 so it will be interesting to see if this trend continues in the light of the prevailing difficult economic conditions.

A number of awards are worth particular mention. The first, by the Norman Wates Family Committee to MyGeneration, supports work with young people inspired by the charismatic Shaun Bailey. The second, by the Ronald Wates Family Committee to the promotion of the Age of Stupid campaigning film, reflects the younger generation of the family's engagement with environmental issues. And thirdly, the Allan Wates Family Committee awards to Chissock Woodcraft and Blue Sky Development are examples of support to social enterprises, rather than registered charities, that offer imaginative ways of addressing traditional needs – in these cases former substance abusers and offenders on release – through skills training, furniture manufacture and recycling and horticulture.

Points to note [...] are that London still maintains a significant presence despite the extension of our area to cover 12 counties; that awards to core or running costs are still a mainstay of awards; and that salaries per se are a minor element as more applicants move to Full Cost Recovery.

Recent grants
Grants payable during 2008/09 included those to:

Cool2Care – Surrey (£50,000), towards an expansion of the service throughout Surrey to support more families with disabled children; Jessie May Trust – Bristol (£45,000), towards the core costs of a qualified nurse home-visiting service for terminally-ill children; Apex Charitable Trust (£40,000), towards core costs of a London programme working with offenders on release; Small Charities Coalition (£36,000), towards start-up funding; FAME – Nottingham (£35,000), towards core costs of running a mediation service for low income families; SuperKidz – South London (£29,000), towards a Volunteer Coordinator's post in a parenting and youth project; Friends of Baale Mane – Gopalapura, India (£23,500), towards a building project at a girls' school; Gardening Leave (£20,000), towards repairing and conserving the Stovehouse; STOP Trafficking UK (£10,000), towards core costs; Art for Youth (£5,000), towards an annual award for new artists.

Exclusions As a general rule we expect that applicants will have considered the Guidance for Applications on the foundation's website.

Our preferred format for initial approaches for funding is laid down in the section How to Apply [see 'Applications']. Applications that make no effort to meet this simple requirement will be rejected automatically.
We cannot fund:
- organisations that are not registered or recognised as charities unless in the process of registering. Applications by regulated not-for-profit social enterprises may be considered
- work that is not legally charitable
- political parties, political lobbying or campaigning
- churches or other religious organisations where an award will be used for religious purposes.

We do not fund:
- individuals for any purpose
- large, well-established or national charities
- organisations whose income in the year preceding an application exceeded £700,000
- statutory bodies including local authorities and their agencies

- grant-making bodies except through partnerships
- heritage, conservation or archival projects unless relevant to the urban or rural built environment
- capital projects
- conferences
- appeals of any kind including for disaster relief, sporting, social or other fundraising events
- animal welfare organisations
- activity taking place overseas
- work delivered outside of the counties of Berkshire, Bristol, Avon & Somerset, Buckinghamshire, Dorset, Gloucestershire, Middlesex, Nottinghamshire, Oxfordshire, Surrey, Sussex and the Greater London Metropolitan Area as defined by the M25 motorway.

Grants will not be made to:
- work that is a public funding or statutory responsibility whether fulfilled or not
- replace cuts in funding by statutory bodies where the foundation becomes the largest single provider
- top up funding on under-priced contracts or other commissioned work
- organisations where we become the largest single income provider.

Applications
What You Should Know
Applications to the foundation are accepted at any time on a rolling basis. An acknowledgement can normally be expected within 14 working days.

We operate a two stage application process that should reduce the time that applicants may spend preparing material and allow us to give a response to the application in a reasonable time. On average, 90% or more of requests are rejected before the second stage.

First Stage
We do not use an application form so that applicants are not constrained in promoting their case for an award. However, we do expect that you comply with our format. Applications that make no effort to meet this simple requirement will be rejected automatically. The basics:

- Initial applications should be of no more than four A4 pages (minimum font size Arial 11 point) addressing the questions below. These are designed to elicit sufficient information to explain your application without having to contact you.
- A budgetary breakdown may be attached additional to the four-page limit. Budgets covering more than one year should include elements for inflation. Salaries should identify NI costs and pensions where appropriate.
- Your application must be accompanied by a signed copy of your latest Annual Report

and Accounts which comply with Charity Commission requirements.

- Additional publicity material including pamphlets, newspaper cuttings, Annual Reviews and DVDs will not be considered.

Tell us:

- who you are and what you do
- about the work you want funded including beneficiaries, location and timescales
- how much you need from us and over what period – one year, two years or three
- where any balance of funding is coming from and how you intend to fund the work when our award ends
- how this work will make a difference to those people you seek to benefit
- how you intend to monitor the work, measure its success and ensure its quality
- how your work benefits the public in accordance with the requirements of the Charities Act 2006.

Your application **MUST** contain the following statement:

We are aware that supplying any deliberately false information or making any deliberately false statement may result in prosecution. To the best of our knowledge and belief, all statements made in this application and its associated documentation are true and accurate. I am authorised to sign on behalf of the organisation.

Name. . . . . Position . . . .

What Happens Next

All requests for support are rigorously filtered. The assessment process includes financial and other due diligence checks to establish the authenticity of your application; this may involve a preliminary visit. Application to the second stage will only be invited after this process.

We send out a letter outlining the broad elements identified in the initial application together with the second stage application questions. You will have assembled much of the information to answer these as part of your initial approach to the foundation. Where appropriate, the completed application questionnaire will be supported by a business or work plan and future funding strategy.

The process of preparing an application that goes to a Grants Committee including arranging a visit to you by a member of the Committee can take three months or more.

If Your Application is Rejected

There is no time limit before unsuccessful applicants at any stage might re-apply. If requested we can provide feedback on why an application was unsuccessful. Before re-applying, however, a telephone call to the foundation is always advisable.

Final Point

Although we have a small staff, we are happy for potential applicants to ring us up and discuss funding opportunities or seek clarification if you are in doubt about whether you are eligible under our guidelines: this often saves on needless correspondence.

The Wellcome Trust

Biomedical research, history of medicine, biomedical ethics and public engagement with science

£598.5 million (2007/08)

Beneficial area UK and overseas.

Gibbs Building, 215 Euston Road, London NW1 2BE

Tel. 020 7611 8888 **Fax** 020 7611 8545

Email grantenquiries@wellcome.ac.uk

Website www.wellcome.ac.uk

Correspondent Grants Information Officer

Trustees *Prof. Adrian Bird; Sir William Castell; Prof. Dame Kay Davies; Prof. Christopher Fairburn; Prof. Richard Hynes; Roderick Kent; Baroness Eliza Manningham-Buller; Prof. Peter Rigby; Prof. Peter Smith; Edward Walker-Arnott.*

CC Number 210183

Information available Extensive information is available from the trust and is accessible through its excellent website.

Summary

The Wellcome Trust is one of the world's leading biomedical research charities and is the UK's largest non-governmental source of funds for biomedical research. It is also the UK's largest charity.

The trust's mission is to foster and promote research with the aim of improving human and animal health. Funding from the trust has supported a number of major successes including:

- sequencing of the human genome
- development of the antimalarial drug artemisinin
- pioneering cognitive behavioural therapies for psychological disorders
- establishing UK Biobank

- building the Wellcome Wing at the Science Museum.

The trust's major activities in 2007/08 are described by its chair, Sir William Castell, in its annual review as follows:

This year saw a substantial increase in the trust's total charitable expenditure – up from £520 million in 2006/07 to £702 million in 2007/08. This was mainly due to significant increases in Strategic Awards and in Technology Transfer investment and £50 million of funds released from the special dividend agreed in 2007.

The majority of our funding is used to support research activities in the UK. During the year we have upped our commitment to the translation of research findings into health benefits by introducing the Medical Engineering initiative (to boost the development of innovative solutions for healthcare), and we announced plans to create with the Department of Health the Health Innovation Challenge Fund, which we hope will facilitate the National Health Service regaining its key role in the development of proven new clinical approaches to disease.

We continue to appreciate that flexible forms of funding are vital to support innovative and productive research, and have a made a number of Strategic Awards this year, across an astonishingly diverse range of areas.

The highlights include:

- The trust's first major Medical Humanities grants: £2 million to Professor Brian Hurwitz at King's College London and around £1.9 million to Professor Martyn Evans at Durham University to establish centres of excellence in the medical humanities.
- A £4 million Strategic Translation Award to Dr Helen McShane to evaluate the tuberculosis vaccine candidate MVA85A in a Phase IIb study in South African infants.
- A £2.8 million renewal of funding for The Wellcome Trust Centre for Molecular Parasitology at the University of Glasgow.

Our long-term investments have continued to make excellent progress, particularly in the area of genomics. The Wellcome Trust Sanger Institute, largely funded by the trust, has moved from identifying the genetic sequences of numerous species to unravelling the biological implications of these findings. In 2007/08, a total of £22.8 million was awarded to the Wellcome Trust Case Control Consortium and other genome-wide association studies to enable researchers to identify and characterise the genetic variants related to common, complex diseases.

Wellcome Collection has continued to enjoy incredible popularity, clocking up over 300,000 visitors in its first year. Among the highlights of the current year were two thought provoking and fascinating temporary exhibitions, Life Before Death and Skeletons, which attracted unprecedented levels of interest, from the press and the general public alike.

Future Challenges

Science has always been one of the foundations underlying humankind's ability to develop and advance. Today, this has not changed, and the numerous and complex challenges currently facing the world demand significant attention from world leaders, policymakers and grantmakers alike. With issues as diverse as energy and biofuels, intellectual property, genetically modified organisms, and information and communication technology among those we must tackle, it is clear that advances in science and technology will undoubtedly play a significant part in how we move forward as a global community, making the trust's global presence more important than ever.

During the year, we have made important progress in building our international influence, in terms of both examining how we contribute to the significant medical challenges facing the world, and how we grasp the opportunities new technologies bring to tackle these issues.

In particular, we recognise the substantial challenge of global climate change and the potential impact of this on, among others, health, agriculture, migration, infrastructure and water supplies. Through a Frontiers Meeting (an expert meeting that explores the current state of science in a particular field) we have identified a number of areas that will form an important part of our agenda over the coming years. In addition, we have moved our partnership focus to see how we can contribute to the nutrition debate, particularly by looking at undernutrition and overnutrition, which are, paradoxically, both growing challenges faced by India and China.

Grantmaking

In 2007/08 the trust had assets of over £12 billion (£14.36 billion in 2006/07) and an income of £305 million. Total charitable expenditure during the year was £701.6 million, including grants totalling £598.5 million (£433.3 million in 2006/07).

Amongst the many grants awarded during the year were those to Universities and other institutes, mainly in the UK, but also elsewhere (these figures represent the total amount awarded during the year, and may comprise many grants):

Institution	Value
University of Oxford	£78,200,000
Imperial College London	£46,900,000
University of Cambridge	£46,900,000
University College London	£34,100,000
King's College London	£25,600,000
University of Edinburgh	£24,800,000
London School of Hygiene and Tropical Medicine	£20,100,000
University of Dundee	£17,500,000
Kenya Medical Research Institute, Kenya	£15,900,000
University of Newcastle upon Tyne	£14,600,000
Liverpool School of Tropical Medicine	£13,300,000
European Molecular Biology Laboratory	£13,100,000
University of Glasgow	£12,700,000
University of Manchester	£10,000,000
Myscience.Co Ltd (National Science Learning Centre)	£10,000,000
University of Bristol	£9,800,000
University of Leicester	£8,100,000
University College Dublin	£7,800,000
Academy of Medical Sciences	£7,700,000
University of Nottingham	£6,800,000
University of Exeter	£6,100,000
University of St Andrews	£6,000,000
International Development Research Council, Canada	£5,100,000
Public Health Foundation of India	£5,000,000
University of Warwick	£4,300,000
Medical Research Council	£4,200,000
University of Cape Town, South Africa	£4,200,000
Massachusetts General Hospital, USA	£4,000,000
Cardiff University	£4,000,000
University of Leeds	£4,000,000
University of Sheffield	£4,000,00
University of Liverpool	£3,800,000
Diamond Light Source Ltd	£3,600,000
Grants to other institutions	£70,000,000

Grantmaking Policy

The trust supports high-quality research across both the breadth of the biomedical sciences and the spectrum of proposals from 'blue skies' to clinical to applied research, and encourages the translation of research findings into medical benefits.

Although the majority of grants are awarded to United Kingdom recipients, there are also a number of schemes designed specifically for overseas applicants.

For the most part grant funding is channeled through a university or similar institution in response to proposals submitted by individual academic researchers. Applications are peer reviewed using referees selected by trust staff from the United Kingdom and international research communities. Expert committees, which also include members from outside the United Kingdom, make most funding decisions, with external experts also brought into Strategic Award Committee meetings to assist in the decision-making process.

Grant awards are made to the employing institution, which is then required to take responsibility for administering a grant in accordance with its purpose and with the terms and conditions attached to the award. Only a limited number of small-scale awards are made directly to individuals. Grant funding is available via a range of schemes including:

- short-term awards for between a few months and three years, and longer-term project and programme grants for research, usually for up to five years
- awards for research training and career development where support is provided for individuals at all stages of their careers
- strategic awards to provide outstanding research groups with significant levels of support.

The trust is aware of the profound impact biomedical research has on society and in its grantmaking also seeks to raise awareness of the medical, ethical and social implications of research and to promote dialogue between scientists, the public and policy makers.

The trust also undertakes activities in and funds research into the history of medicine. The Wellcome Library, which forms part of Wellcome Collection, provides access to resources that support its activities, and the trust also provides grant funding for improved access to and preservation of other medical history collections in the United Kingdom.

In addition to the above, the trust funds its own research institute, the Wellcome Trust Sanger Institute, channelling support through a wholly-owned subsidiary, Genome Research Limited. Led by Allan Bradley, the Director of the Sanger Institute, its researchers are engaged in research programmes using large-scale sequencing, informatics and analysis of genetic variation to further understanding of gene function in health and disease and to generate data and resources of lasting value to biomedical research.

Strategic Plan 2005–2010

The trust set out its first strategic plan for the period 2000–2005. The current strategic plan aims to build on the successes of the first by:

- ensuring that the single biggest element of our total funding is used to support basic, curiosity-driven, investigator-led research and career initiatives – recognising that this underpins future discovery and application
- using around 10 per cent of our spend each year to enable us to respond flexibly to new, unanticipated opportunities
- increasing support for clinical research and training to ensure that the research we support benefits human health
- increasing support for the use of knowledge that arises from biomedical research for health benefit
- expanding activities to engage with the public about biomedical science and the issues it raises for society.

The trust updated its strategic plan in February 2009 to reflect ongoing developments. Although the information provided by the trust is naturally specialist and detailed, it is also accessible and interesting and gives a enlightening summary of this fascinating trust's work. Details of the updated strategic plan are reproduced here:

Aim 1: Advancing Knowledge – to support research to increase understanding of health and disease, and its societal context

Objective 1.1 – To provide funding support across the continuum of biomedical research:

- basic – to encourage an experimental and exploratory approach to increase understanding of the biological basis of health and disease in humans and animals
- clinical – to increase our support for clinical research designed to answer questions about health and disease
- population health – to support research to improve understanding of the determinants of disease and quality of life in populations, and generate a sound evidence base to inform decisions in public health and healthcare delivery
- medical humanities – to improve our understanding of the historical, ethical, social and cultural context in which biomedical research and its application take place.

Progress 2007/08

During the third year of the plan we:

- committed £457 million in response-mode grant funding through our biomedical science funding streams to support outstanding researchers, teams and ideas
- provided an additional £77 million funding over the year for the Wellcome Trust Sanger Institute, a world-leading genomics research centre playing a key role in ground-breaking international initiatives such as the 1000 Genomes Project and the International Cancer Genome Consortium
- continued to use Strategic Awards in Biomedical Science to support major research and training programmes; examples included:
  - an £8.7 million award to support the UK HIV Vaccine Consortium, which brings together research groups developing new HIV vaccine constructs and immunisation strategies
  - awards of £6.5 million to the Oxford Ion Channel Initiative (OXION) and £5 million to the London Pain Consortium to further develop their trust-funded interdisciplinary research and training programmes in integrative physiology
- funded awards in priority research areas through targeted calls for proposals, including:
  - providing £30 million for genome-wide association studies that will expand the number of diseases investigated via the

Wellcome Trust Case Control Consortium
  - awarding £9 million to support 17 projects utilising electronic patient records for biomedical research, in the first round of a joint initiative with the UK Research Councils
- provided significant funding contributions to the UK Clinical Research Collaboration initiatives on Centres for Excellence in Public Health and Translational Infection Research
- developed a successful bid to Government in partnership with the Medical Research Council (MRC), Cancer Research UK and University College London to acquire the land to construct the new world-leading UK Centre for Medical Research and Innovation
- provided £13 million in grant funding via our Medical Humanities funding stream, including support for new Strategic Awards in Medical Humanities and Strategic Awards in Biomedical Ethics.

During 2008/09 we:

- developed strategic focus areas in the biomedical sciences through Strategic Awards and targeted calls for proposals; priorities included:
  - funding interdisciplinary research on neurodegenerative diseases, through a £30 million joint initiative with the MRC
  - progressing further calls for proposals for genome-wide association studies and research using electronic patient records and databases
  - developing new activity to support mouse phenotyping
- continued to use the advice of our strategy committees to explore emerging strategic topics, and develop Frontiers meetings and workshops to engage the wider community – themes for the year ahead will include: childhood obesity and behaviour; emerging infectious diseases; synthetic biology; and health and the built environment
- worked with our partners to progress the UK Centre for Medical Research and Innovation and develop its scientific strategy and governance arrangements
- partnered with other organisations to coordinate research activities to address key global health challenges – such as pandemic influenza, global nutrition and the health consequences of climate change
- developed our history of medicine funding strategies based on the outcomes of a review completed during 2007/08 and take forward a new funding initiative in bioarcheology.

Indicators of progress

- Between 1 October 2007 and 30 September 2008, 4290 scientific papers associated with the Wellcome Trust were

published in journals featuring in the PubMed database.
- The Wellcome Trust Sanger Institute and European Bioinformatics Institute placed first and second respectively in a June 2008 report on the UK's 'citations elite'. In addition, based on publication output over the last decade, seven of world's 12 most highly cited researchers in the field of microbiology are based at the Sanger Institute.
- Examples of our funded research that have contributed to important advances in knowledge include:
  - key studies led by Professor Gabriel Waksman to elucidate the three-dimensional protein structures of the secretion machinery in Gram-negative bacteria
  - research undertaken by Professor David van Heel and colleagues to identify new genetic variants implicated in coeliac disease through genome-wide association studies, transforming our knowledge of the condition
  - research led by Professor Malcolm Parker to examine the role of nuclear receptors in the body's handling of fats – work that could identify new drug targets for the control of body weight and ovulation.

Aim 2: Using Knowledge – to support the development and use of knowledge to create health benefit

Objective 2.1 – To increase the opportunities for the development of products, devices and enabling technologies for health benefit.
Objective 2.2 – To work with relevant partners to ensure that the outcomes of research are considered in changes to clinical practice, healthcare and public policy.

Progress 2007/08

During the third year of the plan we:

- provided a total of £12 million in Technology Transfer grant funding to help to bridge the gap between fundamental research and commercial application, through Translation Awards and Strategic Translation Awards
- awarded £10 million funding through our Seeding Drug Discovery initiative to support early-stage drug discovery projects in a range of therapeutic areas
- supported additional major Strategic Awards for product development activities, including:
  - an award of £5 million to Daniel Henderson and colleagues at PaxVax Inc. to develop an oral tablet vaccine for pandemic avian influenza
  - a grant of £3.5 million to Mike Dawson and colleagues at Novacta Biosystems to develop a bioengineered antibiotic to combat hospital-acquired Clostridium difficile infections

- launched a new £45 million initiative – in partnership with the Engineering and Physical Sciences Research Council – to support centres of excellence in medical engineering, with awards made during 2008/09
- continued to support the network of Clinical Research Facilities as major centres for clinical translation in the UK
- developed a joint initiative with the Alliance for Health Systems and Policy Research to support capacity building for the uptake of research knowledge into policy in developing countries.

During 2008/09 we:

- continued to support the development of innovative technologies products and devices through our Technology Transfer funding schemes
- worked with the UK Department of Health to implement the Health Innovation Challenge Fund, which will provide up to £100 million for up to five years to promote the uptake of new healthcare technologies to benefit patients within the NHS
- expanded the international scope of our technology transfer activities, including through:
  - the further development of global health research and development (R&D) partnerships to develop vaccines and drugs for neglected diseases
  - new product development initiatives in India, working with partners from academia, industry and non-governmental organisations
- used the expert advice of our Technology Transfer Strategy Panel and Challenge Committee to identify and develop new strategic highlight areas for technology transfer
- continued to foster the uptake of research into policy and practice through providing support to grantholders and working with other organisations.

Indicators of progress

- During 2007/08, in follow-up to Wellcome Trust Technology Transfer funding, researchers secured over £119 million in venture capital and industry finance for commercialisation of R&D efforts.
- Recipients of Translation Award funding reported 15 new inventions over the year; nine new projects were developed through licensing deals with commercial partners.
- Examples of trust-funded activities that are contributing to the uptake and use of research knowledge for health benefit include:
  - funding the clinical development of a new single-dose drinkable typhoid vaccine developed by Emergent BioSolutions Inc.

- funding a phase IIb trial in infants to evaluate the protective efficacy of a new candidate booster vaccine for tuberculosis, partnered by the University of Oxford with Emergent BioSolutions Inc.
- providing long-term support to Professor Anke Ehlers, a Wellcome Trust Principal Research Fellow who has developed new cognitive behavioural therapies for anxiety-related disorders and supported their uptake into clinical practice
- supporting the National Survey of Sexual Attitudes and Lifestyles with the MRC, which has gathered invaluable data on sexual behaviour, fertility and sex-related diseases across the UK.

Aim 3: Engaging Society – to engage with society to foster an informed climate within which biomedical research can flourish

Objective 3.1 – To fund public engagement activities and research to:

- promote interest, learning and excitement about biomedical science and its past, present and future impacts on society;
- stimulate an informed debate to raise awareness and understanding of biomedical science, its achievements, applications and implications;
- inform our own – and wider national – debates, research plans and policies, in relation to public interests and concerns, to balance the needs of the research endeavour with those of society.

Progress 2007/08
During the third year of the plan we:

- delivered a highly successful first year of exhibitions and public events at Wellcome Collection, our new public venue, which was shortlisted for the Art Fund Prize
- took forward a range of activities to support and promote science education; highlights included:
  - launching Project Enthuse, a £30 million partnership between the Wellcome Trust, Government and industry to support continuing professional development of science teachers via the National Science Learning Centre
  - supporting key research to inform education policy – publishing the first opinion pieces in the Perspectives on Education series, which focused on science in primary schools
- provided over £3 million in grant funding for innovative public engagement activities, and continued to develop our funding schemes; in particular:
  - we announced a new annual themed competition for Society Awards, with the topic for 2008/09 being 'genetic variations and health

- we launched International Engagement Awards to support public engagement activities relevant to global health issues
- funded three major Capital Awards for public engagement totalling nearly £5 million at the Science Museum, Science Gallery Dublin and At-Bristol
- supported a range of activities to foster the development of broadcast projects on biomedicine – including through funding Broadcast Development Awards, sponsoring key events, and providing training and development opportunities for broadcasters and scientists
- continued to provide training and resources for scientists to engage the public, including launching the Beacons for Public Engagement initiative in partnership with the Higher Education Funding Council for England and Research Councils UK
- launched the Wellcome Trust Book Prize to celebrate the best of medicine in literature.

During 2008/09 we:

- delivered a broad and innovative series of exhibitions, live events and tours at Wellcome Collection and develop new partnerships with other venues internationally. Exhibitions for 2008/09 [included]:
  - War and Medicine (November 2008 to February 2009)
  - Madness and Modernity (April to June 2009)
  - Bobby Baker's Diary Drawings (March to August 2009)
  - Models (June to October 2009)
- continued to strengthen our work to promote science education, providing continued support for the professional development of science teachers, funding research on key education issues and maximising our impact on science education policy
- conducted the first series of Wellcome Monitor surveys to gauge, analyse and disseminate the attitudes of adults and young people to biomedical science
- delivered a range of public engagement activities via the Darwin200 initiative, including:
  - Darwin's Children – producing a series Darwin-inspired experiments that will be made available to every UK schoolchild
  - Darwin and Broadcast – working with broadcast media on programming to engage audiences in Darwin's life and work
  - Darwin and Culture – exploring the cultural impact of Darwin's ideas, including through the Darwin's Poets project

- take forward further broadcast development projects and activities to increase the quality and coverage of science in broadcast media.

Indicators of progress
- Wellcome Collection attracted over 325,000 visitors during 2007/08, and received widespread and positive media coverage.
- Over 1,700 teachers participated in training activities provided by the National Science Learning Centre.
- Activities supported by public engagement grants ending in 2007/08 reached an audience of over 500,000 people.
- Examples of public engagement activities supported via Wellcome Trust funding have included:
  - innovative arts projects such as Project Façade, which tells the story of facial reconstructive surgery undergone by soldiers who were injured in World War I through sculptures constructed from uniforms
  - science education projects, including supporting the development of a new AS-level qualification (Perspectives on Science), which has now been rolled out nationally
  - drama projects such as Playing God, a deaf theatre performance exploring the dilemmas facing parents of deaf babies about whether to allow their children to have cochlear implants.

Aim 4: Developing People – To foster a research community and individual researchers who can contribute to the advancement and use of knowledge
Objective 4.1 – To provide training and career support schemes to attract and retain the highest quality individuals in biomedical research.
Objective 4.2 – To stimulate research capacity building to address priority areas of science, or career gaps, by developing tailored training and career initiatives.
Objective 4.3 – To work with others on key issues related to research careers.

Progress 2007/08
During the third year of the plan we:

- continued to provide career support to outstanding researchers at all levels, including:
  - funding 17 new Sir Henry Wellcome Postdoctoral Fellowships, which support the best newly qualified scientists embarking on independent research careers
  - making the first awards to enable researchers and students to spend time in laboratories at the US National Institutes of Health and the Howard Hughes Medical Institute

- provided new funding schemes to enhance clinical research careers, namely:
  - interdisciplinary Training Programmes for Clinicians in Translational Medicine and Therapeutics – training partnerships between academia and industry to provide clinicians with the expertise to undertake studies to develop and evaluate novel therapies in humans
  - postdoctoral Training Fellowships for MB/PhD Graduates – fellowships for the most promising MB/PhD graduates to embark on research careers
  - start-up funds for clinical lecturers – grants for clinical lecturers to meet research costs through a scheme run in partnership with the Academy of Medical Sciences.
- launched an £80 million initiative to support the careers of Indian scientists, with trust funding of £40 million over five years to be matched by the Indian Government
- supported a series of major Strategic Awards to support research capacity building in developing countries, with four awards totalling £20 million to initiatives in Africa and three awards totalling £15 million to programmes in India
- expanded the scope of our International Senior Research Fellowship scheme to now support researchers in Croatia, Slovenia and the Slovak Republic
- continued to develop our Advanced Courses programme, which provides training courses and workshops in state-of-the-art research techniques at the Wellcome Trust Genome Campus and at centres in developing countries.

During 2008/09 we:

- continued to provide and develop our portfolio of fellowship and studentship schemes to support outstanding researchers in the UK and overseas throughout their research careers
- provided a series of major awards to support the development of African research institutions through north–south and south–south partnerships
- took forward the Wellcome Trust–Department of Biotechnology India Alliance, providing the first round of fellowship schemes for current and future research leaders in India
- continued to foster interdisciplinary research training through the use of Strategic Awards and targeted calls for proposals where appropriate
- led and participate in new initiatives in partnership with others to address issues related to research careers (including through the implementation of the Concordat to Support the Career Development of Researchers) and to enhance systems for career tracking.

Indicators of progress
- During 2007/08 we made a total of 142 fellowship awards to support the careers of researchers (including 135 biomedical science fellows and seven fellows in the medical humanities).
- Mechanisms used by the trust to support training and capacity building include:
  - PhD programmes – such as the four-year PhD programme in neuroscience at University College London, which has been training graduate students since 1996
  - Strategic Awards, including a recent major award to Professor Shah Ebrahim for capacity building and training at the New Delhi Public Health Foundation in India, with a focus on chronic disease.
- Through our fellowship schemes we support outstanding scientists in the UK and overseas, such as:
  - Professor Dorothy Bishop, a Wellcome Trust Principal Research Fellow whose work on language impairment has led to improved diagnosis and treatment for children with language difficulties
  - Dr Cameron Simmons, a Wellcome Trust Senior Research Fellow working in Vietnam to enhance our understanding of the virus that causes dengue, a disease of enormous public health importance in the region.

Aim 5: Facilitating Research – To promote the best conditions for research and the use of knowledge
Objective 5.1 – To support the development of research resources.
Objective 5.2 – To support the development of state-of-the-art laboratories, facilities and buildings.
Objective 5.3 – To work with science and innovation policy makers and others in order to provide a sustainable environment for biomedical research.

Progress 2007/08
During the third year of the plan we:

- announced a series of Capital Awards to nine universities throughout the UK, providing a total of nearly £30 million to support the development of world-class biomedical research infrastructure
- supported research at Wellcome Trust Centres in the UK and Major Overseas Programmes, renewing our core funding for the Malawi–Liverpool–Wellcome Trust Programme for Research in Tropical Medicine and the Wellcome Trust Centre for Molecular Parasitology at the University of Glasgow
- funded key research collections and databases, including through two Strategic Awards to the European Bioinformatics Institute for a trace archive and chemogenomics data resource

- developed existing major partnership initiatives to develop research resources and grasped new opportunities to enhance their scientific potential, including:
  - funding the Membrane Protein Laboratory at the Diamond synchrotron and Imperial College London
  - granting a Strategic Award to the Structural Genomics Consortium to develop a resource providing chemical probes for epigenetic targets
- continued to support the Wellcome Library, enhancing access to its collections
- took forward policy and advocacy on key issues impacting the research environment; highlights included:
  - delivering a range of advocacy and engagement activities around research issues debated in the development of the Human Fertilisation and Embryology Act
  - taking forward discussions with policy makers and general practitioners around the use of electronic patient data in research
  - engaging actively in policy discussions on the use of animals in research.

During 2008/09 we:

- continued to support and develop major research resources in partnership with other funders, with consideration of scientific enhancement of the UK Biobank a key priority for the year ahead
- took forward the development of the Sainsbury–Wellcome Centre for Neural Circuits and Behaviour as a new cutting-edge neuroscience research facility, in partnership with the Gatsby Charitable Foundation and University College London
- initiated a programme of work to develop the Wellcome Library as a major international resource for history of medicine research and enhanced its services for teaching and exploration
- continued to promote activities to maximise access to the outcomes of funded research, exploring the scope to develop a European PubMed Central resource and examining how we can work with others to ensure key research data are sustained for the long term
- develop the Wellcome Trust Conference Centre at Hinxton as a leading international venue for scientific meetings and conferences
- progressed advocacy work around key policy issues at the UK and European levels, with priorities including the future of the dual support system and the EU Directive on the use of animals in research

- partnered with others to support research and advocacy activities on key global health challenges:
  - worked with the World Health Organization and other partners on policy aspects of pandemic influenza preparedness
  - worked with organisations to develop the evidence base around the health impacts of climate change in advance of the Copenhagen Climate Conference in December 2009
  - took forward work with the Gates Foundation on global nutrition and health in the context of best practice within the food industry.

Indicators of progress

- The Wellcome Library attracted over 33,000 user visits over the year ending September 2008.
- The Wellcome Trust provides long-term support for world-class research centres, for example:
  - the Malawi–Liverpool–Wellcome Trust Programme for Research in Tropical Medicine – our Major Overseas Programme in Malawi has helped to develop research capacity in one of the world's poorest countries
  - the Wellcome Unit for the History of Medicine – this Trustfunded Unit at the University of Manchester undertakes research and training in medical history and has developed a range of outreach activities.
- Our funding has helped to develop key research resources, such as the DECIPHER database at the Wellcome Trust Sanger Institute, which enables researchers and clinicians to share information relating to developmental diseases.
- We have taken forward advocacy activities in partnership with others to influence key policy developments impacting research, including:
  - the Human Fertilisation and Embryology Act, where the trust undertook a range of activities to ensure that this new legislation had appropriate provisions to enable stem cell and embryo research to proceed within a robust regulatory framework
  - the EU Physical Agents (Electromagnetic Fields) Directive, where work undertaken by the trust and other organisations to highlight the potential negative consequences of the Directive helped to secure a postponement of the Directive to allow the guidelines to be reassessed.

Aim 6: Developing Our Organisation – To use our resources efficiently and effectively

Objective 6.1 – To adopt investment and finance strategies to maximise the funding available to support our mission, maintaining

a balance between the long term and short term, and providing flexibility to respond to new opportunities.

Objective 6.2 – To ensure that the Wellcome Trust's staff and processes best support the delivery of all our aims and activities.

Objective 6.3 – To increase awareness of the work supported by the Wellcome Trust.

Progress 2007/2008

During the third year of the plan we:

- appointed Baroness Eliza Manningham-Buller to the Trust's Board of Governors; four other new members also joined the Board who were appointed during 2006/2007 (Kay Davies, Chris Fairburn, Rod Kent and Peter Rigby)
- embedded a new organisational structure in order to maximise the effectiveness of our grant-making and grant-management activities
- developed and refined our investments strategies in order to maximise the funding we have been able to provide to biomedical research
- launched the new-look Wellcome Trust corporate website in order to serve our key audiences more effectively
- developed new work to evaluate the impact of our funding, including commissioning a study to measure the economic returns from research in partnership with the Medical Research Council and the Academy of Medical Sciences
- secured extensive positive coverage in the media for the work of the Wellcome Trust and Wellcome Collection.

During 2008/09 we:

- continued to actively develop our investments strategies in order to maximise returns in the face of turbulent global market conditions
- developed our staff in light of our activities and priorities – including our growing international focus – continually ensuring that we have the skill sets we need to deliver our charitable mission
- developed our information technology strategies in order to enhance our internal efficiency and service provision
- maximised the use of new web and other communication technologies in order to engage audiences in the work of the trust and with biomedicine more broadly
- strengthened and expanded the assessment and evaluation of our funded research, including through new approaches to examining different areas of our scientific portfolio
- expanded our work with local communities in the Camden area
- reviewed formally our progress in implementing our current Strategic Plan, and began work on a new five-year plan for the period from 2010 to 2015.

Indicators of progress

- The Wellcome Trust's Annual Report and Financial Statements 2008 provides details of our investments and expenditure for the 2007/08 financial year:
  - the value of the Wellcome Trust's net investment base was £13.1 billion on 30 September 2008 (falling from £15.1 billion on 30 September 2007)
  - our charitable expenditure for 2007/08 was £702 million (compared with an expenditure of £520 million in 2006/07)
  - our support and governance expenditure for 2007/08 was £44 million (compared to £47 million in 2006/07).

Exclusions The trust does not normally consider support for the extension of professional education or experience, the care of patients or clinical trials.

Contributions are not made towards overheads and not normally towards office expenses.

The trust does not supplement support provided by other funding bodies, nor does it donate funds for other charities to use, nor does it respond to general appeals.

Applications

eGrants: online application

The eGrants system enables applicants to apply for grants online. The system provides workflow to steer the application through head of department and university administration approval steps until final submission to the Wellcome Trust.

Most applicants for Science Funding and Medical Humanities grants are required to submit their applications via our eGrants system. However, Word forms are still available for:

- preliminary applications
- Public Engagement grants
- Technology Transfer grants
- applicants who have limited/unreliable access to the internet – please email the eGrants helpdesk – ga-formsupport@wellcome.ac.uk – if this is the case.

If you haven't applied using eGrants before, here is what you need to do:

- make sure your institution (or the institution that would be administering the grant, if you are not already based there) is registered with us
- access eGrants and fill in a home page for yourself (this will include your personal details that can be downloaded onto future application forms).

Other people – such as coapplicants – will need to fill in details too.

The benefits of our eGrants system include:

- better functionality
- clear sign off process through the host institution
- reduced administration at the trust
- helping us to capture management information (useful for us and useful for you).

How to register

You can register with eGrants through the log-in page. Further information on the registration process, help and guidance notes are available by accessing this page.

Registration status of institutions

If you wish to register with eGrants but are not sure whether your institution is registered, you can check the list of registered institutions. If your institution is not on this list you should contact your administration office directly for further information.

Frequently asked questions

A list of frequently asked questions for eGrants is available from the trust's website.

The Welton Foundation

Medical research, health and general

£487,000 (2007/08)

Beneficial area UK.

33 St Mary Axe, London EC3A 8LL

Tel. 020 7342 2630

Correspondent The Trustees

Trustees *D B Vaughan; H A Stevenson; Dr Michael Harding.*

CC Number 245319

Information available Accounts were available from the Charity Commission.

Registered in 1965, the objective of the foundation is 'to provide financial support to other charities at the absolute discretion of the trustees. As a discretionary trust the foundation has no fixed policy for making grants. The current policy of the trustees is in the main to support charitable causes in the fields of health and medicine, but they can exercise their discretion to make donations to any other charities'.

In 2007/08 the foundation had assets of £8.25 million and an income of £381,000. Grants were made to 14

organisations during the year totalling £487,000, categorised as follows:

Health and medicine – 5 grants totalling £445,500

The beneficiaries were: The Healing Foundation (£250,000); National Centre for Young People with Epilepsy (£100,000); Raynaud's and Scleroderma Association (£89,500); Sheffield Institution for Motor Neurone Disease (£5,000); and the Stroke Association (£1,000).

Education and training – 3 grants totalling £18,300

Priors Court Foundation (£10,000); Joint Educational Trust (£5,300); and Kidscape (£3,000).

Community development – 3 grants totalling £11,000

British Association for Adoption and Fostering and the Public Catalogue Foundation (£5,000 each); and Wednesday's Child (£1,000).

Culture and arts – 2 grants totalling £8,000

Worshipful Company of Musicians (£5,000); and the Academy of St Mary's – Wimbledon (£3,000).

Disability

One grant of £5,000 to the Aidis Trust.

Exclusions Grants only to registered charities, and not in response to general appeals.

Applications The foundation has previously stated that 'due to the number of appeals received, the foundation only replies to those that are successful'. However the foundation now also states that grants are not made to unsolicited applicants.

The Westminster Foundation

Social welfare, military charities, education, environment and conservation

£1.5 million (2008)

Beneficial area Unrestricted, in practice mainly UK. Local interests in central London (SW1 and W1 and immediate environs), north-west England, especially rural Lancashire and the Chester area, and the Sutherland area of Scotland.

70 Grosvenor Street, London W1K 3JP

Tel. 020 7408 0988 **Fax** 020 7312 6244

Email westminster.foundation@ grosvenor.com

Website www.grosvenorestate. com/charity

Correspondent Mrs J Sandars, Administrator

Trustees *The Duke of Westminster, Chair; Jeremy H M Newsum; Mark Loveday; Lady Edwina Grosvenor.*

CC Number 267618

Information available Accounts were available from the Charity Commission.

The foundation was established in 1974 for general charitable purposes by the fifth Duke of Westminster and continues to make grants to a wide range of charitable causes. In 1987 the Grosvenor Foundation, a separately registered charity, transferred all its assets to The Westminster Foundation.

The foundation makes over 100 grants a year, mainly for welfare and educational causes but with substantial support for conservation and rather less for medicine and the arts. A new category called 'commemorative' has recently been adopted. Grants appear to be all for UK causes and perhaps half by number, though less by value, are in the areas of church, conservation, young people, education, medical, arts and social welfare.

Grants can be for very large amounts, but generally, all but a handful are usually for amounts of not more than £60,000 and most are between £5,000 and just a few hundred pounds. About half of the beneficiaries were also supported in previous years.

The foundation has previously noted that:

It is usual that the trustees have knowledge of, or connection with, those charities which are successful applicants. The trustees tend to support caring causes and not research.

Grants are directed towards geographical areas in which the Grosvenor family and Grosvenor Group have a particular connection. For example, Grosvenor Group are major stakeholders in the redevelopment of the Paradise Street site in Liverpool [completed in September 2008]. The trustees have previously committed £500,000 over a period of five years to the Liverpool One Foundation [previously known as the Liverpool Paradise Foundation], a registered charity set up by some of the stakeholders involved in the Liverpool

development, and this money will be distributed to a wide range of charities and organisations in the immediate vicinity.

For further information on the Liverpool One Foundation, see the entry for the Community Foundation for Merseyside.

This is assumed to be a largely personal trust, created by the present duke. He is well known in the charity world for his active personal involvement in many organisations, and no doubt a significant number of the regular beneficiaries are organisations with which he has developed a personal connection that goes beyond grantmaking.

In 2008 the foundation had assets of £30.9 million and an income of £2.4 million. Grants were committed to 121 organisations totalling £1.5 million and were broken down as follows:

Category	No. of grants	Amount
Social & Welfare	69	£851,000
Conservation	5	£282,000
Education	15	£201,500
Medical	20	£105,000
Young people	10	£99,000
Arts	2	£11,000

The 2008 accounts also offer details on future plans:

In future, the trustees intend to reduce the number of small grants made so as to increase the money available for larger sums. but not at the expense of grants to smaller, local charities. They are also seeking to be more proactive in identifying causes rather than being responsive to the many appeals received. This will be done by increasing the number of visits to charities to assess their compatibility with the aims of the foundation and the effectiveness of the given charity to deliver to their chosen beneficiaries. Consideration will also be given to funding in connection with other charitable organisations where the whole can be greater than the sum of the parts – an example of this is the Liverpool One Foundation.

Further to this, in 2009 the foundation reduced and clarified its funding categories into the following:

Social care and education – social care: for example, the homeless; prison offenders; those with learning disabilities; facial disfigurements; older people; relief of those with chronic illness. Education: for example, training and retraining to help disadvantaged people; scholarships, apprenticeships or awards in areas of study or expertise relevant to Grosvenor's core business activities.

Military welfare – benevolent funds for serving and former members of the armed services.

Environment and conservation – protection of rural or specific habitats, churches and community centres in Grosvenor locations.

Exclusions Only registered charities will be considered. No grants to individuals, 'holiday' charities, student expeditions, or research projects.

Applications In writing to the secretary, enclosing an up-to-date set of accounts, together with a brief history of the project to date and the current need.

The trustees meet four times a year.

The Garfield Weston Foundation

General

£55 million (2007/08)

Beneficial area UK.

Weston Centre, 10 Grosvenor Street, London W1K 4QY

Tel. 020 7399 6565

Website www.garfieldweston.org

Correspondent Philippa Charles, Administrator

Trustees *Guy H Weston, Chair; Camilla H W Dalglish; Catrina A Hobhouse; Jana R Khayat; Sophia M Mason; Eliza L Mitchell; W Galen Weston; George G Weston: Melissa Murdoch.*

CC Number 230260

Information available Excellent descriptive annual report and accounts with an analysis of a selection of grants, large and small, and a full list of beneficiaries.

Summary

This huge foundation makes about 1,500 one-off grants a year, typically for amounts anywhere between £3,000 and £1 million. Perhaps helped by the fact that the income of the foundation has been rising rapidly, about half of all appeals result in a grant, though not necessarily for the full amount requested. Awards are regularly made in almost all fields except overseas aid and animal welfare.

Probably more than 85% of the money, and an even higher proportion for the largest grants, is for capital or endowment projects.

The published 'criteria' for grantmaking, reported below, are in the most general terms. Compared to the general run of trusts described elsewhere, there are relatively few grants to unconventional causes, or for campaigning or representational activities, and more for institutions such as independent schools and charities connected with private hospitals. Nevertheless, almost all kinds of charitable activity, including the radical, are supported to some extent. Grants are rarely given to major charities with high levels of fundraising costs.

The foundation is one of the few which can consider very large grants, a number of which were made in 2007/08.

The charity's ten trustees (all family members) are backed by a very modest staff, but nevertheless the foundation aims to deal with applications within four months of them being received.

In 2007/08 the foundation had assets standing at over £3.7 billion. Its income totalled £43 million. As in previous years, grants were made far exceeding income, totalling £55 million (£42 million in 2006/07).

Grant-making criteria

What are the trustees looking for in an application?

Applications are considered individually by the Foundation trustees. In assessing applications, the following issues are taken into consideration so please bear this in mind to ensure your application is able to address these things.

1) The financial viability of the organisation

Organisations that are relatively stable financially tend to be in a better position to run effectively and deliver the quality of services for which the charity was created. Therefore the trustees look for signs that the organisation is likely to remain running – these signs include, but are not limited to, past history, local support, an appropriate level of reserves, statutory and local council funding.

2) The degree of need for the project requiring funding

There are many ways to evaluate this, however indicators include the level of local commitment to the project, evidenced by such things as fundraising activity, volunteer effort, local authority support, numbers who will benefit etc.

3) The amount spent on administration and fundraising as compared to the charitable activities

The Charity Commission indicates a target of 10% for administration.

4) The ability to raise sufficient funding to meet the appeal target

The trustees are keen to assist projects where they can have a high degree of confidence that the necessary funds can be secured from relevant sources, therefore it is important to demonstrate the level of funds already secured and from what sources; as well as the likely targets to address any shortfall.

5) Whether the organisation has appropriate priorities and plans in place to manage its activities

This includes ensuring that core services are adequately resourced and stable before expanding into new projects, locations or services. It also refers to the ability of an organisation to secure appropriate funding for key projects & services and that necessary capabilities are available for operational success.

Amount by region

- South Central – £13 million
- London – £10 million
- National (England) – £4.7 million
- Anglia – £3.6 million
- South East – £3.2 million
- Midlands – £3.1 million
- South West – £3.1 million
- North West – £2.7 million
- Scotland – £2.2 million
- North East – £1.6 million
- Northern Ireland – £485,000
- Wales – £348,000.

Arts – £6.4 million distributed in 126 grants

In the arts category, the Royal College of Art received £1,000,000 for the development of their Battersea campus to include studios, workshops, teaching spaces, incubator units for start-up businesses and room for a programme of talks, lectures and exhibitions. The Art Fund received a grant of £1,113,000 in response to the appeal to rescue Dumfries House in Ayrshire for the nation. Completed in 1758, this magnificent Palladian mansion set in a 750 acre estate is one of the grandest and most imposing designs of any house in Scotland. In addition the furniture comprises one of the most outstanding eighteenth century collections in any house in the United Kingdom with magnificent examples of the work of Thomas Chippendale and Scottish craftsmen such as Alexander Peter and William Mathie. It is arguably the most complete and intact collection surviving in any Scottish country house, with the pieces still remaining in-situ in the locations originally designed for them by Robert Adam. A new trust has been set up and it opened to the public in June 2008.

There were two grants made of £500,000, to the Royal Festival Hall at Southbank, and also to the Shakespeare Globe Trust. The grant to the Festival Hall was for a comprehensive refurbishment project which will create riverside and roof terraces with better hospitality spaces, more open access and circulation, an education centre, replacement seating, improved technical and backstage facilities and upgraded acoustics. The grant to the Shakespeare Globe was in contribution to their extensive redevelopment programme to upgrade facilities which will include workshops, a rehearsal studio, viewing gallery and comprehensive disability access. Both grants are reflective of the trustees' continued interest in, and support for, arts projects which are interactive and accessible to their local communities and wider audiences.

Sadlers Wells received a grant of £150,000 which supported the ongoing development of their programme, and in particular their international work. They host some of the world's finest visiting companies and commission new work and are currently extending their production capability with international co-production projects.

There were also a number of grants of £100,000 which included donations to the London Philharmonic Orchestra for its education work, Scottish Ballet towards relocating its premises in Glasgow and the Ruskin Museum in Coniston for the restoration and display of Donald Campbell's ill-fated Bluebird. Additional donations to a range of organisations also reflected the trustees' desire to support arts projects in

---

THE GARFIELD WESTON FOUNDATION
Grants in 2007/08
Summary of grants paid

Category	£20,000 and over	No. of appeals	Less than £20,000	No. of appeals	Total amount	Total no. of appeals
Arts	£5,800,000	44	£523,000	82	£6,400,000	126
Community	£490,000	10	£961,000	185	£1,500,000	195
Education	£34,400,000	59	£511,000	83	£35,000,000	142
Environment	£740,000	15	£102,000	17	£842,000	32
Health	£3,200,000	43	£231,000	35	£3,500,000	78
Religion	£1,000,000	17	£1,600,000	372	£2,600,000	389
Welfare	£2,200,000	46	£1,100,000	192	£3,300,000	238
Young people	£1,100,000	29	£796,000	160	£1,900,000	189
Other	£50,000	1	£10,000	2	£60,000	3
Totals	**£49,000,000**	**264**	**£5,800,000**	**1,128**	**£55,000,000**	**1,392**

locations across the UK, examples of which included Artes Mundi in Cardiff, the National Youth Orchestra of Scotland and the Old Museum Arts Centre in Belfast.

The Royal Court Theatre received a grant of £50,000 for its Rough Cuts programme, which focuses on developing new writers' skills and encouraging the research of new ideas and projects. It will enable writers to work collaboratively with directors, actors and designers in experimenting and taking risks in a supportive and dedicated environment. This grant demonstrates that the trustees are willing to consider all art forms from ancient and traditional to the most contemporary.

A grant of £50,000 was donated towards the redevelopment of Spike Island in Bristol, a large facility for artists with studios, exhibition areas, workshops and education spaces. One end of the building is rented to The University of the West of England's Department of Fine Arts which, added to other commercial rents, help to ensure that the project is self-sustaining.

Community – £1.5 million distributed in 195 grants

The largest grant in this category was for £250,000 to Kingsgate Community Centre in Peterborough. Kingsgate is a church community group that focuses volunteer effort on a wide range of community support activities. These range from furniture recycling to courses on money and debt management, and parenting and relationship skills. The centre also runs daily after-school activity clubs for disadvantaged children, youth groups for teenagers and volunteering days involving litter-picking, repainting run-down community spaces and a companion scheme for older people. They receive referrals from over 65 social agencies across five counties.

A donation of £50,000 was given to Pembroke House which is an active community project in Walworth occupying a substantial Grade II listed property in one of Europe's largest social housing estates. The trustees contributed towards essential renovation and restructuring which will make the building sound and fully accessible and enable a wider range of activities and participants to be involved.

Other grants included £25,000 each to Gracious Street Methodist Church in Knaresborough towards new purpose-built facilities for its community work; Wanstead Flats Playing Fields for new changing rooms and St Agnes Miners & Mechanics Institute for restoring its building into gallery space and multi-use community facilities. Village halls in Mudford, Gretton, Clothall, Glenfarg and Punnetts Town all benefited with grants of £10,000.

Education – £35 million distributed in 142 grants

In this financial year this category received the largest proportion of the distribution, impacted in particular by the grant of £10 million and commitment of a further £15 million over the next two years made to Oxford University for the New Bodleian Library.

The Campaign for the University of Oxford is organised around three major strategic themes; supporting students and the life of the University, supporting academic staff and programmes and supporting infrastructure and buildings. The planned programme of investment by the University is designed to achieve a permanent transformation in the way the Colleges, Divisions and Departments of the University sustain themselves. The upgrading of key buildings and infrastructure will bring important changes to the physical face of Oxford for generations, including new facilities, accommodation and infrastructure to support academic and communal life, and the preservation and enhancement of their historic fabric to the Colleges and Halls. The new Bodleian will open up the site to wider audiences through the use of spaces for events, lectures, exhibitions and readings. Seminar rooms will be created to enable students to handle delicate original materials safely, and multi media resources will be used to build a world-class learning experience.

There will also be a new conservation centre to preserve ancient manuscripts and texts, using both the latest technologies and traditional approaches in concert. In the current age of technology and digitisation, the purpose of the Library is evolving into one where the services it provides and the connections it facilitates are increasingly important, and the fact that it is able to house rare and highly valuable materials will continue to place it in the role of a vital resource for the University and for the United Kingdom. This is the largest single grant ever awarded in the history of the Foundation and reflects the trustees' commitment to supporting excellence.

Museums also feature strongly this year, with a grant of £1,500,000 to the Victoria and Albert Museum for the creation of the Medieval & Renaissance Galleries. £1,000,000 was given to the Mary Rose Trust in Portsmouth for the ongoing conservation of Henry VIII's favourite warship which requires highly specialised preservation techniques to secure the ship and artefacts for future generations. In addition new visitor and educational facilities will be created in a purpose-built home for the Ship, bringing all the artefacts onto the same site as the ship itself.

The National Museums of Scotland received £500,000 for the transformation of access,

facilities and learning space for their outstanding collections in art, science and the natural world, which is visited by over 800,000 people a year. The London Transport Museum, originally supported with a grant of £200,000 in 2004, received a further £100,000 to help complete the redevelopment.

The Universities of Nottingham Trent and Strathclyde both received £500,000 this financial year. The former grant was for the upgrade of dated buildings unsuitable for teaching space. Two of their main buildings, both Grade 2 listed, will be reordered to create new learning spaces and flexible, modern facilities. By demolishing 1960's extensions, and clearing a car park, a new enclosed quadrangle will be created. A further car parking area will be removed and a new hub, the heart of the whole campus, will serve as a student support, community information and public access area.

The grant to the University of Strathclyde was also for a major capital project. The University has created a new Institute to be a pioneering, world-class centre for research and teaching in drug discovery and development. It will bring together leading researchers in the chemical, biological and pharmaceutical sciences to help combat important health issues of the 21st century. The proposed new building will take the work forward, merging five departments onto one site. The building will include laboratory space for 150 researchers, teaching laboratories for 100 students, ancillary laboratories and social learning spaces.

Seven grants of £250,000 were awarded over the course of the year, of which four are for capital projects benefiting people with special needs, namely TreeHouse Trust, a school for children with autism, The Royal School for Deaf Children in Margate, the Royal National College for the Blind and the National Star College in Cheltenham which provides further education for young people with severe & complex disabilities. The trustees remain highly committed to supporting educational attainment for those with specialised needs, enabling people to reach their potential.

The Prior's Court Foundation in Thatcham, another establishment for children with severe autism, received further support towards its capital improvements, this time with a grant of £100,000. A grant of £50,000 was provided to the Red Balloon Learning Centre in Cambridge to develop its work with children who have been the victims of bullying.

The Hansel Foundation in Scotland, which provides supported living and educational projects for people with complex disabilities, was supported with a grant of £30,000 towards the creation of a new four-bedroom bungalow. This facility is intended to help young people to make the transition from school into adult life. In addition, the Amberley Working Museum received a grant of £15,000 towards delivering a programme of lifelong learning for people of all ages, with specific programmes designed to respond to the National Curriculum.

Contributions were also made to bursary funds in a number of establishments, at various levels of learning, to help disadvantaged students to access high quality education.

Grants of £100,000 were provided to Painshill Park Trust, the Woodland Trust and the United Kingdom Antarctic Heritage Trust. In the last fifteen years Painshill Park has researched and restored its 18th century landscape and visitor facilities have been provided, including a purpose built education centre. The final stage of the programme of restoration, the ornamental buildings ('follies'), is now under way and the trustees have agreed to help to complete this work. The grant to the Woodland Trust is towards the cost of purchasing an extension to Elemore Woods together with undertaking a three year programme of tree-planting, conservation work, community engagement and public access works.

£50,000 is provided to the Father Thames Trust for the restoration and conservation of the various historic gardens and public spaces along the river.

The Tree Council was granted £20,000 towards its Tree Warden scheme and The Little Ouse Headwaters Project £10,000 for restoration of grazed wet fen and wet meadow. A similar amount was also provided to the Royal Society for the Protection of Birds for helping to reintroduce the Red Kite into Northern Ireland.

Health – £3.5 million distributed in 78 grants

This financial year the Institute of Cancer Research received £500,000 towards the development of new drugs, and Cancer Research UK the same amount towards the programme of breast cancer research being carried out in their Cambridge Institute.

There were three grants of £250,000, to the Thrombosis Research Institute, Breakthrough Breast Cancer and to Imperial College of Science, Technology and Medicine. The aim of the Thrombosis Research Institute is the detection of those at high risk of thrombosis and the development of effective and affordable therapies. Breakthrough Breast Cancer 's grant was towards their cohort study which will initially cover a ten year time frame and include 100,000 women over the age of 18; the trustees matched their earlier grant towards the project to enable them to meet their targets. The grant to Imperial College was to support a new Chair of

Science and Society, with the aim of improving public engagement with science and to build greater levels of understanding and education in the scientific disciplines.

Changing Faces received £100,000 towards their work in supporting adults with facial disfigurement. This organisation assists both children and adults who experience life with facial differences, whether from birth or acquired in later life through accident or illness – the charity helps individuals navigate the challenges they face in life with confidence, and they also raise awareness of the issues involved to the wider community and to healthcare professionals.

Additionally there were four grants of £100,000 to the School of Health & Social Care at Oxford Brookes University (for osteopathy clinics), Meath Epilepsy Trust (for the modernisation of its facilities), Marie Curie Cancer Care (towards replacing their Glasgow hospice) and Action Medical Research (for research into chronic pain in children).

As in previous years, various other hospices and medical charities across the country benefit with grants ranging from £250 to £50,000.

Religion – £2.6 million distributed in 389 grants

Religion again accounts for the largest number of grants, the majority being for £10,000 or less for fabric repairs and re-ordering. The exceptions are cathedrals and some important churches with major capital appeals towards which the trustees provided more significant support.

Ely Cathedral received the largest grant, £250,000. As with most ancient heritage buildings urgent fabric repairs were required, and they also aim to build an endowment fund to support the Choir. The trustees helped to provide music scholarships.

Grants of £100,000 were provided to the Cathedrals of Hereford, Bristol and Rochester and £50,000 to the Selby Abbey Appeal, all for capital requirements. Selby Abbey has received previous support from the Foundation as the trustees note the ongoing challenge to repair and restore the stonework, much of which has been affected by pollution. The Abbey is the largest parish church in England, founded by William the Conqueror in the 11th century, and is one of the few great monastic churches to survive the Dissolution of the Monasteries.

£50,000 was donated each to St James's Church on Piccadilly, Worcester Cathedral, Clonard Monastery in Belfast, Llandaff Cathedral in Cardiff and Wells Cathedral. The latter topped up an earlier substantial grant towards a £6 million appeal to open up and restore the medieval spaces, including the Undercroft which was previously not

accessible to the public. The appeal aims to improve access throughout, provide purpose-built facilities for music, a dedicated education space and an interactive interpretation centre.

The challenges facing St Pancras Parish Church are typical of many churches throughout the UK and illustrate the commitment of local communities to raise the funding they need to carry out their ministries. In addition to normal Sunday and weekday services Saint Pancras provides advice and support and runs projects for both older people and the young. In addition there are regular recitals, lectures, discussion groups and social welfare activities. The trustees recognise that this level of community activity can put strain on the facilities so a grant of £25,000 was provided towards improved access, toilets, kitchen facilities and meeting space.

Another typical example is the case of St Mary's Church in Chiddingfold, where the cramped Grade I listed building struggles to meet the growing needs of the community, particularly the expanding Sunday School and youth groups. A new church room, specifically designed to minimise the visual impact on the ancient church, is planned to solve these problems and the trustees provided a grant of £5,000 in support of this.

Welfare – £3.3 million distributed in 238 grants

The majority of grants made in this category were under £20,000, however donations of £100,000 each were made to Emmaus UK, Erskine, The Stroke Association and the Royal National Institute for the Blind.

Emmaus helps homeless people to help themselves, providing accommodation, full time work and training in an increasing number of Communities throughout England. Residents are required to work five days a week, collecting, refurbishing and selling donated goods. In return they receive food, clothing, rooms of their own and pay. The scheme aims to reduce dependency on handouts, teach new skills and build self respect and self sufficiency. Once set up, each Community aims to become self-financing and companions sign off primary benefits to work full time within the Community. Emmaus aims to create another six Communities by 2010.

Erskine is the foremost ex-service care facility in Scotland. It includes residential nursing (there are 353 permanent residents in four care homes across central Scotland), a 40 bed specialist dementia care unit, respite care, 56 war pensioners' cottages and a woodwork factory, print shop and Garden Centre providing training, employment and rehabilitation for disabled workers. They provide therapies and support on site, together with social facilities and full programme of events and activities. The trustees' grant was to help set up a new residential facility in Edinburgh.

The Stroke Association sought support for launching a major media campaign to raise awareness amongst the general public that strokes are treatable, can be prevented and that investment into medical research will help save more lives.

The fourth grant for £100,000, to The Royal National Institute for the Blind, was for developing their Finding Your Feet programme nationally. The programme provides emotional and practical support to newly diagnosed blind and partially-sighted people through the delivery of residential workshops covering a wide range of relevant topics.

The Parchment Trust offers day care, leisure, occupation and support to people with very specific needs. Currently, the trust runs a Cooperative for 19-plus school leavers with learning disabilities, a horticultural scheme for people with a variety of disabilities and 1 to 1 day schemes for those with profound and multiple disabilities. Eviction from their premises in Ore became likely so they embarked on an emergency fundraising drive to raise sufficient funds to purchase the premises. This was supported with a grant of £50,000.

£50,000 was given to the Royal National Institute for the Deaf. The RNID has introduced a new service for deaf people with mental health issues aimed at bridging the gap between specialist healthcare provision and independent living. The trustees' contribution is to help with the building of specialist residential units.

A similar grant was provided to Barrowmore in Chester, a residential unit providing vocational training and meaningful employment for 35 people with disabilities. The project is the creation of supported move-on accommodation to encourage those with sufficient potential to achieve the maximum independence.

The Byker Bridge Housing Association in Newcastle received a grant of £30,000 towards the building of a new hostel. Combat Stress also benefited with £30,000 for its work with ex-service men and women suffering from psychological injury such as clinical depression, phobic disorders and Post Traumatic Disorder.

Christians Against Poverty has been supported on a regular basis by the trustees since its inception twelve years ago. Having started in one room the charity now operates its debt counselling service through a network of 72 centres based around the UK, all opened in partnership with a local church. It received a further grant of £25,000.

Home-Start UK is another charity which has been a beneficiary for many years and several branches feature on the list again this year whereby volunteers befriend mothers with young children who are often in challenging situations. An additional grant of £30,000 was provided to the national office for their bespoke training programme for new Scheme staff.

The U-Turn Project in East London was supported with £5,000 for its core costs. This charity provides services to vulnerable women, particularly those involved in street prostitution. Most have multiple needs including housing, health and drug issues.

Young people – £1.9 million distributed in 189 grants

The two largest grants in this category were for the Outward Bound Trust and the Marine Society & Sea Cadets, both of which received £100,000. The Outward Bound Trust is at the forefront of challenging and innovative outdoor learning and has centres located in Fort William, Aberdovey and Ullswater. Young people are introduced to both physical and mental activities, and are encouraged to try new things in a safe and controlled environment. The trustees recognise that outdoor adventure makes a significant contribution towards the development of young people.

The Sea Cadets is the nation's most enduring maritime charity for young people, with 400 units throughout the UK and 15,000 young people engaged in learning nautical and other skills. Fun, friendship, adventure and the acquisition of new skills is at the core of the organisation. This year's grant helped to acquire a new training vessel.

There were several grants of £50,000, mostly for charities organising a range of activities for young people. The Woodlarks Camp Site Trust in Farnham is redeveloping some outdated support buildings, the Rona Trust in Southampton is replacing one of its yachts and TocH in Aylesbury is being supported in its work encouraging young people to volunteer. Lodge Hill Trust activity centre near Chichester received £30,000 for refurbishing overnight accommodation.

£25,000 was donated to Skill Force Development for its work with disadvantaged and vulnerable young people. It aims to build confidence and self-esteem, and also to develop team work, problem solving and leadership skills. It takes place largely within schools and complements the statutory provision. This grant was in support of the ongoing delivery of their work in Islington and Greenwich.

Kids' City received £15,000 to help maintain and grow its frontline work in the inner city boroughs of Lambeth and Wandsworth. Activities range from martial arts to arts and crafts, keeping children engaged and active. An extensive volunteering and training programme for young people and adults with limited work experience has also been introduced.

£15,000 was also received by the Exodus Project in Barnsley, which runs activity clubs for children aged 8 to 11 and separate clubs for older teenagers. It also visits children and their families in their homes in order to support parents and carers as well as the wider community.

The trustees considered a wide range of projects of varying scale, demonstrated by a £1,000 grant made to Holiday Support in Cheltenham, which provides respite holidays for children living in Women's refuges in Gloucestershire. Similarly the 21st Hartshill Scouts was supported with £1,000 for new camping equipment.

Environment – £842,000 distributed in 32 grants

Grants of £100,000 were provided to Painshill Park Trust, the Woodland Trust and the United Kingdom Antarctic Heritage Trust. In the last fifteen years Painshill Park has researched and restored its 18th century landscape and visitor facilities have been provided, including a purpose built education centre. The final stage of the programme of restoration, the ornamental buildings ('follies'), is now under way and the Trustees have agreed to help to complete this work. The grant to the Woodland Trust is towards the cost of purchasing an extension to Elemore Woods together with undertaking a three year programme of tree-planting, conservation work, community engagement and public access works.

£50,000 is provided to the Father Thames Trust for the restoration and conservation of the various historic gardens and public spaces along the river. The Tree Council was granted £20,000 towards its Tree Warden scheme and The Little Ouse Headwaters Project £10,000 for restoration of grazed wet fen and wet meadow. A similar amount was also provided to the Royal Society for the Protection of Birds for helping to reintroduce the Red Kite into Northern Ireland.

Other – £60,000 distributed in 3 grants

The largest grant in this category was to the Landmark Trust which was established to rescue historic and architecturally interesting buildings and their surroundings from neglect and, when restored, to give them new life by letting them out to stay in as places to experience. The trust has now restored almost 200 buildings, with the holiday lets covering the costs of ongoing maintenance. The current £50,000 grant is towards the restoration of the Grade II listed Silverton Park Stables in Devon, a rare example of an unconverted stable block built in the mid-19th century and in itself the size of a large country house.

Friends of Anne of Cleves House in Lewes, Sussex, received £5,000 towards renovation work and a similar amount was provided to the Heritage of London Trust for the restoration of the Minnie Lansbury bracket clock which hangs in Bow Road, Tower Hamlets. This memorial clock commemorates the brave East End suffragette heroine from the 1920s, who was a Labour councillor in Poplar, and who served a six week prison sentence for refusing to levy full rates in the poverty-stricken area.

Exclusions The foundation cannot consider any funding requests made within 12 months of the outcome of a previous application, whether a grant was received or not.

- The foundation only considers applications from UK registered charities and your registration number is required (unless you have exempt status as a church, educational establishment, hospital or housing corporation).
- The foundation does not typically fund projects outside the UK, even if the organisation is a registered charity within Britain.
- The foundation is not able to accept applications from individuals or for individual research or study.
- The foundation does not support animal welfare charities.
- Typically the foundation does not fund one-off events, galas or festivals, even if for fundraising purposes.
- The foundation does not fund specific salaries and positions (although contributing to the core operating costs of charitable organisations will be considered).
- The foundation does not make funding commitments over several years – grants made are typically for a single year.
- It is unusual for the foundation to consider making a grant to organisations who cannot demonstrate significant progress with fundraising, so please bear this in mind when considering the timing of your application. In general, the trustees look for organisations to have raised the majority of funding through local or statutory sources before an approach is made.
- The foundation does not place limits on information sent, however applications should be concise and include only the most relevant details relating to the application.

Applications In writing to the correspondent. A basic details form is available to download from the foundation's website and must be included with a letter of application.

All applications are considered on an individual basis by a committee of trustees. From time to time, more information about a charity or a visit to the project might be requested. Trustees meet monthly and there is no deadline for applications, which are considered in order of receipt. It normally takes three or four months for an application to be processed. All applicants are notified of the outcome by letter.

Grants are normally made by means of a single payment and the foundation does not normally commit to forward funding.

All applicants are asked to include the following information:

- the charity's registration number
- a copy of the most recent report and audited accounts
- an outline description of the charity's activities
- a synopsis of the project requiring funding, with details of who will benefit
- a financial plan
- details of current and proposed fundraising.

The Will Charitable Trust

Environment and conservation, people with sight loss and the prevention and cure of blindness, cancer care and people with mental disability

£714,000 (2007/08)

Beneficial area UK and overseas.

Grants Office, Sunbury International Business Centre, Brooklands Close, Windmill Road, Sunbury on Thames TW16 9DX

Tel. 01932 724148

Email admin@willcharitabletrust.org.uk

Website willcharitabletrust.org.uk

Correspondent Christine Dix, Grants Administrator

Trustees *Mrs Vanessa A Reburn; Alastair J McDonald; Ian C McIntosh; Rodney Luff.*

CC Number 801682

Information available Accounts were available from the Charity Commission.

The trust provides financial assistance to charities, mainly in the UK, supporting the following categories:

- care of and services for blind people, and the prevention and cure of blindness
- care of people with learning disabilities in a way that provides lifelong commitment, a family environment and the maximum choice of activities and lifestyle
- care of and services for people suffering from cancer, and their families
- conservation of the countryside in Britain, including its flora and fauna.

The trust provides the following additional information on its grantmaking:

A small proportion of the trust's income may be allocated to assistance in other fields, but this is rare and reserved for causes that have come to the attention of individual trustees. It is therefore only in very exceptional circumstances that the trustees will respond favourably to requests from organisations whose activities fall outside the categories listed above.

General
Grants are awarded only to UK registered or exempt charities which must have proven track records of successful work in their field of operation or, in the case of newer charities, convincing evidence of ability. Grants will only be awarded in response to direct applications from the charity concerned.

The trust will consider grants to charities of all sizes. Accordingly, grants vary in amount, but generally fall within the range of £5,000 to £20,000. The total amount awarded varies from year to year according to available funds.

In the current financial climate, commitments to make future payments are given only in exceptional circumstances, with grants normally being one-off annual grants. Charities which have received a grant in one year are encouraged to apply in the next and subsequent years, but should note that only in exceptional circumstance will grants be given to the same charity for more than three successive years. This does not however mean that a charity that has received three grants will not be eligible in future years, just that we would not generally award a grant in year four.

Exceptional grants

The trustees may occasionally consider larger exceptional grants, but this is unusual and confined to charities that we know well and have supported for some time. There is no separate grants programme for this, and contenders will be identified from the normal grant round.

Grantmaking in 2007/08

In 2007/08 the trust had assets of £17.1 million and an income of £665,000. Grants were made during the year totalling £714,000, broken down as follows:

Category	No. of grants	Amount
Care of cancer patients	14	£179,000
Blindness	13	£175,000
Mental health	11	£169,000
Conservation	7	£71,000
Other grants	1*	£10,000

In addition to the above, grants were also made to Beacon (£100,000) and Clear Vision (£10,000) for 'special projects'.

Beneficiaries in the above categories included: Bradford Cancer Support Daisy Bank and SeeAbility (£25,000 each); Home Farm Trust and Sightsavers (£20,000 each); Canterbury Oast Trust (£16,000); Cornerstone and Breast Cancer Care (£15,000 each); Nottingham Wildlife Trust, MPS Society* and County Durham Society (£10,000 each); and York Blind and Partially Sighted Society (£5,000).

Exclusions Grants are only given to registered or exempt charities. 'It is unlikely that applications relating to academic or research projects will be successful. The trustees recognise the importance of research, but lack the resources and expertise required to judge its relevance and value.'

Applications Applications in writing to the correspondent. There are no application forms – the trust offers the following advice on its website on how applications should be presented:

We are not necessarily looking for glossy professional bids and understand that your application to us will vary according to the size of organisation you are, and the size of the proposed project. It can be a professionally prepared presentation pack, but can equally be a short letter with supporting information. Both will receive equal consideration.

Whatever the presentation, the following is a guide to the main areas that we like to see covered. This is however intended only as a guide to assist you in preparing an application, it should *not* be seen as a prerequisite for applying for a grant – we understand that some small organisations will not have the sort of project(s) that need detailed treatment. Generally, we expect most applications will contain the following:

- An overview of your organisation. Please tell us in a nutshell who you are and what you do.
- Tell us what you want a grant for/towards. Give us a full description of your project. For instance, what do you hope to achieve/who will benefit from the project and how?
- Costs. Tell us what your project is going to cost, giving details of the main items of expenditure. Tell us how you intend to fund it, and how much you have raised so far.
- A contingency plan. What will you do if you do not raise the funds you need?
- A timetable. Tell us your timescale for raising funds and when you aim to have the project up and running.
- A copy of your latest audited Annual Accounts must be included. A copy of your Annual Review is also useful if you have one.
- Other information. Please include any other information which you feel will assist us in judging your application. This could include for example a copy of any newsletter you produce, or short promotional/advertising leaflets. Such publications often help give a flavour of an organisation.

Deadlines

Blind people and Learning disabilities
- Applications should be submitted from November and by 31 January at the latest. Decisions are made in the following March and successful applicants will be notified by the end of the month.

Cancer care and Conservation
- Applications should be submitted from June and by 31 August at the latest. Decisions are made in the following November and successful applicants will be notified by the end of the month.

The H D H Wills 1965 Charitable Trust

General and wildlife conservation

£990,000 (2007/08)
Beneficial area Mainly UK.

Henley Knapp Barn, Fulwell, Chipping Norton OX7 4EN

Tel. 01608 678051

Email hdhwills@btconnect.com

Correspondent Wendy Cooper, Trust Secretary

Trustees *John Carson; The Lord Killearn; Lady E H Wills; Dr Catherine Wills; Liell Francklin; Martin Fiennes.*

CC Number 1117747

Information available Annual report and accounts were on file at the Charity Commission, but without a full list of beneficiaries.

The trust has been endowed by the family of Sir David Wills, from a fortune derived largely from the tobacco company of that name.

In April 2007 all the assets of the unincorporated charity, The H D H Wills 1965 Charitable Trust (registered charity number 244610) were transferred into this charitable company limited by guarantee.

The trust runs three separate funds: the General Fund, the Knockando Church Fund and the Martin Wills Fund. The three funds operate in different areas of grantmaking and, in the case of the Martin Wills Fund, on a seven-year cycle.

The charitable activities of each fund are described by the trustees as follows:

General Fund – [grants for] such charitable purposes, charitable institutions or charitable foundations in such proportions as the trustees in their absolute discretion see fit, or for the Ditchley Foundation and Atlantic College.

Knockando Church Fund – [grants] shall be applied in the repair, maintenance and upkeep of Knockando Church, Morayshire.

Martin Wills Fund – [grants] to the following institutions in seven year cycles commencing from 6 April 1992:

- 1st year – Magdalen College, Oxford
- 2nd year – Rendcomb College, Gloucestershire
- 3rd and 4th years – organisations dedicated or primarily dedicated to the conservation and protection of wildlife or the conservation, protection and improvement of the physical and natural environment to promote the biodiversity of fauna
- 5th year – the Ditchley Foundation
- 6th and 7th years – such charitable institutions as the trustees shall in their absolute discretion think fit.

The period ending in March 2008 was the 2nd year of the current cycle.

Grantmaking in 2007/08

During the year the trust had assets of £47 million and a consolidated income of £2.4 million. Grants were made totalling just over £990,000 and were broken down as follows:

General Fund – There were 177 grants made in 2007/08 totalling £93,000. The vast majority of grants (175) were for less than £1,000 each. Grants of more than £1,000 went to United World College of the Atlantic (£25,000) and Sandford St Martin PCC (£10,000). No further information was available.

Previous information has indicated that grants are well spread around the country, with Scotland, perhaps, coming nearest to being over represented. A small proportion of the grants have been given to charities working overseas.

Knockando Church Fund – A grant of £3,000 was made towards the upkeep and repair of the church.

Martin Wills Fund – 2007/08, being the 2nd year of the cycle, saw a grant totalling £894,000 being made to Rendcombe College – Gloucestershire.

Exclusions No grants to individuals or national charities.

Applications In writing to the correspondent. The trust considers small appeals monthly and large ones bi-annually from the Martin Wills Fund. Only one application from a given charity will be considered in any 18-month period.

The Community Foundation for Wiltshire and Swindon

Community welfare

£725,000 (2007/08)

Beneficial area Wiltshire and Swindon only.

48 New Park Street, Devizes SN10 1DS
Tel. 01380 729284 **Fax** 01380 729772
Email info@wscf.org.uk
Website www.wscf.org.uk

Correspondent Chan Chitroda, Grants Officer

Trustees *Richard Handover, Chair; David Holder; Clare Evans; Tim Odoire; John Rendell; Sarah Troughton; Simon Wright; Nicky Alberry; Ray Fisher; Angus Macpherson; Dr Fiona Richards; Ram Thaigarajah; Elizabeth Webbe; Geraldine Wimble; John Woodget.*

CC Number 298936

Information available Accounts were available from the Charity Commission.

The Community Foundation was set up in 1991 and is 'dedicated to strengthening local communities by encouraging local giving'. Grant funding is placed where it will make a significant difference to those most in need. The primary focus is on disadvantage including, supporting community care, tackling isolation and investing in young people.

The Community Foundation for Wiltshire and Swindon has particular strengths as a grant-making organisation. We are local. We understand what life is really like for the groups we support- especially the smaller 'grass-roots' groups. We can also offer help with problems, ideas for development, and regularly put groups in touch with other organisations that can offer specialist advice or assistance.

Grants range in size from £50 to £10,000 and are awarded for up to three years.

In 2007/08 the foundation had assets of £7.5 million and an income of £4.4 million. Grants were made totalling £725,000.

The foundation manages a wide range of grant programmes and can provide access to a range of funds.

Its two main programmes are:

Main Grants Fund
Revenue or capital grants to projects meeting the following criteria:

- Supporting Community Care – working especially with people who are older and disabled, and with carers such as those caring at home for older or disabled relatives
- Tackling Isolation – working in particular to improve access to services and information
- Investing in Young People – concentrating on the 12–25 age group.

Grants are for up to £3,000 per year for up to three years or £5,000 per year for two years. Groups that have previously received an award can apply again to support new developments.

Small Grants Fund
One-off grants to small groups working to charitable purpose with a set of rules or a constitution. Grants are for up to £500.

The foundation also works in partnership with other funders to deliver a programme of grants aimed at Wiltshire groups. In 2009 these included:

- the Haydon Wick Fund
- Gazette and Herald Community Fund
- Fair Share.

Please note: grant schemes can change frequently. Please consult the foundation's website for full details of current programmes and their deadlines.

Applications The foundation's website has details of the grant schemes currently being administered.

All applicants must have:

- a constitution or set of rules (if you are applying for a Small Grant it may be possible to receive funding before you have a constitution, but only if you are working towards adopting one)
- a bank account in the group's name, or another eligible organisation that is happy to receive the grant on your behalf.

Applicants should first complete an 'expression of interest' form on the foundation's website. If the project is eligible for funding the foundation will send out an application pack.

The Harold Hyam Wingate Foundation

Jewish life and learning, performing arts, music, education and social exclusion, overseas development and medical

£1 million to organisations (2007/08)

Beneficial area UK and developing world.

2nd Floor, 20–22 Stukeley Street, London WC2B 5LR

Website www.wingatefoundation.org.uk/

Correspondent Karen Marshall, Trust Administrator

Trustees *Roger Wingate; Tony Wingate; Prof. Robert Cassen; Prof. David Wingate; Prof. Jonathon Drori.*

CC Number 264114

Information available Accounts were available from the Charity Commission.

The foundation was established in 1960 and aims to support Jewish life and learning, performing arts, music, education and social exclusion, developing countries and medical organisations. The trust also administers the Wingate Scholarships which makes grants to young people with outstanding potential for educational research.

Guidelines

Medical research – 20% of grants were awarded in this category

The foundation values the influence that new clinical and laboratory techniques can have on the advance of medical science, and is aware of the advantages that may be derived from visits to laboratories for the acquisition of new skills, and for setting up inter-institutional collaborative research. It is prepared to consider applications for funds to cover the expenses of travel and subsistence for such visits up to a maximum of £1,000. Applications should:

- specify the benefit to the applicant of a proposed visit, including the relevance to the applicant's ongoing research programme and career development
- be accompanied by letters of support from the applicant's head of department, and from the corresponding individual in the department to be visited
- include justification of the amount requested and the applicant's CV.

The foundation will not support the costs of travel, subsistence or registration for international or national congresses and symposia.

Jewish life and learning – 20% of grants were awarded in this category

By the selection of projects, institutions and activities the foundation aims to encourage Jewish cultural, academic and educational life in a manner that enhances the Jewish contribution to the life of the wider community.

In particular, applications are invited from academic institutions specialising in Jewish subjects and from bodies promoting Jewish culture, including museums, libraries and literary publications. Applications are also welcomed from organisations able to demonstrate a record in inter-faith dialogue, in the promotion of reconciliation between Jews in Israel and their Arab neighbours and the encouragement of liberal values in both communities.

Music – 10% of grants were awarded in this category

The foundation believes that music is seriously under-funded in the UK and will consider applications for support in those areas of music performance and education which do not readily attract backing from commercial sponsors or other funding bodies, or which are not eligible for public funding. Priority will be directed towards supporting the work or education of musicians based in, or wishing to study in, the UK, but by no means exclusively so. An important criterion will be whether, in the opinion of the trustees, the funding sought will make a significant difference to the applicant's prospects.

The foundation will be prepared to consider applications for support for on-going expenses and will be willing to consider such support for a period up to three years. Priority will be given to those organisations which give opportunities to young professionals and to education projects for young people as well as for new adult audiences. This would include direct assistance as well as funding for organisations which promote their work or performance and support for master classes.

The foundation may draw up particular priorities for a given year such as support for aspiring conductors, young composers, amateur choral work, or the musical education of young people and/or adults. Please contact the foundation for further information.

Performing arts – 10% of grants were awarded in this category

The foundation has been a consistent supporter of the performing arts. This policy will be maintained with particular emphasis on financial support for not-for-profit companies with a record of artistic excellence, that require additional funding, not available from public sources or commercial sponsorship, to broaden their repertoire or develop work of potentially outstanding interest which cannot be funded from usual sources.

Assistance will also be considered for training and professional development for creative talent or the technical professions.

Education and social exclusion – 8% of grants were awarded in this category

The foundation recognises that there are already considerable public resources allocated to these two areas. However, it will be willing to consider support for projects which may not qualify for public funding or attract other major funding bodies. Contributions towards the running expenses of projects for a strictly limited period will be considered. Eligible projects would ideally:

- be innovative
- focus on the disadvantaged
- have lasting effects.

Alternatively they should consist of work (for example, action research, pilot schemes) that would lead to such projects, and preferably they should also be capable of replication if successful.

UK projects which the foundation has supported in the past include those providing for vulnerable and disturbed children, the education of the autistic, homeless children, deaf adults, artists with disabilities, outreach work of arts organisations and help for ex-offenders.

Overseas development – 3% of grants were awarded in this category

Applications are welcome from organisations working in developing countries for projects in any of the foundation's priority fields, including music and the arts. It will be willing to consider support for projects which may not qualify for public funding or attract other major funding bodies. However, the foundation would welcome applications which address the particular problems of water supply.

Projects supported in the past have included education for scheduled castes in India, training for classical musicians in South Africa and water supply in Africa.

Scholarships and literary prizes – 28% and 1% of grants respectively were awarded in these categories

Scholarships are awarded to individuals over the age of 24 who have shown great potential or excellence and are in financial need. The Wingate Scholarship Fund is administered separately and further details can be obtained from the fund's website: www.wingatescholarships.org.uk.

In 2007/08 the foundation had assets of £12 million and an income of £418,000. Grants totalling £1 million were made to organisations.

Beneficiaries of the largest grants were: Centre of the Cell (£173,000); Queen Mary and Westfield College (£155,000); Bradford Media Museum (£75,000); Queen Mary University London (£60,000); Foundation for Conductive Education (£56,000); and Oxford Centre for Hebrew and Jewish Studies (£25,000).

Smaller grants included those to: English National Opera (£10,000); Little Angel Theatre (£8,500); Jerusalem Foundation (£7,800); Live Music Now (£6,000); One World Broadcasting Trust (£5,000); Young Concert Artists Trust (£2,500); Keele University (£1,000); and Anglo Israel Association (£150).

The Scholarship Fund awarded grants totalling £417,000.

Exclusions No grants to individuals (the scholarship fund is administered separately). The foundation will not normally make grants to the general funds of large charitable bodies, wishing instead to focus support on specific projects.

Applications Applicants are advised to write to the trust administrator with full details, including the most recent financial accounts. Applications are only acknowledged if a stamped addressed envelope is enclosed or if the application is successful.

The administrator of the foundation only deals with enquiries by post and it is hoped that the guidelines and examples of previous support for successful applicants, given on the foundation's website, provides sufficient information. There is no email address for the foundation. Trustee meetings are held quarterly and further information on upcoming deadlines can be found on the trust's website.

The Wixamtree Trust

General, in particular, social welfare, environment and conservation, medicine and health, the arts, education, sports and leisure and training and employment

£727,000 (2007/08)

Beneficial area UK, in practice mainly Bedfordshire.

148 The Grove, West Wickham BR4 9JZ

Tel. 020 8777 4140

Email wixamtree@thetrustpartnership. com

Website www.wixamtree.org

Correspondent Paul Patten, Administrator

Trustees *Sam C Whitbread; Mrs J M Whitbread; H F Whitbread; Charles E S Whitbread; Geoff McMullen; I A D Pilkington.*

CC Number 210089

Information available Accounts were available from the Charity Commission.

The trust was established in 1949 for general charitable purposes. It considers requests from registered charities based or operating within Bedfordshire. A small number of national charities with a focus on family social issues are also supported. The trustees are also sympathetic towards applications received from organisations of which the late Humphrey Whitbread was a benefactor.

During 2005/06 the trustees entered into a formal agreement with Bedfordshire and Hertfordshire Historic Churches Trust (BHHCT). BHHCT has undertaken to use its specialist knowledge to review applications received by the Wixamtree Trust from Bedfordshire churches seeking funds for repairs to the fabric of their buildings and other projects. BHHCT visits the projects, assesses the need and makes grant recommendations to the trustees on a quarterly basis.

The trust has set aside an annual sum of £100,000 for such applications, £90,000 of this is to be used to make grants to Bedfordshire churches and the remaining £10,000 is to be donated to BHHCT to establish an endowment fund, subject to an annual review. The usual amount of grant for a church in any one year will be £10,000 and will not normally exceed 10% of the project cost.

In 2007/08 the trust had assets of £23 million and an income of £1.1 million. Grants were made to 139 organisations (many being annual or bi-annual recipients) totalling £727,000. They were categorised as follows:

Category	Value
Social welfare	£339,000
Environment and conservation	£105,000
Medicine and health	£87,000
Education	£83,000
Arts	£61,000
Sports and leisure	£24,000
International	£15,000
Training and employment	£14,000
Miscellaneous	£250

Beneficiaries were not listed in the annual accounts but can be viewed on the trust's website, although individual grant awards are not included. Beneficiaries included: Bedfordshire Body Positive, Hospice at Home Volunteers – Bedford, Hope UK, Guinness Place and Kimble Drive Residents Association, Family Welfare Association, Youth Music Theatre UK, European Squirrel Initiative, National Youth Orchestra of Great Britain, St Gregory's Foundation and Sharnbrook Playing Field Association.

Exclusions No grants to non-registered charities or individuals.

Applications Application forms can be downloaded from the trust's website or requested via email or post. The trust prefers completed forms to be returned by email so that any amendments can be made before they are presented to the trustees for consideration at their quarterly meetings. Future meeting dates and application deadlines are also listed on the website. All requests for support should be accompanied by a current report and accounts.

The Maurice Wohl Charitable Foundation

Jewish, health and welfare

£9.8 million (2007/08)

Beneficial area UK and Israel.

7–8 Conduit Street, London W1S 2XF

Correspondent J Houri, Secretary

Trustees *Mrs Ella Latchman; Prof. David Latchman; Martin D Paisner; Daniel Dover; Sir Ian Gainsford.*

CC Number 244519

Information available Accounts were available from the Charity Commission.

Support is given to organisations in the UK with particular emphasis on the following areas:

- the care, welfare and support of children (including education)
- the promotion of health, welfare and the advancement of medical services
- the relief of poverty, indigence and distress
- the care, welfare and support of the aged, inform, handicapped and disabled
- the support of the arts.

In 2007/08 the foundation received an income of £56 million which mostly came from the revisionary interest of two trusts following the death of Mr Wohl in June 2007. It made grants totalling £9.8 million. Assets stood at £63.8 million at year end.

Donations were broken down as follows:

Category	Value
Care of older people	£5,400,000
Health, welfare and the advancement of medicine	£4,400,000
Care, welfare and support of children	£19,000
Relief of poverty, indigence and distress	£1,100

Beneficiaries included: Jewish Care (£6 million); Shaare Zedek UK (£2 million); Nightingale House (£1.8 million); Ovarian Cancer Action (£1 million); Jewish Care, Medical Aid Trust and Yeshiva Ohel Torah Beth David (£10,000 each); Community Security Trust (£5,000); and Emunah (£3,000).

Exclusions The trustees do not in general entertain applications for grants for ongoing maintenance projects. The trustees do not administer any schemes for individual awards or scholarships and they do not, therefore, entertain any individual applications for grants.

Applications In writing to the correspondent. The trustees meet regularly throughout the year.

The Charles Wolfson Charitable Trust

Medical research, education and welfare

£6.8 million (2007/08)
Beneficial area Unrestricted, mainly UK.

c/o 129 Battenhall Road, Worcester WR5 2BU
Tel. 020 7636 0604
Correspondent Ricky Cohen, Administrator
Trustees *Lord David Wolfson of Sunningdale; Hon. Simon Wolfson; Dr Sara Levene; Hon. Andrew Wolfson.*
CC Number 238043
Information available Accounts were available from the Charity Commission.

The trust was established in 1960 for general charitable purposes with special regard to the encouragement of medical and scientific research and facilities, education or child welfare, the advancement of any religion and the relief of poverty. Particular regard is given to the Jewish community. Grants are mostly for capital or fixed term projects. The trustees tend to support a few large projects over two to three years and make a number of smaller annual grants to other projects.

The bulk of the trust's income derives from grants received from Benesco, which is a registered charity whose

investments are held in property. Benesco is in effect controlled by the trust and the annual accounts present both trust and consolidated financial statements including the combined assets, liabilities and income of the trust, Benesco and its subsidiary companies as a group.

In 2007/08 the trust had assets of £5.4 million and an income of £6.8 million. Over 100 grants were made totalling £6.8 million and were categorised as follows:

Medical research and facilities – 29 grants totalling £2 million
Beneficiaries of the largest grants included: Addenbrookes Charitable Trust (£500,000); Heart Cells Foundation (£300,000); Cure Parkinsons Trust (£200,000); Hadassah UK (£151,000); and Oxford Foundation for Theoretical Neuroscience (£100,000).

Other beneficiaries included: Royal Marsden Cancer Campaign (£50,000); Sir George Pinker Appeal (£30,000); Speech Language and Hearing Centre (£10,000); Tavistock Trust for Aphasia (£5,000); and Cancer Research UK (£500).

Welfare – 64 grants totalling £1.3 million
Beneficiaries of the largest grants included: Jewish Care (£350,000); Nightingale House Home for Aged Jews (£150,000); Policy Exchange (£144,000); and AISH Hatorah (£75,000).

Other beneficiaries included: Council for Christians and Jews (£40,000); Friends of Bnei Akiva (£30,000); Zoological Society of London (£25,000); Victory Services Club (£10,000); Shabaton Choir (£2,000); and SSAFA Forces Help – Central Office (£1,000).

Education – 20 grants totalling £991,000
Beneficiaries of the largest grants included: Yavneh College Trust (£500,000); Huntingdon Foundation (£125,000); Institute for Policy Research (£75,000); and British Friends of the Ariel Institute (£62,000).

Other beneficiaries included: Ellen Tinkham PTFA (£25,000); Priors Court Foundation (£10,000); Federation of Synagogues (£2,000); and the Roundhouse Trust (£1,000).

Exclusions No grants to individuals.

Applications In writing to the correspondent. Whilst all applications will be considered, the trustees do not notify all unsuccessful applicants because of the volume of appeals received.

The Wolfson Family Charitable Trust

Jewish charities

£10 million (2007/08)
Beneficial area Israel and UK.

8 Queen Anne Street, London W1G 9LD
Tel. 020 7323 5730 **Fax** 020 7323 3241
Website www.wolfson.org.uk
Correspondent Paul Ramsbottom, Secretary
Trustees *Sir Eric Ash; The Hon. Janet Wolfson de Botton; Lord Turnberg; Lord Wolfson of Marylebone; Martin D Paisner; Sir Bernard Rix; Lady Wolfson; Sir Ian Gainsford; The Hon. Laura Wolfson Townsley.*
CC Number 228382
Information available Accounts were available from the Charity Commission.

The trust gives a relatively small number of often very large grants, mostly to institutions in Israel, in the fields of science, medical research, health, welfare and, to a lesser extent, arts and humanities. The trust has previously stated that much of its future income is already committed to long-term projects. Offices and administration are shared with the much larger Wolfson Foundation, and an application to one may be considered by the other.

General

The trust operates on a large scale and over an extended time frame, often having sharp changes in the level of new commitments each year.

There is a 'three year rolling plan of grants' which, as a general policy, 'are given to act as a catalyst, to back excellence and talent and to provide support for promising future projects which may currently be underfunded, particularly for research, renovation and equipment'.

In 2007/08 the trust had assets of £29 million which generated an income of £2 million. Grants were made totalling £10 million, with a further £13 million committed in grants to be paid in the following year.

Grantmaking in 2007/08

The following is the list of grants paid during the year:

Science, technology and medical research – 17 grants totalling £9.5 million

The beneficiaries during the year were: Hebrew University of Jerusalem, Tel Aviv University and Weizmann Institute (£750,000 each), for equipment for microRMA research; Soroka Medical Centre – Beer Sheva (£630,000), for a PET CT scanner; Rambam Health Care Centre – Haffa (£615,000), for MRI equipment; Hadassah University Hospital – Jerusalem (£525,000); Edith Wolfson Medical Centre – Holon (£470,000), towards a cardiac catheterisation laboratory and medical camera equipment; Sourasky Medical Centre – Tel Aviv (£420,000), towards a linear accelerator; Chaim Sheba Medical Centre – Tel Hashomer (£350,000), for breast MRI equipment; Rabin Medical Centre – Petah Tivka (£190,000), towards a catheterisation laboratory system; Shaare Zedek Medical Centre – Jerusalem (£85,000), towards an orthopaedic operating theatre and related equipment; Bar Ilan University (£50,000), equipment for biochemistry/molecular biology laboratory; Daniel Turnburg exchange scheme – supporting medical researchers from the UK working in Israeli institutions and Israeli researchers working in the UK; Laniado Hospital- Netanya (£45,000), for an ultra-sound machine; and Christie Hospital – Manchester (£15,000), to support research into salivary gland cancer.

Health and welfare – 16 grants totalling £652,000

The beneficiaries during the year were: Negev Hospice (£150,000), towards the building of a new hospice; Yad Sarah – Jerusalem (£50,000), towards equipment for people with disabilities; St Mary's Hospital – London (£45,000), towards equipment for the baby unit; Donisthorpe Hall – Leeds (£25,000), for refurbishment work; Kav-Or – Northern Israel (£12,000), towards IT equipment for children in hospital; Beit Moriah – Beer Sheva (£11,000), towards refurbishment work to accomodate people with disabilities; Nalaga'at – Jerusalem (£10,000), for specialist equipment in a theatre for people with sensory impairments; Shema Kolenu – Jerusalem (£10,000), towards equipment for children with disabilities; Association for Fighting AT Diseases, Ramat Gan (£10,000), for equipment for a treatment clinic; Akim Israel – Beit Amit Centre (£7,000), for the development of a mulit-sensory room; Centre for Deaf-Blind Persons – Tel Aviv (£6,000) and Centre for the Blind in Israel – Tel Aviv (£6,000), towards IT equipment; Or

Simcha – Kfar Chabad (£5,000), for refurbishment of a residential home; Shalheveth – Jerusalem (£5,000), towards a mini-bus; and Al-Taj – Arraba (£1,000), towards IT equipment.

Education – 8 grants totalling £253,000

The beneficiaries were: Technion – Israel Institute of Technology (£100,000), towards the renovation of the Churchill Auditorium; Youth Aliyah (£75,000), towards the renovation of the Edith Wolfson dormitory; World ORT (£25,000), for science equipment for eight schools in Israel; Peres Centre for Peace (£20,000), towards the development of computer centres in Israel; Emunah – Bnei Brak (£20,000), towards refurbishment at Necha Sarah Wolfson HIgh School; Kedma Youth Village – Shephelah and Maccabim Centre – Tel Aviv (£5,000 each), towards equipment in centres for children and young people; and Tirat Carmel Community Foundation (£3,000), towards equipment in an education centre for vulnerable young people.

Arts and humanities – 4 grants totalling £57,000

The beneficiaries were: The Israel Philharmonic Orchestra (£20,000), towards instruments; Bevis Marks Synagogue – London (£15,000), for conservation costs; Central Synagogue (£12,000), towards building maintenance costs; and Merton College – Oxford (£10,000), towards research assistance.

Exclusions Grants are not made to individuals.

Applications The trust shares its application procedure with the Wolfson Foundation. A brief explanatory letter, with organisation and project details, including costs and current shortfalls, will elicit an up-to-date set of guidelines in return, if the charity is able to consider the project concerned.

The Wolfson Foundation

Medical and scientific research, education, health and welfare, heritage and arts

£39.2 million (2008/09)

Beneficial area Mainly UK, but also Israel.

8 Queen Anne Street, London W1G 9LD
Tel. 020 7323 5730 **Fax** 020 7323 3241
Website www.wolfson.org.uk
Correspondent Paul Ramsbottom, Executive Secretary
Trustees *Lord Wolfson of Marylebone, Chair; Lord Quirk; Hon Mrs Laura Wolfson Townsley; Lord Quinton; Lord McColl; Sir Eric Ash; Lord Turnberg; Lady Wolfson of Marylebone; Sir Derek Roberts; Hon Mrs Janet Wolfson de Botton; Sir David Weatherall.*
CC Number 206495
Information available Accounts were available from the Charity Commission. Further information taken from the foundation's informative website.

Set up in 1955, it is endowed from the fortune created by Sir Isaac Wolfson through the Great Universal Stores company. Grants are for buildings and equipment, but not for revenue or project costs, in four main areas:

- science and technology
- education
- arts and humanities
- health and welfare.

Grants can be very large; few are for amounts of less than £5,000.

The foundation shares offices and administration with the smaller Wolfson Family Charitable Trust, and an application to one may be considered by the other. The foundation provides excellent information on its activities, objectives and achievements, much of which is used in this entry.

Grants policy

The objective of the foundation, through its grantmaking, is the support of excellence in the fields of science and technology, healthcare, education, the arts and humanities.

The foundation pursues its objective through investment in outstanding projects across a wide range of activities, usually by the provision of infrastructure. Four particular factors continue to influence trustees in their decision-making. First, trustees aim to back excellence (both existing and potential). Secondly, attempts are made to identify and support important areas that are under-funded. Thirdly, applicants are encouraged to use Wolfson funds as a catalyst, so that the foundation's funding can lever additional support. Fourthly, collaboration is actively sought with other expert bodies, with benefits accruing to both organisations. The Royal Society and English Heritage are two examples of organisations with whom the foundation collaborates on joint funding programmes.

It is anticipated that the range of activities will remain broadly similar during 2009/10 (within the context of an income that is likely to be lower). The impact of the foundation's funding is monitored through biannual reports on projects provided by recipients during the lifetime of a grant, and also by visits undertaken by trustees and staff.

Trustees make awards twice each year and are advised by panels comprising trustees and specialists which meet before the main board meetings. As well as assessing the merits of the applicants' proposals and their congruence with the foundation's aims and priorities, appraisal criteria include: the anticipated outcome of the project (including public benefit); financial viability; value for money; adequate provision for ongoing costs and maintenance and the aesthetics of any building project.

Priorities [...] are grouped around four funding areas: Science and Technology, Education, Arts and Humanities and Health and Welfare. Funding is made through a number of programmes, including preventive medicine, people with special needs, historic buildings, libraries, the visual arts and education. Grants are made to universities for student accommodation, equipment for research, new buildings and renovations. Awards for university research are normally made under the umbrella of designated programmes in which vice-chancellors are invited to participate.

All applications are assessed by expert external reviewers, and applicants are given an opportunity to respond to queries raised during the review process.

Guidelines

Arts and Humanities
Museums and Galleries
The majority of grants to museums and galleries have in recent years been awarded through a joint programme with the Department for Culture, Media and Sport (DCMS). Museums and galleries with capital projects of national significance may approach the foundation directly [see Applications]. Funding for the purchase of works of art is provided through an annual allocation to the National Art Collections Fund.

Performing Arts
The trustees have over a number of years supported theatre, ballet, opera and music, mainly through grants for capital projects with a national significance. Musical education is also supported through the Wolfson Music Awards, which provide scholarships and funds for the purchase of instruments to students at the major British musical conservatoires. Students should apply directly to their conservatoire.

Historic Buildings
Grants are awarded for repair to the fabric of listed (Grade I or Grade II∗) buildings that are open to the public.

Churches
The foundation has a dedicated programme in support of Anglican churches, awarding grants of up to £4,000. Eligible churches must be listed (Grade I or Grade II∗) and pre-date 1850, and grants are made toward the conservation of the historic fabric. The programme is administered by the Council for the Care of Churches on behalf of the foundation and so enquiries should be sent to: The Conservation Officer, The Council for the Care of Churches, Fifth Floor, Church House, Great Smith Street, London, SW1P 3NZ. Non-Anglican churches and cathedrals that meet the above criteria may be eligible under the general historic buildings programme and should see the general advice for making an application.

War Memorials
The foundation has a joint programme for the conservation of war memorials with English Heritage and the War Memorials Trust. More information is available from the English Heritage website: www.english-heritage.org.uk.

History Prize
The Wolfson History Prizes, which were established in 1972, are awarded annually to promote and encourage standards of excellence in the writing of history for the general public. Prizes are given annually, usually for two exceptional works published during the year, with an occasional oeuvre prize (a general award for an individual's distinguished contribution to the writing of history).

In order to qualify for consideration, a book must be published in the United Kingdom within the current calendar year. The author must be a British subject at the time the award is made and normally resident in the UK. Books should be scholarly but accessible to the lay reader. Books are selected for consideration by the judges. Any suggestions to the judges should come via the publisher and be addressed to the Prize Administrator at the Wolfson Foundation. Suggestions should be detailed in a letter and accompanied by catalogues listing the books in question. Please do not send any books unless requested to do so by the Prize Administrator.

The prize winners of a given year are announced in the summer of the following year. The judges do not release a short list. The judges are Sir Keith Thomas, (Chairman), Prof. Dame Averil Cameron, Prof. Richard Evans and Prof. Sir David Cannadine.

Education
Higher Education
Grants are awarded for higher education buildings, including student accommodation and teaching facilities.

Schools
The schools programme supports the teaching of science and technology in selected categories of secondary schools. Independent, foundation, voluntary-aided and voluntary-controlled schools and sixth form colleges may be eligible to apply. Grants are awarded for capital expenditure and equipment. The main aim of the programme is to support schools with a proven track record of excellent performance. In addition, schools with a clear record of continuing improvement may also be considered.

Science and Technology
Scientific Research (including preventative medicine and clinical research)
Over the past decade, this area has received the highest proportion of the foundation's funding. Grants are made for the capital infrastructure underpinning top quality university research. Initial approaches should come via the Vice-Chancellor's office and be a priority for the university.

Wellcome Wolfson Capital Awards in Biomedical Science
The Wellcome Trust and the Wolfson Foundation are working together to provide up to £30 million of investment in UK research infrastructure. Full details are available via the Wellcome Trust's website: www.wellcome.ac.uk.

Laboratory Refurbishment Programme
This programme, which is administered by the Royal Society, aims to improve the existing physical infrastructure at British universities to promote high quality scientific research. It is focussed on a specific subject area each year.

Further information is available from the Royal Society's website: www.royalsoc.ac.uk.

Healthcare
Medical Education
Capital grants are made for learned societies (particularly in the medical field) and for other medical education projects, both through Medical Schools and NHS Trusts.

Special Needs and Hospices
Grants are made for capital projects at special needs organisations and hospices.

General

In 2008/09 the foundation had assets of £647 million and an income of £32.5 million. Grants were made during the year totalling £39.2 million, broken down as follows:

Category	Amount
Science, technology and medical research	£29,000,000
Arts and humanities	£3,900,000
Health and welfare	£3,300,000
Education	£2,900,000

Grantmaking in 2008/09

This was described by the foundation as follows:

Medical research and health care

Trustees continued their policy of investing in infrastructure supporting high quality research at British universities.

During the year, a joint programme totalling £30 million with the Wellcome Trust was announced. The programme (with decisions on grant applications in 2010) will fund university capital projects in the biomedical sciences. The foundation's contribution is £8 million.

Under the foundation's existing programme of support for medical research an award of £2.25 million was made toward the fitting out of a research area for University of Cambridge researchers embedded within the new MRC Laboratory for Molecular Biology. A grant of £2 million was made for the new School of Medicine and Medical Research Institute at St Andrews University (specifically allocated toward the Biophotonics Laboratory).

Significant grants were also made for medical research projects at University College London (£2 million to restructure the research facilities at the Royal Free campus), the University of Glasgow (£1.75 million for their Beatson Translational Research Centre) and the London School of Hygiene and Tropical Medicine (£1.7 million for the Health Policy Unit in their new Tavistock Place building).

The trustees continued their programmes in the fields of special needs and hospices. Grants totalling over £3.3 million were awarded for new buildings, refurbishment work and equipment.

Science education and research

The major investment in this area was the renewal of the programme for Wolfson research merit awards. The programme aims to provide universities with additional support to enable them to attract to this country (or retain) outstanding research scientists. The programme has been renewed for a further three years at the level of £2 million each year, to be administered by the Royal Society and with matched funding from government. The commitment was made following a review of the existing programme undertaken by the Royal Society.

A number of awards were made for science education: for an education centre at Sumburgh Head in the Shetlands (£300,000), for a science centre at Keele Observatory (£250,000) and for a new Learning Centre at the Royal Horticultural Society's Harlow Carr Botanical Gardens in Yorkshire (£100,000).

Arts and humanities

The largest award during the year of £1 million went to Tate Britain for the renovation of the Millbank Gallery.

A number of other significant awards were made to museums and galleries, including £400,000 to the Natural History Museum for the renovation of the central hall. Grants of £250,000 each were awarded to the Israel Museum (for the refurbishment of their 19th Century/impressionist gallery) and the National Galleries of Scotland (for the refurbishment of the Scottish National Portrait Gallery).

Other awards in this area were made under the seventh year of the joint programme with the Department for Culture, Media and Sport for the renovation of museums and galleries.

In the field of music and the performing arts, the largest grant was £250,000 toward the refurbishment of the Concert Hall at the Royal College of Music. Awards of £50,000 each were made to Leeds Grand Theatre/Opera North and to the Royal Opera House.

During the year, Trustees announced a new partnership with the British Academy to fund four research professorships (a total of £200,000 per annum for three years).

A large number of awards were made for the conservation of historic buildings, landscapes and monuments, including a grant of £75,000 for the conservation of the White Tower at the Tower of London. Other historic buildings funded included Glastonbury Abbey, buildings at Hestercombe Gardens and several dozen Anglican churches through a scheme administered by the Church Buildings Council. Awards were also made through joint programmes with English Heritage (for war memorials and cathedrals) and the National Trust (for historic properties and gardens).

Education

The largest awards were made to learned societies promoting medical education and research: the Academy of Medical Sciences (toward a conference suite at 41 Portland Place, £350,000) and the Royal College of Physicians (toward refurbishing the Wolfson Lecture Theatre, £250,000).

Grants of over £1.6 million were awarded as part of the ongoing programme funding equipment and building projects for the teaching of science and technology at secondary schools.

Exclusions

- Overheads, running or administrative costs
- VAT or professional fees
- non-specific appeals (including circulars)
- endowment funds or conduit organisations
- costs of meetings, exhibitions, concerts, expeditions, etc.
- the purchase of land
- research involving live animals
- film
- video production.

Applications Before submitting an application please write to enquire whether your project is eligible, enclosing a copy of the organisation's audited accounts for the previous two years.

If a project is eligible, further details of the application process will be provided.

The Woodward Charitable Trust

General

£344,000 (2008/09)

Beneficial area Unrestricted.

Allington House, 1st Floor, 150 Victoria Street, London SW1E 5AE

Tel. 020 7410 0330 **Fax** 020 7410 0332

Email contact@woodwardcharitabletrust.org.uk

Website www.woodwardcharitabletrust.org.uk

Correspondent Karin Hooper, Administrator

Trustees *Camilla Woodward; Rt Hon. Shaun A Woodward; Miss Judith Portrait.*

CC Number 299963

Information available Annual report and accounts were available from the Charity Commission. The trust also has a clear and simple website.

This is one of the Sainsbury Family Charitable Trusts, which share a joint administration but it operates quite differently to most others in this group in that it gives a large number of small grants in response to open application. It is the trust of Camila Woodward (nee Sainsbury) and her husband Shaun Woodward MP, Northern Ireland Secretary.

Guidelines

The following guidance is offered by the trust:

The trustees favour small-scale, locally based initiatives. Funding is primarily for one-off projects, but the trustees are willing to consider funding for start-up or running costs (including core costs and salaries).

Please be clear when applying who the target users are and what your projected outcomes are. If this is a continuation of existing work what are your outcomes to date? If your project is on-going, how will it be sustainable? What are your plans for future/ongoing funding? If your request is for a one-off project, what will be its legacy? How many people will benefit from the grant? Trustees are interested in helping smaller organisations which offer direct services. Any participation by past or current users of the service should be mentioned and is encouraged.

The current areas of grantmaking are set out below:

Funding Priorities

1) Social and ethnic minority groups, including young people at risk of exclusion or isolation, refugees, asylum-seekers, gypsies and travellers. Projects that promote integration and community cohesion will be favoured
2) Prisoners and ex-offenders. Projects that help the rehabilitation and resettlement of prisoners and/or ex-offenders are supported as well as requests to help prisoners' families
3) Homelessness, especially affecting young people and women, and covering facilities such as women's refuges
4) People experiencing violence or abuse
5) Arts outreach work by local groups involving disadvantaged people
6) Disability projects; which can include rehabilitation, training or advocacy for people who are either physically disabled or learning disabled as well as help to improve employability
7) Environmental projects, especially with a strong educational element
8) Addiction, including projects tackling the social exclusion elements and preventative programmes and projects supporting families of addicts.

Types of grants

Trustees review grant applications twice a year, usually in January and July. Please consult the diary page for up-to-date deadlines for receipt of applications.

Small grants

£100-£5,000 (around 40–50 grants made per year, to projects within areas 1–8 above on a one-off basis)

Large grants

Over £5,000 (around 5–10 grants made per year, usually to projects within areas 1–5 above and spread over a maximum of three years). Applications for large grants will be rejected unless applications are discussed with the administrator prior to submission.

Children's summer playscheme grants

£500-£1,000 (usually about 30–40 grants made each year on a one-off basis). Applications for these are made separately and considered in May each year.

Grantmaking in 2008/09

In the 16 months to April 2009 the trust had assets of £8.5 million and an income of £491,000. Grants were paid during the year totalling £344,000, and were categorised as follows:

Category	No. of grants	Amount
Community and social welfare	45	£201,500
Disability and health	15	£62,300
Summer schemes	33	£29,500
Education	6	£20,500
Arts	6	£16,400
Environment	5	£14,000

The following are examples of grants that were made during the year, including a description of the trust's interests in each category taken from the accounts.

Community and social welfare

The trustees funded charities such as East Cleveland Housing Trust [£1,300], Porch Steppin' Stone Centre and West London Churches Homeless Concern [£1,500] which help homeless people. The trustees helped refugee groups such as PARCA (Poor African Refugees Community Association) [£2,000] and Refugee Advice Group [£2,000] with rent and funds for volunteers. A grant to SHARP (Support Help and Advice for Relatives of Prisoners) [£4,800] helped fund helpline volunteers. Relate Kent Consortium [£3,000] was funded to provide counsellors that could help prisoners and their partners prior to release. Gypsy and travellers groups have been helped through the charity Friends, Families and Travellers [£15,000] with funds for a family support worker. An inclusive arts and drama project at the Tricycle Theatre [£4,500] gave travellers' children a chance to learn new skills and mix with local children. East Cleveland Youth Housing Trust [£1,300] was given a grant to help train young people in renovating an empty property which, once completed, provided them with affordable accommodation. Small women's refuges were supported with grants to provide playworkers' for children accompanying the women fleeing from domestic violence.

Disability and health

This year the trustees have funded a variety of projects helping disabled people of all ages. Grants have been made to provide family support workers to help families cope with caring for disabled children. Other grants have been made towards the running costs of a cyber café for disabled users; training to enable disabled people set up their own businesses and equipment for sports programmes for disabled users.

Beneficiaries included: Deafness Research UK (£20,000); Association for Research into Stammering in Childhood (£5,000); Root & Branch (£3,500); Oxford Parent-Infant Project (£2,500); and British Heart Foundation (£1,500).

Summer schemes

Every year the trustees make small grants for summer playschemes during the long summer holidays for children between the ages of 5 -16 who come from disadvantaged backgrounds. Only charities whose annual income is £100,000 or less can apply. The playschemes funded are inclusive and encourage integration both by accepting those of differing abilities as well as different social and racial backgrounds. Funds have also been made to train past users to come back as volunteers.

Education

Trustees have supported some literacy projects to help children from disadvantaged backgrounds improve their reading skills. The trustees supported an innovative scheme in the East End which encouraged young BME students to gain skills for employment through creativity scholarships.

The beneficiaries were: The Ideas Foundation (£8,000); Story Museum (£5,000); Reading Quest (£3,000); Pegasus School (£2,000); The Sainsbury Archive (£1,500); and School-Aid UK (£1,000).

Arts

The arts projects which the trustees have funded this year usually have had a dual benefit. By using art or the performing arts, the projects have helped combat social isolation, help change 'at risk' behaviour, and provide an arena or forum in which to address social problems. A notable grant was made this year to help refugees participate in a musical concert inside an immigration removal centre; another grant funded disabled actors who wanted to put on an anti-bullying awareness show. Other grants helped disaffected young people learn new skills and combat anti-social behaviour as well as raise self-esteem.

The beneficiaries were: Reach Inclusive Arts (£5,000); Lewisham Youth Theatre (£3,500); Ithaca (Charity) Ltd (£3,000); Ifa Yoruba Contemporary Arts Trust and Big Brum Theatre in Education Trust (£2,000 each); and Oxford Concert Party (£1,000).

Environment

The trustees have supported schemes to help volunteers recycle goods that might have gone to landfill sites and redistribute them to people suffering from poverty. Other grants have funded programmes in schools to inspire and empower young people to look after their environment for the future as well as encouraging sustainable energy projects.

The beneficiaries were: The Ashden Awards (£5,000); Young People's Trust for the Environment and All Party Parliamentary Group on the Great Lakes Region of Africa (£3,000 each); Chipping Norton Lido Ltd (£2,000); and Blythswood Care – Medway (£800).

Exclusions Trustees will not normally fund:

- charities whose annual turnover exceeds £250,000
- construction projects such as playgrounds, village halls, and disabled accesses
- general school appeals including out of hours provision
- hospices
- medical research
- parish facilities
- playgroups and pre-school groups
- requests for vehicles.

Trustees will definitely not support

- individuals in any capacity
- educational fees.

Applications On simple application forms available from the trust, or via its website. Potential applicants are invited to telephone the administrator in advance to discuss the advisability of making an application.

Main grants are allocated following trustees' meetings in January and July each year, with the exception of summer schemes, which are considered at the beginning of May each year. All application forms are assessed on arrival and if additional information is required you will be contacted further. Applicants must make sure the trust receives a project budget and audited accounts.

The trust's website also has a useful diary of trustees' meetings and of the cut-off dates for applications.

The Worwin UK Foundation

General

£1.3 million (2007/08)

Beneficial area UK and overseas, particularly Canada.

6 New Street Square, London EC4A 3LX

Tel. 020 7427 6400

Correspondent John Ward, Trustee

Trustees *William Hancock; Brian Moore; Mark Musgrave; Nick Dunnell; John Ward.*

CC Number 1037981

Information available Accounts were available from the Charity Commission.

This trust has general charitable purposes but tends to focus its grantmaking on the advancement of education, the promotion of the arts (particularly focused on young people from low-income backgrounds) and the prevention and relief of sickness.

In 2007/08 the trust had assets of £1.7 million and an income of £2.6 million. Grants were made to 120 organisations totalling £1.3 million.

Grants were made during the year in the following categories:

Education and training

Beneficiaries included: Excellence in Literacy Foundation (£54,000); Evergreen (£45,000); Junior Undiscovered Maths Prodigies (£17,000); University of Manitoba (£12,000); L'Arche – Ottawa (£7,300); York Humber High School (£2,400); and Viscount Alexander Public School (£490).

Care of children

Beneficiaries included: Hospital for Sick Children – Clown Programme (£53,000); Theodora Children's Trust (£37,000); Operation Go Home (£19,000); Children's Aid Foundation of Toronto (£7,300); Manitoba Pioneer Camp (£2,900); and AMICI Camping Charity (£1,300).

Promotion of arts

Beneficiaries included: Toronto Symphony Orchestra (£34,000); National Arts Centre Foundation (£27,000); Shakespeare in the Ruins Incorporated (£15,000); Royal Opera House (£10,000); Theatre La Catapulte (£4,600); Urbanarts Community Arts Council (£3,000); and Tricycle Theatre Company (£1,000).

Medical Research

Beneficiaries were: Heart and Stroke Foundation of Ontario (£49,000); Canadian MedicAlert (£12,000); and EORTC Charitable Trust (£4,000).

Other charitable purposes

Mostly in Canada, the beneficiaries included: Paroisse de St Tropez (£35,000); Bereaved Families of Ontario – Toronto Chapter (£26,000); Sleeping Children Around the World (£14,000); Toronto Zoo Foundation (£7,500); and Mooreland's Community Services (£3,000).

Applications In writing to the correspondent.

The South Yorkshire Community Foundation

General

£2.7 million (2007/08)

Beneficial area South Yorkshire wide, with specific reference to Barnsley, Doncaster, Rotherham, Sheffield.

Unit 3 – G1 Building, 6 Leeds Road, Attercliffe, Sheffield S9 3TY

Tel. 0114 242 4294 **Fax** 0114 242 4605

Email grants@sycf.org.uk

Website www.sycf.org.uk

Correspondent Pauline Grice, Chief Executive

Trustees *Jonathan Hunt, Chair; David Moody; Sir Hugh Neill; Peter W Lee; Martin P W Lee; Peter Hollis; Isadora Aiken; Frank Carter; Jackie Drayton; Galen Ives; Christopher Jewitt; Michael Mallett; Sue Scholey; Maureen Shah; Allan Sherriff; Lady R Sykes; R J Giles Bloomer; Timothy M Greenacre; Allan Jackson; Jane Kemp; Jane Marshall.*

CC Number 517714

Information available Accounts were on file at the Charity Commission. The foundation also has a helpful and informative website.

The South Yorkshire Community Foundation, launched in 1986, specialises in funding small community and voluntary groups within the South Yorkshire area. Priority is given to small and medium-sized groups which find it hard to raise money elsewhere. Projects funded include those which help local people in need, such as people who may be homeless, ill, disabled or older, and community life, such as nursery care, arts and culture, nature and heritage and sport.

Applicants do not have to be a registered charity but do have to have a charitable purpose. As well as running its own programme, the foundation also makes grants on behalf of its donors.

The foundation is particularly interested in supporting groups or projects which:

- support people in greatest need
- are locally led and run
- involve people who face particular discrimination or disadvantage for example, young people, people with disabilities or facing mental health issues, black and minority ethnic communities and so on
- respond to local communities' needs
- work well with other local community initiatives
- are innovative
- will benefit from relatively small amounts of funding
- give real value for money.

Grant programmes 2009/10

As the end 2009, the following funds were available for applications – as with other community foundations, funds may close and new ones open, so check the foundation's website for up-to-date information:

SYCF Small Grants Fund
These grants are intended for small, developing and less well-resourced groups and organisations from across South Yorkshire, where small amounts of funding can make a real difference.

Organisations/groups do not have to be a registered charity and the majority of grants are one-off payments of between £50 and £1,500.

We welcome applications from all community and voluntary groups and organisations operating for the benefit of South Yorkshire communities. Groups must therefore have beneficiaries who live in South Yorkshire and be locally led and run. This includes locally constituted and managed branches of national or large charities.

Which groups or activities will be prioritised for funding?
Higher priority will be given to those applications that can demonstrate how they will address some of the following needs. If your group or activity will not meet these

priorities then you can still apply but it is less likely that you will receive funding from us:

- groups that respond to their communities' needs
- activities or projects that will support people whose needs can be clearly demonstrated
- groups whose main activities focus upon the advancement of education, promotion of good health or the relief of poverty and sickness
- groups that work in collaboration with other local community groups
- activities or projects that will engage people who face discrimination or disadvantage
- activities or projects that will produce a wide range of benefits and provide good value for money.

How to apply?
To apply for a grant, simply download the Small Grants Fund overview sheet [from the foundation's website] for more information on eligibility and how the application process works.

Then download the 'Guidelines for Completing Forms' and the application form and return the completed application form to the South Yorkshire Community Foundation to get the process underway.

Grassroots Grants – Small Grants
Small grants aims to reach out to those in our local communities who need assistance most. The foundation is able to distribute grants of £250-£5,000 to grassroots community groups throughout Barnsley, Rotherham and Sheffield.

By downloading the forms below you can make your application for assistance from the fund.

If you are thinking of applying for a Grassroots Grant you must read the 'Overview and Criteria' sheet to check your eligibility for the scheme. If you are eligible and wish to apply, you need to complete both the standard Grant Application Form and the Grassroots Grants Application Form. [All of the forms are available from the foundation's website.]

If your group or project is not eligible to apply to Grassroots Grants small grants, you can still apply to the SYCF Small Grants scheme using the standard Grant Application Form.

It will help us to process your application efficiently if you provide as much detail as you can when completing the form(s), particularly when describing the project you would like funded and the costs of the items you intend to spend the grant on.

Please note: Doncaster Central Development Trust will be administering the fund in Doncaster and prospective applicants should

contact Katie Wall on 01302 735766 for an application pack and further information.

Third Sector ERDF Access Fund
Register your interest for the Third Sector ERDF Access Fund by emailing: **admin@sycf.org.uk.**
Yorkshire Forward has created the Third Sector ERDF Access Fund, offering grants of between £2,000 and £10,000, which will be delivered locally throughout the county by the Yorkshire Community Foundations.

The funding has been made available to help Third Sector organisations prepare themselves to make bids for larger sums from the European Regional Development Fund (ERDF).

Through ERDF, Yorkshire Forward is offering projects costing £1 million and above the chance to apply for a grant to cover up to 50% of the total cost.

Malcolm Taylor, who manages the ERDF Programme for Yorkshire Forward, said: 'We want to give Third Sector organisations throughout the region as great a chance as possible to be successful with bids for funding from ERDF. Support from the Third Sector Access Fund will enable organisations to improve the quality of bids they submit for ERDF funding.

The smaller grants from the Access Fund will help with preparatory tasks such as the carrying out of feasibility studies, exploring possibilities of collaborative working with other local organisations and gaining expert advice on the preparation of bids.

Successful bids for the larger sums from ERDF must be based upon the Fund's Priority 3 objectives:

- part capital (buildings/refurbishment), part transport
- business support
- social enterprise support
- IT development/knowledge.

The grants come from the ERDF operational programme for the Yorkshire and Humber 2007–2013, which had over £500 million available for investment in the region. Over £100 million of which was earmarked to support the Programme's third priority of Sustainable Communities which is of particular relevance to Third Sector organisations..

The Community Foundations for South Yorkshire, Leeds, Calderdale, Wakefield and District and York and North Yorkshire (including the Humber) will be delivering the Access Fund locally for their respective areas.

You can register your interest in the Access Fund by emailing SYCF: **admin@sycf.org.uk.**

Comic Relief
The South Yorkshire Community Foundation has teamed up with Comic Relief to bring

almost £80,000 in grants to local community groups over the next two years.

In the past, SYCF has delivered Sports Relief funding, but this new pot will provide much needed funding for non-sporting groups as well with grants of up to £10,000 available until March 2011.

At least 50% of the funding will be delivered to sporting projects in the region, with the remainder distributed amongst other worthwhile groups.

Successful applications for sporting projects will show how the group increases access to sport and exercise for people who face social exclusion and isolation, and to help people who are experiencing difficulties in their lives.

Non-sporting projects should increase local services, build skills of local people, increase community cohesion or respond to local economic needs.

Further information, including eligibility criteria and application forms will appear on our website [...]

Sir Samuel Osbourne Deed of Gift

The Sir Samuel Osborn Deed of Gift provides grants ranging from £250 to £1,000 for applications that fall in to two main categories: education and special needs.

Sir Samuel Osborn headed one of Sheffield's great tool steelmaking families, who at their peak virtually monopolised the world's manufacture of tool steel back in the 19th century.

The fund has previously only been available to former employees or their dependants of the Osborn company (which ceased to exist in 1978), although now the fund is open to any individual resident in the city of Sheffield.

However due to the current high level of demand, applications received where there is no family connection to a former Samuel Osborn employee [may not be considered].

To find out more information about the fund and eligibility download the information sheet [from the foundation's website].

If you want to make an application to the fund then download the Grant Application form and return it to Karen Alsop at the foundation.

Grantmaking in 2007/08

During the year the foundation had assets of £2.5 million and an income of over £3.6 million. Grants were made totalling £2.7 million and were broken down by area as follows:

Area	Grant total
Sheffield	£647,000
Barnsley	£373,500
Doncaster	£330,400
Rotherham	£323,000
National	£18,000

The foundation also distributed over £1 million in the above areas through its Flood Disaster Relief Fund [now closed].

A wide range of organisations across all of the foundation's areas of operation were supported under various programmes, some of which are no longer running. Many organisations received grants from more than one fund.

The beneficiary of the largest grant during the year was Monk Bretton Cricket Club (£103,000 in total). Other beneficiaries included: North Barnsley Partnership (£65,000 in total); Stainforth Community Partnership (£45,000); Friends of Thornhill School (£18,200 in total); Kiveton Park & Wales Community Development Fund (£16,200); Somali Special Needs Scheme (£12,000 in total); Roughwood Primary School (£11,000); Doncaster Rowing Club (£7,000); Carterknowle and Burngreave Youth Club Group (£6,000); Shiregreen Children & Families Project (£5,000); Owls Trust All Stars (£4,600); Sheffield Disabled Fishing Group (£3,000); Tinsley Parent and Children's Consortium (£2,000); and Beighton Welfare Recreation Ground (£1,500).

Exclusions The following exclusions apply to all funds administered by the foundation:

- groups that have substantial unrestricted funds
- national charities
- activities promoting political or religious beliefs or where people are excluded on political or religious grounds
- statutory bodies for example, schools, local councils, colleges
- projects outside of South Yorkshire
- endowments
- small contributions to large projects
- projects for personal profit
- minibuses or other vehicle purchases
- projects that have already happened
- animals
- sponsorship and fundraising events.

Applications Applications are made by completing a simple form, available for download from the foundation's website. See the additional application information for each fund.

Initial enquiries can be made by email, telephone or fax. Staff at the foundation are happy to talk to you, and can:

- talk through your project idea to assess eligibility and give advice
- provide support in putting together your application
- let you know about other useful support and advice services

- provide more detailed information on all our funds.

All applications are submitted to a grant assessment panel which meets every six weeks. The frequency of meetings means the foundation does not operate an advertised deadline system and applicants are invited to apply at any point during the year. The foundation endeavours to provide applicants with a decision within eight weeks of a completed application form being received.

The Yorkshire Dales Millennium Trust

Conservation and environmental regeneration

£786,000 (2007/08)

Beneficial area The Yorkshire Dales.

The Old Post Office, Main Street, Clapham, Lancaster LA2 8DP

Tel. 01524 251002 **Fax** 01524 251150

Email info@ydmt.org

Website www.ydmt.org

Correspondent David Sharrod, Director

Trustees *Joseph Pearlman; Carl Lis; Brian Braithwaite-Exley; Colin Speakman; Dorothy Fairburn; Hazel Waters; David Sanders Rees-Jones; Jane Roberts; Peter Charlesworth; Steve Macaré; David Joy; Thomas Wheelwright; Lesley Emin; Margaret Billing; Michael Ackrel; Andrew Campbell.*

CC Number 1061687

Information available Annual report and accounts were available from the Charity Commission. The trust also has an informative website detailing current and previous projects.

This trust's patron is HRH The Prince of Wales and the role of the trust is to distribute money to organisations, communities and individuals in the Yorkshire Dales. Grants are made towards the conservation and regeneration of the natural and built heritage and community life of the Yorkshire Dales. It supports, for example, planting new and restoring old woods, the restoration of dry stone walls and field barns, conservation of historical features and community projects.

The trust has adopted the following aims:

1) To conserve or restore the natural, built, scenic and cultural heritage features which together make up the special landscape of the Dales.
2) To develop and encourage opportunities for wider access to and understanding of the Dales.
3) To improve understanding of and wider use of countryside and traditional skills.
4) To support the people and communities of the Dales to live and work in harmony with this special and protected landscape.

The trust raises and distributes its own funds and manages programmes on behalf of external funders, such as the Heritage Lottery Fund and the Learning and Skills Council. Details of the trust's current funding schemes can be found on the website.

The trust makes grants to applicants for up to 70% of their project costs. For every project it supports the trust can pull in matching funding from other sources.

In 2007/08 it had assets of £649,000 and an income of over £1.3 million made up almost entirely from grants and donations. Grants were made to 74 projects during the year totalling £786,000, including grants from the following restricted funds:

Recipient	Value
YDNPA Sustainable Development Fund	£184,000
Dales Woodland Restoration	£92,200
North Yorkshire Aggregate Grants Scheme	£91,300
Hay Time	£82,000
Nidderdale AONB Sustainable Development Fund	£71,600
Modern Apprenticeships	£36,500
Donate to the Dales Project	£6,000
Community Wardens	£3,000
Learning in Limestone Country	£600

Applications In writing to the correspondent.

Elizabeth and Prince Zaiger Trust

Welfare, health and general

£836,000 (2007/08)

Beneficial area UK, some preference for Somerset, Dorset and the South West.

6 Alleyn Road, Dulwich, London SE21 8AL

Correspondent David W Parry, Trustee

Trustees *David J Davidge; Peter J Harvey; Derek G Long; David W Parry.*

CC Number 282096

Information available Accounts were available from the Charity Commission.

As well as supporting general charitable causes, the trust has the following objects:

● relief of older people
● relief of people who are mentally and physically disabled
● advancement of education of children and young people
● provision of care and protection for animals.

In 2007/08 the trust had assets of £14.9 million and an income of £801,000. Grants were made during the year totalling £836,000 to 123 organisations.

Most grants ranged from £1,000 to £7,000. Larger grants included those to: Variety Club of Great Britain and St Margaret's Somerset Hospice (£30,000 each); Centre 70 Community Association (£25,000); Brainwave (£20,000); Kids Company (£15,000); and Home-Start Taunton Deane Ltd, Neuromuscular Centre and St David's Foundation (£10,000 each).

Other beneficiaries included: Abbeyfield UK (£7,000); Design & Manufacture for Disability (£6,000); Action Medical Research, Mission Care and Well Being of Yeovil Community Association (£5,000 each); Marie Curie Cancer Care (£4,000); Spinal Injuries Association (£3,000); and Knight's Youth Centre and Woborns Almshouses (£2,000 each).

Applications 'The only thing people need to know is that we do not respond to unsolicited applications and it is, therefore, useless and a waste of time and money to contact us.'

The Zochonis Charitable Trust

General

£2.1 million (2007/08)

Beneficial area UK, particularly Greater Manchester, and overseas, particularly Africa.

c/o Cobbetts LLP, 58 Mosley Street, Manchester M2 3HZ

Tel. 0845 165 5270 **Fax** 0845 166 6733

Email ruth.barron@cobbetts.com

Correspondent Ruth Barron

Trustees *Sir John Zochonis; Christopher Nigel Green; Archibald G Calder; Joseph J Swift.*

CC Number 274769

Information available Accounts were available from the Charity Commission.

Established in 1977, this is the trust of Sir John Zochonis, former head of PZ Cussons, the soap and toiletries manufacturer. It has general charitable objectives but tends to favour local charities with a particular emphasis on education and the welfare of children. Grants do not appear to be ongoing, but local charities with an established relationship with the trust are supported intermittently, if not regularly, over many years.

In 2007/08 the trust had assets of £92 million and an income of £2.4 million. Grants were made to 106 organisations totalling £2.1 million.

The largest grants included those to: Cancer Research UK (£150,000); Christie Hospital NHS Foundation Trust and VSO (£100,000 each); Greater Manchester High Sheriff's Trust (£60,000); and Big Issue in the North (£50,000).

Other beneficiaries included: Manchester YMCA (£35,000); Smile Train (£25,000); Book Aid International and Manchester Library Theatre Development Trust (£15,000 each); Concern Worldwide (£12,000); Child Victims of Crime (£10,000); Willow Wood Hospice (£3,000); and CHICKS (£2,500).

Exclusions No grants for individuals.

Applications In writing to the correspondent.

Community Foundation Network

Community foundations are a new kind of charitable trust. They work in specific geographical areas as endowment builders, grantmakers and community leaders. They channel funds on behalf of individuals, organisations, companies and other agencies which recognise that their detailed knowledge of local needs puts them in an ideal position to distribute funding.

In England, in particular, many community foundations are the local agents for government programmes such as Grassroots Grants. The foundations are also increasingly called on to help deliver short-term programmes and emergency assistance on behalf of other grantmakers.

Community foundations already exist in most parts of the UK and new ones are being established all the time. At present, approximately 95% of the population live in a community foundation's area of benefit. The foundations are one of the largest independent funders of community organisations in the UK, giving around £70 million a year.

A list of all current community foundations, with basic contact details, follows below. Many are still at early stages of development, while others are well-established grant-making foundations. Contacts that are in italics have their own separate entries in this book.

Community Foundation Network
12 Angel Gate
320–326 City Road
London EC1V 2PT
Tel: 020 7713 9326
Fax: 020 7713 9327
Email: network@communityfoundations.
org.uk
Website: www.communityfoundations.
org.uk

Bedfordshire and Luton Community
Foundation
The Smithy
The Village
Old Warden
SG18 9HQ
Tel: 01767 626459
Contact: Mark West (Chief Executive)
Email: administrator@blcf.org.uk
Website: www.blcf.org.uk

Berkshire Community Foundation
Arlington Business Park
Theale
Reading
RG7 4SA
Tel: 01189 303021
Fax: 01189 304933
Contact: Andrew Middleton (Director)
Email: info@berkshirecommunity
    foundation.org.uk
Website: www.berkshirecommunity
    foundation.org.uk

Birmingham Community Foundation
Nechells Baths
Nechells Park Road
Nechells
Birmingham
B7 5PD
Tel: 0121 322 5560
Fax: 0121 322 5579
Contact: Derek Inman (Chief Executive)
Email: team@bhamfoundation.co.uk
Website: www.bhamfoundation.co.uk

Community Foundation for
Bournemouth, Dorset and Poole
Abchurch Chambers
24 St Peters Road
Bournemouth
BH1 2LN
Tel: 01202 292255
Fax: 01202 292255
Contact: Tina Baker (Chief Executive)
Email: bdpfoundation@btconnect.com
Website: www.localgiving4dorset.org.uk

Bradford District Community Foundation
385 Canal Road
Frizinghall
Bradford
BD2 1AW
Tel: 01274 714144
Fax: 01274 714140
Contact: John Corbishley (Chief Executive)
Email: john@cnet.org.uk

Buckinghamshire Community Foundation
Cavan House
119a Bicester Road
Aylesbury
HP19 9BA
Tel: 01296 330134
Fax: 01296 330158
Contact: Hilary Vickers (Development
    Director)
Email: info@buckscf.org.uk
Website: www.buckscf.org.uk

*Community Foundation for **Calderdale***
Community Foundation House
162a King Cross Road
Halifax
HX1 3LN
Tel: 01422 349700
Fax: 01422 350017
Contact: Steve Duncan (Director)
Email: enquiries@cffc.co.uk
Website: www.cffc.co.uk

Cambridgeshire Community Foundation
The Quorum
Barnwell Road
Cambridge
CB5 8RE
Tel: 01223 410535
Contact: Jane Darlington (Chief Executive)
Email: jane@cambscf.org.uk
Website: www.cambscf.org.uk

Capital Community Foundation
357 Kennington Lane
London
SE11 5QY
Tel: 020 7582 5117
Fax: 020 7582 4020
Contact: Sonal Shah or Rhys Moore
     (Director)
Email: enquiries@capitalcf.org.uk
Website: www.capitalcf.org.uk

Cornwall Community Foundation
The Orchard
Market Street
Lauceston
PL15 8AU
Tel: 01566 779333
Contact: Linda Whittaker (Executive
     Director)
Email: linda.whittaker@cornwall
     foundation.com
Website: www.cornwallfoundation.com

The **Craven** Trust (covers Keighley,
Sedbergh, Grassington, Barnoldswick and
the Trough of Bowland)
c/o Mrs Linda Lee (Hon secretary)
4 Halsteads Way
Steeton
Keighley
BD20 6SN
Contact: Jeremy Mackrell (Chair)
Email: enquiries@craventrust.org.uk
Website: www.craventrust.org.uk

Cumbria Community Foundation
Dovenby Hall
Dovenby
Cockermouth
CA13 0PN
Tel: 01900 825760
Fax: 01900 826527
Contact: Andrew Beeforth (Director)
Email: enquiries@cumbriafoundation.org
Website: www.cumbriafoundation.org

Dacorum Community Trust
Cementaprise Centre
Paradise
Hemel Hempstead
HP2 4TF
Tel: 01442 231396
Contact: Margaret Kingston
     (Administrator)
Email: mk@dctrust.org.uk
Website: www.dctrust.org.uk

Derbyshire Community Foundation
Foundation House
Unicorn Business Park
Wellington Street
Ripley
DE5 3EH
Tel: 01773 514850
Fax: 01773 741410
Contact: Rachael Grime (Executive Director)
Email: info@derbyshirecommunity
     foundation.co.uk
Website: www.derbyshirecommunity
     foundation.co.uk

Devon Community Foundation
The Factory
Leat Street
Tiverton
EX16 5LL
Tel: 01884 235887
Fax: 01884 243824
Contact: Melanie McLoughlin (Director)
Email: admin@devoncf.com
Website: www.devoncf.com

County **Durham** Foundation (includes
Darlington)
Jordan House
Forster Business Centre
Finchale Road
Durham
DH1 5HL
Tel: 0191 383 0055
Fax: 0191 383 2969
Contact: Barbara Gubbins (Chief Executive)
Email: barbara@cdcf.org.uk
Website: www.cdcf.org.uk

East London Community Foundation
LCCM House
Kemp Road
Dagenham
RM8 1ST
Tel: 0300 303 1203
Contact: Anja Beinroth (Acting Chief
     Executive)
Email: anja@elcf.org.uk
Website: www.elcf.org.uk

Essex Community Foundation
121 New London Road
Chelmsford
CM2 0QT
Tel: 01245 355947
Fax: 01245 346391
Contact: Laura Warren (Chief Executive)
Email: general@essexcf.org.uk
Website: www.essexcommunityfoundation.
     org.uk

European Foundation Centre
Community Philanthropy Initiative
Avenue de la Toison d'Or
1060 Brussels
Belgium
Tel: 0032 2 512 8938
Fax: 0032 2 512 3265
Contact: Ana Feder
Email: ana@efc.be
Website: www.efc.be

Fermanagh Trust
County Fermanagh's Community
     Foundation
Fermanagh House
Broadmeadow Place
Enniskillen
BT74 7BT
Tel: 028 6632 0210
Fax: 028 6632 0230
Contact: Lauri McCusker (Director)
Email: info@fermanaghtrust.org
Website: www.fermanaghtrust.org

Gloucestershire Community Foundation
c/o British Energy Plc
Barnett Way
Barnwood
Gloucester
GL4 3RS
Tel: 01452 656385
Fax: 01452 654164
Contact: Darien Parkes (Director)
Email: darien.parkes@british-energy.com
Website: www.gloucestershirecommunity
     foundation.co.uk

Community Foundation for **Greater
Manchester**
5th Floor
Speakers House
Deansgate
Manchester
M3 2BA
Tel: 0161 214 0940
Fax: 0161 214 0941
Contact: Nick Massey (Director)
Email: enquiries@commmunityfoundation.
     co.uk
Website: www.communityfoundation.co.uk

Community Foundation for **Hampshire**
and the Isle of Wight
Sun Alliance House
Wote Street
Basingstoke
RG21 1LU
Tel: 01256 776101
Contact: Toni Shaw (Chief Executive
     Officer)
Email: info@hantscf.org.uk
Website: www.hantscf.org.uk

Heart of England (covers Coventry and
Warwickshire)
Pinley House
HoECF
Coventry
CV3 1ND
Tel: 024 7688 4386
Contact: Kate Mulkern (Director)
Email: info@heartofenglandcf.co.uk
Website: www.heartofenglandcf.co.uk

Herefordshire Community Foundation
The Fred Bulmer Centre
Wall Street
Hereford
HR4 9HP
Tel: 01432 272550
Contact: David Barclay (Director)
Email: dave.barclay@herefordshire-cf.co.uk
Website: www.herefordshirecommunity
     foundation.org

Hertfordshire Community Foundation
2–4 Forum Place
Hatfield
AL10 0RN
Tel: 01707 251351
Fax: 01707 251133
Contact: David Fitzpatrick (Chief Executive)
Email: office@hertscf.org.uk
Website: www.hertscf.org.uk

Community Foundation for **Ireland**
32 Lower O'Connell Street
Dublin 1
Ireland
Tel: 00 353 1874 7354
Fax: 00 353 1874 7637
Contact: Tina Roche (Chief Executive)
Email: troche@bitc.ie
Website: www.communityfoundation.ie

Kent Community Foundation
Evegate Park Barn
Evegate
Smeeth
Ashford
TN25 6SX
Tel: 01303 814500
Fax: 01303 815150
Contact: Eric Watts (Chief Executive)
Email: admin@kentcf.org.uk
Website: www.kentcf.org.uk

Community Foundation for **Lancashire**
12 Richmond Terrace
Blackburn
BB1 7BG
Tel: 01254 585056
Contact: Glen Lockett (Chief Executive)
Email: info@lancsfoundation.org.uk
Website: www.lancsfoundation.org.uk

Leeds Community Foundation
Ground Floor
51a St Paul Street
Leeds
LS1 2TE
Tel: 0113 242 2426
Fax: 0113 242 2432
Contact: Sally-Anne Greenfield (Chief
Executive)
Email: info@leedscommunityfoundation.
org.uk
Website: www.leedscommunityfoundation.
org.uk

Leicestershire, Leicester and Rutland
Community Foundation
Charnwood Court
5a New Walk
Leicester
LE1 6TE
Tel: 0116 257 5694
Contact: Katy Green (Director)
Email: admin@llrcommunityfoundation.
org.uk
Website: www.llrcommunityfoundation.
org.uk

Lincolnshire Community Foundation
4 Mill House
Carre Street
Sleaford
NG34 7TW
Tel: 01529 305825
Fax: 01529 305825
Contact: Gordon Hunter
Email: lincolnshirecf@btconnect.com
Website: www.lincolnshirecf.co.uk

Community Foundation for **Merseyside**
c/o Alliance & Leicester
Bridle Road
Bootle
L30 4GB
Tel: 0151 966 4604
Fax: 0151 966 3384
Contact: Cathy Elliott (Chief Executive)
Email: info@cfmerseyside.org.uk
Website: www.cfmerseyside.org.uk

Milton Keynes Community Foundation
Acorn House
381 Midsummer Boulevard
Central Milton Keynes
MK9 3HP
United Kingdom
Tel: 01908 690276
Fax: 01908 233635
Contact: Julia Upton (Chief Executive)
Email: information@mkcommunity
foundation.co.uk
Website: www.mkcommunityfoundation.
co.uk

Norfolk Community Foundation
St James Mill
Whitefriars
Norwich
NR3 1SH
Tel: 01603 623958
Contact: Graham Tuttle (Director)
Email: grahamtuttle@norfolkfoundation.
com
Website: www.norfolkfoundation.com

Northamptonshire Community
Foundation
Suite 39–42
Burlington House
369 Wellingborough Road
Northampton
NN1 4EU
Tel: 01604 230033
Fax: 01604 639780
Contact: Victoria Miles (Chief Executive)
Email: enquiries@ncf.uk.com
Website: www.ncf.uk.com

Community Foundation for **Northern
Ireland**
Community House
Citylink Business Park
6a Albert Street
Belfast
BT12 4HQ
Tel: 028 9024 5927
Fax: 028 9032 9839
Contact: Avila Kilmurray (Director)
Email: info@communityfoundationni.org
Website: www.communityfoundationni.org

North West London Community
Foundation
Room 1
The Wealdstone Centre
Harrow
HA3 7AE
Tel: 020 8427 3823
Fax: 020 8427 2104
Contact: Patrick Vernon (Interim Director)
Email: patrick.v@nwlondoncf.org.uk
Website: www.nwlcommunityfoundation.
org.uk

Nottinghamshire Community Foundation
Cedar House
Ransom Wood Business Park
Southwell Road West
Mansfield
G21 0HJ
Tel: 01623 636365
Fax: 01623 620204
Contact: Nina Dauban (Chief Executive–
part time)
Email: enquiries@nottscf.org.uk
Website: www.nottscf.org.uk

Oxfordshire Community Foundation
3 Woodins Way
Oxford
OX1 1HD
Tel: 01865 798666
Fax: 01865 245385
Contact: Barry Tanswell (Director)
Email: ocf@oxfordshire.org
Website: www.oxfordshire.org

Quartet Community Foundation (covers
Bristol, north Somerset, south
Gloucestershire, Bath and north east
Somerset)
Royal Oak House
Royal Oak Avenue
Bristol
BS1 4GB
Tel: 0117 989 7700
Fax: 0117 989 7701
Contact: Fran Jones (Chief Executive)
Email: info@quartetcf.org.uk
Website: www.quartetcf.org.uk

St Katharine and Shadwell Trust
1 Pennington Street
London
E1W 2BY
Tel: 020 7782 6962
Fax: 020 7782 6963
Contact: Jenny Dawes (Director)
Email: enquiries@skst.org
Website: www.skst.org

Scottish Community Foundation
2nd Floor Calton House
22 Calton Road
Edinburgh
EH8 8PD
Tel: 0131 524 0300
Fax: 0131 524 0329
Contact: Giles Ruck (Chief Executive)
Email: info@scottishcf.org
Website: www.scottishcf.org

Community Foundation for **Shropshire** and Telford
Trevithick House
Stafford Park 4
Telford
TF3 3BA
Tel: 01952 201858
Fax: 01952 210500
Contact: Mike Lowe (Chair)
Email: contact@cfst.co.uk
Website: www.cfsat.org.uk

Solihull Community Foundation
Block 33
Land Rover
Lode Lane
Solihull
B92 8NW
Tel: 0121 700 3934
Fax: 0121 700 9158
Contact: Eric Baptiste (Director)
Email: director@solihullcf.org
Website: www.solihullcf.org

Somerset Community Foundation
Yeoman House
Royal Bath and West Showground
Shepton Mallet
BA4 6QN
Tel: 01749 344949
Contact: Justin Sargent (Director)
Email: info@somersetcf.org.uk
Website: www.somersetcf.org.uk

South Yorkshire Community Foundation
Clay Street
Sheffield
S9 2PF
Tel: 0114 242 4857
Fax: 0114 242 4605
Contact: Pauline Grice (Chief Executive)
Email: admin@sycf.org.uk
Website: www.sycf.org.uk

Staffordshire Community Foundation
Dudson Centre
Hope Street
Hanley
Stoke-on-Trent
ST1 5DD
Tel: 01782 683000
Fax: 01782 683199
Contact: Terry Walsh (Director)
Email: director@staffsfoundation.org.uk
Website: www.staffsfoundation.org.uk

Stevenage Community Trust
c/o Astrium
Gunnels Wood Road
Stevenage
SG1 2AS
Tel: 01438 773368
Fax: 01438 773341
Contact: June Oldroyd (Director)
Email: info@sct.uk.net
Website: www.sct.uk.net

Suffolk Foundation
Old Reading Rooms
The Green
Grundisburgh
Woodbridge
IP13 6TT
Tel: 01473 734120
Fax: 01473 734121
Contact: Stephen Singleton (Chief Executive)
Email: info@suffolkfoundation.org.uk
Website: www.suffolkfoundation.org.uk

Surrey Community Foundation
1 Bishops Wharf
Walnut Tree Close
Guildford
GU1 4RA
Tel: 01483 409230
Contact: Wendy Varcoe (Director)
Email: info@surreycommunityfoundation.org.uk
Website: www.surreycommunityfoundation.org.uk

Sussex Community Foundation
Suite B
Falcon Wharf
Railway Lane
Lewes
BN7 2AQ
Tel: 01273 409440
Contact: Kevin Richmond (Chief Executive)
Email: info@sussexgiving.org.uk
Website: www.sussexgiving.org.uk

Tees Valley Community Foundation
Southlands Business Centre
Ormesby Road
Middlesbrough
TS3 0HB
Tel: 01642 314200
Fax: 01642 313700
Contact: Hugh McGouran (Chief Executive)
Email: info@teesvalleyfoundation.org
Website: www.teesvalleyfoundation.org

Thames Community Foundation
NPL Building 1, Rooms 201–206
Hampton Road
Teddington
TW11 0LW
Tel: 020 8943 6029
Contact: Nigel Hay (Chief Executive)
Email: tcf@thamescommunityfoundation.org.uk
Website: www.thamescommunityfoundation.org.uk

Community Foundation serving Tyne and Wear and Northumberland
Cale Cross
156 Pilgrim Street
Newcastle upon Tyne
NE1 6SU
Tel: 0191 222 0945
Fax: 0191 230 0689
Contact: Rob Williamson (Chief Executive)
Email: general@communityfoundation.org.uk
Website: www.communityfoundation.org.uk

Community Foundation for **Wakefield** District
Room B29
Wakefield College
Margaret Street
Wakefield
WF21 2DH
Tel: 01924 789166
Contact: Linda Box
Email: info@communityfoundation wakefield.co.uk
Website: www.communityfoundation wakefield.co.uk

Community Foundation in **Wales**
9 Coopers Yard
Curran Road
Cardiff
CF10 5NB
Tel: 02920 536590
Fax: 02920 342118
Contact: Liza Kellett (Executive Director)
Email: mail@cfiw.org.uk
Website: www.cfiw.org.uk

Community Foundation for Wiltshire and Swindon
48 New Park Street
Devizes
SN10 1DS
Tel: 01380 729284
Fax: 01380 729772
Contact: Rosemary MacDonald (Chief Executive)
Email: info@wscf.org.uk
Website: www.wscf.org.uk

Worcestershire Community Foundation
134 Sandy Lane
Stourport on Severn
DY13 9QB
Tel: 01299 826013
Fax: 01299 877008
Contact: Jackie Howorth (Director)
Email: jackie@worcscf.org.uk
Website: www.worcscf.org.uk

York and North Yorkshire Community Foundation
Primrose Hill
Buttercrambe Road
Stamford Bridge
York
YO41 1AW
Tel: 01759 377400
Fax: 01759 377401
Contact: Stephen Beyer (Director)
Email: office@ynycf.plus.com
Website: www.ynycf.org.uk

Subject index

The following subject index begins with a list of categories used. The categories are very wide-ranging to keep the index as simple as possible. DSC's subscription website (www.trustfunding.org.uk) has a much more detailed search facility on the categories. There may be considerable overlap between the categories – for example, children and education, or older people and social welfare.

The list of categories is followed by the index itself. Before using the index, please note the following points.

How the index was compiled

1) The index aims to reflect the most recent grant-making practice. Therefore, it is based on our interpretation of which areas each trust has actually given to, rather than what its policy statement says or its charitable objects allow it to do in principle. For example, where a trust states that it has general charitable purposes, but its grants list shows a strong preference for welfare, we index it under welfare.

2) We have tried to ensure that each trust has given significantly in the areas under which it is indexed (usually at least £15,000). Thus small, apparently untypical grants have been ignored for index purposes.

3) The index has been complied from the latest information available to us.

Limitations

1) Policies may change, and some more frequently than others.

2) Sometimes there will be a geographical restriction on a trust's grantgiving which is not shown in this index, or the trust may not give to the area and the heading under which your specific purposes fall. It is important to read each entry carefully.

You will need to check that:

- the trust gives in your geographical area of operation

- the trust gives for the specific purposes you require

- there is no other reason to prevent you from making an application to this trust.

3) It is worth noting that one or two of the categories list almost half the trusts included in this guide.

Under no circumstances should the index be used as a simple mailing list. Remember that each trust is different and that the policies or interests of a particular trust often do not fit easily into the given categories. Each entry must be read individually before you send off an application. Indiscriminate applications are usually unsuccessful. They waste time and money and greatly annoy trusts.

The categories are as follows:

Arts, culture, sport and recreation *page 412*

This is a very wide category including: performing, written and visual arts; crafts; theatres, museums and galleries; heritage, architecture and archaeology; and sports.

Children and young people *page 413*

This is mainly for welfare and welfare-related activities.

Development, housing and employment *page 413*

This includes specific industries such as leather making or textiles.

Disability *page 414*

Disadvantaged people *page 414*

This includes people who are:

- socially excluded
- socially and economically disadvantaged
- unemployed
- homeless
- offenders
- educationally disadvantaged
- victims of social/natural occurrences, including refugees and asylum seekers.

Education and training *page 415*

Environment and animals *page 416*

This includes:

- agriculture and fishing
- conservation
- animal care
- environment and education
- transport
- sustainable environment.

General charitable purposes *page 417*

This is a very broad category and includes trusts that often have numerous specific strands to their programmes as a well as those that will consider any application (subject to other eligibility criteria).

Illness *page 418*

This includes people who are suffering from specific conditions.

Medicine and health *page 418*

Older people *page 419*

Religion – general *page 419*

This includes inter-faith work and religious understanding.

Christianity *page 420*

Islam *page 420*

Judaism *page 420*

Arts, culture, sport and recreation

The 29th May 1961 Charitable Trust
The Alice Trust
Allchurches Trust Ltd
Arcadia
The Architectural Heritage Fund
The Ashden Trust
The Baring Foundation
The Bedford Charity (The Harpur Trust)
The Big Lottery Fund
The Audrey and Stanley Burton 1960
    Charitable Trust
The Derek Butler Trust
Edward Cadbury Charitable Trust
The William A Cadbury Charitable Trust
The Barrow Cadbury Trust and the
    Barrow Cadbury Fund
The Carpenters' Company Charitable
    Trust
The Clore Duffield Foundation
The R and S Cohen Fondation
The John S Cohen Foundation
Colyer-Fergusson Charitable Trust
The Ernest Cook Trust
The D'Oyly Carte Charitable Trust
The Daiwa Anglo-Japanese Foundation
Peter De Haan Charitable Trust
The Djanogly Foundation
The Drapers' Charitable Fund
The Dulverton Trust
Dunard Fund
The John Ellerman Foundation
The Eranda Foundation
Esmée Fairbairn Foundation
The February Foundation
The Sir John Fisher Foundation
Fisherbeck Charitable Trust
The Fishmongers' Company's Charitable
    Trust
The Football Association Youth Trust
The Football Foundation
The Donald Forrester Trust
The Foyle Foundation
The Hugh Fraser Foundation
The Joseph Strong Frazer Trust
The Gannochy Trust
The Gatsby Charitable Foundation
The Robert Gavron Charitable Trust
J Paul Getty Jr Charitable Trust
Simon Gibson Charitable Trust
The Girdlers' Company Charitable Trust
The Glass-House Trust
The Goldsmiths' Company Charity
The Gosling Foundation Limited
The Great Britain Sasakawa Foundation

The Grocers' Charity
The Gulbenkian Foundation
Paul Hamlyn Foundation
The Helen Hamlyn Trust
The Peter Harrison Foundation
The Charles Hayward Foundation
The Headley Trust
The Hintze Family Charitable
    Foundation
Hobson Charity Limited
Jerwood Charitable Foundation
The Sir James Knott Trust
The Neil Kreitman Foundation
The LankellyChase Foundation
The Leathersellers' Company Charitable
    Fund
Lord Leverhulme's Charitable Trust
The Joseph Levy Charitable Foundation
The Linbury Trust
The George John and Sheilah Livanos
    Charitable Trust
Lloyds TSB Foundation for Northern
    Ireland
The London Marathon Charitable Trust
The Lord's Taverners
John Lyon's Charity
The Mackintosh Foundation
The MacRobert Trust
The Manifold Charitable Trust
The Manoukian Charitable Foundation
Marshall's Charity
The Mercers' Charitable Foundation
Milton Keynes Community Foundation
The Monument Trust
The Henry Moore Foundation
The Peter Moores Foundation
The John R Murray Charitable Trust
The National Art Collections Fund
The National Churches Trust
Network for Social Change
The Northern Rock Foundation
The Northwood Charitable Trust
The Ofenheim Charitable Trust
The Parthenon Trust
The Performing Right Society
    Foundation
The Pilgrim Trust
Polden-Puckham Charitable Foundation
The Prince's Charities Foundation
Mr and Mrs J A Pye's Charitable
    Settlement
The Sigrid Rausing Trust
The Rayne Foundation
The Reed Foundation
The Richmond Parish Lands Charity
The Robertson Trust
Mrs L D Rope Third Charitable
    Settlement
The Rose Foundation
The Rothschild Foundation

Children and young people

Development, housing and employment

Disability

Disadvantaged people

The Barrow Cadbury Trust and the Barrow Cadbury Fund

The Campden Charities

The Charities Advisory Trust

The Church Urban Fund

The City Parochial Foundation

The Clore Duffield Foundation

Closehelm Ltd

Richard Cloudesley's Charity

The R and S Cohen Fondation

Colyer-Fergusson Charitable Trust

Comic Relief

Cumbria Community Foundation

The Diana, Princess of Wales Memorial Fund

The Drapers' Charitable Fund

The EBM Charitable Trust

The John Ellerman Foundation

Euro Charity Trust

The Eveson Charitable Trust

The Execution Charitable Trust

Esmée Fairbairn Foundation

Fisherbeck Charitable Trust

The Fishmongers' Company's Charitable Trust

The Donald Forrester Trust

Four Acre Trust

The Hugh Fraser Foundation

The Freemasons' Grand Charity

The Gannochy Trust

The Gatsby Charitable Foundation

The Robert Gavron Charitable Trust

J Paul Getty Jr Charitable Trust

The Girdlers' Company Charitable Trust

Global Charities

The Grocers' Charity

H C D Memorial Fund

The Hadley Trust

Paul Hamlyn Foundation

Hampton Fuel Allotment Charity

The Haramead Trust

The Peter Harrison Foundation

The Charles Hayward Foundation

The Heart of England Community Foundation

Help the Aged

The Hilden Charitable Fund

The Albert Hunt Trust

The Hunter Foundation

Impetus Trust

The J J Charitable Trust

The Joffe Charitable Trust

The Jones 1986 Charitable Trust

The King's Fund

The Mary Kinross Charitable Trust

Maurice and Hilda Laing Charitable Trust

The Beatrice Laing Trust

The Allen Lane Foundation

The LankellyChase Foundation

The Leathersellers' Company Charitable Fund

The William Leech Charity

The Mark Leonard Trust

The Joseph Levy Charitable Foundation

The Linbury Trust

The Enid Linder Foundation

Lloyds TSB Foundation for England and Wales

Lloyds TSB Foundation for Northern Ireland

John Lyon's Charity

The Mackintosh Foundation

The Mercers' Charitable Foundation

Milton Keynes Community Foundation

John Moores Foundation

The Edith Murphy Foundation

The Nationwide Foundation

Network for Social Change

The North British Hotel Trust

North West London Community Foundation

The Northern Rock Foundation

The Nuffield Foundation

The Parthenon Trust

The Pilgrim Trust

The Pilkington Charities Fund

Mr and Mrs J A Pye's Charitable Settlement

The Rayne Foundation

The Sir James Reckitt Charity

The Richmond Parish Lands Charity

The Robertson Trust

Mrs L D Rope Third Charitable Settlement

The Joseph Rowntree Charitable Trust

Erach and Roshan Sadri Foundation

The Alan and Babette Sainsbury Charitable Fund

The Sandra Charitable Trust

The Severn Trent Water Charitable Trust Fund

The Sovereign Health Care Charitable Trust

The Stone Family Foundation

Sutton Coldfield Municipal Charities

The Tolkien Trust

Trust for London

The Wates Foundation

The Woodward Charitable Trust

The Worwin UK Foundation

Education and training

The 1989 Willan Charitable Trust

The Alliance Family Foundation

The John Armitage Charitable Trust

The Baily Thomas Charitable Fund

The Balcombe Charitable Trust

The Bedford Charity (The Harpur Trust)

The Big Lottery Fund

The Booth Charities

The Bowland Charitable Trust

British Record Industry Trust

Brushmill Ltd

The Audrey and Stanley Burton 1960 Charitable Trust

Edward Cadbury Charitable Trust

The William A Cadbury Charitable Trust

The Campden Charities

The Carpenters' Company Charitable Trust

Sir John Cass's Foundation

CfBT Education Trust

The Childwick Trust

Church Burgesses Trust

The Clore Duffield Foundation

The Coalfields Regeneration Trust

The R and S Cohen Fondation

The John S Cohen Foundation

The Peter Cruddas Foundation

Cullum Family Trust

The Daiwa Anglo-Japanese Foundation

The Djanogly Foundation

The Drapers' Charitable Fund

The James Dyson Foundation

The Sir John Eastwood Foundation

The Equitable Charitable Trust

The Eranda Foundation

Euro Charity Trust

Esmée Fairbairn Foundation

The February Foundation

Allan and Nesta Ferguson Charitable Settlement

Fisherbeck Charitable Trust

The Fishmongers' Company's Charitable Trust

The Football Foundation

The Donald Forrester Trust

Four Acre Trust

The Foyle Foundation

The Hugh Fraser Foundation

The Joseph Strong Frazer Trust

The Freemasons' Grand Charity

The Gatsby Charitable Foundation

The Robert Gavron Charitable Trust

The Girdlers' Company Charitable Trust

The Golden Bottle Trust

The Goldsmiths' Company Charity

The Great Britain Sasakawa Foundation

The Grocers' Charity

The Gulbenkian Foundation

H C D Memorial Fund

Paul Hamlyn Foundation

The Helen Hamlyn Trust

Hampton Fuel Allotment Charity

The Kathleen Hannay Memorial Charity

Environment and animals

General charitable purposes

The 1989 Willan Charitable Trust
The 29th May 1961 Charitable Trust
Allchurches Trust Ltd
The H B Allen Charitable Trust
The Alliance Family Foundation
The Arbib Foundation
AW Charitable Trust
Awards for All
The Band Trust
The Birmingham Community Foundation
The Bluston Charitable Settlement
The Derek Butler Trust
Edward Cadbury Charitable Trust
The Cadogan Charity
Capital Community Foundation
The Carpenters' Company Charitable Trust
The Charities Advisory Trust
CHK Charities Limited
Church Burgesses Trust
Closehelm Ltd
The Clothworkers' Foundation
Clydpride Ltd
The Coalfields Regeneration Trust
The John S Cohen Foundation
Community Foundation for Calderdale
The Community Foundation for Greater Manchester
The Alice Ellen Cooper Dean Charitable Foundation
County Durham Foundation
Cripplegate Foundation
Cullum Family Trust
Peter De Haan Charitable Trust
Derbyshire Community Foundation
Devon Community Foundation
The Djanogly Foundation
The DM Charitable Trust
The Dollond Charitable Trust
The Drapers' Charitable Fund
The Dulverton Trust
The Charles Dunstone Charitable Trust
The James Dyson Foundation
The Maud Elkington Charitable Trust
The Englefield Charitable Trust
Essex Community Foundation
The Fidelity UK Foundation
The Sir John Fisher Foundation
Fisherbeck Charitable Trust
Gwyneth Forrester Trust
The Donald Forrester Trust
Four Acre Trust
The Hugh Fraser Foundation

The Joseph Strong Frazer Trust
The Freemasons' Grand Charity
The Patrick Frost Foundation
The Gatsby Charitable Foundation
The Robert Gavron Charitable Trust
Simon Gibson Charitable Trust
The G C Gibson Charitable Trust
Global Charities
The Golden Bottle Trust
The Goldsmiths' Company Charity
Mike Gooley Trailfinders Charity
The Gosling Foundation Limited
GrantScape
The Grocers' Charity
Hampton Fuel Allotment Charity
The Kathleen Hannay Memorial Charity
The Haramead Trust
The Maurice Hatter Foundation
The Heart of England Community Foundation
Heathside Charitable Trust
The Hertfordshire Community Foundation
The Hilden Charitable Fund
Lady Hind Trust
The Jane Hodge Foundation
The Sir Joseph Hotung Charitable Settlement
Impetus Trust
The Isle of Anglesey Charitable Trust
Isle of Dogs Community Foundation
John James Bristol Foundation
The Jones 1986 Charitable Trust
The Jordan Charitable Foundation
The Joron Charitable Trust
The Anton Jurgens Charitable Trust
The Kennedy Charitable Foundation
Keren Association
Ernest Kleinwort Charitable Trust
The Sir James Knott Trust
The Laing Family Foundations
The Kirby Laing Foundation
The Leathersellers' Company Charitable Fund
The Kennedy Leigh Charitable Trust
The Lennox and Wyfold Foundation
The Mark Leonard Trust
Lord Leverhulme's Charitable Trust
The Linbury Trust
The Enid Linder Foundation
The George John and Sheilah Livanos Charitable Trust
Lloyds TSB Foundation for Northern Ireland
Lloyds TSB Foundation for the Channel Islands
The Mackintosh Foundation
The MacRobert Trust
The Manifold Charitable Trust
The Medlock Charitable Trust

The Mercers' Charitable Foundation
Community Foundation for Merseyside
Milton Keynes Community Foundation
The Brian Mitchell Charitable Settlement
The Monument Trust
The Mulberry Trust
The Northwood Charitable Trust
Oglesby Charitable Trust
The P F Charitable Trust
The Peacock Charitable Trust
The Dowager Countess Eleanor Peel Trust
The Privy Purse Charitable Trust
Quartet Community Foundation
The Queen's Silver Jubilee Trust
Rachel Charitable Trust
The Rank Foundation
The Joseph Rank Trust
The Sir James Reckitt Charity
The Reed Foundation
Reuben Brothers Foundation
The Richmond Parish Lands Charity
Ridgesave Limited
The Robertson Trust
The Gerald Ronson Foundation
Mrs L D Rope Third Charitable Settlement
The Rose Foundation
The Rothschild Foundation
The Rubin Foundation
The Rufford Maurice Laing Foundation
The Saddlers' Company Charitable Fund
The Alan and Babette Sainsbury Charitable Fund
Basil Samuel Charitable Trust
The Schreib Trust
The Schroder Foundation
The Scottish Community Foundation
The Samuel Sebba Charitable Trust
ShareGift (The Orr Mackintosh Foundation)
The Sheepdrove Trust
The Archie Sherman Charitable Trust
The Steel Charitable Trust
Stratford upon Avon Town Trust
The Bernard Sunley Charitable Foundation
Sussex Community Foundation
Sutton Coldfield Municipal Charities
The Charles and Elsie Sykes Trust
The Tedworth Charitable Trust
Tees Valley Community Foundation
The Thompson Family Charitable Trust
The Tolkien Trust
The Constance Travis Charitable Trust
The Triangle Trust (1949) Fund
The Trusthouse Charitable Foundation
The Tudor Trust
The Douglas Turner Trust

Illness

Medicine and health

Older people

Religion – general

Christianity

Islam

Judaism